Cuba

Brendan Sainsbury

HAVANA (p94)
Old forts, fascinating museums and a kicking Caribbean nightlife

LAS TERRAZAS (p222)
Model village and ecolodge nestled in a reforested Unesco Biosphere Reserve

VARADERO (p236)
Gorgeous beaches, swanky resorts and first-class tourist facilities

SANTA CLARA (p277)
Che memorabilia and a buzzing cultural scene

VIÑALES (p210)
Spectacular limestone cliffs, lush green tobacco fields and an expansive network of caves

MARÍA LA GORDA (p208)
World-class diving on Cuba's isolated western tip

NUEVA GERONA (p188)
Sleepy old town on the Isle of Youth

CIÉNAGA DE ZAPATA (p256)
Abundant wildlife in Cuba's largest wilderness area

CIENFUEGOS (p262)
A French-flavored city and a Unesco World Heritage Site

TRINIDAD (p298)
Music houses and museums in Cuba's historic colonial jewel

UNITED STATES OF AMERICA (Florida)
Florida Keys
Straits of Florida

GULF OF MEXICO

Tropic of Cancer

Archipiélago de los Colorados
Archipiélago de Sabana
Archipiélago de los Canarreos

HAVANA
Playas del Este
Varadero
Matanzas
Cárdenas
Las Terrazas
Soroa
Surgidero de Batabanó
Viñales
Pinar del Río
Autopista Habana–Pinar del Río
Carretera Central
Autopista Nacional
Ciénaga de Zapata
Santa Clara
Cienfuegos
Topes de Collantes
Trinidad
Nueva Gerona
Isla de la Juventud
Cayo Largo del Sur

Little Cayman
Cayman Brac
Grand Cayman
CAYMAN ISLANDS (UK)
GEORGE TOWN

CARIBBEAN SEA

ELEVATION
1800m
1500m
1200m
900m
600m
300m
150m
75m
0

LEGEND
Freeway
Primary Road
Secondary Road

LP

0   100 km
0   60 miles

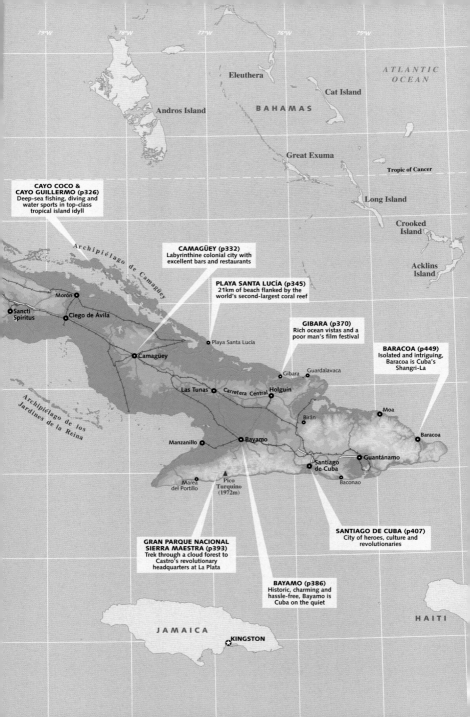

79°W 78°W 77°W 76°W 75°W

Eleuthera

Cat Island

ATLANTIC OCEAN

Andros Island

BAHAMAS

Great Exuma

Tropic of Cancer

Long Island

Crooked Island

Acklins Island

CAYO COCO & CAYO GUILLERMO (p326)
Deep-sea fishing, diving and water sports in top-class tropical island idyll

Archipiélago de Camagüey

CAMAGÜEY (p332)
Labyrinthine colonial city with excellent bars and restaurants

PLAYA SANTA LUCÍA (p345)
21km of beach flanked by the world's second-largest coral reef

GIBARA (p370)
Rich ocean vistas and a poor man's film festival

BARACOA (p449)
Isolated and intriguing, Baracoa is Cuba's Shangri-La

Morón

Sancti Spíritus

Ciego de Ávila

Playa Santa Lucía

Camagüey

Gibara   Guardalavaca

Moa

Baracoa

Las Tunas   Carretera Central   Holguín

Archipiélago de los Jardines de la Reina

Birán

Manzanillo   Bayamo

Marea del Portillo   Pico Turquino (1972m)

Santiago de Cuba   Guantánamo

Baconao

GRAN PARQUE NACIONAL SIERRA MAESTRA (p393)
Trek through a cloud forest to Castro's revolutionary headquarters at La Plata

SANTIAGO DE CUBA (p407)
City of heroes, culture and revolutionaries

BAYAMO (p386)
Historic, charming and hassle-free, Bayamo is Cuba on the quiet

JAMAICA

KINGSTON

HAITI

On the Road

BRENDAN SAINSBURY

This photo, taken by the Lago San Juan in Las Terrazas (p222), belies the hullabaloo of my research. I'd just spent two months gallivanting across Cuba, gate-crashing music venues, trolling around museums, gawping at dive sites and traveling alfresco on antiquated Russian trucks. Las Terrazas was the final chapter, a placid eco-village with nothing to do but sidle up to nature. Boy, did I need it!

MY FAVORITE TRIP

I hit the ground running in Havana (p94) before heading east to the understated and under-appreciated city of Matanzas (p227) for a bit of rousing rumba. Santa Clara's (p277) the next exciting revelation with some excellent casas particulares, and a buoyant and youthful nightlife. You can combine beach, mountains and history in Trinidad (p298), while Gibara (p370) is strictly for loners and tour-circuit escapees. Marea del Portillo's (p402) no Varadero, but it's gloriously spectacular, while hot Santiago (p407), with its colorful *folklórico* troupes, is a Cuban rite of passage. Then there's Baracoa (p449) – my all-time favourite – weird, zany, wild and magical, for reasons far too complicated to explain here.

ABOUT THE AUTHOR

Brendan is a British freelance writer based in British Columbia, Canada. He first went to Cuba on a whim in 1997 and returned, equally serendipitously, five years later to work as a travel guide. In 2006 he researched and wrote the 4th edition of Lonely Planet's *Cuba* guide with his wife and three-month-old son in tow. The following year he went back to research for Lonely Planet's *Havana* guide. When not in Cuba, Brendan likes to run across deserts, play flamenco guitar and hang out with his three-year-old son, Kieran.

VIVA CUBA

Defying all logic, the world's 105th-largest country is also one of its most instantly recognizable. Think psychedelic Che Guevara murals and antediluvian American Buicks, dudes with bongos and old men slapping down dominoes, queues outside ration shops and communist cadres smoking chunky Montecristos. Cuba has a way of going against the grain. It's all part of its historical make-up, part of its dynamism, part of its intrinsic beauty.

Architecture

If Cuba's soul is hidden in its music, then its architecture – in the words of novelist Alejo Carpentier – is its 'music turned to stone.' Running the gamut of styles from baroque to art deco, the country is a museum of soaring architectural eclecticism that, by a trick of historical fate, got spared from the developer's bulldozers.

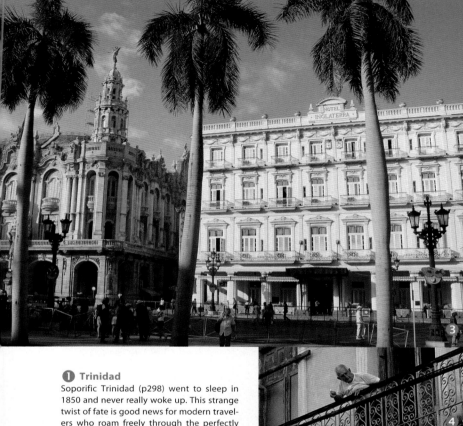

❶ Trinidad

Soporific Trinidad (p298) went to sleep in 1850 and never really woke up. This strange twist of fate is good news for modern travelers who roam freely through the perfectly preserved mid-19th century sugar town like voyeurs from another era.

❷ Cienfuegos

The so-called Perla del Sur (Pearl of the South; p262) is Cuba's most architecturally complete city, a love letter to French neoclassicism that is wrapped picturesquely around one of the Caribbean's best natural bays.

❸ Havana

Shaped by a colorful colonial history and embellished by myriad foreign influences from as far afield as Italy and Morocco, the Cuban capital (p94) gracefully combines *mudéjar*, baroque, neoclassical, art nouveau, art deco and modernist architectural styles into a visually striking whole.

❹ Remedios

A city of legends and mysteries, Remedios (p285) is Cuba's forgotten corner, a colonial secret that glimmers subtly like an undiscovered Trinidad. Sit with a mojito under the winking louvers and keep the good fortune to yourself. Sssssh…

❺ Camagüey

Classical blends with ecclesial in Camagüey (p332) – a city of churches, spires, towers and crosses. Then there are the streets: a network of winding, twisting, sinuous thoroughfares which take you to places that even the locals don't know about.

Music

Cuba's contribution to world music isn't just one band, or even one brand. Characterized by a unique synthesis of African, Spanish, French, indigenous and Caribbean influences, the country has produced enough musical genres to host a global party and still have plenty left over.

❶ Salsa
You can argue all night about who created salsa (p67) but, the truth is, few people can write it and perform it as well as the Cubans. Not really convinced? Take a dance lesson in Havana, or head to one of the city's two Casas de la Música and see the experts in motion.

❷ Nueva Trova
An improbable blend of Bob Dylan, Celia Cruz, John Lennon, Víctor Jara and Joan Manuel Serrat, *nueva trova* (p69) is the Cuban Revolution's lilting musical soundtrack, whose greatest exponents – Pablo Milanés and Carlos Puebla – came from Granma province.

❸ Rumba
An exuberant mix of thumping drums and athletic dancing, rumba (p66) is Cuba's African soul, a musical genre heavy with religious iconography and the painful echoes of slavery. See it at its best in Matanzas, upon whose docks many of the rhythms were first played out.

❹ Son-Changüí
In Santiago they call it *son*, next door in Guantánamo province they call it *son-changüí* (p65), an eastern variation on a traditional Cuban theme that was born in provincial sugar refineries and influenced by slaves.

❺ Reggaetón
Love it or hate it, *reggaetón* (p68) is the sound of the moment in Cuba, a muscular mélange of rap, hip-hop, reggae and dance that emanates ubiquitously from car radios, parks, squares, schoolyards and the hard-nosed streets of its spiritual home – gritty Alamar.

Revolutionaries

Cuba churns out revolutionaries like other countries produce movie stars and, with outside influence from at least three (neo)colonial powers over the last 100 years, their heroics have usually been ecstatically welcomed. Recreated in bronze or emblazoned on hulking billboards, the icons live on.

① Che Guevara

The face that launched a million T-shirts is still omnipresent in Cuba where government propaganda has elevated him into a pantheon of socialist 'saints.' Che pilgrims head straight to Santa Clara (p277), where monuments, museums and the great *guerrillero's* hallowed remains pay homage to the legend.

② Antonio Maceo

Cuba's Bronze Titan led the island's brave Mambí fighters in both Independence Wars before being killed by the Spanish in a skirmish near Havana in 1896. An open-air mausoleum at El Cacahual (p164) marks the spot where he fell.

③ José Martí

Known simply as El Maestro (The Master) to most Cubans, Martí's legacy can be seen all over the island. One of the most poignant monuments is his magnificent mausoleum watched over by a military guard in the Cementerio de Santa Ifigenia in Santiago de Cuba (p418).

④ Camilo Cienfuegos

The second most popular man in Cuba (after Fidel) at the time of the 1959 Revolution, ruggedly handsome Camilo Cienfuegos has since been overshadowed by the more marketable Che. But in Cuba his contribution to the defeat of Batista's army in the town of Yaguajay (p314) has never been forgotten.

⑤ Hatuey

The so-called Rebels' Rebel was an uppity Indian *cacique* (chief) who led Cuba's first anticolonial struggle against the Spanish in 1512. Captured and burned at the stake, his feisty independent spirit is remembered in the main square in Baracoa (p450).

Festivals

Through war, austerity, rationing and hardship, the Cubans have always retained their infectious joie de vivre. Even during the darkest days of the Special Period, the feisty festivals never stopped; a lasting testament to the country's capacity to put politics aside and get on with the very important business of living.

① Las Parrandas

To casual observers, Remedios (p285) suffers from cultural schizophrenia. For 99% of the year it's a sleepy colonial backwater. And then, on December 24, out come the fireworks, costumes, spirit and passion, as the locals show off in Las Parrandas.

② Santiago Carnival

Draw a line between New Orleans and Rio de Janeiro and chances are you'll pass pretty close to Santiago de Cuba (p407), the home of Cuba's colorful carnival and, in many minds, the country's most 'Caribbean' festival.

③ Jazz Festival

Not salsa, not rumba, but jazz. Cuba has an unnerving habit of taking any international musical genre and reinventing it for its own purposes. See the greats congregate in Havana (p127) for this annual festival of improvisation.

④ Fiesta de la Cubanía

Effervescent dancers shoulder up to cerebral chess players in Bayamo's (p386) weekly streetside shindig. Then there are the homemade snacks, the spit-roasted pork, and the quaintly surreal mechanical street organs.

⑤ Festival Internacional de Cine Pobre

Seaside Gibara (p370) – Cuba's antidote to Hollywood – is where mega-poor film makers come to see mega-good movies made on mega-low budgets. Hook up with some of Latin America's cash-strapped but talent-rich movie guerrillas and leave your teary Oscar acceptance speech at home.

Go Eco

During the lean years of the 1990s, the Cubans were ecologists by necessity. But as times changed, so did the public zeitgeist. With 10% of the country's land now under environmental protection, Cuba's eco-credentials have proved to be far from hollow as it faces up to the twin threats of rising tourist numbers and looming climate change.

❶ Isla de la Juventud
In Cuba all underwater roads lead to Punta Francés (p190), a national marine park where the protected coral, water clarity and stunning caves turn snorkelers into divers and divers into budding marine scientists.

❷ Baracoa
Isolated for centuries, the town of Baracoa (p449) sits behind the jungle-like curtain of the Cuchillas de Toa, a mini-Amazon of extraordinary endemism and a thousand different shades of green that beckons like a Cuban Shangri-La.

❸ Pinar del Río Province
Successful environmental projects were rare in the 1960s, which makes the achievements of Las Terrazas (p222) – founded in 1968 – all the more remarkable. Come to Pinar del Río province and meet the artisans and artists that make up Cuba's original 'new model village.'

❹ Península de Zapata
The Caribbean's largest swamp (p254) is a nirvana for fishermen, bird-watchers, tour-circuit escapees and weekend eco-warriors in search of Cuba's only dangerous animal, the snappy *Crocodylus rhombifer* (Cuban crocodile).

❺ Pico Turquino
In a country where the right to roam isn't quite as hallowed as the right to free health care and education, the trek up Cuba's highest mountain (p395) is a rare privilege. Hire a guide and make a side trip to Fidel's wartime jungle HQ on the way up.

Dreamy sea drive past the sun-kissed facades and splashing waves of the Malecón, Havana (p121)
CHRISTOPHER BAKER

Contents

On The Road 4

Viva Cuba 5

Destination Cuba 20

Getting Started 21

Events Calendar 26

Itineraries 28

History 34

The Culture 53

Music 65

Food & Drink 70

Environment 80

Cuba Outdoors 87

Havana 94
History 95
Orientation 96
DOWNTOWN HAVANA 97
Information 97
Dangers & Annoyances 108
Sights & Activities 108
Habana Vieja
Walking Tour 122
Centro Habana
Architectural Tour 123
Courses 125
Havana for Children 126
Tours 126
Sleeping 126
Eating 133
Drinking 140

Entertainment 142
Shopping 147
Getting There & Away 149
Getting Around 150
OUTER HAVANA 152
Playa & Marianao 152
Parque Lenin Area 161
Santiago de las
Vegas Area 164
Regla 164
Guanabacoa 166
San Francisco de Paula 167
Santa María del Rosario 167
Parque Histórico
Militar Morro-Cabaña 167
Casablanca 169
Cojímar Area 170
Playas del Este 170

Havana Province 176
Playa Jibacoa Area 178
Jaruco 180
Surgidero de Batabanó 180
San Antonio de los Baños 181
Bejucal 182
Artemisa 183
Mariel 183

Isla de la Juventud
(Special
Municipality) 185
ISLA DE LA JUVENTUD 186
Nueva Gerona 188
East of Nueva Gerona 193
South of Nueva Gerona 194
The Southern Military Zone 194
CAYO LARGO DEL SUR 195

Pinar del Río
Province 198
PINAR DEL RÍO AREA 200
Pinar del Río 200
Southwest of Pinar del Río 206
PENÍNSULA DE
GUANAHACABIBES 207
Parque Nacional Península
de Guanahacabibes 208

VALLE DE VIÑALES 210
Viñales 210
Parque Nacional Viñales 214
West of Viñales 217
Cayo Jutías 217
NORTHERN PINAR DEL RÍO 217
Puerto Esperanza 217
Cayo Levisa 218
Bahía Honda & Around 218
San Diego de los Baños & Around 219
Soroa 220
Las Terrazas 222

Matanzas Province 225
NORTHERN MATANZAS 227
Matanzas 227
Varadero 236
Cárdenas 251
PENÍNSULA DE ZAPATA 254
Central Australia & Around 255
Boca de Guamá 255
Gran Parque Natural Montemar 256
Playa Larga 257
Playa Girón 258

Cienfuegos Province 261
Cienfuegos 262
Rancho Luna 271
Castillo de Jagua 272
Jardín Botánico de Cienfuegos 272
El Nicho 272
The Caribbean Coast 273

Villa Clara Province 275
Santa Clara 277
Embalse Hanabanilla 285
Remedios 285
Caibarién 287
Cayerías del Norte 288
Baños de Elguea 290

Sancti Spíritus Province 291
Sancti Spíritus 293
Trinidad 298

Playa Ancón & Around 308
Valle de los Ingenios 310
Topes de Collantes 311
Northern Sancti Spíritus 314

Ciego de Ávila Province 316
Ciego de Ávila 318
Morón 323
North of Morón 324
Florencia 326
Cayo Coco 326
Cayo Guillermo 329

Camagüey Province 331
Camagüey 332
Florida 343
Sierra del Chorrillo 344
Guáimaro 344
Minas 344
Nuevitas 344
Cayo Sabinal 345
Playa Santa Lucía 345

Las Tunas Province 349
Las Tunas 351
Puerto Padre 356
Punta Covarrubias 356
Playas La Herradura, La Llanita & Las Bocas 357

Holguín Province 359
Holguín 361
Gibara 370
Playa Pesquero & Around 373
Guardalavaca 374
Banes 378
Birán 380
Sierra del Cristal 381
Cayo Saetía 381
Moa 382

Granma Province 384
Bayamo 386
Around Bayamo 392
Dos Ríos & Around 392
Yara 393
Gran Parque Nacional Sierra Maestra 393

Manzanillo 396
Media Luna 398
Niquero 398
Parque Nacional Desembarco del Granma 400
Pilón 401
Marea del Portillo 402

Santiago de Cuba Province 404
Santiago de Cuba 407
Siboney 429
La Gran Piedra 430
Parque Baconao 433
El Cobre 435
El Saltón 436
West of Santiago de Cuba 436
Chivirico & Around 437
El Uvero 437
Pico Turquino Area 438

Guantánamo Province 440
Guantánamo 442
Around Guantánamo US Naval Base 446
Zoológico de Piedras 447
South Coast 447
Punta de Maisí 447
Boca de Yumurí 447
Baracoa 449
Northwest of Baracoa 455
Parque Nacional Alejandro de Humboldt 456

Directory 458
Accommodation 458
Activities 461
Business Hours 461
Children 461
Climate Charts 462
Courses 462
Customs 463
Dangers & Annoyances 463
Embassies & Consulates 464
Food 464
Gay & Lesbian Travelers 464
Holidays 465
Insurance 465
Internet Access 465

Legal Matters 465
Maps 465
Money 466
Post 467
Shopping 467
Telephone 468
Time 469
Toilets 469
Tourist Information 469
Travelers with Disabilities 469
Visas & Tourist Cards 469
Volunteering 472
Women Travelers 472

Transport 473
GETTING THERE & AWAY 473
Entering the Country 473
Air 473
Sea 477
Tours 477
GETTING AROUND 477
Air 477

Bicycle 478
Bus 478
Car 479
Ferry 481
Hitchhiking 481
Local Transport 481
Tours 482
Train 482
Truck 483

Health 484
BEFORE YOU GO 484
Insurance 484
Medical Checklist 484
Internet Resources 485
Further Reading 485
IN TRANSIT 485
Deep Vein Thrombosis (DVT) 485
Jet Lag & Motion Sickness 485
IN CUBA 486
Availability & Cost of Health Care 486

Infectious Diseases 486
Traveler's Diarrhea 487
Environmental Hazards 488
Traveling with Children 489
Women's Health 489
Traditional Medicine 489

Language 490

Glossary 497

Behind the Scenes 501

Index 506

GreenDex 518

Map Legend 520

Regional Map Contents

CITY OF HAVANA pp99–106
HAVANA p177
PINAR DEL RÍO p199
MATANZAS p226
VILLA CLARA p276
CIENFUEGOS p262
SANCTI SPÍRITUS p292
CIEGO DE ÁVILA p317
ISLA DE LA JUVENTUD (SPECIAL MUNICIPALITY) p187
CAMAGÜEY p332
LAS TUNAS p350
HOLGUÍN pp360–1
GRANMA p385
SANTIAGO DE CUBA p406
GUANTÁNAMO p441

Destination Cuba

Caressed by the warm currents of the Caribbean and lashed by regular destructive hurricanes, Cuba is the ultimate travel contradiction; a dynamic mix of music, history and revolutionary politics that, at times, seems to have had the life sucked out of it by 50 years of austere, unbending socialism. As much as you'll love it (and it's hard not to), there will be occasions when it baffles and frustrates you, raising both your passion and your ire.

To the outside world, life in Cuba has changed little since the 1960s. Castro's isolated island nation remains one of the world's last great Cold War anachronisms, a stubborn contrarian caught in an ideological no-man's-land between an ever-powerful USA on one hand and a long defunct USSR on the other.

But, while gasping 'yank tanks' still splutter unhealthily around the streets of Santiago and Havana, Cuba has been quietly dusting off its communist cobwebs for more than a decade. Aided by a growing medical and pharmaceutical sector and bolstered by a 'new left tide' in Latin American politics, Cuba is no longer the international basket case that it once was.

The first signs of a thaw came in the early 1990s when the post–Cold War economic meltdown forced the Castro administration into making some important free-market concessions. Allowing limited private enterprise and opening up the floodgates to tourism, the Cubans were able to let out their homes to foreigners and mingle freely with visitors from the capitalist West.

Progress was slow at first, but by the mid-2000s subtle signs of the new economic buoyancy were beginning to appear. A veteran of the Special Period returning home today after a 10-year exile would detect a plethora of subtle but important changes. There's a greater choice of consumer goods in the city's shops, the expanding waistlines of the better-off Habaneros and – most noticeably – the traffic: in the late '90s you could have quite conceivably sat down and had your lunch in the middle of Havana's Malecón sea drive; today, it takes a good five minutes to even cross it.

On inheriting the presidency from his brother in February 2008, Raúl Castro initiated a handful of progressive but largely symbolic reforms. In May, the Cuban government passed a law that allowed its citizens access to all tourist hotels (they had previously been barred from all but the cheapest). The same month the Cubans were also legally permitted to own cell phones, buy various electronic goods and own larger tracts of land in private farms.

The Cubans greeted the inauguration of Barack Obama to the White House in January 2009 with guarded optimism. Cautiously they envisaged, if not an immediate end to the embargo, then at least the start of some long-overdue dialogue. But with the country battered by three hurricanes inside two months and bloodied by the global economic downturn, the long-awaited celebrations to mark the 50th anniversary of the Revolution in January 2009 turned out to be muted and low-key.

After half a century of on-off austerity, the Cubans have grown wearily accustomed to false dawns. Placing their hopes in new leaders on both sides of the Straits of Florida, the optimists are hoping that this is not another one.

FAST FACTS

Population: 11.3 million

Area: 110,860 sq km

GNP per capita: US$12,700

Life expectancy: 76 (men); 80 (women)

Adult HIV/AIDS prevalence rate: 0.01%

Ethnicity: 65% white, 24% mixed, 10% black, 1% Chinese

Number of cell phones: 198,000

Total railways: 4226km

First Cuban heart transplant performed: 1985

Ranking on World Press Freedom Index: 169th

Getting Started

Cuba is a unique country with many distinct characteristics. Travel here not only requires a passport, money and a good sturdy rucksack; it also requires flexibility, creativity, good humor, patience and a healthy sense of adventure. Speaking Spanish, though not a prerequisite, is undoubtedly a huge advantage, and will allow you to travel further and dig deeper than the average tourist.

Linguistic dexterity aside, Cuba remains an easy country to travel in and there are few barriers stopping you from wandering around pretty much how and as you choose. A slight loosening of the screws since Raúl Castro took office in February 2008 has allowed Cubans access to cell phones and entry into tourist hotels, meaning interaction with the locals is now simpler and often surprisingly candid.

Legislation under the Bush administration tightened the rules governing travel of US citizens to Cuba, though early signs from the Obama camp suggest many (if not all) of these limitations could soon be lifted. The thaw began in April 2009 when President Obama signed a law permitting unlimited travel to the island for Cuban-American families visiting relatives; they had previously been restricted to one visit every three years. For more information on legal travel to the island check out the Center for Cuban Studies' website at www.cubaupdate.org. For additional advice see the boxed text, p474.

WHEN TO GO

The best time to go to Cuba is between December and April, after the lashing rains of the hurricane season and before the hot and sticky discomfort of the scorching summer months. The downside is that during this period – the high season or *temporada alta* as it is called in Cuba – accommodation prices are hiked up by about 20% (see p458). You'll also find the country a little more crowded at this time, particularly in the resort areas, although, off the beaten track, it is unlikely that you will ever have trouble finding a room in a casa particular.

See Climate Charts (p462) for more information.

Weather aside, Cuba has few other hurdles for visitors. Culture vultures should keep a close eye on the annual arts calendar (p26) for festivals and other events; baseball fans will certainly not want to miss the postseason, which runs from April to May; and political junkies may want to catch important days in the socialist calendar, particularly Labor Day (May 1) and Day of the National Rebellion (July 26).

COSTS & MONEY

For seasoned budget travelers Cuba can be a bit of a financial shock. There's no network of dirt-cheap backpacker hostels here and not a lot of bargaining potential. In fact, compared with, say, Guatemala or Peru, you could feel yourself staring at a veritable financial conundrum with little or no room to maneuver. Furthermore, there is a tendency in Cuba to herd all foreign visitors around in one state-controlled tourist sector. Follow this well-trodden path of organized excursions and prepackaged cultural 'experiences' at your peril. The costs will soon add up.

With a little guile and a certain amount of resilience, however, it needn't all be overpriced hotel rooms and wallet-whacking credit-card bills. Underneath the surface (and contrary to what a lot of tour reps will tell you), Cuba has a whole guidebook's worth of cheaper alternatives. On the accommodation front, the vibrant casa particular scene can cut costs by more than half, while do-it-yourself grocery purchasing and an ability to muck in with the resourceful locals on trucks, buses, trains and bicycles can give you access to a whole new world of interesting food and transport opportunities.

For those more interested in service and comfort, prices are equally variable, from CUC$50 per person at Varadero's cheapest all-inclusive to CUC$200 per person at a swanky Playa Esmeralda resort. If you're interested in getting away to the beach, prearranged air and hotel packages from Canada and Europe can be absurdly affordable (less than US$500 for a week in Varadero from Toronto) and seasoned Cuba travelers often take these deals because it works out cheaper than just the airfare alone. Most resorts and hotels offer big discounts for children under 12 years of age; it's worth asking about. Children also travel half-price on Víazul buses, and many museums and attractions offer a 50% discount for kids. See the Transport chapter for further information on travel agencies (p474) who can arrange travel and tours to Cuba.

As with most islands, Cuba struggles with food supply and prices reflect this – especially if you crave something imported such as canned corn or nuts. Paladares and casas particulares usually offer good value, with monstrous meal portions (no rationing here), including a pork chop, rice and beans, salad and french fries, costing around CUC$8. Add a couple of beers, dessert and a tip and you're looking at CUC$12 (or more). Drinking is considerably more affordable than eating, with a strong mojito costing CUC$2 (in a non-Hemingway-esque bar) and a fresh juice or beer CUC$1.

For tourists to Cuba there are many transport options and as many prices to go with them. From Havana to Santiago de Cuba, for example (a trip of 861km), you will pay around CUC$114 to fly one-way with Cubana, from CUC$50 to CUC$62 to take the train and approximately CUC$52 to do the journey on a Víazul bus. Rental cars are expensive – bank on CUC$70 a day for a small Fiat to CUC$220 a day for a convertible Audi.

There is, of course, the double economy, whereby Convertibles and Cuban pesos circulate simultaneously. In theory, tourists are only supposed to use Convertibles, but in practice, there is nothing to stop you walking into a Cadeca (change booth) and swapping your Convertibles into *moneda nacional* (Cuban pesos). With an exchange rate of 24 pesos per Convertible, there are fantastic saving opportunities with pesos if you're willing to sacrifice a little (or a lot!) in quality, service and/or comfort. For example, a pizza in a fast-food joint costs CUC$1, but street pizzas cost seven pesos (less than CUC$0.25). Pesos are also useful for urban transport and some cultural activities (such as movies), but almost everything else is sold to foreigners only in Convertibles: the symphony or theater, interprovincial transport and taxis are but a few examples where Cubans will pay in pesos, but you won't.

Before you become indignant about the marked price differential, remember that the double economy cuts both ways: while Cubans may sometimes pay less for the same services as foreigners, they also have to stand in line, frequent ration shops and stay in the kind of fly-blown substandard hotels that most foreigners wouldn't poke a stick at. Furthermore, Cubans (who earn between 200 and 400 pesos – or CUC$8 and CUC$15 – a month) have to survive in an entirely different economy from outsiders; a financial minefield where access to valuable Convertibles is a daily crapshoot between tips, personal guile and who you know.

Since April 2009 Cuban-Americans traveling legally to Cuba in order to visit relatives have faced no financial restrictions (they were limited to spending US$50 per day under the Bush administration).

HOW MUCH?

Room in a casa particular
CUC$15-35

Museum entrance
CUC$1-5

Cross-island train ticket
CUC$62

Bike rental per day
CUC$3-5

Internet use per hour
CUC$6

See also Lonely Planet
index, inside front cover.

DON'T LEAVE HOME WITHOUT...

You'll quickly find that basic commodities such as toothpaste, toilet paper and soap are widely available in Cuba. However, condoms, aspirin, dental floss, sunscreen, insect repellant, contact-lens solution, moisturizing lotion and reading material in any language besides Spanish definitely aren't.

Clothing-wise come prepared. Aside from the ubiquitous Che Guevara T-shirts, fashionable beach wear is overpriced or low quality. You might also want to bring your own snorkel gear. A flashlight will be handy during occasional blackouts. An alarm clock for predawn bus departures, a universal plug for sinks and tubs and a little washing powder are all useful. People staying in campismos will need a sheet as linen isn't always provided.

Aside from a scant supply of biscuits and soggy sandwiches, take-out fare is hard to find. Gatorade powder, granola and protein bars, nuts, dried fruit, peanut butter and trail mix provide energy and a break from the vicious pizza/ice-cream/fried-chicken cycle of appetizers. See the boxed text, p76, for more food advice.

Money-wise, your best bet is to bring cash, preferably in Canadian dollars, euros or pound sterling (avoid US dollars as the cost of changing them into Convertibles is a lot higher). A credit card will provide a good emergency backup and traveler's checks from non-American banks are usually acceptable. Unfortunately, few (if any) foreign debit cards will work in Cuban ATMs. For more information see the Directory, p466.

TRAVELING RESPONSIBLY

Cubans are pretty forward-thinking when it comes to the environment. What in the West would be viewed as conscientious eco-practices, are often everyday necessities here (general recycling, public transport, locally grown produce), meaning finding excuses to 'go green' are easy. While hiring a car might make life simpler in some areas, getting a bus or train will lower your footprint and often be more fun. Many of Cuba's newer Chinese-made buses have lower emissions and are far cleaner that the fume-belching monsters of yore.

Staying in casas particulares is a great way to taste the local food, and you can be sure that everything your casa owner cooks will have been produced or reared locally, probably within a few kilometers of your plate. The resort hotels are a different matter, and the exotic out-of-season fruit and vegetables that you enjoy at your fantastic dinnertime buffet will have undoubtedly been flown in from Europe or North America.

Real eco-resorts are in their infancy in Cuba, the two main exceptions being Hotel Moka (p224) in Las Terrazas and El Saltón (p436) in Santiago de Cuba. Many of the newer places in Cayo Coco and Guardalavaca, however, have been built with respect for the local environment and incorporate some sustainable practices.

Undertaking visits to national parks and Unesco Biosphere Reserves is a great way to learn and understand about Cuba's environmental practices and share the passion of its forward-thinking people. For more details see p33.

TRAVEL LITERATURE

Zoë Bran's *Enduring Cuba* (2002), an illuminating and beautifully written book, conveys the daily shortages, slowdowns and *lucha* (struggle) of the Cuban reality with a keen eye for detail. Isadora Tatlin's *Cuba Diaries* (2002) takes an equally eye-opening look at a similarly thought-provoking and contradictory subject.

Even better on the travelogue scene is *Trading with the Enemy: A Yankee Travels through Castro's Cuba* (1992), by Tom Miller, a rich feast of Cuban lore gleaned during eight months of perceptive travel in Cuba. It may be the best travel book about Cuba ever written. Christopher Baker provides

TOP PICKS

CUBA

Havana

Bahamas

CUBA ON THE CHEAP

While ostensibly expensive, Cuba's dual economy ensures that cheaper treats are hiding just beneath the radar – and they're usually more sustainable options too. If you're armed with guile, patience and an open-minded sense of adventure, the following only-in-Cuba innovations are yours for the taking. Check out the Directory (p458) for more information.

- **Amarillos** Line up with the transit officials and pay five centavos to travel 50km
- **Casas particulares** Go local, stay in private rooms, and save money
- **Campismos** Go even more local, stay in rural huts, and save even more money
- **Agropecuarios** Buy local at free-enterprise markets and do your own cooking

- **Cadecas** Swap your Convertibles in the change booths and enter the peso economy
- **Peso pizza** It's not Italian but it's got cheese and tomatoes, and it's cheap
- **Quiet towns** No tourists = lower prices; hit Las Tunas, Gibara, Puerto Esperanza…
- **Spanish lessons** *Se habla español* and suddenly the prices start to drop

FAMOUS NON-CUBAN 'CUBANS'

Relocating to Cuba was an important career move for many of history's famous expats. Make a note of the following names and look out for their colorful legacies as you troll your way around the country (and through this book). See also History (p34) and Culture (p53) chapters.

- **Ernest Hemingway** They loved him so much they named a marina after him
- **Graham Greene** Observant Brit who brought the seediness of 1950s Havana to life
- **Winston Churchill** WWII leader who did his apprenticeship as a journalist in Cuba during the 1895–98 Independence War
- **Diego Maradona** History's greatest soccer player was once treated for cocaine addiction in Holguín
- **Che Guevara** The most famous Argentine (and non-Cuban Cuban) on the planet

- **La Rusa** The Russian émigré from Baracoa who gave Fidel US$25,000 to buy more rifles
- **Meyer Lansky** A Mafia boss who ruled Havana as his personal fiefdom
- **Hatuey** Cuba's first rebel was a Taíno mercenary from Hispaniola with an axe to grind – literally
- **Máximo Gómez** A great Independence War general and native of the Dominican Republic
- **Alexander von Humboldt** The second 'discoverer' of Cuba was an eminent German naturalist

SEMINAL CUBAN MOVIES

They haven't won any Oscars (yet), but cutting-edge cinematic creativity has kept Cuban movies at the forefront of Latin American culture for decades. For more details see p61.

- **Fresa y Chocolate** Robbed of an Oscar in1995, but who cares – it's still brilliant
- **Memorias de Subdesarrollo** In which Tomás Gutiérrez Alea tests the boundaries of Fidel's censorship police
- **Lucía** Humberto Solás' made-in-Gibara classic that inspired a film festival
- **El Benny** The Barbarian of Rhythm in glorious Technicolor

- **Soy Cuba** The director's choice, this 1964 groundbreaker apparently influenced Scorsese
- **Viva Cuba** Award-winning road movie with kids
- **Una Mujer, Un Hombre, Una Ciudad** Obscure, art-house flick about postrevolutionary life in Nuevitas

a slightly different take on the *período especial* (Special Period; Cuba's new economic reality post-1991) in *Mi Moto Fidel* (2001), a book inspired by a cross-island motorcycling odyssey undertaken during the mid-1990s.

Reminiscent of the uncompromising, in-your-face style of Irvine Welsh or Charles Bukowski, Pedro Juan Gutierrez *Dirty Havana Trilogy* (2000) is a fascinating, if sometimes disturbing insider look at life in Havana during the dark days of the Special Period. Carlos Eire's *Waiting for Snow in Havana* (2003), meanwhile, is a nostalgic account of boyhood during the tumultuous days of the Cuban Revolution.

In the literary field, classics include Hemingway's Nobel Prize–winning *Old Man and the Sea* (1952), and his less-heralded but equally compelling *Islands in the Stream* (1970). Graham Greene captures the prerevolutionary essence of Havana in *Our Man in Havana* (1958), while Elmore Leonard documents the events surrounding the explosion of the battleship USS *Maine* and the Cuban-Spanish-American War with thrill-a-minute panache in *Cuba Libre* (2000).

Biographies of Che Guevara abound, although there's no contest when it comes to size, quality and enduring literary legacy. Jon Lee Anderson's *Che Guevara: a Revolutionary Life* (1997) is one of the most groundbreaking biographies ever written, and during the research for the book Mr Anderson initiated the process by which Guevara's remains were found and dug up in Bolivia before being returned to Cuba in 1997. Unauthorized biographies of Castro are equally authoritative: try Volker Skierka's *Fidel Castro: a Biography* (2000) or Tad Szulc's exhaustive *Fidel: A Critical Portrait* (1986). By far the best to date is *My Life: Fidel Castro* (2006), a spoken-word testimony catalogued by Spanish journalist Ignacio Ramonet who spent more than 100 hours interviewing the Cuban leader between 2003 and 2005. It provides a fascinating insight into Castro's life in his own (many) words.

INTERNET RESOURCES

AfroCuba Web (www.afrocubaweb.com) Everything imaginable on Cuban culture, with worldwide concert listings, dance and drum workshops, seminars and encounters in Cuba.

BBC (www.bbc.co.uk) One of the best sites for up-to-date Cuba news stories; BBC Cuba correspondent Michael Voss uncovers some classic journalistic gems. Type 'Cuba' into the search engine on the main page to reveal what's on offer.

Boomers Abroad (www.boomersabroad.com) Choose the Cuba icon on the main page for links galore on everything from caving to Che Guevara.

Cubacasas.net (www.cubacasas.net) Ostensibly a Canadian website containing information, photos and contact details for casas particulares, this colorful website is one of the most comprehensive and consistently accurate sources of Cuba info on the web. There are full versions in English and French.

Granma Internacional (www.granma.cu) Official newspaper of the Cuban Communist Party; news from Cuba in five languages.

LonelyPlanet.com (www.lonelyplanet.com) Summaries on traveling to Cuba, the Thorn Tree bulletin board, travel news and links to useful travel resources elsewhere on the web.

Events Calendar

The Cubans are never shy of holding a fiesta, and through revolution and recession the country's social calendar has always included its fair share of cerebral and celebratory happenings. Indeed, many of Cuba's annual get-togethers are internationally renowned cultural extravaganzas that draw in movers and shakers from around the globe.

JANUARY

DÍA DE LA LIBERACIÓN   Jan 1
As well as seeing in the New Year with roast pork and a bottle of rum, Cubans celebrate the triumph of the Revolution, the anniversary of Fidel's 1959 victory (see p43).

FEBRUARY

FERIA INTERNACIONAL DEL LIBRO
First held in 1930, the International Book Fare is headquartered in Havana's Fortaleza de San Carlos de la Cabaña (p168), but it later goes on the road to other cities. Highlights include book presentations, special readings and the prestigious Casa de las Américas prize.

MARCH

FIESTA DE LA TORONJA
Famous for its citrus plantations, Isla de la Juventud celebrates the annual grapefruit harvest with this animated excuse for a party in Nueva Gerona (p190) where the *guachi* (grapefruit schnapps) flows freely.

APRIL

FESTIVAL INTERNACIONAL DE CINE POBRE
Gibara's celebration of low- and no-budget cinema (see boxed text, p372) has been an annual event since 2003 when it was inaugurated by Cuban film director Humberto Sales. Events include film-showing workshops and discussions on movie-making with limited resources.

BIENAL INTERNACIONAL DEL HUMOR
You can't be serious! Cuba's unique humor festival takes place in San Antonio de los Baños in out-of-the-way Havana province. Headquartered at the celebrated Museo del Humor (p182), talented scribblers try to outdo each other by drawing ridiculous caricatures. Hilarious!

MAY

DÍA DE LOS TRABAJADORES   May 1
Hundreds of thousands of flag-waving Cubans converge on Havana's Plaza de la Revolución (p119) on Labor Day to witness military parades and listen to impassioned annual 'worker's day' speeches. It's a fantastic spectacle, even if you're lukewarm about the polemics.

ROMERÍAS DE MAYO   1st week of May
This religious festival (p366) takes place in the city of Holguín and culminates with a procession to the top of the city's emblematic Loma de la Cruz, a small shrine atop a 275m hill.

JUNE

JORNADA CUCALAMBEANA   late Jun
Cuba's celebration of country music and the witty 10-line *décimas* (stanzas) that go with it takes place about 3km outside unassuming Las Tunas at Motel Cornito (p353), the former home of erstwhile country-music king Juan Fajardo 'El Cucalambé.'

FIESTAS SANJUANERAS   last weekend of Jun
This feisty carnival in Trinidad (p303) is a showcase for the local *vaqueros* (cowboys), who gallop with their horses through the narrow cobbled streets.

JULY

DÍA DE LA REBELDÍA NACIONAL   Jul 26
On this day the Cubans 'celebrate' Fidel Castro's failed 1953 attack on Santiago's Moncada Barracks (see boxed text, p416). The event is a national holiday and – in the days when Castro enjoyed better health – the loquacious leader was famous for making five-hour speeches. Expect *un poco* (a little) politics and *mucho* (much) eating, drinking and being merry.

CARNAVAL DE SANTIAGO
DE CUBA   end of Jul
Arguably the biggest and most colorful carnival in the Caribbean, the famous Santiago shindig (p421) is a riot of floats, dancers, rum, rumba and more. Come and join in the very *caliente* (hot) action.

AUGUST

FESTIVAL INTERNACIONAL
'HABANA HIP-HOP'
Organized by the Asociación Hermanos Saíz – a youth arm of Unión de Escritores y Artistas de Cuba (Uneac; Union of Cuban Writers and Artists) – the annual Havana Hip-Hop Festival is a chance for the island's young musical creators to improvise and swap ideas (see p68).

SEPTEMBER

FESTIVAL INTERNACIONAL DE MÚSICA
BENNY MORÉ
The Barbarian of Rhythm is remembered in this biannual celebration of his suave music, headquartered in the singer's small birth town of Santa Isabel de las Lajas in Cienfuegos province (see boxed text, p270).

FIESTA DE NUESTRA SEÑORA DE
LA CARIDAD   Sep 8
Religious devotees from around Cuba partake in a pilgrimage to the Basílica de Nuestra Señora del Cobre (p435) near Santiago to honor Cuba's venerated patron saint.

OCTOBER

FESTIVAL INTERNACIONAL DE BALLET
DE LA HABANA
Hosted by the Cuban National Ballet (p64), this annual festival brings together dance companies, ballerinas and a mixed audience of foreigners and Cubans for a week of expositions, galas, and classical and contemporary ballet. It has been held in even-numbered years since its inception in 1960.

NOVEMBER

FIESTAS DE LOS BANDAS ROJO Y AZUL
Considered one of the most important manifestations of Cuban *campesino* (country person) culture, this esoteric fiesta in Ciego de Ávila settlement of Majagua splits the town into two teams (red and blue) who compete against each other in boisterous dancing and music contests (see boxed text, p320).

MARABANA   late Nov
The popular Havana marathon draws between 2000 and 3000 competitors from around the globe. It's a two-lap course though there are also races for half-marathon, 10km and 5km distances.

FESTIVAL INTERNACIONAL DE JAZZ
Intrinsically linked to Cuban jazz maestro, Chucho Valdés (p68), the International Jazz Festival is staged in the Karl Marx, Mella and Amadeo Roldán theaters in Havana, and draws in top figures from around the world for some truly memorable concerts.

DECEMBER

FESTIVAL INTERNACIONAL DEL NUEVO
CINE LATINOAMERICANO
The internationally renowned film festival (www.habanafilmfestival.com) held in cinemas across Havana illustrates Cuba's growing influence in Latin American cinema worldwide (see p61).

PROCESIÓN DE SAN LÁZARO   Dec 17
Every year on this day Cubans descend en masse on the venerated Santuario de San Lázaro (p164) in Santiago de las Vegas, on the outskirts of Havana. Some come on bloodied knees, others walk barefoot for kilometers to exorcize evil spirits and pay off debts for miracles granted.

LAS PARRANDAS   Dec 24
A firework frenzy that takes place every Christmas Eve in Remedios (p285) in Villa Clara province, Las Parrandas sees the town divide into two teams who compete against each other to see who can come up with the most colorful floats and the loudest *bangs!*

LAS CHARANGAS DE BEJUCAL   Dec 24
Didn't like Las Parrandas? Then try Las Charangas (p182), Havana province's cacophonous alternative to the firework fever further east. The town splits into the exotically named Espino de Oro (Golden Thorn) and Ceiba de Plata (Silver Ceiba).

Itineraries
CLASSIC ROUTES

CULTURE VULTURE
Two to Three Weeks / Havana to Baracoa

Cuba has certain rites of passage, cultural must-sees which condense the country's confusing kaleidoscope of varied attractions into one succinct, easy-to-understand whole. This tour reigns in the highlights.

Say a big warm *buenos días* to Cuba in **Havana** (p94) with its museums, forts, theaters and rum. Pinar del Río is tobacco country and its scenic highlight is **Viñales** (p210), where farmers grow the stuff with skill and *amor* (love). On most itineraries these days is French-flavored **Cienfuegos** (p262), an architectural monument to 19th-century neoclassicism. A couple of hours down the road is colonial **Trinidad** (p298) with more museums per head than anywhere else in Cuba. **Santa Clara** (p277) is a rite of passage for Che pilgrims but also great for smart private rooms and an upbeat nightlife. Further east, **Camagüey** (p332) is a confusing maze of Catholic churches and giant *tinajones* (clay pots). You can bypass Las Tunas, but you'd be foolish to miss gritty **Holguín** (p361) which is about as *real* as Cuba gets. Laid-back **Bayamo** (p386) is where the Revolution was first ignited, but the cultural nexus of **Santiago de Cuba** (p407) was where it was conceived. Save the best till last with a long but by no means arduous journey over the hills and far away to **Baracoa** (p449) for coconuts, chocolate and other tropical treats.

BEACHES   Two Weeks to One Month / Playa Santa María to Playa Paraíso

From the capital, colorful **Playa Santa María** (p170) is the most easily accessible beach, an exuberant mélange of makeshift fish barbecues, beach-volleyball tournaments and wandering troubadours. Tracking west it's a toss-up between low-key **Cayo Levisa** (p218) and even lower-key **Cayo Jutías** (p217), so why not throw the dice away and hit both. There's a reason why Varadero boasts more tourists than any other resort in the Caribbean and 20km-long diamond-dust **Playa Varadero** (p236) might well be it. Few beaches adorn Cuba's swampy south coast, making platinum blond **Playa Ancón** (p308) all the more gorgeous. Of the few remaining public beaches on Villa Clara's Cayerías del Norte, **Playa Las Salinas** (p289) is a windswept classic. Guarding the biggest sand dunes on the archipelago, **Playa Pilar** (p329) is the one Cuban beach worthy of a 'world top 10' listing. **Playa Santa Lucía** (p345) competes with Varadero as the island's longest beach (20km plus), but beats it hands down on the diving front. Postcard-perfect **Playa Pesquero** (p373) in Guardalavaca is paradise found for many, with a 933-room, five-star resort to match. White sand? What white sand? Granma's southern coast is more Big Sur than Palm Beach, but the wildness of the setting adds romanticism to an evening walk on the beach at **Marea del Portillo** (p402). It rains at least half the year on **Playa Maguana** (p456), but when the sun breaks out, so do the locals, with their swimming costumes, snorkels and Baracoan sense of fun. If you'd rather leave your swimming costume at home, you'll need to jump on a flight to **Playa Paraíso** (p196) on the tiny island of Cayo Largo del Sur, where Cuba's only nudist colony basks in almost perfect seclusion.

Beaches are the lifeblood of Cuba, providing the country with its innate beauty and its premier source of tourist income. Come and see what all the fuss is all about on this sandy sojourn around some of the archipelago's best-served and most secluded coastal spots.

ROADS LESS TRAVELED

CUBA THROUGH THE BACK DOOR

One Month / Playas del Este
to Siboney

These little-known towns and villages have two things in common: a handful of legal casas particulares and a dearth of regular visitors. If you don't mind roughing it on local transport, conversing in barely intelligible Spanish or reading your Lonely Planet by torchlight, read on.

Boycott Havana and head east to the beaches of **Playas del Este** (p170), where private houses and picturesque sunsets abound, or leapfrog straight to **Santa Cruz del Norte** (p178), a worthwhile base camp situated within hiking distance of the golden sands of Playa Jibacoa. Switch west along the beautiful (and deserted) northern coast route to **Puerto Esperanza** (p217) for a few days of turning off, tuning in and dropping out before pressing on to **Sandino** (p207), within striking distance of María la Gorda. The Bahía de Cochinos (Bay of Pigs) area is awash with decent casas particulares, none better than those found on shimmering **Playa Larga** (p257), and you can easily work your way along the coast from here to **Rancho Luna** (p271) and **La Boca** (p309), where assorted private houses offer up an ideal antidote to the tourist hotels of Cienfuegos and Trinidad. The long road east presents ample opportunities to avoid the city hustlers in Ciego de Ávila and Camagüey. Check out unsung **Florida** (p343) with its archetypal sugar mills, or bustling **Guáimaro** (p344) with its groundbreaking constitutional history. Turn left in **Las Tunas** (p351) and detour to the remote northern beach 'resort' of **Playa Las Bocas** (p357), where you'll see no one but a handful of ingratiating casa particular owners. Homing in on Holguín province, check out the pretty town of **Banes** (p378) as a launching pad for Guardalavaca before making one last fling down to Santiago de Cuba, where peace and tranquility await you in sleepy **Siboney** (p429).

THE MUSICAL TOUR   Two Weeks to One Month / Havana to Baracoa

Ease in gently at Havana's **Iglesia de San Francisco de Asís** (p111), where refined
classical music echoes eerily through the cloisters of a converted 18th-century
church. Next shimmy a couple of blocks west to **Mesón de la Flota** (p128), where
rasping vocals and furious flamenco invites listeners to discover the elusive
spirit of what aficionados call *duende* (a term used in flamenco to describe
the ultimate climax to the music). For something more authentically Cuban,
visit Havana's **Casa de la Música** (p144) in El Centro, or forge your way west to
venerable Viñales, home of the *guajira* (a type of flamenco) and location of
the spanking new **Centro Cultural Polo Montañez** (p213). In unsung Matanzas, live
rumba performances reverberate in **Plaza de la Vigía** (p230) while, an hour or
two further on, in Santa Clara's **Club Mejunje** (p283), loose rhythms and heavy
bass mix in one of Cuba's most vibrant and underrated cultural institutions.
Trinidad has *trova* (traditional poetic singing) and *son* (Cuba's popular
music) and a lot more besides in **Palenque de los Congos Reales** (p307), while
the long journey east to Santiago's spit-and-sawdust **Casa de las Tradiciones**
(p426) is a musical homecoming, akin to sailing down the Mississippi to
New Orleans. With the hangover starting to bite, tie in Haitian drums and
voodoo rhythms in Guantánamo's **Tumba Francesa Pompadour** (p445) before
heading over the Sierra Puril Mountains for the grand finale: a frenetic all-out
Cuban knees-up at the amiable **Casa de la Trova** (p454) in Baracoa.

Cuban music is
famous the world
over, but to break
free of the *Buena
Vista Social Club*
ditties that have
become the staple
diet in Cuban res-
taurants, you have
to wander off the
beaten track. This
compact itinerary
details some of
Cuba's eclectic
music venues.

TAILORED TRIPS

BOOK TOUR

Start off in Havana in the **Hotel Sevilla** (p131), which Graham Green borrowed as a setting in his comedic novel *Our Man in Havana*. Head east next through **Centro Habana** (p114), the seedy, mildewed quarter disturbingly brought to life by 'dirty realist' author Pedro Juan Gutiérrez in *Dirty Havana Trilogy*. Stop at the **Monumento a las Víctimas del Maine** (p121) to recall the historical events chronicled so eloquently by Elmore Leonard in *Cuba Libre*. Don't leave town without first calling in at **Uneac** (p98) and **La Casa de las Américas** (p98), where bookish intellectuals trade tall stories. Take a beach break next on **Cayo Guillermo** (p329), a fishing key to which Hemingway paid homage in *Islands in the Stream*. South and a little east is **Camagüey** (p332), birthplace of Cuban national poet and Uneac founder Nicolás Guillén. Low-key **Gibara** (p370) produced and inspired Guillermo Cabrera Infante, the Cuban Joyce whose *Tres Tristes Tigres* is often called 'the Spanish Ulysses.' **Dos Ríos** (p392) provides one of the most poignant monuments to the ubiquitous José Martí – writer, poet, sage and politician. In Santiago de Cuba you'll find the **Casa Natal de José María de Heredia** (p413), another classy Cuban poet. Close the book in **Baracoa** (p449), the magical town that provided both the characters and backdrop for Alejo Carpentier's classic *La Consagración de la Primavera*.

BIRD-WATCHING CUBA

With your binoculars polished, sally forth into the verdant **Valle de Viñales** (p210) where, with a bit of patience and the help of the locals, you can catch glimpses of Cuban bullfinches or chirpy Cuban peewees. The **Península de Guanahacabibes** (p207) has virgin beaches and dense flora that attracts everything from tody flycatchers to migratory ruby-throated hummingbirds. Don't overlook the **Sierra del Rosario Reserve** (p223), where it's possible to spot up to 50% of Cuba's endemic birds, including the often elusive *carpinteros*. The **Gran Parque Natural Montemar** (p256) is a huge protected area encompassing Cuba's largest wetland. Wait around for a few hours (or days) and you might see a *zunzún* – the world's smallest bird. In **Topes de Collantes** (p311) keep an eye out for the bright red, white and blue *tocororo* (Cuba's national bird), then venture into **Cayo Romano** (p347) to get a look at some of the island's more than 30,000 flamingos. **La Hacienda la Belén Reserve** (p344) near Camagüey promises glimpses of Cuban parakeets, giant kingbirds and Antillean palm swifts. While the journey might appear long and the hiking arduous, no Cuban birding adventure is complete without a visit to the almost virgin **Parque Nacional Alejandro de Humboldt** (p456) for viewings of Cuban Amazon parrots, hook-billed kites and – unlikely but not impossible – ivory-billed woodpeckers last spotted here in the early 1980s.

ISLANDS IN THE ARCHIPELAGO

Hotel-free **Cayo Jutías** (p217) is the highlight of the Archipelago de los Colorados, the necklace of quiet keys that stretches west from Havana. If you need a room for the night, catch the boat to **Cayo Levisa** (p218), its more developed but equally beautiful eastern sibling. Leapfrogging Havana, you'll have to go upmarket on **Cayo Ensenachos** (p290), where a plush new resort has embellished (and privatized) one of Cuba's most stunning beaches. Three keys on the huge Sabana-Camagüey archipelago are linked to the mainland by a massive causeway. **Cayo Guillermo** (p329) plays heavily on its Hemingway connections; **Cayo Coco** (p326), Cuba's fourth-largest island, is replete with large resorts; while uninhabited **Cayo Paredón Grande** (p327) guards a solitary lighthouse, a couple of fine beaches and plenty of fishing possibilities. Heading east on another causeway to **Cayo Romano** (p347), the tourists are replaced by flamingos, mosquitoes and plenty of interesting birdlife. **Cayo Sabinal** (p345) with its lighthouse and old Spanish fort is a favorite of many, while tiny **Cayo Saetía** (p381) has a safari park with exotic African fauna. For real Robinson Crusoe–like isolation you'll need to charter a trip to **Jardines de la Reina** (p330), a chain of 600 uninhabited keys where the only accommodation is on a floating hotel. It's not particularly Cuban, but tourists love **Cayo Largo del Sur** (p195) for its visiting turtles and Cuba's only nudist beach.

PARKS & RESERVES

On the island's western tip, the **Parque Nacional Península de Guanahacabibes** (p208) is home to crabs, turtles, archaeological sites and not many humans. Further east but also in Pinar del Río province, the karstic, cave-flecked **Parque Nacional Viñales** (p214) is a Unesco World Heritage Site that exhibits the fine art of Cuban tobacco-growing. Pinar's third Unesco site is the **Sierra del Rosario Reserve** (p223), an oft-lauded biosphere and site of the country's most successful environmental reclamation project. Cuba's biggest protected area, the expansive **Grand Parque Natural Montemar** (p256), is also the Caribbean's largest swamp and ideal for bird-watching, fly-fishing and spotting the odd sunbathing crocodile. **Topes de Collantes** (p311) in the Sierra Escambray is one of the island's most accessible and popular protected parks and has a plethora of waterfalls and junglelike trails. To the north, **Parque Nacional Caguanes** (p314) is a little-visited mix of mangrove and marine park that sits amid the Buenavista Unesco Biosphere Reserve. **Parque Nacional Desembarco del Granma** (p400) is a collection of plunging marine terraces where Fidel Castro mistakenly landed aboard his stricken yacht in 1956. Nearby, Cuba reaches its highest point in the **Gran Parque Nacional Sierra Maestra** (p393), home of 1972m Pico Turquino. **Parque Baconao** (p433) is a strange mix of ruined coffee haciendas, sheltered beaches and surreal stone dinosaurs. Things get clearer in the **Parque Nacional Alejandro de Humboldt** (p456), an almost virgin Caribbean rainforest that registers Cuba's highest levels of endemism.

History

Embellished by breathless feats of revolutionary derring-do, and plagued routinely by meddling armies of foreign invaders, Cuban history has achieved a level of importance way out of proportion to its size. Indeed, with its strategic position slap-bang in the middle of the Caribbean and its geographic closeness to its powerful US neighbor to the north, the historical annals of the Cuban archipelago often read more like the script of an action-packed Hollywood movie production than a dull end-of-year school exam paper. Read on.

PRE-COLUMBIAN HISTORY

Get the Cuba news hot off the press at www .cubaheadlines.com.

According to exhaustive carbon dating, Cuba has been inhabited by humans for over 4000 years. The first known civilization to settle on the island were the Guanahatabeys, a primitive Stone Age people who lived in caves around Viñales in Pinar del Río province and eked out a meager existence as hunter-gatherers. At some point over the ensuing 2000 years the Guanahatabeys were gradually displaced by the arrival of a new preceramic culture known as the Siboneys, a significantly more developed group of fishermen and small-scale farmers who settled down comparatively peacefully on the archipelago's sheltered southern coast.

The island's third and most important pre-Columbian civilization, the Taínos (see boxed text, p451) first started arriving in Cuba around AD 1100 in a series of waves, concluding a migration process that had begun in the Orinoco River delta in South America several centuries earlier. Taíno culture was more developed and sophisticated than that of its two archaic predecessors; the adults practiced a form of cranial transformation by flattening the soft skulls of their young children (flat foreheads were thought to be a sign of great beauty). Related to the Greater Antilles Arawaks, the new natives were skillful farmers, weavers and boat-builders, and their complex society boasted an organized system of participatory government that was overseen by series of local *caciques* (chiefs). Taínos are thought to be responsible for pioneering approximately 60% of the crops still grown in Cuba today and they were the first of the world's pre-Columbian cultures to nurture the delicate tobacco plant into a form that could easily be processed for smoking.

FROM COLONY TO REPUBLIC

When Columbus neared Cuba on October 27, 1492, he described it as 'the most beautiful land human eyes had ever seen,' naming it Juana in honor of a Spanish heiress. But deluded in his search for the kingdom of the Great

TIMELINE

BC 2000	AD 1100	1492
The Guanahatabeys, Cuba's earliest known Stone Age civilization is known to be living in the caves along the coast of present-day Pinar del Río province.	Taíno people start arriving in Cuba after leapfrogging their way across the islands of the Lesser Antilles from the Orinoco River basin in present-day Venezuela.	Christopher Columbus lands in Cuba near modern Gibara in Holguín province. He sails for a month along the coast as far as Baracoa, planting religious crosses and meeting with the indigenous Taínos.

Khan, and finding little gold in Cuba's lush and heavily forested interior, Columbus quickly abandoned the territory in favor of Hispaniola (modern-day Haiti and the Dominican Republic).

The colonization of Cuba didn't begin until nearly 20 years later in 1511, when Diego Velázquez de Cuéllar led a flotilla of four ships and 400 men from Hispaniola destined to conquer the island for the Spanish Crown. Docking near present-day Baracoa, the conquistadors promptly set about establishing seven pioneering settlements throughout their new colony, namely at Baracoa, Bayamo, Trinidad, Sancti Spíritus, Puerto Príncipe (Camagüey), Havana and Santiago de Cuba (see also boxed text, p286). Watching nervously from the safety of their *bohíos* (thatched huts), a scattered population of Taíno Indians looked on with a mixture of fascination and fear.

Despite Velázquez' attempts to protect the local Indians from the gross excesses of the Spanish swordsmen, things quickly got out of hand and the invaders soon found that they had a full-scale rebellion on their hands. Leader of the embittered and short-lived insurgency was the feisty Hatuey, an influential Taíno *cacique* and archetype of the Cuban resistance, who was eventually captured and burned at the stake, inquisition-style, for daring to challenge the iron fist of Spanish rule.

With the resistance decapitated, the Spaniards set about emptying Cuba of its relatively meager gold and mineral reserves using the beleaguered natives as forced labor. As slavery was nominally banned under a papal edict, the Spanish got around the various legal loopholes by introducing a ruthless *encomienda* system, whereby thousands of natives were rounded up and forced to work for Spanish landowners on the pretext that they were receiving free 'lessons' in Christianity. The brutal system lasted 20 years before the 'Apostle of the Indians,' Fray Bartolomé de Las Casas, appealed to the Spanish Crown for more humane treatment, and in 1542 the *encomiendas* were abolished. Catastrophically, for the unfortunate Taínos, the call came too late. Those who had not already been worked to death in the gold mines quickly succumbed to fatal European diseases such as smallpox and by 1550 only about 5000 scattered survivors remained.

For the most comprehensive all-round news about Cuba today, click on the Havana Journal (www .havanajournal.com, in five different languages).

A Taste for Sugar

In 1522, with the local natives perishing fast, the first slaves arrived in Cuba from Africa via Hispaniola. The Spanish colonizers were marginally less repressive in the treatment of their African brethren than the plantation owners further north, a situation that allowed Afro-Cubans greater freedom of expression and more scope to be creative. Cuba's slaves were kept together in tribal groups, enabling them to retain certain elements of their indigenous culture and, in contrast to their counterparts in Haiti or the United States, they retained various legal rights: to own property, get married and even buy their own freedom.

1508	1511	1512
Sebastián de Ocampo circumnavigates Cuba discovering the bays of Havana and Cienfuegos. In doing so he proves that it's an island, not part of Asia as Columbus had died thinking.	Diego Velázquez de Cuéllar lands at Baracoa with four ships and 400 colonizers including Hernán Cortés (the future colonizer of Mexico). The new arrivals construct a fort and quickly make enemies with the local Taínos.	Rebel Indian chief Hatuey leads a brief insurrection against the Spanish before being captured and burnt at the stake for refusing to convert to Catholicism.

Put to work on cattle ranches, tobacco plantations and the fledgling sugar mills that had already started to spring up around the countryside, the slaves were integral to the gradual growth of the Cuban economy over the ensuing 100 years from subsistence colony to grand commercial enterprise. But there were troubles ahead.

From the mid-16th century to the mid-18th century, Cuba became the nexus point for a vicious power struggle between wealthy Spanish traders on the one hand and pirates flying the Jolly Roger on the other. The bountiful booty of New World gold and silver shored up in Cuban harbors was too hard for the corsairs to resist. Santiago de Cuba was plundered in 1554 and Havana was attacked a year later, leading the embattled Spaniards to construct an impressive line of fortifications around the island's most vulnerable harbors. It made little difference. By the 1660s a new generation of marauding pirates led by the wily Welsh governor of Jamaica, Henry Morgan, revealed further holes in Spain's weak naval defenses and, with Spanish power in Europe constantly under threat, the healthy economic future of the Cuban colony looked to be seriously in doubt.

In 1762 Spain joined in the Seven Years' War on the side of France against the British. For Cuba it quickly turned out to be a fatal omen. Unperturbed by their new Spanish foes and sensing an opportunity to disrupt trade in Spain's economically lucrative Caribbean empire, 20,000 British troops homed in on Havana, landing in the village of Cojímar on June 6 and attacking and capturing the seemingly impregnable castle of El Morro (see p167) from the rear. Worn down and under siege, the Spanish reluctantly surrendered Havana two months later, leaving the British to become the city's (and Cuba's) rather unlikely new overlords.

The British occupation turned out to be brief but incisive. Bivouacking themselves inside Havana's formidable city walls for 11 months, the enterprising English flung open the doors to free trade and sparked a new rush of foreign imports into the colony in the form of manufacturing parts and consumer goods. Not surprisingly, it was the sugar industry that benefited most from this economic deregulation, and in the years that followed the British handover (they swapped Havana for Florida at the Treaty of Paris in 1763) the production of sugarcane boomed like never before.

The industry got a further stimulus in the 1790s when a bloody slave rebellion on the neighboring island of Haiti led 30,000 French planters to flee west and seek asylum in Cuba (see boxed text, opposite).

By the 1820s, Cuba was the world's largest sugar producer and the freshly inaugurated United States – hooked on sugar and spice and all things nice – was its most prestigious market. Indeed, so important was Cuban sugar to the American palate that a growing movement inside the US started petitioning the government for annexation of the island during the 19th century. In 1808 Thomas Jefferson became the first of four US presidents to offer to buy Cuba

Essayist and ethno-musicologist, Fernando Ortiz was a dedicated chronicler of Cuba's African heritage who in 1955 was nominated for the Nobel Peace Prize for his 'love for culture and humankind.'

1522	1555	1589
The first slaves arrive in Cuba from Africa, ushering in an era that was to last for 350 years and have a profound effect on the growth and development of Cuban culture.	The age of piracy is inaugurated. French buccaneer, Jaques de Sores, attacks Havana and burns it to the ground. In response, the Spanish start building a huge network of military forts.	Work begins on two forts – Castillo de San Salvador de la Punta, and Castillo de los Tres Santos Reyes Magnos del Morro – on either side of Havana harbor, to protect Spain's prized colony from pirates and foreign invaders.

from its increasingly beleaguered Spanish owners and in 1845 President Polk upped the ante further when he slapped down a massive US$100 million bid for the jewel of the Caribbean.

For better or for worse, Spain refused to sell, preferring instead to import more slaves and bank more pesetas. By 1840 there were 400,000 slaves incarcerated on the island, the bulk of them of West African origin.

On the political front the sugar boom went some way in forestalling the formation of a coherent independence movement in Cuba before 1820.

THE SPECTER OF HAITI

The legacy of Haiti, Cuba's blighted eastern neighbor, and its bloody 1791 slave revolution loomed large over political life on the island in the 19th century and strongly redirected the course of its history.

Colonized by France in the mid-17th century, the western third of the island of Hispaniola – known formerly as Saint-Domingue – quickly prospered as a rich sugar-growing plantation economy built on an inexhaustible supply of African slaves. But, as the colony developed, the ratio between white settlers and black slaves grew dangerously disproportionate.

The spark was lit in August 1791 when, inspired by the overthrow of the *ancien régime* in France, thousands of slaves rose up in violent rebellion. In the space of two bloody months more than 280 sugar plantations were destroyed and 2000 white planters violently killed. In the process the rebels successfully established the new independent state of Haiti, a free republic ruled by blacks, the first of its kind in the Western hemisphere.

Watching from the sidelines 70 miles to the west, Cuba's slave-owning sugar farmers were horrified. Though quick to offer a safe refuge to the 30,000 surviving French planters who had fled the mayhem, they were equally adamant not to import the fragile social conditions that had precipitated Saint-Domingue's collapse.

Historically speaking, the Haitian episode influenced Cuba in a number of important ways. Firstly, it led to a huge influx of skilled French immigrants to the island, a class that brought with them an enterprising mix of farming know-how, plentiful money and a new Francophile culture. These immigrants went on to set up the island's first commercial coffee plantations, establish new cities and add a fresh new dynamic to Cuban culture, particularly music.

Secondly, the sheer violence of the Haitian debacle instilled in Cuba's colonial class an underlying fear – a type of 'black legend' – which resurfaced on numerous occasions in the ensuing years. This fear went a long way in watering down independence demands in Cuba long after the rest of Latin America had broken free from the Spanish rule. It also deferred the abolition of slavery on the island until 1886.

Elements of French and Haitian culture are still traceable in Cuban society today, particularly in the French-founded settlements of Guantánamo and Cienfuegos. Eastern musical forms such as *changüí* and *guaracha* are the bastardized descendants of the French contredanse, while the resplendent neoclassical architecture that characterizes the city of Cienfuegos on the south coast has a definitive Parisian feel.

1607	**1728**	**1741**
Havana is declared capital of Cuba and becomes the annual congregation point for Spain's stinking-rich Caribbean treasure fleet loaded up with silver from Peru and gold from Mexico.	The University of Havana is founded in Cuba's rapidly growing capital, a city of decorative baroque churches and muscular Spanish forts encircled by a 5km-long wall.	A British Navy contingent under the command of Admiral Edward Vernon briefly captures Guantánamo Bay during the War of Jenkin's Ear, but is quickly sent packing after an outbreak of yellow fever.

Curiously, Cuba played little part in the sweeping liberation of South America spearheaded by Simón Bolívar in the 1820s, or the independence movements in Central America starting with Miguel Hidalgo's 1810 *Grito de Dolores* in Mexico, preferring instead to stay loyal to the Spanish Crown – along with Puerto Rico, Guam and the Philippines. Nonetheless, the rumblings of discontent wouldn't be long in coming.

The War for Independence

Fed up with Spain's reactionary policies and enviously eyeing Lincoln's new American dream to the north, criollo (Spaniards born in the Americas) landowners around Bayamo began plotting rebellion in the late 1860s. The spark was auspiciously lit on October 10, 1868, when Carlos Manuel de Céspedes, a budding poet, lawyer and sugar-plantation owner, launched an uprising from his Demajagua sugar mill near Manzanillo in the Oriente (see p396). Calling for the abolition of slavery and freeing his own slaves in an act of solidarity, Céspedes proclaimed the famous *Grito de Yara,* a cry of liberty for an independent Cuba, encouraging other disillusioned separatists to join him. For the colonial administrators in Havana such an audacious bid to wrest control from their incompetent and slippery grasp was an act tantamount to treason. The furious Spanish reacted accordingly.

Fortuitously, for the loosely organized rebels, the cagey Céspedes had done his military homework. Within weeks of the historic *Grito de Yara* the diminutive lawyer-turned-general had raised an army of more than 1500 men and marched defiantly on Bayamo, taking the city in a matter of days. But initial successes soon turned to lengthy deadlock. A tactical decision not to invade western Cuba, along with an alliance between *peninsulares* (Spaniards born in Spain but living in Cuba) and the Spanish, soon put Céspedes on the back foot. Temporary help arrived in the shape of *mulato* general Antonio Maceo, a tough and uncompromising Santiagüero nicknamed the 'Bronze Titan' for his ability to defy death on countless occasions, and the equally formidable Dominican Máximo Gómez, but, despite economic disruption and the periodic destruction of the sugar crop, the rebels lacked a dynamic political leader capable of uniting them behind a singular ideological cause.

In 1824 priest Félix Varela published an independent newspaper called *El Habanero* in Philadelphia. It was considered to be the first Cuban revolutionary publication.

With the loss of Céspedes in battle in 1874, the war dragged on for another four years, reducing the Cuban economy to tatters and leaving an astronomical 200,000 Cubans and 80,000 Spanish dead. Finally, in February 1878 a lackluster pact was signed at El Zanjón between the uncompromising Spanish and the militarily exhausted separatists, a rambling and largely worthless agreement that solved nothing and acceded little to the rebel cause. Maceo, disgusted and disillusioned, made his feelings known in the antidotal 'Protest of Baraguá' but after an abortive attempt to restart the war briefly in 1879, both he and Gómez disappeared into a prolonged exile.

1762	1791	1808
Spain joins France in the Seven Years' War, provoking the British to attack and take Havana. They occupy Cuba for 11 months before exchanging it for Florida at the Treaty of Paris in 1763.	A bloody slave rebellion in Haiti causes thousands of white French planters to flee west to Cuba, where they set up some of the earliest coffee plantations in the New World.	Pre-empting the Monroe Doctrine, US president Thomas Jefferson proclaims Cuba 'the most interesting addition which could be made to our system of states,' thus beginning a 200-year-long US obsession with all things Cuban.

The 1880s brought an end to slavery, a boom in railway construction and Cuba's worst economic crisis for over a century. With the price of sugar falling on the world market, the island's old landowning oligarchy was forced to sell out to a newer and slicker competitor as the US investors started to buy up Cuban land on the cheap. By the end of the 19th century, US trade with Cuba was larger than US trade with the rest of Latin America combined, and Cuba was America's third-largest trading partner (after Britain and Germany). The island's sweet-tasting mono-crop economy was translating into a US monopoly, as much of Cuba's sugar land was owned by US interests, and some wealthy Cuban landowners were readvocating the old annexation argument.

Spanish-Cuban-American War

Cometh the hour, cometh the man: José Martí, poet, patriot, visionary and intellectual, had grown rapidly into a patriotic figure of Bolívarian proportions in the years following his ignominious exile in 1871 (see boxed text, p40), not just in Cuba, but in the whole of Latin America. After his arrest at the age of 16 during the First War of Independence for a minor indiscretion, Martí had spent 20 years formulating his revolutionary ideas abroad in places as diverse as Guatemala, Mexico and the US. Although impressed by American business savvy and industriousness, he was equally repelled by the country's all-consuming materialism and was determined to present a workable Cuban alternative.

Dedicating himself passionately to the cause of the resistance, Martí wrote, spoke, petitioned and organized tirelessly for independence for well over a decade and by 1892 had enough momentum to coax Maceo and Gómez out of exile under the umbrella of the Partido Revolucionario Cubano (PRC; Cuban Revolutionary Party). At last, Cuba had found its Bolívar.

Predicting that the time was right for another revolution, Martí and his compatriots set sail for Cuba in April 1895, landing near Baracoa two months after PRC-sponsored insurrections had tied down Spanish forces in Havana. Raising an army of 40,000 men, the rebels promptly regrouped and headed west, engaging the Spanish for the first time on May 19 in a place called Dos Ríos. It was on this bullet-strafed and strangely anonymous battlefield that Martí, conspicuous on his white horse and dressed in his trademark black dinner suit, was shot and killed as he charged suicidally toward the Spanish lines. Had he lived he would certainly have become Cuba's first president; instead, he became a hero and a martyr whose life and legacy would inspire generations of Cubans in the years to come.

Conscious of mistakes made during the First War of Independence, Gómez and Maceo stormed west in a scorched-earth policy that left everything from the Oriente to Matanzas up in flames. Early victories quickly led to a sustained offensive, and by January 1896 Maceo had broken through to

For one of the most thoughtful re-evaluations of Cuban history in recent years, check out Richard Gott's *Cuba: A New History*. This British academic was one of only two people present in Bolivia in October 1967 to identify the corpse of Che Guevara (he had met Guevara once in the early 1960s).

1850	**1868**	**1878**
Venezuelan filibuster Narciso López raises the Cuban flag for the first time in Cárdenas during an abortive attempt to 'liberate' the colony from Spain.	Céspedes frees his slaves in Manzanillo and proclaims the *Grito de Yara*, Cuba's first independence cry and the beginning of a 10-year-long war against the Spanish.	The Pact of El Zanjón ends the First War of Independence. Cuban general Antonio Maceo issues the Protest of Baraguá and briefly resumes hostilities before disappearing into exile.

JOSÉ MARTÍ

For millions of Cubans worldwide José Martí is a heroic and emblematic figure; a potent unifying symbol in a nation fractiously divided by economy, ideology and 90 miles of shark-infested ocean. In Florida they have named a TV station after him. In Havana, Castro touts his name with an almost religious reverence. Throughout Cuba there is barely a town or village that hasn't got at least one street, square or statue named proudly in his honor. The fact that Martí – who died prematurely at the age of 42 leading a suicidal cavalry charge headlong toward the Spanish lines – spent less that one-third of his life residing in his beloved motherland, is largely academic.

Born in Havana in 1853 to Spanish parents, Martí grew up fast, publishing his first newspaper, *La Patria Libre,* at the age of 16. But his provocative writings, flushed with the fervent prose and lyrical poetry that would one day make him famous, soon landed him in trouble. Tried and convicted in 1870 for penning a letter denouncing a friend who had attended a pro-Spanish rally during the First War of Independence, he was charged with treason and sentenced to six months of hard labor in a Havana stone quarry. Later that year, the still-teenage Martí was moved to Isla de Pinos and in 1871 he was exiled to Spain.

Slightly built, with a well-waxed Dalí-esque moustache and trademark black dinner suit, Martí cut a rather unlikely hero-to-be in his formative years. Graduating with a degree in law from Saragossa University in 1874, he relocated to Mexico City where he tentatively began a career in journalism.

For the next five years Martí was constantly on the move, living successively in Guatemala, Spain, France, Venezuela and Cuba, from where he was exiled for a second time in 1879 for his conspiratorial activities and anticolonial statements.

Gravitating toward the US, the wandering writer based himself in the Big Apple for 13 years with his wife and son, devoting his time to poetry, prose, politics and journalism. He was the New York correspondent for two Latin American newspapers, *La Nación* in Buenos Aires and

Pinar del Río, while Gómez was tying down Spanish forces near Havana. The Spaniards responded with an equally ruthless general named Valeriano Weyler, who built countrywide north–south fortifications to restrict the rebels' movements. In order to break the underground resistance, *guajiros* (country people) were forced into camps in a process called *reconcentración,* and anyone supporting the rebellion became liable for execution. The brutal tactics started to show results and on December 7, 1896 the Mambís (the name for the 19th-century rebels fighting Spain) suffered a major military blow to their confidence when Antonio Maceo was killed south of Havana trying to break out to the east.

By this time Cuba was a mess: thousands were dead, the country was in flames, and William Randolph Hearst and the tub-thumping US tabloid press were leading a hysterical war campaign characterized by sensationalized, often inaccurate reports about Spanish atrocities.

1886	1892	1895
After more than 350 years of exploitation and cross-Atlantic transportation, Cuba becomes the second-last country in the Americas to abolish slavery.	From exile in the US, José Martí galvanizes popular support and forms the Cuban Revolutionary Party, starting to lay the groundwork for the resumption of hostilities against Spain.	José Martí and Antonio Maceo arrive in Cuba to ignite the Second Independence War. Martí is killed at Dos Ríos in May and is quickly elevated to a martyr.

La Opinión Nacional in Caracas, and was later appointed New York consul for the countries of Uruguay, Paraguay and Argentina. Adamant to avoid cultural assimilation in the American melting pot, Martí nurtured a deep-rooted mistrust for the US system of government borne out of insider experience and a canny sense of political calculation. He argued vociferously for Cuban independence, and claimed consistently that the Americans were no better than the Spanish in their neocolonial ambitions. 'I have lived inside the monster and know its entrails,' he once stated portentously.

Never one to rest on his rhetoric, Martí left for Florida in 1892 to set up the Partido Revolucionario Cubano (PRC; Cuban Revolutionary Party), the grassroots political movement that spearheaded the 1895–98 War of Independence against the Spanish.

Landing in Cuba in April 1895 at the remote beach of La Playita in Guantánamo province, Martí's personal war effort lasted precisely 38 days. Destined to be more of a theorist than a man of action, he was cut down in a skirmish at Dos Ríos on May 19, one of the war's first casualties and an instantly recognizable martyr.

Though never ostensibly a socialist during his lifetime, Martí propounded the values of liberty, equality and democracy as central to his fledgling manifesto for an independent Cuba. Unflinching in his hatred of racism and imperialism, he believed in the power of reason, extending friendship to those Spaniards who supported Cuban independence, but calling for war against those who didn't.

The spirit of José Martí is still very much alive in Cuba today. Indeed, it is difficult to imagine the country – with its distinct culture and enviable health and education systems – without his legacy. Artistically speaking, the scope of Martí the writer was, and still is, mind-boggling. From his eloquent political theorizing to his populist *Versos Sencillos* and his best-selling children's magazine *La Edad de Oro*, he was a cultural icon without equal in Latin America. It is little wonder that Cubans today refer to him quite simply as El Maestro.

Preparing perhaps for the worst, the US battleship *Maine* was sent to Havana in January 1898, on the pretext of 'protecting US citizens.' Fatefully, its touted task never saw fruition. On February 15, 1898 the *Maine* exploded out of the blue in Havana Harbor, killing 266 US sailors. The Spanish claimed it was an accident, the Americans blamed the Spanish, and some Cubans accused the US, saying it provided a convenient pretext for intervention. Despite several investigations conducted over the following years, the real cause of the explosion may remain one of history's great mysteries, as the hulk of the ship was scuttled in deep waters in 1911.

After the *Maine* debacle, the US scrambled to take control. They offered Spain US$300 million for Cuba and when this deal was rejected, demanded a full withdrawal of the Spanish from the island. The long-awaited US-Spanish showdown that had been simmering imperceptibly beneath the surface for decades had finally resulted in war.

1896	**1898**	**1902**
After sustaining more than 20 injuries in a military career that spanned four decades and two independence wars, Mambí general Antonio Maceo finally meets his nemesis at El Cacahual near Havana where he is killed in an ambush.	Following the loss of the battleship USS *Maine*, the US declares war on Spain and defeats its forces at land and sea near Santiago de Cuba. A four-year US occupation begins.	Cuba gains nominal independence from the US and elects Tomás Estrada Palma as its first president. But US troops are called back three times within the first 15 years of the republic.

The only important land battle of the conflict was on July 1, when the US Army attacked Spanish positions on San Juan Hill (p417), just east of Santiago de Cuba. Despite vastly inferior numbers and limited, antiquated weaponry, the under-siege Spanish held out bravely for over 24 hours before future US president Theodore Roosevelt broke the deadlock by leading a celebrated cavalry charge of the Rough Riders up San Juan Hill. It was the beginning of the end for the Spaniards and an unconditional surrender was offered to the Americans on July 17, 1898.

On December 12, 1898 a peace treaty ending the Spanish-Cuban-American War was signed in Paris by the Spanish and the Americans. Despite three years of blood, sweat and sacrifice, no Cuban representatives were invited. After a century of trying to buy Cuba from the Spanish, the US – wary of raised voices among shortchanged Cuban nationalists – decided to appease the situation temporarily by offering the island a form of quasi-independence that would dampen internal discontent while keeping any future Cuban governments on a tight leash. In November 1900 US Governor of Cuba, General Leonard Wood, convened a meeting of elected Cuban delegates who drew up a constitution similar to that of the US. The then–Connecticut Senator Orville Platt attached a rider to the US Army Appropriations Bill of 1901 giving the US the right to intervene militarily in Cuba whenever they saw fit. This was approved by President McKinley, and the Cubans were given the choice of accepting what became known as the Platt Amendment, or remaining under a US military occupation indefinitely. The US also used its significant leverage to secure a naval base in Guantánamo Bay in order to protect its strategic interests in the Panama Canal region.

> In the 1880s there were more than 100,000 Chinese living in Cuba, mainly as cheap labor on sugar plantations in and around the Havana region.

BETWEEN REPUBLIC & REVOLUTION

On May 20, 1902 Cuba became an independent republic. Hopelessly unprepared for the system of US-style democracy that its northern neighbors optimistically had in mind, the country quickly descended into five decades of on-off chaos headed up by a succession of weak, corrupt governments that called upon US military aid anytime there was the merest sniff of trouble. Intervening three times militarily in the ensuing years, the US walked a tightrope between benevolent ally and exasperated foreign meddler. There were, however, some coordinated successes, most notably the eradication of yellow fever using the hypotheses of Cuban doctor Carlos Finlay (see p338), and the transformation of the ravaged Cuban economy from postwar wreck into nascent sugar giant.

The postwar economic growth was nothing short of astounding. By the 1920s US companies owned two-thirds of Cuba's farmland and most of its mineral resources. The sugar industry was booming and, with the US gripped by prohibition from 1919 to 1933, the Mafia moved into Havana and gangsters such as Al Capone began to set up a lucrative tourist sector based on drinking,

1903	1920	1933
The controversial Platt Amendment gives the US a 99-year lease on Guantánamo Naval Base, establishing a military presence on the island that continues to this day.	Sharp increases in world sugar prices after WWI spearhead the so-called 'Dance of the Millions' in Cuba when huge fortunes are made overnight. A heavy economic crash quickly follows.	The 1933 revolution is sparked by a 'Sergeant's Revolt' that deposes of the Machado dictatorship and installs Fulgencio Batista in power.

gambling and prostitution. When commodity prices collapsed following the Great Depression, Cuba, like most other Western countries, was plunged into chaos and president-turned-dictator Gerardo Machado y Morales (1925–33) went on a terror campaign to root out detractors. Hoist by his own petard, Machado was toppled during a spontaneous general strike in August 1933 that left a seemingly innocuous army sergeant named Fulgencio Batista (who took no part in Machado's overthrow) to step into the power vacuum.

Batista was a wily and shrewd negotiator who presided over Cuba's best and worst attempts to establish an embryonic democracy in the '40s and '50s. From 1934 onwards he served as the army's chief of staff, and in 1940 in a relatively free and fair election he was duly elected president. Given an official mandate, Batista began to enact a wide variety of social reforms and set about drafting Cuba's most liberal and democratic constitution to date. But neither the liberal honeymoon nor Batista's good humor were to last. Stepping down after the 1944 election, the former army sergeant handed over power to the politically inept President Ramón Grau San Martín, and corruption and inefficiency soon reigned like never before.

Aware of his underlying popularity and sensing an easy opportunity to line his pockets with one last big paycheck, Batista cut a deal with the American Mafia in Daytona Beach, Florida, promising to give them carte blanche in Cuba in return for a cut in their gambling profits, and positioned himself for a comeback. On March 10, 1952, three months before scheduled elections that he looked like losing, Batista staged a military coup. Wildly condemned by opposition politicians inside Cuba but recognized by the US government two weeks later, Batista quickly let it be known that his second incarnation wasn't going to be quite as enlightened as his first by suspending various constitutional guarantees including the right to strike.

THE CUBAN REVOLUTION

After Batista's coup, a revolutionary circle formed in Havana around the charismatic figure of Fidel Castro, a lawyer by profession and gifted orator who had been due to stand in the cancelled 1952 elections. Supported by his younger brother Raúl and aided intellectually by his trusty lieutenant Abel Santamaría (later tortured to death by Batista's thugs), Castro saw no alternative to the use of force in ridding Cuba of its detestable dictator. Low on numbers but adamant to make a political statement, Castro led 119 rebels in an attack on the strategically important Moncada army barracks in Santiago de Cuba on July 26, 1953 (see boxed text, p416). The audacious and poorly planned assault failed dramatically when the rebel's driver (who was from Havana) took the wrong turning in Santiago's badly signposted streets and the alarm was raised.

Fooled, flailing and hopelessly outnumbered, 64 of the Moncada conspirators were rounded up by Batista's army and brutally tortured and executed.

In December 1946 the Mafia convened the biggest ever get-together of the North American mobsters in Havana's Hotel Nacional under the pretence that they were going to see a Frank Sinatra concert.

1940	1952	1953
Cuba's 1940 constitution – one of the most progressive in the world at the time – is implemented by President Federico Laredo Brú. Among other liberal measures, it provides for land reform, a minimum wage and a program of public education.	Batista stages a bloodless military coup cancelling the upcoming Cuban elections in which a young ambitious lawyer named Fidel Castro was due to stand.	Castro leads a band of rebels in a disastrous attack on Moncada army barracks in Santiago. Although unsuccessful, he uses his subsequent trial as a platform to expound his future political plans for Cuba.

Castro and a handful of others managed to escape into the nearby mountains, where they were found a few days later by a sympathetic army lieutenant named Sarría, who had been given instructions to kill them. 'Don't shoot, you can't kill ideas!' Sarría is alleged to have shouted on finding Castro and his exhausted colleagues. By taking him to jail instead of doing away with him, Sarría ruined his military career, but saved Fidel's life. (One of Fidel's first acts after the Revolution triumphed was to release Sarría from the prison where Batista had incarcerated him and give him a commission in the revolutionary army.) Castro's capture soon became national news, and he was put on trial in the full glare of the media spotlight. A lawyer by profession, the loquacious Fidel defended himself in court, writing an eloquent and masterfully executed speech that he later transcribed into a comprehensive political manifesto entitled *History Will Absolve Me*. Basking in his newfound legitimacy and backed by a growing sense of restlessness with the old regime in the country at large, Castro was sentenced to 15 years imprisonment on Isla de Pinos (a former name for Isla de la Juventud). Cuba was well on the way to gaining a new national hero.

In February 1955 Batista won the presidency in what were widely considered to be fraudulent elections and, in an attempt to curry favor with growing internal opposition, agreed to an amnesty for all political prisoners, including Castro. Believing that Batista's real intention was to assassinate him once out of jail, Castro fled to Mexico leaving Baptist schoolteacher Frank País in charge of a fledgling underground resistance campaign that the vengeful Moncada veterans had christened the 26th of July Movement (M-26-7). Another early M-26-7 member was Celia Sánchez Manduley, a formidable female revolutionary who later went on to become Castro's premier confidant and muse (see boxed text, p399).

Of the 12 or so men who survived the disastrous *Granma* landing in December 1956, only four now remain. They are Fidel Castro, Raúl Castro, Juan Almeida and Ramiro Valdés.

Cocooned in Mexico, Fidel and his compatriots plotted and planned afresh, drawing in key new figures such as Camilo Cienfuegos and the Argentine doctor Ernesto 'Che' Guevara, both of whom added strength and panache to the nascent army of disaffected rebel soldiers. On the run from the Mexican police and adamant to arrive in Cuba in time for an uprising that Frank País had planned for late November 1956 in Santiago de Cuba, Castro and 81 companions set sail for the island on November 25 in an old and overcrowded leisure yacht named *Granma*. After seven dire days at sea they arrived at Playa Las Coloradas near Niquero in Oriente (p400) on December 2 (two days late), and after a catastrophic landing – 'it wasn't a disembarkation; it was a shipwreck,' a wry Guevara later commented – they were spotted and routed by Batista's soldiers in a sugarcane field at Alegría de Pío three days later.

Of the 82 rebel soldiers who had left Mexico, only little more than a dozen managed to escape. Splitting into three tiny groups, the survivors wandered around hopelessly for days half-starved, wounded and assuming that the rest of their compatriots had been killed in the initial skirmish. 'At one point

1955	1956	1957
Released from prison, Castro flees to Mexico where he meets Che Guevara and starts to put together the plans that will ultimately dislodge Batista.	The *Granma* yacht lands in eastern Cuba with Castro and 81 rebels aboard. Decimated by the Cuban Army, only about a dozen survive to regroup in the Sierra Maestra.	Embittered university students led by José Antonio Echeverría attack the Presidential Palace in Havana and attempt to assassinate Fulgencio Batista. Batista narrowly escapes and the students are rounded up and executed.

I was Commander in Chief of myself and two other people,' commented Fidel sagely years later (see boxed text, p400). However, with the help of the local peasantry, the dozen or so hapless soldiers finally managed to re-assemble two weeks later in Cinco Palmas, a clearing in the shadows of the Sierra Maestra where a half-delirious Fidel gave a rousing and premature victory speech. 'We will win this war,' he proclaimed confidently, 'we are just beginning the fight!'

The comeback began on January 17, 1957, when the guerrillas scored an important victory by sacking a small army outpost on the south coast called La Plata (p438). This was followed in February by a devastating propaganda coup when Fidel persuaded *New York Times* journalist Herbert Matthews to come up into the Sierra Maestra to interview him. The resulting article made Castro internationally famous and gained him much sympathy among liberal Americans. Suffice to say, by this point, he wasn't the only anti-Batista agitator. On March 13, 1957, university students led by José Antonio Echeverría attacked the Presidential Palace in Havana (now the Museo de la Revolución; see p116) in an unsuccessful attempt to assassinate Batista. Thirty-two of the 35 attackers were shot dead as they fled, and reprisals were meted out on the streets of Havana with a new vengeance. Cuba was rapidly disintegrating into a police state run by military-trained thugs.

> The famous photo of Che Guevara that adorns thousands of T-shirts worldwide was taken by Alberto Korda in March 1960 at the funeral of the victims of *El Coubre*, a French ship purportedly blown up by the CIA in Havana harbor.

Elsewhere passions were running equally high and in September 1957 naval officers in the normally tranquil city of Cienfuegos staged an armed revolt and set about distributing weapons among the disaffected populace. After some bitter door-to-door fighting, the insurrection was brutally crushed and the ringleaders rounded up and killed, but for the revolutionaries the point had been made. Batista's days were numbered.

Back in the Sierra Maestra, Fidel's rebels overwhelmed 53 Batista soldiers at an army post in El Uvero in May and captured more badly needed supplies. The movement seemed to be gaining momentum and despite losing respected underground leader Frank País to a government assassination squad in Santiago de Cuba in July, support and sympathy around the country was starting to mushroom. By the beginning of 1958 Castro had established a fixed headquarters at La Plata, in a cloud forest high up in the Sierra Maestra, and was broadcasting propaganda messages from Radio Rebelde (710AM and 96.7FM) all across Cuba. The tide was starting to turn.

Sensing his popularity waning, Batista sent an army of 10,000 men into the Sierra Maestra in May 1958 on a mission known as Plan FF (*Fin de Fidel* or End of Fidel). The intention was to liquidate Castro and his merry band of loyal guerrillas who had now burgeoned into a solid fighting force of 300 men. Outnumbered 30 to one and fighting desperately for their lives, the offensive became something of a turning point as the rebels – with the help of the local *campesinos* (country people) – gradually halted the onslaught of Batista's young and ill-disciplined conscript army. With the Americans

1958	1959	1960
Che Guevara masterminds an attack against an armored train in Santa Clara, a military victory that finally forces Batista to concede power. The rebels march triumphantly on Havana.	Castro is welcomed ecstatically in Havana. The new government passes the historic First Agrarian Reform Act. Camilo Cienfuegos' plane goes missing over the Cuban coast off Camagüey.	Castro nationalizes US assets on the island, provoking the Americans to cancel their Cuban sugar quota. Castro immediately runs into the arms of the Soviet Union and sells the sugar lock, stock and barrel to Khrushchev.

increasingly embarrassed by the no-holds-barred terror tactics of their one-time Cuban ally, Castro sensed an opportunity to turn defensive into offensive and signed the groundbreaking Caracas Pact with eight leading opposition groups calling on the US to stop all aid to Batista. Che Guevara and Camilo Cienfuegos were promptly dispatched off to the Escambray Mountains to open up new fronts in the west and by December, with Cienfuegos holding down troops in Yaguajay (the garrison finally surrendered after an 11-day siege) and Guevara closing in on Santa Clara, the end was in sight. It was left to Che Guevara to seal the final victory, employing classic guerrilla tactics to derail an armored train in Santa Clara and split the country's battered communications system in two. By New Year's Eve 1958, the game was up: a sense of jubilation filled the country, and Che and Camilo were on their way to Havana unopposed.

In the small hours of January 1, 1959 Batista fled by private plane to the Dominican Republic. Meanwhile, materializing in Santiago de Cuba the same day, Fidel made a rousing victory speech from the town hall in Parque Céspedes before jumping into a jeep and traveling across the breadth of the country to Havana in a Caesar-like cavalcade. The triumph of the Revolution was complete. Or was it?

CONSOLIDATING POWER

On January 5, 1959, the Cuban presidency was assumed by Manuel Urrutia, a judge who had defended the M-26-7 prisoners during the 1953 Moncada trials, though the leadership and real power remained unquestionably with Fidel. Riding on the crest of a popular wave the self-styled Líder Máximo began to mete out revolutionary justice with an iron fist and within a matter of weeks hundreds of Batista's supporters and military henchmen had been rounded up and executed inside the walls of La Cabaña fort (see p168). Already suspicious of Castro's supposed communist leanings, the US viewed these worrying developments with a growing sense of alarm and when Fidel visited Richard Nixon in the White House on a state visit in April 1959 the vice president gave him a decidedly cool and terse reception.

On January 2, 1959 the Cuban government announced that 50% to 60% of all casino profits would be directed to welfare programs.

Among more than 1000 laws and acts passed by revolutionary government in its first year were rent and electricity cost reductions, the abolition of racial discrimination and the much-lauded (among Cubans) First Agrarian Reform Act. This landmark piece of legislation nationalized all rural estates over 400 hectares (without compensation) and infuriated Cuba's largest landholders, the bulk of whom were American. Establishing the embryonic Instituto Nacional de Reforma Agraria (INRA; Agrarian Reform Institute) as an umbrella organization, the government slowly began to piece together the rural apparatus that would later prove decisive in promoting its ambitious literacy and community-doctor programs.

1961	1962	1967
Cuban mercenaries with US backing stage an unsuccessful invasion at the Bay of Pigs. The US declares a full trade embargo. Cuba embarks on a highly successful literacy campaign.	The discovery of medium-range nuclear missiles in Cuba installed by the Soviet Union brings the world to the brink of nuclear war in what becomes known as the Cuban Missile Crisis.	Che Guevara is hunted down and executed in Bolivia in front of CIA observers after a 10-month abortive guerrilla war in the mountains.

Meanwhile, back on the political scene, entities with vested interests in Cuba (ie the US-owned businesses) were growing increasingly bellicose. Perturbed by Castro's intransigent individual style and increasingly alarmed by his gradual and none-too-subtle shift to the left, dissidents started voting with their feet. Between 1959 and 1962 approximately 250,000 judges, lawyers, managers and technicians left Cuba, primarily for the US, and throughout the top professions Cuba began to experience an economically debilitating brain drain. At the same time Fidel hit back at the counterrevolutionaries with stringent press restrictions and the threat of arrest and incarceration for anyone caught being outwardly critical of the new regime.

Crisis begot crisis, and in June 1960 Texaco, Standard Oil and Shell refineries in Cuba buckled under US pressure and refused to refine Soviet petroleum. Sensing an opportunity to score diplomatic points over his embittered American rivals, Castro dutifully nationalized the oil companies. President Eisenhower was left with little choice: he cut 700,000 tons from the Cuban sugar quota in an attempt to get even. Rather worryingly for Cold War relations, the measure played right into the hands of the Soviet Union. Already buttered up by a 1959 visit from Che Guevara, the USSR stepped out of the shadows the following day and promised to buy the Cuban sugar at the same preferential rates. The tit-for-tat war that would come to characterize Cuban-Soviet-US relations for the next 30 years had well and truly begun.

The diplomatic crisis heated up again in August when Cuba nationalized US-owned telephone and electricity companies and 36 sugar mills, including US$800 million in US assets. Outraged, the American government forced through an Organization of American States (OAS) resolution condemning 'extra-continental' (ie Soviet) intervention in the Western hemisphere, while Cuba responded by establishing diplomatic relations with communist China and edging ever closer to its new Soviet ally, via a hastily signed arms deal.

By October 1960, 382 major Cuban-owned firms, the majority of its banks and the whole rental housing market had been nationalized, and both the US and Castro were starting to prepare for the military showdown that by this point seemed inevitable. Turning the screw ever tighter, the US imposed a partial trade embargo on the island as Che Guevara (now Minister of Industry) nationalized all remaining US businesses. In the space of just three short years Fidel had gone from the darling of the American liberals to US public enemy number one. The stage was set.

COLD WAR DEEP FREEZE

The brick finally hit the window in early 1961 when Castro ordered US embassy reductions in Havana. Furious, the US government broke off diplomatic relations with Cuba, banned its citizens from traveling to the island and abolished the remaining Cuban sugar quota. At the same time the government, in collusion with the CIA, began to initiate a covert program of

Che Guevara – whose father's family name was Guevara Lynch – can trace his Celtic roots back to a Patrick Lynch (born in Galway in Ireland in 1715), who emigrated to Buenos Aires via Bilbao in 1749.

1968	1970	1976
The Cuban government nationalizes 58,000 small businesses in a sweeping socialist reform package. Everything from family-run shops to streetside food vendors falls under strict government control.	Castro attempts to achieve a 10-million-ton sugar harvest and encourages the whole country to get behind the task. Not surprisingly, the plan fails and Cuba slowly begins to wean itself off its unhealthy mono-crop.	Terrorists bomb a Cuban jet in Barbados killing all 73 people aboard, including the entire Cuban fencing team. A line is traced back to anti-Castro activists with histories as CIA operatives working out of Venezuela.

action against the Castro regime that, according to various historical sources, included invasion plans, assassination plots and blatant acts of sabotage. Much of this aid was filtered through to counterrevolutionary gangs who – borrowing a tactic from Fidel – had set up in the Escambray Mountains in an attempt to initiate a guerrilla war against the new government. At the center of subterfuge lay the infamous Bay of Pigs invasion (see boxed text, p259), a poorly conceived military plot that honed 1400 disaffected Cuban exiles into a workable fighting force in the jungles of Guatemala. Deemed sufficiently armed and ready to fight, the émigrés sailed on April 14, 1961 with a US Navy escort from Puerto Cabeza in Nicaragua to the southern coast of Cuba. But military glory wasn't forthcoming. Landing at Playa Girón and Playa Larga three days later, the US-backed expeditionary forces took a conclusive drubbing, in part because President Kennedy canceled US air cover during the landings, a decision which has been the subject of much historical analysis (and according to some of the theories that abound about his assessination, might have cost him his life).

Rocked and embarrassed by what had been a grave and politically costly military defeat, the Kennedy administration declared a full trade embargo on Cuba in June 1961, and in January 1962 it used diplomatic pressure to expel the island from the OAS (Organization of American States). To the dismay of the US, its closest neighbors, Mexico and Canada, refused to bow to pressure to sever diplomatic relations with Cuba completely, thus throwing the country a valuable lifeline which – especially in the case of Canada – still exists to this day. Spinning inexorably into the Soviet sphere of influence, Castro began to cement closer relations with Khrushchev and upped the ante even further in April 1962 when, exploiting American weakness after the Bay of Pigs fiasco, he agreed to effect the installation of Soviet-made medium-range missiles on the island.

La Rosa Blanca (the White Rose), the first anti-Castro movement to take hold in the US, was formed in January 1959 by Dr Rafael Díaz-Balart, Fidel's former brother-in-law.

Furious and anxious not to lose any more face on the international scene, the Kennedy administration decided to act quickly and decisively. On October 22, 1962 President Kennedy ordered the US Navy to detain Cuba-bound Soviet ships and search for missiles, provoking the Cuban Missile Crisis, which brought the world closer to the nuclear brink than it has ever been before or since. Six days later, only after receiving a secret assurance from Kennedy that Cuba would not be invaded, Khrushchev ordered the missiles dismantled. Castro, who was not consulted nor informed of the decision until it was a done deal, was livid and reputedly smashed a mirror in his anger. More bad luck was on the way.

BUILDING SOCIALISM WORLDWIDE

The learning curve was steep in the Revolution's first decade. The economy continued to languish in the doldrums despite massive injections of Soviet aid, and production was marked by all of the normal inconsistencies, short-

1977	1980	1988
In a thaw in relations under Jimmy Carter, the US establishes a Special Interests Section in Havana and Cuba opens an equivalent office in Washington DC.	Following an incident at the Peruvian embassy, Castro opens up the Cuban port of Mariel to anyone wanting to leave. Within six months 125,000 have fled the island for the US in the so-called Mariel Boatlift.	Cuban forces play a crucial role in the Battle of Cuito Cuanavale in Angola, a serious defeat for the white South African Army that's considered one of the final nails in the coffin of the apartheid system.

ages and quality issues that characterize uncompetitive socialist markets. As National Bank president and later Minister of Industry, Che Guevara advocated centralization and moral, rather than material, incentives for workers. But despite his own tireless efforts to lead by example and sponsor voluntary work weekends, all attempts to create the New Man (an individual inspired by moral rather than financial rewards), ultimately proved to be unsustainable.

The effort to produce a 10-million-ton sugar harvest in 1970 was equally misguided and almost led to economic catastrophe, as the country ditched everything in pursuit of one all-encompassing obsession.

Adamant to learn from its mistakes, the Cuban government elected to diversify and mechanize after 1970, ushering in a decade of steadier growth and relative economic prosperity. As power was decentralized and a small market economy was permitted to flourish, people's livelihoods gradually began to improve and, for the first time in decades, Cubans started to live more comfortably, due in no small part to burgeoning trade with the Soviet bloc, which increased from 65% of the total in the early 1970s to 87% in 1988.

> Cuba began its developing-world medical assistance by sending 56 doctors to Algeria. It now has ongoing medical programs with 58 developing-world countries.

With the home front starting to reawaken from a deep slumber, Castro turned his attention toward the international stage and his vision for Cuba as leader of a developing-world coalition in global affairs. The idea was nothing new. Covertly, Cuba had been sponsoring guerrilla activity in South America and Africa since the early 1960s, as documented in various historical sources, and in 1965 Che Guevara had spent nine largely fruitless months in the Republic of Congo trying to ignite a popular uprising among a fractious band of antigovernment rebels. Quickly abandoning his plans in frustration, Guevara resurfaced a year later in Bolivia where he launched another equally fruitless campaign aimed at inspiring the Bolivian peasantry to rise up against their oppressive militaristic government. However, the Cuban model didn't translate well to the Bolivian reality and Bolivian troops, with heavy US support, captured Guevara on October 8, 1967. Shot the next day by a nervous alcohol-plied executioner he went down in history much as Martí had done before him – a martyr.

In an interesting footnote to the story, Guevara's remains, which lay in an unmarked grave beneath a Bolivian airfield for nearly 30 years, were rediscovered in 1997 and returned to Cuba amid much ceremony. They now rest in a mausoleum adjacent to the Plaza de la Revolución in Che's adopted Cuban city of Santa Clara (p279).

Another heavy and costly adventure was Cuba's involvement in the Angolan war. Initially invited to send troops to Luanda by Angolan leader Agostinho Neto in November 1975, the Cubans quickly became bogged down in a long and complex bush war that pitted tribe against tribe and Marxist MPLA (Movimento Popular de Libertação de Angola) govern-

1989	**1991**	**1993**
Former M-26-7 loyalist and hero of the Angolan War, General Arnaldo Ochoa is arrested on charges of corruption and drug trafficking. After being found guilty of treason by a military court, he is executed by firing squad.	The Soviet Union collapses and Cuba heads for the worst economic collapse of modern times, entering what Castro calls a 'Special Period in a Time of Peace.'	Attempting to revive itself from its economic coma, Cuba legalizes the US dollar, opens up the country to tourism and allows limited forms of private enterprise.

ment against South Africa's reactionary apartheid regime. Famous for their tenacity in battle and oft-lauded for their bravery under fire, the Cubans slugged it out for over 10 years alongside poorly trained MPLA forces and heavy-duty Soviet weaponry. But, despite a military defeat over the apartheid regime in 1988, the price of the Angolan escapade was inexorably high – for many, too high. Barely mentioned in Cuban history books, the Angolan war conscripted over 300,000 Cubans between 1975 and 1991 and left 14,000 of them dead. And the end result was negligible. The war in Angola dragged on until 2002, killing an estimated 1.5 million Angolans and leaving the country a mess.

In 1976 a third Cuban constitution was drawn up and approved by referendum; Fidel Castro replaced Osvaldo Dorticós as president.

CRISIS AS THE WALL FALLS

The 'wet foot, dry foot' law (Cuban Adjustment Act) signed by Bill Clinton in 1995 means that only Cubans who make it onto US soil can apply for citizenship. Those picked up at sea are summarily sent home.

After almost 25 years of a top-down Soviet-style economy, it was obvious that quality was suffering and ambitious production quotas were becoming increasingly unrealistic. In 1986 Castro initiated the 'rectification of errors' campaign, a process that aimed to reduce malfunctioning bureaucracy and allow more local-level decision-making to wrest control. Just as the process was reaping some rewards the Eastern bloc collapsed in the dramatic events that followed the fall of the Berlin Wall in Europe. As trade and credits amounting to US$5 billion vanished almost overnight from the Cuban balance sheet, Castro – adamant to avoid the fate of East German leader Erich Honecker and Romanian president Ceausescu – declared a five-year *período especial* (Special Period; Cuba's economic reality post-1991) austerity program that sent living standards plummeting and instituted a system of rationing that would make the sacrifices of wartime Europe almost pale in comparison. Any Cuban over the age of 25 can furnish you with painful horror stories from this era, including tales of fried grapefruit skins, micro-jet rice and pigs being reared in the bathroom.

Sniffing the blood of a dying communist animal, the US tightened the noose in 1992 with the harsh Torricelli Act, which forbade foreign subsidiaries of US companies from trading with Cuba and prohibited ships that had called at Cuban ports from docking at US ports for six months. Ninety percent of the trade banned by this law consisted of food, medicine and medical equipment, which led the American Association for World Health to conclude in 1997 that the US embargo had caused a significant rise in suffering – even deaths – in Cuba.

In August 1993, with the country slipping rapidly into an economic coma and Havana on the verge of riot, the US dollar was legalized, allowing Cubans to hold and spend foreign currency and open US-dollar bank accounts. Spearheaded by the unlikely figure of Raúl Castro, other liberal reforms followed including limited private enterprise, self-employment, the opening of

1996	**1998**	**2000**
Miami 'Brothers to the Rescue' planes are shot down by Cuban jets, provoking Bill Clinton to sign the Helms-Burton Act, further tightening the terms of the US embargo.	Pope John Paul II visits Cuba and is watched by more than one million people in Havana. Despite conversing politely with Castro, he diplomatically questions Cuba's human-rights record.	The Elián González affair adds new drama to fraught US-Cuban relations when five-year-old Elián is picked up at sea and brought (illegally) to the US. After an international furor, he is returned to his father in Cuba.

farmers markets and the expansion of the almost nonexistent tourist sector into a mainstay of the new burgeoning economy.

But the recovery was not without its problems. Class differences re-emerged as people with US dollars began to gain access to goods and services not available in pesos, while touts and prostitutes known as *jineteros/jineteras* took up residence in tourist areas where they preyed upon rich foreigners whose designer clothes and comfortable capitalist lifestyles they longed to emulate.

Although some of the worst shortages have been alleviated thanks to the reinvestment of tourist revenue into public services, the *período especial* has left a nasty scar. Much to the popular chagrin, the government also started to go back on some of its earlier liberalization measures in an attempt to reestablish an updated brand of old socialist orthodoxy (eg by raising the taxes in casas particulares and limiting their capacity).

Following the 1994 *balsero* crisis (whereby temporarily loosened restrictions on emigration caused more than 36,000 Cubans to flee to the US, many of them on homemade rafts) and a handful of further shots in the ongoing diplomatic war that had been plaguing US-Cuban relations for decades, the US pulled the embargo a notch tighter in 1996 by signing the Helms-Burton Act into law. Widely condemned by the international community, and energetically leapt upon by Castro as a devastating propaganda tool, the bill allows US investors to take legal action in the American courts against foreign companies utilizing their confiscated property in Cuba. It also prevents any US president from lifting the embargo until a transitional government is in place in Havana.

THE NEW LEFT TIDE

Cuba entered the new millennium in the throes of the Elián González drama, a tragic family crisis that was to become an allegory for the all-pervading senselessness of the ongoing Cuban-American immigration showdown.

Further problems were faced with the new Bush administration across the water who rolled back US policy to resemble the worst of the Cold War years with rigid travel restrictions, economically damaging financial constraints and a hawkish no-compromise political rhetoric.

At home Castro lost vital friends in the EU (who placed sanctions on high-level diplomatic visits) after two crackdowns in 2003 and 2005 that threw more than 100 political dissidents into jail. Castro claimed the dissidents were political agitators sponsored by new US Special Interests Office chief James Cason to spread social unrest across the island. Most human rights groups worldwide, including Amnesty International, agreed to differ.

While ostensibly things have improved immeasurably in Cuba since the dark days of the *período especial*, the subsequent socio-economic changes have set in motion numerous seemingly irreversible trends. By dangling

In 2001 Maine became the first US state to pass a resolution calling for a complete end to the trade and travel ban against Cuba.

2002	2003	2004
Half of Cuba's sugar refineries are closed, signaling the end of a three-century-long addiction to the boom-bust mono-crop. Laid-off sugar workers continue to draw full salaries and are offered free education grants.	The Bush administration tightens the noose for US citizens traveling to Cuba. Many political dissidents are arrested by Cuban authorities in an island-wide crackdown.	In a sharp reaction to the Bush administration's new travel restrictions, Castro takes the US dollar out of circulation and charges all foreign visitors an 11% tax to change money.

the carrot of capitalism in front of the Cuban populace in the form of all-inclusive tourism, limited private enterprise and the legalization of US dollar (1993 to 2004), the psychology of Cuba's 'one size fits all' socialism has been irrevocably damaged.

But it's not all bad news. On the international scene Cuba has successfully managed to wrest itself free from its once near-fatal addiction to sugarcane and has branched out confidently into other areas. Spearheading a mini-economic revival is a clutch of new industries such as tourism, nickel-mining and the island's internationally famous medical sector. The latter service has played a large part in fostering a strong economic and political alliance with Cuba's new friends in Venezuela. In exchange for Cuban doctors and teachers Venezuelan president Hugo Chávez has furnished Cuba with millions of dollars worth of petroleum from his country's abundant oil wells; this deal also enabled him to enact vital social reforms. It doesn't end there. Thanks to the success of a medical exchange program known as Operación Milagros (which offered free laser-eye treatment to Venezuelans in Cuban hospitals), this cooperation has been extended to a number of other countries throughout the region and evidence of a new left tide in Latin American politics, which may one day challenge the hegemony of the United States, is growing.

Much to the chagrin of his avowed enemies, Fidel Castro's eagerly anticipated political demise didn't precipitate the radical 'regime change' that had long been touted. Instead this gnarly veteran of the Revolution, Cold War and the economic chaos that followed was shunted off onto the sidelines relatively quietly in July 2006 following a serious, but not life-threatening, illness. Power was passed temporarily – and, in February 2008, permanently – onto his younger and slightly less dogmatic brother Raúl, whose demeanor was once likened by Castro biographer Tad Szulc to that of a 'self-satisfied Spanish grocer.'

Despite some progressive but largely symbolic early reforms, Raúl's first year in office sprung few big surprises during an *annus horribilis* in which the global economic downturn coupled with a trio of devastating hurricanes largely put the brakes on the country's post–Special Period economic rebirth. Perhaps more important for the future of US-Cuban relations is the political reawakening that greeted the inauguration of Barack Obama in the United States in January 2009. While the Obama administration's initial efforts will surely be devoted to tackling the global economic crisis and the problems faced in the Middle East, the noises made by the new government vis-à-vis better relations with Cuba have been the most open-minded and encouraging for decades. Following the easing of travel restrictions for Cuban-Americans in March 2009, for the first time in nearly 50 years an end to the embargo and a total relaxation of US travel restrictions have started to look like a realistic possibility.

In 2005 *Human Rights Watch* condemned the travel restrictions imposed by both Cuba and the US, saying: 'Both countries are sacrificing people's freedom of movement to promote dead-end policies.'

2006

Castro is taken ill just before his 80th birthday with divertilitus disease and steps down from the day-to-day running of the country. He is replaced by his brother Raúl.

2008

Castro officially steps down as Cuban president after 49 years at the helm. His position is filled by Raúl Castro who spends his first few months in power passing moderate reforms.

2009

The inauguration of Barack Obama in the US signifies a long-awaited thaw in Cuban-US relations. In an early act of rapprochement, Obama loosens restrictions for Cuban-Americans returning to the island to visit relatives.

The Culture

THE NATIONAL PSYCHE

Funny, gracious, generous, tactile and slow to anger, the Cuban people are the Irish of the Americas; a small nation with a big personality, and plenty of rum-fueled backs-to-the-wall boisterousness to go with it. Take the time to get to know them on their own turf and you're halfway to understanding what this most confounding and contradictory of Caribbean countries is all about.

Survivors by nature and necessity, Cubans have long displayed an almost inexhaustible ability to bend the rules and 'work things out' when it matters. In a country where so much is impossible, anything becomes possible, and from the backstreets of Baracoa to the hedonistic heights of Havana nobody's shy about 'giving it a go.'

The two most overused verbs in the national phrasebook are *conseguir* (to get, manage) and *resolver* (to resolve, work out), and Cubans are experts at doing both. Their intuitive ability to bend the rules and make something out of nothing is borne out of economic necessity. In a small nation bucking modern sociopolitical realities, where monthly salaries top out at around the equivalent of US$25, survival can often mean getting innovative as a means of supplementing personal income. Cruise the crumbling streets of Centro Habana and you'll see people *conseguir*-ing and *resolver*-ing wherever you go. There's the casa particular owner offering guided tours using his car as a taxi, or the lady selling lobsters in defiance of government regulations. Other schemes may be ill-gotten or garnered through trickery, such as the *compañero* (comrade) who pockets the odd blemished cigar from the day job to sell to unsuspecting Canadians. Old Cuba hands know one of the most popular ways to make extra cash is working with (or over) tourists.

In Cuba, hard currency (ie Convertible pesos) rules, primarily because it is the only way of procuring the modest luxuries that make living in this austere socialist republic vaguely bearable. Paradoxically, the post-1993 double economy has reinvigorated the class system the Revolution worked so hard to neutralize, and it's no longer rare to see Cubans with access to Convertibles touting designer clothing while others hassle tourists mercilessly for bars of soap. This stark re-emergence of 'haves' and 'have nots' is among the most ticklish issues facing Cuba today.

Other social traits absorbed since the Revolution are more altruistic and less divisive. In Cuba sharing is second nature and helping out your *compañero* with a lift, a square meal or a few Convertibles when they're in trouble is considered a national duty. Check the way that strangers interact in queues or at transport intersections and log how your casa owner always refers you onto someone else, often on the other side of the country.

In such an egalitarian system the notion of fairness is often sacred, and although the image of Che's New Man (an individual inspired by moral rather than financial rewards) might be looking a little worn around the edges these days, the social cohesion that characterized the lean years of the *período especial* (Special Period; Cuba's economic reality post-1991) remains loosely intact. One of the most common arguments you'll see in a Cuban street is over queue-jumping – a fracas that won't just engage the one or two people directly involved, but half the town.

Life in Cuba is open and interactive. Come 10pm, the whole population will be sitting outside on their rocking chairs shooting the breeze over dominoes, cigars, cheap rum or the omnipresent TV sets. Home life is important here and often three generations of the same family can be found living together

For the best up-to-date Cuban cultural news in English go to www.cuba now.net for an easy-to-read and informative exposé on everything and everyone connected with Cuban culture from Frank Sinatra to Graham Greene.

Cuba has 70,000 qualified doctors. The whole of Africa has only 50,000.

under one roof. Such binding ties make the complex question of the embargo all the more painful. One of the saddest effects of the US-Cuban deep freeze is the broken families. Precipitated by prejudicial immigration policies on Washington's part and downright intransigence from the brothers Castro, many Cubans have left home in search of brighter horizons and almost everyone has a long-lost sister, cousin or aunt making it good (or not so good) overseas.

But it's not all bad news. Meager wages have risen in recent years and new economic relations with Venezuela, China and India have taken the sting out of Cuba's ongoing shortages. Nonetheless, the brow-creased refrain of *no es fácil* (it ain't easy) is still widely heard in the streets and bars of Cuba, in response to a government which has an eerie habit of giving with one hand while taking away with the other.

LIFESTYLE

Cuban socialism dances to its own strangely off-beat rhythm. While Cubans technically own their homes, they can't sell them for a profit, only swap them for a house of equivalent size. Though there's no mortgage to pay, housing shortages mean three or even four generations might live under the same roof, which gets tight in a two-bedroom apartment. This also cramps budding love lives, and Cubans will tell you it's the reason the country is one of the world's highest divorce rates. On the flip side, a full house means there's almost always someone to babysit, take care of you when you're sick or do the shopping while you're at work.

Cuban women have been liberated in the sense that they have access to education and training of any sort they desire. In fact, women make up 66% of the professional and technical workforce. But, like everywhere, a glass ceiling still exists in some fields (eg politics) and the home is still largely the woman's responsibility, which translates to a 'double workday' – women go to work and then come home, to work. Thanks to specific government policies, such as one-year guaranteed maternity leave and free day care, it's easier being a mother *and* a career woman in Cuba. Children are an integral part of life and kids are everywhere – the theater, church, restaurants and rock concerts. It's refreshing that Cubans don't drastically alter their lives once they become parents.

That women are turning to hustling to make some extra cash or attain baubles is disturbing. While some *jineteras* (women who attach themselves to male foreigners for monetary or material gain) are straight-up hookers, others are just getting friendly with foreigners for the perks they provide: a ride in a car, a night out in a fancy disco or a new pair of jeans. Some are after more, others nothing at all. It's a complicated state of affairs and can be especially confusing for male travelers who get swept up in it.

Most homes don't have computers or flat-screen TVs, infinitesimally few have internet access and disposable income is an oxymoron. All of this has a huge effect on lifestyle. What makes Cuba different from somewhere like Bolivia or Appalachia though, are the government's heavy subsidies of every facet of life, meaning there is no mortgage, no health-care bills, no college fees and little tax. Expensive nights out cost next to nothing in Cuba where tickets for the theater, the cinema, the ballpark or a music concert are state-subsidized and considered a right of the people. Now if only there was the transport to get there. Still, with a set of dominoes or a guitar, a bottle of rum and a group of friends, who needs baseball or the ballet?

ECONOMY

Nearly destroyed during the economic meltdown that followed the collapse of the Soviet Union in the early 1990s, the Cuban economy has defied all logic by its continued survival. Given new life with a three-pronged recovery plan

Cuban tobacco and cigar exports net approximately CUC$200 million annually, but every year 6000 Cubans die from smoking-related illnesses.

In 2008 the state-owned oil company Cubapetroleo estimated that there may be as much as 21 billion barrels of oil in Cuban waters, a potential haul that would give Cuba a greater capacity than the US and put it in the top 20 oil producers in the world.

INNOVATIONS OF THE SPECIAL PERIOD

When it comes to inventiveness in the face of austerity, the Cubans are world champions – primarily because they've had to be. Burdened with a crippling economic meltdown in the early 1990s, society was forced to mobilize behind what Castro termed a 'Special Period in a Time of Peace.' In an era of drastic shortages, the island threw up some of modern history's unlikeliest innovations, many of which are still going strong nearly 20 years later.

- **Amarillos** When your transportation network collapses overnight, you've only got one option: promote hitchhiking. Even better, make it a legal obligation. *Amarillos* (named for their faded yellow uniforms) are traffic organizers who stand at official hitchhiking points on the periphery of Cuban towns and flag down vehicles for car-less commuters. All cars with government (blue) license plates are legally obliged to stop.

- **Camellos** Though not indigenous to Cuba, camels first arrived on the island in the early 1990s. But far from resembling the graceful 'ships of the desert,' Cuban camels were a cross between a metro bus and a Russian truck. Cuba's 'two-humped' urban buses ran along seven metro routes in Havana that were originally earmarked for an urban subway system that never reached fruition. In 2007 they were finally phased out and replaced by sleeker, more comfortable Chinese 'bendy' buses.

- **Casas particulares** The Cubans were first allowed to let out their houses as bed-and-breakfasts in 1997 and the new laws quickly created a deluge. By the early 2000s there were literally thousands of family homes renting out rooms to both Cubans and foreigners all over the country. While government taxes have tightened over the years and the government inspections have become increasingly stringent, the trend shows no signs of abating.

- **Grapefruit steaks** You might have tried veggie steaks or even – at a stretch – vegan steaks but, during the lean '90s, Cuba's top TV chefs began circulating a recipe for grapefruit steaks. Carefully cut the rind off, cover the fruit in breadcrumbs and hey presto…

- **Paladares** While the initial effect of the Special Period was to send Cuban cuisine (which was already decidedly iffy) plummeting back into the dark age, the long-term consequences for food were surprisingly refreshing. By the early 2000s privately operated family restaurants known as paladares had overcome draconian government regulations and started to produce dishes that were healthy, edible and surprisingly delicious.

- **Peso pizza** In the 1970s, few Cubans knew what a pizza was. By the '90s, they were cooking up more than the Italians. Oven-baked in makeshift kitchens, peso pizzas (so called because you pay for them in Cuban pesos) reinvigorated a hungry nation during the dark days of the Special Period – and made a pleasant change from grapefruit steaks.

- **Stretch Ladas** It took a unique kind of panache to take the world's ugliest car and make it into a sexy limo, but armed with a blowtorch, some metal bashers and a lucid imagination, the Cubans came up with the 'stretch' Lada.

in 1993 that included the legalization of the US dollar (retracted in 2004), the limited opening up of the private sector and the frenzied promotion of the tourist industry in resort areas such as Varadero and Cayo Coco, net advances have been slow but steady with much of the benefits yet to filter down to the average person on the street in Havana or Santiago. Throwing off its heavy reliance on old staples such as sugar and tobacco, Cuba's recent economic development has spun inexorably toward Latin America in the shape of new trade agreements such as the 2004 Bolívarian Alternative for the Americas (ALBA) accords that have exchanged Cuban medical know-how for Venezuelan oil. Other modern economic mainstays include nickel-mining (Cuba is among the world's largest producers) and pharmaceuticals. Along with the rest of the world, at the time of writing Cuba was significantly impacted by the 2008–09 economic downturn.

China is Cuba's second-biggest trading partner (after Venezuela). In 2008 the Chinese extended a US$350-million credit package to repair and renovate Cuban hospitals.

POPULATION

The slave trade and the triumph of the Cuban Revolution are two of the most important factors in Cuba's population mix. From Santería traditions to popular slang, Afro-Cuban culture is an integral part of the national identity. According to the 2002 census, Cuba's racial breakdown is 24% *mulato* (mixed race), 65% white, 10% black and 1% Chinese. Aside from the obvious Spanish legacy, many of the so-called 'white' population are the descendants of French immigrants who arrived on the island in various waves during the early part of the 19th century. Indeed, the cities of Guantánamo, Cienfuegos and Santiago de Cuba were all either pioneered or heavily influenced by French émigrés, and much of Cuba's coffee and sugar industry owes its development to French entrepreneurship.

The black population is also an eclectic mix. Numerous Haitians and Jamaicans came to Cuba to work in the sugar fields in the 1920s and they brought many of their customs and traditions with them. Their descendants can be found in Guantánamo and Santiago in the Oriente or places such as Venezuela in Ciego de Ávila province where Haitian voodoo liturgies are still practiced. Another important immigrant town is Baraguá in Ciego de Ávila, which is famous for its English-speaking West Indian community who still celebrate their annual 'freedom day' each August with a game of cricket.

The invitation to partake in free education up to university level had Cubans pouring into the cities from the countryside after the Revolution, so that today the urban population is a top-heavy 75%. In an effort to stem or reverse this trend, the government offered land incentives to urbanites during the *período especial* to encourage resettling in rural areas, and since May 1998 Cubans have needed official permission to relocate to Havana.

There are no official class breakdowns in Cuba, although class divisions based on income have begun to rear their ugly head since the beginning of the *período especial*. More refreshingly, Cuba is one of the few countries in the world where the notion of doffing your cap to someone of higher social stature is virtually nonexistent.

SPORT

Considered a right of the masses, professional sport was abolished by the government after the Revolution. Performance-wise it was the best thing the new administration could have done. Since 1959 Cuba's Olympic medal haul has rocketed into the stratosphere. The crowning moment came in 1992 when Cuba – a country of 11 million people languishing low on the world's rich list – brought home 14 gold medals and ended fifth on the overall medals table. It's a testament to Cuba's high sporting standards that their 11th-place finish in Athens in 2004 was considered something of a national failure.

Characteristically the sporting obsession starts at the top. Fidel Castro was once renowned for his baseball-hitting prowess, but what is lesser known was his personal commitment to the establishment of a widely accessible national sporting curriculum at all levels. In 1961 the National Institute of Sport, Physical Education and Recreation (Inder) founded a system of sport for the masses that eradicated discrimination and integrated children from a young age. By offering paid leisure-time to workers and dropping entrance fees to major sports events, the organization caused participation in popular sports to multiply tenfold by the 1970s and the knock-on effect to performance was tangible.

Cuban *pelota* (baseball) is legendary and the country is riveted during the October–March regular season, turning rabid for the play-offs in April. You'll see passions running high in the main square of provincial capitals, where fans debate minute details of the game with lots of finger-wagging in what is

Habana Vieja is one of the most crowded quarters in Latin America, with more than 70,000 people living in an area of just 4.5 sq km.

On being offered US$5 million to turn professional and fight Muhammad Ali in the 1970s, Cuban triple heavyweight boxing champion, Teófilo Stevenson, is purported to have said 'Why do I need US$5 million when I already have the love of five million Cubans.'

known as a *peña deportiva* (fan club) or *esquina caliente* (hot corner). These are among the most opinionated venues in Cuba, and the *esquina* in Havana's Parque Central (see boxed text, p116) is highly entertaining, especially in the postseason when funereal wreaths and offerings to *orishas* (Santería deities) appear for eliminated teams and those still contending. Sometimes a Cuban player is lured to the US, like José Ariel Contreras, who pitched for Pinar, but now earns millions playing for the Chicago White Sox (he formerly played for the Yankees). Most players, however, shun the big-money bait and the opportunity to play in baseball's greatest stadiums, opting instead to continue earning the equivalent of around US$20 per month – decisions that make their athletic achievements all the more admirable.

Cuba is also a giant in amateur boxing, as indicated by champions Teófilo Stevenson, who brought home Olympic gold in 1972, 1976 and 1980, and Félix Savón, another triple medal winner, most recently in 2000. Every sizable town has an arena called *sala polivalente,* where big boxing events take place, while training and smaller matches happen at gyms, many of which train Olympic athletes. Travelers interested in sparring lessons or seeing a match should drop in at a gym (see individual regional chapters for information). For boxing shows, ask around at the local *sala polivalente* or keep an eye out for posters advertising upcoming bouts. As with all sporting events in Cuba, entrance to professional-standard (though technically amateur) shows is cheap and relatively hassle-free.

Basketball, volleyball (the national women's team won gold at the 2000 Sydney Olympic Games) and, to a lesser extent, football are all popular in Cuba, but *dominó* (always referred to in the singular) and chess, both considered sports, are national passions. Self-taught José Raúl Capablanca, touted as the greatest ever natural chess player, became World Chess Champion in 1921; you'll see chess matches on the street and read about the masters in the sports pages. *Dominó* is everywhere and you'll find quartets of old men and young boys slugging back shots of rum and slamming down their tiles in every Cuban neighborhood. In March 2003 Havana hosted the first annual Campeonato Mundial de Dominó (World Domino Championship), with 10 countries and thousands of players participating. The finals were held in Ciudad Deportiva, where Cuba won it all. Cockfighting, while technically illegal, is still practiced widely in Cuba with clandestine shows attracting a large number of mainly male spectators who come to gamble away their hard-earned pesos.

Cuban high-jumper Javier Sotomayor is, arguably, the best high-jumper in history. He has held the world record for the event (2.45m) since 1993 and has recorded 17 of the 24 highest jumps ever.

MULTICULTURALISM

Despite the fact that racism was abolished by law after the Revolution, Cuba is still facing up to the difficult challenges of establishing lasting racial equality in a widely cosmopolitan and multicultural society. While there are no ghettos or gangs in Cuba's larger cities, a quick tally of the roaming *jineteros/jineteras* in Vedado and Habana Vieja will reveal a far higher proportion of black participants. On the other side of the coin, over 90% of Cuban exiles are of white descent, and of the victorious rebel army that took control of the government in 1959 only a handful (Juan Almeida being the most obvious example) were of mixed heritage.

MEDIA

In a country replete with writers, sages and poets, Cuba's media is without doubt one of the Revolution's greatest failures. The only daily national newspaper – a dour eight-page tabloid called *Granma* – is an insipid dose of politics, politics and yet more politics, all of which pours forth from the all-pervading, all-encompassing propaganda ministries of the Cuban Communist Party.

The silencing of the press was one of Castro's first political acts on taking power in 1959. Challenged with the crime of speaking out against the Revolution, nearly all of Cuba's once independent newspapers were either closed down or taken over by the state by the summer of 1960. Many freelance operators faced a similar fate. In 1965 Guillermo Cabrera Infante, one of Cuba's most respected writers, left for an ignominious exile in London after serving as a cultural attaché in Brussels; many others followed.

Despite some relaxation of press restrictions since the heavy-handed days of the 1970s and '80s, Cuban journalists must still operate inside strict press laws that prohibit the use of antigovernment propaganda and ban the seemingly innocuous act of 'insulting officials in public,' a crime that carries a three-year jail term.

Other limitations include the prohibition of private ownership of the electronic media and a law that prohibits foreign news agencies from hiring local journalists without first going through official government channels.

Most foreign observers, both in and outside Cuba, agree that the Cuban media situation is an unmitigated disaster. Furthermore, in 2005 the New York–based Committee to Protect Journalists revealed that Cuba was one of the world's leading jailers of journalists.

RELIGION

Religion is among the most misunderstood and complex aspects of Cuban culture. Before the Revolution 85% of Cubans were nominal Roman Catholics, though only 10% attended church regularly. Protestants made up most of the remaining church-going public, though a smattering of Jews and Muslims have always practiced in Cuba and still do. When the Revolution triumphed, 140 Catholic priests were expelled for reactionary political activities and another 400 left voluntarily, while the majority of Protestants, who represented society's poorer sector, had less to lose and stayed.

When the government declared itself Marxist-Leninist and therefore atheist, life for *creyentes* (literally 'believers') took on new difficulties. Though church services were never banned and freedom of religion never revoked, Christians were sent to Unidades Militares de Ayuda a la Producción (UMAPs; Military Production Aid Units), where it was hoped hard labor might reform their religious ways; homosexuals and vagrants were also sent to the fields to work. This was a short-lived experiment, however. More trying for believers were the hard-line Soviet days of the '70s and '80s, when they were prohibited from joining the Communist Party and few, if any, believers held political posts. Certain university careers, notably in the humanities, were off-limits as well.

Things have changed dramatically since then, particularly in 1992 when the constitution was revised, removing all references to the Cuban state as Marxist-Leninist and recapturing the laical nature of the government. This led to an aperture in civil and political spheres of society for religious adherents, and to other reforms (eg believers are now eligible for party membership). Since Cuban Catholicism gained the papal seal of approval with Pope John Paul II's visit in 1998, church attendance has surged and posters welcoming him are still displayed with pride. It's worth noting that church services have a strong youth presence. There are currently 400,000 Catholics regularly attending Mass and 300,000 Protestants from 54 denominations. Other denominations such as the Seventh Day Adventists and Pentecostals are rapidly growing in popularity.

The religious beliefs of Africans brought to Cuba as slaves were originally layered over Catholic iconography and doctrines, eventually forming new belief systems. Santería (also known as Lucumí) – a complicated mix of Catholicism and Yoruba beliefs – is the most widespread of these and is an integrated part of daily life here; you'll see initiates dressed in white everywhere you go and many

In June 2008 the Cuban government legalized sex-change operations and agreed to provide them free to qualifying parties.

homes have altars tucked into the corners. Other hybrids include Abakuá, a se-cret society with ancestry in Cameroon and Nigeria, and Arará, a cross between Lucumí and Voodoo celebrated for its distinctive drumming rituals.

Santería has served as a cultural ambassador of sorts, with new museums and dance and drum performances becoming standard itinerary fare. Some take exception to this 'folkloricization' of the sacred – dressing all in white has now become fashionable whether you're initiated or not, for example – and curious tourists may be taken to consultations with *babalawos* (priests) more interested in your money than your dilemmas.

ARTS

In contrast to some other communist countries, Cuba's reputation as a powerhouse of art and culture is nothing short of staggering. Each provincial town, no matter how small, has a Casa de Cultura that stages everything from traditional salsa music to innovative comedy nights and, on top of this, countless other theaters, organizations and institutions bring highbrow art to the masses completely free of charge.

The quality of what's on offer is equally amazing. The Cubans seem to have made a habit out of taking almost any artistic genre and replicating it perfectly. You'll pick up first-class flamenco, ballet, classical music and Shakespearean theater here in the most mundane of places, not to mention Lorca plays, alternative cinema and illuminating deconstructions of novels by the likes of Márquez and Carpentier.

Several governmental organizations countrywide oversee the work of writers and artists, including the revered Casa de las Américas, the Unión de Escritores y Artistas de Cuba (Uneac; Union of Cuban Writers and Artists; see boxed text, p60) and its junior counterpart, Asociación Hermanos Saíz.

Although art and culture are actively encouraged in Cuban society, writers of all genres are set strict limits. Conformists (national poet Nicolás Guillén was the best example) enjoy prestige, patronage and a certain amount of artistic freedom, while dissidents (Guillermo Cabrera Infante and Herberto Padilla were two notable historical examples) face oppression, incarceration and the knowledge that their hard-won literary reputation will be quickly airbrushed out of Cuban history.

For information on Cuban music styles, check out the dedicated Music chapter (p65).

In June 2008 the EU finally lifted a set of sanctions against Cuba relating to governmental and diplomatic visits. The sanctions had first been imposed in 2003 following Cuba's jailing of more than 100 political dissidents.

Literature

In a country strewn with icons like rice at a wedding, José Martí (1853–95) is the master. Visionary, patriot and rebel, he was also a literary giant whose collected plays, essays and poetry fill 30 volumes. Exiled for his writings before he was 20, Martí lived most of his life outside Cuba, primarily in the US. His last book of poetry, *Versos Sencillos* (Simple Verses), is, as the title proclaims, full of simple verses and is arguably one of his best. Though written more than a century ago, the essays collected in *Nuestra América* (Our America) and *Los Estados Unidos* (The United States) are remarkably forward-thinking, providing a basis for Latin American self-determination in the face of US hegemony. For more on Martí's role as Cuban independence leader, see the History chapter (p40).

Like Martí, *mulato* Nicolás Guillén (1902–89) is considered one of Cuba's world-class poets. Ahead of his time, he was one of the first mainstream champions of Afro-Cuban culture, writing rhythmic poems such as *Sóngoro Cosongo* (1931). A communist who believed in social and racial equality, Guillén lived in exile during Batista's regime, writing *Elegía a Jesús Menéndez* (1951) and *La Paloma de Vuelo Popular: Elegías* (1958). Some of his most famous poems are available in the English collection entitled *New Love Poetry:*

UNEAC

To be a writer in Cuba is to walk a fine line. On the one hand, the arts on this colorful and highly literate island are actively encouraged; on the other, many liberal free-thinkers have, over time, been repeatedly suppressed.

Founded in 1961 by national poet Nicolás Guillén, the Unión de Escritores y Artistas de Cuba (Uneac; Union of Cuban Writers and Artists) has long acted as the island's official literary mouthpiece. Delegated with the task of redefining Cuban intellectualism within a new postrevolutionary paradigm, Uneac laid out its ambitious agenda in the early 1960s by initiating a series of heated debates about the future of art and social expression within a brave new society.

For a brief period the experimentation appeared to work. Far from being ostracized by Western intellectuals, Castro and his poetry-scribbling cohort Che Guevara came to be viewed as romantic and bohemian figures in Europe and America, and few left-leaning writers or artists remained impervious to their mystique and charm. Eschewing his less flamboyant Kremlin comrades, Fidel happily went his own way in the cultural sphere, hobnobbing with literary luminaries such as Jean Paul Sârtre and forming a close lifelong friendship with Nobel Prize–winning author, Gabriel García Márquez (who has occasionally raised his voice to protect writers' freedoms in Cuba).

But it wasn't all wine and roses. Ever adamant to guard his ethos of 'in the Revolution everything, against the Revolution nothing,' Castro's artistic judgment turned increasingly bellicose in the late '60s and early '70s when skeptical writers and critics were treated with growing intolerance and disdain. With the press effectively silenced and any criticism of the Revolution viewed as largely treasonable, many talented writers fled into exile, including respected novelist Guillermo Cabrera Infante and the former editor of the newspaper *Revolución*, Carlos Franqui.

Yet, despite the draconian clampdown, Cuba somehow managed to avoid the artistic asphyxiations of the Soviet Union and Eastern Europe. Part of the reason for this success is the country's consistently high literacy rate (Cubans are avid readers) coupled with its already strong tradition of music and dance. Another underlying bonus has been the continued loyalty of key cultural icons such as Uneac founder Nicolás Guillén and writer Alejo Carpentier, who have gone a long way in promoting Cuba's culture and artistic image abroad.

Headquartered in all of the 14 provinces, Uneac is a welcome sight in any Cuban city. Usually housed in tastefully restored colonial buildings, the centers are friendly and inclusive places that offer fresh and probing art in a variety of different genres. You can catch a music concert here, attend a film debate, see a Lorca play, or view cutting-edge art expos – all for free.

Elegy. He returned after the Revolution and cofounded Uneac (see boxed text, above). Guillén was Cuba's national poet until his death.

Cubans are crazy for poetry, so don't be surprised when someone starts reeling off verses by Dulce María Loynaz (1902–97), recipient of Spain's coveted Miguel de Cervantes literary award; Eliseo Diego (1920–94), the poet's poet, whose words give wings to the human spirit; or singer-songwriter Silvio Rodríguez, who is a good guitar player, but a great poet.

In literature, as in poetry, the Cuban bibliography is awe-inspiring. Novelist Alejo Carpentier (1904–80) was another exiled writer, returning after the Revolution to write *El Recurso del Método* (Reasons of State) and *Concierto Barroco,* both published in 1974. The latter is considered his masterpiece. Havana fans will want to check out his *Ciudad de las Columnas* (The City of Columns; 1970), which juxtaposes B&W photographs of the city's architectural details with insightful prose.

Paradiso by José Lezama Lima (1910–76) was a 'scandalous novel' when it appeared in 1966 because of its erotic (homosexual) scenes. Now it's considered a classic. Lezama was a poet and essayist who cofounded the influential magazine *Orígenes* in 1944.

Notable writers who left Cuba after the Revolution include playwright Reinaldo Arenas (1943–90), whose autobiography *Antes que Anochezca*

(Before Night Falls; 1992) was made into a critically acclaimed drama for the silver screen; and Guillermo Cabrera Infante (1929–2005), whose *Tres Tristes Tigres* (Three Trapped Tigers; 1967) describes cultural decadence during the Batista era. Of course, Cuba's most famous foreign writer-in-residence was Ernest Hemingway, who wrote *For Whom the Bell Tolls* in the Hotel Ambos Mundos in Havana (p129).

Cinema & Television

Cubans are crazy about cinema and this passion is reflected in the plethora of movie houses that exist in all but the smallest towns. Since 1959 the film industry has been run by the Instituto Cubano del Arte e Industria Cinematográficos (Icaic), headed by longtime film sage and former Havana University student, Alfredo Guevara. Guevara is widely recognized, along with other influential filmmakers such as Tomás Gutiérrez Alea (1928–96), as putting cutting-edge Cuban cinema on the international map. Indeed, for years cinema has led the way in cultural experimentation and innovation on the island, exploring themes such as homosexuality, misogyny and bureaucratic paranoia that are generally considered taboo in other parts of Cuban society.

Cuba's first notable postrevolutionary movie, the Cuban-Soviet made *Soy Cuba* (I am Cuba; 1964) dramatized the events leading up to the 1959 Revolution in four interconnecting stories and was once described by an American film critic as 'a unique, insane, exhilarating spectacle.'

Serving his apprenticeship in the 1960s, Cuba's most celebrated director, Tomás Gutiérrez Alea cut his teeth directing art-house movies such as *La Muerte de un Burócrata* (Death of a Bureaucrat; 1966), a satire on excessive socialist bureaucratization; and *Memorias de Subdesarrollo* (Memories of Underdevelopment; 1968), the story of a Cuban intellectual too idealistic for Miami, yet too decadent for the austere life of Havana. Teaming up with fellow director Juan Carlos Tabío in 1993, Gutiérrez went on to make Cuba's all-time movie classic, the Oscar-nominated *Fresa y Chocolate* (Strawberry and Chocolate) – the tale of Diego, a skeptical homosexual who falls in love with a heterosexual communist militant. It remains Cuba's cinematic pinnacle.

Havana's growing influence in the film culture of the American hemisphere is highlighted each year in the Festival Internacional del Nuevo Cine Latinoamericano held every December in Havana. Described alternatively as the ultimate word in Latin American cinema or Cannes without the asskissing, this annual get-together of critics, sages and filmmakers has been fundamental in showcasing recent Cuban classics to the world, such as *Viva Cuba* (2005), a study of class and ideology as seen through the eyes of two children, and *El Benny* (2006), a biopic of mambo king Benny Moré.

To say that Cubans are cinema buffs would be a massive understatement: the crush of a crowd shattered the glass doors of a movie theater during the 2001 film festival in Havana and an adoring mob nearly rioted trying to get into Steven Spielberg's *Minority Report* premier in 2002. If you're headed for a flick, queue early.

Cuban TV has three national channels, no commercials and an obligatory nightly dose of political speeches (infinitely more boring since Fidel stepped down). Elsewhere, educational programming dominates, with Universidad Para Todos (University for All) offering full university-level courses in everything from astronomy to film editing. The news is a predictable litany of good things Cuba has done (eg big tobacco harvest, sending doctors to Africa) and bad things the US is up to (eg mucking around in the Middle East, big corporations buying influence). *Mesa Redonda* (Round Table) is a nightly 'debate' program where several people sharing the same opinion sit around discussing a topic of national or global importance. *Telenovelas* (soap operas) are a national

The 1964 Cuban-Soviet film *Soy Cuba* (I am Cuba) has recently been resurrected as an erstwhile movie classic by a clutch of contemporary directors such as Martin Scorcese for its highly innovative tracking shots and poetic plot.

obsession, and the latest favorite *La Cara Oculta de la Luna* (The Dark Side of the Moon) has been known to bring the country to a virtual standstill.

Architecture

In terms of style, Cuba is a smorgasbord of different architectural genres with influences ranging from Spanish Moorish to French neoclassical to decorative colonial baroque. Emerging relatively unscathed from the turmoil of three revolutionary wars, well-preserved cities such as Camagüey, Santiago de Cuba and Habana Vieja have survived into the 21st century with the bulk of their original colonial features remarkably intact. The preservation has been aided further by the nomination of Trinidad, Cienfuegos and Habana Vieja as Unesco World Heritage Sites.

Some of Cuba's oldest and most engaging architectural creations can be seen in the network of Spanish fortresses erected around the country during the 16th and 17th centuries to deter attacks from pirates and corsairs on the island's coastal cities. Notable examples include Havana's Castillo de la Real Fuerza (p110), the second-oldest fort in the Americas; the labyrinthine Castillo de San Pedro del Morro (p419) in Santiago, designed by Italian military architect Giovanni Bautista Antonelli; and the massive Cabaña (p168) overlooking Havana Bay, the largest fort in the Americas.

Cuban townscapes in the 17th and 18th centuries were dominated by ecclesial architecture, reflected initially in the noble cloisters of Havana's Convento de Santa Clara (p113), built in 1632, and culminating a century or so later in the magnificent Catedral de San Cristóbal (p109), considered by many as the country's most outstanding baroque monument. Some of the best architecture from this period can be viewed in Habana Vieja, whose peculiar layout around *four* main squares – each with its own specific social or religious function – set it apart from other Spanish colonial capitals.

With a booming economy and cash raked in from a series of record-breaking sugarcane harvests, plantation-owners in the small town of Trinidad had money to burn at the start of the 19th century. Ideally positioned to the south of the verdant Valle de los Ingenios and heavily influenced by haute couture furnishings of Italy, France and Georgian England, the city's enterprising sugar merchants ploughed their vast industrial profits into a revitalized new city full of exquisite homes and businesses that juxtaposed popular baroque and neoclassical styles with vernacular Cuban features such as wooden *rejas* (grilles), high ceilings and tiny *postigos* (doors). Isolated on the southern coast and protected by law as part of a Unesco World Heritage Site, the unique and beautiful streets of 19th-century Trinidad remain one of Latin America's most intact colonial cities.

By the mid-19th century sturdy neoclassical buildings were the norm among the country's bourgeoisie in cities such as Cienfuegos and Matanzas, with bold symmetrical lines, grandiose frontages and rows of imposing columns replacing the decorative baroque flourishes of the early colonial period. The style reached its high-water mark in a trio of glittering theaters: the Caridad in Santa Clara (see boxed text, p282), the Sauto in Matanzas (p235) and the Terry Tomás in Cienfuegos (p265). In the 1920s and '30s a neoclassical revival delivered a brand new clutch of towering giants onto the Havana skyline, including the Washington-influenced Capitolio (p114), the monumental Hotel Nacional (p118) and the Athenian Universidad de La Habana (p119).

Eclecticism was the leading style in the new republican era post-1902, with a combination of regurgitated genres such as neo-Gothic, neobaroque, neo-Renaissance and neo-Moorish giving rise to a hotchpotch of groundbreaking buildings that were as eye-catching as they were outrageous. For a wild tour of Cuban eclecticism, check out the Museo de Ciencias Naturales Sandalio

Memorias de Sub-desarrollo (Memories of Underdevelopment), directed by Tomás Gutiérrez Alea, was the first Cuban movie to be shown in the US after the Revolution (in 1968). It chronicles the travails of Sergio, a bourgeois writer undergoing feelings of ambivalence and alienation about Cuba's new revolutionary order.

de Noda in Pinar del Río (p202), the Presidential Palace (now the Museo de la Revolución) in Havana (p116) or the Byzantine-meets-Arabic Palacio de Valle in Cienfuegos (p265).

Bridging the gap between eclecticism and modernism was art deco, a lavish architectural style epitomized in structures such as New York's Chrysler building, and best manifested in Cuba in Havana's opulent Bacardí building (p114) or some of the religious iconography exhibited in the Necrópolis Cristóbal Colón (p120).

Modernism arrived in Havana in the 1950s with a rapid surge of prerevolutionary skyscrapers that eliminated decorative flourishes and merged function rather harmoniously with form. Visitors can observe this rich architectural legacy in the cubic Hotel Habana Libre (p118) or the skyline-hogging Focsa building (p119), an edifice that was constructed – legend has it – without the use of a single crane.

Painting & Sculpture

Painting and sculpture are alive and well in Cuba, despite more than four decades of asphyxiating on-off censorship. From the archaic cave paintings of Cueva Punta del Este on Isla de la Juventud to the vibrant poster art of 1960s Havana, a colorful and broad-ranging artistic pastiche has been painstakingly conserved through arts schools, government sponsorship and an eclectic mix of cross-cultural influences that include everything from Diego Rivera–style murals to European avant-gardism.

Engaging and visceral, modern Cuban art combines lurid Afro–Latin American colors with the harsh reality of the 50-year-old Revolution. For visiting foreign art lovers it's a unique and intoxicating brew. Forced into a corner by the constrictions of the culture-redefining Cuban Revolution, budding artists have invariably found that, by co-opting with (as opposed to confronting) the socialist regime, opportunities for academic training and artistic encouragement are almost unlimited. Encased in such a volatile creative climate, the concept of graphic art in Cuba – well established in its own right before the Revolution – has flourished exponentially.

Serigraphy was first employed on the island at the beginning of the 20th century, but this distinctive style of silk-screen printing didn't gather ground until the 1940s when, in connection with film and political posters, it enjoyed a wide distribution. The genre exploded after the 1959 Revolution when bodies such as Icaic and the propagandist Editora Política were enthusiastically sponsored by the Castro government to create thousands of informative posters designed to rally the Cuban population behind the huge tasks of building a New Society. Eschewing standard Soviet realism, Cuban poster artists mixed inherent Latin American influences with the eye-catching imagery of 1960s pop culture to create a brand new subgenre of their own. This innovative form of poster art can best be viewed at the Taller de Serigrafía René Portocarrero in Habana Vieja (p148).

In the international context, art in Cuba is dominated by the prolific figure of Wilfredo Lam, painter, sculptor and ceramicist of mixed Chinese, African and Spanish ancestry. Born in Sagua La Grande, Villa Clara province in 1902, Lam studied art and law in Havana before departing for Madrid in 1923 to pursue his artistic ambitions in the fertile fields of post-WWI Europe. Displaced by the Spanish Civil War in 1937, he gravitated toward France where he became friends with Pablo Picasso and swapped ideas with the pioneering surrealist André Breton. Having absorbed various cubist and surrealist influences, Lam returned to Cuba in 1941 where he produced his own seminal masterpiece *La Jungla* (The Jungle), considered by critics to be one of the developing world's most representative paintings.

Havana's modernist Edificio Focsa is considered one of the seven wonders of Cuban civil engineering, along with two tunnels, two roads, a bridge and an aqueduct.

Post-Lam Cuba's unique artistic heritage has survived and prospered in Havana's Centro Wilfredo Lam (p109) and the Instituto Superior de Arte (p156) in outlying Cubanacán. The capital is also blessed with a splendid national art museum, the sprawling Museo Nacional de Bellas Artes (p116), housed in two separate buildings. Outside Havana further inspiration can be found in scattered artistic communities in the cities of Santiago, Camagüey and Baracoa. Diehards can also uncover notable artistic work hiding beneath the surface in other less heralded cultural outposts such as Las Tunas (known locally as the 'city of sculptures').

Theater & Dance

Described by aficionados as 'a vertical representation of a horizontal act,' Cuban dancing is famous for its libidinous rhythms and sensuous close-ups. It comes as no surprise to discover that the country has produced some of the most exciting and dexterous dancers in the world. Inheriting a love for dancing from childbirth and able to replicate perfect salsa steps by the age of two or three, Cubans are natural performers who approach dance with a complete lack of self-consciousness; a notion that leaves most visitors from Europe or North America feeling as if they've got two left feet.

Most Cuban dances are connected with a specific genre of music. Rumba is a music style of Afro-Cuban origin in which the rhythm is provided by drums, maracas and a singer. Accompanied by one of three sexually-charged dances, the music provides for a hypnotic and dazzling spectacle that evokes the spirits of Santería *orishas* (deities) who take possession of the dancers and fuel further drumming frenzies. Varieties of rumba dances include the pedestrian *yambú*, the faster *guaguancó* and the acrobatic *columbia*. The latter originated as a devil dance of the Náñigo rite, and today it's performed only by solo males.

Imported into New York in the 1920s, rumba took on big-band credentials and developed into mambo under the influence of Afro-Cuban jazz. Mambo, in turn, sprouted its own distinctive dance pioneered by Cuban bandleader Pérez Prado in the late 1940s. As that was too difficult for many North Americans to master, violinist Enrique Jorrín developed a more straightforward mambo offshoot known as the *chachachá* in the early 1950s and the craze swept America.

On the opposite side of the coin sits *danzón,* a European-influenced ballroom dance that was derived from the French contredanse and the suave strains of the Spanish-influenced *habanera*. A bandleader known as Miguel Failde was responsible for developing the first *danzóns* in the late 1880s when he added syncopated rhythms and a provocative pause to the basic steps. *Danzón* was in vogue from 1880 until 1940, during which time it was progressively Africanized developing such exciting offshoots as *charanga* and *danzón-chá*. It still has a strong influence on Cuban popular music today.

Cuban ballet is synonymous with prima ballerina Alicia Alonso. Now well past her pointe days, Alicia cofounded the Ballet Nacional de Cuba in 1948 and her choreography is still in heavy rotation – classic stuff such as *Don Quixote* and *Giselle*, with few surprises save the powerful dancers themselves. The Festival Internacional de Ballet de La Habana (see boxed text, p127) takes Havana by storm in October every other year, when you can see a *Swan Lake* matinee and an evening performance of *Carmen* – a ballet junkie's dream.

Original Cuban theater is limited, but the Cubans showcase excellent interpretations of classic foreign works including Lorca's plays and Shakespeare's comedies. Havana's theaters also put on surprisingly edgy (and funny) comedy shows, professional rumba dancing and music performed by the Conjunto Folklórico Nacional de Cuba (founded in 1962), and some fantastic children's theater – most big towns have a Teatro Guiñol (puppet theater).

'Described as 'a vertical representation of a horizontal act,' Cuban dancing is famous for its libidinous rhythms and sensuous close-ups.'

Music

'In Cuba the music flows like a river,' wrote Ry Cooder in his sleeve notes to the seminal *Buena Vista Social Club* CD, 'It takes care of you and rebuilds you from the inside out.'

Rich, vibrant, layered and soulful, Cuban music has long acted as a standard-bearer for the sounds and rhythms emanating out of Latin America. From the down-at-heel docks of Matanzas to the bucolic local villages of the Sierra Maestra, everything from *son*, salsa, rumba, mambo, *chachachá*, *charanga* and *danzón* owe at least a part of their existence to the magical musical dynamism that was first ignited here.

Aside from the obvious Spanish and African roots, Cuban music has intermittently called upon a number of other important influences in the process of its embryonic development. Mixed into an already exotic melting pot are genres from France, the US, Haiti and Jamaica. Conversely, Cuban music has also played a key role in developing various melodic styles and movements in other parts of the world. In Spain they called this process *ida y vuelta* (return trip) and it is most clearly evident in a style of flamenco called *guajira*. Elsewhere the 'Cuban effect' can be traced back to forms as diverse as New Orleans jazz, New York salsa, West African Afrobeat, and even the famous Habanera aria in Bizet's opera *Carmen*.

FOLKLORIC ROOTS

Son, Cuba's instantly recognizable signature music, first emerged from the mountains of the Oriente region in the second half of the 19th century, though the earliest known testimonies go back as far as 1570. Famously described by Cuban ethnologist Fernando Ortiz as 'a love affair between the African drum and the Spanish guitar,' the roots of this eclectic and intricately fused rural music lie in two distinct subgenres: rumba and *danzón*.

While drumming in the North American colonies was ostensibly prohibited, the Spanish were slightly less mean-spirited in the treatment of their African brethren. As a result Cuban slaves were able to preserve and pass on many of their musical traditions via influential Santería *cabildos*, religious brotherhoods that re-enacted ancient African percussive music on simple *batá* drums or *chequeré* rattles. Performed at annual festivals or on special Catholic saint's days, this rhythmic yet highly textured dance music was offered up as a form of religious worship to the *orishas* (deities).

Over time the ritualistic drumming of Santería evolved into a more complex genre known as rumba (see boxed text, p66). Rumba first metamorphosed in the dock areas of Havana and Matanzas in the late 19th century and was originally viewed as a lewd and unsophisticated form of entertainment for black Afro-Cubans only. But while the music itself sat well outside the cultural mainstream, the dances and rhythms of rumba gradually permeated more accepted forms of popular Cuban music and it became universally popular.

On the other side of the musical equation sat *danzón*, a type of refined European dance closely associated with the French contredanse or the English 'country dance' of the 19th century. Pioneered by innovative Matanzas band leader Miguel Failde in the 1880s, the Cuban *danzón* quickly developed its own peculiar syncopated rhythm borrowing heavily from Haitian slave influences and, later on, adding such improbable extras as conga drums and vocalists. By the early 20th century Cuban *danzóns* had evolved from a stately ballroom dance played by an *orchestra típica* into a more jazzed-up free-for-all known alternatively as *charanga, danzonete* or *danzón-chá*.

The Empresa de Grabaciones y Ediciones Musicales (Egrem) is Cuba's government-run recording and publishing company. It was formed in 1964 and runs the famous Casas de la Música in Centro Habana, Miramar, Varadero, Trinidad and Santiago de Cuba.

RUMBA

Rumba – Cuba's hypnotic dance music – was first concocted in the docks of Havana and Matanzas during the 1890s when ex-slaves, exposed to a revolving cache of outside influences, began to knock out soulful rhythms on old packing cases in imitation of various African religious rites. As the drumming patterns grew more complex, vocals were added, dances emerged and, before long, the music had grown into a collective form of social expression for all black Cubans.

Spreading in popularity throughout the 1920s and '30s, rumba gradually spawned three different but interrelated dance formats: *guaguancó*, an overtly sexual dance; *yambú*, a slow couple's dance; and *columbia*, a fast, aggressive male dance often involving fire torches and machetes.

Pitched into Cuba's cultural melting pot, these rootsy yet highly addictive musical variants slowly gained acceptance among a new audience of middle-class whites and, by the 1940s, the music had fused with *son* in a new subgenre called *son montuno* which, in turn, provided the building blocks for salsa.

Indeed, so influential was Cuban rumba by the end of WWII that it was transposed back to Africa with experimental Congolese artists such as Sam Mangwana and Franco Luambo (of OK Jazz fame) using ebullient Cuban influences to pioneer their own variation on the rumba theme – a genre popularly known as *soukous*.

Raw, expressive and exciting to watch, Cuban rumba is a spontaneous and often informal affair performed by groups of up to a dozen musicians. Conga drums, claves, *palitos* (sticks), *marugas* (iron shakers) and *cajones* (packing cases) lay out the interlocking rhythms, while the vocals alternate between a wildly improvising lead singer and an answering *coro* (chorus).

The best places to see and hear authentic rumba in Cuba are in its two rumba cities: Havana and Matanzas. The former has great live performances in the Callejón de Hamel (p142) every Sunday at 2pm, El Gran Palenque in Vedado (p142), and Centro Cultural Recreativo Los Orishas in Guanabacoa (p166). The latter showcases the real deal outside the Palacio del Junco (municipal museum) on Friday at 4pm (p232). If you're in Trinidad, check out the 10pm shows at the Palenque de Congos Reales (p307).

Welded together, rumba and *danzón* provided the musical backbone that ultimately paved the way for *son*, a distinctive blend of anticipated African rhythms and melodic rustic guitars over which a singer would improvise from a traditional 10-line Spanish poem known as a *décima*.

In its pure form, *son* was played by a sextet consisting of guitar, *tres* (guitar with three sets of double strings), double bass, bongo and two singers who played maracas and claves (sticks that tap out the beat). Arising from the precipitous mountains of Cuba's influential east, the genre's earliest exponents were the legendary Trio Oriental, who stabilized the sextet format in 1912 when they were reborn as the Sexteto Habanero. Another early *sonero* was singer Miguel Matamoros, whose self-penned *son* classics such as 'Son de la Loma' and 'Lágrimas Negras' are de rigueur among Cuba's ubiquitous musical entertainers, even today.

By the 1930s the sextet had become a septet with the addition of a trumpet, and exciting new musicians such as blind *tres* player Arsenio Rodríguez – a songwriter who Harry Belafonte once called the 'father of salsa' – were paving the way for mambo and *chachachá*.

MAMBO & CHACHACHÁ

In the 1940s and '50s the *son* bands grew from seven pieces to eight and beyond until they became big bands boasting full horn and percussion sections that played rumba, *chachachá* and mambo. The reigning mambo king was Benny Moré (see boxed text, p273), who with his sumptuous voice and rocking 40-piece all-black band was known as El Bárbaro del Ritmo (The Barbarian of Rhythm).

Mambo grew out of *charanga* music which itself was a derivative of *danzón*. Bolder, brassier and altogether more exciting than its two earlier incarnations, the music was characterized by exuberant trumpet riffs, belting saxophones and regular enthusiastic interjections by the singer (usually in the form of the word *dilo!* or 'say it!'). The style's origins are mired in controversy. Some argue that it was invented by native Habanero Orestes López after he penned a new rhythmically dexterous number called 'Mambo' in 1938. Others give the credit to Matanzas band leader Pérez Prado who was the first musician to market his songs under the increasingly lucrative mambo umbrella in the early '40s. Whatever the case, mambo had soon spawned the world's first universal dance craze and, from New York to Buenos Aires, people couldn't get enough of its infectious rhythms.

A variation on the mambo theme, the *chachachá* was first showcased by Havana-based composer and violinist Enrique Jorrín in 1951 while playing with the Orquesta América. Originally known as 'mambo-rumba,' the music was intended to promote a more basic kind of Cuban dance that less coordinated North Americans would be able to master, but it was quickly mambo-ized by overenthusiastic dance competitors who kept adding complicated new steps.

SALSA, TIMBA & JAZZ

Salsa is an umbrella term used to describe a variety of musical genres that emerged out of the fertile Latin New York scene in the 1960s and '70s when jazz, *son* and rumba blended to create a new, brassier sound. While not strictly a product of Cubans living in Cuba, salsa's roots and key influences are descended directly from *son montuno* and owe an enormous debt to innovators such as Pérez Prado, Benny Moré and Miguel Matamoros.

Concocted in the early 1800s, the *habanera* was one of Cuba's earliest hybrid music styles. It was later popularized in Europe by Spanish composer Sebastián Yradier, who wrote the classic song 'La Paloma' after visiting the island in 1860.

The self-styled Queen of Salsa was Grammy award–winning singer and performer Celia Cruz. Born in Havana in 1925, Cruz served the bulk of her musical apprenticeship in Cuba before leaving for self-imposed exile in the US in 1960. But, due to her longstanding opposition to the Castro regime, Cruz' records and music have remained largely unknown on the island despite her enduring legacy elsewhere. Far more influential on their home turf are the legendary salsa outfit Los Van Van, a band formed by Juan Formell in 1969 and one that still performs regularly at venues across Cuba. With Formell at the helm as the group's great improviser, poet, lyricist and social commentator, Los Van Van are one of the few contemporary Cuban groups to have created their own unique musical genre – that of songo-salsa. The band also won top honors in 2000 when they memorably took home a Grammy for their classic album, *Llego Van Van*.

Modern salsa mixed and merged further in the '80s and '90s, allying itself with new cutting-edge musical genres such as hip-hop, *reggaetón* and rap, before coming up with some hot new alternatives, most notably *timba* and songo-salsa.

Timba is, in many ways, Cuba's own experimental and fiery take on traditional salsa. Mixing New York sounds with Latin jazz, *nueva trova*, American funk, disco, hip-hop and even some classical influences, the music is more flexible and aggressive than standard salsa, incorporating greater elements of the island's potent Afro-Cuban culture. Many *timba* bands such as Bambaleo and La Charanga Habanera use funk riffs and rely on less conventional Cuban instruments such as synthesizers and kick drums. Others – such as NG La Banda, formed in 1988 (and often credited as being the inventors of *timba*) – have infused their music with a more jazzy dynamic.

Traditional jazz, considered the music of the enemy in the Revolution's most dogmatic days, has always seeped into Cuban sounds. Jesús 'Chucho'

Valdés' band Irakere, formed in 1973, broke the Cuban music scene wide open with its heavy Afro-Cuban drumming laced with jazz and *son,* and the Cuban capital boasts a number of decent jazz clubs (see p142). Other musicians associated with the Cuban jazz set include pianist Gonzalo Rubalcaba, Isaac Delgado and Adalberto Álvarez y Su Son.

LOS TROVADORES

The original *trovadores* (traditional singers/songwriters) were like wandering medieval minstrels, itinerant songsmiths who plied their musical trade across the Oriente region in the early 20th century, moving from village to village and city to city with the carefree spirit of perennial gypsies. Equipped with simple acoustic guitars and armed with a seemingly limitless repertoire of soft, lilting rural ballads, early Cuban *trovadores* included Sindo Garay, Nico Saquito and Joseíto Fernández, the man responsible for composing the overplayed Cuban *trova* classic, 'Guantanamera.' As the style developed into the 1960s, new advocates such as Carlos Puebla from Bayamo gave the genre a grittier and more political edge penning classic songs such as 'Hasta Siempre Comandante,' his romantic if slightly sycophantic ode to Che Guevara.

Traditional *trova* is still popular in Cuba today though its mantle has been challenged since the '60s and '70s by its more philosophical modern offshoot, *nueva trova* (see boxed text, opposite).

RAP, REGGAETÓN & BEYOND

The contemporary Cuban music scene is an interesting mix of enduring traditions, modern sounds, old hands and new blood. With low production costs, solid urban themes and lots of US-inspired crossover styles, hip-hop and rap are taking the younger generation by storm.

Born in the ugly concrete housing projects of Alamar, Havana, Cuban hip-hop, rather like its US counterpart, has gritty and impoverished roots.

First beamed across the nation in the early 1980s when American rap was picked up on homemade rooftop antennae from Miami-based radio stations, the new music quickly gained ground among a population of young urban blacks culturally redefining themselves during the inquietude of the Special Period. By the '90s groups such as Public Enemy and NWA were de rigueur on the streets of Alamar and by 1995 there was enough hip-hop to throw a festival.

In 2001 Welsh group the Manic Street Preachers became the first Western rock band to play live in Cuba. After the concert, which took place in Havana's Karl Marx theater, Castro commented that their music was very loud, but 'not as loud as war.'

Tempered by Latin influences and censored by the parameters of strict revolutionary thought, Cuban hip-hop – or *reggaetón* as locals prefer to call it – has shied away from US stereotypes taking on a progressive flavor all of its own. Instrumentally the music uses *batá* drums, congas and electric bass, while lyrically the songs tackle important national issues such as sex tourism and the difficulties of the stagnant Cuban economy.

Despite being viewed early on as subversive and antirevolutionary, Cuban hip-hop has gained unlikely support from inside the Cuban government, whose art-conscious legislators consider the music to have played a constructive social role in shaping the future of Cuban youth. Fidel Castro has gone one further, describing hip-hop as 'the vanguard of the Revolution' and – allegedly – once tried his hand at rapping at a Havana baseball game.

Today there are upwards of 800 hip-hop groups in Cuba and the Cuban Rap Festival is well into its second decade. The event even has a sponsor, the fledgling Cuban Rap Agency, a government body formed in 2002 to give official sanction to the country's burgeoning alternative music scene. Groups to look out for include Obsession, 100% Original, Freehole Negro (cofronted by a woman) and Anónimo Consejo, while the best venues are usually the most spontaneous ones.

NUEVA TROVA – THE SOUNDTRACK OF A REVOLUTION

The 1960s were heady days for radical new forms of musical expression. In the US Dylan released *Highway 61 Revisited,* in Britain The Beatles concocted *Sgt Pepper* while, in the Spanish-speaking world, musical activists such as Chilean Víctor Jara and Catalan Joan Manuel Serrat were turning their politically charged poems into passionate protest songs.

Determined to develop their own revolutionary music apart from the capitalist West, the innovative Cubans under the stewardship of Haydee Santamaría, director at the influential Casa de las Américas, came up with *nueva trova.*

A caustic mix of probing philosophical lyrics and folksy melodic tunes, *nueva trova* was a direct descendent of pure *trova,* a bohemian form of guitar music that had originated in the Oriente in the late 19th century.

Post-1959 the genre became increasingly politicized and was taken up by more sophisticated artists such as Manzanillo-born Carlos Puebla, who provided an important bridge between old and new styles with his politically-tinged ode to Che Guevara 'Hasta Siempre Comandante' (1965).

Nueva trova came of age in February 1968 at the Primer Encuentro de la Canción Protesta, a concert organized at the Casa de las Américas in Havana and headlined by such rising stars as Silvio Rodríguez and Pablo Milanés. In cultural context, it was Cuba's mini-Woodstock, an event that resounded forcefully among leftists worldwide as a revolutionary alternative to American rock 'n' roll.

In December 1972 the nascent *nueva trova* movement gained official sanction from the Cuban government during a music festival held in the city of Manzanillo to commemorate the 16th anniversary of the *Granma* landing.

Highly influential throughout the Spanish-speaking world during the '60s and '70s, *nueva trova* has often acted as an inspirational source of protest music for the impoverished and downtrodden populations of Latin America, many of whom looked to Cuba for spiritual leadership in an era of corrupt dictatorships and US cultural hegemony. This solidarity was reciprocated by the likes of Rodríguez who penned numerous internationally lauded classics such as 'Canción Urgente para Nicaragua' (in support of the Sandinistas), 'La Maza' (in support of Salvador Allende in Chile) and 'Canción para mi Soldado' (in support of Cuban soldiers in Angola).

It's hard to categorize Interactivo, a collaboration of young, talented musicians led by pianist Robertico Carcassés. Part funk, jazz and rock, and very 'in the groove,' this band jams to the rafters; a guaranteed good time. Interactivo's bassist is Yusa, a young black woman whose eponymous debut album made it clear she's one of the most innovative musicians on the Cuban scene today. Other difficult-to-categorize modern innovators include X Alfonso, an ex-student of the Conservatorio Amadeo Roldán; and dynamic *nueva trova*–rock duo Buena Fe, whose guitar-based riffs and eloquent lyrics push the boundaries of art and expression within the confines of the Cuban Revolution.

In the late 1990s, US guitar virtuoso Ry Cooder famously breathed new life into Cuban *son* music with his remarkable *Buena Vista Social Club* album. Linking together half a dozen or so long-retired musical sages from the 1940s and '50s, including 90-year-old Compay Segundo (writer of Cuba's second most played song, 'Chan Chan') and the pianist Rúben González (ranked by Cooder as the greatest piano player he had ever heard), the unprepossessing American producer sat back in the studio and let his ragged clutch of old-age pensioners work their erstwhile magic. More than two million albums later, European and North American audiences are still enraptured by the sounds.

Food & Drink

Veterans of WWII rationing could get flashbacks in Cuba. Remember Spam ham, vinegary vegetables, jam from a tin and gristly meat? Well, they're all still alive and kicking in the Caribbean. But, while there's a certain truth in the rumor that the local chickens are born fried and salad is a euphemism for 'whatever raw thing is available,' it's not all rubbery fish and microwaved pizzas. Indeed, many of Cuba's chefs can be extraordinarily creative, and the good old-fashioned home cooking in privately run paladares and casas particulares is both plentiful and delicious.

Moros y cristianos (Moors and Christians) is a typical Cuban meal of white rice cooked with black beans. *Congrí oriental* is rice with red beans sometimes mixed in with crispy pork slices.

The key is to manage your expectations. Don't arrive in Cuba assuming that you'll find New York–standard delis or Singapore-style variety. Food culture here – or the apparent lack of it – is a direct consequence of the country's Special Period when meat was a rare luxury and an average breakfast consisted of sugar mixed with water.

The upside of Cuban cooking is that almost everything is locally produced and organic. Cut into a fish in Havana and you can almost guarantee it was caught in Cuban waters. Slice open a sweet potato in Camagüey and chances are it was grown within about 500m of your plate with no added fertilizers.

STAPLES & SPECIALTIES

Popularly known as *comida criolla* (Creole food), Cuban meals use a base of *congrí* and meat, garnished with fried plantains (green bananas) and salad. *Congrí* is rice flecked with black beans (sometimes called *moros y cristianos,* literally 'Moors and Christians'). Salad, meanwhile, is limited to seasonal ingredients (outside the posh hotels) and consists mostly of a triumvirate of tinned green beans, cucumber slices and/or shredded cabbage.

Protein means pork, and you'll become well acquainted with *lomo ahumado* (aromatic smoked loin), *chuletas* (thin juicy filets) and *fricasé de cerdo* (pork fricassee with peppers and onions). *Filete Uruguayo* is a breaded, deep-fried cutlet stuffed with ham and cheese.

Chicken is readily available in Cuba, though it's often fried to a crisp, while the *pescado* (fish) is variable depending on where you are. Though you'll come across *pargo* (red snapper) and occasionally octopus and crab in some of the specialist seafood places, you're more likely to see lobster or shrimp *ajillo* (sautéed in oil and garlic) or *enchilado* (in tomato sauce). *Ostiones,* small oysters served with tomato sauce and lime juice, are also popular. Cows are government-controlled, so beef products such as steak are only sold (legally) in state-run restaurants.

Cuba imports US$2 billion worth of food a year, over half its total requirement.

Yuca (cassava) and *calabaza* (pumpkinlike squash) are served with an insanely addictive sauce called *mojo* made from oil, garlic and bitter orange. Green beans, beets and avocados (June to August) are likely to cross your lips too.

Few restaurants do breakfast (although pastries are sold at chains such as Doña Neli and Pain de París), so stock up at a hotel buffet or arrange for your casas particulares to provide it. Most casas do huge, hearty breakfasts of eggs, toast, fresh juice, coffee and piles of fruit for CUC$2 to CUC$3.

Desserts

Cubans are aficionados of ice cream and the nuances of different flavors are heatedly debated (they even produced an Oscar-nominated movie on the subject). Coppelia's ice cream is legendary, but ridiculously cheap tubs of other brands (440g for CUC$1) can be procured almost everywhere, and even the

NUEVA COCINA CUBANA

For legions of taste-deprived gastronomes, Cuban cuisine has always been something of an international joke. From the empty-shelved ration shops of Centro Habana, to the depressing ubiquity of soggy cheese and ham sandwiches that seem to serve as the country's only viable lunch option, it's a question of less feast, more famine. But while celebrity chefs might still be in short supply in many of Cuba's uninspiring government-run restaurants, simmering quietly on the sidelines, a whole new pot of tricks is brewing.

'Nueva Cocina Cubana' is a loose term used to describe a new awakening in Cuban cooking. Combining fresh innovative ingredients and exciting new flavors onto a traditional Caribbean base, the ideas have their roots in the US and owe a notable debt to celebrated Cuban-American chefs such as Douglas Rodríguez. But the real engine room of this gourmet-led food revolution lies, not in the US, but in the country's own small clutch of congenial but vastly underrated paladares.

Legalized in 1995, Cuba's paladares faced tough times during the dark days of the Special Period. But by the late 1990s, as tourism increased and food shortages gradually began to ease, some of the restaurants started to use their new private status to experiment and expand. One such innovator was La Guarida (p134), a private paladar housed in a wonderfully eclectic mansion in Centro Habana. Fostering close ties with gastronomic gurus in France, Spain and the US, La Guarida's chefs keenly absorbed passing international influences and slowly began to fuse traditional Cuban food with more exotic European and North American flavors. The results were as tasty as they were unexpected: tuna infused with sugarcane, chicken in a lemon and honey sauce, and *caimanera* (a fish indigenous to the Guantánamo region) pan-fried in onions and white wine. Word of the delicacies spread rapidly and, before long, big names were descending on La Guarida thick and fast in a roll call that read like a 'who's who' of international celebrities: Jack Nicholson, Uma Thurman, Matt Dillon, Queen Sofía of Spain, plus a plethora of US congressmen; soon it wasn't a question of whether you had been to Havana, but whether you had been to Havana *and* eaten at La Guarida.

Not to be outdone, other Havana paladares quickly started jumping on the culinary bandwagon. Based in old grandiose houses in the neighborhoods of Vedado and Playa, places such as La Esperanza (p159) and La Cocina de Lilliam (p159) were soon churning out equally delectable dishes and recipes were developed and expanded.

Thanks largely to Nueva Cocina Cubana, Cuban cuisine – primarily, but not only, in Havana – has slowly edged itself back into international reckoning and visitors to the island are increasingly surprised by the quality of the food on offer. Although the country is still a long way from becoming the gourmet capital of Latin America (let alone the Caribbean), by most measures, that age-old Cuban stereotype of cheap rum and iron rations could soon be confined to the annals of gastronomic history.

machine-dispensed peso stuff ain't half bad. Walk down any Cuban street at any time of the day or night and you'll see somebody coming to grips with a huge tub of Nestlés or enjoying a fast melting cornet. See boxed text, p139.

Flan is baked custard with a caramel glaze served in individual portions. Cubans also make pumpkin and coconut flan of Spanish origin. Huge sickly sweet cakes are wheeled out at the smallest excuse – and usually transported around town on a wobbling bicycle first. Havana and a couple of the larger cities also have some good patisseries. The standard (and only) dessert in all cheap restaurants and Islazul hotels is the incongruous *mermelada con queso* (tinned jam with a slice of stale cheese). It's as vile as it sounds!

DRINKS
Alcoholic Drinks

Cuba's rum cocktails are world-famous. There's the minty mojito, the shaved-ice daiquirí and the sugary Cuba Libres (rum and Coke), to name but three. Havana Club is Cuba's most celebrated *ron* (rum), with Silver Dry (the cheapest) and three-year-old Carta Blanca used for mixed drinks, while five-year-old Carta de Oro and seven-year-old Añejo are best enjoyed in a highball. Cuba's finest rum is Matusalem Añejo Superior, brewed in Santiago de Cuba since 1872. Other top brands include Varadero, Caribbean Club and Caney (made at the old Bacardí factory in Santiago de Cuba, though the name Bacardí is anathema, as the exiled family decided to sue the Cuban government under US embargo laws). Most Cubans drink their rum straight up and, on more informal occasions, straight from the bottle.

> Though it originates in the Canary Islands, *ropa vieja* (old clothes) has become a Cuban signature dish. It is made with shredded beef seasoned with garlic, onion, tomatoes, cumin, bay leaves, oregano and green peppers.

The drink made from fermented cane is called *aguardiente* (fire water) and a few shots will have your eyes watering. In bodegas (stores distributing ration-card products) it's sold as *ron a granel* (rum from the barrel) for about 20 pesos – bring an empty bottle. Local nicknames for this hooch include 'drop her drawers' and 'train spark.' Popular bottled brands are Santero and El Niño. Cubans also make fruit wines from mango, pineapple or raisins. Big city stores usually carry a limited selection of Spanish, Chilean and Cuban wines. Top beer brands include Mayabe (3.8% alcohol), Hatuey (5.4%) and the big two: Cristal (4.9%) and Bucanero (5.4%). Imported beers include Lagarto, Bavaria and Heineken.

Nonalcoholic Drinks

Cubans love their coffee *(cafecito* or *café cubano)* which is served strong, black and sweetened in small espresso-sized cups. Homegrown in the Escambray and Sierra Maestra Mountains, a fresh brew will be brought out as an ice-breaker wherever you go, from a top-end resort bar to a wooden *campesino* (country) hut. *Café con leche* (a mixture of strong coffee and hot milk) is more of a tourist drink and is thus available in nearly all bars and hotels serving foreigners. Havana has some great coffee houses and more are being added all the time. Smaller towns have them too, though here they are usually less fancy and more local (look out for the Cubanitas chain). There isn't much of a *té* (tea) culture in Cuba, but you can always get a pot of hot water at hotels or restaurants. Tea bags are sold in stores that sell items in Convertibles. If you're fussy (or English), bring your own.

An increasing number of places can whip up a refreshing *limonada* (lime-ade). Pure *jugo* (fruit juice), *refresco* (instant-powdered drink) and *batidos* (fruit milkshakes) are sold in street stalls for a few pesos and are tasty and usu-ally safe to drink. Small 250mL juice boxes with attached straws are ubiquitous in Cuba and can be bought in bars and grocery stores for 50 to 80 centavos. They come in about a dozen different flavors from orange to mango.

Guarapo is a pure sugarcane juice mixed with ice and served from quaint little roadside stalls all over Cuba. If you're a long-distance cyclist, forget Gatorade, this is the ultimate energy drink. *Prú* is a special nonalcoholic brew from the Oriente made from spices, fermented *yuca* and secret ingredients *prú*-meisters won't divulge.

Tap-water quality is variable and many Cubans have gory amoebic tales, including giardia. To be safe you can drink *agua natural* (bottled water), but that gets expensive over longer trips. You can also boil it (the local method) or buy bottled chlorine drops called Gotica. Available in most stores that sell products in Convertibles for CUC$1.25, one drop makes 3L of drinkable water; this works well in the provinces, but in Havana it's better to boil or buy bottled water. Don't touch the water in Santiago, even to brush your teeth. It's famously dirty – and brown!

CELEBRATIONS

New Year's Eve, birthdays, family reunions, weddings: whatever the reason, big events are celebrated with *lechón asado* (roast pork). As much about the process and camaraderie as the food, a pig roast is a communal effort where the jokes fly, the rum flows and dancing or *dominó* is de rigueur. Once the pig is killed, cleaned and seasoned, it's slowly pit-roasted over a charcoal fire. Traditional sides include *yuca con mojo* (yuca with garlic and lime sauce), *congrí* and salad.

Pig roast is also the street food of choice for the regular fiestas that enliven numerous Cuban towns at weekends, especially in the Oriente. Classic examples can be observed (and tasted) in Bayamo, Manzanillo, Guantánamo, Ciego de Ávila and other towns.

WHERE TO EAT & DRINK
State-Run Restaurants

Restaurant opening hours are generally 11am to 11pm daily, although staff sometimes drift off for lunch unannounced, or will be too busy counting stock to serve you right away. Government-run restaurants take either Cuban pesos or Convertibles. Peso restaurants are notorious for handing you a nine-page menu (in Spanish), when the only thing available is fried chicken. Obviously, you're supposed to pick up this information via telepathy because you'll sit for half an hour or more before learning this while the waitress falls asleep, wakes up, takes a phone call, files her nails, wipes the bar with a dirty cloth and falls asleep again. But it's not all pain and stomachache. Some peso restaurants are quite good; all are absurdly cheap and they're often your only option off the tourist circuit, so don't discount them altogether (Doña Yulla is a nationwide chain to look out for). Sometimes workers in peso restaurants either won't show you the menu in an effort to overcharge you, or they will charge Convertibles at a one-to-one ratio – making the food ridiculously overpriced. Verify *before* you order that you're looking at peso prices (meals will be in the 15- to 25-peso range). Some peso restaurants have one menu in Convertibles at a reasonable rate and another in pesos.

Restaurants that sell food in Convertibles are generally more reliable, but this isn't capitalism: just because you're paying more doesn't necessarily mean better service. In fact, after a week or two roaming the streets of Cuba's untouristed provincial towns in search of a decent meal, you'll quickly realize that Cuban restaurants are the Achilles' heel of the socialist revolution. Food is often limp and unappetizing and discourses with bored and disinterested waiters worthy of something out of a Monty Python sketch ('we can't do you a cheese sandwich, but we can do you a cheese and ham sandwich'). There are a few highlights in an otherwise dull field. The Palmares group runs a wide variety of excellent restaurants countrywide, from a small shabby hut on Maguana beach, Baracoa, to the *New York Times*–lauded El Aljibe in Miramar, Havana. Another safe, if uninspiring certainty is El Rápido, the Cuban version of McDonald's, which offers a generic menu of microwaved pizzas, hot dogs, sandwiches and – sometimes – excellent yogurt. Cuba would do well to open more La Vicarias, where the service is uniformly good, the prices fair and the food palatable. Havana is, of course, a different ballpark, with many state-run restaurants in Habana Vieja and Miramar of excellent quality. All state-run restaurant employees earn the standard CUC$8 to CUC$13 a month, so tips are highly appreciated (see boxed text, p75).

Paladares

Paladares are small family-run restaurants that are permitted to operate privately on the payment of a monthly tax to the government. First established in 1995 during the economic chaos of the Special Period, paladares owe much of their success to the sharp increase in tourist traffic on the

The farming of cows is state-controlled in Cuba, meaning beef can only legally be sold in state-run restaurants. In the past, beef smugglers were handed stiff jail sentences.

The name paladar (Portuguese for 'taste') is taken from a fictional restaurant of the same name that was depicted in a Brazilian soap opera called *Vale Tudo* in the early 1990s. The soap opera became insanely popular in Cuba and the name stuck.

island, coupled with the bold experimentation of the local chefs who, despite a paucity of decent ingredients, have heroically managed to keep the age-old traditions of Cuban cooking alive.

Legally, paladares are only supposed to offer 12 seats and are prohibited from selling lobster, beef or shrimps (which are a government monopoly). The reality, however, is often rather different. Through secrecy, guile or a surreptitious bending of the rules, many paladares pack well over a dozen people into carefully concealed dining rooms or romantically lit back gardens and, with meal prices hovering in the CUC$15 to CUC$20 bracket, make enough to scrape by.

Although the atmosphere between different paladares can differ significantly, the food is almost always of a superior quality to the rations offered elsewhere. Indeed, following big reviews in the *New York Times,* the *Guardian* and *Cigar Aficionado* magazine, leading Havana paladares such as La Guarida, La Cocina de Lilliam and La Fontana have managed to attract international attention (see boxed text, p71).

To allow readers to easily distinguish between private and state-run restaurants, in this book all privately operated eateries are listed as paladares. Whenever we refer to a 'restaurant,' it means it's a government-operated place.

Quick Eats

Like all private industry, cafeterías (street stalls) are government-regulated so – although they might look a bit grungy – hygiene isn't usually a problem. Cuban street pizza, with its pungent cheese and occasional glob of tomato, is surprisingly good and became the new national dish during the Special Period. Good standards on the street dining scene include *batidos, asado* (roasted) or breaded pork-cutlet sandwiches, fruit cocktails and ice cream. There's also a whole category of *pan con…* (bread with…) – whatever can be put inside bread, from *tortilla* (tasty eggs) to *pasta* (a greasy mayonnaise substance).

Keep an eye out for stalls and windows with *comida criolla* signs. These places sell *cajitas* (literally 'little boxes'): full meals of salad, baked vegetables, *congrí* and pork cutlets that are sold in little take-out boxes with a cardboard spoon cutout on the lid for CUC$1.

Cuban fast-food chains El Rápido and Pollo make McDonald's look like a health-food store and are best avoided unless you are suffering from exceedingly severe hunger pangs.

VEGETARIANS & VEGANS

In a land of rationing and food shortages, strict vegetarians (ie no lard, no meat bullion, no fish) will have a hard time. Cubans don't really understand vegetarianism and, when they do (or when they *say* they do), it can be summarized rather adroitly in one key word: omelette – or, at a stretch, scrambled eggs. The other problem is preparation. Even if your omelette has no meat in it, don't assume that it has been prepared in a manner that is in any way sympathetic to vegetarian requirements. Indeed, Cubans often interpret vegetarianism as 'no meat chunks in the soup.' The solution: pick out the offending items out just before serving. Thankfully change is on the horizon. The opening of a handful of new vegetarian restaurants in Havana has coincided with a nationwide educational campaign about the health benefits of a vegetarian diet. Furthermore, cooks in casas particulares who may already have had experience cooking meatless dishes for other travelers are usually more than happy to accommodate vegetarians; just ask.

Nitza Villapol, Cuban cook and TV personality, carried on rustling up resourceful recipes throughout the darkest days of the Special Period. Indeed, legend has it that her show was once canceled after she tried to present an innovative new menu alternative called 'black-bean dessert.'

TIPPING & RESERVATIONS

Remembering to tip is important in Cuba. In a country where the doctors work as waiters and the waiters double up as musicians serenading mojito-sipping tourists as they tuck tentatively into *moros y cristianos* (rice and beans), a couple of Convertibles left in the bread basket at the end of the meal can effectively make or break a person's week. It is important to bear in mind that most of these people earn their salaries in *moneda nacional* (pesos), which works out to the equivalent of US$10 to US$25 a month. Access to hard currency is necessary to make up the shortfall. However mediocre your food, a Convertible or two isn't just a show of appreciation; it's a vital contribution to the local economy.

In Cuba, a 10% to 15% tip is sufficient, with CUC$1 being the appropriate minimum in a restaurant that accepts Convertibles. Tipping in peso restaurants is not compulsory, but is greatly appreciated. Leaving 10 pesos or CUC$0.50 change is a generous tip.

Unless you're in a large group or want to eat at one of the chic, trendy paladares (such as La Guarida in Havana; see p134), there's no need for a reservation.

Vegans have little choice but to cook for themselves. Many people rent rooms with kitchen privileges or entire self-sufficient apartments. It's not easy, but like all things in Cuba, it's possible. Other options for serious vegans and/or vegetarians:

Agropecuarios Vegetable markets; also sell rice, beans, fruit (for a list of Havana's best markets, see p140).

Organopónicos Organic vegetable markets.

Proteina vegetal Dried soy protein (sold in bodegas).

Spirulina Spirulina powder (an aquatic plant offering high protein and vitamins).

Yogurt de soya Soy yogurt (sold in bodegas; regular yogurt is sold in stores that sell goods in Convertibles).

EATING WITH KIDS

With a dearth of exotic spices and an emphasis on good, plain, nonfancy food, kids in Cuba are often surprisingly well accommodated. The family-orientated nature of life on the island certainly helps. Few eating establishments turn away children, and waiters and waitresses in most cafes and restaurants will, more often than not, dote on your boisterous young offspring and go out of their way to try to accommodate their unadventurous childish tastes. Rice and beans are good staples and chicken and fish are relatively reliable sources of protein. The main lacking ingredient – though your kid probably won't think so – is a regular supply of fresh vegetables. Consider bringing a vitamin supplement, as the paltry cabbage and cucumber salads that pass for spring greens in many Cuban restaurants will challenge even the most mature palates.

Cuba's ubiquitous range of tropical fruit juices available in small cartons with an attached straw are a big hit with kids and come in a dozen different flavors. Even better is raw fruit, a staple at Cuban breakfast tables with delicious plates of chopped banana, papaya, pineapple and orange on offer at most casas particulares (where it's always incredibly fresh). For a treat, hit the ice-cream stores which are evident in even the smallest towns and always riotously popular.

HABITS & CUSTOMS

Food culture in Cuba is another oxymoron. It's as if the population reserves all its gusto for producing rum, rolling cigars and creating innovative music, and has no energy left afterwards for anything but rice and beans. Rationing and the Special Period have obviously done their damage, and a quick glance around the exile community in the US does, at least, prove that Cuban cooks *can* actually cook, given the right freedom and ingredients.

Mealtimes in Cuba aren't the long drawn-out social occasions so common in Europe and North America, and people rarely have the inclination to sit down and quaff wine or discuss the merits of Dolcelatte over Camembert. Eating, rather, is seen as a basic necessity – and a hastily undertaken one at that – that acts as a prelude to drinking, music or some other more exciting form of nighttime entertainment.

In Cuba the taste of the orangey-red *mamey* fruit is loved by almost everybody. So much so, that the word *mamey* has entered the Cuban vocabulary as an oft-used superlative. To describe a woman as *mamey* is to pay her the ultimate compliment.

The speed at which Cubans eat is famous. Hit an all-you-can-eat buffet in a Cuban-patronized hotel and the first rule of thumb is 'move quickly,' or the food will all be gone in an eye blink. À la carte restaurants are a different matter, though people rarely linger romantically. Bars are considered better places for hot dates.

Knowledge of food and food culture is equally thin. There are no Gordon Ramsays or Rachel Rays in Cuba, and don't expect your less-than-eager waiter in a government-run restaurant to know or care about the nuances of what the chef might be secretly concocting.

Cubans love to snack and eat a lot on the go in roughshod streetside peso stalls, often standing up. Change up some coins in the Cadeca and feel free to join them.

EAT YOUR WORDS

Managing a menu in Spanish, making special requests or maneuvering a meal in pesos – your eating options will expand if you can speak the local language. For pronunciation guidelines see the Language chapter, p490.

STAYING FED

In Cuba, someone who is always eating is called a *jamaliche* or *camelón* but, unless you're staying at an all-inclusive resort, there are going to be hours, days – even whole weeks – when you're going to wish you'd stuffed a jar of peanut butter into your rucksack. Here's some advice to keep all you *jamaliches* out there fed:

- Always carry Cuban pesos (which can be easily changed in Cadeca exchange offices). Pesos are good for ice cream, peanuts, egg sandwiches, fruit shakes, bread, fruits, vegetables and, above all, peso pizza.
- Keep a spare plastic bag (a rarity in Cuba) and fill it up at bakeries and fruit markets.
- Keep an eye out for 24-hour peso stalls which usually congregate around hospitals.
- If you are fortunate enough to stumble upon an as-much-as-you-can-eat buffet, wrap up your leftovers in a napkin and smuggle it out for later.
- Cyclists, exercise freaks or any other type of *jamaliche* should come prepared with power bars, nuts, dried fruit and other lightweight, high-protein snacks.
- Be willing to eat fried food, including unidentifiable tidbits sold on the street.
- Stock up on biscuits whenever you see a grocery store.
- Look for good yogurt in gas stations and cafeterías (especially the El Rápido chain).
- Rent a room with kitchen privileges, then hit the *agropecuario* (vegetable market) and have a dinner party.
- Become a Cuban and never waste *anything*.
- Don't forget the peanut butter!

Useful Phrases

Is there food?
¿Hay comida? ai ko·*mee*·da

What kind of food is there?
¿Qué comida hay? ke ko·*mee*·da ai

Table for..., please.
Una mesa para..., por favor. oo·na *me*·sa pa·ra... por fa·*vor*

Can I see the menu, please?
¿Puedo ver la carta, por favor? pwe·do ver la *kar*·ta por fa·*vor*

This menu is in pesos, right?
¿Esta carta está en moneda nacional, verdad? es·ta *kar*·ta es·*ta* en mo·*ne*·da na·syo·*nal* ver·*da*

Do you have a menu in English?
¿Tienen una carta en inglés? tye·nen *oo*·na *kar*·ta en een·*gles*

What is today's special?
¿Cuál es el plato del día? kwal es el *pla*·to del *dee*·a

I'll try what she/he is having.
Probaré lo que ella/él está comiendo. pro·ba·*re* lo ke e·ya/el es·*ta* ko·*myen*·do

I'd like the set lunch.
Quisiera el almuerzo, por favor. kee·*sye*·ra el al·*mwer*·so por fa·*vor*

What's in that dish?
¿De qué es ese plato? de ke es e·se *pla*·to

Thank you, that was delicious.
Muchas gracias, estaba buenísimo. moo·chas *gra*·syas es·*ta*·ba bwe·*nee*·see·mo

The bill, please.
La cuenta, por favor. la *kwen*·ta por fa·*vor*

I'm a vegetarian.
Soy vegetariano/a. soy ve·khe·ta·*rya*·no/a

Do you have any vegetarian dishes?
¿Tienen algún plato vegetariano? tye·nen al·*goon pla*·to ve·khe·ta·*rya*·no

I'm allergic to...
Tengo alergia a... ten·go a·ler·*khee*·ya a...

Menu Decoder

ajiaco	a·*khya*·ko	a 'kitchen sink' stew that has potatoes, squash, *malanga* (root vegetable similar to taro), plantains, corn, meat, tomato paste, spices, old beer, lemon juice and whatever else is around
arroz con pollo	a·*ros* kon *po*·yo	rice and bits of chicken mixed together
bocadito	bo·ka·*dee*·to	sandwich on round bread
café cortado	ka·*fe* kor·*ta*·do	espresso with a shot of milk
cajita	ka·*khee*·ta	take-out meal that comes in a small box
caldosa	kal·*do*·sa	similar to *ajiaco*; literally 'stew'
chicharitas/ mariquitas	chee·cha·*ree*·tas/ ma·ree·*kee*·tas	plantain (green banana) chips; sometimes made from potatoes or *malanga*
chicharrones	chee·cha·*ro*·nes	fried pork rinds
crema de queso	*kre*·ma de *ke*·so	heavy cheese soup that has as much flour as cheese; variations include *crema Aurora* and *crema Virginia*
entremés	en·tre·*mes*	finger food or appetizer, usually with ham and cheese slices and green olives; sometimes quite large servings
filete Canciller	fi·*le*·te kan·*see*·yer	breaded fish stuffed with ham and cheese
filete Monte Toro	fi·*le*·te *mon*·te *to*·ro	delicately breaded fish filet, fried and stuffed with cheese

filete Uruguayo	fi·*le*·te oo·ro·*gwa*·yo	fried, breaded pork cutlet stuffed with ham and cheese
Gordon Bleu	*gor*·don bloo	chicken stuffed with ham and cheese; charming anthropomorphism of Cordon Bleu
guarnición	gwar·nee·*syon*	side dish
hígado a la italiana	ee·ga·do a la ee·tal·*ya*·na	liver sautéed in tomato sauce, with peppers and onions
lomo ahumado	*lo*·mo a·oo·*ma*·do	smoked pork loin
potaje	po·*ta*·khe	subtly spiced black beans with pork bones or chunks, served in its own soupy juices
ropa vieja	*ro*·pa vye·kha	traditional Cuban dish of mounds of shredded beef livened with tomatoes and onions; only available in state-run restaurants
servicio incluído	ser·vee·syo een·kloo·*ee*·do	tip included
table 1, 2…	*ta*·ble *oo*·no dos…	different meal offers (distinguished by the numbers) that include a main dish, salad, side and dessert, usually with smaller portions
tamal en cazuela	ta·*mal* en ka·*swe*·la	ground fresh corn, boiled with meat and spices and served in a pot; called *tamales* when wrapped in corn husks
tostones	tos·*to*·nes	fried plantain patties
vegetales Macedonias	ve·khe·*ta*·les ma·se·*don*·yas	a mix of carrots and green beans boiled to death or canned
vianda	*vyan*·da	any root vegetable (potato, yuca, *malanga*, plantain etc); this appears on many menus as *vianda frita*

Food Glossary
FRUTAS (FRUITS)

fruta bomba	*froo*·ta *bom*·ba	papaya
guayaba	gwa·*ya*·ba	guava
mamey	ma·*mey*	brown-skinned fruit with orange flesh
melón	me·*lon*	watermelon
naranja (agria)	na·*ran*·kha (*a*·gree·a)	orange (bitter)
piña	*pee*·nya	pineapple
plátano fruta	*pla*·ta·no *froo*·ta	banana
toronja	to·*ron*·kha	grapefruit
zapote	sa·*po*·te	brown-skinned fruit with orange flesh

VERDURAS (VEGETABLES)

berenjena	be·ren·*khe*·na	eggplant
boniato	bo·*nya*·to	sweet potato
calabaza	ka·la·*ba*·sa	squash
champiñón	cham·pee·*nyon*	mushroom
espinaca	es·pee·*na*·ka	spinach
maíz	ma·*ees*	corn
malanga	ma·*lan*·ga	root vegetable similar to taro
papa	*pa*·pa	potato
plátano maduro	*pla*·ta·no ma·*doo*·ro	green plantain (sweet)
plátano verde	*pla*·ta·no *ver*·de	green plantain (savory)

ENSALADA (SALAD)

aguacate	a·gwa·*ka*·te	avocado
aliño	a·*lee*·nyo	oil and vinegar dressing/carafes
berro	*be*·ro	watercress

col	kol	cabbage
ensalada de estación	en·sa·*la*·da de es·ta·*syon*	seasonal salad
ensalada mixta	en·sa·*la*·da *meeks*·ta	mixed salad; usually tomatoes, cucumbers and cabbage/lettuce
habichuela	a·bee·*chwe*·la	green beans
lechuga	le·*choo*·ga	lettuce
pepino	pe·*pee*·no	cucumber
remolacha	re·mo·*la*·cha	beets
zanahoria	sa·na·*o*·rya	carrot

CARNE (MEAT)

cerdo	*ser*·do	pork
chorizo	cho·*ree*·so	sausage
jamón	kha·*mon*	ham
lechón asado	le·*chon* a·*sa*·do	roast pork
picadillo	pee·ka·*dee*·yo	ground beef
pollo frito	*po*·yo *free*·to	fried chicken
puerco	*pwer*·ko	pork

PESCADO & MARISCOS (FISH & SHELLFISH)

calamar	ka·la·*mar*	squid
camarones	ka·ma·*ro*·nes	shrimps
cangrejo	kan·*gre*·kho	crab
langosta	lan·*gos*·ta	lobster
mariscos	ma·*rees*·kos	shellfish
ostiones	os·*tyo*·nes	oysters
pargo	*par*·go	red snapper

POSTRES (DESSERTS)

arroz con leche	a·*ros* kon *le*·che	rice and milk pudding
flan	flan	baked custard with caramel glaze
helado (en pote)	e·*la*·do (en *po*·te)	ice cream (cup)
jimagua	khee·*ma*·gwa	two scoops of ice cream
lolita	lo·*lee*·ta	flan à la mode
natilla	na·*tee*·ya	sinful custard made almost entirely of egg yolks
pudín	poo·*deen*	bread pudding
tres gracias	tres *gra*·syas	three scoops of ice cream

COMIDA EN LA CALLE (SNACKS & STREET FOOD)

croqueta	kro·*ke*·ta	fritter
maní en grano	ma·*nee* en *gra*·no	peanut brittle
maní molido	ma·*nee* mo·*lee*·do	peanut paste (similar to peanut butter)
pan con tortilla	pan kon tor·*tee*·ya	bread with egg
pasta	*pas*·ta	mayonnaise
tortica	tor·*tee*·ka	butter cookie (often made with lard)

TÉCNICAS (COOKING TECHNIQUES)

a la plancha	a la *plan*·cha	cooked in a skillet
asado	a·*sa*·do	roasted
empanizado	em·pa·nee·*sa*·do	breaded
parrillada/grille	pa·ree·*ya*·da/*gree*·ye	on the grill
sofrito	so·*free*·to	Cuban seasoning made by sautéing onions, garlic and sweet peppers

Environment

THE LAND

Measuring 1250km from east to west and between 31km and 193km from north to south, Cuba is the Caribbean's largest island with a total land area of 110,860 sq km. Shaped like an alligator and situated just south of the Tropic of Cancer, the country is actually an archipelago made up of 4195 smaller islets and coral reefs, though the bulk of the territory is concentrated on the expansive Isla Grande and its 2200-sq-km smaller cousin, Isla de la Juventud.

Formed by a volatile mixture of volcanic activity, plate tectonics and erosion, the landscape of Cuba is a lush and varied concoction of caves, mountains, plains and *mogotes* (strange flat-topped hills). The highest point, Pico Turquino (1972m), is situated in the east among the lofty triangular peaks of the Sierra Maestra, while further west, in the no less majestic Sierra del Escambray, ruffled hilltops and gushing waterfalls straddle the borders of Cienfuegos, Villa Clara and Sancti Spíritus provinces. Rising like purple shadows in the far west, the 175km-long Cordillera de Guanguanico is a more diminutive range that includes the protected Sierra del Rosario reserve and the distinctive pincushion hills of the Valle de Viñales.

Lapped by the warm turquoise waters of the Caribbean Sea in the south, and the foamy, white chop of the Atlantic Ocean in the north, Cuba's 5746km of coastline shelters more than 300 natural beaches and features one of the largest tracts of coral reef in the world. Home to more than 900 reported species of fish and more than 410 varieties of sponge and coral, the country's unspoiled coastline is a marine wonderland that entices tourists from all over the globe.

The 7200m-deep Cayman Trench between Cuba and Jamaica forms the boundary of the North American and Caribbean plates. Tectonic movements have tilted the island over time, creating uplifted limestone cliffs along parts of the north coast and low mangrove swamps on the south. Over millions of years Cuba's limestone bedrock has been eroded by underground rivers, creating interesting geological features including the 'haystack' hills of Viñales and more than 20,000 caves countrywide.

As a sprawling archipelago, Cuba boasts thousands of islands and keys (most uninhabited) in four major offshore groups: the Archipiélago de los Colorados, off northern Pinar del Río; the Archipiélago de Sabana-Camagüey (or Jardines del Rey), off northern Villa Clara and Ciego de Ávila; the Archipiélago de los Jardines de la Reina, off southern Ciego de Ávila; and the Archipiélago de los Canarreos, around Isla de la Juventud. Most visitors will experience one or more of these island idylls, as the majority of resorts, scuba diving and virgin beaches are found in these regions.

Being a narrow island, never measuring more than 200km north to south, means Cuba's capacity for large lakes and rivers is severely limited (preventing hydroelectricity). Cuba's longest river, the 343km-long Río Cauto that flows from the Sierra Maestra in a rough loop north of Bayamo, is only navigable by small boats for 80km. To compensate, 632 *embalses* (reservoirs) or *presas* (dams), larger than 5km altogether, have been created for irrigation and water supply; these supplement the almost unlimited groundwater held in Cuba's limestone bedrock.

Lying in the Caribbean's main hurricane region, Cuba has been hit by some blinders in recent years including three devastating storms in 2008, its worst year for more than a century (see boxed text, p86).

Cuba's worst ever hurricane in human terms occurred on November 9, 1932 off the southern coast of Camagüey province and left more than 3000 people dead. Hurricane Ike in 2008 was of an equitable strength (Category 4) but killed only seven people.

The Caribbean manatee can grow 4.5m in length and weigh up to 600kg; grazing on seaweed in estuaries and rivers it can consume up to 50kg of plant life a day.

WILDLIFE
Animals

While it isn't exactly the Serengeti, Cuba has its fair share of indigenous fauna and animal lovers won't be disappointed. Birds are probably the biggest drawcard (see p32) and Cuba boasts more than 350 different varieties, 70 of which are indigenous. Head to the mangroves of Ciénaga de Zapata near the Bahía de Cochinos (Bay of Pigs) or to the Península de Guanahacabibes in Pinar del Río for the best sightings of the blink-and-you'll-miss-it *zunzuncito* (bee hummingbird), the world's smallest bird and, at 6.5cm, not much longer than a toothpick. These areas are also home to the *tocororo* (Cuban trogon; see boxed text, p311), Cuba's national bird, which sports the red, white and blue colors of the Cuban flag. Other popular bird species include flamingos (by the thousand), *cartacubas* (a type of bird indigenous to Cuba), herons, spoonbills, parakeets and rarely-spotted Cuban pygmy owls.

Land mammals have been hunted almost to extinction with the largest indigenous survivor the friendly *jutía* (tree rat), a 4kg edible rodent that scavenges on isolated keys living in relative harmony with armies of inquisitive iguanas. Other odd species include the *mariposa de cristal* (Cuban clear-winged butterfly), one of only two clear-winged butterflies in the world; the rare *manjuarí* (Cuban alligator gar), an odd, ancient fish considered a living fossil; and the *polimita*, a unique land snail distinguished by its festive yellow, red and brown bands.

Reptiles are well represented in Cuba. Aside from crocodiles, iguanas and lizards, there are 15 species of snake, none of which is poisonous. Cuba's largest snake is the *majá*, a constrictor related to the anaconda that grows up to 4m in length; it's nocturnal and doesn't usually mess with humans.

Cuba's marine life makes up for what the island lacks in land fauna. The manatee, the world's only herbivorous aquatic mammal, is found in the Bahía de Taco and the Península de Zapata, and whale sharks frequent the María la Gorda area at Cuba's eastern tip from August to November. Four turtle species (leatherback, loggerhead, green and hawksbill) are found in Cuban waters and they nest annually in isolated keys or on the protected western beaches of the Guanahacabibes Peninsula.

UNESCO WORLD HERITAGE & BIOSPHERE RESERVE SITES

There are currently six Unesco Biosphere Reserves in Cuba and nine Unesco World Heritage Sites. The most recent addition was the city of Camagüey, whose splendidly preserved colonial core was deservedly added to the list in July 2008 (see boxed text, p341).

The Biosphere Reserves are: the Reserva Sierra del Rosario (250 sq km; declared in 1984) and the Reserva Península de Guanahacabibes (1015 sq km; 1987), both in Pinar del Río; Ciénaga de Zapata (6282 sq km; 2001) in Matanzas; Buenavista (3135 sq km; 2000) in parts of Villa Clara, Sancti Spíritus and Ciego de Ávila; Parque Baconao (846 sq km; 1987) in Santiago de Cuba; and the Reserva Cuchillas de Toa (1275 sq km; 1987) in Guantánamo. Standards, services and administration of these reserves vary greatly. For example, the Reserva Península de Guanahacabibes is carefully protected, while Parque Baconao has small communities and many tourist installations within its boundaries.

Cuba's nine World Heritage Sites are: Habana Vieja, the historical core of Havana (declared in 1982); Trinidad and adjacent Valle de los Ingenios (1988) in Sancti Spíritus; Castillo de San Pedro del Morro (1997) and the First Coffee Plantations in the Southeast of Cuba (2000), both in Santiago de Cuba; Parque Nacional Desembarco del Granma (1999) in Granma; Valle de Viñales (1999) in Pinar del Río; Parque Nacional Alejandro de Humboldt (2001) in Guantánamo; the Urban Historic Center of Cienfuegos (2005) in Cienfuegos province, and the Historic Center of Camagüey (2008) in Camagüey province.

ENDANGERED SPECIES

Due to habitat loss and persistent hunting by humans, many of Cuba's animals and birds are listed as endangered species. These include the Cuban crocodile, a fearsome reptile that has the smallest habitat of any crocodile, existing only in the Zapata swamps and in the Lanier swamps on Isla de la Juventud. Other vulnerable species include the *jutía,* which was hunted mercilessly during the *período especial* (special period; Cuba's new economic reality post-1991), when hungry Cubans tracked them for their meat (they still do – in fact, it is considered something of a delicacy); the tree boa, a native snake that lives in rapidly diminishing woodland areas; and the elusive *carpintero real* (ivory-billed woodpecker; see boxed text, p456), spotted after a 40-year gap in the Parque Nacional Alejandro de Humboldt near Baracoa in the late 1980s, but not seen since.

The seriously endangered West Indian manatee, while protected from illegal hunting, continues to suffer from a variety of man-made threats, most notably from contact with boat propellers, suffocation caused by fishing nets and poisoning from residues pumped into rivers from sugar factories.

Cuba has an ambiguous attitude toward the hunting of turtles. Hawksbill turtles are protected under the law, though a clause allows for up to 500 of them to be captured per year in certain areas (Camagüey and Isla de la Juventud). Travelers will occasionally encounter *tortuga* (turtle) on the menu in places such as Baracoa. You are advised not to partake as these turtles may have been caught illegally.

THE WORLD'S MOST SUSTAINABLE COUNTRY?

With its antiquated infrastructure and fume-belching city traffic, Cuba might not always seem like a font of innovative environmentalism. But in October 2006, in an environmental report entitled 'The Living Planet,' the World Wildlife Foundation (WWF) named Castro's struggling island nation as the only country in the world with sustainable development.

The WWF based its study on two key criteria: human welfare index (life expectancy, literacy and GDP) and ecological footprint (the amount of land needed to fulfill a person's food and energy needs). Most countries failed to meet their sustainability requirements either because their ecological footprint was too high (the megaconsuming West), or their human welfare index was too low (the poverty-stricken countries of Africa and Asia). Cuba, with its excellent health and education indices and low rates of consumption, proved to be the only exception.

It would be naive to suggest that Cuba achieved its sustainability record through foresight alone. On the contrary, the Cubans are largely ecologists by necessity. The country's sustainability credentials were first laid out in the Special Period when, shorn of Soviet subsidies and marginalized from the world economy by a US trade embargo, rationing and recycling measures were necessary to survive.

To their credit, the Cubans haven't wavered since. Despite a car-ownership ratio of 28 per 1000 (the US is closer to 850 per 1000) and an almost total absence of chemical fertilizers, the country refused to take the easy route toward greater prosperity post–Special Period and, instead, quickly fell in with the new global environmental zeitgeist.

Before his much publicized health relapse, Fidel Castro named 2006 as the 'Year of the Energy Revolution' and gave out free new energy-efficient appliances to millions of Cuban households. Visit a Cuban casa particular these days and you'll find that dinner is made in a pressure cooker, all the lightbulbs are LEDs and the once inefficient 1950s fridge has, more often than not, been replaced by a more ecofriendly (and quieter) Chinese model.

Similarly, both Havana and Santiago have recently received a whole new fleet of Chinese-made 'bendy' buses replacing the famously filthy *camellos* (metro buses) of yore. Suddenly people can breathe again.

Plants

Cuba is synonymous with the palm tree; through songs, symbols, landscapes and legends the two are inextricably linked. The national tree is the *palma real* (royal palm), and it's central to the country's coat of arms and the Cristal beer logo. It's believed there are 20 million royal palms in Cuba and locals will tell you that wherever you stand on the island, you'll always be within sight of one of them. Marching single file by the roadside or clumped on a hill, these majestic trees reach up to 40m in height and are easily identified by their lithesome trunk and green stalk at the top. There are also *cocotero* (coconut palm); *palma barrigona* (big-belly palm) with its characteristic bulge; and the extremely rare *palma corcho* (cork palm). The latter is a link with the Cretaceous period (between 65 and 135 million years ago) and is cherished as a living fossil. You can see examples of it on the grounds of the Museo de Ciencias Naturales Sandalio de Noda (p202) and La Ermita (p213), both in Pinar del Río province. All told, there are 90 palm-tree types in Cuba.

Other important trees include mangroves, in particular the spiderlike mangroves that protect the Cuban shoreline from erosion and provide an important habitat for small fish and birds. Mangroves account for 26% of Cuban forests and cover almost 5% of the island's coast; Cuba ranks ninth in the world in terms of mangrove density, and the most extensive swamps are situated in the Ciénaga de Zapata.

The largest native pine forests grow on Isla de la Juventud (the former Isle of Pines), in western Pinar del Río, in eastern Holguín (or more specifically the Sierra Cristal) and in central Guantánamo. These forests are especially susceptible to fire damage, and pine reforestation has been a particular headache for the island's environmentalists.

Rainforests exist at higher altitudes – between approximately 500m and 1500m – in the Sierra del Escambray, Sierra Maestra and Macizo de Sagua-Baracoa mountains. Original rainforest species include ebony and mahogany, but today most reforestation is in eucalyptus, which is graceful and fragrant, but invasive.

Dotted liberally across the island, ferns, cacti and orchids contribute hundreds of species, many endemic, to Cuba's cornucopia of plant life. For the best concentrations check out the botanical gardens in Santiago de Cuba (p431) for ferns and cacti and Pinar del Río (p220) for orchids. Most orchids bloom from November to January, and one of the best places to see them is in the Reserva Sierra del Rosario. The national flower is the graceful *mariposa* (butterfly jasmine); you'll know it by its white floppy petals and strong perfume.

Medicinal plants are widespread in Cuba due largely to a chronic shortage of prescription medicines (banned under the US embargo). Pharmacies are well stocked with effective tinctures such as aloe (for cough and congestion) and a bee by-product called *propólio*, used for everything from stomach amoebas to respiratory infections. On the home front, every Cuban patio has a pot of *orégano de la tierra* (Cuban oregano) growing and if you start getting a cold you'll be whipped up a wonder elixir made from the fat, flat leaves mixed with lime juice, honey and hot water.

NATIONAL PARKS

In 1978 Cuba established the National Committee for the Protection and Conservation of Natural Resources and the Environment (Comarna). Attempting to reverse 400 years of deforestation and habitat destruction, the body set about designating green belts and initiated ambitious reforestation campaigns. It is estimated that at the time of Columbus' arrival in

Approximately 2% of Cuba's arable land is given over to coffee production and the industry supports a workforce of 265,000 people.

Parque Nacional Alejandro de Humboldt is named after the German naturalist Alexander von Humboldt (1769–1859), who visited the island between 1801 and 1804 to undertake important social and scientific research.

NATIONAL PARKS

Park	Features	Activities	Best time to visit	Page
Gran Parque Natural Montemar	wetland: mangroves, 190 bird species, manatees, crocodile breeding, Taíno village replica	birding, boat tours, fishing	Nov-Apr	p256
Gran Parque Nacional Sierra Maestra	mountains: Cuban Revolution headquarters, cloud forest, high peaks, views, museum	trekking, camping	Oct-May dry season	p393 & p438
Parque Nacional Alejandro de Humboldt	mangrove/forest: well-protected bayside setting, on-site specialists, visitors center, manatees, trails	boat tours, birding, hiking	year-round	p456
Parque Nacional Caguanes	caves, karst systems, mangroves, coral keys, birds, marine life	limited hiking, boat trips	Oct-May	p314
Parque Nacional Desembarco del Granma	forests/beach: rainforest, reef, trails, *Granma* replica, cacti, lighthouse, caves, petroglyphs	hiking, spelunking, swimming, fishing	Sep-Jun	p400
Parque Nacional Península de Guanahacabibes	mangrove/beach: whale sharks, marine turtles, rare birds	scuba diving, hiking, birding	Jun-Oct for nesting turtles, few visitors	p208
Parque Nacional Viñales	verdant valley: caves, pincushion hills, tobacco fields, visitors center	spelunking, hiking, horseback riding, rock climbing	year-round	p214

1492, 95% of Cuba was covered in virgin forest. By 1959 this area had been reduced to just 16%. The implementation of large-scale tree planting and the organization of large tracts of land into protected parks has seen this figure creep back up to 20%, but there is still a lot of work to be done.

As of 2009, there were seven national parks in Cuba: Parque Nacional Península de Guanahacabibes and Parque Nacional Viñales (both in Pinar del Río); Gran Parque Natural Montemar (Matanzas); Gran Parque Nacional Sierra Maestra and Parque Nacional Desembarco del Granma (both in Granma province); Parque Nacional Alejandro de Humboldt (Guantánamo) and Parque Nacional Caguanes (Sancti Spíritus province). Of these, both Desembarco del Granma and Alejandro de Humboldt are also Unesco World Heritage Sites.

On top of these parks there are many more protected areas: natural parks, flora and fauna reserves, areas of managed resources, eco-parks, bio-parks and Ramsar Convention sites. The interconnecting network is often confusing (some parks have two interchangeable names) – and sometimes overlapping – but the sentiment's the same; environmental stewardship with a solid governmental backing.

National conservation policies are directed by Comarna, which acts as a coordinating body, overseeing 15 ministries and ensuring that current national and international environmental legislation is being carried out efficiently and effectively. This includes adherence to the important international treaties that govern Cuba's six Unesco Biosphere Reserves and nine Unesco World Heritage Sites.

ENVIRONMENTAL ISSUES

Cuba's greatest environmental problems are aggravated by an economy struggling to survive. As the country pins its hopes on tourism to save the financial day, a schizophrenic environmental policy has evolved, cutting right to the heart of the dilemma: how can a developing nation provide for its people *and* maintain high (or at least minimal) ecological standards?

One disaster in this struggle, most experts agree, was the 2km-long stone *pedraplén* (causeway) constructed to link offshore Cayo Sabinal with mainland Camagüey. This massive project involved piling boulders in the sea and laying a road on top, which interrupted water currents and caused irreparable damage to bird and marine habitats. Other longer causeways were built connecting Los Jardines del Rey to Ciego de Ávila (27km long; p327) and Cayo Santa María to Villa Clara (a 48km-long monster; p288). The full extent of the ecological damage wreaked by these causeways won't be known for another decade at least.

Building new roads and airports, package tourism that shuttles large groups of people into sensitive habitats and the frenzied construction of giant resorts on virgin beaches exacerbate the clash between human activity and environmental protection. The grossly shrunken extents of the Reserva Ecológica Varahicacos in Varadero due to encroaching resorts is just one example. Rounding up dolphins as entertainers has rankled activists as well. Overfishing (including turtles and lobster for tourist consumption), agricultural runoff, industrial pollution and inadequate sewage treatment have contributed to the decay of coral reefs, and diseases such as yellow band, black band and nuisance algae have begun to appear.

As soon as you arrive in Havana or Santiago de Cuba, you'll realize that air pollution is a problem. Airborne particles, old cars belching black smoke and by-products from burning garbage are some of the culprits. Cement factories, sugar refineries and other heavy industry take their toll. The nickel mines engulfing Moa serve as stark examples of industrial concerns taking precedence: this is some of the prettiest landscape in Cuba, turned into a barren wasteland of lunar proportions.

On the bright side is the enthusiasm the government has shown for reforestation and protecting natural areas – there are several projects on the drawing board (see boxed text, p223) – and its willingness to confront mistakes from the past. Havana Harbor, once Latin America's most polluted, has been undergoing a massive cleanup project, as has the Río Almendares, which cuts through the heart of the city. Both programs are beginning to show positive

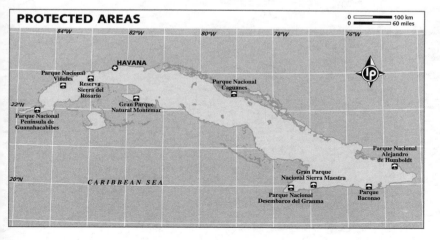

PROTECTED AREAS

0 ————— 100 km
0 ————— 60 miles

HAVANA

Parque Nacional Viñales

Reserva Sierra del Rosario

Parque Nacional Caguanes

22°N

Gran Parque Natural Montemar

Parque Nacional Península de Guanahacabibes

Parque Nacional Alejandro de Humboldt

20°N CARIBBEAN SEA

Gran Parque Nacional Sierra Maestra

Parque Nacional Desembarco del Granma

Parque Baconao

GUSTAV, IKE AND PALOMA – AN UNHOLY TRINITY

The year 2008 was Cuba's worst hurricane season in living memory, with a triple whammy of summer storms – Gustav, Ike and Paloma – pummeling crops, destroying infrastructure and wrecking more than half a million homes. From his sickbed, the normally cool-headed Fidel likened the hurricanes' combined force to the strength of an atomic bomb. Yet, miraculously, only seven people were killed and as few as 30 injured – a glowing testament to the Cuban government's well-organized hurricane evacuation procedures.

Gustav arrived first, a lethal Category 4 storm that slammed into the Isla de la Juventud on August 30 before tracking north through Pinar del Río province where 225km/h winds ripped roofs off homes, downed electricity pylons and destroyed half of the normally lucrative tobacco crop.

After a respite of just seven days, Ike raged in on September 7 causing a devastating storm surge in Baracoa (the whole Malecón was leveled) before making landfall as a Category 4 storm in eastern Holguín province a day later.

The urban centers of Banes and Gibara bore the brunt of the carnage with over 70% of the towns' colonial houses flattened or severely damaged. The storm then blasted southwest cutting a swathe through Las Tunas and Camagüey provinces before regrouping off Cuba's southern coast. The nightmare wasn't over. Amazingly, Ike swung back to the north and slammed into Cuba a second time, hitting the already crippled Pinar del Río province where it caused widespread flooding and power outages.

Cuba's third 2008 storm was a rare late-season hurricane that pitched into the southern shoreline of Camagüey province on November 8 causing a massive storm surge that took out 435 houses in the small fishing village of Santa Cruz del Sur in one hit. Miraculously, Paloma was downsized to a tropical storm a few hours later before fizzling out over the Oriente, but the hurricane had already wrought its damage, adding a couple more digits to a crippling cleanup bill that ultimately cost the Cuban government US$8.4 billion.

results. Sulfur emissions from oil wells near Varadero have been reduced and environmental regulations for developments are now enforced by the Ministry of Science, Technology and the Environment. Fishing regulations, as local fisherman will tell you, have become increasingly strict. Striking the balance between Cuba's immediate needs and the future of its environment is one of the Revolution's increasingly pressing challenges.

Cuba Outdoors

Culture is Cuba's traditional tour de force. But behind the infectious music and cerebral museums lies 5746km of coastline, six Unesco Biosphere Reserves, more than 20,000 caves, three sprawling mountain ranges, 350 bird species, the world's second-largest coral reef, and hectares and hectares of unspoiled countryside.

Adventurers who feel that they've had their fill of rum, cigars and all-night salsa dancing can break loose on a bike, fish (as well as drink) like Hemingway, hike on guerrilla trails, jump out of an airplane or rediscover a sunken Spanish shipwreck off the shimmering south coast.

Thanks to the dearth of modern development, Cuba's outdoors is refreshingly green and free of the smog-filled highways and ugly suburban sprawl that infects many other countries.

While not on a par with North America or Europe in terms of leisure options, Cuba's facilities are well established and improving. Services and infrastructure vary depending on what activity you are looking for. The country's diving centers are generally excellent and its instructors of an international caliber. Naturalists and ornithologists in the various national parks and flora and fauna reserves are similarly conscientious and qualified. Hiking, while limited and frustratingly rule-ridden, is usually expertly guided and well organized, if a little tailored toward beginners and 'conventional tourists.' Cycling is refreshingly DIY, and all the better for it. Canyoning and climbing are new sports in Cuba that have a lot of local support but little official backing – as yet.

It's possible to hire reasonable outdoor gear in Cuba for most of the activities you will do (cycling excepted). But, if you do bring your own supplies, any gear you can donate at the end of your trip to individuals you meet along the way (headlamps, snorkel masks, fins etc) will be greatly appreciated.

Cubamar Viajes (www.cubamarviajes.cu) organizes numerous outdoor adventure trips, tours and courses throughout Cuba and can often tailor things around individual needs and requirements, as long as you arrange this in advance. It handles everything from caving to cycling and can get you well off the beaten path. Government agency **Ecotur** (☎ 7-204-5188) is another good resource.

Cuba's greatest outdoor adventurer was undoubtedly Antonio Núñez Jiménez (1923–98), whose investigations into Cuban geology, geography and anthropology have become standard texts on the island and beyond.

DIVING

If Cuba has a Blue Riband activity, it is scuba diving. Even Fidel in his younger days liked to don a wetsuit and escape beneath the iridescent waters of the Atlantic or Caribbean (his favorite dive site was – apparently – the rarely visited Jardines de la Reina; see boxed text, p330). Indeed, so famous was the Cuban leader's diving addiction that the CIA allegedly once sponsored an assassination plot that involved inserting an explosive device inside a conch and placing it on the seabed.

Excellent dive sites are so numerous in Cuba that you could quite easily plan a whole trip around this one activity alone. Competing for top honors are Punta Francés on the Isla de la Juventud (see boxed text, p190) and María la Gorda (p208) in the far west of Pinar del Río province, both renowned for their calm seas, excellent water clarity (the Isla holds an annual underwater-photography competition) and profusion of all kinds of sea life. Not surprisingly, both areas, though relatively isolated, have excellent international dive centers with recompression chambers and in-house instruction available. Of equitable quality but much harder to

RESPONSIBLE DIVING

Please consider the following tips when diving and help preserve the ecology and beauty of the reefs:

- Never use anchors on the reef, and take care not to ground boats on coral.
- Avoid touching or standing on living marine organisms or dragging equipment across the reef. Polyps can be damaged by even the gentlest contact. If you must hold on to the reef, only touch exposed rock or dead coral.
- Be conscious of your fins. Even without contact, the surge from fin strokes near the reef can damage delicate organisms. Take care not to kick up clouds of sand, which can smother organisms.
- Practice and maintain proper buoyancy control. Major damage can be done by divers descending too fast and colliding with the reef.
- Take great care in underwater caves. Spend as little time within them as possible as your air bubbles may be caught within the roof and thereby leave organisms high and dry. Take turns to inspect the interior of a small cave.
- Resist the temptation to collect or buy corals or shells or to loot marine archaeological sites (mainly shipwrecks).
- Ensure that you take home all your rubbish and any litter you may find as well. Plastics in particular are a serious threat to marine life.
- Do not feed fish.
- Minimize your disturbance of marine animals. *Never* ride on the backs of turtles.

Safety Guidelines for Diving

Before embarking on a scuba-diving, skin-diving or snorkeling trip, carefully consider the following points to ensure a safe and enjoyable experience:

- Possess a current diving certification card from a recognized scuba-diving instructional agency (if scuba diving).
- Be sure you are healthy and feel comfortable diving.
- Obtain reliable information about physical and environmental conditions at the dive site (eg from a reputable local dive operation).
- Be aware of local laws, regulations and etiquette about marine life and the environment.
- Dive only at sites within your realm of experience; if available, engage the services of a competent, professionally trained dive instructor or dive master.
- Be aware that underwater conditions vary significantly from one region, or even site, to another. Seasonal changes can significantly alter any site and dive conditions. These differences influence the way divers dress for a dive and what diving techniques they use.
- Ask about the environmental characteristics that can affect your diving and how locally trained divers deal with these considerations.

reach is the Jardines de la Reina, south of Ciego de Ávila province, where strict environmental protection and limited access has kept the seabed in an almost pristine state. Visiting here will cost more in terms of money and effort; see boxed text, p330.

The Bahía de Cochinos (Bay of Pigs; see boxed text, p260), on the south coast of Matanzas, offers the island's most accessible diving with a plunging 35km-long coral wall located within about 50m of the shore. There are also a number of freshwater or saltwater cenotes (sinkholes) here, providing unique diving opportunities for the curious and the brave.

Cuba's longest (and the world's second-longest) coral reef sits 1.5km off Playa Santa Lucía (p347) on the north coast of Camagüey province, making this another mecca for divers from around the globe. The pièce de résistance here is the underwater shark-feeding show that takes place off nearby Playa Los Cocos.

Guajimico (p274) in Cienfuegos province is a large campismo (with dive outfit) that offers good, cheap accommodation and in excess of 20 diving sites about 20 minutes away by boat. The area is renowned for its coral gardens.

The big north coast resorts of Varadero (p240), Cayo Coco (p327) and Guardalavaca (p375) all have well-organized, professional dive centers that run trips to nearby reefs. Varadero boasts *El Neptuno,* a Russian ship purposefully sunk in the 1940s; Cayo Coco has La Jaula with a profusion of gorgonians; and Guardalavaca offers La Corona (The Crown), a colorful coral wall.

Cuba's best wreck dive is the *Cristóbal Colón,* off the coast of Santiago de Cuba province, a Spanish warship sunk by the Americans in 1898. It is accessible from dive sites in Chivirico and Parque Baconao (p434).

In all, you'll find more than 30 dive centers across Cuba, managed by **Marinas Gaviota** (www.gaviota-grupo.com), **Cubanacán Náutica** (www.cubanacan.cu) or **Cubamar** (www.cubamarviajes.cu). Though equipment does vary between installations, you can generally expect safe, professional and often multilingual service with these operators. Environmentally sensitive diving is where things can get wobbly, and individuals should educate themselves about responsible diving (see boxed text, opposite).

Dives and courses are comparably priced island-wide, from CUC$30 to CUC$45 per dive, with a discount after four or five dives. Full certification courses are CUC$310 to CUC$365, and 'resort' or introductory courses cost CUC$50 to CUC$60. Because of the US embargo laws, Professional Association of Diving Instructors (PADI) certification is generally not offered in Cuba; instead, you'll likely receive American Canadian Underwater Certification (ACUC) credentials.

CYCLING

Riding a bike in Cuba is *the* best way to discover the island in close-up. Some decent roads, wonderful scenery and the opportunity to get off the beaten track and meet Cubans eye-to-eye make cycling here a pleasure whichever route you take. For more mellow pedalers, daily bike rental is sometimes available in hotels, resorts and cafes for a going rate of approximately CUC$3 to CUC$7 a day, but don't always bank on it. The bigger resorts in Varadero are more reliable and will often include bike use as part of the all-inclusive package. Alternatively, if you're staying in a casa particular, your host will generally be able to rig something together (sometimes quite literally) in order to get you from A to B.

The main problem with procuring bikes in Cuba is that their quality is almost always substandard and, with the poor state of some of the roads, you'll often feel more like you're sitting atop an improvised coat hanger than a well-oiled machine. Serious cyclists should bring their boxed bikes from home on the airplane along with plenty of spare parts and reconfigure them in Cuba.

Cycling highlights include the Viñales valley (p212), the spin from Trinidad down to Playa Ancón (p303), the quiet lanes that zigzag through Guardalavaca (p375), and the roads out of Baracoa (p449) to Playa Maguana (northwest) and Boca de Yumurí (southeast). For a bigger challenge try La Farola (see boxed text, p455) between Cajobabo and Baracoa (21km of

The Vuelta a Cuba is a multistage bike race now in its 45th year. The 2009 event covered 1780km in 13 stages beginning in Baracoa.

ascent), the bumpy but spectacular coast road between Santiago and Marea del Portillo – best spread over three days with overnights in Brisas Sierra Mar (p437) and Campismo La Mula (p439) – or, for real wheel warriors, the insanely steep mountain road from Bartolomé Masó to Santo Domingo in Granma province.

With a profusion of casas particulares offering cheap, readily available accommodation, cycle touring is a joy here – just keep off the Autopista and steer clear of Havana and you'll be fine.

Off-road biking has not yet taken off in Cuba and is generally not permitted.

FISHING

Hemingway wasn't wrong. Cuba's fast-moving Gulf Stream along the north coast supports prime game fishing for sailfish, swordfish, tuna, mackerel, barracuda, marlin and shark, pretty much year-round. Fishing is a rite of passage for many and a great way to wind down, make friends, drink beer, watch sunsets and generally leave the troubles of the world behind. Not surprisingly, the country has great facilities for sport anglers and every Cuban boat captain seems to look and talk as if he's walked straight from the pages of a Hemingway classic.

> Gregorio Fuentes, the captain of Hemingway's fishing boat *Pilar*, was often credited as the model for the character of Santiago in the novel *The Old Man and the Sea*. He died at the age of 104 in 2002.

Cuba's best deep-sea fishing center is Cayo Guillermo (p329) – the small island that featured in *Islands in the Stream* (then uninhabited). Papa might have gone, but the fish still swim freely. Another good bet is Havana, which has two marinas, one at Tarará (p171) and the other – better one – at Marina Hemingway (p156) to the west.

Elsewhere, all of Cuba's main resort areas offer deep-sea fishing excursions for similar rates. Count on paying approximately CUC$280/450 per half-/full day for four people including crew and open bar.

Shore casting for bonefish and tarpon is practiced off the south coast at Jardines de la Reina (see boxed text, p330).

Freshwater fishing in Cuba is lesser known but equally rewarding and many Americans and Canadians hone in on the island's many lakes. Fly-fishing is superb in vast Ciénaga de Zapata (p257) in Matanzas, where enthusiasts can arrange multiday catch-and-release trips. *Trucha* (largemouth bass) was first introduced into Cuba in the early 20th century by Americans at King's Ranch and the United Fruit Company. Due to favorable environmental protection, the fish is now abundant in many Cuban lakes and many experts believe the next world-record bass (currently 9.9kg) will come from Cuba. Good places to cast a line are the Laguna del Tesoro (p256) in Matanzas, the Laguna de la Leche and Laguna la Redonda (p324) in Ciego de Ávila province, Embalse Zaza (p296) in Sancti Spíritus and Embalse Hanabanilla (p285) in Villa Clara – 7.6kg specimens have been caught here! To meet other fishermen, head for La Casona in Morón (p324), Hotel Zaza in Sancti Spíritus (p296) or Hotel Hanabanilla in Villa Clara province (p285).

SNORKELING

You don't have to go very deep to enjoy Cuba's tropical aquarium: snorkelers will be thrilled with treasures along the south coast from Playa Larga (p257) to Caleta Buena (Matanzas; see boxed text, p260); around Cienfuegos (p271); Playa Jibacoa (Havana province; p179) and along the Guardalavaca reef (Holguín; p375). In Varadero, daily snorkeling tours sailing to Cayo Blanco (p240) promise abundant tropical fish and good visibility. If you're not into the group thing, you can don a mask at Playa Coral (p233), 20km away.

Good boat dives for snorkeling happen around Isla de la Juventud (see boxed text, p190) and Cayo Largo (p195) especially, but also in Varadero (for sunken wrecks and reef; p240) and in the Cienfuegos (p271) and Guajimico (p273) areas. If you anticipate spending a lot of time snorkeling, bring your own gear as the rental stuff can be tattered and buying it in Cuba will mean you'll sacrifice both price and quality.

BIRD-WATCHING

Cuba offers a bird-watching bonanza year-round and no serious ornithologist should enter the country without their binoculars close at hand. Your experience will be enhanced by the level of expertise shown by many of Cuba's naturalists and guides in the key bird-watching zones. Areas with specialist bird-watching trails or trips include the Cueva Las Perlas trail (p209) in Parque Nacional Península de Guanahacabibes; the Maravillas de Viñales trail (p215) in Parque Nacional Viñales; the Sendero La Serafina (p223) in the Reserva Sierra del Rosario; the Observación de Aves tour (p257) in Gran Parque Natural Montemar; Parque Natural El Bagá (p327), on Cayo Coco; and the Sendero de las Aves (p344) in Hacienda La Belén in Camagüey province.

Must-sees include the *tocororo* (Cuban trogon), the *zunzuncito* (bee hummingbird), the Cuban tody, the Cuban parakeet, the Antillean palm swift, the *cartacuba* (an indigenous Cuban bird) and, of course, the flamingo – preferably in a flock. Good spots for some DIY birding are on Cayo Romano (see boxed text, p347) and adjacent Cayo Sabinal (p345), although you'll need a car to get there. Specialists and ivory-billed woodpecker seekers will enjoy Parque Nacional Alejandro de Humboldt (see boxed text, p456).

For more bird-watching tips, see the Itineraries chapter (p32).

> Cuba is home to both the world's smallest toad, the *ranita de Cuba* (Cuban tree toad; 1cm) and the world's smallest bird, the *zunzuncito* (bee humming-bird; 6.5cm).

HIKING & TREKKING

European hikers and North American wilderness freaks, take note. While Cuba's trekking potential is enormous, the traveler's right to roam is severely restricted by badly maintained trails, poor signage, lack of maps, and rather draconian restrictions about where you can and cannot go without a guide. The Cubans don't really understand hiking in the modern Western sense. They automatically assume that all trekkers want to be led by hand along short, relatively tame trails that are rarely more than 5km or 6km in length. You'll frequently be told that hiking alone is a reckless and dangerous activity, despite the fact that Cuba harbors no big fauna and no poisonous snakes. The best time of year for these activities is outside the rainy season and before it gets too hot (December to April).

The dearth of available hikes isn't always the result of nit-picking restrictions. Much of Cuba's trekkable terrain is in ecologically sensitive areas meaning access is carefully managed and controlled. Another reason is the lack of any real hiking culture (and thus demand) among Cubans themselves. Walking from A to B for the fun of it is often viewed with a certain degree of mirth in many Latin American countries, and Cuba is no exception. Rather than spend all day bushwhacking along a path in order to reach a beautiful waterfall, the Cubans would much rather pack some beers, load up the car and drive there.

For multiday hiking in Cuba, you've basically got two options, the three-day trek to the summit of Pico Turquino (p438) or the overnight San Claudio trail in the Reserva Sierra de Rosario (p223).

More challenging day hikes include El Yunque (p456), Parque Nacional Alejandro de Humboldt (p457) and some of the hikes around Las Terrazas (p223) and Viñales (p215).

Topes de Collantes (p311) probably has the largest concentration of hiking trails in its protected zone (a natural park). Indeed, some overseas groups organize four- to five-day treks here, starting near Lago Hanabanilla and finishing in Parque El Cubano. Inquire in advance at the Carpeta Central information office in Topes de Collantes if you are keen to organize something on behalf of a group.

Other tamer hikes include Cueva Las Perlas and Del Bosque al Mar in the Península de Guanahacabibes (p209); the guided trail in Parque Natural El Bagá (p456); El Guafe trail in Parque Nacional Desembarco del Granma (p457); and the short circuit in Reserva Ecológica Varahicacos (p239) in Varadero. Most of these hikes are guided and all require the payment of an entry fee.

If you want to hike independently, you'll need patience, resolve and an excellent sense of direction. It's also useful to ask the locals in your casa particular. Try experimenting first with Salto del Caburní or La Batata in Topes de Collantes (p312) or the various hikes around Viñales (p215). There's a beautiful little-used DIY hike on a good trail near Marea del Portillo (p402).

HORSEBACK RIDING

With its long-standing cowboy culture, horseback riding is available all over Cuba in both official and unofficial capacities. If you arrange it privately, make sure you check the state of the horses and equipment first. Riding poorly kept horses is both cruel and potentially dangerous.

The Pinto Cubano horse was perfected as a breed in the 1970s. Typically the horse has a suave gait, a well-defined musculature and is obedient and good-natured.

The state-owned catering company Palmares owns numerous rustic ranchos across Cuba that are supposed to give tourists a feel for traditional country life. All of these places offer guided horseback riding, usually for around CUC$5 an hour. You'll find good ranchos in Florencia (p326) in Ciego de Ávila province, Hacienda La Vega (p273) in Cienfuegos province, Finca Mayabe (p366) in Holguín province and Rancho Toa (p455) near Baracoa.

La Guabina (p206) is a horse-breeding center near the city of Pinar del Río that offers both horse shows and horseback-riding adventures.

BOATING & KAYAKING

Kayaking as a sport is pretty low-key in Cuba where it is treated more as a beach activity in the plusher resorts. Most of the tourist beaches will have *náutica* points that rent out simple kayaks, good for splashing around in but not a lot else. Boat rental is also available on many of the island's lakes. Good options include the Laguna de la Leche and Laguna la Redonda (p324), both in Ciego de Ávila province; Embalse Zaza (p296) in Sancti Spíritus province; and the Liberación de Florencia (p326) in Ciego de Ávila.

One of Cuba's best rivers is the Río Canímar (p233) near Matanzas, where you can rent rowboats and head up this mini-Amazon with its jungle-covered banks.

ROCK CLIMBING

The Viñales valley (p210) has been described as having the best sport rock climbing in the Western hemisphere. There are more than 150 routes now open (at all levels of difficulty, with several rated as YDS Class 5.14) and the word is out among the international climbing crowd, who are creating their own scene in one of Cuba's prettiest settings. Independent travelers will appreciate the free reign that climbers enjoy here.

Though you can climb here year-round, the heat can be oppressive, and locals stick to an October-to-April season, with December to January being the optimum months. For more information, visit the **Cuba Climbing** (www .cubaclimbing.com) website or head straight to Viñales.

It is important to note that though widely practiced – and normally without consequence – climbing in Viñales is still not technically legal. Though

ALTERNATIVE ADVENTURES

Las Terrazas has Cuba's first and (to date) only **canopy tour** (p224), a series of three zip lines that shoot adrenalin-junkies through 800m of thin air above Pinar del Río's famous eco-village. If you want to get even higher, try **tandem skydiving** (p241) in Varadero and Guardalavaca, or **ultralight flights** over the famous beaches. Various **boat adventures** are available in Cuba plying the mangrove-filled channels that crisscross the northern keys in small motorboats. Good options exist in Varadero (p243) and Cayo Guillermo (p329). **Aqua bikes** are available in most of the resort areas and you can take them in guided trips along the coastline.

Canyoning is still in its infancy in Cuba, but Topes de Collantes (p313) is the place to go to see how plans are progressing. Currently it is the preserve of preorganized trips only.

In a country that churns out boxers like it produces musicians, you might wish to don a pair of gloves and undertake a bit of 'friendly' **boxing** training. Gyms in Havana (p147) and Holguín (p369) are usually happy to welcome foreigners for a light workout. If you've still got any energy left, enroll in the **Marabana Havana marathon** (p27) that takes place every November in the capital.

you're unlikely to get arrested or even warned, take extreme care and do not under any circumstances do anything that infringes on the delicate Parque Nacional Viñales ecosystem.

CAVING

Cuba is riddled with caves – more than 20,000 and counting – and cave exploration is available to both casual tourists and professional speleologists. The Gran Caverna de Santo Tomás (p217), near Viñales, is Cuba's largest cavern with over 46km of galleries; the Cueva de los Peces (see boxed text, p260), near Playa Girón, is a flooded cenote with colorful snorkeling; and the Cueva de Ambrosio (p239) and Cuevas de Bellamar (p232), both in Matanzas, have tours daily.

Caving specialists have virtually unlimited caves from which to choose. With advance arrangements, you can explore deep into the Gran Caverna de Santo Tomás or visit the Cueva Martín Infierno (p273), which has the world's largest stalagmite. Also ask about San Catalina near Varadero, which has unique mushroom formations. Speleo-diving is also possible, but only for those already highly trained. Interested experts should contact Angel Graña, secretary of the **Sociedad Espeleológica de Cuba** (☎ 7-209-2885; angel@fanj.cult .cu) in Havana. The **Escuela Nacional de Espeleología** (☎ 48-77-10-14) in Moncada, just at the entrance to the Caverna de Santo Tomás, is another good resource for professionals.

Havana

'Anything is possible in Havana,' wrote British novelist Graham Greene of Cuba's rhapsodic capital, echoing the thoughts and dreams of millions. Prophetically, he wasn't far wrong. Truly one of the world's great urban centers, this tough-minded yet ebullient Caribbean metropolis is a riotous mélange of noble monuments and hip-gyrating music that has few cultural equals.

Yet, scarred by its past and flummoxed by one of the worst economic fallouts of modern times, Havana is no Paris. Here, at the proverbial heart of Cuba's great paradox, seductive beauty sidles up to spectacular decay, as life carries on precariously and capriciously, but always passionately.

For most visitors, the jewel in Havana's ruptured crown is Habana Vieja, a fascinating work-in-progress that has taken one of Spain's most beguiling colonial centers and rehabilitated it after years of poverty and neglect. Winking on the sidelines, a statuesque cluster of historical movers and shakers look down in granite and bronze: heroes and villains, colonizers and independence fighters, sugar merchants and mambo kings, hustlers and dreamers.

Enamored Habaneros love their city and it's not difficult to see why. This is the metropolis that inspired Lorca and enchanted Hemingway, a place where Winston Churchill wistfully concluded that he could quite happily 'leave his bones.' But while the setting is mesmerizing and the history like pungent cigar smoke drifting through the louvers, the city is far more than just a museum to rogues and revolutionaries. At least half of Havana's attraction is visceral. You'll fall in love here, but you'll struggle to ever understand why. The city is an impenetrable muse, the ultimate 'riddle wrapped up in a mystery inside an enigma.' Hit the streets and let it work its magic.

HIGHLIGHTS

- **Architecture** Art deco, colonial baroque, neoclassicism, Gaudí-esque experimentation: take a walk through Havana's architectural mosaic (p123)

- **The Malecón** Take in the dramatic sweep of Havana at sunset (p121)

- **The Cañonazo Ceremony** Head across the harbor for a tradition almost as old as the city itself (see boxed text, p169)

- **Cabaret** Rediscover kitsch at a professional cabaret show (p160)

- **Museo de la Revolución** The Revolution will not be televised, it will be brought to you right here – live (p116)

The Malecón
Fortaleza de San
Carlos de la Cabaña
Museo de la Revolución
Tropicana
Nightclub
Centro Habana

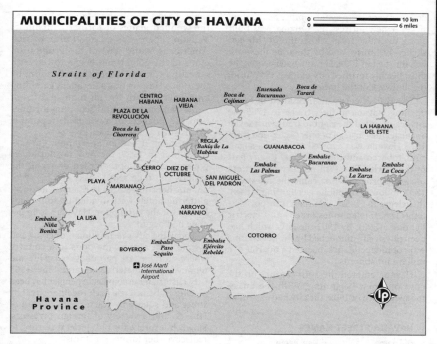

MUNICIPALITIES OF CITY OF HAVANA

0 — 10 km
0 — 6 miles

Straits of Florida

CENTRO HABANA
HABANA VIEJA
PLAZA DE LA REVOLUCIÓN
Boca de la Chorrera
Boca de Cojímar
Ensenada Bacuranao
Boca de Tarará
LA HABANA DEL ESTE
REGLA
Bahía de La Habana
GUANABACOA
Embalse Bacuranao
Embalse La Zarza
Embalse La Coca
CERRO
DIEZ DE OCTUBRE
SAN MIGUEL DEL PADRÓN
Embalse Las Palmas
PLAYA
MARIANAO
ARROYO NARANJO
COTORRO
Embalse Niña Bonita
LA LISA
BOYEROS
Embalse Paso Sequito
Embalse Ejército Rebelde
José Martí International Airport

Havana Province

HISTORY

In 1514 San Cristóbal de la Habana was founded on the south coast of Cuba near the mouth of the Río Mayabeque by Spanish conquistador Pánfilo de Narváez. Named after the daughter of a famous Taíno Indian chief, the city was moved twice during its first five years due to mosquito infestations and wasn't permanently established on its present site until December 17, 1519. According to local legend, the first Mass was said beneath a ceiba tree in present-day Plaza de Armas.

Havana is the most westerly and isolated of Diego Velázquez' original villas and life was hard in the early days. Things didn't get any better in 1538 when French corsairs and local slaves razed the city to the ground.

It took the Spanish conquest of Mexico and Peru to swing the pendulum in Havana's favor. The town's strategic location, at the mouth of the Gulf of Mexico, made it a perfect nexus point for the annual treasure fleets to regroup in the sheltered harbor before heading east. Thus endowed, its ascension was quick and decisive, and in 1607 Havana replaced Santiago as the capital of Cuba.

The city was sacked by French privateers led by Jacques de Sores in 1555; the Spanish replied by building the La Punta and El Morro forts between 1558 and 1630 to reinforce an already formidable protective ring. From 1674 to 1740, a strong wall around the city was added. These defenses kept the pirates at bay but proved ineffective when Spain became embroiled in the Seven Years' War with Britain, the strongest maritime power of the era.

On June 6, 1762, a British army under the Earl of Albemarle attacked Havana, landing at Cojímar and striking inland to Guanabacoa. From there they drove west along the northeastern side of the harbor, and on July 30 they attacked El Morro from the rear. Other troops landed at La Chorrera, west of the city, and by August 13 the Spanish were surrounded and forced to surrender. The British held Havana for 11 months. (The same war cost France almost all its colonies in North America, including Québec and Louisiana – a major paradigm shift.)

When the Spanish regained the city a year later in exchange for Florida, they began a crash building program to upgrade the city's defenses in order to avoid another debilitating siege. A new fortress, La Cabaña, was built along the ridge from which the British had shelled El Morro, and by the time the work was finished in 1774, Havana had become the most heavily fortified city in the New World, the 'bulwark of the Indies.'

The British occupation resulted in Spain opening Havana to freer trade. In 1765 the city was granted the right to trade with seven Spanish cities instead of only Cádiz, and from 1818 Havana was allowed to ship its sugar, rum, tobacco and coffee directly to any part of the world. The 19th century was an era of steady progress: first came the railway in 1837, followed by public gas lighting (1848), the telegraph (1851), an urban transport system (1862), telephones (1888) and electric lighting (1890). By 1902 the city, which had been physically untouched by the devastating wars of independence, boasted a quarter of a million inhabitants.

Havana entered the 20th century on the cusp of a new beginning. With the quasi-independence of 1902, the city had expanded

HAVANA STREET NAMES

Old name	New name
Av de los Presidentes	Calle G
Av de Maceo	Malecón
Av del Puerto	Av Carlos Manuel de Céspedes
Av de Rancho	Av de la Independencia Boyeros (Boyeros)
Belascoaín	Padre Varela
Cárcel	Capdevila
Carlos III (Tercera)	Av Salvador Allende
Cristina	Av de México
Egido & Monserrate	Av de Bélgica
Estrella	Enrique Barnet
Galiano	Av de Italia
La Rampa	Calle 23
Monserrate	Av de las Misiones
Monte	Máximo Gómez
Paseo del Prado	Paseo de Martí
Paula	Leonor Pérez
Reina	Av Simón Bolívar
San José	San Martín
Someruelos	Aponte
Teniente Rey	Brasil
Vives	Av de España
Zulueta	Agramonte

rapidly west along the Malecón and into the wooded glades of formerly off-limits Vedado. There was a large influx of rich Americans at the start of the Prohibition era, and the good times began to roll with a healthy (or not-so-healthy) abandon; by the 1950s Havana was a decadent gambling city frolicking to the all-night parties of American mobsters and scooping fortunes into the pockets of various disreputable hoods such as Meyer Lansky.

For Fidel, it was an aberration. On taking power in 1959, the new revolutionary government promptly closed down all the casinos and then sent Lansky and his sycophantic henchmen back to Miami. The once-glittering hotels were divided up to provide homes for the rural poor. Havana's long decline had begun.

Today the city's restoration is ongoing and a stoic fight against the odds in a country where shortages are part of everyday life and money for raw materials is scarce. Since 1982 City Historian Eusebio Leal Spengler has been piecing Habana Vieja back together street by street and square by square with the aid of Unesco and a variety of foreign investors. Slowly but surely, the old starlet is starting to rediscover her former greatness.

ORIENTATION

Surrounded by Havana province, the City of Havana is divided into 15 municipalities (see Map p95).

Habana Vieja, sometimes referred to as the Old Town, sits on the western side of the harbor in an area once bounded by 17th-century city walls that ran along present Av de Bélgica and Av de las Misiones. In 1863 these walls were demolished and the city spilled west into Centro Habana, bisected by busy San Rafael (the dividing line between the two is still fuzzy). West of Calzada de Infante lies Vedado, the 20th-century hotel and entertainment district that developed after independence in 1902. Near Plaza de la Revolución and between Vedado and Nuevo Vedado, a huge government complex was erected in the 1950s. West of the Río Almendares are Miramar, Marianao and Playa, Havana's most fashionable residential suburbs prior to the 1959 Revolution.

Between 1955 and 1958, a 733m-long tunnel was drilled between Habana Vieja

SCAMS

Well-documented *jinetero* (tout) problem aside, Havana is a remarkably safe city – particularly when compared with other Latin American capitals. Stroll through the atmospheric backstreets of Centro Habana or Habana Vieja of an evening, and your biggest worry is likely to be a badly pitched baseball or a flailing line of household washing.

But innocents beware. Scams do exist, particularly in the more touristy areas where well-practiced hustlers lurk outside the big hotels waiting to prey on unsuspecting foreign visitors.

One popular trick is for young men in the street to offer to change foreign currency into Cuban Convertibles at very favorable rates. Accept this at your peril. The money that you will be given is *moneda nacional* or Cuban pesos, visually similar to Convertibles, but worth approximately one-twenty-fifth of the value when you take them into a shop.

A second scam is the illicit sale of cheap cigars usually perpetuated by hissing street salesmen around Centro Habana and Habana Vieja. It is best to politely ignore these characters. Any bartering is not worth the bother. Cigars sold on the street are almost always substandard – something akin to substituting an expensive French wine with cheap white vinegar. Instead, buy your cigars direct from the factory or visit one of the numerous Casas del Habano that are scattered throughout the city.

and Habana del Este under the harbor mouth, and since 1959 a flurry of ugly high-rise housing blocks have been thrown up in Habana del Este, Cojímar (a former fishing village) and Alamar, northeast of the harbor. South of Habana del Este's endless blocks of flats are the prettier colonial towns of Guanabacoa, San Francisco de Paula and Santa María del Rosario. On the eastern side of the harbor are Regla and Casablanca.

Totally off the beaten track for most tourists are Havana's working-class areas south of Centro Habana, including Cerro, Diez de Octubre and San Miguel del Padrón. Further south still is industrial Boyeros, with the golf course, zoo and international airport, and Arroyo Naranjo with Parque Lenin.

Visitors spend the bulk of their time in Habana Vieja, Centro Habana and Vedado. Important streets here include: Obispo, a pedestrian mall cutting through the center of Habana Vieja; Paseo de Martí (aka Paseo del Prado or just 'Prado'), an elegant 19th-century promenade in Centro Habana; Av de Italia (aka Galiano), Centro Habana's main shopping street for Cubans; Malecón (aka Av de Maceo), Havana's broad coastal boulevard; and Calle 23 (aka La Rampa), the heart of Vedado's commercial district.

Confusingly, many main avenues around Havana have two names in everyday use – a new name that appears on street signs and in this book, and an old name overwhelm-ingly preferred by locals. See the boxed text on opposite to sort it all out.

Maps
The best place to head for maps is the official government information service, Infotur (p108), which has a wide variety of city maps, many of them free.

DOWNTOWN HAVANA

For simplicity's sake downtown Havana can be split into three main areas: Habana Vieja, Centro Habana and Vedado, which between them contain the bulk of the tourist sights. Centrally located Habana Vieja is the city's atmospheric historical masterpiece; Centro Habana, to the west, provides an eye-opening look at the real-life Cuba in close-up; while the more majestic Vedado is the once-notorious Mafia-run district replete with hotels, restaurants and a pulsating nightlife.

INFORMATION
Bookstores
Librería Centenario del Apóstol (Map pp102-3; ☎ 870-7220; Calle 25 No 164, Vedado; ☽ 10am-5pm Mon-Sat, 9am-1pm Sun) Great assortment of used books.
Librería Grijalbo Mondadovi (Map p100; Palacio del Segundo Cabo, O'Reilly No 4, Plaza de Armas, Habana Vieja; ☽ 9am-5pm Mon-Sat) Fantastic mix of magazines, guidebooks, reference, politics and art imprints in English and Spanish.

Librería La Internacional (Map p100; ☎ 861-3283; Obispo No 526, Habana Vieja; ◯ 9am-7pm Mon-Sat, 9am-3pm Sun) Good selection of guides, photography books and Cuban literature in English; next door is Librería Cervantes, an antiquarian bookseller.

Librería Luis Rogelio Nogueras (Map p106; ☎ 863-8101; Av de Italia No 467 btwn Barcelona & San Martín, Centro Habana) Literary magazines and Cuban literature in Spanish.

Librería Rayuela (Map pp102-3; Casa de las Américas, cnr Calles 3 & G, Vedado; ◯ 9am-4:30pm Mon-Fri) Great for contemporary literature, compact discs; some guidebooks.

Moderna Poesía (Map p100; ☎ 861-6640; Obispo 525, Habana Vieja; ◯ 10am-8pm) Perhaps Havana's best spot for Spanish-language books.

Plaza de Armas Secondhand Book Market (Map p100; cnr Obispo & Tacón, Habana Vieja) Old, new and rare books; with plenty of Fidel's written pontifications.

Cultural Centers

Alliance Française (Map pp102-3; ☎ 833-3370; Calle G No 407 btwn Calles 17 & 19, Vedado) Free French films Monday (11am), Wednesday (3pm) and Friday (5pm); good place to meet Cubans interested in French culture.

Casa de la Cultura Centro Habana (Map pp102-3; ☎ 878-4727; Av Salvador Allende No 720); Vedado (Map pp102-3; ☎ 831-2023; Calzada No 909) High-quality concerts and festivals.

Casa de las Américas (Map pp102-3; ☎ 838-2706; cnr Calles 3 & G, Vedado) Powerhouse of Cuban and Latin American culture, with conferences, exhibitions, a gallery, book launches and concerts. The Casa's annual literary award is one of the Spanish-speaking world's most prestigious. Pick up a schedule of weekly events in the library.

Fundación Alejo Carpentier (Map p100; Empedrado No 215, Habana Vieja; ◯ 8am-4pm Mon-Fri) Near the Plaza de la Catedral. Check for cultural events at this baroque former palace of the Condesa de la Reunión (1820s) where Carpentier set his famous novel *El Siglo de las Luces*.

Instituto Cubano de Amistad con los Pueblos (ICAP; Map pp102-3; ☎ 830-3114; Paseo No 416 btwn Calles 17 & 19, Vedado; ◯ 11am-11pm) Rocking cultural and musical events in elegant mansion (1926); restaurant, bar and cigar shop also here.

Union Nacional de Escritores y Artistas de Cuba (Uneac; Map pp102-3; ☎ 832-4551; cnr Calles 17 & H, Vedado) The pulse of the Cuban arts scene, this place is the first point of call for anyone with more than a passing interest in poetry, literature, art and music.

Emergency

Asistur (Map p106; ☎ 886-8339, 866-8920; asisten@ asistur.cu; www.asistur.cu; Paseo de Martí No 208, Centro Habana; ◯ 8:30am-5:30pm Mon-Fri, 8am-2pm Sat) Someone on staff should speak English; the alarm center here is open 24 hours.

Fire Service (☎ 105)

Police (☎ 106)

Internet Access

Havana doesn't have any private internet cafes. Your best bet outside the Etecsa Telepuntos is in the posher hotels. Most Habaguanex hotels in Habana Vieja have internet terminals and sell scratch cards (CUC$6 per hour) that work throughout the chain. You don't have to be a guest to use them.

Cibercafé Capitolio (Map p106; ☎ 862-0485; cnr Paseo de Martí & Brasil, Centro Habana; per hr CUC$5; ◯ 8am-8pm) Inside main entrance.

Etecsa Telepuntos Centro Habana (Map p106; Aguilar No 565; ◯ 8am-9:30pm) The long-promised internet terminals still hadn't arrived at time of writing; check ahead; Habana Vieja (Map p100; Habana 406) Six terminals in a back room.

Hotel Business Centers Hotel Habana Libre (Map pp102-3; Calle L btwn Calles 23 & 25, Vedado); Hotel Inglaterra (Map p106; Paseo de Martí No 416, Centro Habana); Hotel Nacional (Map pp102-3; cnr Calles O & 21, Vedado); Hotel NH Parque Central (Map p106; btwn Agramonte & Paseo de Martí, Centro Habana) Costs vary at these places.

Libraries

Foreign students with a *carnet* (or letter from their academic institution) can get library cards. Each library requires its own card; show up with two passport photos.

Biblioteca José A Echeverría (Map pp102-3; ☎ 838-2705; Casa de las Américas, Calle G No 210, Vedado) Best art, architecture and general-culture collection; books can't leave library.

Biblioteca Nacional José Martí (Map pp102-3; ☎ 881-7657; cnr Paseo & Av de la Independencia, Plaza de la Revolución, Vedado; ◯ 8:30am-6pm Mon-Sat) Havana's biggest library. Book and magazine launches are often held here.

Biblioteca Rubén M Villena (Map p100; ☎ 862-9035; Obispo No 59 cnr Baratillo, Habana Vieja; ◯ 8am-9pm Mon-Sat, 9am-4pm Sat) Nice reading rooms and garden.

Media

Cuba has a fantastic radio culture, where you'll hear everything from salsa to Supertramp, plus live sports broadcasts and soap operas. Radio is also the best source for listings on concerts, plays, movies and dances.

(Continued on page 107)

CITY OF HAVANA

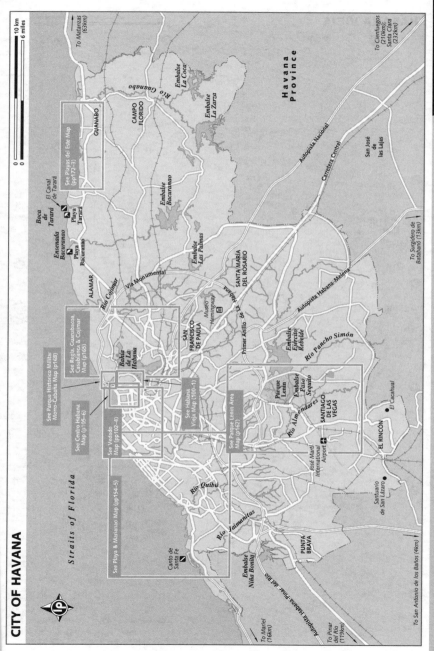

HAVANA

HABANA VIEJA

0 — 400 m
0 — 0.2 miles

Plaza 13 de Marzo

Parque Anfiteatro

Bahía de La Habana

Av Carlos Manuel de Céspedes

Parque Luz Caballero

Plaza de la Catedral

Plaza de Armas

See Enlargement

Obispo

Obrapía

Lamparilla

Amargura

Brasil

Plaza de San Francisco de Asís

Plaza Vieja

Santa Clara

Sol

Luz

Muelle Luz

Plaza del Cristo

Muralla

Parque de los Agrimensores

Estación Central de Ferrocarriles (Central Train Station)

Old City Wall

Bus 400 to Guanabo

Desamparados

La Coubre Train Station

Bahía de La Habana

Plaza de San Francisco de Asís

0 — 100 m

HABANA VIEJA

INFORMATION
Banco Financiero Internacional..**1** D6
Biblioteca Rubén M Villena.......**2** D5
Cadeca.......................................**3** D5
Cambio..**4** B2
Etecsa Telepunto......................**5** B2
Farmacia Taquechel.....................**6** C5
Fundación Alejo Carpentier......**7** B2
Infotur..**8** A2
Infotur..**9** C5
Librería Grijalbo Mondadovi..(see **62**)
Librería La Internacional...........**10** A3
Moderna Poesía.......................**11** A3
Plaza de Armas Secondhand
  Book Market **12** C2
Post Office...............................**13** A2
Post Office...............................**14** D6
San Cristóbal Agencia de
  Viajes..................................**15** D6

SIGHTS & ACTIVITIES
Aquarivm................................**16** D6
Cámara Oscura.......................**17** D6
Casa de África.........................**18** C5
Casa de Asia...........................**19** C5
Casa de la Obra Pía.................**20** C5
Casa de Lombillo....................**21** C1
Casa de México Benito Juárez..**22** C5
Casa Oswaldo Guayasamín....**23** D5
Castillo de la Real Fuerza........**24** C1
Catedral de San Cristóbal
  de la Habana.......................**25** B1
Catedral Ortodoxa Nuestra
  Señora de Kazán................**26** D3
Centro Cultural Pablo de la
  Torriente Brau....................**27** C3
Centro Wilfredo Lam................**28** B1
Coche Mambí..........................**29** D6
Edificio Bacardí......................**30** A2
Edificio Santo Domingo..........**31** C5
El Caballero de París............... **32** D6
Fototeca de Cuba....................**33** C3
Fuente de los Leones **34** D6
Iglesia de San Francisco de
  Paula...................................**35** C5
Iglesia del Santo Ángel
  Custodio.............................**36** A1
Iglesia Parroquial del Espíritu
  Santo...................................**37** C4
Iglesia y Convento de Nuestra
  Señora de Belén.................**38** B4
Iglesia y Convento de Nuestra
  Señora de la Merced...........**39** C5
Iglesia y Convento de Santa
  Clara..................................(see **84**)
Iglesia y Monasterio de San
  Francisco de Asís................**40** D6
La Casona Centro de Arte.......**41** C3
La Maestranza.........................**42** B1
Lonja del Comercio.............. **43** D6
Maqueta de La Habana Vieja..**44** C5
Museo 28 Septiembre de los
  CDR...................................**45** B2

Museo de Arte Colonial...........**46** B2
Museo de Arte Religioso.........(see **40**)
Museo de la Cerámica
  Artística Cubana.................**47** C1
Museo de la Ciudad................**48** C2
Museo de la Farmacia
  Habanera.............................**49** B3
Museo de la Orfebrería...........**50** C5
Museo de Naipes.....................**51** C3
Museo de Numismático...........**52** B2
Museo de Pintura Mural...........**53** C5
Museo de Simón Bolívar.........**54** C6
Museo de Tabaco...................(see **120**)
Museo del Automóvil..............**55** D5
Museo del Ron........................**56** D3
Museo El Templete..................**57** C2
Museo Nacional de Historia
  Natural.................................**58** D5
Museo – Casa Natal de José
  Martí....................................**59** B5
Palacio Cueto..........................**60** B2
Palacio de los Capitanes
  Generales...........................(see **48**)
Palacio de los Condes de
  Casa Bayona......................(see **46**)
Palacio de los Condes de
  Santovenia.........................(see **78**)
Palacio de los Marqueses de
  Aguas Claras......................(see **103**)
Palacio del Marqués de
  Arcos...................................**61** C2
Palacio del Segundo Cabo.......**62** B2
Parroquial del Santo Cristo
  del Buen Viaje.....................**63** A3
Sala Galería Raúl Martínez.....(see **62**)
Statue of Carlos Manuel de
  Céspedes............................**64** C2
Statue of Simón Bolívar.........**65** C5
Taller Experimental de Gráfica...**66** B2
Terminal Sierra Maestra
  (cruise terminal).................**67** D2

SLEEPING
Casa de Pepe y Rafaela...........**68** C4
Hostal Beltrán de la
  Santa Cruz............................**69** C3
Hostal Condes de Villanueva....**70** C6
Hostal Palacio O'Farrill............**71** B1
Hostal Valencia.......................**72** B2
Hotel Ambos Mundos..............**73** C5
Hotel El Comendador.............**74** D5
Hotel Florida...........................**75** B2
Hotel Marqués de Prado
  Ameno................................**76** B2
Hotel Raquel..........................**77** C6
Hotel Santa Isabel..................**78** C2
Juan & Margarita....................**79** A2
Mesón de la Flota...................**80** D6
Migdalia Carraballe.................**81** C4
Noemi Moreno.......................**82** C4
Pablo Rodríguez.....................**83** B3
Residencia Académica
  Convento de Santa Clara....**84** C4

EATING
Agropecuario Sol.....................**85** B4
Al Medina................................ **86** D5
Café de las Infusiones.............. **87** C5
Café de O'Reilly......................**88** C5
Café del Oriente.....................**89** D6
Café El Escorial.......................**90** C3
Café Santo Domingo...............**91** C5
Cafetería Torre La Vega.........**92** D5
El Mecurio.............................(see **43**)
Hanoi......................................**93** A3
Harris Brothers........................**94** A2
Heladería Obispo....................**95** A3
La Julia...................................**96** A2
La Mina..................................**97** D5
La Torre de Marfil....................**98** C5
La Zaragozana........................**99** A3
Museo del Chocolate.............. **100** C4
Paladar La Mulata del Sabor...**101** C4
Paladar Moneda Cubana.......**102** B2
Restaurante El Patio...............**103** B2
Restaurante Europa................**104** B2
Restaurante La Dominica..... **105** C2
Restaurante La Paella...........(see **72**)
Restaurante Puerto
  de Sagua............................**106** A4

DRINKING
Bar Dos Hermanos................ **107** D3
Bar La Marina........................ **108** D6
Café París.............................. **109** C5
Café Taberna......................... **110** D6
El Baturro............................... **111** A5
El Floridita.............................. **112** A3
La Bodeguita del Medio.........**113** B2
La Dichosa.............................**114** B2
La Lluvia de Oro.....................**115** B2
Monserrate Bar...................... **116** A3
Taberna de la Muralla............ **117** C3

ENTERTAINMENT
Basílica Menor de San
  Francisco de Asís..............(see **40**)
Gimnasio de Boxeo Rafael
  Trejo................................... **118** C5

SHOPPING
Casa de Carmen Montilla..... **119** D6
Casa del Habano.................... **120** C5
Estudio Galería Los Oficios... **121** D6
Feria de la Artesanía............**122** B1
Fundación Havana Club
  Shop..................................(see **56**)
Habana 1791........................ **123** C5
Longina Música..................... **124** B2
Palacio de la Artesanía..........**125** B1
Taller de Serigrafía René
  Portocarrero.......................**126** C3

TRANSPORT
Ferries to Regla &
  Casablanca.........................**127** D3
Horse Carriages.....................**128** C5

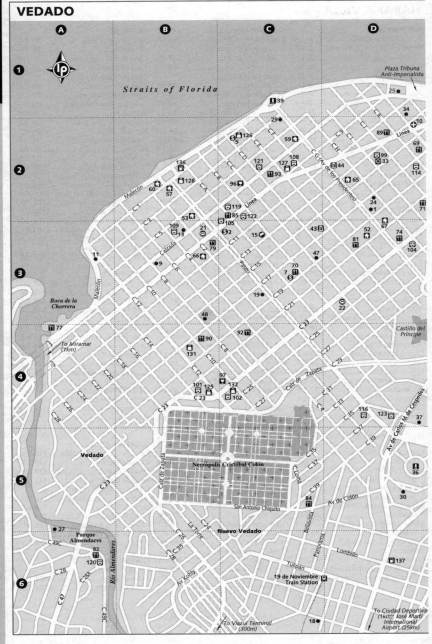

VEDADO

Straits of Florida

Boca de la Chorrera

Plaza Tribuna Anti-Imperialista

To Miramar (1km)

Castillo del Príncipe

Necropolis Cristóbal Colón

San Antonio Chiquito

Vedado

Caliz Zapata

Nuevo Vedado

Parque Almendares

19 de Noviembre Train Station

Tulipán

To Viazul Terminal (300m)

To Ciudad Deportiva (1km); José Martí International Airport (25km)

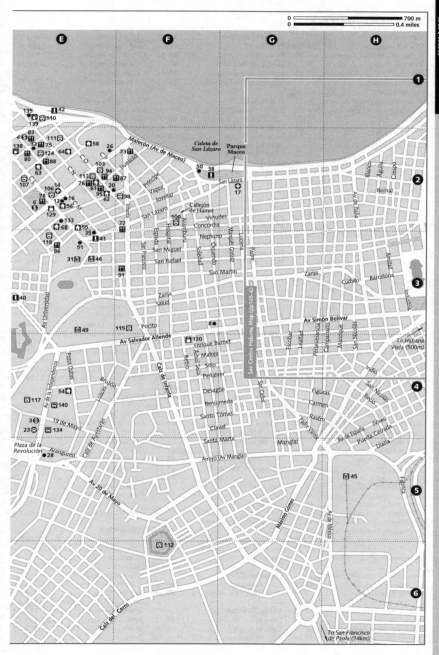

VEDADO (p102-3)

INFORMATION
Alliance Française..................... **1** D2
Banco de Crédito Comercio....(see 26)
Banco de Crédito y Comercio....**2** C3
Banco de Crédito y Comércio.....**3** E4
Banco Financiero
    Internacional.......................(see 56)
Banco Metropolitano................**4** E2
Biblioteca José A Echevarría.....(see 29)
Cadeca.................................**5** C2
Cadeca.................................**6** E2
Cadeca.................................**7** C3
Casa de la Cultura Centro
    Habana...............................**8** F3
Casa de la Cultura de Plaza......**9** B3
Centro Oftalmológico Camilo
    Cienfuegos.........................**10** D2
Cubamar Viajes......................**11** A3
Cubanacán...........................(see 58)
Cubatur...............................**12** C2
DHL....................................**13** B3
DHL...................................(see 58)
Farmacia Homopática...............**14** E2
German Embassy....................**15** D2
Havanatur............................**16** E2
Hospital Nacional Hermanos
    Ameijeiras..........................**17** G2
Inmigración..........................**18** C6
Instituto Cubano de Amistad
    con los Pueblos...................**19** C3
Librería Centenario
    del Apóstol.........................**20** E2
Librería Rayuela.....................(see 29)
Post Office...........................**21** B3
Post Office...........................**22** D3
Post Office...........................**23** E4
Sol y Son.............................(see 26)
Uneac................................**24** D2
US Interests Section................**25** D1

SIGHTS & ACTIVITIES
Airline Building......................**26** E2
Anfiteatro Parque Almendares....**27** A5
Biblioteca Nacional José Martí...**28** E5
Casa de las Américas...............**29** C2
Comité Central del Partido
    Comunista de Cuba..............**30** D5
Edificio Felipe Poey.................**31** B3
Edificio Focsa.......................**32** E2
Gran Synagoga Bet Shalom......**33** D2
López Serrano Building.............**34** D1
Mella portraits.......................**35** D2
Memorial a José Martí..............**36** D5
Ministerio del Interior..............**37** D4
Monumento a Antonio Maceo.**38** F2
Monumento a Calixto García...**39** C1
Monumento a José Miguel
    Gómez.............................**40** E3
Monumento a Julio Antonio
    Mella................................**41** E3
Monumento a las Víctimas del
    Maine...............................**42** E1
Museo Antropológico
    Montané...........................(see 31)
Museo de Artes Decorativas....**43** C3
Museo de Danza....................**44** D2
Museo de Historia Natural......(see 31)
Museo del Ferrocarril.............**45** H5

Museo Napoleónico................**46** E3
Paradiso..............................**47** C3
Parque Lennon......................**48** B3
Quinta de los Molinos.............**49** E3
Torreón de San Lázaro............**50** F2
Universidad de La Habana.......**51** E3

SLEEPING
Basilia Pérez Castro................(see 68)
Eddy Gutiérrez Bouza.............**52** D3
Guillermina & Roberto Abreu...**53** B2
Hotel Bruzón........................**54** E4
Hotel Colina.........................**55** E3
Hotel Habana Libre.................**56** E2
Hotel Meliá Cohiba................**57** B2
Hotel Nacional......................**58** E2
Hotel Presidente....................**59** C2
Hotel Riviera........................**60** B2
Hotel St John's......................**61** E2
Hotel Vedado.......................**62** E2
Hotel Victoria.......................**63** E2
Manuel Martínez....................**64** E2
Marta Vitorte........................**65** D2
Melba Piñeda Bermudez.........**66** B3
Mercedes González................**67** D3
Nelsy Alemán Machado..........**68** E2

EATING
Agropecuario 17 & K...............**69** D2
Agropecuario 19 & A...............**70** C3
Agropecuario 21 & J................**71** D2
Biki....................................**72** F2
Bim Bom.............................**73** F2
Café Literario del 'G'...............**74** D3
Café TV..............................**75** E2
Cafetería Sofía......................**76** E2
Complejo Turístico 1830..........**77** A4
Coppelia.............................**78** E2
Decameron...........................**79** B3
El Conejito...........................**80** E2
El Gringo Viejo......................**81** D3
El Lugar..............................**82** A6
La Casona y 17......................**83** E2
La Torre...............................(see 32)
Organopónico Plaza...............**84** C5
Pain de París.........................**85** C2
Pain de París.........................(see 20)
Paladar Aries........................**86** E3
Paladar El Hurón Azul..............**87** C2
Paladar Los Amigos................**88** E2
Paladar Marpoly....................**89** D2
Pan.com..............................**90** B4
Peso Pizza...........................**91** F3
Peso Stalls...........................**92** C4
Restaurante Vegetariano
    Carmelo............................**93** C2
Restaurante Wakamba.............**94** E2
Supermercado Meridiano......(see 128)
Trattoría Maraka's..................**95** E2

DRINKING
Bar-Club Imágenes.................**96** C2
Café Fresa y Chocolate............**97** C4

ENTERTAINMENT
Cabaret Las Vegas.................**98** F2
Cabaret Parisién....................(see 58)
Cabaret Turquino..................(see 56)

Café Cantante......................(see 123)
Café Teatro Brecht.................**99** D2
Callejón de Hamel..................**100** F2
Casa de la Amistad................(see 19)
Centro Cultural
    Cinematográfico................(see 97)
Cine 23 y 12........................**101** B4
Cine Charles Chaplin..............**102** C4
Cine La Rampa......................**103** E2
Cine Riviera.........................**104** D3
Cine Trianón.........................**105** C3
Cine Yara............................**106** E2
Club La Red..........................**107** E2
Club Tropical........................**108** C2
Conjunto Folklórico
    Nacional de Cuba...............**109** B3
Copa Room..........................(see 60)
Discoteca Amanecer...............**110** E1
El Gato Tuerto......................**111** E2
El Hurón Azul.......................(see 24)
Estadio Latinoamericano.........**112** F6
Habana Café........................(see 57)
Jazz Café.............................(see 128)
Jazz Club La Zorra y
    El Cuervo.........................**113** E2
Karachi Club.........................**114** D2
La Colmenita........................(see 123)
La Madriguera......................**115** F3
Patio de María.......................**116** D4
Piano Bar Delirio Habanero....(see 123)
Pico Blanco..........................(see 61)
Sala Polivalente Ramón Fonst..**117** E4
Sala Teatro El Sótano..............**118** E3
Sala Teatro Hubert de Blanck...**119** C2
Salón Chèvere.......................**120** A6
Teatro Amadeo Roldán............**121** C2
Teatro Mella.........................**122** C2
Teatro Nacional de Cuba.........**123** D4
Teatro Nacional de Guiñol......**124** E2

SHOPPING
ARTex................................(see 106)
Centro de Arte 23 y 12...........**125** B4
Feria de la Artesanía..............**126** C2
Galería de Arte
    Latinoamericano................(see 29)
Galería Habana.....................**127** C2
Galerías de Paseo..................**128** B2
La Habana Sí........................**129** C2
Photo Service........................(see 128)
Plaza Carlos III......................**130** F4
Registro Nacional de Bienes
    Culturales.........................**131** B4
Sevando Galería del Arte........**132** C4

TRANSPORT
Aerocaribbean......................(see 26)
Cubana Airlines.....................(see 26)
Havana Bus Tour....................**133** E2
Havana Bus Tour
    - main interchange
    for buses T1 and T2.............**134** E4
Rex Rent-a-Car......................**135** E1
Servi-Cupet Gas Station..........**136** B2
Servi-Cupet Gas Station..........**137** D6
Servi-Cupet Gas Station..........**138** E2
Servi-Cupet Gas Station..........**139** E1
Terminal de Ómnibus.............**140** E4

CENTRO HABANA (p106)

INFORMATION
Asistur..**1** C3
Banco Metropolitano................**2** B5
Cadeca................................(see 34)
Cibercafé Capitolio...................**3** C5
Denmark Embassy....................**4** C2
Etecsa Telepunto......................**5** C5
Librería Luis Rogelio
    Nogueras..............................**6** B5
Post Office................................**7** C4
Spain Embassy.....................(see 20)

SIGHTS & ACTIVITIES
Asociación Cultural Yoruba de
    Cuba.....................................**8** D5
Cárcel..**9** D2
Castillo de San Salvador de la
    Punta..................................**10** D2
Centro Gallego.....................(see 69)
Centro Hispano Americano de
    Cultura...............................**11** C2
Escuela Nacional de Ballet........**12** D3
Fuente de la India....................**13** D5
Iglesia del Sagrado Corazón de
    Jesús..................................**14** A6
Memorial a los Estudiantes de
    Medicina.............................**15** D2
Museo de la Revolución...........**16** D3
Museo Nacional
    de Bellas Artes (Colección
    de Arte Cubano).................**17** D3
Museo Nacional
    de Bellas Artes (Colección
    de Arte Universal)...............**18** D4
Palacio de los Matrimonios.......**19** C4
Palacio Velasco........................**20** D2
Pavillón Granma......................**21** D3
Real Fábrica de Tabacos
    Partagás..............................**22** C5

Statue of General Máximo
    Gómez................................**23** D2
Statue of José Martí................ **24** D4

SLEEPING 🛏
Casa del Científico...................**25** C3
Dulce Hostal –
    Dulce María González.........**26** C4
Elicio Fernández.......................**27** C4
Esther Cardoso.........................**28** C4
Hotel Caribbean.......................**29** C3
Hotel Deauville.........................**30** B3
Hotel Inglaterra.......................**31** C4
Hotel Lido................................**32** C3
Hotel Lincoln...........................**33** B4
Hotel NH Parque Central..........**34** D4
Hotel Park View.......................**35** D3
Hotel Saratoga.........................**36** D5
Hotel Sevilla............................**37** D3
Hotel Telégrafo........................**38** C4
Juan Carlos..............................**39** C3
Julio y Elsa Roque....................**40** C4
La Casona Colonial –
    Jorge Díaz...........................**41** A4
Martha Obregón......................**42** A4
Niurka O Rey...........................**43** C4

EATING 🍴
Almacenes Ultra......................**44** B6
Café Neruda.............................**45** B3
Centro Andaluz........................**46** C3
Chi Tack Tong..........................**47** B5
El Gran Dragón........................**48** B5
La Época..................................**49** B4
Los Gijones.............................**50** D4
Los Nardos..............................**51** D5
Mercado Agropecuario Egido..**52** D6
Paladar Bellamar......................**53** C4
Paladar Doña Blanquita............**54** C3

Paladar La Guarida...................**55** A4
Paladar Torressón.....................**56** C2
Pastelería Francesa...................**57** C4
Prado y Neptuno......................**58** C4
Rancho Coquito........................**59** C3
Restaurante Tien-Tan...............**60** B5
Supermercado Isla de Cuba......**61** C6

DRINKING 🍷
Prado No 12.............................**62** C2
Prado y Ánimas........................ **63** D4

ENTERTAINMENT 🎭
Cabaret Nacional......................**64** C4
Cine Actualidades.....................**65** D4
Cine Payret..............................**66** D4
Cinecito...................................**67** C4
El Palermo...............................**68** C4
Gran Teatro de La Habana........**69** C4
Kid Chocolate..........................**70** D5
La Casa de la Música Centro
    Habana...............................**71** B4
Teatro América.........................**72** B4
Teatro Fausto...........................**73** D3

SHOPPING 🛍
Area de Vendedores por
    Cuenta Propia......................**74** C6
El Bulevar................................**75** C4
Galería La Acacia......................**76** C4
La Manzana de Gómez.............**77** D4

TRANSPORT
Buses to Havana Province.........**78** D6
CicloBus...................................**79** C5
El Orbe..................................(see 77)
Havana Bus Tour -
    main interchange
    for buses T1 & T3................**80** C4

HAVANA

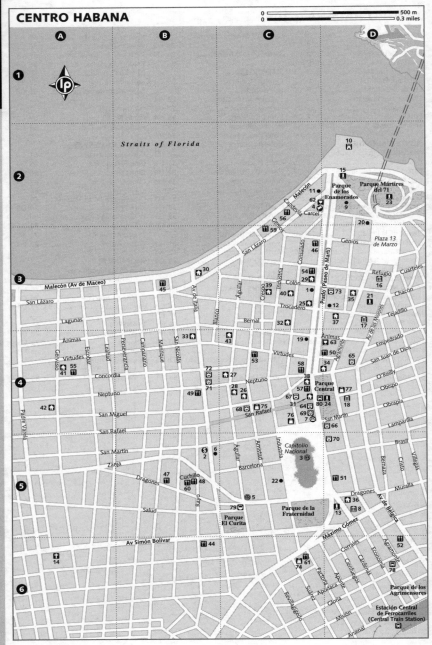

CENTRO HABANA

0 — 500 m
0 — 0.3 miles

A **B** **C** **D**

1

2

Straits of Florida

Parque Mártires del 71

Parque de los Enamorados

Plaza 13 de Marzo

3

Malecón (Av de Maceo)

San Lázaro

Lagunas

Ánimas

Virtudes

Concordia

4

Neptuno

San Miguel

San Rafael

5

San Martín

Zanja

Dragones

Salud

Av Simón Bolívar

6

Parque El Curita

Parque de la Fraternidad

Capitolio Nacional

Parque de los Agrimensores

Estación Central de Ferrocarriles (Central Train Station)

(Continued from page 98)

Radio Ciudad de la Habana (820AM & 94.9FM) Cuban tunes by day, foreign pop at night; great '70s flashback at 8pm on Thursday and Friday.

Radio Metropolitana (910AM & 98.3FM) Jazz and traditional boleros (music in 3/4 time); excellent Sunday afternoon rock show.

Radio Musical Nacional (590AM & 99.1FM) Classical.

Radio Progreso (640AM & 90.3 FM) Soap operas and humor.

Radio Rebelde (640AM, 710AM & 96.7FM) News, interviews, good mixed music, plus baseball games.

Radio Reloj (950AM & 101.5FM) News, plus the time every minute of every day.

Radio Taíno (1290AM & 93.3FM) National tourism station with music, listings and interviews in Spanish and English. Nightly broadcasts (5pm to 7pm) list what's happening around town.

Medical Services

Most of Cuba's specialist hospitals offering services to foreigners are based in Havana; see www.cubanacan.cu for details. Consult the Playa & Marianao section of this chapter (p153) for other international clinics and pharmacies.

Centro Oftalmológico Camilo Cienfuegos (Map pp102-3; ☎ 832-5554; cnr Calle L No 151 & Calle 13, Vedado) Head straight here with eye problems; also has an excellent pharmacy.

Farmacia Homopática (Map pp102-3; cnr Calles 23 & M, Vedado; ☼ 8am-8pm Mon-Fri, 8am-4pm Sat)

Farmacia Taquechel (Map p100; ☎ 862-9286; Obispo No 155, Habana Vieja; ☼ 9am-6pm) Next to the Hotel Ambos Mundos. Cuban wonder drugs such as anticholesterol medication PPG sold in pesos here.

Hospital Nacional Hermanos Ameijeiras (Map pp102-3; ☎ 877-6053; San Lázaro No 701, Centro Habana) Special hard-currency services, general consultations and hospitalization. Enter via the lower level below the parking lot off Padre Varela (ask for CEDA in Section N).

Hotel Pharmacies Hotel Habana Libre (Map pp102-3; ☎ 831-9538; Calle L btwn Calles 23 & 25, Vedado) Products sold in Convertibles; Hotel Sevilla (Map p100; ☎ 861-5703; Prado cnr Trocadero, Habana Vieja)

Money

Banco de Crédito y Comercio Vedado (Map pp102-3; cnr Línea & Paseo); Vedado (Map pp102-3; ☎ 870-2684; Airline Bldg, Calle 23); Vedado (Map pp102-3; ☎ 879-2074; Av Independencia No 101) The last one – in post office between Terminal de Ómnibus and Plaza de la Revolución – is most convenient to immigration for visa extension stamps. Expect lines.

Banco Financiero Internacional Habana Vieja (Map p100; ☎ 860-9369; cnr Oficios & Brasil); Vedado (Map pp102-3; Hotel Habana Libre, Calle L btwn Calles 23 & 25)

Banco Metropolitano Centro Habana (Map p106; ☎ 862-6523; Av de Italia No 452 cnr San Martín); Vedado (Map pp102-3; ☎ 832-2006; cnr Línea & Calle M, Vedado)

Cadeca Centro Habana (Map p106; cnr Neptuno & Agramonte; ☼ 9am-noon & 1-7pm Mon-Sat); Habana Vieja (Map p100; cnr Oficios & Lamparilla; ☼ 8am-7pm Mon-Sat, 8am-1pm Sun); Vedado (Map pp102-3; Calle 23 btwn Calles K & L; ☼ 7am-2:30pm & 3:30-10pm); Vedado (Map pp102-3; Mercado Agropecuario, Calle 19 btwn Calles A & B; ☼ 7am-6pm Mon-Sat, 8am-1pm Sun); Vedado (Map pp102-3; cnr Malecón & Calle D) Cadeca gives cash advances and changes traveler's checks at 3.5% commission Monday to Friday (4% weekends).

Cambio (Map p100; Obispo No 257, Habana Vieja; ☼ 8am-10pm) The best opening hours in town.

Post

DHL Vedado (Map pp102-3; ☎ 832-2112; Calzada No 818 btwn Calles 2 & 4; ☼ 8am-5pm Mon-Fri); Vedado (Map pp102-3; ☎ 836-3564; Hotel Nacional, cnr Calles O & 21)

Post offices Centro Habana (Map p106; Gran Teatro, cnr San Martín & Paseo de Martí); Habana Vieja (Map p100; Plaza de San Francisco de Asís, Oficios No 102); Habana Vieja (Map p100; Unidad de Filatelia, Obispo No 518; ☼ 9am-7pm); Vedado (Map pp102-3; cnr Línea & Paseo; ☼ 8am-8pm Mon-Sat); Vedado (Map pp102-3; cnr Calles 23 & C; ☼ 8am-6pm Mon-Fri, 8am-noon Sat); Vedado (Map pp102-3; Av de la Independencia btwn Plaza de la Revolución & Terminal de Ómnibus; ☼ stamp sales 24hr) The last one has many services, including photo developing, a bank and Cadeca. The Museo Postal Cubano (☎ 870-5581; admission CUC$1; ☼ 10am-5pm Sat & Sun) here has a philatelic shop. The post office at Obispo, Habana Vieja, also has stamps for collectors.

Telephone

Etecsa Telepuntos Centro Habana (Map p106; Aguilar No 565; ☼ 8am-9:30pm) There's also a Museo de las Telecomunicaciones (☼ 9am-6pm Tue-Sat) here if you get bored waiting; Habana Vieja (Map p100; Habana 406)

Toilets

Not overendowed with clean available public toilets, most tourists slip into the upscale hotels if they're caught short. The following establishments are all fairly relaxed about toilet security.

Hotel Ambos Mundos (Map p100; Obispo No 153, Habana Vieja) Tip the attendant.

Hotel Habana Libre (Map pp102-3; Calle L btwn Calles 23 & 25, Vedado) To the left of the elevators.

Hotel Nacional (Map pp102-3; cnr Calles O & 21, Vedado) Right in the lobby and left past the elevators.

Hotel Sevilla (Map p106;Trocadero No 55 btwn Paseo de Martí & Agramonte, Centro Habana) Turn right inside the lobby.

Tourist Information

Infotur Airport (off Map p162; ☎ 642-6101; Terminal 3 Aeropuerto Internacional José Martí; 🕑 24hr); Habana Vieja (Map p100; ☎ 866-3333; Obispo btwn Bernaza & Villegas); Habana Vieja (Map p100; ☎ 863-6884; cnr Obispo & San Ignacio; 🕑 10am-1pm & 2-7pm) Books excursions, sells maps, phone cards and transport schedules.

Travel Agencies

Many of the following agencies also have offices at the airport, in the international arrivals lounge of Terminal 3.

Cubamar Viajes (Map pp102-3; ☎ 833-2523/4; www .cubamarviajes.cu; Calle 3 btwn Calle 12 & Malecón, Vedado; 🕑 8:30am-5pm Mon-Sat) Travel agency for Campismo Popular cabins countrywide. Also rents mobile homes.

Cubanacán (Map pp102-3; ☎ 873-2686; www.cuban acan.cu; Hotel Nacional, cnr Calles O & 21, Vedado; 🕑 8am-7pm) Very helpful; head here if you want to arrange fishing or diving at Marina Hemingway; also in Hotel NH Parque Central, Hotel Inglaterra and Hotel Habana Libre.

Cubatur (Map pp102-3; ☎ 835-4155; cnr Calles 23 & M, Vedado; 🕑 8am-8pm) Below Hotel Habana Libre. This agency pulls a lot of weight and finds rooms where others can't, which goes a long way toward explaining its slacker attitude. It has desks offices in most of the main hotels.

Havanatur (Map pp102-3; ☎ 835-3720; www .havanatur.cu; Calle 23 cnr M, Vedado)

San Cristóbal Agencia de Viajes (Map p100; ☎ 861-9171/2; www.viajessancristobal.cu; Oficios No 110 btwn Lamparilla & Amargura, Habana Vieja; 🕑 8:30am-5:30pm Mon-Fri, 8:30am-2pm Sat, 9am-noon Sun) Habaguanex agency operates Habana Vieja's classic hotels; income helps finance restoration. It offers the best tours in Havana.

Sol y Son (Map pp102-3; ☎ 833-3647; Calle 23 No 64; 🕑 8:30am-7pm Mon-Fri, 8:30am-noon Sat) Sells Cubana flights.

DANGERS & ANNOYANCES

Havana is not a dangerous city, especially when compared to other metropolitan areas in North and South America. There is almost no gun crime, violent robbery, organized gang culture, teenage delinquency, drugs, or dangerous no-go zones. Rather, a heavy police presence on the streets and stiff prison sentences for crimes such as assault have acted as a major deterrent for would-be criminals and kept the dirty tentacles of organized crime at bay.

But it's not all love and peace, man. Petty crime against tourists in Havana – almost nonexistent in the 1990s – is widespread and on the rise, with pickpocketing, bag-snatching by youths mounted on bicycles and the occasional face-to-face mugging all being reported.

Bring a money belt and keep it on you at all times, making sure that you wear it concealed – and tightly secured – around your waist.

In hotels use a safety deposit box (if there is one) and never leave money/passports/credit cards lying around during the day. Theft from hotel rooms is tediously common, with the temptation of earning three times your monthly salary in one fell swoop often too hard to resist.

In bars and restaurants it is wise to check your change. Purposeful overcharging, especially when someone is mildly inebriated, is a favorite (and easy) trick.

Visitors from the well-ordered countries of Europe or litigation-obsessed North America should keep an eye out for crumbling sidewalks, manholes with no covers, inexplicable driving rules, veering cyclists, carelessly lobbed front-door keys (in Centro Habana) and enthusiastically hit baseballs (almost everywhere). Waves cascading over the Malecón sea wall might look pretty, but the resulting slime-fest has been known to throw Lonely Planet–wielding tourists flying unceremoniously onto their asses.

For more popular scams see the boxed text on p97.

SIGHTS & ACTIVITIES
Habana Vieja

Studded with architectural jewels from every era, Habana Vieja offers visitors one of the finest collections of urban edifices in the Americas. At a conservative estimate, the Old Town alone contains over 900 buildings of historical importance with myriad examples of illustrious architecture ranging from intricate baroque to glitzy art deco.

For a whistle-stop introduction to the best parts of the neighborhood, check out the suggested walking tour (p122) or stick closely to the four main squares – Plaza de

HAVANA IN...

Two Days

Go for an early morning caffeine jolt in **Café El Escorial** (p138) overlooking Plaza Vieja before investigating the colonial treasures of the **Museo de la Ciudad** (p110). Clear your head afterwards with a casual stroll down **Calle Mercaderes** (p111), where specialist shops and colonial mansions offer plenty of streetside diversions. Lunchtime snacks can be procured upstairs at the **Café Santo Domingo** (p138), while afternoon entertainment is everywhere in **Calle Obispo** (p112). Line up for a guided tour of the **Capitolio** (p114) before decamping for a predinner daiquirí in **El Floridita** (p141). Have dinner in the legendary **Paladar La Guarida** (p134) and catch a late-night show in **Cabaret Parisién** (p144) in the Hotel Nacional.

Head through Chinatown on day two, stopping for an early lunch in **Tien-Tan** (p136). Admire the architectural wonders on the **Centro Habana Architectural Tour** (p123) before tracking west along the Malecón for a reviving drink in the bar of the **Hotel Habana Libre** (p133). Reach for Havana's culinary heights in **La Torre** (p137) on top of the Focsa building before heading down for a comedy show at **Café TV** (p136).

Four Days

Follow the two-day itinerary, and on the morning of day three board the Havana Bus Tour for the **Plaza de la Revolución** (p119). After the obligatory Che mural photos board a second bus for Miramar, disembarking at the **Acuario Nacional (p156)** for an afternoon dolphin show. Stroll over to the fascinating **Fundación Naturaleza y El Hombre** (p153) before tracking back to **El Aljibe** (p158) for a classic Cuban dinner. For evening entertainment roll the dice and choose between a concert at **Teatro Karl Marx** (p160), hot salsa at the **Casa de la Música** (p160) or full-blown Cuba kitsch at the Tropicana Nightclub (p160). On day four, pack up your beach bag and hop on the Havana Bus Tour to **Playa Santa María del Mar** (p170).

Armas, Plaza Vieja, Plaza de San Francisco de Asís and Plaza de la Catedral.

The renovation of Habana Vieja is overseen by the government-run agency Habaguanex and directed by long-standing City Historian, Eusebio Leal Spengler. Eager to recreate a 'living' historic center that integrates the neighborhood's 70,000-plus inhabitants, Habaguanex splits its US$160 million annual tourist income between further restoration (45%) and other deserving social projects in the city (55%).

PLAZA DE LA CATEDRAL

Habana Vieja's most uniform square is a museum to Cuban baroque with all the surrounding buildings (including the city's magnificent cathedral) dating from the 1700s. Despite this homogeneity, it is actually the newest of the four squares in the Old Town with its present layout dating from the 18th century.

Dominated by two unequal towers and framed by a theatrical baroque facade designed by Italian architect Francesco Borromini, the graceful **Catedral de San Cristóbal de La Habana** (cnr San Ignacio & Empedrado; ☯ before noon) was de-

scribed by novelist Alejo Carpentier as 'music set in stone.' The Jesuits began construction of the church in 1748 and work continued despite their expulsion in 1767. When the building was finished in 1787, the diocese of Havana was created and the church became a cathedral – one of the oldest in the Americas. The remains of Columbus were interred here from 1795 to 1898 when they were moved to Seville. The best time to visit is during Sunday Mass (10:30am).

On the corner to the left of the cathedral is the **Centro Wilfredo Lam** (☎ 862-2611; cnr San Ignacio & Empedrado; admission CUC$3; ☯ 10am-5pm Mon-Sat), a cafe and exhibition center named after the island's most celebrated painter but which usually displays the works of more modern painters.

Situated on the western side of the Plaza is the majestic **Palacio de los Marqueses de Aguas Claras** (San Ignacio No 54), a one-time baroque palace completed in 1760 and widely lauded for the beauty of its shady Andalucian patio. Today it houses the Restaurante El Patio (p135).

Directly opposite are the **Casa de Lombillo** and the **Palacio del Marqués de Arcos**. The former, built in 1741, once served as a post office (a stone-mask ornamental mailbox built into the wall is still in use). Since 2000 it has functioned as the main office for the City Historian, Eusebio Leal Spengler.

The square's southern aspect is taken up by its oldest building, the resplendent **Palacio de los Condes de Casa Bayona** built in 1720. Today it functions as the **Museo de Arte Colonial** (☎ 862-6440; San Ignacio No 61; unguided/guided CUC$2/3, camera CUC$2; ☺ 9am-6:30pm), a small museum displaying colonial furniture and decorative arts. Among the finer exhibits are pieces of china with scenes of colonial Cuba, a collection of ornamental flowers, and many colonial-era dining room sets.

At the end of a short cul-de-sac, the **Taller Experimental de Gráfica** (☎ 862-0979; Callejón del Chorro No 6; admission free; ☺ 10am-4pm Mon-Fri) is Havana's most cutting-edge art workshop, which offers the possibility of engraving classes (see p126).

PLAZA DE ARMAS

Havana's oldest square was laid out in the early 1520s, soon after the city's foundation, and was originally known as Plaza de Iglesia after a church – the Parroquial Mayor – that once stood on the site of the present-day Palacio de los Capitanes Generales. The name Plaza de Armas (Square of Arms) wasn't adopted until the late 16th century, when the colonial governor, then housed in the Castillo de la Real Fuerza, used the site to conduct military exercises. The modern plaza, along with most of the buildings around it, dates from the late 1700s.

In the center of the square, which is lined with royal palms and enlivened by a daily (except Sundays) secondhand book market, is a marble **statue of Carlos Manuel de Céspedes** (1955), the man who set Cuba on the road to independence in 1868.

Filling the whole west side of the Plaza is the **Palacio de los Capitanes Generales** dating from the 1770s. Built on the site of Havana's original church, this muscular baroque beauty has served many purposes over the years. From 1791 until 1898 it was the residence of the Spanish captains general. From 1899 until 1902, the US military governors were based here, and during the first two decades of the 20th century the building briefly became the presidential palace. Since 1968

it has been home to the **Museo de la Ciudad** (☎ 861-6130; Tacón No 1; unguided/guided CUC$3/4, camera CUC$2; ☺ 9am-6pm), one of Havana's most comprehensive and interesting museums that wraps its way regally around a splendid central courtyard adorned with a white marble statue of Christopher Columbus (1862). Artifacts include period furniture, military uniforms and old-fashioned 19th-century horse carriages, while old photos vividly recreate events from Havana's rich history such as the 1898 sinking of US battleship *Maine* in the harbor. It's better to body-swerve the pushy attendants and wander around at your own pace.

Wedged into the square's northwest corner is the **Palacio del Segundo Cabo** (O'Reilly No 4; admission CUC$1), constructed in 1772 as the headquarters of the Spanish vice-governor. After several reincarnations as a post office, palace of the Senate, Supreme Court, the National Academy of Arts and Letters, and the seat of the Cuban Geographical Society, the building is today a well-stocked bookstore (p97). Pop-art fans should take a look at the **Sala Galería Raúl Martínez** (☺ 9am-6pm Mon-Sat).

On the square's seaward side is the **Castillo de la Real Fuerza**, the oldest existing fort in the Americas, built between 1558 and 1577 on the site of an earlier fort destroyed by French privateers in 1555. The west tower is crowned by a copy of a famous bronze weather vane called **La Giraldilla**; the original was cast in Havana in 1632 by Jerónimo Martínez Pinzón and is popularly believed to be of Doña Inés de Bobadilla, the wife of gold explorer Hernando de Soto. It is now kept in the Museo de la Ciudad, and the figure also appears on the Havana Club rum label. Imposing and indomitable, the castle is ringed by an impressive moat and today shelters the **Museo de la Cerámica Artística Cubana** (☎ 861-6130; admission CUC$2; ☺ 9am-6pm), displaying work by some of Cuba's leading artists.

The tiny neoclassical Doric chapel on the east side of the Plaza, known as the **Museo El Templete** (admission CUC$2; ☺ 8:30am-6pm), was erected in 1828 at the point where Havana's first Mass was held beneath a ceiba tree in November 1519. A similar ceiba tree has now replaced the original. Inside the chapel are three large paintings of the event by the French painter Jean Baptiste Vermay (1786–1833).

Adjacent to El Templete is the late-18th-century **Palacio de los Condes de Santovenia**, today the five-star, 27-room Hotel Santa Isabel. Nearby is the **Museo Nacional de Historia Natural** (☎ 863-9361; Obispo No 61; admission CUC$3; ☒ 9:30am-7pm Tue-Sun), which contains examples of Cuba's flora and fauna.

You'd think that the last thing Havana would need is a car museum, but a block down Calle Oficios lies the small, surreal **Museo del Automóvil** (Oficios No 13; admission CUC$1; ☒ 9am-7pm) stuffed with ancient Thunderbirds, Pontiacs and Ford Model Ts, at least half of which appear to be in better shape than the antiquated automobiles that ply the streets outside.

ALONG MERCADERES & OBRAPÍA

Cobbled, car-free Calle Mercaderes (literally: Merchant's Street) has been fully restored to replicate the splendor of its 18th-century high-water mark. Myriad museums along here include the **Casa de Asia** (☎ 863-9740; Mercaderes No 111; admission free; ☒ 10am-6pm Tue-Sat, 9am-1pm Sun), with paintings and sculpture from China and Japan; and the **Museo de Tabaco** (☎ 861-5795; Mercaderes No 120; admission free; ☒ 10am-5pm Mon-Sat), where you can gawp at various indigenous pipes and idols and buy some splendid smokes.

The **Maqueta de La Habana Vieja** (Mercaderes No 114; unguided/guided CUC$1/2; ☒ 9am-6pm) is a 1:500 scale model of Habana Vieja complete with an authentic soundtrack meant to replicate a day in the life of the city. It's incredibly detailed and provides an excellent way of geographically acquainting yourself with the city's historical core. Come here first.

A few doors down, the **Casa de la Obra Pía** (Obrapía No 158; admission CUC$1, camera CUC$2; ☒ 9am-4:30pm Tue-Sat, 9:30am-12:30pm Sun) is a typical Havana aristocratic residence originally built in 1665 and rebuilt in 1780. Baroque decoration – including an intricate portico made in Cádiz, Spain – covers the exterior facade. In addition to its historical value, the house today also contains one of the City Historian's most commendable social projects, a sewing and needlecraft cooperative that has a workshop inside and a small shop selling clothes and textiles on Calle Mercaderes. Across the street, the **Casa de África** (☎ 861-5798; Obrapía No 157; admission CUC$2; ☒ 9:30am-7:30pm) houses sacred objects relating to Santería collected by ethnographer Fernando Ortíz.

The corner of Mercaderes and Obrapía has an international flavor with a bronze **statue of Simón Bolívar**, the Latin America liberator, and a **museum** (☎ 861-3988; Mercaderes No 160; donations accepted; ☒ 9am-5pm Tue-Sun) dedicated to his life across the street. The **Casa de México Benito Juárez** (☎ 861-8166; Obrapía No 116; admission CUC$1; ☒ 10:15am-5:45pm Tue-Sat, 9am-1pm Sun) exhibits Mexican folk art and plenty of books, but not a lot on Señor Juárez (Mexico's first indigenous president) himself. Just east is the **Casa Oswaldo Guayasamín** (☎ 861-3843; Obrapía No 111; donations accepted; ☒ 9am-5pm Tue-Sun), the old studio and now a museum of the great Ecuadorian artist who painted Fidel in numerous poses.

PLAZA DE SAN FRANCISCO DE ASÍS

Facing Havana harbor, the breezy Plaza de San Francisco de Asís first grew up in the 16th century when Spanish galleons stopped by at the quayside on their passage through the Indies to Spain. A market took root in the 1500s followed by a church in 1608, though when the pious monks complained of too much noise the market was moved a few blocks south to Plaza Vieja. The Plaza de San Francisco underwent a full restoration in the late 1990s and is most notable for its uneven cobbles and the white marble **Fuente de los Leones** (Fountain of Lions) carved by the Italian sculptor Giuseppe Gaginni in 1836. A more modern statue outside the square's famous church depicts **El Caballero de París**, a well-known street person who roamed Havana during the 1950s, engaging passers-by with his philosophies on life, religion, politics and current events. On the eastern side of the plaza stands the **Terminal Sierra Maestra** cruise terminal, which dispatches shiploads of weekly tourists, while nearby the domed **Lonja del Comercio** is a former commodities market erected in 1909 and restored in 1996 to provide office space for foreign companies with joint ventures in Cuba.

The southern side of the square is taken up by the impressive **Iglesia y Monasterio de San Francisco de Asís**. Originally constructed in 1608 and rebuilt in the baroque style from 1719 to 1738, San Francisco de Asís was taken over by the Spanish state in 1841 as part of a political move against the powerful religious orders of the day, when it ceased to be a church. Today it's both a **concert hall** (☒ from 5pm or 6pm) hosting classical music and the **Museo de Arte Religioso** (☎ 862-3467; unguided/guided CUC$2/3; ☻ 9am-6pm) replete with religious paintings, silverware, woodcarvings and ceramics.

To the side of the Palacio de Gobierno on Churruca is the **Coche Mambí** (admission free; ☻ 9am-2pm Tue-Sat), a 1900 train car built in the US and brought to Cuba in 1912. Put into service as the Presidential Car, it's a palace on wheels, with a formal dining room, louvered wooden windows and, back in its heyday, fans cooling the car with dry ice.

MUSEO DEL RON

You don't have to be an Añejo Reserva quaffer to enjoy the **Museo del Ron** (☎ 861-8051; San Pedro No 262; admission incl guide CUC$5; ☻ 9am-5pm Mon-Fri, 10am-4pm Sat & Sun) in the Fundación Havana Club, but it probably helps. The museum, with its bilingual guided tour showing rum-making antiquities and the complex brewing process, gets mixed reviews from travelers, though most give a hearty thumbs-up to the popular dancing lessons held here weekday mornings (see p125).

PLAZA VIEJA

Laid out in 1559, Plaza Vieja (Old Square) is Havana's most architecturally eclectic square where Cuban baroque nestles seamlessly next to Gaudí-inspired art nouveau. Originally called Plaza Nueva (New Square), it was initially used for military exercises and later served as an open-air marketplace. During the Batista regime an ugly underground parking lot was constructed here, but the monstrosity was demolished in 1996 to make way for a massive renovation project. Sprinkled liberally with bars, restaurants and cafes, Plaza Vieja today boasts its own micro-brewery, the Angela Landa primary school and a beautiful fenced-in fountain.

On the northwestern corner is Havana's **cámara oscura** (admission CUC$2; ☻ 9am-5pm Tue-Sat, 9am-1pm Sun) providing live, 360-degree views of the city from atop a 35m-tall tower. Explanations are in Spanish and English. In the arcade adjacent is the **Fototeca de Cuba** (☎ 862-2530; Mercaderes No 307; admission free; ☻ 10am-5pm Tue-Fri, 9am-noon Sat), a photo gallery with intriguing exhibits by local and international artists.

Encased in the plaza's oldest building is the quirky **Museo de Naipes** (Muralla No 101; admission free; ☻ 9am-6pm Tue-Sun), a playing-card museum

with a 2000-strong collection that includes rock stars, rum drinks and round cards. Next door is **La Casona Centro de Arte** (☎ 861-8544; Muralla No 107; admission free; ☻ 10am-5pm Mon-Fri, 10am-2pm Sat), with great solo and group shows by up-and-coming Cuban artists.

Down the street, the **Centro Cultural Pablo de la Torriente Brau** (☎ 861-6251; www.centropablo.cult .cu; Muralla No 63; admission free; ☻ 9am-5:30pm Tue-Sat), a leading cultural institution that was formed under the auspices of the Unión de Escritores y Artistas de Cuba (Uneac; Union of Cuban Writers and Artists) in 1996. The center hosts expositions, poetry readings and live acoustic music. Its Salón de Arte Digital is renowned for its groundbreaking digital art.

The square's most distinctive building is the Gaudí-esque **Palacio Cueto** (cnr Muralla & Mercaderes), Havana's finest example of art nouveau that was constructed in 1906. Its outrageously ornate facade once housed a warehouse and a hat factory before it was rented by José Cueto in the 1920s as the Palacio Vienna hotel. Habaguanex has recently pledged to restore the building, empty and unused since the early '90s.

CALLE OBISPO & AROUND

Narrow, car-free Calle Obispo (literally: Bishop's Street), Habana Vieja's main interconnecting artery, is packed with art galleries, shops, music bars and people.

The **Museo de Numismático** (☎ 861-5811; Obispo btwn Aguiar & Habana; admission CUC$1; ☻ 9am-4:45pm) brings together various collections of medals, coins and banknotes from around the world, including a stash of 1000 mainly American gold coins (1869–1928) and a full chronology of Cuban banknotes from the 19th century to the present. Opposite, the new **Museo 28 Septiembre de los CDR** (Obispo btwn Aguiar & Habana; admission CUC$2; ☻ 9am-5pm) dedicates two floors to the nationwide Comites de la Defensa de la Revolución (CDR; Committees for the Defense of the Revolution). Commendable neighborhood-watch schemes, or grassroots spying agencies? You decide. Two blocks further down the **Museo de Pintura Mural** (Obispo btwn Mercaderes & Oficios; admission free; ☻ 10am-6pm) exhibits some beautifully restored original frescoes in the Casa del Mayorazgo de Recio, popularly considered to be Havana's oldest surviving house. Two doors down is the **Museo de** la Orfebrería (☎ 863-9861; Obispo No 113; admission donation; ⏰ 9am-4:30pm Tue-Sat, 9:30am-12:30pm Mon), a silverware museum set out in the house of erstwhile silversmith Gregorio Tabares, who had a workshop here from 1707.

Across Obispo from the Hotel Ambos Mundos lies the **Edificio Santo Domingo** (Mercaderes btwn Obispo & O'Reilly) on the site of Havana's old university between 1728 and 1902. It was originally part of a convent; the current incongruous office block dates from the 1950s when the roof was used as a helicopter landing pad. In 2006 Habaguanex rebuilt the convent's original bell tower and inserted an elaborate baroque doorway onto the building's eastern side. The result provides an interesting juxtaposition of old and new.

PLAZA DEL CRISTO & AROUND
Habana Vieja's fifth (and most overlooked) square lies at the west end of the neighborhood, a little apart from the historical core, and has yet to benefit from the City Historian's makeover. It's worth a look for the **Parroquial del Santo Cristo del Buen Viaje**, a church dating from 1732, although there has been a Franciscan hermitage on this site since 1640. Still only partially renovated, the building is most notable for its intricate stained-glass windows and brightly painted wooden ceiling. The Plaza del Cristo also boasts a primary school (hence the noise) and a microcosmic slice of everyday Cuban life *sin* tourists.

Sidetrack a few blocks up Brasil and you'll stumble upon the **Museo de la Farmacia Habanera** (cnr Brasil & Compostela; admission free; ⏰ 9am-5pm), founded in 1886 by Catalan José Sarrá and once considered the second most important pharmacy in the world. The antique shop still acts as a pharmacy for Cubans, but also as a museum displaying an elegant mock-up of an old drugstore with some interesting historical explanations.

CHURCHES
South of Plaza Vieja is a string of important but little-visited churches. The 1638–43 **Iglesia y Convento de Santa Clara** (☎ 866-9327; Cuba No 610; admission CUC$2; ⏰ 9am-4pm Mon-Fri) stopped being a convent in 1920. Later this complex was the Ministry of Public Works, and today the Habana Vieja restoration team is based here. You can visit the large cloister and nuns' cemetery or even spend the night (with res-

ervations far in advance; see p128). The Old Town's other main convent is the **Iglesia y Convento de Nuestra Señora de Belén** (☎ 861-7283; Compostela btwn Luz & Acosta; admission CUC$2; ⏰ 9am-5pm Mon-Sat, 9am-1pm Sun), completed in 1718 and run by nuns from the Order of Bethlehem and (later) the Jesuits. Today it is a convalescent home for senior citizens funded by the City Historian's office.

Havana's oldest surviving church (built in 1640 and rebuilt in 1674) is the **Iglesia Parroquial del Espíritu Santo** (☎ 862-3140; Acosta 161; ⏰ 8am-noon & 3-6pm), with many burials in the crypt. Built in 1755, the **Iglesia y Convento de Nuestra Señora de la Merced** (Cuba No 806; ⏰ 8am-noon & 3-5:30pm) was reconstructed in the 19th century. Beautiful gilded altars, frescoed vaults and a number of old paintings create a sacrosanct mood; there's a quiet cloister adjacent.

The **Iglesia de San Francisco de Paula** (☎ 41-50-37; cnr Leonor Pérez & Desamparados) is one of Havana's most attractive churches. Fully restored in 2000, it is all that remains of the San Francisco de Paula women's hospital from the mid-1700s. Lit up at night for concerts, the stained glass, heavy cupola and baroque facade are romantic and inviting.

One of Havana's newest buildings is the beautiful gold-domed **Catedral Ortodoxa Nuestra Señora de Kazán** (Av Carlos Manuel de Céspedes btwn Sol & Santa Clara), a Russian Orthodox church built in the early 2000s and consecrated at a ceremony attended by Raúl Castro in October 2008. The church was part of an attempt to reignite Russian-Cuban relations after they went sour in 1991.

MUSEO–CASA NATAL DE JOSÉ MARTÍ
The **Museo–Casa Natal de José Martí** (☎ 861-3778; Leonor Pérez No 314; admission CUC$1, camera CUC$2; ⏰ 9am-5pm Tue-Sat) is a humble, two-story dwelling on the edge of Habana Vieja where the apostle of Cuban independence was born on January 28, 1853. Today it's a small museum that displays letters, manuscripts, photos, books and other mementos of his life. While not as comprehensive as the Martí museum on Plaza de la Revolución, it's a charming little abode and well worth a small detour.

Nearby, to the west across Av de Bélgica, is the longest remaining stretch of the **old city wall** (see boxed text, p114).

THE WALL

Located at the gateway to the New World, colonial Havana was the strategic nexus of Spain's lucrative Latin American empire and the congregation point for its annual trans-Atlantic treasure fleet. In the 17th century, anxious to defend the city from attacks by pirates and overzealous foreign armies, Cuba's perennially paranoid colonial authorities drew up plans for the construction of a 5km-long city wall.

Built on the backs of slave labor, the wall was begun in 1674 and took over 60 years to finish. On its completion in the 1740s, it was 1.5m thick and 10m high, running along a line now occupied by Av de las Misiones and Av de Bélgica.

Among the wall's myriad defenses were nine bastions and 180 big guns aimed toward the sea. The only way in and out of the city was through 11 heavily guarded gates that closed every night and opened every morning to the sound of a solitary gunshot.

As the age of piracy passed and the burgeoning city began to outgrow its 17th-century parameters, the wall's importance gradually diminished. In 1863 the colonial authorities ordered its demolition, though the work began piecemeal and much of the structure remained intact more than half a century later.

EDIFICIO BACARDÍ

Finished in 1929, the magnificent **Edificio Bacardí** (Bacardí building; Av de las Misiones btwn Empedrado & San Juan de Dios; ☺ hours vary) is a triumph of art-deco architecture with a whole host of lavish finishings that somehow manage to make kitschy look cool. Hemmed in by other buildings, it's hard to get a full kaleidoscopic view of the structure from street level, though the opulent bell tower can be glimpsed from all over Havana. There's a bar in the lobby and for a few Convertibles you can travel up to the tower for an eagle's-eye view.

IGLESIA DEL SANTO ANGEL CUSTODIO

Originally constructed in 1695, this **church** (☎ 861-0469; Compostela No 2; ☺ during Mass 7:15am Tue, Wed & Fri, 6pm Thu, Sat & Sun) was pounded by a ferocious hurricane in 1846 after which it was entirely rebuilt in neo-Gothic style. Among the notable historical and literary figures that have passed through its handsome doors are 19th-century Cuban novelist Cirilo Villaverde, who set the main scene of his novel *Cecilia Valdés* here, as well as Félix Varela and José Martí, who were both baptized in the church in 1788 and 1853 respectively.

Centro Habana

CAPITOLIO NACIONAL

The incomparable **Capitolio Nacional** (☎ 863-7861; unguided/guided CUC$3/4; ☺ 9am-8pm) is Havana's most ambitious and grandiose building, constructed after the 'Dance of the Millions' had gifted the Cuban government a seemingly bottomless treasure box of sugar money. Similar to the US Capitol Building in Washington, DC, but (marginally) taller and much richer in detail, the work was initiated by Cuba's US-backed dictator Gerardo Machado in 1926 and took 5000 workers three years, two months and 20 days to build at a cost of US$17 million. Formerly it was the seat of the Cuban Congress but, since 1959, it has housed the Cuban Academy of Sciences and the National Library of Science and Technology.

Constructed with white Capellanía limestone and block granite, the entrance is guarded by six rounded Doric columns atop a staircase that leads up from the Prado. A stone cupola rising 62m and topped with a replica of 16th-century Florentine sculptor Giambologna's bronze statue of Mercury in the Palazzo de Bargello looks out over the Havana skyline. Directly below the dome is a copy of a 24-carat diamond set in the floor. Highway distances between Havana and all sites in Cuba are calculated from this point.

The entryway opens up into the Salón de los Pasos Perdidos (Room of the Lost Steps, so named because of its unusual acoustics), at the center of which is the statue of the republic, an enormous bronze woman standing 11m tall and symbolizing the mythic Guardian of Virtue and Work. In size, it's smaller only than the gold Buddha in Nava, Japan, and the Lincoln Monument in Washington, DC.

REAL FÁBRICA DE TABACOS PARTAGÁS

One of Havana's oldest and most famous cigar factories, the landmark neoclassical **Real Fábrica de Tabacos Partagás** (☎ 862-0086; Industria No

520 btwn Barcelona & Dragones; tours CUC$10; ☺ every 15 min 9:30-11am & 12:30-3pm) was founded in 1845 by a Spaniard named Jaime Partagás. Today some 400 workers toil for up to 12 hours a day in here rolling such famous cigars as Montecristos and Cohibas. As far as tours go, Partagás is the most popular and reliable factory to visit. Tour groups check out the ground floor first, where the leaves are un-bundled and sorted, before proceeding to the upper floors to watch the tobacco get rolled, pressed, adorned with a band and boxed. Though interesting in an educational sense, the tours here are often rushed and a little robotic and some visitors find they smack of a human zoo. Still, if you have even a passing interest in tobacco and/or Cuban work envi-ronments, it's probably worth a peep.

PARQUE DE LA FRATERNIDAD
Leafy Parque de la Fraternidad was established in 1892 to commemorate the fourth centenary of the Spanish landing in the Americas. A few decades later it was remodeled and renamed to mark the 1927 Pan-American Conference. The name is meant to signify American broth-erhood, hence the many busts of Latin and North American leaders that embellish the green areas – including one of US president, Abraham Lincoln. Today the park is the ter-minus of numerous metro bus routes, and is sometimes referred to as 'Jurassic Park' for the plethora of photogenic old American cars now used as *colectivos* (collective taxis) that congregate here.

The **Fuente de la India** (on a traffic island op-posite the Hotel Saratoga) is a white Carrara marble fountain, carved by Giuseppe Gaginni in 1837 for the Count of Villanueva. It por-trays a regal Indian woman adorned with a crown of eagle's feathers and seated on a throne surrounded by four gargoylesque dol-phins. In one hand she holds a horn-shaped basket filled with fruit, in the other a shield bearing the city's coat of arms.

Just east of the sculpture, across Paseo de Martí is the **Asociación Cultural Yoruba de Cuba** (☎ 863-5953; Paseo de Martí No 615; admission CUC$10; ☺ 9am-4pm Mon-Sat). A museum here provides a worthwhile overview of the Santería religion, the saints and their powers, although some travelers have complained that the exhibits don't justify the price. There are *tambores* (Santería drum ceremonies) here on alter-nate Fridays at 4:30pm. Note that there's a

church dress code for the *tambores* (no shorts or tank tops).

A little out on a limb but well worth the walk is the **Iglesia del Sagrado Corazón de Jesús** (Av Simon Bolívar btwn Gervasio & Padre Varela), an inspir-ing marble creation with a distinctive white steeple, where you can enjoy a few precious minutes of quiet and cool contemplation away from the craziness of the street. This church is rightly famous for its magnificent stained-glass windows, and the light that penetrates through the eaves first thing in the morning (when the church is deserted) gives the place an almost ethereal quality.

PARQUE CENTRAL & AROUND
Diminutive Parque Central is a scenic haven from the belching buses and roaring taxis that ply their way along the Prado. The park, long a microcosm of daily Havana life, was expanded to its present size in the late 19th century after the city walls were knocked down, and the marble **statue of José Martí** (1905) at its center was the first of thousands to be erected in Cuba. Raised on the 10th anniversary of the poet's death, the monument is ringed by 28 palm trees planted to signify Martí's birth date: January 28. Hard to miss over to one side is the group of baseball fans who linger 24/7 at the famous **Esquina Caliente** (see boxed text, p116).

On the park's southwest corner is the or-nate neobaroque **Centro Gallego** (Paseo de Martí No 458), erected as a Galician social club between 1907 and 1914. The Centro was built around the existing Teatro Tacón, which opened in 1838 with five masked Carnaval dances. This connection is the basis of claims by the present 2000-seat **Gran Teatro de La Habana** (☎ 861-3077; guided tours CUC$2; ☺ 9am-6pm) that it's the oldest operating theater in the Western hemisphere. History notwithstanding, the architecture is brilliant, as are many of the weekend perform-ances (see p145).

Just across the San Rafael pedestrian mall is the **Hotel Inglaterra**, Havana's oldest hotel, which first opened its doors in 1856 on the site of a popular bar called El Louvre (the ho-tel's alfresco bar still bears the name). Facing leafy Parque Central, the building exhibits neoclassical design features in vogue at the time, although the interior decor is distinctly Moorish. At a banquet here in 1879, José Martí made a speech advocating Cuban in-dependence, and much later US journalists

LA ESQUINA CALIENTE

To the uninitiated, the sight of 30 or more Cuban men remonstrating loudly in a Havana park probably appears more like a malevolent mob than a spontaneous gathering of sports enthusiasts. But ask any of the aggrieved fist-shakers who frequent the boisterous Esquina Caliente (literally 'hot corner') in Parque Central what they're arguing about and you'll get back a rather innocuous reply: baseball.

While the Canadians debate hockey and the Brits bore each other with cricket statistics, the Cubans seek solace in baseball, a sport that inspires more saber-rattling than a May Day rally.

Havana's key baseball rivalry revolves around Los Industriales (the silverware-hogging Manchester United) and Los Metropolitanos (the less successful Manchester City), though the biggest debates are reserved for when the boys from Santiago roll into town and Havana's two sets of opposing supporters form a formidable – if temporary – alliance.

The 'hot corner' is the place to go if you want to discuss form, home runs or the chances of Liván Hernández making a Cuban comeback. It runs from dawn till dusk 365 days a year and, in contrast to cricket, rain never stops play (instead the group reconvenes under the porch of the adjacent Museo Nacional de Bellas Artes).

covering the Spanish-Cuban-American War stayed at the hotel.

A detour along **Calle San Rafael**, a riot of peso stalls, 1950s department store and local cinemas, gives an immediate insight into everyday life in economically challenged Cuba.

MUSEO NACIONAL DE BELLAS ARTES

Cuba has a huge art culture and its dual-site art museum rivals its counterpart in San Juan, Puerto Rico, for the title of 'best art museum in the Caribbean.' You can spend a whole day here viewing everything from Greek ceramics to Cuban pop art.

Arranged inside the fabulously eclectic Centro Asturianas (a work of art in its own right), the **Colección de Arte Universal** (☎ 863-9484; cnr Agramonte & San Rafael; admission CUC$5, children under 14 free; ☉ 10am-6pm Tue-Sat, 10am-2pm Sun) exhibits international art from 500 BC to the present day on three separate floors. Highlights include an extensive Spanish collection (with a canvas by El Greco), some 2000-year-old Roman mosaics, Greek pots from the 5th century BC and a suitably refined Gainsborough canvas (in the British room).

Two blocks away, the **Colección de Arte Cubano** (☎ 861-3858; Trocadero btwn Agramonte & Av de las Misiones; admission CUC$5; ☉ 10am-6pm Tue-Sat, 10am-2pm Sun) displays purely Cuban art and, if you're pressed for time, is the better of the duo. Works are displayed in chronological order starting on the 3rd floor and are surprisingly varied. Artists to look out for are Guillermo Collazo, considered to be the first truly great Cuban artist, Rafael Blanco with

his cartoon-like paintings and sketches, Raúl Martínez, a master of 1960s Cuban pop art, and the Picasso-like Wilfredo Lam.

MUSEO DE LA REVOLUCIÓN

The **Museo de la Revolución** (☎ 862-4093; Refugio No 1; unguided/guided CUC$4/6, camera extra; ☉ 10am-5pm) is housed in the former Presidential Palace, constructed between 1913 and 1920 and used by a string of cash-embezzling Cuban presidents, culminating in Fulgencio Batista. The world-famous Tiffany's of New York decorated the interior, and the shimmering Salón de los Espejos (Room of Mirrors) was designed to resemble the room of the same name at the Palace of Versailles. In March 1957 the palace was the target of an unsuccessful assassination attempt against Batista led by revolutionary student leader José Antonio Echeverría. The museum itself descends chronologically from the top floor starting with Cuba's pre-Columbian culture and extending to the present-day socialist regime (with *mucho* propaganda). The downstairs rooms have some interesting exhibits on the 1953 Moncada attack and the life of Che Guevara, and highlight a Cuban penchant for displaying blood-stained military uniforms. Most of the labels are in English and Spanish. In front of the building is a fragment of the former city wall as well as an SAU-100 tank used by Castro during the 1961 battle of the Bay of Pigs.

In the space behind you'll find the **Pavillón Granma**, a memorial to the 18m yacht that carried Fidel Castro and 81 other revolutionaries from Tuxpán, Mexico to Cuba in December 1956. It's encased in glass and guarded 24 hours a day, presumably to stop anyone from breaking in and making off for Florida in it. The pavilion is surrounded by other vehicles associated with the Revolution and is accessible from the Museo de la Revolución.

PRADO (PASEO DE MARTÍ)

Construction of this stately European-style boulevard (officially known as Paseo de Martí) – the first street outside the old city walls – began in 1770, and the work was completed in the mid-1830s during the term of Captain General Miguel Tacón (1834–38). The original idea was to create a boulevard as splendid as any found in Paris or Barcelona (Prado owes more than a passing nod to Las Ramblas). The famous bronze lions that guard the central promenade at either end were added in 1928.

Notable Prado buildings include the neo-Renaissance **Palacio de los Matrimonios** (Paseo de Martí No 302), the streamline-moderne **Teatro Fausto** (cnr Paseo de Martí & Colón) and the neoclassical **Escuela Nacional de Ballet** (cnr Paseo de Martí & Trocadero), Alicia Alonso's famous ballet school.

PARQUE DE LOS ENAMORADOS

Preserved in Parque de los Enamorados (Lovers' Park), surrounded by streams of speeding traffic, lies a surviving section of the colonial **Cárcel** or Tacón Prison, built in 1838, where many Cuban patriots including José Martí were imprisoned. A brutal place that sent unfortunate prisoners off to perform hard labor in the nearby San Lázaro quarry, the prison was finally demolished in 1939 with the park that took its place dedicated to the memory of those who had suffered so horribly within its walls. Two tiny cells and an equally minute chapel are all that remain. The beautiful wedding cake–like building (art nouveau with a dash of eclecticism) behind the park, flying the Spanish flag, is the old **Palacio Velasco** (1912), now the Spanish embassy.

Beyond that is the **Memorial a los Estudiantes de Medicina**, a fragment of wall encased in marble marking the spot where eight Cuban medical students chosen at random were shot by the Spanish in 1871 as a reprisal for allegedly desecrating the tomb of a Spanish journalist (in fact, they didn't do it).

Across the Malecón is the picturesque **Castillo de San Salvador de la Punta**, designed by the Italian military engineer Giovanni Bautista Antonelli and built between 1589 and 1600. During the colonial era a chain was stretched 250m to the castle of El Morro every night to close the harbor mouth to shipping. The castle's **museum** (admission CUC$5; ⏰ 10am-6pm Wed-Sun) was renovated in 2002 and displays artifacts from sunken Spanish treasure fleets, a collection of model ships and information on the slave trade.

On a large traffic island where Prado merges with the Malecón is a rather grand **statue of General Máximo Gómez** on the right-hand side. Gómez was a war hero from the Dominican Republic who fought tirelessly for Cuban independence in both the 1868 and 1895 conflicts against the Spanish. The impressive statue of him sitting atop a horse was created by Italian artist Aldo Gamba in 1935 and faces heroically out to sea.

Vedado

Vedado is Havana's commercial hub and archetypal residential district, older than Playa but newer than Centro Habana. The first houses penetrated this formerly protected forest reserve in the 1860s, with the real growth spurt beginning in the 1920s and continuing until the 1950s.

Laid out in a near-perfect grid, Vedado has more of a North American feel than other parts of the Cuban capital, and its small clutch of *rascacielos* (skyscrapers) – which draw their inspiration from the art-deco giants of Miami and New York – are largely a product of Cuba's 50-year dance with the US.

During the 1940s and '50s, Vedado was a louche and tawdry place where Havana's pre-revolutionary gambling party reached its heady

---

ASK A LOCAL

If you get a chance, be sure to wander around El Barrio Chino in Centro Habana. Pass through the giant pagoda-shaped arch behind the Capitolio on Calle Dragones and follow the crowds. Although there aren't many Chinese living in the neighborhood these days, the neighborhood retains a distinct atmosphere and has lots of decent restaurants on Calle Cuchillo.

Felipe, Havana

HAVANA

LENNON OUTSHINES LENIN

There are three Lenin statues in Havana. The first, sculpted in utilitarian grey granite, dominates leafy Parque Lenin (p161) near the airport. The second – a 3m-tall bronze face set in stone – sits atop a small hill in the ramshackle suburb of Regla. Both are of Russian communist icon Vladimir Ilyich Ulyanov (better known as Lenin) and were constructed during Cuba's 30-year dalliance with the Soviet Union in the 1960s, '70s and '80s.

But it is Havana's third Lennon statue, a hyper-realistic study of the former Beatle, John, that graces out-of-the-way **Parque Lennon** (Map pp102-3; Calles 15 & 17 btwn Calles 6 & 8) in suburban Vedado, which pulls in the lion's share of the visitors.

Unveiled by Fidel Castro in December 2000 on the 20th anniversary of Lennon's death, the monument marks one of the leader's more dramatic policy U-turns. The Beatles' music was actively discouraged in Cuba in the 1960s for being too 'decadent.' But following Lennon's strong social activism and opposition to US involvement in the Vietnam War, he quickly became a hero among Cuban music fans, causing Castro to belatedly rebrand him as a 'revolutionary.'

A magnet for souvenir hunters, Lennon's 21st-century reincarnation has suffered the ignominy of having his glasses stolen so many times that a 'guard' has now been employed to keep a regular watch. Hiding the famous spectacles in his trouser pocket, he routinely sneaks up unannounced in front of camera-wielding tourists and deftly places them on the Liverpudlian's nose.

climax. The Hotel Nacional once boasted a Las Vegas–style casino, the ritzy Hotel Riviera was the former stomping ground of influential mobster Meyer Lansky, while the now empty Hotel Capri was masterfully managed by Hollywood actor (and sometime mob associate) George Raft. Everything changed in January 1959 when Fidel Castro rolled into town with his army of scruffy bearded rebels in tow and set up shop on the 24th floor of the spanking new Havana Hilton hotel (promptly renamed Hotel Habana Libre).

Today, Vedado boasts a population of approximately 175,000 and its leafy residential pockets are interspersed with myriad theaters, nightspots, paladares and restaurants. Bisected by two wide Parisian-style boulevards, Calle G and Paseo, its geometric grid is embellished by a liberal sprinkling of pleasant parks and the gargantuan Plaza de la Revolución laid out during the Batista era in the 1950s.

HOTEL NACIONAL

Built in 1930 as a copy of the Breakers Hotel in Palm Beach, Florida, the eclectic art-deco/neoclassical **Hotel Nacional** (☎ 873-3564; cnr Calles O & 21) is a national monument and one of Havana's 'postcard' sights.

The hotel's notoriety was cemented in October 1933 when, following a sergeant's coup by Fulgencio Batista which toppled the regime of Gerardo Machado, 300 aggrieved army officers took refuge in the building hoping to curry favor with resident US ambas-

sador Sumner Wells who was staying there. Much to the officers' chagrin, Wells promptly left, allowing Batista's troops to open fire on the hotel killing 14 of them and injuring seven. More were executed later, after they had surrendered.

In December 1946 the hotel gained notoriety of a different kind when US mobsters Meyer Lansky and Lucky Luciano used it to host the largest ever get-together of the North American Mafia, who gathered here under the guise of a Frank Sinatra concert.

These days the hotel maintains a more reputable face and the once famous casino is long gone, though the kitschy Parisién cabaret is still a popular draw. Nonguests are welcome to admire the Moorish lobby, stroll the breezy grounds overlooking the Malecón and examine the famous photos of past guests on the walls inside.

HOTEL HABANA LIBRE

This classic modernist **hotel** (☎ 834-6100; Calle L btwn Calles 23 & 25) – the former Havana Hilton – was commandeered by Castro's revolutionaries in 1959 just nine months after it had opened, and promptly renamed the Habana Libre. During the first few months of the Revolution, Fidel ruled the country from a luxurious suite on the 24th floor.

A 670-sq-m Venetian tile mural by Amelia Peláez is splashed across the front of the building, while upstairs Alfredo Sosa Bravo's *Carro de la Revolución* utilizes 525 ceramic pieces. There are some good shops here and an interesting photo gallery inside displaying snaps of the all-conquering *barbudas* (literally 'bearded ones') lolling around with their guns in the hotel's lobby in January 1959.

EDIFICIO FOCSA

Unmissable on the Havana skyline, the modernist **Edificio Focsa** (Focsa building; cnr Calles 17 & M) was built in 1954–56 in a record 28 months using pioneering computer technology. In 1999 it was listed as one of the seven modern engineering wonders of Cuba. With 39 floors housing 373 apartments it was, on its completion in June 1956, the second-largest concrete structure of its type in the world, constructed in its entirety without the use of cranes. Falling on hard times in the early '90s, the upper floors of the Focsa became nests for vultures and in 2000 an elevator cable snapped killing one person. Sparkling once more after a recent restoration project, this skyline-dominating Havana giant nowadays contains refurbished apartments and – in the shape of top-floor restaurant La Torre (p137) – one of the city's most celebrated eating establishments.

UNIVERSIDAD DE LA HABANA

Founded by Dominican monks in 1728 and secularized in 1842, Havana University began life in Habana Vieja before moving to its present site in 1902. The existing neoclassical complex dates from the second quarter of the 20th century, and today some 30,000 students follow courses in the social sciences, humanities, natural sciences, mathematics and economics here.

Perched on a Vedado hill at the top of the famous *escalinata* (stairway) and **Alma Mater** statue, the university's central quadrangle, the Plaza Ignacio Agramonte, displays a tank captured by Castro's rebels in 1958. Directly in front is the **Librería Alma Mater** (library) and, to the left, the **Museo de Historia Natural Felipe Poey** (admission CUC$1; 9am-noon & 1-4pm Mon-Fri Sep-Jul), the oldest museum in Cuba, founded in 1874 by the Royal Academy of Medical, Physical and Natural Sciences. Many of the stuffed specimens of Cuban flora and fauna date from the 19th century. Upstairs is the **Museo Antropológico Montané** (admission CUC$1; 9am-noon & 1-4pm Mon-Fri Sep-Jul), established in 1903, with a rich collection of pre-Columbian Indian artifacts including the wooden 10th-century Ídolo del Tabaco.

At the bottom of the university steps is the **Monumento a Julio Antonio Mella** (cnr Neptuno & San Lázaro), a monument to the student leader who founded the first Cuban Communist Party in 1925. In 1929 the dictator Machado had Mella assassinated in Mexico City. More interesting than the monument itself are the black-and-white **Mella portraits** permanently mounted in the wall in the little park across San Lázaro.

MUSEO NAPOLEÓNICO

An anomaly – but an interesting one – is the esoteric **Museo Napoleónico** (879-1460; San Miguel No 1159; unguided/guided CUC$3/5; 9am-4:30pm Tue-Sat) situated just outside the university walls. It's a collection of 7000 objects associated with the life of Napoleon Bonaparte amassed by Cuban sugar baron Julio Lobo and politician Orestes Ferrera. Highlights include sketches of Voltaire, paintings of the battle of Waterloo, china, furniture, an interesting recreation of Napoleon's study and bedroom, and one of several bronze Napoleonic death masks made two days after the emperor's death by his personal physician, Dr Francisco Antommarchi.

OTHER MUSEUMS

Two museums further afield in Vedado that are worth checking out if you're in the neighborhood are the **Museo de Artes Decorativas** (830-9848; Calle 17 No 502 btwn Calles D & E; admission CUC$2; 11am-7pm Tue-Sat), with its fancy rococo, oriental and art-deco baubles, and the **Museo de Danza** (831-2198; Línea No 365; admission CUC$2; 11am-6:30pm Tue-Sat), which collects objects from Cuba's rich dance history, including some personal effects of Alicia Alonso.

PARQUE ALMENDARES

Running along the banks of the city's Río Almendares, below the bridge on Calle 23, is this wonderful oasis of green and fresh air in the heart of chaotic Havana. The park was restored in 2003 and they did a beautiful job: benches now line the river promenade, plants grow profusely and there are many facilities here, including an antiquated **miniature golf course**, the **Anfiteatro Parque Almendares** (a small outdoor performance space) and a **playground**. There are several good places to eat.

PLAZA DE LA REVOLUCIÓN

Conceived by French urbanist Jean Claude Forestier in the 1920s, the gigantic Plaza de

---

ART DECO IN HAVANA

Art deco is a distinctive early-20th century architectural style that reached its zenith in the 1920s and '30s in structures such as New York's Chrysler Building. But disguised beneath 50 years of revolutionary dust, Havana hides some of the most quintessential art-deco monuments on the planet.

Financed by a decade-long sugar boom and inspired by the elegant modernist building trends imported into the United States from Europe following WWI, Havana's 20-year flirtation with art deco began in the late 1920s with a flurry of US-backed construction projects.

The city's pièce de résistance was – and still is – the opulent Edificio Bacardí (p114), an exotic early incarnation of the art-deco style that was completed in 1929 using polychrome tiles and multitextured bricks to provide a Havana HQ for the world-famous rum dynasty.

More iconic buildings followed, including the 14-story López Serrano building (opposite) in Vedado, one of Havana's early *rascacielos* (skyscrapers) that doffed a cap to New York's Empire State, and the emblematic Hotel Nacional (p118) which mixed art deco with flashes of Moorish eclecticism. Other, less lavish but more functional, art-deco creations include the geometric Teatro América (p145), the streamline-moderne Teatro Fausto (p145) and the cathedral-like Casa de las Américas (p122).

---

la Revolución (known as Plaza Cívica until 1959) was part of Havana's 'new city' that grew up between 1920 and 1959. As the nexus point of Forestier's ambitious plan, the square was built on a small hill (the Loma de los Catalanes), in the manner of Paris' Place de Étoile, with various avenues fanning out toward the Río Almendares, Vedado and the Parque de la Fraternidad in Centro Habana.

Surrounded by grey, utilitarian buildings constructed in the late 1950s, the square today is the base of the Cuban government and a place where large-scale political rallies are held. In January 1998, one million people (nearly one-tenth of the Cuban population) crammed into the square to hear Pope Jean Paul II say Mass.

Center-stage is the **Memorial a José Martí** (☎ 59-23-47; admission CUC$5; ☺ 9:30am-5pm Mon-Sat), which at 138.5m is Havana's tallest structure. Fronted by an impressive 17m marble statue of a seated Martí in pensive *Thinker* pose, the memorial houses a museum – the definite word on Martí in Cuba – and a 129m lookout (reached via small CUC$2 lift) with fantastic city views.

The ugly concrete block on the northern side of the Plaza is the **Ministerio del Interior**, well known for its huge mural of Che Guevara (a copy of Alberto Korda's famous photograph taken in 1960) with the words *Hasta la Victoria Siempre* (Always Toward Victory) emblazoned underneath.

On the eastern side is the 1957 **Biblioteca Nacional José Martí** (admission free; ☺ 8am-9:45pm Mon-Sat) with a photo exhibit in the lobby, while on the west is the **Teatro Nacional de Cuba** (see p145).

Tucked behind the Martí Memorial are the governmental offices housed in the heavily guarded **Comité Central del Partido Comunista de Cuba**.

Quinta de los Molinos (cnr Av Salvador Allende & Luaces) is the former stately residence of General Máximo Gómez, which sits amid lush botanical gardens on land that once belonged to Havana University. The residence and grounds were halfway through an extensive and long-winded renovation project at the time of writing.

NECRÓPOLIS CRISTÓBAL COLÓN

Declared a national monument in 1987, this **cemetery** (admission CUC$1; ☺ 7am-5pm) is one of Latin America's most fascinating, renowned for its striking religious iconography and elaborate marble statues. Far from being eerie, a walk through these 56 hallowed hectares can be an educational and emotional stroll through the annals of Cuban history. A guidebook with a detailed map (CUC$5) is for sale at the entrance.

After entering the neo-Romanesque **northern gateway** (1870), there's the tomb of independence leader **General Máximo Gómez** (1905) on the right (look for the bronze face in a circular medallion). Further along past the first circle, and also on the right, are the **monument to the firefighters** (1890) and the neo-Romanesque **Capilla Central** (1886) in the center of the cemetery. Just northeast of this chapel is the graveyard's most celebrated (and visited) tomb, that of **Señora Amelia Goyri** (cnr Calles 1 & F), better known as La Milagrosa (the miraculous one), who died while giving birth on May 3, 1901. The marble figure of a woman with a large cross and a baby in her arms is easy to find, due to the many flowers piled on the tomb and the local devotees in attendance. For many years after her death, her heartbroken husband visited the grave several times a day. He always knocked with one of four iron rings on the burial vault and walked away backwards so he could see her for as long as possible. When the bodies were exhumed some years later, Amelia's body was uncorrupted (a sign of sanctity in the Catholic faith) and the baby, who had been buried at its mother's feet, was – allegedly – found in her arms. As a result, La Milagrosa became the focus of a huge spiritual cult in Cuba and thousands of people come here annually with gifts in the hope of fulfilling dreams or solving problems. In keeping with tradition, pilgrims knock with the iron ring on the vault and walk away backwards when they leave.

Also worth seeking out is the tomb of Orthodox Party leader **Eduardo Chibás** (Calle 8 btwn Calles E & F). During the 1940s and early '50s Chibás was a relentless crusader against political corruption, and as a personal protest he committed suicide during a radio broadcast in 1951. At his burial ceremony a young Orthodox Party activist named Fidel Castro jumped atop Chibás' grave and made a fiery speech denouncing the old establishment – the political debut of the most influential Cuban of the 20th century.

Also worth looking out for are the graves of novelist Alejo Carpentier (1904–80), scientist Carlos Finlay (1833–1915), the Martyrs of Granma and the Veterans of the Independence Wars.

ALONG THE MALECÓN

The Malecón, Havana's evocative 8km-long sea drive, is one of the city's most soulful and quintessentially Cuban thoroughfares.

Long a favored meeting place for assorted lovers, philosophers, poets, traveling minstrels, fishermen and wistful Florida-gazers, Malecón's atmosphere is most potent at sunset when the weak yellow light from creamy Vedado filters like a dim torch onto the buildings of Centro Habana, lending their dilapidated facades a distinctly ethereal quality.

Laid out in the early 1900s as a salubrious oceanside boulevard for Havana's pleasure-seeking middle classes, the Malecón expanded rapidly eastward in the century's first decade with a mishmash of eclectic architecture that mixed sturdy neoclassical with whimsical art nouveau. By the 1920s the road had reached the outer limits of burgeoning Vedado and by the early 1950s it had metamorphosed into a busy six-lane traffic highway that carried streams of wave-dodging Buicks and Chevrolets from the grey hulk of the Castillo de San Salvador de la Punta to the borders of Miramar.

Today the Malecón remains Havana's most authentic open-air theater, a real-life 'cabaret of the poor' where the whole city comes to meet, greet, date and debate.

Fighting an ongoing battle with the corrosive effects of the ocean, many of the thoroughfare's magnificent buildings now face decrepitude, demolition or irrevocable damage. To combat the problem, 14 blocks of the Malecón have recently been given special status by the City Historian's office in an attempt to stop the rot.

The Soviet-era 24-story **Hospital Nacional Hermanos Ameijeiras**, built in 1980, dominates the center section of the Malecón. Some of its clinics specialize in treating foreigners (see p107). Lying in its shadow is the **Monumento a Antonio Maceo**, a bronze representation of the *mulato* general who cut a blazing trail across the entire length of Cuba during the First War of Independence. The nearby 18th-century **Torreón de San Lázaro** is a watchtower that quickly fell to the British during the invasion of 1762.

West beyond Hotel Nacional is the **Monumento a las Víctimas del Maine** (1926), monument to the victims of USS *Maine*, the battleship that blew up mysteriously in Havana harbor in 1898. Once crowned by an American eagle, the monument was decapitated during the 1959 Revolution.

The modern seven-story building with the high security fencing at the western end of this open space is the **US Interests Office**, first set up by the Carter administration in the late 1970s. Surrounded by hysterical graffiti, the building is the site of some of the worst tit-for-tat finger-wagging on the island. Facing the office front is the **Plaza Tribuna Anti-Imperialista**, built during the Elián González affair to host major in-your-face protests (earning it the local nickname *protestódromo*). Concerts, protests and marches – some one-million strong – are still held here.

Tucked away behind the square is the **López Serrano building** (Calle L btwn Calles 11 & 13), an art-deco tower that looks like the Empire State with the bottom 70 floors chopped off.

Statues of illustrious Latin American leaders line Calle G (Av de los Presidentes), including Salvador Allende (Chile), Benito Juárez (Mexico) and Simón Bolívar. At the top of the avenue is a huge marble **memorial to José Miguel Gómez**, Cuba's second president. At the other end, the monument to his predecessor – Cuba's first president – Tomás Estrada Palma (long considered a US puppet) has been toppled and all that remains are his shoes.

Guarding the entrance to Calle G on the Malecón is the equestrian **Monumento a Calixto García** (cnr Malecón & Calle G), paying homage to the valiant Cuban general who was prevented by US military leaders in Santiago de Cuba from attending the Spanish surrender in 1898. Twenty-four bronze plaques around the statue provide a history of García's 30-year struggle for Cuban independence. Just behind the monument is the cathedral-like **Casa de las Américas** (☎ 838-2706; www.casa.cult.cu; cnr Calles 3 & G; admission CUC$2; ☺ 10am-4:40pm Tue-Sat, 9am-1pm Sun), a cultural institution set up by Moncada survivor Haydee Santamaría in 1959 that awards one of Latin America's oldest and most prestigious literary prizes. Inside there's an art gallery and bookstore (see p98).

Cuba has three synagogues servicing a Jewish population of approximately 1:500. The main community center and library is at the **Gran Synagoga Bet Shalom** (Calle I No 251 btwn Calles 13 & 15), where the friendly staff would be happy to tell interested visitors about the fascinating history of the Jews in Cuba.

Out on a limb but worth a diversion for railway enthusiasts is the **Museo del Ferrocarril** (☎ 873-4414; cnr Av de México & Arroyo; ☺ 9am-5pm), housed in the old Cristina train station built in 1859. There's a big collection of signaling and communication gear here plus old locos from various eras including *La Junta*, dating from 1843. Train rides are available by prior appointment.

HABANA VIEJA WALKING TOUR

It's unlikely you'll get to do both the Habana Vieja and Centro Habana walking tours in a day, unless you hop on some transport halfway through. You can connect with a horse carriage (CUC$10 per hour) on Mercaderes just off Obispo, a coco-taxi anywhere around Plaza de San Francisco de Asís (horse carriages hang out here, too) or a bici-taxi near the Estación Central de Ferrocarriles (Central Train Station).

Plaza de la Catedral is a moveable feast and you can espy most of what's going on from the lush **Restaurante El Patio** (1; p135) before heading into the **Catedral de San Cristóbal de La Habana** (2; p109). Track southwest next, past the resident fortune teller and the brightly clad ladies in polka-dot dresses (who'll plant a kiss on your cheek for a ludicrous tip) and pop into the alleyway on the right housing the **Taller Experimental de Gráfica** (3; p126). Here, in what must be Havana's funkiest art gallery, Pink Floyd meets Jackson Pollack meets Wilfredo Lam with a bit of Picasso thrown in for good measure. Use your excellent map-reading skills to deliver you in front of the gargantuan **Museo de la Ciudad** (4; p110) on the western side of Plaza de Armas before the crowds arrive. If they've already beaten you to it, take a break outside in the breezy plaza – a bibliophile's nirvana – with an outdoor book fair if it's Wednesday, or if it's not pop into one of Havana's top bookstores in the **Palacio del Segundo Cabo** (5; p110). You might skip the stuffed animals at the Museo Nacional de Historia Natural and head straight to the 5th-floor terrace bar at **Restaurante La Mina** (6; p135), where the burgers are good and the views even better.

Breaking out of the plaza head south on Obispo past some of Havana's oldest surviving houses to the corner of Mercaderes. The lurid pastel-pink building on the left is the **Hotel Ambos Mundos** (7; p129), where Ernest Hemingway stayed on and off during the 1930s. You can visit room 511 (admission CUC$2; open 9am to 5pm Monday to Saturday) where he started writing *For Whom the Bell Tolls*, or enjoy a few romantic tunes from the resident pianist in the lobby downstairs. A few doors south on Mercaderes is the **Maqueta de La Habana Vieja** (8; p111), a darling scale model of everyone's favorite Unesco World Heritage Site. Continuing straight to the intersection with Obrapía at the next corner, drop into **Habana 1791** (9; p148) where

HAVANA

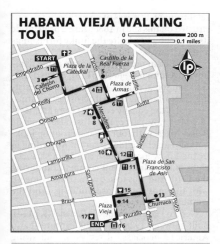

HABANA VIEJA WALKING TOUR

WALK FACTS

Start Restaurante El Patio
Finish Taberna de la Muralla
Distance 1.3km
Duration Three hours

floral fragrances are mixed by hand (you can see all the petals drying in the laboratory out back.) These make a great souvenir for mom or aunty Vera.

Crossing Lamparilla you'll quickly fall upon the **Hostal Condes de Villanueva** (10; p128), an impressively restored Habaguanex hotel with a tranquil inner courtyard and a first-class on-site cigar shop (great presents for uncle Charlie here). Walk past the quirky **Museo del Chocolate** (11; p138) – situated ironically on Calle Amargura which translates as 'Bitterness Street' – and you're either ill or in serious denial. It's a predictably busy melee inside, but you'll get served eventually and when it comes, the hot chocolate with dip-in biscuits is…well, words cannot describe! Jog left down Amargura as the sugar high kicks in and you'll hit the warm sea breezes of Plaza de San Francisco de Asís. The western side of the plaza hosts several art galleries (see p147), some with little gardens out back if you need a break. Or splurge with a cappuccino at **Café del Oriente** (12; p135).

Train lovers will want to detour half a block south on Oficios and turn left on Churruca to check out the **Coche Mambí** (13; p112).

Otherwise, turn right at the corner of Oficios and Brasil and you're headed toward Plaza Vieja. This plaza is captivating: you'll get some of the city's best views from atop the tower housing the **cámara oscura** (14; p112) on the northeastern corner. Peek quickly into **Café Taberna** (15; p140), a temple to the late Benny Moré and other assorted mambo kings, before nosing through the card collection at **Museo de Naipes** (16; p112), on the square's southeastern corner. Finish the tour with a glass of Havana's best beer brewed on the premises at **Taberna de la Muralla** (17; p141). There's an outdoor grill here, too, if you're feeling peckish.

If you want to say goodbye to tourist-brochure Habana Vieja and hello to the real world, continue west on Muralla for one block and then south on Cuba. Here ceilings fall without warning and power outages, water shortages and garbage-strewn streets are the norm. This is one of the roughest parts of the city, so be on your toes. Everyone will see at a glance that you're a tourist, but try not to look like an easy mark. If in doubt, head back toward the Plaza de Armas. Avoid these areas after dark.

CENTRO HABANA ARCHITECTURAL TOUR

This leisurely amble through some of Centro Habana's eclectic architectural sights begins at the end of Paseo de Martí, a salubrious tree-lined avenue known to locals by its old name, **El Prado** (1; p117).

Heading south toward Parque Central, the more interesting buildings lie initially to your left. Exhibiting the sharp lines and pure cubist simplicity of depression-era America, the **Teatro Fausto** (2; p145), on the corner of Prado and Colón, is an art-deco classic. Still a functioning performance venue for a new generation of budding thespians, the theater is famous for its light plays and hilarious comedy shows.

One block further up on the left, the **Casa del Científico** (3; p130), now a budget hotel, is an eclectic masterpiece that was once the residence of former Cuban president, José Miguel Gómez. Furnished with sweeping staircases, elaborate balconies and an eye-catching rooftop lookout, this veritable palace is dripping with diverse architectural influences from art nouveau to Italian Renaissance.

Contrasting sharply with other modern architectural styles on Calle Trocadero, the

HAVANA

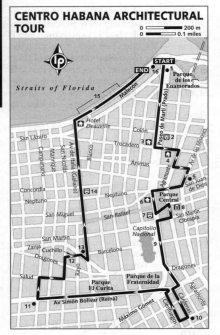

CENTRO HABANA ARCHITECTURAL TOUR

WALK FACTS

Start El Prado
Finish Centro Hispano Americano de Cultura
Distance 4km
Duration Three hours

neo-Moorish **Hotel Sevilla** (4; p131) harks back to a bygone age of Spanish stucco and intricate *mudéjar* craftsmanship. A glimpse inside its gilded lobby with its blue-tinted azulejo tiles and decorative wooden ceilings calls to mind a scene from Granada's Alhambra, though the hotel itself was built in 1908.

Turn right on Agramonte and detour down Ánimas for Havana's – and perhaps Latin America's – most emblematic art-deco building, the kitschy **Edificio Bacardí** (5; p114), a vivid and highly decorative incarnation of this popular interwar architectural genre garnished with granite, Capellanía limestone and multicolored bricks.

On the northwest corner of Parque Central, the royal blue **Hotel Telégrafo** (6; p131), renovated in 2002 by the City Historian's office,

retains many features of an earlier hotel constructed on this site in 1886. Take a peep inside its airy lobby to admire the funky furnishings and intricate bar mosaic.

Eclecticism meets neobaroque at the flamboyant **Centro Gallego** (7; p115), erected as a Galician social club in 1915 around the existing Teatro Tacón. Facing it across leafy Parque Central is the equally eclectic **Centro Asturianas** (8; p116), now part of the Museo Nacional de Bellas Artes, with four separate rooftop lookouts and a richly gilded interior. According to in-the-know locals, these two Spanish social clubs entered into silent competition during the 1910s and '20s to see who could come up with the most grandiose building. And the winner? You decide.

Centro Havana's **Capitolio Nacional** (9; p114), built between 1926 and 1929, captures Latin America's neoclassical revival in full swing with sweeping stairways and Doric columns harking back to a purer and more strident Grecian ideal.

Few travelers venture down Calle Cárdenas behind the Fuente de los Indios, but those who do quickly fall upon some of Havana's most engaging art-nouveau and art-deco townhouses. For pure artistic cheek, check out the pink-and-white wedding cake structure on the southeast corner of **Calles Cárdenas & Apodaca** (10) before doubling back along Calle Cienfuegos to the Parque de la Fraternidad.

Avenida Simón Bolívar, better known to locals as Calle Reina, is another architectural mish-mash that will leave modern-day urban designers blinking in bewilderment. It also contains one of Havana's finest Gaudí-esque buildings, an outrageously ornate apartment dwelling on the southwest corner of **Av Simón Bolívar & Calle Campanario** (11).

Go north on Campanario, right on Salud and left on San Nicolás, and you're in the Barrio Chino, Havana's bustling Chinatown. **Calle Cuchillo** (12) is the main drag here, a short, narrow pedestrian street with plenty of color, but few buildings of architectural note. Merge into Zanja and proceed one block southeast to the next junction. Here on the corner of **Calle Zanja & Av de Italia** (13) is one of Havana's zaniest art-deco creations, a narrow turreted townhouse with cubelike balconies and sharply defined vertical and horizontal lines.

Turn left on Av de Italia (Galiano to locals) and stroll three blocks north to the **Teatro América** (14; p145), one of a trio of classic art-deco *rascacielos* (skyscrapers) put up in the 1920s and '30s to house new shops and apartments. Continue north on Av de Italia for six more blocks and turn right at the Hotel Deauville into the **Malecón** (15; p121). Havana's storm-lashed sea drive is a museum of brilliant eclecticism, with each building differing defiantly from the next. The style reaches its apex two buildings from the junction with Prado (and your starting point) in the faux Egyptian **Centro Hispano Americano de Cultura** (16; right). Admire the gaudy granite gargoyles before heading off for a well-earned drink.

COURSES

Aside from Spanish-language courses, Havana offers a large number of learning activities for aspiring students.

Language

Universidad de La Habana (Map pp102–3; ☎ 832-4245, 831-3751; dpg@uh.cu; www.uh.cu; Edificio Varona, 2nd fl, Calle J No 556, Vedado) offers Spanish courses 12 months a year, beginning on the first Monday of each month. Costs start at CUC$100 for 20 hours (one week), including textbooks, and cover all levels from beginners to advanced. You must first sit a placement test to determine your level. Aspiring candidates can sign up in person at the university or reserve beforehand via email or phone.

Other places to check out Spanish courses include **Uneac** (Map pp102–3; ☎ 832-4551; cnr Calles 17 & H, Vedado), **Paradiso** (Map pp102–3; ☎ 832-9538; Calle 19 No 560, Vedado) and **Cubamar Viajes** (Map pp102–3; ☎ 830-1220; www.cubamarviajes.cu; Calle 3 btwn Calle 12 & Malecón, Vedado; ☺ 8:30am–5pm Mon–Sat).

Private lessons can be arranged by asking around locally – try your casa particular.

Dance

The easiest way to take a dance class is at the **Museo del Ron** (Map p100; ☎ 861-8051; San Pedro No 262, Habana Vieja), which offers on-the-spot lessons Monday to Friday at 9am for CUC$10 for the first two hours; it invariably gets good reports. Another option is the **Teatro América** (Map p106; ☎ 862-5416; Av de Italia No 253 btwn Concordia & Neptuno, Centro Habana), next to the Casa de la Música, which can fix you up with both a class and a partner for CUC$8 per hour.

The **Conjunto Folklórico Nacional de Cuba** (Map pp102–3; ☎ 830-3060; www.folkcuba.cult.cu; Calle 4 No 103 btwn Calzada & Calle 5, Vedado) teaches highly recommended classes in *son*, salsa, rumba, mambo and more. It also teaches percussion. Classes start on the third Monday in January and the first Monday in July, and cost in the vicinity of CUC$400 to CUC$500 for a 15-day course. An admission test places students in classes of four different levels.

Culture

Centro Hispano Americano de Cultura (Map p106; ☎ 860-6282; Malecón No 17 btwn Paseo de Martí & Capdevila, Centro Habana; ☺ 9am–5pm Tue–Sat, 9am–1pm Sun) has all kinds of facilities, including a library, internet cafe and concert venue. Pick up its excellent monthly brochure and ask about the literature courses. Another place worth approaching is **Paradiso** (Map pp102–3; ☎ 832-9538; Calle 19 No 560, Vedado), a cultural agency that can arrange courses on history, architecture, music, theater, dance and more. The University of Havana (see left) runs 60-hour courses on Cuban culture for CUC$360.

Yoga

Yoga classes are offered in the garden of the **Museo de Artes Decorativas** (Map pp102–3; ☎ 830-9848; Calle 17 No 502 btwn Calles D & E, Vedado). Check at the museum for the next session. You may be able to drop in on classes held at the **Teatro Nacional de Cuba** (Map pp102–3; ☎ 879-6011; cnr Paseo & Calle 39, Vedado). Look for the class schedule by the box office.

Music

Typically, Cubans perform flamenco as well as the Spanish, and you can take dance classes or even enquire about the possibility of guitar lessons at the **Centro Andaluz** (Map p106; ☎ 863-6745; Paseo de Martí No 104 btwn Genios & Refugio, Centro Habana).

ASK A LOCAL

If you want a more individualized and in-depth city tour, then book with San Cristóbal Agencia de Viajes. It does tours for small groups of people on topics and routes that no other agencies cover. Highly recommended are both its Architectural and Social Projects Tour. The latter takes you around all of the social projects in Habana Vieja that have benefited directly from tourist money.

Geraldo, Havana

HAVANA

Art

The **Taller Experimental de Gráfica** (Map p100; ☎ 862-0979; fax 824-0391; Callejón del Chorro No 6, Habana Vieja) offers classes in the art of engraving. Individualized instruction lasts one month, during which the student creates an engraving with 15 copies; longer classes can be arranged. The cost is around CUC$250.

HAVANA FOR CHILDREN

Cuba is a child-friendly country. Waiters will ruffle your kid's hair almost instinctively, and walking around with your child(ren) anywhere will act as a great leveler and open doors that would otherwise have remained closed. Staying in casas particulares is especially recommended as it provides the opportunity for cross-cultural family exchanges. Vagaries of the Cuban reality will demand patience and creativity from parents (particularly when it comes to food), but there is no lack of fun things to do here. Playa has two of the best attractions: a big aquarium (see Acuario Nacional, p156), plus a huge new Chinese-built amusement park called **Isla del Coco** (Map pp154-5; Av 5 & Calle 112, Playa) with big wheels, bumper cars, the works. There's another, far inferior, Parque de Diversiones in hard-to-reach Parque Lenin (p161), and a smaller freshwater **Aquarivm** (Map p100; ☎ 863-9493; Brasil No 9 btwn Mercaderes & Oficios, Habana Vieja; 9am-5:30pm Tue-Sun) in the Old Town. Marina Hemingway has a **Bolera** (bowling alley; Map pp154-5; admission CUC$3) and some pinball machines. Head to the **beach** at Playas del Este (p170) to sail, kayak and swim. Young kids will enjoy the inflatable castles and other games at **La Maestranza** (Map p100; Av Carlos Manuel de Céspedes, Habana Vieja; admission CUC$1; under 4yr only).

Culturally, there are loads of things specifically for kids, including **La Colmenita** children's theater (p145) and **Cinecito** (p146) with all-kids' movies all the time.

The **ice-cream parlors** are a delight for children; you could also visit the scale-model **Maqueta** (p111) in Calle Mercaderes. Even the transport here is kid-friendly: hop in an old Chevy, grab a coco-taxi, commission a horse and cart around Habana Vieja or hire a bici-taxi and discover Havana.

TOURS

Most general agencies offer the same tours, with some exceptions noted below. The regular tour diet includes a four-hour city tour (CUC$15), a specialized Hemingway tour (from CUC$20), a *cañonazo* ceremony (shooting of the cannons at the Fortaleza de San Carlos de la Cabaña; without/with dinner CUC$15/25), a Varadero day trip (from CUC$35) and, of course, excursions to Tropicana Nightclub (starting at CUC$65). Other options include tours to Boca de Guamá crocodile farm (CUC$48), Playas del Este (CUC$20 including lunch), Viñales (CUC$44), Cayo Largo del Sur (CUC$137) and a Trinidad-Cienfuegos overnight (CUC$129). Children usually pay a fraction of the price for adults and solo travelers get socked with a CUC$15 supplement. Note that if the minimum number of people don't sign up, the trip will be cancelled. Any of the following agencies can arrange these tours and more:

Cubatur (Map pp102-3; ☎ 835-4155; cnr Calles 23 & M, Vedado; 8am-8pm) Below the Hotel Habana Libre.

Havanatur (Map pp102-3; ☎ 835-3720; cnr Calles 23 & M, Vedado)

Infotur Airport (off Map p162; ☎ 642-6101; Terminal 3 Aeropuerto Internacional José Martí; 24hr); Habana Vieja (Map p100; ☎ 863-6884; cnr Obispo & San Ignacio; 10am-1pm & 2-7pm); Habana Vieja (Map p100; ☎ 866-3333; Obispo btwn Bernaza & Villegas)

Paradiso (Map pp102-3; ☎ 832-9538; Calle 19 No 560, Vedado) Tours with art emphasis in several languages and departing from many cities. Check out Martí's Havana or special concert tours.

San Cristóbal Agencia de Viajes (Map p100; www .viajessancristobal.cu; ☎ 861-9171/2; Oficios No 110 btwn Lamparilla & Amargura, Habana Vieja; 8:30am-5:30pm Mon-Fri, 8:30am-2pm Sat, 9am-noon Sun) Offers the best tours in the city including a Havana archaeological tour (CUC$20 for two people) and a tour of the city's valuable social projects.

SLEEPING

With over 3000 private houses letting out rooms, you'll never struggle to find accommodation in Havana. Casas particulares go for anywhere between CUC$20 and CUC$40 per room, with Centro Habana offering the best bargains. Rock-bottom budget hotels can match casas for price, but not comfort. There's a dearth of decent hotels in the 'mid' price range, while Havana's top-end hotels are plentiful and offer oodles of atmosphere, even if the overall standards can't always match facilities elsewhere in the Caribbean.

HAVANA'S FESTIVALS

Through hell and high water, Havana has always clung proudly to its annual calendar of festivals and events, many of which are internationally renowned cultural extravaganzas that draw in movers and shakers from around the globe.

February

Feria Internacional del Libro de La Habana Hosted at the Fortaleza de San Carlos de la Cabaña, ExpoCuba and various bookstores around the capital, the Havana Book Festival includes book presentations, special readings and the prestigious Premio Casa de las Américas, an award for outstanding writers of Latin American origin.

April

Festival Internacional de Coros Headquartered in the Teatro Amadeo Roldán and held in even-numbered years, the International Choir Festival brings together different choirs from around the world in a series of workshops and performances.

May

Cubadisco An annual get-together of foreign and Cuban record producers and companies, Cubadisco hosts music concerts, a trade fair at the Pabexpo conference center and a Grammy-style awards ceremony that encompasses every musical genre from chamber music to pop.

Festival Internacional de Poesía de La Habana An opportunity for poets from around the world to convene in Cuba as part of an international cultural exchange, this festival is organized by Uneac (Unión de Escritores y Artistas de Cuba) and bivouacked in the Convento de San Francisco de Asís.

June

Festival Internacional 'Boleros de Oro' Organized by Uneac, the Boleros de Oro was created by Cuban composer and musicologist José Loyola Fernández in 1986 as a global celebration of this distinctive Cuban musical genre.

August

Carnaval de La Havana Parades, dancing, music, colorful costumes and striking effigies; Havana's annual summer shindig might not be as famous as its more rootsy Santiago de Cuba counterpart, but the celebrations and processions along the Malecón leave plenty of other city carnivals in the shade.

Festival Internacional 'Habana Hip-Hop' Organized by the Asociación Hermanos Saíz (a youth arm of Uneac), the annual Havana Hip-Hop Festival – headquartered in the rough Havana suburb of Alamar – is a chance for the island's young musical creators to improvise and swap ideas.

October

Festival Internacional de Ballet de La Habana Presided over by long-standing dance diva Alicia Alonso, the International Ballet Festival brings together dance companies, ballerinas and a mixed audience of foreigners and Cubans for a week of expositions, galas and classical and contemporary ballet.

November

Jazz Festival Intrinsically linked to Cuban jazz maestro Chucho Valdés, the International Jazz Festival has been around for nearly a quarter of a century. Staged in the Casa de las Américas, along with the Karl Marx, Mella and Amadeo Roldán theaters, the event draws in top figures from around the world for some truly memorable concerts.

December

Festival Internacional del Nuevo Cine Latinoamericano An internationally renowned film festival held in cinemas across Havana that illustrates Cuba's growing influence in Latin American cinema worldwide. For more information, see www.habanafilmfestival.com.

Many of Havana's hotels are historic monuments in their own right. Worth a look, even if you're not staying over, are the Hotel Sevilla and the Saratoga (located in in Centro Habana), the Raquel, the Hostal Condes de Villanueva and the Hotel Florida (all in Habana Vieja), and the iconic Hotel Nacional in Vedado.

Habana Vieja

BUDGET

Casas Particulares

Noemi Moreno (☎ 862-3809; Cuba No 611 apt 2 btwn Luz & Santa Clara; r CUC$25-30) Two simple, clean rooms sharing a bath, Noemi's got a great location behind the Santa Clara convent. If she's full, apartments 1 and 4 also rent in the same building.

Casa de Pepe & Rafaela (☎ 862-9877; San Ignacio No 454 btwn Sol & Santa Clara; r CUC$30) One of Havana's best: antiques and Moorish tiles throughout, two rooms with balconies and gorgeous new baths, excellent location and great hosts. The son also rents a charming colonial house at San Ignacio No 656 (same price).

Migdalia Carraballe (☎ 861-7352; Santa Clara No 164 btwn Cuba & San Ignacio; r CUC$30) Handily placed two blocks from Plaza Vieja, Migdalia has three rooms available but can only rent two at once. The two with balconies overlook the Santa Clara convent. Climb the staircase to the 1st floor.

Pablo Rodríguez (☎ 861-2111; pablo@sercomar.telemar.cu; Compostela No 532 btwn Brasil & Muralla; r CUC$30) Another lovely old colonial classic, this one with some original frescoes partially uncovered on the walls. It would be worth millions elsewhere, but here you can rent one of venerable Pablo's two rooms with en-suite bath, fan and fridge for a giveaway CUC$30 per night.

Juan & Margarita (☎ 867-9592; Obispo No 522 apt 8 btwn Bernaza & Villegas; apt CUC$60) A two-bedroom apartment on Obispo, no less – Vieja's Fifth Avenue. You can bag the whole place for CUC$60 – sitting room with TV and table, two clean bedrooms with baths, and a balcony. Juan is a gentleman and a scholar who speaks excellent English and has a lot of local knowledge.

Hostels

Residencia Académica Convento de Santa Clara (☎ 866-9327; Cuba No 610 btwn Luz & Sol; r per person CUC$25) Something of a novelty for Havana, this run-down but charmingly atmospheric old nunnery has been partially converted into a hostel to take in travelers. Situated a stone's throw from Plaza Vieja and priced cheaper than the surrounding casas particulares, it's a tempting budget option if you don't mind fairly Spartan facilities and possible room sharing. The Residencia was undergoing renovations at the time of writing.

MIDRANGE

Mesón de la Flota (Habaguanex; ☎ 863-3838; Mercaderes No 257 btwn Amargura & Brasil; s/d incl breakfast CUC$65/100) Habana Vieja's smallest and most reasonably priced period hotel is an old Spanish tavern decked out with maritime motifs and located within spitting distance of gracious Plaza Vieja. Five individually crafted rooms contain all of the modern comforts and amenities, while downstairs a busy restaurant serves up delicious tapas – check out the *garbanzos con chorizo* (chickpeas with sausage) – and scrumptiously prepared *platos principales* (main meals). For music lovers the real drawcard, however, is the nightly *tablaos* (flamenco shows), the quality of which could rival anything in Andalusia. Sit back and soak up the intangible spirit of duende.

Hostal Valencia (Habaguanex; ☎ 867-1037; Oficios No 53; s/d incl breakfast CUC$80/130) The Valencia is decked out like a Spanish *posada* (inn) with hanging vines, doorways big enough to ride a horse through and a popular on-site paella restaurant. With a bit of imagination you can almost see the ghosts of Don Quixote and Sancho Panza floating through the hallways. Slap-bang in the middle of the historical core and with a price that makes it one of the cheapest offerings in the current Habaguanex stable, this hostel is an excellent old-world choice with good service and plenty of atmosphere.

Hotel El Comendador (Habaguanex; ☎ 867-1037; cnr Obrapía & Baratillo; ☒) Situated next door to the Valencia, the El Comendador offers similar facilities and rates.

Hostal Beltrán de la Santa Cruz (☎ 860-8330; San Ignacio No 411 btwn Muralla & Sol; s/d incl breakfast CUC$80/130; ☒) Excellent location, friendly staff and plenty of old-world authenticity make this compact inn just off Plaza Vieja a winning combination. Housed in a sturdy 18th-century building and offering just 11 spacious rooms, intimacy is a premium here and the standard of service has been regularly lauded by both travelers and reviewers.

TOP END

Hostal Condes de Villanueva (Habaguanex; ☎ 862-9293; Mercaderes No 202; s/d low season CUC$67/98, high season CUC$93/150; ☒) If you are going to splash out on one night of luxury in Havana, you'd do well to check out this highly lauded colonial gem. Restored under the watchful eye of City Historian Eusebio Leal Spengler in the late

'90s, the Villanueva has converted a grandiose city mansion into an intimate and thoughtfully decorated hotel with nine bedrooms spread spaciously around an attractive inner courtyard (complete with resident peacock). Upstairs suites contain stained-glass windows, chandeliers, arty sculptures and – best of all – a fully workable whirlpool bathtub.

Hostal Palacio O'Farrill (Habaguanex; ☎ 860-5080; Cuba No 102-108 btwn Chacón & Tejadillo; s/d CUC$95/160; P ❀ 🖳) Not an Irish joke, but one of Havana's most impressive period hotels, the Palacio O'Farrill is a staggeringly beautiful colonial palace that once belonged to Don Ricardo O'Farrill, a Cuban sugar entrepreneur who was descended from a family of Irish nobility. Taking the Emerald Isle as its theme, there's plenty of greenery on the plant-filled 18th-century courtyard. The 2nd floor, which was added in the 19th century, provides grandiose neoclassical touches, while the 20th-century top floor merges seamlessly with the magnificent architecture below.

Hotel Florida (Habaguanex; ☎ 862-4127; Obispo No 252; s/d incl breakfast CUC$95/160; P ❀) They don't make them like this anymore. The Florida is an architectural extravaganza built in the purest colonial style, with arches and pillars clustered around an atmospheric central courtyard. Habaguanex has restored the building (constructed in 1836) with loving attention to detail, with the amply furnished rooms retaining their original high ceilings and wonderfully luxurious finishes. Anyone with even a passing interest in Cuba's architectural heritage will want to check out this colonial jewel, complemented with an elegant cafe and an amiable bar-nightspot (from 8pm).

Hotel Marqués de Prado Ameno (Habaguanex; ☎ 862-4127; cnr O'Reilly & Cuba; s/d incl breakfast CUC$95/160; P ❀) Connected to the Florida by a tunnel, Havana's newest hotel offers similar facilities – thoughtful restoration, eager-to-please staff and plenty of colonial grandiosity.

Hotel Ambos Mundos (Habaguanex; ☎ 860-9529; Obispo No 153; s/d CUC$95/160; ❀ 🖳) Hemingway's Havana hideout and the place where he is said to have penned his seminal guerrilla classic *For Whom the Bell Tolls* (Castro's bedtime reading during the war in the mountains), the pastel-pink Ambos Mundos is a Havana institution and an obligatory pit stop for anyone on a world tour of 'Hemingway-once-fell-over-here' bars. Small, sometimes windowless rooms suggest overpricing, but the lobby bar

is classic enough (follow the romantic piano melody) and drinks on the rooftop restaurant one of the city's finest treats.

our pick **Hotel Raquel** (Habaguanex; ☎ 860-8280; cnr Amargura & San Ignacio; s/d CUC$115/200; ❀) Encased in a dazzling 1908 palace (that was once a bank), the Hotel Raquel takes your breath away with its grandiose columns, sleek marble statues and intricate stained-glass ceiling. Painstakingly restored in 2003, the reception area in this marvelous eclectic building is a tourist sight in its own right; replete with priceless antiques and intricate art-nouveau flourishes. Behind its impressive architecture, the Raquel offers well-presented if noisy rooms, a small gym/sauna, friendly staff and a great central location.

Hotel Santa Isabel (Habaguanex; ☎ 860-8201; Baratillo No 9; s/d incl breakfast CUC$190/240; P ❀ 🖳) Considered one of Havana's finest hotels, as well as one of its oldest (it first began operations in 1867), the Hotel Santa Isabel is housed in the Palacio de los Condes de Santovenia, the former city crash pad of a decadent Spanish count. In 1998 this three-story baroque beauty was upgraded to five-star status but, unlike other posh Cuban hotels, the Santa Isabel actually comes close to justifying the billing. The 17 regular rooms have bundles of historic charm and are all kitted out with attractive Spanish colonial furniture as well as paintings by contemporary Cuban artists. No small wonder ex-US president, Jimmy Carter, stayed here during his visit in 2002.

Centro Habana
BUDGET
Casas Particulares
Dulce Hostal – Dulce María González (☎ 863-2506; Amistad No 220 btwn Neptuno & San Miguel; r CUC$20) The Dulce (sweet) Hostal on Amistad (friendship) Street sounds like a good combination, and sweet and friendly is what you get in this beautiful colonial house with tile floors, soaring ceilings and a quiet, helpful hostess.

Martha Obregón (☎ 870-2095; marthaobregon@yahoo.com; Gervasio No 308 Altos btwn Neptuno & San Miguel; r CUC$20-25) A pleasant family home with little balconies and small street views. You'll get a good sense of life in the crowded central quarter here with its whistling tradesmen, snippets of music and stickball-playing kids.

Niurka O Rey (☎ 863-0278; Águila No 206 btwn Ánimas & Virtudes; r CUC$20-25) A sparkling blue house with slightly less sparkling but adequate interior.

One of the two rooms here comes with a private bath and there's parking close by.

Juan Carlos (☎ 863-6301, 861-8003; Crespo No 107 btwn Colón & Trocadero; r CUC$20-25) Big, spotless house in the middle of the hood that is Centro Habana, this house has two rooms, one with a shared bath and plenty of natural light throughout. It's a good-value central option.

Julio & Elsa Roque (☎ 861-8027; julioroq@yahoo.com; Consulado No 162 apt 2 btwn Colón & Trocadero; r CUC$25) Julio's a pediatrician and rents out two rooms in his friendly family house just a block from Prado. Ring the door bell and a key will be lowered down from a 1st-floor balcony to let you in. The house is cozy and nicely furnished and both Julio and his wife Elsa are superhelpful and a mine of information. English spoken.

Esther Cardoso (☎ 862-0401; esthercv2551@cubarte .cult.cu; Águila No 367 btwn Neptuno & San Miguel; r CUC$25) Esther is an artist, meaning that this little palace shines like an oasis in Centro Habana's dilapidated desert with tasteful decor, funky posters, spick-and-span baths and a spectacular roof terrace. Book early as there are plenty in-the-know.

Elicio Fernández (☎ 861-7447; Águila No 314 apt 405 btwn Neptuno & Concordia; r CUC$25) These two rooms are in a block, meaning you'll have to find the doorman and negotiate the elevator to get in. It's probably worth it: breezy rooms have natural light and there are great rooftop views. The bath is shared.

La Casona Colonial – Jorge Díaz (☎ 870-0489; cuba rooms2000@yahoo.com; Gervasio No 209 btwn Concordia & Virtudes; r CUC$25) A colonial house with a pleasant courtyard, this place has a shared bathroom but plenty of bed space and configurations. It's located in the thick of the Centro Habana action with friendly owners and good access.

Hotels

Casa del Científico (☎ 862-1607/8, Paseo de Martí No 212; s/d with bath CUC$45/55, without bath CUC$25/31; ▢) Eclectic meets eccentric in this eye-catching Prado palace that was once the residence of Cuba's second president, José Miguel Gómez. These days the Casa del Científico's grand stairways, marble columns, hidden courtyards and withered terraces maintain a slightly more abandoned air (expect the odd cobweb and a good coating of dust) but, with its central location and time-warped prerevolutionary atmosphere, it makes an evocative introduction to Havana. The rooms are ordinary but adequate and there's a rather evocative restaurant on the 1st floor.

Hotel Lido (Islazul; ☎ 867-1102; Consulado No 210 btwn Ánimas & Trocadero; s/d CUC$28/38; ☒ ▢) A travelers' institution, the lackluster Lido is Havana's unofficial backpacker's hostel that has been popular for years for its central location, no-frills rooms (with intermittent hot water) and gritty neighborhood feel. It certainly ain't fancy, but there's a handy internet terminal downstairs, breakfast on the roof and a helpful Cubanacán info desk. Then there's the price – cheaper than most of Havana's casas.

Hotel Caribbean (Islazul; ☎ 860-8233; Paseo de Martí No 164 btwn Colón & Refugio; s/d CUC$36/54; ☒) Cheap but not always so cheerful, the Caribbean – which was the recipient of a long-awaited 2006 makeover – offers aspiring Cuban renovators a lesson in how not to decorate. Dark poky rooms contain basic facilities such as shower, TV and air-con, but it's all a bit rough around the edges and the price – while competitive – certainly doesn't justify the facilities. There's a bar in the lobby and the Café del Prado next door is OK for a snack. Budget travelers should try the Lido around the corner first.

Hotel Lincoln (Islazul; ☎ 33-82-09; Av de Italia btwn Virtudes & Ánimas; s/d CUC$39/46; ☒) A peeling nine-story giant on busy Galiano (Av de Italia), the Hotel Lincoln was the second-tallest building in Havana when it was built in 1926. Overshadowed by taller opposition these days, the hotel still offers 135 air-con rooms with bath and TV in an atmosphere that is more 1950s than 2000s. Notoriety hit this hotel in 1958 when Castro's 26th of July Movement kidnapped five-time motor racing world champion Carlos Fangio from the downstairs lobby on the eve of the Cuban Grand Prix. A small 'museum' on the 8th floor records the event for posterity. Otherwise the facilities are friendly but timeworn.

MIDRANGE

Hotel Park View (Habaguanex; Colón No 101; s/d CUC$52/86; ☒ ▢) Built in 1928 with American money, the Park View's reputation as the poor man's 'Sevilla' isn't entirely justified. Its location alone (within baseball-pitching distance of the Museo de la Revolución) is enough to consider this mint-green city charmer a viable option. Chuck in friendly doormen, modern furnishings (the hotel was renovated in 2002 by Habaguanex) and a small but perfectly poised 7th-floor restaurant and you've got yourself a veritable bargain.

Hotel Deauville (Hotetur; ☎ 866-8812; Av de Italia No 1 cnr Malecón; s/d/tr CUC$61/88/99; **P** ⊠ ☎) The Deauville is housed in a kitschy seafront high-rise that sharp-eyed Havana-watchers will recognize from picturesque Malecón-at-sunset postcards. But while the location might be postcard-perfect, the facilities inside this former Mafia gambling den don't quite match up to the stellar views. Currently reborn in peach and red and already showing the effects of the corrosive sea water, the Deauville's handy facilities (money exchange and car rental) and reasonably priced restaurant are ever popular with the mid-priced tour-circuit crowd; plus it's great for an early morning Malecón stroll.

TOP END

Hotel Inglaterra (Gran Caribe; ☎ 860-8595; Paseo de Martí No 416; s/d/tr CUC$84/120/168; **P** ⊠ ☎) It's José Martí's one-time Havana hotel of choice and it's still playing on the fact – which says something about the current state of affairs. The Inglaterra is a better place to hang out than actually to stay in, with its exquisite Moorish lobby and crusty colonial interior easily outshining the lackluster and often viewless rooms. The rooftop bar's a popular watering hole and the downstairs foyer is a hive of bustling activity where there's always music blaring. Beware of the streets outside which are full of overzealous hustlers waiting to pounce.

Hotel Telégrafo (Habaguanex; ☎ 861-1010, 861-4741; Paseo de Martí No 408; s/d from CUC$100/160; **P** ⊠ ☎) A bold royal-blue charmer on the northwest corner of Parque Central, this Habaguanex beauty juxtaposes old-style architectural features (the original building hails from 1888) with futuristic design flourishes that include shiny silver sofas, a huge winding central staircase and an amazingly intricate tile mosaic emblazoned on the wall of the downstairs cafe. The rooms are equally spiffy.

Hotel Sevilla (Gran Caribe; ☎ 860-8560; Trocadero No 55 btwn Paseo de Martí & Agramonte; s/d incl breakfast CUC$150/210; **P** ⊠ ☎ ☎) Al Capone once hired out the whole 6th floor, Graham Greene used it as a setting for his novel *Our Man in Havana* and the Mafia requisitioned it as operations centre for their prerevolutionary North American drugs racket. Refurbished by the French Sofitel group in 2002, the Hotel Sevilla

now sparkles like the colonial jewel of old with large spacious rooms, comfortable beds and a lobby straight out of the Alhambra.

our pick Hotel Saratoga (Habaguanex; ☎ 868-1000; Paseo de Martí No 603; s/d CUC$200/275; **P** ⊠ ☎ ☎) One of Havana's newest, ritziest and most dramatic hotels, the glittering Saratoga is an architectural work-of-art that stands imposingly at the intersection of Prado and Dragones with fantastic views over toward the Capitolio. Sharp, if officious, service is a premium here, as are the extra-comfortable beds, power showers and a truly decadent rooftop swimming pool. Not surprisingly, there's a price for all this luxury. The Saratoga is Havana's most expensive hotel and, while its facilities impress, its service can't quite match up to the marginally cheaper Meliás.

Hotel NH Parque Central (NH Hotels; ☎ 860-6627; www.nh-hotels.com; Neptuno btwn Agramonte & Paseo de Martí; s/d CUC$205/270; **P** ⊠ ☎ ☎) If you have a penchant for hanging out – but not staying – in expensive five-star hotel lobbies sipping mojitos, the Parque Central could fill a vacuum. Reserving a room's another (more expensive) matter. Outside Havana's two Meliás, the NH is, without a doubt, Havana's best international-standard hotel with service and business facilities on a par with top-ranking five-star facilities elsewhere in the Caribbean. Although the fancy lobby and classily furnished rooms may lack the historical riches of the Habaguanex establishments, the ambience here is far from antiseptic. Bonus facilities include a full-service business center, a rooftop swimming pool/fitness center/Jacuzzi, an elegant lobby bar, the celebrated El Paseo restaurant plus excellent international telephone and internet links. Two of the bedrooms are wheelchair-accessible. In late 2006 the Parque Central was in the process of constructing a large new wing directly behind the existing building on Calle Virtudes.

Vedado

BUDGET

Casas Particulares

Nelsy Alemán Machado (☎ 832-8467; Calle 25 No 361 apt 1 btwn Calles K & L; r CUC$25) Nelsy is one of two renters in this house up by the university and a stone's throw from the Hotel Habana Libre. Geographically, it's one of Vedado's better options; safe and secure but within close proximity to most of the main action.

Basilia Pérez Castro (☎ 832-3953; bpcdt@hotmail .com; Calle 25 No 361 apt 7 Bajos btwn Calles K & L; r CUC$25) Basilia rents out two more rooms with independent entrances in the same house as Nelsy. It's a mellow scene and good value.

Eddy Gutiérrez Bouza (☎ 832-5207; Calle 21 No 408 btwn Calles F & G; r CUC$30; (P) (X)) Eddy is a fantastic host with a great knowledge of Havana and his huge colonial house has hosted many visitors over the years. It's an inviting abode with a well-kept garden, grand exterior and Eddy's 1974 Argentinian-made Dodge parked in the driveway. Guests are accommodated out back in comfortable quarters, and one room comes equipped with a kitchenette.

Guillermina & Roberto Abreu (☎ 833-6401; Paseo No 126 apt 13A btwn Calle 5 & Calzada; r CUC$30; (X)) On the 13th floor of a Vedado apartment block built in 1958, this is another 'view' property with two rooms, private baths and plush china furnishings. Hold your breath as you take the clunking elevator from the ground floor up.

Melba Piñeda Bermudez (☎ 832-5929; lienafp@ yahoo.com; Calle 11 No 802 btwn Calles 2 & 4; r CUC$30) This 100-year-old villa in a shady Vedado street would be a millionaire's pad anywhere else. But here in Havana, it's a casa particular with two large rooms and decent meals served (handy as you're more detached here). The front room is the brightest with a tranquil terrace overlooking a street thick with laurel trees.

Mercedes González (☎ 832-5840; mercylupe@ hotmail.com; Calle 21 No 360 apt 2A btwn Calles G & H; r CUC$30-35) One of the most welcoming hosts in Havana, Mercedes comes highly recommended by readers, fellow travelers, other casa owners, you name it. Her lovely art-deco abode is a classic Vedado apartment with two fine rooms, an airy terrace and top-notch five-star service.

Manuel Martínez (☎ 832-6713; Calle 21 No 4 apt 22 btwn Calles N & O; r CUC$30-35) There are 10 to 12 casas in this magnificent art-deco building constructed in 1945 opposite the Hotel Nacional, so if you don't get lucky here look for the blue sign and try again. This one overlooks the hotel gardens; about as close as you can get to Cuba's famous five-star without having to pay the five-star rates.

Marta Vitorte (☎ 832-6475; martavitorte@hotmail .com; Calle G No 301 apt 14 btwn Calles 13 & 15; r CUC$35-40) Marta has lived in this sinuous apartment on Av de los Presidentes since 1960 – one look at the view and you'll see why; it's as if you're standing atop the Martí monument with a glass-fronted wraparound terrace that soaks up 270° of Havana's stunning panorama. Not surprisingly, the two rooms are deluxe with lovely furnishings, minibars and safes. Then there are the breakfasts, the laundry, the parking space, the lift attendant…get the drift?

Hotels

Hotel Bruzón (Islazul; ☎ 877-5684; Bruzón No 217 btwn Pozos Dulces & Av de la Independencia; s/d CUC$26/36; (X)) There are only two reasons to stay at the lackluster Bruzón: you've got an early morning bus to catch (the terminal is a handy 400m around the corner), or everywhere else is full. Otherwise, the claustrophobic rooms, lumpy beds and out-of-the-way location aren't worth it.

MIDRANGE

Hotel Colina (Islazul; ☎ 836-4071; cnr Calles L & 27; s/d CUC$46/60; (X)) The friendliest and least fussy of Vedado's cheaper accommodation options, the Colina is situated directly outside the university and is a good choice if you're studying on a Spanish course. The 80 rooms are basic with air-con, satellite TV and intermittent hot water, plus there's a good people-watching sidewalk cafe just off the reception.

Hotel St John's (Gran Caribe; ☎ 833-3740; Calle O No 216 btwn Calles 23 & 25; s/d incl breakfast CUC$56/80; (X) (X)) A fair to middling Vedado option, the St John's has a rooftop pool, clean bathrooms, reasonable beds and the ever-popular Pico Blanco nightclub (p143) on the 14th floor. If wall-vibrating Cuban discos aren't your thing, you might get more peace at the identically priced Hotel Vedado half a block down the road. Ask for one of the western-facing rooms with killer views over the Malecón.

Hotel Vedado (Gran Caribe; ☎ 836-4072; Calle O No 244 btwn Calles 23 & 25; s/d CUC$63/80; (X) (回) (X)) Ever popular with the tour-bus crowd, the Hotel Vedado is a tough sell. Granted, there's an OK pool (rare in Havana), along with a passable restaurant and not unpleasant rooms. But the patchy service, perennially noisy lobby and almost total lack of character will leave you wondering if you wouldn't have been better off staying in a local casa particular – for half the price.

Hotel Victoria (Gran Caribe; ☎ 833-3510; Calle 19 No 101; s/d incl breakfast CUC$80/100; (P) (X) (回) (X)) A well-heeled and oft-overlooked Vedado option, the Victoria is a diminutive five-story hotel situated within spitting distance of the larger and more expensive Nacional. Deluxe and compact, though (due to its size) invariably full, this venerable Gran Caribe establishment housed in an attractive neoclassical building dating from 1928 contains a swimming pool, a bar and a small shop. A sturdy midrange accommodation option (if you can get in).

TOP END

Hotel Riviera (Gran Caribe; ☎ 836-4051; cnr Paseo & Malecón; s/d incl breakfast CUC$91/130; P 🅿 💻 🛜) Meyer Lansky's magnificent Vegas-style palace has leapt back into fashion with its gloriously retro lobby almost unchanged since 1957 (when it was the height of modernity). It isn't hard to imagine all the old Mafia hoods congregating here with their Cohiba cigars and chauffer-driven Chevrolets parked outside. The trouble for modern-day visitors are the rooms (there are 354 of them) which, though luxurious 50 years ago, are now looking a little rough around the edges and struggle to justify their top-end price tag. You can dampen the dreariness in the fabulous '50s-style pool, good smattering of restaurants or the legendary Copa Room cabaret (p145), far cheaper than Tropicana. The location on a wild and wave-lashed section of the Malecón is spectacular, although a good bus or taxi ride from the Old Town.

Hotel Presidente (Gran Caribe; ☎ 55-18-01; cnr Calzada & Calle G; s/d CUC$90/140; P 🅿 💻 🛜) Fully restored in 2000, this art-deco influenced hotel wouldn't be out of place on a street just off Times Square in New York. Built the same year as the Victoria (1928), the Presidente is similar but larger, with gruffer staff. Unless you're a walker or fancy getting some elbow exercise on Havana's crowded bus system, the location can be awkward.

Hotel Nacional (Gran Caribe; ☎ 836-3564; cnr Calles O & 23; s/d/tr CUC$120/170/238; P 🅿 💻 🛜) The cream of the crop in Cuban hotels and flagship of the government-run Gran Caribe chain, the neoclassical/neocolonial/art-deco (let's call it eclectic) Hotel Nacional is as much a city monument as it is an international accommodation option. Even if you haven't got the money to stay here, chances are you'll find yourself sipping at least one minty mojito in its exquisite oceanside bar. Steeping in history and furnished with rooms with plaques that advertise the details of illustrious occupants past, this towering Havana landmark sports two swimming pools, a sweeping manicured lawn, a couple of lavish restaurants and its own top-class nighttime cabaret show, the Parisién (p144). While the rooms might lack some of the fancy gadgets of deluxe Varadero, the ostentatious communal areas and the erstwhile ghosts of Winston Churchill, Frank Sinatra, Lucky Luciano and Errol Flynn that haunt the Moorish lobby make for a fascinating and unforgettable experience.

Hotel Habana Libre (Gran Caribe; ☎ 834-6100; Calle L btwn Calles 23 & 25; d/ste incl breakfast CUC$200/300; P 🅿 💻 🛜) Havana's biggest and boldest hotel opened in March 1958 on the eve of Batista's last waltz. Once part of the Hilton chain, in January 1959 it was commandeered by Castro's rebels who put their boots over all the plush furnishings and turned it into their temporary HQ (Castro effectively ran the country from a suite on one of the upper floors). Now managed by Spain's Meliá chain as an urban Tryp Hotel, all 574 rooms in this skyline-hogging giant are kitted out to international standard, though the lackluster furnishings could do with an imaginative makeover. The tour desks in the lobby are helpful for out-of-town excursions and the 25th-floor Cabaret Turquino (p144) is a city institution.

Hotel Meliá Cohiba (Cubanacán; ☎ 833-3636; Paseo btwn Calles 1 & 3; r CUC$220; P 🅿 💻 🛜) Royally professional, this oceanside concrete giant built in 1994 (it's the only building from this era on the Malecón) will satisfy the highest of international expectations with its knowledgeable, consistent staff and modern, well-polished facilities. After a few weeks in the Cuban outback, you'll feel like you're on a different planet here, although the ambience is more Houston than Havana. For workaholics there are special 'business-traveler rooms' and 59 units have Jacuzzis. On the lower levels gold-star facilities include a shopping arcade, one of Havana's plushest gyms and the ever-popular Habana Café (p144).

EATING
Paladares
HABANA VIEJA

Many of Habana Vieja's once vibrant paladares have been squeezed out of business in recent years, leaving just a handful of legal places that compete gamefully with the heavily promoted Habaguanex-run restaurants. The following three places are all worth a visit if you want a break from the sometimes mediocre state-sponsored eateries.

Paladar Moneda Cubana (☎ 867-5984; San Ignacio No 77; meals CUC$8-10; ⏰ noon-midnight) There's a soccer obsession going on at this perfectly placed paladar just off Plaza de la Catedral that must be passed by every tourist in Cuba at some point. Underneath the sporty regalia, a quartet of tables offers chicken and pork dishes at very reasonable prices (CUC$8 to CUC$10). Go on, contribute a few Convertibles to the spirit of private enterprise.

La Julia (☎ 862-7438; O'Reilly No 506A btwn Bernaza & Villegas; meals CUC$10; ⏰ noon-midnight) It's been around long enough to be called an institution and outlasted almost all the opposition – except, perhaps, Fidel. La Julia is an unfussy family-run paladar in Calle O'Reilly that serves Cuban comfort food – *comida criolla* – with patience and panache.

Paladar La Mulata del Sabor (☎ 867-5984; Sol No 153 btwn Cuba & San Ignacio; meals CUC$10; ⏰ noon-midnight) Delicious smells emanating from the kitchen in this hole-in-the-wall paladar have lured in many an off-track traveler disorientated after taking a wrong turn out of Plaza Vieja. Thankfully, La Mulata is an amiable hostess and the word-of-mouth reviews from budget travelers are always good.

CENTRO HABANA

Paladar Bellamar (Virtudes No 169; meals from CUC$6; ⏰ noon-10pm) In the gastronomic desert of Centro Habana (La Guarida apart), the family-run Bellamar is a good standby. Sticking to the official rules, it serves classic chicken and pork dishes in a 12-cover front room whose walls have been 'decorated' Bodeguita del Medio–style with the graffiti of punters past.

Paladar Doña Blanquita (Paseo de Martí No 158 btwn Colón & Refugio; meals CUC$7-9; ⏰ noon-10pm) Overlooking the Prado boulevard, this is one of Centro Habana's best-placed paladares, with a proper typewritten menu and meat-biased main plates in the CUC$7 to CUC$9 range. You can dine in the shabby chic salon or on a pleasant terrace overlooking the promenade.

Paladar Torressón (☎ 861-7476; Malecón btwn Capdevila & Genios; meals CUC$7-9; ⏰ noon-midnight) Situated at the eastern end of the Malecón with a great view of El Morro castle, the Torressón takes up the 2nd floor of a suitably dilapidated seafront tenement. Complete meals of meat

or fish cost between CUC$10 and CUC$15, but the stupendous views are free.

ourpick Paladar La Guarida (☎ 866-9047; Concordia No 418 btwn Gervasio & Escobar; ⏰ noon-3pm & 7pm-midnight) Located on the top floor of a spectacularly dilapidated Havana tenement, La Guarida's lofty reputation rests on its movie-location setting (*Fresa y Chocolate* was filmed in this building) and a clutch of swashbuckling newspaper reviews (including the *New York Times* and the *Guardian*). The food, as might be expected, is up there with Havana's best, shoehorning its captivating blend of Nueva Cocina Cubana into dishes such as sea bass in a coconut reduction, and chicken with honey and lemon sauce. Reservations required.

VEDADO

Vedado's once-splendid paladares are fighting a losing battle against high rents and nit-picking government regulations. Although few new places open these days, there are a handful of stalwart survivors.

Paladar Los Amigos (Calle M No 253; ⏰ noon-midnight) Paladar Los Amigos, situated in the back of a prerevolutionary house on the corner of Calles M and 19 near the Hotel Victoria, serves good Cuban meals for CUC$10, including side plates. It's enthusiastically recommended by locals.

El Gringo Viejo (☎ 831-1946; Calle 21 No 454 btwn Calles E & F; ⏰ noon-11pm) The Gringo offers a good atmosphere and large portions of invariably brilliant food. Locals and visitors love it for its speedy service, fine wine list and big portions of more adventurous plates, such as smoked salmon with olives and Gouda or crabmeat in red sauce (CUC$10 to CUC$12).

Paladar Aries (☎ 831-9668; Av Universidad No 456 Bajos btwn Calles J & K; ⏰ noon-midnight) Traditional Cuban fare mixed with what are generously referred to as 'international dishes,' this nicely decked-out, family-run place with occasional wandering *trovadores* (traditional singers/songwriters) is conveniently located behind the university.

Decameron (☎ 832-2444; Línea No 753 btwn Paseo & Calle 2; meals CUC$12-15; ⏰ noon-midnight; Ⓥ) Ugly from the outside, but far prettier within, the Decameron is an intimate Italian-influenced restaurant where you can order from the varied menu with abandon. Veggie pizza, lasagne bolognese, steak au poivre and a divine calabaza soup: it's all good. On top of that, there's a decent wine selection and the kitchen is sympathetic to vegetarians.

Paladar El Hurón Azul (☎ 879-1691; Humboldt No 153; meals CUC$15-20; ☺ noon-midnight Tue-Sun) This place is often touted as one of Havana's best private restaurants and, although the food might be tasty, the windowless interior combined with the preponderance of after-dinner smokers can leave your meal tasting more like nicotine than *comida criolla*. Nonetheless, the Hurón Azul (Blue Ferret) boasts plenty of original food and is locally famous for its adventurous smoked pork served with a pineapple salsa. That said, it's not cheap, averaging CUC$15 a pop plus a 10% service charge added to every bill. Reserve ahead.

Paladar Marpoly (☎ 832-2471; Calle K No 154 btwn Línea & Calle 11; ☺ noon-1am) An unsignposted – and hence hard to find – paladar just off Calle Línea, the Marpoly offers good food, including a seafood platter and a great selection of wines, in luxurious surroundings. Ask a neighbor if in doubt about the location.

Restaurants
HABANA VIEJA
Restaurante Puerto de Sagua (☎ 867-1026; Av de Bélgica No 603; ☺ noon-midnight) This nautical-themed eating joint in Habana Vieja's grittier southern quarter is characterized by its small porthole-style windows and serves mostly seafood at reasonable prices (CUC$5 to CUC$8). The jacketed waiters are courteous and friendly.

Al Medina (☎ 867-1041; Oficios No 12 btwn Obrapía & Obispo; ☺ noon-midnight) Havana takes on the Middle East in this exotic restaurant, appropriately situated in one of the city's 17th-century *mudéjar*-style buildings. Tucked into a beautiful patio off Calle Oficios, Al Medina is where you can dine like a Moroccan sheik on lamb couscous (CUC$10), chicken tagine (CUC$5) and Lebanese sumac (CUC$8) with a spicy twist. It's especially recommended for its voluminous veggie platter that comes with hummus, tabouleh, dolma, pilaf and falafel.

Café del Oriente (☎ 860-6686; Oficios No 112; appetizers CUC$8-12, mains CUC$20-27; ☺ noon-11pm) Havana suddenly becomes posh when you walk through the door at this choice establishment on breezy Plaza de San Francisco de Asís. Smoked salmon, caviar (yes, caviar!), goose liver pâté, lobster thermidor, steak au poivre, cheese plate and a glass of port. Plus service in a tux, no less. There's just

one small problem: the price. But what the hell?

Restaurante El Patio (☎ 867-1034/5; San Ignacio No 54; meals CUC$15-20; ☺ noon-midnight) Possibly one of the most romantic settings on the planet when the hustlers stay away, the mint stalks in your mojito are pressed to perfection and the band breaks spontaneously into your favorite tune. This place – in the Plaza de la Catedral – must be experienced at night alfresco when the atmosphere is almost otherworldly.

Cafetería Torre La Vega (Obrapía No 114a btwn Mercaderes & Oficios; ☺ 9am-9pm) This is the flop-down lunchtime place that everyone hits in the middle of a sightseeing tour. It's perfectly placed in the middle of the Old Town with tables spilling onto the street and into a little park opposite. Diners sit with their noses in guidebooks chomping on 'spag bol,' pizza, chicken and sandwiches, none of it particularly expensive.

Restaurante Europa (Obispo No 112 cnr Aguiar) Fine fin de siècle furnishings lure you into this former Havana sweet shop that recently got a restaurant makeover by the City's Historian's office and Habaguanex. They obviously forgot to makeover the chef. Despite a menu that boasts of prize-winning cuisine (what prize?), the plate doesn't quite live up to the billing, though the ambience is pleasant and the service eager.

Restaurante La Paella (☎ 867-1037; cnr Oficios & Obrapía; ☺ noon-11pm) Known for its paella (CUC$10), this place, attached to the Hostal Valencia, has an authentic ambience, but never really matches the real deal from Spain's famous Mediterranean city. The fish is a good alternative.

Hanoi (☎ 867-1029; cnr Brasil & Bernaza; ☺ noon-11pm) The name might suggest solidarity with 'communist' Vietnam, but don't get too excited – you won't find any Saigon-flavored spring rolls here. Instead, what you get is straight-up Creole cuisine, with a couple of fried-rice dishes thrown in to justify the (rather misleading) name. One of the only fully restored buildings in untouristy Plaza del Cristo, the Hanoi is a backpacker favorite where the foreign clientele usually has its communal nose in a copy of Lonely Planet or Rough Guide.

La Mina (☎ 862-0216; Obispo No 109 btwn Oficios & Mercaderes; ☺ 24hr) A mediocre menu but a top-class location, La Mina graces a scenic corner of Plaza de Armas, meaning every tourist in

Havana walks past it at some point. The food options – displayed on a stand in the street outside and backed up by an army of verbose waiters – include chicken, pork and prawns cooked in a variety of different ways but lacking in culinary panache. There's a tempting Heladería (ice-cream parlor) around the corner in Calle Oficios.

Restaurante La Dominica (☎ 860-2918; O'Reilly No 108; ☽ noon-midnight) Despite a tendency to be a little overgenerous with the olive oil, La Dominica – with its wood-fired pizza oven and al dente pasta – could quite legitimately stake its claim as Havana's finest Italian restaurant. Located in an elegantly restored dining room with alfresco seating on Calle O'Reilly, the menu offers Italy's 'usual suspects' augmented by shrimp and lobster (CUC$10 to CUC$18). Professional house bands serenade diners with a slightly more eclectic set than the obligatory Buena Vista Social Club staples.

La Torre de Marfil (☎ 867-1038; Mercaderes No 111 btwn Obispo & Obrapía; ☽ noon-10pm Mon-Thu, noon-midnight Fri-Sun) Where have all the punters gone? Chinatown, perhaps? You feel sorry for the Marfil. Perfectly placed in Calle Mercaderes with smiling waiting staff and an inviting interior, it somehow always seems to be three-quarters empty. Brave the deserted interior and you'll find that the chop suey and chow mein plates – *when* they arrive – are fresh, crisp and huge.

El Mercurio (☎ 860-6188; Lonja del Comercio; ☽ 24hr) An elegant indoor-outdoor cafe-restaurant with cappuccino machines, intimate booths and waiters in black ties. You can get decent main dishes here such as lobster and steak tartar, but it's also a great place for lunch or a snack. The formidable 'Cuban sandwich' with ham, cheese and pork (CUC$4.50) should keep you going until dinnertime.

La Zaragozana (☎ 867-1040; Av de Bélgica btwn Obispo & Obrapía; ☽ noon-midnight) Established in 1830, this is Havana's oldest restaurant but a long way from being its best. The Spanish-themed food – which includes the obligatory paella – would have kept Don Quijote happy but the ambience, amid assorted Iberian flags and memorabilia, is a little gloomy.

CENTRO HABANA

El Gran Dragón (☎ 861-5396; Cuchillo No 1; ☽ 11am-midnight; Ⓥ) First on the left as you enter Cuchillo from Calle Zanja, this is as good an introduction as any to the energetic pulse of Havana's Barrio Chino. Specialties include wonton soup, chop suey, chow mein and fried rice, and the prices come in at less than CUC$5 a dish. Spread over three floors and with alfresco dining options outside, this is a good place for vegetarians.

Prado & Neptuno (☎ 860-9636; cnr Paseo de Martí & Neptuno; meals CUC$8-12; ☽ noon-5pm & 6:30-11:30pm) Dark lighting and tinted windows lure you into this trusty Italian restaurant on the lively intersection of Prado and Calle Neptuno. Stick to the pizza and pasta and choose from a good selection of Italian wines at the bar.

Chi Tack Tong (☎ 861-8095; Dragones No 356 btwn San Nicolás & Manrique; ☽ noon-midnight) Another aspiring Chinese restaurant situated in a large upstairs room in Calle Dragones, this place wins plenty of kudos for decor, with waitresses in Chinese-style dresses and a large painting of Sun Yatsen hung reverently on the wall. The downside is the menu, which is a little limited, particularly when compared to some of the Cuchillo joints nearby. As if to make amends, portions sizes are absolutely huge. Box up your leftovers.

Restaurante Tien-Tan (☎ 861-5478; Cuchillo No 17 btwn Rayo & San Nicolás; ☽ 11am-11pm) One of the Barrio Chino's best authentic Chinese restaurants, Tien-Tan (the 'Temple of Heaven') is run by a Chinese-Cuban couple and serves up an incredulous 130 different dishes. With such complexity you might have thought that you would be in for a long wait and that the food would, at best, be average. Thankfully, neither is the case. Try chop suey with vegetables or chicken with cashew nuts and sit outside in action-packed Cuchillo, one of Havana's most colorful and fastest-growing 'food streets.'

VEDADO

Café TV (☎ 833-4499; cnr Calles N & 19; ☽ 10am-9pm) Hidden in the bowels of the Focsa building, the goggle box–themed Café TV is a funky dinner/performance venue lauded by those in the know for its cheap food and hilarious comedy nights. If you're willing to brave the frigid air-con and rather foreboding underground entry tunnel, head here for fresh burgers (CUC$2), healthy salad (CUC$1.50), pasta (CUC$4) and *Gordon Bleu* (chicken stuffed with ham and cheese; CUC$5). Televisión Cubana is around the corner, hence the name and theme.

El Lugar (☎ 204-5162; cnr Calles 49C & 28A; ☽ noon-midnight) Set in Parque Almendares just across the road from the river below the bridge, this place is fantastic value offering CUC$5 for a juicy pork filet, a Pico Turquino of *congrí* (rice flecked with black beans), salad, *tostones* (fried plantain patties), ice cream and coffee. There's music in the evenings.

Trattoría Maraka's (Calle 0 No 260 btwn Calles 23 & 25; ☉ 10am-11pm) Don't be put off by the cheap Formica tables and the pictorial map of Italy on the wall. Real olive oil, parmesan and mozzarella cheese, plus a wood oven, mean that the pizza in this Vedado Italian trattoria is among the city's best. Also on offer are Greek salad, tortellini with red sauce, and spinach-stuffed cannelloni – mostly under CUC$10.

Pan.com (cnr Calles 17 & 10; ☉ 10am-2am) Missing home, decent burgers, club sandwiches, ice-cream milkshakes and quick no-nonsense service? Rejuvenate yourself with your cholesterol here at Havana's best-fast-food joint. There's an even better branch in Miramar (see p158).

El Conejito (☎ 832-4671; Calle M No 206; ☉ noon-midnight) A red-bricked Tudor-style mansion with lederhosen-clad waiters that serves rabbit (CUC$8 and up); now that's classic! If the *conejo* (rabbit) doesn't grab you, try the chicken, beef, fish or lobster. The rather surreal ambience is lightened somewhat by a resident pianist serenading romantically in the background.

Complejo Turístico 1830 (☎ 838-3090; Malecón No 1252; ☉ noon-10pm) One of Havana's most elegant restaurants is heavily touted but gets mixed reviews. Try the chicken in lemon and honey sauce and stick around after 10pm when the kitchen closes and there's live music and salsa dancing in the garden behind the restaurant.

La Torre (☎ 838-3088; Edificio Focsa, cnr Calles 17 & M) One of Havana's tallest and most talked-about restaurants is perched high above downtown Vedado atop the skyline-hogging Focsa building. A colossus of both modernist architecture and French/Cuban haute cuisine, this lofty fine-dining extravaganza combines sweeping city views with a progressive French-inspired menu that serves everything from artichokes to foie gras to *tart almandine*. The prices at CUC$30 a pop (and the rest!) are as distinctly non-Cuban as the ingredients, but with this level of service, it's probably worth it.

Biki (cnr Infanta & San Lázaro; ☉ noon-10pm, closed Mon; Ⓥ) This place near the university, on the border between Centro Habana and Vedado,

is a peso vegetarian buffet with a few meat selections thrown in. It's laid out cafetería-style; grab a tray and pick from several fresh juices and salads, veggie paella, fried rice, stuffed peppers and desserts. It all costs peanuts.

Restaurante Vegetariano Carmelo (Calzada btwn Calles D & E; ☉ noon-midnight, closed Mon; Ⓥ) This place has the same menu as Biki, but a much nicer locale opposite the Teatro Amadeo Roldán, with patio dining and a full bar.

Also recommended:

Cafetería Sofía (☎ 832-0740; Calle 23 No 202; ☉ 24hr) Late-night hair-of-the-dog seekers meet annoyingly chirpy early risers at this 24-hour institution on La Rampa.

La Casona & 17 (☎ 838-3136; Calle 17 btwn Calles M & N; ☉ 11am-10pm) Eclectic Vedado residence turned restaurant. Eat in the elegant dining room or outside at the barbecue grill.

Restaurante Wakamba (☎ 878-4526; Calle 0 btwn Calles 23 & 25; ☉ 24hr) An indoor restaurant with a 24-hour outside counter helps stifle those 3am hunger pangs.

Spanish Clubs

Havana's Spanish clubs offer some of the city's tastiest and most affordable food.

ourpick Los Nardos (Map p106; ☎ 863-2985; Paseo de Martí No 563, Centro Habana; ☉ noon-midnight) Directly opposite the Capitolio but easy to miss, Los Nardos is one of a handful of semi-private Havana restaurants operated by the Spanish Asturianas society. Touted in some quarters as one of the best eateries in the city, this unprepossessing place is decked out in mahogany and leather and serves up such astoundingly delicious dishes as lobster in a Catalan sauce, garlic prawns with sautéed vegetables and an authentic Spanish paella. Portions are huge and the prices, which start at around CUC$4 for chicken and pork dishes, are unbelievably cheap.

Los Gijones (Map p106; Paseo de Martí No 309, Centro Habana; ☉ noon-midnight) Melancholy Mozart serenades you here, causing you to weep helplessly into your *ropa vieja* (CUC$5). Dry your eyes and you'll find that you're in another Spanish mutual-aid society, this time the Centro Asturianas, whose dark mahogany dining room is frequented by a charming resident violinist.

Rancho Coquito (Map p106; ☎ 863-2985; Malecón 107 btwn Genios & Crespo, Centro Habana; ☉ 6pm-midnight) At last, a decent restaurant on the Malecón. Run by the local Spanish Asturianas society, this is an inconspicuous food joint with a balcony that overlooks Havana's dreamy 8km sea drive (look for the waiter posted outside) and is frequented mainly by Cubans. Upstairs, the food is tasty and unbelievably cheap. Paella goes for CUC$7, *garbanzos fritos* (fried chickpeas) CUC$5, tortilla CUC$3 and a decent portion of lobster pan-fried in butter for a giveaway CUC$8.

Centro Andaluz (Map p106; ☎ 863-6745; Paseo de Martí No 104 btwn Genios & Refugio, Centro Habana; ☯ 6-11pm Tue-Sun) Another Spanish social club with a restaurant, the Centro Andaluz resembles an old 19th-century Andalucian flamenco bar with a chipped wooden stage and equally chipped azulejo-tiled walls. Aside from the flamenco dancing, the center also serves reasonable meals, including a house paella for two.

Cafes

Café Santo Domingo (Map p100; Obispo No 159 btwn San Ignacio & Mercaderes, Habana Vieja; ☯ 9am-9pm) Tucked away upstairs above Habana Vieja's best bakery – and encased in one of its oldest buildings – this laid-back cafe is aromatic, tasty and light on the wallet. Check out the delicious fruit shakes, huge *sandwich especial*, or smuggle some cakes upstairs to enjoy over a steaming cup of *café con leche* (coffee with warm milk).

Café de las Infusiones (Map p100; Mercaderes btwn Obispo & Obrapía, Habana Vieja; ☯ 8am-11pm) Wedged into Calle Mercaderes, this recently restored Habaguanex coffee house is a caffeine addict's heaven; it boasts a wonderful resident pianist, too. Fancier than your average Cuban coffee bar and more comprehensive than the Escorial (see below), you can order more than a dozen different cuppas here, including Irish coffee (CUC$3.50), punch coffee (CUC$5), mocha (CUC$1), cappuccino (CUC$1.75) and so on.

Pastelería Francesa (Map p106; Parque Central No 411, Centro Habana) This cafe has all the ingredients of a Champs-Élysées classic: a great location in Parque Central, waiters in waistcoats, and myriad pastries displayed in glass cases. But the authentic French flavor is ruined somewhat by the swarming *jineteras* who roll in here with their European sugar daddies for cigarettes and strong coffee.

ourpick Café El Escorial (Map p100; ☎ 868-3545; Mercaderes No 317 cnr Muralla, Habana Vieja; ☯ 9am-9pm) Opening out onto Plaza Vieja and encased in a finely restored colonial mansion, there's something definitively European about El

Escorial. Among some of the best caffeine infusions in the city served here are *café cubano*, *café con leche*, frappé, coffee liquor and even *daiquirí de café*. There's also a sweet selection of delicate pastries.

Pain de París Vedado (Map pp102-3; Calle 25 No 164 btwn Infanta & Calle O; ☯ 8am-midnight); Vedado (Map pp102-3; Línea btwn Paseo & Calle A; ☯ 24hr) With quite possibly the best cakes in Havana – including iced cinnamon buns – this small chain does box-up cakes, cappuccinos, croissants and the odd savory snack. If you've been OD-ing on paltry Cuban desserts, or have hit a sugar low after a super-light breakfast, get your 11 o'clock pick-me-up here.

Café de O'Reilly (Map p100; O'Reilly No 203 btwn Cuba & San Ignacio, Habana Vieja; ☯ 11am-3am) Good old-fashioned 'spit and sawdust' cafe that sells drinks and snacks morning, noon and night. The bar is spread over two floors interconnected by a spiral staircase with most of the action taking place upstairs.

Café Literario del 'G' (Map pp102-3; Calle 23 btwn Av de los Presidentes & Calle H, Vedado) If Havana has a proverbial Left Bank, this is it, a laid-back student hangout full of arty wall scribblings and coffee-quaffing intellectuals discussing the merits of Guillén over Lorca. Kick back in the airy front patio among the green plants and dusty books and magazines (available to read, lend and buy), and keep an ear out for one of the regular *trova* (traditional music), jazz and poetry presentations.

ourpick Museo del Chocolate (Map p100; cnr Amargura & Mercaderes, Habana Vieja; ☯ 9am-8pm) Chocolate addicts beware, this quirky place in the heart of Habana Vieja is a lethal dose of chocolate, truffles and yet more chocolate (and it's all made on the premises). Situated – with no irony intended – in Calle Amargura (literally: Bitterness Street), the sweet-toothed establishment is more a cafe than a museum, with a small cluster of marble tables set amid a sugary mélange of chocolate paraphernalia. Not surprisingly, everything on the rather delicious menu contains one all-pervading ingredient: have it hot, cold, white, dark, rich or smooth, the stuff is divine, whichever way you choose.

Café Neruda (Map p106; Malecón No 203 btwn Manrique & San Nicolás, Centro Habana; ☯ 11am-11pm) Barbecued Chilean ox, Nerudian skewer, Chilean turnover? Poor old Pablo Neruda would be turning in his grave if this wasn't such an inviting place and a rare ray of light

FRESA Y CHOCOLATE

Aficionados of Ben & Jerry's might find it a little lacking in creaminess but, for legions of *helado* (ice cream)–starved Habaneros, the famous Coppelia in Vedado is more than just an ice-cream parlor – it's a full-on social extravaganza. Relationships have been forged here, fledgling novels drafted, birthday parties celebrated and Miami-bound escape plots hatched.

The ultimate accolade came in 1993 when Cuban film director Tomás Gutiérrez Alea shot part of his Oscar-nominated movie *Fresa y Chocolate* in the Coppelia park. Integral to the plot, the film's two central characters, David and Diego, meet for the first time over ice cream when communist student (David) suspects that the cynical artist (Diego) is gay because he chooses a strawberry flavor over the more macho chocolate.

Set in a bizarre flying saucer–shaped building on the corner of Calles 23 and L, the Coppelia is famous for its queues, which spill haphazardly onto the street and continue snaking for at least a block. As a tourist you'll probably be directed by a security guard into a smaller, Convertible-paying outdoor section, but dodge the directives. Queuing is an integral part of Coppelia folklore, an experience as traditional as the table-sharing, the cheap ice cream (you'll pay in pesos if you sit inside), the spontaneous conversation and the uncensored people-watching opportunities that abound upstairs.

First opened in 1966, the state-run Coppelia claims to be the largest ice-cream parlor in the world serving up to 30,000 customers a day. Well known for his micromanagement skills, there was a time in the '70s when it was said that the ice-cream loving Fidel chose the daily flavors himself. These days you generally get a little more choice than the standard strawberry and chocolate, though cookies and cream with a caramel twist would be stretching it.

---

on the otherwise mildewed Malecón. Spend a poetic afternoon watching the waves splash over the sea wall.

Ice-Cream Parlors

Havana has some good ice cream, available both in Convertibles and pesos. Coppelia is the national chain – if you can bear the queues. *Paleticas* are popsicles (usually chocolate-covered), while *bocaditos* are big, delicious ice-cream sandwiches (often handmade). Little mobile ice-cream machines selling the soft, whippy stuff can appear anyplace anytime. Cones are sold for a couple of pesos and melt almost before you can get them in your mouth. Here are some good parlors:

Bim Bom (Map pp102-3; ☎ 879-2892; cnr Calle 23 & Infanta, Vedado) Phenomenally creamy stuff in flavors like coffee, condensed milk (sounds gross, tastes great) and rum raisins; in Convertibles.

Coppelia (Map pp102-3; ☎ 832-6184; cnr Calle 23 & L, Vedado) The original and best. See boxed text, above.

Heladería Obispo (Map p100; Obispo No 58, Habana Vieja) Pleasant parlor in the heart of Habana Vieja; often has fruit flavors (pineapple, strawberry etc).

Takeout

There are some great peso places sprinkled about, though few have names; look for the streets. Some of the most outstanding peso pizza is at San Rafael just off Infanta (look for the lines). Av de la Italia (Galiano to anyone who lives there) also has some holes-in-the-wall. Also try around Calles H and 17 where there are clusters of peso stalls and Calle 21 between Calles 4 and 6; this area is close to the hospital, so there's great variety and long hours.

Cajitas (take-out meals in cardboard boxes) usually cost about CUC$1. Some boxes have cutout spoons on the lid, but most don't, so you'll have to supply your own fork (or use part of the box itself as a shovel). You can usually buy *cajitas* at *agropecuarios* (vegetable markets); Chinatown is known for its *cajitas*.

Cubans haven't really caught onto the idea of coffee 'to go' and you'll get baffled looks if you ask for a coffee *para llevar* (takeout).

Groceries
HABANA VIEJA

Café Santo Domingo (Obispo No 159 btwn San Ignacio & Mercaderes; ⏰ 9am-9pm) Some of the best bread and pastries can be procured at this place, downstairs underneath the cafe.

Harris Brothers (O'Reilly No 526; ⏰ 9am-9pm Mon-Sat) The best-stocked grocery store in Habana Vieja sells everything from fresh pastries to baby's nappies. It's just off Parque Central and is open until late.

HAVANA

The local farmers market is called **Agropecuario Sol** (Sol btwn Habana & Compostela).

CENTRO HABANA
Supermercado Isla de Cuba (cnr Máximo Gómez & Factoría; 🕑 10am-6pm Mon-Sat, 9am-1pm Sun) On the southern side of Parque de la Fraternidad, with yogurt, cereals, pasta etc. You have to check your bag outside, to the right of the entrance.

Almacenes Ultra (Av Simón Bolívar No 109; 🕑 9am-6pm Mon-Sat, 9am-1pm Sun) A decent supermarket in Centro Habana, at the corner of Rayo, near Av de Italia.

La Época (cnr Av de Italia & Neptuno; 🕑 9am-9pm Mon-Sat, 9am-noon Sun) A hard-currency department store with a supermarket in the basement. Check your bags outside before entering this epic Havana emporium.

For fresh produce hit the free-enterprise **Mercado Agropecuario Egido** (Av de Bélgica btwn Corrales & Apodaca).

VEDADO
Supermercado Meridiano (Galerías de Paseo, cnr Calle 1 & Paseo; 🕑 10am-5pm Mon-Fri, 10am-2pm Sun) Across the street from the Hotel Meliá Cohiba, this supermarket has a good wine and liquor selection, lots of yogurt, cheese and chips.

There are numerous *agropecuarios*:

Calles 17 & K (cnr Calles 17 & K) A 'capped' market with cheap prices, but limited selection.

Calles 19 & A (Calle 19 btwn Calles A & B) Havana's 'gourmet' market, with cauliflower, fresh herbs and rarer produce during shoulder seasons.

Calles 21 & J (cnr Calles 21 & J) Good selection, including potted plants.

Organopónico Plaza (cnr Av de Colón & Bellavista) One of Havana's biggest organic farms with a retail market.

Tulipán (Av Tulipán) This is a huge, 'capped' market, with prices set by the government, so it's cheap.

DRINKING
Habana Vieja
La Lluvia de Oro (☎ 862-9870; Obispo No 316; 🕑 24hr) It's on Obispo and there's always live music belting through the doorway – so it's always crowded. But with a higher-than-average *jinetero/jinetera* to tourist ratio, it might not be your most intimate introduction to Havana. Small snacks are available and the musicians 'hat' comes round every three songs.

La Bodeguita del Medio (☎ 86-68-87; Empedrado No 207; 🕑 11am-midnight) Made famous thanks to the rum-swilling exploits of Ernest Hemingway (who by association instantly sends the prices soaring), a visit to Havana's most celebrated bar has become de rigueur for literary sycophants and wannabe writers. Past visitors have included Salvador Allende, Fidel Castro, Nicolás Guillén, Harry Belafonte and Nat King Cole, all of whom have left their autographs on La Bodeguita's wall – along with thousands of others. These days the clientele is less luminous, with package tourists bussed in from Varadero to delight in the bottled bohemian atmosphere and the CUC$4 mojitos (which, though good, have lost their Hemingway-esque shine). The menu specialty is *comida criolla* or 'the Full Monty' Cuban-style (CUC$14).

Café París (Obispo No 202; 🕑 24hr) Jump into the mix by grabbing one of the rough-hewn tables at this Habana Vieja standby, known for its live music and gregarious atmosphere. On good nights, the rum flows, talented musicians jam and spontaneous dancing and singing erupt from the crowd.

Bar La Marina (cnr Oficios & Brasil; 🕑 10am-11pm) This pleasant outdoor courtyard with a 'ceiling' made out of twisted vines is as an agreeable Old Town nook as any. You can grab a bite to eat, feast on popcorn or just sup quietly on a mojito while the resident band strums along.

Bar Dos Hermanos (☎ 861-3436; San Pedro No 304; 🕑 24hr) Despite its erstwhile Hemingway connections, this bar has (so far) managed to remain off the standard Havana tourist itinerary. Out of the way and a little seedy, it was a favorite watering hole of Spanish poet Federico García Lorca during a three-month stopover in 1930. With its long wooden bar and salty seafaring atmosphere, it can't have changed much since.

La Dichosa (cnr Obispo & Compostela; 🕑 10am-midnight) It's hard to miss the rowdy La Dichosa on busy Calle Obispo, despite the fact that it doesn't display its name outside. Small and cramped with at least half the space given over to the resident band, this is a good place to stall for a quick drink before heading off down the road.

Café Taberna (☎ 861-1637; cnr Brasil & Mercaderes) Founded in 1772 and still glowing after a recent 21st-century makeover, this drinking and eating establishment is a great place to prop up the (impressive) bar and sink a few cocktails before dinner. The music – which gets swinging around 8pm – doffs its cap, more often than not, to one-time resident mambo king Benny Moré. Skip the food.

our pick **Taberna de la Muralla** (☎ 866-4453; cnr San Ignacio & Muralla; ☺ 11am-midnight) Havana's only homebrew pub is situated on a boisterous corner of Plaza Vieja. Set up by an Austrian company in 2004, it sells smooth cold homemade beer at sturdy wooden benches set up outside on the cobbles or indoors in an atmospheric beer hall. Get a group together and they'll serve the amber nectar in a tall plastic tube, which you draw out of a tap at the bottom. There's also an outside grill.

El Baturro (cnr Av de Bélgica & Merced; ☺ 11am-11pm) In the long tradition of drinking houses situated next to train stations, El Baturro is a rough-and-ready Spanish bistro with a long wooden bar and an all-male drinking clientele.

El Floridita (☎ 867-1300; Obispo No 557; ☺ 11am-midnight) Promoting itself as the 'cradle of the daiquirí,' El Floridita was a favorite of expat Americans long before Ernest Hemingway dropped by in the 1930s (hence the name, which means 'little Florida'). A bartender named Constante Ribalaigua invented the daiquirí soon after WWI, but it was Hemingway who popularized it and ultimately the bar christened a drink in his honor: the Papa Hemingway Special (basically, a daiquirí made with grapefruit juice). His record – legend has it – was 13 doubles in one sitting. Any attempt to equal it at the current prices (CUC$6 a single shot) will cost you a small fortune – and a huge hangover.

THE SEX TRADE

'The one thing Castro can't ration is sex,' Cuban commentators have been prone to quip, and one look around the bars and clubs of nocturnal Havana, where impossibly attractive Cuban prostitutes stroll arm in arm with ageing 'sugar daddies' from Torino or Düsseldorf, is enough to prove them correct.

It's ironic that in a state where rationing is a given and empty supermarket shelves are a wearisome part of everyday life, there usually seems to be no shortage of young, pretty *señoritas* 'available' for carnal relationships. Indeed, while technically illegal, prostitution in Cuba – which was equally rampant during the Batista era – is one of the few capitalist enterprises that the socialist government has so far failed to stamp out.

In the economic context, the situation is understandable. Contact with foreign men gives interested Cuban women access to interchangeable currency and the opportunity of bagging double a doctor's monthly salary in a week. There's even the not-so-remote possibility of spontaneous nuptials and the promise of a new and better life overseas.

For the planeloads of oversexed foreign males who fly in weekly to find out that they've been suddenly reborn as Brad Pitt, the attractions are equally libidinous. Indeed, Cuba's growing reputation as an exotic mix of sun, sand, socialism and…sex, with no strings attached, has given rise to a whole new (unofficial) sex industry based on the well-tested economic laws of supply and demand.

Not surprisingly, the 'rules of engagement' have a number of peculiarly Cuban characteristics. Unlike in other financially disadvantaged countries in the developing world, Cuban prostitutes – or *jineteras* as they are popularly known – are not part of any highly organized network of pimps. Furthermore, Cuba is not a society where sex is sold to fuel a drug habit or procure the next square meal. On the contrary, many of these illicit rendezvous are innocuous and open-ended couplings perpetuated by young girls looking for friendship, blind opportunity or a free pass into some of Havana's best nightclubs.

Despite the island's generally lax attitude to sexual promiscuity, clampdowns in the sex trade can and do occur. The all-inclusive resort areas are particularly prone to police attention. In 1996 the authorities rounded up legions of prostitutes in Varadero and placed a barring order on the resort's paladares and casas particulares. As a result, tourism in the resort noticeably blipped.

Until recently, the problems associated with the sex trade also served to reinforce Cuba's rather unpleasant system of tourist 'apartheid.' Nearly all of the island's tourist-class hotels used to bar access to their rooms to *all* Cuban guests on the pretext that some of them might be *jineteras*. Raúl Castro reversed this policy soon after taking office in 2008 and, as yet (to the surprise of some), there has been no radical increase in sex tourism in Cuba's tourist hotels.

Alternatively, hit the **Monserrate Bar** (☎ 860-9751; Obrapía No 410) a couple of doors down, where daiquirís are half the price due to the fact that Hemingway never drank here.

Centro Habana

Prado No 12 (Paseo de Martí No 12; ☽ noon-11pm) A slim flat-iron building on the corner of Prado and San Lázaro that serves drinks and simple snacks, Prado 12 still resembles Havana in a 1950s time-warp. Soak up the serendipitous atmosphere of this amazing city here after a sunset stroll along the Malecón.

Prado & Animas (Paseo de Martí cnr Ánimas No 12; ☽ 9am-9pm) Another good old-fashioned Prado place with a time-warped '50s feel. The cafe also serves simple food and coffee but it's best for a beer, sitting at one of the window tables beneath the baseball memorabilia (including a picture of a *pelota*-playing Fidel).

Vedado

ourpick **Café Fresa y Chocolate** (Calle 23 btwn Calles 10 & 12; ☽ 9am-11pm) No ice cream here, just movie memorabilia. This is the HQ of the Cuban Film Institute and a nexus for coffee-quaffing students and art-house movie addicts. You can debate the merits of Almodóvar over Scorcese on the pleasant patio before disappearing next door for a film preview.

Bar-Club Imágenes (☎ 833-3606; Calzada No 602; ☽ 9pm-5am) This upscale piano bar attracts something of an older crowd with its regular diet of boleros (ballads) and *trova*, though there are sometimes comedy shows; check the schedule posted outside. Affordable meals are available (minimum CUC$5).

ENTERTAINMENT
Folk & Traditional Music

Casa de la Amistad (Map pp102-3; ☎ 830-3114; Paseo No 416 btwn Calles 17 & 19, Vedado) Housed in a beautiful rose-colored mansion on leafy Paseo, the Casa de la Amistad mixes traditional *son* sounds with suave Benny Moré music in a classic Italian Renaissance–style garden. Buena Vista Social Club luminary, Compay Segundo, was a regular here before his death in 2003 and there is a weekly 'Chan Chan' night in his honor. Other perks include a restaurant, bar, cigar shop and the house itself – an Italianite masterpiece.

El Hurón Azul (Map pp102-3; ☎ 832-4551; cnr Calles 17 & H, Vedado) If you want to rub shoulders with some socialist celebrities, hang out with the intellectuals at Hurón Azul, the social club of the Unión Nacional de Escritores y Artistas de Cuba (Uneac; Union of Cuban Writers and Artists), Cuba's leading cultural institution. Replete with priceless snippets of Cuba's under-the-radar cultural life, most performances take place outside in the garden. Wednesday is the Afro-Cuban rumba, Saturday is authentic Cuban boleros, and alternate Thursdays there's jazz and *trova*. You'll never pay more than CUC$5.

El Gato Tuerto (Map pp102-3; ☎ 836-0212; Calle 0 No 14 btwn Calles 17 & 19, Vedado; drink minimum CUC$5; ☽ noon-6am) Once the HQ of Havana's alternative artistic and sexual scene, the 'one-eyed cat' (as Gato Tuerto translates into English) is now a nexus for karaoke-crazy baby-boomers who come here to knock out rum-fuelled renditions of traditional Cuban boleros (ballads). Hidden in a quirky two-story house just off the Malecón, with turtles swimming in a front pool, the upper floor is taken up by a restaurant while down below late-night revelers raise the roof in a chic nightclub.

ourpick **Conjunto Folklórico Nacional de Cuba** (Map pp102-3; Calle 4 No 103 btwn Calzada & Calle 5, Vedado; admission CUC$5; ☽ 3pm Sat) Founded in 1962, this high-energy ensemble specializes in Afro-Cuban dancing (all of the drummers are Santería priests). See them perform, and dance along during the regular Sábado de Rumba at El Gran Palenque. This group also performs at Teatro Mella (p145). A major festival called FolkCuba unfolds here biannually during the second half of January.

Callejón de Hamel (Map pp102-3; Vedado; ☽ from noon Sun) Aside from its funky street murals and psychedelic art shops, the main reason to come to Havana's high temple of Afro-Cuban culture is for the frenetic rumba music that kicks off every Sunday at around noon. For aficionados, this is about as raw and hypnotic as it gets, with interlocking drum patterns and lengthy rhythmic chants powerful enough to summon up the spirit of the *orishas* (Santería deities). Due to a liberal sprinkling of tourists these days, some argue that the Callejón has lost much of its basic charm. Don't believe them. This place can still deliver.

Jazz

Jazz Club La Zorra y El Cuervo (Map pp102-3; ☎ 833-2402; cnr Calles 23 & 0, Vedado; admission CUC$5-10; ☽ 10pm) Havana's most famous Jazz Club is La Zorra y El Cuervo (the vixen and the crow) on La Rampa, which opens its doors nightly at 10pm to long lines of committed music fiends. Suitably shoehorned into a cramped, smoky basement, the freestyle jazz showcased is second to none and, in the past, the club has hosted such big names as Chucho Valdés and George Benson.

Jazz Café (Map pp102-3; top fl, Galerías de Paseo, cnr Calle 1 & Paseo, Vedado; drink minimum CUC$10; noon-late) This upscale joint located improbably in a shopping mall overlooking the Malecón is a kind of jazz supper club, with dinner tables and a decent menu. At night, the club swings into action with live jazz, *timba* and, occasionally, straight-up salsa. It attracts plenty of big-name acts.

Rock, Reggae & Rap

Patio de María (Map pp102-3; Calle 37 No 262 btwn Paseo & Calle 2, Vedado; admission 5 pesos) Rather unique in Cuba for a number of reasons, the Patio de María, near the Teatro Nacional de Cuba, is a nexus point for Havana's burgeoning counterculture hosting everything from rock music to poetry readings. Run by María Gattorno, the venue has received heavy media coverage in Cuba and abroad, partly due to Gattorno's AIDS and drug-prevention educational work. You can catch all kinds of entertainment here from videos and debates to workshops and theater, but the real deal are the rock nights (to canned music) that take off most weekends. Check the *cartelera* posted at the door or head to Parque de los Rockeros (Calles 23 and G) to find out what's happening.

La Madriguera (Map pp102-3; 879-8175; cnr Salvador Allende & Luaces; admission 5-10 pesos) Locals bill it as a 'hidden place for open ideas,' while outsiders are bowled over by its musical originality and artistic innovation. Welcome to La Madriguera – home to the Hermanos Saíz organization, the youth wing of Uneac. This is where the pulse of Cuba's young musical innovators beats the strongest. Come here for arts, crafts, spontaneity and the three Rs: *reggaetón* (Cuban hip-hop), rap and rumba.

Dance Clubs

Havana's dance clubs range from suave lounges to wall-vibrating hotel discos that continue well into the small hours. Alternatively you can uncover a more local *caliente* (hot) scene and mingle congenially with Cubans as they dance energetically to *timba*, salsa/jazz, *reggaetón* and rap.

CENTRO HABANA

El Palermo (861-9745; cnr San Miguel & Amistad; admission CUC$2; from 11pm Thu-Sun) A hole in the wall with a heavy rap scene. Fun but *fuerte* (intense).

VEDADO

Cabaret Las Vegas (870-7939; Infanta No 104 btwn Calles 25 & 27; admission CUC$5; 10pm-4am) Don't get duped into thinking this is another Tropicana. On the contrary, Cabaret Las Vegas is a rough and seedy local music dive (with a midnight show) where a little rum and a lot of *No moleste, por favor* will help you withstand the overzealous entreaties of the hordes of haranguing *jineteras*.

Salón Chévere (Parque Almendares, cnr Calles 49C & 28A; admission CUC$6-10; from 10pm) One of Havana's most popular discos, this alfresco place in a lush park setting hosts a good mix of locals and tourists.

Pico Blanco (833-3740; Calle O btwn Calles 23 & 25; admission CUC$5-10; 9pm) An insanely popular nightclub, the Pico Blanco is situated on the 14th floor of the Hotel St John's in Vedado and kicks off nightly at 9pm. The program can be hit or miss. Some nights it's karaoke and cheesy boleros, another it's jamming with some rather famous Cuban musicians.

Café Cantante (879-0710; cnr Paseo & Calle 39; admission CUC$10; 9pm-5am Tue-Sat) Below the Teatro Nacional de Cuba (side entrance), this place is a hip disco that offers live salsa music and dancing, as well as bar snacks and food. The clientele is mainly 'yummies' (young urban Marxist managers) and ageing sugar-daddy tourists with their youthful Cuban girlfriends. And the Café tends to get feistier than the adjacent Piano Bar Delirio Habanero (p144). Musically, there are regular appearances from big-name singers such as Haila María Mompie. No shorts, T-shirts or hats may be worn, and no under-18-year-olds are allowed.

Vedado has a few mixed peso-Convertible discos that are great fun (especially if your budget has blown out), including **Club La Red** (832-5415; cnr Calles 19 & L; admission CUC$3-5) and the ferociously *caliente* **Karachi Club** (832-3485; cnr Calles 17 & K; admission CUC$3-5; 10pm-5am). To the west are **Discoteca Amanecer** (832-9075; Calle 15 No 12 btwn Calles N & O; admission CUC$3-5; 10pm-4am) and **Club Tropical** (832-7361; cnr Línea & Calle F; 9pm-2am). As with all clubs, late-night Friday and Saturday are best.

HAVANA

GAY HAVANA

The Revolution had a rather ambiguous attitude toward homosexuality in its early days. While the Stonewall riots were engulfing New York City, Cuban homosexuals were still being sent to re-education camps by a government that was dominated by macho, bearded ex-guerillas dressed in military fatigues.

But, since the 1990s, the tide has been turning, spearheaded somewhat ironically by Fidel's combative niece Mariela (the daughter of current president, Raúl Castro), the director of the Cuban National Center for Sex Education in Havana.

An important door was opened in 1993 with the release of the Oscar-nominated film *Fresa y Chocolate*, a tale of homosexual love between a young communist student and a skeptical Havana artist. A decade later, gay characters hit the headlines again in a popular government-sponsored Cuban soap opera called *La Cara Oculta de la Luna* (The Dark Side of the Moon).

The unprecedented happened in June 2008 when the Cuban government passed a law permitting free sex-change operations to qualifying citizens courtesy of the country's famously far-sighted health system.

Though Cuba still has no 'official' gay clubs, there are plenty of places where a 'gay scene' has taken root. Havana is the obvious nexus, with the busy junction of Calles 23 and L in Vedado outside the Cine Yara serving as the main nighttime cruising spot. Other meeting places include the Malecón below the Hotel Nacional and the beach at Boca Ciega in Playas del Este.

Hang around at these places in the evening to get word of spontaneous gay parties in private houses, or bigger shindigs in venues such as Parque Lenin. You can now also enjoy gay film nights at the Icaic headquarters (Centro Cultural Cinematográfico; see boxed text, p146) on the corner of Calles 23 and 12.

Nightclubs

Piano Bar Delirio Habanero (Map pp102-3; ☎ 873-5713; cnr Paseo & Calle 39, Vedado; admission CUC$5; ☾ from 6pm Tue-Sun) This suave lounge upstairs in the Teatro Nacional de Cuba hosts everything from young *trovadores* to smooth, improvised jazz. The deep red couches abut a wall of glass overlooking the Plaza de la Revolución, and it's stunning at night with the Martí Memorial alluringly backlit. Escape here when the adjoining Café Cantante nightclub gets too hot.

Habana Café (Map pp102-3; ☎ 833-3636; Paseo btwn Calles 1 & 3, Vedado; admission CUC$10; ☾ from 9:30pm) A hip and trendy nightclub cum cabaret show at the Hotel Meliá Cohiba laid out in 1950s American retro style. After 1am the tables are cleared and the place rocks to 'international music' until the cock crows.

La Casa de la Música Centro Habana (Map p106; ☎ 862-4165; Av de Italia btwn Concordia & Neptuno, Centro Habana; admission CUC$5-25) One of Cuba's best and most popular (check the queues) nightclubs and live-music venues; all the big names play here, from Bamboleo to Los Van Van – and you'll pay peanuts to see them. Of the city's two Casas de la Música, this Centro Habana version is a little edgier than its Miramar counterpart (some have complained it's too edgy), with big salsa bands and little space. Price varies depending on the band.

Cabaret

Cabaret Nacional (Map p106; ☎ 863-2361; San Rafael No 208, Centro Habana; per couple CUC$10; ☾ 9pm-2am) Barely noticeable below the Gran Teatro de La Habana across from Parque Central, this subterranean dance cellar has a show nightly at 11:30pm if enough patrons are present. It's a little camper than other Havana cabarets and the noise – rather annoyingly if you're watching the opera – sometimes filters through into the Lorca auditorium next door. There's a couples-only policy and a 'no shorts/T-shirts' dress code.

Cabaret Turquino (Map pp102-3; Calle L btwn Calles 23 & 25, Vedado; admission CUC$15; ☾ from 10pm) Spectacular shows in a spectacular setting on the 25th floor of the Hotel Habana Libre.

Cabaret Parisién (Map pp102-3; ☎ 836-3564; cnr Calles 23 & O, Vedado; admission CUC$35; ☾ 9pm) One rung down from the Tropicana, in both price and quality, but this nightly cabaret show in the Hotel Nacional is well worth a look, especially if you're staying in or around Vedado. It's the usual mix of frills, feathers and semi-naked women, but the choreography is first class and the whole spectacle has excellent kitsch value.

Copa Room (Map pp102-3; ☎ 836-4051; cnr Paseo & Malecón, Vedado; admission CUC$20; ⏱ 9pm) Doormen in tuxes and an atmosphere that's pure 1950s kitsch make the refurbished Copa Room in Meyer Lansky's Hotel Riviera look like a nostalgic walk through *The Godfather II*.

Theater

With a well-entrenched and influential arts movement, Havana boasts a theater scene unmatched elsewhere in the Caribbean (and possibly Latin America), even if the auditoriums themselves may sometimes look a little run down.

CENTRO HABANA

our pick **Gran Teatro de La Habana** (☎ 861-3077; cnr Paseo de Martí & San Rafael; per person CUC$20; ⏱ box office 9am-6pm Mon-Sat, to 3pm Sun) The amazing neobaroque theater across from Parque Central is the seat of the acclaimed Ballet Nacional de Cuba, founded in 1948 by Alicia Alonso. It is also the home of the Cuban National Opera. A theater since 1838, the building contains the grandiose Teatro García Lorca along with two smaller concert halls, the Sala Alejo Carpentier and the Sala Ernesto Lecuono – where art films are sometimes shown. For upcoming events enquire at the ticket office. Backstage tours of the theater leave throughout the day (CUC$2).

Teatro Fausto (☎ 863-1173; Paseo de Martí No 201) An eye-catching art-deco theater on Prado, rightly renowned for its sidesplitting comedy shows.

Teatro América (☎ 862-5695; Av de Italia No 253 btwn Concordia & Neptuno) Housed in a classic art-deco *rascacielo* (skyscraper) on Galiano (Av de Italia), the América seems to have changed little since its theatrical heyday in the 1930s and '40s. It plays host to vaudeville variety, comedy, dance, jazz and salsa; shows are normally staged on Saturdays at 8:30pm and Sundays at 5pm. You can also enquire about dance lessons here (p125).

VEDADO

Teatro Nacional de Cuba (☎ 879-6011; cnr Paseo & Calle 39; per person CUC$10; ⏱ box office 9am-5pm & before performances) One of the twin pillars of Havana's cultural life, the Teatro Nacional de Cuba on Plaza de la Revolución is the modern rival to the Gran Teatro in Centro Habana. Built in

the 1950s as part of Jean Forestier's grand city expansion, the complex hosts landmark concerts, foreign theater troupes, La Colmenita children's company and the Ballet Nacional de Cuba. The main hall, Sala Avellaneda, stages big events such as musical concerts or plays by Shakespeare, while the smaller Sala Covarrubias along the back side puts on a more daring program (the seating capacity of the two *salas* combined is 3300). The 9th floor is a rehearsal and performance space where the newest, most experimental stuff happens. The ticket office is at the far end of a separate single-story building beside the main theater.

Teatro Mella (☎ 833-5651; Línea No 657 btwn Calles A & B) Occupying the site of the old Rodi Cinema on Línea, the Teatro Mella offers one of Havana's most comprehensive programs, including an International Ballet Festival, comedy shows, theater, dance and intermittent performances from the famous Conjunto Folklórico Nacional. If you have kids, come to the children's show Sunday at 11am.

Sala Teatro Hubert de Blanck (☎ 833-5962; Calzada No 657 btwn Calles A & B) This theater is named for the founder of Havana's first conservatory of music (1885). The Teatro Estudio based here is Cuba's leading theater company. You can usually see plays in Spanish on Saturday at 8:30pm and on Sunday at 7pm. Tickets are sold just prior to the performance.

Teatro Nacional de Guiñol (☎ 832-6262; Calle M btwn Calles 17 & 19) This venue has quality puppet shows and children's theater.

If you understand Spanish, it's well worth attending some of the cutting-edge contemporary theater that's a staple of Grupo Teatro Rita Montaner in the **Sala Teatro El Sótano** (☎ 832-0833; Calle K No 514 btwn Calles 25 & 27; ⏱ 5-8:30pm Fri & Sat, 3-5pm Sun), not far from the Habana Libre. Performances are Friday and Saturday at 8:30pm and Sunday at 5pm. Also check **Café Teatro Brecht** (cnr Calles 13 & I), where varied performances take place (tickets go on sale one hour before the performance).

Classical Music

Teatro Amadeo Roldán (Map pp102-3; ☎ 832-1168; cnr Calzada & Calle D, Vedado; per person CUC$10) Constructed in 1922 and burnt down by an arsonist in 1977, this wonderfully decorative neoclassical theater was rebuilt in 1999 in the exact style of the original. Named after the famous Cuban composer and the man responsible for bringing Afro-Cuban influences into modern classical music, the theater is one of Havana's grandest boasting two different auditoriums. The Orquesta Sinfónica Nacional play in the 886-seat Sala Amadeo Roldán, while soloists and small groups are showcased in the 276-seat Sala García Caturla.

Basílica Menor de San Francisco de Asís (Map p100; Plaza de San Francisco de Asís, Habana Vieja; tickets CUC$3-8; ☺ from 6pm Thu-Sat) Plaza de San Francisco de Asís' glorious church, which dates from 1738, has been reincarnated as a 21st-century museum and concert hall. The old nave hosts choral and chamber music two to three times a week (check the schedule at the door) and the acoustics inside are excellent. It's best to bag your ticket at least a day in advance.

Cinemas

There are about 200 cinemas in Havana. Most have several screenings daily and every theater posts the *Cartelera Icaic*, which lists show times for the entire city. Tickets are usually CUC$2; queue early. Hundreds of movies are screened throughout Havana during the Festival Internacional del Nuevo Cine Latinoamericano in late November/early December. Schedules are published daily in the *Diario del Festival*, available in the morning at big theaters and the Hotel Nacional. Here's a list of the best movie houses:

Cine 23 & 12 (Map pp102-3; ☎ 833-6906; Calle 23 btwn Calles 12 & 14, Vedado) One of a clutch of well-maintained cinemas on Icaic's Vedado movie strip.

Cine Actualidades (Map p106; ☎ 861-5193; Av de Bélgica No 262 btwn Neptuno & Virtudes, Centro Habana) Timeworn place centrally located behind the Hotel Plaza.

Cine Charles Chaplin (Map pp102-3; ☎ 831-1101; Calle 23 No 1157 btwn Calles 10 & 12, Vedado) An arthouse

cinema adjacent to the Icaic HQ. Don't miss the poster gallery of great Cuban classic films next door or the movie grapevine that is the Café Fresa y Chocolate opposite.

Cine La Rampa (Map pp102-3; ☎ 878-6146; Calle 23 No 111, Vedado) De Niro seasons, French classics, film festivals; catch them all at this Vedado staple that houses the Cuban film archive.

Cine Payret (Map p106; ☎ 863-3163; Paseo de Martí No 505, Centro Habana) Opposite the Capitolio, this is Centro Habana's largest and most luxurious cinema, erected in 1878. Plenty of American movies play here.

Cine Riviera (Map pp102-3; ☎ 830-9564; Calle 23 No 507 btwn Calles G & H, Vedado) Big pop, rock and sometimes rap concerts happen here. The movies are a myriad of Latin American, European and North American, and the audience has a strong student demographic.

Cine Trianón (Map pp102-3; ☎ 830-4698; Línea No 706, Vedado) Movies or live theater in a salubrious setting.

Cine Yara (Map pp102-3; ☎ 832-9430; cnr Calles 23 & L, Vedado) One big screen and two video *salas* (cinemas) here at Havana's most famous cinema and the venue for many a hot date.

Cinecito (Map p106; ☎ 863-8051; San Rafael No 68, Centro Habana) Films for kids behind the Hotel Inglaterra. There's another one next to Cine Chaplin on Calles 23 & 12.

Sport

Estadio Latinoamericano (Map pp102-3; ☎ 870-6526; Zequiera No 312, Vedado) From October to April, this 58,000-seat baseball stadium in Cerro is home to Los Industriales and Los Metropolitanos (they alternate home fixtures). Entry costs a few pesos (but they like to charge foreigners CUC$1). Games are 7:30pm Tuesday, Wednesday and Thursday, 1:30pm Saturday and Sunday. The benches are cement – painful after nine innings.

Ciudad Deportiva (Map pp102-3; cnr Av de la Independencia & Vía Blanca, Vedado; admission 5 pesos)

AND NOW FOR SOMETHING COMPLETELY DIFFERENT

To see a different side of Havana, hang out with the arty crowd at the **Centro Cultural Cinematográfico** (Map pp102-3; Calle 23 btwn Calles 10 & 12) in Vedado, a hive of talented creativity and youthful energy. The HQ of the Instituto Cubano del Arte e Industria Cinematográficos (Icaic), the center hosts film premieres, discussion nights, art expos, live music and is home to Havana's best DVD movie outlet. The adjacent Café Fresa y Chocolate (p142) is a great place to get acquainted with the Icaic's movers and shakers, especially on Wednesday nights when there's an excellent live clarinet quartet. The most enlightening shows are the interactive debate nights known as El Último Jueves de Cada Mes (The Last Thursday of Each Month) for when they're held. Hosted by a small panel of academics, intellectuals and experts from the arts magazine *Temas*, respectful but enthusiastic public audiences discuss everything from politics to TV soap operas. It's a fascinating insight into the parameters of public debate in a supposedly totalitarian society. Admission is free and the debates are in Spanish.

KNOW YOUR BASEBALL

To discover the true essence of a country – any country – you first have to understand its sporting rituals, and in Cuba that means baseball.

The Cuban National Series (Serie Nacional de Béisbol), the country's premier baseball tournament, has run in its present format since 1993 when the competition was reorganized into 16 teams: one from each province (including the special municipality of Isla de la Juventud) plus two teams from the city of Havana – Los Industriales and Los Metropolitanos.

Split regionally into four groups of four, the teams play each other over the course of a 90-game season that runs from November to March and culminates in an eight-team play-off to decide top honors.

Historically, Havana's Industriales – known colloquially as Los Leones Azules (Blue Lions) – have the best series record with 11 titles to their name as of 2008. Emulating the New York Yankees – or soccer's Manchester United – they are Cuba's 'glory' team, retaining fans all over the country, but also attracting an equally vociferous contingent of naysayers who'd pay to see them lose.

In the face of weak local opposition (Havana's other team, the Metropolitanos, are perennial underachievers), the Industriales' traditional rivals are the combative Avispas (Wasps) from Santiago de Cuba, who they meet six times a season to replay a grudge match that has been going on ever since Havana stole the mantle of Cuban capital in 1607.

The Havana-Santiago domination was interrupted briefly in the 1990s by strong teams from Villa Clara (who won a hat trick of titles between 1993 and 1995), and Pinar del Río (who logged two straight wins in 1997 and 1998). The biggest surprise in recent years, however, was when a journeyman team from Holguín appeared out of nowhere to steal Cuba's baseball crown in 2002.

'Sport City' is Cuba's premier sports training center and big basketball, volleyball, boxing and track contests happen at the coliseum here. The P-2 metro bus from Línea & Av de los Presidentes (Calle G) stops across the street.

Sala Polivalente Ramón Fonst (Map pp102-3; ☎ 881-4196; Av de la Independencia, Vedado; admission 1 peso) Basketball and volleyball games are held at this tatty-looking stadium opposite the main bus station.

For boxing, try **Kid Chocolate** (Map p106; ☎ 861-1546; Paseo de Martí, Centro Habana), directly opposite the Capitolio, which usually hosts matches on Friday at 7pm, or **Gimnasio de Boxeo Rafael Trejo** (Map p100; ☎ 862-0266; Cuba No 815 btwn Merced & Leonor Pérez, Habana Vieja). Here you can see matches on Friday at 7pm (CUC$1) or drop by any day after 4pm to watch the training. Travelers interested in boxing can find a trainer here. Enquire within; they're very friendly.

Havana, with its spectacular Malecón sea drive, boasts one of the world's most scenic municipal jogging routes. The sidewalk from the Castillo de San Salvador de la Punta to the outer borders of Miramar measures 8km, though you can add on a few extra meters for holes in the pavement, splashing waves, veering *jineteros* and old men with fishing lines.

The recent upsurge in fume-belching traffic has meant that the air along the Malecón has become increasingly polluted. If you can handle it, run first thing in the morning.

SHOPPING
Art Galleries

The art scene in Havana is cutting edge and ever changing, and collectors, browsers and admirers will find many galleries in which to while away hours. The following list is just a pinprick; there are at least a dozen studios in Calle Obispo alone. For gallery events, look for the free *Arte en La Habana*, a triquarterly listings flyer (the San Cristóbal agency on Plaza de San Francisco de Asís usually has them; see p108).

HABANA VIEJA

Casa de Carmen Montilla (☎ 866-8768; Oficios No 164; ◷ 10:30am-5:30pm Tue-Sat, 9am-1pm Sun) An important art gallery named after a celebrated Venezuelan painter who maintained a studio here until her death in 2004. Spread across three floors, the house exhibits the work of Montilla and other popular Cuban and Venezuelan artists. The rear courtyard features a huge ceramic mural by Alfredo Sosabravo.

Estudio Galería Los Oficios (☎ 863-0497; Oficios No 166; ◷ 10am-5:30pm Mon-Sat) Pop into this gallery to see the large, hectic but intriguing canvasses by Nelson Domínguez, whose workshop is upstairs.

Taller de Serigrafía René Portocarrero (☎ 862-3276; Cuba No 513 btwn Brasil & Muralla; ☽ 9am-4pm Mon-Fri) Paintings and prints by young Cuban artists are exhibited and sold here (from CUC$30 to CUC$150). You can also see the artists at work.

CENTRO HABANA

Galería La Acacia (☎ 861-3533; San Martín No 114 btwn Industria & Consulado; ☽ 10am-3:30pm Mon-Fri, 10am-1pm Sat) This important gallery behind the Gran Teatro de La Habana has paintings by leading artists like Zaida del Río, plus antiques. Export permits are arranged.

VEDADO

Sevando Galería del Arte (☎ 833-9399; cnr Calles 23 & 10; ☽ 9am-6pm Tue-Sat) This cool gallery next to the Cine Chaplín and opposite the Icaic headquarters is in an arty part of town and displays some interesting modern paintings and prints. Be sure to check out the Cuban movie-poster gallery on the other side of the cinema (two doors away).

Galería Habana (☎ 832-7101; Línea No 460 btwn Calles E & F; ☽ 10am-5pm Mon-Sat) This wonderful space in the heart of Vedado shows contemporary Cuban art in big, bright galleries. Come here to see what's new and different.

Galería de Arte Latinoamericano (cnr Calles 3 & G; admission CUC$2; ☽ 10am-4:30pm Tue-Sat, 9am-1pm Sun) Situated inside the Casa de las Américas and featuring art from all over Latin America.

Other galleries worth a peek in Vedado are the **Centro de Arte 23 & 12** (cnr Calles 12 & 23; ☽ 10am-5pm Tue-Sat) for contemporary Cuban art and the gallery at **Uneac** (cnr Calles 17 & H).

Shops & Markets

For photo services and camera needs, try outlets in the Hotel Habana Libre and the Hotel Nacional. There's also the Galerías de Paseo (opposite).

HABANA VIEJA

Calle Mercaderes has some fantastic old stores restored by the City Historian's office.

Habana 1791 (☎ 861-3525; Mercaderes No 156 btwn Obrapía & Lamparilla) A specialist shop that sells perfume made from tropical flowers, Havana 1791 retains the air of a working museum. Floral fragrances are mixed by hand and you can see the petals drying in a laboratory out the back.

Palacio de la Artesanía (Cuba No 64; ☽ 9am-7pm) A former 18th-century colonial palace turned into a shopping mall – the Americans could learn from this! Gathered around a shaded central patio is one-stop shopping for souvenirs, cigars, crafts, musical instruments, CDs, clothing and jewelry at fixed prices. Join the gaggles of tour-bus escapees and fill your bag.

Feria de la Artesanía (Tacón btwn Tejadillo & Chacón; ☽ Wed-Sat) Havana's best open-air handicraft market sells all kinds of interesting souvenirs – paintings, *guayabera* shirts, woodwork, leather items, jewelry and numerous apparitions of the highly marketable El Che. If you thought communism had put an end to the fine art of business negotiation, try out your haggling skills with the amiable stall holders here. If you buy paintings, make sure you arrange an export license (see p463).

Longina Música (☎ 862-8371; Obispo No 360 btwn Habana & Compostela; ☽ 10am-7pm Mon-Sat, 10am-1pm Sun) This place on the pedestrian mall has a good selection of CDs, plus musical instruments such as bongos, guitars, maracas, guiros and *tumbadoras* (conga drums). It often places loudspeakers in the street outside to grab the attention of passing tourists.

For rum check out the **Fundación Havana Club shop** (San Pedro No 262; ☽ 9am-9pm); for cigars try the **Casa del Habano** (Mercaderes No 120) in the Museo de Tabaco.

CENTRO HABANA

El Bulevar (San Rafael btwn Paseo de Martí & Av de Italia) This is the pedestrianized part of Calle San Rafael just behind the Hotel Inglaterra. Come here for peso snacks and surprises and 1950s shopping nostalgia.

La Manzana de Gómez (cnr Agramonte & San Rafael) This faded but elegant European-style covered shopping arcade built in 1910 is full of shabby, half-empty stores. Opposite the Plaza hotel is El Orbe bike rentals.

Area de Vendedores por Cuenta Propia (Máximo Gómez No 259; ☽ 9am-5pm Mon-Sat) This is a permanent flea market where you can pick up Santería beads, old books, leather belts etc.

VEDADO

La Habana Sí (cnr Calles 23 & L; ☽ 10am-10pm Mon-Sat, 10am-7pm Sun) This shop opposite the Hotel

Habana Libre has a good selection of CDs, cassettes, books, crafts and postcards.

Feria de la Artesanía (Malecón btwn Calles D & E; ✹ from 10:30am, closed Wed) This artisan market has much of the same as its Habana Vieja counterpart, with a few handmade shoes and sandals, and some old stamps and coins thrown in for good measure.

ARTex (☎ 832-9430; cnr Calles 23 & L) A fabulous selection of old movie posters, antique postcards, T-shirts and, of course, all the greatest Cuban films on videotape are sold at this shop inside the cinema.

Galerías de Paseo (cnr Calle 1 & Paseo; ✹ 9am-6pm Mon-Sat, 9am-1pm Sun) Across the street from the Hotel Meliá Cohiba, this place is a surprisingly upscale shopping center with Adidas and Chanel labels and even a car dealership. It sells designer clothes and other consumer items to tourists and affluent Cubans.

Plaza Carlos III (Av Salvador Allende btwn Arbol Seco & Retiro; ✹ 10am-6pm Mon-Sat) After Plaza América in Varadero, this is probably Cuba's flashiest shopping mall – and there's barely a foreigner in sight. Step in on a Saturday and see the double economy working at a feverish pitch.

GETTING THERE & AWAY

Air

Cubana Airlines (Map pp102-3; ☎ 834-4446; Calle 23 No 64 cnr Infanta, Vedado; ✹ 8:30am-4pm Mon-Fri, 8:30am-noon Sat) has its head office at the Malecón end of the Airline Building on La Rampa. You can buy international or domestic tickets here. If it's packed, try the helpful **Sol y Son** (Map pp102-3; ☎ 833-3647; fax 33-51-50; Calle 23 No 64 btwn Calle P & Infanta, Vedado; ✹ 8:30am-6pm Mon-Fri, 8:30am-noon Sat) travel agency a few doors down.

Aerocaribbean (Map pp102-3; ☎ 832-7584; Airline Bldg, Calle 23 No 64, Vedado) is another airline with domestic services.

Boat

Buses connecting with the hydrofoil service to Isla de la Juventud leave at 9am from the **Terminal de Ómnibus** (Map pp102-3; ☎ 878-1841; cnr Av de la Independencia & 19 de Mayo, Vedado), near the Plaza de la Revolución, but they're often late. You'll be told to arrive at least an hour before the bus to buy your ticket and it's best to take heed of this advice. Bus/boat combo tickets are sold at the kiosk marked 'NCC' between gates 9 and 10 and we found the staff quite unhelpful. Tickets cost CUC$55. Bring your passport.

Bus

Víazul (off Map pp2-3; ☎ 881-1413, 881-5652; www .viazul.com; cnr Calle 26 & Zoológico, Nuevo Vedado) covers most destinations of interest to travelers, in deluxe, air-conditioned coaches. All buses are direct except those to Guantánamo and Baracoa; for these destinations you must change in Santiago de Cuba. You can board all Víazul buses at the inconveniently located terminal 3km southwest of Plaza de la Revolución, or at the Terminal de Ómnibus. Here tickets for Víazul services are sold immediately prior to departure in the Venta de Boletines office. You can get full schedules on the website or at **Infotur** (Map p100; Obispo btwn Bernaza & Villegas, Habana Vieja), which also sells tickets requiring you to board at its originating station in Nuevo Vedado.

Havana-bound, you can usually get off the Víazul bus from Varadero/Matanzas in Centro Habana right after the tunnel (check with the driver beforehand), but if you arrive from most other points you'll be let out at the Nuevo Vedado terminal. From here city bus 27 will take you to Vedado or Centro Habana (ask). Alternatively a taxi will cost you a rip-off CUC$10 – unless you negotiate extra hard. Otherwise, if your bus stops at the Terminal de Ómnibus on Av de la Independencia, jump off there.

The 8am, 10am and 12pm buses to Varadero stop at Varadero airport. The 8am service also makes a scheduled stop at the Infotur office in Guanabo, Playas del Este. The two daily Viñales buses are scheduled to stop at Las Terrazas (at the Rancho Curujey). The 9:30am Santiago de Cuba bus stops at Entronque de Jagüey on the Autopista, as do the 8:15am and 1pm buses to Trinidad. The 8:15am Trinidad bus takes a different route from Jagüey via Playa Girón. It can drop you off (on request) at Playa Larga.

Buses to points in the Havana province leave from Apodaca No 53, off Agramonte, near the main train station in Habana Vieja. They go to Güines, Jaruco, Madruga, Nueva Paz, San José, San Nicolás and Santa Cruz del Norte, but expect large crowds and come early to get a peso ticket.

Taxi

Small Lada taxis, operated by Cubataxi, park on Calle 19 de Mayo beside the Terminal de Ómnibus. They charge approximately CUC$0.50 per kilometer. This translates as

VÍAZUL BUS TIMETABLE

Destination	Cost (CUC$)	Duration	Departure time
Bayamo	44	12hr 50min	9:30am, 3pm, 10pm
Camagüey	33	9hr	8:40am, 9:30am, 3pm, 6:15pm, 8:30pm, 10pm
Ciego de Ávila	27	7hr	8:40am, 9:30am, 3pm, 8:30pm, 10pm
Cienfuegos	20	4hr	8:15am, 1pm
Holguín	44	12hr 10min	8:40am, 3pm, 8:30pm
Las Tunas	39	11hr 30min	8:40am, 9:30am, 3pm, 8:30pm, 10pm
Matanzas	7	2hr	8am, 10am, 12pm, 6pm
Pinar del Río	11	3hr	9am, 2pm
Playa Girón	4	3hr 15min	8:15am
Sancti Spíritus	23	5hr 45min	8:40am, 9:30am, 3pm, 8:30pm, 10pm
Santa Clara	18	3hr 45min	8:40am, 9:30am, 3pm, 10pm
Santiago de Cuba	51	15hr	9:30am, 3pm, 6:15pm, 10pm
Trinidad	25	6hr	8:15am, 1pm
Varadero	10	3hr	8am, 10am, 12pm, 6pm
Viñales	12	3hr 50min	9am, 2pm

CUC$70 to Varadero, CUC$80 to Pinar del Río, CUC$140 to Santa Clara, CUC$125 to Cienfuegos and CUC$165 to Trinidad. Up to four people can go for the price. It's worth considering in a pinch and is perfectly legal.

Train

Trains to most parts of Cuba depart from **Estación Central de Ferrocarriles** (Map p100; ☎ 862-1920, 861-8540; cnr Av de Bélgica & Arsenal), on the southwestern side of Habana Vieja. Foreigners must buy tickets in Convertibles at **La Coubre station** (Map p100; ☎ 862-1006; cnr Av del Puerto & Desamparados, Habana Vieja; ⌚ 9am-3pm Mon-Fri). If it's closed, try the Lista de Espera office adjacent, which sells tickets for trains leaving immediately. Kids under 12 travel half-price.

Cuba's best train, the Tren Francés (an old French SNCF train), runs every other day between Havana and Santiago stopping in Santa Clara (CUC$17) and Camagüey (CUC$32). It leaves Havana at 7pm and arrives in Santiago the following morning at 9am. There are no sleeper cars, but carriages are comfortable and air-conditioned and there's a snack service. Tickets cost CUC$62 for 1st class and CUC$50 for 2nd class.

Slower *coche motor* (cross-island train) services run to Santiago stopping in smaller stations, such as Matanzas (CUC$4), Sancti Spíritus (CUC$13), Ciego de Ávila (CUC$16), Las Tunas (CUC$23), Bayamo (CUC$26), Manzanillo (CUC$28) and Holguín (CUC$27). One train goes as far as Guantánamo (CUC$32). There are separate branch lines to Cienfuegos (CUC$11) and Pinar del Río (CUC$6.50).

The above information is only a rough approximation of what should happen; services are routinely delayed or canceled (including the Tren Francés, which was temporarily out of service at the time of writing). Always double-check scheduling and from which terminal your train will leave.

For information about the electric train from Casablanca to Matanzas, see p169. Suburban trains and local services to points within the Havana province are discussed under Getting Around (below).

GETTING AROUND
To/From the Airport

Aeropuerto Internacional José Martí is at Rancho Boyeros, 25km southwest of Havana via Av de la Independencia. There are four terminals here. Terminal 1, on the southeastern side of the runway, handles only domestic Cubana flights. Three kilometers away, via Av de la Independencia, is Terminal 2, which receives flights and charters from Miami and New York and some to and from the Cayman Islands. All other international flights use Terminal 3, a well-ordered, modern facility at Wajay, 2.5km west of Terminal 2. Charter flights on Aerocaribbean, Aerogaviota, Aerotaxi etc to Cayo Largo del Sur and elsewhere use the Caribbean Terminal (also known as Terminal 5), at the northwestern end of the runway, 2.5km west of Terminal 3. (Terminal 4 hasn't been built yet.) Check carefully which terminal you'll be using.

Public transport from the airport into central Havana is practically nonexistent. A standard taxi will cost you approximately CUC$20 (40 minutes). You can change money at the bank in the arrivals hall.

True adventurers with light luggage and a tight budget can chance their arm on the P-12 metro bus from the Capitolio or the P-15 from the Hospital Hermanos Ameijeiras on the Malecón, both of which go to Santiago de Las Vegas stopping close to the airport (about 1.5km away) on Av Boyeros. This is a lot easier for departing travelers who will have a better knowledge of the local geography.

To/From the Bus Terminal

The Víazul bus terminal is in the suburb of Nuevo Vedado and taxis will charge between CUC$5 and CUC$10 for the ride to central Havana. There are no direct metro buses from central Havana. If you take the P-14 from the Capitolio, you'll have to get off on Av 51 and walk the last 500m or so.

Bici-taxi

Two-seater bici-taxis will take you anywhere around Centro Habana for CUC$1/2 for a short/long trip, after bargaining. It's a lot more than a Cuban would pay, but cheaper and more fun than a tourist taxi. Laws prohibit bici-taxis from taking tourists and they may wish to go via a roundabout route through the back streets to avoid police controls – a cheap tour! If they get stopped, it's them that get the warning/fine, not you.

Bicycle

Havana's (and Cuba's) only official bike rental shop, **El Orbe** (Map p106; ☎ 860-2617; cnr Agramonte & San Rafael, Centro Habana; ☷ 9:30am-4:40pm Mon-Sat) in the La Manzana de Gómez shopping center in Centro Habana, was closed at the time of writing. Whether it opens again was a matter of much speculation. The bikes here were passable imports, mainly from Canada, but don't bank on using them for anything more than a city tour. The best time to cycle in Havana is on a weekend morning when the Malecón is traffic-free and positively sublime. Locks and helmets are a must (El Orbe used to supply them).

Boat

Passenger **ferries** (Map p100; ☎ 867-3726) shuttle across the harbor to Regla and Casablanca, leaving every 10 or 15 minutes from Muelle Luz, at the corner of San Pedro and Santa Clara, on the southeast side of Habana Vieja.

The fare is a flat 10 centavos, but foreigners often get charged CUC$1. Since the ferries were hijacked to Florida in 1994 and again in 2003 (the hijackers never made it outside Cuban waters), security has been tightened. Expect bag searches and airport-style screening.

Car

There are lots of car-rental offices in Havana, so if you're told there are no cars or there isn't one in your price range, just try another office or agency. All agencies have offices at Terminal 3 at Aeropuerto Internacional José Martí. Otherwise, there's a car-rental desk in any three-star (or higher) hotel. Prices for equivalant models are nearly always the same between the companies; it's called *socialismo*.

Cubacar (☎ 835-0000) and/or **Havanautos** (☎ 273-2277) – it's essentially the same government-run company – have desks at most of the big hotels, including: Meliá Cohiba, Meliá Habana, NH Parque Central, Habana Libre, Comodoro and Sevilla.

Rex Rent a Car (Map pp102-3; ☎ 836-7788; cnr Línea & Malecón, Vedado) rents fancy cars for extortionate prices.

Servi-Cupet gas stations are in Vedado at Calles L and 17; Malecón and Calle 15; Malecón and Paseo, near the Riviera and Meliá Cohiba hotels; and on Av de la Independencia (northbound lane) south of Plaza de la Revolución. All are open 24 hours a day.

Guarded parking is available for approximately CUC$1 all over Havana, including in front of the Hotel Sevilla, Hotel Inglaterra and Hotel Nacional.

Public Transport
HAVANA BUS TOUR

The handy new hop on/hop off **Havana Bus Tour** (☎ 831-7333; Calle L No 456 btwn Calles 25 & 27) runs on three routes. The main stop is in Parque Central opposite the Hotel Inglaterra. This is the pickup point for bus T1 running from Habana Vieja to the Plaza de la Revolución (via Centro Habana, the Malecón and Calle 23), and bus T3, which runs from Centro Habana to Playas del Este (via Parque Histórico Militar Morro-Cabaña). Bus T2 runs from the Plaza de la Revolución (where it connects with T1) to Marina Hemingway (via Necrópolis Cristóbal Colón and Playa). Bus T1 is open-top. All-day tickets are CUC$5. Services run from 9am to 9pm and routes and stops are clearly marked on all bus stops.

BUS

Havana's bus service has improved immensely in recent years with the introduction of a brand new fleet of Chinese-made 'bendy' buses that replaced the famously crowded and dirty *camellos* (the city's former metro buses) in 2007. These buses run regularly along 14 different routes, connecting most parts of the city with the suburbs. Fares are 20 centavos (five centavos if you're using Convertibles), which you deposit into a small slot in front of the driver when you enter.

Cuban buses are crowded and little used by tourists. Beware of pickpockets and guard your valuables closely.

All bus routes have the prefix P before their number:

P-1 Diezmero – Playa (via Virgen del Camino, Vedado, Línea, Av 3)

P-2 Diezmero – Línea y G (via Víbora & Ciudad Deportiva)

P-3 Alamar–Túnel de Línea (via Virgen del Camino & Víbora)

P-4 San Agustín – Terminal de Trenes (via Playa, Calle 23, La Rampa)

P-5 San Agustín – Terminal de Trenes (via Lisa, Av 31, Línea, Av de Puerto)

P-6 Calvario – La Rampa (via Víbora)

P-7 Cotorro – Capitolio (via Virgen del Camino)

P-8 Calvario – Villa Panamericano (via Víbora, Capitolio & harbor tunnel)

P-9 Víbora – Lisa (via Cuatro Caminos, La Rampa, Calle 23, Av 41)

P-10 Víbora – Playa (via Altahabana & Calle 100)

P-11 Alamar – G y 27 (via harbor tunnel)

P-12 Santiago de Las Vegas – Capitolio (via Av Boyeros)

P-13 Santiago de Las Vegas – Víbora (via Calabazar)

P-14 San Agustín – Capitolio (via Lisa & Av 51)

P-15 Santiago de Las Vegas – Hermanos Ameijeiras (via Av Boyeros & Calle G)

P-16 Hospital Naval – Playa (via Calle 100 & Lisa)

Older buses still run along some cross-town routes (eg bus 400 to Playas del Este) but there are no printed timetables or route maps. Individual services have been mentioned in this chapter where appropriate.

Taxi

Metered tourist taxis are readily available at all of the upscale hotels, with the air-conditioned Nissan taxis charging higher tariffs than the non-air-conditioned Ladas. The cheapest official taxis are operated by **Panataxi** (☎ 55-55-55), with CUC$1 starting fare, then CUC$0.50 a kilometer. Tourist taxis charge CUC$1 a kilometer and can be

ordered from **Havanautos Taxi** (☎ 73-22-77) and **Transgaviota** (☎ 206-9793). **Taxi OK** (☎ 204-0000, 877-6666) is based in Miramar. Drivers of the tourist taxis are government employees who work for a peso salary.

The cheapest taxis are the older yellow-and-black Ladas, which are state-owned but rented out to private operators. They won't wish to use their meters, as these are set at an unrealistically low rate, but you can bargain over the fare. They're not supposed to pick up passengers within 100m of a tourist hotel.

Private pirate taxis (ie those that aren't supposed to take foreigners) with yellow license plates are a bit cheaper, but you must agree on the fare before getting into the car, and carry exact change. There are usually classic-car taxis parked in front of the Hotel Inglaterra.

Walking

Yes, walking! It's what the gas-starved Habaneros have been doing for decades. Most parts of Habana Vieja, Centro Habana and Vedado can be easily navigated on foot if you're energetic and up for some exercise. You'll see a lot more of of the local street life in the process.

OUTER HAVANA

Splaying out on three sides from the downtown district, Havana's suburbs are full of quirky and easy-to-reach sights and activities that can make interesting day and half-day trips from the city center. Playa boasts a decent aquarium, top-class conference facilities and Cuba's best restaurants; Guanabacoa and Regla are famous for their Afro-Cuban religious culture; and the bayside forts of La Cabaña and El Morro exhibit some of the island's most impressive military architecture.

PLAYA & MARIANAO

The municipality of Playa, west of Vedado across the Río Almendares, is a paradoxical mix of prestigious residential streets and tough proletarian housing schemes.

Gracious Miramar is a leafy neighborhood of broad avenues and weeping laurel trees where the traffic moves more sedately and diplomats' wives – clad in sun visors and Lycra leggings – go for gentle afternoon jogs along Av Quinta (Fifth Avenue). Many of Havana's foreign embassies are housed here in old pre-Revolution mansions, and business travelers and conference attendees flock in from around the globe to make use of some of Cuba's grandest and most luxurious facilities. If you're interested primarily in sightseeing and entertainment, commuting to Vedado or Habana Vieja is a nuisance and an expense. However, some of the best salsa clubs, discos and restaurants are out this way and the casas particulares are positively luxurious.

Cubanacán plays host to many of Havana's business or scientific fairs and conventions, and it is also where several specialized medical institutes are situated. Despite the austerity of the *período especial*, vast resources have been plowed into biotechnological and pharmaceutical research institutes in this area. Yachties, anglers and scuba divers will find themselves using the Marina Hemingway at Playa's west end.

Marianao is world-famous for the Tropicana Nightclub, but locally it's known as a tough, in parts rough neighborhood with a powerful Santería community and a long history of social commitment.

Information

INTERNET ACCESS & TELEPHONE

Hotel Business Centers (Hotel Meliá Habana; Av 3 btwn Calles 76 & 80, Miramar) Meliá Habana charges CUC$7 per half-hour for internet access. Also try the Aparthotel Montehabana (p1570) and the Occidental Miramar (p157).

MEDICAL SERVICES

Clínica Central Cira García (☎ 204-2811; Calle 20 No 4101 cnr Av 41, Playa; ☽ 9am-4pm Mon-Fri, emergencies 24hr) Emergency, dental and medical consultations for foreigners (consultations CUC$25 to CUC$35).

Farmacia Internacional Miramar (☎ 204-4350; cnr Calles 20 & 43, Playa; ☽ 9am-5:45pm) Across the road from Clínica Central Cira García.

Pharmacy (☎ 204-2880; Calle 20 No 4104 cnr Calle 43, Playa; ☽ 24hr) In Clínica Central Cira García; one of the city's best.

Spa Club Comodoro (☎ 204-5049; Hotel El Comodoro, cnr Av 3 & Calle 84, Miramar) Treatments for stress, relaxation, beauty and fitness; also a pharmacy.

MONEY

Banco Financiero Internacional Miramar (☎ 203-9762; Sierra Maestra Bldg, cnr Av 1 & Calle 0); Playa (☎ 267-5500; cnr Av 5 & Calle 92)

Cadeca Miramar (☎ 204-9327; Av 5A btwn Calles 40 & 42; ☽ 9am-5pm Mon-Sat, 9am-noon Sun); Playa (☎ 204-9087; cnr Av 3 & Calle 70)

POST

DHL (☎ 204-1578; cnr Av 1 & Calle 26, Miramar; ☽ 8am-8pm)

Post office (Calle 42 No 112 btwn Avs 1 & 3, Miramar; ☽ 8am-11:30am & 2-6pm Mon-Fri, 8am-11:30am Sat)

TOURIST INFORMATION

Infotur (☎ 204-7036; cnr Av 5 & Calle 112, Playa; ☽ 8:30am-5pm Mon-Sat, 8:30am-noon Sun) Oddly located but informative office.

TRAVEL AGENCIES

All of the following agencies sell the organized tours listed in the Downtown Havana section (see p108).

Cubanacán (☎ 204-8500) Desk in Hotel Meliá Habana.

Gaviota (☎ 204-4411; cnr Av 49 & 36, Kohly)

Havanatur (☎ 204-7541; Sierra Maestra Bldg, cnr Av 1 & Calle 0, Miramar; ☽ 9am-6pm Mon-Sat)

Sights

MIRAMAR

The fascinating museum at the **Fundación Naturaleza y El Hombre** (☎ 204-0438; Av 5B No 6611 btwn Calles 66 & 70, Playa; admission CUC$3; ☽ 10am-4pm Mon-Fri) displays artifacts from the 17,422km canoe trip from the Amazon source to sea led by Cuban intellectual and anthropologist Antonio Nuñez Jiménez in 1987. Other exhibits in a truly astounding museum include one of Cuba's largest photography collections, books written by the prolific Nuñez Jiménez, the famous Fidel portrait by Guayasamín stalactites, and 'the glass house' – glass cases containing all kinds of intriguing ephemera from the founder's life. The museum is a foundation and one of Havana's most rewarding.

If you thought the Maqueta de La Habana Vieja (p111) was impressive, check out the **Pabellón para la Maqueta de la Capital** (☎ 202-7303; Calle 28 No 113 btwn Avs 1 & 3; admission CUC$3; ☽ 9:30am-5pm Tue-Sat), an ultramodern pavilion containing a huge 1:1000 scale model of the whole city originally created for urban-planning purposes, but now a tourist attraction. Nearby, the two **parks** on Av 5,

PLAYA & MARIANAO

INFORMATION
Austrian Embassy................................1 H1
Banco Financiero Internacional........2 E4
Banco Financiero Internacional.......(see 34)
British Embassy....................................3 G2
Cadeca...4 G2
Cadeca...(see 67)
Canadian Embassy..............................5 G2
Clínica Central Cira García..................6 H2
Cubanacán...(see 43)
DHL...7 G2
Farmacía Internacional Miramar........8 H2
French Embassy...................................9 H3
Gaviota..10 H3
Havanatur..(see 34)
Hotel Business Centers.......................(see 43)
Infotur..11 E4
Italian Embassy..................................12 H2
Japanese Embassy..............................13 F3
Mexican Embassy...............................14 H2
Netherlands Embassy..........................15 H2
Pharmacy...(see 6)
Post Office..16 F2
Russian Embassy.................................17 F3
Spa Club Comodoro...........................(see 41)
Swedish Embassy................................18 G2
Swiss Embassy....................................19 G2

SIGHTS & ACTIVITIES
Acuario Nacional...............................20 H3
Centro de Ingeniería Genética y
    Biotecnología................................21 E6
Centro Internacional de
    Restauración Neurológica............22 E5
Centro Nacional de Investigaciones
    Científicas....................................23 E5
Fundación Naturaleza y El Hombre..24 F3

Iglesia Jesús de Miramar....................25 F3
Instituto Superior de Arte..................26 E4
La Aguja Marlin Diving Center...........27 A5
Marlin Náutica...................................28 A5
Museo de la Alfabetización...............29 G5
Museo del Aire...................................30 D6
Pabellón para la Maqueta
    de la Capital.................................31 G2
Pabexpo...32 D5
Palacio de las Convenciones.............33 E5
Sierra Maestra Building......................34 H1

SLEEPING 🏠
Aparthotel Montehabana....................35 F3
Hostal Costa Sol.................................36 F3
Hotel Acuario.....................................37 B4
Hotel Bello Caribe..............................38 E6
Hotel Chateau Miramar......................39 F3
Hotel El Bosque.................................40 H2
Hotel El Comodoro............................41 E3
Hotel Kohly..42 H3
Hotel Meliá Habana...........................43 E3
Hotel Palco..44 E5
Marta Rodríguez................................45 G3
Occidental Miramar...........................46 F3
Panorama Hotel Habana.....................47 F3
Rina & Geraldo..................................48 E3

EATING 🍴
Casa Española....................................(see 51)
Don Cangrejo.....................................49 G2
Dos Gardenias....................................50 G2
El Aljibe..51 G2
El Buganvil...52 D5
El Palenque...53 D5
El Tocororo...54 G2
La Cecilia...55 E4

La Esperanza......................................56 G2
La Ferminia..57 D5
Paladar Calle 10................................58 G2
Paladar La Cocina de Liliam..............59 G3
Paladar La Fontana.............................60 F3
Paladar Los Cactus de 33..................61 H3
Paladar Mi Jardín...............................62 F3
Paladar Vista Mar..............................63 G2
Pan.com...64 G2
Papa's Complejo Turístico..................65 A5
Restaurante La Cova...........................66 B5
Supermercado 70...............................67 F3

ENTERTAINMENT 🎭
Bolera..68 B4
Casa de la Música..............................69 H2
Circo Trompoloco...............................70 E4
Estadio Pedro Marrero.......................71 H3
Isla del Coco......................................72 E4
Salón Rosado Benny Moré
    (El Tropical)..................................73 H3
Teatro Karl Marx................................74 G1
Tropicana Nightclub...........................75 G4

SHOPPING 🛍
Egrem Tienda de Música....................76 G2
La Casa del Habano............................77 G2
La Maison...78 H2
Miramar Trade Center.........................79 F3

TRANSPORT
Havanautos..(see 34)
Servi-Cupet Gas Station.....................80 E4
Servi-Cupet Gas Station.....................81 G4
Servi-Cupet Gas Station.....................82 H2
Oro Negro Gas Station.......................83 E4
Vía Rent a Car...................................84 H2

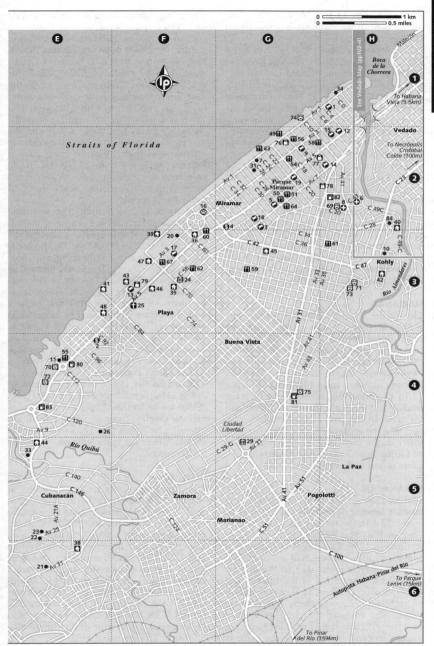

between Calles 24 and 26, with their immense banyan trees and dark lanes, are an atmospheric pocket.

The **Acuario Nacional** (☎ 202-5872; cnr Av 3 & Calle 62; adult/child CUC$5/3; ☉ 10am-10pm Tue-Sun) is a Havana institution founded in 1960 that gets legions of annual visitors, particularly since its 2002 revamp. In the environment context, this place leaves all other Cuban *acuarios* (aquatic centers) and *delfinarios* (dolphin shows) in the shade (which isn't saying much). For a start, it's designed to be both educational and conservationist. Saltwater fish are the specialty, but there are also sea lions, dolphins and lots of running-around room for kids. Dolphin performances are almost hourly from 11am, with the final show at 9pm; admission price includes the show.

The Stalinist obelisk that dominates the skyline halfway down Av Quinta is the **Russian Embassy** (Av 5 No 6402 btwn Calles 62 & 66, Playa). More aesthetically pleasing is the domed **Iglesia Jesús de Miramar** (cnr Av 5 & Calle 82, Playa), a gigantic neo-Romanesque church.

MARIANAO

The former Cuartel Colombia military airfield at Marianao is now a school complex called **Ciudad Libertad**. Pass through the gate to visit the inspiring **Museo de la Alfabetización** (☎ 260-8054; admission free; ☉ 8am-noon & 1-4:30pm Mon-Fri, 8am-noon Sat), which describes the 1961 literacy campaign, when 100,000 youths aged 12 to 18 spread out across Cuba to teach reading and writing to farmers, workers and the aged. In the center of the traffic circle, opposite the entrance to the complex, is a tower in the form of a syringe in memory of Carlos Juan Finlay, who discovered the cause of yellow fever in 1881.

CUBANACÁN

The leading art academy in Cuba is the **Instituto Superior de Arte** (ISA; Calle 120 No 1110), established in the former Havana Country Club in 1961 and elevated to the status of institute in 1976. The cluster of buildings – some unfinished, some half-restored, but all gloriously graceful due to the arches, domes and profuse use of red brick – was the brainchild of Che Guevara and a team of architects. Among them was Ricardo Porro, who designed the striking Facultad de Artes Plásticas (1961) with long curving passageways and domed halls in the shape of

a reclining woman. Some 800 students study here, and foreigners can too (see p463).

Also known as the Havana Convention Center, the **Palacio de las Convenciones** (☎ 208-5199; Calle 146 btwn Avs 11 & 13) is one of Cuba's most dramatic modern buildings. Built for the Nonaligned Conference in 1979, the four interconnecting halls contain a state-of-the-art auditorium with 2101 seats and 11 smaller halls. The 589-member National Assembly meets here twice a year and the complex hosts more than 50,000 conference attendees annually. Not far from here is **Pabexpo** (☎ 271-6614; cnr Av 17 & Calle 180), 20,000 sq meters of exhibition space in four interconnecting pavilions that hosts about 15 trade shows a year.

Many of Cuba's cutting-edge scientific and medical facilities are out here, including **Centro de Ingenería Genética y Biotecnología** (CIGB; ☎ 271-6022; cnr Av 31 & Calle 190), the focus of Cuba's genetic engineering and biotechnology research; the **Centro Nacional de Investigaciones Científicas** (Cenic; ☎ 208-2546; cnr Av 25 & Calle 158), where the anticholesterol wonder drug Ateromixol, or PPG, was created; and the **Centro Internacional de Restauración Neurológica** (Ciren; ☎ 271-6844; cnr Av 25 & Calle 158), where Cuba has developed breakthrough neurological treatments. All these installations are heavily guarded, so unless you're a patient, don't even think about visiting.

Museo del Aire (☎ 271-0632; Calle 212 btwn Avs 29 & 31, La Lisa; unguided/guided CUC$2/3, camera CUC$2; ☉ 9am-4pm Tue-Sun) has 22 planes and helicopters on display, most of them ex-military aircraft. Don't miss Che Guevara's personal Cessna 310, or the space suit used by Cuba's first cosmonaut.

Activities

There are many water activities available at Marina Hemingway in Barlovento, 20km west of central Havana. Fishing trips can be arranged at **Marlin Náutica** (☎ 204-6848; cnr Av 5 & Calle 248, Barlovento) from CUC$150 for four anglers and four hours of bottom fishing, and CUC$280 for four anglers and four hours of deep-sea fishing. Included are a captain, sailor, open bar and tackle. Marlin season is June to October. Scuba packages for CUC$35 per dive and tours of Havana's littoral (CUC$60 in a catamaran) can also be arranged. Hotel tour desks should also be able to arrange these things.

La Aguja Marlin Diving Center (☎ 204-5088; cnr Av 5 & 248, Barlovento), between Cubanacán Náutica and the shopping center, offers scuba diving for CUC$30 per dive, plus CUC$5 for gear. It has one morning and one afternoon departure. A diving excursion to Varadero or Playa Girón can also be arranged. Reader reviews have been favorable.

Sleeping
MIRAMAR
Casas Particulares

Marta Rodríguez (☎ 203-8596; Calle 42 No 914; r CUC$40; **P**) There aren't so many casas in Miramar, but Marta's could be worth the trip. There are art-deco beds, TV, VCR, a music system and lots of space in the two rooms here. Look for the shiny 1959 Mercedes parked outside.

If Marta's full, try **Rina & Geraldo** (☎ 202-4112; Av 3A No 8610 btwn Calles 86 & 88, Playa; r CUC$25-30), who rent two clean rooms, one with a sun terrace.

Hotels

Hostal Costa Sol (☎ 202-8269; Calle 60 No 307, Miramar; s/d CUC$25/36) Operated by the Ministerio de Educación Superior, this small cheap place with 11 rooms is Miramar's only true bargain. Cubans are the premier guests, so don't expect tourist-style luxuries, though there's an OK restaurant and the staff is friendly enough. Phone ahead rather than turn up as this place is sometimes block-booked.

Hotel El Bosque (Gaviota; ☎ 204-9232; Calle 28A btwn Calles 49A & 49B, Kohly; s/d CUC$45/60; ﹩ ﹩) Economical and grossly underrated, El Bosque is the better and less costly arm of the Gaviota-run Kohly-Bosque *complejo* (complex). Clean and friendly, the hotel lies on the banks of the Río Almendares surrounded by the Bosque de La Habana – the city's green lungs – and is a good (and rare) midrange choice in this neck of the woods. The 54 rooms are small but functional, there's 24-hour internet, and out back a pleasant terrace overlooks the wooded slopes of the nearby river.

Hotel Kohly (Gaviota; ☎ 204-0240; cnr Calles 49A & 36, Kohly; s/d CUC$50/65; ﹩ ﹩ ﹩) Just up the road, the Kohly is similarly priced to El Bosque and makes up for its utilitarian exterior with an inviting swimming pool and excellent pizza restaurant which is often open until late.

Aparthotel Montehabana (Gaviota; ☎ 206-9595; Calle 70 btwn Avs 5A & 7, Playa; s/d/tr CUC$60/80/110; **P** ﹩ ﹩) This modern Gaviota giant opened in December 2005 with the promise of something a little different. One hundred and one of the rooms here are apartments with living rooms and fully equipped kitchens – a great opportunity to hit the Havana markets and find out how the Cubans cook. To help you in the kitchen there are microwaves, refrigerators, toasters and coffee machines – even your own cutlery. If you're not up to cooking, the restaurant does a CUC$8 breakfast and a CUC$15 dinner buffet. Elsewhere the facilities are shiny and new with 24-hour internet, car rental and an on-site minimarket. Guests can use the pool at the Hotel Occidental Miramar next door.

Hotel El Comodoro (Cubanacán; ☎ 204-5551; cnr Av 3 & Calle 84, Playa; s/d CUC$65/90; **P** ﹩ ﹩ ﹩) Right on the coast with its own man-made beach (and ugly sea wall), this sprawling complex is a maze of shops, restaurants and accommodation, both old and new. The tatty main four-story building dates from 1952 and was last refurbished in 1987 (it shows). Elsewhere the two-story *cabañas* and bungalows, interspersed with a seemingly endless mishmash of swimming pools, are rather more attractive. There's a tangible resort atmosphere here and with its varied shops and reputable spa, the Comodoro is pretty self-contained.

Hotel Chateau Miramar (Cubanacán; ☎ 204-0224; Av 1 btwn Calles 60 & 70, Playa; s/d CUC$90/125; **P** ﹩ ﹩ ﹩) It's marketed as a 'boutique hotel,' but read between the lines – this château ain't no Loire Valley retreat. Still, techno addicts will appreciate the free internet, flat-screen TV and direct international phone service that come with the otherwise mediocre rooms.

Panorama Hotel Habana (Gaviota; ☎ 204-0100; cnr Av 3 & Calle 70; s/d CUC$95/120; **P** ﹩ ﹩ ﹩) Gaviota's flashy 'glass cathedral' on Playa's rapidly developing hotel strip opened in 2003. The rather strange aesthetics – acres of blue-tinted glass – improve once you step inside the monumental lobby where ultramodern elevators whisk you promptly up to one of 317 airy rooms that offer great views over Miramar and beyond. Extra facilities include a business center, a photo shop, numerous restaurants and a spacious and shapely swimming pool. But, shrinking you in its scale, the Panorama is almost too big, giving the place a rather deserted and antiseptic feel.

Occidental Miramar (Gaviota; ☎ 204-3584; fax 204-3583; cnr Av 5 & Calle 74; s/d CUC$100/130; **P** ﹩ ﹩) Formerly the Novotel, this 427-room colossus was taken over by Gaviota a few years back and has benefited as a result. Professional staff, great business facilities and high standards of service throughout are par for the course here. There are also plenty of sporty extras if the isolated location starts to grate, including tennis courts, a swimming pool, sauna, gym and games room.

our pick Hotel Meliá Habana (Cubanacán; ☎ 204-8500; Av 3 btwn Calles 76 & 80; r CUC$220; P 🅿 🖥 ▣ ▣) Ugly outside but beautiful within, Miramar's gorgeous Hotel Meliá Habana, which opened in 1998, is one of the city's best run and best equipped accommodation options. The 409 rooms (four of which are wheelchair-accessible) are positioned around a salubrious lobby abundant in hanging vines, marble statues and gushing water features, while outside Cuba's largest and most beautiful swimming pool stands next to a desolate, rocky shore. Throw in polite, punchy service, an excellent buffet restaurant, and the occasional room discount, and you could be swayed.

CUBANACÁN

There are two hotels in this neighborhood where you might end up if you're here for an organized activity/conference.

Hotel Bello Caribe (Cubanacán; ☎ 273-9906; cnr Av 31 & Calle 158; s/d CUC$50/67; P 🅿 ▣) Next to the huge Centro de Ingeniería Genética y Biotecnología, this hotel has 120 rooms often used by foreigners undergoing treatment at the nearby medical facilities.

Hotel Palco (Cubanacán; ☎ 204-7235; Calle 146 btwn Avs 11 & 13; s/d CUC$91/111; P 🅿 ▣) Two kilometers to the north and attached to the Palacio de las Convenciones, the Palco is a top business hotel normally block-booked by foreigners in town to attend a conference/symposium/product launch.

MARINA HEMINGWAY

Hotel Acuario (Cubanacán; ☎ 204-6336; cnr Aviota & Calle 248; s/d CUC$60/90; 🅿) You really shouldn't come to Marina Hemingway for the hotels. With the El Viejo y el Mar currently hosting medical patients from Venezuela, the only real option for foreign travelers is the strung-out Acuario, splayed between two of the harbor channels and infested with cheap out-of-date furnishings. If you're booked for an early morning diving excursion, this place might just qualify, otherwise stay in Havana and count your blessings.

Eating

Playa contains some of Havana's and Cuba's best paladares, most of them situated in beautiful early 20th-century mansions with alfresco dining options. There are also some surprisingly good state-run restaurants. It's worth the CUC$5 to CUC$10 taxi fare from the city center to eat out here.

PLAYA & MARIANAO

Paladar Los Cactus de 33 (☎ 203-5139; Av 33 No 3405 btwn Calles 34 & 36, Playa; 🌙 noon-midnight) Reviewed in international lifestyle magazines and used as a setting on Cuban TV, this place has impeccable service, elegant surroundings, well-prepared food and outrageous prices, once you've factored in the taxi fare (it's well out of the way). Bank on a minimum of CUC$20 for the house special, chicken breast with mushrooms, olives and cheese.

MIRAMAR

Pan.com (☎ 204-4232; cnr Av 7 & Calle 26; 🌙 10am-midnight) Not an internet cafe but a haven of Havana comfort food with hearty sandwiches, fantastic burgers and ice-cream milkshakes to die for. Join the diplomats under the airy front canopy.

Casa Española (☎ 206-9644; cnr Calle 26 & Av 7; 🌙 noon-midnight) A medieval parody built in the Batista-era by the silly-rich Gustavo Guitérrez y Sánchez, this crenellated castle in Miramar recently found new life as a Spanish-themed restaurant cashing in on the Don Quijote legend. The ambience is rather fine, if you don't mind suits of armor watching you as you tuck into paella, Spanish omelet or *lanja cerdo al Jerez* (Jerez-style pork fillet).

Dos Gardenias (☎ 204-2353; cnr Av 7 & Calle 28; 🌙 noon-midnight) You can choose from grill, Chinese and pasta restaurants in this complex, which is also famous as a bolero hot spot. Stick around to hear the singers belting out the ballads later on.

Paladar Mi Jardín (☎ 203-4627; Calle 66 No 517; 🌙 noon-midnight) The rare Cuban menu that offers chicken mole or tacos and quesadillas makes this Mexican place a keeper. Dining beneath the vine-covered trellis in the garden is recommended, as is the house special, fish Veracruz.

our pick El Aljibe (☎ 204-1583/4; Av 7 btwn Calles 24 & 26; 🌙 noon-midnight) On paper a humble Palmares restaurant, but in reality a rip-roaring culinary extravaganza, El Aljibe has been delighting both Cuban and foreign diplomatic taste buds for years. The furor surrounds the gastronomic mysteries of just one dish, the obligatory *pollo asado* (roast pork), which is served up with as-much-as-you-can-eat helpings of white rice, black beans, fried plantain, French fries and salad. The accompanying bitter orange sauce is said to be a state secret.

Paladar La Cocina de Lilliam (☎ 209-6514; Calle 48 No 1311 btwn Avs 13 & 15; ☾ noon-midnight) Slick service, secluded ambience and freshly cooked food to die for, La Cocina de Lilliam has all the ingredients of a prize-winning restaurant par excellence. Set in an illustrious villa in Miramar and surrounded by a garden of trickling fountains and lush tropical plants, diners can tuck into such Cuban rarities as chicken mousse and tuna bruschetta in an atmosphere more European than Caribbean. Not a cheese and ham sandwich in sight!

Paladar Calle 10 (☎ 205-3970; Calle 10 No 314 btwn Avs 3 & 5; ☾ noon-3pm & 6-11pm) Paladar Calle 10 is situated in – ur – Calle 10 in the 'posh' Miramar neighborhood and, while the name might be a little unimaginative, the food certainly isn't. Set up barbecue-style in the owner's back garden, the alfresco seating is arranged under an attractive thatched canopy and the printed menu is both varied and adventurous. Delicious main dishes include octopus (CUC$5), *ropa vieja* (CUC$7) and a tempting chicken in balsamic vinegar (CUC$8). Portions are huge and arrive with assorted roasted vegetables and a memorable pureed potato. There are even profiteroles for dessert.

our pick **Paladar La Fontana** (☎ 202-8337; Av 3A No 305) Havana discovers the barbecue or, more to the point, the full-on charcoal grill. Huge portions of meat and fish are served up in this amiable villa-cum-paladar, so go easy on the starters which include crab mixed with eggplant, quail eggs and fried chickpeas. La Fontana specializes in just about everything you'll never see elsewhere in Cuba, from lasagna to huge steaks. Big-shot reviews from the *Cigar Aficionado* and the *Chicago Tribune* testify the burgeoning legend.

Paladar Vista Mar (☎ 203-8328; Av 1 btwn Calles 22 & 24; ☾ noon-midnight) The Paladar Vista Mar is in the 2nd-floor family-room-turned-restaurant of a private residence in Miramar that faces the sea. The oceanside ambience is embellished by a beautiful swimming pool that spills its water into the sea. If enjoying delicious seafood dishes overlooking the crashing ocean sounds enticing, this could be your bag. Most mains run from CUC$8 to CUC$15 with salad.

La Esperanza (☎ 202-4361; Calle 16 No 105 btwn Avs 1 & 3; ☾ 6:30-11pm, closed Thu) Few would disagree that the food, ambience and gastronomic creativity showcased at this unassuming Miramar paladar puts it among Havana's (and undoubtedly Cuba's) best eating establishments. While unspectacular from the street, the interior of this house is a riot of quirky antiques, old portraits and refined 1940s furnishings. The food, which is produced in a standard-sized family kitchen, includes such exquisite dishes as *pollo luna de miel* (chicken flambéed in rum), fish marinated in white wine, lemon and garlic, and a lamb brochette.

Don Cangrejo (☎ 204-4169; Av 1 No 1606 btwn Calles 16 & 18; ☾ noon-midnight) Right on the seafront, this unique seafood restaurant is run by the Ministry of Fisheries and scores high points for atmosphere and service. Fresh fish dishes include red snapper, grouper and prawns (CUC$8 to CUC$12), while lobster plucked from the pit on the terrace comes in at CUC$20 to CUC$25.

El Tocororo (☎ 202-4530; Calle 18 No 302; meals CUC$12-35; ☾ noon-midnight) Once considered (along with El Aljibe) to be one of Havana's finest government-run restaurants, El Tocororo has lost ground to its competitors in recent years and is often criticized for being overpriced. Nonetheless, the candlelit tables and inviting garden are still worth a visit, while the unprinted menu, with such luxuries as lobster's tail and (occasionally) ostrich still has the ability to surprise. El Tocororo also has a small attached sushi bar and restaurant called Sakura.

Supermercado 70 (cnr Av 3 & Calle 70; ☾ 9am-6pm Mon-Sat, 9am-1pm Sun) Still known as the 'Diplomercado' from the days when you had to show a foreign passport to be able to shop here, this place is gigantic by Cuban standards with plenty of selection.

CUBANACÁN

El Buganvil (☎ 271-4791; Calle 190 No 1501 btwn Calles 15 & 17, Siboney; ☾ noon-midnight) A solid paladar with a pleasant outdoor plant and thatch setting, this place has sterling service and good *comida criolla*. The house specialty is *loma ahumado* (smoked pork loin; CUC$4), but if you get a group of six together, they'll smoke a whole pig for you.

La Cecilia (☎ 204-1562; Av 5 No 11010 btwn Calles 110 & 112; ☾ noon-midnight) All-time Havana classic, this classy place is up there with El Aljibe in terms of food quality (check out the *ropa vieja*), but trumps all comers with its big-band music that blasts out on weekend nights inside its large but atmospheric courtyard.

El Palenque (208-8167; cnr Av 17 & Calle 190; Siboney; ☾ 10am-10pm) A huge place next to the Pabexpo exhibition center that sprawls beneath a series of open-sided thatched *bohíos* (traditional Cuban huts), the Palenque offers an extensive menu at prices cheap enough to attract both Cubans and foreigners. The cuisine is Cuban/ Italian, with pizzas starting at CUC$3, steak and fries coming in at CUC$9 and lobster mariposa maxing out at CUC$22.

La Ferminia (☎ 273-6786; Av 5 No 18207, Flores) Havana gets swanky at this memorable restaurant set in an elegant converted colonial mansion in the leafy neighborhood of Flores. Dine inside, in one of a handful of beautifully furnished rooms, or outside on a glorious garden patio – it doesn't matter. The point is the food. Try the mixed grill, pulled straight from the fire, or lobster tails pan-fried in breadcrumbs. There's a strict dress code here: no shorts or sleeveless T-shirts (guys). It's one of the few places where Fidel Castro has dined in public.

MARINA HEMINGWAY

Restaurante La Cova (cnr Av 5 & Calle 248; ☾ noon-midnight) In Marina Hemingway, this place vies with Paladar Piccolo in Playas del Este as Havana's best pizza joint. Part of the Pizza Nova chain, it also does fish, meat and rigatoni a la vodka (CUC$8). The pepperoni topping is purportedly flown in from Canada.

Papa's Complejo Turístico (cnr Av 5 & Calle 248; ☾ noon-3am) There's all sorts of stuff going on here, from beer-swilling boatmen with Hemingway-esque beards to warbling American Idol wannabes hogging the karaoke machine. The eating options are equally varied, with a posh Chinese place (with dress code) and an outdoor *ranchón* (rural restaurant). Good fun if there's enough people.

Entertainment
MIRAMAR

Teatro Karl Marx (☎ 203-0801, 209-1991; cnr Av 1 & Calle 10) Size-wise the Karl Marx puts other Havana

theaters in the shade with a seating capacity of 5500 in a single auditorium. The very biggest events happen here, such as the closing galas for the jazz and film festivals and rare concerts by *trovadores* like Silvio Rodríguez. In 2001 it hosted Welsh rockers The Manic Street Preachers, the first Western rock band to play live on the island (with Fidel Castro in the audience).

Casa de la Música (☎ 202-6147; Calle 20 No 3308; admission CUC$5-20; ☾ 10pm Tue-Sat) Launched with a concert by renowned jazz pianist Chucho Valdés in 1994, this Miramar favorite is run by national Cuban recording company, Egrem, and the programs are generally a lot more authentic than the cabaret entertainment you see at the hotels. Platinum players such as NG La Banda, Los Van Van and Aldaberto Álvarez y Su Son play here regularly; you'll rarely pay more than CUC$20. It has a more relaxed atmosphere than its Centro Habana namesake.

MARIANAO

Tropicana Nightclub (☎ 267-1871; Calle 72 No 4504; ☾ 10pm) A city institution since it opened in 1939, the world-famous Tropicana was one of the few bastions of Havana's Las Vegas–style nightlife to survive the clampdowns of the puritanical Castro Revolution. Immortalized in Graham Greene's 1958 classic *Our Man in Havana*, this open-air cabaret show is little changed since its '50s heyday, featuring a bevy of scantily clad *señoritas* who climb nightly down from the palm trees to dance Latin salsa amid colorful flashing lights on stage. Tickets go for a slightly less than socialistic CUC$70.

Salón Rosado Benny Moré (El Tropical; ☎ 206-1281; cnr Avs 41 & 46, Kohly; admission 10 pesos-CUC$10; ☾ 9pm-late) For something completely different, check out the very *caliente* action at this outdoor venue. The Rosado (aka El Tropical) packs in hot, sexy Cuban youths dancing madly to Los Van Van, Pupi y Su Son Son or Habana Abierta. It's a fierce scene and female travelers should expect aggressive come-ons. Friday to Sunday is best. Some travelers pay pesos, others dollars – more of that Cuban randomness for you.

Circo Trompoloco (cnr Av 5 & Calle 112, Playa; admission CUC$10; ☾ 7pm Thu-Sun) Havana's permanent 'Big Top' with a weekend matinee.

Estadio Pedro Marrero (cnr Av 41 & Calle 46, Kohly) You can see soccer matches on weekends at 3pm at this 15,000-seat stadium.

LA LISA

Sala de Fiesta Macumba Habana (☎ 273-0568; cnr Calle 222 & Av 37; admission CUC$10-20; ☉ 10pm) Cocooned in a residential neighborhood southwest of Cubanacán is Macumba, one of Havana's biggest venues for live salsa. The outdoor setting is refreshing and the sets long, so you'll get a lot of dancing in. You can also dine at La Giradilla in the same complex. This is a great place to catch jazz-salsa combos and *timba* music, a modern extension of salsa mixed with jazz and rap and championed by NG La Banda (who perform here regularly).

Shopping

La Casa del Habano (cnr Av 5 & Calle 16, Miramar; ☉ 10am-6pm Mon-Sat, 10am-1pm Sun) Smokers and souvenir seekers will like La Casa, arguably Havana's top cigar store. There's a comfy smoking lounge and a decent restaurant here as well.

    La Maison (Calle 16 No 701, Miramar) The Cuban fashion fascination is in high gear at this place, with a large boutique selling designer clothing, shoes, handbags, jewelry, cosmetics and souvenirs.

    For CDs head to **Egrem Tienda de Música** (Calle 18 No 103, Miramar; ☉ 9am-6pm Mon-Sat), which has a great selection, or visit the **Casa de la Música** (cnr Av 35 & Calle 20, Miramar; ☉ 10am-10pm). The **Miramar Trade Center** (Av 3 btwn Calles 76 & 80) is Cuba's largest and most modern shopping and business center with myriad stores.

Getting There & Away

The best way to get to Playa from Havana is on the Havana Bus Tour (see p151), which plies most of the neighborhoods' highlights all the way to Marina Hemingway. Coming from Habana Vieja or Centro Habana, you'll need to change buses at Plaza de la Revolución. Plenty of metro buses make the trip, though they often ply the more residential neighborhoods (see p152).

Getting Around

Havanautos (☎ 203-9104; 3rd fl, Sierra Maestra Bldg, cnr Av 1 & Calle 0) can rent out cars for around CUC$70 per day including insurance.

    Cubacar (☎ 204-1707) has offices at the Chateau Miramar and the Meliá Habana hotels.

    Vía Rent a Car (☎ 204-3606; cnr Avs 47 & 36, Kohly) has an office opposite the Hotel El Bosque.

    There are Servi-Cupet gas stations at Av 31 between Calles 18 and 20 in Miramar, on the corner of Calle 72 and Av 41 in Marianao (near the Tropicana), as well as on the traffic circle at Av 5 and Calle 112 in Cubanacán. The Oro Negro gas station is at Av 5 and Calle 120 in Cubanacán. All are open 24 hours.

PARQUE LENIN AREA

Parque Lenin, off the Calzada de Bejucal in Arroyo Naranjo, 20km south of central Havana, is the city's largest recreational area. Constructed between 1969 and 1972 on the orders of Celia Sánchez, it is one of the few developments in Havana from this era. The 670 hectares of green parkland and beautiful old trees surround an artificial lake, the Embalse Paso Sequito, just west of the much larger Embalse Ejército Rebelde, which was formed by damming the Río Almendares.

    Although the park itself is attractive enough, the mishmash of facilities inside has fallen on hard times since the onset of the Special Period. Taxi drivers will wax nostalgic about when 'Lenin' was an idyllic weekend getaway for scores of pleasure-seeking Havana families, though these days the place retains more of a neglected and surreal air. Fortunately, help is on the way. New management and millions of pesos of Chinese investment are currently financing a major renovation project, but it's a big job that's still a long way from completion.

Sights

The main things to see are south of the lake, including the **Galería de Arte Amelia Peláez** (admission CUC$1). Up the hill there's a dramatic white marble **monument to Lenin** (1984) by the Soviet sculptor LE Kerbel, and west along the lake is an overgrown **amphitheater** and an **aquarium** (admission CUC$2; ☉ 10am-5pm Tue-Sun, closed Mon) with freshwater fish and crocodiles. The 1985 bronze **monument to Celia Sánchez**, a long-time associate of Fidel Castro who was instrumental in having Parque Lenin built, is rather hidden beyond the aquarium. A **ceramics workshop** is nearby.

    Most of these attractions are open 9am to 5pm Tuesday to Sunday, and admission to the park itself is free. You can sometimes rent a **rowboat** on the Embalse Paso Sequito from a dock behind the **Rodeo Nacional**. A 9km **narrow-gauge railway** with four stops

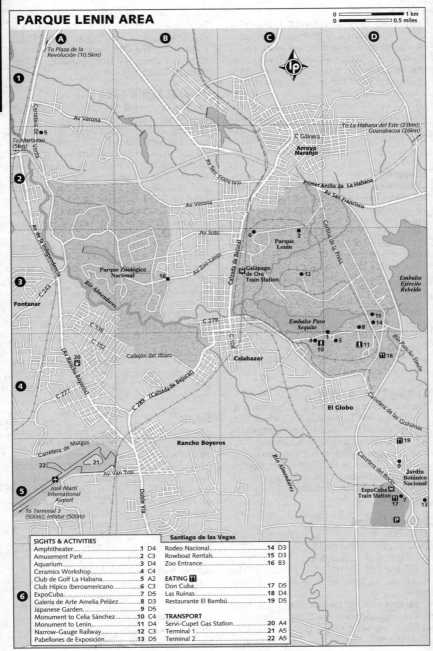

PARQUE LENIN AREA

SIGHTS & ACTIVITIES
Amphitheater	**1** D4
Amusement Park	**2** C3
Aquarium	**3** D4
Ceramics Workshop	**4** C4
Club de Golf La Habana	**5** A2
Club Hípico Iberoamericano	**6** C3
ExpoCuba	**7** D5
Galería de Arte Amelia Peláez	**8** D3
Japanese Garden	**9** D5
Monument to Celia Sánchez	**10** C4
Monument to Lenin	**11** D4
Narrow-Gauge Railway	**12** C3
Pabellones de Exposición	**13** D5

Santiago de las Vegas
Rodeo Nacional	**14** D3
Rowboat Rentals	**15** D3
Zoo Entrance	**16** B3

EATING 🍴
Don Cuba	**17** D5
Las Ruinas	**18** D4
Restaurante El Bambú	**19** D5

TRANSPORT
Servi-Cupet Gas Station	**20** A4
Terminal 1	**21** A5
Terminal 2	**22** A5

operates inside the park from 10am to 3pm Wednesday to Sunday.

A visit to Parque Lenin can be combined with a trip to **ExpoCuba** (☎ 66-42-92; admission CUC$1; 9am-5pm Wed-Sun) at Calabazar on the Carretera del Rocío in Arroyo Naranjo, 3km south of Las Ruinas restaurant. Opened in 1989, this large permanent exhibition showcases Cuba's economic and scientific achievements in 25 pavilions based on themes such as sugar, farming, apiculture, animal science, fishing, construction, food, geology, sports and defense. Cubans visiting ExpoCuba flock to the amusement park at the center of the complex, bypassing the rather dry propaganda displays. **Don Cuba** (☎ 57-82-87), a revolving restaurant, is atop a tower. The Feria Internacional de La Habana, Cuba's largest trade fair, is held at ExpoCuba the first week of November. Parking is available at Gate E, at the south end of the complex (CUC$1).

Across the highway from ExpoCuba is the 600-hectare **Jardín Botánico Nacional** (☎ 54-93-65; admission CUC$1; 8:30am-4:30pm Wed-Sun). The **Pabellones de Exposición** (1987), near the entry gate, is a series of greenhouses with cacti and tropicals, while 2km beyond is the tranquil **Japanese Garden** (1992). Nearby is the celebrated **Restaurante El Bambú** (right), where a vegetarian buffet (a rare treat in Cuba) is CUC$15. The tractor train ride around the park departs four times a day and costs CUC$3, gardens admission included. Parking costs CUC$2.

Let's face it; you don't come to Cuba to see elephants and lions. The Special Period was particularly tough on the island's zoo animals, and a visit to the **Parque Zoológico Nacional** (☎ 881-8195; adult/child CUC$3/2; 9am-3:30pm Wed-Sun), on Av Zoo-Lenin in Boyeros 2km west of the Parque Lenin riding school, only bears out the fact. Though the zoo grounds are extensive and some fauna such as rhinos and hippos roam relatively free, the park is hardly the Serengeti, and many of the big game languish in cramped cages. A trolley bus tours the grounds all day (included in admission price).

Activities

In the northwestern corner of Parque Lenin is the **Club Hípico Iberoamericano** (☎ 44-10-58; 9am-5pm). Horseback riding through the park on a steed rented from the club costs

CUC$12 an hour, but horses rented from boys at the nearby amusement park (undergoing major renovations at the time of writing) or at the entrance to Parque Lenin proper (you'll be besieged) costs CUC$3 per hour, guide included. Watch out for undernourished or maltreated horses.

The **Club de Golf La Habana** (☎ 45-45-78; Carretera de Venta, Km 8, Reparto Capdevila, Boyeros; 8am-8pm) lies between Vedado and the airport. Poor signposting makes it hard to find and most taxi drivers get lost looking: ask locals for directions to the *golfito* or Dilpo Golf Club. Originally titled the Rover's Athletic Club, it was established by a group of British diplomats in the 1920s and the diplomatic corps is largely the clientele today. There are nine holes with 18 tees to allow 18-hole rounds. Green fees start at CUC$20 for nine holes and CUC$30 for 18 holes, with extra for clubs, cart and caddie. In addition, the club has five tennis courts and a bowling alley (open noon to 11pm). Fidel and Che Guevara played a round here once as a publicity stunt soon after the Cuban missile crisis in 1962. The photos of the event are still popular. Che won – apparently.

Sleeping & Eating

Las Ruinas (☎ 57-82-86; Cortina de la Presa; 11am-midnight Tue-Sun) One of Havana's most celebrated restaurants – at least in an architectural sense – is situated on the southeast side of Parque Lenin. Melding off-beat modern architecture – including some eye-catching stained glass by Cuban artist René Portocarrero – onto the ruins of an old sugar mill, this place has an arty and elegant atmosphere, though the food (which is grossly overpriced) doesn't quite live up to the lavish setting. The menu includes lobster plus a selection of Cuban and Italian dishes and you'll be lucky to get much change out of CUC$30. Overrated.

Restaurante El Bambú (Jardín Botánico Nacional; noon-5pm, closed Mon; **V**) This is the first and finest in Havana vegetarian dining and has led the way in education efforts as to the benefits of a meatless diet. The all-you-can-eat lunch buffet is served alfresco deep in the botanical gardens, with the natural setting paralleling the wholesome tastiness of the food. For CUC$15 you can gorge on soups and salads, root vegetables, tamales and eggplant caviar.

Getting There & Away

Your public transport choices to Parque Lenin are bus, car or taxi. The bus isn't easy. The P-13 will get you close, but to catch it you have to first get to Vibora. The best way to do this is to get on the P-9 at Calles 23 and L. Havana taxi drivers are used to this run and it should be easy to negotiate a rate with stops for CUC$25 and up.

Getting Around

There's a Servi-Cupet gas station on the corner of Av de la Independencia and Calle 271 in Boyeros, north of the airport. It's accessible only from the northbound lane and is open 24 hours a day.

SANTIAGO DE LAS VEGAS AREA

While not exactly brimming with tourist potential, downbeat and dusty Santiago de las Vegas offers a fleeting glimpse of Cuba apart from the coffee-table photo spreads. Most visitors encounter this settlement – a curious amalgamation of small town and sleepy city suburb – every December during the 5000-strong devotional crawl to the Santuario de San Lázaro (named after a Christian saint known for his ministrations to lepers and the poor) in the nearby village of El Rincón.

Sights & Activities

On a hilltop at **El Cacahual**, 8km south of Aeropuerto Internacional José Martí via Santiago de las Vegas, is the little-visited mausoleum of the hero of Cuban independence, General Antonio Maceo, who was killed in the Battle of San Pedro near Bauta on December 7, 1896. An open-air pavilion next to the mausoleum shelters a historical exhibit.

Another feature of this area is the well-kept AIDS sanatorium Los Cocos, which opened in 1986 and has helped Cuba maintain an HIV-positive rate that is one of the world's lowest (0.01%).

Getting There & Away

To get here, take bus P-12 from the Capitolio or bus P-16 from outside Hospital Hermanos Ameijeiras just off the Malecón.

REGLA

pop 42,390

The old town of Regla, just across the harbor from Habana Vieja, is an industrial port town known as a center of Afro-Cuban religions, including the all-male secret society Abakúa. Long before the triumph of the 1959 Revolution, Regla was known as the Sierra Chiquita (Little Sierra, after the Sierra Maestra) for its revolutionary traditions. This working-class neighborhood is also notable for a large thermoelectric power plant and shipyard. Regla is almost free of tourist trappings, and makes an easily reachable afternoon trip away from the city; the skyline views from this side of the harbor offer a different perspective.

Sights & Activities

As important as it is diminutive, the **Iglesia de Nuestra Señora de Regla** (☎ 97-62-88; ☻ 7:30am-6pm), which lies just behind the boat dock in the municipality of Regla, has a long and colorful history. Inside on the main altar you'll find *La Santísima Virgen de Regla,* a black Madonna venerated in the Catholic faith and associated in the Santería religion with Yemayá, the *orisha* (spirit) of the ocean and the patron of sailors (always represented in blue). Legend claims that this image was carved by St Augustine 'The African' in the 5th century, and that in the year AD 453 a disciple brought the statue to Spain to safeguard it from barbarians. The small vessel in which the image was traveling survived a storm in the Strait of Gibraltar, so the figure was recognized as the patron of sailors. These days, rafters attempting to reach the US also evoke the protection of the Black Virgin.

A hut was first built on this site in 1687 by a pilgrim named Manuel Antonio to shelter a copy of the image, but this structure was destroyed during a hurricane in 1692. A few years later a Spaniard named Juan de Conyedo built a stronger chapel, and in 1714 Nuestra Señora de Regla was proclaimed patron of the Bahía de La Habana. In 1957 the image was crowned by the Cuban Cardinal in Havana cathedral. Every year on September 8 thousands of pilgrims descend on Regla to celebrate the saint's day and the image is taken out for a procession through the streets.

The current church dates from the early 19th century and is always busy with devotees from both religions stooping in silent prayer before the images of the saints that fill the alcoves. In Havana, there is probably no better (public) place to see the layering and transference between Catholic beliefs and African traditions.

REGLA, GUANABACOA, CASABLANCA & COJIMAR

0 — 500 m
0 — 0.3 miles

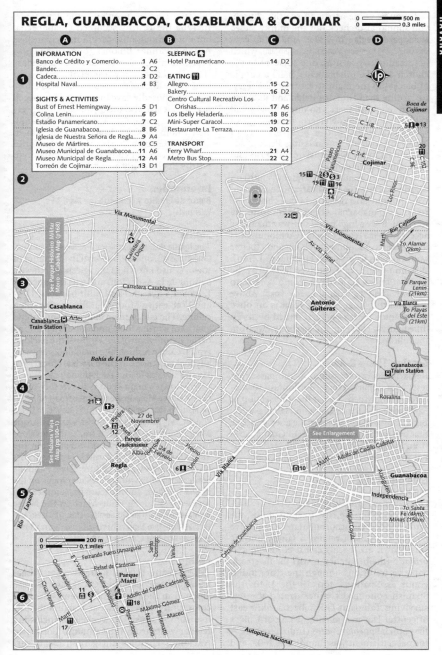

INFORMATION
Banco de Crédito y Comercio..............1 A6
Bandec..2 C2
Cadeca...3 D2
Hospital Naval...................................4 B3

SIGHTS & ACTIVITIES
Bust of Ernest Hemingway.................5 D1
Colina Lenin.....................................6 B5
Estadio Panamericano.......................7 C2
Iglesia de Guanabacoa......................8 B6
Iglesia de Nuestra Señora de Regla....9 A4
Museo de Mártires..........................10 C5
Museo Municipal de Guanabacoa....11 A6
Museo Municipal de Regla...............12 A4
Torreón de Cojimar.........................13 D1

SLEEPING
Hotel Panamericano........................14 D2

EATING
Allegro..15 C2
Bakery..16 D2
Centro Cultural Recreativo Los
    Orishas.......................................17 A6
Los Ibelly Heladería.........................18 B6
Mini-Super Caracol.........................19 C2
Restaurante La Terraza....................20 D2

TRANSPORT
Ferry Wharf.....................................21 A4
Metro Bus Stop...............................22 C2

If you've come across to see the church, you should also check out the quirky **Museo Municipal de Regla** (☎ 97-69-89; Martí No 158; admission CUC$2; ⊙ 9am-5pm Mon-Sat, 9am-1pm Sun), which is spread over two sites, one adjacent to the church and the other (better half) a couple of blocks up the main street from the ferry. Recording the history of Regla and its Afro-Cuban religions, there's an interesting, small exhibit on Remigio Herrero, first *babalawo* (priest) of Regla, and a bizarre statue of Napoleon with his nose missing. Price of admission includes both museum outposts and the Colina Lenin exhibit.

From the museum head straight (south) on Martí past **Parque Guaicanamar**, and turn left on Albuquerque and right on 24 de Febrero, the road to Guanabacoa. About 1.5km from the ferry you'll see a high metal stairway that gives access to **Colina Lenin**. One of two monuments in Havana to Vladimir Ilyich Ulyanov (better known to his friends and enemies as Lenin), this monument was conceived in 1924 by the socialist mayor of Regla, Antonio Borsch, to honor Lenin's death (in the same year). Above a monolithic image of the man is an olive tree planted by Bosch surrounded by seven lithe figures. There are fine harbor views from the hilltop.

Getting There & Away

Regla is easily accessible on the passenger ferry that departs every 10 minutes (10 centavos) from Muelle Luz at the intersection of San Pedro and Santa Clara, in Habana Vieja. Bicycles are readily accepted via a separate line that boards first. Bus 29 runs to Guanabacoa from Parque Maceo between the ferry terminal and the Museo Municipal de Regla.

GUANABACOA

pop 106,374

Guanabacoa is the little village that got swallowed up by the big city. In spite of this, the settlement's main thoroughfare, diminutive Parque Martí, still retains a faintly bucolic small-town air. Locals call it *el pueblo embrujado* (the bewitched town) for its strong Santería traditions, though there are indigenous associations, too. In the 1540s the Spanish conquerors concentrated the few surviving Taínos at Guanabacoa, 5km east of central Havana, making it one of Cuba's first official *pueblos Indios* (Indian towns). A formal settlement was founded in 1607, and

this later became a center of the slave trade. In 1762 the British occupied Guanabacoa, but not without a fight from its mayor, José Antonio Gómez Bulones (better known as Pepe Antonio), who attained almost legendary status by conducting a guerrilla campaign behind the lines of the victorious British. José Martí supposedly gave his first public speech here and it was also the birthplace of the versatile Cuba singer Rita Montaner (1900–58), after whom the Casa de la Cultura is named.

Today, Guanabacoa is a sleepy yet colorful place that can be tied in with an excursion to nearby Regla (easily accessible by ferry).

Information

Banco de Crédito y Comercio (cnr Martí & EV Valenzuela)

Sights

The **Iglesia de Guanabacoa** (cnr Pepe Antonio & Adolfo del Castillo Cadenas), on Parque Martí in the center of town, is also known as the Iglesia de Nuestra Señora de la Asunción, and was designed by Lorenzo Camacho and built between 1721 and 1748 with a Moorish-influenced wooden ceiling. The gilded main altar and nine lateral altars are worth a look, and there is a painting of the *Assumption of the Virgin* at the back. In typical Cuban fashion, the main doors are usually locked; knock at the **parochial office** (⊙ 8-11am & 2-5pm Mon-Fri) out back if you're keen.

The town's main sight is the freshly renovated **Museo Municipal de Guanabacoa** (☎ 97-91-17; Martí No 108; admission CUC$2; ⊙ 10am-6pm Mon & Wed-Sat, 9am-1pm Sun), two blocks west of Parque Martí. Founded in 1964, it tracks the development of the neighborhood throughout the 18th and 19th centuries and is famous for its rooms on Afro-Cuban culture, slavery and the Santería religion with a particular focus on the *orisha* Elegguá. The museum has another arm further west along Calle Martí in the **Museo de Mártires** (Martí No 320; admission free; ⊙ 10am-6pm Tue-Sat, 9am-1pm Sun), which displays material relevant to the Cuban Revolution.

Eating

our pick **Centro Cultural Recreativo Los Orishas** (cnr Martí & Lamas; admission CUC$3; ⊙ 10am-midnight) Situated in the hotbed of Havana's Santería community, this funky bar-restaurant hosts live rumba music at weekends, including regular visits from the Conjunto Folklórico Nacional. The pleasant garden bar is surrounded by colorful Afro-Cuban sculptures that depict various Santería deities such as Babalou Aye, Yemayá and Changó. Well off the beaten track and hard to get to at night, this quirky music venue is usually visited by foreigners in groups. It also does a good selection of food from a CUC$1 pizza to CUC$20 lobster.

Los Ibelly Heladería (Adolfo del Castillo Cadenas No 5a; ☻ 10am-10pm) As close as Guanabacoa gets to the Coppelia, with quick-serve ice cream.

Getting There & Away
Bus P-15 from the Capitolio in Centro Habana goes to Guanabacoa via Av del Puerto. Alternatively, you can walk uphill from Regla, from where the Havana ferry docks, to Guanabacoa (or vice versa) in about 45 minutes, passing Colina Lenin on the way.

SAN FRANCISCO DE PAULA
In 1939 US novelist Ernest Hemingway rented a villa called Finca La Vigía on a hill at San Francisco de Paula, 15km southeast of central Havana. A year later he bought the house (1888) and property and lived there continuously until 1960, when he moved back to the US.

The villa's interior has remained unchanged since the day Hemingway left (there are lots of stuffed trophies), and the wooded estate is now the **Museo Hemingway** (Map p99; ☎ 891-0809; unguided/guided CUC$3/4, camera/video CUC$5/25; ☻ 9am-4:30pm, closed Tue). Hemingway left his house and its contents to the 'Cuban people,' and his house has recently been the stimulus for a rare show of US-Cuban cooperation. In 2002 the Cubans agreed to a US-funded project to digitalize the documents stored in the basement of Finca La Vigía, and in May 2006 Cuba sent 11,000 of Hemingway's private documents to the JFK Presidential Library in America for digitalization. This literary treasure trove (including a previously unseen epilogue for *For Whom the Bell Tolls*) was finally made available online in January 2009.

To prevent the pilfering of objects, visitors are not allowed inside the house, but there are enough open doors and windows to allow a proper glimpse into Papa's universe. There are books everywhere (including beside the toilet), a large Victrola and record collection, and an astounding number of knickknacks. Don't come when it's raining as the house itself will be closed. A stroll through the gar-

den is worthwhile to see the surprisingly sentimental dog cemetery, Hemingway's fishing boat *El Pilar* and the pool where actress Ava Gardner once swam naked. You can chill out on a chaise lounge below whispering palms and bamboo here.

To reach San Francisco de Paula, take metro bus P-7 (Cotorro) from the Capitolio in Centro Habana. Tell the driver you're going to the museum. You get off in San Miguel del Padrón.

SANTA MARÍA DEL ROSARIO
Santa María del Rosario, 19km southeast of central Havana, is an old colonial town founded in 1732. Unlike most other towns from that period, it has not become engulfed in modern suburbs, but stands alone in the countryside. The charms of this area were recognized by one of Cuba's greatest living painters, Manuel Mendive, who selected it for his personal residence. You can also see the countryside of this area in Tomás Gutiérrez Alea's metaphorical critique of slavery in his movie *La Última Cena*.

The **Iglesia de Nuestra Señora del Rosario** (☻ 5:30-7:30pm), also called the Catedral de los Campos de Cuba, on Santa María del Rosario's old town square, was built in 1720 by the Conde de Casa Bayona near the Quiebra Hacha sugar mill, of which nothing remains today. Inside are a gilded mahogany altar and a painting by Veronese. It is one of suburban Havana's most attractive secrets.

From the Capitolio in Centro Habana take the metro bus P-7 to Cotorro and then bus 97, which runs from Guanabacoa to town.

PARQUE HISTÓRICO MILITAR MORRO-CABAÑA
The sweeping views of Havana from the other side of the bay are spectacular, and a trip to the two old forts of the **Parque Histórico Militar Morro-Cabaña** is a must. Despite their location on the opposite side of the harbor, both forts are included in the Habana Vieja Unesco World Heritage Site. Sunset is a good time to visit when you can stay over for the emblematic **cañonazo ceremony** (see boxed text, p169).

CASTILLO DE LOS TRES SANTOS REYES MAGNOS DEL MORRO
The imposing **Castillo de los Tres Santos Reyes Magnos del Morro** (El Morro; per person incl museum entrance CUC$4) was erected between 1589 and

1630 to protect the entrance to Havana harbor from pirates and foreign invaders (French corsair Jacques de Sores had sacked the city in 1555). Perched high on a rocky bluff above the ebbing Atlantic, the fort's irregular polygonal shape, 3m-thick walls and deep protective moat offer a classic example of Renaissance military architecture. For more than a century the fort withstood numerous attacks by French, Dutch and English privateers, but in 1762, after a 44-day siege, a 14,000-strong British force captured El Morro by attacking from the landward side. The Castillo's famous **lighthouse** was added in 1844.

Aside from the fantastic views over the sea and the city, El Morro also hosts a **maritime museum**. To climb to the top of the lighthouse is an additional CUC$2.

FORTALEZA DE SAN CARLOS DE LA CABAÑA

An 18th-century colossus, the **Fortaleza de San Carlos de la Cabaña** (☎ 862-0617; admission day CUC$5, night CUC$8, guide CUC$1; ☼ 8am-11pm) was built between 1763 and 1774 on a long, exposed ridge on the east side of Havana harbor to fill a weakness in the city's defenses. In 1762 the British had taken Havana by gaining control of this strategically important ridge and it was from here that they shelled the city mercilessly into submission. In order to prevent a repeat performance, the Spanish King Carlos III ordered the construction of a massive fort that would repel future invaders. Measuring 700m from end to end and covering a whopping 10 hectares, it is the largest Spanish colonial fortress in the Americas.

The impregnability of the fort meant that no invader ever attacked it, though during the 19th century Cuban patriots faced firing squads here. Dictators Machado and Batista used the fortress as a military prison, and immediately after the Revolution Che Guevara set up his headquarters inside the ramparts to preside over another catalog of grisly executions (this time of Batista's officers).

These days the fort has been restored for visitors and you can spend at least half a day checking out its wealth of attractions. As well as bars, restaurants, souvenir stalls and a cigar shop (containing the world's longest cigar), La Cabaña boasts the **Museo de Fortificaciones y**

PARQUE HISTÓRICO MILITAR MORRO-CABAÑA

0 ———— 200 m
0 ———— 0.1 miles

Straits of Florida

Via Monumental

To Playas del Este (13km)

Castillo de los Tres Santos Reyes Magnos del Morro

Military Cantonment

Dársena de los Franceses

Fortaleza de San Carlos de la Cabaña

Bahía de La Habana

Habana Vieja

To Casablanca (1km)

INFORMATION	
Ticket Booth................1	B1
Ticket Booth................2	B1

SIGHTS & ACTIVITIES	
Batería de la Divina Pastora.....3	B2
Batería de los Doce Apóstoles.4	A2
Batería de Velasco.................5	A1

Cañonazo Ceremony................6	C3
Entrance...................7	A2
Entrance...................8	B2
Estatua de Cristo.................9	D3
Lighthouse...................10	A2
Lookout...................11	C3
Maritime Museum.................12	A1
Museo de Comandancia del Che.................13	C3
Museo de Fortificaciones y Armas.................14	C3
Observatorio Nacional..........15	D3

EATING	
Bar El Polvorín...................16	A2
Paladar Doña Carmela.........17	C1
Restaurante La Divina Pastora.18	B2
Restaurante Los Doce Apóstoles...................19	A2

ASK A LOCAL

The *cañonazo* ceremony in the Fortaleza La Cabaña re-enacts an old tradition carried out since the 18th century, when soldiers used to fire a single cannon shot every night at 9pm to mark the closing of the old city gates. Modern soldiers carrying fire torches and wearing old-style military uniforms have kept the practice alive. It's quite a spectacle.

Augusto, Havana

Armas and the engrossing **Museo de Comandancia del Che**. The nightly 9pm *cañonazo* ceremony is a popular evening excursion (see boxed text, above).

Eating

Paladar Doña Carmela (☎ 863-6048; Calle B No 10; ☉ evenings only) A private eating option that offers quality chicken and pork in a very pleasant alfresco setting (when it's open). Makes a good dinner before or after the *cañonazo*, but check ahead as opening times are sporadic.

Parts of the fortresses have been converted into good restaurants and atmospheric bars. The **Restaurante Los Doce Apóstoles** (☎ 863-8295; ☉ noon–11pm), below El Morro, so named for the battery of 12 cannons atop its ramparts, serves *comida criolla*. It's a better-than-average government-run kitchen, and the prices are fair. **Bar El Polvorín** (☎ 860-9990; ☉ 10am–4am), just beyond Los Doce Apóstoles, offers drinks and light snacks on a patio overlooking the bay. There's zero shade, but it's perfect for those famous Havana sunsets.

Back below La Cabaña, just beyond the Dársena de los Franceses, is another battery of huge 18th-century cannons. The upscale but approachable **Restaurante La Divina Pastora** (☎ 860-8341; ☉ noon–11pm) behind the guns, offers well-prepared seafood, including lobster and fish. You can also just sit and soak in the views with an icy Cristal and some crisp *tostones* (fried plantain patties).

Getting There & Away

Cyclists can get to the fortresses from Havana with the specially designed CicloBus leaving from the corner of Dragones and Águila at Parque El Curita in Centro Habana (Map p106). This seatless bus is accessible via small ramps that lead to the doors. Cyclists are obliged to use it to get to La Habana del Este as riding a bicycle through the tunnel is prohibited. If you don't have a bicycle, you can walk to the head of the line and get on the first bus (ask the person selling bus tickets). Get off at the first stop after the tunnel; it's only a 10-minute walk back to either fortress. You can also get there on the P-15, P-8 or P-11 metro buses (get off at the first stop after the tunnel), but make sure you're near an exit as very few other people get out there. Otherwise, a metered tourist taxi from Habana Vieja should cost around CUC$4.

One of the quickest ways to get here without a car is via the Casablanca ferry. From the entrance to La Cabaña, go down into the moat and follow it around to a gate just below the huge Christ statue.

Parking costs CUC$1 at the fortresses.

CASABLANCA

Casablanca, just across the harbor from Habana Vieja, is dominated by a white marble **statue of Christ** (Map p168) created in 1958 by Jilma Madera. It was allegedly promised to President Batista by his wife after the US-backed dictator survived an attempt on his life in the Presidential Palace in March 1957. As you disembark the Casablanca ferry, follow the road uphill for about 10 minutes until you reach the statue. The views from up here are stupendous and it is a favorite nighttime hangout for locals. Behind the statue is the **Observatorio Nacional** (Map p168; closed to tourists).

Passenger ferries to Casablanca depart Muelle Luz, on the corner of San Pedro and Santa Clara in Habana Vieja, about every 15 minutes (CUC$1). Bicycles are welcome.

The **Casablanca train station** (☎ 862-4888), next to the ferry wharf, is the western terminus of the only electric railway in Cuba. In 1917 the Hershey Chocolate Company of the US state of Pennsylvania built this line to Matanzas (see boxed text, p179). Trains still depart for Matanzas five times a day (at 4:46am, 8:35am, 12:48pm, 4:38pm and 8:46pm). The 8:35am service is an 'express.' You'll travel via Guanabo (CUC$0.80, 25km), Hershey (CUC$1.45, 46km), Jibacoa (CUC$1.65, 54km) and Canasí (CUC$1.95, 65km) to Matanzas (CUC$2.80, 90km) and dozens of smaller stations. No one on a tight schedule should use this train; it usually leaves Casablanca on time but often arrives an hour late. Bikes aren't officially allowed. It's a scenic four- to five-hour trip, and tickets are easily obtainable at the station.

COJÍMAR AREA

Situated 10km east of Havana is the little port town of Cojímar, famous for harboring Ernest Hemingway's fishing boat *El Pilar* in the 1940s and '50s. This picturesque, if slightly run-down harbor community served as the proto-type for the fishing village in Hemingway's novel *The Old Man and the Sea*, which won him the Nobel Prize for Literature in 1954. It was founded in the 17th century at the mouth of the Río Cojímar. In 1762 an in-vading British army landed here on its way through to take Havana; in 1994 thousands of 'rafters' split from the sheltered but rocky bay, lured to Florida by US radio broadcasts and promises of political asylum.

To the southwest of Cojímar just off the Vía Blanca is the rather ugly sporting complex and athletes' village built when Cuba staged the 1991 Pan-American Games.

Information

Bandec (☺ 8:30am-3pm Mon-Fri, 8:30-11am Sat), which is just down the Paseo Panamericano, changes traveler's checks and gives cash advances. For Cuban pesos there's **Cadeca** (☎ 95-15-78; Bldg 46 Btwn Avs 5 & 78), just down the side street, across the avenue from Bandec.

Sights

The huge 55,000-seat **Estadio Panamericano**, on the Vía Monumental between Havana and Cojímar, was built for the 1991 Pan-American Games and is already looking prematurely dilapidated. There are also tennis courts, Olympic-sized swimming pools and other sporting facilities nearby.

Overlooking the harbor is the **Torreón de Cojímar**, an old Spanish fort (1649) presently occupied by the Cuban Coast Guard. It was the first fortification taken by the British when they attacked Havana from the rear in 1762. Next to this tower and framed by a neoclassical archway is a gilded **bust of Ernest Hemingway**, erected by the residents of Cojímar in 1962.

East across the river from Cojímar is **Alamar**, a large housing estate of prefabricated apart-ment blocks built by *micro brigadas* (small

armies of workers responsible for building much of the postrevolutionary housing), beginning in 1971.

Sleeping

Hotel Panamericano (Islazul; ☎ 95-10-00/10; s/d incl breakfast CUC$46/60; P ✷ ✹) If this four-story ugly duckling was the best accommodation Havana could muster for the 1991 Pan-American Games, then thank God they're not hosting the Olympics. Inconveniently located and rough around the edges, the Panamericano establishment was due to re-open at the time of writing after a spell hous-ing Operación Milagros. Call ahead to check the status.

Eating

Restaurante La Terraza (☎ 93-92-32; Calle 152 No 161; ☺ noon-11pm) Another photo-adorned shrine to the ghost of Ernest Hemingway, La Terraza specializes in seafood and does a roaring trade from the hordes of Papa fans who pour in daily. The terrace dining room overlooking the bay is pleasant. More at-mospheric, however, is the old bar out front (10:30am to 11pm) where mojitos haven't yet reached El Floridita rates. The food is surprisingly mediocre.

Just down from the Hotel Panamericano is a **bakery** (☺ 8am-8pm). Across the Paseo Panamericano is a grocery store, the **Mini-Super Caracol** (☺ 9am-8pm), and a clean and reasonably priced Italian restaurant **Allegro** (☺ noon-11pm) with lasagna, risotto, spaghetti and pizza, all for CUC$4.

Getting There & Away

Metro bus P-8 goes to the Villa Panamericano from the Capitolio in Centro Habana. From the hotel it's around 2km downhill through the village to the Hemingway bust.

PLAYAS DEL ESTE

In Cuba you're never far from an idyllic diamond-dust beach, and Havana is no ex-ception. The city's very own pine-fringed Riviera, Playas del Este, begins just 18km to the east of the capital at the small resort of Bacuranao, before continuing east through Tarará, El Mégano, Santa María del Mar and Boca Ciega to the town of Guanabo, 27km from Havana. Although none of these places has so far witnessed the kind of megadevelop-ment redolent of Cancún or Varadero, Playas del Este is still a popular tourist drawcard and, during the summer months of July and August, this is where all of Havana comes to play and relax on the soft white sands and clear aquamarine waters of the beautiful Atlantic coastline.

But while the beaches might be postcard-perfect, Playas del Este can't yet boast the all-round tourist facilities of other Cuban resorts such as Varadero and Cayo Coco, much less the all-out luxury of celebrated Caribbean getaways. Come here in the winter and the place often has a timeworn and slightly abandoned air and, even in the summer, seasoned beach bums might find the tatty restaurants and ugly Soviet-style hotel piles more than a little incongruous.

But for those who dislike modern tourist development or are keen to see how the Cubans get out and enjoy themselves at weekends, Playas del Este is a breath of fresh air.

Each of the six beaches that dot this 9km stretch of attractive coastline has its own distinctive flavor, allowing travelers to shop around until they find something to suit their taste. Tarará is a yacht and diving haven, Santa María del Mar is where the largest concentration of resorts (and foreigners) can be found, Boca Ciega is popular with gay couples, while Guanabo is the rustic Cuban end of the strip, with shops, a nightclub and plenty of cheap casas particulares.

Information
MEDICAL SERVICES
Clínica Internacional Habana del Este (☎ 96-18-19; Av de las Terrazas No 36, Santa María del Mar) Open 24 hours; doctors can make hotel visits. There's also a well-stocked pharmacy on-site. This clinic was being renovated at the time of writing.
Farmacia (cnr Av 5 & Calle 466, Guanabo)

MONEY
Banco Popular de Ahorro (☎ 796-2269; Av 5 No 47810 btwn Calles 478 & 480, Guanabo; ☉ 8:30am-5:30pm Mon-Fri) Changes traveler's checks.
Cadeca (Guanabo (☎ 96-41-34; Av 5 No 47612 btwn Calles 476 & 478; ☉ 8am-6pm); Santa María del Mar (Edificio Los Corales, Av de las Terrazas btwn Calles 10 & 11)

POST
Post office (Av 5 btwn Calles 490 & 492, Guanabo; ☉ 8am-6pm Mon-Sat)

INTERNET ACCESS & TELEPHONE
Etecsa Telepunto (Edificio Los Corales, Av de las Terrazas btwn Calles 10 & 11, Santa María del Mar)

TOURIST INFORMATION
Infotur Guanabo (☎ 96-68-68; Av 5 btwn Calles 468 & 470); Santa María del Mar (☎ 96-11-11; Edificio Los Corales, Av de las Terrazas btwn Calles 10 & 11)

TRAVEL AGENCIES
Cubatur and Havanatur both have desks at Hotel Tropicoco, between Av del Sur and Av de las Terrazas in Santa María del Mar. Their main business is booking bus tours, though they might be willing to help with hotel reservations in other cities.

Activities
Yacht charters, deep-sea fishing and scuba diving are offered by **Cubanacán Náutica Tarará** (☎ 96-15-08/9; VHF channels 16 & 77; cnr Av 8 & Calle 17, Tarará), 22km east of Havana. Ask about this at your hotel tour desk.

There are a number of **Club Náutica** points spaced along the beaches aside from **Club Mégano** at the westernmost end of the Playas. The most central is outside Club Atlántico in the middle of Playa Santa María del Mar. Here you can rent pedal boats (CUC$6 per hour; four to six people), banana boats (CUC$5 per five minutes; maximum five people), one-/two-person kayaks (CUC$2/4 per hour), snorkel gear (CUC$4) and catamarans (CUC$12 per hour; maximum four people plus lifeguard). A paddle around the coast exploring the mangrove-choked canals is a pleasure.

Beach toys such as sailboards, water bikes and badminton gear may also be available; ask. Many people rent similar equipment all along the beach to Guanabo, but check any water vessels and gear carefully as we've received complaints about faulty equipment. Consider leaving a deposit instead of prepaying in full, should anything go awry.

Sleeping
GUANABO
Casas Particulares
Guanabo has dozens of casas, and if one's full they readily recommend somewhere else.

Elena Morina (☎ 796-7975; Calle 472 No 7B11 btwn Avs 7B & 9; r CUC$25-30; 🅿) *Hay Perro* reads the sign, but don't worry, the pit bull that lives here is friendly (really) as is the hostess

PLAYAS DEL ESTE

INFORMATION		
Banco Popular de Ahorro	1	G2
Cadeca	2	B1
Cadeca	3	G2
Clínica Internacional Habana del		
Este	4	B1
Cubacar	(see 13)	
Cubatur	(see 14)	
Etecsa Telepunto	(see 2)	
Farmacia	5	G2
Havanatur	(see 14)	
Infotur	6	G2
Infotur	(see 2)	
Post Office	7	H2

SIGHTS & ACTIVITIES		
Club Mégano	8	A1
Club Náutica	9	C1

SLEEPING		
Club Atlántico – Los Pinos	10	C1
Complejo Atlántico – Las		
Terrazas	11	C1
Elena Morina	12	G2
Hotel Blau Club Arenal	13	D2
Hotel Tropicoco	14	A1
Pablo M Durán Jubiel &		
Rosario Redonda	15	G2
Villa Playa Hermosa	16	G2

EATING		
Bim Bom	17	F2
Don Pepe	18	B1
El Cubano	19	F2
Mini-Super Santa María	20	B1

Minisuper La Barca	21	E2
Paladar El Piccolo	22	H1
Panadería D'Prisa	23	G2
Pizzería al Mare	24	G2
Pizzería Mi Rinconcito	25	A1
Restaurante Maeda	26	G2
Restaurante Mi Casita		
de Coral	27	B1
Restaurante Mi Cayito	28	C1
Tienda Villa Los Pinos	29	A1

ENTERTAINMENT		
Cabaret Guanimar	30	F2
Cine Guanabo	31	G2
La Paté	32	D1
Teatro Avenida	33	G2

Elena who once lived in Italy. The chatty host makes great coffee and rents two decent rooms with a leafy patio a few blocks back from the beach.

Pablo M Durán Jubiel & Rosario Redonda (☎ 796-5281; Calle 476 No 905 btwn Avs 9 & 9B; r CUC$25-30; ⓟ ⓧ) This little house five blocks from the beach comes with a kitchen and patio; there are also rooms at Nos 906 and 9B01 nearby.

Hotels

Villa Playa Hermosa (Islazul; ☎ 796-2774; Av 5D btwn Calles 472 & 474; s/d CUC$22/26; ⓟ ⓧ ⓡ) This unpretentious villa has 47 rooms in small single-story bungalows with shared bath and TV. It's a popular spot with vacationing Cubans, so expect music, dancing and drinking to all hours; the beach is nearby.

SANTA MARÍA DEL MAR

None of Santa María's hotels are knockout and some are downright ugly. The Blau Club Arenal is the closest the strip gets to Varadero levels of comfort.

Complejo Atlántico – Las Terrazas (Islazul; ☎ 797-1494; Av de las Terrazas btwn Calles 11 & 12;

1-/2-/3-bedroom apt CUC$50/75/88; ⓟ ⓧ ⓡ) An amalgamation of two old *aparthotels*, the 60 or so apartments (with kitchenettes) here are mainly the preserve of families. The two-bedroom units sleep four people and the three-bedrooms accommodate six, so it's great for a group. Ask specifically if your unit will have a fridge, as not all of them do. This is a decent-value choice that is just 100m from the beach.

Hotel Tropicoco (Cubanacán; ☎ 797-1371; btwn Avs del Sur & de las Terrazas; s/d all-inclusive CUC$69/99; ⓡ) Picked up by Cubanacán from the now-defunct Horizontes chain, this big blue monster is an architectural disaster both inside and out. Pity the poor Canadians who book this on-line without looking at the photos first. The main (only) benefit for the terribly unfussy is the price (cheap) and the location – you could hit a (big) home run onto the beach from here.

Hotel Blau Club Arenal (Cubanacán; ☎ 797-1272; s/d all-inclusive CUC$95/150; ⓟ ⓧ ⓡ) Playas del Este's most stylish option, this modern hotel is on the Laguna Itabo, between Boca Ciega and Santa María del Mar. It has 166 rooms

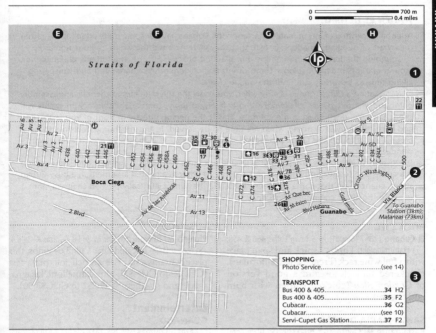

SHOPPING
Photo Service...........................(see 14)

TRANSPORT
Bus 400 & 405...........................**34** H2
Bus 400 & 405...........................**35** F2
Cubacar.....................................**36** G2
Cubacar...................................(see 10)
Servi-Cupet Gas Station.................**37** F2

set around a translucent pool. Ground-floor rooms have patios, but suites are much larger and cost about 20% more. The beach is just 150m away via a wooden footbridge suspended over the lagoon (which you can explore by rowboat).

Club Atlántico – Los Pinos (Gran Caribe; ☎ 797-1085; Av de las Terrazas btwn Calles 11 & 12; s/d/2-bed house all-inclusive CUC$105/150/160; ⓟ ☒ ◻ ☒) Another amalgamation of two of Playas del Este's better resorts, the Atlántico is a 92-room hotel right on the beach, and Los Pinos a collection of little houses (two to four bedrooms) with kitchens and TVs that were holiday homes before the Revolution. Collectively, they're one of the resort's best bets. Extra facilities include tennis courts, a swimming pool, cabaret and a Club Náutica point renting boats etc on the beach.

BACURANAO
Villa Bacuranao (Islazul; ☎ 65-76-45; s/d CUC$38/44) On the Vía Blanca, 18km east of Havana, this is the closest beach resort to Havana. There's a long sandy beach between the resort and mouth of the Río Bacuranao, across which

is the old Torreón de Bacuranao (inside the compound of the military academy and inaccessible). The beach here isn't as nice as its more easterly counterparts, but the price is nice.

Eating
GUANABO
Paladar El Piccolo (☎ 796-4300; cnr Av 5 & Calle 502; ☾ noon-11pm) This paladar is considered by many Habaneros to be the best pizza restaurant in Cuba, and they're not far wrong. Out of the way and a little more expensive than Playas del Este's other numerous pizza joints, it's well worth the walk.

Restaurante Maeda (Av Quebec; ☾ noon-midnight) Guanabo's other paladar is still going strong hidden away on the hill (near Calle 476).

Pizza for CUC$1.50 and up per slice is available at **Pizzería al Mare** (cnr Av 5 & Calle 482; ☾ 24hr), and there's the peso stuff served out of a charcoal-stained shack nearby. For ice cream, head to **Bim Bom** (cnr Av 5 & Calle 464; ☾ 11am-1am). **Panadería D'Prisa** (Av 5 No 47802; ☾ 24hr) is the place for pastries and light snacks.

¿QUIÉN ES ÚLTIMO?

After half a century of interminable shortages, the Cubans have become quite adept at the rather dreary art of queuing; so adept, in fact, that they've reinvented the whole tedious rigmarole.

Shunning the long snaking lineups that plagued postwar Europe, the Cubans prefer to wait around in a less orderly fashion – some sitting and talking, others canoodling and whispering – killing time as best they can until the queue clears.

Negotiating a Cuban queue is easy when you know the rules. Roll up at the relevant assembly point and yell out ¿Quién es último? (Who is last?). In reply, someone within a 90m radius will shout back ¡Yo! (Me!). Make a mental note. This is the person directly in front of you in the line and your two-minute warning when it's time to be served. In the meantime, feel free to pace around, sift through the latest propaganda in *Granma* or – if it looks like an extra-long wait – wander off for a revitalizing mojito.

Despite its lackadaisical appearance, queuing in Cuba is a serious business and line-jumping is a crime akin to breaking and entering. If you ever witness a heated argument in a busy Cuban street, chances are that some impatient bystander has unsocialistically pushed their way into a queue to howls of communal derision.

BOCA CIEGA

El Cubano (☎ 796-4061; Av 5 btwn Calles 456 & 458; ☉ 11am-midnight) This is a spick and span place with a full wine rack (French and Californian), checkered tablecloths and a good version of *Gordon Bleu* (chicken stuffed with ham and cheese).

SANTA MARÍA DEL MAR

Restaurante Mi Cayito (☎ 797-1339; ☉ 10am-6pm) On a tiny island in the Laguna Itabo, this place serves lobster, shrimp and grilled fish in an open-air locale. Nice ambience and cheap pork fillets. There's a live show here every Saturday and Sunday at 3pm, which you can enjoy for the price of a drink.

Restaurante Mi Casita de Coral (cnr Av del Sur & Calle 8; ☉ 10am-11pm) Tucked just off the roundabout by the international clinic, this secluded little place is surprisingly upscale for this neck of the woods and serves good seafood at reasonable prices.

When the Guanabo pizza gets too much, head for **Don Pepe** (Av de las Terrazas; ☉ 10am-11pm), a thatched-roof, beach-style restaurant about 50m from the sand. It specializes in seafood, as the waiters will keenly explain.

Among the many small grocery stores in and around Santa María del Mar are **Minisuper La Barca** (cnr Av 5 & Calle 446; ☉ 9:15am-6:45pm Mon-Sat, 9:15am-2:45pm Sun); **Mini-Super Santa María** (cnr Av de las Terrazas & Calle 7; ☉ 9am-6:45pm), located opposite Hotel Tropicoco; and **Tienda Villa Los Pinos** (Av del Sur btwn Calles 5 & 7; ☉ 9am-6:45pm).

EL MÉGANO

Pizzería Mi Rinconcito (cnr Av de las Terrazas & Calle 4; ☉ noon-9:45pm) Located near Villa Los Pinos, this place contains a surprisingly delicious pizza-fest (CUC$2 to CUC$3), plus cannelloni, lasagna, salads and spaghetti (CUC$2 to CUC$3.50).

Entertainment

GUANABO

Cabaret Guanimar (☎ 796-2947; cnr Av 5 & Calle 468; per couple CUC$10; ☉ 9pm-3am Tue-Sat) An outdoor club with a show at 11pm; if you want to be in the front rows, it's CUC$16 for a couple.

Teatro Avenida (☎ 796-2944; Av 5 No 47612 btwn Calles 476 & 478) has children's matinees at 3pm Saturday and Sunday. For a movie try **Cine Guanabo** (☎ 796-2440; Calle 480; ☉ 5:30pm except Wed) off Av 5.

SANTA MARÍA DEL MAR

Playas del Este's gay scene revolves around a beach bar called **La Paté** (Calle 1), near Restaurante Mi Cayito, at the east end of Santa María del Mar. You might also check all the way west on Playa El Mégano for cruising opportunities.

Shopping

Photo Service (Hotel Tropicoco btwn Avs del Sur & de las Terrazas) This place will satisfy most of your film and camera needs.

Getting There & Away

BUS & TAXI

The Havana Bus Tour (see p151) runs a regular (hourly) service from Parque Central out to Playa Santa María stopping at Villa Bacuranao, Tarará, Club Mégano, Hotel Tropicoco, Club Atlántico and Hotel Blau Arenal Club. It doesn't go as far as Guanabo. All day tickets cost CUC$5.

Bus 400 to Guanabo leaves every hour or so from Calle Agramonte in Centro Habana and stops near the central train station in Habana Vieja. Going the other way, it stops all along Av 5, but it's best to catch it as far east as possible. Bus 405 runs between Guanabacoa and Guanabo.

A tourist taxi using **Taxis OK** (☎ 796-6666) from Playas del Este to Havana will cost around CUC$20.

TRAIN

One of the most novel ways to get to Guanabo is on the Hershey Train, which leaves five times a day from either Casablanca train station or from Matanzas. The train will drop you at Guanabo station (little more than a hut in a field), approximately 2km from the far eastern end of Guanabo. It's a pleasant walk along a quiet road to the beaches.

Getting Around

A large guarded parking area is off Calle 7, between Av de las Terrazas and Av del Sur, near Hotel Tropicoco (CUC$1 a day from 8am to 7pm). Several other paid parking areas are along Playa Santa María del Mar.

Cubacar (Club Atlántico ☎ 797-1650; Hotel Blau Club Arenal ☎ 797-1272; Guanabo ☎ 796-6997; cnr Calle 478 & Av 9) rents average-sized cars for far from average prices – bank on CUC$70 a day with insurance.

Both **Servi-Cupet gas stations** (Guanabo ☎ 96-38-58; cnr Av 5 & Calle 464; west of Bacuranao Vía Blanca) have snack bars and are open 24 hours. The gas station west of Bacuranao is opposite the military academy.

Havana Province

Other provinces have their swanky resorts and their historically compelling colonial cities. Havana province, on the other hand, has…er…well, yes, that's the problem: Havana province doesn't really have a lot. In actual fact, it doesn't even have Havana!

So what can a poor boy/girl do? It all depends on your expectations and, to a lesser extent, your pace. If Cuba, for you, is an unending diet of flamboyant cabaret shows and hulking all-inclusive resorts, head east through Havana province to Varadero and don't get out of the car. But, if you want a warts-and-all insight into the capital's very real rural hinterland where the sight of a tourist is about as rare as a snow shower, then ease your foot off the accelerator and come to a grinding halt.

In fact, you might not even need a car at all. Havana province hosts one of Cuba's greatest rural journeys, the slow jolting Hershey train that stutters and clangs its way to Matanzas through a series of dusty hamlets and cheerful one-horse villages that would have long been swallowed up by sprawling suburbia in any other country.

Geographically speaking, the countryside surrounding Havana is the city's giant vegetable garden. Within easy reach of the capital, a huge variety of crops are grown on the province's fertile and predominantly flat terrain; everything from tobacco and citrus fruit, to sugarcane and grapes for wine (yes, wine!).

Of its numerous small hardworking towns, San Antonio de los Baños is easily the most interesting; a laid-back, quirky place that boasts a world-class film school patronized by Columbian author Gabriel García Márquez, and is the home of what must be Cuba's most esoteric museum; the sardonic Museo del Humor. Havana province boring? You're having a laugh.

HIGHLIGHTS

- **When Sugar Was King** Admire the iron skeleton of a once great sugar mill at Central Camilo Cienfuegos (p178)

- **Campismo Culture** See how the Cubans vacation and book a cabin at the beachside Campismo Los Cocos (p179)

- **Train Trek** Escape the tourist trails on the historic Hershey Electric Railway (p179)

- **Humor House** Have a laugh at the Museo del Humor (p182) in San Antonio de los Baños

- **Coffee Ruins** Join the ghosts of times past at the Antiguo Cafetal Angerona (p183)

■ TELEPHONE CODE: 047   ■ POPULATION: 722,045   ■ AREA: 5731 SQ KM

HAVANA PROVINCE

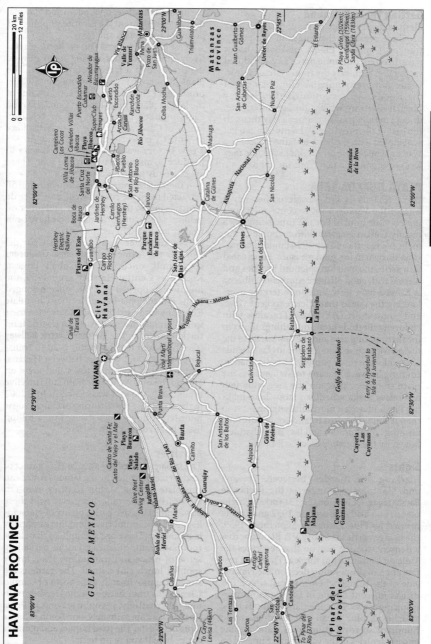

0 20 km
0 12 miles

GULF OF MEXICO

23°00'N
22°45'N

83°00'W
82°30'W
82°00'W

Matanzas

To Playa Girón (202km); Cienfuegos (159km); Santa Clara (183km)

Matanzas Province

Guanábana
Triunvirato
Juan Gualberto Gómez
Unión de Reyes
El Estante
San Antonio de Cabezas
Nueva Paz

Limonar
Mena
Pozo de San Juan
Valle de Yumurí
Villa Blanca
Mirador de Bacunayagua
Puerto Escondido
Camarones Villas Cubanar
Puerto Escondido
Rancho Gaviota
Arcos de Canasí
Ceiba Mocha
Madruga
Catalina de Güines
San Nicolás
Ensenada de la Broa
82°00'W

Campismo Los Cocos
Camaleón Villas Jibacoa
Playa Jibacoa SuperClub Breezes
Villa Loma de Jibacoa
Santa Cruz del Norte
Boca de Jaruco
Jardines de Hershey
Camilo Cienfuegos (Hershey)
Río Jibacoa
Jibacoa Pueblo
San Antonio de Río Blanco
Jaruco
Güines
Melena del Sur
Batabanó
Surgidero de Batabanó
La Playita

Hershey Electric Railway
Canal de Tarará
Playas del Este
Campo Florido
Guanabo
City of Havana
Parque Escaleras de Jaruco
San José de las Lajas
Autopista Habana - Melena

HAVANA
José Martí International Airport
Bejucal
Quivicán
Golfo de Batabanó

Punta Brava
Canto de Santa Fe;
Canto del Viejo y el Mar
Playa Baracoa
Blue Reef Diving Center
Playa Salado
Autopista Habana-Mariel
Bauta
Calimito
San Antonio de los Baños
Güira de Melena
Ferry & Hydrofoil to Isla de Juventud
Cayería Las Cayamas

Mariel
Bahía de Mariel
Cabañas
Guanajay
Carretera Central
Artemisa
Alquízar
Cayos Los Guzmanes
Playa Majana

Autopista Habana-Pinar del Río (A4)
Cayajabos
Antiguo Cafetal Angerona

Las Terrazas
Soroa
San Cristóbal
Candelaria
Pinar del Río Province
To Cayo Levisa (46km)
To Pinar del Río (37km)
23°00'N
22°45'N

HAVANA PROVINCE

HAVANA PROVINCE

Getting There & Around

Despite its proximity to the capital, Havana province presents challenges in the public transport sphere. Plenty of Víazul buses pass through, but none make any scheduled stops here. Similarly the train system is slow, vague and pretty unreliable in this neck of the woods. An exception is the Hershey Electric Railway which, though often late, does generally pass five times a day through the east of the province. Adventurers can get acquainted with the hard-to-fathom local bus system, while those on a tighter schedule may wish to organize a taxi from the capital.

PLAYA JIBACOA AREA

Playa Jibacoa is the Varadero that never was, or the Varadero yet to come – depending on your hunch. For the time being it's a mainly Cuban getaway with a couple of all-inclusive resorts and a hotel-standard campismo thrown in for good measure. Punctuated by a series of small but splendid beaches and blessed with good offshore snorkeling, Jibacoa is backed by a lofty limestone terrace overlooking the ocean that offers excellent views and some short DIY hikes. Travelers with children will find interesting things to do in the surrounding area and the popularity of the region with Cuban families means fast friends are made wherever you go. The Vía Blanca, running between Havana to Matanzas, is the main transport artery in the area, although few buses make scheduled stops here making Playa Jibacoa a more challenging pit stop than it should be. Just inland are picturesque farming communities and tiny dusty hamlets linked by the Hershey Electric Railway.

Sights

Marking the border between Havana and Matanzas provinces is the **Puente de Bacunayagua**, Cuba's longest (314m) and highest (103m) bridge. Begun in 1957 and finally opened by Fidel Castro in September 1959, the bridge carries the busy Vía Blanca across a densely wooded canyon that separates the Valle de Yumurí from the sea. There is a restaurant and observation deck on the Havana side of the bridge where you can sink a few drinks in front of one of Cuba's most awe-inspiring views. Imagine dark, bulbous hills, splashes of blue ocean and hundreds upon hundreds of royal palm trees standing like ghostly sentries in the valley haze. Situated on

the main road between Varadero and Havana, the bridge restaurant is a favorite stopping-off point for tour buses and taxis.

West of here is **Santa Cruz del Norte**, a relatively quiet and unassuming town despite the presence of a famous rum factory. The plant in question is the Ronera Santa Cruz, producer of Havana Club rum and it's one of the largest plants of its kind in Cuba. Havana Club, founded in 1878 by the Arrechabala family of Cárdenas, opened its first distillery at Santa Cruz del Norte in 1919, and in 1973 a new factory was built with the capacity to produce 30 million liters of rum a year. There are currently no tours available.

A thermoelectric power station burning oil extracted from the coastal wells near Boca de Jaruco is just to the west. These and other oil fields west of Santa Cruz del Norte have been heavily exploited in recent years.

Five kilometers south of Santa Cruz del Norte is the former **Central Camilo Cienfuegos** sugar mill, once one of Cuba's largest. Known as Central Hershey until 1959, the mill, which opened in 1916, once belonged to the Philadelphia-based Hershey Chocolate Company who used the sugar to sweeten their world-famous chocolate bars. An electric train track known as the **Hershey Electric Railway** (see the boxed text opposite) used to transport produce and workers between Havana, Matanzas and the small town that grew up around the mill. While the train still runs five times a day, the mill was closed in July 2002 in the economic restructuring of Cuba's sugar industry. It now stands disused on a hilltop like a huge rusting iron skeleton.

Activities

The **Jardines de Hershey** (☎ 20-26-85) is a tract of land formerly owned by the famous American chocolate tycoon, Milton Hershey, who ran the nearby sugar mill. It's pretty wild these days, with attractive paths, plenty of green foliage and a beautiful river, and this essentially is its charm. There are a couple of thatched-roof restaurants on-site and an all-pervading sense of peace and tranquility. It's a lovely spot for lunch and a stroll. The gardens are situated approximately 1km north of Camilo Cienfuegos train station on the Hershey train line. Alternatively, if you're staying in Playa Jibacoa, it's approximately 4km south of Santa Cruz del Norte. The road is quiet and it makes a nice hike if you're up to it.

THE HERSHEY TRAIN

'Cow on the line,' drawls the bored-looking ticket seller. 'Train shut for cleaning' reads a scruffy hand-scrawled notice. To Habaneros, the catalog of daily transport delays is tediously familiar. While the name of the antediluvian Hershey Electric Railway might suggest a sweet treat to most visitors, in Cuba it signifies a more bitter mix of bumpy journeys, hard seats and interminable waits.

Built in 1921 by US chocolate 'czar' Milton S Hershey (1857–1945), the electric-powered railway line was originally designed to link the American mogul's humungous sugar mill in eastern Havana province with stations in Matanzas and the capital. Running along a trailblazing rural route, it soon became a lifeline for isolated communities cut off from the provincial transport network.

In 1959 the Hershey factory was nationalized and renamed Central Camilo Cienfuegos after Cuba's celebrated rebel commander. But the train continued to operate, clinging unofficially to its chocolate-inspired nickname. In the true tradition of the postrevolutionary 'waste not, want not' economy, it also clung to the same tracks, locomotives, carriages, signals and stations.

While a long way from Orient Express–style luxury, an excursion on today's Hershey train is a captivating journey back in time to the days when cars were for rich people and sugar was king. For outsiders, this is Cuba as the Cubans see it; a microcosm of rural life at the sharp end with all its daily frustrations, conversations, foibles and – er – fun.

Seemingly stopping at every house, hut, horse stable and hillock between Havana and Matanzas, getting off is something of a toss-up. Beach bums can disembark at Guanabo and wander 2km north for a taste of Havana's rustic eastern resorts. History buffs can get off at Camilo Cienfuegos and stroll around the ruins of the old Hershey sugar mill. The rest can choose between Playa Jibacoa, Arcos de Canasí and the beautiful Valley of Yumurí.

For more information on train times, stations and prices, see p169.

Puerto Escondido Cubamar (☎ 866-2524; Carretera Panamericana Km 80) has a smallish water sports center at Puerto Escondido, 1.5km off the Vía Blanca, 7km east of Arcos de Canasí. It offers scuba diving at the usual price of CUC$30 per dive and two-hour snorkeling trips for CUC$10 (four-person minimum), both including gear. Deep-sea fishing is also available.

There is good snorkeling from the beach facing Campismo Los Cocos, and heading westward along the coast you'll find unpopulated pockets where you can don a mask or relax under a palm.

Although technically in Havana province, **Ranchón Gaviota** (☎ 61-47-02; admission ind meal CUC$8; ⏰ 9am-6pm), 12km inland from Puerto Escondido, is usually incorporated in day trips from Matanzas and Varadero and approached via a pretty drive through the palm-sprinkled countryside of the Valle de Yumurí. The hilltop ranch overlooking a reservoir offers horseback riding, kayaking, cycling, plus a massive feast of *ajiaco* (meat stew), roasted pork, *congrí* (rice with beans), salad, dessert and coffee. To get to the Ranchón from Havana province take the inland road for 2km to Arcos de Canasí

and turn left at the fork for another 10km to the signpost.

Sleeping & Eating

our pick Campismo Los Cocos (Cubamar; ☎ 29-52-31/-32; s/d CUC$17/28; P ⛽ ⛳ &) The newest and, arguably, the plushest of Cubamar's 80 or more campismo sites, Los Cocos has facilities to match a midrange three-star hotel and a beachside setting that emulates the big shots in Varadero. Ninety self-contained supermodern cabins are clustered around a dazzling pool set in the crock of Havana province's low step-like cliffs. Facilities here include a small library, a medical post, an à la carte restaurant, a games room, rooms for disabled travelers, and plenty of walks and trails that disappear off into the surrounding hills. The only downside is the blaring poolside music – par for the course in Cuban campismos it seems. The campismo is also a fully equipped campervan site. As always it's best to book ahead with Cubamar (see p108) first.

Villa Loma de Jibacoa (Islazul; ☎ 29-53-16; 1-/2-/3-/4-bed apt CUC$38/40/60/70; P ⛳) This hotel stands on a hill overlooking a small beach near the mouth of the Río Jibacoa, just off the Vía Blanca. The perfect place for a family or group beach vacation, it is actually 13 individual houses of one to four rooms each sharing a TV, fridge and bath. As each one is different, you should look at a few before deciding – not always possible at this popular, heavily booked place.

Cameleón Villas Jibacoa (Gran Caribe; ☎ 29-52-05; s/d all-inclusive CUC$70/100; P X R) A little to the east of Campismo Los Cocos, this friendly, well-landscaped resort with great snorkeling and large (if dated) rooms offers good bang for your buck. It's marketed as a three-star and is popular with package tourists from Canada.

SuperClub Breezes (☎ 29-51-22; s/d all-inclusive CUC$151/242; P X R R) Just east of Cameleón Villas Jibacoa, SuperClub Breezes is Jibacoa's one and only swanky choice, a beachfront place that exhibits more panache than Playas del Este but less pretension than Varadero. Laid out in front of a choice nook of sandy beach, guests here are accommodated in attractive two-story bungalows that sit amid a tranquil mélange of blooming flowers, leafy gardens and trickling fountains. SuperClub also has a reputation for good food, entertainment and activities. Children under 16 are not accepted. Coming from Matanzas, the turn-off is 13km west of the Bacunayagua Bridge.

Eating is a grim prospect over this way unless you're in a hotel. There are a couple of dodgy bars around selling microwave pizza. Striking up a friendly conversation with the locals pulling in their fishing nets and arranging a meal might yield better results.

Getting There & Away

The best – some would say the *only* – way to get to Playa Jibacoa is on the Hershey Electric Railway from Casablanca train station in Havana to Jibacoa Pueblo (see p169 for times). There's no bus to the beach from the station and traffic is sporadic, so bank on hiking the last 5km; a not unpleasant walk as long as you haven't got too much gear. The electric train also stops at Arcos de Canasí, but that's still 6km from the beach and it's not a good walking road.

Another option is to take crowded bus 669 from outside **Estación La Coubre** (Desamparados), just south of Havana's Estación Central, to Santa Cruz del Norte. Unfortunately, this bus only operates three times a day and you'd still have to taxi it 9km further east

to Jibacoa. Your best bet is probably to go to the Havana bus station and take any bus headed for Matanzas along the Vía Blanca. Talk to the driver to arrange a drop-off at Playa Jibacoa, just across a long bridge from Villa Loma de Jibacoa.

JARUCO
pop 25,658

Jaruco, set back from the coast halfway between Havana and Matanzas, is a good day trip for travelers with a car/moped/bike who want to give the beaches a body-swerve and capture a bit of quintessential rural quiescence. The **Parque Escaleras de Jaruco**, 6km west of Jaruco village, is a protected area featuring interesting forests, caves, limestone cliffs and a high degree of endemism, and a gander along its hushed unmarked lanes via the small village of Jaruco can make for a highly satisfying scenic sojourn. It's 32km to Jaruco from Guanabo in a southeasterly direction via Campo Florido, and you can make it a loop by returning through Santa Cruz del Norte, 18km northeast of Jaruco via Central Camilo Cienfuegos.

SURGIDERO DE BATABANÓ
pop 25,664

Spanish colonizers founded the original settlement of Havana on the site of present day Surgidero de Batabanó on August 25, 1515, but quickly abandoned it in favor of the north coast. Looking around the decrepit town today, with its ugly apartment blocks and grubby beach-less seafront, it's not difficult to see why. The only reason you're likely to visit this fly-blown port is to catch the daily boat to the Isla de la Juventud. Should there be an unforeseen delay, the patchy **Museo Municipal** (Calle 64 No 7502; 9am-5pm Tue-Sun, closed Mon) will kill 15 minutes. If the wait continues, wander over to **La Playita** (Small Beach) 2km east of the dock, where there's a selection of little eateries selling fried fish by a tiny beach.

If desperation strikes and you need to overnight, your options are limited to the four-story unlisted **Hotel Dos Hermanos** (Calle 68 No 315), an old 29-room peso hotel looming near the port and train station with bad plumbing and the odd bug.

Fidel Castro and the other Moncada prisoners disembarked here on May 15, 1955, after Fulgencio Batista granted them amnesty.

SUGAR – A BITTER-SWEET HISTORY

As synonymous with Cuba as Che Guevara or Havana Club rum, sugarcane was first introduced onto the island by the Spanish in the early 1500s. With its flat rolling plains and fertile limestone soil, the colony quickly provided ideal growing conditions for the new crop and within decades sugar had become Cuba's leading export.

During the 17th and 18th centuries Cuba played second fiddle to French Haiti as a world sugar producer. But, following Toussaint L'Ouverture's 1791 slave rebellion, the pendulum swung inexorably west as thousands of exiled French planters arrived on the island, bringing with them their advanced business know-how and pioneering agro-industrial techniques.

In the two centuries that followed, Cuba metamorphosed from nascent regional sugar economy into the world's biggest exporter with a huge influx of African slaves pushing production through the roof and making vast fortunes for a new class of wealthy landowners.

But the sonic boom wasn't to last. Devastated by the two independence wars in the late 19th century, when huge swathes of cane fields were summarily razed, the industry faced ruin as production fell into a seemingly terminal decline.

Fatefully, it was only a temporary blip. Pulled out of the mire in the early 1900s by profit-hungry American businessmen who bought up struggling Cuban mills and land on the cheap, sugar's unlikely comeback was as dramatic as it was sweet.

Cuba's second big sugar high took place between 1915 and 1920 when the world sugar price hit $0.22 per pound and annual production peaked out at over four million tonnes. Enormous amounts of money were made almost overnight in an era that became known as the 'Dance of the Millions.' Havana reaped the economic benefits with a lavish public works program that saw the construction of such landmark buildings as the US$17 million Capitolio Nacional (p114).

But Cuba's over-reliance on its sweet-tasting mono-crop would come back to haunt it time and again. Following the 1959 Revolution, one of the first retaliatory acts of the US government was to cancel Cuba's preferential sugar quota in response to Castro's radical nationalization campaign. But the 'punishment' soon backfired. The next day the Soviet Union stepped in and bought up the US quota lock, stock and barrel, and a new 30-year Soviet-Cuban alliance was sealed in infamy right under Washington's nose.

Sugar production in Cuba peaked in 1970 when a bumper all-or-nothing harvest hit nearly 10 million tonnes; but thanks to foreign competition, antiquated production techniques and the massive growth of the tourist economy, it's been declining ever since.

In 2002, the government faced the music and shut down 70 of its 150 sugar mills in a drastic restructuring campaign. One notable casualty was the Camilo Cienfuegos (formerly Hershey) mill in Havana province (p178). Here, as in other sugar towns, laid-off workers have been offered graduate study programs and continue to draw their full state salaries (around 400 pesos a month). The aim is to raise the basic level of schooling among ex-sugar workers from ninth to 12th grade and enable them to find new employment elsewhere.

These days Cuba produces a more modest 2.5 million tonnes of sugar a year, and skeletal factories such as Camilo Cienfuegos stand like soot-stained reminders of another era.

Getting There & Away

The ferry from Surgidero de Batabanó to Isla de la Juventud is supposed to leave daily at noon with an additional sailing at 3:30pm on Wednesday, Friday and Sunday (CUC$55, two hours). It is advisable to buy your bus-boat combo ticket in Havana from the office at the main Terminal de Ómnibus (p149) rather than turning up and doing it here. More often than not convertible tickets are sold out to bus passengers.

There's a **Servi-Cupet gas station** (Calle 64 No 7110 btwn Calles 71 & 73) in the center of Batabanó town. The next Servi-Cupet station to the east is in Güines.

SAN ANTONIO DE LOS BAÑOS

pop 46,300

Full of surprises, San Antonio de los Baños, 35km southwest of central Havana, is Cuba on the flip side, a hard-working municipal town where the local college churns out wannabe cinematographers and the museums are more about laughs than crafts.

Founded in 1986 with the help of Nobel Prize–winning Columbian novelist, Gabriel García Márquez, San Antonio's Escuela Internacional de Cine y TV invites film students from around the world to partake in its excellent on-site facilities, including an Olympic-sized swimming pool for practicing underwater shooting techniques. Meanwhile, in the center of town, a unique humor museum makes a ha-ha-happy break from the usual stuffed animal/revolutionary artifact/antique furniture triumvirate.

San Antonio is made all the more amenable by the inclusion of an attractive riverside hotel, Las Yagrumas, which offers a welcome escape from Havana's frenetic pace. The town is also the birthplace of *nueva trova* music giant, Silvio Rodríguez, who was born here in 1946. Rodríguez later went on to write the musical soundtrack to the Cuban Revolution almost single-handed. His best-known songs include 'Ojalá,' 'La Maza' and 'El Necio.'

Sights & Activities

San Antonio de los Baños has several attractive squares; check out the one with the old church at the corner of Calles 66 and 41. Nearby, the **Museo Municipal** (Calle 66 No 4113 btwn Calles 41 & 43; admission CUC$1; ☽ 10am-6pm Tue-Sat, 9am-noon Sun) focuses on art with important works by local born painter Eduardo Abela (1899–1965), a modernist who studied in Paris and rediscovered his homeland with nostalgia from his self-imposed exile.

More local work is displayed at the **Galería Provincial Eduardo Abela** (Calle 58 No 3708 btwn Calles 37 & 39; admission free; ☽ 1-5pm Mon-Fri) nearby.

Unique in Cuba is the side-splitting selection of cartoons, caricatures and other entertaining ephemera at the **Museo del Humor** (cnr Calle 60 & Av 45; admission CUC$2; ☽ 10am-6pm Tue-Sat, 9am-1pm Sun). Among the drawings exhibited in this neoclassical colonial house are saucy cartoons, satirical scribblings and the first known Cuban caricature dating from 1848. Look out for the work of Cuba's foremost caricaturist, Carlos Julio Villar Alemán, a member of Uneac and a one-time judge at the **International Humor Festival** still held here every April (entries remain on display for several weeks during this period).

A footbridge across the river next to La Quintica restaurant leads to a couple of **hiking trails**. Enjoy a drink in the bar, before sallying forth on a DIY adventure around the leafy banks.

Sleeping & Eating

The main shopping strip is Av 41, and there are numerous places to snack on peso treats along this street. You can change your money at the **Cadeca** (☎ 38-28-64; Av 41 No 6003 btwn 60 & 62).

our pick **Hotel Las Yagrumas** (Islazul; ☎ 38-44-60/-61/-62; s/d CUC$30/40; P ☒ ☎) Good enough to be listed as a town highlight, Las Yagrumas is situated 3km north of San Antonio de los Baños, overlooking the picturesque, but polluted Río Ariguanabo. With its 120 rooms with balcony and terrace (some of which face the river) it is generally considered to be one of Islazul's better hotels and is, as a consequence, rather popular with peso-paying Cubans. Buffet meals are surprisingly good and table tennis, a gigantic pool and hilarious karaoke add to a pleasant family atmosphere.

La Quintica (☽ Tue-Sun) A local peso restaurant, situated just past the baseball stadium alongside the river 2km north of town. There's live music Friday and Saturday nights (closed Monday).

Entertainment

Taberna del Tío Cabrera (Calle 56 No 3910 btwn Calles 39 & 41; ☽ 2-5pm Mon-Fri, 2pm-1am Sat & Sun) This is an attractive garden nightclub that puts on the odd humor show (organized in conjunction with the museum). The clientele is an entertaining mix of townies, folk from the surrounding villages and students from the film school.

Getting There & Away

Hard to get to without a car, San Antonio is supposedly connected to Havana's Estación 19 de Noviembre (four trains a day), but check well ahead. Otherwise a taxi should cost you 50 centavos a kilometer.

BEJUCAL

pop 25,425

Though hardly a tourist town in the Varadero sense; tiny Bejucal is famous for two reasons.

Firstly,, there's the jubilant **Charangas de Bejucal**, a cacophonous cross between Santiago's Carnaval and Remedios' Parrandas that takes place every December 24. As in the Parrandas, the town splits into two groups, La Ceiba de Plata (the Silver Ceiba) and La

ASK A LOCAL

Cuba was the sixth country in the world to get a train system and the first in Latin America. Its rail network even preceded that of colonizing power, Spain. It remains the only country in the Caribbean with a fully functioning passenger train system.

Jorge, Havana

Espina de Oro (the Golden Thorn), who hit the streets laughing, dancing and singing among outrageously large, dazzling floats and the famous Bejucal *tambores* (drums). The Charangas date back to the early 1800s when the parading groups were split between creoles and black slaves. The racial distinctions no longer exist.

Bejucal's second claim to fame is its role in the development of the Cuban railway system. Latin America's first ever railway line opened on November 19, 1837, running between Havana and Bejucal. The original station is still here, although it underwent extensive renovation in 1882. The upper floor now serves as a **Railroad Museum** (Calle 7 & Línea de Ferrocarril; 🕑 8am-4pm Mon-Fri, 8am-noon Sat) displaying the history of railways in Cuba.

ARTEMISA
pop 60,477

Known locally as the Villa Roja (Red Town) or the Jardín de Cuba (Garden of Cuba), Artemisa, situated 60km southwest of Havana on the Carretera Central, is famous for the fertility of its soil that produces a rich annual harvest of sugarcane, tobacco and bananas. In days of yore the town grew wealthy on the back of the 19th-century sugar boom and until the 1970s was part of Pinar del Río province. If you're passing, Artemisa contains two national monuments (listed below) along with a **Museo Municipal** (Martí No 2307; admission CUC$1) and a restored section of the Trocha Mariel-Majana, a defensive wall erected by the Spanish during the Wars of Independence.

Revolution buffs may want to doff a cap to the **Mausoleo a los Mártires de Artemisa** (Av 28 de Enero; admission CUC$1; 🕑 9am-6pm Tue-Sun). Of the 119 revolutionaries who accompanied Fidel Castro in the 1953 assault on the Moncada Barracks, 28 were from Artemisa or this region. Fourteen of the men presently buried below the cube-shaped bronze mausoleum

died in the actual assault or were killed soon after by Batista's troops. The other Moncada veterans buried here died later in the Sierra Maestra. There's a small adjacent museum containing photos and personal effects of the combatants.

The **Antiguo Cafetal Angerona**, 17km west of Artemisa on the road to Cayajabos and the Autopista Habana–Pinar del Río (A4), was one of Cuba's earliest *cafetales* (coffee plantations). It is now a national monument. Erected between 1813 and 1820 by Cornelio Sauchay, Angerona once employed 450 slaves tending 750,000 coffee plants. Behind the ruined mansion lie the slave barracks and an old watchtower, from which the slaves' comings and goings were monitored. The estate is mentioned in novels by Cirilo Villaverde and Alejo Carpentier, and James A Michener devotes several pages to it in *Six Days in Havana*. It's a quiet and atmospheric place that has the feel of a latter-day Roman ruin.

The **Artemisa train station** (Av Héroes del Moncada) is four blocks east of the bus station. There are supposed to be two trains a day from Havana at noon and midnight, but don't bank on it.

The bus station is on the Carretera Central in the center of town.

MARIEL
pop 31,922

Mariel, 45km west of Havana, is known mostly for the 125,000 Cubans who left here for Florida in April 1980 (see boxed text, p184). Once you see it, you'll want to flee, too. Founded in 1762, Mariel is a major industrial town and port with the largest cement factory in Cuba, a huge thermoelectric power plant, military airfield and shipyards. There's also a new duty-free industrial zone adding to the action. It sits on the Bahía de Mariel at Cuba's narrowest point, just 31km north of the Caribbean at Playa Majana.

After Moa in Holguín province, Mariel is Cuba's most heavily polluted town. The filthy cement factory at Mariel once belonged to American cement producer Lone Star and was later run by the Mexican cement giant Cemex as a joint venture with the Cuban government.

The local **Museo Municipal de Mariel** (Calle 132 No 6926 cnr Av 71) is opposite the church at the entrance to town and, with its extensive coin collection, will enthrall bored coin collectors. A huge castle-like mansion,

THE MARIEL BOATLIFT

On April 1, 1980, Hector Sanyustic – a disgruntled Cuban dissident – drove a public bus through the fence of the Peruvian embassy in downtown Havana in an audacious escape bid. Despite being fired upon by guards in the street outside (one of whom was killed in the crossfire), Sanyustic and his four accomplices made it safely inside the embassy perimeter where they successfully claimed political asylum.

Hearing the news a furious Castro immediately demanded that Sanyustic and his colleagues be handed back to the Cuban authorities to be tried on charges of manslaughter. When Peru refused, Fidel, in a rare fit of pique, decided to remove the guards from the embassy gates and thus, unwittingly, usher in the biggest human exodus the island had ever seen.

Few observers – Fidel included – could have predicted the chaos that followed. As word of the new security arrangements quickly spread among other disaffected Cubans, the grounds of the Peruvian embassy filled up with over 11,000 Cuban refugees adamant to leave the island in the wake of a worsening economic crisis and an ongoing thaw in US-Cuban relations that had been orchestrated by the Carter administration.

With a major confrontation brewing, Castro did what he always does best: he passed the problem onto the US. On April 9, incensed at a comment by US president Jimmy Carter which had stated that America would 'welcome the refugees with open arms,' Fidel announced that the port of Mariel, 45km west of Havana, would be open to any Cubans wanting to leave, as long as they had someone to pick them up. Moving quickly to bail out their beleaguered compatriots, Cuban exiles in Miami and Key West resourcefully rustled up a Dunkirk-like flotilla of ships that was dispatched off to Mariel on a spontaneous rescue mission.

It was a lengthy and highly disorganized evacuation. Within weeks, the US had been inundated with Cuban refugees, many of whom – it later turned out – had been released from Cuban jails and mental institutions in a cynical bid by Castro to rid the island of its so-called 'undesirables.' Indeed, by the time the two governments finally ended the debacle in October 1980, the US had accepted approximately 125,000 Cuban immigrants from an estimated flotilla of 1700 dangerously overloaded boats. Twenty-seven people died during the sea crossing while over 2700 were denied asylum on the grounds that they were violent felons.

In the US the episode became known as 'the Mariel boatlift' and the refugee crisis that it created – along with the ongoing Iranian hostage affair – played a major part in Jimmy Carter's diminishing popularity. Meanwhile, back across the water, Castro, in a shrewd act of damage limitation, embarked upon a series of fiery nationalistic speeches that lambasted the emigrants as *lumpen* (traitors) and vowed to continue defending the Revolution at all costs.

The Mariel boatlift is fictionally portrayed in the 1983 Brian de Palma movie *Scarface*, which starred Al Pacino in the role of Tony Montana, an unscrupulous cocaine-addicted *marielito* who is let out of a Cuban jail to run amok in Miami.

now a naval academy, stands on a hilltop overlooking Mariel.

Twenty-two kilometers east of Mariel on the Autopista is **Playa Salado**, a popular beach that swarms with locals in summer, but is largely deserted at other times. The shoreline is rocky instead of sandy, but there are 15 dive sites offshore, most of which are utilized via excursion groups from Havana. A few kilometers east of Playa Salado is the more

developed **Playa Baracoa**. This is mainly local turf rarely visited by tourists except for adventurers taking the slow road to northern Pinar del Río province or transfers using the area's small airport (which handles flights to Cayo Largo del Sur). Big dudes near the shoreline lean on old American cars supping beer while fishermen throw lines from the rocky shore. There are a couple of basic beach shacks that sell food.

Isla de la Juventud (Special Municipality)

The Caribbean's sixth-largest land mass is an erstwhile 'Treasure Island' that became a prison and, later on, a giant school. Name-wise it's had as many incarnations as Castro's had assassination plots: Siguanea, Juan El Evangelista, Parrot Island and the Isla de Pinos are just some of the titles that were used before arriving in 1978 at the more topical Isla de la Juventud, a reference to the thousands of students who studied here in the 1960s and '70s.

A sleepy backwater even by Cuban standards, La Isla – as most locals call it – is rarely visited by main island tourists who prefer the more iconic attractions of Havana and the north-coast resorts. The situation isn't helped by poor transport links; the daily flights here are often booked up weeks in advance, and the fickle boat service is a frustrating exercise in exasperation requiring a lot of patience.

Those that do battle through, often come to dive. The dramatic reefs off Punta Francés in the island's sheltered southwest are deemed to be the best in Cuba, and perhaps even the Caribbean.

Downbeat Nueva Gerona is the island's affable but unremarkable capital, a hotchpotch of sleepy squares and even sleepier streets where little has disturbed the afternoon reverie since, oh, 1959.

The Isla's illustrious past residents include a colony of ambitious Americans (who tried unsuccessfully to make the island into an American garden suburb), a young José Martí, tens of thousands of African students, a few hundred crocodiles and prisoner number RN3859, better known to the world and history as Fidel Alejandro Castro Ruz.

The largest island in the Archipiélago de los Cannareos, the Isla's closest cousin is Cayo Largo del Sur, a tourist idyll famous for its turtles and large white (nudist!) beaches.

ISLA DE LA JUVENTUD (SPECIAL MUNICIPALITY)

HIGHLIGHTS

- **Beach Hike** Trek the wide, white (sometimes nudist) beaches from Playa Sirena (p195) back to Playa Lindamar on Cayo Largo del Sur

- **Go Slow** Spend a lazy afternoon in the streets and squares of Nueva Gerona (p188)

- **Crocodile Smile** Investigate an important crocodile conservation project at the Isla's Criadero Cocodrilo (p194)

- **Going Deep** Wrecks, walls, coral gardens and caves; Punta Francés (see boxed text, p190) is *the* best place to dive in Cuba

- **Turtle Watch** Spend the evening watching turtles nesting on the moonlit beaches of Cayo Largo del Sur (p196)

★ Nueva Gerona
★ Punta Francés
★ Criadero Cocodrilo
★ Cayo Largo del Sur
★ Playa Sirena

| ■ TELEPHONE CODE: 046 | ■ POPULATION: 86,637 | ■ AREA: 2398 SQ KM |

History

The first settlers on La Isla were the Siboney Indians, a pre-ceramic civilization who arrived on the island around 1000 BC via the Lesser Antilles and settled down as hunters and fishermen on the coasts. Naming their new-found homeland Siguanea, they made tools from conches and other shells and left a fascinating set of cave paintings in Cueva Punta del Este (p195).

By the time Columbus arrived on these shores in June 1494, the Siboney had long departed (either dying out or returning to the mainland) and the intrepid navigator promptly renamed the island Juan El Evangelista, claiming it for the Spanish crown. But, knotted with mangroves and surrounded by a circle of shallow reefs, the Spanish did little to develop their new possession.

Instead La Isla became a hideout for pirates, including Francis Drake, John Hawkins, Thomas Baskerville and Henry Morgan. They called it Parrot Island, and their exploits are said to have inspired Robert Louis Stevenson's idea for the novel *Treasure Island*.

In December 1830 the Colonia Reina Amalia (now Nueva Gerona) was founded, and throughout the 19th century the island served as a place of imposed exile for independence advocates and rebels, including José Martí. Twentieth-century dictators Gerardo Machado and Fulgencio Batista followed this Spanish example by sending political prisoners – Fidel Castro included – to the island, which had by then reincarnated for a fourth time as Isla de Pinos (Isle of Pines).

Aside from its Spanish heritage, La Isla also has a marked English influence. During the late 19th century, some fishing families from the British colony of the Cayman Islands established a settlement called Jacksonville (now Cocodrilo) on the southwest tip of Isla de Pinos; you'll still occasionally meet people who can converse fluently in English. Additionally, just prior to Cuban independence in 1902, the infamous Platt Amendment included a proviso that placed Isla de Pinos outside the boundaries of the 'mainland' part of the archipelago. Some 300 US colonists established themselves here soon after, and only in March 1925 did the US recognize the island as an integral part of Cuba.

The Americans stayed and thrived making good business from the island's first (but not the last) citrus plantations and building an efficient infrastructure of banks, hotels and public buildings. During WWII, the Presidio Modelo was used by the US to inter Axis prisoners and by the 1950s La Isla had become a favored vacation spot for rich Americans who flew in daily from Miami. The decadent party – which by this point included the age-old staples of gambling and prostitution – ended rather abruptly in 1959 with the ascendancy of Fidel Castro.

Before the Revolution Isla de Pinos was sparsely populated. In the 1960s and 1970s, however, tens of thousands of young people volunteered to study here at specially built 'secondary schools' in the countryside, which now dot the plains in the northern part of the island. Students at these schools worked the fields in shifts, creating the vast citrus plantations that can still be seen today. In 1978 their role in developing the island was officially recognized when the name was changed for the fifth time to Isla de la Juventud (Isle of Youth). Numerous young people from Africa have also studied here, and foreign students still come to the island today, though in smaller numbers.

Parks & Reserves

Punta Francés is a 60-sq-km National Marine Park on the Isla de la Juventud, about two-thirds of which is under the water.

Getting There & Around

Getting to La Isla requires a bit of effort. There are two options; airplane (book early) and boat (a trip that should be straightforward, but rarely is). The boat will take you to capital Nueva Gerona, a town that is easily negotiated on foot; but to see the rest of the island you need to decipher the unreliable local bus service or commission a car or taxi. There are no tourist buses or trains on the Isla.

ISLA DE LA JUVENTUD

One of the most welcoming places you will come across in Cuba, Isla de la Juventud is a world apart from anywhere else on the archipelago. The laid-back pace and opportunities for getting (way) off the beaten track here will appeal to escape artists and adventure types alike. While the hotel scene

ISLA DE LA JUVENTUD

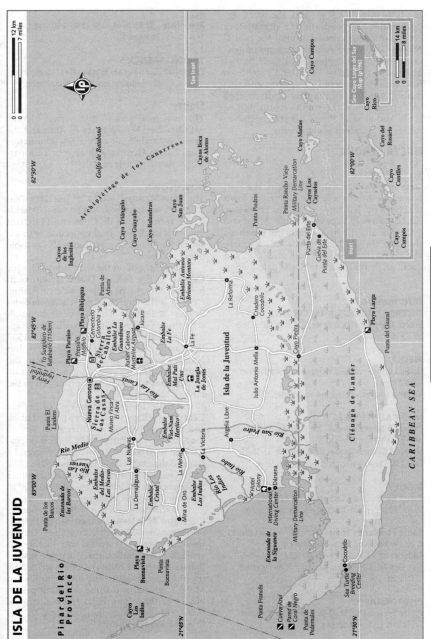

See Cayo Largo del Sur Map (p196)

0 — 14 km
0 — 8 miles

Cayo Rico

Cayo del Rosario

Cayo Campos

Cayo Candiles

Inset

0 — 12 km
0 — 7 miles

Golfo de Batabanó

Cayo Campos

Archipiélago de los Canarreos

Cayos Boca de Alonso

Cayo Triángulo

Cayo Guayabo

Cayo Balandras

Cayo San Juan

Cayos de los Ingleses

Punta de Afuera

See Inset

Cayo Matías

Punta Rancho Viejo

Military Demarcation Line

Cayos Los Cayuelos

Punta Piedras

Playa Paraíso

Playa Bibijagua

Presidio Modelo

Cementerio

Colombia

Sierra de Caballos

Embalse La Guandaba

Júcaro

Embalse La Fe

La Fe

Embalse Antonio Briones Montoto

La Reforma

Punta del Este

Cueva de Punta del Este

To Surgidero de Batabanó (110km)

Ferry & Hydrofoil

Punta de Afuera

Rafael Cabrera Mustelier Airport

Nueva Gerona

Sierra de Las Casas

Río Las Casas

Embalse Mal País Uno

La Jungla de Jones

Isla de la Juventud

Cradero Cocodrilo

Punta El Lindero

Museo Finca El Abra

Embalse Viet-Nam Heróico

Julio Antonio Mella

Cayo Piedra

Playa Larga

Punta del Guanal

Río Medio

Las Nuevas

La Melvis

La Victoria

Argelia Libre

Río San Pedro

Ciénaga de Lanier

Embalse del Medio-Las Nuevas

Río Las Nuevas

Punta de los Barcos

Ensenada de los Barcos

La Demajagua

Embalse Cristal

Mina de Oro

Río Los Indios

Embalse Los Indios

Hotel Colony

Dársena

International Diving Center

Military Demarcation Line

CARIBBEAN SEA

Pinar del Río Province

Cayos Los Indios

Playa Buenavista

Punta Buenavista

Punta Francés

Cueva Azul

Pared de Coral Negro

Ensenada de la Siguanea

Punta de Pedernales

Sea Turtle Breeding Center

Cocodrilo

82°30'W

82°45'W

83°00'W

82°00'W

21°45'N

21°30'N

is a little thin on the ground, the social opportunities are good and the ingratiating casas particulares dotted around the capital Nueva Gerona are run by the kind of generous people who open both their homes and hearts to guests. The island's southern half, with its preserved ecosystems and rich natural wildlife, is a largely undiscovered wilderness while the southwestern part of the island around Punta Francés is known for its magnificent scuba diving.

NUEVA GERONA
☎ 46 / pop 37,300

Flanked by the Sierra de Las Casas to the west and the Sierra de Caballos to the east, Nueva Gerona is a small, unhurried town that hugs the left bank of the Río Las Casas, the island's only large river. Little visited and devoid of any the major historical buildings that dot Cuba's Isla Grande, it's a small, cheap and incredibly friendly place and you could easily find that you're the only foreign face around.

Information

INTERNET ACCESS & TELEPHONE
Etecsa Telepunto (Calle 41 No 2802 btwn Calles 28 & 30; ⏰ 8:30am-7:30pm)

MEDIA
Radio Caribe Broadcasts varied musical programs on 1270AM.
Victoria Local paper published on Saturday.

MEDICAL SERVICES
Farmacia Nueva Gerona (☎ 32-60-84; cnr Calles 39 & 24; ⏰ 8am-11pm Mon-Sat)
Hospital General Héroes de Baire (☎ 32-30-12; Calle 39A) There's a recompression chamber here.

MONEY
Banco de Crédito y Comercio (☎ 32-48-05; Calle 39 No 1802; ⏰ 8am-3pm Mon-Fri) On the corner of Calle 18.
Banco Popular de Ahorro (☎ 32-27-42; cnr Calles 39 & 26; ⏰ 8am-noon & 1:30-5pm Mon-Fri)
Cadeca (☎ 32-34-62; Calle 39 No 2022; ⏰ 8:30am-6pm Mon-Sat, 8:30am-1pm Sun) Located on the corner of Calle 20.

PHOTOGRAPHY
Photo Service (☎ 32-47-66; Calle 39 No 2010 btwn Calles 20 & 22) Buy or develop film.

POST
Post office (☎ 32-26-00; Calle 39 No 1810 btwn Calles 18 & 20; ⏰ 8am-6pm Mon-Sat)

TRAVEL AGENCIES
Ecotur (☎ 32-71-01; Calle 39 btwn Calles 24 & 26) Organizes trips into the militarized zone and to Punta Francés.

Sights

This is a good area to discover on bicycle, with beaches, Museo Finca El Abra and the Presidio Modelo all only a few kilometers from Nueva Gerona. Ask at your casa particular about bicycle rentals.

DOWNTOWN
The **Museo Municipal** (☎ 32-37-91; Calle 30 btwn Calles 37 & 39; ⏰ 9am-1pm & 2-6pm Mon-Sat, 9am-noon Sun) is in the former Casa de Gobierno (1853). It houses a small historical collection with assorted pirate tidbits mixed in with the usual bones and birds.

The art school on the west side of Parque Central is the former **Centro Escolar**, built in 1928. On the northwest side of Parque Central is the church of **Nuestra Señora de los Dolores** (☎ 32-18-35). This Mexican colonial-style church was built in 1926, after the original was destroyed by a hurricane. In 1957 the parish priest, Guillermo Sardiñas, left Nueva Gerona to join Fidel Castro in the Sierra Maestra, the only Cuban priest to do so. Sardiñas was eventually promoted to the rank of *comandante*.

On Calle 28, two blocks east of Parque Central, you'll see a huge ferry painted black and white and set up as a memorial next to the river. This is **El Pinero** (☎ 32-41-62), the original boat used to ferry passengers between La Isla and the main island from the 1920s until 1974. On May 15, 1955, Castro and the other prisoners released from Moncada returned to the main island on El Pinero.

As fascinating as a dusty Beatles bootleg, the **Museo de la Lucha Clandestina** (☎ 32-45-82; Calle 24 btwn Calles 43 & 45; admission CUC$1; ⏰ 9am-5pm Tue-Sat, 8am-noon Sun) is stuffed with rarely seen artifacts of the revolutionary struggle against Batista. There are reams of letters written by the imprisoned Castro and others, timeworn M-26-7 regalia, and some revealing prison photos of the young Fidel and his band of merry Moncadistas hanging out in the Presidio Modelo, c 1954.

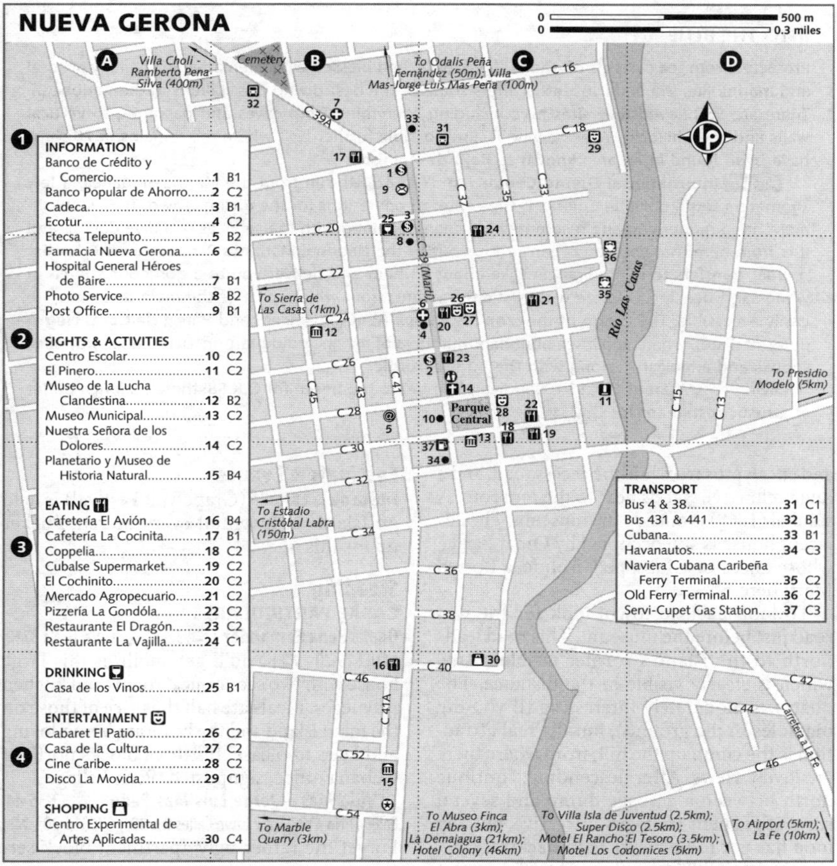
NUEVA GERONA
0 500 m
0 0.3 miles
Villa Choli - Ramberto Pena Silva (400m)
Cemetery
To Odalis Peña Fernández (50m); Villa Mas-Jorge Luis Mas Peña (100m)
To Sierra de Las Casas (1km)
To Estadio Cristóbal Labra (150m)
To Marble Quarry (3km)
To Museo Finca El Abra (3km); La Demajagua (21km); Hotel Colony (46km)
To Villa Isla de Juventud (2.5km); Super Disco (2.5km); Motel El Rancho El Tesoro (3.5km); Motel Los Codornices (5km)
To Airport (5km); La Fe (10km)
To Presidio Modelo (5km)
Río Las Casas
Parque Central
Carretera a La Fe
C 39 (Martí)
INFORMATION
Banco de Crédito y Comercio 1 B1
Banco Popular de Ahorro 2 C2
Cadeca 3 B1
Ecotur 4 C2
Etecsa Telepunto 5 B2
Farmacia Nueva Gerona 6 C2
Hospital General Héroes de Baire 7 B1
Photo Service 8 B2
Post Office 9 B1
SIGHTS & ACTIVITIES
Centro Escolar 10 C2
El Pinero 11 C2
Museo de la Lucha Clandestina 12 B2
Museo Municipal 13 C2
Nuestra Señora de los Dolores 14 C2
Planetario y Museo de Historia Natural 15 B4
EATING
Cafetería El Avión 16 B4
Cafetería La Cocinita 17 B1
Coppelia 18 C2
Cubalse Supermarket 19 C2
El Cochinito 20 C2
Mercado Agropecuario 21 C2
Pizzería La Gondóla 22 C2
Restaurante El Dragón 23 C2
Restaurante La Vajilla 24 C1
DRINKING
Casa de los Vinos 25 B1
ENTERTAINMENT
Cabaret El Patio 26 C2
Casa de la Cultura 27 C2
Cine Caribe 28 C2
Disco La Movida 29 C1
SHOPPING
Centro Experimental de Artes Aplicadas 30 C4
TRANSPORT
Bus 4 & 38 31 C1
Bus 431 & 441 32 B1
Cubana 33 B1
Havanautos 34 C3
Naviera Cubana Caribeña Ferry Terminal 35 C2
Old Ferry Terminal 36 C2
Servi-Cupet Gas Station 37 C3

Astronomers and botanists needn't get too excited about the **Planetario y Museo de Historia Natural** (☎ 32-31-43; cnr Calles 41 & 52; admission CUC$2; 8am-5pm Tue-Sat, 9am-noon Sun). This two-in-one museum/planetarium showcases the natural history, geology and archaeology of the island. There's a replica of the Cueva Punta del Este cave paintings here if you can't make it out there (see p195) and an often out-of-order telescope. Ask a guard and you might get lucky.

MUSEO FINCA EL ABRA

This **museum** (Carretera Siguanea Km 2; 9am-5pm Tue-Sun) is 3km southwest of Nueva Gerona, off the road to La Demajagua (the continuation of Calle 41). Coming from Motel El Rancho El Tesoro, go southwest a few hundred meters on a dirt road to another highway. Turn right and cross a bridge over the Río Las Casas. At the next junction, turn right again and you'll soon come to a sign indicating the access road to Finca El Abra.

The teenage José Martí arrived at Finca El Abra on October 17, 1870, to spend nine weeks of exile on this farm, prior to his deportation to Spain. Legend has it that the shackles he wore here were forged into a ring by his mother, which Martí wore to his death. The old hacienda is directly below the Sierra de Las Casas and it's worth coming as much for the surroundings as for the museum. Cuban oaks

INTO THE BLUE

Protected from sea currents off the Gulf of Mexico and blessed with a remarkable diversity of coral and marine life, Isla de la Juventud offers some of the best diving possibilities in the Caribbean. There are 56 buoyed dive sites here including everything from caves and passages, to vertical walls and coral hillocks. Wreck diving is also possible further east where the remains of 70 ships have been found in an area known as **Bajo de Zambo**.

our pick **International Diving Center** (☎ 39-82-82/-84), run from the Marina Siguanea, a few kilometers south of Hotel Colony, is the center of operations for the diving crowd. The establishment has a modern on-site recompression chamber along with the services of a dive doctor, and it is from here that you can organize trips out to the National Maritime Park at **Punta Francés**.

Boat transfers to Punta Francés take about an hour and deliver you to a gorgeous stretch of white-sand beach (complete with rustic restaurant) from which most of the main dive sites are easily accessible. The cream of the crop are **Cueva Azul** (advanced) and **Pared de Coral Negro** (intermediate), where you'll see abundant numbers of fish including tarpon, barracuda, groupers, snooks and angelfish – along with the odd sea turtle.

Diving costs start at CUC$30. Nondivers can get to the beach for CUC$8; there's a lunch buffet at a rustic restaurant for CUC$12.

and eucalyptus trees line the access road, and a huge ceiba tree stands next to the museum. A sundial (1868) is outside the museum. The adjacent house is still occupied by Omar Sarda, whose ancestor Giuseppe Girondella hosted Martí here.

To loop back to town, look for the dirt road just before the museum. This road leads north to the island's former **marble quarry**, which is clearly visible in the distance. The quarry is moderately interesting (if you dig big holes in the ground), but the real attraction is the climb up the hill, from where there are lovely views. After descending, continue north between a garbage dump and several rows of pig pens (not very attractive, but any loop has got to be better than backtracking, right?) to Calle 54 on the right. This street will bring you into town via the Planetario y Museo de Historia Natural, six blocks to the east.

Activities
HIKING
It's possible to climb the **Sierra de Las Casas** from the west end of Calle 22. A few hundred meters along a dirt track, you will see a trail on the left toward the hills. At the very foot of the hill is a deep cave with a concrete stairway leading down to the local swimming hole. The trail beyond this is fairly obvious, but mark your way mentally so you can return without a worry. A stone on the mountaintop is inscribed 'pilot's seat,' and from here you can see most of the north of the island.

Festivals & Events
Fiesta de la Toronja (Grapefruit Festival) is held on Isla de la Juventud every March. Pucker up for this one.

Sleeping
CASAS PARTICULARES
Odalis Peña Fernández (☎ 32-23-45; Calle 10 No 3710; r CUC$15-20; ❄) You'll get spoilt at this large house with two economical rooms and kitchen privileges. Meals are half the price of those on the main island and the hosts are home-loving and keen to please. It's three blocks north of Cubana office, signposted 'Peña Village'.

Villa Mas – Jorge Luis Mas Peña (☎ 32-35-44; Calle 41 No 4108 Apt 7 btwn Calles 8 & 10; r CUC$15-20; ❄) Forget the rather ugly apartment block setting; there are two above-average rooms here with recently refurbished full marble baths. Jorge and his partner are formidable cooks who'll serve you dinner on their refreshing rooftop terrace. It's just outside the town behind the hospital.

Villa Choli – Ramberto Pena Silva (☎ 32-31-47; Calle C No 4001A btwn Calles 6 & 8; r CUC$20) If Villa Mas is full, try this place instead – it's reader-recommended.

HOTELS
Many people offering private rooms meet the arriving ferries. This is the best way to go, as you'll have a room right in town, and your hosts will provide you with filling meals. Otherwise, Nueva Gerona's state-run hotels are south of town.

Villa Isla de Juventud (Gran Caribe; ☎ 32-32-90; Autopista Nueva Gerona–La Fe Km 1; s/d incl breakfast CUC$29/33; **P** **✷** **☎**) Situated about 5km from the airport and 2.5km from Nueva Gerona, this is the best accommodation option and has friendly staff to boot. There are 20 rooms with fridges in two-story, four-unit blocks. Framed by the island's twin marble mountains, Villa Isla de Juventud has a surprising amount of atmosphere. The villa's reputation is enhanced by a suspension bridge behind the hotel that crosses the Río Las Casas.

Motel El Rancho El Tesoro (Islazul; ☎ 32-30-35; s/d CUC$31/36) This friendly motel lies in a wooded area near the Río Las Casas, 3km south of town, just off the Autopista Nueva Gerona–La Fe. The 60 rooms are in five long blocks of 10 rooms each, with another 10 rooms upstairs in a two-story building near the entrance.

Eating

Casas particulares (most of which are licensed to serve food) serve better-value meals than any of the state-run restaurants. You might try El Doblón, the restaurant in Villa Isla de Juventud.

RESTAURANTS

El Cochinito (☎ 32-28-09; cnr Calles 39 & 24; ☽ noon-11pm, closed Wed) Get your pork steaks, yucca, rice and beans here and eat alfresco out the back.

Restaurante El Dragón (☎ 32-44-79; cnr Calles 39 & 26; meals CUC$3; ☽ noon-10pm, closed Wed) Specializes in Chinese food, but there's little selection and it's not recommended for vegetarians. There's sometimes live music after 8pm and there's always a big gong to beat if the inspiration hits.

Pizzería La Góndola (cnr Calles 30 & 35; ☽ noon-10pm) Offering a break from the pork-chicken-*congrí* (rice flecked with beans) cycle, the pizza here is on par with other Cuban pizza places.

Restaurante La Vajilla (☎ 32-46-92; Calle 37 btwn Calles 20 & 22; mains CUC$4; ☽ noon-9pm, closed Thu) For cheap *comida criolla* (Creole food) try this large hangar-like building that becomes a disco at night.

Cafetería La Cocinita (☎ 32-46-40; Calles 18 & 41; ☽ 24hr) This is a good place for peso sandwiches and juice or more substantial meals in the nicer sit-down section in the back.

Cafetería El Avión (☎ 32-29-70; cnr Calles 41 & 40; ☽ 10am-7pm) Another peso place. The adjacent snack counter is open 24 hours.

Coppelia (☎ 32-22-25; Calle 37 btwn Calles 30 & 32; ☽ noon-10pm Tue-Sun) Just to remind you you're still in Cuba, there's a Coppelia. Head here to satisfy all ice-cream cravings.

GROCERIES

Mercado agropecuario (cnr Calles 24 & 35) Try this large market for fresh vegetables and meat.

Cubalse supermarket (Calle 35 btwn Calles 30 & 32; ☽ 9:30am-6pm Mon-Sat) Sells groceries and sundries.

Drinking

Casa de los Vinos (cnr Calles 20 & 41; ☽ 1-10pm Mon-Wed, 1pm-midnight Fri-Sun, closed Thu) A nice local drinking hole with 'ahoy matey!' nautical decor. Aside from ham sandwiches, you can get wine made from grapefruit, grapes and melon by the glass.

Entertainment

Evening events are often held at the **Casa de la Cultura** (☎ 32-35-91; cnr Calles 37 & 24). Also ask about the famous local *sucu-sucu* (a variation of *son*, Cuba's popular music) group led by Mongo Rives, which sometimes plays at the **Casa de la Cultura** (☎ 39-74-68; cnr Calles 7 & 8) in La Fe.

DANCE CLUBS

Disco La Movida (Calle 18; ☽ from 11pm) For a little atmospheric booty shaking, join the throngs of locals dancing in an open-air locale hidden among the trees near the river.

Cabaret El Patio (☎ 32-23-46; Calle 24 btwn Calles 37 & 39; per couple CUC$3; ☽ 10pm-2am Thu-Sun) Next door to the Casa de la Cultura, this venue has an entertaining floorshow at 11pm. Show up early to get in; official policy is couples only.

Restaurante El Dragón (cnr Calles 39 & 26; ☽ from 10pm Tue & Wed, 8pm Thu-Sun) This restaurant has disco dancing in the rear courtyard.

Super Disco (admission CUC$1; ☽ from 10pm Thu-Sun) You've got to love a place with a name like this. The locals do: this club next to Villa Isla de la Juventud is always packed.

CINEMAS

Cine Caribe (☎ 32-24-16; cnr Calles 37 & 28) For a film or video, check out this cinema on Parque Central.

SPORT

Estadio Cristóbal Labra (☎ 32-10-44; cnr Calles 32 & 53) Nueva Gerona's baseball stadium, Estadio

Cristóbal Labra is six blocks west of the Policlínico Provincial de Emergencia. From October to April, the local team usually plays here daily except Monday and Friday, though not every week. Ask at your local casa particular for details of upcoming games.

Shopping

Calle 39, also known as Calle Martí, is a pleasant pedestrian mall interspersed with small parks.

Centro Experimental de Artes Aplicadas (Calle 40 btwn 39 & 37; ✆ 8am-4pm Mon-Fri, 8am-noon Sat) This center, near the planetarium, makes and sells artistic ceramics.

Getting There & Away

AIR

The most hassle-free and (often) the cheapest way to get to La Isla is to fly. Unfortunately, most other people have already cottoned onto this fact, meaning flights are usually booked up at least a week in advance.

Rafael Cabrera Mustelier Airport (airport code GER) is 5km southeast of Nueva Gerona. **Cubana** (✆ 32-25-31; Calle 39 No 1415 btwn Calles 16 & 18) flies here from Havana three times a day for CUC$35 one-way. There are no international flights. Aerotaxi offers charter flights (you have to buy all the seats on the plane) and you could arrange passage in Havana if you have about CUC$500 to blow.

There's no regular air or sea connection from Isla de la Juventud to Cayo Largo del Sur. It may be possible to charter an 11-passenger Aerotaxi biplane for a day trip for around CUC$500, including waiting time. Otherwise, you must return to Havana to go to Cayo Largo del Sur.

BOAT

Getting to La Isla by boat isn't the piece of cake it ought to be. Tickets for the twice-daily catamaran that plies the route between Surgidero de Batabanó and Nueva Gerona are sold at the **NCC kiosk** (✆ 878-1841; ✆ 7am-noon) in the main (Astro) bus station in Havana, where you can pay for both your bus transfer and ferry reservation in one shot (CUC$55). Due to limited space and perennial popularity it is wise to make a reservation in person one or two days in advance at the NCC kiosk. Check-in for the daily noon boat departure is at 8am at the Astro bus station. Check-in for the second 3:30pm departure (Wednesday, Friday and Sunday only) is at noon.

It's advisable not to show up independently in Batabanó with the intention of buying a ferry ticket direct from the dock. Although technically possible, a number of travelers have come unstuck here, being told, more often than not, that the tickets have been sold out days in advance through the NCC kiosk in Havana. Furthermore, bedding down for the night in Batabanó is not a particularly inspiring experience.

The return leg is equally problematic. Procure your ticket as early as possible in Nueva Gerona's **Naviera Cubana Caribeña (NCC) ferry terminal** (✆ 32-49-77, 32-44-15; cnr Calles 31 & 24), beside the Río Las Casas. The ferry leaves for Surgidero de Batabanó daily at 8am (CUC$50), but you'll need to get there at least two hours beforehand to tackle the infamous queues. A second boat is supposed to leave at noon (with a check-in time of 9:30am).

Before reserving tickets, ask if there's a bus connection from Surgidero de Batabanó to Havana. A connecting bus should cost CUC$5 and you will need to make a reservation as you buy your boat ticket.

True to form, there are no printed schedules for the ferry crossings to and from La Isla. Don't take anything as a given until you have booked your ticket. Isla boat crossings, rather like Cuban trains, have an annoying tendency of being late, breaking down or getting cancelled altogether.

Traveling in either direction you'll need to show your passport. See Surgidero de Batabanó (p181) and Havana City (p149) for more information.

Getting Around

TO/FROM THE AIRPORT

From the airport, look for the bus marked 'Servicio Aéreo,' which will take you into town for one peso. To get to the airport, catch this bus in front of **Cine Caribe** (cnr Calles 28 & 37). A taxi to town will cost about CUC$6, or CUC$35 to the Hotel Colony.

BUS

Ecotur can organize trips/transfers from Nueva Gerona to the diving areas and into the militarized zone. A taxi from Nueva Gerona to Hotel Colony should cost approximately CUC$20. There are less reliable local buses: buses 431 to La Fe (26km) and 441 to the Hotel Colony (45km) leave from a stop opposite the cemetery on Calle 39A, just northwest of the hospital.

OPEN UNIVERSITY

While it might lack the academic credentials of Oxford or Harvard, the Isla de la Juventud's record as an international educator is, arguably, one of the Revolution's greatest triumphs.

The first school on the erstwhile Isla de Pinos (Isle of Pines) opened in 1961 during the Campaña Alfabetización, a government-sponsored campaign that aimed to stamp out illiteracy and provide free and fair education for all Cubans. More schools followed and, by the 1970s, industrious construction brigades had built over 40 junior high schools and eight fully fledged high schools on the Isla, along with night schools, technical institutes and teacher-training colleges.

Castro's long-term aim had always been to share Cuba's successful literacy campaign with other developing countries, and in 1977 the first overseas scholarships were awarded to 2000 seventh-graders from the war-torn African state of Angola. This initial intake was quickly followed by other groups from Angola and Mozambique and, within a few years, there were close to 150,000 students on La Isla studying everything from art to zoology.

Encouraged to give back as much as they took, the overseas students were expected to learn Spanish and socialistically contribute to the annual fruit harvest in the island's famous citrus plantations. In return, they were given free tuition and board, a monthly stipend, and – most importantly – a level and quality of education that, in their own countries, would have been little more than an impossible pipe dream.

Buoyed by its new role as the unofficial mentor of the world's developing nations, Cuba hosted the 11th World Youth Festival in 1978 in Havana, during which a headmaster-like Fidel stood up and announced to the world that he was renaming Cuba's giant offshore classroom, La Isla de la Juventud. No one argued.

Changes to the world order along with the economic chaos that accompanied the Special Period drove a dent in Cuba's international education campaign, but didn't kill it. Today La Isla remains a classroom to over 30,000 students from 123 countries, all of whom are able to enjoy the privilege (or should that be 'right') free of charge.

Bus 38 leaves from the corner of Calles 18 and 37, departing for Chacón (Presidio Modelo), Playa Paraíso and Playa Bibijagua, about four times a day.

CAR

Havanautos (☎ 32-44-32; cnr Calles 32 & 39; ◯ 7am-7pm) rents cars, and can arrange transport into the military zone.

The Servi-Cupet gas station is at the corner of Calles 30 and 39 in the center of town.

HORSE CARTS

Horse *coches* (carts) often park next to the Cubalse supermarket on Calle 35. You can easily rent one at CUC$10 per day for excursions to the Presidio Modelo, Museo Finca El Abra, Playa Bibijagua and other nearby destinations.

EAST OF NUEVA GERONA

The island's most impressive but depressing sight is the **Presidio Modelo** at Reparto Chacón, 5km east of Nueva Gerona. Built between 1926 and 1931, during the repressive regime of Gerardo Machado, the prison's four five-story, yellow circular blocks were modeled after those of a notorious penitentiary in Joliet, Illinois, and could hold 5000 prisoners at a time. During WWII, assorted enemy nationals who happened to find themselves in Cuba (including 350 Japanese, 50 Germans and 25 Italians) were interned in the two rectangular blocks at the north end of the complex.

The Presidio's most famous inmates, however, were Fidel Castro and the other Moncada rebels who were imprisoned here from October 1953 to May 1955. They were held separately from the other prisoners, in the hospital building at the south end of the complex. In 1967, the prison was closed and the section where Castro stayed was converted into a **museum** (☎ 32-51-12; admission CUC$2; ◯ 8am-4pm Tue-Sat, 8am-noon Sun). Admission includes a tour, but cameras/videos are CUC$3/25 extra. Bring exact change. Admission to the circular blocks is free.

Cementerio Colombia, with the graves of Americans who lived and died on the island during the 1920s and 1930s, is about 7km east of Nueva Gerona and 2km east of Presidio Modelo. Bus 38 passes here.

ASK A LOCAL

While Fidel was serving time in Presidio Modelo, President Batista came to visit the prison and its authorities. Fidel used the opportunity to stage a very noisy protest against the Cuban dictator. As a consequence, he was placed in solitary confinement for six months.

Juan, Nueva Gerona

Cabañas Playa Paraíso (☎ 32-52-46), on a beach 2km north of Chacón (about 6km northeast of Nueva Gerona), usually doesn't rent rooms to foreigners, but the **bar & restaurant** (☉ noon-8pm) are open to all. Playa Paraíso itself is no paradise, but more a dirty brown beach. Still, it's in a scenic spot, with a high hill behind and a small island offshore. The wharf here was originally used to unload prisoners for the Presidio Modelo. If you're driving around this way, there's a better beach called Playa Bibijagua 4km to the east of Chacón. Here there are pine trees, a peso restaurant and plenty of low-key Cuban ambience. Nondrivers can catch bus 38 from Nueva Gerona.

SOUTH OF NUEVA GERONA
Sights & Activities

The main reason to come here is for the diving at Punta Francés (see boxed text, p190), but there are a couple of other interesting diversions for those who have time.

Situated 6km west of Santa Fe in the direction of El Colony, **La Jungla de Jones** (☎ 39-62-46; admission CUC$3; ☉ 24hr) is a rich and verdant botanical garden containing more than 80 varieties of tree. Bisected by a network of shaded trails and punctuated by a cornucopia of cacti, bamboo and mangoes, this expansive and recently restored garden once belonged to two American botanists, Helen and Harris Jones, who set up the establishment in 1902 with the intention of studying plants and trees from around the world. The highlight of La Jungla is the aptly named Bamboo Cathedral, an enclosed space surrounded by huge clumps of craning bamboo that only a few strands of sunlight manage to penetrate.

Criadero Cocodrilo (admission CUC$3; ☉ 7am-5pm) has played an important part in crocodile conservation in Cuba over the last few years and the results are interesting to see. Harboring more than 500 crocodiles of all shapes and sizes, the *criadero* (hatchery) acts as a breeding center, similar to the one in Guamá in Matanzas (p255), although the setting here is infinitely wilder. Taken care of until they are seven years old, the center releases groups of crocs back into the wild when they reach a length of about 1m. To get to the *criadero* turn left 12km south of La Fe just past Julio Antonio Mella.

Sleeping & Eating

Hotel Colony (Gran Caribe; ☎ 39-81-81; s/d incl breakfast, CUC$56/84) This hotel on the Ensenada de la Siguanea, 46km southwest of Nueva Gerona, originated in 1958 as part of the Hilton chain but was confiscated by the revolutionary government before it got off the ground. Today the main building's a bit run down but the newer bungalows are in good shape; clean, bright and airy. You might save a few cents by taking a package that includes three meals and scuba diving. The water off the hotel's white-sand beach is shallow, with sea urchins littering the bottom. Take care if you decide to swim. A better (and safer?) bet is the Colony's pleasant pool. A long wharf (with a bar perfect for sunset mojitos) stretches out over the bay, but snorkeling in the immediate vicinity of the hotel is mediocre. The diving, however, is to die for. A Havanautos car-rental office is at the hotel.

Getting There & Away

Transport is tough on La Isla and bus schedules make even the rest of Cuba seem efficient. Try bus 441 from Nueva Gerona. Otherwise, your best bet to get to the hotel is by taxi (approximately CUC$35 from the airport), moped, or rental car (see p193).

THE SOUTHERN MILITARY ZONE

The entire area south of Cayo Piedra is a military zone and to enter you must first procure a one-day pass (CUC$12) from **Ecotur** (☎ 32-71-01; Martí btwn Calles 24 & 26; ☉ 8am-5pm Mon-Sat) in Nueva Gerona. The company will provide you with a Spanish-/English-/German-/French-/Italian-speaking guide, but it is up to you to find your own 4WD transport for within the zone itself. This can be organized with Havanautos in Nueva Gerona (p193). Traveling in the military zone is not possible without a guide or an official pass, so don't arrive at the Cayo Piedra checkpoint without either. As the whole excursion can wind up rather expensive, it's an idea to split the transport costs with other travelers. Good places to fish around for other people are Hotel Colony and the Villa Isla de la Juventud. Both of these places also have tourist information offices that can give you more up-to-date advice on the region.

Cueva de Punta del Este

The Cueva de Punta del Este, a national monument 59km southeast of Nueva Gerona, has been called the 'Sistine Chapel' of Caribbean Indian art. Long before the Spanish conquest (experts estimate around AD 800), Indians painted some 235 pictographs on the walls and ceiling of the cave. The largest has 28 concentric circles of red and black, and the paintings have been interpreted as a solar calendar. Discovered in 1910, they're considered the most important of their kind in the Caribbean. Smaller, similar paintings can be seen in the Cueva de Ambrosio in Varadero (p239). The long, shadeless white beach nearby is another draw (for you and the mosquitoes – bring insect repellent).

Cocodrilo

Cocodrilo, 50km southwest of Cayo Piedra, is a friendly village of 750 residents, still untouched by tourism. Through the lush vegetation beside the potholed road one catches glimpses of cattle, birds, lizards and bee hives. The rocky coastline, with its natural inlets and small, white sandy beaches lapped by crystal-blue water, is magnificent. One kilometer west of this tiny settlement is the **Sea Turtle Breeding Center** (admission CUC$1; 8am-6pm), where visitors can view rows of green-stained glass tanks that teem with turtles of all sizes. While not quite as captivating as watching the creatures nesting in the wild, the breeding center does an excellent job in conserving one of Cuba's rarest and most endangered species.

CAYO LARGO DEL SUR

45

If you came to Cuba to witness historic colonial cities, exotic dancers, straw-hatted *guajiros* (country folk), asthmatic Plymouths and peeling images of Che Guevara, then Cayo Largo del Sur will be a huge disappointment. If, instead, you booked up dreaming of glittering white beaches, teeming coral reefs, fabulous all-inclusive resorts, and lots of fleshy Canadians and Italians wandering around with no clothes on, then this small mangrove-covered tropical paradise is undeniably the place for you.

Cayo Largo del Sur is the second-largest (38 sq km) and easternmost island of the Archipiélago de los Canarreos. It lies between the Golfo de Batabanó and the Caribbean Sea, 114km east of Isla de la Juventud, 80km south of the Península de Zapata and 300km due north of Grand Cayman Island.

No permanent Cuban settlement has ever existed on the Cayo. Instead, the island was developed purely as a tourist enterprise starting in the early 1980s. At least two of its resorts cater exclusively for Italians who book in Europe; the rest are perennially popular with French-speaking Canadians from Québec. The heavenly beaches (26km of 'em) are famous for their size and desolation; during summer turtles come here to nest. There's also a profusion of iguanas and bird life, including cranes, *zunzuncitos* (bee hummingbirds) and flamingos.

Cayo Largo can be done as an expensive day trip from Havana, but most people come here on prebooked packages for one to two weeks at a time. It's a paradisiacal hideaway, even though it neither looks nor feels like Cuba.

Information

There's a good **Cubatur** (24-82-58) office in the Hotel Sol Pelícano; also in Hotel Sol Cayo Largo and Barceló Cayo Largo Beach Resort. Outside of the hotels the main **Bandec** (9am-noon & 2-3:30pm Mon-Fri, 9am-noon Sat & Sun) is in Combinado. Adjacent is a **Casa del Tabaco** (24-82-11) cigar shop and a **Clínica Internacional** (24-82-38; 24hr). Euros are accepted at all the tourist installations here.

Due to dangerous currents, swimming is occasionally forbidden. This will be indicated by red flags on the beach. Mosquitoes can be a nuisance, too; bring repellent!

Sights & Activities

Cayo Largo del Sur's (and, perhaps, Cuba's) finest beach is the broad westward-facing **Playa Sirena**, where 2km of powdery white sand is wide enough to accommodate a couple of football pitches. Tourists on day trips from Havana and Varadero are often brought here. Various nautical activities are available, including kayaks and small catamarans. Set back from the beach there's a *ranchón*-style bar and restaurant along with a small shop, showers and toilets. **Playa Paraíso** is a narrower, less shady strip serviced by a small bar.

The island's other big day-trip destinations are **Cayo del Rosario** and **Cayo Rico** between Cayo Largo del Sur and Isla de la Juventud. Boat excursions to these beaches from the hotels cost around CUC$59 per person. **Cayo Iguana**, off the northwest tip of Cayo Largo del Sur, is home to hundreds of friendly iguanas. A yacht trip there will cost you CUC$73 with lunch.

You can procure a bicycle if you're staying in one of the resorts and head east to **Playa Los Cocos**, where there's good snorkeling, or continue further northeast to **Playa Tortuga**, where sea turtles lay their eggs in the sand (the paved road gives out after Playa Blanca. The **Granja de las Tortugas** (CUC$1; ☉ 9am-6pm) is a small turtle farm in Combinado, on the northwest end of the island beyond the airstrip. From May to September guides here can organize nighttime turtle-watching on the Cayo's beaches. Nearby is the tiny **Casa Museo** (admission CUC$1; ☉ 9am-6pm), which catalogs the damage done to the island by Hurricane Michelle in November 2001 along with further information on turtles and archaeological finds.

Marina Internacional Cayo Largo (☎ 24-82-14) is the disembarkation point for deep-sea fishing trips (CUC$325 for four hours and four people) and diving (CUC$45 for one immersion). Note that prices are more expensive here because you can't shop around.

Other activities available on the island include snorkeling, windsurfing, sailing, kayaking, tennis, horseback riding, cycling and volleyball. Ask at the hotels.

Two international fishing tournaments are held here in September.

Sleeping

All of Cayo Largo del Sur's hotels face the 4km beach on the south side of the island. Though largely shadeless, the beach here is gorgeous and rarely crowded (as no one lives here). If you're on a day trip, a day pass to the Sol resorts is CUC$35 including lunch.

Barceló Cayo Largo Beach Resort (☎ 24-80-80; s/d CUC$135/150; ⓟ ⓧ ⓛ ⓡ) The 306-room Barceló is Cayo Largo's newest resort and is set apart from the other hotels on an expansive stretch of Playa Blanca. Rather drab architecture is augmented by a smorgasbord of different dining options and an impressive array of energetic sporting activities. Good testimonies abound.

Sol Pelícano (☎ 24-82-33; s/d CUC$112/180; ⓟ ⓧ ⓛ ⓡ) This Spanish-style resort, flush on the beach 5km southeast of the airport, has 203 rooms in a series of three-story buildings and two-story duplex *cabañas* (cabins) built in 1993. This is the island's largest resort and facilities include a nightclub and plenty of family-friendly concessions.

our pick Sol Cayo Largo (☎ 24-82-60; s/d CUC$165/270; ⓟ ⓧ ⓛ ⓡ) Sol Meliá's other property is the five-star Sol Cayo Largo, with its Greek-

CAYO LARGO DEL SUR

0 — 8 km
0 — 4 miles

INFORMATION
Bank..................................(see 4)
Cubacar..............................(see 4)
Cubatur..............................(see 6)
Medical Clinic......................(see 4)

SIGHTS & ACTIVITIES
Granja de las Tortugas..............1 B2
Marina Internacional Cayo Largo.2 B2

SLEEPING 🏨
Barceló Cayo Largo Beach Resort.3 C2
Hotel Isla del Sur.....................4 C2
Sol Cayo Largo.........................5 B2
Sol Pelícano............................6 C2
Villa Coral.............................7 C2
Villa Lindamar.........................8 B2
Villa Soledad..........................9 B2

EATING 🍴
Ranchón Playa Sirena................10 B2
Restaurante El Torreón..............11 B2

ENTERTAINMENT
Taberna El Pirata.....................(see 2)

21°45'N

Golfo de Batabanó

Punta del Este
Punta Iguanita
Punta Mangle Prieto
Playa Tortuga

Cayo Rico
Cayería Los Majáes
Cayo Iguana
Cayo Largo
Canalizo Cayo Largo
Punta Gancho
Cayos Los Pájaros

Las Piedras
Playa Luna
Playa Los Cocos
Playa Blanca

Combinado
Villa Acuña Airport
Playa Sirena
Playa Paraíso

CARIBBEAN SEA

Cayo Los Ballenatos
Playa Lindamar

21°40'N

81°40'W   81°35'W   81°30'W   81°25'W

ISLA DE LA JUVENTUD (SPECIAL MUNICIPALITY)

ASK A LOCAL

You can hike from Playa Sirena down to Paraíso and continue all the way around the headland to Hotel Sol Cayo Largo. It's about 7km in total and traverses Cuba's only 'unofficial' nudist beach (the rocky section just east of the hotel).

Fidel, Cayo Largo del Sur

---

temple like lobby and trickling Italianate fountains. The beach out here is fantastic (and nudist) and the brightly painted (but not luxuriant) rooms come with terraces with sea views. To date, it's Cayo Largo's most exclusive resort and great if you want to escape the families and poolside bingo further east. Check out the on-site spa and gym – a trip to Shangri-La.

Villa Coral (Gran Caribe; ☎ 34-81-11; s/d CUC$100/140; ☏ ✗ ☒) Also known as El Pueblito, this villa consists of 10 two-story buildings outfitted to look like colonial villas (eg faux terra-cotta roofs, wooden balconies) arranged around a swimming pool. There are 60 rooms here.

Villa Soledad (Gran Caribe; ☎ 34-81-11; s/d CUC$100/140; ☏ ✗) This adjacent cluster of single-story, plainer bungalows has another 43 rooms (but no restaurant – you have to go to one of the neighboring hotels held by Gran Caribe).

Hotel Isla del Sur (☎ 34-81-11; s/d CUC$100/140; ☏ ✗ ☒) This hotel has 59 rooms with mini-fridges in a long, two-story building. Built in 1981, it was the first hotel on Cayo Largo del Sur and is starting to show its age. All meals are served buffet-style, and there's slightly tacky poolside entertainment nightly (unless you've got a secret penchant for water ballet).

Villa Lindamar (Gran Caribe; ☎ 34-81-11; s/d CUC$112/164; ☏ ✗ ☒) At the time of research the Isla de Sur and the adjacent Villa Lindamar catered exclusively for Italian tourists who book through agencies back home. Check for current situation.

Eating

ourpick **Ranchón Playa Sirena** (☯ 9am-4pm) A rather fetching beach bar with Latino Tom Cruises tossing around the cocktail glasses. Good food is also served here and they stick on a buffet if enough tourists are around. There's no-nonsense, salt-of-the-earth *comida criolla*. There's also a bar on Playa Paraíso.

Restaurante El Torreón (☯ noon-midnight) In Cayo Largo's Combinado settlement, this is the best of the motley eating joints. Encased in a stone fort-like building next to the marina, it serves good old-fashioned Cuban-style grub with a few Spanish surprises (and wine).

Entertainment

Taberna El Pirata (☯ 24hr) You're in all-inclusive land, so almost all of the entertainment is confined to the resorts. One exception is this place next door to the marina. It's primarily a haunt of boat-hands, resort workers and the odd escaped tourist.

Fiesta Marán (admission CUC$15; ☯ 11pm-2:30am) This is a night disco held on a yacht or catamaran off Playa Sirena.

Getting There & Away

Several charter flights arrive directly from Canada weekly, and Cubana has weekly flights from Montreal and Milan.

For pop-by visitors, daily flights from Havana to Cayo Largo del Sur with Cubana cost CUC$80/145 for a one-way/return trip. The island makes a viable day trip from Havana, although you'll have to get up early for the airport transfer (all Cayo Largo flights depart from the airport at Playa Baracoa a few miles west of Marina Hemingway). Another option is to take an organized day trip from Havana or Varadero to Cayo Largo del Sur for in the vicinity of CUC$137, including airport transfers, return flights, lunch, plus trips to Playa Sirena and Cayo Iguana. All the Havana agencies offer this (see p108).

Getting Around

Measuring 37 sq km, getting around Cayo Largo shouldn't present too many challenges. A taxi or transfer bus can transport you the 5km from the airport to the hotel strip. From here a slightly ridiculous mini bus-train (the *trencito*) carts tourists out to the idyllic beaches of Playa Paraíso and Sirena (6km/7km away). The train returns in the afternoon, or you can hike back along the beach (see boxed text, left). The tiny settlement of Combinado with its marina and motley attractions is 1km north of the airport and 6km from the nearest resort. For taxis phone **Taxi OK** (☎ 24-82-45) or hang around outside the hotels/airport.

Pinar del Río Province

Verde, que te quiero verde (green, how I love you green), wrote Lorca in one of his most immortal lines. It's a stanza that springs to mind regularly as you track west through verdant Pinar del Río province where an all-pervading emerald sheen seems to envelop everything you see.

Known popularly as the 'garden of Cuba' for its distinct agricultural heritage, bucolic Pinar protects more land than any other province with two Unesco Biosphere Reserves (the Sierra del Rosario and the Península de Guanahacabibes), a Unesco World Heritage Site (the Valle de Viñales) and a patchwork of carefully managed flora and fauna zones. Long celebrated for the fertility of its rust red soil, this is the best place in the world to grow tobacco, a blessing that has created one of Cuba's most quintessential landscapes, a colorful cornucopia of oxen-furrowed fields and rustic tobacco-drying houses that is guarded jealously by an omnipresent army of sombrero-wearing *guajiros*.

One of Cuba's classic regional stereotypes, the *guajiro* is Pinar del Río personified, an amiable rural hick with a level of generosity that verges on the gullible. Venerable Viñales is the *guajiro's* spiritual home, a serene settlement ringed by craggy *mogotes* (flat-topped hills) which, despite its popularity on the tourist circuit, remains one of Cuba's most friendly and hassle-free towns.

Beyond the countryside, Pinar's beaches are renowned for their quality rather than quantity. Cayo Jutías and Cayo Levisa stand out as highlights, two sandy carpets on the north coast that enjoy minuscule foot traffic compared with the big resorts further east. In-the-know divers head west to Playa María la Gorda on the island's remote tip, while eco-warriors hone in on salubrious Las Terrazas, a groundbreaking 'model village' that took root when environmentalism was still a hobby for hippies.

PINAR DEL RÍO PROVINCE

HIGHLIGHTS

- **Hike or Bike** Get out of the tour bus and see, smell and taste the agricultural beauty of Valle de Viñales (p210)

- **Underwater Odyssey** Experience scuba diving at translucent Playa María la Gorda (p208)

- **Beach Retreat** Recharge your batteries on dreamy Cayo Jutías (p217)

- **Cold War Hideaway** See where Che Guevara played chess during the Cuban Missile Crisis in Cueva de los Portales (p219)

- **Revolutionary Terraces** Visit Las Terrazas, Cuba's primary eco-village where formerly denuded forest slopes have been replanted with trees, orchids, painters and poets (see boxed text, p223)

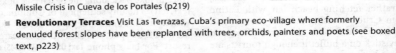

★ Las Terrazas
★ Cayo Jutías
★ Cueva de los Portales
★ Valle de Viñales
★ Playa María la Gorda

■ TELEPHONE CODE: 048　　■ POPULATION: 730,626　　■ AREA: 10,924 SQ KM

PINAR DEL RÍO PROVINCE

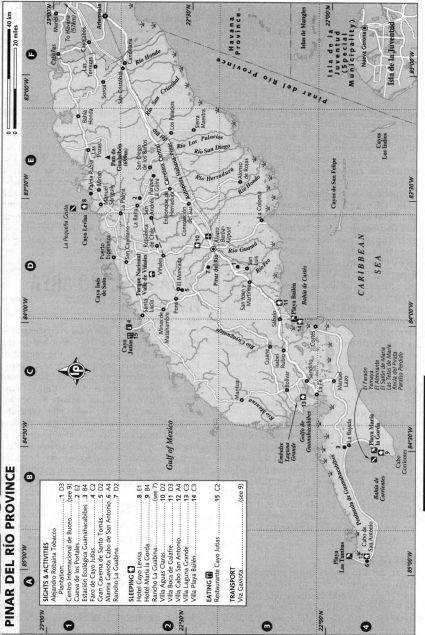

SIGHTS & ACTIVITIES
Alejandro Robaina Tobacco
Plantation............................1 D3
Centro Internacional de Buceo..(see 9)
Cueva de los Portales.................2 E2
Estación Ecológica Guanahacabibes..3 B4
Faro de Cayo Jutías....................4 C2
Gran Caverna de Santo Tomás.....5 D2
Marina Gaviota Cabo de San Antonio..6 A4
Rancho La Guabina.....................7 D2

SLEEPING
Hotel Cayo Levisa.........................8 E1
Hotel María la Gorda.....................9 B4
Rancho La Guabina...................(see 7)
Villa Aguas Claras......................10 D2
Villa Boca de Galafre..................11 D3
Villa Cabo San Antonio...............12 A4
Villa Laguna Grande...................13 C3
Villa Playa Bailén.......................14 C3

EATING
Restaurante Cayo Jutías..............15 C2

TRANSPORT
Vía Gaviota............................(see 9)

PINAR DEL RÍO PROVINCE

History

The pre-Columbian history of western Cuba is synonymous with the Guanahatabeys, a group of nomadic Indians who lived in caves and procured most of their livelihood from the sea. Less advanced than the other indigenous natives who lived on the island, the Guanahatabeys were a peaceful and passive race whose culture had developed, more or less independently of the Taíno and Siboney cultures further east. Extinct by the time the Spanish arrived in 1492, little firsthand documentation remains on how the archaic Guanahatabey society was structured and organized although some archaeological sites have been found on the Guanahacabibes Peninsula.

Post-Columbus the Spanish left rugged Pinar del Río largely to its own devices, and the area developed lackadaisically only after Canary Islanders began arriving in the late 1500s. Originally called Nueva Filipina (New Philippines), the region was renamed Pinar del Río in 1778, supposedly for the pine forests crowded along the Río Guamá. Tobacco plantations and cattle ranches soon sprang up in the rich soil and open grazing land that typifies Pinar, and the fastidious farmers who made a living from the delicate and well-tended crops were colloquially christened *guajiros*, a native word that means – literally – 'one of us.' By the mid-1800s, Europeans were hooked on the fragrant weed and the region flourished. Sea routes opened up and the railway was extended to facilitate the shipping of the perishable product.

These days, tobacco, along with tourism, keep Pinar del Río both profitable and popular. Quiet and laid-back compared with the car-crazy capital 160km or so to the east, the relaxed Pinareños – despite the countless *guajiro* jokes – are some of the friendliest, most ingratiating people you'll meet on the island.

In 2008, Pinar was slammed by two catastrophic hurricanes within a fortnight causing serious damage to local infrastructure (see boxed text, p86).

Parks & Reserves

Pinar del Río boasts more protected land than any other Cuban province, including one Unesco World Heritage Site (the Valle de Viñales) as well as two Unesco Biosphere Reserves – the Sierra del Rosario and the Guanahacabibes. Two of these areas – Guanahacabibes and Viñales – are also national parks. The Área Protegida Mil Cumbres is another expansive reserve that encompasses the mountainous terrain in and around the Hacienda Cortina in the Cordillera de Guaniguanico.

Getting There & Around

Both Pinar del Río and Viñales are well served by twice-daily Víazul buses. Las Terrazas (but not Soroa) was also recently added to this route. An alternative is to hop on one of the many tour buses that head out from Havana to Viñales on a daily basis. The prices often work out the same as Víazul's. Beyond the main hubs, transport can be scant. The train line runs out through the city of Pinar del Río as far as Guane in the west. Beyond this you're off the grid. There are sporadic transfer buses from Havana and Viñales to María la Gorda; if you want more flexibility, hire a taxi or car.

PINAR DEL RÍO AREA

PINAR DEL RÍO
pop 148,295

Pinar del Río is Cuba's tobacco central – it fairly smells of the stuff. Plunked in the middle of the Vuelta Abajo, the capital of Cuba's second-largest province is a sleepy, unprepossessing settlement that feels more like an oversized town than a frenetic city. Not surprisingly, the place boasts its own tobacco factory (open for visits) plus a friendly population of leather-faced cigar-smoking locals. Unfortunately, this affable group is matched by a noticeably less affable contingent of *jineteros* (tourist touts) who have, for some reason, made otherwise tranquil Pinar their unofficial base of operations. Get used to saying *no me moleste, por favor* and watch out for the more aggressive touts on bicycles.

Founded in 1774 by a Spanish army captain, Pinar del Río was one of the last provincial capitals on the island to take root. Neglected by successive central governments who preferred sugarcane to tobacco, the city became an urban backwater and the butt of countless jokes about the supposedly easy-to-fool *guajiros* who were popularly portrayed as simple-minded rural hicks. In 1896 General Antonio Maceo brought the Second War of Independence to Pinar del Río in an

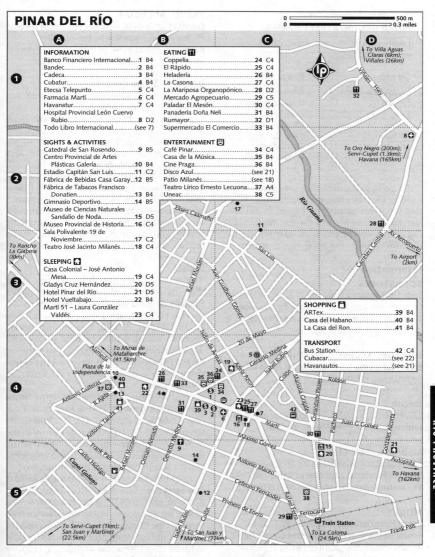

PINAR DEL RÍO

INFORMATION			
Banco Financiero Internacional	1	B4	
Bandec	2	B4	
Cadeca	3	B4	
Cubatur	4	B4	
Etecsa Telepunto	5	C4	
Farmacia Martí	6	C4	
Havanatur	7	C4	
Hospital Provincial León Cuervo Rubio	8	D2	
Todo Libro Internacional	(see 7)		

SIGHTS & ACTIVITIES			
Catedral de San Rosendo	9	B5	
Centro Provincial de Artes Plásticas Galería	10	B4	
Estadio Capitán San Luis	11	C2	
Fábrica de Bebidas Casa Garay	12	B5	
Fábrica de Tabacos Francisco Donatien	13	B4	
Gimnasio Deportivo	14	B5	
Museo de Ciencias Naturales Sandalio de Noda	15	D5	
Museo Provincial de Historia	16	C4	
Sala Polivalente 19 de Noviembre	17	C2	
Teatro José Jacinto Milanés	18	C4	

SLEEPING			
Casa Colonial – José Antonio Mesa	19	C4	
Gladys Cruz Hernández	20	D5	
Hotel Pinar del Río	21	D5	
Hotel Vueltabajo	22	B4	
Martí 51 – Laura González Valdés	23	C4	

EATING			
Coppelia	24	C4	
El Rápido	25	C4	
Heladería	26	C4	
La Casona	27	C4	
La Mariposa Organopónico	28	D2	
Mercado Agropecuario	29	C5	
Paladar El Mesón	30	C4	
Panadería Doña Neli	31	B4	
Rumayor	32	D1	
Supermercado El Comercio	33	B4	

ENTERTAINMENT			
Café Pinar	34	C4	
Casa de la Música	35	B4	
Cine Praga	36	B4	
Disco Azul	(see 21)		
Patio Milanés	(see 18)		
Teatro Lírico Ernesto Lecuona	37	A4	
Uneac	38	C5	

SHOPPING			
ARTex	39	B4	
Casa del Habano	40	B4	
La Casa del Ron	41	B4	

TRANSPORT			
Bus Station	42	C4	
Cubacar	(see 22)		
Havanautos	(see 21)		

PINAR DEL RÍO PROVINCE

ambitious attempt to split the island in two and the town rallied to his wake-up call.

Following the 1959 Revolution Pinar del Río's economic fortunes improved exponentially; this was facilitated further by the building of the Autopista Nacional from Havana and the development of tourism in the 1980s.

Orientation

The main street in Pinar del Río is Martí; there are many facilities on Máximo Gómez and Antonio Maceo, which run parallel to Martí just to the south. A major cross street is Isabel Rubio, which becomes the Carretera Central north of the city toward Havana and on the road to San Juan y Martínez to the southwest.

PINAR DEL RÍO STREET NAMES

Locals stick to the old street names; this chart should help:

Old name	New name
Calzada de la Coloma	Rafael Ferro
Caubada	Comandante Pinares
Recreo	Isabel Rubio
Rosario	Ormani Arenado
San Juan	Rafael Morales
Vélez Caviedes	Gerardo Medina
Virtudes	Ceferino Fernández

To avoid going the wrong way when you're looking for addresses, it's important to know that the street numbering begins at two base streets: Gerardo Medina divides the numbering of east–west streets while Martí marks the division between the north–south streets.

Information

BOOKSTORES

Todo Libro Internacional (☎ 77-84-94; cnr Martí & Colón; ☽ 8am-noon & 1:30-6pm Mon-Fri, 8am-noon & 1-4pm Sat) Selection of maps, books and office supplies in same building as Havanatur office.

INTERNET ACCESS & TELEPHONE

Etecsa Telepunto (cnr Gerardo Medina & Juan Gómez; per hr CUC$6; ☽ 8:30am-7:30pm)

MEDIA

Guerrillero is published on Friday. Radio Guamá airs on 1080AM or 90.2FM.

MEDICAL SERVICES

Farmacia Martí (Martí Este No 50; ☽ 8am-11pm)
Hospital Provincial León Cuervo Rubio (☎ 75-44-43; Carretera Central) Two kilometers north of town.

MONEY

Banco Financiero Internacional (☎ 77-81-53; Gerardo Medina Norte No 46) Opposite Casa de la Música.
Bandec (☎ 75-26-07; Martí Este No 32; ☽ 8:30am-noon & 1:30-3:30pm Mon-Fri) There's another branch on Martí No 53.
Cadeca (☎ 77-83-57; Martí No 46; ☽ 8:30am-5:30pm Mon-Sat)

POST

Post office (Martí Este No 49; ☽ 8am-8pm Mon-Sat)

TRAVEL AGENCIES

Cubatur (☎ 77-84-05; Martí No 51 cnr Ormani Arenado; ☽ 8am-noon & 1-5pm Mon-Fri, 8am-noon Sat)
Havanatur (☎ 77-84-94; cnr Martí & Colón; ☽ 8am-noon & 1:30-6pm Mon-Fri, 8am-noon & 1-4pm Sat)

Dangers & Annoyances

For a relatively untouristed city Pinar del Río has its fair share of unsolicited touts or *jineteros*. The majority are young men who hang around on Calle Martí offering everything from paladar meals to 'guided tours' of tobacco plantations. Most will take your first or second 'no' answer as a sign to back off. However, the bolder ones have been known to mount bicycles and accost tourist cars (identifiable by their purple/brown number plates) when they stop at red traffic lights. Although they're generally nonaggressive, it's best to be firmly polite from the outset and not invite further attention.

Sights

The most interesting sight, at least from the outside, is the **Museo de Ciencias Naturales Sandalio de Noda** (☎ 77-94-83; Martí Este No 202; admission CUC$1, plus camera CUC$1; ☽ 9am-6pm Mon-Sat, 9am-1pm Sun). A wild, neo-Gothic-meets-Moorish mansion built by local doctor and world traveler Francisco Guasch, this museum (called Palacio de Guasch by locals) has everything from a concrete T-Rex to a stuffed baby giraffe.

Nearby is the slightly more riveting **Museo Provincial de Historia** (☎ 75-43-00; Martí Este No 58 btwn Colón & Isabel Rubio; admission CUC$1; ☽ 8:30am-6:30pm Mon-Fri, 9am-1pm Sat), collecting the history of the province from pre-Columbian times to the present. Look for the Enrique Jorrín ephemera (Jorrín was the creator of the *chachachá*).

Four blocks south is the **Fábrica de Bebidas Casa Garay** (Isabel Rubio Sur No 189 btwn Ceferino Fernández & Frank País; admission CUC$1; ☽ 9am-3:30pm Mon-Fri, 9am-12:30pm Sat). Erected in 1892, this factory uses a secret recipe to distill sweet and dry versions of the famous Guayabita del Pinar guava brandy. Whistle-stop 15-minute multilingual factory tours are topped off by a taste of the brew in the sampling room. There's a shop adjacent.

You can observe people busily rolling cigars at the **Fábrica de Tabacos Francisco Donatien** (Maceo Oeste No 157; admission CUC$5; ☽ 9am-noon & 1-4pm Mon-Fri). Until 1961 this building was a jail, but now it's tobacco central on the tourist circuit.

Smaller than the Partagás factory in Havana, you get a more intimate insight here, though the foibles are the same – robotic guides, rushed tours and the nagging notion that it's all a bit voyeuristic. There's an excellent cigar shop opposite.

On Plaza de la Independencia near Alameda and around the corner from the cigar factory is the **Centro Provincial de Artes Plásticas Galería** (Antonio Guiteras; admission free; ☺ 8am-9pm Mon-Sat), Pinar's best art gallery, which houses many local works.

The wooden, 540-seat **Teatro José Jacinto Milanés** (☎ 75-38-71; Martí No 160 btwn Isabel Rubio & Colón) is a gorgeous venue dating from 1845 – making it one of Cuba's oldest. It reopened in 2006 after a lengthy on-off renovation and, with its colorfully painted interiors and Spanish-style patio and cafe, is well worth a look.

Pinar del Río's understated **Catedral de San Rosendo** (Maceo Este No 3) dates from 1883 and its pastel-yellow exterior seems to get a more regular paint job than the rest of the city's buildings. As with most Cuban churches, the interior is often closed. Slip inside for a peek during the Sunday morning service.

Activities

Gym freaks might want to check out the **Gimnasio Deportivo** (Ceferino Fernández No 43 btwn Isabel Rubio & Gerardo Medina) where, with some fumbling Spanish and a bit of deft sign language, you can talk your way into tai chi, weightlifting or somersaulting over a horsebox. Alternatively there's the **Sala Polivalente 19 de Noviembre** (Rafael Morales) for boxing, volleyball and basketball.

From October to April, exciting baseball games happen at the **Estadio Capitán San Luis** (☎ 75-38-95; admission 1 peso), on the north side of town. Pinar del Río is one of the country's best teams, often challenging the Havana-Santiago monopoly. Pop by in the evening to see the players going through a training session.

Festivals & Events

Carnaval in early July features a procession of *carrozas* (carriages) through the streets with couples dancing between the floats. It's a big drunken, dance party.

LADAS EVERYWHERE

Aided by some of the world's most creative mechanics, Cuba has long acted as a giant recycling plant for old American cars. From hectic Havana to sleepy Baracoa, the ailing dowagers of Detroit with their curvaceous art-deco lines and lovingly polished chrome hark back to a brighter, more streamlined age when gas was cheap and a soft-top Oldsmobile was every aspiring teenager's ticket to freedom.

Yet, in reality, one in four cars in Cuba aren't American at all, they're Russian. Even worse, they're Ladas. And of the ones that aren't (the vintage American ones, that is), a good proportion have Lada engines.

An ugly cousin of the Fiat 124 Sedan, the Lada – or VAZ-2101, to give it its proper name – was first concocted in Tolyatti on the banks of the Volga River in 1966. Economical but unattractive, they quickly became a source of ridicule for leery car connoisseurs, most of whom would have rather walked 100 miles than be seen behind the wheel of one.

In Cuba, the reception was a little more enthusiastic. Readily available thanks to a solid economic alliance with the Soviet Union, Ladas quickly became prized possessions in the 1970s and '80s, when they were handed out to model workers as reward for exemplary conduct. Not surprisingly, the car's rugged but ruthlessly efficient VAZ engineering did well on the island's potholed roads and the vehicles prevailed – if not always in the lovingly restored state of their American counterparts.

Ladas today serve multiple purposes in Cuba's hard-to-fathom car economy. Some work industriously as taxis, while others find themselves broken down into their component parts and used to power anything from washing machines to 1951 Plymouths.

The greatest of all Ladas – the classic 'Stretch' – is a peculiarly Cuban invention concocted by hard-up taxi drivers during the 1990s. Armed with blow torches, metal bashers and exceedingly lucid imaginations, these deft DIY kings set out to successfully create one of the world's greatest motoring oxymorons – the Lada limo. Now, that's creativity!

Sleeping

IN TOWN

Casas Particulares

Martí 51 – Laura González Valdés (☎ 75-22-64; Martí Este No 51 Altos btwn Colón & Isabel Rubio; r CUC$20-25; ✷) In a house stuffed with more books than Pinar's main library you won't be stuck for things to read. This lovely senior couple has created a veritable heritage home in this 1928 house with floor-to-ceiling bookshelves and even a small museum with artifacts collected from around the world by the owner's late father. There are two well-appointed rooms, one of which has a huge corner balcony overlooking the full sweep of Calle Martí.

Gladys Cruz Hernández (☎ 77-96-98; Av Comandante Pinares Sur No 15 btwn Martí & Máximo Gómez; r CUC$20; ✷) A splendid house with tasteful colonial furnishings situated near the train station; there are two rooms with baths, fridges, a TV and a big patio.

Casa Colonial – José Antonio Mesa (☎ 75-31-73; Gerardo Medina Norte No 67 btwn Adela Azcuy & Isidro de Armas; r CUC$20; ✷) Loads of space and an improvised Jacuzzi in the backyard. Pinch yourself, this is Pinar del Río! Not surprisingly José's a Pinar stalwart and his two rooms and lovely communal living spaces are perennially popular.

Hotels

Hotel Pinar del Río (Islazul; ☎ 75-50-70; cnr Gonzales Alcorta & Autopista; s/d CUC$29/38; P ✷ ✹) One of the first buildings you hit as you slip off the Autopista Nacional and, frankly, not the best intro to the city. Cold, uninviting and badly-lit, you'd think twice about staying here if it wasn't one of only two hotels in town. There are 136 generic rooms and the usual noise-trap of a swimming pool (with or without water, depending on the season). The disco is popular with locals, but a nightmare for those trying to catch a bit of sleep.

Hotel Vueltabajo (Islazul; ☎ 75-93-81; cnr Martí & Rafael Morales; s/d CUC$45/62; ✷) A rare newcomer in Cuba's stable of midrange hotels this fabulous hotel is as delightful as the Hotel Pinar del Río is drab. Stylishly colonial with high ceilings, and striped Parisian window awnings, the rooms here are so spacious you almost think they must have run out of furniture. Old-fashioned shutters give out onto the street and downstairs there's an OK bar-restaurant; a reasonable breakfast is included in the price.

OUTSIDE TOWN

Villa Aguas Claras (Cubamar; ☎ 77-84-27; s/d incl breakfast CUC$22/36; P ✹) The plushest of all Cuba's 85-plus campismos lies 8km north of town on the Carretera a Viñales and has the facilities of a midrange hotel. The 50 bungalows with hot showers sleep two (10 have air-con). The rooms are adequate, the landscaping lush and the staff congenial, making this a better overall choice than Hotel Pinar del Río. The Villa Aguas Claras also offers horseback riding and day trips. Insect repellent is essential here. Aguas Claras is accessible from Pinar del Río by bus several times a day.

Eating

PALADARES

Paladar El Mesón (Martí Este No 205; ✆ noon-10pm Mon-Sat) This long-standing paladar opposite the Museo de Ciencias Naturales serves chicken, pork and fish in a pleasant colonial atmosphere. Main plates start at CUC$5 with side dishes extra; the service is efficient and friendly.

RESTAURANTS

Coppelia (Gerardo Medina Norte No 33; ✆ noon-midnight Tue-Sun) You'll require the patience of a saint, but the two peso a scoop ice cream (when there *is* ice cream) is cheap and the atmosphere is usually cheerful.

Heladería (cnr Martí & Rafael Morales; ✆ 9am-9pm) Guaranteed to make you even more cheerful is this clean place where you can get a substantial *tres gracias* (three scoops) for the price of half a teaspoon's worth of Haagen Daas.

El Rápido (Martí No 64 btwn Recreo & Colón; ✆ 24hr) Yes, Pinar del Río's struggling restaurant scene might be scant enough to merit a visit to Cuba's proverbial McDonald's where the chickens are born fried and soggy pizzas materialize microwaved.

La Casona (☎ 77-82-63; cnr Martí & Colón; ✆ 11am-11pm) Hard to believe, but this is Pinar's best government-run restaurant outside Rumayor. Encouragingly there are tablecloths and wine glasses, along with steak, chicken and pasta on the menu, but positioned unstrategically on the town's busiest nexus the hissing hustlers are never far away. Get a seat away from the door.

Rumayor (☎ 76-30-51; Carretera a Viñales Km 1; ✆ noon-midnight) The best food in Pinar del Río is probably at Islazul's Rumayor, located 1km north of the town center, off the Carretera a

Viñales. Justly famous for its succulent *pollo ahumado* (smoked chicken), you'll pay a little extra here (CUC$10 to CUC$15), but it is definitely worth it – as is the walk. This is Pinar's premier cabaret spot in the evening (see below).

GROCERIES

Mercado agropecuario (Rafael Ferro; ☾ 8am-6pm Mon-Sat, 8am-1pm Sun) Pinar del Río's colorful open-air market is almost on top of the tracks near the train station. You'll see the odd tour group tramping through here getting a grip on Special Period economics.

La Mariposa organopónico (cnr Carretera Central & Av Aeropuerto) A conveniently located organic fruit and vegetable market; and a good place to get a close-up look at Cuban's urban agriculture program.

Other self-catering options:

Panadería Doña Neli (cnr Gerardo Medina Sur & Máximo Gómez; ☾ 7am-7pm) Gives you each day your daily bread.

Supermercado El Comercio (cnr Martí Oeste & Arenado; ☾ 9am-5pm Mon-Sat, 9am-noon Sun) Believe it or not, one of the best supermarkets in town.

Entertainment

Casa de la Música (Gerardo Medina Norte No 21; admission CUC$1; ☾ concerts start at 9pm nightly) After warming up at Café Pinar, many revelers cross the street for more live music here.

Café Pinar (☎ 77-81-99; Gerardo Medina Norte No 34; admission CUC$1-4; ☾ 10am-2am) This place gets the local youth vote and is also the best place to meet other travelers. Situated on a lively stretch of Calle Gerardo Medina there are live bands at night on the open patio, and light menu items such as pasta, chicken and sandwiches to quench your appetite during the day.

Rumayor (☎ 76-30-51; Carretera a Viñales Km 1; ☾ noon-midnight) As well as serving good food (opposite), this Palmares place metamorphoses at night from Tuesday through Sunday as a kitschy cabaret with a floor show that starts at 11pm (CUC$5 cover). It's not the Tropicana, but it ain't half bad.

Disco Azul (cnr Gonzales Alcorta & Autopista; admission CUC$5; ☾ from 10pm Tue-Sun) A drab hotel, but a kicking disco – this glittery nightclub in Hotel Pinar del Río is the city's most popular.

Teatro Lírico Ernesto Lecuona (Antonio Maceo Oeste No 163) Near the cigar factory, this theater is best for classical music and opera.

Patio Milanés (cnr Martí & Colón) With the Milanés back in business you'd be foolish to miss this theatrical patio alongside the real deal. Check the schedule posted outside for nightly cultural activities.

Cine Praga (☎ 75-32-71; Gerardo Medina Norte No 31) Next to Coppelia restaurant, Cine Praga shows mostly subtitled films; also look here for the video schedule at Uneac (Antonio Maceo No 178 between Rafael Ferro and Comandante Pinares; movies screened at 8:30pm and 10:15pm).

Shopping

ARTex (☎ 77-83-67; Martí Este No 36; ☾ 9am-5pm Mon-Sat, 9am-noon Sun) It sells souvenirs, CDs and T-shirts.

La Casa del Ron (Antonio Maceo Oeste No 151; ☾ 9am-4:30pm Mon-Fri, 9am-1pm Sat & Sun) Near the cigar factory, sells the same merchandise as ARTex, plus plenty of the strong stuff.

Casa del Habano (☎ 77-22-44; Antonio Maceo No 162) Right opposite the tobacco factory, this store is one of this popular government cigar chain's better outlets with a patio bar, frigidly air-conditioned shop, smoking room and Infotur desk.

Getting There & Away

BUS

The city's **bus station** (Adela Azcuy btwn Colón & Comandante Pinares) is conveniently located close to the center. Víazul leaves for Viñales twice daily at 12:05am and 4:30pm (CUC$6) and for Havana at 8:50am and 2:50pm (CUC$11). The afternoon Havana bus also stops in Las Terrazas. Tickets in Convertibles are purchased at the window upstairs (open 8am to 7pm).

Numerous tour buses and excursions leave daily for Havana – a trip that may include a couple of tourist stops. Ask at **Havanatur** (☎ 77-84-94; cnr Martí & Colón; ☾ 8am-noon & 1:30-6pm Mon-Fri, 8am-noon & 1-4pm Sat) about these and other transfers to Cayo Levisa, Cayo Jutías and María la Gorda.

Private taxis hanging around outside the bus station will offer you prices all the way to Havana.

TRAIN

Before planning any train travel, check the blackboards at the station for cancelled, suspended and rescheduled services. From the **train station** (☎ 75-57-34; cnr Ferrocarril & Comandante

PINAR DEL
RÍO PROVINCE

Pinares Sur; ☉ ticket window 6:30am-noon & 1-6:30pm) there's a painfully slow train to Havana (CUC$7, 5½ hours, 9:45am) every other day. You can buy your ticket for this train the day of departure; be at the station between 7am and 8pm. Local trains go southwest to Guane via Sábalo (CUC$2, two hours, 7:18am and 6:30pm). This is the closest you can get by train to the Península de Guanahacabibes.

Getting Around

Cubacar (☎ 75-9381) has a car-rental office at Hotel Vueltabajo (p204) and **Havanautos** (☎ 77-80-15) has one at Hotel Pinar del Río. Mopeds can be rented from La Casona (p204).

Servicentro Oro Negro is two blocks north of the Hospital Provincial on the Carretera Central. The Servi-Cupet gas station is 1.5km further north on the Carretera Central toward Havana; another is on Rafael Morales Sur at the south entrance to town.

Horse carts (one peso) on Isabel Rubio near Adela Azcuy go to the Hospital Provincial and out onto the Carretera Central. Bici-taxis cost five pesos around town.

If you are up for cadging a ride to Viñales Cuban-style, trudge north to the junction of the Carretera a Viñales and the northern extent of Rafael Morales and get talking to the *amarillo* (traffic organizer).

SOUTHWEST OF PINAR DEL RÍO

If Cuba is the world's greatest tobacco producer and Pinar del Río its proverbial jewel box, then the verdant San Luis region southwest of the provincial capital is the diamond in the stash. Few deny that the pancake-flat farming terrain around the town of San Juan y Martínez churns out the crème de la crème of Cuba's (and hence the world's) best tobacco and the rural scenery is typically picturesque. Further on, there are a couple of little-visited southern beaches and the freshwater Embalse Laguna Grande, stocked with largemouth bass.

Sights

Well into his eighties now and threatening to out-live Fidel, Alejandro Robaina is the only surviving Cuban with a brand of cigars named after him. His famous *vegas* (fields), in the rich Vuelta Abajo region southwest of Pinar del Río, have been growing quality tobacco since 1845, but it wasn't until 1997 that a new brand of cigars known as

Vegas Robaina was first launched to wide international acclaim.

An enterprising man in more ways than one, Robaina has also unofficially opened up his tobacco farm to outside visitors, and with a little effort and some deft navigational skills, visitors can roll up at the farm and, for a small fee (CUC$5), get the lowdown on the tobacco-making process from delicate plant to aromatic wrapper.

To get to the **Alejandro Robaina Tobacco Plantation** (☎ 79-74-70) take the Carretera Central southwest out of Pinar del Río for 18km, turn left onto another straight road and then left again (after approximately 4km) onto the rougher track that leads to the farm. Tours are generally available from 10am to 5pm every day bar Sunday, but call ahead to check. The tobacco-growing season runs from October to February and this is obviously the best time to visit.

RANCHO LA GUABINA

A former Spanish farm spread over 1000 hectares of pasture, forest and wetlands, **Rancho La Guabina** (☎ 75-76-16; Carretera de Luis Lazo Km 9.5) is a jack of all trades and a master of at least one. You can partake in horseback riding here, go boating on a lake, enjoy a scrumptious Cuban barbecue, or even see a cockfight. The highlight for most, though, is the fantastic horse shows. The Rancho is a long-standing horse-breeding center that raises fine Pinto Cubano and Apaloosa horses, and mini-rodeo-style shows run on Monday, Wednesday and Friday from 10am to noon and from 4pm to 6pm. Agencies in Viñales and Pinar del Río run excursions here starting at CUC$29, or you can arrive on your own. It's a great place to enjoy the peaceful *guajiro* life. Limited accommodation is available (see opposite).

Sleeping & Eating

Villa Laguna Grande (Islazul; ☎ 84-34-53; Carretera a Ciudad Bolívar; s/d CUC$23/29) Something of an anomaly, this rough-around-the-edges fishing resort, 29km southwest of Guane and 18km off the highway to María la Gorda, is Islazul's most isolated outpost. The 12 rather scruffy thatched cabins sit in woodland directly below the Embalse Laguna Grande, a reservoir stocked with bass where locals come to fish. It's OK for a pit stop, but if it's freshwater fishing you're after, better options are in Embalse Zaza near Sancti Spíritus (p296).

THE CUBAN CIGAR

Groucho Marx, Che Guevara, George Burns, Arnold Schwarzenegger – you don't need to be a monthly subscriber to *Cigar Aficionado* magazine to understand the universal popularity of the aromatic Cuban cigar. Sigmund Freud allegedly puffed his way through a box a day, Winston Churchill had a size named in his honor, while John F Kennedy purportedly told his press secretary Pierre Salinger to order in a thousand of his favorite Petit Upmanns the night before signing the US trade embargo on Cuba into law.

The unsurpassed quality of Cuban cigars in the world market stems from an accidental combination of geography, terrain and fine local workmanship. Grown primarily in the rust-red fields of Pinar del Río province in the island's verdant west, all genuine Cuban cigars are hand-rolled by trained 'experts,' before being packed in tightly sealed cedar boxes and classified into 42 different types and sizes.

Cuba's flagship brand is Cohiba, created in 1966 for diplomatic use and popularized by Fidel Castro who used to puff on Cohiba Espléndidos before he gave up smoking for health reasons in 1985. Other international favorites include the Partagás brand, rolled in Havana since 1845; the superstrong Bolívar, named after South America's formidable liberator; the classic Montecristo 2, another *fuerte* (strong) smoke much admired by Cubans; and the milder Romeo y Julieta brand, invented in 1903 by a Cuban who had traveled widely in Europe.

In terms of purchasing, always avoid the many offers you will receive to buy cigars on the street. These substandard smokes are nearly always of dubious quality, with air pockets and hard wrappings containing protuberances. Indeed, some of them are outright fakes. The best place to wise up on cigars is in the numerous Casas del Habano that are dotted around the country. For factory visits there are three main options, although plenty more if you go as part of an organized tour. Try the Partagás factory in Havana (p114), the Constantino Pérez Carrodegua factory in Santa Clara (p279) or, more appropriately (as it's situated in Cuba's tobacco heartland), the Francisco Donatien factory in Pinar del Río (p202).

Rancho La Guabina (☎ 75-76-16; Carretera de Luis Lazo Km 9.5; r CUC$65; **P** 🞩) Just outside Pinar del Río, this expansive farm (see opposite) offers eight rooms, five in a cottage-style house and three in separate cabins. It's a charming and unhurried place with excellent food and friendly staff.

There are a couple of off-the-beaten-track beach resorts on the Bahía de Cortés halfway between Pinar del Río and María la Gorda, if you don't mind going local. The **Villa Boca de Galafre** (☎ 829-8592; 3/6 beds CUC$15/20), 3km off the main highway, has 32 rock-bottom cabins on a scruffy beach. The train to Guane stops on the access road 2km from the resort, which is often closed in the winter. For a sandier stretch of beach, try **Villa Playa Bailén** (☎ 829-6145; bungalow CUC$15) 8km further on, where basic A-frame bungalows sleep four.

There are also some casas particulares (CUC$15 to CUC$20) available in Sandino, 6km southwest of the Laguna Grande turn-off and 89km from Pinar del Río. Try **Motel Alexis** (☎ 84-32-82; Zona L No 33; r CUC$15-20) or nearby Casa de Estrella; both are signposted just off the main highway.

Getting There & Away

Two trains a day travel between Pinar del Río and Guane stopping at San Luis, San Juan y Martínez, Sábalo and Isabel Rubio (two hours). Passenger trucks run periodically between Guane and Sandino, but southwest of there, public transport is sparse, bar the sporadic Havanatur transfer (p205). Be sure to fill your tank up at the Servi-Cupet gas station in Isabel Rubio if you intend to drive to Cabo de San Antonio, as this is the last gasp for gas.

PENÍNSULA DE GUANAHACABIBES

As the island narrows at its western end, you fall upon the low-lying and ecologically rich Península de Guanahacabibes, one of Cuba's most isolated enclaves that once provided shelter for its earliest inhabitants, the Guanahatabeys. A two-hour drive from Pinar del Río, this region lacks major tourist infrastructure meaning it feels a lot more

PINAR DEL RÍO PROVINCE

isolated than it is. The Guanahacabibes is famous for its national park (also a Unesco Biosphere Reserve) and an international-standard diving center at María la Gorda.

PARQUE NACIONAL PENÍNSULA DE GUANAHACABIBES

Flat and deceptively narrow, the elongated Península de Guanahacabibes begins at La Fe, 94km southwest of Pinar del Río. In 1987, 1015 sq km of this uninhabited sliver of idyllic coastline were declared a Biosphere Reserve by Unesco – one of only six in Cuba. The reasons for the protection measures were manifold. Firstly, the reserve's submerged coastline features a wide variety of different landscapes including broad mangrove swamps, low scrub thicket vegetation and an uplifted shelf of alternating white sand and coral rock. Secondly, the area's distinctive limestone karst formations are home to a plethora of unique flora and fauna including 172 species of bird, 700 species of plant, 18 types of mammal, 35 reptiles, 19 amphibians, 86 types of butterfly and 16 orchid species. Sea turtles, including loggerhead and green turtles, come ashore at night in summer to lay their eggs – the park is the only part of mainland Cuba where this happens. If you're here between May and October, night tours can be arranged to watch the turtles nest. Another curiosity is the swarms of *cangrejos colorados* (red and yellow crabs) that crawl across the peninsula's rough central road only to be unceremoniously crushed under the tires of passing cars. The stench of the smashed shells is memorable.

To date, Guanahacabibes' value as an archaeological goldmine is still in the discovery stage. Suffice to say the area is thought to shelter at least 100 important archaeological sites relating to Cuba's oldest and least-known indigenous inhabitants, the Guanahatabey.

In late 2008 Guanahacabibes was on the verge of opening a long-awaited new visitors center designed to exhibit the park's environmental riches and educate people about its ongoing conservation efforts.

Orientation & Information

Although the park border straddles the tiny community of La Fe, the entry to the reserve proper is at La Bajada where you'll find the Estación Ecológica Guanahacabibes. Just beyond the office the road splits in two with the left-hand branch going south to María la Gorda (14km along a deteriorating coastal road) and the right fork heading west toward the end of the peninsula.

It's a 120km round-trip to Cuba's westernmost point from here. The lonesome Cabo de San Antonio is populated by a solitary lighthouse, the Faro Roncali, inaugurated by the Spanish in 1849, and a Gaviota marina and villa (see opposite). Four kilometers to the northwest lays Playa Las Tumbas, an idyllic beach where visitors to the park are permitted to swim.

There's no charge to visit Hotel María la Gorda and its adjoining 5km beach, both named after a voluptuous Venezuelan who was marooned here by pirates and turned to prostitution to survive. Divers are unanimous about the quality of the reefs here and it's also one of Cuba's prime yachting venues.

Activities

Península de Guanahacabibes is a paradise for eco-travelers, conservationists, divers and bird-watchers – or, at least, it ought to be. Feathered species on display here include parrots, *tocororos,* woodpeckers, owls, tody flycatchers, and *zunzuncitos* (bee hummingbirds) and, with no official settlements, the peninsula is one of Cuba's most untouched. However, thanks to the rather draconian park rules (you can't go anywhere without a guide), some travelers have complained that the experience is too limiting.

DIVING

Diving is **María la Gorda's** raison d'être and the prime reason most people come here. Good visibility and sheltered offshore reefs are highlights, plus the proximity of the 50-plus dive sites to the shore. Couple this with the largest formation of black coral in the archipelago and you've got a recipe for arguably the best diving reefs outside the Isla de la Juventud.

The nerve center is the well-run **Centro Internacional de Buceo** (☎ 77-13-06) dive center based at the Marina Gaviota close to the eponymous hotel. A dive here costs a reasonable CUC$35 (night diving CUC$40), plus CUC$7.50 for equipment. The center offers a full CMAS (Confédération Mondiale des Activités Subaquatiques; World Underwater Activities Federation) scuba certification course (CUC$365; four days) and snorkelers can hop on the dive boat for CUC$12. The dive center also offers four hours of deep-sea fishing for CUC$200 for up to four people and line fishing/trolling at CUC$30 per person, four maximum.

Among the 50 identified dive sites in the vicinity, divers are shown El Valle de Coral Negro, a 100m-long black-coral wall, and El Salón de María, a cave 20m deep containing feather stars and Technicolor corals. The concentrations of migratory fish can be incredible. The furthest entry is only 30 minutes by boat from shore.

Another option is Cuba's most westerly located boat dock, the **Marina Gaviota Cabo de San Antonio** (☎ 75-01-18) on Playa Las Tumbas at the end of the Guanahacabibes Peninsula. The marina has fuel, boat mooring, a small restaurant, shop and easy access to 27 diving sites. The Villa Cabo San Antonio is nearby.

EXCURSIONS

The **Estación Ecológica Guanahacabibes** (☎ 82-75-03-66; www.ecovida.pinar.cu; ☯ 7:30am-3:30pm), opposite the meteorological station at La Bajada, can arrange guides, specialized visits and a five-hour tour to the park's (and Cuba's) western tip at Cabo de San Antonio. The responsibility is yours to supply transport, sufficient gas, water, sunscreen, insect repellent and food, which makes the task for independent travelers a little more difficult. During most of the 120km round-trip you'll have dark, rough *diente de perro* (dog's teeth) rock on one side and the brilliant blue sea on the other. Iguanas will lumber for cover as you approach and you might see small deer, *jutías* (edible tree rats) and lots of birds. Beyond the lighthouse is deserted Playa Las Tumbas where you'll be given 30 minutes for a swim. Any hire car can make this trip though a 4WD is preferable. The five-hour excursion costs CUC$10 per person, plus the CUC$70 or so you'll need to hire a car (there's a Vía rental place at Hotel María la Gorda). There's a possibility of other excursions to local communities in the area and at least four new hikes in the works; call ahead to check developments.

HIKING

The hike to **Cueva las Perlas** (Pearl Cave; CUC$8, three hours, 3km) traverses deciduous woodland replete with a wide variety of birds, including *tocororos, zunzuncitos* and woodpeckers. After 1.5km you come to the cave itself, a multi-gallery cavern of which 300m is accessible to hikers. The **Del Bosque al Mar** trail (CUC$6, 1½ hours, 1.5km) leaves from near the eco-station, passes a lagoon where you can view the resident birdlife, and takes in some interesting flora including orchids. At 90 minutes it's rather short for such an immense park, but the guides are highly trained and knowledgeable, and tours can be conducted in Spanish, English or Italian. There was a new trail called **Guanahacabibes antes de Colón** on the verge of opening as this book was being written. Ask about this and other new trails at the Estación Ecológica Guanahacabibes.

Sleeping & Eating

Hotel María la Gorda (Gaviota; ☎ 77-81-31, 77-30-67; s/d incl breakfast CUC$44/68; **P** 🏊) This is the most remote hotel on the main island of Cuba and the isolation has its advantages. But, while the adjoining palm-fringed beach is pretty, most people come here to dive; there's a dive site with a vertical drop-off just 200m from the hotel. María la Gorda (literally 'Maria the Fatso') is on the Bahía de Corrientes, 150km southwest of Pinar del Río and 14km from the park office at La Bajada along a rough road. Room-wise you get a choice of three pink-concrete, motel-type buildings or 20 newer cabins set back from the beach. The latter are more comfortable and private. Not that luxury is an issue here. Far from being a posh resort, María la Gorda is a place where hammocks are strung between palm trees, cold beers are sipped at sunset and dive talk continues into the small hours.

Buffet meals cost CUC$15 for lunch or dinner; reports on the food vary. Water in the hotel shop is expensive, so bring your own or purify the tap water.

Villa Cabo San Antonio (☎ 75-01-18; Playa Las Tumbas; r CUC$75-120) A 16-villa complex on the almost-virgin Guanahacabibes Peninsula, situated 3km from the Roncali lighthouse and 4km from the new Gaviota Marina, this environment-friendly place has satellite TV, car rental, bike hire and a small cafe.

Restaurante La Bajada (☯ 8:30am-10:30pm) Just next to the meteorological station, this place has (you guessed it) fried chicken, and french fries and sandwiches – when it's open.

PINAR DEL RÍO PROVINCE

Getting There & Away

Without a hire car or a prearranged transfer, getting to Cuba's extreme west can be problematic.

A transfer bus operates between Viñales and María la Gorda, but only with a 10-passenger minimum. Current demand dictates that this bus runs once a week at best. It is scheduled to leave Viñales at 7am and arrive at the peninsula at 9:30am. The return leg leaves María la Gorda at 5pm and arrives in Viñales at 7pm. The cost for a single/return ticket is CUC$15/25. You can inquire at **Cubanacán** (☎ 79-63-93) in Viñales or **Havanatur** (☎ 77-84-94) in Pinar del Río.

Via Gaviota (☎ 77-81-31) has an office at Hotel María la Gorda and offers a jeep taxi service with driver to Cabo de San Antonio at CUC$50 for up to four people. It also offers transfers to/from Pinar del Río at CUC$50 one-way for the whole car (or CUC$120 to/from Havana).

VALLE DE VIÑALES

Embellished by soaring pine trees and scattered with bulbous limestone cliffs that teeter like giant haystacks above the peaceful and well-tended tobacco plantations, Parque Nacional Viñales is one of Cuba's most magnificent natural settings. Wedged spectacularly into the Sierra de los Órganos mountain range, this 11km-by-5km valley was declared a Unesco World Heritage Site in 1999 for its dramatic rocky outcrops (known as *mogotes*), coupled with the vernacular architecture of its traditional farms and villages.

Once upon a time the whole region was several hundred meters higher. Then, during the Cretaceous period 100 million years ago, a network of underground rivers ate away at the limestone bedrock, creating vast caverns. Eventually the roofs collapsed leaving only the eroded walls we see today. It is the finest example of a limestone karst valley in Cuba and contains the Caverna Santo Tomás, the island's largest cave system.

Rock studies aside, Viñales also offers opportunities for fine hiking, history, rock climbing and horseback trekking. On the accommodation front it boasts four first-class hotels and some of the best casas particulares in Cuba. Despite drawing in day-trippers by the busload, the area's well-protected and spread-out natural attractions have somehow managed to escape the frenzied tourist circus of other less well-managed resorts, while the atmosphere in and around the village remains refreshingly hassle-free.

VIÑALES
pop 14,279

Ah…tranquil Viñales where rocking chairs creak on well-swept porches and sombrero-wearing *guajiros* saunter home on horseback after a tough day in the tobacco fields. Despite a double pummeling by hurricanes Gustav and Ike in 2008, this most unhurried and friendly of Cuban towns has lost none of its picturesque charm. Well established on the standard tourist circuit, travelers come here to relax, ruminate and hit the great outdoors in a settlement that has so far managed to avoid the annoying *jinetero*-fest so common elsewhere.

Information

INTERNET ACCESS & TELEPHONE

Etecsa Telepunto (Ceferino Fernández No 3; internet per hr CUC$6; ⊗ 8:30am-4:30pm) One of Cuba's tiniest Telepuntos offices where two computers are squeezed into an office that accommodates three Etecsa clerks.

MEDICAL SERVICES

Farmacia Internacional (☎ 79-63-89) In Hotel Los Jazmines.

MONEY

Banco de Crédito y Comercio (☎ 79-31-30; Salvador Cisneros No 58; ⊗ 8am-noon & 1:30-3pm Mon-Fri, 8-11am Sat)
Cadeca (☎ 93-63-34; cnr Salvador Cisneros & Adela Azcuy; ⊗ 8:30am-5:30pm Mon-Sat)

POST

Post office (cnr Salvador Cisneros & Ceferino Fernández; ⊗ 9am-6pm Mon-Sat) Relocated to a small booth near the park post Hurricane Gustav.

TRAVEL AGENCIES

Cubanacán (☎ 79-63-93; Salvador Cisneros No 63C; ⊗ 9am-7pm Mon-Sat) Arranges tours, excursions and transfer buses.
Havanatur (☎ 79-62-62; Salvador Cisneros No 65; ⊗ 9am-7pm Mon-Sat) Similar to Cubanacán next door but with a few different offers. Browse both before you choose.

PINAR DEL
RÍO PROVINCE

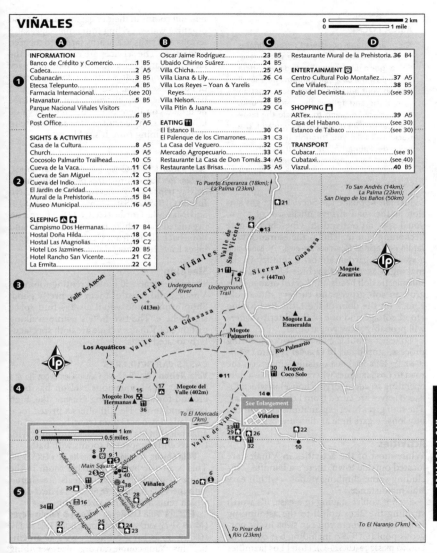

VIÑALES

0 ——— 2 km
0 ——— 1 mile

INFORMATION
Banco de Crédito y Comercio	**1**	B5
Cadeca	**2**	A5
Cubanacán	**3**	B5
Etecsa Telepunto	**4**	B5
Farmacia Internacional	(see 20)	
Havanatur	**5**	B5
Parque Nacional Viñales Visitors		
Center	**6**	B5
Post Office	**7**	A5

SIGHTS & ACTIVITIES
Casa de la Cultura	**8**	A5
Church	**9**	A5
Cocosolo Palmarito Trailhead	**10**	C5
Cueva de la Vaca	**11**	C4
Cueva de San Miguel	**12**	C2
Cueva del Indio	**13**	C3
El Jardín de Caridad	**14**	C4
Mural de la Prehistoria	**15**	B4
Museo Municipal	**16**	A5

SLEEPING
Campismo Dos Hermanas	**17**	B4
Hostal Doña Hilda	**18**	C4
Hostal Las Magnolias	**19**	C2
Hotel Los Jazmines	**20**	B5
Hotel Rancho San Vicente	**21**	C2
La Ermita	**22**	C4

Oscar Jaime Rodríguez	**23**	B5
Ubaido Chirino Suárez	**24**	B5
Villa Chicha	**25**	C4
Villa Liana & Lily	**26**	C4
Villa Los Reyes – Yoan & Yarelis		
Reyes	**27**	A5
Villa Nelson	**28**	B5
Villa Pitín & Juana	**29**	C4

EATING
El Estanco II	**30**	C4
El Palenque de los Cimarrones	**31**	C3
La Casa del Veguero	**32**	C5
Mercado Agropecuario	**33**	C4
Restaurante La Casa de Don Tomás	**34**	A5
Restaurante Las Brisas	**35**	A5

Restaurante Mural de la Prehistoria	**36**	B4

ENTERTAINMENT
Centro Cultural Polo Montañez	**37**	A5
Cine Viñales	**38**	B5
Patio del Decimista	(see 39)	

SHOPPING
ARTex	**39**	A5
Casa del Habano	(see 30)	
Estanco de Tabaco	(see 30)	

TRANSPORT
Cubacar	(see 3)	
Cubataxi	(see 40)	
Víazul	**40**	B5

To Puerto Esperanza (18km);
La Palma (23km)

To San Andrés (14km);
La Palma (22km);
San Diego de los Baños (50km)

Valle de San Vicente

Sierra de Viñales

Sierra La Guasasa
+ (447m)

Mogote Zacarías

Valle de Ancón

Underground River
+ (413m)

Underground Trail

Valle de La Guasasa

Mogote La Esmeralda

Los Aquáticos

Mogote Palmarito

Río Palmarito

Mogote del Valle (402m)

Mogote Dos Hermanas

To El Moncada (7km)

Mogote Coco Solo

See Enlargement

Viñales

Valle de Viñales

To Pinar del Río (23km)

To El Naranjo (7km)

0 ——— 1 km
0 ——— 0.5 miles

Adela Azcuy

Salvador Cisneros

Main Square

Viñales

Celso Maragoto

Rafael Trejo

Cafetal Camilo Cienfuegos

To El Naranjo (7km)

PINAR DEL RÍO PROVINCE

Sights

Founded in 1875, Viñales is more about setting than sights with most of its activities of a lung-stretching outdoor nature. Nevertheless the town has some engaging architecture and a lively main square backed by the sturdy colonial **Casa de la Cultura**, one of the oldest structures in the valley. Next door is a tiny art gallery while to the right is an equally diminutive (and dilapidated) **church**. Positioned halfway down Cisneros, Viñales' pine-lined main street, the **Museo Municipal** (☎ 79-33-95; Salvador Cisneros No 115; ☼ 8am-5pm) occupies the former home of independence heroine Adela Azcuy (1861–1914) and tracks the local history. Four different hikes leave from here daily.

ASK A LOCAL

There are many good walks from Viñales town though none of them are signposted. For a good initiation, head down Adela Azcuy past the baseball stadium and a small lake on your left. At the first main junction turn right and follow the track around. Imagine you're going to encircle the large *mogotes* in front of you (which you are). The tracks will take you through the beautiful Valle de Palmarito and you'll eventually come out by Campismo Dos Hermanas.

Alberto, Viñales

Just left opposite the Servi-Cupet gas station as the road swings north out of town, you'll spot an outlandish, vine-choked gate beckoning you in. This is the entrance to **El Jardín de Caridad** (donations accepted; ✆ 8am-5pm), a sprawling garden almost a century in the making. Cascades of orchids bloom alongside plastic doll heads, thickets of orange lilies grow in soft groves and turkeys run amok. Knock on the door of the Little Red Riding Hood cottage and one of the elderly owners will probably show you around.

To learn about the local tobacco-growing process, stop by at **La Casa del Veguero** (✆ 97-60-80; ✆ 10am-5pm) just outside Viñales on the road to Los Jazmines where you can see a fully operating *secadero* (drying house) in which tobacco leaves are cured from February to May. The staff gives brief explanations and you can buy loose cigars here at discount prices.

Activities

While most of the activities in Viñales are located outside town, there's a handful – including some climbing routes – within easy walking distance.

Even if you're staying in a casa, it's worth strolling the 2km uphill to the astounding Hotel Ermita where you can **swim** in the gorgeous pool (CUC$7, including bar cover) or book a **massage** (CUC$20-35). Hotel Los Jazmines has an equally amazing pool (CUC$5) though the ubiquitous tour buses can sometimes kill the tranquility.

Casa owners in Viñales are particularly adept at being able to rustle up all number of activities more or less on demand. One particularly resourceful couple is **Yoan & Yarelis Reyes** (✆ 79-32-63; Rafael Trejo No 134) who not only rent out rooms in their engaging casa but also organize walks, cycling tours, massage, salsa lessons and visits to a nearby farm and tobacco plantation. The services are enhanced by the fact that Yarelis is a qualified national park biologist and Yoan's father owns a Garden of Eden–like Finca, 1km out of town, nestled beneath the steep *mogotes*. For a small fee he'll take you there (and onto the Cueva de la Vaca) to sample fruit, coffee and a dose of throat-warming rum. It's sublime.

Tours

Cubanacán (✆ 79-63-93; Salvador Cisneros No 63C; ✆ 9am-7pm Mon-Sat) organizes perennially popular day trips to Cayo Levisa (CUC$29), Cayo Jutías (CUC$22), San Tomás Cave (CUC$10) and María la Gorda (CUC$32). There's an organized valley bike tour for CUC$20 and horseback riding from CUC$5. Official park hikes leave from here daily (CUC$8).

Sleeping

There are some 250 houses renting rooms in Viñales, and most of them are pretty good. Shop around and you'll always find space somewhere. The two hotels within walking distance of Viñales village are both spectacularly located gems.

CASAS PARTICULARES

Villa Nelson (✆ 79-32-68; Camilo Cienfuegos No 4; r CUC$15-20; ✆) Loquacious Nelson has been around for ages surviving Gustav, Ike, high taxes and more. He still offers a prized local cocktail known as Ochún (rum, honey and orange juice) in his homely backyard along with two recently renovated rooms with baths.

Villa Chicha (Camilo Cienfuegos No 22; r CUC$15-20) This is a basic but comfortable room in the home of gracious *señora*. Meals are shared with the Villa Blanca (✆ 69-69-44) next door, which rents a similarly-sized room.

our pick **'Villa Los Reyes' – Yoan & Yarelis Reyes** (✆ 69-52-25; yarelis@pnvinales.co.cu; Rafael Trejo No 134; r CUC$20; P ✆) A great house with all amenities; this young couple can organize everything from salsa dancing to Spanish lessons. Yarelis is a biologist at the national park and Yoan has Viñales running through his veins.

Oscar Jaime Rodríguez (✆ 79-33-81; Adela Azcuy No 43; r CUC$20; ✆) Oscar's something of a local legend, not so much for his casa (though he rents two rooms), but for his role as the king of climbing in Viñales (and consequently Cuba).

Not surprisingly, there's plenty of room out back for nonguests to mix, mingle and plan sorties up the *mogotes*.

Ubaido Chirino Suárez (☎ 79-32-26; Adela Azcuy No 35; r CUC$20; ✿) After having chunks ripped out of her house by Hurricane Gustav, Ubaido was planning a 2009 relaunch. This place is a separate apartment with its own entry, terrace, lounge, rocking chairs, kitchen and two bedrooms.

Hostal Doña Hilda (☎ 79-60-53; Carretera Pinar del Río Km 25 No 4; r CUC$20-25; ✿) One of the first houses in town on the road from Pinar del Río, Hilda's house is small, unpretentious, and classic Viñales – just like the perennially smiling hostess.

Villa Pitín & Juana (☎ 79-33-38; Carretera Pinar del Río Km 25 No 2; r CUC$25; Ⓟ ✿) Two rooms on separate floors and a fantastic family atmosphere make this a great place to stay. But the highlight is the food, cooked with true *amor* (love), and ranking among the best in Cuba.

Villa Liana & Lily (☎ 69-53-54; liana86@correode cuba.cu; Carretera Pinar del Río Km 25 No 7; r CUC$25; Ⓟ ✿) The same family as above and the same wonderful hospitality. Liana is new to the game and rents one room with private entry and cooks meals made with vegetables plucked straight from the garden out back.

HOTELS

ourpick **La Ermita** (Cubanacán; ☎ 79-60-71; s/d incl breakfast CUC$56/70; Ⓟ ✿ ✿) While Los Jazmines might edge the prize for best view, La Ermita takes top honors for architecture, interior furnishings and all-round services and quality. It's also a lot less frenetic, thanks to the absence of any tour buses. Among a plethora of extracurricular attractions are an excellent pool, skillfully mixed cocktails, tennis courts, a shop, horseback riding and massage. Rooms with views are housed in handsome two-story colonial edifices and the restaurant is an ideal perch for breakfast. You can walk the 2km downhill to the village or the Viñales tour bus (p214) stops outside.

Hotel Los Jazmines (Cubanacán; ☎ 79-62-05; s/d incl breakfast CUC$56/70; Ⓟ ✿ ✿) Inhale deeply and prepare yourself. The vista from this pastel-pink colonial-style hotel is one of the best and most quintessential in Cuba. Open the shutters of your classic valley-facing room and drink in the sight of magnificent *mogotes*, rust-red fields and palm frond–covered tobacco drying houses shimmering in the early morning mist. While no five-star palace, the Jazmines benefits from its unrivaled location, gloriously inviting swimming pool and a host of handy extras such as international clinic, massage room and small shop/market. The setting comes at a cost: bus tours stop off here every hour or two destroying a little of the ethereal ambience. The hotel is 4km south of Viñales on the road to Pinar del Río.

Eating & Drinking

Viñales home-cooking is some of the best in Cuba – eat at your casa particular! The following places are OK if you're stuck for lunch.

El Estanco II (⏱ 10am-11pm) A simple pizza and beer place 1km out of town on the road north, and a decent pit stop. A pizza costs a couple of Convertibles, a plate of spaghetti slightly more.

Restaurante Las Brisas (☎ 79-33-53; Salvador Cisneros No 96; ⏱ 11am-2pm & 6-9pm) This place serves deep-fried chicken and *congrí* (rice) for peanuts, or you can pick up a lunchtime grilled cheese sandwich at either the Patio del Decimista or the Centro Cultural Polo Montañez (see below).

Restaurante La Casa de Don Tomás (☎ 79-63-00; Salvador Cisneros No 140; ⏱ 10am-11pm) The oldest house in Viñales is also its best restaurant – by default (there's no real opposition). The casa, with its terra-cotta roof and exuberant flowering vines, is suitably salubrious and the food's OK if you stick to the house special, *las delicias de Don Tomás,* a rich mélange of rice, lobster, fish, pork, chicken and sausage with an egg on top (CUC$10). There's an atmospheric deck out back.

Viñales' *mercado agropecuario* (agricultural market) is about 100m from town at the west end of Salvador Cisneros down the road toward Dos Hermanas. Get your peso rum and Convertible bread here.

Entertainment

Centro Cultural Polo Montañez (cnr Salvador Cisneros & Joaquín Pérez; admission after 9pm CUC$2) Named for the late Pinar del Río resident turned *guajiro* hero, Polo Montañez, this open-to-the-elements patio off the main plaza is a bar-restaurant with a full-blown stage and lighting rig that comes alive after 9pm.

Patio del Decimista (Salvador Cisneros No 102; admission free; ⏱ music at 9pm) Smaller but equally ebullient is this long-standing place that serves live music and cold beers.

Cine Viñales (cnr Ceferino Fernández & Rafael Trejo) The settlement's only cinema is a block south of the main square.

Shopping

ARTex (Salvador Cisneros No 102) You can get postcards, T-shirts and CDs here. It's attached to the Patio Decimista.

Estanco de Tabaco (Carretera de Puerto Esperanza Km 1; 🕑 9am-5pm) A good choice for cigar shopping, next to Estanco II.

Getting There & Around

BUS

The **Víazul ticket office** (Salvador Cisneros No 63A; 🕑 8am-noon & 1-3pm) is opposite the main square in the same building as Cubataxi (below). The daily Víazul bus for Havana via Pinar del Río departs at 8am and 2pm daily (CUC$12). At the time of writing only the second bus stopped in Las Terrazas.

There are also daily transfer buses to Havana (CUC$15), Soroa (CUC$12) and Las Terrazas (CUC$12); and a daily – except Tuesday – service to Cienfuegos (CUC$25) and Trinidad (CUC$40). The transfers to Cayo Levisa (CUC$29, two person minimum), Cayo Jutías (CUC$22, six minimum) and María la Gorda (CUC$32, six minimum) run if enough people book. Cayo Levisa departs most days while María la Gorda runs approximately once a week. Transfers can be booked through Havanatur or Cubanacán (p212).

CAR & MOPED

To reach Viñales from the south, you take the long and winding road from Pinar del Río; the roads from the north coast are not as sinuous, but are pretty drives. The wildly scenic mountain road from the Península de Guanahacabibes through Guane and Pons is one of Cuba's most spectacular routes. Allow a lot of travel time.

Car hire can be arranged at **Cubacar** (☎ 79-60-90; Salvador Cisneros No 63C; 🕑 9am-7pm) in the Cubanacán office and **Havanautos** (☎ 76-63-30; Salvador Cisneros final) opposite the gas station.

Mopeds can be rented for CUC$24 a day at Restaurante La Casa de Don Tomás.

There's a Servi-Cupet gas station at the northeast end of Viñales town.

TAXI

Cubataxi (☎ 79-31-95; Salvador Cisneros No 63A) shares an office with Víazul. Drivers hanging around outside will take you to Pinar del Río for approximately CUC$15, Palma Rubia (for the boat to Cayo Levisa) for CUC$28 or Gran Caverna de Santo Tomás for CUC$13.

VIÑALES BUS TOUR

The Viñales Bus Tour is a hop-on/hop-off minibus that runs nine times a day between the valley's spread-out sites. Starting and finishing in the village's main park, the whole circuit takes an hour and five minutes with the first bus leaving at 9am and the last at 4:50pm (with a one-hour break for lunch). There are 18 stops along the route and all are clearly marked with route maps and timetables. All-day tickets cost CUC$5 and can be purchased on the bus.

PARQUE NACIONAL VIÑALES

Parque Nacional Viñales' extraordinary cultural landscape covers 150 sq km and supports a population of 25,000 people. A mosaic of communities grows coffee, tobacco, sugarcane, oranges, avocados and bananas on some of the oldest landscape in Cuba. The park is administered through the highly informative **Parque Nacional Viñales visitors center** (Carretera a Pinar del Río Km 2) on the hill just before you reach Hotel Los Jazmines. Inside, colorful displays (in Spanish and English) map out the park's main features. Hiking, information and guides are also on hand.

Sights

Four kilometers west of Viñales village is the **Mural de la Prehistoria** (admission CUC$1). On a cliff at the foot of the 617m-high Sierra de Viñales, the highest portion of the Sierra de los Órganos, this 120m-long painting on the side of Mogote Dos Hermanas was designed in 1961 by Leovigildo González Morillo, a follower of Mexican artist Diego Rivera (the idea was hatched by Celia Sánchez, Alicia Alonso and Antonio Núñez Jiménez). It took 15 people five years to complete it. The huge snail, dinosaurs, sea monsters and humans on the cliff symbolize the theory of evolution and are either impressively psychedelic or monumentally horrific, depending on your point of view. You don't really have to get up close to appreciate the mural, but the admission fee is waived if you take the delicious, if a little overpriced, CUC$15 lunch at the site restaurant (see p216). Horses are usually available here for a short ride around the park or a longer excursion through the valley.

A kilometer beyond the turn-off to Dos Hermanas, a dirt road leads toward the mountain community of **Los Aquáticos**. Los Aquáticos was founded in 1943 by followers of visionary Antoñica Izquierdo, who discovered the healing power of water when the *campesinos* of this area had no access to conventional medicine. They colonized the mountain slopes and several families still live there. Unfortunately, the last patriarch practicing the water cure died in 2002, taking the tradition with him, but you can still visit. Los Aquáticos is accessible only by horse or on foot. Ask at your casa for guide contacts; horses can be hired from farmers living near the trailhead (CUC$10 per person for a three-hour tour with a Spanish-speaking guide). From the main road it's 1km inland to the trailhead (just across the stream) of La Ruta de las Aguas. After your visit, you can make this a loop by continuing on this road (fork left at the same stream, recrossing it a few hundred meters to the east) another 3km to Campismo Dos Hermanas and the cliff paintings; it's a wonderfully scenic route (the complete Los Aquáticos–Dos Hermanas circuit totals 6km from the main highway).

North from the **Cueva del Indio** (☎ 79-62-80; admission CUC$5; ☉ 9am-5:30pm) is the prettiest part of Viñales, although the cave itself, 5.5km north of Viñales village, is a little over-populated with tourists. An ancient indigenous dwelling, it was rediscovered in 1920 and motor boats now ply the underground river through the electrically lit cave.

The **Cueva de San Miguel** is a smaller cave at the jaws of the Valle de San Vicente. You pay CUC$1 to enter a gaping cave that engulfs you for five minutes or so before dumping you a tad cynically in the El Palenque de los Cimarrones restaurant (see p216).

Activities

CYCLING

Despite the sometimes hilly terrain, Viñales is one of the best places in Cuba to cycle (note: there are no off-road routes). La Casa de Don Tomás usually rents bikes (p213). If they're all out, inquire at your casa particular. Viñales residents have a habit of making marvelous two-wheeled cycling machines appear out of thin air.

> **ASK A LOCAL**
>
> If you book one of the park hikes through the official visitors center up by Hotel Los Jazmines, you'll get a better price (CUC$6 versus CUC$8) and the money will go directly into helping the park infrastructure.
>
> *Alejandro, Viñales*

HIKING

The Parque Nacional has three official hikes (four if you count the Gran Caverna de Santo Tomás) and approximately 10 more under 'consideration.' All of them can be arranged directly at the visitors center, the Museo Municipal, or any of the town's tour agencies. The cost is CUC$6 to CUC$8 per person.

The **Cocosolo Palmarito** starts on a spur road just before La Ermita hotel and progresses for 8km past the Coco Solo and Palmarito *mogotes* and the Mural de la Prehistoria. There are good views here and plenty of opportunities to discover the local flora and fauna including a visit to a tobacco *finca* (farmhouse; ask about lunch with one of the families there). It returns you to the main road back to Viñales.

The **Maravillas de Viñales** trail is a 5km loop beginning 1km before El Moncada, 13km from the Dos Hermanas turn-off. This hike takes in endemic plants, orchids and the biggest ant cutter hive in Cuba (so they say).

The **San Vicente/Ancón** trail takes you on an 8km circuit around the more remote Valle Ancón where you can check out still functioning coffee communities in a valley surrounded by *mogotes*.

These are just the official hikes. There are many more unofficial treks available and asking around at your casa particular will elicit further suggestions. Try the Aquáticos walk with its incredible vistas, the Cueva de la Vaca, a cave that forms a tunnel through the *mogotes* and is easily accessible (1.5km) from Viñales village, and the Palmerito Valley, infamous among those in the know for its high-stakes cockfights.

SWIMMING

There is the possibility to swim in a natural pool at La Cueva de Palmerito in the Palmerito Valley. This place is hike-able from Viñales. Ask the locals for directions.

PINAR DEL RIO PROVINCE

CLIMBING IN VIÑALES

You don't need to be Reinhold Messner to recognize the unique climbing potential of Viñales, Cuba's mini-Yosemite. Sprinkled with steep-sided *mogotes* (limestone monoliths) and bequeathed with whole photo-albums' worth of stunning natural vistas, climbers from around the world have been coming here for over a decade to indulge in a sport that has yet to be officially sanctioned by the Cuban government.

Thanks to the numerous grey areas, Viñales climbing remains very much a word-of-mouth affair. There are no printed route maps and no official on-the-ground information (indeed, most state-employed tourist reps will deny all knowledge of it). If you are keen to get up onto the rock-face, your first point of reference should be the comprehensive website of **Cuba Climbing** (www.cubaclimbing.com). Once on the ground, the best nexus for climbers is the Casa de Oscar (p212), which, aside from offering comfortable accommodation, acts as an unofficial HQ for climbers of all types.

Viñales has numerous well-known climbing routes and a handful of skillful Cuban guides, but there is no reliable equipment hire (bring your own) and no adequate safety procedures in place. Everything you do, you do at your own risk, and that includes any sticky situations you may encounter with the authorities (although they generally tend to turn a blind eye). Also bear in mind that unregulated climbing in a national park area has the potential to damage endangered flora and ecosystems. Proceed with caution and care.

Tours

Cubanacán (☎ 79-63-93; Salvador Cisneros No 63C; 🕐 8:30am-7pm Mon-Sat) is conveniently located in the center of Viñales village opposite the main square and organizes excursions everywhere from Cayo Levisa to the Gran Caverna de Santo Tomás. The staff is helpful. Havanatur is next door.

Sleeping

Campismo Dos Hermanas (Cubamar; ☎ 79-32-23; s/d CUC$9.5/13; 🐕) This place, trapped between the sheer-sided jaws of the Dos Hermanas (literally 'two sisters') *mogotes* and in view of the Mural de la Prehistoria, is (along with Aguas Claras) one of Cubamar's best international campismos. The 54 two- and four-bed concrete cabins are frequented by campers, climbers and cyclists and the facilities easily rival those of a two-star hotel. Bonuses include a restaurant, pool and horseback riding, and a couple of trails start outside the gate. The only incongruity is the loud music that spoils the tranquil ambience of this beautiful valley. The campismo is a full Campertour facility.

Hostal Las Magnolias (☎ 79-62-80; Carretera a Esperanza Km 38; CUC$25; 🅿 🔀) Under renovations at the time of writing, this small building with three rooms (restaurant attached) opposite the Cueva del Indio offers a cheap alternative to Hotel Rancho San Vicente.

Hotel Rancho San Vicente (Cubanacán; ☎ 79-62-01; Carretera a Esperanza Km 38.5; s/d CUC$35/55; 🅿 🔀 🐕)

After Viñales' two spectacularly located hotels, you probably thought it couldn't get any better, but Rancho San Vicente does a good job trying. Situated 7km north of the village, this highly attractive hotel nestled in a grove with two dozen or more wooden cabins is lush and – for once – the interior furnishings match the magnificent setting. There's a restaurant, pool, massage facility and short bird-watching hike on-site.

Eating & Drinking

La Casa del Veguero (☎ 97-60-80; 🕐 10am-5pm) Just outside Viñales toward Pinar del Río, this *ranchón* (rural restaurant) serves mediocre à la carte items. It's a stop on the Viñales bus tour and also popular on the tour bus circuit; there's a *secadero* (drying house) adjacent.

Mural de la Prehistoria Restaurant (☎ 79-62-60; 🕐 8am-7pm) Steep but almost worth it, the Mural's humungous CUC$15 set lunch – tasty pork roasted and smoked over natural charcoal – ought to keep you going until tomorrow's breakfast.

El Palenque de los Cimarrones (☎ 79-62-90; 🕐 noon-4pm) If you're exploring the murky Cueva de San Miguel, you'll be unsubtly ushered through this restaurant as you grope for the exit. It's an odd combination of folklore show, eating joint and plantation slavery museum, but the young Cubans dressed as *cimarrones* (runaway slaves) don't really stimulate the appetite.

ourpick El Ranchón (☎ 79-61-10; Carretera a Esperanza Km 38; ⏱ 8am-5pm) Eat here! You won't forget the experience. The set meal, which is (judging by the crowds) a proverbial rite of passage on the tour bus circuit, is melt-in-your-mouth delicious. You pay CUC$11 for a huge traditional spread of roast pork and all the trimmings, and it trumps almost anything else you'll eat in Cuba.

Entertainment
Unesco World Heritage Sites aren't renowned for their nightlife, hence Viñales' nocturnal tranquility. Your one sporadic option is the Cueva San Miguel (p215), where the bar in the entrance cave sometimes puts on a reasonable cabaret show.

Getting Around
Bike, car, moped or the Viñales Bus Tour (p214); take your pick.

WEST OF VIÑALES
El Moncada, a pioneering postrevolutionary workers' settlement 14km west of Dos Hermanas and 1.5km off the road to Minas de Matahambre, is also the site of the **Gran Caverna de Santo Tomás** (admission CUC$8; ⏱ 8:30am-5pm), Cuba's largest cave system and the second-largest on the American continent. There are over 46km of galleries on eight levels, with a 1km section accessible to visitors. There's no artificial lighting, but headlamps are provided for the 90-minute guided tour. Highlights include bats, stalagmites and stalactites, underground pools, interesting rock formations and a replica of an ancient native Indian mural. Specialists should contact the **Escuela de Espeleología** (☎ 79-31-45) for more information. The visitors center contains a small **museum** (admission CUC$1; ⏱ 10am-10pm) with ephemera relating to Cuban scientist Antonio Núñez Jiménez. Most people visit the cave on an organized trip from Viñales (see p212).

CAYO JUTÍAS
Pinar del Río's most discovered 'undiscovered' beach is the 3km-long blanket of sand that adorns the northern coast of Cayo Jutías, a tiny mangrove-covered key situated approximately 65km northwest of Viñales and attached to the mainland by a short *pedraplén* (causeway). Jutías – named for its indigenous tree rats – vies with Cayo Levisa to the east for the title of the prov-

ince's most picturesque beach and, while the latter might be prettier, the former has less crowds and more tranquility.

The serenity is thanks to the lack of any permanent accommodation (unlike Levisa). The only facilities on the island are the airy oceanside **Restaurante Cayo Jutías** (⏱ 11am-5pm), specializing in local seafood, and a small beach hut that rents out kayaks for CUC$1 per hour and runs snorkeling trips to an offshore reef for CUC$12. Beyond the initial arc of sand the beach continues for 3km; you can hike barefoot through the mangroves. The Cayo's access road starts about 4km west of Santa Lucía. Four kilometers further on you'll come to a control post at the beginning of the causeway where you'll need to pay a CUC$5 per person entry fee. Ten minutes later the **Faro de Cayo Jutías** appears, a metal lighthouse built by the US in 1902. The route ends at the white Jutías beach caressed by crystal-clear water, 12.5km from the coastal highway.

Tours from Viñales (basically just transport and a snack lunch) cost CUC$22 and will give you an adequate six hours' beach time. Otherwise you will have to make your own transport arrangements. The fastest and by far the prettiest route is via El Moncada and Minas de Matahambre through rolling pine-clad hills.

NORTHERN PINAR DEL RÍO

Considering its relative proximity to Havana, northern Pinar del Río province is a remote and largely unexplored area. Facilities are sparse and roads are rutted on the isolated Gulf of Mexico coast, though visitors who take the time to make the journey out have reported memorable DIY adventures and famously hospitable locals.

PUERTO ESPERANZA
Puerto Esperanza (Port of Hope), 6km north of San Cayetano and 25km north of Viñales, is a sleepy fishing village visited by yachts sailing around the country. According to town lore, the giant mango trees lining the entry road were planted by slaves in the 1800s. A long pier pointing out into the bay is decent for a jump in the ocean. Otherwise the clocks haven't worked here since…oh…1951.

Sights & Activities

Puerto Esperanza's sights are not the domain of guidebook listings. Rather, this is the kind of low-key, put-down-the-Lonely-Planet sort of place where it's more fun to unravel the social life on your own. Discover some weirdly transcendental Santería ritual or take a spontaneous tour around your neighbor's tobacco plantation in search of pungent peso cigars.

Sleeping & Eating

Villa Leonila Blanco (☎ 79-36-48; Hermanos Caballeros No 41; r CUC$15; ☒) The town has six legal casas including this one. A supernice couple rent two big rooms with bath, garage and meals. They also have the option of an independent house out back with a bath.

Villa Dora González Fuentes (☎ 79-38-72; Pelayo Cuervo No 5; r CUC$15; ☒) This is enthusiastically recommended by readers. It has two rooms with bath and great food.

Getting There & Away

There's a handy Servi-Cupet gas station at San Cayetano. The road to Santa Lucía and Cayo Jutías deteriorates to dirt outside of San Cayetano: expect a throbbing backside if you're on a bike or moped.

CAYO LEVISA

More frequented than Cayo Jutías but just as beautiful, Cayo Levisa sports a beach bungalow–style hotel, basic restaurant and a fully equipped diving center, yet it still manages to feel relatively isolated. Separation from the mainland obviously helps. Unlike other Cuban keys, there's no causeway here and visitors must make the 35-minute journey by boat from Palma Rubia. Most of them agree the trip is worth it. Three kilometers of sugar-white sand and sapphire waters earmark Cayo Levisa as Pinar del Río's best beach. American writer Ernest Hemingway first 'discovered' the area, part of the Archipiélago de los Colorados, in the early 1940s after he set up a fishing camp on Cayo Paraíso, a smaller coral island 10km to the east. These days Levisa attracts up to 100 visitors daily as well as the 50-plus hotel guests and, while you won't feel like an errant Robinson Crusoe here, you should find time (and space) for plenty of R & R.

Sights & Activities

Larger and busier than Cayo Jutías, Levisa has a small marina offering scuba diving for CUC$35 per immersion, including gear and transport to the dive site. Snorkeling plus gear costs CUC$12 and a sunset cruise goes for the same price.

Sleeping & Eating

Hotel Cayo Levisa (Cubanacán; ☎ 52-35-54; s/d CUC$46/67; ☒) With an idyllic tropical beach just outside your front door, you won't really worry about the slightly outdated cabañas (cabins) and dull food choices here. Expanded to a 40-room capacity in 2006, the Levisa's newer wooden cabins (all with bath) are an improvement on the old concrete blocks and the service has pulled its socks up too. Book ahead as this place is understandably popular.

Getting There & Away

The landing for Cayo Levisa is around 21km northeast of La Palma or 40km west of Bahía Honda. Take the turn-off to Mirian and proceed 4km through a large banana plantation to reach the coast-guard station at Palma Rubia, from which the boat to the island departs. The Cayo Levisa boat leaves at 10am and returns at 5pm, and costs CUC$25 per person round-trip (CUC$10 one-way) including lunch. From the Cayo Levisa dock you cross the mangroves on a wooden walkway to the resort and gorgeous beach along the island's north side. If you are without a car, the easiest way to get here is via a day excursion from Viñales, good value at CUC$29 including the boat.

BAHÍA HONDA & AROUND

The wild, whirling road to Havana through northern Pinar del Río province is surprisingly low-key and bucolic. You'll feel as if you're 1000 miles from the busy capital here. Sugarcane gives way to rice paddies in the shaded river valleys as you breeze past a picturesque succession of thatched farmhouses, craning royal palms and machete-wielding guajiros. It makes a tough but highly rewarding cycling route.

Bahía Honda itself is a small bustling town with a pretty church. Close by the purple shadow of the Pan de Guajaibón (699m) marks the highest point for miles around. Despite your relative proximity to Havana you'll feel strangely isolated here, particularly as the road deteriorates after the Palma Rubia turn-off.

Your nearest accommodation options are Cayo Levisa to the west and Soroa to the southeast.

SAN DIEGO DE LOS BAÑOS & AROUND

San Diego de los Baños, 130km southwest of Havana, is a small nondescript town just north of the Carretera Central popularly considered to be Cuba's best spa. In common with other Cuban spas, its medicinal waters were supposedly 'discovered' in the early colonial period when a sick slave stumbled upon a sulfurous spring, took a revitalizing bath and was miraculously cured. Thanks to its proximity to Havana, San Diego's fame spread quickly and a permanent spa was established here in 1891. During the early 20th century American tourists flocked here in their thousands leading to the development of the current hotel and bathhouse facilities built in the early 1950s.

Sitting aside the Río San Diego, the village enjoys an attractive natural setting; with the Sierra de los Órganos to the west, and the higher Sierra del Rosario to the east. The Sierra de Güira on the Pinar del Río side of San Diego de los Baños is a nature reserve with pine, mahogany and cedar forests, and a favorite spot for bird-watchers.

Sights & Activities

BALNEARIO SAN DIEGO

The **balneario** (☎ 73-78-80; ⏰ 8am-5pm) is a decrepit-looking bathing complex where thermal waters of 30°C to 40°C are used to treat all number of muscular and skin afflictions. The sulfurous waters of these mineral springs are potent and immersions of only 20 minutes per day are allowed (CUC\$4/6 for collective/private pools). Mud from the Río San Diego is also used here for revitalizing mud baths (CUC\$20). Other health services include massage (CUC\$25) and a 15-day course of acupuncture; but don't expect fluffy towels and complementary cups of coffee. The Balneario San Diego is more like a Moroccan hammam than a five-star hotel facility, though it's perennially popular with Cubans undergoing courses of medical treatment, plus the odd curious tourist.

If you're looking for cold water, you can swim at the Hotel Mirador **pool** (admission CUC\$1; ⏰ 9am-6pm). Two blocks over from the Hotel Mirador is the gracious old **Hotel Saratoga**

(1924), complete with columns, mosaic tiling and elderly Cubans oiling the rocking chairs on the porch.

PARQUE LA GÜIRA

Five kilometers west of San Diego de los Baños lies the surreal **Parque La Güira**, an abandoned – and vaguely spooky – country mansion surrounded by 219 sq km of protected parkland. Known formerly as the Hacienda Cortina, this rich man's fantasy-made-reality was built in the style of a giant urban park during the 1920s and '30s by wealthy lawyer José Manuel Cortina who plunked a stately home in its midst. Various remnants of the estate remain – most notably the grand crenellated entry gate, along with a gatehouse, the ruins of a Chinese pavilion and large clusters of bamboo – but there's little structure to the surrealism. Wander round on your own and soak up the atmosphere or head for the unimpressive state-operated restaurant 1km beyond the gate for great views (the facilities were closed at time of writing). The complex behind is reserved for vacationing military personnel. You'll need a car, bike or taxi to get here.

CABAÑAS LOS PINOS

Twelve kilometers west of San Diego de los Baños via Parque La Güira is the Cabañas Los Pinos, an abandoned mountain retreat used by Castro's secretary Celia Sánchez in the 1960s. The cabins are built like tree houses above the ground with Sánchez' circular abode standing in the center of the eerie, shuttered complex. It's another rather surreal curiosity that gets few visitors but is worth a spare hour or two of silent contemplation. Ask at Hotel Mirador in San Diego de los Baños for directions.

CUEVA DE LOS PORTALES

During the October 1962 Cuban Missile Crisis, Ernesto 'Che' Guevara transferred the headquarters of the Western Army to this rather spectacular **cave** (admission CUC\$1), 11km west of Parque La Güira and 16km north of Entronque de Herradura on the Carretera Central. The cave is set in a beautiful remote area among steep-sided vine-covered *mogotes* and was declared a national monument in the 1980s. A small outdoor museum contains a few of Che's roughshod artifacts including his bed and the table where he played chess (while the rest of the world stood at the brink of nuclear Armageddon). Three other caves called El Espejo, El Salvador and Cueva Oscura are up on the hillside. This area is excellent for bird-watching. Trips can be arranged at the Hotel Mirador (below) in San Diego de los Baños or you can ask the staff at the cave entrance. There's a campismo and small restaurant just outside the cave. Both were closed at the time of writing in the aftermath of Hurricanes Gustav and Ike.

Sleeping

Hotel Mirador (Islazul; ☎ 77-83-38; s/d CUC$34/41; P ⚡ ⚡) In contrast to the usual ugly two-star Islazul establishments, the Mirador is a low-key gem. Predating the Revolution by five years, the hotel was built in 1954 to accommodate spa-seekers headed for the adjacent Balneario San Diego. The rooms are comfortable with fridges (some have views) while downstairs there's a pleasant swimming pool and an outdoor grill that does whole roast pig. Inquire with the helpful front desk staff about bird-watching trips to the Parque La Güira.

There are two or three proper casas particulares in San Diego de los Baños. Another highly recommended place is the house of **Carlos Alberto González** (Calle 21A No 3003 btwn 30 & 32; r CUC$20). If this is full, the owners can point you in the direction of a few others.

Eating

Hotel Mirador restaurants (Islazul; ☎ 77-83-38; meals under CUC$8) The open-air *parrillada* (grill restaurant) at the Hotel Mirador is rather good and it'll barbecue whole roast pig on a spit if it can muster up enough people. There's also a proper restaurant inside serving Cuban cuisine.

Getting Around

There's a Servi-Cupet gas station at the entrance to San Diego de los Baños from Havana. The road across the mountains from Cabañas Los Pinos and Che Guevara's cave is beautiful, but precariously narrow and full of potholes. That said; a brave driver or superfit (and careful) cyclist should make it.

SOROA

Soroa, 95km west of Havana, is the closest mountain resort area to the capital and makes a popular day trip. It's above Candelaria in the Sierra del Rosario, the easternmost and highest section of the Cordillera de Guaniguanico.

Soroa is nicknamed the 'rainbow of Cuba,' and the region's heavy rainfall (more than 1300mm annually) promotes the growth of tall trees and orchids. The area gets its name from Jean-Pierre Soroa, a Frenchman who owned a 19th-century coffee plantation in these hills. One of his descendants, Ignacio Soroa, created the park as a personal retreat in the 1920s, and only since the Revolution has this luxuriant region been developed for tourism. This is another great area to explore by bike.

Sights & Activities

All Soroa's sights are conveniently near Hotel & Villas Soroa, where you can also organize horseback riding and a couple of otherwise impossible-to-find hikes into the surrounding forest. Next door to the hotel is **Orquideario Soroa** (☎ 57-25-58; admission CUC$3, plus camera CUC$2; ☉ 9am-4pm), a labor of love built by Spanish lawyer Tomás Felipe Camacho in the late 1940s in memory of his wife and daughter. Camacho traveled the world to amass his collection of 700 orchid species (the largest in Cuba), 6000 ornamentals and various growing houses and research facilities. Though he died in the 1960s, the Orquideario lives on with guided tours in Spanish or English; although some orchid enthusiasts have expressed disappointment at the quality and quantity of what's on show. The Orquideario is connected to the University of Pinar del Río.

Down the road is the entrance to a park featuring the **Salto del Arco Iris** (admission CUC$3), a 22m waterfall on the Arroyo Manantiales. It's at its most impressive in the May-to-October rainy season, otherwise it's a trickle. You can swim at the foot of the falls. Entry is free for Hotel & Villas Soroa guests.

On the opposite side of the stream from the waterfall car park is the **Baños Romanos** (per hr CUC$5; ☉ 9am-4pm), a stone bathhouse with a pool of cold sulfurous water. Ask at Villas Soroa about the baths and massage treatments. It's a half-hour steep scramble up the hill from the bathhouse to the **Mirador**, a rocky crag with a sweeping view of all Soroa.

Castillo de las Nubes is a romantic castle with a circular tower on a hilltop above the Orquideario. There are good views of the Valle de Soroa and the coastal plain from the ridge beyond the bar, but the interior – formerly a restaurant – is currently closed to visitors.

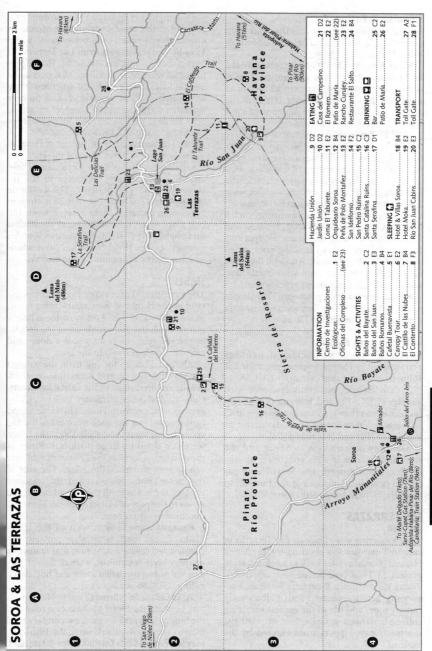

SOROA & LAS TERRAZAS

0 ___ 2 km
0 ___ 1 mile

INFORMATION
Centro de Investigaciones		
Ecológicas......	**1**	E2
Oficinas del Complejo......	(see 23)	

SIGHTS & ACTIVITIES
Baños del Bayate......	**2**	C2
Baños del San Juan......	**3**	E3
Baños Romanos......	**4**	B4
Cafetal Buenavista......	**5**	E1
Canopy Tour......	**6**	E2
El Castillo de las Nubes......	**7**	B4
El Contento......	**8**	F3

Hacienda Unión......	**9**	D2
Jardín Unión......	**10**	D2
Loma El Taburete......	**11**	E2
Orquideario Soroa......	**12**	B4
Peña de Polo Montañez......	**13**	E2
San Ildefonso......	**14**	F2
San Pedro Ruins......	**15**	C2
Santa Catalina Ruins......	**16**	C3
Santa Serafina......	**17**	D1

SLEEPING
Hotel & Villas Soroa......	**18**	B4
Hotel Moka......	**19**	E2
Río San Juan Cabins......	**20**	E3

EATING
Casa del Campesino......	**21**	D2
El Romero......	**22**	E2
Patio de María......	(see 22)	
Rancho Curujey......	**23**	E2
Restaurante El Salto......	**24**	B4

DRINKING
Bar......	**25**	C2
Patio de María......	**26**	E2

TRANSPORT
Toll Gate......	**27**	A2
Toll Gate......	**28**	F1

PINAR DEL
RÍO PROVINCE

Sleeping & Eating

Several signposted houses on the road from Candelaria to Soroa, 3km below the Hotel & Villas Soroa, rent rooms.

Maité Delgado (☎ 522-70069; Carretera a Soroa Km 7; r CUC$20; P ✗) This accommodation is within easy walking distance of all the Soroa sights and the family is pleasant. If it's full, the owners will point you in the direction of a few others further down the road.

Hotel & Villas Soroa (Cubanacán; ☎ 52-35-34; s/d inc breakfast CUC$56/70; P ✗ ✉) Nestled in a narrow valley amid stately trees and verdant hills, you can't knock the setting of this place. But, if you've just drifted over from eco-friendly La Moka (see p224) you might wonder what the architect was thinking when he juxtaposed these scattered blocklike cabins against such a breathtaking natural backdrop. Isolated and tranquil, there are 80 rooms on this spacious complex, along with an inviting pool, small shop and an OK restaurant. And with the forest just shouting distance from your front door, you're never far from an easy escape route.

Restaurante El Salto (⏱ 9am-9pm) This simple place next to the Baños Romanos is your only eating option outside the Hotel.

Getting There & Away

The Havana–Viñales Víazul bus stops in Las Terrazas, but not Soroa; you can cover the last 16km in a taxi for approximately CUC$8.

A daily transfer bus connects Soroa with Viñales (CUC$12) and Havana (CUC$10). Inquire about times (which can be sporadic) at Hotel & Villas Soroa, or at Havanatur in Viñales (p210) and Havana (p108).

The only other access to Soroa and the surrounding area is with your own wheels: car, bicycle or moped. The Servi-Cupet gas station is on the Autopista at the turn-off to Candelaria, 8km below Villas Soroa.

LAS TERRAZAS

pop 1200

The pioneering eco-village of Las Terrazas in eastern Pinar del Río abutting the border of Havana province dates back to a reforestation project in 1968 (see boxed text, opposite). Today it's a Unesco Biosphere Reserve, burgeoning activity center (with Cuba's only canopy tour) and site of the earliest surviving coffee plantations in Cuba. Not surprisingly, it attracts day-trippers from Havana by the busload.

Overnighters can stay in the community's sole hotel, the mold-breaking La Moka, an upmarket eco-resort built between 1992 and 1994 by workers drawn from Las Terrazas to attract foreign tourists. Close by, in the picturesque whitewashed village that overlooks a small lake, there's a vibrant art community with open studios, woodwork and pottery workshops. But the region's biggest attraction is its verdant natural surroundings; ideal for hiking, relaxing and bird-watching.

Las Terrazas is 20km northeast of Hotel & Villas Soroa and 13km west of the Havana–Pinar del Río Autopista at Cayajabos. There are toll gates at both entrances to the reserve (CUC$3 per person). The **Centro de Investigaciones Ecológicas** (☎ 77-29-21) is close to the eastern entrance of the reserve, while the best place to get information is at the **Oficinas del Complejo** (☎ 57-85-55), adjacent to Rancho Curujey, or the Hotel Moka (p224), both of which act as nexus points for the reserve.

Sights

The Las Terrazas area supported 54 coffee estates at the height of the Cuban coffee boom in the 1820s and '30s. Today, coffee is barely grown at all, but you can discover the jungle-immersed ruins of at least half a dozen old *cafetales* (coffee farms) in the area.

About 1.5km up the hill from the gate on the Cayajabos side and accessible by road, are the restored ruins of the **Cafetal Buenavista**, Cuba's oldest coffee plantation built in 1801 by French refugees from Haiti. The huge *tajona* (grindstone) out the back once extracted the coffee beans from their shells. Next the beans were sun-dried on huge platforms. Ruins of the quarters of some of the 126 slaves held here can be seen alongside the driers. The attic of the master's house (now a restaurant) was used to store the beans until they could be carried down to the port of Mariel by mule. There are decent views from here.

Hacienda Unión, 3.5km west of the Hotel Moka access road, is another partially reconstructed coffee-estate ruin that features a country-style restaurant, a small flower garden known as the **Jardín Unión** and horseback riding (CUC$6 per hour).

At **La Cañada del Infierno** (Trail to Hell), midway between the Hotel Moka access road and the Soroa side entrance gate, a secondary road follows the Río Bayate down to the 19th-century **San Pedro & Santa Catalina coffee-estate ruins**.

NEW MODEL VILLAGE

Back in 1968, when Al Gore was still cramming at Harvard and the nascent environmental movement was a prickly protest group for renegades with names like 'Swampy,' the forward-thinking Cubans – concerned about the ecological cost of island-wide deforestation – came up with a prophetic idea.

The plan involved taking a 5000-hectare tract of degraded land in Pinar del Río province around the remains of some old French *cafetales* (coffee farms) and reforesting it on terraced, erosion-resistant slopes. In 1971, with the first phase of the plan completed, the workers on the project created a man-made reservoir and on its shores constructed a groundbreaking new model village to provide much needed housing for eastern Pinar's disparate inhabitants.

The result was Las Terrazas, Cuba's first eco-village, a thriving community of 1200 inhabitants whose self-supporting sustainable settlement includes a hotel, myriad artisan shops, a vegetarian restaurant and small-scale organic farming techniques.

The project was so successful that, in 1985, the land around Las Terrazas was incorporated into Cuba's first Unesco Biosphere Reserve, the Sierra del Rosario.

In 1994, as the tourist industry was expanded to counteract the economic effects of the Special Period, Las Terrazas opened La Moka, an environmentally congruous hotel designed by minister of tourism and green architect, Osmani Cienfuegos, brother of the late revolutionary hero, Camilo.

Now established as Cuba's most authentic eco-resort, Las Terrazas operates on guiding principles that include energy efficiency, sustainable agriculture, environmental education and a sense of harmony between buildings and landscape.

The area is also the site of an important ecological research center.

A kilometer off the main road, a bar overlooks a popular swimming spot.

Looming elsewhere in the fecund forest and only accessible by hiking trails are the **Santa Serafina**, the **San Idelfonso** and **El Contento** coffee-estate ruins.

The former lakeside house of local *guajiro* singer Polo Montañez is now a small museum called **Peña de Polo Montañez** containing various gold records and assorted memorabilia. It's right in the village overlooking the lake.

Activities

HIKING

First the good news: the Sierra del Rosario boasts some of the best hikes in Cuba. Now the bad: they're all guided, ie you can't officially do any of them on your own (and non-existent signposting deters all but the hardiest from trying). On the upside, most of the area's guides are highly trained experts which means you'll emerge from the experience both a fitter *and* wiser person. The cost of the hikes varies depending on the number of people and length of walk. Bank on anything between CUC$15 and CUC$25 per person. Book at the Oficinas del Complejo (opposite) or Hotel Moka.

The biosphere's toughest hike is the 13km **San Claudio trail**, which traverses the hills to the northwest of the community culminating in the 20m-high San Claudio waterfall. It

is sometimes offered as an overnighter with the opportunity to camp out in the forest (equipment provided).

El Contento is an 8km ramble through the reserve's foothills between the Campismo El Taburete (for Cubans only) and the Baños del San Juan taking in two coffee-estate ruins; San Idelfonso and El Contento. **El Taburete** (6.5km) has the same start and finish point but follows a more direct route over the 452m Loma El Taburete where a poignant **monument** is dedicated to the 38 Cuban guerrillas who trained in these hills for Che Guevara's ill-fated Bolivian adventure.

The **Sendero La Serafina** is a 4km loop starting and finishing near the Rancho Curujey and a well-known paradise for bird-watchers (there are more than 70 species on show). **Sendero Las Delicias** (3km) runs from Rancho Curujey to the Cafetal Buenavista and incorporates some fantastic views.

Finally, the **Valle del Bayate trail** (7km) kicks off near the San Pedro coffee-estate ruins and tracks downriver to the Santa Catalina *cafetal*. There's sometimes a possibility of continuing all the way to Soroa; ask when booking.

SWIMMING

It's hard to envisage more idyllic natural swimming pools than those at the **Baños del San Juan** (admission with/without lunch CUC$10/4), situated

3km to the south of Hotel Moka down an undulating paved road. The *baños* (baths) are surrounded by naturally terraced rocks where the clean, bracing waters cascade into a series of pools. Riverside, there are a handful of open-air eating places along with changing rooms, showers and some overnight cabins (below), though the place still manages to retain a sense of rustic isolation.

The **Baños del Bayate** (admission CUC$4) offers a similar idyll on the Río Bayate near the San Pedro coffee-estate ruins. Alternatively you can knock out a few lengths in the Hotel Moka swimming pool.

CYCLING

A 30km guided cycling tour takes in most of the area's highlights for CUC$22 (CUC$20 with your own bike). Inquire at Hotel Moka.

CANOPY TOUR

Cuba's only **canopy tour** (per person CUC$25) maintains three zip lines that catapult you over Las Terrazas village and the Lago del San Juan like an eagle in flight. The total 'flying' distance is 800m. Professional instructors maintain high safety standards.

Sleeping & Eating

our pick **Hotel Moka** (☎ 77-86-00; s/d CUC$75/110; P ✗ ☎) Cuba's only *real* eco-hotel might not qualify for the four stars it advertises, but who's arguing? With its trickling fountains, blooming flower garden and resident tree growing through the lobby, Moka would be a catch in any country. The 26 bright, spacious rooms have fridges, satellite TV and bathtubs with a stupendous view (there are blinds for the shy). Equipped with a bar, restaurant, shop, pool and tennis court, the hotel also acts as an information center for the reserve and can organize everything from hiking to fishing.

our pick **El Romero** (☎ 57-87-00; ☯ 9am-10pm) The most interesting place to grab a bite, this full-blown eco-restaurant (unique in Cuba) specializes in vegetarian fare. El Romero uses home-grown organic vegetables and herbs, solar energy and keeps its own bees. You'll think you've woken up in San Francisco when you browse a menu replete with hummus, bean pancake, pumpkin and onion soup, and extra virgin olive oil.

our pick **Patio de María** (☯ 9am-11pm) A couple of doors down is the Patio de María, a small,

ASK A LOCAL

Las Terrazas is full of local artists and most of them are more than happy for you to pop in and browse around their studios. Lester Campa has a beautiful place overlooking the lake and his work has been exhibited in galleries around the world. Another good spot to hang out in the village is La Plaza where you'll find a cinema, library and small museum.

Juan Carlos, Las Terrazas

brightly painted coffee bar, which might just qualify as the best brew in Cuba. The secret comes in the expert confection (María lives upstairs) and the fact that the beans are grown about 20m away from your cup in front of the airy terrace.

Casa del Campesino (☎ 57-87-00; ☯ 9am-9pm) Of the *ranchón*-style restaurants dotted around, this one adjacent to the Hacienda Unión is the best.

You'll find other *ranchóns* at Cafetal Buenavista, Baños del Bayate and Baños de San Juan. The Rancho Curujey offers beer and snacks under a small thatched canopy overlooking a small lake.

Through the Moka you can also book five rustic cabins 3km away in Río San Juan (single/double CUC$15/25) or arrange tent camping (own tent/rented tent CUC$5/12). There are also three villas (single/double CUC$60/85) available for rent in the village.

Getting There & Away

At the time of writing two Víazul buses a day were stopping at the Rancho Curujey next door to Las Terrazas; one at around 11am from Havana to Pinar del Río and Viñales, the other at 4pm heading in the opposite direction. Daily transfer buses run between Viñales and Las Terrazas (CUC$12) and Las Terrazas and Havana (CUC$10). Inquire at Hotel Moka or contact **Havanatur** (☎ 79-62-62) in Viñales.

Getting Around

The 1950s-style Essto station, 1.5km west of the Hotel Moka access road, is one of Cuba's quirkiest gas stations. Fill up here before heading east to Havana or west to Pinar del Río. Most excursions organize transport. Otherwise you'll have to rely on hire car, taxi or your own two feet to get around.

Matanzas Province

For a province whose name means 'massacres,' Matanzas presents a surprisingly innocuous face. It hasn't always been this way. In the 17th and 18th centuries pillaging pirates ravaged the region's prized north coast, burning property and terrorizing the early Spanish settlers. Two hundred years later, in April 1961, another group of political mercenaries grappled ashore in the Bay of Pigs under the dreamy notion that they had arrived to liberate the nation.

The province's dreams these days are made in Varadero, the Caribbean's largest beach resort, a skillfully manufactured modern Xanadu, which stretches for 20 idyllic kilometers along the sandy Hicacos Peninsula and provides a comfortable tropical haven for tourists from all over the globe.

But Matanzas' Cuban soul lies not here, but some 32km to the west in its eponymous provincial capital, a down-at-heel port city that few visitors see and fewer still appreciate. While glitzy Varadero has spawned high-rise hotels, all-inclusive vacation deals and tandem-skydiving packages, the city of Matanzas has sculpted more subtle creations, giving the world rumba and *danzón* (traditional Cuban ballroom dance) and harboring some of its most grandiose neoclassical buildings.

Traditionally a bastion of the sugar industry, Matanzas' economy has diversified in recent years to include tourism and citrus production. Glimmering in the south is the largely un-inhabited Zapata Peninsula, the Caribbean's largest swamp and a protected area that guards rare birds, crocodiles and a wide variety of different ecosystems. Shimmering nearby, the Bay of Pigs is a more peaceful retreat these days where vertical underwater drop-offs and fantastical coral walls are more popular with divers than invaders.

HIGHLIGHTS

- **Gritty City** Unlock the buried secrets of dusty Matanzas (p227), the 'Athens of Cuba'
- **High Life** Go tandem skydiving over diamond-dust Varadero beach (p240)
- **Ecosystems** Discover the amazingly varied vegetation zones in the Ciénaga de Zapata (p256)
- **Drop Off** Discover the plunging drop-offs and colorful coral walls diving off Playa Larga (see boxed text, p260)
- **Ghost Town** Kick through the ruins of San Miguel de los Baños (see boxed text, p250)

■ TELEPHONE CODE: 045　　■ POPULATION: 675,980　　■ AREA: 11,978 SQ KM

MATANZAS PROVINCE

MATANZAS PROVINCE

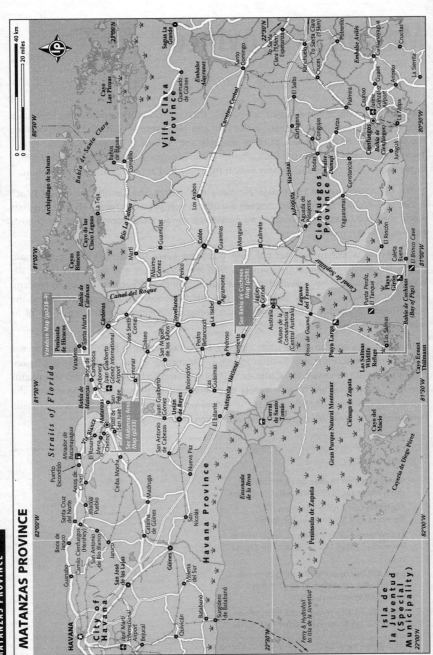

Parks & Reserves

Matanzas contains Cuba's largest protected tract of land, the Gran Parque Natural Montemar, a National Park, Unesco Biosphere Reserve and Ramsar Convention Site. Within the park there are further protected areas such as the Las Salinas Wildlife Refuge. In the north of the province, three areas enjoy protected status: the region bordering the Río Canímar, the Laguna Maya Flora and Fauna Reserve by Playa Coral, and the Reserva Ecológica Varahicacos in Varadero.

Getting There & Around

Because of its position in the Havana/Varadero tourist corridor, northern Matanzas has the best transport connections in Cuba with eight buses a day plying the Vía Blanca to and from the capital. From Varadero there are direct connections to Santa Clara, Trinidad and Cienfuegos while Matanzas has good rail links with Havana and the rest of the country, including the slow but quirky Hershey Train. The south of the province isn't served so well, although entry to the Zapata Peninsula and Playa Girón was recently improved with the rerouting of the Havana–Trinidad Víazul bus.

NORTHERN MATANZAS

Northern Matanzas boasts an attractive rural landscape punctuated by low hills and lush valleys – most notably the Valle del Yumurí. Home to Cuba's largest resort area (Varadero) and one of its biggest ports (Matanzas), the northern coastline is also the province's main population center and is also the national center for industry and commerce.

MATANZAS

pop 143,706

Splayed like a ruined Sparta beside its eponymous bay, Matanzas is a city riddled with dichotomies. Ostensibly one of Cuba's most dilapidated urban centers, it is also one of its most interesting. White culture flourished here in the mid-19th century when influential men of letters concocted great works of literature and the city earned its kiss-of-death euphemism, the 'Athens of Cuba.' Meanwhile on the other side of the Río Yumurí in the humble neighborhood

of Versalles, freed slaves united in secret brotherhoods or *cabildos* began to measure out the drum patterns that gave birth to rumba.

A port settlement that played a pivotal role in Cuba's once dynamic sugar industry, early 20th-century Matanzas was a striking amalgam of bridges (17 in total) and theaters that rivaled Havana as a center of culture and learning. But the salad days didn't last. Virtually ignored since the Revolution, modern Matanzas has long been overshadowed by antiseptic Varadero, 32km to the east, and few of the resort's million or so annual visitors bother to give it a glance.

What they're missing isn't always visible to the naked eye. Many of Matanzas' attractions are visceral, hidden beneath 50 years of postrevolutionary dust. If it's five-star comforts you're after, hop on a Víazul bus straight back to Planet Varadero. But if the thought of ritualistic drumming, beer over dominoes or the chance to meet some genuinely hospitable locals makes you fidget on your beachside sun-lounger, gritty, in-your-face Matanzas could be the place for you. Welcome to the *real* Cuba, amigos!

History

In 1508 Sebastián de Ocampo sighted a bay that the Indians called Guanima. Now known as the Bahía de Matanzas, it's said the name recalls the *matanza* (massacre) of a group of Spaniards during an early indigenous uprising. In 1628 the Dutch pirate Piet Heyn captured a Spanish treasure fleet carrying 12 million gold florins, ushering in a lengthy era of smuggling and piracy. Undeterred by the pirate threat, 30 families from the Canary Islands arrived in 1693, on the orders of King Carlos III of Spain, to found the town of San Carlos y Severino de Matanzas. The first fort went up in 1734 and the original Plaza de Armas still remains as Plaza de la Vigía.

For a decade starting in 1817 Matanzas flourished economically with the building of numerous sugar mills. The export of coffee added further equity to the city's bank balance and in 1843, with the laying of the first railway to Havana, the floodgates were opened. The second half of the 19th century was a golden age in Matanzas' history when the city set new standards in the cultural sphere with the development of a newspaper, a public library,

MATANZAS PROVINCE

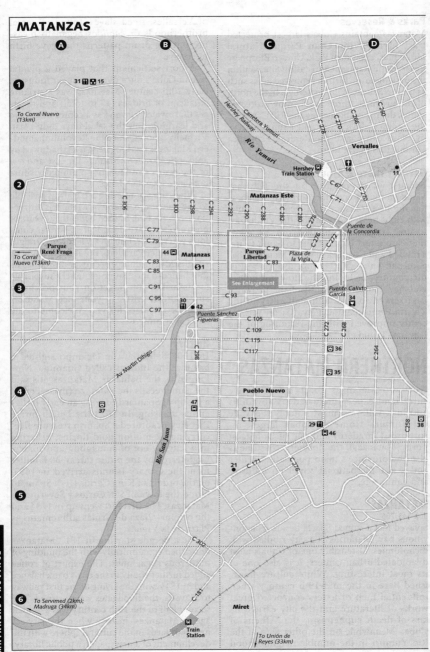

MATANZAS

To Corral Nuevo (13km)

31

15

Carretera Yumurí

Hershey Railway

Río Yumurí

C 306

C 300

C 298

C 294

C 292

C 290

C 288

C 282

C 280

C 278

C 270

C 266

C 240

Versalles

Hershey Train Station

16

11

C 67

C 71

C 270

Matanzas Este

Puente de la Concordia

C 77

C 79

Parque René Fraga

To Corral Nuevo (13km)

44 **Matanzas**

1

Parque Libertad

C 79

C 83

Plaza de la Vigía

C 83

C 85

C 91

C 95

C 97

C 276

C 272

See Enlargement

C 93

30

42

Puente Sánchez Figueras

Puente Calixto García

34

C 105

C 109

C 115

C 117

C 272

C 268

36

35

C 264

Av Martín Dihigo

Río San Juan

C 298

37

Pueblo Nuevo

47

C 127

C 131

29

46

C 258

38

21

C 171

C 276

C 302

To Servimed (2km); Madruga (34km)

C 181

Miret

Train Station

To Unión de Reyes (33km)

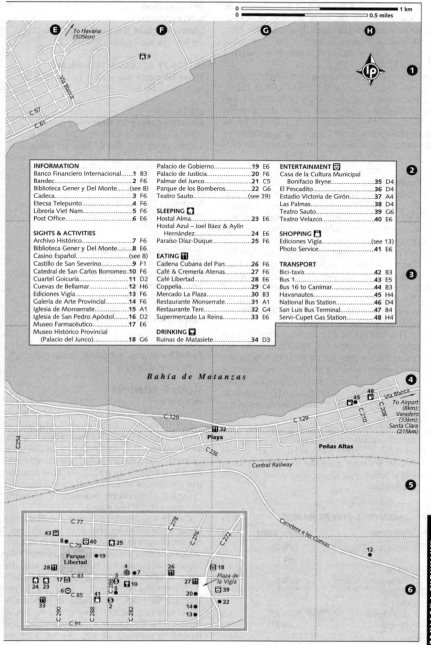

0 ——————— 1 km
0 ——————— 0.5 miles

To Havana
(105km)

E **F** **G** **H**

INFORMATION
Banco Financiero Internacional......**1** B3
Bandec...**2** F6
Biblioteca Gener y Del Monte.......(see 8)
Cadeca..**3** F6
Etecsa Telepunto............................**4** F6
Librería Viet Nam...........................**5** F6
Post Office......................................**6** E6

SIGHTS & ACTIVITIES
Archivo Histórico...........................**7** F6
Biblioteca Gener y Del Monte.......**8** E6
Casino Español...............................(see 8)
Castillo de San Severino.................**9** F1
Catedral de San Carlos Borromeo..**10** F6
Cuartel Goicuría.............................**11** D2
Cuevas de Bellamar........................**12** H6
Ediciones Vigía...............................**13** F6
Galería de Arte Provincial..............**14** F6
Iglesia de Monserrate.....................**15** A1
Iglesia de San Pedro Apóstol.........**16** D2
Museo Farmacéutico.......................**17** E6
Museo Histórico Provincial
 (Palacio del Junco)......................**18** G6

Palacio de Gobierno......................**19** E6
Palacio de Justicia..........................**20** F6
Palmar del Junco............................**21** C5
Parque de los Bomberos.................**22** G6
Teatro Sauto.................................(see 39)

SLEEPING
Hostal Alma....................................**23** E6
Hostal Azul – Joel Báez & Aylín
 Hernández....................................**24** E6
Paraíso Díaz-Duque........................**25** F6

EATING
Cadena Cubana del Pan.................**26** F6
Café & Cremería Atenas..................**27** F6
Café Libertad..................................**28** E6
Coppelia...**29** C4
Mercado La Plaza...........................**30** B3
Restaurante Monserrate..................**31** A1
Restaurante Teni.............................**32** G4
Supermercado La Reina...................**33** E6

DRINKING
Ruinas de Matasiete........................**34** D3

ENTERTAINMENT
Casa de la Cultura Municipal
 Bonifacio Bryne...........................**35** D4
El Pescadito...................................**36** D4
Estadio Victoria de Girón...............**37** A4
Las Palmas.....................................**38** D4
Teatro Sauto..................................**39** G6
Teatro Velazco...............................**40** E6

SHOPPING
Ediciones Vigía.............................(see 13)
Photo Service.................................**41** E6

TRANSPORT
Bici-taxis..**42** B3
Bus 1..**43** E5
Bus 16 to Canímar..........................**44** B3
Havanautos.....................................**45** H4
National Bus Station........................**46** D4
San Luis Bus Terminal.....................**47** B4
Servi-Cupet Gas Station..................**48** H4

Bahía de Matanzas

Vía Blanca
To Airport
(8km);
Varadero
(33km);
Santa Clara
(215km)

Playa

Peñas Altas

Central Railway

Carretera a las Cuevas

C 77
C 79
Parque
Libertad
Plaza de
la Vigía

a high school, a theater and a philharmonic society. Due to the large number of artists, writers and intellectuals living in the area, Matanzas became known as the 'Athens of Cuba' with a cultural scene that dwarfed even Havana.

Home to several modern poets including Cintio Vitier and Carilda Oliver Labra, Matanzas is where Cuba's first *danzón* was performed in 1879 and is also the spiritual home of the rumba. With a long history of slave occupation, there are a number of Santería *cabildos* (associations) here, the oldest of which dates back to 1808.

Orientation

Matanzas lies on the Vía Blanca 42km west of Varadero and 98km east of central Havana. The Carretera Central from Pinar del Río to Santiago de Cuba also passes through the city.

The compact old town is sandwiched between the Río Yumurí and the Río San Juan with the historic Versalles quarter situated to the north. Most of the industry is east of Versalles. The Hershey Railway terminates in Versalles, but all other transport facilities are south of the Río San Juan.

The streets of Matanzas suffer from a capricious numbering system. In the old town the north–south streets bear even numbers, beginning at Calle 268 near the bay. The east–west streets increase from Calle 75 at the Yumurí bridge (Puente de la Concordia) to Calle 97 along the banks of the San Juan.

Matanzas residents just ignore these arbitrary numbers and continue using the old colonial street names. However, in this chapter we have used the numbers because that's what you'll see on street corners (see below).

MATANZAS STREET NAMES

Old name	New name
Contreras	Calle 79
Daoíz	Calle 75
Maceo	Calle 77
Medio/Independencia	Calle 85
Milanés	Calle 83
San Luis	Calle 298
Santa Teresa	Calle 290
Zaragoza	Calle 292

Information

BOOKSTORES

Librería Viet Nam (Map pp228-9; Calle 85 No 28612; 9am-5pm Mon-Fri, 10am-2pm Sat)

INTERNET ACCESS & TELEPHONE

Etecsa Telepunto (Map pp228-9; cnr Calles 83 & 282; per hr CUC$6; 8:30am-7:30pm)

LIBRARIES

Biblioteca Gener y Del Monte (Map pp228-9; ☎ 24-41-34; Calles 79 & 290; 8:30am-10pm Mon-Fri, 8:30am- 3:30pm Sat, 8:30am-12:30pm Sun) Appropriately for the 'Athens of Cuba' this is one of the oldest libraries on the island (1835), housed in the former Casino Español.

MEDICAL SERVICES

Servimed (☎ 25-31-70; Hospital Faustino Pérez, Carretera Central Km 101) Clinic just southwest of town.

MONEY

Banco Financiero Internacional (Map pp228-9; ☎ 25-34-00; cnr Calles 85 & 298)
Bandec (Map pp228-9; ☎ 24-27-81; Calle 85 No 28604 btwn Calles 286 & 288)
Cadeca (Map pp228-9; ☎ 25-35-58; Calle 286 btwn Calles 83 & 85; 8am-6pm Mon-Sat, 8am-noon Sun) Two portable kiosks here behind the cathedral.

POST

Post office (Map pp228-9; Calle 85 No 28813; 24hr) On the corner of Calle 290.

Sights & Activities

IN TOWN

If you've only got time to see *one* bridge (there are 21 in total) in Cuba's celebrated 'city of bridges,' get an eye-full of **Puente Calixto García**, an impressive steel structure built in 1899 that spans the Río San Juan and leads directly into **Plaza de la Vigía** (Map pp228–9). This diminutive square was where Matanzas was founded in the late 17th century and numerous historic buildings still stand guard.

On the southeastern corner, the Matanzas fire brigade is headquartered in the 1897 neoclassical **Parque de los Bomberos** (Map pp228–9), which poses as a museum but will only take a couple of minutes of your time. Across the street is **Ediciones Vigía** (Map pp228-9; ☎ 24-48-45; 8am-4pm Mon-Fri), a unique book publisher, founded in 1985, that produces handmade paper and first-edition books on a variety of topics. The books are typed, stenciled and pasted in editions of 200 copies. Visitors

CABILDOS

Matanzas has played a unique balancing act in the development of Cuban culture. Dubbed the 'Athens of Cuba' in the mid-19th century for its abundance of poets and writers, the city's erudite white intellectuals obscured an underlying 'African-ness,' a cultural force that found expression in the roots music of rumba and the mysterious *cabildos* that helped to shape it.

Afro-Cuban *cabildos* trace their origins back to the beginning of the colonial period when African slaves of similar ethnic backgrounds formed 'brotherhoods' that came together on feast days to worship the *orishas* (deities) and keep their ancient traditions alive.

These loose social organizations imitated the Masonic lodges and mutual aid societies of the ruling colonizers, and were widely encouraged by Spanish authorities who used them as a means of subjugating a potentially restless slave underclass.

By the mid-19th century there were an estimated 100 different *cabildos* in Cuba incorporating enslaved and freed blacks from the same African 'nations.' In the 1920s, Cuban scholar Fernando Ortiz identified four broad 'nations' on the island: the Lucumí, from Nigeria's Yoruba tribe; the Arará, from Dahomey in present-day Benin; the Abakuá, from southwestern Cameroon; and the Kongo, from Angola.

One of Matanzas' earliest *cabildos* was the Lucumí-led Santa Barbara brotherhood, established in 1827 by a freed slave named Remigio Herrera. A Yoruba priest from the Óyo tribe who had been transported from Africa in the early 1820s, Herrera's freedom was bought by his Óyo-Cuban 'brothers' soon after he arrived in Cuba allowing him to establish a powerful and influential priesthood.

When slavery was abolished in 1886, *cabildos* were gradually suppressed and required to officially register with the Catholic Church. But many shirked the draconian new rules and continued to operate beneath the radar.

Pursuing a more secretive existence, associations began to re-evaluate their unique African culture and add new ingredients to a traditional ancestral base.

Examples of this synthesis can be seen in the sacred rites of Regla de Ocha (Santería), a hybrid Catholic-Yoruba religion that grew out of the Lucumí *cabildos* in Versalles, or the dynamic new musical forms forged in the working-class dock districts of Matanzas and Havana, popularly known as rumba.

A number of *cabildos* are still active in Matanzas today. The Iyesá Cabildo of San Juan de Bautista, a branch of Lucumí dating from 1854, is known for its distinctive ritualistic drumming. The Cabildo Arará Sabalú Nonjó, founded in 1880, is a small Arará offshoot that traces its roots back to slaves transported from the Dahomean city of Savalu. The Cabildo Santa Teresa Lucumí is an arm of the influential Villamil family whose members have gone on to play in numerous musical groups including the legendary Muñequitos de Matanzas.

are welcome in the workshop and you can purchase numbered and signed copies (from CUC$5 to CUC$15 each). Next door is the rather scant **Galería de Arte Provincial** (Map pp228-9; Calle 272 btwn Calles 85 & 91; admission CUC$1; 10am-2pm Mon, 10am-6pm Tue-Sat).

Wilting from the outside, the **Teatro Sauto** (Map pp228-9; 24-27-21), back on the plaza's south side is, nonetheless, one of Cuba's finest theaters (1863) and famous for its superb acoustics. The lobby is graced by marble Greek goddesses and the main hall ceiling bears paintings of the muses. Three balconies enclose this 775-seat theater, which features a floor that can be raised to convert the auditorium into a ballroom. A work of art, the original theater curtain is a painting of the Puente de la Concordia over the Río Yumurí. Enrico Caruso performed here, as did the Soviet dancer Anna Pavlova in 1945. Your best chance of catching a performance is on Friday, Saturday or Sunday nights.

Other impressive buildings on Plaza de Vigía include the imposing **Palacio de Justicia** (Map pp228–9) opposite the Teatro Sauto, first erected in 1826 and rebuilt between 1908 and 1911, and the double-arcaded **Museo Histórico Provincial** (Map pp228-9; cnr Calles 83 & 272; admission CUC$2; 10am-noon & 1-5pm Tue-Sun), aka Palacio del Junco (1840), which showcases the full sweep of Matanzas' history from 1693 to the present.

MATANZAS PROVINCE

A few blocks west is **Parque Libertad** (Map pp228–9), Matanzas' modern nexus with a bronze statue (1909) of José Martí in its center. Head to the south side for beer with the locals in Café Libertad, opposite the now closed Hotel Louvre (1894), before visiting the city's showcase sight, the **Museo Farmacéutico** (Map pp228–9; ☎ 25-31-79; Calle 83 No 4951; admission CUC$3; ☺ 10am-5pm Mon-Sun). Founded in 1882 by the Triolett family, this antique pharmacy was the first of its type in Latin America and continued to function until 1964 when it became a museum. The fine displays include all the odd bottles, instruments, porcelain jars and medical recipes used in the trade.

The eastern side of the rather dilapidated park is dominated by the muscular **Palacio de Gobierno** (Map pp228–9) dating from 1853, now the seat of the Poder Popular (Popular Power). On the northern side are the defunct Hotel Velazco and the former **Casino Español** (cnr Calles 79 & 290), where the first performance of the *danzonete* (ballroom dance) *Rompiendo La Rutina*, by Anceto Díaz, took place. It's now the **Biblioteca Gener y Del Monte** (Map pp228–9).

Nearby is the city's **Archivo Histórico** (Map pp228–9; ☎ 24-42-12; Calle 83 No 28013 btwn Calles 280 & 282), in the former residence of local poet José Jacinto Milanés (1814–63). A bronze statue of Milanés stands on the Plaza de la Iglesia in front of the nearby **Catedral de San Carlos Borromeo** (Map pp228–9; Calle 282 btwn Calles 83 & 85; donation welcome; ☺ 8am-noon, 3-5pm Mon-Fri, 9am-noon Sun), a once-great neoclassical cathedral constructed in 1693 and rebuilt in the 1750s that has suffered terribly after years of neglect.

The **Versalles quarter** (Map pp228–9), north of the Río Yumurí, was where the province's freed slaves first settled in the 19th century, and by the 1890s the area had become the font of an exciting new musical genre called rumba. From the Plaza de la Vigía you enter the *barrio* (neighborhood) by taking Calle 272 across the graceful **Puente de la Concordia** (Map pp228–9). The neoclassical **Iglesia de San Pedro Apóstol** (Map pp228–9; cnr Calles 57 & 270) is another Matanzas jewel in need of a makeover. Four blocks east, on the corner of Calles 63 and 260, stands the sinister-looking **Cuartel Goicuría** (Map pp228–9), a former barracks of Batista's army that was assaulted on April 29, 1956 by a group of rebels led by Reinold T García. Today it's a school.

Northeast of Versalles lies the formidable **Castillo de San Severino** (Map pp228–9; ☎ 28-32-59; Av del Muelle; admission CUC$2; ☺ 9am-5pm), built by the Spanish in 1735 as part of Cuba's defensive ring. Slaves were offloaded here in the 18th century and, later, Cuban patriots were imprisoned within the walls – and sometimes executed. San Severino remained a prison until the 1970s and in more recent times became the **Museo de la Ruta de los Esclavos** (admission CUC$2; ☺ 9am-5pm), a rather scant slavery museum. More interesting is the castle itself with its well-preserved central square and great views of Matanzas Bay. A taxi from the city center will costs CUC$2.

For an excellent view of Matanzas and the picturesque Valle del Yumurí, climb north up Calle 306 to the recently renovated **Iglesia de Monserrate** (Map pp228–9). Dating from 1875, this lofty bastion perched high above the city was built by colonists from Catalonia in Spain as a symbol of their power in the region. A new *ranchón*-style restaurant (p234) has recently improved the ambience.

Baseball fans can make the pilgrimage to **Palmar del Junco** (Map pp228–9) in the south of the city, the site of Cuba's first baseball field (1904) and a source of much civic pride.

OUTSIDE TOWN
Cuevas de Bellamar

The **Cuevas de Bellamar** (Map pp228–9; ☎ 25-35-38; admission CUC$5, camera CUC$5; ☺ 9am-6pm), 5km southeast of Matanzas, are 300,000 years old and are promoted locally as the oldest tourist attraction in Cuba. The 2500m-long caves were discovered in 1861 by a Chinese workman in the employ of Don Manual Santos Parga. There's an underground stream inside; two restaurants, a pool and playground outside. One-hour visits into the cave leave every hour seven times a day starting at 9:30am. To get there, take bus 16, 17 or 20 east toward Canímar and ask the driver to let you out near Calle 226. From there it's a 30-minute walk uphill to the caves.

ASK A LOCAL

The city of Matanzas has some of the best rumba on the island. Great alfresco performances take place at 4pm on the third Friday of every month outside the Museo Histórico Provincial (p231) in Plaza de la Vigía. The people to look out for are Afrocuba de Matanzas, a top Cuban *folklórico* group.

Lydia, Matanzas

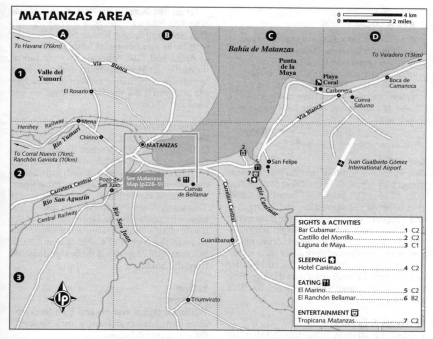

MATANZAS AREA

SIGHTS & ACTIVITIES
Bar Cubamar.............................1 C2
Castillo del Morrillo.....................2 C2
Laguna de Maya........................3 C1

SLEEPING
Hotel Canimao..........................4 C2

EATING
El Marino.................................5 C2
El Ranchón Bellamar...................6 B2

ENTERTAINMENT
Tropicana Matanzas....................7 C2

Río Canímar & Around

Boat trips on the Río Canímar, 8km east of Matanzas, are a truly magical experience. Though little evident from the Vía Blanca bridge, the scenery here is jaw-dropping. Gnarly mangroves dip their jungle-like branches into the ebbing water and a warm haze caresses the regal palm trees as your boat slides silently 12km upstream. Cubamar (p237) in Varadero offers this wonderful excursion with lunch, horseback riding, fishing and snorkeling for CUC$25, or you can chance your arm by showing up at the landing just below the bridge. Rowboats are for rent (CUC$2 per hour) at the colorful **Bar Cubamar** (Map p233; ☎ 26-15-16) any time.

From the same turn-off, a road runs 1km down the western (ocean) side of the river to a cove where the four guns of the **Castillo del Morrillo** (1720) overlook a small beach. This castle is now a **museum** (Map p233; admission CUC$1; ☒ 9am-4pm Tue-Sun) dedicated to the student leader Antonio Guiteras Holmes (1906–35), who founded the revolutionary group Joven Cuba (Young Cuba) in 1934. After serving briefly in the post-Machado government, Guiteras was forced out by army chief Fulgencio Batista and shot on May 8, 1935. A bronze bust marks the spot where he was executed.

Playa Coral

With no reefs accessible from the coast in Varadero, your closest bet for a bit of shore snorkeling is the aptly named **Playa Coral** (Map p233) on the old coastal road (and about 3km off the Vía Blanca) halfway between Matanzas and Varadero. Although you can snorkel solo from the beach itself, it's far better (and safer) to enter via the **Laguna de Maya** (Map p233; ☒ 8am-5pm) Flora and Fauna Reserve 400m to the east where professional Ecotur guides can rent you snorkeling gear and guide you out to the reef for a bargain CUC$5. There are a reported 300 species of fish here and visibility is a decent 15m to 20m. The Laguna de Maya also incorporates a snack bar, a *ranchón*-style restaurant overlooking a small lake with boat rental and opportunities for horseback riding. A package including all the activities is offered for CUC$25. You can hike 2.5km to the Cueva Saturno from here.

MATANZAS PROVINCE

Cueva Saturno

One kilometer south of the Vía Blanca, near the airport turn-off, is the **Cueva Saturno** (Map p233; ☎ 25-32-72; admission incl snorkel gear CUC$5; ⏱ 8am-6pm). It's promoted as a snorkeling spot and Varadero companies include it on many tours, but don't believe the hype: it's really just a ho-hum cave with limited access, unless you're an experienced cave diver with all the relevant equipment. Beware the odd hustler or three and the screaming crowds clamoring to get into the water. There's a snack bar here that sells good coffee.

Festivals & Events

During the 10 days following October 10, Matanzas rediscovers its rumba roots with talented local musicians at the **Festival del Bailador Rumbero** in the Teatro Sauto.

Sleeping

IN TOWN

While beach-embellished Varadero, 32km to the east, has over 50 hotels, Matanzas boasts a total of zero. If you haven't yet sampled the delights of a Cuban casa particular, this could be the place.

Hostal Alma (Map pp228-9; ☎ 24-78-10; Calle 83 No 29008 btwn Calles 290 & 292; r CUC$20-25; ⏱) Two rooms in a mid-19th-century colonial house both with baths, a roof terrace, sun loungers and a pleasant central courtyard. It's a magnificent place tucked away behind Parque Libertad and with oodles of *alma* (soul).

'Hostal Azul' Joel Báez & Aylín Hernández (Map pp228-9; ☎ 24-78-10; joelmatan@gmail.com; Calle 83 No 29012 btwn Calles 290 & 292; r CUC$20-25; ⏱) Next door to the 'Alma' and of the same vintage, the 'Azul' is the type of fine colonial house that once made Matanzas a cultural tour de force. The hosts are attentive, the rooms huge and the food *delicioso* (delicious).

Paraíso Díaz-Duque (Map pp228-9; ☎ 24-33-97; Calle 79 No 28205 2nd fl btwn Calles 282 & 288; r CUC$25; ⏱) This excellent house boasts two bedrooms with baths and congenial hosts in the shape of Anita and Luís Alberto, who are full of the exuberant Matanzas spirit. Delicious food appears as if by magic (where do they buy it?) and you'll get the full lowdown on the local attractions.

OUTSIDE TOWN

Hotel Canimao (Islazul; Map p233; ☎ 26-10-14; s/d CUC$28/38; ⓟ ⏱ ⏱) Perched above the Río Canímar 8km east of Matanzas, the Canimao has 120 comfortable rooms with little balconies. It's handy for Río Canímar excursions, the Cuevas de Bellamar, or the Matanzas Tropicana (literally outside the door), but otherwise you're isolated from the rest of the north coast's multifarious attractions. Bus 16 from the corner of Calles 300 and 83 in Matanzas will drop you at the bridge downhill from the hotel.

Eating

IN TOWN

While Matanzas has no real paladares, the casas particulares can usually rustle up something suitably delicious.

Café Libertad (Map pp228-9; cnr Calles 290 & 83) If you're going Cuban in Matanzas, this cafe on the main square is a fairly painless introduction, though the peso *hamburguesas* (hamburgers) could do with a little bit of extra garnish.

Café Atenas (Map pp228-9; ☎ 25-34-93; Calle 83 No 8301; ⏱ 10am-11pm) Atenas is used to receiving the odd stray tourist on a moped-trip from Varadero and can rustle up a rather delicious bruschetta at short notice. Settle down in the clean, if bland, interior with the local students, taxi drivers and hotel workers on a day off, and contemplate the everyday occurrences of Plaza Vigía outside. Dessert is available next door in an adjoining Cremería (open from 9am to 9pm).

Restaurante Monserrate (Map pp228-9; Calle 312 al final; ⏱ 10am-10pm) Included in the rejuvenation and restoration of the Ermita de Monserrate viewpoint is this *ranchón*-style restaurant designed to lure tourists to the city's best overlook. In the culinary desert of Matanzas it goes straight in at number one.

our pick **Restaurante Teni** (Map pp228-9; Calles 129 & 224; ⏱ 10am-11:30pm) A large thatched roof affair alongside the beach in Reparto Playa on the road to Varadero, this pleasant place with keen service offers a substantial set *comida criolla* (Creole food) meal, with rice, root vegetables, salad and meat, for just CUC$5.

The best cheap peso take-out windows are on Calle 272 in Versalles, just across the bridge from Matanzas. The rather lackluster **Coppelia** (Map pp228-9; cnr Calles 272 & 127; 10am-10pm) is situated near the bus station.

Groceries
For all your self-catering needs hit **Cadena Cubana del Pan** (Map pp228-9; Calle 83 btwn Calles 278 & 280; 24hr) for bread, **Supermercado La Reina** (Map pp228-9; Calle 85 No 29006 btwn Calles 290 & 292; 8:30am-4:30pm Mon-Sat, 8:30am-12:30pm Sun) for groceries and **Mercado La Plaza** (Map pp228-9; cnr Calles 97 & 298) near the Puente Sánchez Figueras (1916) for produce and peso stalls.

OUTSIDE TOWN
El Ranchón Bellamar (Map p233; noon-8:30pm) If you're visiting the caves, you'd do well to grab a *comida criolla* lunch at this *ranchón*-style restaurant before heading back into town. Good pork or chicken meals with the trimmings go for between CUC$7 and CUC$8.

El Marino (Map p233; 26-14-83; noon-9pm) On the main Varadero road next to the turn-off for the Hotel Canimao, El Marino specializes in seafood, including lobster and shrimp, but has delusions of grandeur. Don't be fooled by the fancy decor.

Drinking
Ruinas de Matasiete (Map pp228-9; 25-33-87; cnr Vía Blanca & Calle 101; 24hr) Want to find the town's best drinking hole? Then ask a local. Even better, ask five. Chances are they'll all reply Ruinas de Matasiete, an engaging convertible bar housed in the ruins of a 19th-century warehouse, next to the bay. Drinks and grilled meats are served on an open-air terrace, but a better reason to come is to hear live music (from 9pm Friday, Saturday and Sunday). There's a minimum cover charge of CUC$3.

Entertainment
ourpick **Teatro Sauto** (Map pp228-9; 24-27-21) Across Plaza de la Vigía Teatro Sauto is a national landmark and one of Cuba's premier theaters. Performances have been held here since 1863 and you might catch the Ballet Nacional de Cuba or the Conjunto Folklórico Nacional de Cuba. Performances are at 8:30pm with Sunday matinees at 3pm (see p231).

Teatro Velazco (Map pp228-9; cnr Calles 79 & 288) On Parque Libertad, Teatro Velazco is Matanzas' main movie house.

Casa de la Cultura Municipal Bonifacio Bryne (Map pp228-9; 29-27-09; Calle 272 No 11916 btwn Calles 119 & 121) This is a font of all things cultural and always good for a musical romp.

Las Palmas (Map pp228-9; 25-32-52; cnr Calles 254 & 127; admission CUC$1; noon-midnight Mon-Wed, noon-2am Fri-Sun) A good starlit night out for a fraction of the price of the Tropicana shindig can be had at this ARTex place.

El Pescadito (Map pp228-9; Calle 272 btwn Calles 115 & 117) The 'Little Fish' is similar to Las Palmas but more central and local.

Tropicana Matanzas (Map p233; 26-53-80; admission CUC$35; 10pm-2am Tue-Sat) Capitalizing on its success in Havana and Santiago de Cuba, the famous Tropicana cabaret has a branch 8km east of Matanzas, next to the Hotel Canimao. You can mingle with the Varadero bus crowds and enjoy the same entertaining formula of lights, feathers, flesh and frivolity in the open air. Rather like a cricket match, rain stops play here if the weather cracks.

From October to April, baseball games take place at the **Estadio Victoria de Girón** (Map pp228-9), located 1km southwest of the market. Once one of the country's leading teams, Los Cocodrilos (Crocodiles) struggle to beat La Isla de la Juventud these days.

Shopping
Shopaholics, you'd better look elsewhere. Checking out the stores (what stores?) in Matanzas makes a car boot sale look like Hollywood Boulevard.

Ediciones Vigía (Map pp228-9; 24-48-45; 8am-4pm Mon-Fri) Incurables can browse here for original handmade books.

Photo Service (Map pp228-9; Calle 288 No 8311 btwn Calles 83 & 85) This is the place for all your photo-related needs.

Getting There & Away
AIR
Matanzas is connected to the outside world through Juan Gualberto Gómez International Airport, located 20km east of town. See p249 for details.

BICYCLE

For someone of good fitness, Matanzas is easy to reach on a bike from Varadero. The road is well-paved and completely flat, bar the last 3km into the city starting at the Río Canímar bridge (a relatively easy uphill climb if you're heading east). Bike hire is available at most Varadero all-inclusive hotels.

BUS

Long-distance buses use the **National Bus Station** (Map pp228-9; ☎ 91-64-45) in the old train station on the corner of Calles 131 and 272 in Pueblo Nuevo south of the Río San Juan. Matanzas has good connections to the rest of the country. **Víazul** (www.viazul.com) has four daily departures to Havana (CUC$7; two hours; 9am, 12:15pm, 4:30pm, 7pm) and Varadero (CUC$6; one hour; 10:15am, 12:10pm, 2:10pm, 8:20pm). The first three Varadero departures also call in at the airport.

Buses within Matanzas province use the **San Luis Bus Terminal** (Map pp228-9; ☎ 29-27-01; cnr Calles 298 & 127) and fan out to the province's main cities including Canasí, Cárdenas, Colón, Jagüey Grande and Jovellanos.

TRAIN

The **train station** (Map pp228-9; ☎ 29-16-45; Calle 181) is in Miret, at the southern edge of the city. Foreigners usually pay the peso price in Convertibles to the *jefe de turno* (shift manager). Most trains between Havana and Santiago de Cuba stop here (except the fast Tren Francés). In theory, there are eight daily trains to Havana beginning at 3:25am (CUC$3, 1½ hours) and a Cienfuegos departure at 8:05pm, alternate days (CUC$6, three hours). Eastbound, there are trains that terminate at Manzanillo and Sancti Spíritus. The daily Santiago train (CUC$27) is supposed to leave early evening (5pm-ish, but check) stopping at Santa Clara, Ciego de Ávila, Camagüey, and Las Tunas.

The **Hershey Train Station** (Map pp228-9; ☎ 24-48-05; cnr Calles 55 & 67) is in Versalles, an easy 10-minute walk from Parque Libertad. There are five trains a day to Casablanca station in Havana (CUC$2.80, four hours) via San Antonio (CUC$0.40), Canasí (CUC$0.85), Jibacoa (CUC$1.10), Hershey (CUC$1.40) and Guanabo (CUC$2). Departure times from Matanzas are 4:34am, 8:26am, 12:30pm, 5:12pm and 9:08pm (the 12:30pm train is an express and takes three hours instead of

four). Ticket sales begin an hour before the scheduled departure time and, except on weekends and holidays, there's no problem getting aboard. Bicycles may not be allowed (ask). The train usually leaves on time, but it often arrives in Havana's Casablanca station (just below La Cabaña fort on the east side of the harbor) one hour late. This is the only electric railway in Cuba, and during thunderstorms the train doesn't run. It's a scenic trip if you're not in a hurry.

Getting Around

To get to the train station from the center, bus 1 leaves from Calle 79 between Calles 290 and 292. Buses 16 and 17 go from Calle 300 in the center to the Río Canímar. The Oro Negro gas station is on the corner of Calles 129 and 210, 4km outside the city of Matanzas on the road to Varadero. The Servi-Cupet gas station and **Havanautos** (Map pp228-9; ☎ 25-32-94; cnr Calles 129 & 210) are a block further on. If you're driving to Varadero, you will pay a CUC$2 highway toll between Boca de Camarioca and Santa Marta (no toll between Matanzas and the airport). Bici-taxis congregate next to the Mercado La Plaza and can take you to most of the city's destinations for one to two Cuban pesos.

VARADERO

pop 20,000

Varadero – make of it what you will. Here on the island's idyllic north coast lies a radically different Cuba to the one that most Cubans see, a sanitized 20km-long peninsula wrapped up for tourist consumption and packaged as a cheap alternative to Cancún.

But, kissed by gentle tropical breezes and lapped by the iridescent waters of the ebbing Atlantic, it's not all bad. Varadero's hallowed beach is, arguably, the best in the archipelago and the weighty cache of 50 or more three-, four- and five-star hotels acts as a tantalizing magnet to the hordes of midrange vacationers who descend here annually from the frozen north (Canada mainly). For those on a more serendipitous voyage of discovery, Varadero lacks one vital ingredient: magic. Not just any old magic, but that esoteric Cuban kind, the sort that can't be replicated in fancy air-conditioned cocktail lounges or grandiose faux-Greek hotel lobbies, however many mojitos you sink.

Contrary to popular belief, Cubans have never been banned from Varadero. In fact, in contrast to other more cut-off resorts such as Cayo Coco, integration is higher than you might first expect. At least one third of the peninsula is given over to a Cuban town of the same name, which, while lacking the atmosphere of Havana or Santiago, still retains a rough semblance of everyday Cuban life.

Orientation

Varadero begins at the western end of the Península de Hicacos, where a channel called the Laguna de Paso Malo links the Bahía de Cárdenas to the Atlantic Ocean. After crossing the Puente Bascular (Lift Bridge) over this waterway, the Vía Blanca becomes the Autopista Sur and runs up the peninsula's spine 20km to Marina Gaviota at Varadero's easternmost point. From the same bridge Av Kawama heads west along the channel toward a couple more big resorts. In general, the Atlantic side of the peninsula (with the 20km of bright white sands for which Varadero is famous) is devoted to tourism, while the Bahía de Cárdenas side is where locals live (another Cuban community is in Santa Marta at the western end of the peninsula). The largest and most expensive resorts are to the east on Punta Hicacos. The quietest section of beach in the center of Varadero is between Calles 46 and 65.

Information

BOOKSTORES
Librería Hanoi (Map pp240-1; ☎ 61-26-94; cnr Av 1 & Calle 44; ◷ 9am-9pm) A good selection of books in English, from poetry to politics.

EMERGENCY
Asistur (Map pp240-1; ☎ 66-72-77; Av 1 No 4201 btwn Calles 42 & 43; ◷ 9am-4:30pm Mon-Fri)

INTERNET ACCESS & TELEPHONE
Most hotels have internet access for CUC$6 an hour. Buy a scratch card from the reception. If you're in a cheaper place, use the public **Etecsa Telepunto** (Map pp240-1; cnr Av 1 & Calle 30).

LIBRARIES
Biblioteca José Smith Comas (Map pp240-1; ☎ 61-23-58; Calle 33 No 104 btwn Avs 1 & 3; ◷ 9am-8pm Mon-Fri, 9am-5pm Sat) Present your hotel guest card to withdraw books (free); book donations happily accepted.

MEDICAL SERVICES
Many large hotels have infirmaries that can provide free basic first aid.

Clínica Internacional Servimed (Map pp240-1; ☎ 66-77-11; cnr Av 1 & Calle 60; ◷ 24hr) Medical or dental consultations (CUC$25 to CUC$5) and hotel calls (CUC$50 to CUC$60). There's also a good pharmacy (open 24 hours) here with items in Convertibles.
Farmacia Internacional Marina Chapelín (Map pp238-9; ☎ 61-85-56; Autopista Sur Km 11; ◷ 9am-9pm); Kawama (Map pp240-1; ☎ 61-44-70; Av a Kawama; ◷ 9am-9pm); Plaza América (Map pp238-9; ☎ 66-80-42; Av Las Américas Km 6; ◷ 9am-9pm)

MONEY
In Varadero, European visitors can pay for hotels and meals in euros. If you change money at your hotel front desk, you'll sacrifice 1% more than at a bank.
Banco de Ahorro Popular (Map pp240-1; Calle 36 btwn Av 1 & Autopista Sur; ◷ 8:30am-4pm Mon-Fri) Probably the slowest option.
Banco de Crédito y Comercio (Map pp240-1; ☎ 66-70-02; cnr Av 1 & Calle 36; ◷ 9am-1:30pm & 3-5pm Mon-Fri) Changes traveler's checks; expect queues.
Banco Financiero Internacional Av 1 (Map pp240-1; ☎ 66-70-02; cnr Av 1 & Calle 32; ◷ 9am-3pm Mon-Fri, 9am-5pm Sat & Sun); Plaza América (Map pp238-9; ☎ 66-82-72; Plaza América, cnr Av Las Américas & Calle 61; ◷ 9am-noon & 1-6pm Mon-Fri, 9am-6pm Sat & Sun) Traveler's checks and cash advances on Visa and MasterCard.
Cadeca (Map pp240-1; ☎ 66-78-59; cnr Av de la Playa & Calle 41; ◷ 8:30am-6pm Mon-Sat, 8:30am-noon Sun)

POST
Many of the larger hotels have branch post offices in the reception area.
DHL (Map pp240-1; ☎ 66-44-51; Av 1 btwn Calles 39 & 40; ◷ 8am-noon & 1-5pm Mon-Fri, 8am-noon Sat)
Post office (Map pp240-1; cnr Av 1 & Calle 36; ◷ 8am-6pm Mon-Sat)

TRAVEL AGENCIES
Almost every hotel has a tourism desk where staff will book adventure tours, skydiving, scuba diving, whatever. It's almost always cheaper, however, to go directly to the tour agency or outfit.
Cubamar (Map pp240-1; ☎ 66-88-55; Av 1 btwn Calles 14 & 15) Office on ground floor of Aparthotel Varazul. Arranges trips to Río Canímar.
Cubana (Map pp240-1; ☎ 61-18-23; Av 1 btwn 54 & 55)
Cubatur (Map pp240-1; ☎ 66-72-16; cnr Av 1 & Calle 33; ◷ 8:30am-6pm) Reserves hotel rooms nationally; organizes Varadero excursions and bus transfers to Havana hotels.
Gaviota (Map pp240-1; ☎ 61-18-44; cnr Calle 56 & Playa)

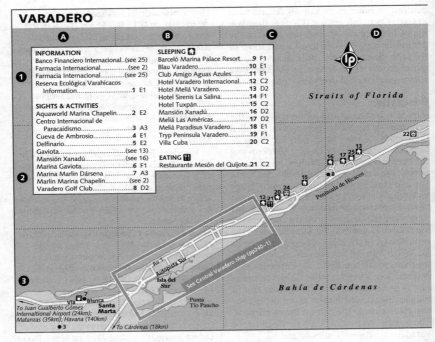

VARADERO

INFORMATION
Banco Financiero Internacional..(see 25)
Farmacia Internacional...............(see 2)
Farmacia Internacional...............(see 25)
Reserva Ecológica Varahicacos
Information.............................**1** E1

SIGHTS & ACTIVITIES
Aquaworld Marina Chapelín........**2** E2
Centro Internacional de
Paracaidismo..........................**3** A3
Cueva de Ambrosio....................**4** E1
Delfinario...................................**5** E2
Gaviota....................................(see 13)
Mansión Xanadú......................(see 16)
Marina Gaviota..........................**6** F1
Marina Marlin Dársena **7** A3
Marlin Marina Chapelín.............(see 2)
Varadero Golf Club....................**8** D2

SLEEPING
Barceló Marina Palace Resort......**9** F1
Blau Varadero...........................**10** E1
Club Amigo Aguas Azules..........**11** E1
Hotel Varadero Internacional.....**12** C2
Hotel Meliá Varadero.................**13** D2
Hotel Sirenis La Salina...............**14** F1
Hotel Tuxpán...........................**15** C2
Mansión Xanadú.......................**16** D2
Meliá Las Américas...................**17** D2
Meliá Paradisus Varadero..........**18** E1
Tryp Península Varadero............**19** F1
Villa Cuba................................**20** C2

EATING
Restaurante Mesón del Quijote..**21** C2

Straits of Florida

Península de Hicacos

Av 1
Autopista Sur
Isla del
Sur

See Central Varadero Map (pp240-1)

Bahía de Cárdenas

Vía Blanca
Santa Marta
Punta
Tío Pancho
To Juan Gualberto Gómez
International Airport (24km);
Matanzas (35km); Havana (140km)
To Cárdenas (18km)

Havanatur (Map pp240-1; ☎ 66-70-27; Av 3 btwn
Calles 33 & 34; ☺ 8am-6pm)

Infotur (☎ 66-29-66; cnr Av 1 & Calle 13) Next to Hotel
Acuazul.

Dangers & Annoyances

Crime-wise Varadero's dangers are minimal.
Aside from getting drunk at the all-inclusive
bar and tripping over your bath mat on the
way to the toilet, you haven't got too much to
worry about. Watch out for mismatched electrical outlets in hotels. In some rooms, a 110V
socket might sit right next to a 220V one. They
should be labeled, but aren't always.

Out on the beach, a red flag means no
swimming allowed due to the undertow or
some other danger. A blue jellyfish known as
the Portuguese man-of-war can produce a bad
reaction if you come in contact with its long
tentacles. Wash the stung area with sea water
and seek medical help if the pain becomes intense or you have difficulty breathing. They're
most common in summer when you'll see
them washed up on the beach; tread carefully. Theft of unguarded shoes, sunglasses
and towels is routine along this beach.

Sights

If it's art and history you're after, you've
come to the wrong place. Varadero is no
Havana. Nevertheless, there are a few sights
worth pondering over if the beach life starts
to bore you.

Varadero's **Parque Central** and **Parque de las
8000 Taquillas** stand side by side between Avs
44 and 46. Once the center of the town's social life, the area was neglected in the 1990s
and early 2000s as bigger resorts sprouted up
further east. Lifted out of its slumber, Parque
de las 8000 Taquillas was recently redeveloped
and now sports a brand new shopping center
beneath the ever-popular Coppelia ice-cream
parlor. Just east is tiny colonial-style **Iglesia de
Santa Elvira** (Map pp240-1; cnr Av 1 & Calle 47), which
resembles a displaced alpine chapel.

Working up the beach from Hotel Acuazul, you'll see many typical wooden beach
houses with elegant wraparound porches.
The most attractive of the bunch has been
turned into the **Museo Municipal de Varadero**
(Map pp240-1; Calle 57; admission CUC$1; ☺ 10am-
7pm), which displays period furniture and
a snapshot of Varadero's relatively short

DRINKING
Bar Mirador..............................(see 16)

ENTERTAINMENT ⬚
Cabaret Continental....................(see 12)
Cabaret Cueva del Pirata..............**22** D2
Club Mambo................................**23** E1
Discoteca La Bamba.....................(see 15)
Habana Café................................**24** C2

SHOPPING 🛍
Plaza América...............................**25** D2

history. There's a fine beach view from the balcony upstairs.

Parque Josone (Map pp240-1; cnr Av 1 & Calle 58; admission free; ☽ 9am-midnight) is a green oasis that's more enclosed and much prettier than Parque Central. The gardens date back to 1940, when the owner of the Arrechabala rum distillery in nearby Cárdenas built a neoclassical mansion here, the Retiro Josone (now a restaurant). Expropriated after the Revolution, the mansion became a guest house for visiting foreign dignitaries. Now a public space – Cuban girls celebrate their *quinciñeras* (15th birthday) here – for the enjoyment of all, Josone's expansive, shady grounds feature an attractive lake (with rowboats for CUC$0.50 per person an hour), resident geese, myriad tree species and a minitrain. There's a public **swimming pool** (admission CUC$2) in the southern part of the park and the odd ostrich lurking nearby. Good music can be heard here nightly.

Everything east of the small stone water tower (it looks like an old Spanish fort, but was actually built in the 1930s), next to the Restaurant Mesón del Quijote, once belonged to the Dupont family. Here the millionaire

American entrepreneur Irenée built the three-story **Mansión Xanadu** (see boxed text, p242), now a B&B that sits abreast Varadero's 18-hole golf course, with a restaurant downstairs and a bar on the top floor – a choice spot for sunset cocktails. On the other side of Meliá Las Américas is the **Plaza América** (Map pp238-9; btwn Meliá Las Américas & Varadero), Varadero's (and Cuba's) only real shopping mall.

Beyond Marina Chapelín, Varadero sprawls east like a displaced North American suburb with scrubby mangroves interspersed with megahotel complexes and the odd iron crane. The much hyped **Delfinario** (Map pp238-9; ☎ 66-80-31; admission CUC$10, camera CUC$5, video camera CUC$10; ☽ 9am-5pm) gets mixed reviews. Dolphin shows happen here daily in a natural pool and swimming with the friendly aquatic mammals costs a steep CUC$65. You're allowed to grab the dolphin's fin and let it drag you around. Ride of a lifetime or cruel aqua-zoo? You decide.

East on Autopista Sur and 500m beyond the Club Amigo Varadero you'll find the **Cueva de Ambrosio** (Map pp238-9; admission CUC$3; ☽ 9am-4:30pm). Some 47 pre-Columbian drawings were discovered in this 300m cave in 1961. The black and red drawings feature the same concentric circles seen in similar paintings on the Isla de la Juventud, perhaps a form of solar calendar. The cave was also used as a refuge by escaped slaves.

A few hundred meters beyond the cave is the entrance to the **Reserva Ecológica Varahicacos** (Map pp238-9; ☽ 9am-4:30pm), Varadero's nominal green zone and a wildlife reserve that's about as 'wild' as New York's Central Park. Bulldozers have been chomping away at its edges for years. There are three short trails (CUC$3, 45 minutes each), none of which are ever out of earshot of the noisy Autopista. The highlight is the **Cueva de Musalmanes** with 2500-year-old human remains and a giant cactus tree nicknamed El Patriarca (patriarch).

Cayo Piedras del Norte, 5km north of Playa Las Calaveras (one hour by boat), has been made into a 'marine park' by the deliberate sinking of an assortment of military equipment in 15m to 30m of water. The yacht *Coral Negro* was sunk here in 1997, followed by frigate 383 in 1998. Also scuttled for the benefit of divers and glass-bottom boat passengers are a towboat, a missile launching gunboat (with missiles intact) and an AN-24 aircraft.

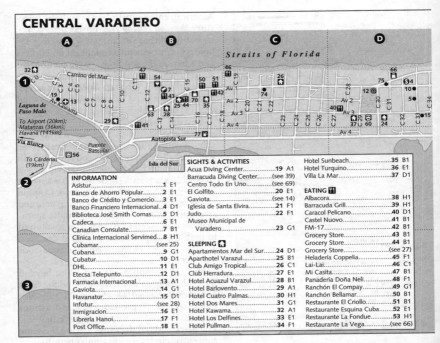

CENTRAL VARADERO

Straits of Florida

INFORMATION	
Asistur	1 E1
Banco de Ahorro Popular	2 E1
Banco de Crédito y Comercio	3 E1
Banco Financiero Internacional	4 D1
Biblioteca José Smith Comas	5 E1
Cadeca	6 E1
Canadian Consulate	7 B1
Clínica Internacional Servimed	8 H1
Cubamar	(see 25)
Cubana	9 G1
Cubatur	10 D1
DHL	11 E1
Etecsa Telepunto	12 D1
Farmacia Internacional	13 A1
Gaviota	14 G1
Havanatur	15 D1
Infotur	(see 28)
Inmigración	16 E1
Librería Hanoi	17 F1
Post Office	18 E1

SIGHTS & ACTIVITIES	
Acua Diving Center	19 A1
Barracuda Diving Center	(see 39)
Centro Todo En Uno	(see 69)
El Golfito	20 E1
Gaviota	(see 14)
Iglesia de Santa Elvira	21 F1
Judo	22 F1
Museo Municipal de Varadero	23 G1

SLEEPING	
Apartamentos Mar del Sur	24 D1
Aparthotel Varazul	25 B1
Club Amigo Tropical	26 C1
Club Herradura	27 E1
Hotel Acuazul Varazul	28 B1
Hotel Barlovento	29 A1
Hotel Cuatro Palmas	30 H1
Hotel Dos Mares	31 B1
Hotel Kawama	32 A1
Hotel Los Delfines	33 H1
Hotel Pullman	34 F1

Hotel Sunbeach	35 B1
Hotel Turquino	36 E1
Villa La Mar	37 D1

EATING	
Albacora	38 H1
Barracuda Grill	39 H1
Caracol Pelicano	40 D1
Castel Nuovo	41 B1
FM-17	42 B1
Grocery Store	43 B1
Grocery Store	44 B1
Grocery Store	(see 27)
Heladería Coppelia	45 F1
Lai-Lai	46 C1
Mi Casita	47 B1
Panadería Doña Neli	48 F1
Ranchón El Compay	49 G1
Ranchón Bellamar	50 B1
Restaurante El Criollo	51 B1
Restaurante Esquina Cuba	52 F1
Restaurante La Fondue	53 H1
Restaurante La Vega	(see 66)

At least half a dozen Varadero hotels are worthy of a visit in their own right – if you can get past the omnipresent security guards. Top favorites include '50s retro Hotel Internacional, the art-deco Mansión Xanadu and the spectacularly modernist Meliá duo.

Activities

SCUBA DIVING & SNORKELING

While not the best location in Cuba for easily accessible diving, Varadero *does* have four excellent dive centers offering competitively priced immersions and courses. All of the 21 dive sites around the Hicacos Peninsula require a boat transfer of approximately one hour minimum. Highlights include reefs, caverns, pitchers and a Russian patrol boat sunk for diving purposes in 1997. The nearest shore diving is at Playa Coral 20km to the west. The centers also offer day excursions to superior sites at the Bay of Pigs in the south of the province (one/two immersions CUC$50/70, with transfer).

Varadero's top scuba facility is the megafriendly, multilingual **Barracuda Diving Center**

(Map pp240-1; ☎ 61-34-81; cnr Av 1 & Calle 58; ⊙ 8am-6pm). Diving costs CUC$40 per dive with equipment, cave diving is CUC$60 and night diving costs CUC$50. Packages of multiple dives work out cheaper. Snorkelers can join the divers for CUC$25. Barracuda conducts introductory resort courses for CUC$70 and ACUC (American Canadian Underwater Certifications) courses for CUC$365, plus many advanced courses. A brand new recompression facility is installed on site and there's also a training pool, resident doctor and popular seafood restaurant on the premises (p246). Barracuda has a daily capacity for 70 divers in three 12m boats.

As a secondary option you have the **Acua Diving Center** (Map pp240-1; ☎ 66-80-63; Av Kawama btwn Calles 2 & 3; ⊙ 8am-5pm) in western Varadero near the Hotel Kawama. It charges much the same prices as Barracuda, but doesn't have quite the facilities, or volume. When a north wind is blowing and diving isn't possible in the Atlantic, you can be transferred to the Caribbean coast in a minibus (90-minute drive); this costs a total of CUC$55/75 for one/two dives.

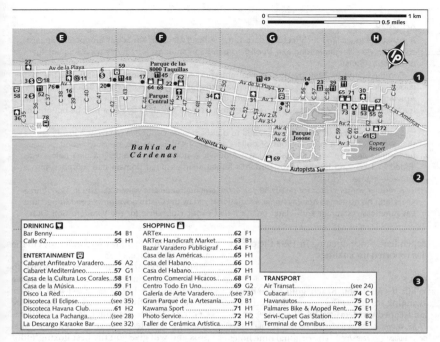

DRINKING 🍸
Bar Benny.....................................**54** B1
Calle 62...................................**55** H1

ENTERTAINMENT 🎭
Cabaret Anfiteatro Varadero.....**56** A2
Cabaret Mediterráneo...............**57** G1
Casa de la Cultura Los Corales...**58** E1
Casa de la Música.....................**59** F1
Disco La Red.............................**60** D1
Discoteca El Eclipse...............(see 35)
Discoteca Havana Club..............**61** H2
Discoteca La Pachanga...........(see 28)
La Descargo Karaoke Bar........(see 32)

SHOPPING 🛍
ARTex.....................................**62** F1
ARTex Handicraft Market...........**63** B1
Bazar Varadero Publicigraf........**64** F1
Casa de las Américas................**65** H1
Casa del Habano.......................**66** D1
Casa del Habano.......................**67** H1
Centro Comercial Hicacos..........**68** F1
Centro Todo En Uno..................**69** G2
Galería de Arte Varadero........(see 73)
Gran Parque de la Artesanía......**70** B1
Kawama Sport **71** H1
Photo Service...........................**72** H1
Taller de Cerámica Artística.......**73** H1

TRANSPORT
Air Transat..............................(see 24)
Cubacar...................................**74** C1
Havanautos...............................**75** D1
Palmares Bike & Moped Rent....**76** H1
Servi-Cupet Gas Station............**77** B2
Terminal de Ómnibus................**78** E1

Aquaworld Diving Center (Map pp238-9; ☎ 66-75-50; Autopista Sur Km 12) at the Marlin Marina Chapelín also organizes snorkeling and diving trips.

Marina Gaviota (Map pp238-9; ☎ 66-77-55; Autopista Sur y Final), at the eastern end of Autopista Sur, also offers scuba diving at similar prices and has snorkeling excursions.

DEEP-SEA FISHING
Varadero has three marinas, all of which offer a variety of nautical activities and facilities. Situated close to the Delfinario and the entrance to Hotel Riu Turquesa is the **Marlin Marina Chapelín** (Map pp238-9; ☎ 66-75-50) where five hours of deep-sea fishing costs CUC$290 for four people (price includes hotel transfers, open bar and licenses; non-fishing companions pay CUC$30). **Marina Gaviota** (Map pp238-9; ☎ 66-77-55), at the eastern end of Autopista Sur, and **Marlin Marina Dársena** (Map pp238-9; ☎ 66-80-62), just west of Varadero, have similar packages. You can book the latter through the **Acua Diving Center** (Map pp240-1; ☎ 66-80-64; Av Kawama btwn Calles 2 & 3).

SKYDIVING
For those with a head for heights, Varadero's greatest thrill has to be skydiving with the **Centro Internacional de Paracaidismo** (Map pp238-9; ☎ 66-72-56, 66-72-60; skygators@cubairsports.itgo .com), based at the old airport just west of Varadero. The terminal is 1km up a dirt road, opposite Marina Acua. Skydivers take off in an Antonov AN-2 biplane of WWII design (don't worry, it's a replica) and jump from 3000m using a two-harness parachute with an instructor strapped in tandem on your back. After 35 seconds of free fall the parachute opens and you float tranquilly for 10 minutes down onto Varadero's white sandy beach. The center also offers less spectacular (but equally thrilling) ultralight flights at various points on the beach. Prices for skydiving are CUC$150 per person with an extra CUC$45 for photos and CUC$50 for video. Ultralight flights start at CUC$30 and go up to CUC$300 depending on the length of time. If you are already a qualified skydiver, solo jumps are also available on production of the relevant certification.

A day's notice is usually required for skydiving and jumps are (obviously) weather

XANADU

A rare jewel in a bland architectural desert, the striking Mansión Xanadu is an opulent Spanish colonial-style villa glimmering like a polished pantheon amongst Varadero's sprawling amalgam of big-box hotels.

Commissioned in 1930 by US chemical entrepreneur Irenée Dupont, Xanadu was the first large-scale building to go up on the wilder eastern end of the now crowded Hicacos Peninsula. Arriving in search of paradise, Dupont found it rather serendipitously on an expansive 180-acre tract of land on the San Bernadino crags just meters from Varadero beach, a plot he bought for a giveaway 90,000 pesos in 1927.

Sparing no expense, Dupont proceeded to build a private Caribbean getaway, a luxury abode that was decked out with millions of dollars' worth of Cuban marble, precious wood, antique furnishings and the largest organ in Latin America. A golf course – initially a nine-hole – was added in 1933, and by the 1950s Dupont's Kublai Khan–inspired domain had morphed into a 540-acre estate.

A regular winter visitor for nearly 30 years, the ageing Irenée last visited Xanadu in 1957. Three years later his esteemed holiday home was nationalized by the Castro government and turned into Las Américas restaurant and – later on – a rather exotic clubhouse for the Varadero Golf Club.

dependent. Since opening in 1993 the center has reported no fatalities.

GOLF

While it's no Pebble Beach, golfers can have a swinging session at the uncrowded and well-landscaped **Varadero Golf Club** (Map pp238-9; ☎ 66-77-88; www.varaderogolfclub.com; Mansión Xanadu Dupont de Nemours; ☯ 7am-7pm). The original nine holes created by the Duponts are between Hotel Bella Costa and the Dupont Mansion, and in 1998 the course was extended to 18 holes (par 72) by adding another nine holes along the southern side of the three Meliá resorts. Bookings are made through the Pro shop next to the Dupont Mansion (now a cozy B&B with free, unlimited tee time). Green fees go for CUC$48/77 nine/18 holes. A 50-minute lesson costs CUC$30.

Golf neophytes can play the miniature version at **El Golfito** (Map pp240-1; cnr Av 1 & Calle 42; per person CUC$3; ☯ 24hr).

OTHER ACTIVITIES

Bowling alleys are popular in Cuba and the *bolera* inside the **Centro Todo En Uno** (Map pp240-1; cnr Calle 54 & Autopista Sur; per game CUC$2.50; ☯ 24hr), a small shopping/games complex on Autopista Sur, is usually full of Cuban families who also come to enjoy the adjacent kids' playground and fast-food joints.

Sailboards are available for rent at various points along the public beach (CUC$10 per hour), as are small catamarans, parasails, banana boats, sea kayaks etc. The upmarket resorts usually include these water toys in the all-inclusive price.

For a workout to remember, pay a visit to the tiny sports club inauspiciously named **Judo** (Map pp240-1; cnr Av 1 & Calle 46; ☯ 9am-noon, 2-5:30pm Mon-Fri, 9-11am Sat) on the east side of Parque Central. Despite the rough facilities and decidedly poky interior, the trainers here are real pros and will give you the best boxing/judo/karate/jujitsu session you've ever had.

Courses

Varadero is not the best place in Cuba to learn Spanish. That said, many of the all-inclusive hotels lay on free Spanish lessons for guests. If you're staying in cheaper digs, ask at the reception of one of these larger hotels and see if you can worm your way onto an in-house language course by offering to pay a small fee.

Tours

Tour desks at the main hotels book most of the nautical or sporting activities mentioned earlier and arrange organized sightseeing excursions from Varadero. You'll pay a surcharge (usually CUC$5 per person) if you book at these desks instead of going directly to the tour operator.

Among the many off-peninsula tours offered are a half-day trip to the Cuevas de Bellamar (see p232) near Matanzas, a bus tour to the Bahía de Cochinos (Bay of Pigs) and a whole range of other bus tours to places as far away as Santa Clara, Trinidad, Viñales and, of course, Havana.

Gaviota (Map p241; ☎ 61-18-44; cnr Calles 56 & Playa) has a variety of helicopter tours in Russian M1-8 choppers; the Trinidad trip (CUC$229) is popular. The Tour de Azúcar (sugarcane tour) visits a disused sugar mill and takes a steam train ride to Cárdenas station. Prices are CUC$39/30 per adult/child. It also organizes jeep safaris to the scenic Valle del Yumurí. The excursion (adult/child CUC$45/34) includes a visit to a *campesino* family and a huge, delicious meal at Ranchón Gaviota (p179).

BOAT TOURS
If you want to enjoy snorkeling without getting wet, book an excursion on the *Varasub*, a 48-berth glass-bottomed boat that allows you to peer out at the fantastic marine life from windows set below the water line. This 90-minute underwater adventure leaves approximately six times a day (adult/child CUC$35/20), and includes unlimited alcoholic or nonalcoholic beverages and transfers. Book through any information desk or office.

Varadero's nautical highlight in the popularity stakes is the **Seafari Cayo Blanco**, a seven-hour sojourn (CUC$75) from Marina Chapelín to nearby Cayo Blanco and its idyllic beach. The trip includes an open bar, lobster lunch, two snorkeling stops, live music and hotel transfers. There's also a shorter CUC$45 catamaran tour with snorkeling, open bar and a chicken lunch. The **Fiesta en el Cayo** is a sunset cruise (CUC$39) to Cayo Blanco with dinner, music and more free-flowing rum at the key. The two-hour guided **Boat Adventure** (☎ 66-84-40; per person CUC$39; ⏰ 9am-4pm) is another perennial favorite. Leaving from the Marina Chapelín, it's a speedy sortie through the adjacent mangroves on two-person jet skis or motorboats to view myriad wildlife including friendly crocs. Bookings for any of these can be made directly at **Aquaworld Marina Chapelín** (Map pp238-9; ☎ 66-75-50; Autopista Sur Km 12) or at hotel tour desks (for a surcharge).

Marina Gaviota has a seven-hour **Seafari Especial Tour**, which is similar to the Cayo Blanco excursion, but includes a chance to swim with dolphins held in an enclosure on a coral key called Rancho Cangrejo (CUC$85).

Festivals & Events
Golf tournaments are held at the Varadero Golf Club in June and October and the annual regatta is in May. Varadero also hosts the annual tourism convention the first week in May when accommodation is tight and some places are reserved solely for conference participants.

Sleeping
Varadero is huge – there are at least 50 hotels. For budget travelers, traipsing around on foot looking for available rooms is a sport akin to marathon running. Book ahead or concentrate your efforts on the southwest end of the peninsula where hotels are cheaper and the town retains a semblance of Cuban life.

As with all other resort areas in Cuba, it is illegal to rent private rooms in Varadero and the law is strictly enforced.

BUDGET
Hotel Turquino (Formatur; Map pp240-1; Av 3 btwn Calles 33 & 34; s/d CUC$15/30; ⌘) This Hotel Escuela, which acts as a training ground for Cuban students vying to work in the tourist industry is the best bargain in town, barring a night out on the beach, and is handily situated two blocks from the Víazul bus station. Some of the rooms are mini-suites with a fridge, microwave and seating area and, although the furnishings are a bit drab, everything is clean, functional and spacious.

Villa La Mar (Islazul; Map pp240-1; ☎ 61-45-17; Av 3 btwn Calles 28 & 30; s/d CUC$37/42; ⌘) Varadero's best budget deal is the no-frills, no-pretensions Villa la Mar where you'll dine on fried chicken, meet paying (in pesos) *Cuban* tourists and fall asleep to the not-so-romantic sound of the in-house disco belting out the Cuban version of Britney Spears.

MIDRANGE
Hotel Dos Mares-Pullman (Islazul; Map pp240-1; ☎ 61-27-02; cnr Av 1 & Calle 53; s/d breakfast only CUC$50/60) This complex is actually made up of two hotels situated three blocks apart. The Pullman is the more striking building, a turreted castle-like abode with heavy wooden furniture and rocking chairs on the front porch overlooking the street. Old-fashioned but comfortable rooms include a quadruple. Dos Mares is a more modern three-story building 70m from a cracking niche of beach. Rooms are a little on the dark side.

Club Herradura (Islazul; Map pp240-1; ☎ 61-37-03; Av de la Playa btwn Calles 35 & 36; s/d breakfast only CUC$50/67; ⌘ ⏰) Plain from the front, but infinitely more attractive on the oceanside, this four-story, crescent-shaped hotel is right on a recently replenished section of the beach. Accommodation is spacious, if a little dog-eared, with timeless wicker furniture and some good balcony view rooms facing the beach. A pleasant all-round unpretentious vibe.

Hotel Acuazul Varazul (Islazul; Map pp240-1; ☎ 66-71-32; Av 1 btwn Calles 13 & 14; s/d breakfast only CUC$55/70, all-inclusive CUC$75/110; ✆ ◻ ✆) This old stalwart stands like a royal blue sentinel at the entrance to Varadero, tempting all who pass. With its 78 rooms having benefited from a recent face-lift and the food buffet looking like it's had a *Hell's Kitchen* revamp, things are looking up at this once-austere prerevolutionary concrete pile. Other benefits include a swimming pool, 24-hour internet and a fantastic Infotur office on-site. The downside is the nightly show, which is tacky even by Varadero standards. Next door the Varazul has one-bedroom apartments with kitchenettes and small balconies.

Apartamentos Mar del Sur (Islazul; Map pp240-1; ☎ 66-74-81; cnr Av 3 & Calle 30; 1-/2-bedroom d incl breakfast CUC$55/82, hotel s/d CUC$42/62; ✆ ◻ ✆) Affording some semblance of independence, the one- and two-bedroom apartments in this scattered complex have cooking facilities and living rooms. It's all several hundred meters from the beach (a long way in Varadero), but decent value.

Hotel Los Delfines (Islazul; Map pp240-1; ☎ 66-77-20; cnr Av de la Playa & Calle 38; s/d CUC$55/88; ✆ ✆) Islazul goes (almost) all-inclusive in this friendlier, cozier copy of the big resorts further northeast. The 100 rooms come packed with additional extras such as satellite TV, minibar and safe deposit box, and there's a lovely scoop of wide protected beach.

TOP END

Rates in these resorts are all-inclusive, and discounted if you take a package.

Hotel Barlovento (Gran Caribe; Map pp240-1; ☎ 66-71-40; Av 1 btwn Calles 10 & 12; s/d CUC$64/88, ocean view CUC$133/190; ✆ ✆ ◻ ✆) The first hotel you encounter when driving into Varadero is an attractive enough place with a lovely palm-fringed pool, integrated colonial-style architecture, and a choice stretch of beach. Popular with Canadians in the winter, the food here is purportedly good though points get deducted for the nighttime entertainment – water ballet and magic shows – which are not a patch on the standard Cuban knees-up.

Hotel Sunbeach (Hotetur; Map pp240-1; ☎ 61-34-46; Calle 17 btwn Avs 1 & 3; s/d CUC$70/140; ✆ ✆) Formerly known as Hotel Bellamar (locals still call it that), this place is one block from the beach. The 282 no-frills rooms are serviceable, but with its worn aquamarine sofas and ugly '60s-style architecture this hotel has delusions of grandeur.

Hotel Cuatro Palmas (Gran Caribe; Map pp240-1; ☎ 66-70-40; Av 1 btwn Calles 60 & 62; r CUC$75/170; ✆ ✆ ◻ ✆) This large resort right on the beach now run by the French Accor chain was once a personal residence of dictator Fulgencio Batista. Jammed together across the street are a series of shared two-story villas with another 122 rooms with fridges and toilet only (shower is shared). This is the first of the real 'posher' all-inclusives as you head east, though it's still close enough to town for getting around on foot.

Hotel Kawama (Gran Caribe; Map pp240-1; ☎ 61-44-16; Av 1 & Calle 1; s/d CUC$89/129; ✆ ✆ ◻ ✆) A venerable old hacienda-style building from the 1930s, the Kawama is, by definition, a piece of Varadero history. It was the first of the 50-plus hotels to inhabit this once-deserted peninsula more than 70 years ago and, as far as character and architectural ingenuity go, it's still one of the best. Even by today's standards the property is huge, with some 235 colorful rooms blended artfully into the thin sliver of beach that makes up Varadero's western extremity. All-inclusive prices include everything from tennis to aqua-bike usage.

Club Amigo Tropical (Cubanacán; Map pp240-1; ☎ 61-39-15; Av 1 btwn Calles 22 & 23; s/d CUC$90/129; ✆ ✆) Right on a great piece of beach, this activities-oriented hotel attracts youthful package tourists and a few married Cubans. It's well located right in the center but, at 40 years of age, the slightly tatty rooms don't merit the asking price.

Club Amigo Aguas Azules (Cubanacán; Map pp238-9; ☎ 66-82-43; Av Las Morlas Km 1.5; s/d CUC$100/160; ✆ ✆ ◻ ✆) Formerly the Gran Hotel, Club Amigo's lurid pinks, yellows and greens suggest Disneyland, Vegas or worse; but the place has perked up since its Aguas Azules reincarnation at the turn of 2008–09. Clean rooms and an excellent slice of beach enhance the three-star rating.

Hotel Tuxpán (Cubanacán; Map pp238-9; ☎ 66-75-60; Av Las Américas; s/d CUC$102/150; ✆ ✆ ◻ ✆) The '60s concrete-block architecture make this all-inclusive one of Varadero's ugliest tourist shrines, but the Tuxpán is famous for other reasons, such as its disco, La Bamba, purportedly one of the resort's hottest. For those not enamored with Soviet architectonics, the beautiful beach is never far away.

Hotel Varadero Internacional (Gran Caribe; Map pp238-9; ☎ 66-70-38; Av Las Américas; s/d CUC$110/157; Ⓟ Ⓧ ⬛ ☎) Opened in December 1950 as a sister hotel to Miami's Fontainebleau, the four-story Internacional is Varadero's most famous and fabulously retro resort. While retaining its '50s charm, the rooms have been regularly upgraded and the extensive facilities include tennis courts, massages and Varadero's best cabaret (p248). Unlike some of Varadero's sprawlers it's also right on the beach. Bonuses at the Internacional include cool art (there's a large René Portocarrero mural in the lobby) and superfriendly staff. If you're rolling a dice on the Varadero all-inclusive options, weight your chances toward here.

Mansión Xanadu (Map pp238-9; ☎ 66-84-82; Av Las Américas; s/d low season CUC$120/150, high season CUC$160/210; Ⓟ Ⓧ ⬛) Rated by many as Varadero's most intriguing and intimate lodging are the six deluxe rooms in the Dupont Mansion. This was once a museum and it still effectively is with the five-star rooms retaining the 1930s furniture and plush decor first commissioned by Dupont. Rates here include unlimited tee time. It's built on a small bluff, and beach access is just alongside.

Blau Varadero (Map pp238-9; ☎ 66-75-45; Av Las Morlas Km 15; s/d CUC$125/155; Ⓟ Ⓧ ⬛ ☎) Built in the shape of a pre-Columbian Mexican pyramid, the Blau seems to have taken the Cancún comparisons too far. Though the room quality and service here are unquestionable, the Blau falls down in its minimalist furnishings and surgical cleanliness, which engender an impassive, airport-like feel.

Villa Cuba (Gran Caribe; Map pp238-9; ☎ 66-82-80; cnr Av 1 & Calle C; s/d CUC$132/189; Ⓟ Ⓧ ⬛ ☎) This 1970s Legoland structure is never going to win any architectural prizes and, up against Varadero's other all-inclusive giants, it seems a bit like a dated dinosaur. Nonetheless, there's a variety of accommodation options and loads of activities here making it a popular family choice. Try the one- to two-bedroom villas (singles/doubles in low season CUC$199/249) which all feature communal living areas, fridge, TV and a patio. There are four rooms designed for disabled guests.

Hotel Sirenis La Salina (Gaviota; Map pp238-9; ☎ 66-70-09; Autopista del Sur Km 8; standard s/d/ste CUC$172/236/278; Ⓟ Ⓧ ⬛ ☎) Welcome to Cuba's biggest hotel. The 1025-room Sirenis opened in 2007 and it's a true monster of a resort (you'd need a book to list even half of the facilities). While the temple-like lobby is beautiful and the grounds rather pleasantly manicured, you have to question the ambience of a place this large. There's a 900-seat theater, almost a dozen restaurants and it's a 1km walk just to get from one end of the resort to the other! Big, yes – the best, no.

Tryp Península Varadero (Gaviota; Map pp238-9; ☎ 66-88-00; Varahicacos Ecological Reserve; r from CUC$180; Ⓟ Ⓧ ⬛ ☎) Paradise or *The Prisoner?* While some people will revel in Tryp's four-star luxuries, others will feel more like they've turned up in an episode of the 1960s allegorical serial *The Prisoner,* where actor Patrick McGoohan wanders around a fanciful Welsh village trying to find a way out. The facilities here are admittedly plush, but there's not much cross-fertilizing with the real Cuba.

ourpick Hotel Meliá Varadero (Cubanacán; Map pp238-9; ☎ 66-70-13; Autopista del Sur Km 7; s/d CUC$195/305; Ⓟ Ⓧ ⬛ ☎) This stunning resort wins the prize for Varadero's most impressive lobby (and there's some pretty ostentatious competition), with its seven-story, vine-dripping atrium creating a natural curtain from the open dome down to the reception area. Rooms overlook the golf course or the beach and it's a popular honeymoon spot. The Meliá Varadero sits on a rocky headland, so you have to walk a bit to reach the beach, but what the hell! Kids aged 12 and under stay here for 50%.

Barceló Marina Palace Resort (Gaviota; Map pp238-9; ☎ 61-44-99; s/d CUC$198/220; Ⓟ Ⓧ ⬛ ☎) You get to a point in Varadero where all the all-inclusives begin to merge into one giant garden suburb of painted bungalows and smiling holiday reps. The Barceló is certainly beautiful, with thoughtful architectural features such as the mock lighthouse and stilted bar perched above the ocean, but at this end of the peninsula it's a long way from central Varadero and a million cultural miles from Cuba.

Meliá Las Américas (Cubanacán; Map pp238-9; ☎ 66-76-00; Autopista del Sur Km 7; s/d CUC$225/340; Ⓟ Ⓧ ⬛ ☎) You've arrived at the luxury end of the peninsula. Everything that went before was small-fry compared to these proverbial giants. Parked on the eastern side of the golf course, this upscale resort is on a choice stretch of beach with plush decor and swanky fittings. The rooms are big, the pool overlooks the beach, and the meals are lavish. Golfers, especially, will have fun here.

Meliá Paradisus Varadero (Gaviota; Map pp238-9; ☎ 66-87-00; Punta Rincón Francés; s/d CUC$225/360; P ⓧ ☐ ⓠ ⓡ) The eastern tip of the peninsula at Punta Hicacos is five-star territory and this Meliá wins the Oscar for Varadero's most expensive hotel (no mean feat). It has shapely pillars and shaded courtyards blending subtlety into a choice stretch of paradisiacal beach.

Eating

You can eat well for under CUC$10 in Varadero in a variety of state restaurants (paladares are banned). As 95% of the hotels on the eastern end of the peninsula are all-inclusive, you'll find the bulk of the independent eating joints west of Calle 64. The prices are fairly generic so the following reviews are listed roughly west to east.

RESTAURANTS

Castel Nuovo (Map pp240-1; ☎ 66-78-45; cnr Av 1 & Calle 11; ☾ noon-11pm) At the gateway to the peninsula stands one of the town's best pizza and pasta restaurants, a cheap, no-nonsense place where atmosphere is lively and the food comes fast. Skip the chicken, beef and fish dishes and go with the Italian fare.

Mi Casita (Map pp240-1; Camino del Mar btwn Calles 11 & 12) Perched over a lovely strip of beach, this cozy restaurant looks and feels more like a paladar than a government-run enterprise. Encased in a charming glass-fronted dining room you can enjoy lobster, spicy chicken and succulent fish – all excellent, if a little overzealous with the garlic.

Ranchón Bellamar (Map pp240-1; Av 1 btwn Calles 16 & 17; meals under CUC$5; ☾ 10am-10pm) Wedged between the main avenue and the beach, this open-sided thatched *ranchón* is part of the Hotel Sunbeach. With its cheap lunches and maracas-shaking musicians, it's a good bet when it's quiet, though the staff struggles to cope when the clientele hits double figures.

FM−17 (Map pp240-1; ☎ 61-48-31; cnr Av 1 & Calle 17; ☾ 8am-2am) With more local vibe than most Varadero visitors ever see, this simple place has sandwiches and burgers for CUC$1 to CUC$2, plus a free cabaret show nightly at 9pm.

Restaurante El Criollo (Map pp240-1; ☎ 61-47-94; cnr Av 1 & Calle 18; ☾ noon-midnight) This is one of the more enjoyable state-run places serving what its name suggests, typical *comida criolla*. Give it a whirl for a lazy lunch.

Lai-Lai (Map pp240-1; ☎ 66-77-93; cnr Av 1 & Calle 18; meals CUC$6-8; ☾ noon-11pm) An old stalwart set in a two-story mansion on the beach, Lai Lai has traditional Chinese set menus with several courses. If you've been craving some wonton soup, crave no more.

Restaurante Mesón del Quijote (Map pp238-9; ☎ 66-77-96; Reparto La Torre; ☾ noon-midnight) Next to a statue of Cervantes' famous Don who seems to be making off rather keenly toward the all-inclusives, this restaurant is one of the eastern peninsula's only non-resort options. Perched on a grassy knoll above the Av las Américas, its Spanish-tinged menu makes a refreshing change from the all-you-can-eat buffet.

Restaurante La Vega (Map pp240-1; ☎ 61-47-19; Av de la Playa btwn Calles 31 & 32; ☾ noon-11pm) They've diminished the seating at this place to a few tables on a wraparound porch, but the paella's still good, along with the tempting *flan al ron* (crème caramel with rum; CUC$3) and strong coffee. Connected to the Casa del Habano, there's an upstairs cigar lounge for after-dinner smokes (replete with beach views).

our pick **Restaurante Esquina Cuba** (Map pp240-1; ☎ 61-40-19; cnr Av 1 & Calle 36; ☾ noon-11:45pm) Notable for the 1950s-era soft-top that sits regally in the middle of the dining room, this place was one-time favorite of Buena Vista Social Club luminary, Compay Segundo. The man obviously had taste. With lashings of beans, rice, plantain chips and chicken, the food here has the aura of Havana's famous El Aljibe (see p158). Great Cuban ephemera line the walls, including black-and-white photos of Varadero back in its Mafia hangout heyday.

Ranchón El Compay (Map pp240-1; Av de la Playa & Calle 54; ☾ 10:30am-10pm) There are not so many Varadero restaurants facing the beach, which makes this chirpy thatched-roof affair all the more alluring. Set just off the central parks, it serves lobster, shrimp and a mean filet mignon.

Barracuda Grill (Map pp240-1; cnr Av 1 & Calle 58; complete meals CUC$7; ☾ 11am-7pm) Set in a thatched pavilion overlooking the beach on the grounds of the Barracuda Diving Center, this popular place has tasty fish and shellfish and it has satisfied many a post-dive appetite.

Albacora (Map pp240-1; ☎ 61-36-50; cnr Av 1 & Calle 59; ☻ 10am-11pm) Fish, squid, shrimp and lobster are available at beachside Albacora. Check out the open bar offer (noon to 4pm).

A few more upscale restaurants are opposite the Hotel Cuatro Palmas, Av 1 and Calle 62, including small and intimate **Restaurante La Fondue** (Map pp240-1; ☎ 66-77-47; ☻ noon-11pm) with beef fillet fondue for CUC$10.

There are several upscale restaurants in **Parque Josone** (Map pp240-1; Av 1 btwn Calles 56 & 59). These include **El Retiro** (☎ 66-73-16; ☻ noon-10pm), with international cuisine and good lobster; **Dante** (☎ 66-77-38), with Italian food; and **Restaurante La Campana** (☎ 66-72-24) with Cuban dishes. On the edge of the park is **La Casa de Antigüedades** (☎ 66-73-29; cnr Av 1 & Calle 59), an old mansion crammed with antiques where beef, fish and shellfish dishes are served beneath chandeliers.

ICE-CREAM PARLORS
Heladería Coppelia (Map pp240-1; Av 1 btwn Calles 44 & 46; ☻ 3-11pm) What, a Coppelia with no queues? Set above the new shopping complex in Parque de las 8000 Taquillas, Varadero's ice-cream cathedral is bright, airy and surprisingly uncrowded.

GROCERIES
There's a handy grocery store beside **Aparthotel Varazul** (Map pp240-1; Calle 15; ☻ 9am-7pm), and also at **Caracol Pelicano** (Map pp240-1; cnr Calle 27 & Av 3; ☻ 9am-7:45pm), **Club Herradura** (Map pp240-1; cnr Av de la Playa & Calle 36; ☻ 9am-7pm) and **Cabañas del Sol** (Map pp238-9; Av Las Américas; ☻ 9am-7:45pm).

The only place where you can always find bread and pastries is **Panadería Doña Neli** (Map pp240-1; cnr Av 1 & Calle 43; ☻ 24hr).

Drinking
Bar Benny (Map pp240-1; Camino del Mar btwn Calles 12 & 13; ☻ noon-midnight) A tribute to Benny Moré, this place has a jazz-den energy, with black-and-white photos of the legendary musician lining the walls and his velvety voice oozing from the sound system. Post-beach cocktails and olives are recommended.

Bar Mirador (Map pp238-9; Av Las Américas; admission CUC$2) On the top floor of the Dupont Mansion, Bar Mirador is Varadero's ultimate romantic hangout where 'happy hour' conveniently coincides with sunset cocktails.

Calle 62 (Map pp240-1; cnr Av 1 & Calle 62) Set in the transition zone between old and new Varadero, this simple snack bar attracts clientele from both ends. It's good for a cheese sandwich during the day, and the ambience becomes feistier after dark with live music going on until midnight.

Entertainment
While Varadero's nightlife might look enticing on paper, there's no real entertainment 'scene' as such, and the concept of bar-hopping à la Cancún or Miami Beach is almost nonexistent, unless you're prepared to incorporate some long-distance hiking into your drinking schedule. Here's a rough rundown of what's on offer.

TROVA & TRADITIONAL MUSIC
Casa de la Cultura Los Corales (Map pp240-1; ☎ 61-25-62; cnr Av 1 & Calle 34) A place where the locals still hold sway. You can catch 'filin' (feeling) matinees here, where singers pour their heart into Neil Sedaka–style crooning. There are also instructors available for Cuban music; or take dance lessons for around CUC$2 an hour.

DANCE CLUBS
Casa de la Música (Map pp240-1; ☎ 61-38-88; cnr Av de la Playa & Calle 42; admission CUC$10; ☻ 10:30pm-3am Wed-Sun) Aping its two popular Havana namesakes, this place has quality live acts and a definitive Cuban feel. It's in town and attracts a local crowd who pay in pesos.

Discoteca Havana Club (Map pp240-1; ☎ 61-18-07; cnr Av 3 & Calle 62; admission CUC$5) Near the Centro Comercial Copey, this is another tourist disco that welcomes Cubans. Expect big, boisterous crowds and plenty of male posturing.

Discoteca La Bamba (Map pp238-9; guests/nonguests free/CUC$10; ☻ 10pm-4am) Varadero's most modern video disco is at Hotel Tuxpán, in eastern Varadero. It plays mostly Latin music and is considered 'hot.'

Club Mambo (Map pp238-9; ☎ 66-86-65; Av Las Américas; open bar, admission CUC$10; ☻ 10am-2am Mon-Fri, 10am-3am Sat & Sun) Cuba's '50s mambo craze lives on at this quality live music venue – arguably one of Varadero's hippest and best. Situated next to Club Amigo Varadero in the eastern part of town, the CUC$10 entry includes all your drinks. A DJ spins when the band takes a break, but this place is all about live music. There's a pool table if you don't feel like dancing.

There are other options, though they're often more international disco than Cuban:

Disco La Red (Map pp240-1; ☎ 61-31-30; Av 3 btwn Calles 29 & 30; admission CUC$1; ☙ from 11pm) When people actually turn out, good local atmosphere is to be had at this place.

Discoteca El Eclipse (Map pp240-1; cnr Av 1 & Calle 17) On the 14th floor at Hotel Sunbeach.

Discoteca La Pachanga (Map pp240-1; ☎ 61-45-71; cnr Av 1 & Calle 13; ☙ 11pm-3am) This disco at Hotel Acuazul is one of Varadero's hottest clubs.

La Descarga Karaoke Bar (Map pp240-1; admission CUC$3; ☙ 10pm-5am) You can check the mic, one, two, at this karaoke place in the strip mall next to the Hotel Kawama.

CABARET

Cabaret Anfiteatro Varadero (Map pp240-1; ☎ 61-99-38; cnr Vía Blanca & Carretera Sur) Just west of the bridge into Varadero, this cabaret has a gala open-air floor show similar to that of the Tropicana. Used mostly for special occasions, it doesn't open every week.

Hotel Kawama (Map pp240-1; Calle 0; admission incl 2 drinks CUC$5; ☙ 11pm nightly except Sun) A cabaret show happens on a stage below the restaurant at Hotel Kawama.

Cabaret Mediterráneo (Islazul; Map pp240-1; ☎ 61-24-60; cnr Av 1 & Calle 54; admission CUC$10; ☙ doors 8:30pm, show 10pm) A professional two-hour show in an open-air location beneath thatched roofs nightly at 10pm. On a good night, it's worth the money.

our pick **Cabaret Continental** (Map pp238-9; Av Las Américas; admission incl drink CUC$35; ☙ show 10pm) There's a coolness to the kitsch at the retro Hotel Internacional, which stages a shamelessly over-the-top Tropicana-style floor show (Tuesday to Sunday) that is, arguably, second only to 'the one' (in Havana). Book dinner at 8pm, catch the singers and dancers strutting their stuff, and stay after midnight for the tie-loosening disco. Enquire at your hotel tour desk about advance bookings. This place is popular.

Habana Café (Map pp238-9; Av Las Américas; admission CUC$10; ☙ 9pm-2am) Done up like Planet Hollywood meets the Tropicana, this place has a talented floor show followed by disco dancing. Expect the 35 plus set and a preponderance of *guayabera* shirts.

Cabaret Cueva del Pirata (Map pp238-9; ☎ 66-77-51; Autopista Sur; open bar CUC$10; ☙ 10pm-3am except Sun) A kilometer east of the Hotel Sol Elite Palmeras, Cabaret Cueva del Pirata presents scantily clad dancers in a Cuban-style floor show with a buccaneer twist (eye patches, swashbuckling moves etc). This cabaret is inside a natural cave and once the show is over, the disco begins. Most hotel tour desks can arrange return hotel transfers. It's a popular place, attracting a young crowd.

Shopping

Parque de las 8000 Taquillas has been the recipient of an extensive remodeling with a new mall tucked under a reborn (and plusher) Coppelia. Called the **Centro Comercial Hicacos** (Map pp240-1; ☙ 10am-10pm), there are a variety of shops here including souvenirs, cigars and photo developing, and an Infotur office. The open-air artisans' market that once stood here has been reborn further down Av 1 as the **Gran Parque de la Artesanía** (Map pp240-1; Av 1 btwn Calles 15 & 16). There's a smaller handicraft market at Av 1 between Calles 51 and 52.

Casa de las Américas (Map pp240-1; cnr Av 1 & Calle 59) A retail outlet of the famous Havana cultural institution, this place sells CDs, books and art, and is one of the few places in the country where a (very) old copy of Lonely Planet's *Cuba* guide has been spotted on sale.

Casa del Habano Av de la Playa btwn Calles 31 & 32 (Map pp240-1; ☙ 9am-6pm); cnr Av 1 & Calle 63 (Map pp240-1; ☎ 66-78-43; ☙ 9am-7pm) The place for cigars: it has top-quality merchandise and helpful service.

Galería de Arte Varadero (Map pp240-1; Av 1 btwn Calles 59 & 60; ☙ 9am-7pm) Antique jewelry, museum-quality silver and glass, paintings and other heirlooms from Varadero's bygone bourgeois days are sold here. As most items are of patrimonial importance, everything is already conveniently tagged with export permission.

Taller de Cerámica Artística (Map pp240-1; ☙ 9am-7pm) Next door to Galería de Arte Varadero, here you can buy fine artistic pottery (they're made on the premises). Most items are in the CUC$200 to CUC$250 range.

Bazar Varadero Publicigraf (Map pp240-1; cnr Av 1 & Calle 44; ☙ 9am-7pm) In Parque Central. It's a good place for ceramics, reproductions of famous paintings, artistic postcards, dolls, wall hangings, T-shirts and books. A clothing boutique is adjacent.

Kawama Sport (Map pp240-1; cnr Av 1 & Calle 60; ☙ 9am-8pm) Forgot your swimming trucks, snorkel, running shoes? Look no further.

Centro Todo en Uno (Map pp240-1; cnr Autopista Sur & Calle 54) A medium-sized mall with a bowling alley and amusements for kids.

Photo Service (Map pp240-1; ☎ 66-72-91; Calle 63 btwn Avs 2 & 3; ☺ 9am-10pm) Come here for all your photo needs.

A small flea market opposite the Hotel Acuazul, **ARTex Handicraft Market** (Map pp240-1; cnr Av 1 & Calle 12; ☺ 9am-9pm) has an excellent selection of CDs, cassettes, T-shirts and even a few musical instruments. Also check out the proper **ARTex store** (Map pp240-1; Av 1 between Calles 46 and 47).

For a hint of American-style consumerism and the shape of things to come, head to **Plaza América** (Map pp238–9), Varadero's and Cuba's largest shopping complex. Here you'll find fancy boutiques, music shops, cigar store, bars, restaurants, a bank, a post office, a **minimarket** (☺ 10am-8:30pm), car rental desks, absolutely everything – oh, and the Varadero Convention Center.

Caracol shops in the main hotels sell souvenirs, postcards, T-shirts, clothes, alcohol and some snack foods. The prices are usually as good as those elsewhere.

Getting There & Away
AIR
Juan Gualberto Gómez International Airport (airport code VRA; Map p233; ☎ 61-30-16) is 20km from central Varadero toward Matanzas and another 4km off the main highway. Airlines here include Cubana from Buenos Aires and Toronto; LTU International Airways from Düsseldorf and four other German cities; Martinair from Amsterdam; and Air Transat and Skyservice from various Canadian cities. The check-in time at Varadero is 90 minutes before flight time.

Note that there are no domestic flights into Varadero.

BUS
Terminal de Ómnibus (Map pp240-1; ☎ 61-26-26; cnr Calle 36 & Autopista Sur) has daily air-con **Víazul** (☎ 61-48-86; ☺ 7am-noon & 1-7pm) buses to a few destinations.

All Havana buses stop at Juan Gualberto Gómez International Airport (CUC$6, 25 minutes) and Matanzas (CUC$6, one hour). The Trinidad bus calls in at Santa Clara and Cienfuegos (CUC$17, four hours 30 minutes). The Santiago bus stops in Cárdenas (CUC$6, 20 minutes), Colón (CUC$6, one hour 30 minutes), Santa Clara, Sancti Spíritus (CUC$17, five hours), Ciego de Ávila (CUC$19, six hours 15 minutes), Camagüey (CUC$25), Las Tunas (CUC$33), Holguín (CUC$38) and Bayamo (CUC$41).

If you have the time, you can get to Havana by catching the Víazul bus to Matanzas and taking the Hershey Railway from there.

Aside from the new 9:25pm Víazul bus to Cárdenas, you can go local on bus 236, which departs every hour or so from next to a small tunnel marked 'Ómnibus de Cárdenas' outside the main bus station. You can also catch this bus at the corner of Av 1 and Calle 13 (CUC$1).

Another easy way to get to Havana is on one of the regular tour buses booked through the tour desk at your hotel or at any Havanatur/Cubanacán office. It's possible to buy just transport between Varadero and Havana for CUC$25/30 for one way/round-trip. These buses collect passengers right at the hotel door, so you'll save money on taxi links.

CAR
You can hire a car from practically every hotel in town and prices are pretty generic between the different makes and models. Once you've factored in fuel and insurance, a standard car will cost you approximately CUC$80 a day – not cheap!

Aside from the hotel reps, you can try **Havanautos** (Map pp240-1; ☎ 61-44-09; cnr Av 1 & Calle 31) or **Cubacar** (Map pp240-1; ☎ 66-73-26; cnr Av 1 & Calle 21).

Havanautos (☎ 25-36-30), **Transtur** (☎ 25-36-21), **Vía** (☎ 61-47-83) and **Cubacar** (☎ 61-44-10) all have car-rental offices in the airport car park. Expect to pay at least CUC$75 a day

BUS TIMETABLE

Destination	Cost (CUC$)	Duration	Departure time
Havana	10	3hr	8am, 11:25am, 3:30pm, 6pm
Santa Clara	11	3hr 20min	9:25pm, 7:30am, 2:25pm
Santiago de Cuba	49	15hr	9:25pm
Trinidad	20	6hr	7:30am, 2:25pm

MATANZAS PROVINCE

for the smallest car (or CUC$50 daily on a two-week basis).

Luxury cars are available at **Rex** (Meliá Las Américas Map pp238-9; ☎ 66-77-39; Autopista del Sur Km 7; Juan Gualberto Gómez International Airport ☎ 66-75-39). It rents Audi and automatic-transmission (rare in Cuba) cars starting from CUC$100 per day.

There's a **Servi-Cupet gas station** (Map pp240-1; cnr Autopista Sur & Calle 17; ☽ 24hr) on the Vía Blanca at the entrance to Marina Acua near Hotel Sunbeach, and one at **Centro Todo En Uno** (Map p364; cnr Calle 54 & Autopista Sur).

If heading to Havana, you'll have to pay the CUC$2 toll at the booth on the Vía Blanca upon leaving.

TRAIN
The nearest train stations are 18km southeast in Cárdenas and 42km west in Matanzas. See the town sections for details.

Getting Around
TO/FROM THE AIRPORT
Varadero and Matanzas are each about 20km from the spur road to Juan Gualberto Gómez International Airport; it's another 6km from the highway to the airport terminal. A tourist taxi costs CUC$20 to Matanzas and around CUC$25 for the ride from the airport to Varadero. Convince the driver to use the meter and it should work out cheaper. Unlicensed private taxis are prohibited from picking up or delivering passengers to the airport. All Víazul buses bound for Havana call at the airport, leaving at 8am, 11:25am, 3:30pm and 6pm and arriving 25 minutes later. Tickets cost CUC$6.

BUS
Varadero Beach Tour (all-day ticket CUC$5; ☽ 9:30am-9pm) is a handy open-top double-decker tourist bus with 45 hop-on/hop-off stops linking all the resorts and shopping centers along the entire length of the peninsula. It passes every half-hour at well-marked stops with route and distance information. You can buy tickets on the bus itself. There's also a free shuttle connecting the three large Meliá resorts.

Local buses 47 and 48 run from Calle 64 to Santa Marta, south of Varadero on the Autopista Sur; bus 220 runs from Santa Marta to the far eastern end of the peninsula. There are no fixed schedules. Fares are a giveaway 20 centavos. You can also utilize bus 236 to and from Cárdenas, which runs the length of the peninsula.

THE TOWN THAT TIME FORGOT
It's hard to miss in-your-face Varadero, but only a trickle of visitors seek out **San Miguel de los Baños**, its less celebrated inland cousin, an atmospheric spa town situated 48km to the south that once rivaled Havana for elegance and opulence.

Hidden away in the center of Matanzas province, barely one hour's drive from the ritzy hotels of the northern coast, this former grand resort is a curious mix of abandoned ghost town and life-sized architectural museum.

Set amid rolling hills and punctuated by vivid splashes of bougainvillea, San Miguel first became popular in the early 20th century when its soothing medicinal waters encouraged wealthy spa seekers to open bath houses in ostentatious buildings such as the ornate **Gran Hotel**, a replica of the Great Casino at Monte Carlo.

The building flurry included a smattering of lavish neoclassical villas that still line the town's arterial Avenida de Abril. But, the salad days didn't last. A few years before the Revolution the bath houses fell into disuse after the local water supply was polluted by waste from a nearby sugar mill, and town quickly faded from prominence.

Today parts of San Miguel de los Baños are still populated while others resemble a scene from a postapocalyptic John Wyndham novel. Passing visitors can stop by at the surreal but now disused Gran Hotel (plans to reopen it have yet to materialize) or negotiate a steep hike up the nearby **Loma de Jacán**, a glowering hill with 448 steps embellished by faded murals of the Stations of the Cross where you can drink in the town's best views.

To get to San Miguel de los Baños, follow Rte 101 from Cárdenas to Colesio where you cross the Carretera Central; the town is situated a further 8km to the southwest.

HORSE CARTS

A state-owned horse and cart around Varadero costs CUC$5 per person for a 45-minute tour or CUC$10 for a full two-hour tour – plenty of time to see the sights.

MOPED & BICYCLE

Mopeds and bikes are an excellent way of getting off the peninsula and discovering a little of the Cuba outside. Rentals are available at most of the all-inclusive resorts, and bikes are usually lent as part of the package. The generic price is CUC$9/24 per hour/day, with gas included in hourly rates (though a levy of CUC$6 may be charged on a 24-hour basis; ask). There's one **Palmares rental post** (Map pp240-1; cnr Av 1 & Calle 38) in the center of town with mopeds for those not staying at an all-inclusive. This guy also has a couple of rickety bikes with no gears and 'pedal-backwards' brakes. Go for a test run first and pay no more than CUC$2/15 per hour/day.

TAXI

Metered tourist taxis charge a CUC$1 starting fee plus CUC$1 per kilometer (same tariff day and night). Coco-taxis (*coquitos* or *huevitos* in Spanish) charge less with no starting fee. A taxi to Cárdenas/Havana will be about CUC$20/85 one way. Taxis hang around all the main hotels or you can phone **Cuba Taxi** (☎ 61-05-55) or **Transgaviota** (☎ 61-97-62). The latter uses large cars if you're traveling with a bike or big luggage. Tourists are not supposed to use the older Lada taxis.

CÁRDENAS

pop 98, 644

It's hard to imagine a more jarring juxtaposition. Twenty kilometers east of the bright lights of Varadero lays shabby Cárdenas, home to countless resort-based waiters, taxi drivers and front-desk clerks; but with barely a hotel, restaurant or motorized cab to serve it.

Threadbare after 50 years of austerity, Cárdenas is the Miss Havisham of Cuba: an ageing dowager, once beautiful, but now looking more like a sepia-toned photo from another era. Streets once filled with illustrious buildings have suffered irrevocably since the Revolution, leaving this former sugar port a shadow of its former self.

It hasn't always been like this. Though spurned these days by most modern travelers,

once gentile Cárdenas has played an episodic role in Cuban history. In 1850 Venezuelan adventurer Narciso López and a ragtag army of American mercenaries raised the Cuban flag here for the first time in a vain attempt to free the colony from its complacent Spanish colonizers. Other history-making inhabitants followed, including revolutionary student leader Antonio Echeverría, shot during an abortive raid to assassinate President Batista in 1957.

Famous for its pioneering spirit, Cárdenas was the first city in Cuba to have electric lighting and a leading player in the early railway industry. These days the pace has slackened somewhat and the dilapidated facades can be a shock to travelers on a brief sojourn from Varadero. If you want to see a picture of real Cuban life, it doesn't get more eye-opening than this. If it's minty mojitos and all-day volleyball you're after, stick to the tourist beaches.

Orientation

The northeast–southwest streets are called Avenidas and streets running northwest–southeast are called Calles. Av Céspedes (Av Real to locals) is Cárdenas' main drag; the avenues to the northwest are labeled *oeste* (west), and those to the southeast are labeled *este* (east). The city's main northwest–southeast street is Calle 13 (Calzada); Calles are numbered consecutively beginning at the bay.

Cárdenas residents (confusingly) use the old street names.

Information

BOOKSTORES

Librería La Concha de Venus (☎ 52-38-06; Av Céspedes No 551 cnr Calle 12; ☑ 9am-5pm Mon-Fri, 8am-noon Sat) Has a decent selection of books in Spanish.

INTERNET ACCESS & TELEPHONE

Etecsa Telepunto (cnr Av Céspedes & Calle 12; ☑ 8:30am-7:30pm)

MEDICAL SERVICES

Centro Médico Sub Acuática (☎ 52-21-14; channel 16 VHF; Calle 13; per hr CUC$80; ☑ 8am-4pm Mon-Sat, doctors on-call 24hr) It's 2km northwest on the road to Varadero at Hospital Julio M Aristegui. Has a Soviet recompression chamber dating from 1981.
Pharmacy (☎ 52-15-67; Calle 12 No 60; ☑ 24hr)

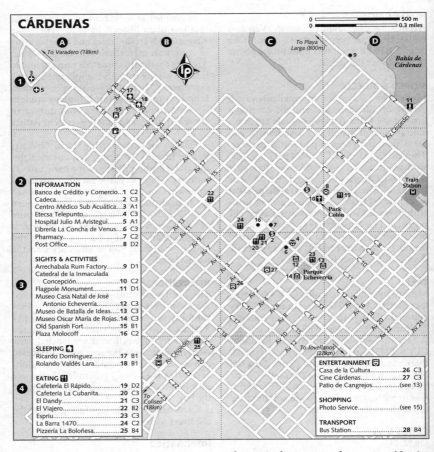

CÁRDENAS

INFORMATION
Banco de Crédito y Comercio...**1** C2
Cadeca.....................................**2** C3
Centro Médico Sub Acuática..**3** A1
Etecsa Telepunto...................**4** C3
Hospital Julio M Aristegui......**5** A1
Librería La Concha de Venus...**6** C3
Pharmacy...............................**7** C2
Post Office............................**8** D2

SIGHTS & ACTIVITIES
Arrechabala Rum Factory........**9** D1
Catedral de la Inmaculada
    Concepción........................**10** C2
Flagpole Monument...............**11** D1
Museo Casa Natal de José
    Antonio Echeverría..........**12** C3
Museo de Batalla de Ideas.....**13** C3
Museo Oscar María de Rojas...**14** C3
Old Spanish Fort...................**15** B1
Plaza Molocoff......................**16** C2

SLEEPING
Ricardo Domínguez................**17** B1
Rolando Valdés Lara..............**18** B1

EATING
Cafetería El Rápido................**19** D2
Cafetería La Cubanita............**20** C3
El Dandy...............................**21** C3
El Viajero.............................**22** B2
Espriu..................................**23** C3
La Barra 1470.......................**24** C2
Pizzería La Boloñesa.............**25** B4

ENTERTAINMENT
Casa de la Cultura................**26** C3
Cine Cárdenas......................**27** C3
Patio de Cangrejos..........(see 13)

SHOPPING
Photo Service....................(see 15)

TRANSPORT
Bus Station..........................**28** B4

MONEY

Banco de Crédito y Comercio (cnr Calle 9 & Av 3)
Cadeca (☎ 52-14-92; cnr Av 1 Oeste & Calle 12)

POST

Post office (cnr Av Céspedes & Calle 8; 8am-6pm
Mon-Sat)

Sights

First impressions lie. In among the battered buildings and dingy peso restaurants
Cárdenas harbors three excellent museums
all situated in the same city square, the pretty
Parque Echeverría. The **Museo Casa Natal de
José Antonio Echeverría** (Av 4 Este No 560; admission
free, but tip the guide; 10am-5pm Tue-Sat, 9am-noon Sun)
has a macabre historical collection including

the original garrote used to execute Narciso
López by strangulation in 1851. Objects relating to the 19th-century independence wars are
downstairs, while the 20th-century Revolution
is covered upstairs. A spiral staircase with 36
steps links the two levels of this house dating
from 1703. In 1932 José Echeverría was born
here, a student leader slain by Batista's police
in 1957 after a botched assassination attempt
in Havana's Presidential Palace. There's a
statue of him in the eponymous square outside. The nearby **Museo Oscar María de Rojas** (cnr
Av 4 Este & Calle 12; admission CUC$5; 10am-6pm Mon-Sat,
9am-noon Sun) is Cuba's second-oldest museum,
after the Museo Bacardí in Santiago. Its extensive, if rather incongruous, collection of artifacts include a fossilized tree, a strangulation

chair from 1830, a face mask of Napoleon, the tail of Antonio Maceo's horse, Cuba's largest collection of snails and, last but by no means least, some preserved fleas – yes fleas – from 1912. Set in a lovely colonial building and staffed with knowledgeable official guides, the museum makes a good side trip.

Around the corner is the newer **Museo de Batalla de Ideas** (Av 6 btwn Calles 11 & 12; admission CUC$2; 9am-5pm Tue-Sun), with a well-designed and organized overview of the history of US-Cuban relations, replete with sophisticated graphics.

Parque Colón is the city's other interesting square containing the **Catedral de la Inmaculada Concepción** (Av Céspedes btwn Calles 8 & 9), built in 1846 and noted for its stained glass and purportedly the oldest statue of Christopher Columbus in the Western hemisphere. Dating from 1862, Colón, as he's known in Cuba, stands rather authoritatively with his face fixed in a thoughtful frown and a globe resting at his feet. It's the closest Cárdenas gets to a decent photo op.

At the northeast end of Av Céspedes is a monument with a huge **flagpole** commemorating the first raising of the Cuban flag on May 19, 1850. It's a simple, but moving memorial with good views of the bay and Varadero. To the northwest in the industrial zone is the **Arrechabala Rum Factory** where Varadero rum is distilled. The Havana Club rum company was founded here in 1878; there are sporadic tours here between 9am and 4pm for a cost of CUC$3; ask in town.

An architectural fantasy that now serves as the font of Cárdenas' city life, **Plaza Molocoff** (cnr Av 3 Oeste & Calle 12) is a whimsical two-story cast-iron market hall with a glittery 16m-high silver dome built in 1859. It's still the city **vegetable market** (8am-5pm Mon-Sat, 8am-2pm Sun) but is crying out for face-lift.

Sleeping

Down the road Varadero flaunts more than 50 hotels. Here in humble Cárdenas there are precisely zero now that the once-grand Hotel Dominica (next to the cathedral) has closed indefinitely (the much-touted renovation never materialized). Fortunately Cárdenas is home to about half a dozen casas particulares and they'll be very keen for your business.

Rolando Valdés Lara (072-703-155; cnr Av 30 & Calle 12; r CUC$30;) The thinnest house in Cuba? Come here for your ultimate anti-

Varadero vacation; breakfast is the standard CUC$3 extra.

Ricardo Domínguez (528-944-31; cnr Avs 31 & 12; r CUC$35; P) Cárdenas dilapidated? Not here. Ricardo's place could have been plucked out of one of Miami's more tasteful suburbs with its leafy garden, plush tile-work and bathrooms befitting a North American show home.

Eating

Half the chefs in Varadero probably come from Cárdenas, which adds irony to the city's dire restaurant scene. Grim, scant and hard to find are the three phrases that spring to mind when discussing the local eating houses. There are three El Rápidos if that's any measuring stick. If you're allergic to soggy microwaved cheese and spam sandwiches, bring a packed lunch.

Espriu (Calle 12 btwn Avs 4 & 6; dishes CUC$1-3; 24hr) The best in town and handily located on Parque Echeverría, Espriu is an OK restaurant among uninspired choices. Choose from espresso, shrimp cocktails, fish fillets, burgers and sandwiches.

Cafetería El Rápido (Av Céspedes btwn Calles 7 & 8; 24hr) After tramping the streets in search of something more inspiring, most tourists end up here swearing to never complain about their Varadero hotel buffet again. There are two more branches around town.

Cafetería La Cubanita (cnr Av 3 Oeste & Calle 13; 24hr) Situated near Plaza Molocoff, Cafetería La Cubanita has a pleasant outdoor setting where you can consume drinks for Convertibles.

La Barra 1470 (Calle 13 btwn Avs 6 & 7) Tablecloths and wine glasses and a nice inner decor raise expectations that probably won't be met when it comes to the food.

Pizzería La Boloñesa (Av Céspedes No 901; 10am-10pm) Peso pizza's always an option, but don't bank on any *boloñesa*.

El Viajero (cnr Calle 13 & Av 13) The address might sound fateful, but you could get lucky at this cheerful peso place long touted by the locals as the best eating joint in town.

There are many Convertible supermarkets and stores along Av 3 Oeste near Plaza Molocoff, including **El Dandy** (Av 3 on Plaza Molocoff; 9am-5pm Mon-Sat, 9am-noon Sun), selling drinks and groceries. You can get cheap peso snacks in the market itself and the area surrounding, where merchants peddle everything from fake hair to plastic Buddhas.

Entertainment

Casa de la Cultura (☎ 52-12-92; Av Céspedes No 706 btwn Calles 15 & 16) Housed in a beautiful but faded colonial building with stained glass, iron awnings and an interior patio with rockers. Search the hand-written advertising posters for rap *peñas* (performances), theater and literature events.

Cine Cárdenas (cnr Av Céspedes & Calle 14) Has daily movie screenings.

Shopping

Photo service (cnr Calle 13 & Av 31) This is housed inside an old Spanish fort. All your standard camera needs can be met here.

Getting There & Away

The Varadero–Santiago **Víazul** (www.viazul.com) bus stops in Cárdenas once daily in either direction. The eastbound service leaves Varadero at 9:25pm and arrives in Cárdenas at 9:45pm. It then heads east via Colón (CUC$6, one hour), Santa Clara (CUC$11, three hours), Sancti Spíritus (CUC$16, four hours 30 minutes), Ciego de Ávila (CUC$17, five hours 50 minutes), Camagüey (CUC$23, seven hours 45 minutes), Las Tunas (CUC$31, 10 hours), Holguín (CUC$35, 11 hours 10 minutes) and Bayamo (CUC$41, 12 hours 30 minutes) to Santiago (CUC$48, 15 hours 30 minutes). The return bus leaves Cárdenas at 10:40am and arrives in Varadero at 11am.

Local buses leave from the **bus station** (cnr Av Céspedes & Calle 22) to Havana and Santa Clara daily, but they're often full upon reaching Cárdenas. There are also trucks to Jovellanos/Perico, which puts you 12km from Colón and possible onward transport to the east. The ticket office is at the rear of the station.

Bus 236 to/from Varadero leaves hourly from the corner of Av 13 Oeste and Calle

---

ASK A LOCAL

Cárdenas has a couple of interesting public spaces that can get lively if you come on the right day. Plaza Roja (Red Square) at Calle 13 and Av 15 has a private grocery market twice a month on Saturdays. Then there's the Patio de Cangrejos in front of the Museo de Batalla de Ideas that hosts occasional live music at weekends.

María, Varadero

---

13 (50 centavos, but they like to charge tourists CUC$1).

Getting Around

The main horse-carriage (one peso) route through Cárdenas is northeast on Av Céspedes from the bus station and then northwest on Calle 13 to the hospital, passing the stop of bus 236 (to Varadero) on the way.

The **Servi-Cupet gas station** (cnr Calle 13 & Av 31 Oeste) is opposite an old Spanish fort on the northwest side of town, on the road to Varadero.

PENÍNSULA DE ZAPATA

pop 8267

Most of the 4520-sq-km Península de Zapata in southern Matanzas is included in Gran Parque Natural Montemar, formerly known as Parque Nacional Ciénaga de Zapata. In 2001, it was declared a Unesco Biosphere Reserve and, despite being one of Cuba's largest municipalities, it's also one of its most uninhabited.

To the east of this swampy wilderness lies the elongated Bahía de Cochinos (Bay of Pigs) where propaganda billboards still laud Cuba's historic victory over the *Yanqui* imperialists in 1961. There are two worthwhile beaches here, Playa Larga at the bay's curvaceous head and the more southerly Playa Girón. Both beaches are fronted by slightly moth-eaten resort hotels that are popular with divers. Aside from its reputation as a proverbial banana-skin for US imperialism, the Bay of Pigs also boasts some of the best cave diving in the Caribbean (see boxed text, p260).

Situated to the northeast of the peninsula lies the sugar-mill town of Australia, along with the cheesy tourist circus of Boca de Guamá, a reconstructed Taíno village.

Transport in the area is limited to a daily Víazul bus. Accommodation outside of the resorts is surprisingly abundant. You can check out excellent casa options in Jagüey Grande, Central Australia, Playa Larga and Playa Girón.

Information

La Finquita (☎ 91-32-24; ⏱ 9am-noon & 1-5pm Mon-Sat), a snack bar and information center run by Cubanacán just before the turn-off toward

MATANZAS PROVINCE

Playa Larga from the Autopista, arranges trips into the Zapata Peninsula (see p257) and books rooms at the Villa Guamá.

Etecsa, the post office and Convertible stores are across the Autopista in bustling Jagüey Grande. Insect repellent is absolutely essential on the peninsula and while Cuban repellent is available locally, it's like wasabi on sushi for the ravenous buggers here.

CENTRAL AUSTRALIA & AROUND

No, you haven't just arrived in Alice Springs. About 1.5km south of the Autopista Nacional on the way to Boca de Guamá, is the large Central Australia sugar mill, built in 1904. During the 1961 Bay of Pigs invasion, Fidel Castro had his headquarters in the former office of the sugar mill. Today it's the **Museo de la Comandancia** (☎ 2504; admission CUC$1; ☺ 8am-5pm Tue-Sun). This municipal museum contains a few stuffed birds and animals, and a good historical collection starting from prehistory, but surprisingly little about the Bay of Pigs episode itself (the Museo de Playa Girón is far better; see p258). Outside is the wreck of an invading aircraft shot down by Fidel's troops. The concrete memorials lining the road to the Bahía de Cochinos mark the spots where defenders were killed in 1961.

Approximately 400m on your right after the Central Australia exit is the **Finca Fiesta Campesina** (admission CUC$1; ☺ 9am-6pm), a kind of wildlife park–meets–country fair with labeled examples of Cuba's typical flora and fauna. The highlights of this strangely engaging place are the coffee (some of the best in Cuba and served with a sweet wedge of sugarcane) and the hilarious if slightly infantile games of guinea-pig roulette overseen with much pizzazz by the gentleman at the gate. It's the only place in Cuba – outside the cockfighting – where you encounter any form of open gambling.

Sleeping & Eating

Motel Batey Don Pedro (Cubanacán; ☎ 91-28-25; Peninsula de Zapata; s/d CUC$25/50) This motel is just south of the turn-off to the Península de Zapata, from Km 142 on the Autopista Nacional at Jagüey Grande, and is really just a glorified campismo. The eight thatched double units are comfortable enough with ceiling fans and crackling TVs. Beware of the frogs in the bathroom. The motel is designed to resemble a peasant settlement, and the on-

site restaurant, though friendly and intimate, serves pretty ropey food. A better bet is the adjacent Fiesta Campesino, which sells energy-boosting *guarapo* (sugarcane juice) and coffee that's positively divine.

Pío Cuá (☎ 91-33-43; Carretera de Playa Larga Km 8; meals CUC$6-20; ☺ 9am-9pm) A favorite with Guamá-bound tour buses, this huge place is set up for big groups, but retains a fancy decor with lots of stained glass. Shrimp, lobster or chicken meals are pretty good. It's 8km from the Autopista turn-off.

If you just can't drive any further, there are a number of legal casas particulares in the area including *Orlando Caballero Hernández* (☎ 91-32-75; Calle 20 No 5; r CUC$20; ℗ ☒), at the Central Australia sugar mill, with small, clean rooms and some great testimonies, and the more convenient **Casa de Zuleida** (☎ 91-36-74; Calle 15A No 7211 btwn 72 & 74; r CUC$15-20; ℗ ☒) in Jagüey Grande behind the hospital. There are more casas in Playa Larga (32km) and Playa Girón (48km).

BOCA DE GUAMÁ

Boca de Guamá is a tourist creation situated about halfway between the Autopista Nacional at Jagüey Grande and the famous Bahía de Cochinos (Bay of Pigs). Named after native Taíno chief Guamá, who made a last stand against the Spanish in 1532 (in Baracoa), a cluster of restaurants, expensive snack bars, knick-knack shops along with a crocodile farm crowd around a small dock. Here boats wait to take you across Laguna del Tesoro (Treasure Lake) to the main attraction: an Indian-themed resort built to resemble an authentic Taíno village. Tour buses crowd the car park and loud rap music welcomes your passage back in time to the hidden mysteries of pre-Columbian Cuba. You'll need an extremely hyperactive imagination to make anything out of it.

Sights

Don't confuse the real **Criadero de Cocodrilos** (guided visit CUC$5; ☺ 8am-5pm) with the faux farm inside Boca de Guamá's tourist complex. On your right as you come from the Autopista, the Criadero de Cocodrilos is an actual breeding facility, run by the Ministerio de Industrias Pesqueras, where two species of crocodiles are raised: the native *Crocodylus rhombifer* (*cocodrilo* in Spanish), and the *Crocodylus acutus* (*caimán* in Spanish), which is found throughout the tropical Americas. Sometimes security guards will try to point you across the road to the Guamá zoo, but if you're persistent you can get a guided tour here (in Spanish), taking you through every stage of the breeding program, from eggs and hatchlings to big, bad crocs. Prior to the establishment of this program in 1962 (considered the first environmental protection act undertaken by the revolutionary government), these two species of marsh-dwelling crocodiles were almost extinct.

The breeding has been so successful that across the road in the Boca de Guamá complex you can buy stuffed baby crocodiles or dine, perfectly legally, on crocodile steak.

The **park/zoo** (adult/child CUC$5/3; ☽ 9am-6pm) has two crocodiles that are often under water trying to beat the stifling 85% humidity. There are other caged animals here.

If you buy anything made from crocodile leather at Boca de Guamá, be sure to ask for an invoice (for the customs authorities) proving that the material came from a crocodile farm and not wild crocodiles. A less controversial purchase would be one of the attractive ceramic bracelets sold at the nearby **Taller de Cerámica** (☽ 9am-6pm Mon-Sat) where you can see five kilns in operation.

Aside from the crocodile farm, the main attraction is the **Laguna del Tesoro**, 8km east of Boca de Guamá via the Canal de la Laguna and accessible only by boat (see right). On the east side of this 92-sq-km lake is a tourist resort named Villa Guamá, built to resemble a Taíno village, on a dozen small islands. A sculpture park next to the mock village has 32 life-size figures of Taíno villagers in a variety of idealized poses. The lake is called 'Treasure Lake' due to a legend about some treasure the Taíno are said to have thrown into the water just prior to the Spanish conquest (not dissimilar to South American El Dorado legends). The name Guamá comes from a rebel Taíno *cacique* (chief) who led a partially successful rebellion against the Spanish in the 1530s near Baracoa. The lake is stocked with largemouth bass, which makes it popular with fishermen.

Sleeping & Eating

Villa Guamá (Cubanacán; ☎ 91-55-15; s/d CUC$22/44) This place was built in 1963 on the east side of the Laguna del Tesoro, about 5km from Boca de Guamá by boat (cars can be left at the crocodile farm; CUC$1). The 50 thatched *cabañas*

(cabins) with bath and TV are on piles over the shallow waters. The six small islands bearing the units are connected by wooden footbridges to other islands with a bar, cafetería, overpriced restaurant and a swimming pool containing chlorinated lake water. Rowboats are for rent. Noise from the on-site disco will leave you questioning this place's authenticity (there are no known records of discos in Taíno Indian villages), and the tranquility is further broken by the ubiquitous day-trippers who come and go by speedboat from dawn till dusk. Bird-watching at sunrise, however, is reputedly fantastic. You'll need insect repellent if you decide to stay. The ferry transfer is not included in the room price (see below).

At the boat dock you'll find **Bar La Rionda** (☽ 9:30am-5pm), Restaurante Colibrí and **Restaurante La Boca** (set meals CUC$12).

Getting There & Away

The Havana–Trinidad Víazul bus passes daily in either direction. Guamá isn't an official stop but a word with the driver and you may be able to negotiate a drop-off at Boca de Guamá. There are regular tours from Varadero to Boca de Guamá.

Getting Around

A passenger ferry (adult/child CUC$10/5, 20 minutes) departs Boca de Guamá for Villa Guamá across Laguna del Tesoro four times a day. Speedboats depart more frequently and whisk you across to the pseudo-Indian village in just 10 minutes any time during the day for CUC$10 per person round-trip (with 40 minutes waiting time at Villa Guamá; two persons minimum). In the morning you can allow yourself more time on the island by going one way by launch and returning by ferry.

GRAN PARQUE NATURAL MONTEMAR

The largest *ciénaga* (swamp) in Cuba, **Ciénaga de Zapata** is also one of the country's most diverse ecosystems. Crowded into this vast wetland (which is essentially two swamps divided by a rocky central tract) are 14 different vegetation formations including mangroves, wood, dry wood, cactus, savannah, selva and semideciduous. There are also extensive salt pans. The marshes support more than 190 bird species, 31 types of reptiles, 12 species of mammals, plus countless amphibians, fish and insects (including the insatiable mosquito). There are more than 900 plant species here, some 115 of them endemic. It is also an important habitat for the endangered *manatí* (manatee), the Cuban *cocodrilo* (crocodile; *Crocodylus rhombifer*), and the *manjuarí* (alligator gar; *Atractosteus tristoechus*), Cuba's most primitive fish.

The Zapata is the place to come to see *zunzuncitos* (bee hummingbirds; the world's smallest bird), cormorants, cranes, ducks, flamingos, hawks, herons, ibis, owls, parrots, partridges, sparrows, *tocororos* (Cuba's national bird) and wrens. Numerous migratory birds from North America winter here, making November to April the best birding season. It's also the number-one spot in Cuba for catch-and-release sport fishing and fly-fishing, where the *palometa*, *sábalo* and *robalo* are jumping (bonefish too!).

Communications in Zapata, unsuitable for agriculture, were almost nonexistent before the Revolution when poverty was the rule. Charcoal makers burn wood from the region's semideciduous forests, and *turba* (peat) dug from the swamps is an important source of fuel. The main industry today is tourism and ecotourists are arriving in increasing numbers.

Information
The **National Park Office** (☎ 98-72-49; ⏰ 8am-4:30pm Mon-Fri, 8am-noon Sat) is at the north entrance to Playa Larga on the road from Boca de Guamá. The staff here is knowledgeable and helpful. Alternatively you can try the Cubanacán office (p254) on the Autopista near Central Australia or the Playa Larga or Girón hotels.

Sights & Activities
There are four main excursions into the park, although the itineraries (particularly for birdwatching) are flexible. Transport is not usually laid on, so it is best to arrange beforehand. Cars (including chauffeur-driven jeeps) can be rented from **Havanautos** (☎ 98-41-23) in Playa Girón. One of the most popular excursions is to **Laguna de las Salinas** where large numbers of migratory waterfowl can be seen from November to April: we're talking 10,000 pink flamingos at a time, plus 190 other feathered species. The first half of the road to Las Salinas is through the forest, while the second half passes swamps and lagoons. Here, aquatic birds can be observed. Guides are mandatory to explore the refuge. The 22km visit lasts over four hours but you may be able to negotiate for longer; costs start at CUC$10 per person.

For avid bird-watchers **Observación de Aves** (per person CUC$19) offers an extremely flexible itinerary and the right to roam (with a qualified park ornithologist) around a number of different sites, including the Reserva de Bermejas. Among 18 species of endemic bird found here you can see prized *ferminins, cabreritos* and *gallinuelas de Santo Tomás* – found only on the Zapata Peninsula.

Switching from land to boat, the **Río Hatiguanico** (per person CUC$19) takes you on a three-hour 12km river trip through the densely forested northwestern part of the peninsula. You'll have to duck to avoid the branches at some points while at others the river opens out into a wide delta-like estuary. Birdlife is abundant in this part of the peninsula and if you're lucky you may also see turtles and crocodiles.

It's also worth asking about the **Santo Tomás** trip, an excursion (CUC$10) that begins 30km west of Playa Larga in the park's only real settlement (Santo Tomás) and proceeds along a tributary of the Hatiguanico – walking or boating, depending on the season. It's another good option for birders.

Aspiring fishermen can arrange excellent **fly-fishing** at either Las Salinas or Hatiguanico. Ask at the National Park Office.

PLAYA LARGA
Continuing south from Boca de Guamá you reach Playa Larga, on the Bahía de Cochinos (Bay of Pigs), after 13km (or 32km from where you left the Autopista Nacional). Larga was one of two beaches invaded by US-backed exiles on April 17, 1961 (although Playa Girón 35km further south saw far bigger landings). There's a cheapish resort here, a scuba diving center, and a smattering of casas particulares. It is also the headquarters of the Ciénaga de Zapata National Park and a good base for environmental excursions around the peninsula.

Activities
Playa Larga is a diver's paradise. Check out the boxed text, p260, for more details.

Sleeping & Eating
Villa Playa Larga (Cubanacán; ☎ 98-72-94; s/d low season incl breakfast CUC$27/54; Ⓟ 🍽 🏊) On a small scimitar of white-sand beach by the road, just east of the village, this hotel has huge rooms with bath, sitting room, fridge

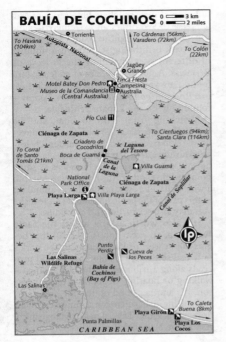

BAHÍA DE COCHINOS

PLAYA GIRÓN

The sandy arc of Playa Girón nestles peacefully on the eastern side of the infamous Bahía de Cochinos (Bay of Pigs), 48km south of Boca de Guamá. Notorious as the place where the Cold War almost got hot, the beach is actually named for a French pirate, Gilbert Girón, who met his nemesis here by decapitation in the early 1600s at the hands of embittered locals. In April 1961 it was the scene of another botched raid, the ill-fated, CIA-sponsored invasion that tried to land on these remote sandy beaches in one of modern history's classic David and Goliath struggles. Lest we forget, there are still plenty of propaganda-spouting billboards dotted around rehashing past glories, though these days Girón, with its clear Caribbean waters and precipitous off-shore drop-off, is a favorite destination for scuba divers and snorkelers.

In addition to some decent private houses, Playa Girón's one and only resort is the modest Villa Girón, a low-key all-inclusive that is perennially popular among the diving fraternity. Long, shady Playa Los Cocos, where the snorkeling is good, is just a five-minute walk south along the shore. But Varadero this is not. In common with many of Cuba's southern coastal areas, there's often more *diente de perro* (dog's tooth) than soft white sand.

Information

On the main entry road to the hotel there's a pharmacy, a post office, an international post office and a Caracol shop selling groceries. The settlement of Playa Girón is a tiny one-horse town, so if you need any goods or services, the hotel is the most likely place to look.

Sights

The **Museo de Playa Girón** (admission CUC$2, cameras CUC$1; ☼ 9am-5pm) has gleaming glass display cases and a tangible sense of history. Housed across the street from Villa Playa Girón, it offers two rooms of artifacts from Bahía de Cochinos plus numerous photos with (some) bilingual captions. The mural of victims and their personal items is eye-catching and the tactical genius of the Cuban forces comes through in the graphic depictions of how the battle unfolded. The 15-minute film about the 'first defeat of US imperialism in the Americas' is CUC$1 extra. A British Hawker Sea Fury aircraft used by the Cuban Air Force is parked outside the museum and round the

and TV. There are also eight two-bedroom family bungalows, though the restaurant is legendary in its bleakness (and in total contrast to the setting). The villa was closed for some long-overdue renovations at the time of writing.

Casa Fefa (☎ 98-71-33; r CUC$20-25; ❄) There are some affable casas particulares in Playa Larga. Start your search at Casa Fefa, run by Josefa Pita Cobas and Osnedy González Pita, near Caleton beach. Osnedy can put you in touch with hiking and bird-watching guides.

Palmares restaurant (meals CUC$2-7) Across the road from Villa Playa Larga, Palmares has hearty ham-and-cheese sandwiches, fish meals and can cook up a respectable vegetarian plate.

Getting There & Away

The reliable Havana–Trinidad Víazul bus passes through daily in either direction and will pick up/drop off on request outside Villa Playa Larga. Approximate arrival times are 11am for the Playa Girón, Cienfuegos and Trinidad service; and 6:45pm for the Jagüey Grande and Havana service.

back are other vessels used in the battle that you can look at.

Sleeping & Eating
CASAS PARTICULARES
The small settlement of Playa Girón has half a dozen decent casas particulares, most of which serve meals.

KS Abella (☎ 98-43-83; r CUC$20; ✖) This *señor* is a former chef at Villa Playa Girón who is now trying out his seafood specialties on his casa guests. He's situated on the corner of the main road.

Villa Merci – Mercedes Blanco Pérez (☎ 98-43-04; r CUC$20; P ✖) *Hay Perro* (meaning 'beware of the dog'), says the sign, but don't be put off by the warning. The dog's as friendly as Merci, the congenial casa owner. Adorned with a lovely garden and porch, this house has two rooms with all the standard amenities plus a TV room complete with a decent stash of videos. It's on the road to Caleta Buena (the last house).

Hostal Luis (☎ 99-42-58; r incl breakfast CUC$25; P ✖) The first house on the road to Cienfuegos is also the village's premier casa. Instantly recognizable by the two stone lions that guard the gate, youthful Luis and his wife offer two spotless rooms on a large lot with plenty of room for parking.

THE BAY OF PIGS

What the Cubans call Playa Girón, the rest of the world has come to know as the Bay of Pigs 'fiasco,' a shoddily planned comedy of errors that made a laughing stock out of the Kennedy administration and elevated Fidel Castro into the role of unassailable national hero.

Conceived in 1959 by the Eisenhower administration and headed up by deputy director of the CIA, Richard Bissell, the plan to initiate a program of covert action against the Castro regime was given official sanction on March 17, 1960. There was but one proviso: no US troops were to be used in combat.

Setting about their task with zeal, the CIA modeled their operation on the 1954 overthrow of the left-leaning government of Jacobo Arbenz in Guatemala. But ambition soon got the better of ardor.

By the time President Kennedy was briefed on the proceedings in November 1960, the project had mushroomed into a full-scale invasion backed by a 1400-strong force of CIA-trained Cuban exiles and financed with a military budget of US$13 million.

Activated on April 15, 1961, the invasion was an unmitigated disaster from start to finish. Intending to wipe out the Cuban Air Force on the ground, US planes painted in Cuban Air Force colors (and flown by Cuban exile pilots) comically missed most of their intended targets. Castro, who had been forewarned of the plans, had scrambled his air force the previous week. Hence when the invaders landed at Playa Girón two days later, Cuban sea furies were able to promptly sink two of their supply ships and leave a force of 1400 men stranded on the beach.

To add insult to injury, a countrywide Cuban rebellion that had been much touted by the CIA never materialized. Meanwhile a vacillating Kennedy told a furious Bissell that he would not provide the marooned exile soldiers with US air cover.

Abandoned on the beaches, without supplies or military back up, the disconsolate invaders were doomed. There were 114 killed in skirmishes and a further 1189 captured. The prisoners were returned to the US a year later in return for US$53 million worth of food and medicine. For the US, the humiliation was palpable.

The Bay of Pigs failed due to a multitude of factors. Firstly, the CIA had overestimated the depth of Kennedy's personal commitment and had made similarly inaccurate assumptions about the strength of the fragmented anti-Castro movement inside Cuba. Secondly, Kennedy himself, adamant all along to make a low-key landing, had chosen a site on an exposed strip of beach close to the Zapata swamps. Thirdly, no one had given enough credit to the political and military know-how of Fidel Castro or to the extent to which the Cuban Intelligence Service had infiltrated the CIA's supposedly covert operation.

The consequences for the US were far reaching. 'Socialism or death!' a defiant Castro proclaimed at a funeral service for seven Cuban 'martyrs' on April 16, 1961. The Revolution had swung irrevocably toward the Soviet Union.

DIVING IN THE BAHÍA DE COCHINOS

While the Isla de la Juventud and María la Gorda lead most Cuban divers' wish lists, the Bahía de Cochinos has some equally impressive underwater treats. There's a huge drop-off here running 30m to 40m offshore for over 30km from Playa Larga down to Playa Girón, a fantastic natural feature that has created a 300m-high coral-encrusted wall with amazing swim-throughs, caves, gorgonians and marine life. Even better, the proximity of this wall to the coastline means that the region's 30-plus dive sites can be easily accessed without a boat – you just glide out from the shore. Good south coast visibility stretches from 30m to 40m and there are a handful of wrecks scattered around, including one from the infamous 1961 Bay of Pigs landing.

Organizationally, Playa Girón is well set up with highly professional instructors bivouacked at five different locations along the coast. Generic prices (CUC$25 per immersion, CUC$100 for five or CUC$365 for an open-water course) are some of the cheapest in Cuba.

The **International Scuba Center** (☎ 98-41-18), at Villa Playa Girón, is the main diving head-quarters. It is complemented by the **Club Octopus International Diving Center** (☎ 98-72-25), 200m west of Villa Playa Larga.

Eight kilometers southeast of Playa Girón is **Caleta Buena** (☺ 10am-6pm), a lovely protected cove perfect for snorkeling and kitted out with another diving office. Admission to the beach is CUC$12 and includes an all-you-can-eat lunch buffet and open bar. There are beach chairs and thatched umbrellas dotting the rocky shoreline and enough space in this remote place to have a little privacy. Snorkel gear is CUC$3.

More underwater treasures can be seen at the **Cueva de los Peces** (admission CUC$1; ☺ 9am-6pm), a flooded tectonic fault (or cenote), about 70m deep on the inland side of the road, almost exactly midway between Playa Larga and Playa Girón. There are lots of bright, tropical fish, plus you can explore back into the darker, spookier parts of the cenote with snorkel or dive gear. Hammocks swing languidly around the cenote and the beach facing back is good snorkeling too, making it a nice afternoon jaunt. There's a handy restaurant and an on-site dive outfit.

Just beyond the Cueva is **Punto Perdiz**, another phenomenal snorkeling and scuba-diving spot with a smaller on-site diving concession. The shallow water is gemstone-blue here and there's good snorkeling right from the shore. It costs CUC$1 to use the thatched umbrellas, beach chairs and showers, and there's another decent restaurant.

HOTELS

Villa Playa Girón (Cubanacán; ☎ 98-41-10; s/d all-inclusive high season CUC$33/66; P ❄ ☎) On a beach im-bued with historical significance lies this rather ordinary hotel – an all-inclusive although, with its spartan bungalows and spatially challenged dining room, it rarely feels like one. Always busy with divers, the villa is an unpretentious kind of place with helpful staff and clean, basic rooms that are often a long walk from the main block. The beach, however, is invariably a mere 50m dash away, though its allure has been spoiled somewhat by the construction of a giant wave-breaking wall.

Getting There & Away

The reliable Havana–Trinidad Víazul bus makes two scheduled daily stops in Playa Girón (one in either direction). You must wait on the main road next to the entrance road to the Villa Playa Girón. The bus for Jagüey Grande/Havana arrives at 6:15pm and the bus for Cienfuegos/Trinidad pulls in at 11:30am. Arrive a good 15 minutes in advance in case it's early. You can buy tickets on the bus.

There's a (very) early morning passenger truck to Cienfuegos. A taxi should cost approximately CUC$40 for the same trip. From Playa Girón to Playa Larga, the fare will be closer to CUC$20.

Getting Around

Havanautos (☎ 98-41-23) has a car-rental office at Villa Playa Girón or you can hire a moto for CUC$24 per day.

Servi-Cupet gas stations are located on the Carretera Central at Jovellanos and on Colón at Jagüey Grande, as well as on the Autopista Nacional at Aguada de Pasajeros in Cienfuegos province.

East of Caleta Buena (southeast of Playa Girón), the coastal road toward Cienfuegos is potholed and not passable in a normal car; backtrack and take the inland road via Rodas.

Cienfuegos Province

Bienvenido (welcome) to Cienfuegos province – or should that be *Bienvenue*? If Cuba has a Gaelic heart, it's hidden here in the lee of the crinkled Escambray Mountains; and if it has a Paris, it is enshrined in the finely sculpted provincial capital that glistens like a polished pearl beside the island's best natural bay.

While Cuba's Gaelic infusions have traditionally come via Haiti, Cienfuegos' lineage is traced back to Louisiana in the US and Bordeaux in France. Undaunted by fickle weather and impervious to the squalid conditions, the original French colonizers arrived in 1819. They brought with them the ideas and manners of the European Enlightenment, which they industriously incorporated into their fledgling neoclassical city with creativity and zest.

The setting helped. Caught dramatically between mountains and sea, the province's southern coast is a minirainbow of emerald greens and iridescent blues that reaches its apex at El Nicho, an outpost of the Topes de Collantes Natural Park, and a fine place to cool off after a strenuous jungle hike. Lapped by the warm Caribbean, the surrounding shoreline is flecked with coves and caves, while out at sea teeming coral reefs beckon at Guajimico.

Though ostensibly white, Cienfuegos' once-muted African 'soul' gained a loquacious mouthpiece in the 1940s and '50s in one of Cuba's most versatile musicians, the incomparable Benny Moré, a great-great-grandson of a king of the Congo who hailed from the small provincial village of San Isabel de las Lajas. Emerging from a brutal slave history, Moré wasn't Cienfuegos' only Afro-Cuban improviser, and close by in the settlement of Palmira, a handful of Santería brotherhoods continue to keep the traditions and beliefs of Cuba's hybrid Catholic-Yoruba religious culture alive.

HIGHLIGHTS

- **Graveyard Fascination** View the classical finery in Cienfuegos' two monumental cemeteries (p266)
- **Benny in Lajas** Track the legend of Benny Moré in Santa Isabel de las Lajas (p270)
- **Punta Life** Stay in an amazing casa particular in Cienfuegos' classic Punta Gorda neighborhood (p267)
- **Cooling Down** Hike to bracing El Nicho (p272) and cool down in an invigorating waterfall
- **Beach Break** Stay in a cool hotel next to the beach in Rancho Luna (p271)

- TELEPHONE CODE: 043
- POPULATION: 398,569
- AREA: 4180 SQ KM

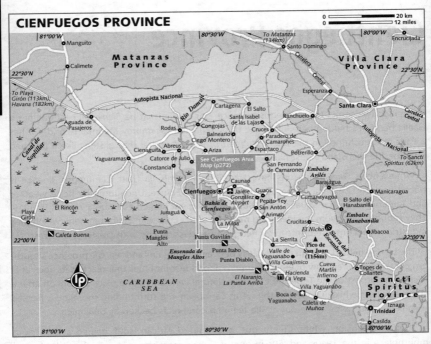

CIENFUEGOS PROVINCE

History

The first settlers in the Cienfuegos area were Taíno Indians who called their fledgling principality, Cacicazgo de Jagua – a native word for 'beauty.' In 1494 Columbus 'discovered' the Bahía de Cienfuegos (Cuba's third-largest bay, with a surface area of 88 sq km) on his second voyage to the New World and 14 years later Sebastián de Ocampo passed by during his pioneering circumnavigation of the island. With the onset of the era of piracy in the 16th and 17th centuries the Spanish built a bayside fort, the imposing Castillo de Jagua (p272), one of the most important military structures on Cuba's south coast.

Parks & Reserves

Parque El Nicho in the Escambray Mountains is managed by the state tourist company Gaviota as an outpost of the Topes de Collantes Natural Park in adjacent Sancti Spíritus province.

Getting There & Around

The city of Cienfuegos is linked to Trinidad and Havana by twice-daily Víazul buses. The train service out of the city is less reliable with sporadic services to Santa Clara and Havana. The province's smaller towns can be reached via truck, local buses or your own wheels. For shorter distances, consider a taxi.

CIENFUEGOS
pop 139,137

La ciudad que más me gusta a mí (the city I like the best), reads a billboard on the Bahía de Cienfuegos quoting the words of native singer Benny Moré. He wasn't the settlement's only cheerleader. Refined, elegant, genteel and hassle-free, Cuba's so-called Perla del Sur (Pearl of the South) has long seduced travelers from around the island with its enlightened French spirit and feisty Caribbean panache. If Cuba has a Paris this is most definitely it.

Arranged around a calm natural bay, Cienfuegos is a nautical city with a superb waterside setting. Founded in 1819, it's one of Cuba's newest settlements, but also one of its most architecturally homogeneous, a factor that earned it a Unesco World Heritage Site listing in 2005. Geographically, the city is split into two distinct parts: the colonnaded central zone with its elegant Prado and salubrious

Parque Martí; and Punta Gorda, a thin knife of land that slices into the southern waters of the bay and contains a clutch of eclectic early 20th-century palaces along with some of Cuba's prettiest casas particulares.

While the city's 19th-century architecture and tranquil seaside setting help create a pleasant atmosphere, the churn of outlying industry does not. Ringing the Bahía de Cienfuegos is a giant shipyard, the bulk of Cuba's shrimp fishing fleet, a nitrogen fertilizer factory, a cement works, an oil refinery, a thermoelectric plant and the ghostlike dome of Cuba's only (unfinished) nuclear power station (the plan was abandoned in the early '90s when Soviet money dried up). Fortunately for travelers, the pollution has yet to penetrate the city center.

History

Cienfuegos was founded in 1819 by a pioneering French émigré from Louisiana named Don Louis D'Clouet. Sponsoring a scheme to increase the population of whites on the island, D'Clouet invited 40 families from New Orleans and Philadelphia, and Bordeaux in France to establish a fledgling settlement known initially as San Fernandina de Jagua. Setting up tents in what is now Parque Martí, the encampment city got off to a bad start when it was destroyed by a hurricane in 1821. Unperturbed, the French settlers rebuilt their homes and – suspicious, perhaps, that their first name had brought them bad luck – rechristened the city Cienfuegos after the then governor of Cuba.

With the arrival of the railway in 1850 and the drift west of Cuban sugar growers after the First War of Independence, Cienfuegos' fortunes grew exponentially. Basking in a period of relative economic prosperity, the local merchants pumped their fortunes into a dazzling array of eclectic architecture that harked back to the neoclassicism of their French forefathers.

D-Day in Cienfuegos' history came in September 1957 when officers at the local naval base staged a revolt against the Batista dictatorship. The uprising was brutally crushed, but the city's place in revolutionary history was sealed in infamy.

Modern-day Cienfuegos retains a slightly plusher and more polished look than many of its urban counterparts. And with some much-needed Unesco money now filtering through, the future for the city's fine array of 19th-century architecture can only be bright.

Orientation

Despite its haphazard geography, the city is laid out in an easy-to-understand grid system with even-numbered Avenidas that run east–west and odd-numbered Calles running north–south. Downtown Cienfuegos, or Pueblo Nuevo, is the area bounded by Avs 46 and 62 and bisected by Calle 37 (popularly called El Prado). Avenida 54 is often called El Bulevar and is a pedestrian mall stretching from Calle 37 to Parque Martí. Calle 37 (or El Prado), meanwhile, runs 3km south to seaside Punta Gorda (where it's called Malecón). Rancho Luna is 18km south of the city via Av 5 de Septiembre.

Information

BOOKSTORES

Librería Bohemia (Map p264; ☎ 52-51-63; Av 56 No 3318 btwn Calles 33 & 35)
Librería Dionisio San Román (Map p264; ☎ 52-55-92; Av 54 No 3526) Well-stocked, modern place on the corner of Calle 37.

EMERGENCY

Asistur (Map p264; ☎ 51-16-24; Av 54 No 3111 btwn Calles 32 & 34)

INTERNET ACCESS & TELEPHONE

Etecsa Telepunto (Map p264; ☎ 51-92-66; Calle 31 No 5402 btwn Avs 54 & 56; per hr CUC$6; ☑ 8:30am-7:30pm)

LIBRARIES

Biblioteca Roberto García Valdés (Calle 37 No 5615) Far more than just books; check out the cultural programs offered here.

MEDIA

Radio Ciudad del Mar 1350AM and 98.9 FM.

MEDICAL SERVICES

Clínica Internacional (Map p264; ☎ 55-16-22; Calle 37 No 202, Punta Gorda) Caters to foreigners, handles dental emergencies and has a 24-hour pharmacy.
Farmacia Principal Municipal (Map p264; ☎ 51-57-37; Av 54 No 3524 btwn Calles 35 & 37)

MONEY

Banco de Crédito y Comercio (Map p264; ☎ 51-57-47; cnr Av 56 & Calle 31)
Banco Financiero Internacional (Map p264; ☎ 55-16-57; cnr Av 54 & Calle 29)

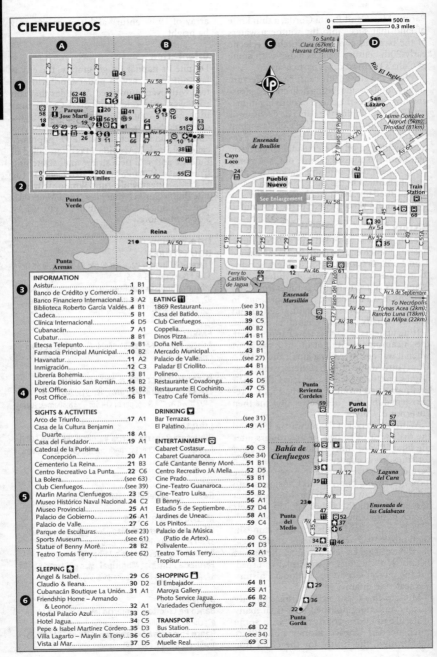

CIENFUEGOS

INFORMATION
Asistur.....................................1 B1
Banco de Crédito y Comercio.....2 B1
Banco Financiero Internacional....3 A2
Biblioteca Roberto García Valdés..4 B1
Cadeca.....................................5 B1
Clínica Internacional.................6 D5
Cubanacán..............................7 A1
Cubatur...................................8 B1
Etecsa Telepunto.....................9 B1
Farmacia Principal Municipal....10 B2
Havanatur..............................11 A2
Inmigración............................12 C3
Librería Bohemia.....................13 B1
Librería Dionisio San Román.....14 B2
Post Office.............................15 B2
Post Office.............................16 B1

SIGHTS & ACTIVITIES
Arco de Triunfo......................17 A1
Casa de la Cultura Benjamin
  Duarte................................18 A1
Casa del Fundador..................19 A1
Catedral de la Purísima
  Concepción..........................20 A1
Cementerio La Reina................21 B3
Centro Recreativo La Punta.....22 C6
La Bolera............................(see 63)
Club Cienfuegos.....................23 C5
Marlin Marina Cienfuegos........23 C5
Museo Histórico Naval Nacional..24 C2
Museo Provincial.....................25 A1
Palacio de Gobierno................26 A1
Palacio de Valle.....................27 C6
Parque de Esculturas..........(see 23)
Sports Museum....................(see 61)
Statue of Benny Moré.............28 B2
Teatro Tomás Terry..............(see 62)

SLEEPING
Angel & Isabel.......................29 C6
Claudio & Ileana....................30 D2
Cubanacán Boutique La Unión..31 A1
Friendship Home – Armando
  & Leonor............................32 A1
Hostal Palacio Azul.................33 C5
Hotel Jagua..........................34 C5
Pepe & Isabel Martínez Cordero.35 D3
Villa Lagarto – Maylin & Tony..36 C6
Vista al Mar..........................37 D5

EATING
1869 Restaurant..................(see 31)
Casa del Batido......................38 B2
Club Cienfuegos.....................39 C5
Coppelia...............................40 B2
Dinos Pizza...........................41 B1
Doña Neli..............................42 D2
Mercado Municipal.................43 B1
Palacio de Valle..................(see 27)
Paladar El Criollito.................44 B1
Polineso................................45 A1
Restaurante Covadonga...........46 A1
Restaurante El Cochinito.........47 C5
Teatro Café Tomás.................48 A1

DRINKING
Bar Terrazas......................(see 31)
El Palatino............................49 A1

ENTERTAINMENT
Cabaret Costasur....................50 C3
Cabaret Guanaroca..............(see 34)
Café Cantante Benny Moré.......51 B1
Centro Recreativo JA Mella......52 D5
Cine Prado............................53 B1
Cine-Teatro Guanaroca...........54 D2
Cine-Teatro Luisa...................55 B1
El Benny...............................56 A1
Estadio 5 de Septiembre.........57 D4
Jardines de Uneac..................58 A1
Los Pinitos............................59 C4
Palacio de la Música
  (Patio de Artex)..................60 C5
Polivalente............................61 D3
Teatro Tomás Terry................62 A1
Tropisur...............................63 D3

SHOPPING
El Embajador.........................64 B1
Maroya Gallery......................65 A1
Photo Service Jagua................66 B2
Variedades Cienfuegos............67 B2

TRANSPORT
Bus Station...........................68 D2
Cubacar............................(see 34)
Muelle Real...........................69 C3

Cadeca (Map p264; ☎ 45-22-82; Av 56 No 3316 btwn Calles 33 & 35)

POST
Post office cnr Av 56 & Calle 35 (Map p264; ☎ 51-82-84); Av 54 No 3514 (Map p264; btwn Calles 35 & 37)

TRAVEL AGENCIES
Cubanacán (Map p264; ☎ 55-16-80; Av 54 btwn Calles 29 & 31) Friendly and efficient service here in English.
Cubatur (Map p264; ☎ 55-12-42; Calle 37 No 5399 btwn Avs 54 & 56)
Havanatur (Map p264; ☎ 51-11-50; fax 55 13 70; Av 54 No 2906 btwn Calles 29 & 31)

Sights
PARQUE JOSÉ MARTÍ
Cienfuegos' serene central park is notable for its **Arco de Triunfo** (Arch of Triumph), the only one of its kind in Cuba. Dedicated to Cuban independence, the Francophile monument on the park's western edge ushers you through its gilded gateway toward a marble statue of José Martí.

Swapping French influences for Italian, the **Teatro Tomás Terry** (Map p264; ☎ 51-33-61; Av 56 No 270 btwn Calle 27 & 29; tours CUC$1; ⊙ 9am-6pm), on the northern side of the Parque, is grand from the outside, but even grander within. Built between 1887 and 1889 to honor Venezuelan industrialist Tomás Terry, the 950-seat auditorium is embellished with Carrara marble, hand-carved Cuban hardwoods and whimsical ceiling frescoes. In 1895 the theater opened with a performance of Verdi's *Aïda* and it has witnessed numerous landmarks in Cuban music and dance in the years since.

On the western side of Parque Martí is the former Palacio de Ferrer (1918), now the **Casa de la Cultura Benjamin Duarte** (Map p264; ☎ 51-65-84; Calle 25 No 5401; admission free; ⊙ 8:30am-midnight), an eye-catching neoclassical building with Italian marble floors and – most noticeably – a domed rooftop cupola equipped with a wrought-iron staircase. For a tip of CUC$1 you can climb up for unparalleled city views. On the opposite side of the park is the singular **Catedral de la Purísima Concepción** (Map p264; ☎ 52-52-97; Av 56 No 2902; donations accepted; ⊙ 7am-noon), dating from 1869 and distinguished by its French stained-glass windows. Surprise – it's nearly always open. The southern side of Parque Martí is dominated by the silvery grey walls and red dome of the **Palacio de Gobierno**, where the provincial government (Poder Popular Provincial) holds forth. It doesn't allow visitors, but you can steal a look at the palatial main staircase through the front door. The **Museo Provincial** (Map p264; ☎ 51-97-22; cnr Av 54 & Calle 27; admission CUC$2; ⊙ 10am-6pm Tue-Sat, 10am-noon Sun) next door offers a microcosm of Cienfuegos' history and displays the frilly furnishings of refined 19th-century French-Cuban society, as well as other assorted knickknacks.

On the park's southeastern corner stands the city's oldest building, the **Casa del Fundador** (Map p264; cnr Calle 29 & Av 54), once the residence of city founder Louis D'Clouet, later a bank and now a souvenir shop. **El Bulevar** (Calle 54), Cienfuegos' quintessential shopping street, heads east from here to link up with the Paseo del Prado.

PASEO DEL PRADO & THE MALECÓN
The stately **Paseo del Prado** (Calle 37), stretching from the Río El Inglés in the north to Punta Gorda in the south, is the longest street of its kind in Cuba and a great place to see Cienfuegueños going about their daily business. The boulevard is a veritable smorgasbord of fine neoclassical buildings and pastel-painted columns, and at the intersection of Av 54 you can pay your respects to a life-sized **statue of Benny Moré** (Map p264).

Next to the Polivalente sports center at the intersection of Prado and Av 48, there's a small **sports museum** (Map p264; cnr Calle 37 & Av 48; admission free) containing hockey, fencing and baseball paraphernalia as well as the boots and T-shirt of local boxing hero, Julio González Valladores, who brought back a gold medal from the 1996 Atlanta Olympics.

Heading south on the Prado, the street becomes the **Malecón** as it cuts alongside the bay offering exquisite vistas of what is considered to be one of the world's finest natural bays. Like all sea drives (Havana's being the archetype), this area later comes alive in the evening when poets come to muse and couples to canoodle.

PUNTA GORDA
When the Malecón sea wall runs out, you will know you have landed in Punta Gorda, Cienfuegos' old upper-class neighborhood characterized by its bright clapboard homes and turreted palaces. Highlighting a 1920s penchant for grandiosity are the cupola-topped **Palacio Azul** (now the Hostal Palacio Azul) and the **Club Cienfuegos**, once an exclusive yacht

club. Nearby an inventive **Parque de Esculturas** throws some interesting modern sculpture into the already eclectic surroundings.

The ultimate in kitsch is yet to come. Continue south on Calle 37 and, with a sharp intake of breath, you'll stumble upon the Arabian Nights–like **Palacio de Valle** (Map p264; ☎ 51-12-26; cnr Calle 37 & Av 2; ⏱ 9:30am-11pm). Built in 1917 by Alcisclo Valle Blanco, a Spaniard from Asturias, the structure resembles an outrageously ornate Moroccan Kasbah. Batista planned to convert this colorful riot of tiles, turrets and stucco into a casino, but today it's an (aspiring) upscale restaurant, with an inviting terrace bar (p268).

The **Centro Recreativo La Punta** (Map p264; ⏱ 10am-10pm) has a gazebo on the point's extreme southern tip and this is where lovers go to watch the sunset. You can also grab a beer or mojito at the bar. Live music sometimes breaks the tranquility.

CEMETERIES

Cienfuegos has a rather morbid fascination with burial grounds, with two of its cemeteries listed as national monuments. The older of the two is **Cementerio La Reina** (Map p264; cnr Av 50 & Calle 7; ⏱ 8am-6pm), founded in 1837 and lined with the graves of Spanish soldiers who died in the Wars of Independence. La Reina is the only cemetery in Cuba where bodies are interred above ground (in the walls) due to the high groundwater levels. It also has a marble statue called *Bella Durmiente*: a tribute to a 24-year-old woman who died in 1907 of a broken heart. It's an evocative place if you're into graveyards.

The **Necrópolis Tomás Acea** (Map p272; Carretera de Rancho Luna Km 2; admission CUC$1; ⏱ 8am-6pm) is classed as a 'garden cemetery' and is entered through a huge neoclassical pavilion (1926) flanked by 64 Doric columns modeled on the Parthenon in Greece. This cemetery contains a monument to the marine martyrs who died during the abortive 1957 Cienfuegos naval uprising.

MUSEO HISTÓRICO NAVAL NACIONAL

A little out of the way, the **Museo Histórico Naval Nacional** (Map p264; ☎ 51-91-43; cnr Av 60 & Calle 21; admission CUC$1; ⏱ 10am-6pm Tue-Fri, 9am-noon Sun) is housed in the former headquarters of the Distrito Naval del Sur (1950). It was here in September 1957 that a group of sailors

and civilians staged an unsuccessful uprising against the Batista government. The revolt is the central theme of the museum.

Activities

The **Marlin Marina Cienfuegos** (Base Náutica; Map p264; ☎ 55-12-41; cnr Av 8 & Calle 35; ⏱ 7am-5pm) is a 36-berth marina a few blocks north of Hotel Jagua. You can organize deep-sea fishing trips here for CUC$200 for four people for four hours. Multiday trips cost CUC$400/680 for one/two nights (gear and crew included). A classic bay cruise costs CUC$16 for the day or CUC$10 for a two-hour sunset cruise (stopping briefly at Castillo de Jagua). Book through Cubatur or Cubanacán (p265).

Nearby, in **Club Cienfuegos** (Map p264; ☎ 52-65-10; Calle 35 btwn Avs 10 & 12; ⏱ 9am-1am Sun-Fri, 9am-2am Sat), you can organize water sports including kayaking and windsurfing (there's a small dock out back). There's also a tennis court and a small amusement center with bumper cars, go-carts and video games.

If you're into billiards or bowling, go to **La Bolera** (Map p264; Calle 37 btwn Avs 46 & 48; per hr CUC$1-2; ⏱ 11am-2am), where there's an ice-cream parlor and occasional live music. Nonguests can use the beautiful Italianate **swimming pool** at Cubanacán Boutique La Unión on the corner of Av 54 and Calle 31 for CUC$5.

Courses

The **Universidad de Cienfuegos** (Map p272; ☎ 52-15-21; Carretera Las Rodas Km 4, Cuatro Caminos; www.ucf .edu.cu) offers Spanish courses for beginners to advanced. The courses last one month and incorporate 64 hours of study (CUC$340). It also offers courses in 'Cuban Culture' (CUC$340). Language courses run monthly, culture courses every other month. Check out its website for more details.

Tours

Cubanacán organizes some interesting local tours, including the three-hour **Along the Paths of the Orishas** (CUC$12) and the ever-popular **El Nicho** (p272) excursion (CUC$30, eight hours; includes lunch).

Festivals & Events

Local festivals in Cienfuegos include the cultural events marking the foundation of the city on April 22, 1819, the **Carnaval** in August and the **Benny Moré International Music Festival** in September of odd-numbered years.

Sleeping

Cienfuegos has a plethora of quality private rooms – your best bet for budget accommodation. Those at Punta Gorda are more removed, but generally more atmospheric. There are three excellent hotels in Cienfuegos proper, and a cheaper Islazul outfit a few kilometers to the east.

IN TOWN
Casas Particulares

Friendship Home – Armando & Leonor (Map p264; ☎ 51-61-43; Av 56 No 2927 btwn Calles 29 & 31; r CUC$20; **P** **⊠**) Friendship's the word in this venerable colonial house stuffed full of family heirlooms just off Parque Martí. Legendary food includes the exotic Cola chicken (yes, *pollo* cooked in the *real thing*). The chatty hosts offer two well-kept rooms and a lovely roof terrace reached via a spiral staircase.

Pepe & Isabel Martínez Cordero (Map p264; ☎ 51-82-76; Av 52 No 4318 btwn 43 & 45; r CUC$20-25; **⊠**) Run by two teachers in a colonial house near the bus station, there are two very clean rooms, a fountain out back and a guaranteed open-arms welcome.

Claudio & Ileana (Map p264; ☎ 51-97-74; Av 54 No 4121 btwn Calles 41 & 43; r CUC$20-25; **⊠**) Another hospitable couple renting a polished place with two bedrooms and all mod cons near the bus station and within walking distance of the Unesco-listed center.

Hotels

our pick **Cubanacán Boutique La Unión** (Cubanacán; Map p264; ☎ 45-10-20; cnr Av 54 & Calle 31; s/d CUC$80/100; **⊠** **⊠**) Barcelona, Naples, Paris? There are echoes of all of them in this plush colonial-style hotel with its European aspirations and splendid Italianate pool fit for a Roman emperor. Tucked away in a small maze of marble pillars, antique furnishings and two tranquil inner courtyards, are 46 well-furnished rooms with balconies either opening to the street or facing in over a colonial patio lined with mosaics. Service is refreshingly efficient and there's an airy roof terrace that showcases live salsa.

PUNTA GORDA
Casas Particulares

Vista Al Mar (Map p264; ☎ 51-83-78; www.vistaalmarcuba .com; Calle 37 No 210 btwn 2 & 4; r CUC$25; **P** **⊠**) It really is a *vista al mar* (sea view) – in fact, this highly professional casa has even got its own private scoop of beach out back with hammocks. The owners have great local knowledge and a website.

our pick **Villa Lagarto – Maylin & Tony** (Map p264; ☎ 51-99-66; Calle 35 No 4B btwn Avs 0 & Litoral; r CUC$30-35; **⊠** **⊠**) When your casa comes with a luxuriant Italianate swimming pool, you know you're onto something. Throw in welcome mojitos, swinging hammocks, king-sized beds, fine food, and a beautiful bayside setting and we're talking top 10 – in Cuba. If it's full (highly likely), no sweat; head next door to Villa Las Estancias (Calle 35 No 10), a gorgeous gingerbread beach house with one comfortable room up for grabs.

Angel & Isabel (Map p264; ☎ 51-15-19; Calle 35 No 24 btwn Av 0 & Litoral; r CUC$30-35; **⊠**) Two nicely furnished rooms and another of those waterfront Punta Gorda gardens with distant mountain views, Angel & Isabel's house is well worth the investment.

Hotels

Hostal Palacio Azul (Map p264; ☎ 58-28-28; Calle 37 No 201 btwn Avs 12 & 14; d/tr CUC$60/71; **P** **⊠**) This striking blue palace was built in 1921 and reopened as a seven-room (16 person capacity) hotel in 2004. One of the first big buildings to grace Punta Gorda, the hotel's huge rooms are named after flowers and, after a recent renovation, sparkle with plenty of prerevolutionary character. Other features include an intimate on-site restaurant called El Chelo and an eye-catching rooftop cupola with gorgeous views.

Hotel Jagua (Gran Caribe; Map p264; ☎ 55-10-03; Calle 37 No 1; s/d CUC$74/105; **P** **⊠** **⊠** **⊠**) It's not clear what Batista's brother had in mind when he erected this modern concrete giant on Punta Gorda in the 1950s, though making money was probably the prime motivation. That said the Jagua is actually a jolly good hotel; airy, hospital surgery–clean and surprisingly plush. Any lack of historical credentials is made up for with a whole host of other amenities including a fine restaurant, an inviting pool, large bright rooms, an in-house cabaret show and a fantastic bay-side setting. There's always at least one tour group staying here.

OUTSIDE TOWN

Hotel Punta La Cueva (Islazul; Map p272; ☎ 51-39-56; s/d CUC$21/28; **P** **⊠** **⊠**) After La Unión and the Jagua, Punta La Cueva is the city's Achilles heel – a scruffy Islazul place situated 3.5km outside town, east across the bay from Punta Gorda. The 67 rooms are a bit run-down, but cheap. There's a small beach, but it doesn't compensate for such a removed location.

Eating

IN TOWN

Polinesio (Map p264; Calle 29 btwn Calles 54 & 56; snacks CUC$2-4) Qualifies in the 'OK for a snack' bracket by right of its fine location under the portals on the eastern side of Parque Martí.

Teatro Café Tomás (Map p264; Av 56 No 2703 btwn Calles 27 & 29) Cafe, souvenir stall and nightly music venue, this delightful place wedged between the Teatro Tomás Terry and the neoclassical Colegio San Lorenzo is the best place to flop down and observe the morning exercisers in Parque Martí. The flower canopy–covered patio to the side comes alive in the evenings with *trova* (traditional singing) duos.

Dinos Pizza (Map p264; ☎ 51-12-26; Calle 31 No 5418 btwn Avs 54 & 56; ☻ noon-3pm & 6pm-midnight) Locals will point you in the direction of this reliable government chain opposite Cubanacán Boutique La Unión with pizzas starting at CUC$4 (with toppings such as mushrooms, black olives and sausage, no less!) and lasagna at CUC$7. The big salads, bruschetta and soups ought to satisfy vegetarians tired of the tortillas.

Paladar El Criollito (Map p264; Calle 33 btwn Avs 56 & 58) You'll feel like you're eating in someone's front room – probably because you are. El Criollito is a salt-of-the-earth, old-school paladar: a decent no-frills family-run restaurant business that makes do with limited ingredients and not a lot of encouragement (or help) from the government. Standard fish and meat meals are plentiful, if not memorable.

1869 Restaurant (Map p264; cnr Av 54 & Calle 31; mains CUC$10; ☻ breakfast, lunch & dinner) Cienfuegos' best city-center dining experience can be found in this elegant restaurant in the La Unión hotel (p267). Although the food doesn't quite match the lush furnishings, a varied international menu makes a welcome change from rice/beans/pork staples offered elsewhere.

Mercado Municipal (Map p264; Calle 31 No 5805 btwn Avs 58 & 60) If you feel like cooking or having a picnic, head to the market for fruits and vegetables in pesos.

For a quick stand-up breakfast, try the **Casa del Batido** (Map p264; Calle 37 No 5211 btwn Avs 52 & 54; ☻ 6am-11pm) on the Prado, where you can sip banana and papaya fruitshakes with work-bound locals for one peso. The ubiquitous **Doña Neli** (Map p264; cnr Calle 41 & Av 62; ☻ 9am-10:15pm) dispatches pastries and bread in Convertibles. **Coppelia** (Map p264; cnr Calle 37 & Av 52) practically gives away its ice cream for two pesos a scoop.

PUNTA GORDA

Restaurante El Cochinito (Map p264; ☎ 51-86-11; Calle 37 & Av 4; ☻ noon-3pm & 7-10pm, closed Tue) Cheap pork for tight budgets.

Restaurante Covadonga (Map p264; ☎ 59-64-20; Calle 37 btwn Avs 2 & 0) Legend has it that Castro and his guerrillas ate here in January 1959 during their triumphant march to Havana. The food probably tasted delicious after two years up in the Sierra Maestra but, if you've just flown in from Canada, you may not appreciate the rubbery fish. Enjoy a relaxing sunset cocktail and see if the paella's on offer. If not, head elsewhere.

Club Cienfuegos (Map p264; ☎ 51-28-91; Calle 37 btwn Avs 10 & 12; ☻ noon-3pm & 6-9pm) With a setting this good, it's easy for the food to fall short, which it often does. But there are plenty of options here, with the Bar Terraza for cocktails and chicken sandwiches; El Marinero, a 1st-floor seafood establishment; and Restaurante Café Cienfuegos, a more refined adventurous place up on the top floor where you'll pay CUC$10 for a steak and CUC$6 for a fine paella. The yacht-club vibe and wraparound dining terraces make for a memorable experience even if the food doesn't.

Palacio de Valle (Map p264; ☎ 51-12-26; cnr Calle 37 & Av 2; ☻ 10am-10pm) While the food doesn't have as many decorative flourishes as the eclectic architecture, the setting is so unique it would be a shame to miss it. Seafood dominates the menu downstairs, but if you still aren't convinced on the quality, eat in the La Jagua next door and use the rooftop bar here for a predinner cocktail or a postdinner cigar.

Drinking

Bar Terrazas (Map p264; ☎ 45-10-20; cnr Av 54 & Calle 31) Cienfuegos was built with the word refinement in mind and you can recreate it here with a mojito upstairs at the Cubanacán Boutique La Unión; live music starts at 10pm. Other excellent drinking perches (especially at sunset) can be found at Club Cienfuegos (p265) and the Palacio de Valle (p265).

El Palatino (Map p264; ☎ 55-12-44; Av 54 No 2514) Liquid lunches were invented with El Palatino in mind – a dark-wood bar set in one of the city's oldest buildings on the southern side of salubrious Parque Martí. Impromptu jazz sets sometimes erupt, but be prepared to be hit up for alms at the end of song number three.

Entertainment
LIVE MUSIC
ourpick Jardines de Uneac (Map p264; ☎ 51-61-17; Calle 25 No 5413 btwn Avs 54 & 56; admission CUC$2) Uneac's a good bet in any Cuban city for its laid-back unpretentious vibe and Cienfuegos is no exception. In fact, this is quite possibly the city's best music venue with a salubrious outdoor patio hosting Afro-Cuban *peñas* (musical performances), *trova* and top local bands such as the perennially popular Los Novos.

Centro Recreativo JA Mella (Map p264; ☎ 55-23-20; Calle 37 btwn Avs 4 & 6) The former Casa de la Música has toned down its act considerably since its conversion into a rec center (much to the relief of many of the tinnitus-suffering local residents); but you can still catch the occasional Disco Temba ('70s and '80s music) here.

Los Pinitos (Map p264; Calle 37 & Av 22) A playground for kids during the day, Los Pinitos matures tenfold by nightfall with decent weekend music shows that have a Benny Moré bias.

Patio de ARTex (Map p264; ☎ 55-12-55; cnr Calle 35 & Av 16) A highly recommendable patio in Punta Gorda where you can catch *son* (Cuba's popular music), salsa, *trova* and a touch of Benny Moré nostalgia live in the evenings as you mingle with true Cienfuegueños.

Café Cantante Benny Moré (Map p264; cnr Av 54 & Calle 37) This is where you might get some suave Benny tunes, especially after hours. A restaurant by day this place undergoes

a metamorphosis in the evenings when it mixes up mean cocktails and tunes into live traditional music.

DANCE CLUBS
El Benny (Map p264; ☎ 55-11-05; Av 54 No 2907 btwn Calles 29 & 31; admission per couple CUC$8; 🕙 10pm-3am Tue-Sun) It's difficult to say what the 'Barbarian of Rhythm' would have made of this disco/club named in his honor. Bring your dancing shoes, stock up on the rum and Cokes and come prepared for more techno than Benny Moré.

Two open-air venues with a more traditional Cuban vibe are the feisty **Tropisur** (Map p264; cnr Calle 37 & Av 48; 🕙 Sat only), on the Prado, and **Cabaret Costasur** (Map p264; Av 40 btwn Calles 33 & 35; 🕙 Fri & Sat), whose beat has been known to rattle buildings on Saturday nights. **Club Cienfuegos** (Map p264; ☎ 51-28-91; Calle 37 btwn Avs 10 & 12) has some good salsa on the terrace as does the rooftop bar at **Cubanacán Boutique La Unión** (Cubanacán; Map p264; ☎ 45-10-20; cnr Av 54 & Calle 31). The **Cabaret Guanaroca** (Map p264; Calle 37 No 1; admission CUC$5; 🕙 9:30pm Tue-Fir, 10pm Sat) in the Hotel Jagua offers a more professional tourist-orientated show.

THEATER
ourpick Teatro Tomás Terry (Map p264; ☎ 51-33-61; Av 56 No 270 btwn Calles 27 & 29) Worth a visit in its own right, you'll really get to appreciate this architectural showpiece if you come for a concert or play; the box office is open 11am to 3pm daily and 90 minutes before show time.

The **Casa de la Cultura Benjamin Duarte** (Map p264; Calle 25 No 5403), on Parque Martí, offers various events to match its grandiose setting, while the **Biblioteca Roberto García Valdés** (Map p264; Calle 37 No 5615) holds classical-music concerts, discussions on Martí and flamenco-inspired searches for *duende*.

CINEMAS
It's a three-way choice in Cienfuegos. Check the movie schedules on display at any of the following: **Cine-Teatro Luisa** (Map p264; Calle 37 No 5001); **Cine Prado** (Map p264; Calle 37 No 5402); and **Cine-Teatro Guanaroca** (Map p264; cnr Calle 49 & Av 58), opposite the bus station.

SPORT
From October to April, the provincial baseball team – nicknamed Los Camaroneros (the Shrimpers) – plays matches at **Estadio 5 de Septiembre** (Map p264; ☎ 51-36-44; Av 20 btwn Calles

45 & 55). Its best ever national series finish was fourth in 1979. Weekend box testing matches and other sporting events occur at Polivalente.

Shopping

Cienfuegos' main drag – known officially as Calle 54, but colloquially as El Bulevar – is a quintessential Cuban shopping street with not a chain store in sight. The best traffic-free stretch runs from Calle 37 (Prado) to Parque Martí and is chock-a-block with shops of all shapes and sizes.

Check out the **Maroya Gallery** (Map p264; Av 54 btwn Calles 25 & 27) for folk art, **Variedades Cienfuegos** (Map p264; cnr Av 54 & Calle 33) for peso paraphernalia or **Casa del Habano 'El Embajador'** (Map p264; cnr Av 54 & Calle 33) for cigars.

Photo Service Jagua (Map p264; Av 54 No 3118 btwn Calles 31 & 33; 8am-10pm) is well stocked with digital cameras, lithium batteries and Agfa film.

Getting There & Away

AIR

Jaime González Airport, 5km northeast of Cienfuegos, receives weekly international flights from Toronto and Montreal. There are no connections to Havana.

BUS

The **bus station** (☎ 51-57-20) is on Calle 49 between Avs 56 and 58. There are Víazul buses to Havana twice a day (CUC$20, four to five hours, 9:10am and 4:30pm) and Trinidad twice a day (CUC$6, one hour 35 minutes, 1:20pm and 5:10pm). The 4:30pm Havana bus also stops at Playa Girón (just outside the Villa Playa Girón) at 6:15pm (CUC$12). To reach any other destinations you have to connect in Trinidad or Havana. Cienfuegos' bus station is clean and well organized. It also offers cheap and safe luggage storage (CUC$1 per item). Bus tickets must be purchased from the *jefe de turno* (shift manager) downstairs.

For local buses to Rancho Luna (CUC$1) or Pasacaballo (CUC$1), check the blackboard on the lower level.

TRAIN

The **train station** (☎ 52-54-95; cnr Av 58 & Calle 49; ticket window 8am-3:30pm Mon-Fri, 8am-11:30am Sat) is across from the bus station. Trains are often canceled. When they do run, trains travel to Havana (CUC$9.50, 10 hours, daily), Santa Clara (CUC$2.10, two hours, two daily) and Sancti Spíritus (CUC$5.20, five hours, two daily).

Getting Around

BOAT

When there's fuel, a 120-passenger ferry runs to the Castillo de Jagua (CUC$1, 40 minutes) from the **Muelle Real** (Map p264; cnr Av 46 & Calle 25). Take note – this is a Cuban commuter boat, not a sunset cruise. Check at the port for current schedules. It's supposed to run three times a day in each direction. A

DAY-TRIPPER

The settlement of **Santa Isabel de las Lajas**, a few kilometers west of Cruces on the Cienfuegos–Santa Clara road, was where Bartolomé (Benny) Moré was born on August 24, 1919 (see boxed text, p273). Easily accessible in a half-day trip from Cienfuegos, this pleasant village hosts the biannual **Benny Moré International Music Festival** every other September. Curiosities include a **Municipal Museum** with assorted Moré memorabilia and the **Casino de los Congos**, a music venue where you can view *tambores* (drums) and Santería rituals in the hallowed confines of where the self-styled Bárbaro del Ritmo (Barbarian of Rhythm) allegedly banged his first drum.

On the way back you may want to stop off briefly in the town of **Cruces** on the Santa Clara road. This settlement was the site of one of the most important battles of the Independence Wars in 1895 – the historic Battle of Mal Tiempo – in which Mambí generals Antonio Maceo and Máximo Gómez inflicted a crushing defeat on the Spanish forces. A needlelike **obelisk** in the middle of a pleasant colonial park commemorates the great battle. The park was declared a national monument in 1981.

Also worth a visit is **Palmira**, 8km north of Cienfuegos, a town famous for its Santería brotherhoods including the societies of Cristo, San Roque and Santa Barbara. Further information can be procured at the centrally located **Museo Municipal de Palmira** (☎ 54-45-33; admission CUC$1; 10am-6pm Tue-Sat).

better bet is the smaller ferry that makes the short hop between the Castillo and the Hotel Pasacaballo (right).

CAR & MOPED

Club Cienfuegos (Map p264; ☎ 52-65-10; Calle 37 btwn Avs 10 & 12) hires mopeds for CUC$24 per day. **Cubacar** (Hotel Rancho Luna Map p272; ☎ 54-80-26; Carretera de Rancho Luna Km 16; Hotel Unión Map p264; ☎ 55-16-45; cnr Av 51 & Calle 31; Punta Gorda Map p264; ☎ 55-20-14; Hotel Jagua) hires cars.

The Servi-Cupet gas station is on Calle 37 at the corner of Av 16, in Punta Gorda. There's another station 5km northeast of Hotel Rancho Luna.

HORSE CARTS

Horse carts and bici-taxis ply Calle 37 charging Cubans one peso a ride, foreigners CUC$1 (though Spanish speakers might be able to 'pass' and pay a peso). It's a pleasant way to travel between town and Punta Gorda.

TAXI

There are plenty of cabs in Cienfuegos. Most hang around outside Hotel Jagua and Cubanacán Boutique La Unión, or linger around the bus station. If you get no luck there phone **Cubataxi** (☎ 51-91-45).

RANCHO LUNA

Rancho Luna is a small but picturesque beach resort 18km south of Cienfuegos close to the jaws of the eponymous bay. It has three large hotels, but it's also possible to stay in private rooms here, one of the few resort areas in Cuba where this is allowed. Protected by a coral reef, the coast is good for snorkeling and close to the hotels you'll also find what, arguably, is Cuba's best *delfinario* (dolphin park). The local post office is in Hotel Rancho Luna. In the small village facing Hotel Club Amigo Faro Luna you'll find a handful of casas particulares and a beach bar.

Sights & Activities

Like most Cuban resort areas, Rancho Luna has its **Delfinario** (Map p272; ☎ 54-81-20; adult/child CUC$10/6; ⏱ 9am-5pm Tue-Sun) – actually one of Cuba's better ones – where you can see dolphins jump through hoops or swim with them for a rip-off CUC$50.

It is possible to organize **scuba diving** with the dive centers at Hotels Rancho Luna and Club Amigo Faro Luna, which visit 30 sites

ASK A LOCAL

Rancho Luna is one of Cuba's most low-key resorts and a great place to chill out. The hotels here are popular with Canadians who come to study on two-week Spanish immersion courses with www.edutourstocuba .com.

Carmen, Cienfuegos

within a 20-minute boat ride. Caves, sunken ships, profuse marine life and dazzling coral gardens are among the attractions. From November to February harmless whale sharks frequent these waters. For more details check out **Cubanacán Náutica** (☎ 54-80-40; Hotel Club Amigo Faro Luna, Carretera de Rancho Luna Km 18; dives CUC$30, open water certification CUC$365) and **Whale Shark** (☎ 54-80-12; mpsolcfg@ip.etecsa.cu; Hotel Rancho Luna, Carretera de Rancho Luna Km 16; 1/2 dives from CUC$30/40, night dives CUC$36).

Sleeping

Hotel Pasacaballo (Islazul; Map p272; ☎ 54-80-13; Carretera de Rancho Luna Km 22; s/d CUC$34/45; P ⏺ ⏺) A five-story monster sitting on a headland opposite the Castillo de Jagua, this Islazul offering is as architecturally ugly as the rest of the scenery. Shoe-stringers only!

Hotel Club Amigo Faro Luna (Cubanacán; Map p272; ☎ 54-80-30; Carretera de Rancho Luna Km 18; s/d all-inclusive CUC$100; P ⏺ ⏺) This intimate resort on a bluff overlooking the sea is the best on the beach. Not all rooms are the same and the newer units in the 200 and 300 blocks have bathtubs. The swimming pool (with separate children's unit) is sweet and the food buffet is surprisingly good. A long beach is only a few minutes' walk away.

Hotel Rancho Luna (Cubanacán; Map p272; ☎ 54-81-31; Carretera de Rancho Luna Km 17.5; s/d all-inclusive CUC$100; P ⏺ ⏺) This beachfront resort – now linked to the Faro Luna in a Cubanacán *complejo* (complex) – is a favorite among Canadian package tourists, who dig the all-inclusive deal, private beach and big pool. A horse and buggy can be hired for rides along the coast.

Recommended casas particulares in Rancho Luna:

'Villa Sol' – Diana Gavio Caso (☎ 0152-27-24-48; Carretera Faro Luna; r CUC$20-30) On the approach road to Hotel Faro Luna. Beautiful house overlooking the ocean; bougainvillea in the garden.

Casa de Julio (☎ 51-57-44; Carretera de Faro Luna; r CUC$25) Last (blue) house on left before Hotel Faro Luna. Nice setting.

Eating

Aside from the hotels, your dining options are limited. Try the beach snack bar or one of the private houses that rent rooms. The Servi-Cupet gas station 5km north of town serves microwave pizza 24 hours a day.

Getting There & Away

Theoretically, there are local buses from Cienfuegos seven times a day. Equally sporadic is the Jagua ferry to Cienfuegos, which calls at the dock directly below Hotel Pasacaballo several times daily. More reliable is a taxi; a one-way fare to Cienfuegos should cost around CUC$8 to CUC$10 – bargain hard.

An even better way to get here is zipping along from Cienfuegos on a rented moped.

CASTILLO DE JAGUA

Predating the city of Cienfuegos by nearly a century, the **Castillo de Nuestra Señora de los Ángeles de Jagua** (Map p272; admission CUC$1; ☑ 8am-4pm), to the west of the mouth of Bahía de Cienfuegos, was designed by José Tontete in 1738 and completed in 1745. At the time it was the third most important fortress in Cuba, after those of Havana and Santiago de Cuba. Built to keep pirates (and the British) out, the castle now shelters a modest museum and boasts a pleasant bayside view.

You can get to the castle via a passenger ferry from Cienfuegos, but it's easier to take a smaller ferry from a landing just below the Hotel Pasacaballo. It operates frequently throughout the day, charging one peso one-way. Tourists pay CUC$1. The Cienfuegos ferry is similarly cheap but takes almost an hour.

JARDÍN BOTÁNICO DE CIENFUEGOS

The 94-hectare **botanic garden** (Map p272; admission CUC$5; ☑ 8am-5pm), near the Pepito Tey sugar mill, 17km east of Cienfuegos, is one of Cuba's biggest gardens. It houses 2000 species of plants, including 23 types of bamboo, 65 of fig and 280 different palms. The botanic garden was founded in 1901 by US sugar baron Edwin F Atkins who initially intended to use it to study different varieties of sugarcane, but instead began planting exotic tropical trees from around the world.

To reach the gardens you'll need a hire car or taxi. The cheapest method is to go with an organized excursion; Cubanacán (p265) in Cienfuegos runs trips for CUC$10. Drivers coming from Cienfuegos should turn right (south) at the junction to Pepito Tey.

EL NICHO

While Cienfuegos province's share of the verdant Escambray Mountains is extensive (and includes the range's highest summit, 1156m Pico de San Juan), access is limited to a small protected area around **El Nicho** (Map p262; admission CUC$5; ☑ 8:30am-6:30pm), an outpost of the Topes de Collantes Natural Park managed by Gaviota.

El Nicho is actually the name of a beautiful waterfall on the Río Hanabanilla, but the area also offers a 1.5km nature trail (Reino de las Aguas), swimming in natural pools, caves, excellent bird-watching opportunities, camping and a *ranchón*-style Palmares restaurant.

Getting to El Nicho can be problematic unless you are partaking in an organized excursion. The 55km journey from Cienfuegos via a rough road through Crucecitas is only negotiable in a 4WD, a vehicle you can rent

CIENFUEGOS AREA

0 ——— 3 km
0 ——— 2 miles

To Autopista Nacional (34km)

Río Salado

To Santa Clara (50km) · Palmira · San Fernando de Camarones

Río Caunao

Caunao · To Cumanayagua (9km)

Jaime González Airport

Bahía de Cienfuegos · Cienfuegos · Pepito Tey · Guaos

See Cienfuegos Map (p264)

San Antón

Arimao

Río Arimao

To Trinidad (38km)

La Corona El Coral, El Laberinto, Camaronero 2, El Bajo · Playa Rancho Luna · Punta Gavilán

CARIBBEAN SEA

SIGHTS & ACTIVITIES
Castillo de Jagua......1	A2
Delfinario......2	A2
Jardín Botánico de Cienfuegos......3	B2
Necrópolis Tomás Acea......4	A2

Universidad de Cienfuegos......5 A1

SLEEPING 🏠
Hotel Club Amigo Faro Luna......6	A2
Hotel Pasacaballo......7	A2
Hotel Punta La Cueva......8	A2
Hotel Rancho Luna......9	A2

TRANSPORT
Ferry to Castillo de Jagua......10	A2

for a stiff CUC$85 a day from Cubacar (p271). The twice-daily truck that serves the small local community leaves at ridiculously inconvenient hours meaning your best bet is the eight-hour day tour from Cienfuegos that costs $30 (book through the excellent Cubanacán office).

THE CARIBBEAN COAST

Heading east toward Trinidad, postcard views of the Escambray Mountains loom ever closer until their ruffled foothills almost engulf the coast road. Hidden coral reefs offshore offer excellent diving.

Sights & Activities

On the main road approximately 8km east of Villa Guajimico, the bucolic **Hacienda La Vega** is a small cattle farm surrounded by fruit trees with an attached Palmares restaurant. After the city, it's a good place to relax over a shady lunch. Unhurried travelers can hire horses and scamper down to a nearby beach called Caleta de Castro.

The **Cueva Martín Infierno** in the Valle de Yaganabo, 56km from Cienfuegos via the shore hamlet of Caleta de Muñoz, contains a 67m stalagmite said to be the world's tallest. This cave is not always open for general

---

BENNY MORÉ

No one singer encapsulates the full gamut of Cuban music more eloquently than Bartolomé 'Benny' Moré, a legendary vocalist and showman who blended African rhythms and Spanish melodies with effortless ease, and successfully mastered every musical genre of his age.

Born in the small village of Santa Isabel de las Lajas in Cienfuegos province in 1919, Moré gravitated to Havana in 1936 where he earned a precarious living selling damaged fruit on the streets of Cuba's swinging capital. Saving up enough cash to buy a cheap guitar, he graduated to playing and singing in the smoky bars and restaurants of Habana Vieja's tough dockside neighborhood where he passed the hat and made just enough money to get by.

His first big break came in 1943 when his velvety voice and pitch-perfect delivery won him first prize in a local radio singing competition and landed him a regular job as lead vocalist for a Havana-based mariachi band called the Cauto Quartet.

His meteoric rise was confirmed two years later when, while singing at a regular gig in Havana's El Temple bar, he was spotted by Siro Rodríguez of the famed Trío Matamoros, then Cuba's biggest son-bolero band. Rodríguez was so impressed by what he heard and saw that he asked Moré to join the band as lead vocalist for an imminent tour of Mexico.

In the late 1940s, Mexico City was a proverbial Hollywood for young Spanish-speaking Cuban performers and Moré wasted no time in making a name for himself. Staying behind when the rest of the band returned home, he was promptly signed up by RCA records and his fame rapidly spread.

Moré returned to Cuba in 1950 a star, and was quickly baptized the Prince of Mambo and the Barbarian of Rhythm by an adoring public who claimed him as their own. Never one to rest on his laurels, he kept obsessively busy in the ensuing years, inventing a brand new hybrid sound called batanga and putting together his own 40-piece backing orchestra, the explosive Banda Gigante. Along with the Banda, Moré toured Venezuela, Jamaica, Mexico and the US in 1956–57, culminating with a performance at the 1957 Oscars ceremony. But the singer's real passion was always Cuba and, from Santiago to Cienfuegos, his beloved countrymen couldn't get enough of him. Indeed, legend has it that whenever Benny performed in Havana's Centro Gallego hundreds of people would fill the parks and streets around the Capitolio in the hope of hearing him sing.

With his multitextured voice and signature scale-sliding glissando, Moré's real talent lay in his ability to adapt and seemingly switch genres at will. As comfortable with a tear-jerking bolero as he was with a hip-gyrating rumba, Moré could convey tenderness, exuberance, emotion and soul, all in the space of five tantalizing minutes. Although he couldn't read music, Moré composed many of his most famous numbers, including 'Bonito y Sabroso' and the big hit 'Que Bueno Baila Usted.' When he died in 1963 of cirrhosis of the liver brought on by a lifelong penchant for rum, more than 100,000 people turned up at his funeral. Not surprisingly, no one in Cuba has yet been able to fill his shoes.

CIENFUEGOS PROVINCE

NUCLEAR GHOSTS

Gaze wistfully across the placid Bay of Cienfuegos from Punta Gorda on a clear summer's evening and you'll spot an incongruous-looking silver dome glistening on the opposite shoreline. This semiabandoned architectural oddity is the infamous Juragua nuclear power plant; a joint government venture between Cuba and the Soviet Union that was conceived in 1976, but which – to date – has never reached completion.

Dogged by controversy from its inception, Juragua was originally designed to accommodate two 440-megawatt nuclear reactors that would ultimately power 15% of Cuba's energy needs. But, situated just 288km from Florida Keys, the plan quickly came up against strong opposition in the US where the federal government cited it as a national-security issue and voiced valid safety concerns in the light of the 1986 Chernobyl disaster.

Fatefully, thanks to the collapse of communism in Eastern Europe, a US-Iranian-style nuclear standoff was never reached. Construction at Juragua began in earnest in 1983 but by 1992, with the USSR disbanded and the Cuban economy in freefall, the project was put on hold with work on the first reactor nearly 90% complete. With US$800 million required to finish the project, the Cubans tried vainly to revive Juragua in the ensuing years but in 1997 the plan was shelved indefinitely.

Today Juragua's dome sits frozen in time, towering over the disused apartment blocks of the Ciudad Nuclear, the city that never was – and probably never will be. It takes a sizeable workforce just to keep the plant from deteriorating, but foreigners can't visit: the site is well guarded and best left to the salvage crews, a testament to Cuba's thwarted nuclear ambitions.

---

tourism. Check with Cubanacán (p265) in Cienfuegos first. The valley is also a good bird-watching area.

Unusually for a campismo, Villa Guajimico has its own **Dive Center** (☎ 54-09-46) serving 16 dive sites situated atop an offshore coral ridge. Dive packages with five immersions go for CUC$125.

Sleeping & Eating

Villa Yaguanabo (Islazul; Map p262; ☎ 54-00-99; Carretera de Trinidad Km 55; s/d CUC$20/26) Twenty-six kilometers west of Trinidad and 52km east of Cienfuegos, the Yaguanabo has 30 nicely situated Islazul cabins and offers horseback riding, boating on the Yaguanabo

River as well as short walks along the Villa Yaguanabo trail.

our pick **Villa Guajimico** (Cubamar; Map p262; ☎ 54-09-46; Carretera de Trinidad Km 42; s/d CUC$22/36; P ❄ ⑬) This is one of Cubamar's most luxurious campismos and the 51 attractive cabins and idyllic seaside setting could easily compete with a medium-priced (three-star) hotel. The villa is a nexus for scuba divers and also offers bike hire, car rental, various catamaran/kayaking options and a couple of short hiking trails. It is also a fully equipped Campertour site.

Both accommodations have restaurants, but there's a nicer option at Hacienda La Vega nearby (p273).

Villa Clara Province

He wasn't born here, never lived here and died thousands of miles away in the remote mountains of Bolivia, yet cocksure Villa Clara will always be synonymous with Che Guevara, its proudly adopted Argentine son.

For many people, the Che connection is the only reason to visit this undulating and surprisingly diverse province. But Villa Clara existed long before history's most marketable *guerrillero* rolled into the city of Santa Clara and sabotaged an armored train.

Known formerly as Las Villas province, the land wedged between the Escambray Mountains and Cuba's northern keys is a pretty pastiche of misty tobacco fields and placid lakes, originally colonized by farmers from the Canary Islands. Emerging above the coastal plains is Remedios, the region's oldest settlement, a tranquil, picturesque town whose somnolence is rudely interrupted every December by a rousing, cacophonous firework party known locally as Las Parrandas.

Stuck in the middle and long an important junction for cross-country travelers, the city of Santa Clara hides a sharp youthful energy beneath its grandiose Che veneer. Home of the most prestigious university outside Havana, the social scene here is animated and cutting edge with a nightlife that includes Cuba's first (and only) official drag show.

To the south the lofty peaks of the Escambray glimmer with outdoor adventure possibilities. Access here is by boat across Cuba's largest upland lake, the mirror-like Lago Hanabanilla, stocked to the brim with largemouth bass.

North is the Cayerías del Norte, the island's newest and fastest-growing tourist resort, though a network of flora and fauna reserves and the presence of the adjacent Buena Vista Unesco Biosphere Reserve have meant that development has been relatively sustainable – so far.

HIGHLIGHTS

- **Che City** Trace the legend of Ernesto 'Che' Guevara in Santa Clara's mausoleum (p279) and Tren Blindado (p279)

- **Quiet Corner** Relax beneath the louvers in the unspoiled colonial pocket of Remedios (p285)

- **Nights on the Town** Plug into the electric nightlife in Santa Clara's Club Mejunje (p283)

- **Witches Villa** Find plenty of magic but no *brujas* (witches) at Villa Las Brujas (p289)

- **Cuban Cure** Submerge yourself in the sulfur springs at Baños de Elguea (p290)

Baños de Elguea ★

Villa Las Brujas ★

Remedios ★

Santa Clara ★

- TELEPHONE CODE: 042
- POPULATION: 817,070
- AREA: 8662 SQ KM

VILLA CLARA PROVINCE

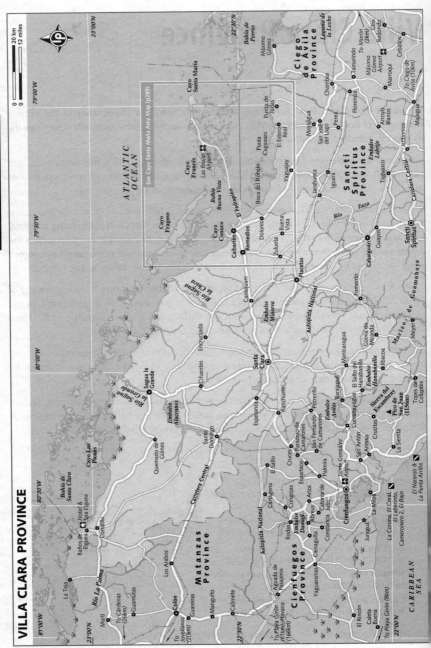

History

Located strategically in the island's geographical center, Villa Clara has long been a focal point for corsairs, colonizers and revolutionaries intent on slicing the country divisively in two. Pirates were a perennial headache in the early years, with the province's first town, Remedios, being moved twice and then abandoned altogether in the late 1600s by a group of families who escaped inland to what is now Santa Clara. Later the population was diluted further by emigrant Canary Islanders who brought their agricultural know-how and distinctive lilting Spanish accents to the tobacco fields of the picturesque Vuelta Arriba region. In December 1958 Ernesto 'Che' Guevara – aided by a motley crew of scruffy *barbudas* (bearded ones) – masterfully orchestrated the fall of the city of Santa Clara, by derailing an armored train carrying more than 350 government troops and weaponry to the east. The victory rang the death knell for Fulgencio Batista's grisly dictatorship and the triumph of Cuba's nationalistic Revolution.

Parks & Reserves

Villa Clara's northern keys – part of the Sabana-Camagüey Archipelago – are heavily protected in a patchwork of flora and fauna reserves. Much of the marine area to the east falls inside the Buenavista Unesco Biosphere Reserve.

Getting There & Around

Located in the center of the island, Santa Clara has excellent transport connections heading east or west. Daily Víazul buses pass through to and from Trinidad, Varadero, Havana and Santiago via Camagüey and Bayamo. The fast Tren Francés stops in Santa Clara, as do numerous slower trains. Both Remedios and Caibarién are accessible via local bus or train. The Cayerías del Norte and Lago Hanabanilla are hard to reach without your own wheels or a taxi.

SANTA CLARA

pop 210,680

Che city has long been hallowed turf for hero-worshiping, beret-wearing Guevara buffs, but away from the bombastic monuments lies a less evident Cuban essence. Santa Clara isn't pretty like Trinidad or particularly cosmopolitan like Matanzas, but it does boast Cuba's second most prestigious university, a feature that lends it academic airs and a brash, youthful vitality. Upbeat and full of life, this is a city that gradually crawls under your skin the longer you stay.

History

Christopher Columbus believed that Cubanacán (or Cubana Khan; an Indian name that meant 'the middle of Cuba'), an Indian village once located near Santa Clara, was the seat of the khans of Mongolia; hence, his misguided notion that he was exploring the Asian coast. Santa Clara proper was founded in 1689 by 13 families from Remedios who were tired of the unwanted attention of passing pirates. The town grew quickly after a fire emptied Remedios in 1692, and in 1867 it became the capital of Las Villas province. A notable industrial center, Santa Clara was famous for its prerevolutionary Coca-Cola factory and its pivotal role in Cuba's island-wide communications network. Today it continues to support a textile mill, a marble quarry and the Constantino Pérez Carrodegua tobacco factory. Santa Clara was the first major city to be liberated from Batista's army in December 1958.

Orientation

Monuments relating to the 1958 battle for Santa Clara are on the east and west sides of the city. The train station is seven blocks north of Parque Vidal; the two bus stations are less conveniently located on the Carretera Central west of town.

In common with many Cuban cities, Santa Clara has a dual street-naming system: see p279 if you're confused.

Information

BOOKSTORES

Librería Viet Nam (Independencia Este btwn Plácido & Luis Estévez) Sells books in Convertibles and pesos.

INTERNET ACCESS & TELEPHONE

Dinos Pizza (Marta Abreu No 10 btwn Villuendas & Cuba; internet access per hr CUC$5) Three terminals.

Etecsa Telepunto (Marta Abreu No 55 btwn Máximo Gómez & Villuendas; internet access per hr CUC$6)

LIBRARIES

Biblioteca José Martí (Colón on Parque Vidal) Inside the stunning Palacio Provincial.

VILLA CLARA PROVINCE

SANTA CLARA

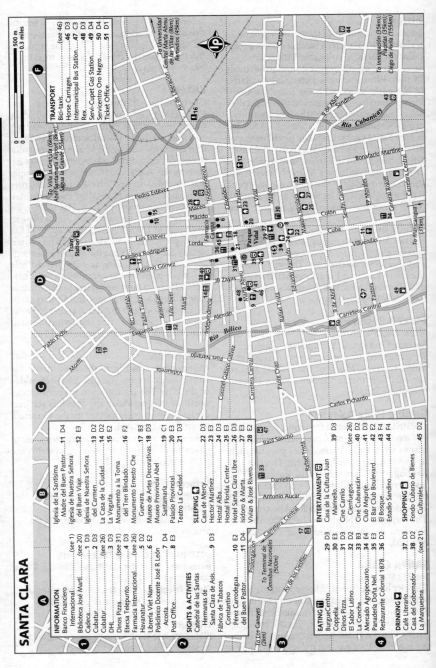

INFORMATION
Banco Financiero
Internacional..........................(see 1)
Biblioteca José Martí..............(see 20)
Cadeca....................................**1** D3
Cubatur..................................**2** D3
Cubatur..............................(see 26)
DHL...**3** D3
Dinos Pizza..........................(see 31)
Etecsa Telepunto.................**4** D3
Farmacia Internacional.....(see 26)
Havanatur.............................**5** D2
Librería Viet Nam..................**6** E2
Policlínico Docente José R León
Acosta....................................**7** D4
Post Office.............................**8** E3

SIGHTS & ACTIVITIES
Catedral de las Santas
Hermanas de
Santa Clara de Asís..............**9** D3
Fábrica de Tabacos
Constantino.......................**10** E2
Pérez Carrodegua...............**10** E2
del Buen Pastor...................**11** D4

Iglesia de la Santísima
Madre del Buen Pastor......**11** D4
Iglesia de Nuestra Señora
del Buen Viaje.....................**12** E3
Iglesia de Nuestra Señora
del Carmen...........................**13** D2
La Casa de la Ciudad...........**14** D2
La Veguita............................**15** E2
Monumento a la Toma
del Tren Blindado...............**16** F2
Monumento Ernesto Che
Guevara.................................**17** B3
Museo de Artes Decorativas..**18** D3
Museo Provincial Abel
Santamaría............................**19** C1
Palacio Provincial.................**20** E3
Teatro La Caridad..................**21** D3

SLEEPING
Casa de Mercy......................**22** D3
Hector Martínez....................**23** D3
Hostal Alba............................**24** D3
Hostal Florida Center............**25** E3
Hotel Santa Clara Libre........**26** D3
Isidoro & Marta......................**27** E3
Vivian & José Rivero............**28** E2

EATING
BurgueCentro.......................**29** D3
Coppelia...............................**30** E3
Dinos Pizza...........................**31** D3
El Sabor Latino......................**32** D2
La Concha..............................**33** B3
Mercado Agropecuario........**34** F4
Panadería Doña Neli............**35** E3
Restaurante Colonial 1878...**36** D2

DRINKING
Café Literario.......................**37** D3
Casa del Gobernador...........**38** D2
La Marquesina.....................(see 21)

ENTERTAINMENT
Casa de la Cultura Juan
Marinello..............................**39** D3
Cine Camilo
Cienfuegos.......................(see 26)
Cine Cubanacán...................**40** D2
Club Mejunje.......................**41** D3
El Bar Club Boulevard..........**42** E2
El Bosque..............................**43** F4
Estadio Sandino...................**44** F4

SHOPPING
Fondo Cubano de Bienes
Culturales.............................**45** D2

TRANSPORT
Bici-taxis.............................(see 46)
Horse Carriages....................**46** D3
Intermunicipal Bus Station...**47** C3
Rex.......................................**48** D3
Servi-Cupet Gas Station......**49** D4
Servicentro Oro Negro.........**50** D4
Ticket Office..........................**51** D1

MEDIA

Radio CMHW broadcasts on 840AM and 93.5FM. The *Vanguardia Santa Clara* newspaper is published Saturday.

MEDICAL SERVICES

Farmacia Internacional (Parque Vidal No 6; ☺ 9am-6pm) In the Hotel Santa Clara Libre.

Policlínico Docente José R León Acosta (☎ 20-22-44; Serafín García Oeste No 167 btwn Alemán & Carretera Central)

MONEY

Banco Financiero Internacional (☎ 20-74-50; Cuba No 6 cnr Rafael Tristá)

Cadeca (☎ 20-56-90; cnr Rafael Tristá & Cuba; ☺ 8:30am-6pm Mon-Sat, 8:30am-12:30pm Sun) On Parque Vidal.

POST

DHL (☎ 21-40-69; Cuba No 7 btwn Rafael Tristá & Eduardo Machado; ☺ 8am-6pm Mon-Sat, 8am-noon Sun)

Post office (Colón No 10; ☺ 8am-6pm Mon-Sat, 8am-noon Sun)

TRAVEL AGENCIES

Cubatur (☎ 20-89-80; Marta Abreu No 10; ☺ 9am-6pm) Near Máximo Gómez.

Havanatur (☎ 20-40-01; Máximo Gómez No 9B; ☺ 8:30am-noon & 1-5:30pm Mon-Fri, 8:30am-12:30pm Sat) Near Independencia.

Sights

MONUMENTO ERNESTO CHE GUEVARA

The site of many a Che 'pilgrimage,' this **monument, mausoleum & museum complex** (Av de los Desfiles; admission free; ☺ 8am-9pm Tue-Sat, to 6pm Sun), 2km west of Parque Vidal via Rafael Tristá, is in a vast square guarded by a bronze statue of 'El Che.' The statue was erected in 1987 to mark the 20th anniversary of Guevara's murder in Bolivia, and the sublime mausoleum below (entry from the rear) contains 38 stone-carved niches dedicated to the other guerillas killed in that failed revolutionary attempt. In 1997 the remains of 17 of them, including Guevara, were recovered from a secret mass grave in Bolivia and reburied in this memorial. Fidel Castro lit the eternal flame on October 17, 1997. The adjacent museum collects the details and ephemera of Che's life and death.

The best way to get to the monument (aside from walking) is to hop on a horse carriage in Calle Marta Abreu outside the Catedral for a

SANTA CLARA STREET NAMES	
Old name	**New name**
Candelaria	Maestra Nicolasa
Caridad	General Roloff
Nazareno	Serafín García
San Miguel	9 de Abril
Sindico	Morales

couple of pesos. The mausoleum and museum are shut on Mondays.

MONUMENTO A LA TOMA DEL TREN BLINDADO

History was made here on December 29, 1958, when Ernesto 'Che' Guevara and a band of 18 rifle-wielding revolutionaries barely out of their teens derailed an armored train using a borrowed bulldozer and some homemade Molotov cocktails. The battle lasted 90 minutes, and it effectively sealed the fate of the Batista dictatorship and ushered in 50 years of Fidel Castro. The event is remembered with a **boxcar museum** (admission CUC$1; ☺ 8am-6pm Tue-Fri) east on Independencia, just over the river, which marks the spot where the train derailed and ejected its 350 heavily armed government troops.

MUSEO PROVINCIAL ABEL SANTAMARÍA

Not actually a memorial to Señor Santamaría (Fidel's right-hand man at Moncada), but rather a small provincial **museum** (☎ 20-30-41; admission CUC$1; ☺ 9am-5pm Mon-Fri, to 1pm Sat) quartered in a former military barracks when Batista's troops surrendered to Che Guevara on January 1, 1959. It contains a room on natural history and a room dedicated to Cuban women throughout history. The museum is situated on a hilltop at the north end of Esquerra, just across the Río Bélico in Reparto Osvaldo Herrera.

FÁBRICA DE TABACOS CONSTANTINO PÉREZ CARRODEGUA

Santa Clara's **tobacco factory** (☎ 20-22-11; Maceo No 181 btwn Julio Jover & Berenguer; admission CUC$4; ☺ 7am-noon & 1-4pm) is one of the best in Cuba and makes a quality range of Montecristos, Partagás and Romeo y Julieta cigars. Tours here are lower key than in Havana and, as a result, the experience is a lot more interesting and less rushed. Rather than turn up you should book tickets through the Cubatur

VILLA CLARA PROVINCE

CHE COMANDANTE, AMIGO

Few 20th-century figures have successfully divided public opinion as deeply as Ernesto Guevara de la Serna, better known to his friends (and enemies) as 'El Che.' From enduring symbol of third-world freedom, to the celebrated hero of the Sierra Maestra, to the most wanted man on the CIA hit-list; the image of this handsome and often misunderstood Argentine physician-turned-*guerrillero* can still be seen all over Cuba, on everything from key rings to blow-up posters to chart-topping album covers. But what would the man himself have made of such rampant commercialization?

Born in Rosario, Argentina, in June 1928 to a bourgeois family of Irish-Spanish descent, Guevara was a delicate and sickly child who developed asthma at the age of two. It was an early desire to overcome this debilitating illness that instilled in the young Ernesto a willpower that would dramatically set him apart from other men.

A pugnacious competitor in his youth, Ernesto earned the name 'Fuser' at school for his combative nature on the rugby field. Graduating from the University of Buenos Aires in 1953 with a medical degree, he shunned a conventional medical career in favor of a cross-continental motorcycling odyssey, accompanied by his old friend and colleague Alberto Granado. Their nomadic wanderings – well documented in a series of posthumously published diaries – would open Ernesto's eyes to the grinding poverty and stark political injustices that were all too common in 1950s Latin America.

By the time Guevara arrived in Guatemala in 1954 on the eve of a US-backed coup against Jacobo Arbenz' leftist government, he was enthusiastically devouring the works of Marx and nurturing a deep-rooted hatred of the US. Deported to Mexico for his pro-Arbenz activities in 1955, Guevara fell in with a group of Cubans that included Moncada veteran Raúl Castro. Impressed by the Argentine's sharp intellect and never-failing political convictions, Raúl – a long-standing Communist party member himself – determined to introduce Che to his charismatic brother, Fidel.

office (p279). Across the street you'll find **La Veguita** (☎ 20-89-52; ⏰ 8:30am-5:30pm), the factory's diminutive sales outlet that is staffed by a friendly team of cigar experts. You can also buy cheap rum here and the bar out the back brews good coffee.

CHURCHES

Santa Clara's four main ecclesial buildings lie at compass points a few blocks from Parque Vidal. South of the center is the colonial-style **Iglesia de la Santísima Madre del Buen Pastor** (EP Morales No 4 btwn Cuba & Villuendas), while to the east lies **Iglesia de Nuestra Señora del Buen Viaje** (cnr Pedro Estévez & R Pardo), a riotous mix of Gothic, Romanesque and neoclassical architecture. The **Catedral de las Santas Hermanas de Santa Clara de Asís** (Marta Abreu), two blocks west of the square, was constructed amid huge controversy in 1923 after the demolition of Santa Clara's original church in Parque Vidal. It contains a fantastic collection of stained-glass windows and a mythical statue of Mother Mary known as *La Virgen del Camino* (Traveler's Virgin).

The city's oldest and most interesting church, the **Iglesia de Nuestra Señora del Carmen** (Carolina Rodríguez), four blocks north of Parque Vidal, was built in 1748, with a tower added in 1846. During the First War of Independence it was used as a jail for Cuban patriots. A modern cylindrical monument facing the church commemorates the spot where Santa Clara was founded in 1689 by 13 refugee families from Remedios.

LA CASA DE LA CIUDAD

The pulse of the city's progressive cultural life is at **La Casa de la Ciudad** (cnr Independencia & JB Zayas; admission CUC$1; ⏰ 8am-5pm), northwest of Parque Vidal. If you want to see another side to Santa Clara aside from the obligatory Che memorabilia, get chatting to the young artists here. The historic building hosts art expositions (including an original Wilfredo Lam sketch), Noches del Danzón and a film museum; but the real buzz of this place is hanging out with the local culture vultures and finding out what makes this most unprepossessing of Cuban cities tick.

Courses

Santa Clara boasts Cuba's second most prestigious university, **Universidad Central Marta**

The meeting between the two men at Maria Antonia's house in Mexico City in June 1955 lasted 10 hours and ultimately changed the course of history. Rarely had two characters needed each other as much as the hot-headed Castro and the calmer and more ideologically polished Che. Both were favored children from large families who shunned the quiet life to fight courageously for a revolutionary cause. Similarly, both men had little to gain and much to throw away by abandoning professional careers for what most would have regarded as narrow-minded folly. 'In a revolution one either wins or dies,' wrote Guevara prophetically years later, 'if it is a *real* one.'

In December 1956 Che left for Cuba on the *Granma* yacht, joining the rebels as the group medic. One of only 12 or so of the original 82 rebel soldiers to survive the catastrophic landing at Las Coloradas, he proved himself to be a brave and intrepid fighter who led by example and quickly won the trust of his less reckless Cuban comrades. As a result Castro rewarded him with the rank of Comandante in July 1957, and in December 1958 Che repaid Fidel's faith when he masterminded the battle of Santa Clara, an action that effectively sealed a historic revolutionary victory.

Guevara was granted Cuban citizenship in February 1959 and soon assumed a leading role in Cuba's economic reforms as president of the National Bank and minister of industry. His insatiable work ethic and regular appearance at enthusiastically organized volunteer worker weekends quickly saw him cast heroically as the living embodiment of Cuba's New Man.

But the honeymoon wasn't to last. Disappearing from the Cuban political scene in 1965, Guevara eventually materialized again in Bolivia in late 1966 at the head of a small band of Cuban *guerrilleros*. After the successful ambush of a Bolivian detachment in March 1967, he issued a call for 'two, three, many Vietnams in the Americas.' Such bold proclamations could only prove to be his undoing. On October 8, 1967, Guevara was captured by the Bolivian army, and after consultation with military leaders in La Paz and Washington DC, he was shot the next day in front of US advisors. His remains were eventually returned to Cuba in 1997 and reburied in Santa Clara.

Abreu de las Villas (☎ 28-14-10; www.uclv.edu.cu; Carretera de Camajuaní Km 5.5). Non-Cubans have, on occasion, been able to study Spanish here. Check the website for current details.

La Casa de la Ciudad (cnr Independencia & JB Zayas) is another good learning center. You might be able to pick up dancing and percussion lessons here if you probe hard.

Sleeping

IN TOWN

Casas Particulares

our pick **Hostal Florida Center** (☎ 20-81-61; Maestra Nicolasa Este No 56 btwn Colón & Maceo; r CUC$20-25; ⊠) The Florida is a national treasure. It boasts more antiques than the local decorative arts museum and serves better food than most Havana paladares (in a jaw-dropping central patio replete with plants). Your main dilemma is which room to choose: the grandiose colonial suite, or the gloriously retro art-deco digs?

Héctor Martínez (☎ 21-74-63; R Pardo No 8 btwn Maceo & Parque Vidal; r CUC$20-25; ⊠) Recline on a rocker on the patio counting the innumerable plants, ferns and blooming flowers. The two huge rooms have two beds (one double),

fridge, private bath and a writing/domino-playing table. A quiet haven just half a block from Parque Vidal.

Casa de Mercy (☎ 21-69-41; Eduardo Machado No 4 btwn Cuba & Colón; r CUC$20-25; ⊠) There are two rooms with private bath available in this beautiful family house with a terrace, a dining room, a multilingual library and a tempting cocktail menu. English, French and Italian are spoken.

Hostal Alba (☎ 29-41-08; Eduardo Machado No 7 btwn Cuba & Colón; r CUC$20-25; ⊠) Another architectural stunner with lovely antique beds, original tilework and a patio, serving amazing food and situated just one block from the main square.

Isidoro & Marta (☎ 20-38-13; Maestra Nicolasa No 74 btwn Colón & Maceo; r CUC$20-25; ⊠) This couple's more modern house is kept *muy limpia* (very clean). A long thin patio leads to two fine bedrooms with super-modern bathrooms. Breakfast and dinner is served.

Vivian & José Rivero (☎ 20-37-81; Maceo No 64 btwn Martí & Independencia; r CUC$20; ⊠) Two rooms with TV, fridge and private bath are available in this lovely colonial house dating from 1908. The unassuming front facade hides a

---

DOWNTIME IN PARQUE VIDAL

The old man in the starched-white *guayabera* shirt inhales deeply on his well-chewed cigar and lazily contemplates the weekend theater of Parque Vidal. It's Saturday evening and the whole town has come out to celebrate. An enterprising ice-cream vendor dispatches cheap peso cones from a tatty patched-together machine; an overworked goat pulls a cart of giggling children around leafy walkways in endless circuits; while, sheltered under a splendid gazebo, members from the local philharmonic band tune up their instruments ready for an impromptu early-evening concert.

Tempered by the gentle rhythms of daily life, there are few places on the archipelago as quintessentially Cuban as Parque Vidal. Named for Colonel Leoncio Vidal y Caro, who was killed here on March 23, 1896, the park is shaded by palm trees and embellished by monuments to noted city luminaries. There's a noble statue of the valiant Vidal, another of local philanthropist Marta Abreu (who helped finance the Teatro La Caridad) and a third depicting the emblematic El Niño de la Bota (Boy with a Boot), a long-standing city symbol.

During the colonial era, Santa Clara's main square was encircled by twin sidewalks, with a fence separating blacks and whites. In its center sat the hallowed Iglesia Mayor, a historic church that was demolished amid much controversy in 1923 and replaced by a Gothic cathedral two blocks to the west.

Plenty of iconic buildings remain, including the 1885 **Teatro La Caridad** (Máximo Gómez), one of the three great rural theaters of the colonial era, with an imposing front facade and frescoes inside by Camilo Zalaya; the **Museo de Artes Decorativas** (☎ 20-53-68; Parque Vidal No 27; admission CUC$2; ☽ 9am-6pm Wed & Thu, 1-10pm Fri & Sat, 6-10pm Sun), an 18th-century museum packed with period furniture; and the muscular **Palacio Provincial** (1902–12), a neoclassical beauty that is now home to the Martí library (with a rare-book collection).

But the real treat is the inherent Cuban-ness of the setting – no cars, no stressed-out shoppers and no hurrying crowds. Sit down next to the gent in the *guayabera* and enjoy the moment.

---

beautiful quiet terrace overlooking a colorful inner garden.

Hotels

Hotel Santa Clara Libre (Islazul; ☎ 20-75-48; Parque Vidal No 6; s/d CUC$27/36; ☒) Santa Clara's only tourist hotel is accommodated in the city's tallest building, the minty-green 168-room Santa Clara Libre. Opened in 1956, this lofty establishment played a key role in the December 1958 battle for the town between Che Guevara and Batista's government troops. You can still see some of the bullet holes on the building's none-too-attractive facade that overlooks Parque Vidal. Inside, the pokey rooms and tired furnishings appear rather worn these days, although prices are cheap and you can enjoy the best views in town from the 10th-floor restaurant.

OUTSIDE TOWN

Villa la Granjita (Cubanacán; ☎ 21-81-90; Carretera de Maleza Km 21.5; s/d CUC$37/46; P ☒ ☐ ☒) Posing as a native Taíno village, La Granjita does well with its *bohío*-style (thatched) huts, equipped with all mod-cons, but loses authenticity at

nighttime when a cheesy poolside show and blaring disco remind you you're still very much in 21st-century Cuba. But, the hotel is a pleasant place and, with its outdoor pool and well-manicured grounds, is a step up from the usual out-of-town Islazul pile. There's a good on-site restaurant, a massage therapist and horseback riding. Try to get a room well away from the noisy swimming-pool area.

Los Caneyes (Cubanacán; ☎ 20-45-13; cnr Av de los Eucaliptos & Circunvalación de Santa Clara; s/d CUC$45/60; P ☒ ☒) Another mock-indigenous village, Los Caneyes has 95 thatched bungalows to la Granjita's 75 and the price tag is a little more expensive. Built in equally verdant grounds replete with abundant birdlife it's a fair out-of-town option that is a favorite with organized coach tours. There's an on-site restaurant and pool.

Eating

RESTAURANTS

BurgueCentro (Parque Vidal No 31; ☽ 24hr) The burgers aren't quite steakhouse standard but the upstairs bar overlooking Parque Vidal is a good drinking perch.

Coppelia (cnr Colón & Mujica; ⊙ 10:30am-midnight Tue-Sun) Stock up on peso ice cream at this architecturally hideous construction.

Dinos Pizza (Marta Abreu No 10 btwn Villuendas & Cuba; ⊙ 9am-11pm; ▢) Smarter than the average Dinos, the Santa Clara branch has three computer terminals for internet access (CUC$5 an hour), a pleasant bar, air-conditioning and friendly, helpful staff. Oh – and it serves good pizza, too.

La Concha (☎ 21-81-24; cnr Carretera Central & Danielito) The town's best restaurant is an easy-to-miss place on the outskirts of town that does a good trade in capturing coach parties on their way to and from the Che memorial. There are some classy lunchtime bands here, though the highlight is generally considered to be the cheap but tasty pizza (from CUC$4).

Restaurante Colonial 1878 (Máximo Gómez btwn Marta Abreu & Independencia; ⊙ noon-2pm & 7-10:30pm) Hold onto the table when you cut your steak here, or you might lose it on the floor. Tough meat aside, 1878 is an amiable enough place, even if the food struggles to emulate the dusty colonial setting. Pop in for a cocktail or a light lunch.

El Sabor Latino (☎ 20-65-39; Esquerra No 157 btwn Julio Jover & Berenguer; ⊙ noon-midnight) Santa Clara's only real paladar is easily trumped by many of the city's casa particular chefs, but still lures plenty of clients into its well-maintained midst with its improbable Rolling Stones' 'Glimmer Twins' logo. The menu offers complete pork or chicken meals with rice, salad, *tostones* (fried plantain patties) and bread for CUC$10 (or fish for CUC$12).

Several peso bars and cafeterías are near the corner of Independencia Oeste and Zayas around Cine Cubanacán and your ever-faithful ice-cream man sometimes operates out of a window on Abreu.

GROCERIES

Mercado agropecuario (Cuba No 269 btwn EP Morales & General Roloff) This market is small, but well stocked with produce. It's in the center of the city.

Panadería Doña Neli (cnr Maceo Sur & 9 de Abril; ⊙ 7am-6pm) This joyous bakery amid the austere shopfronts of Calle Maceo will have your stomach rumbling with its aromatic fruit cakes, bread and pastries. Arrive early and celebrate breakfast.

Drinking

La Marquesina (⊙ 9am-1am) Glued onto the corner of the wondrous Teatro La Caridad building, this lively bar is where the young intelligentsia go to down cocktails and listen to local bands.

Casa del Gobernador (cnr Independencia & JB Zayas; ⊙ noon-11pm) Push your way through the swinging saloon-style doors and you'll uncover one of the city's most understated go-local gathering spots. More noted for its throat-warming rum than its piping hot cuisine, the Gobernador (yes, it was once a provincial government office) is Santa Clara in a bottle in more ways than one.

Café Literario (cnr Rafael Tristá & Colón; ⊙ 9am-9pm) What, a student coffee bar with no laptops? Revisit the pre-Microsoft years with strong espresso, piles of books and plenty of pent-up undergraduate idealism.

Entertainment

Aside from the places listed below, don't discount the Biblioteca José Martí (p277) for refined classical music, La Casa de la Ciudad (p280) for boleros, *trova* (verse) and more, and vibrant Parque Vidal, which presents everything from mime artists to full-scale orchestras.

ourpick **Club Mejunje** (Marta Abreu No 107; ⊙ 4pm-1am Tue-Sun) Set in the ruins of a roofless building given over to sprouting greenery, Club Mejunje is Havana-hip and more. Among the plethora of nighttime attractions here is Cuba's only official drag show every Saturday night – a must-see! Other items on an eclectic entertainment menu include regular *trova*, bolero and *son* (Cuba's popular music) concerts, children's theater and disco nights. If you've only got one night, this is the place.

El Bar Club Boulevard (☎ 21-62-36; Independencia No 2 btwn Maceo & Pedro Estévez; admission CUC$2; ⊙ 10pm-2am Mon-Sat) Another nexus for Santa Clara's musical youth, this much-talked-about cocktail lounge has live bands, dancing plus the odd humor show. It generally gets swinging about 11pm-ish.

Casa de la Cultura Juan Marinello (☎ 20-71-81; Parque Vidal No 5) It looks a bit hollow inside, but concerts in this colonial casa often spill out into the adjacent park.

El Bosque (cnr Carretera Central & Calle Primera; ☽ 9pm-1am Wed-Sun) Santa Clara's cabaret scene begins and ends here.

Cine Camilo Cienfuegos (Parque Vidal), below the Santa Clara Libre, and **Cine Cubanacán** (Independencia Oeste No 60) show large-screen films in English.

The Estadio Sandino, east of the center via 9 de Abril, is the venue for baseball games from October to April. Villa Clara, nicknamed Las Naranjas (the Oranges) for their team strip, won a trio of championships from 1993 to 1995 and were losing finalists to their nemesis, Los Industriales (Havana), in 1996, 2003 and 2004. They are Cuba's third-biggest baseball team, after the heavyweights from Havana and Santiago.

Shopping

Independencia, between Maceo and JB Zayas, is the pedestrian shopping street called the Boulevard by locals. It's littered with all kind of shops and restaurants and is the bustling hub of city life, especially at weekends. **Fondo Cubano de Bienes Culturales** (Luis Estévez Norte No 9 btwn Parque Vidal & Independencia) sells handicrafts and is the main tourist shop here.

Don't forget La Veguita (p280) for some of the best cigars outside Havana.

Getting There & Away

Santa Clara's Abel Santamaría Airport receives weekly flights from Montreal and Toronto. There is no connection to Havana.

BUS

The **Terminal de Ómnibus Nacionales** (☎ 20-34-70) is 2.5km out on the Carretera Central

toward Matanzas, 500m north of the Che monument.

Tickets for air-conditioned **Víazul** (www.viazul .com) buses are sold at a special ticket window for foreigners next to the station entrance.

The Santiago de Cuba–bound bus also stops at Bayamo (CUC$26, nine hours 10 minutes), Camagüey (CUC$15, four hours 25 minutes), Ciego de Ávila (CUC$9, two hours 35 minutes), Holguín (CUC$26, seven hours 50 minutes), Las Tunas (CUC$22, six hours 35 minutes) and Sancti Spíritus (CUC$6, one hour 15 minutes). The Havana bus stops at Entronque de Jagüey (CUC$6, one hour 30 minutes).

The **intermunicipal bus station** (Carretera Central), west of the center via Calle Marta Abreu, has daily buses to Remedios (CUC$1.45), where you can catch a cheaper taxi to the Cayos.

TRAIN

The **train station** (☎ 20-28-95) is straight up Luis Estévez from Parque Vidal on the north side of town. The **ticket office** (Luis Estévez Norte No 323) is across the park from the train station. The comparatively luxurious Tren Francés passes through the city on odd-numbered days heading for Santiago de Cuba (12 hours 45 minutes) via Camagüey (CUC$13, four hours 15 minutes). The Havana-bound train leaves on even-numbered days. There's an additional long-distance service to Santiago (CUC$33, 12¼ hours) stopping in Ciego de Ávila, Camagüey and Las Tunas. Going in the opposite direction there are approximately five daily trains to Havana (CUC$14, five hours), most of which stop in Matanzas (CUC$8, 3½ hours). The train to Cienfuegos (CUC$3, 2½ hours) and Sancti Spíritus (CUC$4, three hours) runs Fridays to Sundays only. The Línea Norte runs three daily trains to Morón (CUC$5, three hours 40 minutes) via Florencia and Chambas. The Remedios and Caibarién service leaves twice daily. It is wise to double-check all of this information at the station a day or two before departing.

VÍAZUL DAILY DEPARTURES			
Destination	**Cost (CUC$)**	**Duration**	**Departure time**
Havana	18	3hr 45min	3:15am, 8:20am, 5:50pm
Holguín	26	7hr 45min	12:50am, 1:50am, 12:55pm, 2pm, 7:30pm
Santiago de Cuba	33	11hr 40min	12:50am, 1:50am, 2pm, 7:30pm
Varadero	11	3hr 20min	7:40am, 5:15pm

Getting Around

You can take a horse carriage from outside the church on Calle Marta Abreu to the Che memorial for a couple of pesos. Bici-taxis (from the northwest of the park) cost CUC$1 a ride.

CAR & MOPED

Parque Vidal is thankfully closed to traffic (and cyclists must also dismount and walk their bikes).

Agencies renting wheels around the town:

Cubacar (☎ 20-81-77; Hotel Santa Clara Libre, Parque Vidal No 6)

Rex (☎ 22-22-44; Marta Abreu; ☷ 9am-6pm) Rents luxury cars and mopeds for around CUC$80 per day.

The **Servi-Cupet gas station** (cnr Carretera Central & General Roloff) is south of the center. Just north is **Servicentro Oro Negro** (cnr Carretera Central & 9 de Abril).

TAXI

Private cabs (not technically legal) hang around in front of the national bus station and will offer you lifts to Remedios and Caibarién. A state taxi to the same destinations will cost approximately CUC$25 and CUC$30 respectively. To get out to Cayo Las Brujas bank on CUC$50; drivers generally congregate in Parque Vidal outside the Hotel Santa Clara Libre or you can call **Cubataxi** (☎ 20-68-56).

EMBALSE HANABANILLA

Embalse Hanabanilla, Villa Clara's main gateway to Sierra del Escambray, is a 36-sq-km reservoir that nestles picturesquely amid traditional rural farms and broccoli-green hills. Aside from hosting Cuba's largest hydroelectric generating station, the lake is stocked with an ample supply of record-breaking bass, making it something of a nexus for fishermen and boaters. Due to its proximity to the Escambray, there are also (limited) hiking opportunities. The area is best accessed via the dowdy Hotel Hanabanilla on the reservoir's northwestern shore, which lies approximately 80km south of Santa Clara.

Activities

The lake is world-famous for its largemouth bass (9kg bass have been caught here) and fishing trips can be organized at the hotel starting at around CUC$40. Boats also ferry passengers over to the Río Negro Restaurant,

perched atop a steep stone staircase overlooking the lake shore 7km away. You can enjoy *comida criolla* (Creole food) here surrounded by nature and tour groups. Nearby is Casa del Campesino, offering coffee, fresh fruit and a taste of bucolic Cuban life. You'll need to hike 1.5km through forest replete with ferns and birdlife to reach the **Arroyo Trinitario waterfall**. There's a pool for swimming. You can organize these activities at Hotel Hanabanilla or book a day excursion (CUC$33 from Santa Clara; CUC$69 from Cayo Santa María).

Sleeping & Eating

Hotel Hanabanilla (Islazul; ☎ 20-85-50; s/d CUC$21/28; P ☒ ☷) Incongruous and lacking any subtlety, this four-story, 125-room hotel is an ugly 1970s anachronism that glowers like an unsightly blemish across Hanabanilla's glistening waters. Facilities inside are a little less hard on the eye with an à la carte restaurant, a swimming pool, a vista-laden bar and lake-facing rooms equipped with small balconies. Peaceful during the week but packed with mainly Cuban guests at weekends, it's your only accommodation for miles and the best base for lakeside hikes and fishing.

Getting There & Away

Theoretically there are buses from Manicaragua, but the only practical access is by car, bike or moped. Taxi drivers will energetically offer the trip. Bank on CUC$25 one way in a state cab. Negotiate hard if you want them to wait over while you participate in an excursion.

REMEDIOS

pop 48,908

Historic Remedios suffers from cultural schizophrenia. Blissfully quiet for 51 weeks of the year, the city's tranquility is blown apart for seven days each December when the exuberant citizens take sides and face off against each other with floats, fireworks and dancing competitions in the legendary Las Parrandas, a street party that makes Mardi Gras seem second-rate.

Laid-back and pretty, with a personality to match, Remedios (when it isn't *parranda*-ing) is used as both a cheap base for the Cayerías del Norte and a cool, colonial getaway in its own right. Despite losing half its citizens to Santa Clara in 1689 in an exodus that left it decimated, the town has managed to maintain

---

THE FOUNDATION OF REMEDIOS

Was it or wasn't it? Historical debate rages about the foundation of Remedios and whether or not it qualifies as one of Cuba's seven original colonial settlements. Popular consensus suggests that it doesn't, placing it in a humiliating eighth place after Havana (which was founded in 1515). The city, traditionalists claim, was inaugurated in 1524 by energetic Spanish conquistador Vasco Porcallo de Figueroa, a captain in Diego Velázquez' army who married the daughter of the Taíno *cacique* (chief) of Sabaneque and went on to sire 200 children.

But die-hard locals agree to differ. While acknowledging that Remedios wasn't *legally* registered as a city until as late as 1550, they maintain that the settlement was founded 37 years earlier in 1513 (making it Cuba's third-oldest, after Baracoa and Bayamo). The savvy Figueroa – so the story goes – founded Remedios (then known as Santa Cruz de la Sabana de Vasco Porcallo) with money gained from a sizable land grant that he had inherited through his marriage to the local *cacique's* daughter. Slyly, he kept his new village a secret from the Spanish crown in order to avoid hefty tax payments.

---

its unique cultural charisma – an atmosphere that is best enjoyed in a clutch of decent casas particulares and its striking but somnolent central square.

Sights

Remedios is the only city in Cuba with two churches in its main square, Plaza Martí. The **Parroquia de San Juan Bautista de Remedios** (Camilo Cienfuegos No 20; ☉ 9am-11am Mon-Sat) is one of the island's finest ecclesial buildings. Though a church was founded here in 1545, this building dates from the late 18th century; the campanile was erected between 1848 and 1858 and its famous gilded high altar and mahogany ceiling are thanks to a restoration project (1944–46) financed by millionaire philanthropist Eutimio Falla Bonet. The pregnant Inmaculada Concepción on the first side altar to the left of the entrance is said to be the only one of its kind in Cuba. If the front doors are closed, go around to the rear or attend 7:30pm mass.

Also on Parque Martí is the 18th-century **Iglesia de Nuestra Señora del Buen Viaje** (Alejandro del Río No 66), still awaiting a long-overdue restoration.

Between these churches is the **Museo de Música Alejandro García Caturla** (Parque Martí No 5; admission CUC$1; ☉ 9am-noon & 1-6pm Mon-Thu, 7-11pm Fri, 2pm-midnight Sat), commemorating García Caturla, a Cuban composer and musician who lived here from 1920 until his murder in 1940. Look for occasional impromptu concerts.

Visiting the **Museo de las Parrandas Remedianas** (Máximo Gómez No 71; admission CUC$1; ☉ 9am-6pm), two blocks off Parque Martí, is probably a poor substitute for partying here on December 24,

but what the hell? The downstairs photo gallery usually recaps the previous year's shenanigans, while the upstairs rooms outline the history of this tradition, including scale models of floats and detailed depictions of how the fireworks are made. Another room is jammed with feathers, headdresses and tassels from celebrations past.

You can muse for a few minutes at the friendly **Galería del Arte Carlos Enríquez** (Parque Martí No 2; admission free; ☉ 9am-noon & 1-5pm), also in the main park. A gifted painter hailing from the small Villa Clara town of Zulueta, Enríquez called his studio 'Hurón Azul,' a name later adopted by Uneac (Union of Cuban Writers and Artists).

Sleeping

CASAS PARTICULARES

ourpick **'Villa Colonial' – Frank & Arelys** (☎ 39-62-74; felicialr@uclv.edu.cu; Maceo No 43 cnr Av General Carrillo; r CUC$20-25; 🌂) A truly elegant villa with high ceilings and huge wrought-iron window guards, this place has been restored with a meticulous eye for history. For as little as CUC$20 you get your own private entrance and lobby, an antique-stuffed sitting room, a gorgeous patio and spacious bedrooms with modern baths. The young hosts are charming and passionate about their town and its history.

La China & Richard (☎ 39-66-49; Maceo No 68 btwn Fe del Valle & Cupertino Garcia; r CUC$20-25; P 🌂) This friendly young couple rent two rooms with a terrace and decent meals. Richard can give you the lowdown on local history.

La Paloma (☎ 39-54-90; Balmaseda No 4 btwn Capablanca & Máximo Gómez; r CUC$20-25; P 🌂)

Another grand Remedios casa with tilework and furnishings that would be worth zillions anywhere else, La Paloma dates from 1875 and is right on the main square. The two rooms have massive shower units, art-deco beds, and doors big enough to ride a horse through.

HOTELS

OUR PICK Hotel Mascotte (Cubanacán; ☎ 39-51-44; Parque Martí; r CUC$49) Remedios makes up for its lack of tourist hotels by the quality of this one, housed in a beautiful colonial building dating from 1869. Run by the Cubanacán chain as one of its boutique hotels, the Mascotte was undergoing a renovation at the time of writing. When it's finished its 10 spacious rooms, five of which overlook the main square, promise plenty of romantic Remedios evenings.

Eating

Driver's Bar (José A Peña No 61; ⏰ 8am-10pm) Way down the desperation stakes, this place serves peso meals on one side and is a no-nonsense saloon on the other.

Las Arcadas (Parque Martí) If you're staying in the Mascotte, you'll probably end up eating here, as it's the only visible restaurant in town that sells anything resembling a square meal. If you're staying in a casa particular, you'll know better.

El Louvre (☎ 39-56-39; Máximo Gómez No 122) Acting with a gravitational pull on Remedios' small scattering of tourists, El Louvre has cleaned its act up in recent years to fulfill the expectations of its more demanding clientele. Locals will tell you it's the oldest bar in the country in continuous service (since 1866) but, longevity awards aside, the fried-chicken-and-sandwiches menu still can't quite match up to the quaint parkside location. If you're looking for

a room/paladar/taxi, park yourself here, have a drink and wait for the offers.

Entertainment

Dancers should head to **Bar Juvenil** (Adel Río No 47; ⏰ 9pm-1am Sat & Sun), a courtyard disco near Máximo Gómez (enter via park), with palms, pillars and Moorish tiles. During the day there's table tennis and dominoes; at night it's an alcohol-free party. **El Güije** (☎ 20-09-54; cnr Independencia & Maceo; ⏰ 2pm-2am) is another newer nexus; bank on open-air shows at night and ask about dancing classes during the day.

Next door to El Louvre is **Centro Cultural Las Leyendas** (Máximo Gómez btwn Margali & Independencia), an ARTex cultural center with music till 1am Wednesday to Saturday. A block east of the park is the elegant old **Teatro Rubén M Villena** (Cienfuegos No 30), with dance performances, plays and Theater Guiñol for kids. The schedule is posted in the window and tickets are in pesos. Additional cultural activities can be found in the **Casa de Cultura Agustín J Crespo** (José A Peña No 67), opposite the Parroquia, **Uneac** (Maceo No 25), and – in the city that invented Las Parrandas – outside in the parks and squares.

Getting There & Away

The bus station is on the southern side of town at the beginning of the 45km road to Santa Clara. There are half a dozen daily buses to Santa Clara (one hour), three daily services to Caibarién (20 minutes) and two departures Monday, Wednesday and Friday to Zulueta (30 minutes). Fares are negligible. Remedios is not on the Víazul network; the closest you can get is Santa Clara.

There are three daily trains to Caibarién and two to Santa Clara. The bus and train services aren't always 100% reliable.

A state taxi from the bus station to Caibarién will cost CUC$5(ish) one way, and CUC$25 to Santa Clara. A bici-taxi from the bus station to Parque Martí is two pesos.

CAIBARIÉN
pop 40,798

This once-busy shipping port situated on Cuba's Atlantic coast 9km east of Remedios has slipped into deep stupor since the provincial sugar mills closed down and the old piers fell crumbling into the sea. These days the main commercial activity is fishing, though the colorful seafront retains a quaint, ramshackle feel despite the dilapidated architecture.

ASK A LOCAL

Remedios is famous for Las Parrandas, but there are plenty of other festivals here. In May and June we have a Semana de la Cultura (Week of Culture) in the main square. In June it's the Fiesta de San Juan to commemorate the founding of Remedios with theater put on in the evenings. Then in early December (around the 15th or 16th) there is a special *parrandas* for children with activities and – of course – fireworks.

Richard, Remedios

Open-minded travelers can get eye to eye with the real Cuba in Caibarién where serendipitous treats include a restored Malecón seawall, a local *cangrejo* (crab) dinner and December *parrandas,* which are – allegedly – second only to Remedios in their explosiveness. With a handful of casas particulares, the town also makes a cheap base for those keen to catch a glimpse of the pristine cayos without shelling out the expensive all-inclusive prices.

Havanatur (☎ 35-11-71; Av 9 btwn Calles 8 & 10) can arrange accommodation on Cayo Santa María. Next door the **Museo Municipal María Escobar Laredo** (☎ 36-47-31; cnr Av 9 & Calle 10) is worth a once-over. There's a **Cadeca** (Calle 10 No 907 btwn 9 & 10) nearby.

Sleeping & Eating

An economical launching pad for the resort-strewn, casa particular–free zone of the Cayerías del Norte, Caibarién has a small number of legal private houses.

Virginia's Pension (☎ 36-33-03; www.virginias pension.com; Ciudad Pesquera No 73; r CUC$20-25; ⓟ ⓧ) Among the handful, this is the most popular; it's a reputable professional joint run by Virginia and Osmany Rodríguez and has received several recommendations.

Complejo Brisas del Mar (☎ 35-16-99; Reparto Mar Azul; s/d CUC$29/38; ⓟ ⓧ ⓡ) Also known as Villa Blanca, this 17-room Islazul hotel is located 4km east of the town right by Caibarién beach (seven rooms face the sea). Facilities include a bar, a restaurant, a swimming pool and satellite TV.

There are a couple of passable places to eat in Convertibles, including the venerable **Restaurante La Vicaria** (☎ 35-10-85; Calle 10 & Av 9; ⏱ 10am-10:30pm), which specializes in fish, and **La Ruina** (cnr Avs 15 & 6), a Palmares place that also hosts a nightly cabaret. There's an **agropecuario** (Calle 6) near the train station.

Entertainment

Piste de Baile (Calle 4; admission 2 pesos) Surprisingly, Caibarién has a hot, happening disco near the train station. It's known by a generic name (*piste de baile* means dance floor) and it jumps with hundreds of young locals on weekends.

Getting There & Away

Four buses a day go to Remedios (CUC$1, 20 minutes), two carry on to Santa Clara (CUC$2, 90 minutes) and three go to Yaguajay (CUC$1.50, 45 minutes) from Caibarién's old blue-and-white **bus & train station** (Calle 6) on the western side of town. There are two listed daily trains to Santa Clara, one leaving in the small hours and the other just after lunch. The journey, via Remedios, is scheduled to take two hours. The Servi-Cupet gas station is at the entrance to town from Remedios, behind the huge crab statue by Florencio Gelabert Pérez (1983). **Cubacar** (☎ 35-19-60; Av 11 btwn 6 & 8) rents cars at the standard rates.

CAYERÍAS DEL NORTE

The hundreds of small keys that lie off the north coast of Villa Clara province – known communally as the Cayerías del Norte – are Cuba's next big tourism project. There are currently five resorts splayed out here (including one of the archipelago's newest), scattered over three of the largest keys, Cayo Las Brujas, Cayo Ensenachos and Cayo Santa María, but plans are on the table for as many as 20 more. The existing hotels are all linked by an impressive 48km causeway called **El Pedraplén** that runs across the shallow Bahía de Buenavista from the fishing port of Caibarién crossing 45 bridges en route. The bridges were incorporated in the mid-1990s to allow the exchange of tidal waters after studies on an older bridgeless *pedraplén* (causeway) in Cayo Coco revealed significant environmental damage.

To date, tourist development on the Cayerías del Norte has been thoughtful and carefully managed. Protecting 248 species of flora and incorporating parts of the Unesco-listed Buenavista Biosphere Reserve, the government has wisely earmarked large tracts of land as protected flora and fauna reserves.

ASK A LOCAL

If you're going for a day trip to the Cayos, beware, as many of the beaches are flora and fauna reserves or the exclusive property of big hotels. The best two to aim for are Perla Blanca (shadeless), on the far tip of Cayo Santa María, and Playa Las Salinas, next door to Villa Las Brujas. To avoid paying an entry fee to the latter, take the left turn just after the gas station on Cayo Las Brujas and follow the track to the public entry point.

Juan, Remedios

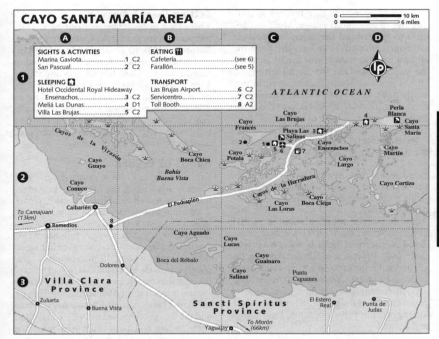

CAYO SANTA MARÍA AREA

SIGHTS & ACTIVITIES	
Marina Gaviota.....................1 C2	
San Pascual.........................2 C2	

SLEEPING	
Hotel Occidental Royal Hideaway	
Ensenachos..................3 C2	
Meliá Las Dunas...................4 D1	
Villa Las Brujas....................5 C2	

EATING	
Cafetería...........................(see 6)	
Farallón............................(see 5)	

TRANSPORT	
Las Brujas Airport.................6 C2	
Servicentro........................7 C2	
Toll Booth.........................8 A2	

These measures have ensured that the area's fine white beaches have (so far) retained a more pristine and detached feel noticeably absent in other resort complexes such as Cayo Coco and Varadero.

Sights & Activities

Most water-based activities can be arranged at **Marina Gaviota** (☎ 35-00-13), next to Villa Las Brujas. Highlights include a one-hour catamaran excursion with snorkeling (CUC$15), a half-day catamaran cruise (CUC$36), a sunset cruise (CUC$49), deep-sea fishing (CUC$260 for four people) and a two-hour Aqua bike excursion (CUC$60). Diving to one of 24 offshore sites is offered for an expensive CUC$40 per immersion. Most water activities are cancelled if there is a cold weather front.

One of the area's oldest curiosities is the wreck of the **San Pascual**, a San Diego tanker built in 1920 that got wrecked in 1933 on the opposite side of nearby Cayo Francés. Later the ship was used to store molasses, and later still it was opened up as a rather surreal hotel-restaurant (it closed in 2004). The journey out to see the ship is included in the snorkeling excursions and sunset cruises.

Sleeping

There are five hotels here. The following three run the gamut of price ranges.

our pick Villa Las Brujas (Gaviota; ☎ 35-01-99; s/d CUC$80/85; P ☒) Wild and still relatively untamed atop a small headland that is crowned by a statue of a *bruja* (witch), Villa Las Brujas has the air of a tropical *Wuthering Heights* when a cold front blows in. It all adds to the unique atmosphere of this comfortable but affordable small resort that rises subtly among the mangroves on one of Cuba's prettiest northern keys. The 24 spacious *cabañas* equipped with coffee machines, cable TV and massive beds have killer views, while the friendly Farallón restaurant overlooks a magnificent scoop of private beach (part of paradisiacal Playa Las Salinas). The nearest resort to the mainland, Villa Las Brujas lies adjacent to the marina and 3km from the airport.

Meliá Las Dunas (☎ 35-01-00; s/d CUC$122/193; P ☒ ☐ ☒) The mind-boggling 925-room Meliá is one of Cuba's newest and biggest resorts and opened to rave reviews in 2007. The size of an English village, Meliá has golf carts to get around the extensive grounds, although, after tucking into the generous all-you-can-eat buffet, you might welcome the walk. Encased in a wonderful setting, Las Dunas is a Caribbean beach paradise personified but, unless you book for a guided day excursion (or drive/cycle 45km to the mainland), the most you'll see of everyday Cuba is on the way to and from the airport.

Hotel Occidental Royal Hideaway Ensenachos (s/d CUC$232/301; P X 🔲 🔁) If you're an all-inclusive type, you'll love this top-end paradise which is on a par with some of the five-star resorts in Puerto Rico and Cancún (with a Canadian rather than an American demographic). Refined and tranquil with Alhambra-esque fountains and attractive natural foliage, guests here are accommodated in pretty 20-unit blocks, each with their own private concierge. Among the all-inclusive luxuries are king-sized beds, bathrobes, water toys, tennis coaching, myriad restaurants, and golf carts to drive you around. But the highlight is the two absolutely gorgeous private beaches, Ensenachos and Mégano.

Eating

For nonhotel guests the best bet for a decent meal is in the Farallón restaurant, perched like a bird's nest overlooking blissful Las Salinas beach. Access is via the Gaviota Villa Las Brujas. Lunch with use of beach, bathrooms and parking costs CUC$20. Otherwise your only food/drink option is at the airport cafetería (not much beyond biscuits and coffee) or an expensive all-inclusive day pass to the Hotel Occidental or the Meliá Las Dunas.

Getting There & Away

There's no public transport out here. Daytrippers can zoom in from Caibarién (56km), Remedios (65km) or Santa Clara (110km) by rental car or taxi. A taxi from Remedios should cost CUC$30 to CUC$35 one way to Villa Las Brujas. **Las Brujas airport** (☎ 35-00-09) has mainly charter flights to Havana. There's a Servicentro gas station opposite. The causeway is accessed from Caibarién and there's a toll booth (CUC$2 each way) where you'll need to show your passport/visa.

BAÑOS DE ELGUEA

Baños de Elguea, 136km northwest of Santa Clara nearly kissing the Matanzas provincial border, is a well-established health resort. According to local legend, a slave who had contracted a serious skin disease in 1860 was banished by his master, sugar-mill owner Don Francisco Elguea, so that he wouldn't infect others. Sometime later the man returned completely cured. He explained that he had relieved his affliction merely by bathing in the region's natural mineral spring. Somewhat surprisingly, his master believed him. A bathhouse was built and the first hotel opened in 1917. Today these sulfur springs and the mud are used by medical professionals to treat skin irritations, arthritis and rheumatism. The waters here reach a temperature of 50°C and are rich in bromide, chlorine, radon, sodium and sulfur.

Situated north of Coralillo, **Hotel & Spa Elguea** (☎ 68-62-90; s/d incl breakfast low season CUC$30/40, high season CUC$36/48; P X 🔁) has 139 rooms with numerous spa treatments, such as mud therapy, hydrotherapy and massages available at the nearby thermal pools. Regulars claim that its rejuvenating powers are among the best in Latin America.

Sancti Spíritus Province

Sancti Spíritus is the province of good fortune. Spend a day trekking through its rolling Jatibonico hills or crested Sierra del Escambray and you'll quickly discover that there's more of everything here, and all of it squeezed into an area half the size of Camagüey or Pinar del Río.

The cities are a perennial highlight. Sancti Spíritus is the only province that hosts two of Cuba's seven founding settlements: in the east is the understated provincial capital, a soporific mix of weather-beaten buildings and bruised Ladas. South, and within sight of the coast, is ethereal Trinidad, Cuba's – and Latin America's – colonial jewel that is second only to Havana as a tourist magnet.

Unlike other colonial belles, Trinidad has beaches – nearby Ancón is a stunner, easily the best on Cuba's southern coast – and mountains. Within mirror-glinting distance of the city's colonial core lie the haunting Escambray, Cuba's best hiking area with an actual network of decent trails, a couple of which can be done – officially – *without a guide!*

Sandwiched in between is the once-formidable Valle de los Ingenios, the industrial heartland upon which Trinidad's fortunes were once laid out in sugar. But, while the valley's economic riches depleted, its tourist value sky-rocketed; it's now a Unesco World Heritage Site and best explored on a steam train.

The rest of the province hides a surprisingly varied cache of oft-overlooked curiosities. There's a great fishing lake at Zaza, a seminal museum to Cuba's guerrilla icon Camilo Cienfuegos in Yaguajay, and a barely visited Unesco Biosphere Reserve in the beautiful Bahía de Buenavista.

SANCTI SPÍRITUS PROVINCE

HIGHLIGHTS

- **Time-warp in Trinidad** Peel off the layers in Cuba's colonial jewel (p298)
- **Hook a Line** Go fishing in Embalse Zaza (p296)
- **Life by the Lago** Watch the flamingos in the lake and relax in mineral springs in Villa San José del Lago (p315)
- **Beach Break** Rent a house in La Boca and stroll the sands of Playa Ancón (p309)
- **Heavenly Hike** Discover the hikes, waterfalls and swimming holes of beautiful Parque La Guanayara (p312)

- TELEPHONE CODE: 041
- POPULATION: 463,258
- AREA: 6744 SQ KM

SANCTI SPÍRITUS PROVINCE

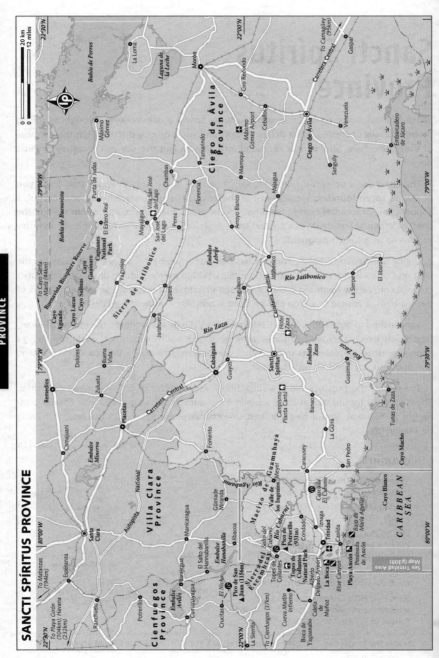

See Trinidad Area Map (p309)

Parks & Reserves

Approximately 300 sq km of Sancti Spíritus' north coast is protected in the Unesco Buenavista Biosphere Reserve. Encased inside the reserve is the pristine Parque Nacional Caguanes and the whole area has been designated a Ramsar Convention Site. In the south of the province, the ecologically important Sierra del Escambray is incorporated in the Topes de Collantes Natural Park, a carefully managed recreation area run by government-owned tourist company Gaviota.

Getting There & Around

Thanks to its popularity on the tourist circuit, Trinidad maintains good bus connections with the rest of the island, with Víazul coaches pulling in and out of its well-organized terminal daily. Train travel is a different matter and, since 1992, the city has been cut off from the rest of the island's rail network by a damaged bridge. Sancti Spíritus has better train connections, though on occasion you'll have to change in Guayos, 15km to the north. The north of the province is more remote, though a good road runs from Remedios to Morón via Yaguajay. There are no Víazul buses on this route.

SANCTI SPÍRITUS

pop 105,815

Poor Sancti Spíritus. In any other country this attractive colonial city would be a cultural tour de force. But cocooned inside illustrious Sancti Spíritus province and destined to always play second fiddle to Trinidad, it barely gets a look-in. Of course, for many visitors therein lies the attraction. Sancti Spíritus is Trinidad without the tourist hassle. You can get served in a restaurant here and search for a casa particular without an uninvited assemblage of pushy 'guides' telling you that the owner is deceased, on vacation, or living in Miami. You can also get decidedly comfortable sitting on a metal chair in Parque Serafín Sánchez watching the kids play stickball while plaintive boleros (romantic love songs) infiltrate streets that never quite earned a Unesco listing.

Founded in 1514 as one of Diego Velázquez' seven original 'villas,' Sancti Spíritus was moved to its present site on the Río Yayabo in 1522. But the relocation didn't stop audacious corsairs, who continued to loot the town until well into the 1660s.

While Trinidad gave the world Playa Ancón, filthy-rich sugar barons and *jineteros* (touts) on bicycles, Sancti Spíritus concocted the dapper *guayabera* shirt, the *guayaba* (guava) fruit, and a rather quaint humped-back bridge that wouldn't look out of place in Yorkshire, England.

Orientation

The bus and train stations are on opposite sides of town. Of the two, the train station is more convenient. It's an easy five-minute walk to the old Puente Yayabo and then another five minutes to Parque Serafín Sánchez in the heart of the town. The bus station is a couple of kilometers east of the center on Carretera Central (called Bartolomé Masó as it passes through Sancti Spíritus).

Information

BOOKSTORES

Librería Julio Antonio Mella (☎ 32-74-16; Independencia Sur No 29; ◷ 8am-5pm Mon-Sat) Opposite the post office.

INTERNET ACCESS & TELEPHONE

Etecsa Telepunto (Independencia Sur; internet access per hr CUC$6; ◷ 8:30am-7:30pm) Spanking new place in the main pedestrian shopping street.

LIBRARIES

Biblioteca Provincial Rubén Martínez Villena (☎ 32-77-17; Máximo Gómez Norte No 1) On Parque Serafín Sánchez.

MEDIA

Radio Sancti Spíritus CMHT Airing on 1200AM and 97.3FM.

MEDICAL SERVICES

Farmacia Especial (☎ 32-46-60; Independencia Norte No 123; ◷ 24hr) Pharmacy on Parque Maceo.
Hospital Provincial Camilo Cienfuegos (☎ 32-40-17; Bartolomé Masó) Five hundred meters north of Plaza de la Revolución.
Policlínico Los Olivos (☎ 32-63-62; Circunvalación Olivos No 1) Near the bus station. Will treat foreigners in an emergency.

MONEY

Banco Financiero Internacional (☎ 32-75-78; Independencia Sur No 2) On Parque Serafín Sánchez.
Cadeca (☎ 32-85-35; Independencia Sur No 31; ◷ 8am-6pm Mon-Sat, 8am-noon Sun) Lose your youth in this line.

SANCTI SPÍRITUS

INFORMATION
Banco Financiero Internacional..**1**	C2
Biblioteca Provincial	
Rubén Martínez Villena......**2**	C2
Cadeca....................................**3**	C3
Cubatur.................................**4**	C1
Etecsa Telepunto....................**5**	C3
Farmacia Especial...................**6**	B2
Havanatur......................(see 30)	
Inmigración...........................**7**	B2
Librería Julio Antonio Mella....**8**	C3
Post Office.............................**9**	C3

SIGHTS & ACTIVITIES
Colonia Española Building......**10**	C4
Fundación de la Naturaleza	
y El Hombre....................**11**	B2
Galería de Arte.....................**12**	C2
Iglesia de Nuestra Señora	
de la Caridad..................**13**	B1
Iglesia Parroquial Mayor	
del Espíritu Santo...........**14**	B4
Museo Casa Natal de	
Serafín Sánchez..............**15**	B2
Museo de Arte Colonial........**16**	B4
Museo de Ciencias Naturales..**17**	C2
Museo Provincial..................**18**	C2
Puente Yayabo.....................**19**	B4
Teatro Principal....................**20**	B4

SLEEPING
Hostal del Rijo....................**21**	B3
Hostal Los Pinos.................**22**	C1
Hostal Paraíso.....................**23**	B3
Hotel Plaza.........................**24**	C1
'Los Richards' – Ricardo	
Rodríguez.......................**25**	C1

EATING
Cremería El Kikiri................**26**	C1
La Época......................(see 40)	
Las Arcadas.................(see 24)	
Mercado Agropecuario........**27**	C3
Mesón de la Plaza...............**28**	B3
Panadería El Fenix..............**29**	B2
Quinta Santa Elena.............**30**	B4
Restaurante Hostal del Rijo..(see 21)	

ENTERTAINMENT
Cafe ARTex........................**31**	C2
Casa de la Cultura...............**32**	C2
Casa de la Trova Miguel	
Companioni.....................**33**	B3
Casa del Joven Creador........**34**	B2
Cine Conrado Benítez..........**35**	C1
Cine Serafín Sánchez...........**36**	C2
Teatro Principal............(see 20)	
Uneac................................**37**	C3

SHOPPING
Casa de Comisiones.............**38**	C2
Galería La Arcada................**39**	C4
VideCuba...........................**40**	B2

TRANSPORT
Bici-taxis...........................**41**	C1
Cubacar............................**42**	C1

POST
Post office (⏰ 9am-6pm Mon-Sat) There are two branches: one at Independencia Sur No 8; the other at the Etecsa building, Bartolomé Masó No 167.

TRAVEL AGENCIES
Cubatur (☎ 32-85-18; Máximo Gómez Norte No 7; ⏰ 9am-5pm Mon-Sat) On Parque Serafín Sánchez.
Havanatur (☎ 32-83-08; Padre Quintero No 60) Offices in Quinta Santa Elena restaurant.

Sights
Looking like something out of an English country village, the quadruple-arched **Puente Yayabo** is Sancti Spíritus' signature sight. Built by the Spanish in 1815, it carries traffic across the Yayabo and is now a national monument.

For the best view (and a mirror-like reflection) hit the outdoor terrace at the Quinta Santa Elena. The **Teatro Principal**, alongside the bridge, dates from 1876, and the sun-bleached cobbled streets that lead uphill toward the city center from here are some of the settlement's oldest. The most quintessential is narrow **Calle Llano**, a sinuous side street where old ladies peddle live chickens door to door, and feisty neighbors gossip noisily in front of their sky-blue or lemon-yellow houses.

Turning left on Pancho Jiménez you come to the **Museo de Arte Colonial** (☎ 2-5455; Plácido Sur No 74; admission CUC$2; ⏰ 9am-5pm Tue-Sat, 8am-noon Sun), with 19th-century furniture and decorations displayed in an imposing 17th-century building that once belonged to the sugar-rich

Valle-Iznaga family. Further up the hill is the verging-on-decrepit **Iglesia Parroquial Mayor del Espíritu Santo** (Agramonte Oeste No 58; ⌚ 9-11am & 2-5pm Tue-Sat). Originally constructed of wood in 1522 and rebuilt in stone in 1680, it's said to be the oldest church in Cuba still standing on its original foundations (although the clock seems to have given out in recent years). While the interior isn't particularly interesting, locals are proud of this place and the best time to peek is during Sunday morning Mass.

Formerly known as Plaza de Jesús, tiny **Plaza Honorato** was where the Spanish authorities once conducted grisly public hangings. Later on it hosted a produce market and scruffy peso stalls still line the small connecting lane to the east.

Independencia Sur, the city's newly revived shopping mall, is traffic-free and lined with statues, sculptures and myriad curiosity shops. Check out the junk store/antiques den Casa de Comisiones (p298) and catch a glimpse of the opulent **Colonia Española Building**, once a whites-only gentlemen's club. The **Galería de Arte** (Céspedes Sur No 26; admission free; ⌚ 8am-noon & 2-5pm Tue-Sat, 8am-noon Sun), next to the *agropecuario* (vegetable market; enter via Independencia Sur), houses numerous works by local painter Oscar Fernández Morera (1890–1946).

While not Cuba's shadiest or most atmospheric square, pretty **Parque Serafín Sánchez** is full of understated Sancti Spíritus elegance. Metal chairs laid out inside the pedestrianized central domain are usually commandeered by cigar-smoking grandpas and flirty young couples with their sights set on some ebul-lient local nightlife. There's plenty to whet the appetite on the square's south side where the impressive Casa de la Cultura often exports its music onto the street. Next door the columned Hellenic beauty that today serves as the **Biblioteca Provincial Rubén Martínez Villena** was built originally in 1929 by the Progress Society. Sport and coins make improbable bedfellows in the obligatory **Museo Provincial** (Máximo Gómez Norte No 3; admission CUC$1; ⌚ 9am-6pm Mon-Thu, 9am-6pm & 8-10pm Sat, 8am-noon Sun) on Parque Serafín Sánchez, which might appeal to numismatically minded baseball fanatics, but few others. Nearby, the **Museo de Ciencias Naturales** (☎ 2-6365; Máximo Gómez Sur No 2; admission CUC$1; ⌚ 8:30am-5pm Tue-Fri, 8-10pm Sat, 8:30am-noon Sun), off Parque Serafín Sánchez, has a stuffed crocodile that will scare your three-year-old and some shiny rock collections.

A few blocks north of the park is the **Museo Casa Natal de Serafín Sánchez** (Céspedes Norte No 112; admission CUC$0.50; ⌚ 8am-5pm). Serafín Sánchez was a local patriot who took part in both Wars of Independence and went down fighting in November 1896.

Replicating its equally diminutive name-sake in Miramar, Havana, the **Fundación de la Naturaleza y El Hombre** (☎ 2-8342; Cruz Pérez No 1; admission CUC$1; ⌚ 10am-5pm Mon-Fri, 10am-noon Sat) on Parque Maceo chronicles the 17,422km canoe odyssey 'from the Amazon to the Caribbean' in 1987 led by Cuban writer and Renaissance man Antonio Nuñez Jiménez (1923–98). Some 432 explorers made the journey through 10 countries, from Ecuador to the Bahamas, in the twin dugout canoes *Simón Bolívar*

THE GUAYABERA

No Mexican beach wedding would be complete without one, but according to popular legend, the *guayabera* shirt originated not in Puerto Vallarta, but in Sancti Spíritus in the late 1800s where people who lived close to the Yayabo River were known colloquially as Yayaberos. Crafting com-fortable work-shirts for their menfolk to wear out in the fields, the local women took to calling their deftly sewn homemade garments *guayaberas* when their husbands started coming home with their pockets full of *guayabas* (guavas).

With its distinctive *alforzas* (pleats) and rustic retro elegance, the *guayabera's* popularity quickly spread and by the 1880s it was being worn at official events in towns and cities throughout the Sancti Spíritus area. By the early 20th century the *guayabera* had arrived in Havana and, in the mid-1940s, the trend went national when Cuban President Ramón Grau San Martín was seen sporting one.

These days, *guayaberas* are ubiquitous all over Latin America from backstreet bars in Mexico to smart Miami business meetings. Usually worn casually untucked at the waist, the shirt comes in a variety of pastel colors (though white is the standard) and is noted for its four large pockets and numerous decorative buttons.

and *Hatuey*. The latter measures over 13m and is the collection's central, prized piece. Across from the Fundación is the handsome old **Iglesia de Nuestra Señora de la Caridad** (Céspedes Norte No 207), the city's second church whose internal arches are a favored nesting spot for Cuban sparrows.

Sleeping
IN TOWN
Casas Particulares
Hostal Los Pinos (☎ 32-93-14; Carretera Central Norte No 157 btwn Mirto Milián & Coronel Lagón; r CUC$20-25; ❄) Good for travelers in transit, this museum to art deco is on Carretera Central and has a garage, delicious dinners and two comfy rooms.

'Los Richards' – Ricardo Rodríguez (☎ 32-30-29; Independencia Norte No 28 Altos; r CUC$25; ❄) The small stairway off the main square belies the size of this place. The front room is enormous, dwarfing the two beds, rocking chairs, full bar area and fridge. There's a smaller room out back.

Hostal Paraíso (☎ 5271-1257; Máximo Gómez Sur No 11 btwn Honorato & Cervantes; r CUC$25; ❄) Hang out amid the hanging plants with this new kid on the block. The house itself dates from 1838 and, although the rooms are a little dark, bathrooms are huge and the surrounding greenery spirit-lifting.

Hotels
Sancti Spíritus' two city-center hotels are set in attractive restored colonial buildings. They form part of a *complejo* that charges the same prices, though the Rijo is recommended as the best nook.

our pick Hostal del Rijo (Cubanacán; ☎ 32-85-88; Honorato No 12; r CUC$49; ❄ ☎) Even committed casa particular fans will have trouble resisting this meticulously restored 1818 mansion situated on quiet (until the Casa de la Trova opens) Plaza Honorato. Sixteen huge, plush rooms – many with plaza-facing balconies – are equipped with everything a romance-seeking Cuba-phile could wish for, including satellite TV, complimentary shampoos, and chunky colonial furnishings. Downstairs in the elegant courtyard restaurant you'll get served the kind of sumptuous, unhurried breakfast that'll have you lingering until eleven. Oh, what the hell, might as well stay another night.

Hotel Plaza (☎ 32-71-02; Independencia Norte No 1; r CUC$49; ❄) The Rijo's smaller and slightly less

attractive younger sister, the Plaza is a block north on Parque Serafín Sánchez. Spreading 28 rooms over two stories, the hotel is embellished by hanging wicker chairs suspended from the rafters and European-style statues and tiles surrounding a cozy downstairs bar. There's a *mirador* (lookout) on the roof and great service throughout. If the Rijo's full, look no further.

NORTH OF TOWN
There are two very agreeable hotels along Carretera Central as you head north; either one makes a good choice if you don't want to bother with the city center.

Villa Los Laureles (Islazul; ☎ 32-73-45; Carretera Central Km 383; s/d CUC$30/38; P ❄ ☎) Not content to rest on them, Los Laureles lines its laurel trees up along a shady entrance drive that beckons visitors into a surprisingly classy Islazul out-of-towner. There's no dodgy Soviet architectonics here. In fact, even those with in-the-clouds expectations might fill out a favorable comments card here. Supplementing big, bright rooms with fridges, satellite TV and patio/balcony, are an attractive pool, leafy flower-studded gardens and colorful in-house cabaret, the Tropi, with a nightly show at 9pm.

Villa Rancho Hatuey (Islazul; ☎ 32-83-15; Carretera Central Km 384; s/d CUC$36/53; P ❄ ☐ ☎) Here's the dilemma. Not 1km from Los Laureles' row of gnarly laurel trees lies another veritable Islazul gem accessible from the southbound lane of Carretera Central. Probably the more peaceful of the two options, Rancho Hatuey spreads 76 rooms in two-story cabins across expansive landscaped grounds set back a good 500m from the road. Catching some rays around the swimming pool or grabbing a bite in the serviceable on-site restaurant you'll see bus groups from Canada and Communist Party officials from Havana mingling in awkward juxtaposition.

EAST OF TOWN
Hotel Zaza (Islazul; ☎ 32-85-12; s/d incl breakfast CUC$30/40; P ❄ ☎) It's the fish – in the nearby lake, not in the restaurant – that dominate the menu here. Perched above expansive Embalse Zaza, this scruffy rural retreat looks more like a utilitarian apartment block transplanted from Moscow than a hotel – not that this discourages the armies of bass fishermen who descend on here in their droves (four-hour fishing trips on the lake go for CUC$30). For

nonfishermen there's a swimming pool, and friendly staff who can organize boat trips on the lake without the fishing rod (one-hour cruise CUC$20 for two people). To get here, go east 5km on Carretera Central toward Ciego de Ávila, then south 5km to the lake.

Eating

You'll burn vital calories searching for a square meal in Sancti Spíritus. Outside of the casas particulares and duo of Cubanacán hotels, there are just two places to seriously test your taste buds, both of which are run by state-run restaurant group Palmares.

RESTAURANTS

Cremería El Kikiri (Independencia Norte & Laborni) What, no Coppelia? Kikiri is Sancti Spíritus' long-standing provincial stand-in. Alternatively, hang around long enough in Parque Serafín Sánchez and a DIY ice-cream man will turn up with his ice-cream maker powered by a washing-machine motor.

Quinta Santa Elena (☎ 32-81-67; Padre Quintero No 60; dishes CUC$4-8; ☯ 10am-midnight) 'Old clothes' is a name that has never really done justice to Cuba's famous shredded-beef dinner (ropa vieja). There's certainly nothing 'old' or 'clothes-like' about the dish here, or the equally tasty shrimps in red sauce for that matter. While the Mesón (below) has the edge on food, the Santa Elena wins the Oscar for location, set on a charming riverside patio in front of the city's famous packhorse bridge.

Mesón de la Plaza (☎ 32-85-46; Máximo Gómez Sur No 34; ☯ noon-2:30pm & 6-10pm) The best food in town and the best location after the Santa Elena. Encased in a 19th-century mansion that once belonged to a rich Spanish tycoon you can tuck in to classic Spanish staples such as potaje de garbanzos (chickpeas with pork) and paella here while appetizing music drifts in from the Casa de la Trova next door.

Restaurante Hostal del Rijo (Cubanacán; ☎ 32-85-8; Honorato No 12) You could come here on a first date, so alluring is the quiet colonial ambience in the hotel's impressive central courtyard. Service is equally good and the food does its best in a city not renowned for its cuisine.

Las Arcadas (☎ 32-71-02; Independencia Norte No 1) Based at Hotel Plaza, Las Arcadas restaurant is another place where the refined colonial surroundings seem to add taste layers to the all-too-familiar comida criolla (Creole food) dishes. There's good coffee, too.

GROCERIES

Mercado agropecuario (cnr Independencia Sur & Honorato) Cuba's most centrally located agropecuario is situated just off the main shopping boulevard. Stick you head in and see how the Cubans shop.

Panadería El Fenix (cnr Máximo Gomez Norte & Frank País; ☯ 6am-6pm) Follow the aroma. Cuban bread might taste like the host at Sunday Mass, but it sure smells good.

La Época (Independencia Norte No 50C) Good for groceries.

Entertainment

Sancti Spíritus has a wonderful evening ambience: cool, inclusive and unpretentious. You can sample it in any of the following places.

Casa de la Cultura (☎ 32-37-72; M Solano No 11) Numerous cultural events that at weekends spill out into the street and render the pavement impassable.

our pick **Uneac** (Unión Nacional de Escritores y Artistas de Cuba; National Union of Cuban Writers & Artists; ☎ 32-63-75; Independencia Sur No 10) There are friendly nods as you enter, handshakes offered by people you've never even met, while the starry-eyed crooner on stage blows kisses to his girlfriend(s) in the audience. Uneac concerts always feel more like family gatherings than organized cultural events and Sancti Spíritus' is one of the nicest 'families' you'll meet.

Casa del Joven Creador (Céspedes Norte No 118) Instead of hanging around on street corners peddling dodgy substances, Sancti Spíritus' youth head to this happening cultural venue near the Museo Casa Natal de Serafín Sánchez for rock and rap concerts.

Casa de la Trova Miguel Companioni (☎ 32-68-02; Máximo Gómez Sur No 26) Kicking folk-music venue off Plaza Honorato on a par with Trinidad. But here the crowds are 90% local and 10% tourist.

Café ARTex (M Solano; admission CUC$1; ☯ 10pm-2am Tue-Sun) On an upper floor in Parque Serafín Sánchez, this place has more of a nightclub feel than the usual ARTex patio. There's dancing, live music and karaoke nightly and a Sunday matinee at 2pm (admission CUC$3). Thursday is reggaetón (Cuban hip-hop) night and the cafe also hosts comedy. Good groups to look out for in Sancti Spíritus are the Septeto Espirituanao and the Septeto de Son del Yayabo.

Estadio José A Huelga (Circunvalación) From October to April, baseball games are held at this stadium, 1km north of the bus station.

SANCTI SPÍRITUS PROVINCE

Teatro Principal (☎ 232-5755; Av Jesús Menéndez No 102) This landmark architectural icon next to the Puente Yayabo has weekend matinees (at 10am) with kids' theater.

The city's two main cinemas are **Cine Conrado Benítez** (☎ 32-53-27; Máximo Gómez Norte No 13) and **Cine Serafín Sánchez** (☎ 32-38-39; M Solano No 7), both on Parque Serafín Sánchez.

Shopping

Anything you might need – from batteries to frying pans – is sold at street stalls along the pedestrian mall on Independencia Sur, which recently benefited from a handsome refurbishment.

Casa de Comisiones (Independencia Sur No 6; ☒ 9am-4pm) Serious retro freaks will love this combination of pawn shop and flea market, a riot of prerevolutionary cameras, vintage jewelry, and stuff your Grandma never got around to throwing out.

Galería La Arcada (Independencia Sur) This place has Cuban crafts and paintings.

VideCuba (Independencia Norte No 50; ☒ 9am-9pm) Replace your well-worn batteries next door to La Época grocery store.

Getting There & Away

BUS

The provincial **bus station** (☎ 2-4142; Carretera Central) is 2km east of town. Punctual and air-conditioned **Víazul** (☎ 2-4142; www.viazul.com) buses serve numerous destinations.

The Santiago de Cuba departure also stops in Ciego de Ávila (CUC$6, 1¼ hours), Camagüey (CUC$10, three hours), Las Tunas (CUC$17, five hours 40 minutes) and Bayamo (CUC$21, seven hours). The Havana bus stops at Santa Clara (CUC$6, 1¼ hours) and Entronque de Jagüey (CUC$10, three hours).

TRAIN

There are two train stations serving Sancti Spíritus. For Havana (CUC$14, eight hours, 9pm alternate days), via Santa Clara (CUC$4,

two hours), and to Cienfuegos (CUC$5.50, five hours, 4am Monday) use the main **train station** (☎ 32-47-90; Av Jesús Menéndez al final; ☒ ticket window 7am-2pm Mon-Sat), southwest of the Puente Yayabo, an easy 10-minute walk from the city center.

Points east are served out of Guayos, 15km north of Sancti Spíritus, including Holguín (CUC$14, 8½ hours, 9:30am), Santiago de Cuba (CUC$21, 10¼ hours, 8:45am) and Bayamo (CUC$13, 8¼ hours). If you're on the Havana–Santiago de Cuba cross-country express and going to Sancti Spíritus or Trinidad, you have to get off at Guayos.

The ticket office at the Sancti Spíritus train station can sell you tickets for the trains from Guayos, but you must find your own way there (CUC$8 to CUC$10 in a taxi, but bargain hard).

TRUCKS & TAXIS

Trucks to Trinidad, Jatibonico and elsewhere depart from the bus station. A state taxi to Trinidad will cost you around CUC$35.

Getting Around

Horse carts on Carretera Central, opposite the bus station, run to Parque Serafín Sánchez when full (one peso). Bici-taxis gather at the corner of Laborni and Céspedes Norte. There is a **Cubacar** (☎ 32-85-33) booth on the northeast corner of Parque Serafín Sánchez; prices for daily car hire start at around CUC$70. The **Servi-Cupet gas station** (Carretera Central) is 1.5km north of Villa Los Laureles, on the Carretera Central toward Santa Clara. Parking in Parque Serafín Sánchez is relatively safe. Ask in hotels Rijo and Plaza and they will often find a man to stand guard overnight for CUC$1.

TRINIDAD
pop 52,896

Trinidad is special; a perfectly preserved Spanish colonial settlement where the clock stopped ticking in 1850 and – bar the odd

VÍAZUL DEPARTURES

Destination	Cost (CUC$)	Duration	Departure time
Havana	23	5hr	1:55am, 3:05am, 6:45am, 4:30pm, 8:25pm
Holguín	21	6hr	1:05am, 2:25am, 2:15pm, 8:50pm
Santiago de Cuba	28	9hr 15min	2:25am, 3:10am, 9:25am, 3:20pm, 8:50pm
Trinidad	6	1hr 20min	5:25am
Varadero	17	5hr	5:55am

THE ROAD TO NOWHERE

To the experienced motorist, Cuba's arterial Autopista is no ordinary freeway. Home to vintage Buicks, grazing cattle, onion sellers, hitchhikers, hovering vultures and the odd runaway steam train or two, the road – originally designated to stretch from Pinar del Río in the west to Guantánamo in the east – comes to an abrupt halt at Jatibonico in Sancti Spíritus province after 650km of badly paved purgatory.

Financed with Soviet money during the 1980s, construction of the island's ambitiously planned Autopista Nacional barely got beyond the halfway stage thanks to the ignominious fall of communism in Eastern Europe in 1991 and the resulting demise of Cuba's once-illustrious superpower patron.

Indeed, so sudden was the Soviet pullout that, even today, lane markings remain unpainted, slip roads end in sugarcane fields and an odd assortment of half-finished bridges dangle like crumbling beacons above the surreally deserted eight-lane highway.

---

gaggle of tourists – have yet to restart. Built on huge sugar fortunes amassed in the adjacent Valle de Ingenios during the early 19th century, the riches of the town's pre–War of Independence heyday are still very much in evidence in illustrious colonial-style mansions bedecked with Italian frescoes, Wedgewood china, Spanish furniture and French chandeliers.

Declared a World Heritage Site by Unesco in 1988, Trinidad's secrets quickly became public property and it wasn't long before busloads of visitors started arriving to sample the beauty of Cuba's oldest and most enchanting 'outdoor museum.' Yet tourism has done little to deaden Trinidad's gentle southern sheen. The town retains a quiet, almost soporific air in its rambling cobbled streets replete with leather-faced *guajiros* (country folk), snorting donkeys and melodic guitar-wielding troubadours.

But, ringed by sparkling natural attractions, Trinidad is more than just a potential PhD thesis for history buffs. Twelve kilometers to the south lies platinum-blond Ancón, the south coast's best beach, while, looming 18km to the north, the purple-hued shadows of the Sierra del Escambray offer a lush adventure playground.

With its Unesco price tag and a steady stream of overseas visitors, Trinidad, not surprisingly, has an above-average quota of prowling *jineteros*, though mostly they're more annoying than aggressive. If you get worn down by the constant unwanted attention, head for a friendly casa particular in the small town of La Boca, 5km to the south, and bike or hike back in for the day-time and evening attractions.

History

In 1514 pioneering conquistador Diego Velázquez de Cuéllar founded La Villa de la Santísima Trinidad on Cuba's south coast, the island's third settlement, after Baracoa and Bayamo. Legend has it that erstwhile 'Apostle of the Indians' Fray Bartolomé de las Casas held Trinidad's first Mass under a Calabash tree in present-day Plazuela Real del Jigüe. In 1518 Velázquez' former secretary, Hernán Cortés, passed through the town recruiting mercenaries for his all-conquering expedition to Mexico and the settlement was all but emptied of its original inhabitants. Over the ensuing 60 years it was left to a smattering of local Taíno Indians to keep the ailing economy alive through a mixture of farming, cattle-rearing and a little outside trade.

Reduced to a small rural backwater by the 17th century and cut off from the colonial authorities in Havana by dire communications, Trinidad became a haven for pirates and smugglers who controlled a lucrative contraband slave trade with British-controlled Jamaica.

Things began to change in the early 19th century when the town became the capital of the Departamento Central and hundreds of French refugees fleeing a slave rebellion in Haiti arrived, setting up more than 50 small sugar mills in the nearby Valle de los Ingenios. Sugar soon replaced leather and salted beef as the region's most important product and by the mid-19th century the area around Trinidad was producing a third of Cuba's sugar, generating enough wealth to finance the rich cluster of opulent buildings that characterize the town today.

The boom ended rather abruptly during the two Wars of Independence, when the

SANCTI SPÍRITUS PROVINCE

TRINIDAD

0 —— 500 m
0 —— 0.3 miles

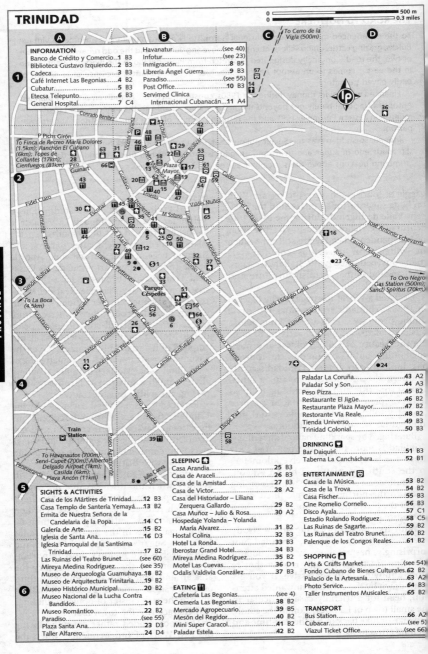

INFORMATION
Banco de Crédito y Comercio....1 B3
Biblioteca Gustavo Izquierdo...2 B3
Cadeca....................................3 B3
Café Internet Las Begonias.....4 B2
Cubatur...................................5 B3
Etecsa Telepunto.....................6 B3
General Hospital......................7 C4
Havanatur.........................(see 40)
Infotur..............................(see 23)
Inmigración...........................8 B5
Librería Ángel Guerra..............9 B3
Paradiso............................(see 55)
Post Office..........................10 B3
Servimed Clínica
Internacional Cubanacán...11 A4

To Cerro de la Vigía (500m)

To Finca de Recreo María Dolores
(1.5km); Ranchón El Cubano
(6km); Topes de
Collantes (17km);
Cienfuegos (81km)

To Oro Negro
Gas Station (500m);
Sancti Spíritus (70km)

To La Boca
(4.5km)

Train
Station

To Havanautos (700m);
Servi-Cupet (700m); Alberto
Delgado Airport (1km);
Casilda (6km);
Playa Ancón (11km)

SIGHTS & ACTIVITIES
Casa de los Mártires de Trinidad......12 B3
Casa Templo de Santería Yemayá...13 B2
Ermita de Nuestra Señora de la
Candelaria de la Popa............14 C1
Galería de Arte.........................15 B2
Iglesia de Santa Ana.................16 D3
Iglesia Parroquial de la Santísima
Trinidad..................................17 B2
Las Ruinas del Teatro Brunet....(see 60)
Mireya Medina Rodríguez.......(see 35)
Museo de Arqueología Guamuhaya..18 B2
Museo de Arquitectura Trinitaria.....19 B2
Museo Histórico Municipal......20 B2
Museo Nacional de la Lucha Contra
Bandidos...............................21 B2
Museo Romántico....................22 B2
Paradiso...............................(see 55)
Plaza Santa Ana.......................23 D3
Taller Alfarero.........................24 D4

SLEEPING
Casa Arandia...........................25 B3
Casa de Araceli........................26 B3
Casa de la Amistad...................27 B3
Casa de Victor..........................28 A2
Casa del Historiador – Liliana
Zerquera Gallardo.................29 B2
Casa Muñoz – Julio & Rosa......30 A2
Hospedaje Yolanda – Yolanda
María Alvarez.........................31 B2
Hostal Colina............................32 B3
Hotel La Ronda.........................33 B3
Iberostar Grand Hotel...............34 B3
Mireya Medina Rodríguez.........35 B3
Motel Las Cuevas......................36 D1
Odalis Valdivia González...........37 B3

EATING
Cafetería Las Begonias...........(see 4)
Cremería Las Begonias.............38 B3
Mercado Agropecuario.............39 B5
Mesón del Regidor...................40 B2
Mini Super Caracol...................41 B2
Paladar Estela..........................42 B2
Paladar La Coruña....................43 A2
Paladar Sol y Son.....................44 A3
Peso Pizza...............................45 B2
Restaurante El Jigüe.................46 B2
Restaurante Plaza Mayor..........47 B2
Restorante Vía Reale................48 B2
Tienda Universo.......................49 B3
Trinidad Colonial.....................50 B3

DRINKING
Bar Daiquirí.............................51 B3
Taberna La Canchánchara........52 B1

ENTERTAINMENT
Casa de la Música....................53 B2
Casa de la Trova.......................54 B2
Casa Fischer.............................55 B3
Cine Romelio Cornelio..............56 B3
Disco Ayala..............................57 C1
Estadio Rolando Rodríguez.......58 C5
Las Ruinas de Sagarte...............59 B2
Las Ruinas del Teatro Brunet.....60 B2
Palenque de los Congos Reales..61 B2

SHOPPING
Arts & Crafts Market..............(see 54)
Fondo Cubano de Bienes Culturales.62 B2
Palacio de la Artesanía..............63 A2
Photo Service...........................64 B3
Taller Instrumentos Musicales...65 B2

TRANSPORT
Bus Station..............................66 A2
Cubacar................................(see 5)
Víazul Ticket Office................(see 66)

surrounding sugar plantations were devastated by fire and fighting. Floundering in the years that followed, the industry never fully recovered. By the late 19th century the focus of the sugar trade had shifted to Cienfuegos and Matanzas provinces and Trinidad, cut off by the Sierra del Escambray from the other parts of Cuba, slipped into a somnolent and life-threatening economic coma. Trinidad's tourist renaissance began in the 1950s when President Batista passed a preservation law that recognized the town's historical value. In 1965 the town was declared a national monument and in 1988 it became a Unesco World Heritage Site.

Orientation

Trinidad turns on two hubs. The museums and churches of the *casco histórico* (old town) are focused around Plaza Mayor, while the everyday facilities serving the local people are on – or near – Parque Céspedes. The bus station is west of Plaza Mayor. Everything is walking distance.

Information

BOOKSTORES

Librería Ángel Guerra (☎ 99-37-48; José Martí No 273 btwn Colón & Zerquera; ☺ 8am-3pm Mon-Sat)

INTERNET ACCESS & TELEPHONE

Café Internet Las Begonias (Antonio Maceo No 473; internet access per half hr CUC$3; ☺ 9am-9pm) On the corner of Simón Bolívar. Crowded.

Etecsa Telepunto (cnr General Lino Pérez & Francisco Pettersen; internet access per hr CUC$6; ☺ 7am-11pm) Freshly refurbished Telepunto with brand-new computer terminals.

LIBRARIES

Biblioteca Gustavo Izquierdo (José Martí No 265 btwn Colón & Zerquera; ☺ 8am-9pm Mon-Fri, to 6pm Sat, to 1pm Sun)

MEDIA

Radio Trinidad Broadcasts over 1200AM.

MEDICAL SERVICES

General Hospital (☎ 99-32-01; Antonio Maceo No 6) Southeast of the center.

Servimed Clínica Internacional Cubanacán (☎ 99-62-40; General Lino Pérez No 103; ☺ 24hr) On the corner of Anastasio Cárdenas. There is an on-site pharmacy selling products in Convertibles.

MONEY

Banco de Crédito y Comercio (☎ 99-24-05; José Martí No 264)

Cadeca (☎ 99-62-63; José Martí No 164) Between Parque Céspedes and Camilo Cienfuegos.

POST

Post office (Antonio Maceo No 418) Between Colón and Zerquera.

TRAVEL AGENCIES

Cubatur (☎ 99-63-14; Antonio Maceo No 447; ☺ 9am-8pm) On the corner of Zerquera. Good for general tourist information, plus hotel bookings, car rentals, excursions etc. State taxis congregate outside.

Havanatur (☎ 99-61-83; Simón Bolívar No 424) In the Mesón del Regidor cafe.

Infotur (☎ 99-82-57; Plaza Santa Ana, Camilo Cienfuegos)

Paradiso (☎ 99-64-86; General Lino Pérez No 306) Cultural and general tours in English, Spanish and French.

Dangers & Annoyances

Thefts, though still uncommon, are on the rise in Trinidad. Incidents usually occur late at night and the victims are, more often than not, inebriated. Be on your guard, particularly when returning to your hotel or casa after a night out on the drink.

Sights

In Trinidad, all roads lead to **Plaza Mayor**, the town's remarkably peaceful main square, located at the heart of the *casco histórico* and ringed by a quartet of impressive buildings.

The showpiece museum here is the grandiose **Museo Histórico Municipal** (☎ 99-44-60; Simón Bolívar No 423; admission CUC$2; ☺ 9am-5pm Sat-Thu), just off Plaza Mayor, housed in a mansion that belonged to the Borrell family from 1827 to

1830. Later the building passed to a German planter named Kanter or Cantero, and it's still called Casa Cantero. Reputedly Dr Justo Cantero acquired vast sugar estates by poisoning an old slave trader and marrying his widow, who also suffered an untimely death. Cantero's ill-gotten wealth is well displayed in the stylish neoclassical decoration of the rooms. The view of Trinidad from the top of the tower alone is worth the price of admission. Visit before 11am, when the tour buses start rolling in.

Despite its rather unremarkable outer facade, the **Iglesia Parroquial de la Santísima Trinidad** (11am-12:30pm Mon-Sat), on the northeastern side of Plaza Mayor, graces countless Trinidad postcard views. Rebuilt in 1892 on the site of an earlier church destroyed in a storm, the church mixes 20th-century touch-ups with older artifacts from as far back as the 18th century, such as the venerated Christ of the True Cross (1713), which occupies the second altar from the front to the left. Your best chance of seeing it is during Mass at 8pm weekdays, 4pm Saturday, and 9am and 5pm Sunday.

Across Calle Simón Bolívar is the **Museo Romántico** (99-43-63; Echerri No 52; admission CUC$2; 9am-5pm Tue-Sun) in the glittering Palacio Brunet. The ground floor was built in 1740, and the upstairs was added in 1808. In 1974 the mansion was converted into a museum with 19th-century furnishings, a fine collection of china and various other period pieces. Pushy museum staff will materialize out of the shadows for a tip. The shop adjacent has a good selection of photos and books in English.

Another public display of wealth is in the **Museo de Arquitectura Trinitaria** (99-32-08; Ripalda No 83; admission CUC$1; 9am-5pm Sat-Thu), on the southeastern side of Plaza Mayor, showcasing upper-class domestic architecture of the 18th and 19th centuries. The museum is housed in buildings erected in 1738 and 1785 that were joined together in 1819. It was once the residence of the wealthy Iznaga family.

On the northwestern side of Plaza Mayor is the **Museo de Arqueología Guamuhaya** (99-34-20; Simón Bolívar No 457; admission CUC$1; 9am-5pm Tue-Sat), an odd mix of stuffed animals, native bones, and vaguely incongruous 19th-century kitchen furniture. Don't make it your first priority.

Admission is completely free at the 19th-century Palacio Ortiz, which today houses the **Galería de Arte** (cnr Rubén Martínez Villena & Simón Bolívar; 9am-5pm), on the southwestern side of Plaza Mayor. Worth a look for its quality local art, particularly the embroidery, pottery and jewelry; there's also a pleasant courtyard.

No Santería museum can replicate the ethereal spiritual experience of Regla de Ocha, though the **Casa Templo de Santería Yemayá** (Rubén Martínez Villena No 59 btwn Simón Bolívar & Piro Guinart) has a try. Containing a Santería altar to Yemayá, Goddess of the Sea with myriad offerings of fruit, water and stones, the house is presided over by *santeros* (priests of the Afro-Cuban religion Santería) who'll emerge from the back patio and surprise you with some well-rehearsed tourist spiel. On the saint's anniversary, March 19, ceremonies are performed day and night.

Perhaps the most recognizable building in Trinidad is the withered pastel-yellow bell-tower of the former convent of San Francisco de Asís. Since 1986 the building has housed the **Museo Nacional de la Lucha Contra Bandidos** (99-41-21; Echerri No 59; admission CUC$1; 9am-5pm Tue-Sun). The displays are mostly photos, maps, weapons and other objects relating to the struggle against the various counterrevolutionary bands that took a leaf out of Fidel's book and operated illicitly out of the Sierra del Escambray between 1960 and 1965. The fuselage of a US U-2 spy plane shot down over Cuba is also on display. You can climb the tower for good views.

It's easy to miss the small **Casa de los Mártires de Trinidad** (Zerquera No 254 btwn Antonio Maceo & José Martí; guided/unguided CUC$1/free; 9am-5pm), dedicated to 72 Trinidad residents who died in the struggle against Fulgencio Batista, the campaign against the counterrevolutionaries, and the little-mentioned war in Angola.

Grass grows around the domed bell-tower and the arched doorways were bricked up long ago, but the shell of the ruined **Iglesia de Santa Ana** (1812) still defiantly remains. Looming like a time-worn ecclesial stencil, it looks quite ghostly after dark. Across the eponymous square that delineates Trinidad's northeastern reaches is a former Spanish prison (1844) that has been converted into a tourist center the **Plaza Santa Ana** (Camilo Cienfuegos; admission free 11am-10pm). The complex includes an art gallery, a handicraft market, a ceramics shop, a bar and a restaurant.

Five blocks south is **Taller Alfarero** (Andrés Berro admission free; 8am-noon & 2-5pm Mon-Fri), a large factory where teams of workers make trademark Trinidad ceramics from local clay using a traditional potter's wheel. You can watch them at work and buy the finished product.

Activities

There are a couple of DIY hikes worth doing if you can take the heat and the uphill gradients. For views and a workout, walk straight up the street between the Iglesia Parroquial and the Museo Romántico (Calle Simón Bolívar) to the destroyed 18th-century **Ermita de Nuestra Señora de la Candelaria de la Popa**, part of a former Spanish military hospital situated on a hill to the north of the town (use insect repellent). From here it's a 30-minute hike further up the hill to the radio transmitter atop 180m-high **Cerro de la Vigía**, which delivers broad vistas of Trinidad, Playa Ancón and the entire littoral.

Another option is to hike west out of town on the (quiet) road to Cienfuegos. Pass the 'Welcome to Trinidad' sign and cross a bridge over the Río Guaurabo. A track on your left now leads back under the bridge and up a narrow, poorly paved road for 5km to **Ranchón El Cubano** (Map p309; admission CUC$6.50). This pleasant spot within a protected park consists of a *ranchón*-style restaurant that specializes in *pez gato* (catfish), a fish farm, and a 2km trail to a refreshing waterfall. There are also stables here and opportunities to partake in horseback riding. If you hike to El Cubano from Trinidad, you'll clock up a total of approximately 16km. With a stop for lunch in the *ranchón*, it can make an excellent day trip. Alternatively, for CUC$15 you can organize a day excursion with Cubatur (p301) including motor transport.

Closer to town is the **Finca de Recreo María Dolores** (☎ 99-64-81; Carretera de Cienfuegos Km 1.5), a rustic Cubanacán hotel that runs horseback-riding trips to El Cubano (CUC$15, four hours) and boat trips down the Río Guaurabo to La Boca (CUC$5), and hosts sporadic *fiestas campesinas* (country fairs).

The bike ride to **Playa Ancón** is another great outdoor adventure. Once there you can snorkel, catch some rays or use the swimming pool or ping-pong table. The best route by far is via the small seaside village of La Boca. See p308 for information about bike rental.

Courses

At **Las Ruinas del Teatro Brunet** (Antonio Maceo No 461 btwn Simón Bolívar & Zerquera) you can take drumming lessons (9am to 11am Saturday) and

dance lessons (1pm to 4pm Saturday). Dance lessons are also available with popular local teacher **Mireya Medina Rodríguez** (☎ 99-39-94; Antonio Maceo No 472 btwn Simon Bolivar & Zerquera), who instructs everything from *chachachá* to rumba in her front room. Another option is the travel agent **Paradiso** (☎ 99-64-86; paradisotr@sctd.artex.cu; Casa ARTex, General Lino Pérez No 306), which offers salsa lessons from CUC$5 for 90 minutes.

Paradiso has incorporated a number of interesting courses into its cultural program including Cuban architecture (CUC$20), Afro-Cuban culture (CUC$30), *artes plásticas* (visual arts; CUC$30) and popular music (CUC$30). These courses last four hours and are taught by cultural specialists. They require a minimum number of six to 10 people to take place, but you can always negotiate. At the same venue there are guitar lessons for CUC$5 an hour and courses in Spanish language/Cuban culture for CUC$8 an hour.

Tours

With its sketchy public transport and steep road gradients (making cycling arduous), it's easiest to visit Topes de Collantes (p311) via a day tour. A tour to Topes de Collantes by state taxi shouldn't cost more than CUC$25 with the wait time; bargain hard. **Cubatur** (☎ 99-63-14; Antonio Maceo No 447; ☯ 9am-8pm), just outside the *casco histórico*, organizes a variety of hiking/nature trips from between CUC$23 and CUC$43 per person depending on the excursion. Also available are horseback-riding tours to Ranchón El Cubano.

Paradiso has the best-value day tour to the Valle de los Ingenios, for CUC$9 per person, and an artist-studio tour in Trinidad for CUC$10 per person.

If you're staying in a private house, your hosts will usually know someone renting horses. Julio Muñoz, proprietor of Casa Muñoz (p304), is a horse whisperer who specializes in the humane treatment of animals.

For diving, fishing, sailing and snorkeling tours, see Playa Ancón, p309; any of Trinidad's agencies (p301) can organize the same excursions.

Festivals & Events

The three-day **Fiestas Sanjuaneras** in the last weekend in June is a local Carnaval where rum-fuelled horsemen gallop through the streets: take cover. The **Semana de la Cultura Trinitaria** (Trinidad Culture Week) is during

ASK A LOCAL

If you choose to go horseback riding around Trinidad, be sure to check the condition of your horse and equipment first. Some of the illegal guides offer horses in a poor state of health, which is not only cruel for the horses, but dangerous for the rider too.

Julio, Trinidad

the second week in January to coincide with the city's anniversary. **Semana Santa** is also important in Trinidad and on Good Friday thousands of people form a procession.

Sleeping

Trinidad has approximately 400 casas particulares and competition is hot: arriving by bus or walking the streets with luggage, you'll be besieged by hustlers working for commissions or by the casa owners themselves. With so many beautiful homes and hospitable families renting, there's no reason to be rushed. Take your time to shop around.

IN TOWN
Casas Particulares

Mireya Medina Rodríguez (☎ 99-39-94; miretrini@yahoo.es; Antonio Maceo No 472 btwn Simón Bolívar & Zerquera; r CUC$20-25; 🔀) Right in the center of things, Mireya is a popular dance teacher who rents out one room with private bath in her well-kept colonial house. Expect excellent dinners, hospitable service and plenty of salsa in the front room.

our pick Casa Muñoz – Julio & Rosa (☎ 99-36-73; www.trinidadphoto.com; José Martí No 401; r CUC$25; 🅿 🔀) Julio is an accomplished published photographer who runs workshops and courses out of his stunning colonial home (which has been featured in *National Geographic*). He's also a horse whisperer – his beautiful mare lives out back next to a slightly less attractive Russian Moskvich. There are two huge rooms here, but book early, it's insanely popular.

Casa de Victor (☎ 99-64-44; Maceo btwn Piro Guinart & P Pichs Girón; r CUC$20-25; 🔀) If Casa Muñoz is full you can keep it in the family down the road at Victor's place, where two self-contained upstairs rooms share a couple of spacious *salas*, a balcony overlooking the street, and a fine *terraza* decorated rather ingeniously with recycled ceramic pots.

Odalis Valdivia González (☎ 99-33-09; Callejón Smith No 3 btwn Maceo & Av Jesús Menéndez; r CUC$20-25; 🔀) With two independent rooms off a back patio this place is clean and relaxing with welcoming hosts.

Casa del Historiador – Liliana Zerquera Gallardo (☎ 99-36-34; Echerri No 54 btwn Piro Guinart & Simón Bolívar; r CUC$20-25; 🔀) On the corner of Plaza Mayor, this place could (should) be a museum. Instead it's the home of the octogenarian city historian whose wife lets out a couple of rooms in this classic 1808 sugar-merchant's house. The fine accommodation is complemented by a huge rear terrace adorned with a grand terra-cotta staircase and signature Trinidadian *aljibe* (water-storage well).

Casa de Araceli (☎ 99-35-58; General Lino Pérez No 207 btwn Frank País & Miguel Calzada; r CUC$20-25; 🔀) Had enough of the colonial splendor? Head away from the tourist frenzy to General Lino Pérez, where Araceli rents two upstairs rooms with a private entrance and a very quiet flower-bedecked terrace.

Casa Arandia (☎ 99-32-40; Antonio Maceo No 438 btwn Colón & Zerquera; r CUC$20-25; 🔀) Another Trinidad dream home that comes with a loft room, a terrace and views.

'Hospedaje Yolanda' – Yolanda María Alvarez (☎ 99-30-51; yolimar56@yahoo.com; Piro Guinart No 227; r CUC$25-30) This isn't a casa; it's a palace! There are eight rooms for starters, though only two can be rented at one time. Dating from the 1700s, its dazzling interior makes the Museo Romántico look like a jumble sale. Take the Italian tiles, the French frescoes, the rare Mexican spiral staircase, the fabulous terrace views; the list goes on…

Hostal Colina (☎ 99-23-19; Antonio Maceo No 374 btwn General Lino Pérez & Colón; r CUC$25-35; 🔀) Another place that leaves you struggling for superlatives. Although the house dates from the 1830s, it's got a definitive modern touch, giving one the feeling of being in a plush Mexican hacienda. Two pastel-yellow rooms give out onto a patio where you can sit at the plush wooden bar and catch mangos and avocados as they fall from the trees.

Hotels

Trinidad also has four in-town hotels, one for every price bracket.

Casa de la Amistad (amistur@ceniai.inf.cu; Zerquera btwn José Martí & Frank País; r CUC$25) This hostel, run by the Instituto Cubano de la Amistad, is popular among visitors politically sympathetic to Cuba. It has six clean and well-equipped rooms with brand-new showers and TVs, plus a small eating area and patio out the back. It's a decent budget option in the center of town.

Hotel La Ronda (Cubanacán; ☎ 99-61-33; José Martí No 238; r CUC$46; 🖳) A boutique hotel that never really deserved its classification, the centrally located La Ronda has always struggled to compete with the scores of better-run, more comfortably attired casas particulares nearby. Aware perhaps of their predicament, state owners Cubanacán were giving this former Islazul-run crash-pad a face-lift at the time of writing. With 19 rooms and a great location there's plenty of potential.

Motel Las Cuevas (Cubanacán; ☎ 99-61-33; s/d with breakfast CUC$80/100; 🅿 🕱 🖳) Perched on a hill above town, Las Cuevas is more hotel than motel with bus tours being the main drive-by clientele. While the setting's lush, the rooms – which are arranged in scattered two-storied units – are a little less memorable, as is the breakfast. Value is added with a swimming pool, well-maintained gardens, panoramic views and the murky Cueva La Maravillosa, accessible down a stairway, where you'll see a huge tree growing out of a cavern (entry CUC$1).

our pick Iberostar Grand Hotel (Gran Caribe; ☎ 99-60-70; cnr José Martí & General Lino Pérez; s/d CUC$141/172; 🕱 🖳) Look out, Habaguanex! One in a trio of Spanish-run Iberostar's Cuban hotels, the five-star Grand oozes luxury the moment you arrive in its fern-filled, tile-embellished lobby. Clearing another hurdle is the service, which is as sleek as the fittings are flash. Maintaining 36 classy rooms in a remodeled 19th-century building, the Grand shies away from the standard all-inclusive tourist tattle, preferring to press privacy, refinement and an appreciation of history (you are, after all, in Trinidad).

OUTSIDE TOWN

Villa de Recreo María Dolores (Cubanacán; Map p309; ☎ 99-64-10 Carretera de Cienfuegos Km 1.5; s/d CUC$59/74; 🅿 🕱 🖳) Trinidad goes rustic with the out-of-town Recreo María Dolores, situated 1.5km west on the road to Cienfuegos and Topes de Collantes. Equipped with hotel-style rooms and cabins, the latter are the better option (try for one with a porch overlooking the Río Guaurabo). On nights when groups are present, there's a *fiesta campesina* (country

fair) with country-style Cuban folk dancing at 9:30pm, (free/CUC$5 for guests/nonguests, including one drink). There's also a swimming pool, a *ranchón* restaurant and boat and horseback-riding tours. One kilometer west of the Recreo María Dolores is a monument to Alberto Delgado, a teacher murdered by counterrevolutionaries.

Eating

In truth, the casas particulares are Trinidad's best restaurants. Dinners usually cost from CUC$6 to CUC$10, depending on what you eat, and they're nearly always more accommodating for vegetarians. Nonetheless, the lure of Trinidad's nightlife is strong and the small stash of colonial restaurants is pretty, even if the food isn't.

PALADARES

Trinidad has three long-standing legal paladares. Innumerable hustlers will accost you around Plaza Mayor claiming otherwise. Don't believe them.

Paladar Sol y Son (☎ 99-29-26; Simón Bolívar No 283 btwn Frank País & José Martí; mains CUC$8-10; 🕒 noon-2pm & 7:30-11pm) All the ingredients of a fine Trinidad evening – think antiques, an elegant patio and the dulcet strains of an eloquent *trovador* – plus good food thrown in. Even the waiting room (yes, it gets busy) is a veritable museum piece. The house special is roast chicken and it's worth the wait. English is spoken here.

Paladar Estela (☎ 99-43-29; Simón Bolívar No 557; 🕒 2-11:30pm) You can choose the dining room or pretty rear garden to take your meals in this popular place located above the Plaza Mayor (the owner also rents rooms). *Cordero* (lamb) served shredded is the house specialty, and the portions are large.

Paladar La Coruña (José Martí No 428; 🕒 11am-11pm) A battling third after Sol y Son and Estela. Eager-to-please and friendly staff at this no-frills paladar serve chicken and pork, and the occasional fish.

RESTAURANTS

Housed in an attractive array of colonial mansions, Trinidad's government restaurants are full of the standard state-run foibles: average food, bored staff, and menus where most of the dishes have gone AWOL. These places are OK for an un-fancy lunch but, for a filling dinner, you might want to stick to the home cooking in your casa particular.

Restaurante Plaza Mayor (☎ 99-64-70; cnr Rubén Martínez Villena & Zerquera; dishes from CUC$4; ⏰ 11am-10pm) The best bet courtesy of its on-off lunchtime buffet, which, for around CUC$10, ought to fill you up until dinnertime. Nighttime offerings aren't bad either if you stick to the chicken and beef, though the atmosphere can be a little flat.

Trinidad Colonial (☎ 99-64-73; Antonio Maceo No 402; ⏰ 11:30am-10pm) Here you'll dine on good portions of Cuban cuisine in the elegant 19th-century Casa Bidegaray. Meals are reasonable, even if the service is a bit frosty, with smoked pork topping out at CUC$6. The store attached has a good selection of books.

Restorante Vía Reale (Rubén Martínez Villena No 74 btwn Piro Guinart & Pablo Pichs Girón; lunch CUC$4; ⏰ noon-4pm) Break the chicken-and-pork grind at this Italian place with good pizza and spaghetti lunches. This is a viable vegetarian option.

Restaurante El Jigüe (☎ 99-64-76; cnr Rubén Martínez Villena & Piro Guinart; ⏰ 11am-10pm) Stunning setting with less-than-stunning food. Bank on the house specialty, the aptly-named *pollo al Jigüe*; it's baked at least, offering savory flavors distinct from the usual *frito* (fried).

QUICK EATS

Mesón del Regidor (☎ 99-65-72; Simón Bolívar No 424; ⏰ 10am-10pm) A cafe-cum-restaurant with a friendly ambience and a revolving lineup of local musicians, including the town's best *trovador*, Israel Moreno, who'll drop by during the day and serenade you with a song over grilled cheese sandwiches and *café con leche* (coffee with milk). Savor the surprise.

Cafetería Las Begonias (☎ 99-64-73; cnr Antonio Maceo & Simón Bolívar; ⏰ 9am-10pm; 🖳) The daytime nexus for Trinidad's transient backpacker crowd, meaning it's a good font of local information and the best place in town to meet other travelers over sandwiches, espresso and ice cream. There's a bar behind a partition wall, clean(ish) toilets in a rear courtyard, and four or five cheap – but always crowded – internet terminals.

Just across the street is an ever-popular **Cremería Las Begonias** (Antonio Maceo) that doubles up as a Cubatur office, and opposite from it a little old man does a flying trade in **peso pizza** (Simón Bolívar).

Look out for more peso food on the corner of Piro Guinart and Antonio Maceo, not far from the bus station, and also around the Camilo Cienfuegos–Paseo Agramonte–Anastasio Cárdenas intersection on the road south out of town.

GROCERIES

Mercado agropecuario (cnr Pedro Zerquera & Manuel Fajardo; ⏰ 8am-6pm Mon-Sat, to noon Sun) Trinidad's *agropecuario* (vegetable market) isn't Covent Garden, but you should still be able to get basic fruits and vegetables.

Tienda Universo (José Martí) This shop, near Zerquera in the Galería Comercial Universo, is Trinidad's best (and most expensive) grocery store. Head here for yogurt, nuts and those lifesaving cookies.

Mini Super Caracol (cnr Gustavo Izquierdo & Zerquera; ⏰ 9am-9pm) This store has a decent selection of groceries and a resident hawker outside plying cigars.

Drinking

Bar Daiquirí (General Lino Pérez No 313; ⏰ 24hr) Presumably Papa Hemingway never dropped by this cozy joint named after the drink he so famously popularized because the prices are extremely reasonable. Shoehorned into lively Lino Pérez, this is where locals and backpackers warm up on their way to an all-night salsa binge. There are snacks, if you've got the stomach.

Taberna La Canchánchara (cnr Rubén Martínez Villena & Ciro Redondo). This place is famous for its eponymous house cocktail made from rum, honey, lemon and water. Local musicians regularly drop by for off-the-cuff jam sessions and it's not unusual for the Canchánchara-inebriated crowd to break into spontaneous dancing.

Entertainment

Casa Fischer (General Lino Pérez No 312 btwn José Martí & Francisco Codania; admission CUC$1) This is the local ARTex patio, which cranks up at 10pm with a salsa orchestra (on Tuesday, Wednesday, Thursday, Saturday and Sunday) or a folklore show (Friday). If you're early, kill time at its art gallery (free) and chat to the staff at the on-site Paradiso office about salsa lessons and other courses (p303).

Casa de la Trova (Echerri No 29; admission CUC$1; ⏰ 9pm-2am) Trinidad's spirited casa retains its earthy essence despite the high package-tourist-to-Cuban ratio. Local musicians to look out for here are Semillas del Son, Santa Palabra and the town's best *trovador*, Israel Moreno.

Las Ruinas del Teatro Brunet (Antonio Maceo No 461 btwn Simón Bolívar & Zerquera; admission CUC$1) Thi jazzed-up ruin has an athletic Afro-Cuban show on its pleasant patio at 9:30pm nightly.

Casa de la Música (☎ 99-34-14; admission free) One of Trinidad's and Cuba's classic venues, this casa is an alfresco affair that congregates on the sweeping staircase beside the Iglesia Parroquial off Plaza Mayor. A good mix of tourists and locals take in the 10pm salsa/dance show here. Alternatively, full-on salsa concerts are held in the casa's rear courtyard (also accessible from Juan Manuel Márquez; cover CUC$2).

ourpick Palenque de los Congos Reales (cnr Echerri & Av Jesús Menéndez; admission free) A must for rumba fans, this open patio on Trinidad's music alley has an eclectic menu incorporating salsa, *son* (Cuban popular music) and *trova* (traditional poetic singing). The highlight, however, is the 10pm rumba drums with soulful African rhythms and energetic fire-eating dancers.

Las Ruinas de Sagarte (Av Jesús Menéndez; admission free; 24hr) Another ruin (Trinidad's full of them) with a good house band and a high-energy, low-pressure dance scene.

Disco Ayala (admission CUC$10; 10pm-3am) It might not be the first time you've gone jiving in a cave, but this surreal place up by the Ermita Popa church beats all others for atmosphere and animation. While it's mainly a place to let rip and dance J-Lo style in the semi-darkness with as many mojitos as you care to sink, this disco also puts on a decent cabaret show with a pre-Columbian Indian theme.

Cine Romelio Cornelio (8pm Tue-Sun) This cinema, on the southwestern side of Parque Céspedes, shows films nightly.

Estadio Rolando Rodríguez (Eliope Paz; Oct-Apr) This stadium, at the southeastern end of Frank País, hosts baseball games.

Shopping

You can shop until you almost drop in Trinidad, at least at the open-air markets that are set up all over town. If you're looking for good souvenirs you've come to the right place.

Arts & Crafts Market (Av Jesús Menéndez) This excellent open-air market situated in front of the Casa de la Trova is the place to buy souvenirs, especially textiles and crochet work – just avoid the black coral and turtle-shell items that are made from endangered species and are forbidden entry into many countries.

Fondo Cubano de Bienes Culturales (Simón Bolívar No 418; 9am-5pm Mon-Fri, 9am-3pm Sat & Sun) Just down from Plaza Mayor, this store has a good selection of Cuban handicrafts.

You can see local painters at work – and you can buy their paintings too – at various points along Calles Francisco Toro, Valdés and Muñoz.

Other shopping options:

Palacio de la Artesanía (Piro Guinart No 221) This store, located opposite the bus station, also sells handicrafts.
Photo Service (José Martí No 192 btwn Camilo Cienfuegos & General Lino Pérez) Servicing all your photographic needs.
Taller Instrumentos Musicales (cnr Av Jesús Menéndez & Valdés Muñoz) Musical instruments are made here and sold in the adjacent shop.

Getting There & Away

AIR
Alberto Delgado Airport is 1km south of Trinidad, off the road to Casilda. Only Aerotaxi charters fly here.

BUS
The **bus station** (☎ 99-24-04; Piro Guinart No 224), runs provincial buses to Sancti Spíritus and Cienfuegos, though most foreigners use the more reliable Víazul service. Tickets are sold at a small window marked Taquilla Campo near the station entrance. Check the blackboard for the current schedule.

The **Víazul ticket office** (☎ 4448; 8-11:30am & 1-5pm) is further back in the station. It sells Víazul tickets to the following places (this

VÍAZUL DEPARTURES

Destination	Cost (CUC$)	Duration	Departure time
Cienfuegos	6	1½hr	7:30am, 9am, 3:00pm, 3:30pm
Havana	25	6hr 20min	7:30am, 3:00pm
Playa Girón	12	3hr 15min	3pm
Santa Clara	8	3hr	3:30pm
Santiago de Cuba	33	12hr	8:00am
Varadero	20	6hr	9am, 3:30pm

office is well organized and you can usually book tickets a couple of days in advance).

The Varadero departures can deposit you in Jagüey Grande (CUC$15, three hours) with request stops in Jovellanos, Colesio and Cárdenas. The Santiago de Cuba departure goes through Sancti Spíritus (CUC$6, 1½ hours), Ciego de Ávila (CUC$9, two hours 40 minutes), Camagüey (CUC$15, five hours 20 minutes), Las Tunas (CUC$22, 7½ hours), Holguín (CUC$26, eight hours) and Bayamo (CUC$26, 10 hours). There are request stops in Jatibonico, Florida, Sibanicú, Guáimaro and Palma Soriano.

TRAIN

Train transport out of Trinidad is awful even by Cuban standards. The town hasn't been connected to the main rail network since a hurricane in the early 1990s, meaning the only functioning line runs up the Valle de Ingenios, stopping in Iznaga (35 minutes) and terminating at Meyer (one hour 10 minutes). There are supposedly four trains a day, the most reliable leaving Trinidad at 9am and 1pm, but they often don't run; always check ahead at the **terminal** (☎ 99-42-23) in a pink house across the train tracks on the western side of the station.

For information on train tours, see p311.

Getting Around
BICYCLE

You can hire bikes at **Las Ruinas del Teatro Brunet** (Antonio Maceo No 461 btwn Simón Bolívar & Zerquera; per day CUC$3) or you can ask around at your casa particular. These are fine for getting to Playa Ancón, but nowhere near adequate for the steep climbs up to Topes de Collantes.

TRINIDAD TOUR BUS

Trinidad now has a handy hop-on/hop-off **minibus** (☎ 99-64-54) similar to Havana and Viñales linking its outlying sights. It plies a route from outside the Cubatur office in Antonio Maceo to Finca Ma Dolores, Playa La Boca, Bar Las Caletas, and the three Playa Ancón hotels. It runs approximately five times a day in either direction starting at 9am and terminating at 6pm. Cost is CUC$5 for an all-day ticket.

CAR & TAXI

The rental agencies at the Playa Ancón hotels rent mopeds (CUC$27 per day); or you can try the **Las Ruinas del Teatro Brunet** (Antonio Maceo No 461 btwn Simón Bolívar & Zerquera).

Cubacar (Trinidad/Cubatur office ☎ 99-62-57; cnr Antonio Maceo & Zerquera; Hotel Ancón ☎ 99-65-57) rents cars for approximately CUC$70 per day.

The **Servi-Cupet gas station** (⏱ 24hr), 500m south of town on the road to Casilda, has an El Rápido snack bar attached. The Oro Negro gas station is at the entrance to Trinidad from Sancti Spíritus, 1km east of Plaza Santa Ana.

Guarded parking is available in certain areas around the *casco histórico*. Ask at your hotel or casa particular and they can arrange it.

Trinidad has Havana-style coco-taxis; they cost approximately CUC$5 to Playa Ancón. A car costs from CUC$6 to CUC$8 both ways. State-owned taxis tend to congregate outside the Cubatur office in Antonio Maceo. A cab to Sancti Spíritus will cost approximately CUC$35.

HORSE CARTS

Horse carts (costing two pesos) leave for Casilda from Paseo Agramonte at the southern end of town.

PLAYA ANCÓN & AROUND

Playa Ancón, a precious ribbon of white beach on Sancti Spíritus' iridescent Caribbean shoreline, is usually touted – with good merit – to be the finest arc of sand on Cuba's south coast.

While not comparable in all-round quality to the north-coast giants of Varadero, Cayo Coco and Guardalavaca, Ancón has one important trump card: Trinidad, Latin America's sparkling colonial diamond shimmering just 12km to the north. You can get here in less than 15 minutes in a car or a leisurely 40 on a bike. Alternatively, Ancón has three all-inclusive hotels and a well-equipped marina that runs catamaran trips to a couple of nearby coral keys.

Beach bums who want to be near the water but don't have the money or inclination to stay at one of the resorts, might consider a private home in the seaside village of La Boca. What Ancón's gushing tourist brochures fail to mention are the sand fleas: they're famously ferocious at sunrise and sunset. Be warned.

The old fishing port of **Casilda**, 6km due south of Trinidad, is a friendly village with one paved road that was devastated during the 2005 hurricane season. On August 17 the **Fiesta de Santa Elena** engulfs little Casilda with feasting, competitions, horse races and

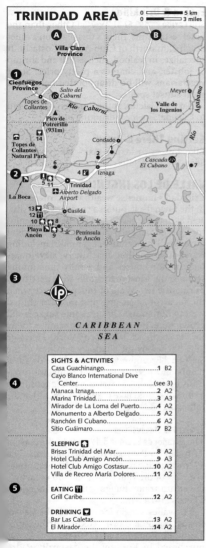

TRINIDAD AREA

0 ___ 5 km
0 ___ 3 miles

Villa Clara Province

1 Cienfuegos Province

Salto del Caburní

Meyer

Topes de Collantes

Río Caburní

Valle de los Ingenios

Pico de Potrerillo (931m)

Condado

2 Topes de Collantes Natural Park

6

Cascada El Cubano

7

4

Iznaga

2 La Boca

5 11 Trinidad

Alberto Delgado Airport

13
12
10
Playa Ancón
8
9
3

Casilda

Península de Ancón

3

CARIBBEAN SEA

SIGHTS & ACTIVITIES
Casa Guachinango...........................1 B2
Cayo Blanco International Dive
  Center.................................(see 3)
Manaca Iznaga.................................2 A2
Marina Trinidad...............................3 A3
Mirador de La Loma del Puerto........4 A2
Monumento a Alberto Delgado.........5 A2
Ranchón El Cubano..........................6 A2
Sitio Guáimaro.................................7 B2

SLEEPING
Brisas Trinidad del Mar.....................8 A2
Hotel Club Amigo Ancón...................9 A3
Hotel Club Amigo Costasur.............10 A2
Villa de Recreo María Dolores.........11 A2

EATING
Grill Caribe.....................................12 A2

DRINKING
Bar Las Caletas...............................13 A2
El Mirador.......................................14 A2

oads of rum. The road from Ancón to Casilda rosses a tidal flat, meaning abundant birdlife s visible in the early morning.

Activities

From Hotel Ancón, it's 18km to Trinidad via Casilda, or 16km on the much nicer coastal oad via La Boca. The Hotel Ancón pool is also open to nonguests and you can usually nab the ping-pong table undetected.

FISHING

The **Marina Trinidad** (☎ 99-62-05) is a few hundred meters north of Hotel Ancón. Four hours of deep-sea fishing, including transport, gear and guide, costs CUC$400 per boat (minimum six people), or a cheaper CUC$180 for bottom-fishing (from a moored boat off Cayo Blanco). Fly-fishing is also possible around the rich mangrove forests of Península de Ancón (CUC$400 for four hours, maximum six people).

SNORKELING & SCUBA DIVING

Cayo Blanco, a reef islet 25km southeast of Playa Ancón, has 22 marked scuba sites where you'll see black coral and bountiful marine life. Diving with the **Cayo Blanco International Dive Center** (☎ 99-62-05), located at Marina Trinidad, costs CUC$30 a dive and CUC$299 for an open-water course. The Marina also runs a seven-hour snorkeling-and-beach tour to Cayo Blanco for CUC$40 per person with lunch. There are similar trips to the equally pristine **Cayo Macho**.

Romantic types might want to check out the **sunset catamaran cruise** (cruise with/without dinner CUC$28/15), which has been enthusiastically recommended. There is a minimum of eight passengers. Inquire at the marina or ask at the Cubatur office in Trinidad.

SAILING

The **Windward Islands Cruising Company** (☎ in US 1-650-343-0717, in UK 44-20-3080-1023; www.caribbean-adventure.com) charters crewed and bareboat monohulls and catamarans out of the Marina to the Jardines de la Reina (p330). You can sail with or without guides, on a partial package or an all-inclusive tour. Interested parties should inquire using contact details on the website.

Sleeping

CASAS PARTICULARES

The small village of La Boca, a few clicks up the coast from Ancón, has about a dozen lovely casas.

'Villa Río Mar' – Nestor Manresa (☎ 99-31-08; San José No 65, La Boca; r CUC$20-25; P) There are further treats at Río Mar, where two rooms with shared bath give out onto a lovely tiled verandah. If it's full, there's more next door.

'Villa Sonia' – Sonia Santos Barrera (☎ 99-29-23; Av del Mar No 11, La Boca; r CUC$25-30; P ⏰) If you need an excuse to stay in La Boca, here it is. A beautiful house with a wraparound porch all to yourself, complete with polished-wood dining area, private kitchen, hammocks, rocking chairs and a thatched gazebo. Situated right opposite the (rocky) beach.

HOTELS

Ancón's three hotels offer all-inclusive rates.

Hotel Club Amigo Costasur (Cubanacán; ☎ 99-61-74; s/d all-inclusive CUC$75/94; P ⏰ ⏰) Playa Ancón's oldest and humblest resort, this hotel is at the base of the peninsula, 9km from Casilda. For about CUC$10 more, you can upgrade to a superior room, which gives you better location and views (but not decor unfortunately). There are also 20 rooms in duplex bungalows that are better still. From here you can scuba dive and ride horses. The hotel faces a rocky shore, but a white, sandy beach is just to the right. Swimming is difficult on the shallow reef. This place is popular with Canadian package tourists.

Hotel Club Amigo Ancón (Cubanacán; ☎ 99-61-23, 99-61-27; s/d all-inclusive CUC$88/100; P ⏰ ⏰ ⏰) Built during Cuba's 30-year flirtation with Soviet architectonics, the Ancón wouldn't win any beauty contests. Indeed, this steamship-shaped seven-story concrete pile looks more than a little incongruous next to the natural beauty of Ancón beach. But, if it's location you're after, coupled with close proximity to the historic delights of Trinidad, the deal could cut ice. Even better, you're just a short walk from the marina where you can fish, learn to scuba dive or enjoy a sunset cruise. Additionally, nonguests can use the facilities, which is exceptional for a resort.

Brisas Trinidad del Mar (Cubanacán; ☎ 99-65-00; s/d all-inclusive CUC$150/190; P ⏰ ⏰ ⏰) A kitschy attempt to recreate Trinidad in an all-inclusive resort environment, Brisas wins kudos for rejecting the monolithic architecture of Club Amigo Ancón in favor of low-rise colonial-style villas. But after barely half a decade in operation the quality of this place has begun to suffer from poor maintenance and decidedly iffy service. Though the swath of beach is stunning and the massage, sauna, gym and tennis courts handy for the sports-minded, you might be better off saving a few dollars and opting for one of the Club Amigos.

Eating & Drinking

Grill Caribe (☎ 99-62-41; ⏰ 24hr) Other than the hotel restaurants, there's this place on a quiet beach 2km north of Club Amigo Costasur. It specializes in seafood, such as fish and shrimp or lobster, and charges a pretty price. Strict vegetarians will be disappointed here. It's a great sunset spot.

Bar Las Caletas, at the junction of the road to Casilda, is a local drinking place.

Getting There & Away

Bike, bus, coco-taxi or taxi – take your pick. See p308 for details.

VALLE DE LOS INGENIOS

Trinidad's immense wealth was garnered not in the town itself, but in a verdant valley situated 8km to the east. The Valle de los Ingenios (or Valle de San Luis) still contains the ruins of dozens of 19th-century sugar mills, including warehouses, milling machinery, slave quarters, manor houses and a fully functioning steam train. Most of the mills were destroyed during the two Wars of Independence when the focus of sugar-growing in Cuba shifted west to Matanzas. Though some sugar is still grown here, the valley is more famous today for its status as a Unesco World Heritage Site. Backed by the shadowy sentinels of the Sierra del Escambray, the pastoral fields, royal palms and peeling colonial ruins are timelessly beautiful. A horseback-riding tour from Trinidad should take in most (if not all) of the following sites.

Sights & Activities

The **Mirador de La Loma del Puerto** is 6km east of Trinidad on the road to Sancti Spíritus. The 192m-high lookout provides the best eagle-eye view of the valley with – if you're lucky – the steam train chugging through its midst. There's also a bar.

The valley's main focal point is the **Manaca Iznaga** (admission CUC$1), 16km northeast of Trinidad. Founded in 1750, the estate was purchased in 1795 by the dastardly Pedro Iznaga, who became one of the wealthiest men in Cuba by the unscrupulous business of slave trafficking. The 44m-high tower next to the hacienda was used to watch the slaves, and the bell in front of the house served to summon them. Today you can climb to the top of the tower for pretty views, followed by a reasonable lunch (from noon to 2:30pm) in the restaurant-bar in Iznaga's former colonial mansion. Don't miss the huge sugar press out back.

Three kilometers beyond the Manaca Iznaga, on the valley's inland road, is the **Casa Guachinango**, an old hacienda built by Don Mariano Borrell toward the end of the 18th century (now a restaurant). The Río Ay is just below, and the surrounding landscape is wonderful. To get to Casa Guachinango, take the paved road to the right just beyond the second bridge as you come from Manaca Iznaga. The Meyer train stops right beside the house every morning, and you can walk back to Iznaga from Guachinango along the railway line in less than an hour.

Seven kilometers east of the Manaca Iznaga turn-off, then 2km south, is the **Sitio Guáimaro**, the former estate of Don Mariano Borrell. The seven stone arches on the facade lead to frescoed rooms, now a restaurant.

Getting There & Away

There are two train options – both equally unreliable. The tourist steam train goes at the speed of Thomas the Tank Engine, but it's a sublime journey when it's running through an impossibly green valley full of munching cows and slender bridges. The train is pulled by the indomitable and classic engine No 52204, built by the Baldwin Locomotive Company of Philadelphia in August 1919. Organized as an excursion (CUC$10), passengers pay for their own lunch separately at the Manaca Iznaga where they can visit the Manaca Iznaga and the famous bell-tower. **Cubatur** (☎ 99-63-14; Antonio Maceo No 447; ☼ 9am-8pm) in Trinidad will know when the next tourist train trip is scheduled and if it's working.

Tour desks at the Ancón hotels sell the same train tour for CUC$17, including bus transfers to Trinidad. For details of the daily local train from Trinidad see p308.

Horseback tours can be arranged at the travel agencies in Trinidad or Playa Ancón, or contract a horse and guide privately in Trinidad for CUC$15 per six hours.

TOPES DE COLLANTES
Elevation 771m

The crenellated, 90km-long Sierra del Escambray is Cuba's second-largest mountain range and it straddles the borders of three provinces: Sancti Spíritus, Cienfuegos and Villa Clara. Though not particularly high (the loftiest point, Pico de San Juan, measures just 1156m), the mountain slopes are rich in flora and surprisingly isolated. In late 1958 Che Guevara set up camp in these hills on his way to Santa Clara and, less than three years later, CIA-sponsored counterrevolutionary groups operated their own cat-and-mouse guerrilla campaign from the same vantage point.

Though not strictly a national park, Topes is, nonetheless, a heavily protected area. The umbrella park, comprising 200 sq km, overlays four smaller parks – Parque Altiplano, Parque Codina, Parque Guanayara and Parque El Cubano (see p303) – while a fifth enclave, El Nicho (p272) in Cienfuegos province, is also administered by park authority Gaviota.

The park takes its name from its largest settlement, an ugly health resort founded in 1937 by dictator Fulgencio Batista to placate his sick wife, for whom he built a quaint rural cottage. The architecture went downhill thereafter with the construction of a grotesque tuberculosis sanatorium (now

---

TOCORORO

In the forested mountains of rural Cuba, there are few birds as striking or emblematic as the *tocororo*.

Endemic to the island, the *tocororo* – or Cuban trogon, to give it its scientific name – is a medium-sized black-and-white bird with a bright red belly and a blueish-green patch between the wings. Other distinctive features include a sharp serrated bill and a sweeping concave tail.

Easy to spot if you know where to look, the bird is widely distributed throughout Cuba in heavily forested areas, especially near rivers and streams. The unusual name is derived from its distinctive call which sounds out: *to-co-ro-ro*.

Long venerated for its striking plumage, the *tocororo* was chosen as Cuba's national bird due to its coloring (which replicates the red, white and blue of the Cuban flag) and its apparent resistance to captivity. Nationalistically minded Cubans will tell you that *tocororos* are instinctively libertarian, and if you cage one, it will quickly die.

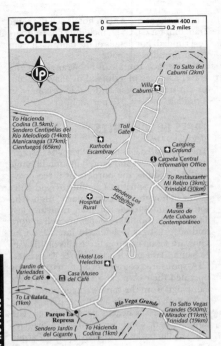

the Kurhotel) begun in the late '30s but not opened until 1954.

Topes de Collantes has three hotels open to foreigners, plus excellent guided and unguided hiking. Its jungle-like forests harboring vines, lichens, mosses, ferns and eye-catching epiphytes are akin to a giant outdoor biological classroom.

The **Carpeta Central information office** (☎ 54-02-31; ⏱ 8am-5pm), near the sundial at the entrance to Topes de Collantes, is the best place to procure maps, guides and trail info.

Sights

Believe it or not, Topes de Collantes' monstrous sanitarium once harbored a treasure trove of Cuban art boasting works by Cuban masters such as Tomás Sánchez and Rubén Torres Llorca. Raiding the old collection in 2008, inspired provincial officials opened **Museo de Arte Cubano Contemporáneo** (☎ 54-02-31; admission CUC$3), an infinitely more attractive museum that displays over 70 works in six *salas* (rooms) spread over three floors.

Coffee has been grown in these mountains for over two centuries and in the small rustic

Casa Museo del Café (☎ 54-02-31) you can fill in the gaps on its boom-bust history while sipping the aromatic local brew (called Cristal Mountain). Just up the road there is the **Jardín de Variedades de Café**, a short hike around 25 different varieties of coffee plant.

Activities

HIKING

The Blue Riband hike, and the one most easily accessed on foot from the hotels, is to the 62m **Salto del Caburní** (entry CUC$6.50), cascading over rocks into cool swimming holes before plunging into a chasm where macho locals dare each other to jump. At the height of the dry season (March to May) you may be disappointed by these falls. The entry fee is collected at the toll gate to Villa Caburní, just down the hill from the Kurhotel near the Carpeta Central (it's a long approach on foot). Allow an hour down and an hour and a half back up for this 2.5km hike. Some slopes are steep and can be slippery after rain.

The 1km **Sendero Los Helechos** (entry free), billed rather ambitiously as an eco-walk, is basically just a shortcut between the Kurhotel and the Hotel Los Helechos. Look out for snow-white mariposas and multiple species of fern along the route.

Parque La Represa on the Río Vega Grande, just downhill from La Batata trail entry, contains 300 species of trees and ferns, including the largest *caoba* (mahogany) tree in Cuba. You can take it all in on the 1km **Sendero Jardín del Gigante** (entry CUC$7). The small restaurant at the entrance to the Jardín is in a villa built by Fulgencio Batista's wife, whose love for the area inspired her husband to build the Topes resort.

The 6km out and back trail to **La Batata** (entry CUC$3), a large cave containing an underground

---

ASK A LOCAL

Topes has the most extensive trail network in Cuba. You can actually cobble together about 50km worth of trails here from Lago Hanabanilla all the way down to Parque El Cubano to make one long five- to six-day hike. At present this trek is only undertaken by foreigners who prebook trips overseas, but ask at the Carpeta to see if this situation has changed.

Humberto, Trinidad

river, starts at a parking sign just downhill from Casa Museo del Café. When you reach another highway, go around the right side of the concrete embankment and down the hill. Keep straight or right after this point (avoid trails to the left). Allow an hour each way. It's possible to swim in the cave's pools.

The **Vegas Grandes** (entry CUC$5) trail begins at the apartment blocks known as Reparto El Chorrito on the southern side of Topes de Collantes, near the entrance to the resort as you arrive from Trinidad. Allow a bit less than an hour each way to cover the 2km to the waterfall. It's possible to continue to the Salto del Caburní, though consider hiring a guide.

Another destination is **Hacienda Codina** (entry CUC$5). The 3.5km jeep track begins on a hilltop 2.5km down the road toward Cienfuegos and Manicaragua, 1km before the point at which these roads divide. There's a shorter trail to the hacienda from below Hotel Los Helechos that links for part of the way with La Batata, but you'll need a guide to use it. At the hacienda itself there's a 1.2km circular trail through orchid and bamboo gardens and past the Cueva del Altar. Also here are mud baths, a restaurant and a scenic viewpoint.

The least accessible but infinitely most rewarding hike from Topes de Collantes is the 2.5km (5km return) **Sendero 'Centinelas del Río Melodioso'** (entry CUC$5) in the Parque Guanayara, situated 15km from the Carpeta Central along a series of rough and heavily rutted tracks. For logistical reasons this excursion is best organized with a guide from the Carpeta, or as part of an organized tour from Trinidad with Cubatur (CUC$43 with lunch). The trail itself begins in cool, moist coffee plantations and descends steeply to the **El Rocio** waterfall, where you can strip off and have a bracing shower. Following the course of the Río Melodioso (Melodic River), you pass another inviting waterfall and swimming pool before emerging into the salubrious gardens of the riverside Casa La Gallega, a traditional rural hacienda where a light lunch can be organized and camping is sometimes permitted in the lush grounds.

CANYONING

Topes is the only place in Cuba where you can participate in the burgeoning sport of canyoning, but there are limitations and you'd be wise to do your homework first. The up-and-coming scene focuses on four main rivers, the Calburni, Vegas Grandes, Cabagan and Gruta Nengoa, where canyoners travel spectacularly downstream with ropes, wetsuits, helmets and harnesses. The highlight of the trip is a 200m series of vertical cascades over Salto Vegas Grandes. One experienced Canadian outfit offering excursions is **Canyoning Quebec** (www .canyoning-quebec.com), which runs eight-day trips into the Sierra del Escambray. There are currently no organized tours in-country and no equipment available for hire. At the time of writing there was at least one Gaviota parks guide who was a qualified canyon guide. Ask at the Carpeta Central information office (opposite) for more up-to-date information.

Sleeping & Eating

Hotel Los Helechos (Gaviota; ☎ 54-02-31; s/d CUC$40/50; ⓟ ⌧ ⓡ) For years the Achilles heel of the Gaviota chain, Los Helechos has recently undergone extensive refurbishments to pull it out of its 1970s stupor. Never 100% at home in its verdant natural surroundings, the clumsy chocolate-box building with its wicker furnishings and holiday camp–style villas still looks a bit awkward. Not helping matters is the unattractive indoor pool, poky steam baths (if they're working), journeyman restaurant, and kitschy local disco (in a natural park of all places!). The saving grace is the restaurant's delicious homebaked bread – surely the best in Cuba.

Villa Caburní (Gaviota; ☎ 54-01-80; s/d CUC$40/50; ⌧ ⓟ) This place is a veritable rural gem that offers one- or two-story Swiss-style chalets with kitchenettes and private baths in a small park next to the Kurhotel.

Kurhotel Escambray (Gaviota; ☎ 54-02-31; s/d CUC$40/50) Doing a good impersonation of the 'mental institution' in *One Flew Over the Cuckoo's Nest*, this eight-story architectural monster dreamt up by Batista in the 1930s would be an eyesore anywhere, let alone in a jaw-droppingly beautiful natural park. Judging by the grotesque Stalinist design of the exterior, the wily Cuban dictator must have sensed that the Russians were already on the way. Conceived originally as a sanitarium, the complex still serves as a therapeutic treatment center and you can book in for a session if you're up to donning the obligatory tracksuit. The rest of the building acts as a very scary-looking hotel.

Restaurante Mi Retiro (Carretera de Trinidad), situated 3km back down the road to Trinidad, does fair-to-middling *comida criolla* to the sound of the occasional traveling 'minstrel.' Three other eating options exist on the trails: the Hacienda Codina, Restaurante La Represa and Casa La Gallega (in Parque Guanayara). **El Mirador** (Map p309; Carretera de Trinidad) is a simple bar with a stunning view halfway up the ascent road from Trinidad.

Getting There & Away

It's very difficult to get here without a car and harder still to get around to the various trailheads. Your best bet is a taxi (CUC\$25 return with a two- to three-hour wait), an excursion from Trinidad (p303) or a hire car.

The road between Trinidad and Topes de Collantes is paved, but it's very steep. When wet, it becomes slippery and should be driven with caution. There's also a spectacular 44km road that continues right over the mountains from Topes de Collantes to Manicaragua via Jibacoa (occasionally closed, so check in Trinidad before setting out). It's also possible to drive to and from Cienfuegos via San Blas on a partly paved, partly gravel road (4WD only).

NORTHERN SANCTI SPÍRITUS

For every 1000 tourists that visit Trinidad, a small handful gets to see the province's narrow northern corridor that runs between Remedios, in Villa Clara, and Morón, in Ciego de Ávila. For the minority who do pass through there's a trio of worthwhile stop-offs plus an excellent Islazul hotel.

The **Museo Nacional Camilo Cienfuegos** (admission CUC\$1; 8am-4pm Tue-Sat, 9am-1pm Sun), at Yaguajay, 36km southeast of Caibarién, was opened in 1989 and is eerily reminiscent of the Che Guevara monument in Santa Clara. Camilo fought a crucial battle in this town on the eve of the Revolution's triumph, taking control of a local military barracks (now the Hospital Docente General opposite the museum). The museum is directly below a modernist plaza embellished with a 5m-high statue of *El Señor de la Vanguardia* (The Man at the Vanguard). It contains an interesting expose of Cienfuegos' life intermingled with facts and mementos from the revolutionary struggle. A replica of the small tank 'Dragon I,' converted from a tractor for use in the battle, stands in front of the hospital.

The **Sierra de Jatibonico** is a range of hills that runs across the entire north of the province and offers great views over toward the Bahía de Buenavista. Guided hikes can be organized at Villa San José del Lago (p315). Highlights include a three-hour excursion

---

PARQUE NACIONAL CAGUANES

Northern Sancti Spíritus province is one of Cuba's most heavily protected areas dominated by the 313-sq-km Buenavista Unesco Biosphere Reserve, also a Ramsar Convention Site (important wetlands area).

The nucleus of this reserve is the rarely mentioned (in tourist literature) Parque Nacional Caguanes, made up of the sinuous Caguanes Peninsula, the Guayabera swamps and 10 tiny islets known collectively as Cayos de Piedra.

The park is unique for its unusual karst formations; there are over 75 caves here and a pristine ecosystem that guards manatees, flamingos and the world's only freshwater cave sponge.

Indigenous people once frequented this area; so far 263 pictographs have been discovered in 40 different archaeological sites. In the late 19th and early 20th centuries hunters and charcoal burners made sporadic incursions, but they showed little long-term interest and these days the human population is minimal.

Strict conservation measures mean public access is limited, but not impossible. There is a basic visitors center and eco-station on the coast due north of Yaguajay but, rather than just turn up, your best bet is to check details first at the Villa San José del Lago (opposite).

The one advertised excursion is **Las Maravillas que Atesora Caguanes**, which incorporates a path to the Humboldt and Los Chivos caves and a boat trip around the Cayos de Piedra.

Refreshingly, the park has logged some landmark successes in environmental regeneration in recent years. Pollution in the Bahía de Buenavista bay from inefficient sugar mills had driven numerous bird species away from Caguanes by the late 1990s, but the closure of the mills in 2002, coupled with sustained environmental efforts on the part of park authorities, has seen many species start to return.

along the **Río Jatibonico**, the 1km **La Solapa de Genaro** hike through tropical savannah to the ruins of a slave wall, and the 800m **Cueva de Valdés** walk through semideciduous woodland to the cave.

Sleeping & Eating

Villa San José del Lago (☎ 55-61-08; Antonio Guiteras, Mayajigua; s/d CUC$25/32; P ✶ ≋) This novel spa, once popular with vacationing Americans, is situated just outside Mayajigua in northern Sancti Spíritus province. The tiny rooms set in a variety of two-story villas nestle beside a small palm-fringed lake (with pedal boats and resident flamingos). The complex is famous for its thermal waters first utilized by injured slaves in the 19th century but now mainly the preserve of holidaying Cubans. The 67 rooms are no-frills, but the setting, wedged between the Sierra Jatibonico and Parque Nacional Caguanes, is magnificent and makes a good base for some of Cuba's lesser-known excursions. There's a restaurant and snack bar on-site.

SANCTI SPÍRITUS
PROVINCE

Ciego de Ávila Province

For centuries Ciego de Ávila was little more than an overnight stop on Cuba's arterial east–west highway. Then came the immigrants, from Haiti, Jamaica, the Dominican Republic and Barbados, bringing with them their myriad cultural quirks: cricket in Baraguá, voodoo in Venezuela, country dancing in Majagua and explosive fireworks in Chambas. Within a century this boring former drive-by had become a potentially exciting drive-*in*.

Chopped off the western flank of Camagüey province in 1975, Ciego de Ávila set about carving its new regional identity with characteristic aplomb. Maybe that's why its resilient citizens take such commendable pride in their less-than-illustrious history (Ciego – founded in 1840 – is Cuba's newest provincial capital). Encased in the so-called 'city of porches' you'll find ingratiating casa particular owners, a smattering of good cheap restaurants and one of Cuba's best municipal museums.

Morón is Ciego's oldest town, but it's no Trinidad. More notable are the attractions to the immediate north: a patchwork of nature reserves, a hunting ground, and Cuba's largest lake, the lime-filled Laguna de la Leche.

Follow the road further still and you'll hit the sea, quite literally, on a huge man-made causeway that takes tourists (and now Cubans, if they can afford it) across the Bahía de Perros to the paradise island of Cayo Coco. Often given a bad rap during the 'tourist apartheid' era, Coco and its smaller western cousin Cayo Guillermo were the bright tropical pearls that once seduced Hemingway. Laced with gorgeous beaches and bedizened with nearly a dozen exclusive tourist resorts, they're now seducing the vacation-bound readers of his books.

HIGHLIGHTS

- **Branch Out** Uncover the traditions and festivals of Majagua (p320)
- **Scuba Cuba** Dive from a live-aboard in the secluded Jardines de la Reina (see boxed text, p330)
- **Environmental Rehab** See how an old airport has been made into a successful nature reserve at Parque Natural El Bagá (p327) on Cayo Coco and rub shoulders with the all-inclusive crowd
- **Provincial Highlight** Pay a visit to the Museo Provincial Simón Reyes (p320), one of Cuba's best small museums
- **Hemingway-esque** Attempt to emulate Papa with a bit of deep-sea fishing off Cayo Guillermo (p329)

★ Cayo Guillermo
★ Parque Natural El Bagá

Majagua ★

★ Ciego de Ávila

★ Jardines de la Reina

■ TELEPHONE CODE: 033 ■ POPULATION: 416,370 ■ AREA: 6910 SQ KM

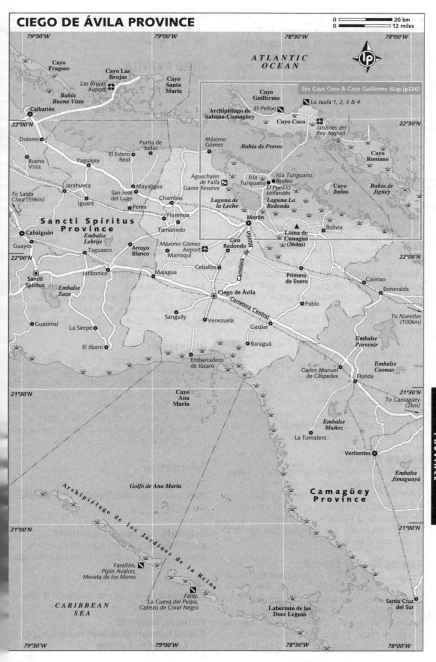

CIEGO DE ÁVILA PROVINCE

ATLANTIC OCEAN

See Cayo Coco & Cayo Guillermo Map (p326)

History

The area now known as Ciego de Ávila province was first prospected by Spanish adventurer Pánfilo de Narváez in 1513, who set out to explore the expansive forests and plains of the north coast, then presided over by a local Indian chief called Ornofay. Integrating itself into the new Spanish colony of Cuba in the early 1500s, the province got its present name from a local merchant, Jacomé de Ávila, who was granted an *encomienda* (indigenous workforce) in San Antonio de la Palma in 1538. A small *ciego* (clearing) on Ávila's estate was put aside as a resting place for tired travelers heading east–west and it quickly became a nexus for a burgeoning settlement.

Throughout the 16th and 17th centuries the northern keys provided a valuable refuge for buccaneering pirates fresh from their lucrative raids on cities such as Havana and Puerto Príncipe. Two hundred years later a buccaneer of a different kind arrived, in the shape of American writer Ernest Hemingway, who played his own game of cat-and-mouse tracking German submarines in the waters off Cayo Guillermo.

During the Wars of Independence in the latter half of the 19th century, the area was infamous for its 67km-long Morón–Júcaro defensive line, better known to historians as La Trocha. Characterized by its sturdy military installations and manned by a voluminous force of up to 20,000 men, the defense system was built up by the ruling Spanish administrators in the 1870s and designed to stop the marauding Mambís (19th-century rebels) from forging a passage west.

Parks & Reserves

Though there are no major parks in Ciego de Ávila province, Cayo Coco has a patchwork of flora and fauna reserves including Parque Natural El Bagá, a highly successful environmental reclamation project. Jardines de la Reina in the south constitutes another huge natural park.

Getting There & Around

Long a nexus on the cross-island transport routes, Ciego de Ávila is well served by Víazul buses. Trains also stop here on their way through to Havana and Santiago. Morón has relatively good train connections, but no Víazul service. If you haven't arrived here on a package, getting to Cayo Coco is more challenging. There are no regular scheduled buses, meaning a hire car or taxi is probably the best option.

CIEGO DE ÁVILA
pop 104,850

A small city of shady colonnaded shopfronts, Ciego de Ávila is the most modern of Cuba's provincial capitals, founded in 1840. Growing up originally in the 1860s and '70s as a military town behind the defensive Morón–Júcaro (Trocha) line, it later became an important processing center for the region's lucrative sugarcane and pineapple crop (the pineapple is the city mascot). Although a minor-league attraction compared to Trinidad and Camagüey, Ciego's inhabitants are innately proud of their modest city (which they refer to affectionately as 'the city of porches') and their understated enthusiasm is infectious.

Famous Avileñas include Cuban pop-art exponent Raúl Martínez and local socialite Ángela Hernández Viuda de Jímenenz, a rich widow who helped finance many of the city's early-20th-century neoclassical buildings, including the 500-seat Teatro Principal.

Orientation

The streets of Ciego de Ávila are divided between Norte (north) and Sur (south) at Calle Independencia. Marcial Gómez marks the transition from Este (east) to Oeste (west). This is important to remember, as the compass points are often part of an address. The Carretera Central turns into Chicho Valdés as it cuts across town.

Information

BOOKSTORES
Bookstore (Independencia Oeste No 153) On the corner of Simón Reyes.

INTERNET ACCESS & TELEPHONE
Etecsa Telepunto (Joaquín Agüero No 62; internet access per hr CUC$6; ☉ 8:30am-7:30pm) Three terminals.

MEDIA
Radio Surco Broadcasting over 1440AM and 98.1FM.

MEDICAL SERVICES
General Hospital (☎ 22-24-29; Máximo Gómez No 257) Not far from the bus station.

CIEGO DE ÁVILA

0   500 m
0   0.3 miles

INFORMATION	
Banco Financiero Internacional.1	B4
Bandec...................................2	B4
Bookstore...............................3	B3
Cadeca..................................4	B3
Etecsa Telepunto....................5	B4
General Hospital......................6	D4
Havanatur..............................7	B3
Immigración...........................8	B4
Infotur..................................9	B3
Post Office............................10	B4

SIGHTS & ACTIVITIES	
Ayuntamiento.......................11	B4
Centro Raúl Martínez Galería	
de Arte Provincial.............12	B4
Doce Plantas.....................(see 9)	
Estadio José R Cepero..........13	A2
Fábrica de Tabacos El Surco...14	B3
Museo de Artes Decorativas...15	B4
Museo Provincial Simón	
Reyes..............................16	B3
Parque Zoológico..................17	C4
Plano-Mural de Ciego de	
Ávila...............................18	B4
Teatro Principal....................19	B4

SLEEPING	
Belkis de Caridad Jiménez......20	B4
Hotel Ciego de Ávila..............21	B2
Hotel Santiago-Habana..........22	B4
Leonarda Guitierrez...............23	B4

EATING	
Fonda La Estrella..................24	B3
La Vicaria...........................25	D4
Mercado Agropecuario..........26	A3
Panadería Doña Neli..........(see 9)	
Restaurante Don Pepe..........27	B3
Solaris.............................(see 9)	
Supermercado Cruz Verde......28	B4

DRINKING	
La Confronta.......................29	B4
La Fontana.........................30	B3

ENTERTAINMENT	
Casa de la Cultura.................31	B3
Casa de la Trova Miguel	
Angel Luna.......................32	B3
Cine Carmen.......................33	B3
Cine Iriondo........................34	B4
Discoteca Colibrí..................35	B3
El Batanga.......................(see 21)	
La Macarena.......................36	B4
Patio de ARTex....................37	B3

SHOPPING	
Vide Cuba..........................38	B3

TRANSPORT	
Bus Station.........................39	D4
Cubacar.............................40	D4
Cubacar..........................(see 21)	
Cubana.............................41	B4
Ferro Ómnibus Bus Station....42	A4
Oro Negro..........................43	D4

MONEY

Banco Financiero Internacional (☎ 22-52-74; cnr Honorato del Castillo & Joaquín Agüero Oeste)

Bandec (☎ 22-23-32; cnr Independencia Oeste & Antonio Maceo)

Cadeca (☎ 26-64-18; Independencia Oeste No 118 btwn Antonio Maceo & Simón Reyes; ☻ 8:30am-6pm Mon-Sat, 8:30am-12:30pm Sun)

POST

Post office (cnr Chicho Valdés & Marcial Gómez)

TOURIST INFORMATION

Havanatur (☎ 26-63-42; Libertad btwn Antonio Maceo & Honorato del Castillo; ☻ 9am-5pm Mon-Fri, 9am-noon Sat)

Infotur (☎ 20-91-09; Doce Plantas, cnr Honorato del Castillo & Libertad; ☻ 9am-noon & 1-6pm Mon-Sun)

Cuba's premier information outlet offers advice on less-heralded attractions.

Sights & Activities

Manageable and friendly, Ciego de Ávila engenders a leisurely pace. The city has worked hard to make its relatively low-key history appear interesting and relevant and *deserves* at least a two-hour visit!

Check out **Parque Martí** first – with the inevitable monument to José Martí (1925) – which is overlooked by the 1911 **Ayuntamiento** (City Hall; no visitors), now the provincial government headquarters, and the **Museo de Artes Decorativas** (☎ 20-16-61; cnr Independencia & Marcial Gómez; admission CUC$1; ☻ 8am-5pm Mon & Tue, 8am-10pm Wed-Sat, 8am-noon & 6-10pm Sun). This

---

FESTIVALS & FIREWORKS

New Orleans' Mardi Gras might win the populist vote, but if you're the type of traveler who likes sniffing out obscure festivals in even more obscure places, Ciego de Ávila could be your nirvana.

Every November the rural town of Majagua celebrates the **Fiesta de los Bandos Rojo y Azul**, when the populace splits into two teams – one red and one blue – to re-enact an old *caringa* dancing competition played out to a background of traditional *guajiro* (country) music.

Meanwhile in Baraguá, the **Fiesta del 1 de Agosto** on slave emancipation day includes an 80-year-old cricket tournament (p323), a legacy of West Indian immigrants from Jamaica who came here in the 1920s to work on the sugar plantations, bringing their googlies, reverse sweeps and silly mid-offs with them.

Remedios in Villa Clara isn't the only place to catch a cacophonous fireworks party. The towns of Chambas and Punta Alegre in the northwest of Ciego de Ávila province host their own version of the ebullient **Parrandas**, with papier-mâché effigies, colorful floats, winding processions and *mucho* rum.

Festivities take a Haitian turn further east where immigrants from the former French colony have recreated their voodoo-influenced liturgies in annual ceremonies in the towns of Bolivia, Venezuela and Primero de Enero.

For more information on the above try the helpful staff at the Infotur office in Ciego de Ávila (p319).

---

thoughtful collection contains quirky items from a bygone age, such as a working Victrola (Benny Moré serenades your visit), antique pocket watches and ornate canopy beds with mother-of-pearl inlays. A CUC$1 tip gets you a typically enthusiastic local guide (in English or Spanish). The only other notable building is the grand **Teatro Principal** (☎ 22-20-86; cnr Joaquín Agüero Oeste & Honorato del Castillo), built in 1927 with the help of local financier Angela Jiménez.

Duck under the signature Ciego porches along Calle Independencia to reach the **Centro Raúl Martínez Galería de Arte Provincial** (Independencia Oeste No 65 btwn Honorato del Castillo & Antonio Maceo; ◷ 8am-noon & 1-5pm Mon & Wed, 1-9pm Thu & Fri, 2-10pm Sat, 8am-noon Sun), where works by Cuba's king of pop art are on permanent display, along with many new works by local artists.

The newly renovated **Museo Provincial Simón Reyes** (☎ 20-44-88; cnr Honorato del Castillo & Máximo Gómez; admission CUC$1; ◷ 8am-10pm) is quite possibly the best-presented municipal museum in Cuba and one buck well spent. Fascinating exhibits include a scale model of La Trocha (p325), detailed information on Afro-Cuban culture and religion, and explanations on the province's rich collection of traditional festivals. Afterwards it's worth wandering down to the **Plano-Mural de Ciego de Ávila** (cnr Marcial Gómez & Joaquín de Agüero), where a bronze map

of the city in the late 19th century marks the site of its founding in 1840.

There's a tobacco factory, **Fábrica de Tabacos El Sucro** (cnr Libertad & Maceo), in town, though tours are normally group-only. Ask at the Havanatur office (p319) and you may be able to tag along.

If you're faced with a long wait for the bus or have a posse of hyperactive kids to amuse, the small **Parque Zoológico** (Independencia Este; admission free; ◷ Tue-Sun) might fill a vacant half-hour.

October to April, baseball games take place at the **Estadio José R Cepero** (☎ 22-82-83; Máximo Gómez), northwest of the center. Ciego's Tigres (Tigers) aren't as fierce as their name suggests and rarely qualify for the play-offs.

Sleeping

CASAS PARTICULARES

Ciego has some decent, well-signposted casas particulares and not much demand.

Belkis de Caridad Jiménez (☎ 22-46-09; Carretera Central No 76 btwn Antonio Maceo & Honorato del Castillo; r CUC$15-20; ✷) A private entrance from the Carretera Central (and two blocks from the city center) makes this place easy to find, but it's surprisingly quiet once you're inside. The hosts are friendly, no-pressure Avileñas who'll cook you good meals.

Leonarda Guitierrez (☎ 20-27-22; Honorato del Castillo No 64 btwn Chicho Valdés & Joaquín Agüero; r CUC$15-20; P ✷) Another house with independent entry and two rooms spread over two floors. It's one block from the main square and the owner knows other casas if you're stuck.

HOTELS

Hotel Santiago-Habana (Islazul; ☎ 22-57-03; cnr Chicho Valdés & Honorato del Castillo; s/d CUC$27/36; ☒) Your one-and-only town-center option is this musty but serviceable 76-room hotel, well-placed for most of the city's sights. The rooms are 1970s motel-style and there's a restaurant along with the Disco Centro Nocturno La Cima on the top floor.

Hotel Ciego de Ávila (Islazul; ☎ 22-80-13; Carretera a de Ceballos Km 1.5; s/d CUC$29/38; Ⓟ ☒ ☒) Where have all the tourists gone? Cayo Coco probably, leaving this Islazul staple 2km from the city center overlooking a small lake that's the domain of Cuban sports teams and workers on government-sponsored vacation time. Nothing unusual here except for, perhaps, the solar panels on the roof which deflect from the monotony of the bog-standard rooms, noisy swimming-pool area and boring breakfasts. The friendly staff add a bit of much-needed color.

Eating

RESTAURANTS

ourpick Fonda La Estrella (☎ 26-61-86; Honorato del Castillo No 34 cnr Máximo Gómez; ☺ 10am-midnight) Quite possibly the cheapest quality food in Cuba, this small airy place serves four set dishes for just CUC$1.50. But it's far tastier than your standard fried-chicken ration. For a few Convertibles more you can bag paella and a delicious *ropa vieja*.

La Vicaria (☎ 26-64-77; Carretera Central; ☺ 24hr) A safe haven next to the bus terminal, La Vicaria is a dependable national chain with affordable food and efficient service. The open-fronted sitting area on the Carretera Central is less than salubrious, but the food's more than adequate for a pre–bus journey snack.

Yisan (Carretera Central btwn Calles 8 & 13; ☺ Wed-Mon) Alright, so it's not dim sum; but if you haven't yet tried chicken chow mien with a mysterious Cuban twist then you haven't really been to Ciego de Ávila.

Restaurante Don Pepe (☎ 22-37-13; Independencia Oeste No 103 btwn Antonio Maceo & Simón Reyes; ☺ 8-11:45pm Wed-Mon) A bartender named Eladio invented the Coctel Don Pepe (two shots of orange juice, 1.5 shots of white rum, and half a shot of crème de menthe, stirred) here back in

the day. They're still serving them, along with the good old pork and chicken dishes, in this pleasant colonial building. There's occasional live music.

Solaris (☎ 22-34-24; Doce Plantas Bldg, Honorato del Castillo) Enthusiastically recommended by the locals, this city-center joint, on the 12th floor of the rather ugly Doce Plantas building, offers excellent city views and has a menu that includes a special cordon bleu. Ask to try the unique Solaris cocktail.

GROCERIES

Mercado agropecuario (Chicho Valdés Oeste btwn Agramonte & Fernando Callejas) There is a vegetable market located in a blemished part of town below the overpass.

Supermercado Cruz Verde (cnr Independencia & Marcial Gómez; ☺ 9am-6pm Mon-Sat, 9am-noon Sun) Sells groceries in one of Ciego's grandest fin de siècle buildings.

For bread, look no further than **Panadería Doña Neli** (Doce Plantas, cnr Honorato del Castillo & Libertad), which also displays tempting sweet pastries.

Drinking

ourpick La Confronta (cnr Marcial Gómez & Joaquín Agüero) Amid the well-worn bar stools and Benny Moré paraphernalia you can sample 25 different varieties of cocktail and all the prices are in Cuban pesos, a tempting proposition for a Convertible-loaded traveler. There's also a limited food menu.

La Fontana (☎ 20-21-79; cnr Independencia & Antonio Maceo; ☺ 6am-2pm & 3-11pm) Ciego's famous coffee institution has lost its shine since a recent renovation failed to evoke the atmosphere of yore. For the caffeine-starved, it's OK – if you don't mind drinking your coffee in a thick fog of cigarette smoke.

Entertainment

For traditional music it's a dice-roll. **Casa de la Trova Miguel Angel Luna** (Libertad No 130) has Thursday night regional *trovadores*, the **Casa de la Cultura** (☎ 22-39-74; Independencia No 76 btwn Antonio Maceo & Honorato del Castillo) has a Wednesday *danzón* club, and the **Patio de ARTex** (Libertad btwn Antonio Maceo & Honorato del Castillo; admission 5 pesos) has a bit of everything; check the *cartelera* (culture calendar) out front.

For total spontaneity hit the streets on a Saturday night for the wonderful Noches Avileñas spread over various venues including the main park and Museo de Artes

Decorativas (p319). Every Sunday morning at 10am a brass band plays in Parque Martí.

If you're in the mood to catch a film, try **Cine Carmen** (☎ 22-33-87; Antonio Maceo No 51), on the corner of Calle Libertad, with big-screen and video offerings daily (don't miss the big movie projector spilling film on the Libertad side of the building), or **Cine Iriondo** (☎ 22-33-04; cnr Joaquín Agüero Oeste & Antonio Maceo).

Slightly tacky discos haunt the hotels: there's **La Macarena** (☎ 22-56-03; Independencia Oeste No 57 btwn Antonio Maceo & Honorato del Castillo) in the Cuban-only Hotel Sevilla and the **El Batanga** (admission per couple CUC$3; ◷ 10pm-2am) in the Hotel Ciego de Ávila (p321). If you have delusions of stardom, head straight for the karaoke scene at **Discoteca Colibrí** (☎ 26-62-19; cnr Máximo Gómez & Honorato del Castillo; admission CUC$1; ◷ 10pm-3am).

Shopping

Vide Cuba (Independencia No 171 btwn Agramonte & Simón Reyes; ◷ 8:30am-8:30pm, closed Sun) This store will service all your basic camera needs.

Getting There & Away

AIR

Ciego de Ávila's **Máximo Gómez Airport** (airport code AVI; ☎ 26-66-26; Carretera a Virginia) is 10km northwest of Ceballos, 23km north of Ciego de Ávila and 23km south of Morón. **Cubana** (☎ 33-25-31; Chicho Valdés No 83 btwn Honorato del Castillo & Antonio Maceo) has weekly flights to Havana (CUC$78 one way, 1½ hours).

International flights arrive daily from Canada, Argentina, France, the UK and Italy and visitors are bussed off to Cayo Coco.

BUS

The **bus station** (☎ 22-24-07; Carretera Central), situated about 1.5km east of the center, has daily Víazul services.

The Santiago de Cuba departure also stops at Camagüey (CUC$6, one hour 35 minutes), Las Tunas (CUC$13, four hours 25 minutes),

Holguín (CUC$17, five hours 40 minutes) and Bayamo (CUC$17, seven hours). The Havana bus stops at Sancti Spíritus (CUC$6, two hours) and Santa Clara (CUC$9, three hours 20 minutes). For Víazul tickets, see the *jefe de turno* (shift manager); the office is right near the normal ticket window.

TRAIN

The **train station** (☎ 22-33-13) is located six blocks southwest of the center. Ciego de Ávila is on the main Havana–Santiago railway line. There are nightly trains to Bayamo (CUC$11, seven hours), Camagüey (CUC$3, two hours 10 minutes), Guantánamo (CUC$17, 9½ hours), Havana (CUC$16, 7½ hours), Holguín (CUC$11, seven hours), Manzanillo (CUC$12, 8½ hours) and Santiago de Cuba (CUC$15, 9¼ hours). Different train numbers run on alternate nights, so make sure you check the latest timetable before you leave. There are three trains daily to Morón (CUC$1, one hour).

TRUCK

Private passenger trucks leave from the Ferro Ómnibus bus station adjacent to the train station heading in the direction of Morón and Camagüey. Check the blackboards for current details.

Getting Around

CAR & MOPED

The **Carretera a Morón gas station** (Carretera de Morón) is just before the bypass road, northeast of the town center. The **Oro Negro gas station** (Carretera Central) is near the bus station.

You can park safely in front of the Hotel Santiago-Habana overnight.

Cubacar (Hotel Ciego de Ávila ☎ 20-01-02; Carretera a Ceballos; Terminal de Ómnibus ☎ 22-51-05) can help with vehicle rental for around CUC$70 per day. The branch at the Hotel also rents out mopeds for CUC$24 a day.

VÍAZUL DAILY DEPARTURES

Destination	Cost (CUC$)	Duration	Departure time
Havana	27	7hr	3:10pm, 6:20pm, 12:35am, 1:55am, 5:25am
Holguín	26	5hr 50min	2:20am, 3:45am, 10:45am, 3:35pm, 10:10pm
Santiago de Cuba	24	8hr 45min	3:45am, 4:25am, 10:45am, 4:35pm, 10:10pm
Trinidad	9	2hr 40min	4:05am
Varadero	19	6hr 20min	4:40am

LEATHER ON WILLOW

In 1895 a young Winston Churchill, fresh from a journalistic posting in Havana, lamented whimsically over what might have been had the British held onto Cuba after the short-lived occupation of 1762–63. In romantic undertones he imagined a 'free and prosperous' Anglo-Saxon colony that 'sent its ponies to Hurlingham and its cricketers to Lords.'

But the cricket wasn't to be – at least, not immediately. After dispatching the Spanish in 1898, Cuba spun inexorably into US orbit and Churchill's dream of hearing the thud of leather on willow was quickly replaced by the heavy swish of a baseball bat. Or was it?

Ingrained in the culture of its English-speaking neighbors, cricket never strayed far from Cuba's shores. Entering the island through the back door in the 1920s, the game first took root among immigrants from the cricket-playing nations of Jamaica and Barbados who came to work on Cuba's booming sugar plantations. Creating their own teams, the new arrivals were soon competing in prestigious local tournaments, the most important of which was an annual cricket festival held in Baraguá in Ciego de Ávila province on slave emancipation day every August 1. In 1952 Cuba even staged its first international against an all-star team from Jamaica.

But in the 1960s and '70s, under the direction of new leader and one-time baseball protégée Fidel Castro, Cuban cricket almost died out. The revival came in 1998 after Leona Ford, the daughter of a cricket-playing Barbadian immigrant, proposed a six-week cricket-coaching course with representatives from Trinidad and Tobago. Interest quickly spread and, within a couple of years, cricket had gained the support of a Cuban government anxious to re-emphasize its Caribbean heritage in a post–Cold War world.

Today there are almost 4000 practising cricket players in Cuba and the country is an affiliate member of the International Cricket Council (ICC). In February 2007 the Cubans were invited to form their own national team, which competed for the first time against guest teams from England, Jamaica and India in Havana.

Meanwhile, in sleepy Baraguá, the annual August cricket tournament continues to spin its esoteric magic just as it has done for the last 80 years.

TAXI

A taxi ride to the airport will cost around CUC$12; bargain if they're asking more. You can book a cab at Hotel Ciego de Ávila or find one in Parque Martí. A one-way ride to Cayo Coco should cost in the vicinity of CUC$60.

MORÓN
pop 59,194

Morón is a dull town with a wealth of interesting sights surrounding it. Situated about 40km north of Ciego de Ávila across a flat sea of sugarcane, it acts as a kind of base camp for people heading north toward Cayo Coco, as well as a hometown for the hundreds of Cubans who work there.

Founded in 1643, two centuries before provincial capital Ciego de Ávila, it's known as the Ciudad del Gallo (City of the Cockerel) island-wide for a verse about a cockerel that continued to crow after being defeathered. The offending bird stands recreated in bronze on a pedestal at the entrance to the Hotel Morón; a town mascot and one of its more notable sights.

Compact and easygoing, Morón is a plausible base for shoestringers who want to enjoy the beaches of Cayo Coco and Guillermo without having to fork out half a month's salary for the privilege. It's also a favorite among fishermen and hunters headed for the Laguna de la Leche.

Information

You'll find internet at **Etecsa** (Martí; ☻ 8:30am-7:30pm), and there are money-changing facilities at the **Cadeca** (Martí No 346) in the same street. Information on the Laguna La Redonda and Laguna de la Leche can be procured at **Cubatur** (☎ 50-55-19; cnr Martí & Dimas Daniel; ☻ 9am-5pm).

Sights

Ponder the cockerel, the historic railway station and animated Calle Martí, and you've pretty much covered Morón in a short morning. You can round things off with a visit to the **Museo de Arqueología e Historia** (Martí; admission CUC$1; ☻ 9am-noon & 6-10pm). Shoehorned in among the busy sidewalks and peeling colonnades, this well-laid-out museum is spread

CIEGO DE ÁVILA PROVINCE

over two floors, the upper of which is given over to the city's history. There is a *mirador* (lookout) on the roof with a good view out over the town.

Sleeping

CASAS PARTICULARES

'Hospedaje Liberluz' – Carlos Manuel Baez (☎ 50-50-54; Libertad No 148 btwn Luz Caballero & Padre Cabo; r CUC$20-25; ❄) Flowers, rockers, a patio and two well-equipped rooms spread over two floors. Morón has its pleasant escapes and this is one of them.

Tamara Companioni Medina (☎ 50-36-30; Martí No 247 btwn Serafín Sánchez & Sergio Antuña; r CUC$20-25; P ❄) An old stalwart in the center of town where you'll bump into the odd (American) fisherman. One of the rooms is in a converted garage out back; the other more spick-and-span option is inside the house.

HOTELS

Hotel Morón (Cubanacán; ☎ 50-22-30; Av de Tarafa; s/d CUC$33/42; P ❄ ☎) Morón is famous for its cockerel, but it's the in-house disco that's more likely to keep you awake at this modern-ish, four-story hotel at the south entrance to town. Package tourists are the main clientele with the odd stray fisherman thrown in for good measure. The pool is a rare highlight; nonguests can ask about day passes. Maintain low expectations for the restaurant and you might be pleasantly surprised.

Casona de Morón (☎ 50-22-36; Colón No 41; s/d CUC$40/50; ❄) Catering mainly to the hunting and fishing crowd, Casona, near the train station, is a cozy enough place for those on a budget, and trumps Hotel Morón in many respects with its colonial features and cheery ambience. There are seven rooms and a small restaurant on-site.

Eating

Las Fuentes (☎ 50-57-58; Martí No 189 btwn Agramonte & Libertad; ⏱ 10am-midnight) The surest bet for a solid meal in Morón is this place: you can get everything from a very basic salad to grilled lobster here. Fish dinners start at CUC$5 – if you can't face another dose of fried-to-a-cinder chicken.

La Casona (Colón No 43; ⏱ noon-midnight) Attached to the hunting lodge, this place can rustle up something hot and palatable at relatively short notice.

Paraíso Palmares (☎ 50-21-94; Martí No 382; ⏱ noon-2pm & 7-9pm) This restaurant has standard chicken fare with the obligatory *arroz congrí* (rice and beans). The house specialty is Valencian paella.

Coppelia (cnr Callejas & Martí) While the Coppelia chain invariably offers good ice cream, the setting is often dire, and never more so than in this hollowed-out shell of a building. Get a take-out and head to the park.

On the self-catering front there's the dependable **Doña Neli Dulcería** (Serafín Sánchez No 86 btwn Narciso López & Martí) for bread and pastries and **La Mina de Oro** (Martí) for groceries.

Entertainment

A night out in Morón is a toss-up between the traditional **Casa de la Trova Pablo Bernal** (Libertad No 74 btwn Martí & Narciso López) or the younger, more raucous Discoteca Morón at the hotel of the same name (left).

Getting There & Away

Five buses a day leave from the hectic **train station** (☎ 3683; cnr Martí & JF Poey) for Ciego de Ávila. Trains depart for Santiago de Cuba (CUC$22, alternate days) via Ciego de Ávila (CUC$1, twice daily) and Camagüey (CUC$4, twice daily). The line from Santa Clara to Nuevitas also passes through Morón via Chambas. A *coche motor* (cross-island) railcar to Havana (CUC$24, 6½ hours) operates on alternate days.

Getting Around

The roads from Morón northwest to Caibarién (112km) and southeast Nuevitas (168km) are both good.

Cubacar (☎ 50-22-22; Hotel Morón, Av de Tarafa) rents cars and mopeds.

The **Servi-Cupet gas station** (⏱ 24hr) is near Hotel Morón.

NORTH OF MORÓN

Far more interesting than Morón itself is the grab-bag of attractions to the north.

Laguna de la Leche & Laguna La Redonda

These two freshwater lakes a few kilometers north of Morón are hot spots for fishermen. Measuring 67 sq km, the **Laguna de la Leche** (Milk Lake) is named for its reflective underwater lime deposits and is the largest natural lake in Cuba. Accessed from the south via

---

TROCHA DE JÚCARO A MORÓN

Shaped by a volatile history, many of Ciego de Ávila's provincial towns grew up in the mid-19th century around the formidable Trocha, a 68km-long line of fortifications that stretched from Morón in the north to Júcaro in the south, splitting the island divisively in two.

Constructed by the Spanish in the early 1870s using a mixture of black slaves and poorly paid Chinese laborers, the gargantuan Trocha was designed to contain the rebellious armies of the Oriente and stop the seeds of anarchy from spreading west during the First War of Independence.

By the time of the construction's completion in 1872, the Trocha was the most sophisticated military defense system in the colonies, a seemingly unbreakable bastion that included 17 forts, 5000 full-time military guards and a parallel railway line.

Armed to the hilt, it held firm during the First War of Independence, preventing the rebel armies of Antonio Maceo and Máximo Gómez from causing widespread destruction in the richer western provinces of Matanzas and Pinar del Río, where more conservative sugar planters held sway.

But, despite renovations that doubled the number of forts and tripled the number of armed guards by 1895, the Trocha proved to be more porous during the Spanish-Cuban-American War, enabling the audacious Maceo to break through and march his army as far west as Pinar del Río.

A handful of old military towers that once acted as lookouts and guard houses on the Trocha still scatter the countryside between Ciego de Ávila and Morón. While none are, as yet, official museums, they stand as timeworn testaments to a more divisive and violent era.

---

a link road from Morón (3km), the lake is popular among budding anglers who flock here to take advantage of its abundant stocks of carp, tarpon, snook and tilapia. Situated on the southern shoreline you'll find **La Atarraya** (☎ 50-53-51), a restaurant specializing in fish dishes, as well as an entertainment venue known as **Cabaret Cueva** (☎ 50-22-39). You can rent boats here as well. Every year Laguna de la Leche is the venue for the **Morón Aquatic Carnival**. The area has also twice hosted the Jardines del Rey **F-1 speedboat competition**.

The next world record largemouth bass will come from Cuba, if fishing around **Laguna La Redonda** is anything to go by. The lake has already yielded a humongous 9½kg-er. Situated 18km north of Morón, off the road to Cayo Coco, the mangroves surrounding this 4-sq-km lake have the best square-kilometer density of bass and trout on the island. Four/eight hours of fishing costs CUC$35/70 or a 45-minute boat trip without rods costs CUC$16. There's a decent, rustic bar-restaurant combo here if you only want to stop for a drink with a lake view. Try the house specialty, a fillet of fish called *calentico* – great with ketchup and Tabasco.

The **Aguachales de Falla Game Reserve** is a hunting area containing seven natural lakes and abundant flocks of pigeons, ducks and doves. If you really feel the urge, you can take the Hemingway tour to its natu-

ral conclusion (Papa loved firing guns at feathered targets).

Loma de Cunagua

Rising like a huge termite mound above the surrounding flatlands, the **Loma de Cunagua** (admission CUC$5; ☻ 9am-4pm), 18km east of Morón on the Carretera de Bolivia, is a protected flora and fauna reserve that harbors a *ranchón*-style restaurant, a small network of trails, and excellent bird-watching opportunities. Turn left off the main road at the sign, pay your fee at the gate, and proceed up the steep unpaved road to the summit. At 364m above sea level, the Loma is the province's highest point and the views over land and ocean are excellent. You can arrange horseback riding here or stroll along short bushy trails in search of *to-cororos*, *zunzúns* and plenty more. The restaurant whips up a decent all-in pork lunch for CUC$10 and a couple of **cabins** (r CUC$30) offer rustic overnight accommodation for those in search of some rural tranquility.

Isla Turiguano

In rodeo-land Cuba is right up there with the Calgary Stampede, and one of the island's best cattle-fests can be seen at Isla Turiguano on the road out of Morón, a kilometer or two before the Cayo Coco checkpoint. Cowboys, bulls, horses and lassos are in evidence every weekend at around 2pm for exciting

90-minute *espectáculos* (shows). Alternatively you can drop by for a look at the animals any time. There's a small bar out front.

EL PUEBLO HOLANDÉS

El Pueblo Holandés, a small community with 49 red-roofed, Dutch-style dwellings, is on a hill next to the highway, 4km north of La Redonda. It was built by Celia Sánchez in 1960 as a home for area cattle workers. It's an interesting blip on the landscape, but not worth a detour.

FLORENCIA

Ringed by gentle hills, the town of Florencia, 40km west of Morón, was named after Florence in Italy by early settlers who claimed that the surrounding countryside reminded them of Tuscany. The town itself grew up around the Santa Clara–Nuevitas railway in the 1920s when local farmers began transporting their products to more lucrative markets in the west. In the early 1990s the Cuban government constructed a hydroelectric dam, the Liberación de Florencia, on the Río Chambas and the re-

sulting lake has become a recreational magnet for nature lovers. There are a number of activities available here, including horseback riding through the Florencia hills, kayaking, aqua-biking, and a boat ride on the lake to a tiny key called La Presa with a restaurant and small animal 'zoo.' The nexus is a Palmares rancho called **La Esquinita** (☎ 6-9294; ⏰ 9am-5pm) by the side of the lake in Florencia. You can get more details at Infotur in Ciego de Ávila (p319) or at **Palmares** (☎ 50-21-12; Martí No 306) in Morón. For a place to stay you may get lucky in the lovely Campismo Boquerón, 5km west of Florencia, normally only available to Cubans but sometimes able to take in foreigners. Enquire at La Esquinita.

CAYO COCO

Cayo Coco is Cuba's fourth-largest island and the main tourist destination after Varadero. Situated in the Archipiélago de Sabana-Camagüey, or the Jardines del Rey, as travel brochures prefer to call it, the area north of the Bahía de Perros (Bay of Dogs) was uninhabited before 1992, when the first hotel – the Cojímar – went up on adjoin-

CAYO COCO & CAYO GUILLERMO

0 —— 10 km
0 —— 6 miles

ATLANTIC OCEAN

Cayo Media Luna
Playa Pilar
Cayo Guillermo
Punta del Perro
El Penón
Playa Flamenco
La Jaula 1, 2, 3 & 4
Punta Coco
Casasa
Cayo Coco
Parque Natural El Bagá
Jardines del Rey Internacional Airport
Cayo Paredón Grande
Bahía de Perros
Cayo Romano
Máximo Gómez
Isla Turiguano
La Loma
San Rafael
Toll Gate
El Pueblo Holandés
Manatí
El Salado
Laguna de La Leche
Laguna La Redonda
Ranchuelo
Morón
Canal de la Yana
Loma de Cunagua (364m)
To Chambas (19km)
To Ciego de Ávila (38km)

INFORMATION
Banco Financiero Internacional.....1 B1
Banco Financiero
   Internacional..................(see 10)
Clínica Internacional Cayo
   Coco...............................2 B1
Havanatur........................(see 1)
Infotur............................3 C1

SIGHTS & ACTIVITIES
Blue Diving.......................(see 11)
Boat Adventure.................4 A1
Coco Diving.......................(see 9)
Cubanacán Náutica – Sol
   Club Cayo Guillermo.......5 A1
Faro Diego Velázquez.........6 C1
Marina Marlin Aguas
   Tranquilas.....................(see 11)
Marlin Dive Centre.............(see 8)
Marlin Marina....................7 A1

SLEEPING
Hotel Blau Colonial..............8 B1
Hotel Tryp Cayo Coco...........9 B1
Iberostar Daiquirí...............10 A1
Meliá Cayo Coco................11 C1
Motel Villa Jardín Los Cocos...12 C1
NH Krystal Laguna..............13 C1
Sitio La Güira....................14 B1
Villa Cojímar.....................15 B1
Villa Gaviota Cayo Coco.......16 B1

EATING
Parador La Silla.................17 B2
Ranchón Las Coloradas.........18 C1
Ranchón Playa Flamenco.......19 B1
Ranchón Playa Pilar.............20 A1
Restaurant Sitio La Güira......(see 14)

ENTERTAINMENT
La Cueva del Jabalí.............21 B1

TRANSPORT
Cubacar...........................22 B1
Cubacar...........................(see 5)
Cubacar...........................(see 15)

ASK A LOCAL

Cayo Coco actually has some good environmental credentials. Hotels can be no more than three-story in height and have to be situated a designated distance from the beach with wooden walkways built over the various lagoons. There is also controlled fishing in the area. To find out more about the island's eco-efforts, visit Parque Natural El Bagá.

Diego, Cayo Coco

---

ing Cayo Guillermo. The bulldozers haven't stopped buzzing since.

While the beauty of the beaches on these islands is world-famous, Cayo Coco pre-1990 was little more than a mosquito-infested mangrove swamp. French corsair Jacques de Sores was one of the earliest visitors, fresh from successful raids on Havana and Puerto Príncipe, and he was followed in 1752 by the island's first landowner, an opportunistic Spaniard named Santiago Abuero Castañeda. Between 1927 and 1955 a community of 600 people scraped a living by producing charcoal for use as domestic fuel on the island, but with the rise of electrical power after the Revolution this too died.

Since 1988 Cayo Coco has been connected to the mainland by a 27km causeway slicing across the Bahía de Perros. There are also causeways from Cayo Coco to Cayo Guillermo in the west and to Cayo Romano in the east.

Information

Euros are accepted in all the Cayo Coco and Cayo Guillermo resorts.

Banco Financiero Internacional At the Servi-Cupet gas station and Hotel Iberostar Daiquirí.

Clínica Internacional Cayo Coco (☎ 30-21-58; Av de los Hoteles al final) Provides medical treatment, and is located next to Villa Gaviota Cayo Coco.

Havanatur (☎ 30-13-29) This travel agency is on the main roundabout next to the Servi-Cupet gas station. There's a small, handy store (read: insect repellent) and an El Rápido here too.

Infotur (☎ 30-91-09) Has a helpful office at the Jardines del Rey airport. There are also desks at most of the main hotels.

Sights

Parque Natural El Bagá (☎ 30-10-63; admission CUC$12) is a commendable eco-project where

the Cuban government has juxtaposed environmental reclamation alongside lucrative but controlled tourist development. Sited on what was Cayo Coco's original airport, this 769-hectare natural park is a sublime mix of dense mangroves, small lakes, idyllic coastline and winding trails. A three-hour tour with a guide costs CUC$25 (no minimum), but these guys are flexible, knowledgeable and passionate about their subject. You can see *jutías* (tree rats) and iguanas here and handle a live croc (mouth taped of course), but the real highlight is the 130 species of bird that frequent the area. Slightly lower down the authenticity stakes are a reconstructed native village (including shows) and the on-site restaurant, which specializes in rabbit.

East of Cayo Coco, a road crosses Cayo Romano and turns north to Cayo Paredón Grande and **Faro Diego Velázquez**, a 52m working lighthouse that dates from 1859. This area has a couple of beaches and is good for fishing.

Activities

The **Marina Marlin Aguas Tranquilas** (☎ 30-13-24), near the Meliá Cayo Coco, offers deep-sea fishing outings (CUC$290 per four hours).

The **Marlin Dive Center** (☎ 30-12-21), on the west side of Hotel Tryp Cayo Coco, is accessible via a dirt road to the beach. Scuba diving costs CUC$35, plus CUC$5 for gear. The open-water certification course costs CUC$365, less in low season. The diving area stretches for over 10km mainly to the east, and there are six certified instructors with the capacity for 30 divers per day. **Blue Diving** (☎ 30-81-79; Meliá Cayo Coco), and **Coco Diving** (☎ 30-13-23; Hotel Tryp Cayo Coco) offer similar services. Dive masters are multilingual and there are live-aboard options here.

Tours

There's no shortage of day excursions available from the main hotel information desks, which are usually staffed by Cubatur or Cubanacán representatives. Highlights include Por la Ruta de Hemingway (CUC$29), a journey through the keys mentioned in Hemingway's novel *Islands in the Stream*, a motorboat cruise around Cayo Paredón Grande (CUC$25), as well as a flamingo-spotting tour (CUC$29).

Sleeping

BUDGET

Sitio La Güira (☎ 30-12-08; cabaña with/without bath CUC$25/20) A simple abode situated on a small farm 8km west of the Servi-Cupet gas station, La Güira rents two rooms sharing a bath and a couple of Cuban *bohíos* (thatched huts) with private bath. Facilities are rustic and there's a *ranchón*-style restaurant on-site.

Motel Villa Jardín Los Cocos (☎ 30-21-80; s/d/tr CUC$30/35/45) This is one of Cayo Coco's few cheap options. Don't expect much – it's primarily designed for Cuban workers – but, if budget's your main consideration, one of the cheap musty rooms here could work.

TOP END

Cayo Coco's all-inclusive resorts are policed pretty diligently. Unless you're wearing the 'access all areas' plastic wristband, think twice about sneaking in to use the toilets. Room rates are all-inclusive.

Hotel Tryp Cayo Coco (Cubanacán; ☎ 30-13-00; s/d CUC$108/172; P ✗ ☐ ☎) The Tryp is a quintessential all-inclusive resort with a meandering pool, myriad bars, a nightly tourist show, and the obligatory plastic wristband. While the facilities are of a good quality, over-zealous poolside 'entertainers' lend the place a holiday-camp feel at times. The 500-plus rooms – housed in sunny three-story apartment blocks – are big, with balconies and huge beds, although the finishes are sometimes a little worn considering the room price. The hotel is immensely popular with families and European travelers.

NH Krystal Laguna (☎ 30-14-70; s/d CUC$110/170; P ✗ ☐ ☎) The same chain that runs Parque Central in Havana also tends to this low-rise resort spread spaciously between the Meliás and the Tryp. It's run as a complex with the Emperador located next door, and sports 80 villas on a lagoon behind the beach and sea. Novelties aside, the NH gets mixed reviews with many travelers citing its (relative) inferiority compared to its spiffy Havana cousin.

Villa Gaviota Cayo Coco (Gaviota; ☎ 30-21-80; d/tr CUC$130/185; P ✗ ☐ ☎) An amiable low-key place, Villa Gaviota has friendly service and a degree of intimacy missing from most of the larger resorts. It's right on the beach.

Hotel Blau Colonial (☎ 30-13-11; r from CUC$130; P ✗ ☐ ☎) Formerly known as the Guitart Cayo Coco, this well-designed resort was the island's first hotel when it opened in 1993 (ancient history by Cayo Coco standards). The hotel gained notoriety in 1994 when, according to Cuban media, gunmen from the right-wing Cuban exile movement Alpha 66 opened fire on the building in a blatant act of provocation. Fortunately, no one was hurt. Refurbished under new management in 2003, the Blau boasts attractive Spanish colonial-style villas that lend it a more cloistered and refined air than the Tryp next door.

Meliá Cayo Coco (☎ 30-11-80; s/d CUC$132/208; P ✗ ☐ ☎) This stellar resort on Playa Las Coloradas, at the eastern end of the hotel strip, is everything you'd expect from the business-like Spanish Meliá chain. For a luxury twist try staying in one of the elegant white bungalows that stand perched on stilts in the middle of a lagoon. Though the prices are high, the Meliá is a romantic haven, and a 'no-kids' policy enhances the tranquility.

Eating

Amid the ubiquitous as-much-as-you-can-eat hotel buffets there are a few independent restaurants – mainly thatched roof, *ranchón*-style places on or near the beach.

Restaurant Sitio La Güira (☼ 8am-11pm) Set in the old reconstructed charcoal burners' camp, La Güira's food is fresh, plentiful and not too charcoaly. Try the big, fresh sandwiches for CUC$2 or the shrimp plates for CUC$12. Strumming music trios do the rounds.

Parador La Silla (☎ 30-11-67; ☼ 9am-6pm) A thatched-roof snack bar halfway along the causeway into Cayo Coco that seems to almost float on the shallow Bahía de Perros. After a full plate of *comida criolla* (Creole food) you can climb up an adjacent lookout tower and try to spot distant specks of pink (flamingos).

Ranchón Playa Flamenco (☼ 9am-4pm) Eat exquisite seafood, drink cold beer, swim, snorkel, sunbathe, eat more seafood, drink more beer…you get the picture.

Ranchón Las Coloradas (☎ 30-11-74; ☼ 9am-4pm) Seafood again in an even more paradisiacal setting – can it be possible?

There's an additional bar-*parrillada* (grill restaurant) at the Parque Natural El Bagá.

Drinking & Entertainment

All the *ranchóns* reviewed have attached bars and all the all-inclusive hotels have a full nightly entertainment program (usually only available to hotel guests). Otherwise it's…

La Cueva del Jabalí (☎ 30-12-06; admission CUC$5; ✆ Tue-Sat) For those bored of the all-inclusive floor show, this is the only independent entertainment venue in Cayo Coco. It's 5km west of the Tryp complex, in a natural cave. The place features a cabaret show and it's free all day to visit the bar.

Getting There & Around

Opened in 2001, Cayo Coco's **Aeropuerto Internacional Jardines del Rey** (☎ 30-91-65) boasts a modern 3000m-runway facility that can process 1.2 million visitors annually. Weekly flights arrive here from Canada, Mexico, Spain, the UK, Germany and more. There's a twice-daily service to and from Havana (CUC$105) with **Aerogaviota** (☎ 7-203-0686).

Although getting to Cayo Coco is nigh on impossible without a car or taxi (or bike), getting around has got infinitely easier with the introduction of a **Transtur** (☎ 30-11-75) hop-on/hop-off minibus. The service is still in its infancy and varies according to season, but expect a minimal service of two buses per day in either direction. The bus ferries east to west between Meliá Cayo Coco and Playa Pilar, stopping at all Cayo Coco and Cayo Guillermo hotels as well as El Parque Bagá. Tickets cost CUC$5 for an all-day pass.

A taxi to Cayo Coco from Morón will cost in the region of CUC$30; from Ciego de Ávila closer to CUC$55. You pay a CUC$2 fee to enter the causeway.

You can rent a car or moped independently at **Cubacar** (☎ 30-12-75) on the second roundabout between the Meliá and Tryp complexes. Cubacar also has a desk at all the major hotels.

Bicycles are in short supply at Cayo Coco's hotels. The NH Krystal Laguna (opposite) is your best bet.

CAYO GUILLERMO

Cayo Guillermo is the definitive 'island in the stream.' Linked eternally with the name of Ernest Hemingway – who, though he didn't discover it, inadvertently stuck a CUC$3 'levy' on every drink – Cayo Guillermo was a prized deep-sea fishing spot long before its first hotel opened in 1993. Just west of Cayo Coco, to which it is connected by a causeway, 3-sq-km Guillermo is a much smaller key that supports four all-inclusive hotels and the jaw-droppingly beautiful Playa Pilar, arguably Cuba's finest beach. The mangroves off

the south coast are home to pink flamingos and pelicans, and there's a tremendous diversity of tropical fish and crustaceans on the Atlantic reef.

Cayo Guillermo remains the number-one sport-fishing destination in Cuba. The deep-sea fishing facilities are unequalled, and several freshwater lakes on the mainland are within commuting distance.

Activities

The **Marlin Marina** (☎ 30-17-38) on the right of the causeway as you arrive from Cayo Coco is a certified international entry port with 36 boat berths. You can organize deep-sea fishing for mackerel, pike, barracuda, red snapper and marlin here on large boats that troll five kilometers to 13km off-shore. It's CUC$290/450 for a half-/full day, and you can keep some of the fish. There's also a professional dive center charging CUC$45 for a dive with equipment. You can book at the hotels or go directly to the marina. **Cubanacán Náutica** (☎ 30-17-60) has two dive centers running dives for around the same price.

The popular **Boat Adventure** (☎ 30-15-16) has its own separate dock on the left-hand side of the causeway as you enter Guillermo. For CUC$41 you are treated to a two-hour motorboat trip (with a chance to man the controls) through the key's natural mangrove channels. Trips leave four times daily starting from 9am.

Cayo Guillermo was a favorite fishing spot of writer Ernest Hemingway, who mentioned it in his book *Islands in the Stream*. Its best beach (and possibly the best in Cuba) is **Playa Pilar**, named after Papa's famous boat. It's a lovely, unspoiled strip of sand backed by huge sand dunes and situated at the far western end of the key. You can sail and snorkel off nearby **Cayo Media Luna**; regular boats provide passage (CUC$11), or you can partake in a day-long catamaran excursion for CUC$49 including

JARDINES DE LA REINA

Jardines de la Reina are a 120km-long mangrove and coral island system situated 80km off the south coast of Ciego de Ávila province and 120km north of the Cayman Islands. The local marine park measures 3800 sq km with virgin territory left more or less untouched since the time of Columbus. Commercial fishing in the area has been banned and, with a permanent local population of precisely zero inhabitants, visitors must stay on board a two-story, seven-bedroom houseboat called **Hotel Flotante Tortuga** (☎ 339-8104) or venture in from the port of Embarcadero de Júcaro on one of two yachts, the six-cabin *Halcon* or the four-cabin *Explorador*.

The flora consists of palm trees, pines, sea grapes and mangroves, while the fauna – aside from tree rats and iguanas – contains an interesting variety of resident birds including ospreys, pelicans, spoonbills and egrets. Below the waves the main attraction is sharks (both whale and hammerhead) and this, along with the pristine coral and unequaled clarity of the water, is what draws in divers from all over the world.

Getting to the Jardines is not easy – or cheap. The only company currently offering excursions is the Italian-run **Avalon** (www.avalons.net). One-week dive packages, which include equipment, six nights of accommodation, a guide, a park license, 12 dives and transfer from Embarcadero de Júcaro, cost in the vicinity of CUC$1500. Another option is to sail with the Windward Islands Cruising Company departing from Trinidad (for details, see p309).

bus and boat transfers, snorkeling and lobster lunch. The hop-on/hop-off bus (p329) stops at Pilar twice daily in either direction and there's also a bar-restaurant (right).

Sleeping & Eating

Guillermo has four hotels at present, lined up on its northern shore; there are plans for two more. As well as the Daiquirí and Cojímar (following), you'll find the familiar luxury Sol/Meliá combo.

Villa Cojímar (Gran Caribe; ☎ 30-17-12; s/d CUC$102/145; ［P］［✖］［▢］［▣］) The oldest hotel on the Sabana-Camagüey archipelago opened back in 1993 and it comprises a rather low-key collection of bungalows in a quiet beachside location. The advertising blurb refers to it as a 'Cuban-style hotel,' but the only Cubans you're likely to meet are the people who make your room up.

Iberostar Daiquirí (Gran Caribe; ☎ 30-16-50; s/d CUC$105/150; ［P］［✖］［▢］［▣］) Plenty of shade, a lily pond, and a curtain of water cascading in front of the pool bar add up to make the Daiquirí the pick of the bunch in Guillermo. The 312 rooms are encased in attractive colonial-style apartment blocks and the thin slice of paradisiacal beach is straight out of the brochure. Extensive gardens are a bonus.

our pick **Ranchón Playa Pilar** (⏱ 9am-4pm) Not staying here? Worry not – Cuba's greatest beach also has a rather decent bar and restaurant to keep you fed and watered while you indulge in a bit of R and R.

Getting There & Around

Access information is the same as for Cayo Coco (see p329). The twice-daily hop-on hop-off bus carries people to and from Cayo Coco, stopping at all four Cayo Guillermo hotels and terminating at Playa Pilar. The cost is CUC$5 for an all-day ticket.

Cars can be hired with **Cubacar** (Villa Cojímar ☎ 30-17-43; Hotel Sol Cayo Guillermo ☎ 30-17-72).

CIEGO DE ÁVILA PROVINCE

Camagüey Province

Neither Occidente nor Oriente, Camagüey is Cuba's provincial contrarian, a region that likes to go its own way in political and cultural matters – and usually does – much to the chagrin of its neighbors in Havana and Santiago.

The seeds were sown in the colonial era when Camagüey's preference for cattle ranching over sugarcane meant a less heavy reliance on slave labor and more enthusiasm to get rid of a system that bred malevolence and misery. In answer to Céspedes' independence cry, the Camagüeyanos produced their own swashbuckling war hero, the feisty Ignacio Agramonte, a 32-year-old lawyer who questioned his eastern cohorts at every turn and ultimately managed to get Cuba's first (unofficial) constitution signed in the town of Guáimaro on home turf.

Today, Cuba's largest province is a pastoral mix of grazing cattle and soot-stained sugar mills. Devoid of any mountains of note, the region is flanked by Cuba's two largest archipelagos: the Sabana-Camagüey in the north and the isolated Jardines de la Reina in the south. Underdeveloped and almost virgin in places, these sprawling keys are Cuba's last true wilderness areas, cherished for their abundant marine life and unrivaled bird-watching opportunities.

Colonial Camagüey, Cuba's third-largest city, is the province as a microcosm. Staunchly Catholic and often just as staunchly against the status quo in the rest of the country, the city was the first to risk Castro's wrath in 1959 when its loose-cannon governor Huber Matos questioned the leftward drift of the still nascent Revolution. The province made amends by producing loyal revolutionary poet Nicolas Guillén, groundbreaking scientist Carlos Finlay and an internationally famous ballet company. Nowadays you're just as likely to see Camagüeyanos kicking back at a rodeo as enjoying a performance of Swan Lake in a province where the 'cowboy culture' is historically ingrained.

HIGHLIGHTS

- **Colonial Cartography** Get lost in Camagüey's wickedly twisted streets (p332)
- **Get Sharky** Watch dive instructors fearlessly feed sharks off Playa Santa Lucía (p347)
- **Nowhere Land** Escape to Cuba's last wilderness on Cayo Romano (p347)
- **Catholic Soul** Say your penance in Camagüey and sally forth to find Cuba's Catholic soul (p338)
- **Constitutional Landmark** Make a pit stop in Guáimaro and see where Cuba's first constitution was signed (p344)

- TELEPHONE CODE: 032
- POPULATION: 786,657
- AREA: 15,900 SQ KM

CAMAGÜEY PROVINCE

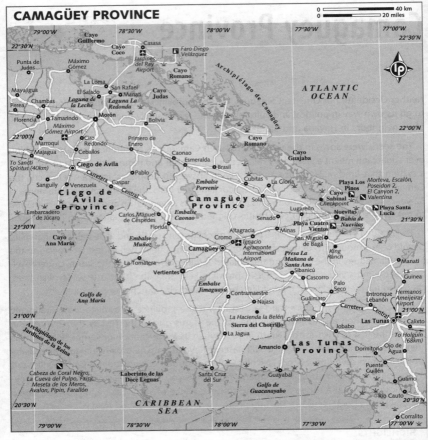

CAMAGÜEY PROVINCE

Parks & Reserves

Fifty-four hectares of central Camagüey are a Unesco World Heritage Site, dedicated in 2008. Thirty-six kilometers southeast of the provincial capital lies the Sierra del Chorrillo, a protected nature reserve run by government travel agency Ecotur.

Getting There & Around

As Cuba's third-largest population center, Camagüey is served well by daily Víazul buses and a better-than-average train service (the fast and comfortable Havana–Santiago Tren Francés stops here). A train line also links Camagüey with Nuevitas. Heading north to the keys and Playa Santa Lucía you'll need your own car or an aptitude for deciphering local Cuban truck/bus schedules.

CAMAGÜEY
pop 324,921

Welcome to the maze. Caught inadvertently in the tide of history, Camagüey is a Latin American city without precedent. The oddities lie in its unique urban layout. Two centuries spent fighting off musket-toting pirates such as Henry Morgan led the fledgling settlement to develop a peculiar labyrinthine street pattern designed to confuse pillaging invaders and provide cover for its long-suffering residents. As a result, Camagüey's sinuous streets and narrow winding alleys are more reminiscent of a Moroccan medina than the geometric grids of Lima or Mexico City.

Sandwiched on Carretera Central halfway between Ciego de Ávila and Las Tunas, the city of *tinajones* (clay pots), as Camagüey is sometimes known, is Cuba's third-largest city and the bastion of the Catholic Church on the island. Well known for going their own way in times of crisis, the resilient citizens are popularly called 'Agramontinos' by other Cubans, after local War of Independence hero Ignacio Agramonte, coauthor of the Guáimaro constitution and courageous leader of Cuba's finest cavalry brigade.

Some travelers love Camagüey with its secret nooks and crannies. Others are not so enamored with its unsavory reputation for bike thieves and *jineteros* (touts). Take to the maze and find out for yourself.

History

Founded in February 1514 as one of Diego Velázquez' hallowed seven 'villas,' Santa María del Puerto Príncipe was originally established on the coast near the site of present-day Nuevitas. Due to a series of bloody rebellions by the local Taíno Indians, the site of the city was moved twice in the early 16th century, finally taking up its present location in 1528. Its name was changed to Camagüey in 1903.

Camagüey developed quickly in the 1600s – despite continued attacks by corsairs – with an economy based on sugar production and cattle-rearing. Due to acute water shortages in the area the townsfolk were forced to make *tinajones* in order to collect rainwater and even today Camagüey is known as the city of *tinajones* – although the pots now serve a strictly ornamental purpose.

Aside from swashbuckling independence hero Ignacio Agramonte, Camagüey has produced several local personalities of note, including poet and patriot Nicolas Guillén and eminent doctor Carlos J Finlay, the man who was largely responsible for discovering the causes of yellow fever. In 1959 the prosperous citizens quickly fell foul of the Castro revolutionaries when local military commander Huber Matos (Fidel's one-time ally) accused El Líder Máximo of burying the Revolution. He was duly arrested and later thrown in prison for his pains.

CAMAGÜEY STREET NAMES

To make things even more confusing, locals doggedly stick to using the old names of streets, even though signs and maps (including those in this book) carry the new names. Here's a cheat sheet:

Old name	New name
Estrada Palma	Agramonte
Francisquito	Quiñones
Pobre	Padre Olallo
Rosario	Enrique Villuendas
San Estéban	Oscar Primelles
San Fernando	Bartolomé Masó
San José	José Ramón Silva
Santa Rita	El Solitario

Loyally Catholic Camagüey welcomed the Pope in 1998 and in 2008 it was declared a Unesco World Heritage Site.

Orientation

The irregular street layout makes getting around Camagüey as confusing to visitors as it was to pirates. Luckily, friendly Camagüeyanos are used to baffled travelers asking the way and they've recently put up a series of easy-to-decipher billboards that map out the best historical walking routes.

The train station is on the northern side of town, and several inexpensive hotels are clustered nearby. The city's north–south axis is República, which meets Av Agramonte at the historic La Soledad church. Most of the other hotels, churches and museums are just southwest of the church, in the city center. The Río Hatibonico crosses the southern side of the city center, and the main bus station is on Carretera Central, about 3km southeast of the river.

Information

BOOKSTORES

Librería Antonio Suárez (Maceo btwn General Gómez & Plaza Maceo) Carries a large selection of books in Spanish.
Librería Ateneo (República No 418 btwn El Solitario & San Martín)

INTERNET ACCESS & TELEPHONE

Etecsa Telepunto (República btwn San Martin & José Ramón Silva; internet access per hr CUC$6)

THE DISAPPEARANCE OF CAMILO CIENFUEGOS

With a bushier beard than Fidel's and a countenance as rugged as a handsome Hollywood cowboy, Camilo Cienfuegos cut a dashing figure when he marched triumphantly into Havana atop a horse in 1959. Had he lived, Cuban history might have been very different.

Born into a humble Havana family in 1932, Camilo was an unremarkable youth who dropped out of art school in his late teens to work in a tailor's shop. In 1953 he traveled with a friend to the US where he drifted for a time between New York, Chicago and San Francisco working as a waiter and dishwasher. Deported for visa irregularities in 1955, Cienfuegos returned to Cuba where he was shot in the leg and hospitalized during an anti-Batista demonstration in Havana. The revolutionary spark was inauspiciously lit.

By the time the Revolution triumphed in 1959, Cienfuegos' iconic status and meteoric rise largely paralleled that of Che Guevara. Like the Argentine, he had been a late addition to the *Granma* expedition, allegedly only being allowed to board the boat in Mexico due to his exceedingly lean physique. Surviving the debacle of the rebels' initial disembarkation, he escaped into the mountains in a party that included Juan Almeida and Che. *Nadie se rinde aquí* (No one surrenders here), he is said to have shouted at the height of the chaos.

Cienfuegos quickly attained the rank of Comandante in the Sierra Maestra and was instrumental in the final rebel victory in Las Villas province in December 1958. Leading the victory parade west, he was the first rebel commander to enter Havana, a few hours before Che and a full week before Fidel.

Along with Fidel, Raúl and Che Guevara, Camilo was considered one of the four great icons of the Cuban Revolution and his image is still omnipresent on billboards and photographs throughout the island. Though never ostensibly communist, he was always fiercely loyal to the Castro brothers and risked his life many times for the revolutionary cause.

In October 1959 Fidel sent Cienfuegos to Camagüey to arrest Huber Matos, a vacillating commander in the rebel army who objected to Castro's increasingly leftist leanings. Though partly sympathetic to Matos' cause, Camilo carried out his task as ordered before boarding a plane back to Havana. On the way home his Cessna aircraft mysteriously disappeared into thin air over the ocean. For more than a week all political activity was suspended as a frantic search was mounted for the missing *comandante,* but Cienfuegos' body was never found. The national shock was palpable.

Before long a whole host of conspiracy theories arose relating to Camilo's disappearance. Some allege that Fidel did away with Cienfuegos as the young *comandante's* snowballing popularity was starting to threaten his own. Others suggest that the less conspicuous Raúl had him killed in a jealous rage. Both theories seem unlikely and were vigorously denied at the time by Che Guevara, one of Camilo's closest confidantes.

Cubans today still reserve a tremendous affection for Cienfuegos – especially young people. Each October 28, on the anniversary of his death, every schoolchild in the country symbolically throws a flower into the sea to invoke his memory.

LIBRARIES

Biblioteca Provincial Julio A Mella (Parque Ignacio Agramonte; ☼ Mon-Sat)

MEDIA

The local newspaper *Adelante* is published every Saturday. Radio Cadena Agramonte broadcasts in the city over frequencies 910AM and 93.5FM; it's located south of the city by tuning to 1340AM, and to the north, by tuning your radio to 1380AM.

MEDICAL SERVICES

Farmacia Internacional (Av Agramonte No 449 btwn Independencia & República)

Policlínico Integral Rodolfo Ramirez Esquival (☎ 28-14-81; cnr Ignacio Sánchez & Joaquín de Agüero) North of the level crossing from the Hotel Plaza; it will treat foreigners in an emergency.

MONEY

Banco de Crédito y Comercio (cnr Av Agramonte & Cisneros)

Banco Financiero Internacional (☎ 29-48-46; Independencia btwn Hermanos Agüero & Martí)
Cadeca (☎ 29-52-20; República No 353 btwn Oscar Primelles & El Solitario; ⏲ 8:30am-6pm Mon-Sat, 8:30am-1pm Sun)

POST
Post office (Av Agramonte No 461 btwn Independencia & Cisneros; ⏲ 8am-6pm)

TRAVEL AGENCIES
Cubanacán (☎ 29-73-74; Hotel Plaza, Van Horne No 1) The best place for information on Playa Santa Lucia (Cubanacán runs all the hotels at the resort).
Cubatur (☎ 25-47-85; Av Agramonte No 421 btwn República & Independencia)

Dangers & Annoyances
Camagüey invites more hassle than other cities. Thefts have been reported in its narrow, winding streets, mainly from bag-snatchers who then jump onto the back of a waiting bicycle for a quick getaway. Keep your money belt tied firmly around your waist and don't invite attention.

Sights & Activities
Named – like half the city – after the exalted local War of Independence hero, the **Museo Provincial Ignacio Agramonte** (☎ 28-24-25; Av de los Mártires No 2; admission CUC$2; ⏲ 10am-6pm Tue-Thu & Sat, 2:30-10pm Fri, 9am-1pm Sun), just north of the train station, is housed in a building first erected in 1848 as a Spanish cavalry barracks. In 1902 the structure became a hotel and in 1948 it changed to its present function. Large and full of minuscule detail, the museum, like many in Cuba, has plenty of interesting artifacts but no thematic glue. Consequently, you'll find yourself wandering listlessly through a hazy mishmash of local history, natural history, fine arts, antique furniture, family heirlooms; the list goes on. All very interesting, but…

Wide-open **Plaza San Juan de Dios** (cnr Hurtado & Paco Recio) is Camagüey's most picturesque corner and the only town plaza to retain its original layout and buildings. Its eastern aspect is dominated by the **Museo de San Juan de Dios** (admission CUC$1; ⏲ 9am-5pm Tue-Sat, to 1pm Sun), housed in what was once a hospital administered by Father José Olallo, a Cuban friar who became Cuba's first saint when he was beatified at a ceremony attended by Raúl Castro in Camagüey in November 2008. The hospital

has a front cloister dating from 1728 and a unique triangular rear patio with Moorish touches, built in 1840. Since ceasing to function as a hospital in 1902, the building has served as a teacher's college, a refuge during the 1932 cyclone, and the Centro Provincial de Patrimonio directing the restoration of Camagüey's monuments. The museum chronicles Camagüey's history and exhibits some local paintings.

Also in Plaza San Juan de Dios is the **Estudio-Galería Jover** (Paco Recio; ⏲ 9am-noon & 3-5pm Mon-Sat), the working studio of Joel Jover. Joel, along with his wife Ileana Sánchez, are Camagüey's most accomplished contemporary artists with a whole gallery's worth of probing, inspirational exhibits. You can see plenty more at their magnificent home, **Casa de Arte Jover** (☎ 29-23-05; Martí No 154 btwn Independencia & Cisneros), in Plaza Agramonte.

Plaza del Carmen (Hermanos Agüero btwn Honda & Carmen), 600m west of the frenzy of Av República, is Camagüey's prettiest (and least visited) square. Little more than 10 years ago this whole place was a ruin, but local foresight and some canny restoration work has restored it to a state better than the original. The eastern half of the square is dominated by the Iglesia de Nuestra Señora de Carmen (see boxed text, p338) but, juxtaposing new against old, the cobbled central space has been infused with giant *tinajones*, atmospheric street lamps and unique life-sized sculptures of Camagüeyanos going about their daily business.

Just north of the Iglesia de Nuestra Señora de la Soledad is the quaint **Callejón de la Soledad**, a quintessential Camagüey alley with an outdoor cafe and live music most nights.

If you visit just one market in Cuba, make sure it's the **Mercado Agropecuario El Río**. Glued (by mud) beside the murky Río Hatibonico and characterized by its *pregones* (singsong, often comic, offering of wares) ringing through the stalls, this open-air piece of Camagüeyan theater is a classic example of Cuban-style free enterprise at work. Check out the *herberos* (purveyors of herbs, potions and secret elixirs), huge avocados (in season) and bundles of garlic, and sample one of the delicious *batidos* (fruitshakes) served with crushed ice in recycled jam jars. Be sure to keep a tight hold on your money belt.

The dazzling **Parque Ignacio Agramonte** (cnr Martí & Independencia) in the heart of the city lures

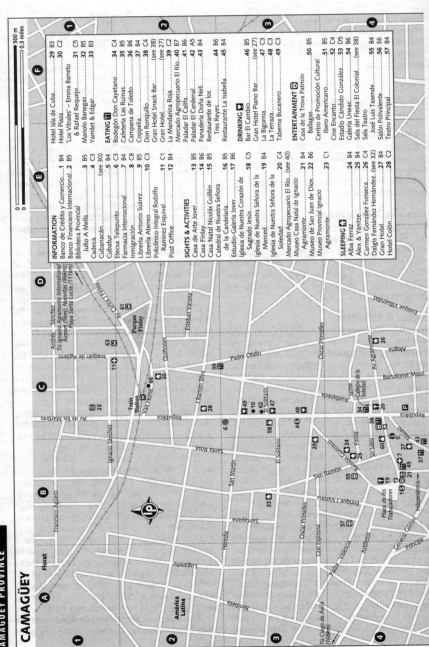

CAMAGÜEY

INFORMATION
Banco de Crédito y Comercio...**1** B4
Banco Financiero Internacional...**2** B5
Biblioteca Provincial
  Julio A Mella...........................**3** B5
Cadeca...................................**4** C3
Cubanacán............................(see 30)
Cubatur..................................**5** B4
Etecsa Telepunto....................**6** C3
Farmacia Internacional...........**7** B4
Inmigración...........................**8** C8
Librería Antonio Suárez..........**9** B5
Librería Ateneo....................**10** C3
Policlínico Integral Rodolfo
  Ramírez Esquival................**11** C1
Post Office...........................**12** B4

SIGHTS & ACTIVITIES
Casa de Arte Jover................**13** B5
Casa Finlay..........................**14** B6
Casa Natal Nicolás Guillén....**15** B5
Catedral de Nuestra Señora
  de la Candelaria.................**16** B5
Estudio-Galería Jover.............**17** B6
Iglesia de Nuestra Corazón de
  Sagrado Jesús....................**18** C5
Iglesia de Nuestra Señora de la
  Merced..............................**19** B4
Iglesia de Nuestra Señora de la
  Soledad.............................**20** C4
Mercado Agropecuario El Río...(see 40)
Museo Casa Natal de Ignacio
  Agramonte.........................**21** B4
Museo de San Juan de Dios...**22** B6
Museo Provincial Ignacio
  Agramonte.........................**23** C1

SLEEPING
Alba Ferraz..........................**24** B4
Alex & Yanitze.....................**25** B4
Carmen González Fonseca....**26** C4
Dalgis Fernández Hernández...(see 32)
Gran Hotel...........................**27** B4
Hotel Colón..........................**28** C2

Hotel Isla de Cuba...............**29** B3
Hotel Plaza..........................**30** C2
'Los Vitrales' – Emma Barreto
  & Rafael Requelo..............**31** C5
Manolo Banegas...................**32** B5
Yamilet & Edgar...................**33** B3

EATING
Bodegón Don Cayetano........**34** C4
Cafetería Las Ruinas.............**35** B5
Campana de Toledo.............**36** B6
Coppelia..............................**37** B4
Don Ronquillo......................**38** C4
Gran Hotel Snack Bar...........(see 38)
Gran Hotel...........................(see 27)
La Mandarina Roja...............**39** C2
Mercado Agropecuario El Río...**40** B7
Paladar El Califa...................**41** B6
Paladar El Cardenal..............**42** A5
Panadería Doña Nel.............**43** B4
Restaurante de los
  Tres Reyes.........................**44** B6
Restaurante La Isabella.........**45** B4

DRINKING
Bar El Cambio.......................**46** B5
Gran Hotel Piano Bar............(see 27)
La Bigornia..........................**47** C3
La Terraza............................**48** C3
Taberna Bucanero................**49** C3

ENTERTAINMENT
Casa de la Trova Patricio
  Ballagas............................**50** B5
Centro de Promoción Cultural
  Ibero Americano................**51** B5
Cine Encanto........................**52** C4
Estadio Cándido González.....**53** D5
Galería Uneac.......................**54** B6
José Luis Tasende.................**55** B4
Sala del Fiesta El Colonial......(see 38)
Sala Teatro...........................**56** E6
Salón Polivalente...................**57** B4
Teatro Principal....................**57** B4

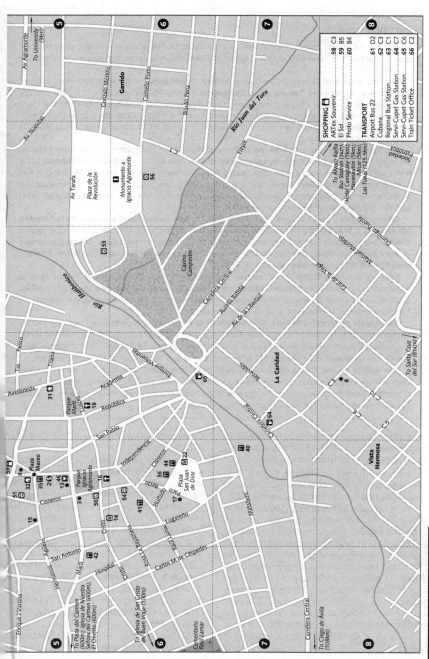

SHOPPING
ARTex Souvenir............58 C3
El Sol............59 B5
Photo Service............60 B4

TRANSPORT
Airport Bus 22............61 D2
Cubana............62 C3
Regional Bus Station............63 C1
Servi-Cupet Gas Station............64 C7
Servi-Cupet Gas Station............65 G6
Train Ticket Office............66 C2

CATHOLIC SOUL

If Cuba has a Catholic soul, it undoubtedly resides in Camagüey; a city of baroque churches and gilded altars, where haunting ecclesial spires rise like minarets above the narrow, labyrinthine streets.

Any exploration of Camagüey's religious history should begin at its most important church, the **Catedral de Nuestra Señora de la Candelaria** (Cisneros No 168), rebuilt in the 19th century on the site of an earlier chapel dating from 1530. The cathedral, which is named for the city's patron saint, was fully restored with funds raised from the 1998 visit of Pope John Paul II and, while not Camagüey's most eye-catching church, it is noted for its noble Christ statue that sits atop a craning bell tower.

The **Iglesia de Nuestra Señora de la Merced** (Plaza de los Trabajadores), dating from 1748, is, arguably, Camagüey's most impressive colonial church with a history imbued with legend. Local myth tells of a miraculous figure that floated from the watery depths here in 1601 and it has been a spot of worship ever since. The active convent in the attached cloister is distinguished by its two-level arched interior, spooky catacombs (where church faithful were buried until 1814) and the dazzling Santo Sepulcro, a solid-silver coffin.

Gleaming after a much-lauded 2007 renovation, the **Iglesia de Nuestra Señora de la Soledad** (cnr República & Av Agramonte) is a massive brick structure dating from 1779. Its picturesque cream-and-terra-cotta tower actually predates the rest of the structure and is an eye-catching landmark on the city skyline. Inside there are ornate baroque frescoes and the hallowed font where patriotic hero Ignacio Agramonte was baptized in 1841.

Baroque becomes Gothic in rectangular Parque Martí, a few blocks east of Parque Ignacio Agramonte, where the triple-spired **Iglesia de Nuestra Corazón de Sagrado Jesús** (cnr República & Luaces) dazzles with its ornate stained glass, iron work and updated interpretation of Europe's favorite medieval architectural style (a rarity in Cuba).

The **Iglesia de Nuestra Señora del Carmen** (Plaza del Carmen), a twin-towered baroque beauty dating from 1825, is another church that shares digs with a former convent. The Monasterio de las Ursalinas is a sturdy arched colonial building with a pretty cloistered courtyard that once provided shelter for victims of the furious 1932 hurricane. Today it is the offices of the City Historian.

The **Iglesia de San Cristo del Buen Viaje** (Plaza del Cristo), next door from the necropolis and overlooking a quiet square, is probably the least visited of Camagüey's ecclesial sextet, but it is worth a peek if you're visiting the graveyard. An original chapel was raised here in 1723, but the current structure is of mainly 19th-century vintage.

visitors with rings of marble benches and an equestrian statue (from 1950) of Camagüey's precocious War of Independence hero.

Opposite Iglesia de Nuestra Señora de la Merced, on the corner of Independencia, is the **Museo Casa Natal de Ignacio Agramonte** (☎ 29-71-16; Av Agramonte No 459; admission CUC$2; ☒ 10am-5:45pm Tue-Thu, 8am-noon Sun), the birthplace of the independence hero Ignacio Agramonte (1841–73), the cattle rancher who led the revolt against Spain in this area in 1868. In July 1869 rebel forces under Agramonte bombarded Camagüey, and four years later he was killed in action (aged only 32) fighting bravely against the Spanish. Nicknamed 'El Mayor' (the Major), you can hear Silvio Rodríguez' anthem to this hero on his disc *Días y Flores*. The house – an elegant colonial building in its own right – tells the oft-overlooked role of Camagüey and Agramonte in the First War of Independence.

Camagüey's other hero, Dr Carlos J Finlay, was more concerned with saving lives than taking them. His small birth-house at **Casa Finlay** (☎ 29-67-45; Cristo btwn Cisneros & Lugareño; ☒ 10am-6pm Tue-Thu & Sat) documents his life and scientific feats, most notably his medical breakthrough that discovered how mosquitoes transmit yellow fever. There's a splendid indoor patio and cafetería.

Nearby, the modest **Casa Natal Nicolás Guillén** (Hermanos Agüero No 58; admission free; ☒ 8:30am-4:30pm) gives visitors a small insight into Cuba's late national poet and his books, and today doubles up as the **Instituto Superior de Arte**, where local students come to study music.

Across the bridge over the Río Hatibonico is the **Casino Campestre**, one of Cuba's larg-

---

ASK A LOCAL

In 1998 Pope John Paul II chose Camagüey as the site of one of his four Cuban Masses. Now, 10 years later, we have been honored with Cuba's first saint, Camagüeyan friar José Olallo, a member of the Order of Saint John who aided the wounded of both sides in the 1868–78 War of Independence.

Ramiro, Camagüey

---

est urban parks with lots of shaded benches, a baseball stadium, concerts and activities. Get one of the ubiquitous bici-taxis to pedal you around.

Festivals & Events

The **Jornadas de la Cultura Camagüeyana** festival, commemorating the founding of the city, takes place during the first two weeks of February. The annual carnival, known as the **San Juan Camagüeyano**, is from June 24 to 29 and includes dancers, floats and African roots music.

Sleeping

IN TOWN

Casas Particulares

our pick **'Los Vitrales' – Emma Barreto & Rafael Requejo** (☎ 29-58-66; Avellaneda No 3 btwn General Gómez & Martí; r CUC$20-25; P ⊠) This painstakingly restored colonial house was once a convent and sports broad arches, high ceilings and dozens of antiques. Two rooms are arranged around a shady patio embellished with 50 different types of plants and a fantastic tile mural. Owner Rafael is an architect and it shows.

Alba Ferraz (☎ 28-30-30; misleydis2000@yahoo.com; Ramón Guerrero No 106 btwn San Ramón & Oscar Primelles; r CUC$20-25; ⊠) Two rooms sharing a bath open onto a rather grand colonial courtyard bedecked with plants. There's a roof terrace, of course, and Alba can arrange dance and guitar lessons for guests.

Alex & Yanitze (☎ 29-78-97; Ramón Guerrero No 104 btwn San Ramón & Oscar Primelles; r CUC$20-25). A huge bath, along with a TV and a comfortable bed. The room might be small, but the welcome's huge.

Manolo Banegas (☎ 29-46-06; Independencia No 251 altos, btwn Hermanos Agüero & General Gómez; r CUC$20-25) Great expectations spring to mind with this place (think Mrs Havisham's house) and, mostly, they're fulfilled. There are some

seriously valuable antiques, including the bed you'll be sleeping in, plus an amazing roof terrace overlooking intimate Plaza Maceo. If it's full, try the house of Dalgis Fernández Hernández (☎ 28-57-32) next door, which shares the same stairway and roof terrace.

Yamilet & Edgar (☎ 25-29-91; San Ramón No 209 btwn El Solitario & Heredia; r CUC$20-25) Edgar is a *maletero* (porter) in the Gran Hotel by day, and a casa-owner by night, running this inviting place just northwest of the center with his wife Yamilet. There's one pleasant room with private bath, plus meals and access to a comfortable sitting area.

Carmen González Fonseca (☎ 29-69-30; Av Agramonte No 229 btwn Padre Ollalo & Alegría; r CUC$20-25; P ⊠) A well-equipped self-contained room on the top floor with its own terrace and fridge. Daredevil drivers who have already negotiated the confusing Camagüeyan maze ought to have no problem reversing into the tight-fitting garage (a rarity here).

Hotels

Hotel Isla de Cuba (Islazul; ☎ 28-15-14; Oscar Primelles No 453 cnr Ramón Guerrero; s/d incl breakfast CUC$25/32; P ⊠) An often overlooked bargain bang in the center of town, the Isla de Cuba is cheap, friendly and keen to please – and because tour groups tend to shun it in favor of the Gran or Colón it's usually half-empty. Budget backpackers, look no further.

Hotel Plaza (Islazul; ☎ 28-24-13; Van Horne No 1; s/d/tr incl breakfast CUC$27/38/42; P ⊠) No two rooms are alike in this rough-around-the-edges colonial hotel built in the dying days of the Spanish era, so peek inside a few to see what's on offer. All have sitting areas, TVs and big fridges – and you can't argue with the price. Its location opposite the station makes it a logical spot for brutally early train departures (the 5:07am to Santiago, for instance).

our pick **Hotel Colón** (Islazul; ☎ 28-11-85; República No 472 btwn J Ramón Silva & San Martín; s/d incl breakfast CUC$36/44; ⊠) A classic long mahogany bar, colorful tile-flanked walls, and a stained-glass portrait of Christopher Columbus over the lobby door give this place a mixed colonial/fin-de-siècle feel. Sandwiched between shops on busy República, the Colón is both a good base for exploring and a good place to relax; there are rocking chairs on the upstairs balcony and a sheltered colonial patio out back.

Gran Hotel (Islazul; ☎ 29-20-93; Maceo No 67 btwn Av Agramonte & General Gómez; s/d incl breakfast CUC$50/58;

(P) (X) (□) (≋) For amenities and charm in the heart of the city, this hotel dating from 1939 is the place. The 72 clean rooms are reached by a worn marble staircase or ancient lift replete with cap-doffing attendants and antique gate. There are bird's-eye citywide views from the 5th-floor restaurant or you can brave the frenzy in the downstairs street-side snack bar. A *jinetera*-friendly piano bar is accessed through the lobby and an elegant renaissance-style swimming pool shimmers out back.

OUTSIDE TOWN

Hotel Camagüey (Islazul; ☎ 28-72-67; Carretera Central Este Km 4.5; s/d incl buffet breakfast CUC$36/42; (P) (X) (≋)) A built-to-spec Islazul out-of-towner 5km southeast of the center, the Camagüey presents that all-too-familiar mix of dodgy architecture, noisy disco and tacky 1970s furnishings. On the plus side, it's cheap, clean and relatively friendly.

Eating

RESTAURANTS

With restaurants specializing in Italian and Spanish fare, and another offering a Cuban rarity, lamb, Camagüey has an up-and-coming selection of eating establishments. The bars are equally eclectic.

La Mandarina Roja (☎ 29-02-67; Padre Olalla No 731 btwn San Martín & José Ramón Silva; dishes 20-25 pesos; ☺ noon-3pm & 7-10pm Thu-Tue) For a real peso paladar experience, head to this Chinese-inspired place serving large portions of chop suey, soup or fried rice. The food is as good as it is at any Cuban-Chinese crossover restaurant.

our pick **Restaurante La Isabella** (cnr Av Agramonte & Independencia; ☺ 11am-4pm & 6:30-10pm) Cool, cinematic and perennially crowded, Camagüey's newest restaurant was opened during a visit by delegates from Gibara's Festival Internacional del Cine Pobre in April 2008. Mixing Italian food with a maverick movie-themed decor (each of the 32 director-style seats is emblazoned with the name of a different Cuban 'star'), the restaurant occupies the site of Camagüey's first ever cinema and is named after local actress Isabella Santos. Hungry gastronomes won't be disappointed by the ample plates of pizza, lasagne and fettuccine.

Bodegón Don Cayetano (☎ 26-19-61; República No 79) Of Camagüey's handful of Spanish-style taverns, this is undoubtedly the best – and the only one that serves food. Nestled in the shadow of the Iglesia de Nuestra Señora de la Soledad, with tables spilling into the adjacent alley, the food is primarily Spanish with quality tapas such as tortilla, chorizo and garbanzos. For something more substantial try the chef's special: beef steak in red wine and mushroom sauce (CUC$5.50).

Restaurante de los Tres Reyes (Plaza San Juan de Dios No 18; meals CUC$7; ☺ 10am-10pm) Was that chicken really roasted – or was it fried? Such are the questions that beset you in this handsome state-run place set in beautiful colonial digs on Plaza San Juan de Dios. You ruminate over the answer in one the giant iron-grilled windows out front or enjoy greater privacy on a plant-bedecked patio behind. The equally romantic Campana de Toledo is next door.

Don Ronquillo (cnr Av Agramonte & República) A rather inviting restaurant hidden in the pretty Galería El Colonial with polished wine glasses and OK *comida criolla* (Creole food). Stick around for the cabaret (opposite).

Paladar El Cardenal (Martí No 309; dishes CUC$7-8; ☺ 11am-11pm) This old Camagüey standby is popular for a reason: seriously good *comida criolla* and lots of it. Try the pork steak, salad, *tostones* (fried plantains) and *congrí* (rice flecked with beans).

Paladar El Califa (Raúl Lamar No 49a btwn Cisneros & Lugareño; meals CUC$8; ☺ noon-midnight) Boy, the food here is fantastic – and such big portions. Hard to pick out in old-fashioned Calle Raúl Lamar, El Califa has been around for donkey's years and is rightly renowned for its huge plates of *uruguayano* (a type of pork fillet) and cordon bleu.

El Ovejito (☎ 29-25-24; Hermanos Agüero btwn Honda & Carmen; ☺ noon-10pm Wed-Mon) No, the name isn't a joke, state-run El Ovejito does actually serve 'little sheep' (as the name translates). Even better, it's situated on sublime Plaza del Carmen with nary a hustler to bother you. Try the lamb chops or the lamb fricassee.

Gran Hotel (Maceo No 67 btwn Av Agramonte & General Gómez; dinner buffet CUC$12) The 5th-floor restaurant here has superb city views and a rather nice buffet; get here early and watch the sun set over the church towers.

CAFETERÍAS

Gran Hotel snack bar (Maceo No 67 btwn Av Agramonte & General Gómez; ☺ 9am-11pm) This generally lively snack bar accessible off Maceo has coffee, sandwiches, chicken and ice cream. The hamburgers (when available) are good and the atmosphere is 1950s retro.

Cafetería Las Ruinas (Plaza Maceo) A fern-filled colonial patio with a bargain-basement menu of fried chicken and pizza. Order a margarita and strike up a conversation with the local street hawkers through the iron railings.

Coppelia (Maceo btwn Av Agramonte & General Gómez). Ice cream wasn't meant to be eaten in dark, cavernous canteens, but sometimes you've got to integrate. Join the queue and toss a coin – *fresa* (strawberry) or chocolate?

GROCERIES

Mercado Agropecuario El Río (Matadero; ☾ 7am-6pm) Above the fetid Río Hatibonico, this place is a classic example of a Cuban market where everything is grown within 500m of the stalls. Chew heartily on peso sandwiches and fresh *batidos* (fruit shakes, sold in jam jars); also sells an excellent selection of fruit and vegetables. Watch out for pickpockets.

For bread and delicate cakes, try the **Panadería Doña Neli** (Maceo; ☾ 7am-7pm), which is opposite the Gran Hotel.

Drinking

Maybe it's the pirate past, but Camagüey has some great tavern-style drinking houses.

Bar El Cambio (cnr Independencia & Martí; ☾ 7am until late) The Hunter S Thompson choice. A dive bar with graffiti-splattered walls and interestingly named cocktails, this place consists of one room, four tables and bags of atmosphere.

La Terraza (Av República No 352; ☾ 8am-midnight) The local choice. An open-air peso place full of carefree Camagüeyanos getting smashed on cheap beer and rum.

Taberna Bucanero (República btwn El Solitario & San Martín; ☾ 2-11pm) The buccaneer's choice. Fake pirate figures and Bucanero beer on tap characterize this swashbuckling tavern more reminiscent of an English pub.

La Bigornia (República btwn El Solitario & Oscar Primelles) The young person's choice. A lurid purple boutique bar-restaurant with a sports store on its mezzanine level, this is where the city's well-dressed (read scantily-dressed) 18 to 25s come for date nights and Noche Camagüeyana (see below) warm-ups.

Gran Hotel piano bar (Maceo No 67 btwn Av Agramonte & General Gómez; ☾ 1pm-2am) The *jinetera's* choice. An atmospheric hotel bar (in the stately 'Gran') with a long wooden bar, vintage juke-box and grand piano allows cross-cultural fertilization between Cubans and tourists. Live music happens nightly after 9pm.

Entertainment

Every Saturday night, the raucous Noche Camagüeyana spreads up República from La Soledad to the train station with food and alcohol stalls, music and crowds. Often a rock or *reggaetón* (Cuban hip-hop) concert takes place in the square next to La Soledad.

FOLK MUSIC

Casa de la Trova Patricio Ballagas (☎ 29-13-57; Cisneros No 171 btwn Martí & Cristo; admission CUC$3; ☾ Tue-Sun) An ornate entrance hall gives way to an atmospheric patio where old crooners sing and young couples *chachachá*. One of Cuba's best *trova* houses, where the regular tourist traffic takes nothing away from the old-world authenticity.

Galería Uneac (Cisneros No 159; ☾ 5pm & 9pm Sat) Folk singing and Afro-Cuban dancing happen at this place, just south of the cathedral.

Centro de Promoción Cultural Ibero Americano (Cisneros btwn General Gómez & Hermanos Agüero) Check out what's happening at this under-the-tourist-radar cultural center housed in the former Spanish Club, which hosts tango nights and the like.

CABARET

Sala del Fiesta El Colonial (cnr Av Agramonte & República) A restaurant by day and Camagüey's only cabaret by night. Part with CUC$7 at the door to witness an intoxicating dose of perfectly enacted Cuban kitsch.

THEATER

ourpick **Teatro Principal** (☎ 29-30-48; Padre Valencia No 64; admission CUC$5-10; ☽ 8:30pm Fri & Sat, 5pm Sun) If it's on – GO! Second only to Havana in its ballet credentials, the Camagüey Ballet Company, founded in 1971 by Fernando Alonso (ex-husband of number-one Cuban dancing diva Alicia Alonso), is internationally renowned and performances, when they run, are the talk of the town. Also of interest is the wonderful theater building, of 1850 vintage, bedizened with majestic chandeliers and stained glass.

Sala Teatro José Luis Tasende (☎ 29-21-64; Ramón Guerrero No 51; ☽ 8:30pm Sat & Sun) For serious live theater, it's this venue with quality Spanish-language performances.

CINEMA

Big-screen showings take place at the city's one reliable movie house, the crumbling **Cine Encanto** (Av Agramonte).

SPORT

Estadio Cándido González (Av Tarafa) From October to April baseball games are held here alongside Casino Campestre. Team Camagüey, known as the Alfareros (the Ceramists), play in Group C with Ciego de Ávila, Las Tunas and Villa Clara.

Salón Polivalente (Plaza de la Revolución) This place is nearby Estadio Cándido González, behind

the huge Monumento a Ignacio Agramonte, and hosts other athletic matches.

Shopping

Calle Maceo is Camagüey's top shopping street, with a number of souvenir shops, bookstores and department stores.

Other stores:

ARTex Souvenir (República No 381; ☽ 9am-5pm) On the main drag.

Photo Service (Av Agramonte 430 btwn República & San Ramón) Sells instant cameras and batteries and develops prints.

El Sol (Maceo No 53; ☽ 9am-5pm Mon-Sat, 8:30am-12:30pm Sun) Che T-shirts, mini-*tinajones*, Che key-rings, compact discs, Che mugs. Get the picture?

Getting There & Away

AIR

Ignacio Agramonte International Airport (airport code CBG ; Carretera Nuevitas Km 7) is 9km northeast of town on the road to Nuevitas and Playa Santa Lucía.

Cubana (☎ 29-13-38; República No 400) has daily flights to Havana (CUC$93 one way, one hour 35 minutes). **Air Transat** (www.airtransat.com) and **Skyservice** (www.skyserviceairlines.com) fly in the all-inclusive crowd from Toronto, who are hastily bussed off to Playa Santa Lucía.

BUS & TRUCK

The **regional bus station** (Av Carlos J Finlay), near the train station, has trucks to Nuevitas (87km, twice daily) and Santa Cruz del Sur (82km, three daily). You pay in Cuban pesos. Trucks toward Playa Santa Lucía (109km, three daily) leave from here as well: ask for *el último* (last in the queue) inside the station and you'll be given a paper with a number; line up at the appropriate door and wait for your number to come up.

Long-distance **Víazul** (☎ 27-01-94; www.viazul .com) buses depart **Álvaro Barba Bus Station** (☎ 27-24-80; Carretera Central), 3km southeast of the center.

VÍAZUL DEPARTURES

Destination	Cost (CUC$)	Duration	Departure time
Havana	33	7hr 45min	4:30pm, 10:45pm, 11:20pm, 3:35am
Holguín	11	3hr	1:20pm, midnight, 4am, 5:35am
Santiago de Cuba	18	6hr	1:20pm, 6:25pm, midnight, 1:25am, 5:35am, 6:15am
Trinidad	15	4hr 30min	2:15am
Varadero	24	8hr 10min	2:50am

The Santiago de Cuba departure also stops at Las Tunas (CUC$7, two hours), Holguín (CUC$11, three hours 10 minutes) and Bayamo (CUC$11, 4½ hours). The Havana bus stops at Ciego de Ávila (CUC$6, one hour 45 minutes), Sancti Spíritus (CUC$10, four hours), Santa Clara (CUC$15, four hours 35 minutes) and Entronque de Jagüey (CUC$25, six hours 10 minutes). For Víazul tickets, see the *jefe de turno* (shift manager).

Passenger trucks to nearby towns including Las Tunas and Ciego de Ávila also leave from this station. Arriving before 9am will greatly increase your chances of getting on one of these trucks.

Public transport to Playa Santa Lucía is scant unless you're on a prearranged package. Expect to pay between CUC$55 and CUC$70 for a taxi one-way from Camagüey.

TRAIN

The **train station** (☎ 28-32-14; cnr Avellaneda & Finlay) is more conveniently located than the bus station – though the service isn't. Foreigners buy tickets in Convertibles from an unmarked office across the street from the entrance to Hotel Plaza. The Tren Francés leaves for Santiago at 3am-ish on alternate days and for Havana (stopping in Santa Clara) at 11pm-ish, also on alternate days. Slower *coche motor* (cross-island) trains also serve the Havana–Santiago route, stopping at places such as Matanzas, Sancti Spíritus and Ciego de Ávila. Going east there are daily services to Las Tunas, Manzanillo and Bayamo. Heading north there are (theoretically) four daily trains to Nuevitas and four to Morón.

Getting Around
TO/FROM THE AIRPORT

A taxi to the airport should cost CUC$5 from town or you can hang around for the local bus (No 22) from Parque Finlay (opposite the regional bus station) that runs every 30 minutes on weekdays and hourly on weekends.

BICI-TAXIS

Bicycle taxis are found on the square beside La Soledad or in Plaza Maceo. Technically, bici-taxis aren't permitted to carry tourists, but they do (including organized tour groups); they should cost five pesos, but they'll probably ask for payment in Convertibles.

CAR

Car-hire prices start at around CUC$70 a day plus gas depending on make of car and duration of hire. Hire companies include **Havanautos** (Hotel Camagüey ☎ 27-22-39; Carretera Central Este Km 4.5; Ignacio Agramonte International Airport ☎ 28-70-67).

Guarded parking (CUC$2 for 24 hours) is available for those brave enough to attempt Camagüey's maze in a car. Ask at your hotel/casa particular for details.

There are two **Servi-Cupet gas stations** (Carretera Central; ☽ 24hr) near Av de la Libertad. Driving in Camagüey's narrow one-way streets is a sport akin to Olympic tobogganing. Avoid it if you possibly can.

HORSE CARTS

Horse carts shuttle along a fixed route between the bus station and the train station, though you may have to change carts at Casino Campestre, near the river.

FLORIDA
pop 53,441

A million metaphoric miles from Miami, the hard-working sugar-mill town of Florida, 46km northwest of Camagüey on the way to Ciego de Ávila, is a viable overnighter if you're driving around central Cuba and are too tired to negotiate the labyrinthine streets of Camagüey after dark (a bad idea, whatever your physical or mental state is). There's a working rodeo, a hospital and an Etecsa telephone office.

Sleeping & Eating

Hotel Florida (Islazul; ☎ 5-3011; Carretera Central Km 534; s/d CUC$24/32; P ⊠ ⊠) This two-story hotel, 2km west of the center of town, has 74 adequate rooms. The entry drive is potholed, which sort of sets the tone for the place, but the staff are friendly and the price no more than a local casa particular.

Next to the Hotel Florida is Cafetería Caney, a thatched restaurant that's better value than the fly-blown hotel restaurant.

Getting There & Away

A **Servi-Cupet gas station** (Carretera Central) is in the center of town. Passenger trucks run from Florida to Camagüey where you can connect with Víazul.

SIERRA DEL CHORRILLO

This protected area 36km southeast of Camagüey contains three low-hill ranges: the Sierra del Chorrillo, the Sierra del Najasa and the Guaicanámar (highest point 324m). Nestled in their grassy uplands is **La Hacienda la Belén** (admission CUC$6; ☎ 27-49-95), a handsome country ranch that was built by a Peruvian architect during WWII and is now run as a nature reserve by travel agency **Ecotur** (☎ 27-49-95). As well as boasting an interesting display of (nonindigenous) exotic animals such as zebras, deer, bulls and horses, the park functions as a **bird reserve**, and is one of the best places in Cuba to view rare species such as the Cuban parakeet, the giant kingbird and the Antillean palm swift. Another curiosity is a three-million-year-old **petrified forest** of fossilized tree stumps spread over one hectare.

There is a swimming pool and a restaurant on-site, as well as accommodation provided in a rustic **hacienda** (r with bath CUC$35) with a 16-person capacity. Treks can be arranged around the reserve by jeep or on horseback and there are two guided walks: the **Sendero Santa Gertrudis** (4.5km) covering flora, fauna and a cave, and the **Sendero de las Aves** (1.8km), which reveals a cornucopia of birdlife. You'll need your own wheels to get here (drive 24km east of Camagüey on Carretera Central, then 12km southeast toward Najasa) or you can negotiate a rate with a taxi in Camagüey.

GUÁIMARO
pop 35,813

Guáimaro would be just another nameless Cuban town if it wasn't for the famous Guáimaro Assembly of April 1869, which approved the first Cuban constitution and called for emancipation of slaves. The assembly also elected Carlos Manuel de Céspedes as president. These events are commemorated by a large **monument** erected in 1940 on Parque Constitución in the center of town. Around the base of the monument are bronze plaques with the likenesses of José Martí, Máximo Gómez, Carlos Manuel de Céspedes, Ignacio Agramonte, Calixto García and Antonio Maceo, the stars of Cuban independence. If you're making a pit stop there's a small **museum** (Constitución No 83 btwn Libertad & Máximo Gómez; admission CUC$1) with a couple of rooms given to art and history. Guáimaro is also famous for its sculpture culture.

There is a Servi-Cupet gas station on your entry into town from Camagüey with an El Rápido snack bar attached. There are also seven legal casas in town. One of the better ones is **Casa de Magalis** (☎ 8-2891; Olimpo No 5 btwn Benito Morell & Carretera Central; r CUC$20-25), a super upper-floor apartment with, quite possibly, the largest bathroom in Cuba.

MINAS
pop 21,708

Minas, 60km northeast of Camagüey en route to Nuevitas, is notable only for the musical-instrument factory that opened here in 1976. The **Fábrica de Violines** (Camilo Cienfuegos; admission CUC$2; Mon-Sat), at the eastern entrance to town, carves beautiful instruments out of local hardwoods.

NUEVITAS
pop 40,607

Nuevitas, 87km northeast of Camagüey, is a 27km jaunt north off the Camagüey–Playa Santa Lucía road. It's an industrial town and sugar-exporting port with friendly locals and easy shore access, but not worth a major detour. In 1978 Cuban movie director Manual Octavio Gómez filmed his revolutionary classic *Una Mujer, Un Hombre, Una Ciudad* here, giving the city its first and – to date – only brush with fame.

Sights

The only specific sight in Nuevitas is the **Museo Histórico Municipal** (Máximo Gómez No 66; admission CUC$1; Tue-Sun), near Parque del Cañón in the center of town. It has the standard semi-interesting mix of stuffed animals and sepia-toned photographs; you can hike up the steps in the town center for a sweeping view of the bay and industry in ironic juxtaposition.

Below the Hotel Caonaba there's a shaggy amusement park/playground, which you may or may not want your kids to negotiate. A bit further along the coast is **Playa Cuatro Vientos**, a local beach, from where you can see two of the three small islands, called Los Tres Ballenatos, in the Bahía de Nuevitas. If you snake along the coast for 2km, you'll come to **Santa Rita** at the end of the road, a friendly place with a pier jutting into the bay.

Texans will be flummoxed by such a familiar-sounding name in the wilds of northern Camagüey, but this Wild West apparition is no phony. **King Ranch** (☎ 4-8115; Carretera de Santa Lucía Km 35; ☒ 10am-10pm), en route to Playa Santa Lucía, 4km beyond the crossroads where you join the main highway from Camagüey, was once an offshoot of its legendary Texas namesake (the largest ranch in the US). Expropriated after the Revolution, the Cubans have kept the name and broadened its appeal to include a restaurant, a rodeo show and horses for rent. It mostly caters for tour groups from Playa Santa Lucía, but you can turn up unannounced.

Sleeping & Eating

Hotel Caonaba (Islazul; ☎ 4-4803; cnr Martí & Albisa; s/d CUC$24/32; ☒) This friendly, three-story hotel is on a rise overlooking the sea. It's at the entrance to town as you arrive from Camagüey. The rooms have fridges and some have views; but don't expect the Ritz – or even the Rex. In summer you can eat at the restaurant, 200m along the coast from the amusement park. This is a favorite local swimming spot. The hotel also has a terrace bar (open from noon till late).

Getting There & Away

Nuevitas is the terminus of railway lines from Camagüey via Minas and Santa Clara via Chambas and Morón. The station is near the waterfront on the northern side of town. There should be up to four trains a day to Camagüey (CUC$2), and a service on alternate days to Santa Clara, but they are often canceled. Trucks are more reliable than buses. Trucks to Camagüey leave around 4:30am and 9am.

A Servi-Cupet gas station is at the entrance to town, a block from Hotel Caonaba. There's a Transtur taxi office nearby.

CAYO SABINAL

Cayo Sabinal, 22km to the north of Nuevitas, is virgin territory, a 30km-long coral key with marshes favored by flamingos and iguanas. The land cover is mainly flat and characterized by marshland and lagoons. The fauna consists of tree rats, wild boar and a large variety of butterflies. It's astoundingly beautiful.

Cayo Sabinal has quite some history for a wilderness area. Due to repeated pirate attacks in the 17th and 18th centuries, the Spanish built the **San Hilario fort** here in 1831 to restore order and keep the marauding corsairs at bay. Some years later the fort became a prison and in 1875 it was witness to the only Carlist uprising (a counterrevolutionary movement in Spain that opposed the reigning monarchy) in Cuba. There is also a lighthouse, **Faro Colón** (Punta Maternillo), erected in 1848 and one of the oldest still in operation on the Cuban archipelago. As a result of various naval battles fought in the area during the colonial era, a couple of Spanish shipwrecks – *Nuestra Señora de Alta Gracia* and the *Pizarro* – rest in shallow waters nearby, providing great fodder for divers.

Of Cayo Sabinal's 30km of beaches, **Playa Los Pinos** is undoubtedly the best. There's no accommodation at present (five basic cabins were recently closed), though a small snack bar can rustle up something resembling a meal. Any other activities are strictly of the do-it-yourself variety. Try hiking, strolling, swimming, stretching, writing, thinking, philosophizing or meditating. Everything seems to be more accentuated here.

Getting There & Away

There are three options: private car, taxi or boat. The dirt road to Cayo Sabinal begins 6km south of Nuevitas, off the road to Camagüey. You must show your passport at the bridge to the key and pay CUC$5. The 2km causeway linking the key to the mainland was the first of its kind constructed in Cuba and the most environmentally destructive. The Playa Santa Lucía tour agencies all offer day trips to Cayo Sabinal: by boat from around CUC$69 including transfers and lunch, or by jeep for CUC$75. Book through the hotels.

PLAYA SANTA LUCÍA

Playa Santa Lucía is an isolated resort 112km northeast of Camagüey situated on an unbroken 20km-long stretch of white-sand beach that competes with Varadero as Cuba's longest. The bulk of travelers come here to scuba dive on one of the island's best and most accessible coral reefs that lies just a few kilometers offshore. Another highlight is the beach itself, a tropical gem, still deserted in places, and on a par with Varadero in terms of size and quality.

The area around Playa Santa Lucía is flat and featureless, the preserve of flamingos, scrubby bushes and the odd grazing cow. Aside from a small micro-village that serves as lodging for itinerant hotel workers, there are no Cuban settlements of note. History seekers will be disappointed – Trinidad this is not! The swimming, snorkeling and diving are a different story, however, and the large hotels lay on plenty of activities for those with the time and inclination to explore. Packages to Playa Santa Lucía are usually cheaper than those to Cayo Coco and the resorts themselves have a more laid-back and relaxed feel. You're also within easy reach of Camagüey here, which is infinitely more interesting than Morón, Cayo Coco's gateway city.

Information

The Bandec bank where you can change money is in the Cuban residential area between the Servi-Cupet gas station at the southeastern entrance to Playa Santa Lucía and the hotel strip. Nearby is **Clínica Internacional de Santa Lucía** (☎ 36-53-00; Residencia 4), a well-equipped Cubanacán clinic for emergencies and medical issues. There's also a pharmacy here. Etecsa, 1.5km further along near the entrance to the hotel zone, has internet access for CUC$6 per hour and international phone capabilities. For tour agencies, Cubanacán, which owns four of the five hotels here, is well represented. Try the desk in the Gran Club Santa Lucía.

Sights

The arched comma of beach at the end of 20km-long Playa Santa Lucía, **Playa Los Cocos**, 7km from the hotels at the mouth of the Bahía de Nuevitas, is another stunner, with white sand and iridescent jade water. Sometimes flocks of pink flamingos are visible in Laguna El Real, behind this beach. A horse and carriage from the Santa Lucía hotels to Playa Los Cocos is CUC$6 each way for one or two persons, or you can walk it, jog it, bike it, taxi it, or jump on the twice-daily bus service that calls at all the tourist hotels. This is a fine swimming spot with views of the Faro Colón lighthouse on Cayo Sabinal but beware of tidal currents further out.

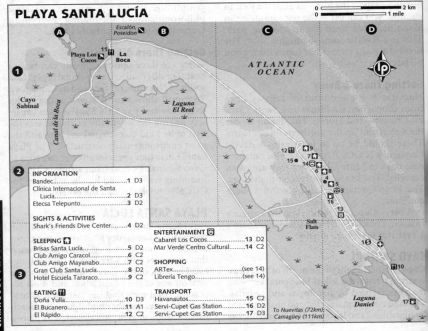

PLAYA SANTA LUCÍA

ATLANTIC OCEAN

Escalón, Poseidon

Playa Los Cocos · La Boca

Cayo Sabinal

Canal de la Boca

Laguna El Real

Salt Flats

To Nuevitas (72km); Camagüey (111km)

Laguna Daniel

INFORMATION	
Bandec	1 D3
Clínica Internacional de Santa Lucía	2 D3
Etecsa Telepunto	3 D2

SIGHTS & ACTIVITIES	
Shark's Friends Dive Center	4 D2

SLEEPING	
Brisas Santa Lucía	5 D2
Club Amigo Caracol	6 C2
Club Amigo Mayanabo	7 C2
Gran Club Santa Lucía	8 D2
Hotel Escuela Tararaco	9 C2

EATING	
Doña Yulla	10 D3
El Bucanero	11 A1
El Rápido	12 C2

ENTERTAINMENT	
Cabaret Los Cocos	13 D2
Mar Verde Centro Cultural	14 C2

SHOPPING	
ARTex	(see 14)
Librería Tengo	(see 14)

TRANSPORT	
Havanautos	15 C2
Servi-Cupet Gas Station	16 D2
Servi-Cupet Gas Station	17 D3

CUBA'S LAST WILDERNESS

Carpeted by expansive mangrove swamps and home to an estimated 30,000 flamingos, Cayo Romano is one of Cuba's last true wilderness areas. Largely ignored by contemporary travelers and virtually unvisited, save for the odd binocular-wielding ornithologist, two causeways link this most lonesome and untamed of northern keys with Cayo Coco in the west and Camagüey province to the south. Ernest Hemingway first championed the island's desolate and barren beaches in his posthumously published Cuban classic *Islands in the Stream* in the early '40s, and in 1947 a young Fidel Castro hid out in adjoining Cayo Confites for 52 days training for an abortive plot to overthrow the dictatorial Trujillo regime in the Dominican Republic. Other than that, not much has ignited the party here since Columbus first rolled by in 1494.

Targeted for future tourist development along the lines of Cayo Coco and Cayo Guillermo, Cayo Romano – the Cuban government claims – could one day play host to more than 5000 hotel rooms. For the time being, however, if you're equipped with a set of wheels, a large dose of mosquito repellent and a true sense of do-it-yourself adventure, the place is all yours.

Activities

Playa Santa Lucía is a diving destination extraordinaire that sits alongside what is, purportedly, the world's second-longest coral reef (after Australia's Great Barrier Reef). The 35 scuba sites take in six Poseidon ridges, the Cueva Honda dive site, shipwrecks, several types of rays and the abundant marine life at the entrance to the Bahía de Nuevitas. The much-promoted highlight is the hand-feeding of bull sharks between 3m and 4m long (June to January).

Shark's Friends Dive Center (Cubanacán Náutica; ☎ 36-51-82; Av Tararaco) is a professional outfit with dive masters who speak English, Italian and French. The center, on the beach between Brisas Santa Lucía and Gran Club Santa Lucía, offers dives for CUC$30, plus night dives (CUC$40) and the famous shark feeds (CUC$65) where cool-as-cucumber dive guides chuck food into the mouths of 3m-long bull sharks. It has boats going out every two hours between 9am and 3pm daily, though the last dive is contingent on demand. The open-water course costs CUC$360; a resort course is CUC$60. It also has snorkeling excursions.

The hotels can organize other water activities including a full-day catamaran cruise along the littoral (CUC$57 with lunch and snorkeling), a Flamingo Tour (CUC$59) and deep-sea fishing (CUC$200 for the boat for 3½ hours).

Sleeping

The small hotel strip begins 6km west of the roundabout at the entrance to Santa Lucía. The four big ones are Cubanacán all-inclusives with not much to choose between them. Due to Playa Santa Lucía's size and isolation, it's a good idea to book a room beforehand. Private rooms are prohibited here.

Hotel Escuela Tararaco (Formatur; ☎ 33-63-10; r CUC$35; ✷) There are no casas particulares in Playa Santa Lucia, so thank Changó for the Tararaco, one of those life-saving Escuela hotels where the staff are keen and every room has a TV and a little patio and is within stone-chucking distance of the beach. With a dearth of budget options, the 30 basic but comfortable digs fill up here fast here; book ahead.

Club Amigo Mayanabo (Cubanacán; ☎ 36-51-68; CUC$65/100; P ✷ ▯ ▣) You are the weakest link here – goodbye! Actually, there's nothing wrong with the Mayanabo, where regular renovations have kept pace with heavy usage.

Club Amigo Caracol (Cubanacán; ☎ 36-51-58; s/d CUC$65/100; P ✷ ▯ ▣) A newer version of the Mayanabo, the Caracol has the edge on its more worn partner, and with its large kids' program it is usually promoted as the beach's family favorite.

Brisas Santa Lucía (Cubanacán; ☎ 33-63-02; s/d CUC$75/120; P ✷ ▯ ▣) This all-inclusive resort has 412 rooms in several three-story buildings. In all, it covers a monstrous 11 hectares and gets the strip's top rating: four stars. Rooms in the 200 to 800 range are closest to the beach, while those in the 100 block kiss up against the Laberinto Disco. There is special kids' programming. Shark's Friend Dive Center (left) is next door.

Gran Club Santa Lucía (Cubanacán; ☎ 33-61-09; fax 36-51-47; s/d CUC$75/120; P ✷ ▯ ▣) Colorfully painted and still in good nick, the 249 rooms in this amiable resort-village all have minifridges and balconies or patios and they are accommodated in a series of tile-roofed two-story blocks. Prices quoted are for the cheap rooms furthest from the beach with parking-lot views. Discoteca La Jungla is the not overly inspiring nightclub, plus there's an evening music/comedy show with *mucho* audience participation.

Eating

Aside from the hotel buffets your choices are limited to El Rápido, opposite Hotel Escuela Santa Lucía, which serves cheap (for a reason) fast food, and Doña Yulla, right before the roundabout entrance to Santa Lucía serving simple, filling meals in pesos.

our pick **El Bucanero** (☎ 36-52-26; Playa los Cocos; 🕙 10am-10pm) Located on Playa los Cocos at the Santa Lucía end of the beach, this place is in a different class, serving seafood, meat and salads, all of which are enhanced by the setting.

Drinking & Entertainment

Outside of the resort entertainment, nothing much happens here. If you want a taste of something different, stroll east into the micro-village and take a look at Cabaret Los Cocos, a spit-and-sawdust Cuban place where hotel workers go on their night off.

The **Mar Verde Centro Cultural** (☎ 33-62-05; admission CUC$1) has a pleasant patio bar and a cabaret with live music nightly.

Shopping

Just before the Club Amigo Mayanabo, the Mar Verde Centro Cultural has an ARTex store with compact discs and Librería Tengo with high-quality art books and photographs for sale.

Getting There & Around

Anything is possible in Cuba, even getting to Playa Santa Lucía without your own transport, but it's a hard day's night full of dull waits, overcrowded *camiones* (trucks) and much local grumbling (mostly in Spanish). Some trucks go in this direction, but they are sporadic and a taxi will cost you CUC$70 one way. The cheapest option is to chat up the driver of one of the daily transfer buses laid on for the all-inclusive crowd and work out a deal. Start at CUC$10 and head north.

The **Servi-Cupet gas station** (Playa Santa Lucía) is at the southeastern end of the strip, near the access road from Camagüey. Another large Servi-Cupet station, with a Servi-Soda snack bar, is just south of Brisas Santa Lucía.

You can rent cars or mopeds (CUC$24 per day, including a tank of gas) at **Havanautos** (☎ 33-64-01; Tararaco) or at any of the hotels.

Las Tunas Province

It's an onerous label, but some place has to live with it. Wedged between uppity Camagüey to the west and the cultural powerhouse of the Oriente to the east, Las Tunas is Cuba's least touristy province and, for most travelers, its least interesting. Overlooked for centuries, its historical legacy rests on two longstanding myths: the mastery of Victoria de Las Tunas, a 1897 War of Independence battle won by Mambí general Calixto García; plus a flimsy but not totally disproved notion that Columbus actually anchored in Puerto Padre before he moved on to Gibara and Baracoa.

With such a lackluster role of honor, it would be easy to forgive the unassuming Tuneros a little pique. But the inhabitants of this most down-to-earth province aren't the wallowing sort. Check out the provincial capital on Saturday night when there's a rodeo in town, or drive-by Puerto Padre on any given Sunday to shoot the breeze with the salt-of-the-earth locals.

In the fame game, Las Tunas has produced two national heroes of note: Cuba's greatest ever boxing champion, Teófilo Stevenson, the man who once – with typical Tunero modesty – turned down a US$5 million offer to fight Muhammad Ali; and the witty musician-cum-poet Juan Cristóbal Nápoles Fajardo, better known as El Cucalambé, whose *décima* (10-stanza) verses brought to life the day-to-day travails of the rural Cuban peasant.

Marshy in the south, Las Tunas' north coast is a largely undiscovered nirvana of colorful coral reefs and deserted eco-beaches that, to date, hosts just one all-inclusive resort. Long may it continue!

HIGHLIGHTS

- **Sculpture Vulture** Stroll the streets of sleepy Las Tunas (p351), where imaginative sculptures embellish the cityscape
- **Rustic Rodeo** Check out the dudes with lassos at the Feria Ganado (p355), Las Tunas' celebrated traveling rodeo
- **Eco-beach** Enjoy the unkempt beaches of Playa La Herradura et al (p357), before resort developers shatter the tranquility
- **Pit Stop** Linger awhile in friendly Puerto Padre (p356), where the locals have always got time to talk
- **Folk Fest** Roll into Las Tunas in June to enjoy some country crooning at the Jornada Cucalambeana music festival (p353)

| TELEPHONE CODE: 031 | POPULATION: 529,850 | AREA: 6589 SQ KM |

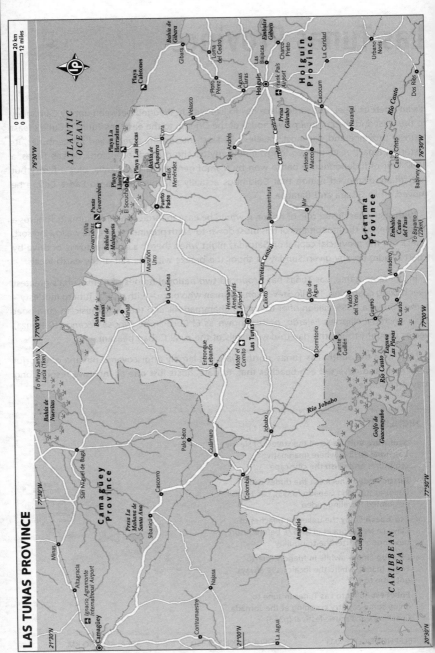

LAS TUNAS PROVINCE

History

The settlement of Las Tunas was founded in 1759 but wasn't given the title of 'city' until 1853. In 1876 Cuban General Vicente García briefly captured the city during the First War of Independence, but repeated Spanish successes in the area soon led the colonizers to rename it La Victoria de Las Tunas. During the Spanish-Cuban-American War the Spanish burned Las Tunas to the ground, but the Mambís fought back bravely, and in 1897 General Calixto García forced the local Spanish garrison to surrender in a pivotal Cuban victory.

Las Tunas became a provincial capital in 1975 during Cuba's postrevolutionary geographic reorganization. Its population has mushroomed in the years since.

Getting There & Around

Las Tunas is on the Carretera Central and Cuba's main west–east railway line. Víazul buses stop in the provincial capital daily as do a more limited selection of cross-country trains. The north of the province is the preserve of trucks and local buses, and roads here are often rutted and slow.

LAS TUNAS

pop 139,637

First impressions matter – but they're not always right. If it was down to sights and historical attractions alone, it's doubtful that many people would bother with Las Tunas. But, thanks to its handy location on Cuba's arterial Carretera Central, handfuls of road-weary travelers drop by. Some give it a once-over and quickly rejoin the highway, bound for Santiago or Havana; others, swept up in one of the city's riotous Saturday-night shindigs, come over all affectionate and book another night.

Referred to euphemistically as the 'city of sculptures,' Cuba's least-heralded provincial capital is certainly no Florence. But what it lacks in grandiosity it makes up for in small-town quirks. You can see a thigh-slapping rodeo here, admire a statue of a two-headed Taíno chief, or wax lyrical at the weird and witty Cucalambeana, Cuba's leading country-music festival. Go on, give it a whirl.

Orientation

The train station is on the northeastern side of town and the bus station is east of the center. Most of the things to see are in the center. A *circunvalación* (bypass road) runs around the south side of the city if you want to avoid Las Tunas altogether.

Information

BOOKSTORES
Librería Fulgencio Oroz (Colón No 151)

INTERNET ACCESS & TELEPHONE
Etecsa Telepunto (Francisco Vega btwn Vicente García & Lucas Ortiz; ⏰ 8:30am-7:30pm) Spanking new air-conditioned haven on the shopping boulevard.

LIBRARIES
Biblioteca Provincial José Martí (☎ 34-27-10; Vicente García No 4; ⏰ Mon-Sat)

MEDICAL SERVICES
Hospital Che Guevara (☎ 34-50-12; cnr Avs CJ Finlay & 2 de Diciembre) One kilometer from the highway exit toward Holguín.

MONEY
Banco de Crédito y Comercio (Vicente García No 69; ⏰ 8am-2pm Mon-Fri, 8-10.20am Sat)
Banco Financiero Internacional (☎ 34-62-02; cnr Vicente García & 24 de Febrero)
Cadeca (☎ 34-63-63; Colón No 41; ⏰ 8:30am-6pm Mon-Sat, 8:30am-1pm Sun)

POST
Post office (☎ 34-27-38; Vicente García No 6; ⏰ 8am-8pm) There are internet terminals here too.

TRAVEL AGENCIES
Cubana (☎ 34-27-02; cnr Lucas Ortíz & 24 de Febrero)

Sights

Las Tunas' most evocative sight, **Memorial a los Mártires de Barbados** (Lucas Ortíz No 344; admission free; ⏰ 10am-6pm Mon-Sat), is located in the former home of Carlos Leyva González, an Olympic fencer who was killed in the nation's worst terrorist atrocity: the bombing of Cubana Flight 455 in 1976 (see boxed text, p354). Individual photos of the victims of the attack, which included the entire 24-member Cuban Olympic fencing team, line the museum walls and provide a poignant reminder of the fated Flight 455.

Housed in the royal-blue town hall with a clock mounted on the front facade, the **Museo Provincial General Vicente García** (☎ 34-82-01; cnr Francisco Varona & Ángel Guardia; admission CUC$1;

LAS TUNAS

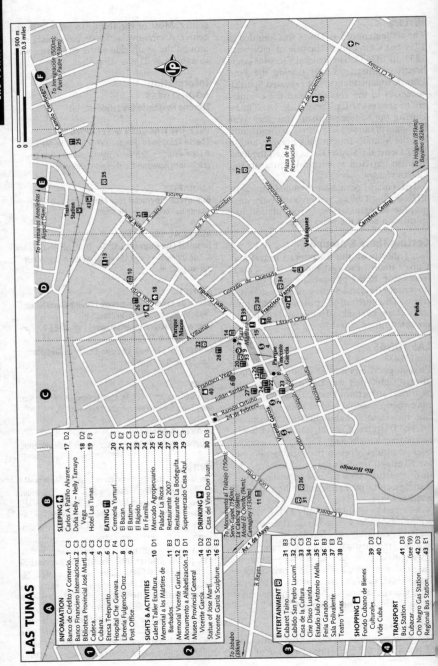

INFORMATION
Banco de Crédito y Comercio....1 C3
Banco Financiero Internacional..2 C3
Biblioteca Provincial José Martí..3 C3
Cadeca.............................4 C3
Cubana............................5 C2
Etecsa Telepunto.................6 C2
Hospital Che Guevara.............7 F4
Librería Fulgencio Oroz..........8 C3
Post Office.......................9 C3

SIGHTS & ACTIVITIES
Galería Taller Escultura........10 D1
Memorial a los Mártires de
  Barbados......................11 B3
Memorial Vicente García.........12 C3
Monumento a Alfabetización.....13 D1
Museo Provincial General
  Vicente García................14 D2
Statue of José Martí............15 D3
Vincente García Sculpture......16 E3

SLEEPING
Carlos A Patiño Alvarez.........17 D2
Doña Nelly – Nelly Tamayo
  Vega..........................18 D2
Hotel Las Tunas.................19 F3

EATING
Cremería Yumurí.................20 C3
El Bacan........................21 E2
El Baturro......................22 C3
El Rápido.......................23 C3
En Familia......................24 C3
Mercado Agropecuario...........25 E1
Paladar La Roca.................26 D2
Restaurante 2007...............27 C2
Restaurante La Bodeguita.......28 C2
Supermercado Casa Azul.........29 C3

DRINKING
Casa del Vino Don Juan.........30 D3

ENTERTAINMENT
Cabaret Taíno...................31 B3
Cabildo San Pedro Lucumí.......32 C2
Casa de la Cultura.............33 D3
Cine Disco Luanda..............34 D3
Estadio Julio Antonio Mella....35 E1
Feria Ganado...................36 B3
Sala Polivalente...............37 E3
Teatro Tunas...................38 D3

SHOPPING
Fondo Cubano de Bienes
  Culturales....................39 D3
Vide Cuba......................40 C2

TRANSPORT
Bus Station....................41 D3
Cubacar....................(see 19)
Oro Negro Gas Station..........42 D3
Regional Bus Station...........43 E1

🕙 11am-7pm Tue-Thu, 2-10pm Fri & Sat, 3-7pm Sun) documents local history. Congenial guides will fill in the gaps.

Nearby is the **Memorial Vicente García** (Vicente García No 7; admission CUC$1; 🕙 3-7pm Mon, 11am-7pm Tue-Sat), a colonial-era structure that commemorates Las Tunas' great War of Independence hero who captured the town from the Spanish in 1876 and torched it 21 years later when the colonizers sought to reclaim it. The limited exhibits include antique weapons and some grainy photos.

Popularly called the 'city of sculptures' (there are more than 100 in town), Las Tunas' alfresco art is dotted around the city. In Plaza Martiana, opened in 1995 to commemorate the 100th anniversary of José Martí's death, you'll see an inventive bronze **statue** of the apostle by Rita Longa, that also acts as a solar clock. Other notables include the **Monumento al Trabajo** (Carretera Central & Martí), commemorating Cuban workers, and the pencil-like **Monumento a Alfabetización** (Lucas Ortiz), marking the act passed in Las Tunas on November 16, 1961 to stamp out illiteracy. You'll have to get out to Motel El Cornito to see the emblematic Janus-inspired **Cacique Maniabo y Jibacoa**, a double-headed Taíno chief looking in opposite directions. Back in town the small **Galería Taller Escultura** (cnr Av 2 de Diciembre & Lucas Ortiz) pulls together some fine local work.

Las Tunas' **Plaza de la Revolución** is huge, bombastic and worth a once-over. Check out the huge Lenin-esque **sculpture of Vicente García**, sword raised.

Festivals & Events

Lovers of Cuban country music gather at Motel El Cornito in late June for the **Jornada Cucalambeana**, Cuba's greatest celebration of rural culture. The town hosts a **National Sculpture Exhibition** in February and the rather

---

ASK A LOCAL

There's plenty to do in Las Tunas, if you know where to look. The highlight is the annual Cucalambé festival that honors our greatest country musician. Not too far away there's a pleasant lake called Lago Azul where the locals like to hang out. Then there's 'our' beaches on the north coast – the most eco-friendly on the island.

Ana, Las Tunas

---

esoteric **Festival Internacional de Magia** (Magic Festival) in November.

Sleeping

Unless you're up for a night in the grim and gritty Hotel Las Tunas, a private room is your best bet for accommodation. Several houses rent clean, affordable rooms along Calle Lucas Ortíz, between the train station and the center.

CASAS PARTICULARES

'Doña Nelly' – Nelly Tamayo Vega (🕿 34-25-26; Lucas Ortíz No 111; r CUC$20-25; 🟦) Doña Nelly runs a pleasant colonial house with rockers on the front porch. Setting the scene for a tranquil few nights in Las Tunas, she rents one room with a private bathroom separated from the bedroom. There's a fridge and you can use some of the house's facilities.

Carlos A Patiño Alvarez (🕿 34-22-88; Lucas Ortíz No 120; r CUC$20-25; 🟦) There are two apartments here, each with their own kitchen, bathroom and sitting room. The upstairs one is brighter and has its kitchen on a terrace equipped with pots and pans.

HOTELS

Motel El Cornito (🕿 34-50-14; Carretera Central Km 8; r CUC$20) A Cuban-oriented place located outside of town near the site of El Cucalambé's old farm. The annual country music festival takes place here. You might get lucky with one of the basic bungalows. Phone ahead.

Hotel Las Tunas (Islazul; 🕿 34-50-14; Av 2 de Diciembre; s/d CUC$28/40; 🅿 🟦 🔲) What you see is what you get: unimaginative architecture, austere interiors, out-of-the-way location, dodgy restaurant and rooms that feel more like rabbit hutches than comfortable crash-pads. Then there's the noise from the late-night disco.

Eating
PALADARES

For a small and little-visited city, Las Tunas has a couple of surprisingly good paladares.

Paladar La Roca (Lucas Ortíz No 108; meals CUC$7-8; 🕙 noon-midnight) The pick of the bunch, for its luscious leg of lamb in gravy, a rarity in Cuba and something akin to a desert mirage in Las Tunas. Order it while you can.

El Bacan (F Suárez No 12; dishes 25-50 pesos) A peso place with big portions of *comida criolla* (Creole food) that mainly caters to Cubans.

FLIGHT 455

Blink and you'll miss it. The tiny bronze monument beside the Río Hormiguero in unfashionable Las Tunas is Cuba's sole memorial to one of the country's darkest hours.

On October 6, 1976, Cubana de Aviación Flight 455, on its way back to Havana from Guyana, took off after a stopover in Barbados' Seawell airport. Nine minutes after clearing the runway, two bombs went off in the cabin's rear toilet causing the plane to crash into the Atlantic Ocean. All 73 people on board – 57 of whom were Cuban – were killed. The toll included the entire Cuban fencing team fresh from a clean sweep of gold medals at the Central American Championships. At the time, the tragedy of Flight 455 was the worst ever terrorist attack in the Western hemisphere.

Hours after the bombing, two Venezuelan men were arrested in Barbados and a line was quickly traced back to Luis Posada Carriles and Orlando Bosch, two Cuban-born anti-Castro activists with histories as CIA operatives.

Arrested in Venezuela in 1977, the men were tried by both civilian and military courts and spent the best part of 10 years in Venezuelan prisons. Bosch was released in 1987 and went to live in the US. Carriles, meanwhile, broke out of jail in 1985 in a daring escape in which he dressed up as a priest. A year later he re-emerged in Nicaragua coordinating military supply drops for US-sponsored Contra rebels.

Despite worsening relations with the CIA and a failed attempt on his life in Guatemala City in 1990, Carriles remained active. In 1997 he was implicated in a series of bombings directed against tourist sites in Havana, and in 2000 he was arrested in Panama City for allegedly attempting to assassinate Fidel Castro.

Pardoned in 2004 by outgoing Panamanian president Mireya Moscoso, Carriles sought asylum in the US after the Venezuelan Supreme Court filed an extradition request for him. The US has so far refused to hand him over claiming that he faces the threat of torture in Venezuela.

As of 2009 Carriles and Bosch – both now in their 80s – were still living freely in the US. Among some anti-Castro extremists they are hailed as freedom fighters, while to most Cubans they are Latin America's Osama bin Ladens.

RESTAURANTS

Cremería Yumurí (cnr Francisco Vega & Vicente García; ☉ 10am-4pm & 5-11pm) Las Tunas' substitute Coppelia; queue up with your pesos for sundaes or *tres gracias* (three scoops) in flavors such as coconut and *café con leche* (espresso with milk). Not surprisingly, it's insanely popular.

En Familia (☎ 37-15-23; Vicente García btwn Ramon Ortuño & Julián Santana; ☉ 11am-11pm) Promising sign, morbid surroundings, scant menu; but if you can rouse the pizza man from his catatonic slumber you might just get lucky.

Restaurante 2007 (Vicente García btwn Julián Santana & Ramón Ortuño; ☉ noon-2:45pm & 6-10:45pm) A new attempt at fine dining in Las Tunas (albeit in pesos), this place claims to be 'reservations only' and doesn't exactly encourage non-Cubans. The plush interior and besuited waiters look promising, but you'll get a friendlier welcome at El Baturro across the road.

our pick **El Baturro** (☎ 34-90-11; Av Francisco Varona btwn Julián Santana & Ramón Ortuño; ☉ 11am-11pm) The walls are covered in scribbled prose – love notes and eulogies to murdered Chilean troubadour Victor Jara – and the plates are stuffed with better-than-average Cuban cooking, including a surprise rabbit dish, making this the best restaurant in Las Tunas – hands down!

Restaurante La Bodeguita (☎ 34-90-11; Francisco Varona No 293; ☉ 11am-11pm) A Palmares joint, meaning that it's a better bet than the usual peso parlors. You'll get checkered tablecloths here, a limited wine list and what the Cuban government calls 'international cuisine' – read spaghetti and pizza. Try the chicken breast with mushroom sauce for around CUC$5.

GROCERIES

To stock up on groceries (or to break bigger bills), try **Supermercado Casa Azul** (cnr Vicente García & Francisco Vega; ☉ 9am-6pm Mon-Sat, 9am-noon Sun). **Mercado agropecuario** (Av Camilo Cienfuegos) is a small market not far from the train station.

Drinking

Casa del Vino Don Juan (cnr Francisco Varona & Joaquín Agüero; ☉ 9am-midnight) Wine-tasting in Las

Tunas probably sounds about as credible as food rationing in Beverley Hills, yet here it is; and only seven pesos for a shot of Cuba's – er – finest wine, the slightly vinegary Soroa (red or white). The Don Juan is a down-to-earth corner bar with large open doors, a handful of tables and only one product on sale. Go just to say you've been there.

Entertainment

Las Tunas comes alive on Saturday nights when packed streets and fun-seeking locals defy the city's 'boring' image. The main hubs are: Parque Vicente García, where alfresco *son* music competes with more modern *reggaetón* (Cuban hip-hop); and the Feria Ganado.

our pick **Feria Ganado** (Farm Fair; admission free; 9am-6pm Sat & Sun) Located in Parque Julio 26 where Vicente García bends into Av 1 de Mayo, it kicks off every weekend with a market, music, food stalls, kids' activities and, if you're lucky, a full-scale rodeo (you'll see the large permanent arena as you walk in).

Cabildo San Pedro Lucumí (☎ 34-64-61; Francisco Varona btwn Vicente García & Lucas Ortíz; admission free; from 9pm Sun) Cultural activities happen at this friendly Afro-Caribbean association, HQ of the Compañía Folklórica Onilé. Drop in on Sunday for some dancing and drumming.

Teatro Tunas (Francisco Varona btwn Joaquín Agüero & Nicolas Heredia) A recently revitalized theater that shows quality movies and some of Cuba's best touring entertainment including flamenco, ballet and plays.

Cine Disco Luanda (Francisco Varona No 256; 10pm-2am Sun-Fri, 10pm-3am Sat) The most popular disco in Las Tunas. There's also a cinema here.

Cabaret Taino (☎ 34-38-23; cnr Vicente García & A Cabrera; admission per couple CUC$10; 9pm-2am Tue-Sun) This large thatched venue at the west entrance to town has the standard feathers, salsa and pasties show. Cover charge includes a bottle of rum and cola.

Casa de la Cultura (☎ 34-35-00; Vicente García No 8) The best place for the traditional stuff with concerts, poetry, dance etc. The action spills out into the street on weekend nights.

From October to April is baseball season. Las Tunas plays at the Estadio Julio Antonio Mella near the train station. Los Magos (the Wizards) haven't produced much magic of late and usually compete with Ciego de Ávila for bottom place in Group C. Other sports happen at the Sala Polivalente, an indoor arena near Hotel Las Tunas.

Shopping

Fondo Cubano de Bienes Culturales (cnr Angel Guardia & Francisco Varona; 9am-noon & 1:30-5pm Mon-Fri, 8:30am-noon Sat) This store sells fine artwork, ceramics and embroidered items.

Vide Cuba (cnr Lucas Ortiz & Francisco Vega; 8:30am-9pm Mon-Sat) For your photographic needs, try this place.

RODEOS

Despite spawning John Wayne, Lee Marvin and a whole generation of square-jawed Hollywood gunslingers, the US doesn't have a monopoly on cowboys – or those most boisterous of cowboy shindigs: rodeos. In fact, rather like with baseball, the Cubans have taken a peculiarly American obsession and given it their own Caribbean twist.

Cattle-herding has a long history in Cuba. Before the Revolution, Cuban cows produced some of the best beef in the Western hemisphere and, although the succulence of the streaks might have suffered since Castro nationalized the ranches, the skill and dexterity of the *vaqueros* (cowboys) has gone from strength to strength.

The cathedral of Cuban rodeo is the National Rodeo Arena in Parque Lenin in Havana – the host, since 1996, of the annual Boyeros Cattleman's Fair. But for a more authentic look at cowboy culture in the island's untrammeled hinterland, head first to the prime cattle-rearing provinces of Camagüey and Las Tunas where wildly contested rodeos take place every weekend in season.

Cuban rodeos exhibit all of the standard equestrian attractions with a few quirky Caribbean extras thrown in. Expect myriad horseback-riding events, obnoxious clowns, dexterous *vaqueros* lassoing steers, and rugged Benicio del Toro look-a-likes bolting out of rusty paddocks atop ill-tempered 680kg bulls to rapturous cheers from a noisy audience.

Held in tandem with its alfresco Saturday-night street parties, the Las Tunas rodeo is reason alone to visit this small, underestimated city. Entrance to the arena in Parque Julio 26 is normally free and the atmosphere inside refreshingly congenial.

Getting There & Away

BUS & TRUCK

The main bus station (☎ 34-30-60; Francisco Varona) is 1km southeast of the main square. Víazul (www.viazul.com) buses have daily departures; tickets are sold by the *jefe de turno* (shift manager).

Havana buses also stop at Camagüey (CUC$7, two hours 30 minutes), Ciego de Ávila (CUC$13, four hours 15 minutes), Sancti Spíritus (CUC$17, six hours 40 minutes), Santa Clara (CUC$22, seven hours 15 minutes) and Entronque de Jagüey (CUC$26, nine hours 20 minutes). Santiago buses stop at Bayamo (CUC$6, one hour 15 minutes). To get to Guantánamo or Baracoa, you have to connect through Santiago de Cuba.

Passenger trucks to other parts of the province, including Puerto Padre, pick up passengers on the main street near the train station, with the last departure before 2pm. Buy your tickets at the window. It's easier to reach Playa La Herradura from Holguín, but you can take a truck to Puerto Padre and connect with ongoing trucks there.

TRAIN

The train station (☎ 34-81-40) is near Estadio Julio Antonio Mella on the northeast side of town. See the *jefe de turno* for tickets. The fast Havana–Santiago Tren Francés doesn't stop in Las Tunas so you're left with slower, less reliable services. Trains to Havana (via Camagüey and Santa Clara) leave on odd-numbered days; the service to Santiago leaves on even-numbered days. There are daily services to Camagüey and Holguín. As ever, double-check these times and prices before you depart.

Getting Around

A taxi from the bus station to Hotel Las Tunas should cost approximately CUC$2, or you can walk. You can hail a cab here or anywhere around the main square. Horse carts run along Frank País near the baseball stadium to the town center; it costs 10 pesos.

Cubacar (☎ 37-15-06; Av 2 de Diciembre) is at Hotel Las Tunas. An Oro Negro gas station (cnr Francisco Varona & Lora) is a block west of the bus station. The Servi-Cupet gas station (Carretera Central; ◷ 24hr) is at the exit from Las Tunas toward Camagüey.

PUERTO PADRE

Languishing in a half-forgotten corner of Cuba's least spectacular province, the sizable town of Puerto Padre – or the 'city of mills' as it is locally known – is hardly a tourist mecca. But for the die-hard traveler therein lies the attraction. Blessed with a Las Ramblas–style boulevard, a miniature Malecón, and an emaciated statue of Don Quixote standing rather forlornly beneath a small windmill, the town is the sort of place where you stop to ask the way at lunchtime and end up, five hours later, tucking into fresh lobster at a bayside eating joint.

Unshakable Cuba junkies can scratch beneath the surface at the Museo Fernando García Grave de Peralta (Yara No 45 btwn Libertad & Maceo; admission CUC$1), effectively the municipal museum, or search the ruins of the Fuerte de la Loma (Libertad), also known as the Salcedo Castle. There is a Casa de la Cultura for nighttime activities or you can just surf the streets in search of friends, conversation or overnight accommodation in a *casa particular*.

Puerto Padre is best accessed by truck leaving from Las Tunas train station, or with your own wheels.

PUNTA COVARRUBIAS

Las Tunas province's only all-inclusive resort is also one of the island's most isolated, situated 49 rutted kilometers northwest of Puerto Padre on a spotless sandy beach at Punta Covarrubias. Sitting aside the blue-green Atlantic, the Brisas Covarrubias (Gran Caribe; ☎ 51-55-30; s/d from CUC$70/110; P ⊠ ⊠ ⅙) has

VÍAZUL DEPARTURES			
Destination	**Cost (CUC$)**	**Duration**	**Departure time**
Havana	39	11hr	9pm, 10:10pm, 1:55am, 8:25am, 10:30am
Holguín	6	1hr 10min	5:55am, 7:50am, 7:25pm
Santiago de Cuba	11	4hr 45min	1:40pm, 3:20pm, 7:55pm, 1:25am, 7:50am
Trinidad	21	6hr 30min	12:10am
Varadero	33	11hr	11:55pm

THE BALCONY OF THE ORIENTE

A long, sinuous island measuring 1250km from Cabo San Antonio to Punta de Maisí, Cuba exhibits an interesting cocktail of regional peculiarities with the two main camps dividing up west–east, or in the local jargon Occidente–Oriente.

Most Cubans will tell you that the Oriente begins in Las Tunas, a city often referred to as El Balcón del Oriente (The Balcony of the Oriente) for its location on the cusp of two colorful regional cultures. Prior to 1976 the area to the east of the settlement was a province in its own right, a large, culturally distinct region that encompassed the five present-day provinces of Guantánamo, Santiago de Cuba, Granma, Holguín and Las Tunas.

Geographically closer to Haiti than Havana, the Oriente has often preferred to look east rather than west in its bid to cement an alternative Cuban identity, absorbing myriad influences from Hispaniola, Jamaica and elsewhere. It is this soul-searching, in part, which accounts for the region's rich ethnic diversity and long-standing penchant for rebellion.

In the historical context, all of Cuba's revolutionary movements have been ignited in the Oriente, inspired by such fiery easterners as Carlos Manuel de Céspedes (from Bayamo), Antonio Maceo (from Santiago) and Fidel Castro (from Birán near Holguín). The region has also been a standard-bearer for the lion's share of Cuba's musical genres, from *son* and *changüí* to *nueva trova*.

Today, Cuba's long-standing east-west rivals continue to trade humorous insults on topics such as language (easterners have a distinctive 'singsong' accent), baseball (Los Industriales versus Santiago is an event akin to Real Madrid versus Barcelona), history (Santiagueros have never forgiven Habaneros for stealing the mantle of capital city in 1607) and economics (poorer easterners have tended to migrate west for work). While high-and-mighty Habaneros will tell you that the rest of Cuba is just a 'green field' and jokingly refer to people from Santiago as Palestinos, the proud citizens of the Oriente like to think of themselves as feisty historical liberators and jealous guardians of Cuba's world-famous musical heritage.

122 comfortable rooms in cabin-blocks (one room is designed for disabled guests). Scuba diving at the coral reef 1.5km off-shore is the highlight. Packages of two dives per day start at CUC$45 at the Marina Covarrubias. There are 12 dive sites here. Almost all guests arrive on all-inclusive tours and are bussed in from Frank País Airport in Holguín, 115km to the southeast. It's very secluded.

Self-sufficient travelers can turn in to the beach at the **mirador** (a tower with fantastic panoramic views), 200m before the hotel, or procure a hotel day pass for CUC$20.

PLAYAS LA HERRADURA, LA LLANITA & LAS BOCAS

Congratulations! You've made it to the end of the road. A captivating alternative to the comforts of Covarrubias can be found in this string of northern beaches hugging the Atlantic coast 30km north of Puerto Padre and 55km from Holguín. There's not much to do here apart from read, relax, ruminate and get lost in the vivid colors of traditional Cuban life.

From Puerto Padre it's 30km around the eastern shore of Bahía de Chaparra to **Playa La Herradura**. The beach is a scoop of golden sand that will one day undoubtedly host an all-inclusive resort. Enjoy it while you can – by yourself. There are a handful of houses legally renting rooms (look for the blue-and-white Arrendador Divisa sign). A long-standing choice is **Villa Papachongo** (in Holguín ☎ 24-42-41-74; Casa No 137; r CUC$15; ❄), right on the beach with a great porch for catching the sunset. Other options are Villa Rocío and Villa Pedro Hidalgo. Ask around. The place isn't big and everybody knows everybody else. If you want to explore more, push on to Playa Las Bocas where there are several more houses for rent along with a small snack store and an open-air bar at the entrance to town.

Continue west on this road for 11km to **Playa La Llanita**. The sand here is softer and whiter than in La Herradura, but the beach lies on an unprotected bend and there's sometimes a vicious chop.

Just 1km beyond, you come to the end of the road at **Playa Las Bocas**. Wedged between the coast and Bahía de Chaparra, you can usually catch a local ferry to El Socucho and continue to Puerto Padre or rent a room in a casa particular.

Getting There & Away

There are trucks that can take you as far as Puerto Padre from Las Tunas, from where you'll have to connect with another ride to the junction at Lora before heading north to the beaches. It's much easier to get up this way from Holguín, but even this way there are only regular trucks to the junction at Velasco, from where you'll have to connect with another ride north.

Driving is the best shot. Head out of Las Tunas 52km north to Puerto Padre (gas up at the Servi-Cupet here), east to the junction at Lora, then north to Playa La Herradura. A hired taxi should cost between CUC$40 and CUC$50 one-way. From Holguín, leave town on the Gibara road, then head northwest in Aguas Claras on Rte 123. Proceed through the town of Velasco and in Lora turn north on the rutted road to Playa La Herradura.

Holguín Province

With native sons as polar opposite as Fidel Castro and Fulgencio Batista, it's no surprise that Holguín is a region of extremes, and if you delve a little deeper you'll find a few more. There's the pine-scented purity of the Sierra del Cristal versus the environmental degradation of the Moa nickel mines; the tranquility of Cayo Saetía versus the bustle of the provincial capital; or the inherent Cuban-ness of Gibara versus the tourist swank of Guardalavaca.

Outside its dazzling north coast resorts, few non-Cubans know much about this hard-working but hard-to-fathom province. It's a sad, if excusable, oversight. Native Holguiñeros have been ruling over Cuba since 1934 (Batista-Castro-Castro). Not bad for a province that only registered its first city in 1752 and, until the late 1950s, was a virtual fiefdom of the American-owned United Fruit Company.

Holguín's beauty was first spotted by Christopher Columbus who, by most historical accounts, docked here in October 1492, describing the region's broccoli-green forests and shapely coastal hills as the 'most beautiful land he had ever laid eyes on.'

Timeless and benevolent in their mystery, the hills are still here, though the forests were cleared long ago by United Fruit and other sugar-hungry plantation owners. In more recent times sprawling resorts have sprung up along the coast forming three distinct enclaves – Guardalavaca, Esmeralda and the superposh Playa Pesquero.

Further south the hills become craggier before giving way to the purple-hued Sierra del Cristal, a fresh-scented alpine-flavored wilderness where an adventure-seeking Castro roamed as a child. Pine-clad and bursting with wild orchids, the area around the Parque Nacional La Mensura guards a mountain research center and the island's highest waterfall.

HIGHLIGHTS

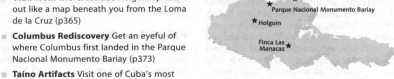

- **View from the Cross** See Holguín spread out like a map beneath you from the Loma de la Cruz (p365)
- **Columbus Rediscovery** Get an eyeful of where Columbus first landed in the Parque Nacional Monumento Bariay (p373)
- **Taíno Artifacts** Visit one of Cuba's most important archaeological sites at Museo Chorro de Maita (p375)
- **Casa del Comandante** Take a peep behind the mask at Fidel's childhood home, the Finca Las Manacas (p380)
- **Film Festival** Go to Gibara in April for the cutting-edge Festival Internacional de Cine Pobre (see boxed text, p372)

■ TELEPHONE CODE: 024   ■ POPULATION: 1.04 MILLION   ■ AREA: 9300 SQ KM

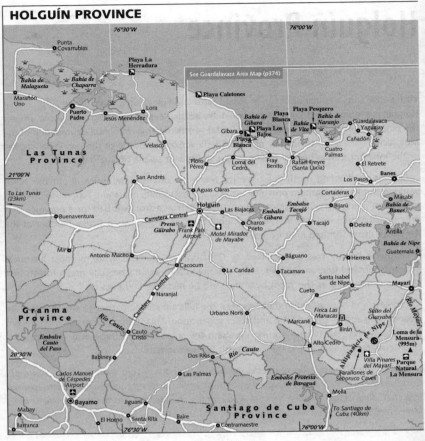

HOLGUÍN PROVINCE

History

Most historians and experts agree that Christopher Columbus first made landfall in Cuba on October 28, 1492 at Cayo Bariay near Playa Blanca, just west of Playa Don Lino (now in Holguín province). The gold-seeking Spaniards were welcomed ashore by Seboruco Indians and they captured 13 of them to take back to Europe as scientific 'specimens.' Boycotting Bariay in favor of Guantánamo 20 years later when they set up their new colonial capital in Baracoa, Spanish explorer Diego Velázquez de Cuéllar gifted the hilly terrain north of Bayamo to Captain García Holguín, a Mexican conquistador. The province became an important sugar-growing area at the end of the 19th century when much of the land was bought up and cleared of forest by the US-owned United Fruit Company. Formerly part of the Oriente territory, Holguín became a province in its own right in 1975.

Parks & Reserves

Holguín's mountainous southern region is protected in the Sierra Cristal and La Mensura National Parks. Rocazul is a small bio-park near Playa Pesquero.

Getting There & Around

The city of Holguín is well served by Víazul buses, trucks and slower trains heading to Havana, Santiago and all the main cities in between. Gibara and Banes can be reached by less comfortable local buses or trucks.

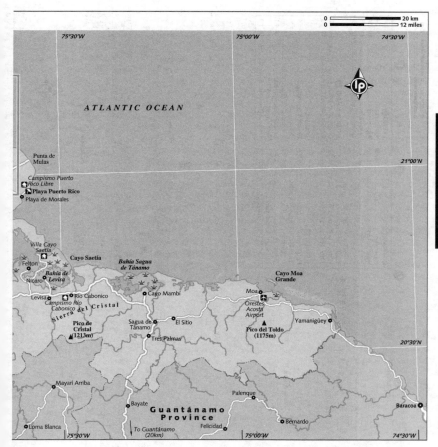

Guardalavaca has a handy hop-on/hop-off tourist bus linking the sights along the coast. The east of the province is off the main transport grid and getting around here without a car or bike is both slow and uncomfortable.

HOLGUÍN
pop 264,927

Although it can't claim a World Heritage Site listing or compete with the likes of Havana and Santiago for culture and music, the city of San Isidoro de Holguín has an imperceptible Cuban energy. Things just sort of happen here – a spontaneous shindig in the main square, a solemn religious procession to the Calvary-like Loma de la Cruz, a surprise victory in the National Baseball Series.

Known euphemistically as 'the city of parks,' Cuba's fourth-largest urban center retains a laid-back and friendly atmosphere that puts visitors instantly at ease. You won't see too many of your fellow tourists here, but you probably won't miss them either. There's too much reality to witness, too many rhythms to absorb. Flop down in a cafe on Parque Calixto García and soak up the sights and sounds of a city of stalwart survivors going industriously about their daily business.

History

In 1515 Diego Velázquez de Cuéllar, Cuba's first governor, conferred the lands north of Bayamo to Captain García Holguín, an officer

HOLGUÍN

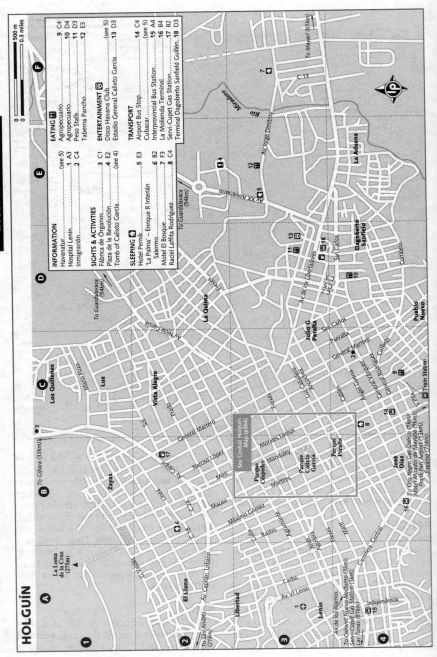

INFORMATION

Havanatur..................	(see 5)
Hospital Lenin............	1 A3
Inmigración...............	2 C4

SIGHTS & ACTIVITIES

Fábrica de Órganos..........	3 C1
Plaza de la Revolución.......	4 E2
Tomb of Calixto García.......	(see 4)

SLEEPING 🏠

Hotel Pernik...............................	5 E3
'La Palma' – Enrique R Interián	
Salermo...........................	6 B2
Motel El Bosque..................	7 F3
Raciel Laffita Rodríguez.......	8 C4

EATING 🍴

Agropecuario..........	9 C4
Agropecuario..........	10 D4
Peso Stalls.............	11 D3
Taberna Pancho.....	12 E3

ENTERTAINMENT 🎭

Disco Havana Club..............	(see 5)
Estadio General Calixto García.	13 D3

TRANSPORT 🚌

Airport Bus Stop.............................	14 C4
Cubacar..	(see 5)
Interprovincial Bus Station..........	15 A4
La Molienda Terminal....................	16 B4
Servi-Cupet Gas Station................	17 B2
Terminal Dagoberto Sanfield Guillén.	18 D3

in the Spanish army and one of island's original colonizers. Setting up a cattle ranch in the province's verdant and fertile hinterland, Holguín and his descendants presided over a burgeoning agricultural settlement that by 1720 had sprouted a small wooden church and more than 450 inhabitants. In 1752 San Isidoro de Holguín (the settlement was renamed after the church) was granted the title of city and by 1790 the population had expanded tenfold to 12,000.

Holguín was the setting of much fighting during the two wars of independence when ferocious Mambí warriors laid siege to the heavily fortified Spanish barracks at La Periquera (now the Museo de Historia Provincial; p365). Captured and lost by Julio Grave de Peralta (after whom one of the squares is named), the city was taken for a second time on December 19, 1872, by Cuban general and native son Calixto García, Holguín's posthumous local hero.

With the division of Oriente into five separate provinces in 1975, the city of Holguín became a provincial capital. It suffered a severe mauling from Hurricane Ike in 2008.

Orientation

Parque Calixto García is Holguín's most important central square; to the north is Parque Céspedes and to the south is Parque Peralta. Manduley (aka Libertad) and Maceo are the main north–south thoroughfares, running between the train station and the hills that border the city's northern limits. The main bus station is to the southwest of the center, the main tourist hotels to the east.

Information

BOOKSTORES
ARTex (Map p364; Manduley No 193A) Sells books, CDs, posters and Che T-shirts on Parque Calixto García.

INTERNET ACCESS & TELEPHONE
Etecsa Telepunto (Map p364; cnr Martí & Maceo; per hr CUC$6; ☉ 8:30am-7:30pm) Three computer terminals in Parque Calixto García.

LIBRARIES
Biblioteca Alex Urquiola (Map p364; ☎ 42-44-63; Maceo No 178; ☉ 8:30am-9pm Mon-Fri, 8:30am-4:30pm Sat) On Parque Calixto García.

MEDIA
The local newspaper *Ahora* is published on Saturday. Radio Ángulo CMKO can be heard on 1110AM and 97.9FM.

MEDICAL SERVICES
Farmacia Turno Especial (Map p364; Maceo No 170; ☉ 8am-10pm Mon-Sat) On Parque Calixto García.
Hospital Lenin (Map p362; ☎ 42-53-02; Av VI Lenin) Will treat foreigners in an emergency.

MONEY
Banco de Crédito y Comercio (Map p364; ☎ 42-25-12; Arias) On Parque Céspedes.
Banco Financiero Internacional (Map p364; ☎ 46-85-02; Manduley No 167 btwn Frexes & Aguilera)
Cadeca (Map p364; ☎ 46-85-03; Manduley No 205 btwn Martí & Luz Caballero; ☉ 8:30am-6pm Mon-Sat, 8am-1pm Sun)

POST
Post office Manduley No 183 (Map p364; ☎ 46-82-54; ☉ 10am-noon & 1-6pm Mon-Fri); Parque Céspedes (Map p364; Maceo No 114; ☉ 8am-6pm Mon-Sat) There's a DHL office at the first branch, on Parque Calixto García.

TRAVEL AGENCIES
Havanatur Frexes (Map p364; ☎ 46-80-91; Frexes No 172 btwn Morales Lemus & Narciso López); Hotel Pernik (Map p362; cnr Avs Jorge Dimitrov & XX Aniversario)

Sights

Base yourself around the four central squares and you'll see most of what's on offer. Of course, no walk is complete without a climb up to La Loma de la Cruz (p365), a little off the grid, but well worth the detour.

PARQUE CÉSPEDES
Holguín's youngest park is also its shadiest. Named for 'Father of the Motherland,' Carlos Manuel de Céspedes – his statue stands center-stage next to a monument honoring the heroes of the War of Independence – the cobbled central square is dominated by the **Iglesia de San José** (Map p364; Manduley No 116) with its distinctive dome and bell tower (1842) that was once used by the Independistas as a lookout tower. Locals still refer to the park by its old name, San José.

In a colonial building behind the church is the **Galería Holguín** (Map p364; ☎ 42-23-92; Manduley No 137; admission free; ☉ 8am-6pm Tue-Wed, 8am-10pm Thu-Sun) displaying a revolving cache of good local art. The small **Museo Eduardo García Feria y**

HOLGUÍN PROVINCE

CENTRAL HOLGUÍN

0   200 m
0   0.1 miles

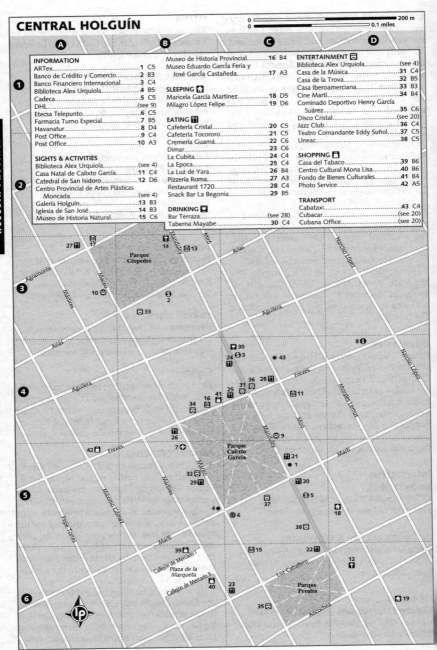

INFORMATION
ARTex...1 C5
Banco de Crédito y Comercio..........2 B3
Banco Financiero Internacional........3 C4
Biblioteca Alex Urquiola....................4 B5
Cadeca..5 C5
DHL...(see 9)
Etecsa Telepunto...............................7 B5
Farmacia Turno Especial....................8 D4
Havanatur..9 C4
Post Office..10 A3

SIGHTS & ACTIVITIES
Biblioteca Alex Urquiola.............(see 4)
Casa Natal de Calixto García..........11 C4
Catedral de San Isidoro.................12 D6
Centro Provincial de Artes Plásticas
   Moncada.................................(see 4)
Galería Holguín................................13 B3
Iglesia de San José...........................14 B3
Museo de Historia Natural..............15 C6

Museo de Historia Provincial...........16 B4
Museo Eduardo García Feria y
   José García Castañeda.................17 A3

SLEEPING
Maricela García Martínez................18 D5
Milagro López Felipe.......................19 D6

EATING
Cafetería Cristal................................20 C5
Cafetería Tocororo............................21 C5
Cremería Guamá................................22 C6
Dimar...24 C4
La Cubita...25 C4
La Época...26 B4
La Luz de Yara..................................26 B4
Pizzería Roma....................................27 A3
Restaurant 1720................................28 C4
Snack Bar La Begonia.......................29 B5

DRINKING
Bar Terraza...................................(see 28)
Taberna Mayabe...............................30 C4

ENTERTAINMENT
Biblioteca Alex Urquiola.............(see 4)
Casa de la Música............................31 C4
Casa de la Trova...............................32 B5
Casa Iberoamerciana........................33 B3
Cine Martí...34 B4
Cominado Deportivo Henry García
   Suárez...35 C6
Disco Cristal...............................(see 20)
Jazz Club...36 C4
Teatro Comandante Eddy Suñol......37 C5
Uneac..38 C5

SHOPPING
Casa del Tabaco...............................39 B6
Centro Cultural Mona Lisa...............40 B6
Fondo de Bienes Culturales.............41 B4
Photo Service....................................42 A5

TRANSPORT
Cabataxi..43 C4
Cubacar.......................................(see 20)
Cubana Office.............................(see 20)

José García Castañeda (Map p364; cnr Agramonte & Maceo; admission free) on the square's northwestern corner documents the life and work of two local archaeologists and naturalists. Eduardo was responsible for creating Holguín's first museum and he once boasted the largest snail collection in Cuba.

PARQUE CALIXTO GARCÍA
Wide, expansive 'El Parque,' as it's known among the Holguiñeros, is more visceral than visual. It was laid out in 1719 as the original Plaza de Armas and served for many years as the town's meeting point and marketplace. The centerpiece today is a 1912 statue of General Calixto García, around which congregate a multifarious mixture of old sages, baseball naysayers and teenagers on the prowl.

To learn more about the militaristic deeds of Holguín's local hero, head to the **Casa Natal de Calixto García** (Map p364; ☎ 42-56-10; Miró No 147; admission CUC$1; ☺ 9am-9pm Tue-Sat), situated two blocks east of the park. The hugely underestimated García – who stole the cities of Las Tunas, Holguín and Bayamo from Spanish control between 1896 and 1898 – was born here in 1839 and this small collection gives a reasonable overview of his life.

On the park's northern side is the **Museo de Historia Provincial** (Map p364; ☎ 46-33-95; Frexes No 198; admission CUC$1; ☺ 8am-5pm). Now a national monument, the building was constructed between 1860 and 1868 and used as a Spanish army barracks during the independence wars. It was nicknamed La Periquera (parrot cage) for the red, yellow and green uniforms of the Spanish soldiers who stood guard outside. The prize exhibit is an old axe-head carved in the likeness of a man, known as the Hacha de Holguín (Holguín Axe), thought to have been made by indigenous inhabitants in the early 1400s and discovered in 1860. Looking even sharper in its polished glass case is a sword that once belonged to national hero and poet, José Martí.

In the southwestern corner of Parque Calixto García is the **Centro Provincial de Artes Plásticas Moncada** (Map p364; ☎ 42-23-92; Maceo No 180; admission free; ☺ 9am-4pm Mon-Sat), a bright gallery that shares space with **Biblioteca Alex Urquiola** (Map p364; ☎ 46-25-62; Maceo No 180), named after a local revolutionary and housing Holguín's biggest book collection.

The **Museo de Historia Natural** (Map p364; ☎ 42-39-35; Maceo No 129 btwn Parques Calixto García & Peralta; admission/camera CUC$1/1; ☺ 9am-10pm Tue-Sat, 9am-9pm Sun) has more stuffed animals than a New York toy store – everything from the world's smallest frog to the world's smallest hummingbird.

PARQUE PERALTA
This square (called Parque de las Flores locally) is named for General Julio Grave de Peralta (1834–72), who led an uprising against Spain in Holguín in October 1868. His marble statue (1916) faces the cathedral. Dazzling white and characterized by its twin domed towers, the **Catedral de San Isidoro** (Map p364; Manduley) dates from 1720 and was one of the town's original constructions. Added piecemeal over the years, the towers are of 20th-century vintage and in 1979 it became a cathedral. A hyperrealistic statue of Pope Jean Paul II stands to the right of the main doors.

PLAZA DE LA MARQUETA
Long earmarked for major renovation, hopelessly ruined Plaza de la Marqueta is a plaza of possibilities that have, so far, remained unfulfilled. Laid out in 1848 and rebuilt in 1918, the square is dominated by an impressive covered marketplace that is supposed to be undergoing a transformation into a top-notch concert hall (after nearly a decade of rumors, the work has yet to start). Running along the north and south sides of the plaza are myriad shops that are meant to provide quality shopping but, at the time of writing, only a couple of music and cigar outlets were open and even they were poorly stocked (see Shopping, p369). For the time being the most interesting sights are the telephone poles turned into totems that anchor the plaza's corners and the numerous bronze statues of well-known Holguiñeros that decorate the sidewalks.

BEYOND THE CENTER
At the northern end of Maceo is a stairway built in 1950, with 465 steps ascending **La Loma de la Cruz** (Map p362), a 275m-high hill with panoramic views. A cross was raised here in 1790 in hope of relieving a drought, and every May 3 during Romerías de Mayo (p366) devotees climb to the summit where a special Mass is held. It's a 20-minute walk from town or you can flag a bici-taxi to the foot of the hill for around 10 pesos. This walk is best tackled

HOLGUÍN PROVINCE

early in the morning when the light is pristine and the heat not too debilitating.

Holguín is a city most *fiel* (faithful), and the **Plaza de la Revolución** (Map p362) east of the center is a huge monument to the heroes of Cuban independence, bearing quotations from José Martí and Fidel Castro. Massive rallies are held here every May 1 (Labor Day). The **tomb of Calixto García** (Map p362) is also here, as is a smaller monument to García's mother.

Fábrica de Órganos (Map p362; Carretera de Gibara No 301; ☺ 8am-4pm Mon-Fri) is the only mechanical music-organ factory in Cuba. This small factory produces about six organs a year, as well as guitars and other instruments. A good organ costs between the equivalent of US$10,000 and US$25,000. Eight professional organ groups exist in Holguín (including the Familia Cuayo, based at the factory), and, if you're lucky, you can hear one playing on Parque Céspedes on Thursday afternoons or Sunday mornings.

Festivals & Events

The **Romerías de Mayo**, in the first week of May, is a week-long art party with exhibitions, music, poetry and festivities; the national rap competition and La Loma de la Cruz pilgrimage are among the highlights. Holguín's **Carnaval** happens in the third week of August with outdoor concerts and copious amounts of dancing, roast pork and potent potables.

Sleeping
IN TOWN
Casas Particulares

Maricela García Martínez (Map p364; ☎ 47-10-49; Miró No 110 btwn Martí & Luz Caballero; r CUC$20-25) If you can negotiate your way around the motorbike in the front room, the place is yours. The downstairs bedroom is a little on the dark side, but it has an en suite bath and is a block from the central parks.

'La Palma' – Enrique R Interián Salermo (Map p362; ☎ 42-46-83; Maceo No 52A btwn Calles 16 & 18, El Llano; r CUC$25; ⊠) Poor Enrique's neocolonial house dating from 1945 near the Loma de la Cruz was caught in the eye of Hurricane Ike and his beautiful garden patio was flattened. Nonetheless, he's stoically rebuilding. His son is a talented painter and sculptor and you can check out the terra-cotta bust of Che Guevara

in the living room next to a 3m-long canvas of the last supper (with St John as a woman). Truly fantastic hosts.

Milagro López Felipe (Map p364; Miró No 207; r CUC$25) The blue-and-white sign outside makes this place difficult to miss. One upstairs room with all mod cons and terrace is shielded from the street by a pretty curtain of begonias.

Raciel Laffita Rodríguez (Map p362; ☎ 42-59-30; cnr Cables & Manduley; r CUC$25) A friendly Holguiñero who rents two small upstairs rooms *con terraza* slap-bang in the middle of town. The TVs here can (unusually) pick up a couple of English-language channels.

Hotels

Hotel Pernik (Islazul; Map p362; ☎ 48-10-11; cnr Avs Jorge Dimitrov & XX Aniversario; s/d with breakfast CUC$45/60; ⓟ ⊠ 🖳 🖵) Holguín's only tourist hotel is a notch above its Soviet-inspired competitors and of late has countered its 'overpriced' reputation with some quirky improvements. On a whim, a handful of the rooms were given over to a group of local artists who ran amok covering every available space (including the sinks and toilets) with colorful art. As for the basics, the breakfast buffet is plentiful and the information desk helpful enough; but the hotel suffers from the usual foibles of interminable renovations and blaring late-night music.

OUTSIDE TOWN

Motel Mirador de Mayabe (Islazul; off Map p362; ☎ 42-54-98; Alturas de Mayabe; s/d CUC$45/60; ⓟ ⊠ 🖵) This motel, high up on the Loma de Mayabe 10km southeast of Holguín, has 24 rooms tucked into lush grounds. The views, taking in vast mango plantations, are especially good from the pool. The Mirador de Mayabe's claim to fame is a beer-drinking donkey named Pancho, who hangs out near the bar. Typical Cuban lunches are served at the Finca Mayabe, just above the motel, where there's also a cockfighting ring. A bus runs to Holguín from the bottom of the hill, 1.5km from the motel, three times a day.

Motel El Bosque (Islazul; Map p362; ☎ 48-11-40; Av Jorge Dimitrov; s/d incl breakfast CUC$45/60; ⓟ ⊠ 🖵) One kilometer beyond Hotel Pernik, the 69 duplex bungalows here are set among extensive green grounds, making it feel more removed than it is. There's a relaxing bar beside the swimming pool (nonguests can use it for a small fee). El Bosque is perennially popular on the tour bus circuit.

Eating
RESTAURANTS

Dimar (Map p364; cnr Mártires & Luz Caballero; dishes CUC$2-5; ☻ 10am-11pm) Cuba's mediocre seafood chain doesn't get a look-in in other cities where tastier options abound, but here in Holguín you might find yourself popping in for a cheap shrimp cocktail and grilled fish.

Taberna Pancho (Map p362; ☎ 48-18-68; Av Jorge Dimitrov; ☻ noon-10pm) This is a lively Cuban place between Hotel Pernik and Motel El Bosque with some original menu choices. Nothing on the list, including hamburgers and draft Mayabe beer, costs more than CUC$3. Try the sausage special.

our pick **Restaurant 1720** (Map p364; ☎ 46-81-50; Frexes btwn Manduley & Miró; ☻ 12:30-10:30pm) Holguín's finest dining is in this painstakingly restored wedding cake mansion where you can tuck into paella (CUC$6) or chicken stuffed with vegetables and cheese (CUC$8); there's even complementary crackers. In the same colonial-style complex there's a cigar shop, a bar, a boutique, car rental and a terrace with nighttime music. Check out the wall plaques that give interesting insights into Holguín's history.

CAFETERÍAS

While the chefs might be gastronomically challenged, Holguín boasts some great street-side cafes and is a mesmerizing place to slump down with a beer or coffee and watch half the city troop by.

Cremería Guamá (Map p364; cnr Luz Caballero & Manduley; ☻ 10am-10:45pm) A Coppelia in all but name. Waste an hour or three underneath the striped red-and-white awning overlooking pedestrianized Calle Manduley and enjoy peso ice-cream alfresco.

Cafetería Cristal (Map p364; ☎ 42-58-55; ground fl, Edificio Pico de Cristal, cnr Manduley & Martí; ☻ 24hr) Reliable, affordable chicken meals are served at the chilly Cristal where the air-con does its best to replicate a frigid day in Vancouver. A more upscale restaurant is upstairs (open noon to 10pm).

Cafetería Tocororo (Map p364; Manduley No 189; ☻ 24hr) So the lackluster menu may give you

a sneaking sense of déjà vu (think spaghetti, pizza, chicken and sandwiches), but to enjoy Parque Calixto García in all its glory you've got to get in on the act. Pull up a seat at this park-side cafe and get down to some serious square-spotting with the local barflies and the odd stray Guardalavaca tourist.

La Cubita (Map p364; Manduley btwn Frexes & Aguilera; ☻ 9am-11pm) Formica tables, some local gossip and cheap shots of strong coffee slammed down on the bar for two pesos. Give yourself enough rocket fuel to last the rest of the day.

Snack Bar La Begonia (Map p364; ☎ 46-85-86; Maceo No 176; ☻ 9am-10pm) With ice cream (CUC$1), sandwiches (CUC$2 to CUC$3) and drinks served beneath flowering trellises on Parque Calixto García, this is a relaxed place to meet other travelers. It's also popular with wedding parties and *quinciñera* (15th-birthday celebrations for Cuban girls) photo shoots.

Pizzería Roma (Map p364; cnr Maceo & Agramonte) It's a long way from Rome, let alone Naples. You don't need to cross the threshold of this popular local place by Parque Céspedes; just get the guy on the stall by the door to hand you over a slice of thick dough smeared with cheese and tomatoes for six pesos.

GROCERIES

La Luz de Yara (Map p364; cnr Frexes & Maceo; ☻ 8:30am-7pm Mon-Sat, 8:30am-noon Sun) Spartan department store/supermarket with a bakery section on Parque Calixto García.

La Epoca (Map p364; Frexes No 194) Another make-your-own-picnic option on Parque Calixto García.

There are two *agropecuarios* (vegetable markets; Map p362): one is off Calle 19, the continuation of Morales Lemus near the train station, the other on Calle 3 in Dagoberto Sanfield. There are plenty of peso stalls beside the baseball stadium.

Drinking

Taberna Mayabe (Map p364; Manduley btwn Aguilera & Frexes; ☻ 3-6pm & 8pm-midnight Tue-Sun, closed Mon) Newish place on pedestrianized Manduley with wooden tables, ceramic mugs and a hearty pub atmosphere. Tip your sombrero to the doorman on the way in.

Bar Terraza (Map p364; ☎ 46-81-50; Frexes btwn Manduley & Miró; ☻ 9pm-2am) Perched above

Restaurant 1720, this is the poshest spot to sip a mojito (cocktail made from rum, mint, sugar, seltzer and fresh lime juice) with views over Parque Calixto García and regular musical interludes.

Entertainment

Teatro Comandante Eddy Suñol (Map p364; ☎ 46-31-61; Martí No 111) Holguín's premier theater is an architectural treat from 1939 on Parque Calixto García. It hosts both the Teatro Lírico Rodrigo Prats and the Ballet Nacional de Cuba and is renowned both nationally and internationally for its operettas, dance performances and Spanish musicals. Check here for details of performances by the famous children's theater Alas Buenas.

our pick **Uneac** (Map p364; Manduley btwn Luz Caballero & Martí) If you only visit one Uneac (Unión Nacional de Escritores y Artistas de Cuba; National Union of Cuban Writers and Artists) center in Cuba – there are 14 of them in all (one in each province) – make sure it's this one. Situated in a lovingly restored house on pedestrianized Calle Manduley, this friendly establishment offers everything from literary evenings (with famous authors) and music nights, to patio theater (including Lorca), and cultural reviews. Everyone is welcome.

Biblioteca Alex Urquiola (Map p364; ☎ 46-25-62; Maceo No 180) Culture vultures steam the creases out of their evening dresses to come here to see live theater, and performances by the Orquesta Sinfónica de Holguín.

Casa de la Trova (Map p364; Maceo No 174; ☿ Tue-Sun) Old guys in Panama hats croon under the rafters, musicians in *guayaberas* (pleated, buttoned shirts) blast on trumpets, while ancient couples in their Sunday best map out a perfect *danzón* (traditional Cuban ballroom dance colored with African influences). So timeless, so Holguín.

Casa de la Música (Map p364; cnr Frexes & Manduley; ☿ Tue-Sun) There's a young trendy vibe along the line outside this place on Parque Calixto García. If you can't dance, stay static sinking beers on the adjacent Terraza Bucanero (entry via Calle Manduley).

Casa Iberoamericana (Map p364; ☎ 42-25-33; Arias No 161) Situated on quieter Parque Céspedes, this paint-peeled place frequently hosts *peñas* (musical performances).

ON THE ROAD WITH THE AMARILLOS

'The road is life,' wrote seminal American author Jack Kerouac in the 1950s, inadvertently summing up Cuba's post–Special Period transport system in one succinct sentence. Hitchhiking around the country with the *amarillos*, the state-sanctioned traffic officials (so named for their mustard-yellow uniforms), is about as real life as Cuba gets. To do it you'll need oodles of patience, a sense of humor and an innate ability to wait interminably at the side of the road for hours on end. In the process, it could turn out to be your greatest in-country adventure or your worst Cuban nightmare.

In Cuba, *hacer botella* (hitchhiking) using the *amarillo* system is legally enforced making it socially acceptable and generally safe. All cars with blue (government-owned) license plates are obliged to stop and take on passengers if they have room. Drivers who unsocialistically whizz past risk a stiff fine.

Though the waiting system appears disorganized to the uninitiated, there's a certain method to the madness. First, proceed to the edge of town and find the local transit point. Second, approach the authoritative-looking person in the mustard-yellow uniform and tell them which direction you're heading. Third, take the colored scrap of card they give you, join the haphazard queue at the side of the road (for hints on queuing see boxed text, p174) and pray it's not a long wait.

Far from being a desperation measure for impoverished backpackers, hitchhiking in Cuba is the preserve of everyone from doctors to students who gather patiently by the highway to trade gossip, grumbles, jokes and jibes. Caught up in the melee, your tales from the road will rarely be dull. Fatefully, you might spend your morning sitting Houdini-like in the backseat of a Fiat Uno, and the afternoon wedged cheek to jowl in a *camión particular* (private truck). Alternatively, there are the easy days when a plush new tour coach pulls up fresh from dumping its wealthy tourist cargo in an expensive north-coast all-inclusive and invites you to step on board. Ah, if only life could always be so serendipitous!

Jazz Club (Map p364; 42-47-16; cnr Frexes & Manduley; 11am-3am) The jazz jams get moving around 8pm-ish and continue weaving their magic until 11pm. Then there's taped music until 3am. During the daytime you can choose from the cafe or restaurant downstairs.

DANCE CLUBS
Disco Cristal (Map p364; ☎ 42-58-55; 3rd fl, Edificio Pico de Cristal, Manduley No 199; admission CUC$2; 9pm-2am Tue-Thu) A nexus for Holguín's dexterous dancers (most of whom are young, cool and determined to have a good time), this place is insanely popular at weekends when you'll find lots of inspiration for the salsa/rap/*reggaetón* (Cuban hip-hop) repertoire.

Disco Havana Club (Map p362; ☎ 48-10-11; Hotel Pernik, cnr Avs Jorge Dimitrov & XX Aniversario; guests/nonguests CUC$2/4; 10pm-2am Tue-Sun) Holguín's premier disco. If you're staying at Hotel Pernik the music will visit you – in your room! – like it or not, until 1am.

Cabaret Nuevo Nocturno (off Map p362; ☎ 42-51-85; admission CUC$10; 10pm-2am) There's always one. This is a Tropicana-style cabaret club beyond the Servi-Cupet gas station 3km out on the road to Las Tunas. Rather like a cricket match, there's no show if it's raining.

CINEMAS
Cine Martí (Map p364; Frexes No 204; 1-2 pesos) For big-screen movies, head to this cinema on Parque Calixto García.

SPORT
Holguín is one of the best places on the island to view Cuba's two national sports: baseball and boxing.

Estadio General Calixto García (Map p362; admission 1 peso) The excitement (disbelief?) has died down somewhat since Holguín's feisty Perros came out of nowhere to snatch the national baseball championship from under the noses of the 'big two' in 2002. But they're still a team to be watched. Mosey on down to this stadium, just off Av de los Libertadores, near the Hotel Pernik to see the giant-killers confidently swing their bats at pitchers from across the island. The stadium also houses a small but interesting sport museum.

Cominado Deportivo Henry García Suárez (Map p364; Maceo; admission 1 peso; 8pm Wed, 2pm Sat) You can catch boxing matches at this spit-and-sawdust gym on the western side of Parque Peralta, where three Olympic medalists have

trained. You can also pluck up the courage to ask about some (noncontact) training sessions. They're very friendly.

Shopping
The much vaunted shopper's paradise of Plaza de la Marqueta has yet to take off (see p365). At the time of writing the square was a virtual ruin except for the **Casa del Tabaco** (Map p364; cnr Callejón de Mercado I & Mártires) and the lackluster **Centro Cultural Mona Lisa** (Map p364; cnr Callejón de Mercado II & Mártires). If ambitious plans are ever realized, this place could be a stunner.

Fondo de Bienes Culturales (Map p364; ☎ 42-37-82; Frexes No 196) This shop on Parque Calixto García has one of the best selections of Cuban handicrafts.

Photo Service (Map p364; Frexes btwn Máximo Gomez & Mártires) Can cater for all your camera needs.

Getting There & Away
AIR
There are 16 international flights a week into Holguín's well-organized **Frank País Airport** (airport code HOG; off Map p362; ☎ 42-52-71), 13km south of the city, including from Amsterdam, Düsseldorf, London, Montreal and Toronto. Almost all arrivals get bussed directly off to Guardalavaca and see little of Holguín city.

Domestic destinations are served by **Cubana** (Map p364; ☎ 46-81-11; Edificio Pico de Cristal, cnr Manduley & Martí), which flies daily to Havana (CUC$103 one-way, one hour 20 minutes).

BUS
The **Interprovincial Bus Station** (Map p362; ☎ 46-10-36; cnr Carretera Central & Independencia), west of the center near Hospital Lenin, has air-conditioned **Víazul** (www.viazul.com) buses leaving daily; see the table on the next page.

You can take the Havana bus as far as Las Tunas (CUC$6), Camagüey (CUC$11), Ciego de Ávila (CUC$17), Sancti Spíritus

VÍAZUL DEPARTURES

Destination	Cost (CUC$)	Duration	Departure time
Havana	44	12hr 45min	9:20am, 12:30pm, 6:35pm, 9pm
Santiago de Cuba	11	3hr 30min	3:15am, 9:05am, 4:35pm
Trinidad	26	7hr 45min	11pm
Varadero	38	11hr 20min	11:40pm

(CUC$21) or Santa Clara (CUC$26). The Santiago departure also stops in Bayamo (CUC$6), but to reach Guantánamo or Baracoa, you have to change in Santiago de Cuba.

TRAIN

The **train station** (Map p362; ☎ 42-23-11; Calle V Pita) is on the southern side of town. Foreigners must purchase tickets in Convertibles at the special **Ladis ticket office** (7:30am-3pm). The ticket office is marked 'U/B Ferrocuba Provincial Holguín' on the corner of Manduley opposite the train station.

Theoretically, there's one daily morning train to Las Tunas (CUC$4, two hours), a daily afternoon train to Santiago de Cuba (CUC$5, 3½ hours), and a daily 6:15pm train to Havana (CUC$31, 15 hours). This train stops in Camagüey (CUC$9), Ciego de Ávila (CUC$13), Guayos (CUC$17), Santa Clara (CUC$20) and Matanzas (CUC$20). You may have to change trains at the Santiago–Havana mainline junction in Cacocum, 17km south of Holguín.

The only service that operates with any regularity is the train to Havana. The service to Santiago de Cuba is rather irregular; ask before planning your trip around it.

TRUCK

Trucks to points south and west operate from **La Molienda Terminal** (Map p362; ☎ 46-20-11; Carretera Central No 46), between the bus and train stations. Trucks leave when full for Las Tunas and Bayamo; mornings are best. No trucks go directly to Santiago de Cuba or Camagüey, so you must make the journey in stages.

The **Terminal Dagoberto Sanfield Guillén** (Map p362; Av de los Libertadores), opposite Estadio General Calixto García, has at least two daily trucks to Gibara, Banes and Moa. To reach Guardalavaca, take a truck to Rafael Freyre (aka Santa Lucía) and look for something else there.

Getting Around

TO/FROM THE AIRPORT

The public bus to the airport leaves daily around 2pm from the **airport bus stop** (Map p362; General Rodríguez No 84) on Parque Martí near the train station. A tourist taxi to the airport costs from CUC$8 to CUC$10. It's also possible to spend your last night in Bayamo, then catch a taxi (CUC$18 to CUC$20) to Holguín airport.

BICI-TAXI

Holguín's bici-taxis are ubiquitous. They charge five pesos for a short trip, 10 pesos for a long one.

CAR

You can rent or return a car at these places: **Cubacar** Hotel Pernik (Map p362; ☎ 46-81-96; Av Jorge Dimitrov); Aeropuerto Frank País (☎ 46-84-14); Cafetería Cristal (Map p364; ☎ 46-85-88; cnr Manduley & Martí)

A **Servi-Cupet gas station** (off Map p362; Carretera Central; 24hr) is 3km out toward Las Tunas; another station (off Map p362) is just outside town on the road to Gibara. An **Oro Negro gas station** (off Map p362; Carretera Central) is on the southern edge of town. The road to Gibara is north on Av Cajígal; also take this road and fork left after 5km to reach Playa La Herradura.

TAXI

A **Cubataxi** (Map p364; ☎ 42-32-90; Miró No 133) to Guardalavaca (54km) costs around CUC$35. To Gibara one-way should cost no more than CUC$20.

GIBARA

pop 28,826

Everyone knows about Hurricane Katrina and the destruction of New Orleans, but less known is Gibara's equally desperate fight against Hurricane Ike three years later. A Category 4 storm when it smashed into Holguín's northern coast on September 8, 2008, Ike's cruel winds ripped through Gibara, damaging 70% of the buildings and almost wiping the city off the map. Almost, but not quite…

Gibara is Holguín's outlet to the sea, a once-important sugar-export town that was linked to the provincial capital via a railway. With the construction of the Carretera Central in the 1920s, Gibara lost its mercantile importance and after the last train service was axed in 1958, the town fell into a sleepy slumber from which it has yet to awaken.

Columbus first arrived in the area in 1492 and called it Río de Mares (River of Seas) for the Ríos Cacoyugüín and Yabazón that drain into the Bahía de Gibara. The current name comes from *jiba*, the indigenous word for a bush that still grows along the shore.

Refounded in 1817, Gibara prospered in the 19th century as the sugar industry expanded and the trade rolled in. To protect the settlement from pirates, barracks were built and a 2km wall was constructed around the town in the early 1800s, making Gibara Cuba's second walled city (after Havana). The once sparkling-white facades earned Gibara its nickname, La Villa Blanca.

Situated 33km from Holguín via a scenic road that undulates through friendly, eye-catching villages, Gibara is a small, intimate place whose unique oceanside atmosphere gives it a distinct, almost non-Cuban, flavor. Redolent of a small Baracoa, the town's beautiful bayside setting is characterized by pretty plazas, crumbling Spanish ruins and a postcard view of the saddle-shaped Silla de Gibara that so captivated Columbus.

Each year in April Gibara hosts the **Festival Internacional de Cine Pobre** (International Low-Budget Film Festival; see boxed text, p372), which draws films and filmmakers from all over the world.

Information

Most services line Calle Independencia.

Banco Popular de Ahorro (cnr Independencia & Cuba) Changes traveler's checks.

Bandec (cnr Independencia & J Peralta) Also changes traveler's checks.

Post office (Independencia No 15) There are few public phones here.

Sights

At the time of writing, Gibara was still recovering from Hurricane Ike, and many of the sights mentioned below were closed due to storm damage. Hopefully, it won't be too long before they are revived and reopened.

At the top of Calle Cabada is **El Cuartelón**, a crumbling-brick Spanish fort with graceful arches that provides stunning town and bay views. Continue on this street for 200m to Restaurante El Mirador for an even better vantage point. You'll see remnants of the old fortresses here and at the **Fuerte Fernando VII**, on the point beyond Parque de las Madres, a block over from Parque Calixto García.

The centerpiece of **Parque Calixto García** (lined with weird *robles africanos* – African oaks with large penis-shaped pods) is **Iglesia de San Fulgencio** (1850). The Statue of Liberty in front commemorates the Spanish-Cuban-American War. On the western side of the square, in a beautiful colonial palace (more interesting than the stuffed stuff it collects), is the **Museo de Historia Natural** (Luz Caballero No 23; admission CUC$1; ☼ 8am-noon & 1-5pm Mon-Wed, 8am-noon, 1-5pm & 8-10pm Thu-Sun). Through barred windows you can watch women rolling cheroots in the cigar factory across the square.

Two museums share the colonial mansion (1872) at Independencia No 19: the **Museo de Historia Municipal** (admission CUC$1; ☼ 8am-noon & 1-5pm Mon-Wed, 8am-noon, 1-5pm & 8-10pm Thu-Sun) downstairs and the **Museo de Artes Decorativas** (☎ 84-44-07; admission CUC$2; ☼ 8am-noon & 1-5pm Mon-Wed, 8am-noon, 1-5pm & 8-10pm Thu-Sun) upstairs. The latter is more interesting, with nearly 800 pieces collected from Gibara's colonial heyday. Across the street is **Galería Cosme Proenza** (Independencia No 32), with wall-to-wall works by one of Cuba's foremost painters.

Activities

There are three decent beaches within striking distance of Gibara. **Playa Los Bajos** is usually accessible by local *lancha* (ferry), costing a few pesos, from the fishing pier on La Enramada, the waterfront road leading out of town. These boats cross the Bahía de Gibara to **Playa Blanca**, from where it's 3km east to Playa Los Bajos. Should the ferry be out of action, Los Bajos is a rough 30km drive via Floro Pérez and Fray Benito. For more on Playa Blanca, see p373.

You'll need some sort of transport (bike, taxi, rental car) to get to lovely, little **Playa Caletones**, 17km to the west of Gibara. The apostrophe of white sand and azure sea here is a favorite of vacationers from Holguín. The

---

THE POOR MAN'S FILM FESTIVAL

There's no red carpet, no paparazzi and no Brangelina, but what the Festival Internacional de Cine Pobre (International Low-Budget Film Festival) lacks in glitz it makes up for in raw, undiscovered talent. Then there's the setting – ethereal Gibara, Cuba's crumbling Villa Blanca, a perfect antidote to the opulence of Hollywood and Cannes.

Inaugurated in 2003, the Cine Pobre was the brainchild of late Cuban director Humberto Solás, who fell in love with this quintessential fisherman's town after shooting his seminal movie *Lucía* here in 1968.

Open to independent filmmakers of limited means, the festival takes place in April and, despite limited advertising, attracts up to US$100,000 in prize money. Lasting for seven days, proceedings kick off with a gala in the Cine Jiba followed by film showings, art expositions and nightly music concerts. The competition is friendly but hotly contested, with prizes used to reward and recognize an eclectic cache of digital movie guerrillas drawn from countries as varied as Iran and the US.

---

town is ramshackle, with no services except the thatched place guarded by a palm tree that serves as a bar in summer. The beach suffered damage from Hurricane Ike.

Sleeping

There are no hotels in Gibara at present, but with half a dozen magnificent casas particulares, who needs them?

Odalys & Luis (☎ 84-45-42; Céspedes No 13 btwn Luz Caballero & J Peralta; r with air-con CUC$20; 🅿) More colonial splendor here with big rooms, a salubrious patio and fountain, signature Gibara stained glass and delicious meals – all located a block and a half from Parque Calixto García.

ourpick La Casa de los Amigos (☎ 84-41-15; lacasa delosamigos@yahoo.fr; Céspedes No 15 btwn J Peralta & Luz Caballero; r CUC$20-25; 🅿) One of the most amazing casas particulares you'll find in Cuba with frescoes, wood carvings, gazebo and a huge, colorful open courtyard/patio. The rooms are boutique-hotel standard with antique sinks and the food a French-Cuban fusion.

Eating

Gibara is still in the Special Period as far as restaurants go. Stick to your casa particular or, if you're excruciatingly hungry/curious, choose from this lackluster list of two.

Restaurante El Faro (☎ 84-45-96; La Concha; 🕙 10am-10pm) This place, on Parque de las Madres, serves chicken and fish meals overlooking the bay. It's a simple, potentially romantic spot that was damaged by Hurricane Ike.

Restaurante El Mirador (🕙 24hr) Perched high above town near El Cuartelón, this place has a view to die for but not much in the way of good food. Quench your thirst after a romp up the hill and head back to your casa particular for dinner.

Drinking & Entertainment

Cine Jiba (Parque Calixto García) Cuba's improbable poor man's film festival hosts most of its cutting-edge movies in this small but quirky cinema bedizened with colorful art-house movie posters. If you're going to go to the cinema anywhere in Cuba, it should be in Gibara – it's a local rite of passage.

Casa de Cultura (Parque Colón) You might catch a salsa night here or gain an appreciation of the poetry of Nicolas Guillén in the pleasant inner courtyard.

For theater and dance, it's the historic Casino Español (1889). Patio Colonial, wedged between the Museo de Historia Natural and Casino Español, is an atmospheric outdoor cafetería that hosts regular musical performances.

Getting There & Away

There are no Víazul buses to Gibara. Travelers can tackle the route with Cuban transport on a truck or bus from Holguín. The bus station is 1km out on the road to Holguín. There are two daily buses in each direction. A taxi (to Holguín) should cost no more than CUC$20.

For drivers heading toward Guardalavaca, the link road from the junction at Flores Pérez is hell at first, but improves just out side Rafael Freyre. There's an Oro Negro gas station at the entrance to town.

PLAYA PESQUERO & AROUND

Of Holguín's three northern resort areas, Playa Pesquero (Fishermen's Beach) is the most high-end. There are four tourist colossi here, including the Hotel Playa Pesquero (until recently the largest hotel in Cuba), and the strip has a luxury Caribbean sheen missing elsewhere on the island. Not surprisingly, the adjacent beach is sublime, with golden sand, shallow, warm water and great opportunities for snorkeling. The resorts and beaches are accessible off the main Holguín–Guardalavaca road via a spur road just before the Cuatro Palmas junction.

Ten kilometers west of Playa Pesquero and 3km west of Villa Don Lino is **Playa Blanca**; Columbus is thought to have landed somewhere near here in 1492, and this great meeting of two cultures is commemorated in **Parque Nacional Monumento Bariay** (Parque Natural Cristóbal Colón; Map p374; admission CUC$8), a varied mix of sights and memorabilia, the centerpiece of which is an impressive Hellenic-style monument designed by Holguín artist Caridad Ramos for the 500th anniversary of the landing in 1992. Other points of interest here include an information center, the remains of a 19th-century Spanish fort, three reconstructed **Taíno Indian huts**, an **archaeological museum** and the reasonable Restaurante 'Columbo.' It makes a pleasant afternoon's sojourn.

Parque Rocazul (Map p374; ☎ 43-08-33), off the link road that joins Playa Turquesa with the other Pesquero resorts, is a protected bio-park that offers the usual hand-holding array of outdoor activities under the supervision of a nonnegotiable government guide. It's a commendable environmental effort in a major resort area, but the limitations on your right to roam can be a little stifling (and costly). Leisurely walking excursions go for CUC$8/10/12 for one/two/three hours. You can go horseback riding for CUC$16 an hour or fishing for CUC$25. An all-inclusive package costs CUC$40. The park is extensive with hills, trails, ocean access and an ostrich farm. There's a friendly bar at the entrance where you weigh can up the financial pros and cons.

Sleeping & Eating

PLAYA PESQUERO

Playa Costa Verde (Gaviota; Map p374; ☎ 43-05-10; s/d/tr all-inclusive CUC$150/230/327; P ⛶ 🖳 ⛶) Stuck somewhere between the elegance of Hotel Playa Pesquero and the simplicity of Villa Don Lino, the Costa Verde feels a bit faux, not that top-notch facilities are lacking. There's a Japanese restaurant, a gym, colorful gardens and a lagoon you cross to get to the beach. Good diving trips are run out of the confusingly named Blau Costa Verde next door.

Hotel Playa Pesquero (Gaviota; Map p374; ☎ 43-35-30; s/d CUC$175/300; P ⛶ 🖳 ⛶) Once upon a time Cuba's biggest hotel, Playa Pesquero had its mantle stolen in 2007 by the precocious Sirenis La Salina in Varadero, but who cares? With 933 rooms, the Pesquero is no slouch and no ugly duckling either. Beautifully landscaped grounds spread over 30 hectares include Italianate fountains, fancy shops, seven restaurants, a classy spa, a floodlit basketball court, and enough swimming pool space to accommodate a school of whales. And then there's the beach…in a word, beautiful. Opened in 2003 by Fidel Castro, the great leader's speech is reprinted on a wall in the reception area. Fortunately, it was one of his shorter efforts.

The other two resorts on this strip are Grand Playa Turquesa and Blau Costa Verde, both all-inclusive four-star establishments in a similar price range.

WEST OF PLAYA PESQUERO

Campismo Silla de Gibara (Cubamar; Map p374; ☎ 42-15-86; s/d CUC$11.50/17; ⛶) This rustic campismo (camping installation) sits on sloping ground beneath Gibara's signature saddle-shaped hill. Reached via a rough road between Floro Pérez and Rafael Freyre, it's 35km southeast of Gibara itself and 1.5km off the main road. There are 42 rooms sleeping two, four or six people, but come for the views, not the comfort. There's also a cave you can hike to, 1.5km hike up the hill, and horses for rent. It's best to make reservations with Cubamar (www.cubamarviajes.cu) in Havana rather than just turn up.

Villa Don Lino (Islazul; Map p374; ☎ 43-03-08; s/d CUC$50/60; ⛶) The cheap alternative to Playa Pesquero's 'big four,' Don Lino's 36 single-story *cabañas* (bungalows) are planted right on a small white beach, and make for a romantic retreat. There's a small pool, night-time entertainment and an element of Cuban-ness missing in the bigger resorts. Villa Don Lino is 8.5km north of Rafael Freyre along a spur road.

GUARDALAVACA

Guardalavaca is a string of megaresorts draped along a succession of idyllic beaches 54km northeast of Holguín. Glimmering in the background, a landscape of rough green fields and haystack-shaped hills remind you that rural Cuba is never far away.

In the days before towel-covered sun loung-ers and poolside bingo, Columbus described this stretch of coast as the most beautiful place he had ever laid eyes on. Few modern-day visitors would disagree. Love it or hate it, Guardalavaca's enduring popularity has a solid Caribbean base: enviable tropical beaches, ver-dant green hills and sheltered turquoise coral reefs that teem with aquatic action. More spread out than Varadero and less isolated than Cayo Coco, for many discerning travel-ers Guardalavaca gets the balance just right – R and R (read: relaxation and realism).

In the early 20th century this region was an important cattle-rearing area and the site of a small rural village (Guardalavaca means, quite literally, 'guard the cow'). The tour-ism boom moved into first gear in the late 1970s when local Holguiñero Fidel Castro inaugurated Guardalavaca's first resort – the sprawling Atlántico – by going for a quick dip in the hotel pool. The local economy hasn't looked back since.

The resort area is split into three separate enclaves: Playa Pesquero (see p373), Playa Esmeralda and, 7km to the east, Guardalavaca proper, the original hotel strip that is al-ready starting to peel around the edges. Guardalavaca has long allowed beach access to Cubans, meaning it is less snooty and flecked with a dash of local color.

Information

EMERGENCY
Asistur (Map p376; ☎ 43-01-48; Centro Comercial Guardalavaca; ☼ 8:30am-5pm Mon-Fri, 8:30am-noon Sat)
Canadian Consulate (☎ 43-03-20; Club Amigo Atlántico – Guardalavaca, Suite 1)

MEDICAL SERVICES
Clínica Internacional (Map p376; ☎ 43-02-91) A 24-hour pharmacy on the same site as Villa Cabañas.

MONEY
Euros are accepted in all the Guardalavaca, Playa Esmeralda and Pesquero resorts. Additionally, all the big hotels have money-changing facilities.
Banco Financiero Internacional (Map p376; ☎ 43-02-72; Centro Comercial Guardalavaca) In the complex just west of Club Amigo Atlántico – Guardalavaca.

TRAVEL AGENCIES
Cubatur (Map p376; ☎ 43-01-71; ☼ 8am-4pm) Just behind the Centro Comercial Los Flamboyanes.

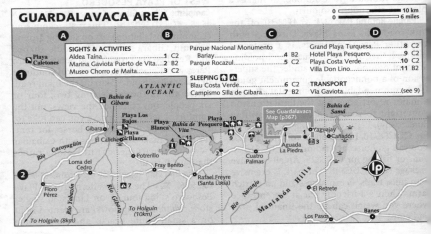

GUARDALAVACA AREA

SIGHTS & ACTIVITIES		
Aldea Taína	1	C2
Marina Gaviota Puerto de Vita	2	B2
Museo Chorro de Maita	3	C2
Parque Nacional Monumento Bariay	4	B2
Parque Rocazul	5	C2

SLEEPING		
Blau Costa Verde	6	C2
Campismo Silla de Gibara	7	B2

Grand Playa Turquesa	8	C2
Hotel Playa Pesquero	9	C2
Playa Costa Verde	10	C2
Villa Don Lino	11	B2

TRANSPORT		
Vía Gaviota	(see 9)	

Ecotur (Map p376; ☎ 43-01-55; Centro Comercial Guardalavaca) Runs trips with a nature bias to places such as Cayo Saetía, Baracoa and Gran Piedra.

Havanatur (Map p376; ☎ 43-02-60; Centro Comercial Los Flamboyanes)

Sights & Activities

You can arrange **horseback riding** (☎ 43-01-17) at the horseback-riding center opposite Club Amigo Atlántico. You can rent **mopeds** at all the hotels for up to CUC$30 per day. Most all-inclusive packages include bicycle use, but the bikes are basic. The road between Guardalavaca and Playa Esmeralda, and on to Playa Pesquero is flat and quiet and makes an excellent day excursion. For a bit more sweat you can make it to Banes and back (62km round-trip).

Paracaidismo Guardalavaca (☎ 43-06-95), aping Varadero, offers tandem skydiving for CUC$150 per person, including hotel transfer (a video of your jump is CUC$45 extra). You can also soar in Zodiac hang-glider rigs called 'ultralights' for CUC$45. There's no office as such. It's best to enquire through the hotels. There's a two-person minimum.

Guardalavaca has some excellent diving (better than Varadero and up there with Cayo Coco). The reef is 200m out and there are 32 dive sites, most of which are accessed by boat. Highlights include caves, wrecks, walls and La Corona, a giant coral formation said to resemble a crown. Guardalavaca has two diving centers: **Eagle Ray Marlin Dive Center** (Cubanacán Náutica; Map p376; ☎ 43-01-85), on the beach behind Disco Club La Roca; and **Center Coral Reef** (Map p376; ☎ 43-07-74), beside Brisas Guardalavaca Hotel. There's another outlet in Playa Esmeralda (it's called Delphis; ask at the hotels). All the outfits offer generic prices and facilities. There are open-water certification courses for CUC$365, resort courses for CUC$40 and dives for CUC$35, with discounts for multiple dives.

Many other water-based excursions leave from the **Marina Gaviota Puerto de Vita** (Map p374; ☎ 43-04-45) and can be booked through the hotels. There's the ubiquitous sunset cruise (CUC$69), deep-sea fishing (CUC$270 for up to six people) and – the highlight – a catamaran trip to Cayo Saetía in the Bahía de Nipe with snorkeling and lunch (CUC$79).

BAHÍA DE NARANJO

The **Parque Natural Bahía de Naranjo** (Map p376), 4km southwest of Playa Esmeralda and about 8km from the main Guardalavaca strip, is an island complex designed to keep the resort crowds entertained. An **aquarium** (☎ 43-01-32; 9am-9pm) is on a tiny island in the bay and your entry fee includes a zippy boat tour of the islands included in the complex, and a sea lion and dolphin show (noon daily). There are various packages starting at around CUC$40, depending on what you want to do – yacht trips, seafaris etc – so check around before you embark. For an extra CUC$50 or so, you can swim with the dolphins for 20 minutes. All of Guardalavaca's (and Playa Esmeralda's) hotel tour desks sell aquarium excursions. Boats to the aquarium leave from the Marina Bahía de Naranjo.

At the end of the Playa Esmeralda road is the self-guided **Las Guanas Eco-archaeological Trail** (Map p376; admission CUC$6; 8am-4:30pm), which, at CUC$6 for 1km of trail (that's CUC$1 per 170m), is quite possibly Cuba's (and one of the world's) most expensive walks. You'd better walk slowly to get your money's worth! The marked route (with several more kilometers of bushwhacking on fire trails leading to a picturesque bluff with a lighthouse) apparently boasts 14 endemic plant species.

Cheaper, but pretty barren post–Hurricane Ike, is the **Eco-parque Cristóbal Colón** (Map p376), reachable via a track off the hotel access road. There's supposedly a small animal 'zoo' here, but on our last visit most of it appeared to have been blown away.

MUSEO CHORRO DE MAITA

This archaeological site–based **museum** (Map p374; ☎ 43-04-21; admission CUC$2; 9am-5pm Tue-Sat, 9am-1pm Sun) protects the remains of an excavated Indian village and cemetery, including the well-preserved remains of 62 human skeletons and the bones of a barkless dog. The village dates from the early 16th century and is one of nearly 100 archaeological sites in the area. Across from the museum is a reconstructed **Aldea Taína** (Taíno village; Map p374; admission CUC$3) that features life-sized models of native dwellings and figures in a replicated indigenous village. Shows of native dance rituals are staged here and there's also a restaurant.

Sleeping

There are no casas particulares here, as renting rooms is banned. Banes, 33km to the southeast, is the closest town with private rooms.

GUARDALAVACA

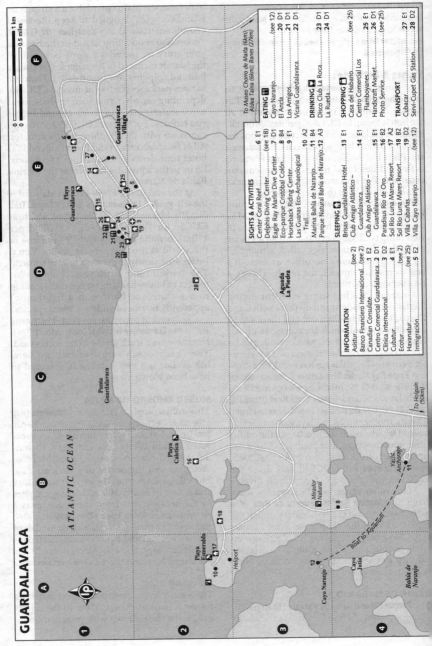

INFORMATION
Asistur......................................(see 2)
Banco Financiero Internacional......(see 2)
Canadian Consulate........................**1** E2
Centro Comercial Guardalavaca........**2** D1
Clínica Internacional......................**3** D2
Cubatur......................................**4** E1
Ecotur......................................(see 25)
Havanatur....................................(see 25)
Inmigración..................................**5** E2

SIGHTS & ACTIVITIES
Center Coral Reef............................**6** E1
Delphis Diving Center......................(see 18)
Eagle Ray Marlin Dive Center............**7** D1
Eco-parque Cristóbal Colón..............**8** B4
Horseback Riding Center..................**9** E1
Las Guanas Eco-Archaeological	
Trail....................................**10** A2
Marina Bahía de Naranjo..................**11** B4
Parque Natural Bahía de Naranjo..**12** A3

SLEEPING
Brisas Guardalavaca Hotel................**13** E1
Club Amigo Atlántico –	
Guardalavaca..........................**14** E1
Club Amigo Atlántico –	
Guardalavaca..........................**15** E1
Paradisus Río de Oro......................**16** B2
Sol Río Luna Mares Resort................**17** A2
Sol Río Luna Mares Resort................**18** B2
Villa Cabañas................................**19** D2
Villa Cayo Naranjo..........................(see 12)

EATING
Cayo Naranjo................................(see 12)
El Ancla......................................**20** D1
Los Amigos..................................**21** D1
Vicaria Guardalavaca......................**22** D1

DRINKING
Disco Club La Roca..........................**23** D1
La Rueda......................................**24** D1

SHOPPING
Casa del Habano............................(see 25)
Centro Comercial Los	
Flamboyanes..........................**25** E1
Handicraft Market..........................**26** D1
Photo Service..............................(see 25)

TRANSPORT
Cubacar......................................**27** E1
Servi-Cupet Gas Station..................**28** D2

To Museo Chorro de Malta (6km);
Aldea Taína (6km); Banes (27km)

ATLANTIC OCEAN

Playa Guardalavaca

Guardalavaca Village

Punta Guardalavaca

Playa Caletica

Playa Esmeralda

Heliport

Mirador Natural

Aguada La Piedra

To Holguín (50km)

Yacht Anchorage

Boat to Aquarium

Cayo Naranjo

Cayo Judía

Bahía de Naranjo

1 km
0.5 miles

ASK A LOCAL

From the Guardalavaca hotels you can organize an excellent trip to the town of Rafael Freyre, where you travel on a narrow gauge stream locomotive following the route of an old sugar train. The train is over 80 years old and is a real Cuban classic.

Gerardo, Guardalavaca

GUARDALAVACA

Villa Cabañas (Map p376; ☎ 43-01-64; r CUC$40; 🎿) There are no private rooms on Holguín's north coast, but you can still shoestring it by decamping in one of these comfortable cabins at the end of Guardalavaca's main resort strip. The 20 rooms have double beds, TVs, hot water, kitchenettes and the odd resident frog (provided free of charge). Also on-site is the Cubanacán Clínica Internacional. A lively stretch of beach with a couple of passable snack bar restaurants is two minutes' walk away.

Club Amigo Atlántico – Guardalavaca (Cubanacán; Map p376; ☎ 43-01-21, s/d all-inclusive CUC$69/99; 🅿 🎿 🖳 🛋) This hard-to-fathom resort is a fusion of the former Guardalavaca and Atlántico hotels, the latter of which is the resort's oldest, completed in 1976 and christened by Fidel Castro, who went for a quick dip in the pool. The architecture in this small 'village' (there are an astounding 600 rooms here in total) is a mishmash of villas, bungalows and standard rooms, and is ever popular with families for its extensive kids' activities program. Expect bingo around the pool and microphone-happy 'entertainers.'

Brisas Guardalavaca Hotel (Cubanacán; Map p376; ☎ 43-02-18; s/d all-inclusive CUC$129/178; 🅿 🎿 🖳 🛋) This *über*-resort made up of the Villa las Brisas and Hotel las Brisas at the eastern end of the beach is a package-tour paradise that stirs memories of 1970s British holiday camps. Bonuses are the huge comfortable rooms, floodlit tennis courts and general lack of pretension. But with its fake pink flamingos and cheesy violinist serenading the buffet crowd with old Abba hits, the kitsch is never far from the surface.

PLAYA ESMERALDA

Three megaresorts line this superior stretch of beach 6km to the west of Guardalavaca and accessed by a spur just east of the Cayo Naranjo boat launch. Esmeralda occupies the middle ground between Guardalavaca's economy and Playa Pesquero's opulence.

Sol Río Luna Mares Resort (Gaviota; Map p376; ☎ 43-00-60; s/d CUC$104/170; 🅿 🎿 🖳 🛋) This two-in-one hotel is an amalgamation of the former Sol Club Río de Luna and the Meliá Río de Mares. Rooms are large and come with a few additional extras (such as coffee machines), but the main advantages for luxury seekers over Guardalavaca is the superior food (Mexican and Italian restaurants) and the better beach (beach toys are included in the price).

Paradisus Río de Oro (Gaviota; Map p376; ☎ 43-00-90; s/d CUC$185/311; 🅿 🎿 🖳 🛋) Elegant and environmentally conscious (a tough combination), this 292-room resort has five-star written all over it, and would stand up against anything in the Caribbean. There's massage available in a cliffside hut, a Japanese restaurant floating on a koi pond, and garden villas with private pools. Paradise is the word.

Rooms are also available in cabins at Villa Cayo Naranjo. Enquire at the hotel desks for details.

Eating

Los Amigos (Map p376; 🕙 9am-9pm) At the epicenter of Guardalavaca's liveliest strip of beach (accessed via the flea market just west of Club Amigo Atlántico), Los Amigos is a bog-standard beach shack with beer, music and enough ingredients to muster up a sand-free fish and rice lunch.

Vicaria Guardalavaca (Map p376; 🕙 9am-9:45pm) You'll feel like an outcast eating at this place, beside Centro Comercial Guardalavaca, while everyone else tucks into the all-you-can-eat buffets a couple of hundred meters away. Nevertheless, pizzas are big and service is quick and amiable. A good meal for two won't break CUC$10.

El Ancla (Map p376; ☎ 43-03-81; 🕙 9am-10:30pm) Somehow El Ancla, which is situated on a rocky promontory of land at the far western end of Guardalavaca beach, didn't get blown away by Hurricane Ike and has survived to serve its excellent lobster in front of magnificent sea views.

Cayo Naranjo (Map p376; ☎ 43-04-33; Cayo Naranjo) On Gaviota's theme park of a *cayo* (coral key), this will be your only lunch option. Fortunately, it's pretty good with a signature plate of Marinera Especial pushing the fish theme.

HOLGUÍN PROVINCE

Drinking & Entertainment

Disco Club La Roca (Map p376; ☎ 43-01-67; admission CUC$1; ⏰ 1-5pm & 9:30pm-3am) This establishment just west of the Centro Comercial Guardalavaca has a pleasant open-air locale overlooking the beach. It's a bar-restaurant by day with video games and karaoke. On weekend evenings it hosts cabaret shows good enough to lure clientele from the posh resorts.

La Rueda (Map p376; ⏰ 7am-11pm) A Palmares bar (next to the craft market) that provides a welcome haven from the resorts. Small snacks and ice cream are also available.

Shopping

There's a small handicraft market next to Club Amigo Atlántico – Guardalavaca and a couple of shopping arcades, the Centro Comercial Guardalavaca and Centro Los Flamboyanes.

Other options:

Casa del Habano (Map p376; Centro Comercial Los Flamboyanes) All the smoke you need and then some.

Photo service (Map p376; Centro Comercial Los Flamboyanes) Does everything from film processing to passport shots.

Getting There & Away

Club Amigo Atlántico – Guardalavaca can sometimes arrange transfers to Holguín for CUC$10; ask around. A taxi from Guardalavaca to Holguín will cost a heftier CUC$35 one way for the car. For radio taxis, call **Cubataxi** (☎ 43-01-39) or **Transgaviota** (☎ 43-49-66).

Marina Gaviota Puerto de Vita (Map p374; ☎ 43-04-45) is an international entry port for yachts and boats and has 38 berths. There's a hardware store, restaurant, electricity and customs authorities on-site.

Getting Around

A new hop-on/hop-off minibus has been installed in Guardalavaca to link the three beach areas and surrounding sights. The red-and-blue bus is run by Transtur. Theoretically it runs every 30 minutes daily between 9am and 7pm, but check at your hotel to see if there are any glitches. Drop-offs include Rocazul, Yuraguanal, Playa Pesquero, Playa Costa Verde, the Acuario, Playa Esmeralda hotels, Club Amigo Atlántico – Guardalavaca and the Aldea Taína. Tickets cost CUC$5 for an all-day pass.

Coches de caballo (horse carriages) run between Playas Esmeralda and Guardalavaca or

you can rent a moped (CUC$24 per day) or bike (free if you're staying at an all-inclusive) at all of the resort hotels.

A **Servi-Cupet gas station** (⏰ 24hr) is situated between Guardalavaca and Playa Esmeralda.

All the rental agencies have offices in Guardalavaca and can also rent mopeds.

Cubacar (Map p376; ☎ 43-01-34; Club Amigo Atlántico – Guardalavaca)

Vía Gaviota (Map p374; ☎ 43-05-55; Hotel Playa Pesquero)

BANES
pop 44,983

The sugar town of Banes, just north of the Bahía de Banes, is the site of one of Cuba's biggest oxymorons. Cuban president Fulgencio Batista was born here in 1901. Then, 47 years later, in the local clapboard church of Nuestra Señora de la Caridad, another fiery leader-in-waiting, Fidel Castro, tied the knot with the blushing Birta Díaz Balart. A generous Batista gave them a US$500 gift for their honeymoon. Ah, how history could have been so different.

Founded in 1887, this effervescent company town was a virtual fiefdom of the US-run United Fruit Company until the 1950s and many of the old American company houses still remain. These days in the sun-streaked streets and squares you're more likely to encounter cigar-smoking cronies slamming dominoes and mums carrying meter-long loaves of bread; in short, everything Cuban that is missing from the all-inclusive resorts.

In September 2008 Banes was pummeled by Hurricane Ike, which damaged or destroyed 70% of its buildings. At the time of writing it was still picking up the pieces.

Information

There's an **immigration office** (Av de Cárdenas No 314A) here if you need a visa extension. Banes is one of those towns with no street signs and locals who don't know street names, so prepare to get lost.

Sights & Activities

If you're coming from the resorts, Banes' biggest attraction may be enjoying the street life provided by a stroll through town.

On October 12, 1948, Fidel Castro Ruz and Birta Díaz Balart were married in the **Iglesia de Nuestra Señora de la Caridad** on Parque Mart

BRUISED FRUIT

United Fruit is a name riddled with historical contradictions. On one hand, the company gave the world the 'Big Mike,' the first mass-produced imported banana; on the other, it developed a reputation for meddling covertly in the internal affairs of successive Latin American 'banana republics' – including Cuba.

Formed back in 1899 when Minor C Keith's Costa Rican–based banana-growing company merged with Andrew Preston's Boston fruit import business, United Fruit quickly morphed into a huge global monolith that went on to become one of the world's first multinational corporations.

Spreading its tentacles in the early 1900s, the company invested in 36 hectares of sugar plantations in eastern Cuba, where they constructed 544km of railroad and two large sugar mills – the Boston and the Preston – in what is now Holguín province. One of the company's early laborers was Ángel Castro (father of Fidel), who helped clear land for the company's burgeoning plantations before setting up on his own in Birán in 1915. Encased in an expansive new rural estate, Castro Senior began hiring out labor to United Fruit for a tidy profit and quickly became a wealthy man.

Holguín was soon the darling scion of United Fruit in Cuba, with provincial towns such as Banes and Mayarí sporting prosperous Americanized enclaves that owed both their existence and wealth to the omnipresent US-owned conglomerate. But dissatisfaction among Cubans was quietly growing.

Like many nationalistically minded leftists, Fidel Castro was incensed with the clandestine role United Fruit played in the 1954 overthrow of Jacobo Arbenz' socialist government in Guatemala and, spurred on by other radicals such as Che Guevara, was determined to make amends.

The payback began during the revolutionary war when Fidel's rebel army famously burned the fields of his late father's Birán estate in a portentous taste of things to come.

On taking power in 1959, Castro nationalized all United Fruit land and property in Cuba and sent its rich bosses scampering back to the US. Unable to gain financial compensation from the Cuban government, the company attempted to get even two years later by lending two ships from its 'Great White Fleet' (the largest private navy in the world) to Cuban mercenaries taking part in the abortive Bay of Pigs landings (see boxed text, p259). But the invasion was unsuccessful.

United Fruit's demise was exacerbated in 1975 when CEO Eli Black spectacularly committed suicide by jumping from the 44th floor of New York's PanAm building after it was alleged he had bribed the Honduran president US$1.2 million to pull out of a banana cartel hostile to UF's interests.

The company rebranded in 1984 and was reincarnated as Chiquita Brands. Meanwhile, in Cuba, the legacy of United Fruit can still be seen in the peeling colonial houses of Banes and – more ironically – at the former Castro farm in Birán.

in the center of Banes. After their divorce in 1954, Birta remarried and moved to Spain; through their only child, Fidelito, Fidel has several grandchildren.

Banes is better known for the **Museo Indocubano Bani** (☎ 80-24-87; General Marrero No 305; admission with/without guide CUC$2/1; ⏰ 9am-5pm Tue-Sat, 8am-noon & 7-9pm Sun). The museum's small but rich collection of Indian artifacts is one of the best on the island. Don't miss the tiny golden fertility idol unearthed near Banes (one of only 20 gold artifacts ever found in Cuba).

Railway enthusiasts shouldn't miss **steam locomotive 964** (El Panchito; Calle Tráfico), built at the HK Porter Locomotive Works in Pittsburgh, Pennsylvania, in 1888, now on display 400m east of the bus station. **Playa de Morales**, 13km east of Banes along the paved continuation of Tráfico, is a fishing village where you can while away an afternoon dining with locals and watching the men mend their nets. A few kilometers to the north is the even quieter **Playa Puerto Rico**.

Sleeping

IN TOWN

There are no hotels in the town proper, but Banes has some good private rooms.

Sergio Aguilera (☎ 80-24-12; Iglesias No 4089, Reparto Nicaragua; r CUC$20; 🔀) A lovely detached villa with a great family atmosphere and tasty meals served.

Casa Evelin Feria (☎ 80-31-50; Bruno Meriño No 3401A btwn Delfin Pupo & JMH, Reparto Cárdenas; r CUC$20-25; 🔀) A town center location, bright modern baths and an attentive hostess/cook make any stay in Evelin's house a pleasure.

OUTSIDE TOWN

Campismo Puerto Rico Libre (Cubamar; per person CUC$5) A mainly Cuban enclave near deserted Playa de Morales 13km north from Banes, the Puerto Rico has basic cabins that line the rocky shore. There's a restaurant, and people in the nearby fishing villages will happily cook seafood meals for you. Ask about the caves (about 1km from the campismo), and bring insect repellent. It's best to enquire with Cubamar (see p108) before arriving.

Motel Brisas de Banes (Map p374; cabins CUC$30) This place, on a hill overlooking a reservoir 10km northwest of Banes off the road to Guardalavaca, has eight cabins, each sleeping two people. There are nice views, and it's a pleasant out-of-the-way place for a beer.

Eating & Drinking

Coctelera (General Marrero No 327A) Several peso bars dotted around town are jumping with atmosphere and cheap hooch, including this one, as well as the superpopular Doña Yulla next door.

Restaurant El Latino (General Marrero No 710; 🕙 11am-11pm) A top Banes choice is this Palmares place with all the usual Creole dishes delivered with a little extra flair and charm. Service is good and the accompanying musicians unusually talented and discreet.

La Vicaria (🕙 24hr) Across the street from El Latino is yet another reliable La Vicaria, with pasta, burgers and Gordon Bleu (chicken stuffed with ham and cheese), plus eggs and coffee for breakfast (everything is less than CUC$4).

Alternatively, head down the street to Las 400 Rosas, an outdoor Convertible place that sells sodas, beer and snacks, and is situated next to the Museo Indocubano Bani.

Entertainment

Cafe Cantante (General Marrero No 320) This gregarious, music-filled patio is the top spot in Banes with honking municipal band rehearsals, discos, *son* (Cuba's basic form of popular music) septets and zen-inducing jazz jams.

Casa de Cultura (☎ 80-21-11; General Marrero No 320) Next door to Cafe Cantante this venue, housed in the former Casino Español (1926), has a regular Sunday *trova* (traditional poetic songs) matinee at 3pm and Saturday *peña del rap* (rap music session) at 9pm.

Getting There & Away

From the bus station at the corner of Tráfico and Los Ángeles, one morning bus goes to Holguín (72km) daily (supposedly). An afternoon bus connects with the train to Havana. Trucks leave Banes for Holguín more frequently. A taxi from Guardalavaca will cost around CUC$20 one-way, or you can tackle it from a bike or moped in an easy day trip.

BIRÁN

Fidel Castro Ruz was born on August 13, 1926, at the **Finca Las Manacas** (aka Casa de Fidel) near the village of Birán, south of Cueto. The farm, which was bought by Fidel's father Ángel in 1915, is huge, and includes its own workers' village (a cluster of small thatched huts for the mainly Haitian laborers), a cockfighting ring, a post office, a store and a telegraph. The several large yellow wooden houses that can be glimpsed through the cedar trees are where the Castro family lived.

The Finca opened as a museum in 2002 under the unassuming name of **Sitio Histórico de Birán** (admission/camera/video CUC$10/20/40; 🕙 9am-noon & 1:30-4pm Tue-Sat, 9am-noon Sun), supposedly to downplay any Castro 'personality cult.' The modesty extends to the signage, which is nonexistent. Nonetheless, the museum is an interesting excursion containing more than a hundred photos, assorted clothes, Fidel's childhood bed and his father's 1918 Ford motorcar. With 27 installations, the place constitutes a *pueblito* (small town) and, if nothing else, shows the extent of the inheritance that this hot-headed ex-lawyer gave up when he lived in the Sierra Maestra for two years surviving on a diet of crushed crabs and raw horse meat.

You'll find the graves of Fidel's parents Ángel Castro and Lina Ruz, to the right of the entrance gate.

To get here, take the southern turnoff 7km west of Cueto, and drive 7km south to the Central Loynaz Hechevarría sugar mill at Marcané. From there a road runs 8km east to Birán, from which it's another 3km northeast to Finca Las Manacas.

SIERRA DEL CRISTAL

Cuba's own 'Little Switzerland' is a rugged amalgam of the Sierra del Cristal and the Altiplanicie de Nipe that contains two important national parks. **Parque Nacional Sierra Cristal**, Cuba's oldest, was founded in 1930 and harbors 1213m Pico de Cristal, the province's highest summit. Of more interest to travelers is the 5300-hectare **Parque Nacional La Mensura**, 30km south of Mayarí, which protects the island's highest waterfall, yields copious Caribbean pines and hosts a mountain research center run by the Academia de Ciencias de Cuba (Cuban Academy of Sciences). Notable for its cool alpine microclimate and 100 or more species of endemic plants, La Mensura offers hiking and horseback-riding activities and accommodation in an economical Gaviota-run hotel.

Sights & Activities

Most activities can be organized at Villa Pinares del Mayarí (right) or via excursions from Guardalavaca's hotels (CUC$78 by jeep or CUC$110 by helicopter; see p377).

At just over 100m in height, the **Salto del Guayabo** is the highest waterfall in Cuba. The guided 1.2km hike to its base through fecund tropical forest costs CUC$5 and includes swimming in a natural pool.

La Plancha (admission free), on the left on the access road a few kilometers before the hotel, is a small flower and crop garden containing everything from mariposas to sugarcane. More flora can be observed on the **Sendero La Sabina**, a short interpretive trail at the Centro Investigaciones para la Montaña (1km from the hotel), which exhibits the vegetation of eight different ecosystems and guards some rare orchids.

Eight kilometers from the hotel is the **Hacienda La Mensura**, a breeding center for exotic animals such as antelope and *guapeti*. Horseback riding can be arranged here.

Speleologists may want to ask about trips to the ghostly **Farallones de Seboruco**, which contain aboriginal cave paintings.

Sleeping & Eating

our pick **Villa Pinares del Mayarí** (Gaviota; ☎ 5-3308; s/d CUC$30/35, cabins CUC$35/40; Ⓟ 🕍 🔊) One in a duo of classic Gaviota Holguín hideaways (Cayo Saetía is the other; see p382), Pinares del Mayarí stands at 600m elevation between the Altiplanicie de Nipe and Sierra del Cristal, 30km south of Mayarí on a rough dirt road. Part Swiss-chalet resort, part mountain retreat, this isolated rural gem is situated in one of Cuba's largest pine forests and the two- and three-bedroom cabins, with hot showers and comfortable beds, make it seem almost alpine-esque. There's also a large restaurant, bar, tennis court and horses for hire.

Getting There & Away

The only way to get to Villa Pinares del Mayarí and Parque Nacional La Mensura outside an organized tour is via car, taxi or bike (if you're adventurous and it's not a Cuban one). The access road is rough and in a poor state of repair, but it's passable in a hire car if driven with care. If arriving from Santiago the best route is via the small settlement of Mella.

CAYO SAETÍA

East of Mayarí the road becomes increasingly potholed and the surroundings, while never losing their dusty rural charm, progressively more remote. The culmination of this rustic drive is lovely Cayo Saetía, a small, flat wooded island in the Bahía de Nipe that's connected to the mainland by a small bridge. During the 1970s and '80s this was a favored hunting ground for communist apparatchiks who enjoyed spraying lead into the local wildlife. Fortunately, those days are now gone. Indeed, ironic as it may sound, Cayo Saetía is now a protected wildlife park with 19 species of exotic animals, including camels, zebras, antelopes, ostriches and deer. Bisected by grassy meadows and adorned by hidden coves and beaches, it's the closet Cuba gets to an African wildlife reserve. Well worth a visit.

Sleeping & Eating

Campismo Río Cabonico (☎ 59-41-18; r per person from CUC$5) This place is at Pueblo Nuevo, 9km east of Levisa and 73km west of Moa, about 900m south of the main road. The 23 cabins with baths and fans on a low terrace beside the Río Cabonico (decent swimming) have four or six beds. It may accept foreigners, if there's space; check ahead or contact Cubamar in Havana.

WILL HISTORY ABSOLVE HIM?

Has the world misunderstood Fidel Castro? Is this rugged survivor of the Cold War and the catastrophic economic meltdown that followed just a Machiavellian dictator responsible for driving an immovable wedge into US-Cuban relations? Or is he the de facto leader of an unofficial Third World alliance pioneering the fight for equal rights and social justice on the world stage? To get closer to the personality that lies behind the public mask we must (as every good Freudian knows) delve back into his childhood.

Born near the village of Birán in Holguín province on August 13, 1926, the illegitimate product of a relationship between Spanish-born landowner Ángel Castro and his cook and housemaid Lina Ruz (they later married), Fidel grew up as a favored child in a large and relatively wealthy family of sugar farmers. Educated at a Jesuit school and sent away to study in the city of Santiago at the age of seven, the young Castro was an exceptional student whose prodigious talents included a photographic memory and an extraordinary aptitude for sport. Indeed, legend has it that at the age of 21, Fidel – by then a skilled left-arm pitcher – was offered a professional baseball contract with the Washington Senators.

At the age of 13 Fidel staged his first insurrection, a strike organized among his father's sugarcane workers against their exploitative boss, a gesture that did little to endear him to the fraternal fold.

One year later the still teenage Castro penned a letter to US president FD Roosevelt congratulating him on his re-election and asking the American leader for a US$10 bill 'because I have not seen a US$10 bill and I would like to have one of them.' Rather ominously for future US-Cuban relations, the request was politely turned down.

Undeterred, Fidel marched on. On the completion of his high school certificate in 1945, his teacher and mentor Father Francisco Barbeito predicted sagely that his bullish star pupil would 'fill with brilliant pages the book of his life.' With the benefit of hindsight, he wasn't far wrong. Armed with tremendous personal charisma, a wrought-iron will and a natural ability to pontificate

ourpick **Villa Cayo Saetía** (Gaviota; ☎ 42-53-20; s/d CUC$58/70; ❄) This wonderfully rustic but comfortable resort on a 42-sq-km island at the entrance to the Bahía de Nipe is small, remote and more upmarket than the price suggests. The 12 rooms are split into rustic and standard *cabañas* with a minimal price differential, while the in-house restaurant La Güira – decked out Hemingway-style with hunting trophies mounted on the wall like gory art – serves exotic meats such as antelope. You'll feel as if you're a thousand miles from anywhere.

Getting There & Around

There are three ways to explore Cayo Saetía aside from the obvious two-legged sorties from the villa itself. A one-hour jeep safari costs CUC$9, while excursions by horse and boat are CUC$6 and CUC$5 respectively. Though isolated you can secure passage on a twice-weekly Gaviota helicopter from Guardalavaca (CUC$124, Saturday and Monday) or a bus-boat combo from the town of Antilles. If arriving by car, the control post is 15km off the

main road. Then it's another 8km along a rough, unpaved road to the resort. A hire car will make it – with care.

MOA

pop 57,484

Important economically and horrendous ecologically, Moa is a big, ugly mine at the foot of the verdant Cuchillas de Moa that has covered the entire region in a film of dirty red dust. Unless you're a Canadian mining technician, or an environmentalist investigating impending ecological disasters, there's absolutely no reason to come here. 'A better world is possible' proclaims one of the billboards as you leave the town behind. Absolutely!

Sleeping

Hotel Miraflores (Islazul; ☎ 60-61-25; Av Amistad, Rpto Miraflores; s/d CUC$36/48; Ⓟ ⚏) If you must stay – and it's a viable pit stop if you're heading south for Baracoa and the Parque Nacional Alejandro de Humboldt – this bog-standard Islazul offering perched on a hillside on the western side of town will do the business. Its interminably for hours on end, Fidel made tracks for Havana University where his forthright and unyielding personality quickly ensured he excelled at everything he did.

Training ostensibly as a lawyer, Castro spent the next three years embroiled in political activity amid an academic forum that was riddled with gang violence and petty corruption. 'My impetuosity, my desire to excel, fed and inspired the character of my struggle,' he recalled candidly years later.

Blessed with more lives than a cat, Castro has survived a failed putsch, 15 months in prison, exile in Mexico, a two-year guerrilla war in the mountains and a reported 617 attempts on his life. His sense of optimism in the face of defeat is nothing short of astounding. With his rebel army reduced to a ragged band of 12 men after the Granma landing (see p43), he astonished his beleaguered colleagues with a fiery victory speech. 'We will win this war,' he trumpeted confidently, 'We are just beginning the fight!'

As an international personality who has outlasted 11 American presidents, the 21st-century incarnation of Fidel Castro that emerged following the Special Period (p50) was no less enigmatic than the revolutionary leader of yore. Fostering his own peculiar brand of Caribbean socialism with an unflinching desire to 'defend the Revolution at all costs,' the ever-changing ideology that Castro so famously preached is perhaps best summarized by biographer Volker Skierka as 'a pragmatic mixture of a little Marx, Engels and Lenin, slightly more of Che Guevara, a lot of José Martí, and a great deal indeed of Fidel Castro.'

Castro stepped out of public life in July 2006 after a serious bout of diverticulitis and handed the reins of power to his younger brother Raúl. Despite penning regular articles for national newspaper *Granma* and making the odd jarring public statement on world affairs, he looks destined to see out his final years like a Caribbean Napoleon wistfully pondering his historical legacy from his lonely island prison. Whether history will absolve him is still anybody's guess.

on-site restaurant is your only real eating option. The airport is 5km distant, and getting there costs about CUC$3 in a taxi.

Getting There & Around

Moa's Orestes Acosta Airport is conveniently located beside the highway to Baracoa, just 3km east of downtown Moa. **Cubana** (☎ 60-73-70; Av del Puerto, Rolo Monterrey) has flights to/from Havana on Monday (CUC$124 one way, three hours).

The bus station is near the center of town, 3km east of the Hotel Miraflores. A daily bus leaves for Holguín and another goes to Santiago de Cuba, but there's no bus to Baracoa. You may be prevented from using the regular passenger trucks that leave the bus station for Holguín and Baracoa, as foreigners are officially prohibited. This means that there's no legal public transport except for hitchhiking and tourist taxis between Moa and Baracoa. Taxi drivers will ask CUC$25 to Baracoa. The road, incidentally, is a potholed nightmare, but just about passable in a standard car.

Cubacar (☎ 60-22-32) has an office at Hotel Miraflores. The Servi-Cupet gas station is at the entrance to Moa from Mayarí, not far from the Hotel Miraflores.

Granma Province

Granma has 'made in Cuba' stamped all over it. This is the land where José Martí died, where Fidel Castro landed with his band of shipwrecked revolutionaries, and where Granma native Carlos Manuel de Céspedes freed his slaves and formally declared Cuban independence in 1868. And, if history doesn't swing it, you can always ponder over the geographical significance of Cuba's longest river (the Cauto), its most pristine coastal marine terraces (in Parque Nacional Desembarco del Granma) and its third-highest mountain (Pico Bayamesa, 1730m).

With much of its interior and southwestern coastal areas cut off from the main transport grid, one of Granma's primary attractions is its isolation and the feisty individualism that goes with it. Street parties in towns such as Bayamo, Manzanillo and Pilón are a weekly occurrence here and are uniquely enlivened with homemade street snacks, hotly contested games of chess, and the kind of archaic street organs that were last seen in Europe when Cuba was still the property of Spain.

Juxtaposing pancake-flat rice fields with the soaring peaks of the Sierra Maestra, Granma is more rural than urban and even the two main cities of Bayamo and Manzanillo retain a faintly bucolic air.

But far from sucking on sugar stalks in the safety of their remote backcountry refuges, the resourceful locals are renowned for their creativity, particularly in the field of music. Two of the giants of Cuban *nueva trova* (philosophical folk guitar music) were born in Granma (Pablo Milanés in Bayamo and Carlos Puebla in Manzanillo), and in 1972 the province hosted a groundbreaking music festival that helped put this revolutionary new music style on Cuba's – and Latin America's – cultural map.

HIGHLIGHTS

- **DIY Hike** Break out of the Marea del Portillo hotels and hike up to El Salto (see boxed text, p402)
- **Guerrilla Watching** Trek up to La Plata in Gran Parque Nacional Sierra Maestra (p393)
- **The Flower of the Revolution** Drop by Media Luna and learn about the life of Celia Sánchez, Castro's longtime muse and confidante (see boxed text, p399)
- **The Roof of the Nation** Stand atop Pico Turquino and admire the bust of José Martí (see boxed text, p395)
- **Street Party** Make time for pork roast, street organs and a game of chess in Bayamo's Fiesta de la Cubanía (p389)

★ Bayamo

Gran Parque Nacional Sierra Maestra

Media Luna ★

★ ★ Pico Turquino

★ El Salto

| TELEPHONE CODE: 023 | POPULATION: 829,333 | AREA: 8372 SQ KM |

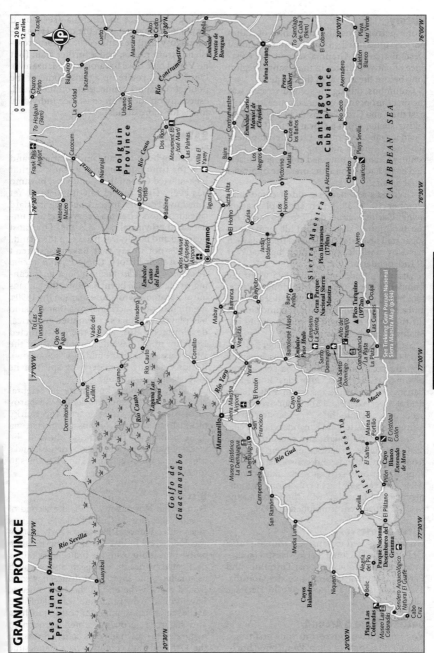

GRANMA PROVINCE

GRANMA PROVINCE

History

Stone petroglyphs and remnants of Taíno pottery unearthed in the Parque Nacional Desembarco del Granma suggest the existence of native cultures in the Granma region long before the arrival of the Spanish.

Columbus, during his second voyage, was the first European to explore the area, tracking past the Cabo Cruz Peninsula in 1494, before taking shelter from a storm in the Golfo de Guanacayabo. All other early development schemes came to nothing and by the 17th century Granma's untamed and largely unsettled coast had become the preserve of pirates and corsairs.

Granma's real nemesis didn't come until October 10, 1868, when sugar-plantation owner Carlos Manuel de Céspedes called for the abolition of slavery from his Demajagua sugar mill near Manzanillo and freed his own slaves by example, thus inciting the First War of Independence.

Drama unfolded again in 1895 when the founder of the Cuban Revolutionary Party, José Martí, was killed in Dos Ríos just a month and a half after landing with Máximo Gómez off the coast of Guantánamo to ignite the Spanish-Cuban-American War.

Sixty-one years later, on December 2, 1956, Fidel Castro and 81 rebel soldiers disembarked from the yacht *Granma* off the coast of Granma province at Playa Las Coloradas. Routed by Batista's troops while resting in a sugarcane field at Alegría del Pío, 12 or so survivors managed to escape into the Sierra Maestra, establishing headquarters at Comandancia La Plata. From there they fought and coordinated the armed struggle, broadcasting their progress from Radio Rebelde and consolidating their support among sympathizers nationwide. After two years of harsh conditions and unprecedented beard growth, the forces of the M-26-7 Movement triumphed in 1959.

Parks & Reserves

Granma has two expansive national parks: Gran Parque Nacional Sierra Maestra (sometimes called Parque Nacional Turquino) and Parque Nacional Desembarco del Granma. The latter is also a Unesco World Heritage Site.

Getting There & Around

You might have to resort to your first truck, *guagua* (local bus) or *amarillo*-inspired hitch-hiking experience in Granma (see boxed text, p368). Bayamo is on the main Havana–Santiago Víazul bus and *coche motor* (cross-island) train routes, and a further train (but no Víazul bus) links Bayamo with Manzanillo. Outside this, you're up against some of the poorest transport connections on the island, especially on the south coast. See individual towns for more details.

BAYAMO
pop 143,844

Predating both Havana and Santiago, and cast for time immemorial as the city that kick-started Cuban independence, Bayamo has every right to feel self-important. Yet somehow it doesn't. Instead, bucking standard categorization, Granma's easygoing and understated provincial capital is one of the most peaceful and hassle-free places on the island.

That's not to say that Bayameses aren't aware of their history. *Como España quemó a Sagunto, así Cuba quemó a Bayamo* (meaning 'as the Spanish burnt Sagunto, the Cubans burnt Bayamo'), wrote José Martí in the 1890s, highlighting the sacrificial role that Bayamo has played in Cuba's convoluted historical development. But, while the self-inflicted 1869 fire might have destroyed most of the city's classic colonial buildings (see below), it didn't destroy its underlying spirit or its long-standing traditions.

Today, Bayamo is known for its cerebral chess players (Céspedes was the Kasparov of his day), tasty street snacks and quirky old-fashioned street organs (imported via Manzanillo). All three are on show at the weekly Fiesta de la Cubanía, one of the island's most authentic street shows and Bayamés to the core.

History

Founded in November 1513 as the second of Diego Velázquez de Cuellar's seven original villas (after Baracoa), Bayamo's early history was marred by Indian uprisings and bristling native unrest. But with the indigenous Taínos decimated by deadly European diseases such as smallpox, the short-lived insurgency soon fizzled out. By the end of the 16th century, Bayamo had grown rich and was established as the region's most important cattle-ranching and sugarcane-growing center. Frequented by pirates, the town filled its coffers further in the 17th and 18th centuries via a clandestine

BAYAMO

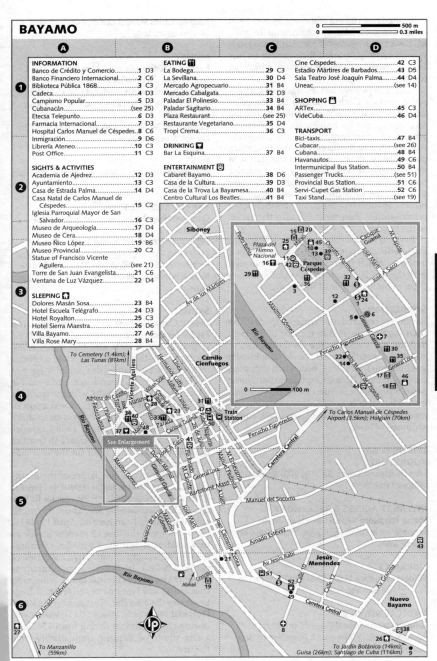

0 — 500 m
0 — 0.3 miles

A

INFORMATION
Banco de Crédito y Comercio.............1 D3
Banco Financiero Internacional..........2 C6
Biblioteca Pública 1868.....................3 C3
Cadeca...4 D3
Campismo Popular..............................5 D3
Cubanacán......................................(see 25)
Etecsa Telepunto...............................6 D3
Farmacia Internacional.......................7 D3
Hospital Carlos Manuel de Céspedes..8 C6
Inmigración.......................................9 D6
Librería Ateneo.................................10 C3
Post Office......................................11 C3

SIGHTS & ACTIVITIES
Academia de Ajedrez.......................12 D3
Ayuntamiento..................................13 D4
Casa de Estrada Palma.....................14 D4
Casa Natal de Carlos Manuel de
  Céspedes......................................15 C2
Iglesia Parroquial Mayor de San
  Salvador.......................................16 C3
Museo de Arqueología.....................17 D4
Museo de Cera................................18 D4
Museo Ñico López............................19 B6
Museo Provincial..............................20 C2
Statue of Francisco Vicente
  Aguilera.....................................(see 21)
Torre de San Juan Evangelista..........21 C6
Ventana de Luz Vázquez..................22 D4

SLEEPING
Dolores Masán Sosa.........................23 B4
Hotel Escuela Telégrafo....................24 D3
Hotel Royalton.................................25 C3
Hotel Sierra Maestra........................26 D6
Villa Bayamo...................................27 A6
Villa Rose Mary...............................28 B4

B

EATING
La Bodega..29 C3
La Sevillana.....................................30 D4
Mercado Agropecuario.....................31 B4
Mercado Cabalgata..........................32 D3
Paladar El Polinesio..........................33 B4
Paladar Sagitario..............................34 B4
Plaza Restaurant...........................(see 25)
Restaurante Vegetariano..................35 D4
Tropi Crema....................................36 C3

DRINKING
Bar La Esquina.................................37 B4

ENTERTAINMENT
Cabaret Bayamo..............................38 D6
Casa de la Cultura............................39 D3
Casa de la Trova La Bayamesa..........40 B4
Centro Cultural Los Beatles..............41 B4

C

Cine Céspedes.................................42 C3
Estadio Mártires de Barbados...........43 D5
Sala Teatro José Joaquín Palma.......44 D4
Uneac...(see 14)

SHOPPING
ARTex...45 C3
VideCuba..46 D4

TRANSPORT
Bici-taxis...47 B4
Cubacar.......................................(see 26)
Cubana..48 B4
Havanautos.....................................49 C6
Intermunicipal Bus Station................50 B4
Passenger Trucks..........................(see 51)
Provincial Bus Station......................51 C6
Servi-Cupet Gas Station...................52 C6
Taxi Stand....................................(see 19)

GRANMA PROVINCE

smuggling ring run out of the nearby port town of Manzanillo. Zealously counting up the profits, Bayamo's new class of merchants and landowners lavishly invested their money in fine houses and an expensive overseas education for their offspring.

One such protégé was local lawyer-turned-revolutionary Carlos Manuel de Céspedes, who, defying the traditional colonial will, led an army against his hometown in 1868 in an attempt to wrest control from the conservative Spanish authorities. But the liberation proved to be short-lived. After the defeat of an ill-prepared rebel army by 3000 regular Spanish troops near the Río Cauto on January 12, 1869, the townspeople – sensing an imminent Spanish reoccupation – set their town on fire rather than see it fall into the hands of the enemy.

Bayamo was also the birthplace of Perucho Figueredo, composer of the Cuban national anthem, which begins, rather patriotically, with the words *Al combate corred, Bayameses* (Run to battle, people of Bayamo).

Orientation

Bayamo is centered on Parque Céspedes. The train station is located to the east of the park and the bus station to the southeast; they're about 2km apart. General García (also known as El Bulevar), a bustling pedestrian shopping mall, leads from Parque Céspedes to Bartolomé Masó. Many of the facilities for tourists (including the bus station, Servi-Cupet gas station and main hotel) are along the Carretera Central, southeast of town.

Information

BOOKSTORES
Librería Ateneo (General García No 9) On the east side of Parque Céspedes.

INTERNET ACCESS & TELEPHONE
Etecsa Telepunto (General García btwn Saco & Figueredo; per hr CUC$6; 🕿 8:30am-7:30pm) Quick, easy internet access.

LIBRARIES
Biblioteca Pública 1868 (☎ 42-64-87; Céspedes No 352; 🕿 9am-6pm Mon-Sat)

MEDICAL SERVICES
Farmacia Internacional (General García btwn Figueredo & Lora; 🕿 8am-noon & 1-5pm Mon-Fri, 8am-noon Sat & Sun)

Hospital Carlos Manuel de Céspedes (☎ 42-50-12; Carretera Central Km1)

MONEY
Banco de Crédito y Comercio (cnr General García & Saco; 🕿 8am-3pm Mon-Fri, 8-10am Sat)
Banco Financiero Internacional (☎ 42-73-60; Carretera Central Km 1) In a big white building near the bus terminal.
Cadeca (Saco No 101; 🕿 8:30am-noon & 12:30-5:30pm Mon-Sat, 8am-noon Sun)

POST
Post office (cnr Maceo & Parque Céspedes; 🕿 8am-8pm Mon-Sat)

TRAVEL AGENCIES
Campismo Popular (☎ 42-42-00; General García No 112)
Cubanacán (☎ 42-22-90; Hotel Royalton, Maceo No 53) Arranges hikes to Pico Turquino (two/three/four days per person CUC$45/65/99), El Yarey (CUC$19) and Parque Nacional Desembarco del Granma (CUC$45), among other places.

Sights

One of Cuba's leafiest and friendliest squares, **Parque Céspedes** is an attractive smorgasbord of grand monuments and big, shady trees. Facing each other in the center are a bronze statue of Carlos Manuel de Céspedes, hero of the First War of Independence, and a marble bust of Perucho Figueredo, with the words of the Cuban national anthem carved upon it. Marble benches and friendly Bayameses make this a nice place to linger. In 1868 Céspedes proclaimed Cuba's independence in front of the **Ayuntamiento** (city hall) on the east side of the square.

The birthplace of the 'father of the motherlands,' **Casa Natal de Carlos Manuel de Céspedes** (Maceo No 57; admission CUC$1; 🕿 9am-5pm Tue-Fri, 9am-2pm & 8-10pm Sat, 10am-1pm Sun), is on the north side of the park. Born here on April 18, 1819, Céspedes spent the first 12 years of his life in this residence, and the Céspedes memorabilia inside is complemented by a collection of period furniture. It's notable architecturally as the only two-story colonial house remaining in Bayamo and was one of the few buildings to survive the 1869 fire. Next door is the **Museo Provincial** (Maceo No 55; admission CUC$1) with a yellowing city document dating from 1567 and a rare photo of Bayamo immediately after the fire.

There's been a church on the site of the **Iglesia Parroquial Mayor de San Salvador** since 1514. The current edifice dates from 1740 and the section known as the **Capilla de la Dolorosa** (donations accepted; ☉ 9am–noon & 3-5pm Mon-Fri, 9am-noon Sat) was another building to survive the 1869 fire. A highlight of the main church is the central arch, which exhibits a mural depicting the blessing of the Cuban flag in front of the revolutionary army on October 20, 1868. Outside, Plaza del Himno Nacional is where the Cuban national anthem, 'La Bayamesa,' was sung for the first time in 1868.

A forerunner of the national anthem, co-written by Céspedes (and also, confusingly, called 'La Bayamesa') was first sung from the **Ventana de Luz Vázquez** (Céspedes btwn Figueredo & Luz Vázquez) on March 27, 1851. A memorial plaque has been emblazoned onto the wall next to the wood-barred colonial window.

Next door is the **Casa de Estrada Palma** (Céspedes No 158), where Cuba's first postindependence president, Tomás Estrada Palma, was born in 1835. A one-time friend of José Martí, Estrada Palma was disgraced after the Revolution for his perceived complicity with the US over the Platt Amendment. His birth house is now the seat of Uneac (Unión Nacional de Escritores y Artistas de Cuba; National Union of Cuban Writers and Artists), but you'll find little about the famous former occupant inside.

The **Torre de San Juan Evangelista** (cnr José Martí & Amado Estévez) is to the southeast. A church dating from Bayamo's earliest years stood at this busy intersection until it was destroyed in the great fire of 1869. Later, the church's tower served as the entrance to the first cemetery in Cuba, which closed in 1919. The cemetery was demolished in 1940, but the tower survived. A **monument** to local poet José Joaquín Palma (1844–1911) stands in the tower in the park diagonally across the street from the tower, and beside the tower is a bronze **statue of Francisco Vicente Aguilera** (1821–77), who led the independence struggle in Bayamo.

Not far away, just off the main road, is the **Museo Ñico López** (Abihail González; admission CUC$1; ☉ 8am–noon & 2-5:30pm Tue-Sat, 9am–noon Sun) in the former officers' club of the Carlos Manuel de Céspedes military barracks. On July 26, 1953, this garrison was attacked by 25 revolutionaries in tandem with the assault on Moncada Barracks in Santiago de Cuba in order to prevent reinforcements from being sent. Though a failure, Ñico López, who led the Bayamo attack, escaped to Guatemala, and he was the

> **ASK A LOCAL**
>
> Take a state-run horse and cart ride (CUC$4) on an untouristy 45-minute tour of the city with verbal explanations about the sights. Afterwards you can stroll along pedestrianized Calle General García and around Parque Céspedes.
>
> *Eddy, Bayamo*

first Cuban to befriend Ernesto 'Che' Guevara in 1954. López was killed shortly after the *Granma* landed in 1956.

Bayamo's main shopping street, Calle General García (also known as **Paseo Bayamés**) was pedestrianized and reconfigured with funky murals in the late 1990s. It's a great place to catch the nuances of city life. Halfway along its course you'll find the tiny **Museo de Cera** (☎ 42-65-25; General García No 261; admission CUC$1; ☉ 9am–noon & 1-5pm Mon-Fri, 2-9pm Sat, 9am–noon Sun), Bayamo's version of Madame Tussaud's, with convincing waxworks of personalities such as Polo Montañez, Benny Moré and local hero Carlos Puebla. Next door is an equally tiny **Museo de Arqueología** (cnr General García & General Lora; admission CUC$1).

Activities

The Cubans love chess, and nowhere more so than in Bayamo. Check out the streetside chess aficionados who set up on Saturday nights during the Fiesta de la Cubanía. The **Academia de Ajedrez** (José A Saco No 63 btwn General García & Céspedes) is the place to go to improve your pawn-king-four technique. Emblazoned on the wall of this cerebral institution, pictures of Che, Fidel and Carlos Manuel de Céspedes offer plenty of inspiration.

Forty-five-minute **horse & cart tours** can be arranged at the Cubanacán desk in the Hotel Royalton (p390) for CUC$4 per person.

Festivals & Events

Bayamo's quintessential nighttime attraction is its weekly **Fiesta de la Cubanía** on Saturday at 8pm. This ebullient and long-standing street party is like nothing else in Cuba. Set up willynilly along Calle Saco, it includes the locally famous pipe organs, whole roast pig, a local oyster drink called *ostiones* and – incongruously in the middle of it all – rows of tables laid out diligently with chess sets. Dancing is, of course, de rigueur.

GRANMA PROVINCE

Sleeping

CASAS PARTICULARES

Rooms are spread around, but Calle Pío Rosada a good place to start looking.

Villa Rose Mary (☎ 42-39-84; reas61@gmail.com; Pío Rosado No 22 btwn Ramirez & Av Aguilera; r CUC$25; P 🐾) Don't be fooled by the name, Ramón's the man in charge here and his house is kitted out like a mini hotel with two bedrooms, big baths, safe security boxes, and a patio/roof terrace ripe for a spot of afternoon R and R. Get Ramón to brew you up a *cafecito* and quiz him on his excellent local knowledge.

Dolores Masán Sosa (☎ 42-29-74; Pío Rosado No 171 btwn Parada & William Soler; r CUC$25; P 🐾) The freshly painted mint-green facade lures you toward Dolores Sosa's house on Pío Rosado. Proceed up the outside staircase, past the well-polished relic of Detroit in the car port, to where two rooms with an independent entrance and an interconnecting door (if required) enjoy pride of place above the street action below. If it's full, try Frank Licea Milan (☎ 42-58-16) at No 73 or Juan Valdes (☎ 42-33-24) at No 64.

HOTELS

Hotel Escuela Telégrafo (Formatur; ☎ 42-55-10; Saco No 108; s/d CUC$15/20; 🐾) Always a good bet for budget travelers, the Telégrafo is one of Cuba's best *hotel escuelas* (hotel schools) staffed by students learning the ropes in the tourist trade. This one is housed in a beautiful old colonial building on busy Calle Saco where big shuttered windows open out onto the street. Rooms are basic but clean, service is suitably perky, and there's a decent restaurant adjacent to the bustling lobby downstairs. Ask here about the possibility of taking Spanish lessons.

our pick Hotel Royalton (Islazul; ☎ 42-22-90; Maceo No 53; s/d CUC$26/33; 🐾) Melting in with the colonial ambience of Parque Céspedes, the Royalton is Bayamo's best hotel – and best bargain. The 33 rooms, though small, are cozy and well maintained with the four at the front opening out over the leafy central square. Downstairs there's an attractive sidewalk terrace and the Plaza restaurant, and you can sunbathe in private on the roof. Handy water machines furnish the corridors.

Villa Bayamo (Islazul; ☎ 42-31-02; s/d CUC$30/35; P 🐾 🐾) This out-of-town option (it's 3km southwest of the center on the road to Manzanillo) has a definitive rural feel and a rather pleasant swimming pool overlooking fields at the back. Well-appointed rooms are in a larger main block or detached cabins off to the side. There's a reasonable restaurant on-site.

Hotel Sierra Maestra (Islazul; ☎ 42-79-70; Carretera Central; s/d CUC$36/41; P 🐾 🐾) Check before you jump in the pool here – there may be no water in it. With a ring of the Soviet '70s about the place, the Sierra Maestra hardly merits the three stars it professes, although the rooms have had some much-needed attention in the last three years and the coffee and TV reception are better. Three kilometers from the town center, it's OK for an overnighter.

Eating

There's some unique street food in Bayamo, sold from the stores along Calle Saco and in Plaza Céspedes. Aside from the places reviewed here, you'll find decent *comida criolla* (Creole food) in the two city-center hotels, the Royalton (left) and the Telégrafo (left), both of which have atmospheric restaurants.

PALADARES

Paladar Sagitario (Donato Marmol No 107 btwn Maceo & Vicente Aguilera; meals CUC$7-9; 🕘 noon-midnight) The Sagitario's been in the game for 13 years, knocking out such delicacies as chicken cordon bleu and pork chops topped with cheese on an attractive back patio with occasional musical accompaniment.

Paladar El Polinesio (☎ 42-24-49; Parada No 125 btwn Pío Rosado & Cisnero) The cheaper and cozier Polinesio has meals served upstairs in what used to be the family dining room.

RESTAURANTS

Tropi Crema (☎ 42-41-69; 🕘 9am-9:45pm) In the absence of a Coppelia, the Tropi, on the southwest corner of Parque Céspedes, does its best – in pesos, of course.

Restaurante Vegetariano (General García No 173; 🕘 7-9am, noon-2:30pm & 6-9pm; V) Manage your expectations before you check out this peso place. This is Cuba where *vegetarianismo* is still in its infancy. Don't expect nut roast, but you should be able to order something other than the ubiquitous omelette.

La Sevillana (☎ 42-14-95; General García btwn General Lora & Perucho Figueredo; 🕘 noon-2pm & 6-10:30pm) Cuban chefs have a go at Spanish cuisine – paella and *garbanzos* (chickpeas). This is a new kind of peso restaurant, with a dress code (no shorts), a doorman in a suit, and a reservations policy. It's OK, if you don't mind the formalities.

our pick La Bodega (☎ 42-79-11; Plaza del Himno Nacional No 34; cover after 9pm CUC$3; ☼ 11am-1am) The best of both worlds. The front door opens out onto Bayamo's main square; the rear terrace overlooks Río Bayamo and is fringed by a bucolic backdrop that will leave you wondering if you've been transported to an isolated country villa. La Bodega is Bayamo's best restaurant and not only for its urban-rural juxtapositions. Try the beef and taste the coffee, or relax on the open terrace before the traveling troubadours arrive at 9pm.

GROCERIES
Mercado agropecuario (Línea) The vegetable market is in front of the train station. There are many peso food stalls along here also.

Mercado Cabalgata (General García No 65; ☼ 9am-9pm Mon-Sat, 9am-noon Sun) This store on the main pedestrian street sells basic groceries.

Drinking
Bar La Esquina (☎ 42-17-31; cnr Donato Marmol & Maceo; ☼ 11am-1am) International cocktails are served in this tiny corner bar replete with plenty of local atmosphere.

Entertainment
Cine Céspedes (☎ 42-42-67; admission CUC$2) This cinema is on the western side of Parque Céspedes, next to the post office. It offers everything from Gutiérrez Alea to the latest Hollywood blockbuster.

our pick Centro Cultural Los Beatles (42-17-99; Zenea btwn Figueredo & Saco; admission 10 pesos; ☼ 6am-midnight) Just as the West fell for the exoticism of the Buena Vista Social Club, the Cubans fell for the downright brilliance of the Fab Four. Guarded by life-size statues of John, Paul, George and Ringo, this quirky place hosts Beatles tribute bands (in Spanish) every weekend. Unmissable!

Uneac (Céspedes No 158; admission free; ☼ 4pm) You can catch heartfelt boleros on the flowery patio here in the former home of disgraced first president Tomás Estrada Palma, who is largely blamed for handing Guantánamo to the *Yanquis*.

Sala Teatro José Joaquín Palma (☎ 42-44-23; Céspedes No 164) In a stylish old church, this venue presents theater on Friday, Saturday and Sunday nights, while the Teatro Guiñol, also here, hosts children's theater on Saturday and Sunday mornings.

Cabaret Bayamo (☎ 42-51-11; Carretera Central Km 2; ☼ 9pm Fri-Sun) Bayamo's glittery nightclub/cabaret opposite the Hotel Sierra Maestra draws out the locals on weekends in their equally glittery attire.

Casa de la Trova La Bayamesa (cnr Maceo & Martí; admission CUC$1; ☼ 9pm) One of Cuba's best in a lovely colonial building; closed Mondays.

Casa de la Cultura (☎ 42-59-17; General García No 15) Wide-ranging cultural events, including art expos, on the east side of Parque Céspedes.

Estadio Mártires de Barbados (Av Granma) From October to April, there are baseball games at this stadium, approximately 1km northeast of the Hotel Sierra Maestra.

Shopping
ARTex (General García No 7) The usual mix of Che Guevara T-shirts and bogus Santería dolls on Parque Céspedes.

VideCuba (General García No 225; ☼ 8am-10pm) This outlet should meet your photographic requirements.

Getting There & Away
AIR
Bayamo's **Carlos Manuel de Céspedes Airport** (airport code BYM; ☎ 42-75-14) is about 4km northeast of town, on the road to Holguín. **Cubana** (☎ 42-75-07; Martí No 52) flies to Bayamo from Havana twice a week (CUC$103 one way, two hours). There are no international flights to or from Bayamo.

BUS & TRUCK
The **provincial bus station** (cnr Carretera Central & Av Jesús Rabí) has **Víazul** (www.viazul.com) buses to several destinations.

GRANMA PROVINCE

VÍAZUL DEPARTURES

Destination	Cost (CUC$)	Duration	Departure
Havana	44	13hr 30min	11:10am, 5:25pm, 12:10am
Santiago de Cuba	6	2hr	5:55pm, 10:25pm, 4:35am, 9:50am, 10:25am
Trinidad	7	9hr	9:40pm
Varadero	41	12hr 30min	10:25pm

The service to Havana also stops at Holguín (CUC$6, two hours 10 minutes), Las Tunas (CUC$6, 2½ hours), Camagüey (CUC$11, 5½ hours), Ciego de Ávila (CUC$17, seven hours 20 minutes), Sancti Spíritus (CUC$21, 9½ hours) and Santa Clara (CUC$26, 10¾ hours).

Passenger trucks leave from an adjacent terminal for Santiago de Cuba, Holguín, Manzanillo and Pilón. You can get a truck to Bartolomé Masó, as close as you can get on public transport to the Sierra Maestra trailhead. Ask which line is waiting for the truck you want, then join. The trucks leave when full and you pay as you board.

The **intermunicipal bus station** (cnr Saco & Línea), opposite the train station, receives mostly local buses of little use to travelers. However, trucks to Las Tunas and Guisa leave from here.

State taxis can be procured for hard-to-reach destinations such as Manzanillo (CUC$30), Pilón (CUC$70) and Niquero (CUC$65). Prices are estimates and will depend on the current price of gas. Nonetheless, at the time of writing it was cheaper to reach all these places by taxi than by hired car.

TRAIN
The **train station** (☎ 42-49-55; cnr Saco & Línea) is 1km east of the center. There are three local trains a day to Manzanillo (via Yara). Other daily trains serve Santiago and Camagüey. The long-distance Havana–Manzanillo train passes through Bayamo every other day (CUC$28).

Getting Around
Cubataxi (☎ 42-43-13) can supply a taxi to Bayamo airport for CUC$3, or to Aeropuerto Frank País in Holguín for CUC$25. A taxi to Villa Santo Domingo (setting-off point for the Alto del Naranjo trailhead for Sierra Maestra hikes) or Comandancia La Plata will cost approximately CUC$35 one way. There's a taxi stand in the south of town near Museo Ñico López.

Havanautos (☎ 42-73-75) is adjacent to the Servi-Cupet, while **Cubacar** (☎ 42-79-70; Carretera Central) is at the Hotel Sierra Maestra.

The **Servi-Cupet gas station** (Carretera Central) is between Hotel Sierra Maestra and the bus terminal as you arrive from Santiago de Cuba.

The main horse-cart route (one peso) runs between the train station and the hospital,

via the bus station. Bici-taxis (a few pesos a ride) are also useful for getting around town. There's a stand near the train station.

AROUND BAYAMO
For a floral appreciation of Bayamo's evergreen hinterland, head to the **Jardín Botánico de Cupaynicu** (Carretera de Guisa Km 10; admission with/without guide CUC$2/1), about 16km outside the city off the Guisa road. It's on very few itineraries, so you can have the 104 hectares of the tranquil botanic gardens to yourself. There are 74 types of palms, scores of cacti, blooming orchids and sections for endangered and medicinal plants. The guided tour (Spanish only) gains you access to greenhouses, notable for the showy ornamentals.

To get here, take the road to Santiago de Cuba for 6km and turn left at the signposted junction for Guisa. After 10km you'll see the botanic gardens sign on the right. Trucks in this direction leave from the intermunicipal bus station in front of the train station.

DOS RÍOS & AROUND
At Dos Ríos, 52km northeast of Bayamo, almost in Holguín, a white obelisk overlooking the Río Cauto marks the spot where José Martí was shot and killed on May 19, 1895. In contrast to other Martí memorials, it's surprisingly simple and low-key. Go 22km northeast of Jiguaní on the road to San Germán and take the unmarked road to the right after crossing the Cauto.

Sleeping & Eating
Villa El Yarey (Cubanacán; ☎ 42-76-84; s/d CUC$31/46) Back toward Jiguaní, 23km southwest of Dos Ríos, is this relaxed, attractive hotel with 16 rooms on a ridge with an excellent view of the Sierra Maestra. This accommodation is perfect for those who want tranquility in verdant natural surroundings. Cubanacán organizes bird-watching trips here. Book through its office in Bayamo (p388).

To get to Villa El Yarey from Jiguaní, go 4km east of town on the Carretera Central and then 6km north on a side road. From Dos Ríos proceed southwest on the road toward Jiguaní and turn left 2km the other side of Las Palmas. It makes an ideal stop for anyone caught between Bayamo and Santiago de Cuba, or for those taking the backdoor Bayamo–Holguín route. Note that public transport here is scant.

YARA

pop 29,237

A small town with a big history, Yara – sandwiched halfway between Bayamo and Manzanillo amid vast fields of sugarcane – is barely mentioned in most travel literature. While ostensibly agricultural, the town's soul is defiantly Indian. The early Spanish colonizers earmarked it as one of their *pueblos Indios* (Indian towns) and a **statue** of rebel *cacique* (chief) Hatuey in the main square supports claims that the Spanish burned the dissenting Taíno chief here rather than in Baracoa. Chapter two of Yara's history began on October 11, 1868, when it became the first town to be wrested from Spanish control by rebel forces led by Carlos Manuel de Céspedes. A second **monument** in the main square recalls this important event and the famous *Grito de Yara* (Yara Declaration) that followed, in which Céspedes proclaimed Cuba's independence for the first time.

Just off the square, the **Museo Municipal** (Grito de Yara No 107; admission CUC$1; ☺ 8am-noon & 2-6pm Mon-Sat, 9am-noon Sun) chronicles Yara's historical legacy along with the town's role as a key supply center during the revolutionary war in the 1950s.

There's a Servi-Cupet here if you need a gas top-up. The Bayamo–Manzanillo train stops here three times a day.

GRAN PARQUE NACIONAL SIERRA MAESTRA

Comprising a sublime mountainscape of broccoli-green peaks and humid cloud forest, and home to honest, hardworking *campesinos* (country folk), the Gran Parque Nacional Sierra Maestra is an alluring natural sanctuary that still echoes with the gunshots of Castro's guerrilla campaign of the late 1950s. Situated 40km south of Yara, up a very steep 24km concrete road from Bartolomé Masó, this precipitous and untamed region contains the country's highest peak, Pico Turquino (just over the border in Santiago de Cuba province), unlimited birdlife and flora, and the rebels' one-time wartime headquarters, Comandancia La Plata.

History

History resonates throughout these mountains, the bulk of it linked indelibly to the guerrilla war that raged throughout this region between December 1956 and December 1958. For the first year of the conflict Fidel and his growing band of supporters remained on the move, never staying in one place for more than a few days. It was only in mid-1958 that the rebels established a permanent base on a ridge in the shadow of Pico Turquino. This headquarters became known as La Plata and it was from here that the combative Castro drafted many of the early revolutionary laws while he orchestrated the military strikes that finally brought about the ultimate demise of the Batista government.

Information

Aspiring visitors should check the current situation before arriving in the national park. Tropical storms and/or government bureaucracy have been known to put the place temporarily out of action. The best source of information is **Cubamar** (☎ 7-833-2523/4) in Havana, or you can go straight to the horse's mouth by directly contacting **Villa Santo Domingo** (☎ 56-53-02). These guys can put you in touch with the Centro de Información de Flora y Fauna next door (see p395). Additional information can be gleaned at the Cubanacán desk at the Hotel Royalton in Bayamo (see p390).

Sights & Activities

Santo Domingo is a tiny village that nestles in a deep green valley beside the gushing Río Yara. Communally it provides a wonderful slice of peaceful Cuban *campesino* life that has carried on pretty much unchanged since Fidel and Che prowled these shadowy mountains in the late 1950s. If you decide to stick around, you can get a taste of rural socialism at the local school and medical clinic, or ask at Villa Santo Domingo about the tiny village **museum**. The locals have also been known to offer horseback riding, pedicure treatments, hikes to natural swimming pools and some classic old first-hand tales from the annals of revolutionary history.

The park closes at 4pm but rangers won't let you pass after mid-morning, so set off early to maximize your visit.

All trips into the park begin at the end of the near-vertical, corrugated-concrete access road at **Alto del Naranjo** (after Villa Santo Domingo the road gains 750 vertical meters

TREKKING GRAN PARQUE NACIONAL SIERRA MAESTRA

in 5km). To get there, it's an arduous two-hour walk, or you can ask about passage in a bone-rattling Russian truck (formerly used by the military in Angola). There's a good view of the plains of Granma from this 950m-high lookout, otherwise it's just a launching pad for La Plata (3km) and Pico Turquino (13km).

Situated atop a crenellated mountain ridge amid thick cloud forest, **Comandancia La Plata** was first established by Fidel Castro in 1958 after a year on the run in the Sierra Maestra. Well camouflaged and remote, the rebel HQ was chosen for its inaccessibility and it served its purpose well – Batista's soldiers never found it. Today it remains much as it was left in the '50s, with 16 simple wooden buildings (including a small museum) providing an evocative reminder of one of the most successful guerrilla campaigns in history.

Comandancia La Plata is controlled by the Centro de Información de Flora y Fauna in the village of Santo Domingo. Aspiring guerrilla-watchers must first hire a guide at the park headquarters (CUC$11), get transport (or walk) 5km up to Alto del Naranjo, and then proceed on foot along a muddy track for the

final 3km. For further information, contact Villa Santo Domingo (p393) or Cubanacán in Bayamo (p388).

Sleeping & Eating

There are three accommodation options for park-bound visitors.

Campismo La Sierrita (Cubamar; ☎ 59-33-26; s/d CUC$9/14) Situated 8km south of Bartolomé Masó you start to feel the slanting shadow of the mountains here. The campismo (camping installation) is 1km off the main highway on a very rough road and boasts 27 cabins with bunks, baths and electricity. There's a restaurant, and a river for swimming. Ask at the desk about trips to the national park. To ensure it's open and has space, reserve in advance with **Cubamar** (☎ 7-833-2523/4) in Havana or at the **Campismo Popular** (☎ 42-42-00; General García No 112) office in Bayamo.

Motel Balcón de la Sierra (Islazul; ☎ 59-51-80; s/d CUC$22/28; P ☒ ☒) One kilometer south of Bartolomé Masó and 16km north of Santo Domingo, this attractively located place nestled in the mountain foothills is a little distant for easy access to the park. A swimming pool and restaurant lie perched on a small hill with killer mountain views, while 20 air-conditioned cabins are scattered below. A lovely natural ambience is juxtaposed with the usual basic but functional Islazul furnishings.

our pick **Villa Santo Domingo** (Islazul; ☎ 56-53-68; s/d with breakfast CUC$32/37; ❄) This villa, 24km south of Bartolomé Masó, sits at the gateway to Gran Parque Nacional Sierra Maestra. There are 20 separate cabins next to the Río Yara and the setting, among cascading mountains and *campesino* huts, is idyllic. From a geographical aspect, this is the best jumping-off point for the La Plata and Turquino hikes. You can also test your lungs going for a challenging early morning hike

up a painfully steep road to Alto del Naranjo (5km; 750m of ascent). Other attractions include horseback riding, river swimming and traditional music in the villa's restaurant. If you're lucky, you might even catch the wizened old Rebel Quintet, a group of musicians who serenaded the revolutionary army in the late 1950s. Fidel stayed here on various occasions (in hut 6) and Raúl Castro dropped by briefly in 2001 after scaling Pico Turquino at the ripe old age of 70.

Getting There & Around

There's no public transport from Bartolomé Masó to Alto del Naranjo. A taxi from Bayamo to Villa Santo Domingo should cost from CUC$30 to CUC$35 one-way. Ensure it can

---

PICO TURQUINO

Towering 1972m above the azure Caribbean, Pico Turquino – so named for the turquoise hue that colors its steep upper slopes – is Cuba's highest and most regularly climbed mountain.

Carpeted in lush cloud forest and protected in a 140-sq-km national park, the peak's lofty summit is embellished by a bronze bust of national hero José Martí, the work of Cuban sculptor Jilma Madera (Madera also fashioned the famous Christ statue that stands on the eastern side of Havana harbor; see p169). In a patriotic test of endurance, the statue was dragged to the top in 1953 by a young Celia Sánchez and her father, Manuel Sánchez Silveira, to mark the centennial of the apostle's birth.

Four years later, Sánchez visited the summit again, this time with a rifle-wielding Fidel Castro in tow to record an interview with American news network, CBS. Not long afterwards, the rebel army pitched their permanent headquarters in the mountain's imposing shadow, atop a tree-protected ridge near La Plata.

Best tackled as a through trek from the Santo Domingo side, the rugged, two- to three-day grind up Turquino starts from Alto del Naranjo near La Plata and ends at Las Cuevas on the Caribbean coast. Guides are mandatory and can be arranged through Flora y Fauna employees at Villa Santo Domingo or at the small hut at Las Cuevas. The cost varies, depending on how many days you take. If you organize it through Cubanacán in Bayamo (p388), bank on CUC$45/65/99 per person for two/three/four days. You'll also need to stock up on food, warm clothing, candles and some kind of sleeping roll or sheet. Even in August it gets cold at the shelters, so be prepared. Sufficient water is available along the trail.

The trail through the mountains from Alto del Naranjo passes the village of La Platica (water), Palma Mocha (campsite), Lima (campsite), Pico Joachín (shelter and water), El Cojo (shelter), Pico Joachín, Regino, Paso de los Monos, Loma Redonda, Pico Turquino (1972m), Pico Cuba (1872m; with a shelter and water at 1650m), Pico Cardero (1265m) and La Esmajagua (600m) before dropping down to Las Cuevas on the coast. The first two days are spent on the 13km section to Pico Turquino (overnighting at the Pico Joachín and/or Pico Cuba shelters), where a prearranged guide takes over and leads you down to Las Cuevas. As with all guide services, tips are in order. Prearranging the second leg from Pico Cuba to Las Cuevas is straightforward and handled by park staff.

These hikes are well coordinated and the guides efficient. The sanest way to begin is by spending the night at Villa Santo Domingo and setting out in the morning (you should enter the park gate by 10am). Transport from Las Cuevas along the coast is sparse with one scheduled truck on alternate days. Arrange a taxi in advance.

See p438 for a description of the Las Cuevas–Pico Turquino leg.

take you all the way; the last 7km before Villa Santo Domingo is extremely steep but passable in a normal car. Returning, the hotel should be able to arrange onward transport for you to Bartolomé Masó, Bayamo or Manzanillo.

A 4WD vehicle with good brakes is necessary to drive the last 5km from Santo Domingo to Alto del Naranjo; it's the steepest road in Cuba with 45% gradients near the top. Russian trucks pass regularly, usually for adventurous tour groups, and you may be able to find a space on board for approximately CUC$7 (ask at Villa Santo Domingo). Alternatively, it's a tough but rewarding 5km hike.

MANZANILLO

pop 110,952

Bayside Manzanillo might not be pretty but – like most low-key Granma towns – it has an infectious vibe. Sit for 10 minutes in the dilapidated central park with its old-fashioned street organs and distinctive neo-Moorish architecture and you'll quickly make a friend or three. With bare-bones transport links and only one grim state-run hotel, not many travelers make it out this far. As a result, Manzanillo is a good place to get off the standard guidebook trail and see how Cubans have learned to live with 50 years of rationing, austerity and school playground–style politics with their big neighbor in the north.

Founded in 1784 as a small fishing port, Manzanillo's early history was dominated by smugglers and pirates trading in contraband goods. The subterfuge continued into the late 1950s, when the city's proximity to the Sierra Maestra made it an important supply center for arms and men heading up to Castro's revolutionaries in their secret mountaintop headquarters.

Manzanillo is famous for its hand-operated street organs, which were first imported into Cuba from France by the local Fornaris and Borbolla families in the early 20th century (and are still widely in use). The city's musical legacy was solidified further in 1972 when it hosted a government-sponsored *nueva trova* festival that culminated in a solidarity march to Playa Las Coloradas (see p400).

Information

Banco de Crédito y Comercio (cnr Merchán & Saco; 8:30am-3:30pm Mon-Fri, 8am-noon Sat)

Cadeca (57-71-25; Martí No 188; 8:30am-6pm Mon-Sat, 8am-1pm Sun) Two blocks from the main square.

With few places accepting Convertibles here, you'll need some Cuban pesos.

Post office (cnr Martí & Codina) One block from Parque Céspedes.

Sights

IN TOWN

Although it may be a little dingy these days, Manzanillo is well known for its striking architecture, a psychedelic mélange of wooden beach shacks, Andalusian-style townhouses and intricate neo-Moorish facades. Check out the old **City Bank of NY building** (cnr Merchán & Doctor Codina), dating from 1913, or the ramshackle wooden abodes around Perucho Figueredo, between Merchán and JM Gómez.

Manzanillo's central square, **Parque Céspedes**, is notable for its priceless **glorieta** (gazebo/bandstand), where Moorish mosaics, a scalloped cupola and arabesque columns set off a theme that's replicated elsewhere. Completely restored a decade ago, the bandstand – an imitation of the Patio de los Leones in Spain's Alhambra – shines brightly amid the urban decay. Nearby, a permanent **statue of Carlos Puebla**, Manzanillo's famous homegrown troubadour, sits contemplatively on a bench admiring the surrounding cityscape.

On the eastern side of Parque Céspedes is the **Museo Histórico Municipal** (Martí No 226; admission free; 8am-noon & 2-6pm Tue-Fri, 8am-noon & 6-10pm Sat & Sun), giving the usual local history lesson with a revolutionary twist. There's an art gallery next door. The city's neoclassical **Iglesia de la Purísima Concepción** was initiated in 1805, but the twin bell towers were added in 1918. The church, named after Manzanillo's patron saint, is notable for its impressive gilded altarpiece.

About eight blocks southwest of the park lies Manzanillo's most evocative sight, the **Celia Sánchez Monument**. Built in 1990, this terra-cotta tiled staircase embellished with colorful ceramic murals runs up Calle Caridad between Martí and Luz Caballero. The birds and flowers on the reliefs represent Sánchez, lynchpin of the M-26-7 Movement and longtime aid to Castro, whose visage appears on the central mural near the top of the stairs. It's a moving memorial with excellent views out over the city and bay.

OUTSIDE TOWN

The **Museo Histórico La Demajagua** (admission CUC$1; 8am-6pm Mon-Fri, 8am-noon Sun) started with a

ASK A LOCAL

Manzanillo is a tranquil city. There are no *jineteros* (tourist touts) here. By contrast, the people are more like country folk. Although we don't get many tourists, those that do come are impressed by the *glorieta* (opposite). It's unique in the world. Once upon a time, there was a similar one in Spain, but it no longer exists.

Guillermo, Manzanillo

cry. Ten kilometers south of Manzanillo across the grassy expanses of western Granma lies La Demajagua, the site of the sugar estate of Carlos Manuel de Céspedes whose *Grito de Yara* and subsequent freeing of his slaves on October 10, 1868, marked the opening shot of Cuba's independence wars. There's a small museum here along with the remains of Céspedes' *ingenio* (sugar mill), a poignant monument (with a quote from Castro) and the famous Demajagua bell that Céspedes tolled to announce Cuba's (then unofficial) independence. In 1947, a then unknown Fidel Castro 'kidnapped' the bell and took it to Havana in a publicity stunt to protest against the corrupt Cuban government. To get to La Demajagua, travel south 10km from the Servi-Cupet gas station in Manzanillo, in the direction of Media Luna, and then another 2.5km off the main road, toward the sea.

Sleeping

Manzanillo – thank heavens – has a smattering of private rooms, as there's not much happening on the hotel scene.

CASAS PARTICULARES

our pick **Adrián & Tonia** (☎ 57-30-28; Mártires de Vietnam No 49; r CUC$20-25; ✺) This attractive casa, full of clever workmanship (double-glazed windows) and weeping plants, would stand out in any city, let alone Manzanillo. The position, on the terracotta staircase that leads to the Celia Sánchez monument, obviously helps. But youthful Adrián and Tonia have gone beyond the call of duty with a vista-laden terrace, Jacuzzi-sized cool-off pool and dinner provided in a paladar (privately owned restaurant) next door.

Villa Luisa (☎ 57-27-38; Rabena No 172 btwn Maceo & Masó; r CUC$20-25; P ✺) Two newly renovated rooms in a clean, open house with coco palms and a small pool in the garden.

HOTELS

Hotel Guacanayabo (Islazul; ☎ 57-40-12; Circunvalación Camilo Cienfuegos; s/d low season CUC$17/22, high season CUC$18/24; ✺ ⌨) The cheapest and most austere of Islazul's Cuban hotels, the Guacanayabo looks like a tropical reincarnation of a Gulag camp. The fake flamingos in the lobby fail to lighten the mood, although the affable staff tries its best. Rooms are badly lit, if relatively clean, and the restaurant's awaiting a visit from Gordon Ramsay's *Kitchen Nightmares*.

Eating & Drinking

Manzanillo is known for its fish, though strangely not a lot of the fresh seafood seems to find its way onto the plates in the restaurants. In common with many untouristed Cuban cities, the culinary scene here is grim. If in doubt, eat in your casa particular, or drop in on the weekend Sábado en la Calle (see below) where the locals cook up traditional whole roast pig.

Restaurante Licetera (☎ 57-52-42; Av Masó btwn Calles 9 & 10; ✺ noon-9:45pm) A decent indoor-outdoor place down near the seafront that specializes in local fish served with the head and bones on but still rather tasty. Prices are in *moneda nacional* (Cuban pesos).

Restaurante Yang Tsé (☎ 57-30-57; Merchán btwn Masó & Saco; ✺ 7am-10pm) *Comida China* is served for *moneda nacional* in this centrally located place with delusions of grandeur (there's a dress code!). It overlooks Parque Céspedes and gets good reports from locals.

Cafetería La Fuente (☎ 57-82-54; cnr Avs Jesús Menéndez & Masó; ✺ 8am-midnight) The Cubans are as stalwart about their ice cream as the British are about their cups of tea. Come what may, the scooper's always in the tub. Join the line here to sweeten up your views of surrounding Parque Céspedes.

Cafetería Piropo Kikiri (☎ 57-78-13; Martí btwn Maceo & Saco; ✺ 10am-10pm) This place has everything from ice-cream sandwiches to sundaes, available for Convertibles.

Dinos Pizza La Glorieta (☎ 57-34-57; Merchán No 221 btwn Maceo & Masó; ✺ 8am-midnight) This small Cuba pizza chain could come in handy here. Perched on the main square, it's run by the government restaurant group, Palmares, and accepts Convertibles.

Entertainment

As in most Cuban cities, Manzanillo's best 'gig' takes place on Saturday evenings in the famed Sábado en la Calle, a riot of piping organs, roasted pigs, throat-burning rum and, of course, dancing locals. Don't miss it!

Teatro Manzanillo (Villuendas btwn Maceo & Saco; admission 5 pesos; ☉ shows 8pm Fri-Sun) Touring companies such as the Ballet de Camagüey and Danza Contemporánea de Cuba perform at this lovingly restored venue. Built in 1856 and restored in 1926 and again in 2002, this 430-seat beauty is packed with oil paintings, red flocking and original detail.

Casa de la Trova (☎ 57-54-23; Merchán No 213; admission 1 peso) In the spiritual home of *nueva trova*, this is not the hallowed musical shrine it ought to be. In fact, it was being renovated at the time of writing.

Uneac (cnr Merchán & Concession) For traditional music you're better off heading for this more dependable option, which has Saturday and Sunday night *peñas* (musical performances) and painting expos.

Cabaret Salón Rojo (☎ 57-51-17; ☉ 8pm-midnight Tue-Sat, 8pm-1am Sun) This place on the north side of Parque Céspedes has an upstairs terrace overlooking the square, for drinks (pay in pesos) and dancing.

Cine Popular (Av 1 de Mayo; ☉ Tue-Sun) This is the town's top movie house.

Getting There & Away

AIR
Manzanillo's **Sierra Maestra Airport** (airport code MZO; ☎ 57-75-20) is on the road to Cayo Espino, 8km south of the Servi-Cupet gas station in Manzanillo. **Cubana** (☎ 57-49-84) has a nonstop flight from Havana once a week on Saturday (CUC$103, two hours). **Skyservice** (www.skyserviceairlines.com) flies directly from Toronto in winter and transfers people directly to Marea del Portillo.

A taxi between the airport and the center of town should cost approximately CUC$6.

BUS & TRUCK
The **bus station** (☎ 57-34-04) is northeast of the city center. There are no Víazul services to or from Manzanillo. This narrows your options down to local Cuban *guaguas* or trucks (no reliable schedules and long queues). Services run several times a day to Yara and Bayamo in the east and Pilón and Niquero in the south. For the latter destinations you can also board at the crossroads near the Servi-Cupet gas station and the hospital (which is also where you'll find the *amarillos*).

TRAIN TIMETABLE

Destination	Cost (CUC$)	Departure time
Bayamo	1.75	10:40am, 2:15pm, 7:40pm
Havana	28	7:20pm (alternate days)
Jiguaní	2.35	10:40am, 2:15pm
Santiago de Cuba	5.50	2:15pm

TRAIN
All services from the train station on the north side of town are via Yara and Bayamo. Trains go to several destinations but they are painfully slow.

Getting Around
Cubacar (☎ 57-77-36) has an office at the Hotel Guacanayabo (p397). There's a sturdy road running through Corralito up into Holguín, making this the quickest exit from Manzanillo toward points north and east.

Horse carts (one peso) to the bus station leave from Doctor Codina between Plácido and Luz Caballero. Horse carts along the Malecón to the shipyard leave from the bottom of Saco.

MEDIA LUNA
pop 15,493

One of a handful of small towns that punctuate the swaying sugar fields between Manzanillo and Cabo Cruz, Media Luna is worth a pit stop on the basis of its Celia Sánchez connections (see boxed text, opposite). The Revolution's 'first lady' was born here in 1920 in a small clapboard house that is now the **Celia Sánchez Museum** (Paúl Podio No 111; admission CUC$1; ☉ 9am-noon & 2-5pm Tue-Sat, 9am-1pm Sun).

If you have time, take a stroll around this quintessential Cuban sugar town dominated by a tall soot-stained mill and characteristic clapboard houses decorated with gingerbread embellishments. Aside from the Sánchez museum, Media Luna showcases a lovely **glorieta**, almost as outlandish as the one in Manzanillo. The main park is the place to get a take on the local street theater while supping on peso fruit shakes and quick-melting ice cream.

NIQUERO
pop 20,273

Niquero, a small fishing port and sugar town in the isolated southwest corner of Granma,

CELIA SÁNCHEZ – FLOWER OF THE REVOLUTION

Much is made of Castro's 1955 meeting with Che Guevara in Mexico City and its importance in the subsequent success of the Cuban Revolution. But it wasn't the only political game-changer. Less heralded, but equally epiphanic, was Fidel's introduction in February 1957 to a small, determined doctor's daughter from Media Luna, a woman who would ultimately go on to become his secretary, muse, confidante and sometime lover.

Celia Sánchez Manduley had been a revolutionary activist long before the ill-fated *Granma* ran aground off Playa Las Coloradas in 1956. In 1953 she and her left-leaning father had dragged a bust of José Martí to the summit of Pico Turquino, Cuba's highest mountain, and by the mid-'50s she was an active member of the M-26-7 Movement in Manzanillo. In November 1956 it was the stalwart Sánchez who camped patiently near Niquero in the Oriente with transport and supplies waiting for the stricken *Granma* to arrive. Undeterred by its delay, she returned to Manzanillo where she continued coordinating the dangerous underground resistance, providing the lifeline that ultimately ensured Fidel's survival and subsequent triumph over Batista.

In February 1957 Sánchez played an integral role in the organization and transport of American journalist Herbert Matthews up into the Sierra Maestra to interview Fidel. The next day, she came face to face with Castro for the first time at a revolutionary 'summit' at La Montería farm, a meeting that included Frank País (leader of the Santiago resistance), Moncada veteran Haydee Santamaría, and Vilma Espín (future wife of Raúl Castro).

Celia's skills and loyalty were quickly recognized by the savvy Castro and, by July 1957, she was living permanently in the Sierra Maestra where she helped form the revolutionary Mariana Grajales brigade, a rebel combat unit made up entirely of women. Utilizing her hard-won contacts in the Manzanillo underground, Sánchez worked hard coordinating supply drops and dispatching crucial messages to leaders in the *llano* (flatlands), often concealing tiny telegrams inside the petals of a mariposa, Cuba's national flower.

After the Revolution Sánchez was appointed secretary to the Council of State and Council of Ministers. But, far more important was her role as Fidel's primary confidante and unofficial adviser. Unfazed by his legendary pigheadedness, it was said that only Celia could tell Cuba's famously stubborn leader news he didn't want to hear – and she often did.

When Sánchez succumbed to cancer, aged 59, in January 1980, the whole nation mourned and a small piece of Fidel Castro (and Cuba) died with her.

Celia Sánchez' legacy is plastered all over her native Granma province. Check out the beautiful terra-cotta staircase in Manzanillo (p396), her quaint clapboard birth house in the sugar town of Media Luna (opposite), and the Casa Museo Celia Sánchez Manduley in the south-coast settlement of Pilón (p401).

is dominated by the local Roberto Ramírez Delgado sugar mill, built in 1905 and nationalized in 1960 (you'll smell it before you see it). Like many Granma settlements, it is characterized by its distinctive clapboard houses and has a lively *noche de Cubanilla*, when the streets are closed off and dining is at sidewalk tables. Live bands replete with organ grinders entertain the locals.

Ostensibly, there isn't much to do in Niquero, but you can explore the park, where there's a **cinema**, and visit the town's small **museum**. Look out for a **monument** commemorating the oft-forgotten victims of the *Granma* landing, who were hunted down and killed by Batista's troops in December 1956.

Niquero makes a good base from which to visit the Parque Nacional Desembarco del Granma (p400). There's a Servi-Cupet gas station in the center of town and another on the outskirts toward Cabo Cruz.

Sleeping & Eating

Hotel Niquero (Islazul; ☎ 59-24-98; Esquina Martí; s/d CUC$22/29; Ⓟ ⊠) Nestled in the middle of the small town, this low-key, out-on-a-limb hotel situated opposite the local sugar factory has dark, slightly tatty rooms with little balconies that overlook the street. The service here is variable, though the affordable on-site restaurant has been known to rustle up a reasonable beef steak with sauce. Better hunker

AND THEN THERE WERE THREE...

It seemed like an ignominious defeat. Three days after landing in a crippled leisure yacht on Cuba's southeastern coast, Castro's expeditionary force of 82 soldiers had been decimated by Batista's superior army. Some of the rebels had fled, others had been captured and killed. Escaping from the ambush, Castro found himself cowering in a sugarcane field along with two ragged companions; his 'bodyguard,' Universo Sánchez, and diminutive Havana doctor, Faustino Pérez. 'There was a moment when I was commander-in-chief of myself and two others,' said the man who would one day go on to overthrow the Cuban government, thwart a US-sponsored invasion, incite a nuclear standoff and become one of the most enduring political figures of the 20th century.

Hunted by ground troops and bombed from the air by military planes, the trio lay trapped in the cane field for four days and three nights. The hapless Pérez had inadvertently discarded his weapon; Sánchez, meanwhile, had lost his shoes. Wracked by fatigue and plagued by hunger, Fidel continued to do what he always did best. He whispered incessantly to his beleaguered colleagues – about the Revolution, about the philosophies of José Martí. Ebulliently he pontificated about how 'all the glory of the world would fit inside a grain of maize.' Sánchez, not unwisely, concluded that his delirious leader had gone crazy and that their grisly fate was sealed – it was just a matter of time.

At night, Fidel – determined not to be caught alive – slept with his rifle cocked against his throat, the safety catch released. One squeeze of the finger and it would have been over. No Cuban Revolution, no Bay of Pigs, no Cuban Missile Crisis, no Battle of Cuito Cuanavale.

Fatefully, the moment didn't arrive. With the army concluding that the rebels had been wiped out, the search was called off. Choosing their moment, Fidel and his two companions crept stealthily northeast toward the safety of the Sierra Maestra, sucking on stalks of sugarcane for nutrition.

It was a desperate fight for survival. For a further eight days the rebel army remained a bedraggled trio as the three fugitive soldiers dodged army patrols, crawled through sewers and drank their own urine. It wasn't until December 13 that they met up with Guillermo García, a *campesino* sympathetic to the rebel cause, and a corner was turned.

On December 15 at a safe meeting house Fidel's brother, Raúl, materialized out of the jungle with three men and four weapons. Castro was ecstatic. Three days later a third exhausted band of eight soldiers – including Che Guevara and Camilo Cienfuegos – turned up, swelling the rebel army to an abject 15.

'We can win this war,' proclaimed an ebullient Fidel to his small band of not-so-merry men, 'We have just begun the fight.'

down because it's the only accommodation in town.

PARQUE NACIONAL DESEMBARCO DEL GRANMA

Mixing unique environmental diversity with heavy historical significance, the **Parque Nacional Desembarco del Granma** (admission CUC$3) consists of 275 sq km of teeming forests, peculiar karst topography and uplifted marine terraces. It is also a spiritual shrine to the Cuban Revolution – the spot where Castro's stricken leisure yacht *Granma* limped ashore in December 1956 to be met with a barrage of gunfire from Batista's waiting army.

Named a Unesco World Heritage Site in 1999, the park protects some of the most pristine coastal cliffs in the Americas. Of the 512 plant species identified thus far, about 60%

are endemic and a dozen of them are found only here. The fauna is equally rich, with 25 species of mollusk, seven species of amphibian, 44 types of reptile, 110 bird species and 13 types of mammal.

In El Guafe, archaeologists have uncovered the second-most important community of ancient agriculturists and ceramic-makers discovered in Cuba. Approximately 1000 years old, the artifacts discovered include altars, carved stones and earthen vessels along with six idols guarding a water goddess inside a ceremonial cave. As far as archaeologists are concerned, it's probably just the tip of the iceberg.

Sights & Activities

The area is famous as the landing place of the yacht *Granma*, which brought Fidel and Revolution to Cuba in 1956 (see boxed text, opposite). A large monument and the **Museo Las Coloradas** (admission CUC$1; ☺ 8am-6pm Tue-Sat, 8am-noon Sun) just beyond the park gate marks the landing spot. The museum outlines the routes taken by Castro, Guevara and the others into the Sierra Maestra, and there's a full-scale replica of the *Granma*.

About eight kilometers southwest of Las Coloradas is the easy 3km-long **Sendero Arqueológico Natural El Guafe** (admission CUC$3), the park's only advertised nature/archaeological trail. An underground river here has created 20 large caverns, one of which contains the famous Ídolo del Agua, carved from stalagmites by pre-Columbian Indians. You should allow two hours for the stroll in order to take in the butterflies, 170 different species of birds (including the tiny *colibrí*), and multiple orchids. There's also a 500-year-old cactus. A park guard can guide you through the more interesting features for an extra CUC$2.

The park is flecked with other trails, but access to them is limited. Inquire about guided excursion with Cubamar in Havana (p108). Cuban students have recounted fascinating expeditions retracing the footsteps of the *Granma* survivors from Alegrío del Pío into the Sierra Maestra.

Three kilometers beyond the El Guafe trailhead is **Cabo Cruz**, a classic fishing port with skiffs bobbing offshore and sinewy men gutting their catch on the golden beach. There's not much to see here except the 33m-tall Vargas lighthouse, which was erected in 1871. An **exhibition room** labeled 'Historia del Faro,' inside the adjacent building, has lighthouse memorabilia and is open sporadically.

There's good swimming and shore snorkeling east of the lighthouse; watch out for strong currents.

Sleeping & Eating
Campismo Las Coloradas (Cubamar; Carretera de Niquero Km 17; s/d CUC$8/12; ⊠) A Category 3 campismo with 28 duplex cabins standing on 500m of murky beach, 5km southwest of Belic, just outside the park. All cabins have air-con and baths and there's a restaurant, a games hall and water-sport rental on-site. Las Coloradas underwent a lengthy reconstruction following damage inflicted by Hurricane Dennis in 2005. You can book through Cubamar (p108) in Havana.

Getting There & Away
Ten kilometers southwest of Media Luna the road divides, with Pilón 30km to the southeast and Niquero 10km to the southwest. Belic is 16km southwest of Niquero. It's another 6km from Belic to the national park entry gate.

If you don't have your own transport, getting here can be tough. Irregular buses go as far as the Campismo Las Coloradas daily and there are equally infrequent trucks from Belic. As a last resort, you can try the *amarillos* in Niquero (p398). The closest gas stations are in Niquero.

PILÓN
pop 11,904

Pilón is a small, isolated settlement wedged between the Marea del Portillo resorts and the Parque Nacional Desembarco del Granma. It is the last coastal town of any note before Chivirico over 150km to the east. Since its sugar mill shut down nearly a decade ago, Pilón has lost much of its raison d'être, though the people still eek out a living despite almost nonexistent transport links and a merciless bludgeoning from Hurricane Dennis in 2005.

Inspired by Fidel's revolutionary call, the town's inhabitants were quick to provide aid to the disparate rebel army after the *Granma* yacht landed nearby in 1956, and Castro muse Celia Sánchez briefly based herself here. The tiny **Casa Museo Celia Sánchez Manduley** (admission CUC$1; ☺ 9am-5pm Mon-Sat, 9am-1pm Sun) has been named in her honor – though it functions mainly as a local history museum.

There's a popular dance in Cuba called the *pilón* (named after the town), which imitates the rhythms of pounding sugar. Your best chance of seeing it is to attend a festive **Sábado de Rumba**, Pilón's weekly street party – similar to those in Manzanillo and Bayamo – with whole roast pig, shots of rum and plenty of live music. The hotels at Marea del Portillo run a weekly Saturday evening transfer bus to Pilón for CUC$5 return.

Sleeping & Eating
Villa Turística Punta Piedra (Cubanacán; ☎ 59-70-62; s/d CUC$26/45; P ⊠ ▣) On the main road 11km east of Pilón and 5km west of Marea del Portillo, this small low-key resort, comprising 13 rooms in two single-story blocks, makes an interesting alternative to the larger hotel complexes to the east. There's a restaurant

here and an intermittent disco located on a secluded saber of sandy beach. The staff, once they've recovered from the surprise of seeing you, will be mighty pleased with your custom.

Getting There & Around

Public transport in and out of Pilón is dire in both directions. The only regular bus is the Astro to Santiago de Cuba via Bayamo on alternate days – but this is no longer available to non-Cubans. Otherwise it's car, long-distance bike, or winging it with the *amarillos* (for tips, see boxed text, p368).

The Servi-Cupet gas station is by the highway at the entrance to Pilón and sells snacks and drinks. Drivers should be sure to fill up here; the next gas station is in Santiago de Cuba nearly 200km away.

MAREA DEL PORTILLO

There's something infectious about Marea del Portillo, a tiny south-coast village bordered by two low-key all-inclusive resorts. Wedged into a narrow strip of dry land between the glistening Caribbean and the cascading Sierra Maestra, it occupies a spot of great natural beauty – and great history.

The problem for independent travelers is getting here. There is no regular public transport, which means that you may, for the first time, have to go local and travel with the *amarillos*. Another issue for beach lovers

is the sand, which is of a light gray color and may disappoint those more attuned to the brilliant whites of Cayo Coco.

The resorts themselves are affordable and well maintained places but they are isolated; the nearest town of any size is lackluster Manzanillo 100km to the north. Real rustic Cuba, however, is a hop, skip and a jump outside the hotel gates.

Activities

There's plenty to do here, despite the area's apparent isolation. Both hotels operate horseback riding for CUC$5 per hour (usually to El Salto; see boxed text, below) or a horse-and-carriage sojourn along the deserted coast road for CUC$4. A jeep tour to Las Jaguas waterfall is CUC$49 and trips to Parque Nacional Desembarco del Granma start at about the same price. Trips can be booked at Cubanacán desks in either hotel.

The **Marlin Dive Center** (☎ 59-70-34), adjacent to Hotel Marea del Portillo, offers scuba diving for a giveaway CUC$25/49 per one/two immersions. A more exciting dive to the *Cristóbal Colón* wreck (sunk in the 1898 Spanish-Cuban-American War) costs CUC$70 for two immersions. Deep-sea fishing starts at CUC$200 for a boat (four anglers) plus crew and gear.

Other water excursions include a seafari (with snorkeling) for CUC$35, a sunset cruise for CUC$15 and a trip to uninhabited Cayo Blanco for CUC$25.

GO FURTHER INTO THE COUNTRYSIDE

If you want to escape – like the *Granma* survivors did – into the wild and wonderful Sierra Maestra with nary a guide, tour rep or *jinetero* (tout) to bother you, then try this 20km (out-and-back) DIY **hike** heading from Marea del Portillo into the undulating mountain foothills.

Starting at the hotel complex, load up on food, water and sun cream, and proceed on foot toward the coast road. Once there, turn right and then, after approximately 400m, hang left onto an unpaved track just before a bridge. The track winds through some fields, joins another wider road and then winds again through a dusty, scattered settlement. On the far side of the village a dam rises above you. Rather than take the paved road up the embankment to the left, branch right and, after 200m, pick up a clear path that rises steeply up above the dam and into view of the lake behind. This beautiful path tracks alongside the lake before crossing one of its river feeds on a wooden bridge. Go straight on and uphill here and, when the path forks on the crest, bear right. Heading down into a verdant tranquil valley, you'll soon arrive at a **casa de campesino** (the friendly owners keep bees and will give you honey, coffee, and a geographical reorientation for a small tip). The path continues on here to a river (cross it and continue on) and then another river; follow it this time upstream. You'll pass a second *campesino* house, and after a few more minutes heading upstream you'll reach **El Salto** (name inscribed on a rock), where there's a shady thatched shelter and an inviting swimming hole. Have a dip, enjoy a leisurely picnic and then head back by the same route.

Sleeping & Eating

our pick **Hotel Marea del Portillo** (Cubanacán; ☎ 59-70-08; s/d all-inclusive CUC$70/100; P ⊠ 🖳 🖳) It's not Cayo Coco, but it barely seems to matter here. In fact, Marea's all-round functionalism and lack of big-resort pretension seem to work well in this traditional corner of Cuba. The 74 rooms are perfectly adequate, the food buffet does a good job, and the dark sandy arc of beach set in the warm rain shadow of the Sierra Maestra is within baseball-pitching of your balcony/patio. Servicing older Canadians and some Cuban families means there is a mix of people here; plus plenty of interesting excursions to some of the island's lesser heralded sights.

Hotel Farallón del Caribe (Cubanacán; ☎ 59-70-09; s/d all-inclusive CUC$95/120; P ⊠ 🖳 🖳) Perched on a low hill with the Caribbean on one side and the Sierra Maestra on the other, the Farallón is Marea's bigger and richer sibling. Cozy and comfortable all-inclusive facilities are complemented by five-star surroundings and truly magical views across Granma's hilly hinterland. Exciting excursions can be organized at the Cubanacán desk here into the Parque Nacional Desembarco del Granma, or you can simply sit by the pool/beach and do absolutely nothing. The resort is popular with package-tour Canadians and is only open April through October.

Getting There & Away

The journey east to Santiago is one of Cuba's most spectacular, but also one of its most difficult (there aren't even any *amarillos* here). Public transport is sporadic to say the least and you'll undoubtedly have to undertake the trip in stages. The occasional Cuban buses do pass; ask around in Pilón or Marea. **Cubacar** (☎ 59-70-05) has a desk at Hotel Marea del Portillo.

Getting Around

The hotels rent out scooters for approximately CUC$24 a day. Cars are available from Cubacar, or you can join in an excursion with Cubanacán (see left). The route to El Salto can be covered on foot (see boxed text, opposite).

Santiago de Cuba Province

It all started here. Well…almost. Serving as the hinterland to Cuba's second-largest city, Santiago de Cuba province is a mountainous mix of jungle-covered peaks and ruined coffee haciendas where all roads lead to the provincial capital. While Cuba's first insurrection might have been sparked in Granma, this is where the revolutionary die was first cast, a hotbed of rebellion and sedition that produced warriors such as Antonio Maceo and Frank País, and patriotic poets such as José María de Heredia.

Traditionally, at least half of Santiago's cultural influences have come from the east, imported via Haiti, Jamaica, Barbados and Africa. For this reason the province is often cited as being Cuba's most 'Caribbean' enclave, with a carnival that is distinctly West Indian and a cache of *folklórico* dance groups that owe as much to French culture as they do to Spanish.

Indomitable in the early colonial era, Santiago de Cuba enjoyed a brief spell as Cuba's capital in the 16th century and it has retained a capital city's pride and presence. But, with a population of just under half a million and little in the way of heavy industry, the city has fallen way behind Havana in terms of economic importance.

Fortuitously, the slower pace of development has some distinct advantages. Drive 20km or so along the coast in either direction from Santiago de Cuba and you're on a different planet; a rugged chain of lonely coves and crashing surf that meets spectacularly in perfect aqueous harmony. Parque Baconao winks in the east, a mishmash of open-air museums and historical coffee plantations set against hills full of riotous endemism. Glowering to the west, you'll find Cuba's highest peak, the wreck of an old Spanish frigate and the splendid El Saltón eco-resort.

HIGHLIGHTS

- **African Folklore** Explore Cuba's numerous Afro-Cuban dance genres at a *folklórico* show in Santiago de Cuba (see boxed text, p426)
- **Spectacular Drive** Take the coast road west toward Chivirico (p437) amid rolling mountains and crashing surf
- **It's All in the Coffee** Get the lowdown on Cuba's French-inspired coffee culture at Cafetal La Isabelica (p431)
- **Fort Thoughts** Wonder at how Henry Morgan breached the ramparts at the Castillo de San Pedro de la Roca del Morro (see boxed text, p419)
- **Eco-tour** Shower beneath a waterfall at the eco-friendly Hotel Carrusel El Saltón (p436)

Hotel Carrusel El Saltón ★   Santiago de Cuba ★   Cafetal La Isabelica ★   Chivirico ★   Castillo de San Pedro de la Roca del Morro ★

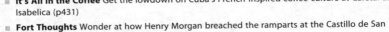

■ TELEPHONE CODE: 022	■ POPULATION: 1.04 MILLION	■ AREA: 6170 SQ KM

History

Illuminated by a rich cast of revolutionary heroes and characterized by a cultural legacy that has infiltrated everything from music and language to sculpture and art, the history of Santiago is inseparable from the history of Cuba itself.

Founded in 1514 by Diego Velázquez de Cuéllar (his bones purportedly lie underneath the cathedral), the city of Santiago de Cuba moved to its present site in 1522 on a sharp horseshoe of harbor in the lee of the Sierra Maestra. Its first mayor was Hernán Cortés – Velázquez' wayward secretary – who departed from the deep yet tranquil bay in 1518 en route to Mexico.

Installed as the colony's new capital, after the abandonment of Baracoa in 1515, Santiago enjoyed a brief renaissance as a center for the copper-mining industry and a disembarkation point for slaves arriving from West Africa via Hispaniola. But the glory wasn't to last.

In 1556 the Spanish captains-general departed for Havana and in 1607 the capital was transferred permanently to the west. Raided by pirates and reduced at one point to a small village of only several hundred people, embattled Santiago barely survived the ignominy.

The tide turned in 1655 when Spanish settlers arrived from the nearby colony of Jamaica, and this influx was augmented further in the 1790s as French plantation owners on the run from a slave revolt in Haiti settled down in the city's Tivolí district. Always one step ahead of the capital in the cultural sphere, Santiago founded the Seminario de San Basilio Magno as an educational establishment in 1722 (six years before the founding of the Universidad de La Habana) and in 1804 wrested ecclesiastical dominance from the capital by ensuring that the city's top cleric was promoted to the post of archbishop.

Individuality and isolation from Havana soon gave Santiago a noticeably distinct cultural heritage and went a long way in fueling its insatiable passion for rebellion and revolt. Much of the fighting in both Wars of Independence took place in the Oriente, and one of the era's most illustrious fighters, the great *mulato* general Antonio Maceo, was born in Santiago de Cuba in 1845.

In 1898, just as Cuba seemed about to triumph in its long struggle for independence, the US intervened in the Spanish-Cuban-American War, landing a flotilla of troops on nearby Daiquirí beach. Subsequently, decisive land and sea battles of both Wars of Independence were fought in and around Santiago. The first was played out on July 1 when a victorious cavalry charge led by Teddy Roosevelt on outlying Loma de San Juan (San Juan Hill) sealed a famous victory. The second ended in a highly one-sided naval battle in Santiago harbor between US and Spanish ships, which led to the almost total destruction of the Spanish fleet.

A construction boom characterized the first few years of the new, quasi-independent Cuban state, but after three successive US military interventions (the last of which, in 1917, saw US troops stationed in the Oriente until 1923), things started to turn sour. Despite its ongoing influence as a cultural and musical powerhouse, Santiago began to earn a slightly less respectable reputation as a center for rebellion and strife, and it was here on July 26, 1953, that Fidel Castro and his companions launched an assault on the Moncada Barracks (see boxed text, p416). This was the start of a number of events that changed the course of Cuban history. At his trial in Santiago, Castro made his famous *History Will Absolve Me* speech, which became the basic platform of the Cuban Revolution.

On November 30, 1956, the people of Santiago de Cuba rose up in rebellion against Batista's troops in a futile attempt to distract attention from the landing of Castro's guerrillas on the western shores of Oriente. Although not initially successful, an underground movement led by Frank and Josué País quickly established a secret supply line that ran vital armaments up to the fighters in the Oriente's Sierra Maestra. Despite the murder of the País brothers and many others in 1957–58, the struggle continued unabated, and it was in Santiago de Cuba, on the evening of January 1, 1959, that Castro first appeared publicly to declare the success of the Revolution. All these events have earned Santiago the title 'Hero City of the Republic of Cuba.'

Santiago continued to grow rapidly in the years that followed the Revolution, as new housing was provided for impoverished workers in outlying suburban districts. Further progress was made in the early 1990s when a construction boom gifted the city a new theater, a train station and a five-star Meliá hotel.

SANTIAGO DE CUBA PROVINCE

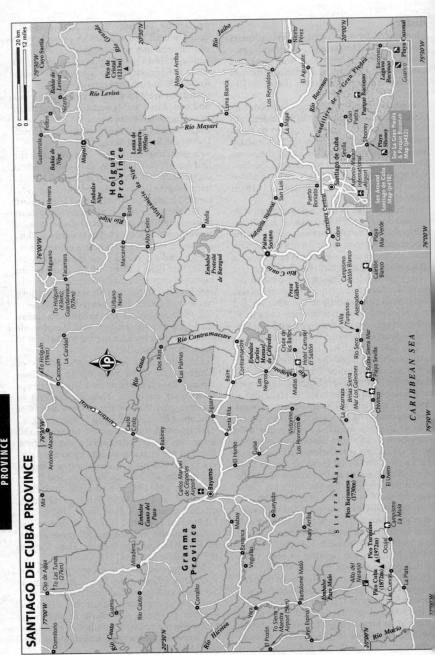

Parks & Reserves

Parque Baconao, east of the city of Santiago, is one of only two areas in Cuba (the other is Parque Nacional Alejandro de Humboldt) that has a double Unesco listing. It's a Unesco Biosphere Reserve and a part of it is also a Unesco World Heritage Site, known as the 'Archaeological Landscape of the First Coffee Plantations in the Southeast of Cuba.' In the west the area around Pico Turquino is part of the Gran Parque Nacional Sierra Maestra (the rest is in Granma province; see p393).

Getting There & Around

Getting to the provincial capital from outside the province is easy with regular Víazul and fast train links to Havana and all points in between. The rest of the province is frustratingly poorly served, especially along the coast. Links west from Santiago, particularly beyond Chivirico, are notoriously bad. Heading east into Parque Baconao you will be relying largely on rental cars, bikes or taxis.

SANTIAGO DE CUBA

pop 443,926

Santiago de Cuba is the island's second-largest city and a glittering cultural capital in its own right. Anyone with even a passing interest in Cuban literature, music, architecture, politics or ethnology should spend at least a day or two kicking through the myriad assorted attractions here.

Enlivened by a cosmopolitan mix of Afro-Caribbean culture and situated closer to Haiti and the Dominican Republic than to Havana, Santiago's influences tend to come as much from the east as from the west, a factor that has been crucial in shaping the city's distinct identity. Nowhere else in Cuba will you find such a colorful combination of people or such a resounding sense of historical destiny. Diego Velázquez de Cuéllar made the city his second capital, Fidel Castro used it to launch his embryonic nationalist Revolution, Don Facundo Bacardí based his first-ever rum factory here, and just about every Cuban music genre from salsa to *son* first emanated from somewhere in these dusty, rhythmic and sensuous streets.

Setting-wise Santiago could rival any of the world's great urban centers. Caught dramatically between the indomitable Sierra Maestra and the azure Caribbean, the city's *casco histórico* (historical center) retains a time-worn and slightly neglected air that's vaguely reminiscent of Barbados, Salvador in Brazil, or New Orleans.

Santiago is also hot, in more ways than one. While the temperature rises into the 30s out on the street, *jineteros* (touts) go about their business in the shadows with a level of ferocity unmatched elsewhere in Cuba. Then there's the pollution, particularly bad in the central district, where cacophonous motorcycles swarm up and down narrow streets better designed for horses or pedestrians. Travelers should beware. While never particularly unsafe, everything in Santiago feels a little madder, more frenetic, a tad more desperate, and visitors should be prepared to adjust their pace accordingly.

Orientation

The city's main attractions are in a narrow corridor running east from Parque Céspedes to Plaza de Dolores and Plaza de Marte along Calle José A Saco, the city's most important shopping street (which becomes a pedestrian mall and street fair on Saturday night). The old residential neighborhoods north and south of this strip also contain some interesting sights. Taken together, this is the city's *casco histórico*. The main monuments to the Revolution are along Av de los Libertadores.

The big hotels are in Vista Alegre, 3.5km east of the train station, 2km southeast of the National Bus Station and 1.5km southeast of the Intermunicipal Bus Station. Antonio Maceo International Airport is 7km to the south.

SANTIAGO DE CUBA STREET NAMES

Welcome to another city where the streets have two names:

Old name	New name
Calvario	Porfirio Valiente
Carniceria	Pío Rosado
Enramada	José A Saco
José Miguel Gómez	Havana
Paraíso	Plácido
Reloj	Mayía Rodríguez
Rey Pelayo	Joaquín Castillo Duany
San Félix	Hartmann
San Francisco	Sagarra
San Gerónimo	Sánchez Hechavarría
San Mateo	Sao del Indio
Santa Rita	Diego Palacios
Santo Tómas	Felix Peña
Trinidad	General Portuondo

SANTIAGO DE CUBA PROVINCE

SANTIAGO DE CUBA

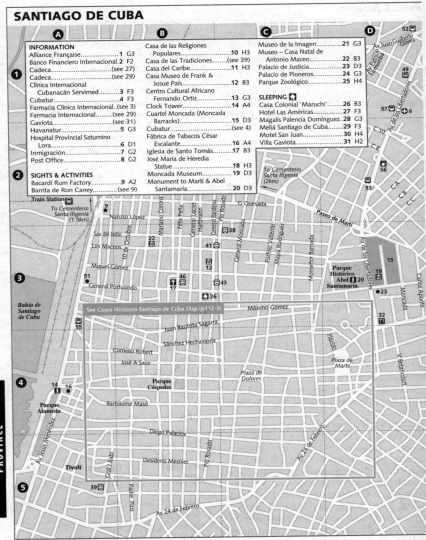

INFORMATION
Alliance Française...................1 G3
Banco Financiero Internacional.2 F2
Cadeca..............................(see 27)
Cadeca..............................(see 29)
Clinica Internacional
  Cubanacán Servimed...........3 F3
Cubatur.................................4 F3
Farmacia Clínica Internacional..(see 3)
Farmacia Internacional.........(see 29)
Gaviota.............................(see 31)
Havanatur.............................5 G3
Hospital Provincial Saturnino
  Lora...................................6 D1
Inmigración...........................7 G2
Post Office............................8 G2

SIGHTS & ACTIVITIES
Bacardi Rum Factory.................9 A2
Barrita de Ron Caney............(see 9)

Casa de las Religiones
  Populares..........................10 H3
Casa de las Tradiciones.........(see 39)
Casa del Caribe....................11 H3
Casa Museo de Frank &
  Josue País..........................12 B3
Centro Cultural Africano
  Fernando Ortiz...................13 G3
Clock Tower.........................14 A4
Cuartel Moncada (Moncada
  Barracks)..........................15 D3
Cubatur.............................(see 4)
Fábrica de Tabacos César
  Escalante..........................16 A4
Iglesia de Santo Tomás.........17 B3
José María de Heredia
  Statue...............................18 H3
Moncada Museum..................19 D3
Monument to Martí & Abel
  Santamaría........................20 D3

Museo de la Imagen..............21 G3
Museo – Casa Natal de
  Antonio Maceo...................22 B3
Palacio de Justicia.................23 D3
Palacio de Pioneros...............24 G3
Parque Zoológico..................25 H4

SLEEPING
Casa Colonial 'Maruchi'.........26 B3
Hotel Las Américas................27 F3
Magalis Palencia Domínguez..28 G3
Meliá Santiago de Cuba.........29 F3
Motel San Juan.....................30 H4
Villa Gaviota........................31 H2

Information
BOOKSTORES
Librería Internacional (Map p412; ☎ 68-71-47; Heredia btwn General Lacret & Félix Peña) On the southern side of Parque Céspedes. Decent selection of political titles in English; sells postcards and stamps.
Librería La Escalera (Map p412; Heredia No 265; ⏰ 10am-11pm) A veritable museum of old and rare

books stacked ceiling high. Sombrero-clad *trovadores* (traditional singers) often sit on the stairway and strum.
Librería Manolito del Toro (Map p412; Saco No 411; ⏰ 8am-4:30pm Mon-Fri, 8am-4pm Sat) Good for politica literature.
Librería Viet Nam (Map p412; Aguilera No 567; ⏰ 9am-5pm Mon-Fri) A top bookstore; it's also open on alternate Saturdays.

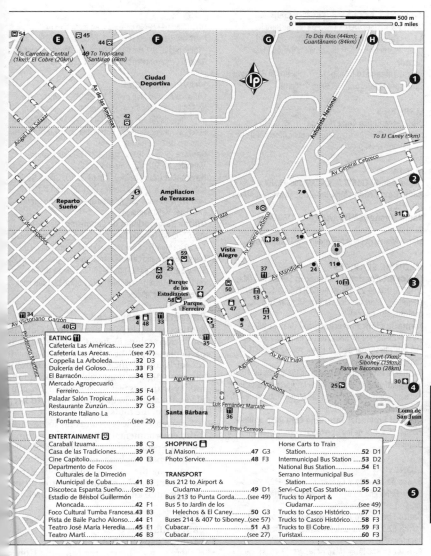

0	500 m
0	0.3 miles

To Dos Ríos (44km);
Guantánamo (84km)

To Carretera Central
(1km); El Cobre (20km)

To Tropicana
Santiago (6km)

Ciudad
Deportiva

To El Caney (5km)

Reparto
Sueño

Ampliación
de Terazzas

Vista
Alegre

Parque
de los
Estudiantes

Parque
Ferreiro

To Airport (7km);
Siboney (19km);
Parque Baconao (28km)

Av Victoriano Garzón

Santa Bárbara

Loma de
San Juan

EATING 🍴
Cafetería Las Américas..........(see 27)
Cafetería Las Arecas............(see 47)
Coppelia La Arboleda............**32** D3
Dulcería del Goloso..............**33** F3
El Barracón..........................**34** E3
Mercado Agropecuario
  Ferreiro............................**35** F4
Paladar Salón Tropical..........**36** G4
Restaurante Zunzún...............**37** G3
Ristorante Italiano La
  Fontana...........................(see 29)

ENTERTAINMENT 🎭
Carabalí Izuama.....................**38** C3
Casa de las Tradiciones..........**39** A5
Cine Capitolio.......................**40** E3
Departamento de Focos
  Culturales de la Dirreción
  Municipal de Cuba.............**41** B3
Discoteca Espanta Sueño.....(see 29)
Estadio de Béisbol Guillermón
  Moncada..........................**42** F1
Foco Cultural Tumba Francesa..**43** B3
Pista de Baile Pacho Alonso...**44** E1
Teatro José María Heredia......**45** E1
Teatro Martí..........................**46** B3

SHOPPING 🛍
La Maison............................**47** G3
Photo Service......................**48** F3

TRANSPORT
Bus 212 to Airport &
  Ciudamar.........................**49** D1
Bus 213 to Punta Gorda........(see 49)
Bus 5 to Jardín de los
  Helechos & El Caney..........**50** G3
Buses 214 & 407 to Siboney..(see 57)
Cubacar................................**51** A3
Cubacar...............................(see 27)

Horse Carts to Train
  Station.............................**52** D1
Intermunicipal Bus Station.....**53** D2
National Bus Station..............**54** E1
Serrano Intermunicipal Bus
  Station.............................**55** A3
Servi-Cupet Gas Station........**56** D2
Trucks to Airport &
  Ciudamar........................(see 49)
Trucks to Casco Histórico......**57** D1
Trucks to Casco Histórico......**58** F3
Trucks to El Cobre................**59** F3
Turistaxi..............................**60** F3

CULTURAL CENTERS

Alliance Française (Map pp408-9; ☎ 64-15-03; Calle 8 No 253, Vista Alegre; ⏰ 9am-7pm Mon-Fri, 9am-noon Sat) French cultural center with photo exhibitions and a French library. Free films are shown here weekly. Native French speakers are in short supply and are encouraged to pursue cross-cultural exchanges with the Alliance.

EMERGENCY

Asistur (Map p412; ☎ 68-61-28; www.asistur .cu; Heredia No 201) Situated under the Casa Granda Hotel, specializes in offering assistance to foreigners, mainly in the insurance and financial fields.

Police (Map p412; ☎ 116; cnr Corona & Sánchez Hechavarría)

INTERNET ACCESS & TELEPHONE

Etecsa Multiservicios (Map p412; cnr Heredia & Félix Peña; per hr CUC$6; ☒ 8:30am-7:30pm) Three internet terminals in a small office on Plaza Céspedes.

Etecsa Telepunto (Map p412; cnr Hartmann & Tamayo Fleites; per hr CUC$6; ☒ 8:30am-7:30pm)

LIBRARIES

Biblioteca Elvira Cape (Map p412; ☎ 62-46-69; Heredia No 258) The city's largest public library and one of the nation's most prestigious.

MEDIA

Radio Mambí CMKW At 1240AM and 93.7FM.
Radio Revolución CMKC Broadcasting over 840AM and 101.4FM.
Radio Siboney CMDV Available at 1180AM and 95.1FM.
Sierra Maestra Local paper published Saturday.

MEDICAL SERVICES

Clínica Internacional Cubanacán Servimed (Map pp408-9; ☎ 64-25-89; cnr Av Raúl Pujol & Calle 10, Vista Alegre; ☒ 24hr) Capable staff speak some English. A dentist is also present.

Farmacia Clínica Internacional (Map pp408-9; ☎ 64-25-89; cnr Av Raúl Pujol & Calle 10; ☒ 24hr) Best pharmacy in town, selling products in Convertibles.

Farmacia Internacional (Map pp408-9; ☎ 68-70-70; Meliá Santiago de Cuba, cnr Av de las Américas & Calle M; ☒ 8am-6pm) In the lobby of the Meliá Santiago de Cuba, it sells products in Convertibles.

Hospital Provincial Saturnino Lora (Map pp408-9; ☎ 64-56-51; Av de los Libertadores) With recompression chamber.

MONEY

Banco de Crédito y Comercio (Map p412; ☎ 62-80-06; Felix Peña No 614) Housed in the jarring modern building in Plaza Céspedes.

Banco Financiero Internacional (Map pp408-9; ☎ 68-62-52; cnr Av de las Américas & Calle I; ☒ 8am-4pm Mon-Fri)

Bandec General Lacret (Map p412; ☎ 62-75-81; cnr General Lacret & Aguilera; ☒ 8am-5pm Mon-Fri); Saco (Map p412; cnr Saco & Mariano Corona)

Cadeca Aguilera (Map p412; ☎ 65-13-83; Aguilera No 508; ☒ 8:30am-6pm Mon-Sat, 8:30am-noon Sun); Hotel Las Américas (Map pp408-9; cnr Avs de las Américas & General Cebreco); Meliá Santiago de Cuba (Map pp408-9; cnr Av de las Américas & Calle M)

POST

DHL (Map p412; ☎ 68-63-23; Aguilera No 310)
Post office Aguilera (Map p412; Aguilera No 519); Calle 9 (Map pp408-9; Calle 9, Ampliación de Terrazas) Near Av General Cebreco; telephones are here too.

TRAVEL AGENCIES

Cubatur Garzón (Map pp408-9; ☎ 65-25-60; Av Garzón No 364 btwn Calles 3 & 4; ☒ 8am-8pm); Heredia (Map p412; Heredia No 701 cnr General Lacret) Also has desks in Hotel Las Américas (p423), Hotel Libertad (p422) and Meliá Santiago de Cuba (p423).

Gaviota (Map pp408-9; ☎ 68-71-35; Villa Gaviota, Manduley No 502, Vista Alegre)

Havanatur (Map pp408-9; ☎ 64-36-03; Calle 8 No 54 btwn Calles 1 & 3, Vista Alegre; ☒ 8am-noon & 1-5pm Mon-Fri, 8am-noon Sat) Additional offices in the airport and Hotel Meliá Santiago.

Oficina Reservaciones de Campismo (Map p412; ☎ 62-90-00; Cornelio Robert No 163; ☒ 8:30am-noon & 1-4:30pm Mon-Fri, 8am-1pm Sat) For information on the Caletón Blanco and La Mula campismos, see p437 and p439.

Sol y Son (Map p412; ☎ 68-70-96; Heredia No 701 cnr General Lacret) Superinformative office that can book hotels and offer advice.

Dangers & Annoyances

Santiago is well known, even among Cubans, for its overzealous *jineteros*, all working their particular angle – be it cigars, paladares, *chicas* (girls) or unofficial 'tours.' Sometimes it can seem nigh on impossible to shake off the money-with-legs feeling, but a firm 'no' coupled with a little light humor ought to keep the worst of the touts at bay.

Santiago's traffic is second only to Havana's in its environmental fallout. Making things worse for pedestrians is the plethora of noisy motorcyclists bobbing and weaving for position along the city's sinuous 1950s streets. Narrow or nonexistent sidewalks throw further obstacles into an already hazardous brew.

Sights

CASCO HISTÓRICO

Parque Céspedes & Around

If there's an archetype for romantic Cuban street life, **Parque Céspedes** (Map p412) is it. A throbbing kaleidoscope of walking, talking, hustling, flirting, guitar-strumming humanity, this most ebullient of city squares is a sight to behold any time of day or night. Old ladies gossip sagely on shady park benches, a guy in a panama hat drags his dilapidated double-bass over toward the Casa de la Trova, while sultry *señoritas* in skin-tight lycra flutter their eye-lashes at the male tourists on the terrace of the Hotel Casa Granda. Meanwhile, standing statuesque in the middle of it all, is a bronze **bust of Carlos Manuel de Céspedes**, the man who started it all when he issued the *Grito de Yara* declaring Cuban independence in 1868.

Aside from a jarring modernist bank on its west side, Parque Céspedes is a treasure trove of colonial architecture. The **Casa de la Cultura Miguel Matamoros** (Map p412; General Lacret 651), on the square's eastern aspect, is the former San Carlos Club, a social center for wealthy Santiagüeros until the Revolution. Next door British novelist Graham Greene once sought literary inspiration in the Parisian terrace bar of the **Hotel Casa Granda** (1914). The neoclassical **Ayuntamiento** (Map p412; cnr General Lacret & Aguilera), on the northern side of the square, was erected in the 1950s using a design from 1783 and was once the site of Hernán Cortés' mayoral office. Fidel Castro appeared on the balcony of the present building on the night of January 2, 1959, trumpeting the Revolution's triumph.

In the park's northwestern corner lies the **Casa de Diego Velázquez** (Map p412; Felix Peña No 602). The oldest house still standing in Cuba, this early colonial abode dating from 1522 was the official residence of the island's first governor. Restored in the late 1960s, the Andalusian-style facade with fine, wooden lattice windows was inaugurated in 1970 as the **Museo de Ambiente Histórico Cubano** (Map p412; ☎ 65-26-52; with/without guide CUC$5/2; ☼ 9am-1pm & 2-4:45pm Mon-Thu, 2-4:45pm Fri, 9am-9pm Sat & Sun). The ground floor was originally a trading house and gold foundry, while the upstairs was where Velázquez lived. Today, rooms display period furnishings and decoration from the 16th to 19th centuries. Visitors are also taken through an adjacent 19th-century neoclassical house.

It might not be particularly old, but Santiago's most important church, the imposing, five-nave **Catedral de Nuestra Señora de la Asunción** (Map p412; ☼ Mass 6:30pm Mon & Wed-Fri, 5pm Sat, 9am & 6:30pm Sun) is stunning both inside and out. There has been a cathedral on this site since the city's inception in the 1520s, though a series of pirate raids, earthquakes and dodgy architects put paid to at least three previous incarnations. The present cathedral, characterized by its two neoclassical towers and open-winged trumpeting archangel, was completed in 1922 and it is believed that the remains of first colonial governor, Diego Velázquez, are still buried underneath. Meticulously restored, the cathedral's interior is a magnificent mélange of intricate ceiling frescoes, hand-carved choir stalls and an altar honoring the venerated Virgen de la Caridad. The adjacent **Museo Arquidiocesano** (Map p412; ☎ 62-21-43; ☼ 9am-5pm Mon-Fri, 9am-2pm Sat, 9am-noon Sun) is rather a disappointment by comparison, housing a dullish collection of furniture, liturgical objects and paintings including the *Ecce Homo*, believed to be Cuba's oldest painting. Behind the cathedral and two blocks downhill from the park is the airy **Balcón de Velázquez** (Map p412; cnr Bartolomé Masó & Mariano Corona), the site of an old Spanish fort which offers ethereal views over the terra-cotta-tiled roofs of the Tivolí neighborhood toward the harbor.

You can dig deeper into Santiago's ecclesiastical history in two more churches in the vicinity of Parque Céspedes. The **Iglesia de Nuestra Señora del Carmen** (Map p412; Félix Peña No 505) is a hall church dating from the 1700s that is the final resting place of Christmas-carol composer Esteban Salas (1725–1803), choir master of Santiago de Cuba's cathedral from 1764 until his death. The three-nave **Iglesia de San Francisco** (Map p412; Juan Bautista Sagarra No 121) is another understated 18th-century gem, situated two blocks to the north.

Calle Heredia & Around

The music never stops on Calle Heredia, Santiago's most sensuous street, and also one of its oldest. The melodies start in the paint-peeled **Casa del Estudiante** (Map p412; ☎ 62-78-04; Heredia No 204), where *danzón*-strutting pensioners mix with svelte rap artists barely out of their teens. One door up is Cuba's original **Casa de la Trova** (Map p412; ☎ 65-26-89; Heredia No 208), a beautiful balconied townhouse redolent of New Orleans' French quarter that is dedicated to pioneering Cuban *trovador*, José 'Pepe' Sánchez (1856–1928). It first opened as a *trova*

ASK A LOCAL

Santiago might have its *jineteros,* but don't let that put you off. This is a great city of music, culture, religion and history. And most Santiagüeros are educated, welcoming people who are only too keen to share their unique heritage with outside visitors.

Pepe, Santiago de Cuba

CASCO HISTÓRICO SANTIAGO DE CUBA

INFORMATION
Asistur...(see 42)
Banco de Crédito y Comercio................1 B2
Bandec..2 B2
Bandec..3 C2
Biblioteca Elvira Cape...........................4 C2
Cadeca...5 D2
Cubatur..6 C2
DHL..7 C2
Etecsa Multiservicios............................8 B2
Etecsa Telepunto....................................9 C1
Librería Internacional..........................10 C2
Librería La Escalera..............................11 C2
Librería Manolito del Toro...................12 D2
Librería Viet Nam.................................13 E2
Oficina Reservaciones de Campismo....14 B1
Police...15 B1
Post Office..16 E2
Sol y Son..(see 6)

SIGHTS & ACTIVITIES
Ateneo..17 B4
Ayuntamiento......................................18 C2
Balcón de Velázquez.............................19 B3
Casa de Diego Velázquez......................20 B2
Casa de la Cultura
    Cultura Miguel Matamoros............21 C2
Casa de la Trova................................(see 61)
Casa del Estudiante............................(see 62)
Casa Natal de José María de Heredia....22 C2
Catedral de Nuestra Señora de la
    Asunción...23 B2
Cubatur..(see 6)
Gobierno Provincial.............................24 C2
Hotel Casa Granda..............................(see 42)
House Where Castro Lived....................25 A3
Iglesia de Nuestra Señora de los
    Dolores..26 D2
Iglesia de Nuestra Señora
    del Carmen......................................27 B2

Iglesia de San Francisco.......................28 B1
Museo Arquidiocesano......................(see 23)
Museo de Ambiente Histórico
    Cubano..(see 20)
Museo de la Lucha Clandestina...........29 A3
Museo del Carnaval.............................30 C2
Museo del Ron....................................31 C3
Museo Municipal Emilio Bacardí
    Moreau..32 C2
Museo Tomás Romay...........................33 E2
Padre Pico Steps..................................34 A3
Unión Nacional de Escritores y
    Artistas de Cuba (Uneac)................35 C2

SLEEPING
Aida & Ali..36 D2
Arelis González...................................37 F2
Casa Nenita..38 D1
Casa Yisel..39 B3
Gran Hotel Escuela..............................40 C2
Hostal San Basilio................................41 C3
Hotel Casa Granda...............................42 C2
Hotel Libertad.....................................43 F2
Lourdes de la Caridad
    Gómez Beaton.................................44 B1
Raimundo Ocana &
    Bertha Pena....................................45 C2

EATING
Café de la Catedral..............................46 C3
Café La Isabelica..................................47 D2
Hotel Casa Granda...........................(see 42)
La Perla del Dragón..............................48 D2
La Teresina..49 D2
Municipal Market.................................50 A2
Paladar Las Gallegas............................51 C3
Pan.com..52 C2
Panadería Doña Neli............................53 F2
Santiago 1900......................................54 C3
Supermercado Plaza de Marte.............55 F1

DRINKING
Bar La Fontana di Trevi........................56 C2
Marylin...57 C2
Santiago 1900...................................(see 54)
Taberna de Dolores..............................58 D2

ENTERTAINMENT
Ballet Folklórico Cutumba....................59 E3
Casa de la Cultura Miguel
    Matamoros....................................(see 21)
Casa de la Música.................................60 B2
Casa de la Trova...................................61 C2
Casa del Estudiante..............................62 C2
Cine Cuba...63 C2
Cine Rialto..64 B3
Club El Iris..65 F2
Conjunto Folklórico de Oriente............66 C1
Coro Madrigalista.................................67 C2
Foco Cultural El Tivolí..........................68 A4
Gimnasio Cultura Física........................69 C1
Orfeón Santiago...................................70 B2
Patio ARTex......................................(see 74)
Patio Los Dos Abuelos..........................71 F2
Sala de Conciertos Dolores...............(see 26)

SHOPPING
ARTex...(see 42)
ARTex...(see 61)
Discoteca Egrem..................................72 C2
Galería de Arte de Oriente...................73 C2
Galería Santiago...............................(see 23)
Patio ARTex...74 D2
Photo Service......................................75 C3

TRANSPORT
AeroCaribbean.....................................76 C3
Bus No 212 to Airport & Ciudamar......77 B4
Bus No 5 to El Caney............................78 F1
Cubana...79 C2
Guarded Parking...............................(see 42)

(traditional poetic singing/songwriting) house in March 1968.

A block east, the **Casa Natal de José María de Heredia** (Map p412; Heredia No 260; with/without guide CUC$2/1; ⏰ 9am-6pm Tue-Sat, 9am-9pm Sun) contains a small museum illustrating the life of one of Cuba's greatest Romantic poets (1803–39) and the man after whom the street is named. Heredia's most notable work, *Ode to Niagara*, is inscribed on the wall outside, and attempts to parallel the beauty of Canada's Niagara Falls with his personal feelings of loss about his homeland. In common with many Cuban independence advocates, Heredia was forced into exile, dying in Mexico in 1839.

Next stop for art fiends is the **Unión Nacional de Escritores y Artistas de Cuba** (Uneac; Union of Cuban Writers & Artists; Map p412; Heredia No 266), where you can seek intellectual solace in talks, workshops, encounters and performances in a gorgeous colonial courtyard. The colorful **Museo del Carnaval** (Map p412; ☎ 62-69-55; Heredia No 303; admission CUC$1; ⏰ 9am-5pm Tue-Sun) displays the history of Santiago's carnival tradition, the oldest and biggest between Río and Mardi Gras. Drop in for the occasional *folklórico* dance show on the patio. While nowhere near as informative as its Havana equivalent (p112), the diminutive

Museo del Ron (Map p412; Bartolomé Masó 358; admission CUC$2; ⏰ 9am-5pm Mon-Sat) offers a rough outline of the history of Cuban rum along with a potent shot of the hard stuff (*añejo*). Encased in a handsome townhouse on Calle Masó, there's also less tourist tittle-tattle here.

Narrow Pío Rosado links Calle Heredia to Calle Aguilera and the fabulous Grecian facade of the **Museo Municipal Emilio Bacardí Moreau** (Map p412; ☎ 62-84-02; admission CUC$2; ⏰ 10am-6pm). Founded in 1899 by the rum magnate/war hero/city mayor, Emilio Bacardí y Moreau (the palatial building was built to spec), the museum is one of Cuba's oldest and most eclectic. Artifacts amassed from Bacardí's travels include an extensive weapons collection, paintings from the Spanish *costumbrismo* (19th-century artistic movement that predated Romanticism) school and the only Egyptian mummy on the island. Situated opposite, the equally Hellenic **Gobierno Provincial** (Poder Popular; Map p412; cnr Pío Rosado & Aguilera) is another building from Cuba's 20th-century neoclassical revival. It's still the seat of the provincial assembly.

Plaza de Dolores

East of Parque Céspedes is the pleasant and shady **Plaza de Dolores** (Map p412; cnr Aguilera

& Porfirio Valiente), a former marketplace now dominated by the 18th-century **Iglesia de Nuestra Señora de los Dolores** (Map p412). After a fire in the 1970s, the church was rebuilt as a concert hall (Sala de Conciertos Dolores; p427). Many restaurants and cafes flank this square. It's also Santiago's most popular gay cruising spot.

Plaza de Marte

Guarding the entrance to the *casco histórico*, the motorcycle-infested Plaza de Marte was formerly a macabre 19th-century Spanish parade ground, where prisoners were executed publicly by firing squad for revolutionary activities. Today, the plaza is the site of Santiago de Cuba's *esquina caliente* (hot corner), where local baseball fans plot the imminent downfall of Havana's glory-hunting Industriales. Among the flowering plants rises a tall column with a red cap perched on top, symbolizing liberty. A block west is the **Museo Tomás Romay** (Map p412; ☎ 65-35-39; cnr José A Saco & Monseñor Barnada; admission CUC$1; ⏱ 8:30am-5:30pm Tue-Fri, 9am-2pm Sat), a natural-science museum collecting natural history and archaeology artifacts, with some modern art thrown in.

SANTIAGO DE CUBA
Tivolí

Santiago's old French quarter was first settled by colonists from Haiti in the late 18th and early 19th centuries. Set on a south-facing hillside overlooking the shimmering harbor, its red-tiled roofs and hidden patios are a tranquil haven these days, with old men pushing around dominoes and ebullient kids playing stickball amid pink splashes of bougainvillea. The century-old **Padre Pico steps** (Map p412), cut into the steepest part of Calle Padre Pico, stand at the neighborhood's gateway.

Up the slope and to the right is a former police station attacked by M-26-7 activists on November 30, 1956, to divert attention from the arrival of the tardy yacht *Granma*, carrying Fidel Castro and 81 others. The gorgeous colonial-style building now houses the **Museo de la Lucha Clandestina** (Map p412; ☎ 62-46-89; admission CUC$1; General Jesús Rabí No 1; ⏱ 9am-5pm Tue-Sun), detailing the underground struggle against Batista in the 1950s. It's a fascinating, if macabre, story enhanced by far-reaching views from the balcony. Across the street is the **house** (Map p412; General Jesús Rabí No 6) where

Fidel Castro lived from 1931 to 1933, while a student in Santiago de Cuba (not open for visits).

Downhill from the Padre Pico steps, on General Jesús Rabí, is the legendary **Casa de las Tradiciones** (Map pp408-9; General Jesús Rabí No 154), known as 'La Casona' to locals. Once the savvy traveler's alternative to the Casa de la Trova, it's now pretty well known to all and sundry. There's some colorful art and a gritty bar but, to get a real taste, come back after dark. One block west, via José de Diego, the street opens out onto another superb Tivolí view over Bahía de Santiago de Cuba.

Rounding the next corner north of this viewpoint, Desiderio Mesnier descends to **Parque Alameda** (Map pp408-9), a dockside promenade that opened in 1840 and was redesigned in 1893. Opposite the old **clock tower** (Map pp408-9) and *aduana* (customs house) at the north end of Parque Alameda is the **Fábrica de Tabacos César Escalante** (Map pp408-9; ☎ 62-23-66; Av Jesús Menéndez No 703; admission CUC$5; ⏱ 9-11am & 1-3pm), a cigar factory sometimes open for visits. The factory shop sells the finished product.

North of Casco Histórico

North of the historic center, Santiago de Cuba turns residential. Tracking up Calle Felix Peña, you can orientate yourself by the baroque bell tower of **Iglesia de Santo Tomás** (Map pp408-9; Félix Peña No 308), one in a trio of notable, if dilapidated, 18th-century churches in this neighborhood.

Two long blocks northwest of the church is the important but little visited **Museo–Casa Natal de Antonio Maceo** (Map pp408-9; ☎ 62-37-50; Los Maceos No 207; admission CUC$1; ⏱ 9am-5pm Mon-Sat) where the *mulato* general and hero of both Wars of Independence was born on June 14, 1845. Known as the Bronze Titan in Cuba for his bravery in battle, Maceo was the definitive 'man of action' to Martí's 'man of ideas.' In his 1878 *Protest of Baraguá*, he rejected any compromise with the colonial authorities and went into exile rather than sell out to the Spanish. Landing at Playa Duaba in 1895, he marched his army as far west as Pinar del Río before being killed in action near Havana in 1896. This simple museum exhibits highlights of Maceo's life with photos, letters and a tattered flag that was flown in battle.

Another home-turned-museum is the **Casa Museo de Frank y Josué País** (Map pp408-9; General

BACARDÍ – RUM GOINGS-ON IN CUBA

Today the world-famous Bacardí brand retains its headquarters in the Bahamas and runs the largest rum factory in the world in San Juan, Puerto Rico. But, with brutal irony, the company's roots were sown more auspiciously several hundred kilometers to the west, in Cuba, a country with which Bacardí has been at loggerheads for the last 50 years.

Founded in 1862 in the city of Santiago de Cuba, the world's largest rum dynasty was the brainchild of Don Facundo Bacardí, an immigrant from Catalonia, Spain, who had arrived on the island in 1830 at the tender age of 16. Recognizing the unusual qualities of the sugarcane in Cuba's verdant east, Facundo began experimenting with distillation techniques using molasses until he was able to produce the world's first 'clear' rum, a liquid that was filtered through charcoal and subsequently aged in oak barrels.

The new refined drink quickly caught on among Cuba's burgeoning middle class and, in time, the wealthy Facundo was able to pass his profitable business down to his sons Emilio and Facundo Jnr.

Facundo Jnr gallantly steered the company through a difficult period of conflict during the Spanish-Cuban-American War, while the more feisty Emilio went on to become a well-known Cuban patriot who was exiled by Spanish authorities for his 'revolutionary activities.' Emilio returned to Cuba a hero in 1898 and was promptly named Santiago's first mayor by American general Leonard Wood. It was during this tempestuous new era that Bacardí concocted its two famous rum cocktails, the daiquirí (named after a Cuban beach) and the Cuba Libre (literally 'free Cuba'), both mixed with their signature clear rum.

After the repeal of the US prohibition laws in 1932, Bacardí began expanding its operation overseas, opening up a bottling plant in Mexico and establishing the Cataño distillery in Puerto Rico, a move that enabled them to combine cheap labor costs with direct entry into the American market. But, post-WWII, with the whiff of Revolution in the air, far more ominous changes loomed. Although the family initially supported Castro and his rugged band of Cuban patriots in the late 1950s (a banner on Bacardí's Havana HQ greeted the rebels with a cordial *Gracias Fidel!*), they quickly changed tack when the new Cuban leader began nationalizing businesses island-wide in 1960. Abandoning a 100-year tradition, the company was promptly relocated overseas, lock, stock and rum-filled barrel.

From self-imposed exile, the Bacardí clan has become a vociferous voice in the powerful anti-Castro movement in the US and gained rum-slinging notoriety for their alleged sponsorship of dubious far-right groups and other clandestine political operations.

In the early 1960s, the family purportedly attempted to sponsor a plot to bomb Cuban oil refineries and thus spark a countrywide insurrection, until their cover was blown by a front-page story in the *New York Times*. A couple of years later, Bacardí boss and one-time Fidel pal, José Pepin Bosch, is alleged to have bankrolled a CIA plot to assassinate the Castro brothers and Che Guevara using Mafia hit men.

Despite the ongoing political fisticuffs, Bacardí has remained the world's most popular rum, selling more than 240 million bottles annually in 170 countries. Ironically, one of the few countries where you still won't find any of its alcoholic beverages is Cuba.

Banderas No 226; admission CUC$1; ⏰ 9am-5pm Mon-Sat), about five blocks southeast. Integral to the success of the Revolution, the young País brothers organized the underground section of the M-26-7 in Santiago de Cuba until Frank's murder by the police on July 30, 1957. The exhibits tell the story.

While it's not as swanky as its modern Bahamas HQ, the original **Bacardí Rum Factory** (Fábrica de Ron; Map pp408-9; Av Jesús Menéndez), opened in 1868, oozes history. Spanish-born founder

Don Facundo dreamt up the world-famous Bacardí bat symbol after finding a colony of the winged mammals living in the factory's rafters. Although the family fled the island after the Revolution, the Cuban government has continued to make traditional rum here – the signature Ron Caney brand coupled with smaller amounts of Ron Santiago and Ron Varadero. In total, the factory knocks out nine million liters a year, 70% of which is exported. There are currently no factory tours, but the

Barrita de Ron Caney (Map pp408-9; 62-55-76; Av Jesús Menéndez No 703; ☻ 9am-6pm), a tourist bar attached to the factory, offers rum sales and tastings. A great billboard opposite the station announces Santiago's modern battle cry: *Rebelde ayer, hospitalaria hoy, heroica siempre* (Rebellious yesterday, hospitable today, heroic always).

Cuartel Moncada & Around

Santiago's famous **Cuartel Moncada** (Moncada Barracks; Map pp408–9) is named after Guillermón Moncada, a War of Independence fighter who was held prisoner here in 1874, though these days the name is more synonymous with one of history's greatest failed putsches.

MONCADA – 26/7

Glorious call to arms or poorly enacted putsch – the 1953 attack on Santiago's Moncada Barracks, while big on bravado, came to within a hair's breadth of destroying Castro's nascent revolutionary movement before the ink was even dry on the manifesto.

With his political ambitions decimated by Batista's 1952 coup, Castro – who had been due to represent the Orthodox Party in the canceled elections – quickly decided to pursue a more direct path to power by swapping the ballot box for a rifle.

Handpicking and training 116 men and two women from Havana and its environs, the combative Fidel, along with his trusty lieutenant, Abel Santamaría, began to put together a plan so secret that even his younger brother Raúl was initially kept in the dark.

The aim was to storm the Cuartel Moncada, a sprawling military barracks in Santiago in Cuba's seditious Oriente region with a shabby history as a Spanish prison. Rather than make an immediate grab for power, Castro's more savvy plan was to capture enough ammunition to escape up into the Sierra Maestra from where he and Santamaría planned to spearhead a wider popular uprising against Batista's malignant Mafia-backed government.

Castro chose Moncada because it was the second-biggest army barracks in the country, yet distant enough from Havana to ensure it was poorly defended. With equal sagacity, the date was set for July 26, the day after Santiago's annual carnival when both police and soldiers would be tired and hungover from the boisterous revelries.

But as the day of attack dawned, things quickly started to go wrong. The plan's underlying secrecy didn't help. Meeting in a quiet rural farmhouse near the village of Siboney, many recruits arrived with no idea that they were expected to fire guns at armed soldiers and they nervously baulked. Secondly, with all but one of the Moncadistas drawn from the Havana region (the only native Santiagüero was an 18-year-old local fixer named Renato Guitart), few were familiar with Santiago's complex street layout and, after setting out at 5am in convoy from the Siboney farm, at least two cars became temporarily lost.

The attack, when it finally began, lasted approximately 10 minutes from start to finish and was little short of a debacle. Splitting into three groups, a small contingent led by Raúl Castro took the adjacent Palacio de Justicia, another headed up by Abel Santamaría stormed a nearby military hospital, while the largest group led by Fidel attempted to enter the barracks itself.

Though the first two groups were initially successful, Fidel's convoy, poorly disguised in stolen military uniforms, was spotted by an outlying guard patrol and only one of the cars made it into the compound before the alarm was raised.

In the ensuing chaos, five rebels were killed in an exchange of gunfire before Castro, seeing the attack was futile, beat a disorganized retreat. Raúl's group also managed to escape, but the group in the hospital (including Abel Santamaría) were captured and later tortured and executed.

Fidel escaped briefly into the surrounding mountains and was captured a few days later; but, due to public revulsion surrounding the other brutal executions, his life was spared and the path of history radically altered.

Had it not been for the Revolution's ultimate success, this shambolic attempt at an insurrection would have gone down in history as a military nonevent. But viewed through the prism of the 1959 Revolution, it has been depicted as the first glorious shot on the road to power.

It also provided Fidel with the political pulpit he so badly needed. 'History will absolve me,' he trumpeted confidently at his subsequent trial. Within six years it effectively had.

The first barracks on this site was constructed by the Spanish in 1859, and in 1938 the present crenellated building was completed. Moncada earned immortality on the morning of July 26, 1953, when more than 100 revolutionaries led by then little known Fidel Castro stormed Batista's troops at what was then Cuba's second-most important military garrison (see boxed text, opposite).

After the Revolution, the barracks, like all others in Cuba, was converted into a school called Ciudad Escolar 26 de Julio, and in 1967 a **museum** (Map pp408–9; ☎ 62-01-57; admission CUC$2, guide/camera/video CUC$1/1/5; ⏰ 9am-5pm Mon-Sat, 9am-1pm Sun) was installed near gate 3, where the main attack took place. As Batista's soldiers had cemented over the original bullet holes from the attack, the Castro government remade them (this time without guns) years later as a poignant reminder. The museum contains a scale model of the barracks plus interesting and sometimes grisly artifacts of the attack, its planning and its aftermath. It's one of Cuba's best.

The **Parque Histórico Abel Santamaría** (Map pp408–9; cnr General Portuondo & Av de los Libertadores) is the site of the former Saturnino Lora Civil Hospital, stormed by Abel Santamaría and 60 others on that fateful July day. On October 16, 1953, Fidel Castro was tried in the Escuela de Enfermeras for leading the Moncada attack. It was here that he made his famous *History Will Absolve Me* speech. The park contains a giant cubist fountain engraved with the countenances of Abel Santamaría and José Martí that gushes out a veritable Niagara Falls of water.

The **Palacio de Justicia** (Map pp408–9; cnr Av de los Libertadores & General Portuondo), on the opposite side of the street, was taken by fighters led by Raúl Castro during the Moncada attack. They were supposed to provide cover fire to Fidel's group from the rooftop but were never needed. Many of them came back two months later to be tried and sentenced in the court.

Vista Alegre

In any other city, Vista Alegre would be a leafy upper-middle-class neighborhood; but in revolutionary Cuba the dappled avenues and whimsical early-20th-century architecture are the domain of clinics, cultural centers, government offices and state-run restaurants. With most of their former owners either underground or drawing their pensions in Miami,

the rough triangle of properties that fans out from Parque Ferreiro between Av Raúl Pujol and Av General Cebreco today hides a handful of esoteric points of interest. The **Centro Cultural Africano Fernando Ortiz** (Map pp408–9; Av Manduley No 106; admission free; ⏰ 9am-5pm Mon-Fri) contains African artifacts, handicrafts and fine art, collected by Cuba's most important ethnologist. It was being renovated at time of writing. A block away is the **Museo de la Imagen** (Map pp408–9; ☎ 64-22-34; Calle 8 No 106; admission CUC$1; ⏰ 9am-5pm Mon-Sat), a fascinating journey through the history of Cuban photography from Kodak to Korda, with little CIA spy cameras and lots of old and contemporary photos.

Nearby, there's a large eclectic palace now used as the **Palacio de Pioneros** (Map pp408–9; cnr Av Manduley & Calle 11). Parked in a corner patch of grass outside, you can spy an old MiG fighter plane on which the younger pioneers play. The traffic circle at the corner of Av Manduley and Calle 13 contains an impressive marble **statue** (Map pp408–9) of poet José María de Heredia.

Around the corner is the **Casa del Caribe** (Map pp408–9; ☎ 64-22-85; Calle 13 No 154; admission free; ⏰ 9am-5pm Mon-Fri), founded in 1982 to study Caribbean life. It organizes the Festival del Caribe and the Fiesta del Fuego every July, and also hosts various concert nights. Interested parties can organize percussion courses here or studies in Afro-Cuban culture (p421).

A block south is the affiliated **Casa de las Religiones Populares** (Map pp408–9; Calle 13 No 206; admission with/without guide CUC$2/1; ⏰ 9am-6pm Mon-Sat), with a large, if haphazard, collection of all things Santería.

Loma de San Juan

Future American president Teddy Roosevelt forged his reputation on Loma de San Juan where, flanked by the immortal rough-riders, he supposedly led a fearless cavalry charge against the Spanish to seal a famous US victory. In reality, it is doubtful that Roosevelt even mounted his horse in Santiago, while the purportedly clueless Spanish garrison – outnumbered 10 to one – managed to hold off more than 6000 American troops for 24 hours. Protected on pleasantly manicured grounds adjacent to the modern-day Motel San Juan, the **Loma de San Juan** (San Juan Hill; Map pp408–9; admission free) marks the spot of the Spanish-Cuban-American War's only land battle, which took place on July 1, 1898. Cannons, trenches and numerous US monuments, including a bronze figure of a Rough Rider, enhance the classy gardening, while the only acknowledgement of a Cuban presence is the rather understated monument to the unknown Mambí soldier.

Just west of the hill is Santiago's doleful **Parque Zoológico** (Map pp408-9; Av Raúl Pujol; admission CUC$1; 10am-5pm Tue-Sun), good only if you're hopelessly bored or have seriously hyperactive children.

Cementerio Santa Ifigenia

Nestled peacefully on the western edge of the city, the **Cementerio Santa Ifigenia** (Map p418; Av Crombet; admission CUC$1, camera CUC$1; 8am-6pm) is second only to Havana's Necrópolis Cristóbal Colón in its importance and grandiosity.

Created in 1868 to accommodate the victims of the War of Independence and a simultaneous yellow-fever outbreak, the Santa Ifigenia includes many great historical figures among its 8000-plus tombs. Names to look out for include Tomás Estrada Palma (1835–1908), Cuba's now disgraced first president; Emilio Bacardí y Moreau (1844–1922) of the famous rum dynasty; María Grajales, the widow of independence hero Antonio Maceo, and Mariana Grajales, Maceo's mother; 11 of the 31 generals of the independence struggles; the Spanish soldiers who died in the battles of San Juan Hill and Caney; the 'martyrs' of the 1953 Moncada Barracks attack; M-26-7 activists, Frank and Josue País; father of Cuban independence, Carlos Manuel de Céspedes (1819–74); and

AROUND SANTIAGO DE CUBA

0 — 4 km
0 — 2 miles

INFORMATION	
UniversiTUR	**1** B1

SIGHTS & ACTIVITIES	
Castillo de San Pedro de la Roca del Morro	**2** A4
Cementerio Santa Ifigenia	**3** A4
Iglesia de San Rafael	**4** B2
Jardín de los Helechos	**5** D2

SLEEPING	
Hotel Balcón del Caribe	**6** A4
Hotel Versalles	**7** B3

EATING	
Restaurante El Cayo	**8** A4
Restaurante El Morro	**9** A4

ENTERTAINMENT	
Tropicana Santiago	**10** C1

TRANSPORT	
Oro Negro Gas Station	**11** C1
Oro Negro Gas Station	**12** B2
Punta Gorda Ferry Route	**13** A4

SANTIAGO DE CUBA PROVINCE

BETWEEN A ROCK & A HARD PLACE

A Unesco World Heritage Site since 1997, the **Castillo de San Pedro de la Roca del Morro** (Map p418; ☎ 69-15-69; admission CUC$4, camera CUC$1; 🕑 9am-5pm Mon-Fri, 8am-4pm Sat & Sun) sits like an impregnable citadel atop a 60m-high promontory at the entrance to Santiago harbor, 10km southwest of the city. But, caught between a rock and a hard place, impregnable it wasn't!

The fort was designed in 1587 by famous Italian military engineer Giovanni Bautista Antonelli (who also designed La Punta and El Morro forts in Havana) to protect Santiago from pillaging pirates who had successfully sacked the city in 1554. Due to financial constraints, the building work didn't start until 1633 (17 years after Antonelli's death) and it carried on sporadically for the next 60 years. But, before it was even finished, El Morro had been overrun and partly destroyed by British privateer Henry Morgan, who rampaged through on his way to Santiago in 1664 where he mockingly set up court for two weeks. Further delays were caused by disruptive changes in architects and a series of damaging earthquakes in the 1680s.

Finally finished in the early 1700s, El Morro's massive batteries, bastions, magazines and walls got little opportunity to serve their true purpose. With the era of piracy in decline, the fort was converted into a prison in the 1800s and it stayed that way – bar a brief interlude during the 1898 Spanish-Cuban-American War – until Cuban architect Francisco Prat Puig mustered up a restoration plan in the late 1960s.

Revived and reinvigorated over the following two decades, El Morro was adopted by Unesco in 1997, who lauded it as the 'most complete and best-preserved example of Spanish-American military architecture based on Italian and Renaissance design principles.'

Today, the fort hosts the swashbuckling **Museo de Piratería**, with another room given over to the US-Spanish naval battle that took place in the bay in 1898. The stupendous views from the upper terrace take in the wild western ribbon of Santiago's coastline backed by the velvety Sierra Maestra.

To get to El Morro from the city center, you can take bus 212 to Ciudamar and cover the final 20 minutes on foot. Alternatively, a round-trip taxi ride from Parque Céspedes with wait should cost CUC$12 to CUC$15.

---

international celebrity-cum-popular-musical-rake, Compay Segundo (1907–2003), of Buena Vista Social Club fame.

The highlight of the cemetery, for most, is the quasi-religious mausoleum to national hero, José Martí (1853–95). Erected in 1951 during the Batista era, the imposing hexagonal structure is positioned so that Martí's wooden casket (draped solemnly in a Cuban flag) receives daily shafts of sunlight. This is in response to a comment Martí made in one of his poems that he would like to die not as a traitor in darkness, but with his visage facing the sun. A round-the-clock guard of the mausoleum is changed, amid much pomp and ceremony, every 30 minutes.

Horse carts go along Av Jesús Menéndez, from Parque Alameda to Cementerio Santa Ifigenia (one peso); otherwise it's a good leg-stretching walk.

AROUND SANTIAGO DE CUBA

Cayo Granma

A small, populated key near the jaws of the bay, **Cayo Granma** (formerly known as Cayo Smith; Map p418) is a little fantasy island of red-roofed wooden houses – many of them on stilts above the water – that guard a traditional fishing community. Come here to enjoy a slower, more hassle-free Santiago. You can hike the short route up to the small whitewashed **Iglesia de San Rafael** (Map p418), at the key's highest point, or circumvent the whole island in 15 minutes, but the best thing about this place is just hanging out, soaking up a bit of the real Cuba.

The only official eating establishment is the seafood-biased Restaurante El Cayo (p424), but local families often offer to cook up excellent fish dinners.

To get to the key, take the regular (leaving every 30 minutes or so) ferry from Punta Gorda just below El Morro castle.

Jardín de los Helechos

Two kilometers from downtown Santiago de Cuba on the road to El Caney, the peaceful **Jardín de los Helechos** (Map p418; ☎ 64-83-35; Carretera de El Caney No 129; admission CUC$1;

⊗ 9am-5pm Mon-Fri) is a lush haven of 350 types of ferns and 90 types of orchids that started life in 1976 as the private collection of Santiagüero Manuel Caluff. In 1984 Caluff donated his collection of 1000-plus plants to the Academia de Ciencias de Cuba (Cuban Academy of Science), which continues to keep the 3000-sq-meter garden in psychedelic bloom (the best time for orchids is November to January). The center of the garden has an inviting dense copsecum-sanctuary dotted with benches.

Bus 5 (20 centavos) from Plaza de Marte (Map p412) in central Santiago passes this way, or you can hire a taxi.

Walking Tour

With a song on your lips and a salsa in your step, a short walking tour of Santiago's *casco histórico* is an obligatory rite of passage for first-time visitors keen to uncover the steamy tropical sensations that make this city tick.

Start where the governor did, surveying the sweeping mountains and sparkling bay from the balmy **Balcón de Velázquez** (1; p411), site of an ancient fort. Head east next, avoiding the angry roar of the motorbikes that swarm like wasps in the streets around, until you resurface in **Parque Céspedes** (2; p410), Santiago's pulsating heart with its resident *jineteras* and craggy-faced old men in Panama hats who strum their way through old Carlos Puebla favorites with the exuberance of 18-year-olds. The **Casa de Diego Velázquez** (3; p411), with its Moorish fringes and intricate wooden arcades, is believed to be the oldest house still standing in Cuba and it contrasts impressively with the mighty, mustard facade of the **Catedral de Nuestra Señora de la Asunción** (4; p411) over to stage right. This building has been ransacked, burned, rocked by earthquakes and rebuilt, remodeled and restored and ransacked again. Statues of Christopher Columbus and Fray Bartolomé de las Casas flank the entrance in ironic juxtaposition. Supposing you're into religious art, the **Museo Arquidiocesano** (5; p411) – say that three times fast! – is somewhere out back.

If you're tired already, you can step out onto the lazy terrace bar at the **Hotel Casa Granda** (6; p423) on the southeastern corner of the park, for mojitos or Montecristo cigars, or both. Graham Greene came here in the 1950s on a clandestine mission to interview Fidel Castro. The interview never came off, but he managed instead to smuggle a suitcase of clothes up to the rebels in the mountains.

Follow the music as you exit past the paint-peeled **Casa del Estudiante** (7; p411) and onto the infamous **Casa de la Trova** (8; p411), where, come 10pm, everything starts to get a shade more *caliente* (hot) with people winking at you lewdly from the overcrowded upstairs balcony.

Heading upstream on Heredia, you'll pass street stalls, cigar peddlers, a guy dragging a double bass, and countless motorbikes. That yellowish house on the right with the poem emblazoned on the wall is **Casa Natal de José María de Heredia** (9; p413), birthplace of one of Cuba's greatest poets. You might find a living scribe in **Uneac** (10; p413), the famous national writers' union a few doors down, or plenty more dead legends offered up in print in funky **Librería La Escalera** (11; p408), a bookstore across the street. You can break loose at the

SANTIAGO DE CUBA PROVINCE

WALK FACTS

Start Balcón de Velázquez
Finish Museo Municipal Emilio Bacardí Moreau
Distance 800m
Duration Two hours

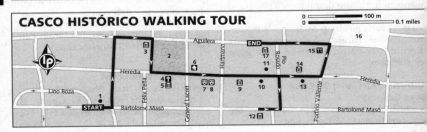

CASCO HISTÓRICO WALKING TOUR

corner of Pío Rosado and head to the south in search of the **Museo del Ron** (12; p413) until temptation gets the better of you and you drift off in the direction of Tivolí or Santa Barbara or Reparto Sueño. Stay on the safer path and you'll stumble upon **Patio ARTex** (13; p426), where boleros are de rigueur and tourists browse through the CDs. Cross the street next (mind that motorbike) and stick your nose into the **Museo del Carnaval** (14; p413), which aims to demonstrate how Santiago de Cuba lets loose when it lets its hair down (more than usual) every July in the best carnival between here and – oh – anywhere.

At the corner of Porfirio Valiente, turn right and see how far 20 centavos get you in the atmospherically austere **Café La Isabelica** (15; p425). It's amazing how tranquil **Plaza de Dolores** (16; p413) can be considering the ongoing motorcycle mania. Maybe it's something they put in the ice cream. Grab one and find out. There are benches to relax on underneath the trees while you weigh up if you've got enough energy to check out the **Museo Municipal Emilio Bacardí Moreau** (17; p413), Santiago's – as well as Cuba's – oldest functioning museum.

Courses

Opportunities for courses abound in Santiago; everything from architecture to music, either official or unofficial. You can sign up for something beforehand, or jump on the bandwagon when you arrive.

LANGUAGE

UniversiTUR (Map p418; ☎ 64-31-86; www.uo.edu.cu; Universidad de Oriente, cnr Calle L & Ampliación de Terrazas) arranges Spanish courses. Monthly rates for 60-hour courses (three hours a day, five days a week) start at CUC$250.

MUSIC & DANCE

Spanish courses, dancing classes and various other specialist activities can be organized at **Ateneo** (Map p412; Felix Peña No 755), a cultural organization set up in the late 19th century by lawyer Antonio Bravo Correoso. Bank on CUC$5 for two-hour lessons on salsa dancing, percussion or guitar/*tres* (a guitar with seven strings and an integral part of *son*). Another central option is the **Casa del Estudiante** (Map p412; ☎ 62-78-04; Heredia No 204), where you can organize singing, dancing or percussion lessons under the auspices of Carlos Bourbon of Ballet Folklórico

Cutumba fame. There are 11 or so teachers here and classes start at CUC$8 per hour.

The **Casa del Caribe** (Map pp408-9; ☎ 64-22-85; fax 64-23-87; Calle 13 No 154) organizes dance lessons in conga, *son* and salsa; it's CUC$10 for two hours or CUC$5 for one. Resident staff member Juan Eduardo Castillo can also organize lessons in percussion. Real aficionados can inquire about in-depth courses on Afro-Cuban religions and culture. These guys are experts and they're very flexible.

Another interesting option is an organization called **Cuban Rhythm** (www.cubanrhythm.com). Take a look at its excellent website and make arrangements beforehand.

Tours

Cubatur (Garzón Map pp408-9; ☎ 65-25-60; fax 68-61-06; Av Garzón No 364 btwn Calles 3 & 4; ☺ 8am-8pm; Heredia Map p412; ☎ 68-60-33; Heredia No 701) sells all number of excursions, for everything from La Gran Piedra (p430) to El Cobre (p435).

Alternatively, you can arrange your own tour to some of the out-of-town sights with one of the ubiquitous taxis that park in Parque Céspedes in front of the cathedral. Cubataxi cabs should charge approximately CUC$0.50 per kilometer for longer trips. Tot up your expected mileage, factor in some waiting time, and get ready to bargain.

Festivals & Events

Few cities can match the variety and vivacity of Santiago de Cuba's annual festivals. The summer season begins with the **Fiesta de San Juan** (June 24), celebrated with processions and conga dancing by cultural associations called *focos culturales*. Mid- to late June is the time for the **Boleros de Oro** extravaganza. It's followed by the **Festival del Caribe, Fiesta del Fuego** (Festival of Caribbean Culture, Fire Celebration) in early July with exhibitions, song and dance from all around the Caribbean. Santiago de Cuba's **Carnaval**, held in the last week of July, is the hottest in Cuba (and possibly the Caribbean), with open-air grandstands erected along Av Garzón. The **International Chorus Festival** is in late November and the **Festival Internacional de Trova** is in mid-March.

Sleeping
BUDGET
Casas Particulares
Magalis Palencia Domínguez (Map pp408-9; ☎ 64-10-87; Calle 4 No 204, Reparto Vista Alegre; r CUC$20) For

a break from the motorbike noise you may want to consider this tranquil place out in once posh Vista Alegre where Magalis' 1930s detached house rents out one room upstairs with en suite bath and rear-facing balcony.

Raimundo Ocana & Bertha Pena (Map p412; ☎ 62-40-97; Heredia No 308 btwn Pío Rosado & Porfirio Valiente; r CUC$20-25; 🗷) A classic 200-year-old house right in the thick of the action on Calle Heredia meaning you can literally shimmy out of your front door and be inside one of half a dozen legendary music houses within seconds.

Arelis González (Map p412; ☎ 65-29-88; Aguilera No 615; r CUC$20-25) This striking blue classical facade on Aguilera is just off Plaza de Marte. It's a noisy street, but the house has a nice ambience. There are two rooms and a three-level terrace, the top of which constitutes a towerlike *mirador* (lookout) that provides great views over the rooftops to the mountains beyond. The gnarly vines on level two are used to make grape juice.

Aida & Ali (Map p412; ☎ 62-27-47; Saco No 516 btwn Mayía Rodríguez & Donato Mármol; r CUC$20-25; 🗷) A thick-in-the-action house on Saco (Enramadas) with two rooms perched on a terrace high above the street. The one at the front is the spiffiest.

our pick **Casa Colonial 'Maruchi'** (Map pp408-9; ☎ 62-07-67; Hartmann No 357 btwn General Portuondo & Máximo Gómez; r CUC$25; 🗷) Maruchi is quintessential Santiago and is the best advert the city could give. For a start it's a hive of all things Santería. You'll meet all types here: sage *santeros* (priests of Santería), bemused backpackers, foreign students studying for PhDs on the Regla de Ocha. The food's legendary and the fecund courtyard equally sublime. So what if the two rooms share a bath?

Casa Yisel (Map p412; ☎ 62-05-22; Diego Palacios No 177 btwn Padre Pico & Mariano Corona; r CUC$20-25; 🅿 🗷) These young hosts run a surgically clean house three blocks from Céspedes and one from the Padre Pico steps. It's an apartment of sorts with a living room, bedroom and superbig bath. There's a little patio and they make great coffee. Guarded parking is nearby.

Casa Nenita (Map p412; ☎ 65-41-10; Sánchez Hechavarría No 472 btwn Pío Rosado & Porfirio Valiente; r CUC$20-25) Santiago throws up another *palacio* of colonial splendor that gives away little from its streetside appearance. Dating from 1850, Nenita's house has soaring ceilings,

original floor tiles and a truly amazing back patio. Sit back beneath the louvers and soak up the history.

Lourdes de la Caridad Gómez Beaton (Map p412; ☎ 65-44-68; Félix Peña No 454 btwn Sagarra & Sánchez Hechavarría; r CUC$20-25) Another colonial gem that has huge bedrooms with baths and typical Santiago features.

Hotels

Gran Hotel Escuela (Formatur; Map p412; ☎ 65-30-20; Saco No 310; s/d CUC$26/32; 🗷) Shoehorned like a 1950s relic into the retro-fest that is Calle Saco, this old four-story establishment has huge rough-edged rooms that fairly dwarf the single beds and wall-mounted small-screen TVs. Despite its bargain-basement apparel, the Gran is an Escuela hotel, meaning service is keen and welcomes are generally warm. And at these prices you're almost undercutting the casas particulares.

Hotel Libertad (Islazul; Map p412; ☎ 62-77-10; Aguilera No 658; s/d CUC$32/38; 🗷) Cheap Cuban hotel chain Islazul breaks out of its ugly Soviet-themed concrete block obsession and goes colonial in this venerable sky-blue beauty on Plaza de Marte. Eighteen clean (if sometimes windowless) high-ceiling rooms and a pleasant streetside restaurant are a bonus. The belting (until 1am) rooftop disco isn't.

MIDRANGE

Hotel Versalles (Cubanacán; Map p418; ☎ 68-70-70; Alturas de Versalles; s/d with breakfast CUC$45/65; 🅿 🗷 🗷) Not to be confused with the namesake rumba district of Matanzas, or the resplendent home of Louis XIV, this modest hotel is on the outskirts of town off the road to El Morro and the airport. It's one of Cubanacán's cheaper options but has a pool and comfortable, if dated, rooms with small terraces.

Villa Gaviota (Gaviota; Map pp408-9; ☎ 64-13-70; Av Manduley No 502 btwn Calles 19 & 21, Vista Alegre; s/d CUC$49/59; 🅿 🗷 🗷) Sitting pretty in an oasis of calm in Santiago's salubrious Vista Alegre district, Villa Gaviota has been upgraded from the tacky holiday camp of yore to embrace a sharper, edgier look. Features include a swimming pool, restaurant, three bars, billiards room and laundry. It's a good bet if you want to escape the motorcycle madness of the city center.

Hotel Balcón del Caribe (Islazul; Map p418; ☎ 69-10-11; Carretera del Morro Km 7.5; s/d with breakfast CUC$53/69; 🗷 🗷) The tremendous setting next to E

SANTIAGO DE CUBA PROVINCE

Morro castle is countered by all the usual Islazul foibles: flowery curtains, ancient bed mattresses and furnishings salvaged from a 1970s garage sale. But you'll feel better after a dip in the pool and an hour or two spent contemplating the stunning Caribbean view. Situated 10km from the city center you'll need your own wheels if you're staying here.

Hotel Las Américas (Islazul; Map pp408-9; ☎ 64-20-11; cnr Avs de las Américas & General Cebreco; s/d CUC$53/69; P ⊠ ⬛) Cheap and normally pretty cheerful, Las Américas sits opposite the Meliá but is a long way from it in price and quality. The 70 rooms offer the usual Islazul interiors though the general facilities – restaurant, 24-hour cafetería, small pool, nightly entertainment, and car rental are comprehensive for the price. The downside is the distance to the historical center (20 to 30 minutes on foot).

Motel San Juan (Islazul; Map pp408-9; ☎ 68-72-00; San Juan Hill; s/d CUC$53/69; P ⊠ ⬛) Surrounded by beautiful grounds on historic Loma de San Juan, with lots of lawn and a children's pool, this place is great if you don't mind some long walks (or taxi rides) into the city center. The rooms are laid out in small blocks and have good amenities with welcome little extras such as radios. Service is friendly. Drive 1km east of Hotel Las Américas via Av Raúl Pujol to get here.

our pick Hostal San Basilio (Cubanacán; Map p412; ☎ 65-17-02; Bartolomé Masó No 403 btwn Pío Rosado & Porfirio Valiente; r CUC$60; ⊠) At last, a boutique hotel that deserves it title. The lovely eight-room San Basilio (named for the original name of the street in which it lies) is one of only four of Cubanacán's so-called Encanto hotels. Think intimate, comfortable and refreshingly contemporary within a romantic colonial setting. Rooms have cable TVs and modern beds and the communal patio is a riot of dripping ferns. There's a small restaurant serving breakfast and lunch.

TOP END

Hotel Casa Granda (Gran Caribe; Map p412; ☎ 65-30-24; Heredia No 201; s/d CUC$78/112; ⊠) This elegant hotel (1914), artfully described by Graham Greene in his book *Our Man in Havana*, has 58 rooms and a classic red-and-white-striped front awning. Greene used to stay here in the late 1950s where he enjoyed relaxing on the streetside terrace, while his famous pen captured the nocturnal essence of the city as it wafted up from the bustling square below.

Half a century later and – aside from the Che Guevara posters and some seriously erratic service on reception – not much has changed. The hotel's 5th-floor Roof Garden Bar (open 11am to 1am) is well worth the CUC$2 minimum consumption charge and the upstairs terrace is an obligatory photo stop for foreign tourists on the lookout for bird's-eye city views. There's music here most nights and an occasional buffet on the roof. It's like *Fawlty Towers* without the laughs.

Meliá Santiago de Cuba (Cubanacán; Map pp408-9; ☎ 68-70-70; cnr Av de las Américas & Calle M; r CUC$115; P ⊠ ⬛ ⬛) A blue-mirrored monster (or marvel, depending on your taste) dreamt up by respected Cuban architect José A Choy in the early '90s, the Meliá is Santiago's only 'international' hotel. Raising its game for the business crowd, there are real bath tubs (in every room), three pools, four restaurants, various shopping facilities, a fancy bar on the 15th floor, and rooms for nonsmokers. The downsides are its out-of-center location and lack of genuine Cuban charm.

Eating

For a city of such fine cultural traditions, Santiago's restaurant scene is surprisingly lean. You'll find no hidden Havana-style experimentation here. Instead, the outlook is generally mediocre with the odd get-out-of-jail card.

PALADARES

Santiago's paladar scene is a bit of a damp squib. High taxes and draconian regulations have done their work and only a handful of old stalwarts remain.

Paladar Las Gallegas (Map p412; Bartolomé Masó No 305; meals CUC$8-10; ⏰ 1-11pm) Around the corner from the cathedral, this place has been here for donkey's years in Santiago-paladar terms, bashing out OK potions of pork, chicken and sometimes *carnero* (lamb). There are a couple of tables on a narrow balcony overlooking the street.

our pick Paladar Salón Tropical (Map pp408-9; ☎ 64-11-61; Fernández Marcané No 310, Reparto Santa Barbara; ⏰ 5pm-midnight Mon-Sat, noon-midnight Sun) The city's best paladar is a few blocks south of Hotel Las Américas on a pleasant rooftop terrace with fairy lights and decent views. The food is plentiful and tasty with a varying menu of succulent smoked pork, chicken and sometimes lamb, served with *congrí* (rice

SANTIAGO DE CUBA PROVINCE

flecked with black beans), salad and plantains (green bananas) and delicious *yuca con mojo* (starchy root vegetable with garlic lime sauce). Reservations are a good idea as this is a favorite spot for young Cuban women who come here with their 50-plus-year-old foreign sugar daddies.

RESTAURANTS

Santiago 1900 (Map p412; ☎ 62-35-07; Bartolomé Masó No 354; ☽ noon-midnight) In the former Bacardí residence you can dine on the standard chicken, fish or pork in a lush dining room replete with a slightly abandoned colonial air. The menu's in pesos, meaning few dishes should cost you more than the equivalent of CUC$2. There are also, not surprisingly, a couple of good bars here selling mojitos etc.

Pan.com (Map p412; Aguilera btwn General Lacret & Hartmann; snacks CUC$3; ☽ 11am-11pm) Havana's refreshingly efficient fast(ish)-food chain has just opened a small branch in Santiago, but the staff has yet to cotton onto the chain's slick service. Arrive with low expectations and see what's available on the ostensibly long menu.

Ristorante Italiano La Fontana (Map pp408-9; Meliá Santiago de Cuba, cnr Av de las Américas & Calle M; ☽ 11am-11pm) Pizza *deliciosa* (CUC$5 and up) and lasagna *formidable* (CUC$8), ravioli and garlic bread (CUC$1); *mamma mía*, this has to be the number-one option for breaking away from all that chicken and pork!

Cafetería Las Américas (Map pp408-9; ☎ 64-59-23; ☽ 24hr) A local hangout of sorts, on the traffic circle near Hotel Las Américas, this cafetería terrace does good basics: chicken, spaghetti and pork for under CUC$2. Inside is the affiliated restaurant with decent full meals of *comida criolla* (Creole food, usually rice, beans and pork) for CUC$5.

La Teresina (Map p412; ☎ 68-64-84; Aguilera btwn Porfirio Valiente & Mayía Rodríguez; ☽ 11am-11pm) One in a triumvirate of inviting-looking restaurants along the north side of Plaza de Dolores, La Teresina doesn't quite live up to its splendid colonial setting. But the terrace is shady, the beers affordable and the food – a familiar mix of spaghetti, pizza and chicken – plentiful enough to take the edge off a hungry appetite.

La Perla del Dragón (Map p412; ☎ 65-30-82; Aguilera btwn Porfirio Valiente & Mayía Rodríguez; ☽ 11am-11pm) Santiago's token Chinese restaurant doesn't quite match up to the diversity of Havana's

Barrio Chino, but it's a change from the standard chicken, pork, fish triumvirate and enjoys a pleasant setting on shady Plaza de Dolores.

Cafetería Las Arecas (Map pp408-9; Av Manduley No 52; dishes around CUC$3; ☽ 10am-1am) Nestled in the garden patio of La Maison, the mansion-turned-mod-shopping-center, this cafetería has an inexpensive menu with spaghetti, pizzas and chicken dishes. Fish filets start at CUC$5.50. The fancier dining-room restaurant in the rear part of the main building is open until 10pm.

Restaurante El Cayo (Map p418; lunch CUC$6-20) If the congenial fishermen on Cayo Granma don't corner you beforehand, this is the island's only state-run place, serving seafood for lunch.

our pick El Barracón (Map pp408-9; ☎ 64-32-42; Av Victoriano Garzón; ☽ noon-midnight) Spanking new, and already competing for the title of Santiago's finest food house, El Barracón opened its doors, amid much fanfare, in August 2008 to reignite the roots of Afro-Cuban culture and cuisine. Early portents are good. The restaurant's interior, a mix of atmospheric Santería shrine and *cimarrón* (runaway slave), is intriguing and the creative food is even better. Try the delicious *tostones* (fried plantain patties) filled with chorizo and cheese.

Restaurante Zunzún (Tocororo; Map pp408-9; ☎ 64-15-28; Av Manduley No 159; ☽ noon-10pm Mon-Sat, noon-3pm Sun) Dine in bygone bourgeois style in this urban mansion-turned-restaurant. Zunzún, in the once upscale Vista Alegre neighborhood, has always been one of Santiago's best restaurants when it comes to food and ambience. Exotic dishes include chicken curry, paella or a formidable cheese plate and cognac. Expect professional, attentive service and entertaining troubadours.

Restaurante El Morro (Map p418; ☎ 69-15-76; Castillo del Morro; ☽ noon-9pm) A gleaming, white plate mounted in a glass case on the wall announces that Paul McCartney once ate here during a whistle-stop 2000 visit (he flew in for four hours from the Turks and Caicos). According to the waiters, the world's most famous vegetarian made do with an omelette. For meat-eaters, the complete *comida criolla* lunch (CUC$12) is a better bet, a filling spread that includes soup, roast pork, a small dessert and one drink. The spectacular cliff-side location offers occasional views of breaching whales.

CAFES

Hotel Casa Granda (Map p412; Casa Granda, Heredia No 201; ☺ 9am-midnight) Positioned like a white-washed theater box overlooking the colorful cabaret of Parque Céspedes, the Casa Granda's Parisian-style terrace cafe has to be one of the best people-watching locations in Cuba. Food-wise, you're talking snacks (burgers, hot dogs, sandwiches etc) and service-wise you're talking impassive, verging on the grumpy; but with this setting, who cares?

Café de la Catedral (Map p412; General Lacret btwn Heredia & Bartolomé Masó; ☺ 8am-9pm) A frigidly air-conditioned new cafe sheltered beneath the cathedral that offers 24 different types of coffee – with a biscuit, if you're lucky. There are some coffee-farming artifacts scattered around the interior and a colorful *cafetal* (coffee farm) mural emblazoned on the wall.

Café La Isabelica (Map p412; cnr Aguilera & Porfirio Valiente; ☺ 9am-9pm) Stronger, smokier, darker cantina-type equivalent of Café de la Catedral, with the prices in pesos.

ICE-CREAM PARLORS

Coppelia La Arboleda (Map pp408-9; ☎ 62-04-35; cnr Avs de los Libertadores & Victoriano Garzón; ☺ 10am-11:40pm Tue-Sun) Santiago's ice-cream cathedral is a little out of the center, not that this lessens the queue-length. Yell out *¿Quién es último?* (who is last?) and take your place on the Av de los Libertadores side of the parlor. Milkshakes are sometimes sold from the outside window.

Dulcería del Goloso (Map pp408-9; cnr Av Victoriano Garzón & Calle 6) Got bored waiting in the queues at Coppelia? Head a few blocks along Victoriano Garzón, to this less-frenetic pit stop where you should be enjoying your *copa de helado* within minutes.

GROCERIES

Supermercado Plaza de Marte (Map p412; Av Garzón; ☺ 9am-6pm Mon-Sat, 9am-noon Sun) One of the better-stocked supermarkets in town, with a great ice-cream selection and cheap bottled water. It's in the northeastern corner of Plaza de Marte.

Panadería Doña Neli (Map p412; cnr Aguilera & Sánchez; ☺ 7:30am-8pm) Nice early morning aromas will send you in the direction off this hard-currency bakery on Plaza de Marte.

Municipal market (Map p412; cnr Aguilera & Padre Pico), the main market, two blocks west of Parque Céspedes, has a poor selection considering the size of the city. There's another option at

Mercado Agropecuario Ferreiro (Map pp408-9; Nuñez de Balboa) across the traffic circle from Hotel Las Américas and up the side street beside the gas station.

Drinking

Bar La Fontana di Trevi (Map p412; General Lacret; ☺ noon-2am) Could it be that the lounge trend has hit Santiago de Cuba? You might think so walking into this cocoon off José A Saco with low stools grouped around individual tables lining the wall. Just don't order any apple martinis; it's strictly peso beer and rum at this cool saloon.

Marylin (Map p412; ☎ 65-45-75; cnr General Lacret & Saco; ☺ 24hr) Standing room only at this rough-hewn counter on Saco where you can quickly fortify yourself with an eye-watering shot of Ron Caney before walking in a straight line up the street.

Taberna de Dolores (Map p412; ☎ 62-39-13; Aguilera No 468) Classic local place on Plaza de Dolores that serves light food but is much better for its beer and rum. The patio tables are the best.

Entertainment

For what's happening, look for the bi-weekly *Cartelera Cultural*. The reception desk at Hotel Casa Granda (p423) usually has copies. Every Saturday night Calle José A Saco becomes a happening place called Noche Santiagüera, where street food, music and crowds make an all-night outdoor party; beware of pickpockets.

FOLK & TRADITIONAL MUSIC

Calle Heredia is Santiago's Bourbon Street, a musical cacophony of stabbing trumpets, multilayered bongos and lilting guitars. For the more secretive corners, prowl the streets with your ears open and let the sounds lure you in.

Casa de la Trova (Map p412; ☎ 65-26-89; Heredia No 208; admission from CUC$2; ☺ 11am-3pm & 8:30-11pm Tue-Sun) Nearly 40 years after its initial incarnation, Santiago's shrine to the power of traditional music is still going strong and continuing to attract big names such as Buena Vista Social Club singer, Eliades Ochoa. Warming up on the ground floor in the late afternoon, the action slowly gravitates upstairs where, come 10-ish, everything starts to get a shade more *caliente*. Arrive with a good pair of shoes and prepare to be – quite literally – whisked off your feet.

FOLKLÓRICO DANCE GROUPS

Santiago de Cuba is home to more than a dozen *folklórico* dance groups, which exist to teach and perform traditional Afro-Cuban *bailes* (dances) and pass their traditions onto future generations. Most of the groups date from the early 1960s and all enjoy strong patronage from the Cuban government.

A good place to find out about upcoming *folklórico* events is at the **Departamento de Focos Culturales de la Dirección Municipal de Cuba** (Map pp408-9; ☎ 65-69-82; Los Maceos No 501 btwn General Bandera & Pío Rosada), which acts as a kind of HQ for the various *cabildos* (Afro-Cuban brotherhoods) and dance groups, most of which are bivouacked nearby. Another good nexus is the Casa del Caribe (p421) in Vista Alegre.

our pick **Ballet Folklórico Cutumba** (Map p412; ☎ 65-51-73; Teatro Galaxia, cnr Avs 24 de Febrero & Valeriano Hierrezuelo; admission CUC$2) This internationally known Afro-Cuban-Franco-Haitian *folklórico* dance group was founded in 1960 and currently appears at Teatro Galaxia (while its home base, the Teatro Oriente, is being renovated). You can pop in to see the group practice between 9am and 1pm Tuesday to Friday or attend an electrifying *café teatro* at 10pm every Saturday. The 55-strong troupe perform such dances as the *tumba francesa, columbia, gagá, guaguancó, yagüetó, tajona* and *conga oriental*. It's one of the finest programs of its kind in Cuba and has toured the world from New York to New Zealand.

Foco Cultural El Tívoli (Map p412; Desiderio Mesnier No 208; ☺ 8pm Mon-Fri) Carnaval practice for the Sarabanda Mayombe happens weekly at this Tívolí Foco (a show that takes place in Tívolí). Saturdays at 5pm it performs a *mágica religiosa* program of *orishas* (Afro-Cuban religious deities), *bembé* (Afro-Cuban drumming ritual) and *palo monte* (Bantu-derived Afro-Cuban religion) at the nearby Casa de las Tradiciones (below).

Also worth seeking out are the **Conjunto Folklórico de Oriente** (Map p412; Hartmann No 407), the **Carabalí Izuama** (Map pp408-9; Pío Rosado No 107) and the **Foco Cultural Tumba Francesa** (Map pp408-9; Pío Rosado No 268), a colorful group of French-Haitian drumming masters who can be seen in their rehearsal rooms on Tuesdays and Thursdays at 8pm.

Casa del Estudiante (Map p412; ☎ 62-78-04; Heredia No 204; admission CUC$1; ☺ 9pm Wed, Fri & Sat, 1pm Sun) Grab a seat (or stand in the street) and settle down for whatever this spontaneous place can throw at you. Orchestral *danzón*, folkloric rumba, lovelorn *trovadores* or rhythmic *reggaetón* (Cuban hip-hop): you never know what you're going to get. See also Courses, p421.

Patio ARTex (Map p412; ☎ 65-48-14; Heredia No 304; admission free; ☺ 11am-11pm) Art lines the walls of this shop-and-club combo that hosts live music both day and night in a quaint inner courtyard; a good bet if the Casa de la Trova is full, or too frenetic.

Patio Los Dos Abuelos (Map p412; ☎ 62-33-02; Francisco Pérez Carbo No 5; admission CUC$2; ☺ 10pm-1am Mon-Sat) The old-timers label (*abuelos* means grandparents) carries a certain amount of truth. This relaxed live-music house is a bastion for traditional *son* sung the old-fashioned way. The musicians are seasoned pros and most of the patrons are perfect ladies and gentlemen.

Casa de la Cultura Miguel Matamoros (Map p412; ☎ 62-57-10; General Lacret btwn Aguilera & Heredia; admission CUC$1) This cultural stalwart in historic digs on Parque Céspedes hosts many crowded musical events, including rumba and *son;* check the *cartelera* (calendar) posted at the door. It also presents some good art expos.

our pick **Casa de las Tradiciones** (Map pp408-9; Rab... No 154; admission CUC$1; ☺ from 8:30pm) The mos... discovered 'undiscovered' spot in Santiago... still retains its smoke-filled, foot-stomping front-room feel. Hidden in the gentle Tívol... district, some of Santiago de Cuba's most ex... citing ensembles, singers and soloists tak... turns improvising. Friday nights are reserve... for straight-up, classic *trova*, à la Ñico Saquit... and the like.

Casa de la Música (Map p412; Corona No 564; admis... sion CUC$5; ☺ 10pm-4am) Similar to the venues i... Havana, this Casa de la Música features a mi... of live salsa and taped disco and is usually... cracking night out.

DANCE CLUBS

Club El Iris (Map p412; ☎ 65-35-00; Aguilera No 617; admi... sion CUC$3; ☺ 10pm-2am) Just off Plaza de Mart... with an old-fashioned neon sign (which rarel... works), the Iris is Santiago de Cuba's loud...

est, hottest and most 'happening' disco. The cover includes one drink, but at night it's couples only. Things generally get moving around midnight.

Discoteca Espanta Sueño (Map pp408-9; cnr Av de las Américas & Calle M; ☑ 10:30pm-3am Fri-Sun) This is the Meliá Santiago de Cuba's house disco; entry is through the hotel lobby, ostensibly to keep out *jineteras*, though they're more relaxed these days.

Pista de Baile Pacho Alonso (Map pp408-9; admission CUC$5; ☑ 8:30pm Sat, 5pm Sun) Check out the *charanga* (brass band) orchestra playing alfresco at this place behind Teatro José María Heredia.

CABARET

Tropicana Santiago (Map p418; ☎ 68-70-90; door prices from CUC$35; ☑ 10pm Wed-Sun) Anything Havana can do, Santiago can do better – or at least cheaper. Styled on the Tropicana original, this 'feathers and baubles' Las Vegas–style floor show is heavily hyped by all the city's tour agencies who offer it for CUC$35 plus transport (Havana's show is twice the price, but no way twice as good). Located out of town, 3km north of the Hotel Las Américas, a taxi or rental car is the only independent transport option, making the tour-agency deals a good bet. The Saturday night show is superior.

THEATER

Teatro José María Heredia (Map pp408-9; ☎ 64-31-90; cnr Avs de las Américas & de los Desfiles; ☑ box office 9am-noon & 1-4:30pm) Santiago's huge, modern theater and convention center went up during the city refurbishment in the early 1990s. Rock and folk concerts often take place in the 2459-seat Sala Principal, while the 120-seat Café Cantante Niagara hosts more esoteric events. Ask about performances by the Compañía Teatro Danza del Caribe.

Teatro Martí (Map pp408-9; ☎ 2-0507; Félix Peña No 313) Children's shows are staged at 5pm on Saturday and Sunday at this theater near General Portuondo, opposite the Iglesia de Santo Tomás.

CLASSICAL MUSIC

Sala de Conciertos Dolores (Map p412; ☎ 65-38-57; cnr Aguilera & Mayía Rodríguez; ☑ 8:30pm) Housed in a former church on Plaza de Dolores, you can catch the Sinfónica del Oriente here, plus the impressive children's choir (at 5pm). The *cartelera* is posted outside.

Orfeón Santiago (Map p412; Heredia No 68) This classical choir sometimes allows visitors to attend its practice sessions from 9am to 11:30am Monday to Friday.

Coro Madrigalista (Map p412; Pio Rosado No 555) This choir, across from the Museo Bacardí, is similar to Orfeón Santiago.

CINEMAS

Cine Rialto (Map p412; ☎ 62-30-35; Félix Peña No 654) This cinema, next to the cathedral, is one of Santiago de Cuba's favorites, showing large-screen films and video.

Cine Capitolio (Map pp408-9; ☎ 62-71-64; Av Victoriano Garzón No 256) Videos are also the usual fare here.

Cine Cuba (Map p412; cnr Saco & General Lacret) Recipient of a recent refurbishment, this place is the best in town with an inviting lobby, decent array of movies and plenty of crowds.

SPORT

Estadio de Béisbol Guillermón Moncada (Map pp408-9; ☎ 64-26-40; Av de las Américas) This stadium is on the northeastern side of town within walking distance of the main hotels. During the baseball season, from October to April, there are games at 7:30pm Tuesday, Wednesday, Thursday and Saturday, and 1:30pm Sunday (one peso). The Avispas (Wasps) have had the edge on Havana's Industriales of late with National Series victories in 2005, 2007 and 2008.

Gimnasio Cultura Física (Map p412; Pio Rosado No 455 btwn Saco & Hechavarría; ☑ 6am-6:45pm Mon-Fri, 8am-4pm Sat, 8am-noon Sun) No manicures here! For a wicked workout drop into this gym with its well-pummeled punching bags, rusty old weights and cold showers.

Shopping

Discoteca Egrem (Map p412; Saco No 309; ☑ 9am-6pm Mon-Sat, 9am-2pm Sun) The definitive Cuban specialist music store; this retail outlet of Egrem Studios has a good selection of local musicians.

ARTex (General Lacret Map p412; General Lacret btwn Aguilera & Heredia; Heredia Map p412; Heredia No 304; ☑ 11am-11pm; Patio ARTex Map p412; Heredia No 208; ☑ 11am-7pm Tue-Sun) From mouse pads to Che trinkets, the branch of ARTex below Hotel Casa Granda collects any type of Cuban souvenir imaginable. The other branches – in the Casa de la Trova and at Patio ARTex one block further up Calle Heredia – focus more on music, with a respectable selection of CDs and cassettes.

La Maison (Map pp408-9; ☎ 64-11-17; Av Manduley No 52; ☻ 10am-6pm Mon-Sat) The Santiago version of the famous Havana fashion house located in an appropriately grand Vista Alegre *maison* (house).

ART GALLERIES

Innovative creativity is inscribed into the louvers in colonial Santiago, and a brief sortie around the *casco histórico* will reveal exciting snippets of eye-catching art. The following places in Parque Céspedes are just the tip of the iceberg.

Galería de Arte de Oriente (Map p412; General Lacret No 656) Probably the best gallery in Santiago de Cuba, the art here is consistently good.

Galería Santiago (Map p412; Heredia) This gallery, below the cathedral on the southern side of Parque Céspedes, is another one with quality art and there are several more galleries along Heredia east of here.

PHOTOGRAPHY

Photo Service Av Garzón (Map pp408-9; ☎ 65-19-91; cnr Av Garzón & Calle 4); General Lacret (Map p412; ☎ 62-35-90; General Lacret No 728)

Getting There & Away
AIR

Antonio Maceo International Airport (Map p418; airport code SCU; ☎ 69-10-14) is 7km south of Santiago de Cuba, off the Carretera del Morro. International flights arrive from Paris-Orly, Madrid, Toronto and Montreal on **Cubana** (Map p412; ☎ 65-15-77; cnr Saco & General Lacret). Toronto, Montreal and Ottawa are also served by **Sunwing** (www.sunwing.ca) and **Skyservice** (www.skyserviceairlines.com). **AeroCaribbean** (☎ 68-72-55; General Lacret btwn Bartolomé Masó & Heredia) flies weekly between here and Port Au Prince, Haiti and twice weekly to Santo Domingo.

Internally, Cubana flies nonstop from Havana to Santiago de Cuba two or three times a day (CUC$114 one-way, 1½ hours). There are also services to Varadero and Holguín and charters to Miami.

BUS

The **National Bus Station** (Map pp408-9; cnr Av de los Libertadores & Calle 9), opposite the Heredia Monument, is 3km northeast of Parque Céspedes. **Víazul** (☎ 62-84-84) buses leave from the same station.

The Havana bus stops at Bayamo (CUC$7, two hours), Holguín (CUC$11, four hours 20 minutes), Las Tunas (CUC$11, five hours 35 minutes), Camagüey (CUC$18, seven hours 35 minutes), Ciego de Ávila (CUC$24, 9½ hours), Sancti Spíritus (CUC$28, 11 hours 35 minutes) and Santa Clara (CUC$33, 13 hours). The Trinidad bus can drop you at Bayamo, Las Tunas, Camagüey, Ciego de Ávila and Sancti Spíritus.

TRAIN

The modern French-style **train station** (Map pp408-9; ☎ 62-28-36; Av Jesús Menéndez) is situated near the rum factory northwest of the center. The Tren Francés leaves at 5:35pm on alternate days for Havana (CUC$62, 16 hours) stopping at Camagüey (CUC$11) and Santa Clara (CUC$20) en route.

Other, slower *coche motor* (cross-island) trains also ply the route to Havana daily stopping at Bayamo (CUC$4), Holguín (CUC$5), Ciego de Ávila (CUC$14), Guayos (CUC$17) and Matanzas (CUC$27).

Cuban train schedules are fickle, so you should always verify beforehand what train leaves when and get your ticket as soon as possible thereafter.

TRUCK

Intermittent passenger trucks leave **Serrano Intermunicipal Bus Station** (Map pp408-9; ☎ 62-43-25; cnr Av Jesús Menéndez & Sánchez Hechavarría) near the train station to Guantánamo and Bayamo throughout the day. Prices are a few pesos and early mornings are the best time to board. For these destinations, don't fuss with the ticket window; just find the truck parked out front going your way. Trucks for Caletón Blanco and Chivirico also leave from here.

The **Intermunicipal Bus Station** (Terminal Cuatro Map pp408-9; ☎ 62-43-29; cnr Av de los Libertadores & Calle 4), 2km northeast of Parque Céspedes, has two buses a day to El Cobre. Two daily buses also leave for Baconao from here.

Getting Around
TO/FROM THE AIRPORT

A taxi to or from the airport should cost around CUC$7, but drivers will often try to charge you more. Haggle hard before you get in. You can also get to the airport on bus 212, which leaves from Av de los Libertadores opposite the Hospital de Maternidad (Map pp408–9). Bus 213 also goes to the airport from the same stop, but visits Punta Gorda first. Both buses stop just beyond the west end of the airport parking lot to the left of the entrances.

TO/FROM THE TRAIN STATION

To get into town from the train station, catch a southbound horse cart (one peso) to the clock tower at the north end of Parque Alameda (Map pp408–9), from which Aguilera (to the left) climbs straight up to Parque Céspedes. Horse carts between the National Bus Station (they'll shout 'Alameda') and train station (one peso) run along Av Juan Gualberto Gómez and Av Jesús Menéndez (Map pp408–9).

BUS & TRUCK

Useful city buses include bus 212 to the airport and Ciudamar, bus 213 to Punta Gorda (both of these buses start from Av de los Libertadores, opposite the Hospital de Maternidad, and head south on Felix Peña in the *casco histórico*), and bus 214 or 407 to Siboney (from near Av de los Libertadores No 425; Map pp408–9). Bus 5 to El Caney stops on the northwestern corner of Plaza de Marte (Map p412) and at Gral Cebreco and Calle 3 in Vista Alegre (Map pp408–9). These buses (20 centavos) run every hour or so; more frequent trucks (one peso) serve the same routes.

Trucks to El Cobre and points north leave from Av de las Américas near Calle M (Map p408–9). On trucks and buses you should be aware of pickpockets and wear your backpack in front.

CAR & MOPED

Santiago de Cuba suffers from a chronic shortage of rental cars (especially in peak season) and you might find there are none available; though the locals have an indefatigable Cuban ability to *conseguir* (to manage, to get) and *resolver* (to resolve, work out). The airport offices usually have better availability than those in town. If you're completely stuck, you can usually rent one at the Hotel Guantánamo, two hours to the east (p444).

Cubacar Airport (☎ 68 61 60; Antonio Maceo International Airport); Hotel Las Américas (Map pp408–9; cnr Avs de las Américas & General Cebreco; ☎ 68-71-60; ☷ 8am-10pm); Jesús Menéndez (Map pp408–9; ☎ 62-62-66; cnr Av Jesús Menéndez & General Portuondo) The

Hotel Las Américas office rents out mopeds for CUC$24 per day.
Rex (☎ 68-64-45; ☷ 9am-8:30pm) Rents the deluxe stuff.

Guarded parking is available in Parque Céspedes, directly below the Hotel Casa Granda. Official attendants, complete with small badges, charge CUC$1 a day and CUC$1 a night.

The **Servi-Cupet gas station** (Map pp408-9; cnr Avs de los Libertadores & de Céspedes) is open 24 hours. There's an **Oro Negro gas station** (Map p418; cnr Av 24 de Febrero & Carretera del Morro) on the Carretera del Morro and another Oro Negro (Map p418) on the Carretera Central at the northern entrance to Santiago de Cuba.

TAXI

There's a Turistaxi stand in front of Meliá Santiago de Cuba (Map p418). Taxis also wait on Parque Céspedes in front of the cathedral and hiss at you expectantly as you walk past. Always insist the driver uses the *taxímetro* (meter) or hammer out a price beforehand. To the airport, it will be between CUC$5 and CUC$7 depending on the state of the car.

Bici-taxis charge about five pesos per person per ride, but it's illegal to carry tourists, so they'll drop you a couple of blocks from Parque Céspedes.

SIBONEY

Playa Siboney is Santiago's Playas del Este, an exuberant seaside town 19km to the east that's more rustic village than deluxe resort. Guarded by precipitous cliffs and dotted with a mixture of craning palms and weather-beaten clapboard houses, the setting here is laid-back and charming, with a beach scene that mixes fun-seeking Cuban families and young, nubile Santiagüeras with their older and balder foreign sugar daddies in tow.

In terms of quality, Siboney's small crescent of grayish sand isn't in Varadero's league and the hotel choice (there *is* no choice, just one rock-bottom villa) is none too inspiring either. But what Siboney lacks in facilities it makes up for in price, location (it's on the doorstep of Parque Baconao) and all-embracing Cuban atmosphere. There's a plethora of legal casas particulares here (more than 30, which in a settlement of this size constitutes half the village) and a decent sit-down restaurant on a hill overlooking the beach. For those in need of a break from the culture-jamming and street hassle of sweltering Santiago, it makes a good little hideaway.

Sights

Had the Revolution been unsuccessful, the insignificant **Granjita Siboney** (admission CUC$1; 9am-5pm), a simple red-and-white farmhouse 2km inland from Playa Siboney on the road to Santiago de Cuba, would be the forgotten site of an unsuccessful and rather futile putsch. As it is, it's another shrine to the glorious national episode that is Moncada. It was from this place, at 5:15am on July 26, 1953, that 26 cars under the command of Fidel Castro left to attack the military barracks in Santiago de Cuba. The house retains many of its original details, including the dainty room used by the two *compañeras* (female revolutionaries) who saw action, Haydee Santamaría and Melba Hernández. There are also displays of weapons, interesting documents, photos and personal effects related to the attack. Notice the well beside the building, where weapons were hidden prior to the attack. In 1973, 26 monuments were erected along the highway between the Granjita Siboney and Santiago de Cuba to commemorate the assault.

The adjacent **Museo de la Guerra Hispano-Cubano-Norteamericano** displays objects related to the 1898 American military intervention at Santiago de Cuba. Several scale models of both the land and sea battles are provided.

Overlooking the stony shoreline is an American **war memorial** dated 1907, which recalls the US landing here on June 24, 1898.

Sleeping

CASAS PARTICULARES

There's an abundance of casas particulares in this small seaside settlement.

Ángel Figuredo Zolórzano (39-91-81; dgarrido1961@yahoo.es; Av Serrano No 63; r CUC$15-20) Nicely outfitted little pad, with a patio, at the end of the street.

Marlene Pérez (3-9219; r CUC$15-20) A seaside apartment with a balcony perched on the coast a block south of the post office. This place has a modern sheen and easy parking.

Ovidio González Salgado (39-93-40; Av Serrano; r CUC$20-25) A reader-recommended place above the pharmacy, serving great meals.

HOTELS

Villa Siboney (39-93-21; bungalow CUC$23) You're wiser heading for the casas particulares first in this neck of the woods, but if for some reason they're all full there's always the bog-standard Villa Siboney; seven independent rustic cabins on the beach that sleep up to four people. Ask at the *carpeta* (reception desk), below the apartment building beside the commercial center.

Eating & Drinking

Restaurante La Rueda (39-93-25) Take note, dear diner, you are sitting in the former house of musical sage–turned–international icon, Francisco Repilado the man responsible for writing the immortal song 'Chan Chan,' which you've probably already heard at least a dozen times since your plane landed. Born in a small shack on this site in 1907, Compay Segundo, as he was more commonly known, shot to superstardom at the advanced age of 90 as the guitarist and winking joker in Ry Cooder's *Buena Vista Social Club*. Despite predictions that he would make 115, Segundo died in 2003 aged 95. La Rueda is Siboney's only real dining option and would have kept old Francisco happy with its no-frills *comida criolla*, friendly service and good beach views.

A number of cheap peso food stalls over look the beach. There is also an open-air bar selling drinks in Convertibles on the beach itself.

Getting There & Away

Bus 214 runs to Siboney from near Av de los Libertadores 425, opposite Empresa Universa with a second stop at Av de Céspedes 110 in Santiago de Cuba. It leaves about once a hour, and bus 407 carries on to Juraguá three times a day. Passenger trucks also shuttle between Santiago de Cuba and Siboney.

A taxi to Playa Siboney will cost in the vicinity of CUC$20 to CUC$25, depending o whether it's state or private.

LA GRAN PIEDRA

Crowned by a 63,000-tonne boulder that perches like a grounded asteroid high above the Caribbean Sea, the Cordillera de la Gran Piedra forms part of Cuba's oddest, greenest and most bio-diverse mountain rang Not only does the range have a refreshing cool microclimate, it also boasts an incredibly unique historical heritage based on the legacy of some 60 or more coffee plantations set up by French farmers in the latter part of the 18th century. On the run from

CAFETALES

The Cubans have always been enthusiastic coffee drinkers. But, while the shade-loving national coffee crop thrives in the cool tree-covered glades of the Sierra del Escambray and Sierra Maestra, it's not indigenous to the island.

Coffee was first introduced into Cuba in 1748 from the neighboring colony of Santo Domingo, yet it wasn't until the arrival of French planters from Haiti in the early 1800s that the crop was grown commercially.

On the run from Toussaint Louverture's slave revolution, the displaced French found solace in the mountains of Pinar del Río and the Sierra Maestra, where they switched from sugarcane production to the more profitable and durable coffee plant.

Constructed in 1801 in what is now the Sierra del Rosario Reserve in Pinar del Río province, the Cafetal Buenavista (p222) was the first major coffee plantation in the New World. Not long afterward, planters living in the heavily forested hills around La Gran Piedra began constructing a network of more than 60 *cafetales* (coffee farms) using pioneering agricultural techniques to overcome the difficult terrain. Their stoic efforts paid off and, by the second decade of the 19th century, Cuba's nascent coffee industry was thriving.

Buoyed by high world coffee prices and aided by sophisticated new growing techniques, the coffee boom lasted from 1800 to about 1820, when the crop consumed more land than sugarcane. At its peak, there were more than 2000 *cafetales* in Cuba, concentrated primarily in the Sierra de Rosario region and the Sierra Maestra to the east of Santiago de Cuba.

Production began to slump in the 1840s with competition from vigorous new economies (most notably Brazil) and a string of devastating hurricanes. The industry took another hit during the War of Independence, though the crop survived and is still harvested to this day on a smaller scale using mainly traditional methods.

The legacy of Cuba's pioneering coffee industry is best evidenced in the Archaeological Landscape of the First Coffee Plantations in the Southeast of Cuba, a Unesco World Heritage Site dedicated in 2000 that sits in the foothills of the Sierra Maestra close to La Gran Piedra (opposite).

bloody slave rebellion in Haiti in 1791, the enterprising Gallic immigrants overcame arduous living conditions and difficult terrain to turn Cuba into the world's number-one coffee producer by the early 19th century. Their workmanship and ingenuity have been reserved for posterity in a Unesco World Heritage Site that is centered on the Cafetal La Isabelica. The area is also included in the Baconao Unesco Biosphere Reserve, instituted in 1987.

Sights & Activities

Near the beginning of the access road to La Gran Piedra, 16km southeast of Santiago de Cuba, is the **Prado de las Esculturas** (admission CUC$1; 8am-4pm). Strewn along a 1km loop road, here are 20 monumental sculptures of metal, wood, concrete, brick and stone by the artists of 10 countries. It's the first of this region's numerous artistic oddities.

The steep, 12km road up the mountain range itself is beautiful, as the trees close and the valley opens up below. Mango trees are ubiquitous here. One kilometer be-

fore Villa La Gran Piedra and 800m down a muddy road is the **Jardín Botánico** (admission CUC$3; 8am-4:30pm Tue-Sun), with orchids (best November to January) and other flowers. Look for the showy yellow, orange and violet *ave de paraíso* (bird of paradise).

You don't need to be Tenzing Norgay to climb the 459 stone steps to the summit of **La Gran Piedra** (admission CUC$1) at 1234m. The huge rock on top measures 51m in length and 25m in height and weighs…a lot. On a clear day there are excellent views out across the Caribbean and on a dark night you are supposedly able to see the lights of Jamaica.

Cafetal La Isabelica (admission CUC$2; 8am-4pm) is part of the Unesco World Heritage Site bestowed in 2000 upon the First Coffee Plantations in the Southeast of Cuba. Two kilometers beyond La Gran Piedra on a rough road, there's a museum describing the coffee-processing technology of a century ago. The impressive two-story stone mansion, with its three large coffee-drying platforms, was built in the early 19th century by French émigrés

LA GRAN PIEDRA & PARQUE BACONAO

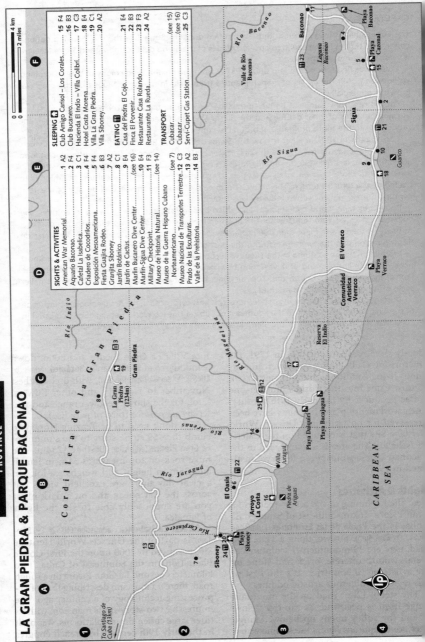

SIGHTS & ACTIVITIES
American War Memorial.....................1 A2
Aquario Baconao................................2 F4
Cafetal La Isabelica...........................3 C1
Criadero de Cocodrilos......................4 F4
Exposición Mesoamericana................5 F4
Fiesta Guajira Rodeo.........................6 B3
Granjita Siboney................................7 A2
Jardín Botánico..................................8 C1
Jardín de Cactus...............................9 E4
Marlin Bucanero Dive Center.........(see 16)
Marlin-Sigua Dive Center................10 E4
Military Checkpoint...........................11 F3
Museo de Historia Natural.............(see 14)
Museo de la Guerra Hispano Cubano
  Norteamericano.........................(see 7)
Museo Nacional de Transportes Terrestre.12 C3
Prado de las Esculturas...................13 A2
Valle de la Prehistoria......................14 B3

SLEEPING
Club Amigo Carisol – Los Corales.....15 F4
Club Bucanero...................................16 B3
Hacienda El Indio – Villa Colibrí........17 C3
Hotel Costa Morena...........................18 E4
Villa La Gran Piedra...........................19 C1
Villa Siboney.....................................20 A2

EATING
Casa del Piedra El Cojo......................21 E4
Finca El Porvenir...............................22 B3
Restaurante Casa Rolando.................23 B3
Restaurante La Rueda........................24 A2

TRANSPORT
Cubacar...(see 15)
Cubacar...(see 16)
Servi-Cupet Gas Station...................25 C3

from Haiti and was once one of more than 60 in the area. There's a workshop, furniture and some slave artifacts, and you can stroll around the pine-covered plantation grounds at will.

Sleeping & Eating

Villa La Gran Piedra (Islazul; ☎ 65-12-05; s/d CUC$34/42; P ✺) It might not be the biggest or the best, but Villa La Gran Piedra has at least one claim to fame – it is the highest hotel in Cuba. Situated at 1225m, near the mountain's summit, there are 17 cabins and five bungalows here with red-tiled roofs and local stone walls. Rooms are basic but perfectly adequate and the verdant setting surrounded by ferns, orchids and wondrous vistas makes up for a lot. There's an on-site restaurant and various short hiking trips are available.

Getting There & Away

A steep, winding paved road climbs 12km up the mountain's spine. It's not always possible to visit by public transport, as the bus arrives only once a week. A taxi from Santiago de Cuba will cost approximately CUC$40 for the round trip.

PARQUE BACONAO

Parque Baconao, covering 800 sq km between Santiago de Cuba and the Río Baconao, is as wondrous as it is weird. A Unesco Biosphere Reserve that is also home to an outdoor car museum, a run-down aquarium and a rather odd collection of 240 life-size dinosaur sculptures, it looks like a historically displaced Jurassic Park, yet in reality acts as an important haven for a whole ecosystem of flora and fauna.

Not surprisingly, the Unesco tag wasn't earned for a museum full of old cars (or for a field full of concrete dinosaurs, for that matter). According to biological experts, Baconao boasts more than 1800 endemic species of flora and numerous types of endangered bats and spiders. Encased in a shallow chasm with the imposing Sierra Maestra on one side and the placid Caribbean on the other, the biodiversity of the area (which includes everything from craning royal palms to prickly cliffside cacti) is nothing short of remarkable.

The beaches are smaller here than those on the northern coast and not quite as white, but the fishing is good and there are 73 scuba-diving sites to choose from nearby, including the *Guarico*, a small steel wreck just south of Playa Sigua.

Baconao is also famous for its crabs. From mid-March to early May, tens of thousands of large land crabs congregate along the coast beyond Playa Verraco, getting unceremoniously squashed under the tires of passing cars and sending up a rare stench as they bake in the sun.

Sights

A dozen painters have studios where their works are displayed and sold in the small artistic community of **El Oasis** at the turn-off to Club Bucanero, 3km east of the Playa Siboney road.

One of the oddest in a plethora of odd attractions is the **Valle de la Prehistoria** (☎ 63-90-39; admission CUC$1; ☯ 8am-6pm), a kind of Cuban Jurassic Park cast in stone that materializes rather serendipitously beside the meandering coastal road. Here giant brontosaurs mix with concrete cavemen, seemingly oblivious to the fact that 57 million years separated the two species' colonization of planet Earth. With your tongue planted firmly in your cheek, you can take in the full 11 hectares of this surreal kitsch park with its 200 life-size concrete dinosaurs built by inmates from a nearby prison. The **Museo de Historia Natural** (☎ 63-93-29; admission CUC$1; ☯ 8am-4pm Tue-Sun) is also here, but something of an anticlimax after the surrealism of the prehistoric beasts.

What's the point, is the question that springs to mind when you stumble upon the **Museo Nacional de Transporte Terrestre** (☎ 63-91-97; admission CUC$1, camera/video CUC$1/2; ☯ 8am-5pm), 2km east of the Valle de la Prehistoria. All very impressive that they've nabbed Benny Moré's 1958 Cadillac and the Chevrolet Raúl Castro got lost in on the way to the Moncada Barracks; but in Cuba where '50s car relics are as common as cheap cigars, it's the equivalent of a Toyota Yaris museum in Kyoto.

The main US landings during the Spanish-Cuban-American War took place on June 24, 1898 at **Playa Daiquirí**, 2km down a side road from the museum. Although they named a cocktail after it, the area is now a holiday camp for military personnel and entry is prohibited.

Ten kilometers further on is the **Comunidad Artística Verraco** (admission free; ☯ 9am-6pm), another village of painters, ceramicists and sculptors who maintain open studios. Here you can visit the artists and buy original works of art.

After a couple of bends in the road you burst onto the coast, where the hotels begin.

Jardín de Cactus (admission CUC$5; ⏰ 8am-3pm), 600m east of Hotel Costa Morena, has 200 kinds of cactus beautifully arrayed along the rocky hillside, with a large cave at the rear of the garden. Keep your eyes peeled for tiny green *colibrí* (hummingbird) suckling nectar from flowering cacti.

Aquario Baconao (☎ 63-51-45; admission CUC$7; ⏰ 9am-5pm), between the Costa Morena and Hotel Carisol, has dolphin shows (with sultry narration) a couple of times a day. It's a rather tacky spectacle, although you can swim with the animals – if you so desire – for CUC$46.

Every Cuban resort area seems to have an attraction replicating indigenous scenes. Here it's the **Exposición Mesoamericana** (admission CUC$1), just east of Club Amigo Carisol – Los Corales. Indigenous cave art from Central and South America is arranged in caves along the coastal cliffs.

At the Laguna Baconao, 2km northeast of Los Corales, you'll find the **Criadero de Cocodrilos** (admission CUC$1; ⏰ 8am-5pm), a dozen crocodiles kept in pens below a restaurant, plus other caged animals such as lizards and *jutías* (tree rats). Horses are (supposedly) for hire here, as well as boats to ply the lake.

From Playa Baconao, 5km northeast of Los Corales, the paved road continues 3.5km up beautiful **Valle de Río Baconao** before turning into a dirt track. A dam up the Río Baconao burst in 1994, inundating Baconao village. Soldiers at a checkpoint at the village turn back people trying to use the direct coastal road to Guantánamo because it passes alongside the US Naval Base. To continue east, you must backtrack to Santiago de Cuba and take the inland road.

Activities

The **Fiesta Guajira Rodeo** (admission CUC$5; ⏰ 9am & 2pm Wed & Sun) at El Oasis, opposite the turn-off to Club Bucanero, stages rodeos with *vaqueros* (Cuban cowboys) four times a week. Horseback riding is available for CUC$5 for the first hour. The rodeo's restaurant serves typical Cuban food from noon to 2pm daily.

Marlin-Sigua Dive Center (Cubanacán Náutica; ☎ 69-14-46) is a 10-minute walk along the beach from Hotel Costa Morena and picks divers up at the hotels daily. Scuba diving costs CUC$30 with gear, and two boats can take up to 20 people to any of 24 local dive sites. Marlin's open-water certification course is CUC$300. There are shipwrecks close to shore here and

you can feed black groupers by hand. **Marlin Bucanero Dive Center** (☎ 68-61-08) offers similar services at Club Bucanero. The water off this bit of coast is some of Cuba's warmest (25°C to 28°C); best visibility is between February and June.

Generally considered to be the best public beach in the area, **Playa Cazonal** offers lots of tawny sand, natural shade and a big sandy swimming hole (much of the coast here is clogged with seaweed forests). Turn into the Club Amigo Carisol – Los Corales and then it's a quick left to the beach access road.

Sleeping

MIDRANGE

Hacienda El Indio – Villa Colibrí (Islazul; ☎ 64-13-70; s/d with breakfast low season CUC$30/40) The former El Indio hunting reserve about 20 minutes' drive out of Santiago is now the Reserva El Indio 'ecotourism park.' There are two clusters of villas, simple chalets set in enticing natural surroundings. The group inland has an attractive rock-hewn swimming pool, while the ones near the beach have a seawater pool. This place is the turf of outdoor types who like to snorkel, horseback ride and hike in the surrounding area.

Hotel Costa Morena (Islazul; ☎ 35-61-35; s/d CUC$53/69; P ❄ 🖳) This place is at Sigua, 44km southeast of Santiago de Cuba and 17km east of the Complejo La Punta Servi-Cupet gas station. It has attractive architecture, a large terrace right on the cliffs, but no direct beach access. A two-star Islazul, it's popular with Cubans and the odd vacationing Canadian.

TOP END

Club Amigo Carisol – Los Corales (Cubanacán; ☎ 35-61-21; s/d all-inclusive CUC$75/105; P ❄ 🖳) There's the swim-up bar, umbrellas in the piña coladas, and the government-sponsored band knocking out the 65th rendition of 'Guantanamera' as you tuck into your lukewarm buffet dinner. You must be back in all-inclusive land on the Parque Baconao version of it to be more precise. The Carisol – Los Corales is a two-piece Cubanacán resort situated 44km east of Santiago on the coast's best section of beach (though parts of it have been damaged by successive hurricanes). There's a tennis court, a disco, multiple day trips on offer, and bright spacious clean rooms (if you get bivouacked in Los Corales). Nonguests can purchase a day pass for CUC$15 including lunch.

Club Bucanero (Gran Caribe; ☎ 68-63-63; Carretera de Baconao Km 4; s/d all-inclusive CUC$84/120; P ⊠ ⊠) Tucked beneath low limestone cliffs with a small scratch of beach, this resort at Arroyo La Costa, 25km southeast of Santiago de Cuba, is a beautiful little haven away from the bustle of the city. The rooms are set in a series of attractive gray stone villas and are within earshot of the ocean. A lovely pool area boasts El Morro–like *garitas* (look-out posts) and the lush mountains beckon invitingly behind.

Eating

Finca El Porvenir (☎ 62-90-64; Carretera de Baconao Km 18; ⊗ noon-7pm) Probably the best place to eat out in this neck of the woods, the Finca knocks out no-frills *comida criolla* specializing in *puerco asado en púa* (pork roasted Oriente-style on a skewer). It's finger-licking good.

Casa del Piedra El Cojo (☎ 35-62-10) The most reliable year-round restaurant out this way – aside from the Fiesta Guajira Rodeo (opposite) – is this peso place just beyond Sigua on the coast. Try the prawn cocktail for about eight pesos.

Restaurante Casa Rolando (☎ 35-00-04; Carretera Baconao Km 53; ⊗ 10:30am-5pm) This joint on the north shore of Laguna Baconao serves mainly seafood.

Getting There & Away

Baconao is poorly served by public transport – frustratingly so. You might get as far as Siboney on bus 214 but after that you'll struggle without a car/bike/taxi. The resolute could try asking about the hotel worker buses that ply this route and might let you squeeze on board. Alternatively, try negotiating a rate with a tourist hotel transfer. Cubataxi usually charges approximately CUC$0.50 per kilometer out this way or you can hire a moped from Cubacar (below) for CUC$24 per day.

When planning your visit to this area, remember that the coastal road from Baconao to Guantánamo is closed to nonresidents.

Getting Around

Cubacar (☎ 68-63-63; Club Bucanero) has cars and mopeds. There's also a branch at Los Corales.

The **Servi-Cupet gas station** (Complejo La Punta; ⊗ 24hr) is 28km southeast of Santiago de Cuba.

EL COBRE

The Basílica de Nuestra Señora del Cobre, high on a hill 20km northwest of Santiago de Cuba on the old road to Bayamo, is Cuba's most sacred pilgrimage site. In Santería, La Virgen de la Caridad is associated with the beautiful *orisha* Ochún, the Yoruba goddess of love and dancing, who is represented by the color yellow. In the minds of many worshipers, devotion to the two religious figures is intertwined.

The copper mine at El Cobre has been active since pre-Columbian times and was once the oldest European-operated mine in the Western hemisphere (by 1530 the Spanish had a mine here). However, it was shut in 2000. Many young villagers, who previously worked in the mine, now work over tourists in the parking lot of the basilica, offering to 'give' you shiny but worthless chalcopyrite stones from the mine. You'll find that a firm but polite *'No, gracias!'* usually does the trick. The road to the basilica is lined with sellers of elaborate flower wreaths, intended as offerings to La Virgen, and hawkers of miniature 'Cachitas,' the popular name for The Virgin.

Sights

Stunning as it materializes above the village of El Cobre, the **Basílica de Nuestra Señora del Cobre** (⊗ 6:30am-6pm) shimmers against the verdant hills behind. Apart from during Mass (8am except on Wednesday, with additional Sunday services at 10am and 4:30pm), La Virgen lives in a small chapel above the visitors center on the side of the basilica. To see her, take the stairs on either side of the entry door. For such a powerful entity, she's amazingly diminutive, some 40cm from crown to the hem of her golden robe. Check out the fine Cuban coat of arms in the center; it's an amazing work of embroidery. During Mass, Nuestra Señora de

ASK A LOCAL

The Virgen of El Cobre is known as 'Cachita' in Cuba and holds an intense spiritual power over the people. Legend says the statue was first found floating in the Bahía de Nipe by three fishermen caught in a storm in the early 1600s. The fishermen survived and brought the virgin back to El Cobre where she became a venerated figure.

Yarelis, El Cobre

la Caridad faces the congregation from atop the altar inside the basilica.

The 'room of miracles' downstairs in the visitors center contains thousands of offerings giving thanks for favors bestowed by the virgin. Clumps of hair, a TV, a thesis, a tangle of stethoscopes, a raft and inner-tube sculpture (suggesting they made it across the Florida Straits safely) and floor-to-ceiling clusters of teeny metal body parts crowd the room. The most notable is a small golden guerrilla fighter donated by Lina Ruz, Fidel Castro's mother, to protect her son during his Sierra Maestra campaign against Batista. Until 1986, the 1954 Nobel Prize won by Ernest Hemingway for his novel *The Old Man and the Sea* was also on display, but in that year a visitor smashed the showcase's glass and carried the medal off. The police recovered the medal two days later, but it has since been kept in a vault, out of sight and reach.

Follow the signs through the town of El Cobre to the **Monumento al Cimarrón**. A 10-minute hike up a stone staircase brings you to this anthropomorphic sculpture commemorating the 17th-century copper-mine slave revolt. The views are superb from up here; walk to the far side of the sculpture for a vista of copper-colored cliffs hanging over the aqua-green reservoir.

Sleeping & Eating

Hospedaría El Cobre (3-6246) This large two-story building behind the basilica has 15 basic rooms with one, two or three beds, all with bath, at eight pesos per person, plus two 40-bed dormitories at five pesos per person. Meals are served punctually at 7am, 11am and 6pm, and there's a pleasant large sitting room with comfortable chairs. The nuns here are very hospitable. House rules include no drinking and no unmarried couples. A Convertible donation to the sanctuary equivalent to what you pay to stay in pesos is the classy thing to do. Foreigners must reserve at least 15 days in advance.

There are several peso stalls in town where you can get *batidos* (fruit shakes), pizza and smoked-pork sandwiches.

Getting There & Away

Bus 2 goes to El Cobre twice a day from the **Intermunicipal Bus Station** (cnr Av de los Libertadores & Calle 4), in Santiago de Cuba. Trucks are more frequent on this route.

A Cubataxi from Santiago de Cuba costs around CUC$20 for a round-trip.

If you're driving toward Santiago de Cuba from the west, you can join the Autopista Nacional near Palma Soriano, but unless you're in a big hurry, it's better to continue on the Carretera Central via El Cobre, which winds through picturesque hilly countryside.

EL SALTÓN

Basking in its well-earned eco-credentials, **Hotel Carrusel El Saltón** (Cubanacán; 56-63-23; Carretera Puerto Rico a File; s/d with breakfast CUC$45/65;) is a tranquil mountain escape in the Tercer Frente municipality, where hills that once echoed with the sound of crackling rifle fire now reverberate to the twitter of tropical birds. Secluded and hard to reach (that's the whole point), the 22-room lodge is spread over three separate blocks that nestle like hidden tree houses amid the thick foliage. Spirit-lifting extras include a sauna, hot tub, massage facilities, a hilltop *mirador* and the hotel's defining feature, a 30m cascading waterfall with an adjacent natural pool ideal for swimming. Eco-guides can offer horseback riding or hiking into the nearby cocoa plantations at Delicias del Saltón. Alternatively, you can just wander off on your own through myriad mountain villages with alluring names like Filé and Cruce de los Baños. The hotel has an OK restaurant and bar with a popular pool table, both of which reside just meters from a gushing mountain river.

To get to El Saltón, continue west from El Cobre to Cruce de los Baños, 4km east of Filé village. El Saltón is 3km south of Filé. With some tough negotiating in Santiago de Cuba a sturdy taxi will take you here for CUC$40 Money well spent.

You may hear about a road over the Sierra Maestra from Cruce de los Baños to Río Seco on the south coast. Southbound from Cruce de los Baños, the first 10km are OK, passing through hamlets in coffee-growing country Then the road goes south, becoming a very rough jeep track with extremely slippery steep sections that can only be covered by a 4WD vehicle in dry weather. In a regular car or in rainy weather, the last 20km to Río Seco would be impossible, although eco-tour jeeps regularly use this road. Good luck.

WEST OF SANTIAGO DE CUBA

Existing as a vital transport artery between the escarpment and the sea, the rutted road west out of Santiago toward Marea de Portillo, 181km away, is a roller coaster of crinkled mountains, hidden bays and crashing surf. This is, without doubt, one of the most breathtaking routes in Cuba, if not the Caribbean. There are countless remote beaches where you can stop along the way, all of them spectacular, and most without a soul within loud-hailing distance. The main problem in this region is that public transport barely exists; a headache for convenience freaks but a blessing in disguise for DIY adventurers.

CHIVIRICO & AROUND
pop 4000

Chivirico, 75km southwest of Santiago de Cuba and 106km east of Marea del Portillo, is the only town of any significance on the south-coast highway. Transport links are relatively good up until this point but, heading west, they quickly deteriorate.

In terms of atmosphere, Chivirico feels like a town from another era, even by Cuban standards, and, while there's not much to do here in the traditional tourist sense, it's a good place to pick up on the nuances of everyday Cuban life. The deep, clear waters of the Cayman Trench just offshore wash the many beaches along this portion of the south coast.

There's a challenging trek that begins at Calentura 4km west of Chivirico and passes through La Alcarraza (12km), crossing the Sierra Maestra to Los Horneros (20km), from where truck transport to Guisa is usually available. Whether skittish local authorities will let you loose in the area is another matter. Don't just turn up – do your homework in Santiago or Chivirico first. Try asking at Cubatur in Santiago or at one of the two Cubanacán Brisas hotels.

Sleeping

Campismo Caletón Blanco (Cubamar; ☎ 62-57-97; Caletón Blanco Km 30, Guamá; s/d CUC$16/26; P 😠) One of two handy campismos situated along this route (the other is La Mula; see p439), Caletón Blanco is the closest to Santiago (30km) and the newest. Open to both international visitors and Cubans are 22 bungalows sleeping two to our people. There's also a restaurant, snack bar and bike rental available. Campervans are accommodated at this site, which is one of Cubamar's top picks. Make your reservations with Cubamar's Havana office (p108) before arrival.

Brisas Sierra Mar Los Galeones (Cubanacán; ☎ 32-61-60; Carretera Chivirico Km 72; s/d all-inclusive high season CUC$82/118; P 😠 😩) This is a small hotel with big surprises; the setting for instance – high on a bluff with shadowy mountains behind and bucolic life mooing and crowing all around. Then there's the steep 296-step stairway that takes you down 100m to the tiny beach. Compared with its sister hotel, the Sierra Mar, Los Galeones is quiet (no kids under 16 here) and secluded, but not posh. All in all, a nice place to relax.

Brisas Sierra Mar (Cubanacán; ☎ 32-91-10; s/d all-inclusive CUC$104/148; P 😠 😩 😩) This isolated and rather inviting place is at Playa Sevilla, 63km west of Santiago de Cuba and a two-hour drive from the airport. The big, pyramid-shaped hotel is built into a terraced hillside with a novel elevator to take you down to a brown-sand beach famous for its sand fleas. Get into the water quickly and discover a remarkable coral wall great for snorkeling just 50m offshore (dolphins sometimes frequent these waters too). Horseback riding is available, there's a Marlin Dive Center on the premises, and plenty of special kids' programs (kids under 13 stay free). The hotel is popular with Canadians and gets a lot of repeat visits. Nonguests can buy a CUC$35 day pass that includes lunch, drinks and sport until 5pm. If you're doing the south coast by bike, it's a nice indulgence.

Getting There & Away

Trucks run to Chivirico throughout the day from the Serrano Intermunicipal Bus Station opposite the train station in Santiago de Cuba. There are also three buses a day.

Theoretically, buses and private trucks operate along the south coast from Chivirico to Campismo La Mula, Río Macío (on the border with Granma province) and Pilón, but they are sporadic. Ask around at Chivirico's bus and truck station 700m up off the coastal road from Cine Guamá.

EL UVERO

A major turning point in the revolutionary war took place in this nondescript settlement situated 23km west of Chivirico, on May 28, 1957, when Castro's rebel army – still numbering less than 50 – audaciously took out a government position guarded by 53 of Batista's soldiers. By the main road are two red trucks taken by the rebels and nearby a double row of royal palms leads to a large monument commemorating the brief but incisive battle. It's a poignant but little-visited spot.

PICO TURQUINO AREA

Five kilometers west of Las Cuevas (which is 40km west of El Uvero) is the **Museo de la Plata** (admission CUC$1; ⏱ Tue-Sat) at La Plata, next to the river just below the highway. The first successful skirmish of the Cuban Revolution took place here on January 17, 1957. The museum has three rooms with photos and artifacts from the campaign, including a piece of paper signed by the 15 *Granma* survivors who met up at Cinco Palmas in late 1956. Marea del Portillo is 46km to the west (see p402). Don't confuse this La Plata with the Comandancia La Plata, Fidel Castro's revolutionary headquarters high up in the Sierra Maestra (p393).

The well-preserved wreck of the Spanish cruiser *Cristóbal Colón* lies where it sank in 1898, about 15m down and only 30m offshore near La Mula. No scuba gear is available here, but you can see the wreck with a mask and snorkel. (Divers from the Brisas Sierra Mar resort are brought here by bus for a shore dive on the wreck.) If you have the time, hike up the Río Turquino to Las Posas de los Morones, which has a few nice pools where you can swim (allow four hours round-trip). You must wade across the river at least three times unless it's dry.

Activities

The emblematic **Pico Turquino trek** is often tackled from Las Cuevas on the remote coast road 130km west of Santiago de Cuba. If summiting the mountain is your main aim, this is probably the quickest and easiest route. If you also want to immerse yourself in the area's history and hike from Comandancia La Plata through and/or across the Sierra Maestra, you should set out from Alto del Naranjo in adjacent Granma province (see boxed text, p395). Bear in mind that both options can be linked in a spectacular through trek (note that onward transport is better from the Alto del Naranjo side).

The hike from Las Cuevas can be organized at relatively short notice at the trailhead. A good option is to book through **Ecotur** (☎ 65-38-59) in Santiago de Cuba. See p394 for the map of this hike.

The trail from Las Cuevas begins on the south-coast highway, 7km west of Ocujal

and 51km east of Marea del Portillo. This trek also passes Cuba's second-highest peak, Pico Cuba (1872m). Allow at least six hours to go up and another four hours to come down, more if it has been raining as the trail floods in parts and becomes a mud slick in others. Most climbers set out at 4am (but if you're on the trail by 6:30am, you'll be OK), having slept at the Campismo La Mula, 12km east; self-sufficient hikers also have the option of pitching camp at Las Cuevas visitors center. The CUC$15 per person fee (camera CUC$5 extra) that you pay at the visitors center/trailhead includes a compulsory Cuban guide. You can overnight at the shelter on Pico Cuba if you don't want to descend the same day (two days/one night CUC$30). Alternatively, you can do the entire Las Cuevas–Alto del Naranjo three-day hike by arranging to be met by a new team of guides at Pico Turquino (three days/two nights CUC$48). Add an extra CUC$5 onto the latter two options if you wish to include a side trip to Castro's former headquarters at Comandancia La Plata (p394).

This hike is grueling because you're gaining almost 2km in elevation across only 9.6km of trail. But shade and peek-a-boo views provide plenty of respite. Fill up on water before setting out. The well-marked route leads from Las Cuevas to La Esmajagua (600m; 3km; there's water here and a hospitable country family) Pico Cardero (1265m; quickly followed by a series of nearly vertical steps called Saca La Lengua, literally 'flops your tongue out'), Pico Cuba (1872m; 2km; water and shelter here) and Pico Turquino (1972m; 1.7km). When the fog parts and you catch your breath, you'll behold a bronze bust of José Martí that stands on the summit of Cuba's highest mountain. You can overnight at either Pico Cuba on the ascent or La Esmajagua on the descent. The Pico Cuba shelter has a rudimentary kitchen and a wood-fire stove, plank beds (no mattresses) or, if those are taken, floor space. For the Alto del Naranjo–Santo Domingo continuation, see boxed text, p395.

Alternatively, walkers with less lofty ambitions can arrange a short four-hour, 6km trek from Las Cuevas to La Esmajagua and back for CUC$13 (camera CUC$5 extra).

Trekkers should bring sufficient food, warm clothing, a sleeping bag and a poncho; precipitation is common up here (some 2200mm annually), from a soft drizzle to pelt ing hail. Except for water, you'll have to carry everything you'll need, including extra food to share if you can carry it and a little something for the *compañeros* (comrades) who take 15-day shifts up on Pico Cuba.

Ask ahead if you would like an English-speaking guide (park officials claim they now have at least one). Also ask about food provision at Pico Cuba. Drinks are available for purchase at the trailhead in Las Cuevas. Tipping the guides is mandatory – CUC$3 to CUC$5 is sufficient. For competitive types, the (unofficial) summit record by a guide is two hours, 45 minutes. So if you're feeling energetic…

Sleeping & Eating

Campismo La Mula (Cubamar; s/d low season CUC$7/10, high season CUC$11/16) On a remote pebble beach at the mouth of Río La Mula, 12km east of the Pico Turquino trailhead, La Mula has 50 small cabins popular with holidaying Cubans, hikers destined for Turquino and the odd hitchhiking south-coast adventurer short on lifts. It's pretty much the only option on this isolated stretch of coast. It's wise to check with Cubamar or the Oficina Reservaciones de Campismo (see p410) in Santiago de Cuba before pitching up. If it's full, you *may* be able to pitch a tent.

There's also a rustic cafe and restaurant on-site.

Getting There & Away

Private trucks and the odd rickety bus connect La Mula to Chivirico, but they are sporadic and don't run on any fixed schedules. A taxi from Santiago should cost CUC$50 to CUC$60. Traffic is almost nonexistent in this neck of the woods and even the *amarillos* are sparse.

Guantánamo Province

Say you're from Guantánamo to anyone outside Cuba, and they'll probably assume that you're either a US Navy Seal on annual leave, or an ex-inmate from one of the world's most notorious jails. But Cuba's wettest, driest, hottest, oldest and most mountainous province is far more than an anachronistic US naval base. Cuba in the modern sense started here in August 1511, when Diego Velázquez de Cuéllar and his band of 400 colonizers landed uninvited on the rain-lashed eastern coastline. Making camp near a mysterious flat-topped mountain known to the natives as El Yunque, they christened their new settlement Villa de Nuestra Señora de la Asunción de Baracoa and quickly made enemies with the local Taínos.

Baracoa lives on, of course; no longer the island's capital, but still one of its most beguiling settlements, cut off for centuries by the shadowy Sierra del Puril – Cuba's Himalayas – and beautifully unique as a consequence.

To get there you'll need to take La Farola, the province's rugged transport artery and one of the seven engineering marvels of modern Cuba, a weaving roller coaster that travels from the dry cacti-littered southern coast up into the humid Cuchillas de Toa mountains. Overlaid by the fecund Parque Nacional Alejandro de Humboldt (a Unesco World Heritage Site), this heavily protected zone is considered to be one of the last few swathes of virgin rainforest left in the Caribbean and guards an incredible array of endemic species.

Closer to sea level, Cuba's eastern extremity is scattered with myriad archaeological sites that exhibit important vestiges of the island's pre-Columbian cultural jigsaw. Separated from the country's cosmopolitan urban centers, the native bloodlines are purer here and, around the isolated Boca de Yumurí, you'll find people who still claim indigenous Indian ancestry.

HIGHLIGHTS

- **River Journey** Take a boat ride on the wondrous Río Yumurí (p447)
- **Coffee, Coconuts and Cacao** Sample the culinary secrets of oceanside Baracoa (p453)
- **Roller-coaster Ride** Up and over La Farola (see boxed text, p455), take the high road to Baracoa on a bicycle
- **Surreal Stones** Get an eyeful of the stony statues at the Zoológico de Piedras (p447)
- **Flat Top** Hike through the tropical jungle to the top of Baracoa's mysterious flat-topped mountain, El Yunque (p456)

El Yunque ★ ★ Baracoa
Zoológico ★ ★ Río Yumurí
de Piedras ★ La Farola

TELEPHONE CODE: 021	POPULATION: 516,311	AREA: 6186 SQ KM

GUANTÁNAMO PROVINCE

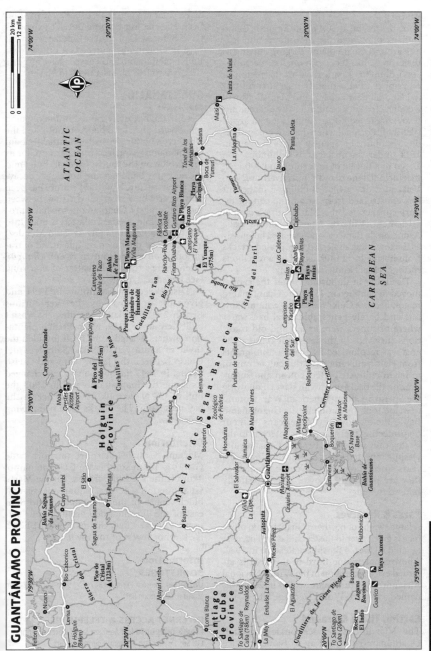

History

Long before the arrival of the Spanish, Taíno Indians populated the mountains and forests around Guantánamo forging a living as fishermen, hunters and small-scale farmers. Columbus first arrived in the region in November 1492, a month or so after his initial landfall near Gibara, and planted a small wooden cross in a beautiful bay he ceremoniously christened Porto Santo – after an idyllic island off Portugal where he had enjoyed his honeymoon. The Spanish returned again in 1511 under the auspices of Columbus' son Diego in a flotilla of four ships and 400 men that included the island's first governor Diego Velázquez de Cuéllar. Building a makeshift fort constructed from wood, the conquistadors consecrated the island's first colonial settlement, Villa de Nuestra Señora de la Asunción de Baracoa, and watched helplessly as the town was subjected to repeated attacks from hostile local Indians led by a rebellious cacique (chief) known as Hatuey.

Declining in importance after the capital moved to Santiago in 1515, the Guantánamo region became Cuba's Siberia – a mountainous and barely penetrable rural backwater where prisoners were exiled and old traditions survived. In the late 18th century the area was recolonized by French immigrants from Haiti who tamed the difficult terrain in order to cultivate coffee, cotton and sugarcane on the backs of African slaves. Following the Spanish-Cuban-American War, a brand new foe took up residence in Guantánamo Bay – the all-powerful Americans – intent on protecting their economic interests in the strategically important Panama Canal region. Despite repeated bouts of mudslinging in the years since, the not-so-welcome Yanquis, as they are popularly known, have repeatedly refused to budge.

Parks & Reserves

A large swathe of northern Guantánamo province is given over to the Cuchillas de Toa, designated a Unesco Biosphere Reserve in 1987. Approximately one-third of this area is afforded extra protection in the Parque Nacional Alejandro de Humboldt, which in 2001 was named a Unesco World Heritage Site.

Getting There & Around

The Víazul bus service passes through Guantánamo all the way to Baracoa twice daily. Guantánamo is also accessible by train from Havana but the line doesn't extend as far as Baracoa. Daily trucks link Baracoa with Moa in Holguín province via a rutted road. Both Guantánamo and Baracoa have airports with two to five flights a week to Havana.

GUANTÁNAMO

pop 244,603

Despite the notoriety gained in the ongoing schoolyard-style feud between Cuba and the US, there's nothing visually remarkable about Guantánamo – which accounts, in part, for its low profile on the tourist 'circuit.' But, amid the ugly grey buildings and hopelessly decaying infrastructure a buoyant culture has been putting up a brave rearguard action. Between them, the feisty Guantanameros have produced 11 gold medals, blasted a man into orbit (Cuban cosmonaut, Arnaldo Méndez) and spawned their own unique brand of traditional son music known as son-changüí. Then there's the small matter of that song (see boxed text, p445).

'Discovered' by Columbus in 1494 and given the once-over by the ever curious British 250 years later, a settlement wasn't built here until 1819, when French plantation owners evicted from Haiti founded the town of Santa Catalina del Saltadero del Guaso between the Jaibo, Bano and Guaso Rivers. In 1843 the burgeoning city changed its name to Guantánamo and in 1903 the bullish US Navy took up residence in the bay next door. The sparks have been flying ever since.

Orientation

Mariana Grajales Airport (airport code GAO) is 16km southeast of Guantánamo, 4km off the road to Baracoa. Parque Martí, Guantánamo's central square, is several blocks south of the train station and 5km east of the Terminal de Ómnibus (bus station). Villa La Lupe, the main tourist hotel, is 5km northwest of the town.

Information

BOOKSTORES

Universal (Pedro A Pérez No 907; ⊙ 9am-noon & 2-5pm Mon-Fri, 9am-noon Sat)

INTERNET ACCESS & TELEPHONE

Etecsa Telepunto (cnr Aguilera & Los Maceos; per hr CUC$6; ⊙ 8:30am-7:30pm) Four computers.

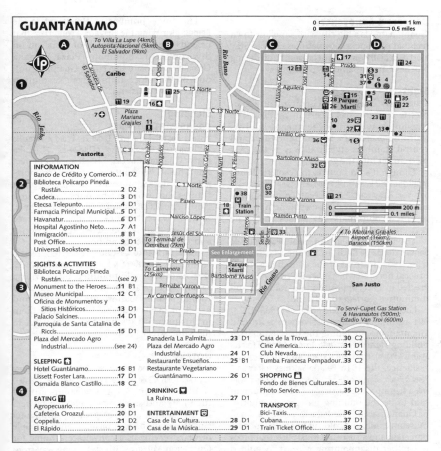

GUANTÁNAMO

	0 1 km
	0 0.5 miles

To Villa La Lupe (4km);
Autopista Nacional (5km);
El Salvador (9km)

INFORMATION
Banco de Crédito y Comercio...**1** D2
Biblioteca Policarpo Pineda
  Rustán.........................**2** D2
Cadeca...........................**3** D1
Etecsa Telepunto...............**4** D1
Farmacia Principal Municipal...**5** D1
Havanatur.......................**6** D1
Hospital Agostinho Neto.......**7** A1
Inmigración.....................**8** B1
Post Office......................**9** D1
Universal Bookstore.............**10** D1

SIGHTS & ACTIVITIES
Biblioteca Policarpo Pineda
  Rustán........................(see 2)
Monument to the Heroes.......**11** B1
Museo Municipal...............**12** C1
Oficina de Monumentos y
  Sitios Históricos.............**13** D1
Palacio Salcines................**14** D1
Parroquia de Santa Catalina de
  Riccis.........................**15** D1
Plaza del Mercado Agro
  Industrial....................(see 24)

SLEEPING
Hotel Guantánamo..............**16** B1
Lissett Foster Lara.............**17** D1
Osmaida Blanco Castillo........**18** C2

EATING
Agropecuario...................**19** B1
Cafetería Oroazul.............**20** D1
Coppelia.......................**21** D2
El Rápido......................**22** D1

Panadería La Palmita...........**23** D1
Plaza del Mercado Agro
  Industrial....................**24** D1
Restaurante Ensueños..........**25** B1
Restaurante Vegetariano
  Guantánamo..................**26** D1

DRINKING
La Ruina.......................**27** D1

ENTERTAINMENT
Casa de la Cultura............**28** D1
Casa de la Música.............**29** D1

Casa de la Trova...............**30** C2
Cine America...................**31** D1
Club Nevada...................**32** C2
Tumba Francesa Pompadour....**33** C2

SHOPPING
Fondo de Bienes Culturales...**34** D1
Photo Service..................**35** D1

TRANSPORT
Bici-Taxis......................**36** C2
Cubana.........................**37** D1
Train Ticket Office..............**38** C2

To Mariana Grajales
Airport (16km);
Baracoa (150km)

To Servi-Cupet Gas Station
& Havanautos (500m);
Estadio Van Troi (600m)

LIBRARIES
Biblioteca Policarpo Pineda Rustán (cnr Los Maceos & Emilio Giro; 8am-9pm Mon-Fri, 8am-5pm Sat, 9am-noon Sun) An architectural landmark.

MEDIA
Radio Trinchera Antimperialista CMKS Trumpets the word over 1070AM.
Venceremos & Lomería Two local newspapers published on Saturday.

MEDICAL SERVICES
Farmacia Principal Municipal (cnr Calixto García & Aguilera; 24hr) On the northeast corner of Parque Martí.
Hospital Agostinho Neto (35-54-50; Carretera de El Salvador Km 1; 24hr) At the west end of Plaza Mariana Grajales near Hotel Guantánamo. It will help foreigners in an emergency.

MONEY
Banco de Crédito y Comercio (Calixto García btwn Emilio Giro & Bartolomé Masó)
Cadeca (32-65-33; cnr Calixto García & Prado; 8:30am-6pm Mon-Sat, 8am-1pm Sun)

POST
Post office (Pedro A Pérez; 8am-1pm & 2-6pm Mon-Sat) On the west side of Parque Martí. There's also a DHL office here.

TRAVEL AGENCIES
Havanatur (32-63-65; Aguilera btwn Calixto García & Los Maceos; 9am-noon & 1-4pm Mon-Fri)

GUANTÁNAMO PROVINCE

Dangers & Annoyances

Guantánamo is a big city with a mellow town feel that pickpockets sometimes exploit. Stay alert especially on public transport and during Noches Guantanameras (p446).

Sights

Ostensibly unexciting, Guantánamo's geometric city grid has a certain rhythm. The tree-lined Av Camilo Cienfuegos with its morning exercisers, bizarre sculptures and central Ramblas-style walkway is the best place to get into the groove.

Though it's no Louvre, the esoteric **Museo Municipal** (cnr José Martí & Prado; admission CUC$1; 2-6pm Mon, 8am-noon & 3-7pm Tue-Sat) contains some interesting US Naval Base ephemera including prerevolutionary day passes and some revealing photos.

The unspectacular but noble **Parroquia de Santa Catalina de Riccis**, in Parque Martí, dates from 1863. In front of the church is a statue of local hero, Mayor General Pedro A Pérez, erected in 1928, opposite a tulip fountain and diminutive *glorieta* (bandstand).

Local architect Leticio Salcines (1888–1973) left a number of impressive works around Guantánamo, including the turreted market building **Plaza del Mercado Agro Industrial** (cnr Los Maceos & Prado), the **train station**, and his personal residence, the 1916 **Palacio Salcines** (cnr Pedro A Pérez & Prado; admission CUC$1; 8am-noon & 2-6pm Mon-Fri), a triumph of eclecticism and a monument said to be the building most representative of Guantánamo. The Palacio is now a small museum exhibiting colorful frescoes, Japanese porcelain and a rusty old music box that pipes out rather disappointing Mozart. A guided tour (CUC$1) makes the dull exhibits infinitely more interesting. On the palace's turret is *La Fama,* a sculpture designed by Italian artist Americo Chine that serves as the symbol of Guantánamo, her trumpet announcing good and evil. Salcines also designed the beautiful provincial library **Biblioteca Policarpo Pineda Rustán** (cnr Los Maceos & Emilio Giro), which was once the city hall (1934–51). Trials of Fulgencio Batista's thugs were held here in 1959, and a number were killed when they snatched a rifle and tried to escape.

For a fuller exposé of Guantánamo's interesting architectural heritage you might want to stop by at the **Oficina de Monumentos y Sitios Históricos** (Los Maceos btwn Emilio Giro & Flor Crombet). Ask about a map of city walking trails.

The huge bombastic **Monument to the Heroes**, glorifying the Brigada Fronteriza 'that defends the forward trench of socialism on this continent,' dominates Plaza Mariana Grajales (opposite the Hotel Guantánamo), one of the more impressive 'Revolution squares' on the island.

Sleeping

CASAS PARTICULARES

Lissett Foster Lara (32-59-70; Pedro A Pérez No 761 btwn Prado & Jesús del Sol; r CUC$20-25;) Like many Guantanameras, Lissett speaks perfect English and her house is polished, comfortable and decked out with the kind of plush fittings that wouldn't be out of place in a North American suburb. The highlight here, in more ways than one, is the roof terrace where you can recline above the car honks and street hassle for an hour or three.

Osmaida Blanco Castillo (32-51-93; Pedro A Pérez No 664 btwn Paseo & Narciso López; r CUC$20-25;) Another well-appointed place with a superb roof terrace (with bar!), two spacious rooms, a shady patio (with fish tank) and excellent meals available (you'll need them in this town). If it's full, try house 670A in the same street.

HOTELS

Hotel Guantánamo (Islazul; 38-10-15; Calle 13 Norte btwn Ahogados & 2 de Octubre; s/d CUC$23/30;) A lick of paint, a quick cleanup around the lobby and some newly planted flowers in the garden, and hey presto – the Hotel Guantánamo's back in business after a couple of years serving as a convalescent home for Operación Milagros. It's still a long way from the Ritz, but at least the generic rooms are clean, the pool has water in it, and there's a good reception bar-cafe mixing up tempting mojitos and serving coffee.

Villa La Lupe (Islazul; 38-26-12; Carretera de El Salvador Km 3.5; s/d CUC$23/30;) Located 5km north of the city on the road to El Salvador, Villa La Lupe – named after a song by Moncada and Granma survivor, Juan Almeida – is Guantánamo's best lodging option, despite its out-of-town location. Attractive, spacious cabins are arranged around a clean central swimming pool and the adjacent restaurant, which serves the usual staples of pork and rice, overlooks a leafy river where young girls celebrate their *quinciñeras* (15th birthdays). For music geeks the words of Almeida's famous song are emblazoned onto a granite wall.

Eating
RESTAURANTS
Restaurante Vegetariano Guantánamo (Pedro A Pérez; ☺ noon-2:30pm & 5-10:30pm; **V**) Vegetarians needn't get too excited; this is a slightly scruffy-looking local peso place situated by the main park, though it could help you jump off the daily cheese-sandwich and tortilla treadmill.

Cafetería Oroazul (cnr Los Maceos & Aguilera) A good place to catch a breather, feel the cool ceiling fan on your face and grab a revitalizing plate of spaghetti cooked a good 10 minutes past al dente. There are cleanish toilets inside.

El Rápido (cnr Flor Crombet & Los Maceos; ☺ 10am-10pm) It's a testament to Guantánamo's dire dining scene that you may have to resort to Cuba's gastronomically challenged fast-food chain. Rapid it ain't.

ourpick Restaurante Ensueños (Calle 15 Norte; ☺ noon-midnight) There's no sign; just a nude statue denoting the entrance to what is, by process of elimination, Guantánamo's best restaurant. Housed in a diminutive modern house tucked away behind the Hotel Guantánamo, the Palmares-run Ensueños serves up chicken, lobster and fish in some interesting sauces. Your *agua con gas* (mineral water) will probably go flat waiting for the meal to emerge from the kitchen, but who cares; for once it's worth the wait.

GROCERIES
Plaza del Mercado Agro Industrial (cnr Los Maceos & Prado; ☺ 7am-7pm Mon-Sat, 7am-2pm Sun) The town's public vegetable market is a red-domed Leticio Salcines creation and rather striking – both inside and out.

Agropecuario (Calle 13) The city's other outdoor market is opposite Plaza Mariana Grajales, just west of the Hotel Guantánamo; it sells bananas, yucca and onions by the truckload, plus plenty of peso snacks.

Panadería La Palmita (Flor Crombet No 305 btwn Calixto García & Los Maceos; ☺ 7:30am-5pm Mon-Sat) sells fresh bread, while the **Coppelia** (cnr Pedro A Pérez & Bernabe Varona) dishes out ice cream.

Drinking
La Ruina (cnr Calixto García & Emilio Giro; ☺ 10am-1am) This shell of a ruined colonial building has 9m ceilings and a crusty feet-on-the-table kind of

---

ASK A LOCAL
The word *Guantanamera* means 'woman from Guantánamo,' while *Guajira* means 'from the countryside.' The famous song was written by a popular *trovador* (singer/songwriter) called Joesito Fernández who allegedly had a romantic entanglement with a girl from the province. Most of the original lyrics have been replaced with words taken from José Martí's *Versos Sencillos*.

Rafael, Guantánamo

---

ambience. There are plenty of benches to prop you up after you've downed yet another bottle of beer and a popular karaoke scene for those with reality-TV ambitions. The bar menu's good for a snack lunch.

Entertainment
Guantánamo has its own distinctive musical culture, a subgenre of *son* known as *son-changüí* that mixes traditional riffs with Spanish, Afro-Cuban and even French influences. Its main exponent was Guantánamo-born Elio Revé (1930–97), former leader of the Orquesta Revé. You can get a taste at the following venues.

Casa de la Trova (Máximo Gómez No 1062; admission CUC$1; ☺ 8pm-1am) Guantánamo has two of these casas, although only this one was functioning at the time of writing. A bright royal-blue building on a quiet urban street, it offers the usual blend of traditional sounds with a *son-changüí* bias. Closed Monday.

Casa de la Música (Calixto García btwn Flor Crombet & Emilio Giro) Another well-maintained, more concert-orientated venue, with Thursday rap *peñas* (performances) and Sunday *trova* (traditional music) matinees.

ourpick Tumba Francesa Pompadour (Serafín Sánchez No 715) This peculiarly Guantánamo nightspot situated four blocks east of the train station specializes in a unique form of Haitian-style dancing. Programs (generally listed on the door) include *mi tumba baile* (*tumba* dance), *encuentro tradicional* (traditional get-together) and *peña campesina* (country music).

Casa de la Cultura (☎ 32-63-91; Pedro A Pérez; admission free) In the former Casino Español, on the west side of Parque Martí, this venue holds classical concerts and Afro-Cuban dance performances.

GUANTÁNAMO PROVINCE

Club Nevada (☎ 35-54-47; Pedro A Pérez No 1008 Altos cnr Bartolomé Masó; admission CUC$1) For the city's funkiest disco, head to this tiled-terrace rooftop, which blasts out salsa mixed with disco standards.

Cine America (Calixto García) A block north of Parque Martí, this is the city's best movie house. Check the taped-up posters outside.

Saturday nights are reserved for Noches Guantanameras, when Calle Pedro A Pérez is closed to traffic and stalls are set up in the street. Locals enjoy whole roast pig, belting music and copious amounts of rum. Watch out for the *borrachos* (drunks)!

Baseball games are played from October to April at the Estadio Van Troi in Reparto San Justo, 1.5km south of the Servi-Cupet gas station. Despite a strong sporting tradition, Guantánamo – nicknamed Los Indios – are perennial underachievers who haven't made the play-offs since 1999.

Shopping

No one comes to Guantánamo to shop but, if you want a local souvenir that doesn't have a US flag emblazoned on it, try the **Fondo de Bienes Culturales** (1st fl, Calixto García No 855) on the east side of Parque Martí.

Photo Service (Los Maceos btwn Aguilera & Flor Crombet) sells film, prints and batteries.

Getting There & Away

AIR

Cubana (☎ 35-45-33; Calixto García No 817) flies five times a week (CUC$124 one-way, 2½ hours) from Havana to **Mariana Grajales Airport** (☎ 35-54-54). There are no international flights to this airport.

BUS & TRUCK

The rather inconveniently placed Terminal de Ómnibus (bus station) is 5km west of the center on the old road to Santiago (a continuation of Av Camilo Cienfuegos). A taxi from the Hotel Guantánamo should cost CUC$3.

There are daily **Víazul** (www.viazul.com) buses daily to Baracoa (CUC$10, 9:30am) and Santiago de Cuba (CUC$6, 5:25pm).

Trucks to Santiago de Cuba and Baracoa also leave from the Terminal de Ómnibus. These will allow you to disembark in the smaller towns in between.

Trucks for Moa park on the road to El Salvador north of town near the entrance to the Autopista.

CAR

The Autopista Nacional to Santiago de Cuba ends near Embalse La Yaya, 25km west of Guantánamo, where the road joins the Carretera Central (at the time of writing work had begun to extend this road). At El Cristo, 12km outside Santiago de Cuba, you rejoin the Autopista. To drive to Guantánamo from Santiago de Cuba, follow the Autopista Nacional north about 12km to the top of the grade, then take the first turn to the right. Signposts are sporadic and vague, so take a good map and keep alert.

TRAIN

The **train station** (☎ 32-55-18; Pedro A Pérez), several blocks north of Parque Martí, has one departure for Havana (CUC$32, 9:05pm) on alternate days. This train also stops at Camagüey (CUC$13), Ciego de Ávila (CUC$16), Guayos (CUC$20; you should disembark here for Sancti Spíritus), Santa Clara (CUC$22) and Matanzas (CUC$29). There was no service to Santiago de Cuba at the time of writing. Purchase tickets in the morning of the day the train departs at the office on Pedro A Pérez.

Getting Around

Havanautos (☎ 35-54-05; Cupet Guantánamo) is by the Servi-Cupet gas station on the way out of town toward Baracoa. If you couldn't get a car in Santiago, you should be able to pick one up here.

The **Oro Negro gas station** (cnr Los Maceos & Jesús del Sol) is another option to fill up on gas before the 150km trek east to Baracoa.

Taxis hang out around Parque Martí or you can call **CubaTaxi** (☎ 32-36-36). The bus 48 (20 centavos) runs between the center and the Hotel Guantánamo every 40 minutes or so. There are also plenty of bici-taxis.

AROUND GUANTÁNAMO US NAVAL BASE

Traditionally, it has been possible to enjoy a distant view of the base from the isolated **Mirador de Malones** (admission incl drink CUC$5; ☼ 8am-3pm), a Gaviota-run restaurant perched on a 320m-high hill just east of the complex. At the time of writing, visits here had been suspended with no reliable information as to when (or if) they would be reinstated. Check the current status beforehand at Hotel Guantánamo (p444) or one of the Gaviota-run hotels in Baracoa (p453).

Should you get lucky, the entrance to the Mirador is at a Cuban military checkpoint on the main Baracoa highway, 27km southeast of Guantánamo. You then ascend 15km up a steep, severely rutted road to the restaurant where you can peer through a telescope at the surprisingly tranquil base below. Sharp-eyed observers should look out for a US flag fluttering at the northeast gate and the sinister glassy sheen of Camp Delta. Contrary to popular belief, there is no visible sign of Cuba's only Golden Arches.

Sleeping

Hotel Caimanera (Islazul; ☎ 9-9414; s/d with breakfast CUC$23/30; P ✗ ≋) This hotel is on a hilltop at Caimanera, near the perimeter of the US Naval Base, 21km south of Guantánamo. It has peculiar rules which permit only groups of seven or more on prearranged tours with an official Cuban guide to stay and enjoy the lookout – which isn't as good as the Mirador de Malones anyway. Ask at the Hotel Guantánamo about joining a trip.

ZOOLÓGICO DE PIEDRAS

A surreal spectacle even by Cuban standards, the **Zoológico de Piedras** (☎ 86-51-43; admission CUC$1; ☾ 9am-6pm Mon-Sat) is an animal sculpture park set amid thick foliage in the grounds of a mountain coffee farm, 20km northeast of Guantánamo. Carved quite literally out of the existing rock by sculptor Angel Iñigo Blanco starting in the late '70s, the animal sculptures now number more than 300 and range from hippos to giant serpents. A 1km path covers the highlights. To get here you'll need your own wheels or a taxi. Head east out of town and fork left toward Jamaica and Honduras. The 'zoo' is in the settlement of Boquerón.

SOUTH COAST

Leaving Guantánamo in a cloud of dust, you quickly hit the long, dry coastal road to the island's eastern extremity, Punta de Maisí. This is Cuba's spectacular semidesert region where cacti nestle on rocky ocean terraces and prickly aloe vera poke out from the dry scrub. Several little stone beaches between Playa Yacabo and Cajobabo make refreshing pit stops for those with time to linger, while the diverse roadside scenery – punctuated at intervals by rugged purple mountains and impossibly verdant riverside oases – impresses throughout.

At the far end of deserted Playita de Cajobabo, just before the main road bends inland, there is a **monument** commemorating José Martí's 1895 landing here to launch the Second War of Independence. A colorful billboard depicts the bobbing rowboat making for shore with Martí sitting calmly inside, dressed rather improbably in trademark dinner suit, not a hair out of place. It's a good snorkeling spot, flanked by dramatic cliffs. The famous **La Farola** (the lighthouse road) starts here (see boxed text, p455). Cyclists, take a deep breath…

Sleeping & Eating

Campismo Yacabo (s/d CUC$7.5/11) This place, by the highway 10km west of Imías, has 18 well-maintained cabins overlooking the sea near the mouth of the river. The cabins sleep four to six people and make a great beach getaway for groups on a budget. It's supposed to accept foreigners, but check ahead.

Cabañas Playa Imías (1-2 people CUC$10; ✗) This place, 2km east of Imías midway between Guantánamo and Baracoa, is near a long dark beach that drops off quickly into deep water. The 15 cement cabins have baths, fridges and TVs. It doesn't guarantee foreign admission but, as ever in Cuba, the rules are flexible.

PUNTA DE MAISÍ

From Cajobabo, the coastal road continues 51km northeast to La Máquina. As far as Jauco, the road is good; thereafter it's not so good. Coming from Baracoa to La Máquina (55km), it's a good road as far as Sabana, then rough in places from Sabana to La Máquina. Either way, La Máquina is the starting point of the very rough 13km track down to Punta de Maisí; it's best covered in a 4WD.

This is Cuba's easternmost point and there's a **lighthouse** (1862) and a small fine white-sand beach. You can see Haiti 70km away on a clear day.

At the time of writing the Maisí area was designated a military zone and not open to travelers.

BOCA DE YUMURÍ

Five kilometers south of Baracoa a road branches left off La Farola and travels 28km along the coast to Boca de Yumurí at the mouth of Río Yumurí. Near the bridge over the river is the Túnel de los Alemanes (German Tunnel), an amazing natural arch

GITMO – A SHORT HISTORY

If the early Spanish settlers could have chosen one piece of their fledgling colony to give away, chances are it would have been Guantánamo Bay, or Gitmo, as generations of homesick US Marines have unsentimentally dubbed it. Insufferably hot, mosquito-ridden and covered in a carpet of prickly bushes, this 116-sq-km nodule of land that hangs like an awkward aberration off Cuba's southeastern shoreline is a long way from Varadero-style paradise, as early settlers quickly discovered.

Columbus was the first arrival, dropping anchor at Fisherman's Point in 1494 when he shared a brief seafood barbecue with the indigenous Taíno. The British followed in 1741, during the long-winded War of Jenkin's Ear, but quickly withdrew after a deadly outbreak of yellow fever.

Procured via the infamous Platt Amendment in 1903 – ostensibly to protect Cuban independence in the aftermath of the Spanish-Cuban-American War – the US' initial reason for annexing Guantánamo was primarily to protect the eastern approach to the strategically important Panama Canal. In 1934 an upgrade of the original treaty reaffirmed the lease terms and agreed to honor them indefinitely unless both governments accorded otherwise. It also set an annual rent of approximately US$4000, a sum that the US generously continues to cough up but which the Cubans defiantly won't bank on the grounds that the occupation is illegal (Castro allegedly stored the checks in the top drawer of his office desk). Until 1958, when motorized traffic was officially cut off between Guantánamo and the outside world, hundreds of Cubans used to travel daily into the base for work, and there were still a handful of workers making the commute up until the turn of the 21st century. Expanded post-WWII, the oldest US military base on foreign soil has gone through many metamorphoses in the last 50 years, from tense Cold War battleground to the most virulent surviving political anachronism in the Western hemisphere. Castro was quick to demand the unconditional return of Guantánamo to Cuban sovereignty in 1959 but, locked in a Cold War deadlock with the Soviet Union and fearing the Cuban leader's imminent flight to Moscow, the US steadfastly refused. As relations between the countries deteriorated, Cuba cut off water and electricity to the base while the Americans surrounded it with the biggest minefield in the Western hemisphere (the mines were removed in 1996).

The recent history of the facility has been equally notorious. In January 1992, 11,000 Haitian migrants were temporarily held here, and in August 1994 the base was used as a dumping ground for 32,000 Cubans picked up by the US Coast Guard while trying to reach Florida. In May 1995 the Cuban and US governments signed an agreement allowing these refugees to enter the US but, since then, illegal Cuban immigrants picked up by the US Coast Guard at sea have been returned to Cuba under the 'wet foot, dry foot' policy.

Since 2002 the US has held more than 750 prisoners with suspected Al-Qaeda or Taliban links at the infamous Camp Delta in Guantánamo Bay without pressing criminal charges. Denied legal counsel and family contact while facing rigorous interrogations, the detainees mounted hunger strikes and at least four are known to have committed suicide. Following calls from Amnesty International and the UN in 2004 to close the base down and reports from the Red Cross that certain aspects of the camp regime were tantamount to torture, the US released 420 prisoners and charged just three of them. Of the remaining 245 prisoners (as of 2009), the US government intended to repatriate some to other countries for rehab or release, and transfer the rest to prisons in the US.

On taking office in January 2009, President Barack Obama promised to shut down Guantánamo's detention camps and thus end what he termed 'a sad chapter in US history.' The chances of the naval base being returned to Cuban sovereignty any time soon, however, remain thin.

of trees and foliage. Though lovely, the dark sand beach here has become the day trip from Baracoa. Hustlers hard-sell fried fish meals, while other people peddle colorful land snails called *polymitas*. They have become rare as a result of being harvested wholesale for tour-

ists, so refuse all offers. From the end of the beach a boat taxi (CUC$2) heads upstream to where the steep river banks narrow into a haunting natural gorge.

Boca de Yumurí makes a superb bike jaunt from Baracoa (56km round-trip): hot, but smooth and flat with great views and many potential stopovers (try Playa Bariguá at Km 25). You can arrange bikes in Baracoa – ask at your casa particular. Taxis will also take you here from Baracoa, or you can organize an excursion with Cubatur (CUC$22; see right).

BARACOA
pop 42,285

Take a pinch of Tolkein, a dash of Gabriel García Márquez, mix in a large cup of 1960s psychedelia and temper with a tranquilizing dose of Cold War–era socialism. Leave to stand for 400 years in a geographically isolated tropical wilderness with little or no contact with the outside world. The result: Baracoa – Cuba's weirdest, wildest, zaniest and most unique settlement that materializes like a surreal apparition after the long dry plod along Guantánamo's southern coast.

Cut off by land and sea for nearly half a millennium, Cuba's oldest city is, for most visitors, one of its most interesting. Founded in 1511 by Diego Velázquez de Cuéllar, Baracoa is a visceral place of fickle weather and haunting legends. After being semiabandoned in the mid-16th century, the town became a Cuban Siberia where rebellious revolutionaries were sent as prisoners. In the early 19th century French planters crossed the 70km-wide Windward Passage from Haiti and began farming the local staples of coconut, cocoa and coffee in the mountains and the economic wheels began to turn.

Baracoa developed in relative isolation from the rest of Cuba until the opening of La Farola (see boxed text, p455) in 1964, a factor that has strongly influenced its singular culture and traditions. Today its premier attractions include trekking up mysterious El Yunque, the region's signature flat-topped mountain, or indulging in some inspired local cooking using ingredients and flavors found nowhere else in Cuba.

Orientation

Gustavo Rizo Airport (airport code BCA) is 1km off the road to Moa beside Hotel Puerto Santo, 4km from central Baracoa. Baracoa's two bus stations are on opposite sides of town. There are three good hotels in or near the old town and another one next to the airport. Most of Baracoa can be explored on foot, but a bicycle is useful for visiting nearby beaches and rural pockets.

Information
INTERNET ACCESS & TELEPHONE

Etecsa Telepunto (cnr Antonio Maceo & Rafael Trejo; per hr CUC$6; ☑ 8:30am-7:30pm) Internet and international calls.

LIBRARIES

Biblioteca Raúl Gómez García (José Martí No 130; ☑ 8am-noon & 2-9pm Mon-Fri, 8am-4pm Sat)

MEDIA

Radio CMDX 'La Voz del Toa' Broadcasts over 650AM.

MEDICAL SERVICES

Clínica Internacional (☎ 64-10-37; cnr José Martí & Roberto Reyes; ☎ 24hr) A new place that treats foreigners; there's also a hospital 2km out of town on the road to Guantánamo.
Farmacia Principal Municipal (Antonio Maceo No 132; ☑ 24hr)

MONEY

Banco de Crédito y Comercio (☎ 64-27-71; Antonio Maceo No 99; ☑ 8am-2:30pm Mon-Fri)
Banco Popular de Ahorro (José Martí No 166; ☑ 8-11:30am & 2-4:30pm Mon-Fri) Cashes traveler's checks.
Cadeca (☎ 64-33-04; José Martí No 241)

POST

Post office (Antonio Maceo No 136; ☑ 8am-8pm)

TRAVEL AGENCIES

Cubatur (☎ 64-53-06; Antonio Maceo; ☑ 8am-noon & 2-5pm Mon-Fri) Helpful office that organizes tours to El Yunque and Parque Nacional Alejandro de Humboldt.
Ecotur (☎ 64-36-65; Coronel Cardoso No 24; ☑ 9am-5pm) Organizes nature tours to Duaba, Toa and Yumurí Rivers.

Sights & Activities
IN TOWN

Crying out for a major renovation, the rapidly disintegrating **Catedral de Nuestra Señora de la Asunción** (Antonio Maceo No 152) was built in 1833 on the site of a much older church. Its most famous artifact is the priceless Cruz de La Parra, a wooden cross said to have been erected by Columbus near Baracoa in 1492. Carbon dating has authenticated the cross' age (it dates from the late 1400s), but has indicated that it was originally made out of indigenous Cuban wood, thus disproving the legend that Columbus brought the cross from Europe. The church was closed at the time of writing and the cross was being displayed

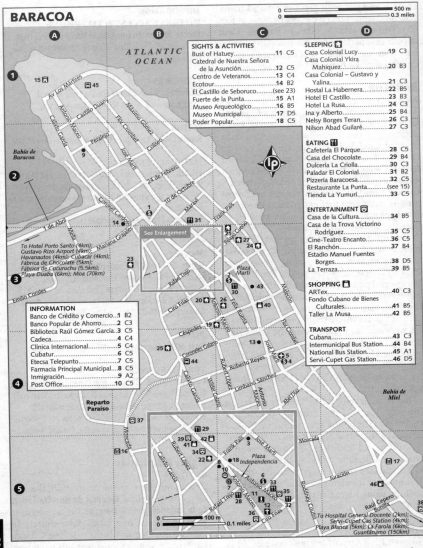

BARACOA

0 ────────── 500 m
0 ────────── 0.3 miles

SIGHTS & ACTIVITIES
Bust of Hatuey	11 C5
Catedral de Nuestra Señora de la Asunción	12 C5
Centro de Veteranos	13 C4
Ecotour	14 B2
El Castillo de Seboruco	(see 23)
Fuerte de la Punta	15 A1
Museo Arqueológico	16 A5
Museo Municipal	17 D5
Poder Popular	18 C5

SLEEPING
Casa Colonial Lucy	19 C3
Casa Colonial Ykira Mahiquez	20 B3
Casa Colonial – Gustavo y Yalina	21 C3
Hostal La Habernera	22 B5
Hotel El Castillo	23 C3
Hotel La Rusa	24 D3
Ina y Alberto	25 B4
Nelsy Borges Teran	26 C3
Nilson Abad Guilaré	27 C3

EATING
Cafetería El Parque	28 C5
Casa del Chocolate	29 B4
Dulcería La Criolla	30 C5
Paladar El Colonial	31 B2
Pizzería Baracoesa	32 C5
Restaurante La Punta	(see 15)
Tienda La Yumurí	33 C5

ENTERTAINMENT
Casa de la Cultura	34 B5
Casa de la Trova Victorino Rodríguez	35 C5
Cine-Teatro Encanto	36 B4
El Ranchón	37 B4
Estadio Manuel Fuentes Borges	38 D5
La Terraza	39 B5

SHOPPING
ARTex	40 C3
Fondo Cubano de Bienes Culturales	41 B5
Taller La Musa	42 B5

TRANSPORT
Cubana	43 C3
Intermunicipal Bus Station	44 B4
National Bus Station	45 A1
Servi-Cupet Gas Station	46 D5

INFORMATION
Banco de Crédito y Comercio	1 B2
Banco Popular de Ahorro	2 C3
Biblioteca Raúl Gómez García	3 C5
Cadeca	4 C4
Clínica Internacional	5 C4
Cubatur	6 C5
Etecsa Telepunto	7 C5
Farmacia Principal Municipal	8 C5
Inmigración	9 A2
Post Office	10 C5

To Hotel Porto Santo (4km); Gustavo Rizo Airport (4km); Havanautos (4km); Cubacar (4km); Fábrica de Chocolate (5km); Fábrica de Cucuruchu (5.5km); Playa Duaba (6km); Moa (70km)

To Hospital General Docente (2km); Servi-Cupet Gas Station (4km); Playa Blanca (5km); La Farola (6km); Guantánamo (150km)

0 ────── 100 m
0 ────── 0.1 miles

GUANTÁNAMO PROVINCE

in the last house on Calle Antonio Maceo, behind the church to the right.

Facing the cathedral is the **Bust of Hatuey**, a rebellious Indian *cacique* (chief) who fell out with the Spanish and was burned at the stake near Baracoa in 1512 after refusing to convert to Catholicism. Also on triangular Plaza Independencia (this being Baracoa, they couldn't have a *square* plaza) is the neoclassical **Poder Popular** (Antonio Maceo No 137), a municipal government building which you can admire from the outside.

The **Centro de Veteranos** (José Martí No 216; admission free) displays photos of those who perished in the 1959 Revolution and in the barely talked-about conflict in Angola.

Baracoa is protected by a trio of muscular Spanish forts. The **Fuerte Matachín** (1802) at the southern entrance to town, now houses the **Museo Municipal** (cnr José Martí & Malecón; admission CUC$1; ☻ 8am-noon & 2-6pm). Though small, this museum showcases an engaging chronology of Cuba's oldest settlement including *polymita* snail shells, the story of Che Guevara and the chocolate factory, and exhibits relating to pouty Magdalena Menasse (née Rovieskuya, 'La Rusa') after whom Alejo Carpentier based his famous book, *La Consagración de la Primavera* (The Rite of Spring).

A second Spanish fort, the **Fuerte de la Punta**, has watched over the harbor entrance at the other end of town since 1803. Today it's a Gaviota restaurant that was temporarily closed after 2008's Hurricane Ike.

Baracoa's third fort, **El Castillo de Seboruco**, begun by the Spanish in 1739 and finished by the Americans in 1900, is now Hotel El Castillo (p453). There's an excellent view of El Yunque's flat top over the shimmering swimming pool. A steep stairway at the southwest end of Calle Frank País climbs directly up.

Baracoa's newest and most impressive museum is the **Museo Arqueológico** (Moncada; admission CUC$3; ☻ 8am-5pm), situated in Las Cuevas del Paraíso 800m southeast of the Hotel El Castillo. The exhibits here are showcased in a series of caves that once acted as Taíno burial chambers. Among nearly 2000 authentic Taíno pieces are unearthed skeletons, ceramics, 3000-year-old petroglyphs and a replica of the *Ídolo de Tabaco*, a sculpture found in Maisí in 1903 that is considered to be one of the most important Taíno finds in the Caribbean.

THE TAÍNO MYTH

Historical consensus maintains that Cuba's pre-Columbian people, the Taínos, were all but eradicated within 50 years of Velázquez' colonization, wiped out by a mix of Spanish brutality and European disease. But in more recent times, this long-standing myth has come under increasing scrutiny.

In his 2004 book *Cuba: A New History,* British historian Richard Gott argues that thousands of Indians could have survived for decades, even centuries, after the official Spanish censuses had written them off. And he wasn't the first doubter.

The re-evaluation of Taíno culture began in 1901 when American anthropologist Stewart Culin found credible evidence of Indian people still living in the isolated mountains of the Oriente. Half a century later, respected Cuban scientist Antonio Núñez Jiménez reported similarly significant remnants of a 'lost' Taíno culture in the Sierra Maestra.

Seen through the prism of history, these finds aren't surprising. Throughout the first three centuries of Spanish colonization, vast swathes of Cuba remained uncharted and unconquered. Retreating into the impenetrable southeastern mountains and northern coral keys, disparate indigenous groups teamed up with runaway slaves in independent fugitive communities known as *cimarrones* or *palenques.*

Meanwhile, in the growing urban areas, less rebellious indigenous populations were herded into official towns earmarked by the Spanish as *pueblos Indios.* The best-known of these was Guanabacoa, now a suburb of Havana; another was Jiguaní, in modern-day Granma province. Existing side by side in these settlements, Old and New World cultures mixed and cross-fertilized, allowing Indian practices and words to seep into everyday Cuban life.

Indian culture was also passed through bloodlines. With European females in short supply during the early colonial period, it is estimated that at least one in three Spanish males took Indian women as their wives, a practice which saw the gradual dissipation of Indian blood through successive generations of Cuban criollos. Some of these mixed-race people eventually rose to positions of prominence in Cuban society, the most notable example being 20th-century president, Fulgencio Batista, a *mulato* from Holguín whose mixed Taíno, black and Chinese heritage was well known.

Today many people in and around Baracoa claim Indian blood although, as yet, no DNA-testing has been able to verify these pronouncements (similar tests in Puerto Rico have revealed that 60% of the population has some Taíno blood). Easier to confirm are the various cultural traditions passed on by the indigenous people, from the small *bohíos* (thatched huts), to the traditional food and the multinational Cuban *cohiba* (cigar).

ASK A LOCAL

Coming into Baracoa you'll get many people approaching you on La Farola selling all kinds of wares. Take the *cucuruchu* – a sweet, locally concocted blend of honey, mango, coconuts, banana and more (not one mix is ever the same), but bypass the *polymita* snail shells which are an endangered species.

José, Baracoa

One of the staff will enthusiastically show you around.

SOUTHEAST OF TOWN

Southeast of town are a couple of magical **hikes** that can only be done on foot. Passing the Fuerte Matachín, hike southeast past the baseball stadium and along the dark-sand beach for about 20 minutes to a rickety wooden bridge over the Río Miel. After crossing the bridge turn left, and follow a track up through a cluster of rustic houses to another junction. Turn left again and continue along the vehicle track until the houses clear and you see a fainter single-track path leading off left to **Playa Blanca**, an idyllic spot for a picnic.

Staying straight on the track, you'll come to a trio of wooden homesteads. The third of these houses belongs to the Fuentes family. Do not continue alone past this point as you are entering a military zone. For a donation (CUC$3 to CUC$5 per person), Señor Fuentes will lead you on a hike to his family **finca**, where you can stop for coffee, coconuts and tropical fruit. Further on he'll show you the **Cueva de Aguas**, a cave with a sparkling, freshwater swimming hole inside, and tracking back up the hillside (a sure pair of feet are required for this bit) you'll come to an **archaeological trail** with some more caves and marvelous views over the ocean.

NORTHWEST OF TOWN

Heading northwest on the Moa road, take the Hotel Porto Santo and airport turning (right) and continue for 2km past the airport runway to **Playa Duaba**, a black-sand beach at the mouth of the river where Antonio Maceo, Flor Crombet and a score of men landed in 1895 to start the Second War of Independence. There's a memorial monument here, but the

beach itself is nothing special and the sand flies can be ferocious.

The delicious sweet smells filling the air in this neck of the woods are concocted in the famous **Fábrica de Chocolate**, 1km past the airport turnoff, opened not by Willy Wonka but by Che Guevara in 1963. Half a kilometer further on you'll pass the equally tempting **Fábrica de Cucuruchu** where you can buy Baracoa's sweetest treat, wrapped in an environmentally friendly palm frond, for a few centavos.

Tours

Organized tours are a good way to view Baracoa's hard-to-reach outlying sights, and the Cubatur office (p449) on Plaza Independencia can book most of them. Highlights include: El Yunque (CUC$18), Playa Maguana (CUC$18), Parque Nacional Alejandro de Humboldt (CUC$28), Río Toa (CUC$11) and Boca de Yumurí (CUC$22).

Festivals & Events

During the first week of April, Baracoa commemorates the landing of Antonio Maceo at Duaba on April 1, 1895, with a raucous **Carnaval** along the Malecón. Every Saturday night, Calle Antonio Maceo is closed off for **Noche Baracuensa**, when food, drink and music take over.

Sleeping

CASAS PARTICULARES

Casa Colonial – Gustavo & Yalina (☎ 64-25-36; Flor Crombet No 125 btwn Frank País & Pelayo Cuervo; r CUC$15-20; 🞲) This grand house was built in 1898 by a French sugar baron from Marseille, an esteemed ancestor of the current residents. The big windowless rooms have antique furnishings, and culinary treats include local freshwater prawns and hot (Baracoan) chocolate for breakfast.

Casa Colonial Lucy (☎ 64-35-48; Céspedes No 29 btwn Rubert López & Antonio Maceo; r CUC$20; 🞲) A perennial favorite, Casa Lucy – which dates from 1840 – has a lovely local character with patios, porches and flowering begonias. There are two rooms as well as terraces here on different levels and the atmosphere is quiet and secluded. Lucy's son is trilingual and offers salsa lessons and massage.

Nelsy Borges Teran (☎ 64-35-69; Antonio Maceo No 171 btwn Ciro Frías & Céspedes; r CUC$20; 🞲) The food is better than the room – and the room ain't half bad. You'll have no culinary worries at Nelsy's with plenty of vegetarian options and adventurous deserts. The rooms have TV and stocked fridge (including chocolate) and there's a great terrace upstairs with rocking chairs overlooking the street.

Casa Colonial Ykira Mahiquez (☎ 64-24-66; Antonio Maceo No 168A btwn Ciro Frías & Céspedes; r CUC$20; ▨) Welcoming and hospitable, Ykira is Baracoa's hostess with the mostess and serves a mean dinner made with homegrown herbs. Her cozy house is one block from the cathedral and full of local charm.

Ina & Alberto (☎ 64-27-29; Calixto García No 158; r CUC$20-25; ▨) Perched on a hill at the back of town, this place has good views, two terraces and private entry. Alberto is something of a local guide who knows the region like the back of his hand.

Nilson Abad Guilaré (☎ 64-31-23; nilson@santiago caribe.com; Flor Crombet No 143 btwn Ciro Frías & Pelayo Cuervo; r CUC$25; ▨) Nilson's a real gent who keeps what must be one of the cleanest houses in Cuba. This fantastic self-contained apartment has a huge bathroom, kitchen access and roof terrace with sea views. The fish dinners with coconut sauce are to die for.

HOTELS

Hotel El Castillo (Gaviota; ☎ 64-51-64; Loma del Paraíso; s/d CUC$42/58; ▨ ▨) You could recline like a colonial-era conquistador in this historic place housed in the hilltop Castillo de Seboruco, except that conquistadors didn't have access to swimming pools, satellite TV or a room maid who folds towels into ships, swans and other advanced forms of origami. While the 34 rooms at this fine Gaviota-run hotel might be a little dilapidated and damp, the jaw-dropping El Yunque views and all-pervading Baracoan friendliness more than make up for it.

Hotel Porto Santo (Gaviota; ☎ 64-51-06; Carretera del Aeropuerto; s/d CUC$42/58; P ▨ ▨) On the bay where Columbus, allegedly, planted his first cross, this well-integrated low-rise hotel has the feel of a small resort. Situated 4km from the town center and 200m from the airport, there are 36 more-than-adequate rooms all within earshot of the sea. Lie awake with the windows open and let the ethereal essence of Baracoa transport you. A steep stairway leads down to a tiny, wave-lashed beach.

Hotel La Rusa (Gaviota; ☎ 64-30-11; Máximo Gómez No 161; r CUC$49; ▨) Khrushchev wasn't the first Russian to hedge his bets with Fidel Castro. Long before the Bay of Pigs sent the Cubans running into the arms of the Soviets, Russian émigré Magdalena Rovieskuya was posting aid to Castro's rebels up in the Sierra Maestra. Rovieskuya – known affectionately as 'La Rusa' – first came to Baracoa in the 1930s where she built a 12-room hotel and quickly became a local celebrity receiving such esteemed guests as Errol Flynn, Che Guevara and Fidel Castro. After her death in 1978, La Rusa became a more modest government-run joint that was all but washed away in Hurricane Ike. It was undergoing a thorough renovation at the time of writing.

our pick Hostal La Habanera (Gaviota; ☎ 64-23-37; Antonio Maceo No 126; r CUC$49; ▨) Atmospheric and inviting in a way only Baracoa can muster, La Habanera sits in a restored pastel-pink colonial mansion where the cries of passing street hawkers compete with an effusive mix of hip-gyrating music emanating from the Casa de la Cultura next door. The four front bedrooms share a street-facing balcony replete with tiled floor and rocking chairs, while the downstairs lobby boasts a bar, the 1511 restaurant, and an interesting selection of local books.

Eating

After the dull monotony of just about everywhere else, eating in Baracoa is a full-on sensory experience. Cooking here is creative, tasty and – above all – different. Local delicacies include *cucuruchu* (grated coconut mixed with sugar, honey and guava, wrapped in a palm frond), fish with coconut sauce, *bacán* (pulped plantain and coconut milk) and *teti* (a tiny red fish indigenous to the Río Toa). To experience the real deal, eat in your casa particular.

PALADARES

Paladar El Colonial (José Martí No 123; mains CUC$10; ♡ lunch & dinner) The town's only surviving paladar has been knocking out good food for years with an exotic Baracoan twist. Still run out of a handsome wooden clapboard house on Calle José Martí, the menu has become a bit more limited in recent times (less octopus and more chicken), though you still get the down-to-earth service and the delicious coconut sauce.

RESTAURANTS

Casa del Chocolate (Antonio Maceo No 123; ♡ 7:20am-11pm) It's enough to make even Willy Wonka wonder. You're sitting next to a chocolate factory but, more often than not, there's none to be had in this bizarre little casa just off the main square. The quickest way to check out Baracoa's on-off supply situation is to stick your head around the door and utter the word 'chocolate' to one of the bored-looking waitresses. *No hay* equals 'no,' a faint nod equals 'yes.' On a good day it sells chocolate ice cream and the hot stuff in mugs. For all its foibles, it's a Baracoa rite of passage.

Pizzería Baracoesa (Antonio Maceo No 155) A recent renovation (ie new tablecloths) have upped the ante a little at this peso place, but it's still got a long way to go to tempt you out of your casa particular.

Cafetería El Parque (Antonio Maceo No 142; 24hr) This open terrace gets regularly drenched in those familiar Baracoa rain showers, but that doesn't seem to detract from its popularity. The favored meeting place of just about everyone in town, you're bound to end up here at some point tucking into spaghetti and pizza as you watch the world go by.

Restaurante La Punta (Fuerte de la Punta; 10am-11pm) In an old fort overlooking the Atlantic, this historic restaurant now run by Gaviota was temporarily closed at the time of writing after the havoc wreaked by Hurricane Ike. It was due to reopen in 2009.

GROCERIES

Tienda La Yumurí (Antonio Maceo No 149; 8:30am-noon & 1:30-5pm Mon-Sat, 9am-noon Sun) Get in line for the good selection of groceries here.

Dulcería La Criolla (José Martí No 178) This place sells bread, pastries and – when it feels like it – the famous Baracoan chocolate.

Drinking & Entertainment

our pick **Casa de la Trova Victorino Rodríguez** (Antonio Maceo No 149A) Cuba's smallest, zaniest, wildest and most atmospheric *casa de la trova* (*trova* house) rocks nightly to the voodoolike rhythms of *changüí-son*. Order a mojito in a jam jar and sit back and enjoy the show.

El Ranchón (admission CUC$1; from 9pm) Atop a long flight of stairs at the western end of Coroneles Galano, El Ranchón mixes an exhilarating hilltop setting with taped disco and salsa music and legions of resident *jineteras* (women who attach themselves to male foreigners for monetary or material gain). Maybe that's why it's so insanely popular. Watch your step on the way down – it's a scary 146-step drunken tumble.

Casa de la Cultura (64-23-49; Antonio Maceo No 124 btwn Frank País & Maraví) This venue does a wide variety of shows including some good rumba incorporating the textbook Cuban styles of *guaguancó, yambú* and *columbia* (subgenres of rumba). Go prepared for *mucho* audience participation.

La Terraza (Antonio Maceo btwn Maraví & Frank País; admission CUC$1; 9pm-2am Mon-Thu, 9pm-4am Fri-Sun) A rooftop disco with occasional hot salsa septets that you'll hear all over town.

Cine-Teatro Encanto (Antonio Maceo No 148) The town's only cinema is in front of the cathedral. It looks disused but you'll probably find it's open.

From October to April, baseball games are held at the Estadio Manuel Fuentes Borges, southeast along the beach from the Museo Municipal.

Shopping

Good art is easy to find in Baracoa and, like most things in this whimsical seaside town, it has its own distinctive flavor.

Fondo Cubano de Bienes Culturales (Antonio Maceo No 120; 9am-5pm Mon-Fri, 9am-noon Sat & Sun) This shop sells Hatuey woodcarvings and T-shirts with indigenous designs.

ARTex (José Martí btwn Céspedes & Coroneles Galano) For the usual tourist fare check out this place.

Taller La Musa (Antonio Maceo No 124) Call by this place opposite the Casa de la Cultura where you can seek out typically imaginative Baracoan art.

Getting There & Away

The closest train station is in Guantánamo, 150km southwest.

AIR

Gustavo Rizo Airport (64-53-76) is 4km northwest of the town, just behind the Hotel Porto Santo. **Cubana** (64-21-71; José Martí No 181; 8am-noon & 2-4pm Mon-Fri) has two weekly flights from Havana to Baracoa (CUC$135 one-way, Thursday and Sunday).

Be aware that the planes and buses out of Baracoa are sometimes fully booked, so don't come here on a tight schedule without outbound reservations.

BUS & TRUCK

The **national bus station** (64-36-70; cnr Av Los Mártires & José Martí) has **Víazul** (www.viazul.com) buses to Guantánamo (CUC$10, three hours), continu-

LA FAROLA

Cut from the rest of the island by the velvety peaks of the Cuchillas de Toa, the only way in or out of Baracoa before the 1960s was by sea.

Four hundred and fifty years of solitude finally came to an end in 1964 with the opening of La Farola (the lighthouse road), a present from a grateful Fidel Castro to Baracoa's loyal revolutionaries who had supported him during the war in the mountains.

Fifty-five kilometers in length, La Farola traverses the steep-sided Sierra del Puril before snaking its way precipitously down through a landscape of grey granite cliffs and pine-scented cloud forest and falling, with eerie suddenness, upon the lush tropical paradise of the Atlantic coastline.

Giant ferns sprout from lichen-covered rocks; small wooden *campesino* (country) huts cling to sharp bends; and local hawkers appear, seemingly out of nowhere, holding up bananas, oranges and a sweet-tasting local delicacy wrapped in a palm frond known as *cucuruchu*.

Construction of La Farola actually began during the Batista era, but the project was indefinitely shelved when it ran into problems with engineering and funds (workers weren't paid). Reignited after the Revolution, the ambitious highway ultimately took 500 workers more than four years to build and consumed 300kg of concrete per square meter.

Today, La Farola remains the only fully paved route into Baracoa and is responsible for 75% of the town's supplies. Listed as one of the seven civil-engineering wonders of modern Cuba (and the only one outside Havana), it crosses from the island's driest zone to its wettest and deposits travelers in what, for many, is its most magical and serendipitous destination.

ing to Santiago de Cuba (CUC$16, five hours) daily at 2:15pm. Bus tickets can be reserved in advance through **Cubatur** (☎ 64-53-06; Antonio Maceo No 181) for a CUC$5 commission, or you can usually stick your name on the list a day or so beforehand.

The **intermunicipal bus station** (cnr Coroneles Galano & Calixto García) has two or three trucks a day to Moa (90 minutes, departures from 6am) and Guantánamo (four hours, departures from 2am). Bank on big crowds and bad roads. Prices are a few Cuban pesos.

Getting Around

The best way to get to and from the airport is by taxi (CUC$2) or bici-taxi (CUC$1), if you're traveling light.

There's a helpful **Havanautos** (☎ 64-53-44) car-rental office at the airport. **Cubacar** (☎ 64-51-55) is at the Hotel Porto Santo. The **Servi-Cupet gas station** (José Martí; ☉ 24hr) is at the entrance to town and also 4km from the center, on the road to Guantánamo. If you're driving to Havana, note that the northern route through Moa and Holguín is fastest but the road disintegrates rapidly after Playa Maguana. Most locals prefer the La Farola route.

Bici-taxis around Baracoa should charge five pesos a ride, but they often ask 10 to 15 pesos from foreigners.

Most casas particulares will be able to procure you a bicycle for CUC$3 per day. The ultimate bike ride is the 20km ramble down to Playa Maguana, one of the most scenic roads in Cuba. Lazy daisies can rent mopeds for CUC$24 either at Cafetería El Parque (opposite) or Hotel El Castillo (p453).

NORTHWEST OF BARACOA
Sights & Activities

The **Finca Duaba** (☉ noon-4pm Tue-Sun), 5km out of Baracoa on the road to Moa and then 1km inland, offers a fleeting taste of the Baracoan countryside. It's a verdant farm surrounded with profuse tropical plants and embellished with a short Cacao (cocoa) trail that explains the history and characteristics of the plant with some interactive displays. There's also a good *ranchón*-style restaurant and the opportunity to swim in the Río Duaba. A bici-taxi can drop you at the road junction.

The **Río Toa**, 10km northwest of Baracoa, is the third-longest river on the north coast of Cuba and the country's most voluminous. It is also an important bird and plant habitat. Cocoa trees and the ubiquitous coconut palm are grown in the Valle de Toa. A vast hydroelectric project on the Río Toa was abandoned after a persuasive campaign led by the Fundación de la Naturaleza y El Hombre convinced authorities it would do irreparable ecological damage; engineering and economic reasons also played a part. **Rancho Toa** is a Palmares restaurant reached via a right-hand turnoff just before the Toa Bridge. You can organize boat or kayak trips here for CUC$3 to CUC$10 and watch acrobatic Baracoans scale *cocotero* (coconut palm). A traditional Cuban feast of whole roast pig is available if you can rustle up enough people (eight usually).

Most of this region lies within the Cuchillas de Toa Unesco Biosphere Reserve, an area of 2083 sq km that incorporates the Alejandro de Humboldt World Heritage Site. This region contains the largest rainforest in Cuba, with trees exhibiting many precious woods, and has a high number of endemic species.

Baracoa's rite of passage is the 8km (up and down) hike to **El Yunque**. At 575m it's not Kilimanjaro, but the views from the summit and the flora and birdlife along the way are stupendous. **Cubatur** (☎ 64-53-06; José Martí No 181, Baracoa) offers this tour almost daily (CUC$18 per person, minimum two people). The fee covers admission, guide, transport and a sandwich. The hike is hot (bring sufficient water) and usually muddy. It starts from a campismo 3km past the Finca Duaba (4km from the Baracoa–Moa road). Bank on seeing *tocororo* (Cuba's national bird), *zunzún* (the world's smallest bird), butterflies and *polymitas*.

On **Playa Maguana** snorkeling is available from boats at a nearby reef. There's no hire kiosk as such; the local boatman just works the strip.

Sleeping & Eating

our pick **Villa Maguana** (Gaviota; ☎ 64-53-72; Carretera a Moa; s/d CUC$60/75; P X) Good old Gaviota renovated this delightful place, 22km north of Baracoa, adding a trio of rustic wooden villas to the original four-room building. Environmental foresight has meant that it still retains its famously dreamy setting above a bite-sized scoop of sand guarded by two rocky promontories. There's a restaurant and some less rustic luxuries in the rooms such as satellite TV, fridge and air-con.

The main strip of Playa Maguana is served by a small Palmares **snack bar** (☉ 9am-5pm) that sells cold drinks, fried chicken and sandwiches. The local fishermen have been known to fire up an excellent fish barbecue.

PARQUE NACIONAL ALEJANDRO DE HUMBOLDT

'Unmatched in the Caribbean' is a phrase often used to describe this most dramatic and diverse of Cuban national parks, named after German naturalist and explorer Alexander von Humboldt who first came here in 1801. The accolade is largely true. Designated a Unesco World Heritage Site in 2001, Humboldt's steep pine-clad mountains and creeping morning mists protect an unmatched ecosystem that is, according to Unesco, 'one of the most biologically diverse tropical island sites on earth.' Perched above the Bahía de Taco, 40km northwest of Baracoa, lie 594 sq km of pristine forest and 2641 hectares of lagoon and mangroves. With 1000 flowering plant species and 145 types of fern, it is far and away the most diverse plant habitat in the entire Caribbean. Due to the toxic nature of the

---

THE IVORY-BILLED WOODPECKER

Considered the Holy Grail for binocular-wielding ornithologists, sightings of the *carpintero real* (ivory-billed woodpecker) are so rare that US-based twitchers have been known to break the travel embargo in an attempt to see it.

Native to both eastern Cuba and parts of the American South, the last verified sighting of this striking black-and-white bird was by Cuban scientists in Guantánamo province in 1987 (in what is now the Parque Nacional Alejandro de Humboldt) and many observers now consider it extinct.

Hope was restored briefly in 2005 when a male woodpecker – distinguishable by its prominent head crest – was allegedly spotted in the US state of Arkansas, but these reports have so far remained unverified.

The species' decline is linked directly to deforestation in both Cuba and the US. Ivory-billed woodpeckers inhabit hardwood forests and require a spacious 25 sq km per pair to feed and survive.

If you want to join the search, head for the mountains around Baracoa where you'll need to look out for the bird's shiny black-and-white plumage, and 75cm wingspan (the ivory-billed woodpecker is the second-largest member of the woodpecker family). Even more distinctive is its characteristic bill drum, said to sound like a toy trumpet.

underlying rocks in the area, plants have been forced to adapt in order to survive. As a result, endemism in the area is high. Seventy percent of the plants found here are endemic, as are many vertebrates and invertebrates. Several endangered species also survive, including Cuban Amazon parrots, hook-billed kites and – arguably – the ivory-billed woodpecker (see boxed text, opposite). Lauded for its unique evolutionary processes, the park is heavily protected and acts as a paradigm for Cuba's environmental protection efforts elsewhere.

Activities

The park contains a small **visitors center** (☎ 38-14-31) staffed with biologists plus a network of trails leading to waterfalls, a *mirador* (lookout) and a massive karst system with caves around the Farallones de Moa. Three trails are currently open to the public and take in only a tiny segment of the park's 594 sq km. Typically, you can't just wander around on your own. The available hikes are: **Balcón de Iberia**, at 5km the park's most challenging loop; **El Recrea**, a 2km stroll around the bay; and the **Bahía de Taco circuit**, which incorporates a boat tour (with a manatee-friendly motor developed by scientists here) through the mangroves and the bay, plus the 2km hike. Each option is accompanied by a highly professional guide. Prices range from CUC$5 to CUC$10, depending on the hike, but it's far better to organize an excursion through Cubatur (p449) in Baracoa.

Sleeping

Lodging is periodically available at the barebones Campismo Bahía de Taco. Phone ahead or inquire at Hostal La Habanera (p453) in Baracoa.

Getting There & Away

You can arrange a tour through an agency in Baracoa or get here independently. The road is rough but passable in a hire car if driven with care.

Directory

CONTENTS

Accommodation	458
Activities	461
Business Hours	461
Children	461
Climate Charts	462
Courses	462
Customs	463
Dangers & Annoyances	463
Embassies & Consulates	464
Food	464
Gay & Lesbian Travelers	464
Holidays	465
Insurance	465
Internet Access	465
Legal Matters	465
Maps	465
Money	466
Post	467
Shopping	467
Telephone	468
Time	469
Toilets	469
Tourist Information	469
Travelers with Disabilities	469
Visas & Tourist Cards	469
Volunteering	472
Women Travelers	472

ACCOMMODATION

Cuban accommodation runs the gamut from CUC$10 beach cabins to five-star resorts. Solo travelers are penalized price-wise, paying 75% of the price of a double room.

In this book, budget means anything under CUC$40 for two people. In this range, casas particulares are almost always better value than a hotel. Only the most deluxe casas particulares in Havana will be anything over CUC$35, where you're assured quality amenities and attention. In cheaper casas particulares (CUC$15), you may have to share a bath and will have a fan instead of air-con. In the rock-bottom places (campismos, mostly), you'll be lucky if there are sheets and running water, though there are usually private baths. If you're staying in a place intended for Cubans, you'll compromise materially, but the memories are guaranteed to be platinum.

The midrange category (from CUC$40 to CUC$80) is a lottery, with some stylish colonial hotels and some awful places. In midrange hotels, you can expect air-con, private hot-water bath, clean linens, satellite TV, a restaurant and a swimming pool – although the architecture's often uninspiring and the food not exactly gourmet.

Unsurprisingly, the most comfortable top-end hotels cost CUC$80 and up for two people. These are usually partly foreign-owned and maintain international standards (although service can sometimes be a bit lax). Rooms have everything that a midrange hotel has, plus big, quality beds and linens; a minibar; international phone service; and perhaps a terrace or view. Havana has some real gems.

Factors influencing rates are time of year, location and hotel chain (in this book the chain is listed after the hotel to give you an idea of what standard and services to expect). Low season is generally mid-September to early December and February to May (except for Easter week). Christmas and New Year is what's called extreme high season, when rates are 25% more than high-season rates. Bargaining is sometimes possible in casas particulares – though as far as foreigners go, it's not really the done thing. The casa owners in any given area pay generic taxes and the prices you will be quoted reflect this. You'll find very few casas in Cuba that aren't priced between CUC$15 to CUC$35, unless you're up for a long stay. Prearranging Cuban accommodation has become easier now that more Cubans (unofficially) have access to the internet.

BOOK YOUR STAY ONLINE

For more accommodation reviews and recommendations by Lonely Planet authors, check out the online booking service at www .lonelyplanet.com/hotels. You'll find the true, insider low-down on the best places to stay. Reviews are thorough and independent. Best of all, you can book online.

The following chains and internet agencies offer online booking and/or information:

Casa Particular Organization (www.casaparticular cuba.org) Reader-recommended for prebooking private rooms.

Cubacasas (www.cubacasas.net) The best online source for casa particular information and booking; up to date, accurate and with colorful links to hundreds of private rooms across the island (in English and French).

Cubalinda.com (www.cubalinda.com) Havana-based, so it knows its business.

Gran Caribe (www.grancaribe.cu)

Islazul (www.islazul.cu)

Sol Meliá (www.solmeliacuba.com) Also offers discounts.

Vacacionar (www.dtcuba.com) Official site of Directorio Turístico de Cuba.

Campismos

Campismos are where Cubans go on vacation. There are more than 80 of them sprinkled throughout the country and they are wildly popular (an estimated one million Cubans use them annually). Hardly 'camping,' most of these installations are simple concrete cabins with bunk beds, foam mattresses and cold showers. Campismos are the best place to meet Cubans, make friends and party in a natural setting.

Campismos are ranked either *nacional* or *internacional*. The former are (technically) only for Cubans, while the latter host both Cubans and foreigners and are more upscale, with air-con and/or linens. There are currently a dozen international campismos in Cuba

ranging from the hotel-standard Aguas Claras (Pinar del Río) to the more basic Puerto Rico Libre (Holguín). In practice, campismo staff may rent out a *nacional* cabin (or tent space) to a foreigner pending availability, but it depends on the installation, and many foreigners are turned away (not helpful when you've traveled to a way-out place on the pretext of getting in). To avoid this situation, we've listed only international campismos in this book.

For a full list of all the country's campismos (both *nacional* and *internacional*), you can pick up an excellent *Guía de Campismo* (CUC$2.50) from any of the Reservaciones de Campismo offices.

As far as international campismos go, contact the excellent **Cubamar** (☎ 7-833-2523/4; www .cubamarviajes.cu; Calle 3 btwn Calle 12 & Malecón, Vedado; ✆ 8:30am-5pm Mon-Sat) in Havana for reservations. If you're adamant to try winging it in a *campismo nacional,* try the provincial Campismo Popular office to make a reservation closer to the installation proper (some office addresses can be found in the relevant regional chapters). Cabin accommodation in international campismos costs from CUC$10 to CUC$20 per bed. Prices at the plush cabins of Villas Aguas Claras (Pinar del Río province; p204) and Guajimico (Cienfuegos province; p274) are higher.

Cubamar also rents mobile homes (campervans) called *autocaravanas,* which sleep four adults and two children. Prices are around CUC$165 per day (but vary according to type, season and number of days required) including insurance (plus CUC$400 refundable deposit). You can park these campers wherever it's legal to park a regular car. There are 21 campismos or hotels that have Campertour facilities giving you access to electricity and water. These are a great alternative for families.

Renegade cyclists aside, few tourists tent camp in Cuba. Yet, the abundance of beaches, plus the helpfulness and generosity of Cubans make camping surprisingly easy and rewarding. Beach camping means insanely aggressive *jejenes* (sand fleas) and mosquitoes. The repellent sold locally just acts as a marinade for your flesh, so bring something strong – DEET-based if you're down with chemicals. Camping supplies per se don't exist; bring your own or improvise.

Casas Particulares

Private rooms are the best option for independent travelers in Cuba and a great way of meeting the locals on their home turf. Furthermore, staying in these venerable, family-orientated establishments will give you a far more open and less censored view of the country with its guard down, and your understanding (and appreciation) of Cuba will grow far richer as a result. Casa owners also often make excellent tour guides.

You'll know houses renting rooms by the blue insignia on the door marked 'Arrendador Divisa.' There are thousands of casas particulares all over Cuba; 3000 in Havana alone and nearly 400 in Trinidad. From penthouses to historical homes, all manner of rooms are available from CUC$15 to CUC$35. Although some houses will treat you like a business paycheck, the vast majority of casa owners are warm, open and impeccable hosts.

Government regulation of casas is intense and it's illegal to rent out private rooms in resort areas. Owners pay CUC$100 to CUC$250 per room per month depending on location; plus extra for off-street parking, to post a sign advertising their rooms and to serve meals. These taxes must be paid whether the rooms are rented or not. Owners must keep a register of all guests and report each new arrival within 24 hours. For these reasons, you will find it hard to bargain for rooms. You will also be requested to produce your passport (not a photocopy). Penalties are high for infractions, and updated regulations in 2004 restricted casas to two people (excluding minors under 17) per room and only two rooms per house. Regular government inspections ensure that conditions inside casas remain clean, safe and secure. Most proprietors offer breakfast and dinner for an extra rate. Hot showers are a prerequisite. In general, rooms these days provide at least two beds (one is usually a double), a fridge, air-con, a fan and private bath. Bonuses could include a terrace or patio, private entrance, TV, security box, kitchenette and parking space.

Due to the plethora of casas particulares in Cuba, it has been impossible to include even a fraction of the total in this book. The ones chosen are a combination of reader recommendations and local research. If one casa is full, they'll almost always be able to recommend you to someone else down the road.

Hotels

All tourist hotels and resorts are at least 51% owned by the Cuban government and are administered by one of five main organizations. Islazul is the cheapest and most popular with Cubans (who pay in Cuban pesos). Although the facilities can be variable at these establishments and the architecture a tad Sovietesque, Islazul hotels are invariably clean, cheap, friendly and, above all, Cuban. They're also more likely to be situated in the island's smaller provincial towns. One downside is the blaring on-site discos that often keep guests awake until the small hours. Cubanacán is a step up and offers a nice mix of budget and midrange options in both cities and resort areas. The company has recently developed a new clutch of affordable boutique-style hotels (the Encanto brand) in attractive city centers such as Sancti Spíritus, Baracoa, Remedios and Santiago. Gaviota manages higher-end resorts including glittering 933-room Playa Pesquero, though the chain also has a smattering of cheaper 'villas' in places such as Santiago and Cayo Coco. Gran Caribe does midrange to top-end hotels, including many of the all-inclusives in Havana and Varadero. Lastly, Habaguanex is based solely in Havana and manages most of the fastidiously restored historic hotels in Habana Vieja. The profits from these ventures go toward restoring the Unesco World Heritage Site. Because each group has its own niche, throughout this book we mention the chain to which a hotel belongs to give you some idea of what to expect at that particular installation. Except for Islazul properties, tourist hotels are for guests paying in Convertibles only. Since May 2008 Cubans have been allowed to stay in any tourist hotels although financially most of them are still out of reach.

At the top end of the hotel chain you'll often find foreign chains such as Sol Meliá and Superclubs running hotels in tandem with Cubanacán, Gaviota or Gran Caribe – mainly in the resort areas. The standards and service at these types of places are not unlike resorts in Mexico and the rest of the Caribbean.

ACTIVITIES

Cuba offers a wealth of exciting outdoor activities. For a full rundown, see the Outdoors chapter, p87.

BUSINESS HOURS

Cuban business hours are hardly etched in stone, but offices are generally open from 9am to 5pm Monday to Friday. Cubans don't take a siesta like people in other Latin American countries, so places normally don't close at midday. Museums and *agropecuarios* (vegetable markets) are usually closed Monday.

Post offices are open from 8am to 6pm Monday to Saturday, with some main post offices keeping later hours. Banks are usually open from 9am to 3pm weekdays, closing at noon on the last working day of each month. Cadeca exchange offices are generally open from 9am to 6pm Monday to Saturday, and from 9am to noon Sunday.

Pharmacies are generally open from 8am to 8pm, but those marked *turno permanente* or *pilotos* are open 24 hours.

In retail outlets everything grinds to a halt during the *cambio de turno* (shift change) and you won't be able to order a beer or buy cigarettes until they're done doing inventory (which can take anywhere from 10 minutes to one hour). Shops are usually closed after noon on Sunday.

Throughout this book, any exceptions to these hours are given in specific listings.

CHILDREN

Children are encouraged to talk, sing, dance, think, dream and play, and are integrated into all parts of society: you'll see them at concerts, restaurants, church, political rallies giving speeches even!) and parties. Travelers with children will find this embracing attitude heaped upon them, too.

In Cuba there are many travelers with kids, especially Cuban-Americans visiting family with their children; these will be your best sources for on-the-ground information. One aspect of the local culture that parents may find foreign (aside from the material shortages) is the physical contact and human warmth that is so typically Cuban: strangers ruffle kids' hair, give them kisses or take their hands with regularity. For more general advice, see Lonely Planet's *Travel with Children*.

Practicalities

Many simple things aren't available in Cuba or are hard to find, including baby formula, diaper wipes, disposable diapers, crayons, any medicine, clothing, sunblock etc. On the upside, Cubans are very resourceful and will happily whip up some squash-and-bean baby food or fashion a cloth diaper. In restaurants, there are no high chairs because Cubans cleverly turn one chair around and stack it on another, providing a balanced chair at the right height. Cribs are available in the fancier hotels and resorts, and in casas particulares one will be found. Good baby-sitting abounds: your hotel concierge or casa owner can connect you with good child care. What you won't find are car seats (or even seat belts in some cases), so bring your own from home.

The key to traveling in Cuba is simply to ask for what you need and some kind person will help you out.

Sights & Activities

Like any great city, Havana has plenty for kids (see p126). It has kids' theater and cinema, two aquariums, two zoos, a couple of great parks and the massive new Isla del Coco amusement park. Resorts are packed with kids' programs, from special outings to designated kiddy pools. Guardalavaca has the added advantage of being near many other interesting sights such as the aquarium at Bahía de Naranjo (p375). Parque Baconao in Santiago de Cuba (p433) has everything from old cars to dinosaur sculptures and is a fantasy land for kids of all ages.

Other activities kids will love include horseback riding, baseball games, cigar-factory tours, snorkeling, miniature golf, exploring caves, and the waterfalls at El Nicho (p272) and Topes de Collantes (p311).

CLIMATE CHARTS

Cuba is hot, with humidity ranging from 81% in summer to 79% in winter. Luckily the heat is nicely moderated by the gentle Northeast Tradewinds and the highest temperature ever recorded on the island was less than 40°C. Beware of cold fronts passing in the winter when evenings can be cool in the west of the island. Cuba's hurricane season (June to November) should also be considered when planning; see also When to Go (p21).

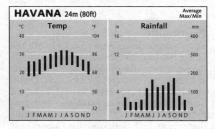

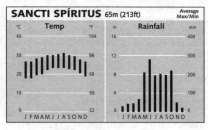

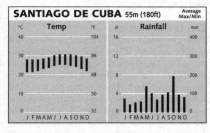

COURSES

Cuba's rich cultural tradition and the abundance of highly talented, trained professionals make it a great place to study. Officially matriculating students are afforded longer visas and issued a *carnet* – the identification document that allows foreigners to pay for museums, transport (including *colectivos* – collective taxis) and theater performances in pesos. Technological and linguistic glitches plus general unresponsiveness, make it hard to set up courses before arriving, but you can arrange everything once you arrive. In Cuba things are always better done face to face.

Private one-on-one lessons are available in everything from *batá* drumming to advanced Spanish grammar. Classes are easily arranged typically for CUC$5 to CUC$10 an hour at the institutions specializing in your area of interest. Other travelers are a great source of up-to-date information in this regard. See also individual chapters for details on specific courses.

While US citizens can still study in Cuba, their options shrank dramatically when the Bush administration discontinued people-to-people (educational) travel licenses in 2003.

Language

The largest organization offering study visits for foreigners is **UniversiTUR SA** (☎ 7-261-4939, 7-55-55-77; agencia@universitur.com; Calle 30 No 768-1 btwn Calle 41 & Av Kohly, Nuevo Vedado, Havana). UniversiTUR arranges regular study and working holidays at any of Cuba's universities and at many higher education or research institutes. Its most popular programs are intensive courses in Spanish language and Cuban culture at Universidad de La Habana (p119). UniversiTUR has 17 branch offices at various universities throughout Cuba, all providing the same services though prices vary. While US students can study anywhere in the country, they must arrange study programs for the provinces (except Havana or Matanzas) through Havanatur (see p108).

Students heading to Cuba should bring a good bilingual dictionary and a basic 'learn Spanish' textbook, as such books are scarce or expensive in Cuba. You might sign up for a two-week course at a university to get your feet wet and then jump into private classes once you've made some contacts.

Culture & Dance

Dance classes are available all over Cuba, although Havana and Santiago are your best bets. Institutions to try include the **Casa del Caribe** (Map pp408-9; ☎ 22-64-22-85; Calle 13 No 154, Vista Alegre, 90100 Santiago de Cuba), the **Conjunto Folklórico Nacional** (Map pp102-3; ☎ 7-830-3060; Calle 4 No 103, btwn Calzada & Calle 5, Vedado, Havana) and the **Centro Andaluz** (Map p106; ☎ 7-863-6745; fax 7-66-69-01; Paseo de Martí No 104 btwn Genios & Refugio

Centro Habana). See the individual chapters for details.

Art & Film

Courses for foreigners can be arranged throughout the year by the Oficina de Relaciones Internacionales of the **Instituto Superior de Arte** (Map pp154-5; ☎ 7-208-0017; isa@ cubarte.cult.cu, www.isa.cult.cu; Calle 120 No 1110, Cubanacán, Playa, Havana 11600). Courses in percussion and dance are available almost anytime, but other subjects, such as the visual arts, music, theater and aesthetics, are offered when professors are available.

Courses usually involve four hours of classes a week and cost between CUC$10 and CUC$15 per hour. Prospective students must apply in the last week of August for the fall semester or the last three weeks of January for spring. The school is closed for holidays throughout July and until the third week in August. The institute also accepts graduate students for its regular winter courses, and an entire year of study here (beginning in September) as part of the regular five-year program costs CUC$2500. Accommodation in student dormitories can be arranged.

The **Escuela Internacional de Cine, Televisión y Video** (☎ 47-38-22-46, 47-38-23-68; Apartado Aéreo 4041, San Antonio de los Baños, Provincia de La Habana) educates broadcasting professionals from all over the world (especially developing countries). Under the patronage of novelist Gabriel García Márquez, it's run by the foundation that also organizes the annual film festival in Havana. The campus is at Finca San Tranquilino, Carretera de Vereda Nueva, 5km northwest of San Antonio de los Baños. Prospective filmmaking students should apply in writing in advance (personal inquiries at the gate are not welcome).

CUSTOMS

Cuban customs regulations are complicated. For the full scoop see www.aduana.co.cu. Travelers are allowed to bring in personal belongings (including photography equipment, binoculars, musical instrument, tape recorder, radio, personal computer, tent, fishing rod, bicycle, canoe and other sporting gear), and gifts up to CUC$50.

Items that do not fit into the categories mentioned above are subject to a 100% customs duty to a maximum of CUC$1000.

Items prohibited entry into Cuba include narcotics, explosives, pornography, electrical appliances broadly defined, global positioning systems, prerecorded video cassettes and 'any item attempting against the security and internal order of the country,' including some books. Canned, processed and dried food are no problem, nor are pets.

Exporting undocumented art and items of cultural patrimony is restricted and involves fees. If you didn't get an official certificate at point of sale, you'll need to obtain one from the **Registro Nacional de Bienes Culturales** (Map pp102-3; Calle 17 No 1009 btwn Calles 10 & 12, Vedado, Havana; ☾ 9am-noon Mon-Fri). Bring the objects here for inspection; fill in a form; pay a fee of between CUC$10 and CUC$30, which covers from one to five pieces of artwork; and return 24 hours later to pick up the certificate.

You are allowed to export 50 boxed cigars duty-free (or 23 singles), US$5000 (or equivalent) in cash and only CUC$200.

DANGERS & ANNOYANCES

Cuba is generally safer than most countries, and violent attacks are extremely rare. Petty theft (eg rifled luggage in hotel rooms or unattended shoes disappearing from the beach) is common, but preventative measures work wonders. Pickpocketing is preventable: wear your bag in front of you on crowded buses and at busy markets, and only take what money you'll need to the disco.

Begging is more widespread and is exacerbated by tourists who amuse themselves by handing out money, soap, pens, chewing gum and other things to people on the street. Sadly, it seems that some Cubans have dropped out of productive jobs because they've found it is more lucrative to hustle tourists or beg than to work. It's painful for everyone when beggars earn more money than doctors. If you truly want to do something to help, pharmacies and hospitals will accept medicine donations, schools happily take pens, paper, crayons etc, and libraries will gratefully accept books. Alternatively pass stuff onto to your casa particular owner. Hustlers are called *jineteros/jineteras* (male/female touts), and can be a real nuisance.

If you're sensitive to smoke, you'll choke in Cuba, and despite government laws supposedly banning smoking in public places, people appear to light wherever and whenever they like.

GOVERNMENT TRAVEL ADVICE

The following government websites offer travel advisories and information on current hot spots.

Australian Department of Foreign Affairs (☎ 1300 139 281; www.smarttraveller .gov.au)

British Foreign Office (☎ 0845-850-2829; www.fco.gov.uk)

Canadian Department of Foreign Affairs (☎ 800-267-6788; www.dfait-maeci.gc.ca)

US State Department (☎ 888-407-4747; http://travel.state.gov)

Despite the many strides Cuba has made since the Revolution in stamping out racial discrimination, traces still linger and visitors of non-European origin are more likely to attract the attention of the police than those that look obviously non-Cuban. Latin, South Asian or black visitors may have to show passports to enter hotels and other places from which ordinary Cubans are barred (under the pretext that they think you're Cuban). Likewise, racially mixed pairs (especially black-white couples) will usually encounter more questions, demanding of papers and hassle than other travelers.

EMBASSIES & CONSULATES

Most embassies are open from 8am to noon on weekdays.

Australia See Canada.

Austria (Map pp154–5; ☎ 7-204-2825; Calle 4 No 101, Miramar, Havana)

Canada Havana (Map pp154–5; ☎ 7-204-2517; Calle 30 No 518, Playa); Varadero (Map pp240–1; ☎ 45-61-20-78; Calle 13 No 422 btwn Av 1 & Camino del Mar) Also represents Australia.

Denmark (Map p106; ☎ 7-33-81-28; 4th fl, Paseo de Martí No 20, Centro Habana, Havana)

France (Map pp154–5; ☎ 7-204-2308; Calle 14 No 312 btwn Avs 3 & 5, Miramar, Havana)

Germany (Map pp102–3; ☎ 7-833-2539; Calle 13 No 652, Vedado, Havana)

Italy (Map pp154–5; ☎ 7-204-5615; Av 5 No 402, Miramar, Havana)

Japan (Map pp154–5; ☎ 7-204-3508; Miramar Trade Center, cnr Av 3 & Calle 80, Playa, Havana)

Mexico (Map pp154–5; ☎ 7-204-7722; Calle 12 No 518, Miramar, Havana)

Netherlands (Map pp154–5; ☎ 7-204-2511; Calle 8 No 307 btwn Avs 3 & 5, Miramar, Havana)

New Zealand See UK.

Russia (Map pp154–5; Av 5 No 6402 btwn Calles 62 & 66, Playa, Havana)

Spain (Map p106; ☎ 7-866-8029; Cárcel No 51, Centro Habana, Havana)

Sweden (Map pp154–5; ☎ 7-204-2831; fax 7-204-1194; Calle 34 No 510, Miramar, Havana)

Switzerland (Map pp154–5; ☎ 7-204-2611; Av 5 No 2005, btwn Avs 20 & 22, Miramar, Havana)

UK (Map pp154–5; ☎ 7-204-1771; Calle 34 No 708, Miramar, Havana) Also represents New Zealand.

USA (Map pp102–3; ☎ 7-833-3026; US Interests Section, Calzada btwn Calles L & M, Vedado, Havana)

FOOD

It will be a very rare meal in Cuba that cost over CUC$25. In this book, restaurant listing are presented in the following order: budge (meals for under CUC$5), midrange (meal for CUC$5 to CUC$10) and top end (meal for over CUC$10). Restaurant are generall open from 11am to 11pm daily. Before yo dig in, check out the detailed information i the Food & Drink chapter (p70).

GAY & LESBIAN TRAVELERS

While Cuba can't be called a queer destina tion (yet), it's more tolerant than many othe Latin American countries. The hit movi *Fresa y Chocolate* (Strawberry and Chocolate 1994) sparked a national dialogue about ho mosexuality, and Cuba is pretty tolerant, a things considered. People from more ac cepting societies may find this tolerance to 'don't ask, don't tell' or tokenistic (every body has a gay friend/relative/coworke whom they'll mention when the topi arises), but what the hell, you have to star somewhere and Cuba is moving in the righ direction.

Machismo shows an ugly face when i comes to lesbians and female homosexualit has not enjoyed the aperture of male homo sexuality. For this reason, female lovers ca share rooms and otherwise 'pass' with facility However Jurassic you might find that, it's workable solution to a sticky problem. Ther are occasional *fiestas para chicas* (not neces sarily all-girl parties, but close); ask around a the **Cine Yara** (Map pp102–3; ☎ 7-832-9430; cnr Calles 2 & L, Vedado, Havana).

Cubans are physical with each other an you'll see men hugging, women holding hand and lots of friendly caressing. This type o casual touching shouldn't be a problem, bu take care when that hug among friends turns overtly sensual in public.

See also boxed text, p144.

HOLIDAYS

The Cuban calendar is loaded with holidays, but there are only a few that might affect your travel plans; among them are December 25 (not declared an official holiday until after the Pope visited in 1998), January 1, May 1 and July 26. On these days, stores will be closed and transport (except for planes) erratic. On May 1, especially, buses are dedicated to shuttling people to the Plaza de la Revolución in every major city and town and you can just forget about getting inner-city transport.

July and August mean crowded beaches and sold-out campismos and hotels.

INSURANCE

Insurance pays off only if something serious happens, but that's what insurance is for, so you'd be foolish to travel without cover. Outpatient treatment at international clinics designed for foreigners is reasonably priced, but emergency and prolonged hospitalization get expensive (the free medical system for Cubans should only be used when there is no other option).

If you're really concerned about your health, consider purchasing travel insurance once you arrive at **Asistur** (Map p106; ☎ 7-866-4499, alarm 7-866-8527; www.asistur.cu; Paseo de Martí No 208, Centro Havana, Havana). It has two types of coverage. For non-Americans the policy costs CUC$2.50 per day and covers up to CUC$400 in lost luggage, CUC$7000 in medical expenses and CUC$5000 each for repatriation of remains or jail bail. For Americans, similar coverage costs CUC$8 per day and provides up to CUC$25,000 in health-care costs, plus CUC$7000 to repatriate remains or evacuate you. See also p484.

It's strongly recommended that you take car insurance for a variety of reasons; see p479 for details.

Worldwide travel insurance is available at www.lonelyplanet.com/travel_services.

INTERNET ACCESS

With state-run telecommunications company Etecsa re-establishing its monopoly as service providers, internet access is available all over the country in Etecsa's spanking new *telepuntos*. You'll find one of its swish, air-conditioned sales offices in almost every provincial town and it is your best point of call for fast and reliable internet access. The drill is to buy a one-hour user card (CUC$6) with scratch-off *usuario* (code) and *contraseña* (password) and help yourself to an available computer. These cards are interchangeable in any *telepunto* across the country so you don't have to use up your whole hour in one go.

The downside of the Etecsa monopoly is that there are few, if any, independent internet cafes outside of the *telepuntos* and many of the smaller hotels – unable to afford the service fee – have had to dispense of their computers. As a general rule, most four- and five-star hotels (and all resort hotels) will have their own internet cafes although the fees here are often higher (sometimes as much as CUC$12 per hour).

As internet access for Cubans is restricted (they're only allowed internet under supervision, eg in educational programs or if their job deems it necessary), you may be asked to show your passport when using a *telepunto* (although if you look obviously foreign, they won't bother). On the plus side, the Etecsa places are open long hours and not often that crowded.

See also Getting Started, p25, for a list of useful internet resources on Cuba.

LEGAL MATTERS

Cuban police are everywhere and they're usually very friendly – more likely to ask you for a date than a bribe. Corruption is a serious offense in Cuba and typically no one wants to get messed up in it. Getting caught out without identification is never good; carry some around just in case (a driver's license, a copy of your passport or student ID card should be sufficient).

Drugs are prohibited in Cuba though you may still get offered marijuana and cocaine on the streets of Havana. Penalties for buying, selling, holding or taking drugs are serious, and Cuba is making a concerted effort to treat demand and curtail supply; it is only the foolish traveler who partakes while on a Cuban vacation.

MAPS

Signage is awful in Cuba so a good map is essential for drivers and cyclists alike. The comprehensive *Guía de Carreteras* (CUC$6), published in Italy, includes the best maps available in Cuba. It has a complete index, a detailed Havana map and useful information in English, Spanish, Italian and French. Handier is the all-purpose *Automapa Nacional,* available at hotel shops and car-rental offices.

The best map published outside Cuba is the Freytag & Berndt 1:1.25 million *Cuba* map. The island map is good, and it has indexed town plans of Havana, Playas del Este, Varadero, Cienfuegos, Camagüey and Santiago de Cuba.

For good basic maps, pick up one of the provincial *Guías* available in Infotur offices.

MONEY

This is a tricky part of any Cuban trip and the double economy takes some getting used to. Two currencies circulate in Cuba: Convertible pesos (CUC$) and Cuban pesos (referred to as *moneda nacional,* abbreviated MN). Most things tourists pay for are in Convertibles (eg accommodation, rental cars, bus tickets, museum admission and internet access). At the time of writing, Cuban pesos were selling at 25 to one Convertible, and while there are many things you can't buy with *moneda nacional,* using them on certain occasions means you'll see a bigger slice of authentic Cuba. The prices in this book are in Convertibles unless otherwise stated.

Making everything a little more confusing, euros are also accepted at the Varadero, Guardalavaca, Cayo Largo del Sur, as well as Cayo Coco and Cayo Guillermo resorts, but once you leave the resort grounds, you'll still need Convertibles. For information on costs, see p21, and for exchange rates go to the Quick Reference on the inside front cover of this book.

The best currencies to bring to Cuba are euros, Canadian dollars or pounds sterling (all liable to an 8% to 11.25% commission). The worst is US dollars and – despite the prices you might see posted up in bank windows – the commission you'll get charged is a whopping 20% (the normal 10% commission plus an extra 10% penalty – often not displayed). At the time of writing, traveler's checks issued by US banks could be exchanged at branches of Banco Financiero Internacional, but credit cards issued by US banks could not be used at all. Note that Australian dollars are not accepted anywhere in Cuba.

Cadeca branches in every city and town sell Cuban pesos. You won't need more than

CUC$10 worth of pesos a week. In addition to the offices located on the maps in this book, there is almost always a branch at the local *agropecuario* (vegetable market). If you get caught without Cuban pesos and are drooling for that ice-cream cone, you can always use Convertibles; in street transactions such as these, CUC$1 is equal to 25 pesos and you'll receive change in pesos. There is no black market in Cuba, only hustlers trying to fleece you with money-changing scams (see boxed text, p97).

ATMs & Credit Cards

When the banks are open, the machines are working and the phone lines are live, credit cards are an option – as long as the cards are not issued by US banks. You will be charged an 11.25% fee on every credit-card transaction. This is made up of the 8% levy charged for all foreign currency exchanges (which must first be converted into US dollars) plus a standard 3.25% conversion fee. However, in reality, credit card and cash payments work out roughly the same; with cash you pay the 11.25% levy when you exchange your foreign money into Convertibles at the bank. Nonetheless, due to poor processing facilities, lack of electronic equipment and nonacceptance of many US-linked cards, cash is still by far the best option in Cuba.

Cash advances can be drawn from credit cards but the commission's the same. Check with your home bank before you leave, as many banks won't authorize large withdrawals in foreign countries unless you notify them of your travel plans first.

ATMs are good for credit cards only and are the equivalent to obtaining a cash advance over the counter. In reality it is best to avoid them altogether (especially when the banks are closed), as they are notorious for eating up people's cards.

Some, but not all, debit cards work in Cuba. Take care as machines sometimes 'eat' cards.

Cash

Cuba is a cash economy and credit cards don't have the importance or ubiquity that they do elsewhere in the western hemisphere. Although carrying just cash is far riskier than the usual cash/credit-card/traveler's-check mix, it's infinitely more convenient. As long as you use a concealed money belt and keep the cash on you or in your hotel's safe deposit box at all times, you should be OK.

It's better to ask for CUC$20/10/5/3/1 bills when you're changing money, as many smaller Cuban businesses (taxis, restaurants etc) can't change anything bigger (ie CUC$50 or CUC$100 bills) and the words *no hay cambio* (no change) resonate everywhere. If desperate, you can always break big bills at hotels.

Denominations & Lingo

One of the most confusing parts of a double economy is terminology. Cuban pesos are called *moneda nacional* (abbreviated MN) or *pesos Cubanos* or simply pesos, while Convertible pesos are called *pesos convertibles* (abbreviated CUC) or often just simply…pesos. Sometimes you'll be negotiating in pesos (Cubanos) and your counterpart will be negotiating in pesos (Convertibles). It doesn't help that the notes look similar as well. Worse, the symbol for both Convertibles and Cuban pesos is $. You can imagine the potential scams just working these combinations.

The Cuban peso comes in notes of one, five, 10, 20, 50 and 100 pesos; and coins of one (rare), five and 20 centavos, and one and three pesos. The five-centavo coin is called a *medio*, the 20-centavo coin a *peseta*. Centavos are also called *kilos*.

The Convertible peso comes in multicolored notes of one, three, five, 10, 20, 50 and 100 pesos; and coins of five, 10, 25 and 50 centavos, and one peso.

Tipping

If you're not in the habit of tipping, you'll learn fast in Cuba. Wandering *son* (Cuban popular music) septets, parking guards, ladies at bathroom entrances, restaurant wait staff, tour guides – they all work for hard-currency tips. Musicians who besiege tourists while they dine, converse or flirt will want a Convertible, but only give what you feel the music is worth. Washroom attendants expect CUC$0.05 to CUC$0.10, while *parqueadores* (parking attendants) should get CUC$0.25 for a short watch and CUC$1 for each 12 hours. For a day tour, CUC$2 per person is appropriate for a tour guide. Taxi drivers will appreciate 10% of the meter fare, but if you've negotiated a ride without the meter, don't tip as the whole fare is going straight into their wallets.

Tipping can quickly *resolver las cosas* (fix things up). If you want to stay beyond the hotel check-out time or enter a site after hours, for instance, small tips (CUC$1 to CUC$5) bend rules, open doors and send people looking the other way. For tipping in restaurants and other advice, see the Food & Drink chapter (see boxed text, p75).

Traveler's Checks

While they add security and it makes sense to carry a few for that purpose, traveler's checks are a hassle in Cuba although they work out better value than credit cards. Bear in mind that you'll pay commission at both the buying and selling ends (3% to 6%) and also be aware that some hotels and banks won't accept them (especially in the provinces). The Banco Financiero Internacional is your best bet for changing Amex checks, though a much safer all-round option is to bring Thomas Cook.

POST

Letters and postcards sent to Europe and the US take about a month to arrive. While *sellos* (stamps) are sold in Cuban pesos and Convertibles, correspondence bearing the latter has a better chance of arriving. Postcards cost CUC$0.65 to all countries. Letters cost CUC$0.65 to the Americas, CUC$0.75 to Europe and CUC$0.85 to all other countries. Prepaid postcards, including international postage, are available at most hotel shops and post offices and are the surest bet for successful delivery. For important mail, you're better off using DHL, located in all the major cities; it costs CUC$55 for a 900g letter pack to Australia, or CUC$50 to Europe.

SHOPPING

If shopping's one of your favorite vacation pastimes, don't make a special trip to Cuba. To the relief of many and the disappointment of a few, Western-style consumerism hasn't yet reached the time-warped streets of Cuba's austere capital. That's not to say you have to walk away empty-handed. Pampering to a growing number of well-off travelers, Cuba's tourist industry has upped the ante considerably in recent years and specialist shops are spreading fast.

The Holy Grail for most foreign souvenirhunters is a box of Cuban cigars, closely followed by a bottle of Cuban rum, both of which are significantly cheaper than in stores in

Europe or Canada. Another often overlooked bargain is a bag of Cuban coffee, a potent and aromatic brew made from organically grown beans and best served espresso-style with a dash of sugar.

Elsewhere memorabilia is thin on the ground. Aimed strictly at the tourist market, you'll find cheap dolls, flimsy trinkets, mediocre woodcarvings and low-quality leather goods, but Cuba is a world leader in none of these things. Far better as long-lasting souvenirs are salsa CDs, arty movie posters, musical instruments or a quirky string of Santería beads.

Paintings are another of Cuba's fortes and local artists selling their work from small private studios are both numerous and talented. If you buy an original painting, print or sculpture, be sure to ask for a receipt to prove you bought it at an official sales outlet; otherwise, it could be confiscated by customs upon departure (see p463).

In a country where clothes were – until recently – rationed, and lycra is still considered to be the height of cool, finding the latest pair of Tommy Hilfiger jeans could prove a little difficult. Incurable fashion junkies can spend their Convertibles on pleated *guayabera* shirts or a yawningly predictable Che Guevara T-shirt (if you don't mind being reduced to a walking cliché). Take your pick.

Cigars

Visitors are allowed to export CUC$2000 worth of documented cigars per person. Amounts in excess of this, or black-market cigars without receipts, will be confiscated (Cuban customs is serious about this, with an ongoing investigation into cigar rings and more than half a million seizures of undocumented cigars annually). The tax-free limit without a receipt is two boxes (50 cigars) or 23 singles of any size or cost. Of course, you can buy additional cigars in the airport departure lounge once you've passed Cuban customs, but beware of your limits when entering other countries. (Mexican customs in Cancún, for instance, conducts rigorous cigar searches.) If you traveled without a license to Cuba, US customs will seize any tobacco you have upon entering; licensed travelers are permitted to bring the equivalent of US$100 worth of cigars into the US. (Imitation Cuban cigars sold in the US contain no Cuban tobacco.)

La Casa del Habano (www.habanos.net) is the national cigar store chain, where the staff is well informed, there's a wide selection and sometimes a smoking lounge.

For more information on Cuban cigars, see the boxed text, p207.

TELEPHONE

The Cuban phone system is still undergoing some upgrading, so beware of phone-number changes. Normally a recorded message will inform you of any recent upgrades. Most of the country's Etecsa *telepuntos* have now been completely refurbished, which means there will be a spick-and-span (as well as air-conditioned) phone and internet office in almost every provincial town.

Mobile Phones

Cuba's two mobile-phone companies are **c.com** (☎ 7-264-2266) and **Cubacel** (www.cubacel.com). While you may be able to use your own equipment, you have to prebuy their services. Cubacel has more than 15 offices around the country (including the Havana airport) where you can do this. Its plan costs approximately CUC$3 per day and each local call costs from CUC$0.52 to CUC$0.70. Note that you pay for incoming as well as outgoing calls. International rates are CUC$2.70 per minute to the US and CUC$5.85 per minute to Europe.

Phone Codes

To call Cuba from abroad, dial your international access code, Cuba's country code (☎ 53), the city or area code (minus '0' which is used when dialing domestically between provinces), and the local number. In this book, area codes are indicated at the start of each chapter. To call internationally from Cuba, dial Cuba's international access code (☎ 119), the country code, the area code and the number. To the US, you just dial ☎ 119, then 1, the area code and the number.

To place a call through an international operator, dial ☎ 09, except to the US, which can be reached with an operator on ☎ 66-12-12. Not all private phones in Cuba have international service, in which case you'll want to call collect (reverse charges or *cobro revertido*). This service is available only to Argentina, Brazil, Canada, Chile, Colombia, Costa Rica, Dominican Republic, France, Italy, Mexico, Panama, Spain, UK, US and Venezuela. International operators are available 24 hours and speak English. You cannot call collect from public phones.

Phonecards

Etecsa is where you buy phonecards, send and receive faxes, use the internet and make international calls. Blue public Etecsa phones accepting magnetized or computer-chip cards are everywhere. The cards are sold in Convertibles: CUC$5, CUC$10 and CUC$20, and Cuban pesos: three, five and seven pesos. You can call nationally with either, but you can call internationally only with Convertible cards. If you are mostly going to be making national and local calls, buy a peso card as it's much more economical.

The best cards for calls from Havana are called Propia. They come in pesos (five- and 10-peso denominations) and Convertibles (CUC$10 and CUC$25 denominations) and allow you to call from any phone – even ones permitting only emergency calls – using a personal code. The rates are the cheapest as well.

Phone Rates

Local calls cost five centavos per minute, while interprovincial calls cost from 35 centavos to one peso per minute (note that only the peso coins with the star work in pay phones). Since most coin phones don't return change, common courtesy asks that you push the 'R' button so that the next person in line can make their call with your remaining money.

International calls made with a card cost from CUC$2 per minute to the US and Canada and CUC$5 to Europe and Oceania. Calls placed through an operator cost slightly more.

TIME

Cuba is on UTC/GMT minus five between October and April and UTC/GMT minus four (daylight-saving time) between April and October – the same as New York or Washington.

TOILETS

Look for public toilets at bus stations, tourist hotels or restaurants, and gas stations. It is unlikely you'll meet a Cuban who would deny a needy traveler the use of their bathroom. In public restrooms there often won't be water or toilet paper and never a toilet seat. The faster you learn to squat and carry your own supply

of paper, the happier you'll be. Frequently there will be an attendant outside bathrooms supplying toilet paper and you're expected to leave CUC$0.05 or CUC$0.10 in the plate provided. If the bathrooms are dirty or the attendant doesn't supply paper, you shouldn't feel compelled to leave money.

Cuban sewer systems are not designed to take toilet paper and every bathroom has a small waste basket beside the toilet for this purpose. Aside from at top-end hotels and resorts, you should discard your paper in this basket or risk an embarrassing backup.

TOURIST INFORMATION

At the time of writing, **Infotur** (www.infotur .cu), Cuba's official tourist information bureau, had offices in Havana (Habana Vieja, Miramar, Playas del Este, Expocuba, the José Martí Airport), Trinidad and Ciego de Ávila (in the city and at Jardines del Rey airport, Cayo Coco). Travel agencies, such as Cubanacán or Cubatur, can usually supply some general information.

TRAVELERS WITH DISABILITIES

Cuba's inclusive culture translates to disabled travelers, and while facilities may be lacking, the generous nature of Cubans generally compensates. Sight-impaired travelers will be helped across streets and given priority in lines. The same holds true for travelers in wheelchairs, who will find the few ramps ridiculously steep and will have trouble in colonial parts of town where sidewalks are narrow and streets are cobblestone. Elevators are often out of order. Etecsa phone centers have telephone equipment for the hearing-impaired and TV programs are broadcast with closed captioning.

VISAS & TOURIST CARDS

Regular tourists who plan to spend up to two months in Cuba do not need visas. Instead, you get a *tarjeta de turista* (tourist card) valid for 30 days (Canadians get 90 days), which can be extended for another 30 days once you're in Cuba. Those going 'air only' usually buy the tourist card from the travel agency or airline office that sells them the plane ticket (equivalent of US$15 extra). Package tourists receive their card with their other travel documents.

Unlicensed tourists originating in the US buy their tourist card at the airline desk in the country through which they're traveling en route to Cuba (equivalent of US$25). You are usually not allowed to board a plane to Cuba without this card, but if by some chance you are, you should be able to buy one at Aeropuerto Internacional José Martí in Havana – although this is a hassle (and risk) best avoided. Once in Havana, tourist-card extensions or replacements cost another CUC$25. You cannot leave Cuba without presenting your tourist card, so don't lose it. You are not permitted entry to Cuba without an onward ticket. Note that Cubans don't stamp your passport on either entry or exit; instead they stamp your tourist card.

The 'address in Cuba' line should be filled in, if only to avoid unnecessary questioning. As long as you are staying in a legal casa particular or hotel, you shouldn't have problems.

Business travelers and journalists need visas. Applications should be made through a consulate at least three weeks in advance (longer if you apply through a consulate in a country other than your own).

Visitors with visas or anyone who has stayed in Cuba longer than 90 days must apply for an exit permit from an immigration office. The Cuban consulate in London issues official visas (£32 plus two photos). They take two weeks to process, and the name of an official contact in Cuba is necessary.

Extensions

For most travelers, obtaining an extension once in Cuba is easy: you just go to the *inmigración* (immigration office) and present your documents and CUC$25 in stamps. Obtain these stamps from a branch of Bandec or Banco Financiero Internacional beforehand. You'll only receive an additional 30 days after your original 30 days, but you can exit and re-enter the country for 24 hours and start over again (some travel agencies in Havana have special deals for this type of trip; see p108). Attend to extensions at least a few business days before your visa is due to expire and never attempt travel around Cuba with an expired visa. Nearly all provincial towns have an immigration office (closed Wednesday, Saturday and Sunday) though the staff rarely speak English and they aren't always overhelpful. Try to avoid Havana's office if you can as it gets ridiculously crowded.

Baracoa (Map p450; Antonio Maceo No 48; 8am-noon & 2-4pm Mon-Fri)

Bayamo (Map p387; Carretera Central Km 2; 9am-noon & 1:30-4pm Tue & Thu-Fri) In a big complex 200m south of the Hotel Sierra Maestra.

Camagüey (Map pp336-7; Calle 3 No 156 btwn Calles 8 & 10, Reparto Vista Hermosa; 8am-11:30am & 1-3pm Mon-Fri, except Wed)

Ciego de Ávila (Map p319; cnr Delgado & Independencia; 8am-noon & 1-5pm Mon & Tue, 8am-noon Wed-Fri)

Cienfuegos (Map p264; 43-52-10-17; Av 46 btwn Calles 29 & 31)

Guantánamo (Map p443; Calle 1 Oeste btwn Calles 14 & 15 Norte; 8:30am-noon & 2-4pm Mon-Thu) Directly behind Hotel Guantánamo.

Guardalavaca (Map p376; 24-43-02-26/7) In the police station at the entrance to the resort. Head here for visa extensions; there's also an immigration office in Banes (p378).

Havana (Map pp102-3; cnr Calle Factor al final & Santa Ana, Nuevo Vedado) This office is specifically for extensions and has long queues. Get there early. It has no phone, but you can direct questions to immigration proper at 7-203-0307.

Holguín (Map p362; cnr General Marrero & General Vázquez; 8am-noon & 2-4pm Mon-Fri) Arrive early – it gets crowded here.

Las Tunas (off Map p352; Av Camilo Cienfuegos, Reparto Buenavista) Northeast of the train station.

Sancti Spíritus (Map p294; 41-32-47-29; Independencia Norte No 107; 8:30am-noon & 1:30-3:30pm Mon-Thu)

Santa Clara (off Map p278; cnr Av Sandino & Sexta; 8am-noon & 1-3pm Mon-Thu) Three blocks east of Estadio Sandino.

Santiago de Cuba (Map pp408-9; 22-69-36-07; Calle 13 No 6 btwn Av General Cebreco & Calle 4; 8:30am-noon & 2-4pm Mon, Tue, Thu & Fri) Stamps for visa extensions are sold at the Banco de Crédito y Comercio at Felix Peña No 614 on Parque Céspedes.

Trinidad (Map p300; Julio Cueva Díaz; 8am-5pm Tue-Thu) Off Paseo Agramonte.

Varadero (Map pp240-1; cnr Av 1 & Calle 39; 8am-3:30pm Mon-Fri)

Entry Permits for Cubans & Naturalized Citizens

Naturalized citizens of other countries who were born in Cuba require an *autorización de entrada* (entry permit) issued by a Cuban embassy or consulate. Called a Vigencia de Viaje, it allows Cubans resident abroad to visit Cuba as many times as they like over a two-year period. Persons hostile to the Revolution or with a criminal record are not eligible.

The Cuban government does not recognize dual citizenship. All persons born in Cuba are considered Cuban citizens unless they have formally renounced their citizenship at a Cuban diplomatic mission and the renunciation has been accepted. Cuban-Americans with questions about dual nationality can contact the Office of Overseas Citizens Services, Department of State, Washington, DC 20520.

Licenses for US Visitors

In 1961 the US government imposed an order limiting the freedom of its citizens to visit Cuba, and airline offices and travel agencies in the US are forbidden to book tourist travel to Cuba via third countries. However, the Cuban government has never banned Americans from visiting Cuba, and it continues to welcome US passport holders under exactly the same terms as any other visitor.

Americans traditionally go to Cuba via Canada, Mexico, the Bahamas, Jamaica or any other third country. Since American travel agents are prohibited from handling tourism arrangements, most Americans go through a foreign travel agency. Travel agents in those countries (see p474) routinely arrange Cuban tourist cards, flight reservations and accommodation packages.

The immigration officials in Cuba know very well that a Cuban stamp in a US passport can create problems. However, many Americans request that immigration officers not stamp their passport before they hand it over. The officer will instead stamp their tourist card, which is collected upon departure from Cuba. Those who don't ask usually get a tiny stamp on page 16 or the last page in the shape of a plane, barn, moon or some other random symbol that doesn't mention Cuba.

The US government has an 'Interests Section' in Havana, but American visitors are advised to go there only if something goes terribly wrong. Therefore, unofficial US visitors are especially careful not to lose their passports while in Cuba, as this would put them in a very difficult position. Many Cuban hotels rent security boxes (CUC$2 per day) to guests and nonguests alike, and you can carry a photocopy of your passport for identification on the street.

At the time of writing there were two types of licenses issued by the US government to visit Cuba: general licenses (typically for government officials, journalists and professional researchers) and specific licenses (for visiting family members, humanitarian projects,

public performances, religious activities and educational activities). The Bush administration cut back on both types of licenses in 2003 cutting off 70% of the travel that had previously been deemed 'legal.' Early moves by the Obama administration have been less asphyxiating and in April 2009 the 'visiting family members' category was opened up. Cuban-Americans now face neither time stipulations nor financial restrictions when visiting extended family members on the island.

For more information, contact the **Licensing Division** (☎ 202-622-2480; www.treas.gov/ofac; Office of Foreign Assets Control, US Department of the Treasury, 2nd fl, Annex Bldg, 1500 Pennsylvania Ave NW, Washington, DC 20220). Travel arrangements for those eligible for a license can be made by specialized US companies such as Marazul or ABC Charters (see p477).

Under the Trading with the Enemy Act, goods originating in Cuba are prohibited from being brought into the US by anyone but licensed travelers. Cuban cigars, rum, coffee etc will be confiscated by US customs, and officials can create additional problems if they feel so inclined. Possession of Cuban goods inside the US or bringing them in from a third country is also banned.

American travelers who choose to go to Cuba (and wish to avoid unnecessary hassles with the US border guards) get rid of anything related to their trip to Cuba, including used airline tickets, baggage tags, travel documents, receipts and souvenirs, before returning to the US. If Cuban officials don't stamp their passport, there will be no official record of their trip. They also use a prepaid Cuban telephone card to make calls to the US in order to avoid there being records of collect or operator-assisted telephone calls.

Since September 11, 2001, all international travel issues have taken on new import, and there has been a crackdown on 'illegal' travel to Cuba. Though it has nothing to do with terrorism, some Americans returning from Cuba have had 'transit to Cuba' written in their passports by Jamaican customs officials. Customs officials at major US entry points (eg New York, Houston, Miami) are onto backpackers coming off Cancún and Montego Bay flights with throngs of honeymoon couples, or tanned gentlemen arriving from Toronto in January. They're starting to ask questions, reminding travelers that it's a felony to lie to a customs agent as they do so.

DIRECTORY

The maximum penalty for 'unauthorized' Americans traveling to Cuba is US$250,000 and 10 years in prison. In practice, people are usually fined US$7500. Under the Bush administration, the number of people threatened with legal action had more than tripled, however the early signs from the Obama administration indicate these numbers are likely to fall. More than 100,000 US citizens a year travel to Cuba with no consequences. However, as long as these regulations remain in place, visiting Cuba certainly qualifies as soft adventure travel for Americans. There are many organizations, including a group of congresspeople on Capitol Hill, working to lift the travel ban (see www.cubacentral .com for more information).

VOLUNTEERING

There are a number of bodies offering volunteer work in Cuba though it is always best to organize things in your home country first. Just turning up in Havana and volunteering can be difficult, if not impossible. Take a look at the following:

Canada-Cuba Farmer to Farmer Project (www .farmertofarmer.ca) Vancouver-based sustainable agriculture organization.

Canada World Youth (☎ 514-931-3526; www.cwy -jcm.org) Head office in Montreal, Canada.

Cuban Solidarity Campaign (☎ 020 8800 0155; www.cuba-solidarity.org) Head office in London, UK.

National Network on Cuba (www.cubasolidarity.com) US-based solidarity group.

Pastors for Peace (PFP; ☎ 212-926-5757; www.ifco news.org) Collects donations across the US to take to Cuba.

Witness for Peace (WFP; ☎ 202-588-1471; www .witnessforpeace.org) Looking for Spanish-speakers with a two-year commitment.

WOMEN TRAVELERS

In terms of personal safety, Cuba is a dream destination for women travelers. Most streets can be walked alone at night, violent crime is rare and the chivalrous part of machismo means you'll never step into oncoming traffic. But machismo cuts both ways, with protecting on one side and pursuing – relentlessly – on the other. Cuban women are used to *piropos* (the whistles, kissing sounds and compliments constantly ringing in their ears), and might even reply with their own if they're feeling frisky. For foreign women, however, it can feel like an invasion.

Ignoring *piropos* is the first step. But sometimes ignoring them isn't enough. Learn some rejoinders in Spanish so you can shut men up: *No me moleste* (don't bother me), *está bueno ya* (all right already) or *que falta respeto* (how disrespectful) are good ones, as is the withering 'don't you dare' stare that is also part of the Cuban woman's arsenal. Wearing plain modest clothes might help lessen unwanted attention; topless sunbathing is out. An absent husband, invented or not, seldom has any effect. If you go to a disco, be very clear with Cuban dance partners what you are and are not interested in. Dancing is a kind of foreplay in Cuba and may be viewed as an invitation for something more. Cubans appreciate directness and as long as you set the boundaries, you'll have a fabulous time. Being in the company of a Cuban man is the best way to prevent *piropos*, and if all else fails, retire to the pool for a day out of the line of fire and re-energize.

Traveling alone can be seen as an invitation for all kinds of come-ons; solo women travelers won't have an easy time of it. Hooking up with a male traveler (or another woman, at least to deflect the barrage) can do wonders.

Transport

CONTENTS

Getting There & Away	**473**
Entering the Country	473
Air	473
Sea	477
Tours	477
Getting Around	**477**
Air	477
Bicycle	478
Bus	478
Car	479
Ferry	481
Hitchhiking	481
Local Transport	481
Tours	482
Train	482
Truck	483

GETTING THERE & AWAY

ENTERING THE COUNTRY

Whether it's your first time or 50th, descending low into José Martí International Airport, over rust-red tobacco fields, is an exciting and unforgettable experience. Fortunately, entry procedures are straightforward, as long as you have a passport valid for six months, an onward ticket and your tourist card filled out (be sure to put something under 'Address in Cuba'; see p469).

Outside Cuba, the capital city is called Havana, and this is how travel agents, airlines and other professionals will refer to it. Within Cuba, it's almost always called Habana or La Habana by everyone. For the sake of consistency, we have used the former spelling throughout this book.

Flights, tours and rail tickets can be booked online at www.lonelyplanet.com /travel_services.

AIR

Airports & Airlines

Cuba has 11 international airports and more than 60 carriers serving the island. Most travelers fly into Aeropuerto Internacional José Martí in **Havana** (HAV; ☎ 7-266-4644), Aeropuerto Juan Gualberto Gómez in **Varadero**

(VRA; ☎ 45-61-30-16) or Aeropuerto Antonio Maceo in **Santiago de Cuba** (SCU; ☎ 22-69-10-14). Travelers on package tours might fly into **Holguín** (HOG; ☎ 24-42-52-71), **Ciego de Ávila** (AVI; ☎ 33-26-66-26), **Cayo Largo del Sur** (CYO; ☎ 46-34-82-07) or **Aeropuerto Jardines del Rey** (CCC; ☎ 33-30-91-27).

The national airline of Cuba is **Cubana de Aviación** (www.cubana.cu). Its modern fleet flies major routes and its airfares are usually among the cheapest. However, overbooking and delays are nagging problems you may well encounter. In addition, the airline has a zero-tolerance attitude towards overweight luggage, charging stiffly for every kilogram above the 20kg baggage allowance. In terms of safety, Cubana's reputation precedes it (it had back-to-back crashes in December 1999, with 39 fatalities), but it hasn't had any incidents since. Still, you might want to check the latest at www.airsafe.com.

AIRLINES FLYING TO/FROM CUBA

Most airlines have offices in the **Airline Building** (Calle 23 No 64) in Vedado or, alternatively, in the **Miramar Trade Center** (Av 3 btwn Calles 76 & 80) in Playa, Havana.

Aerocaribbean (7L; ☎ 7-832-7584; www.aerocaribbean.com; Airline Bldg, Calle 23 No 64, Vedado, Havana)

Aeroflot Russian International Airlines (AFL; ☎ 7-204-3200; www.aeroflot.com; hub Moscow; Miramar Trade Center, Av 3 btwn Calles 76 & 80, Playa, Havana)

Aeropostal (LAV; ☎ 7-55-40-00; www.aeropostal.com; hub Caracas; Hotel Habana Libre, cnr Calles 23 & L, Havana)

Air Canada (ACA; ☎ 7-834-4949; www.aircanada.com; hub Montréal; Airline Bldg, Calle 23 No 64, Vedado, Havana)

THINGS CHANGE...

The information in this chapter is particularly vulnerable to change. Check directly with the airline or a travel agent to make sure you understand how a fare (and ticket you may buy) works and be aware of the security requirements for international travel. Shop carefully. The details given in this chapter should be regarded as pointers and are not a substitute for your own careful, up-to-date research.

TRANSPORT

> **DEPARTURE TAX**
>
> Everyone must pay a CUC$25 departure tax at the airport. It's payable in cash only.

Air Europa (AEA; ☎ 7-204-6905/6/7/8; www.air-europa.com; hub Madrid; Miramar Trade Center, Av 3 btwn Calles 76 & 80, Playa, Havana)

Air France (AFR; ☎ 7-833-2644; www.airfrance.com; hub Paris; Airline Bldg, Calle 23 No 64, Vedado, Havana)

Air Jamaica (AJM; ☎ 7-833-2447; www.airjamaica.com; hub Montego Bay; Airline Bldg, Calle 23 No 64, Vedado, Havana)

Air Transat (TSC; ☎ 1-877-872-6728; www.airtransat.com; hub Montréal)

Copa Airlines (CMP; ☎ 7-204-7857; www.copaair.com; hub Panama City; Miramar Trade Center, Av 3 btwn Calles 76 & 80, Playa, Havana)

Cubana (CU; ☎ 7-834-4446; www.cubana.cu; hub Havana; Airline Bldg, Calle 23 No 64, Vedado, Havana)

Iberia (IBE; ☎ 7-204-3443; www.iberia.com; hub Madrid; Airline Bldg, Calle 23 No 64, Vedado, Havana)

Lacsa (LRC; ☎ 7-833-3114; www.grupotaca.com; hub San José, Costa Rica; Hotel Habana Libre, cnr Calles 23 & L, Havana) Also represents Taca.

LanChile (LAN; ☎ 7-833-3626; www.lanchile.com; hub Santiago de Chile; Airline Bldg, Calle 23 No 64, Vedado, Havana)

Martinair (MPH; ☎ 7-832-6649; www.martinair.com; hub Amsterdam; cnr Calles E & 23, Vedado, Havana)

Mexicana de Aviación (MXA; ☎ 7-833-3533; www.mexicana.com.mx; hub Mexico City; Airline Bldg, Calle 23 No 64, Vedado, Havana) Also represents the regional carrier Aerocaribe.

Skyservice (SSV; ☎ 1-416-679-8330; www.skyserviceairlines.com; hub Toronto)

Virgin Atlantic (VIR; ☎ 7-204-0747; www.virginatlantic.com; hub London Gatwick)

Tickets

Since Americans can't buy tickets to Cuba and can't use US-based travel agents, a host of businesses in Mexico (p476), Canada (below) and the Caribbean (opposite) specialize in air-only deals. They sometimes won't sell you the first leg of your trip to the 'gateway' country for fear of embargo-related repercussions. When booking online or if an agency requires financial acrobatics to steer clear of US embargo laws (which sometimes happens), be sure to confirm details, take contact names and clarify the procedure. You will need a Cuban tourist card and these agencies should arrange that. Except during peak holiday seasons, you can usually just arrive in Mexico, Jamaica or whatever gateway country and buy your round-trip ticket to Cuba there.

The choice for non-Americans is varied, straightforward, cheap and accessible. Often, an air-and-hotel package deal to one of the beach resorts is cheaper than airfare alone.

Canada

Cubana flies to Havana from Montréal four times weekly (via Cayo Coco, Camagüey, Holguín, Santiago or Varadero). From Toronto, it's pretty much the same deal. Lacsa (the good Costa Rican carrier) also has several weekly flights from Toronto and Montréal to Havana. Air Canada is another option. Mexicana flies from Vancouver to Havana via Mexico City five times weekly.

You might find a cheaper fare, though, with the reliable charter lines Air Transat and Skyservice, flying weekly from Toronto and Montréal to almost all international airports in Cuba (even Manzanillo). Some of these flights operate only from mid-December to April,

> **US CITIZENS & CUBA**
>
> In conjunction with the US embargo against Cuba, the US government currently enforces a 'travel ban,' preventing its citizens from visiting Cuba. Technically a treasury law prohibiting Americans from spending money in Cuba, it has largely squelched leisure travel for more than 45 years.
>
> The 1996 Helms-Burton Act, which was signed into law by President Clinton on March 12, 1996, imposes *without judicial review* fines of up to US$50,000 on US citizens who visit Cuba without US government permission. It also allows for confiscation of their property. In addition, under the Trading with the Enemy Act, violators may face up to US$250,000 in fines and up to 10 years in prison. Although fines were only occasionally levied when Clinton was in the White House, the number of individuals stung under the Bush administration more than tripled, and fewer licenses were issued too. Early portents from the Obama administration, such as the April 2009 easing of travel restrictions for Cuban-Americans, suggested a less hard-line approach.
>
> Visit www.cubacentral.com to inform yourself of the latest legislation on Capitol Hill.

CLIMATE CHANGE & TRAVEL

Climate change is a serious threat to the ecosystems that humans rely upon, and air travel is the fastest-growing contributor to the problem. Lonely Planet regards travel, overall, as a global benefit, but believes we all have a responsibility to limit our personal impact on global warming.

Flying & Climate Change

Pretty much every form of motor travel generates CO_2 (the main cause of human-induced climate change) but planes are far and away the worst offenders, not just because of the sheer distances they allow us to travel, but because they release greenhouse gases high into the atmosphere. The statistics are frightening: two people taking a return flight between Europe and the US will contribute as much to climate change as an average household's gas and electricity consumption over a whole year.

Carbon Offset Schemes

Climatecare.org and other websites use 'carbon calculators' that allow jetsetters to offset the greenhouse gases they are responsible for with contributions to energy-saving projects and other climate-friendly initiatives in the developing world – including projects in India, Honduras, Kazakhstan and Uganda.

Lonely Planet, together with Rough Guides and other concerned partners in the travel industry, supports the carbon offset scheme run by climatecare.org. Lonely Planet offsets all of its staff and author travel.

For more information check out our website: lonelyplanet.com.

---

when Canadian flights go directly to Cuba from as far afield as Vancouver and Halifax.

Unfortunately, 'open jaw' ticket arrangements, which allow you to fly into one airport and out of another, are usually not available. The maximum stay on most Canadian charters is 28 days. If you wish to stay longer than that, the price soars. Flight dates cannot be changed and there are heavy cancellation penalties. Always be sure to compare the price of a tour package as it may be only a few hundred dollars more and airport transfers, accommodation and often meals will be included.

The following are reliable agencies selling packages and air-only tickets:

A Nash Travel (☎ 905-755-0647, toll-free 1-800-818-2004; www.anashtravel.com)

Go Cuba Plus (www.gocubaplus.net)

Netssa (☎ 1-866-504-9988; www.netssa.com) Last-minute flight specials, plus multilingual staff.

STA Travel (☎ 1-888-427-5639; www.statravel.ca)

WoWCuba (☎ 1-902-368-2453; toll-free 1-800-969-2822; www.wowcuba.com)

The Caribbean

Cubana has flights to Havana from Nassau, Fort de France, Kingston, Montego Bay, Pointe-à-Pitre and Santo Domingo. The Cuban regional carrier Aerocaribbean flies from Port au Prince, Haiti, and Santo Domingo, Dominican Republic, to Santiago de Cuba weekly, and from Santo Domingo and Grand Cayman to Havana weekly.

Air Jamaica (www.airjamaica.com) flies from Montego Bay and Kingston to Havana daily, with numerous convenient connections from the US. Air Jamaica also has a liberal baggage policy, often allowing you to bring oversized and overweight luggage without problems.

The agency **CubaLinda.com** (www.cubalinda.com) is a Havana-based online agency selling gateway tickets from Mexico and the Caribbean.

From the Bahamas, Cubana flies daily between Nassau and Havana; the Cuban tourist card and the US$15 Nassau airport departure tax should be included in the ticket price, but ask. Due to US embargo laws, these agencies may not accept online payment or credit-card guarantees with cards issued by US banks or their subsidiaries. The financial rigmarole for Americans (mailing certified checks, paying in cash or wiring funds through Western Union, for example) may not be worth the time and energy if that's the case. Check on the payment system before settling on the Bahamas as a gateway. Nassau bookings can be made through the following companies:

Havanatur Bahamas (☎ 1-242-393-5281/2/3/4; fax 393-5280) Offices in the Bahamas.

Majestic Holidays (☎ 1-242-342-322-2606; www
.majesticholidays.com) Offices in the Bahamas.

Europe

Continental Europe is a good gateway to
Cuba. Virgin Atlantic fly twice weekly to
Havana (Thursday and Sunday) out of
London's Gatwick Airport, while Air Europa
flies into Havana daily from Barcelona,
Bilbao, Las Palmas, London, Madrid, Milan,
Paris and Rome. Iberia flies to Havana from
Madrid four times weekly and connects
through most European capitals; check out
its reasonable fares with a maximum three-
month stay. Air France arrives from Paris–
Charles De Gaulle five times a week.

From Amsterdam, Martinair has twice
weekly flights to Havana and one flight
weekly to both Varadero and Holguín. It's
possible to book Martinair flights into one
Cuban airport and out of the other: convenient if you want to travel overland without
backtracking. Also look into Air France and
Iberia flights from Amsterdam, connecting
through Paris or Madrid.

From Russia, Aeroflot flies from Moscow-
Sheremetyevo to Havana.

Cubana flies to Havana from Copenhagen,
Las Palmas, London, Madrid, Milan, Moscow,
Paris-Orly and Rome. Other Cubana flights
go from Madrid, Milan, Paris-Orly and Rome
to Santiago de Cuba. London to Holguín
and Milan to Cayo Largo are also served.
Most operate only once or twice a week, except Havana–Paris, which runs three times
weekly. Cubana sometimes offers reduced
last-minute fares. There are Cubana offices
all over Europe, including **Rome** (☎ 06-700
0714), **Paris** (☎ 01 53 63 23 23), **Madrid** (☎ 91 758
7751) and **London** (☎ 020 7538 5933).

The following European-based agencies
can help arrange your details:
Guamá Havanatur (☎ 91 782 3785) In Madrid.
Havanatour Holanda (☎ 104-12 73 07) In Rotterdam.
Havanatour Paris (☎ 01 48 01 44 55; www.havana
tour.fr)
Havanatour UK (☎ 01707 665 570; www.havanatour
.co.uk) In Hertfordshire, England.
Havanatur Italia (☎ 02-676 0691; www.havanatur.it)
Journey Latin America (☎ 020 8747 3108; www
.journeylatinamerica.co.uk) Based in Britain, this is a
professional company which usually has good deals.
Sol y Son Moscú (☎ 495 931 9964) Sells Cubana flights
from Moscow.

Sol y Son Roma (☎ 06-7720 3421; www
.it.solysonviajes.com) Handles Cubana flights from Italy.
Trailfinders (☎ 020 7938 3366; www.trailfinders.com)
Offices throughout the UK.

Mexico

Mexico is a direct and convenient gateway to
Cuba, with many flights to choose from. Both
Cubana and Aerocaribe (the regional airline
of Mexicana de Aviación) fly from Cancún
to Havana daily. Cancún itself is easily accessible on cheap charter flights, and Aerocaribe
connects with Mexicana flights from many
US cities. If space is available, you can buy
same-day tickets to Havana at the Cubana and
Aerocaribe offices at the Cancún airport.

Mexicana also has frequent flights from
another dozen cities to Havana including
Mexico City, Mérida and Tijuana. Cubana
flies to Havana from Mexico City daily.

From Mexico City to Havana, a round-trip
fare will cost around US$450, from Cancún
about US$275. Mexicana has reservations of-
fices in **Mexico City** (☎ 5-448-0990, 1-800-502-2000,
www.mexicana.com) and **Cancún** (☎ 98-87-4444).
Mexicana offices in the US are prohibited
from booking these flights.

Cubana also has offices in **Mexico City** (☎ 5-
250-6355) and **Cancún** (☎ /fax 98-86-0192).

Also check these agencies:
Acuario Tours (www.acuariotours.com); Acapulco
(☎ 74-85-6100); Mexico City (☎ 5-575-5922)
Divermex (☎ 99-8884-2325; www.divermex.com)
Sol y Son México (☎ 98-87-7017; www.mx.solyson
viajes.com)
Taíno Tours (☎ 5-259-3907; www.tainotours.com.mx)

South & Central America

From Caracas, Venezuela, Aeropostal flies to
Havana five times weekly. Cubana flies from
Caracas to Havana six times weekly. Book in
Caracas through **Ideal Tours** (☎ 2-793-0037/1822
idealtours@cantv.net) or go straight to **Cubana** (☎ 2
12-286-8639; cubana@intercon.net.ve).

Cubana flies to Havana from Bogotá
Buenos Aires and Saõ Paulo. There's also
a weekly flight from Buenos Aires to Cayo
Coco and Varadero. Cubana has offices in
Buenos Aires (☎ 1-326-5291; cubana@tournet.com.ar)
Quito (☎ 59-32-243-073; cubana@hoy.net) and **Bogotá**
(☎ 571-610-1676; solyson@colomsat.net.co).

Cubana flies to Havana from San José
Costa Rica, and Guatemala City twice weekly
and from Panama City three times a week
Lacsa (Líneas Aéreas de Costa Rica) has flights

to Havana from San José, Guatemala City and San Salvador several times a week. Copa Airlines also has frequent flights between Central America and Cuba.

The Cuban regional airline Aerocaribbean flies from Managua to Havana weekly.

SEA

Thanks to the US embargo, which prohibits vessels calling at Cuban ports from visiting the US for six months, few cruise ships include Cuba on their itineraries. European lines, however, tired of being locked out, are starting to trickle in. A specialist travel agent will be able to tell you what cruise ships currently call at Cuban ports.

If you have your own private yacht or cruiser, Cuba has seven international entry ports equipped with customs facilities. They are Havana (Marina Hemingway), Varadero (Marina Dársena), Cayo Guillermo, Santiago de Cuba, Cienfuegos, Cayo Largo del Sur, and Puerto de Vita (near Guardalavaca in Holguín province).

There are no scheduled ferry services to Cuba.

TOURS

A quick internet search delivers scads of tours focusing on the beach, culture, the environment, adventure, cycling, bird-watching, architecture, hiking, you name it… Note that many outfitters anxious to sell packages to Americans aren't always providing 'legal' travel; Americans are still subject to Treasury

laws; see the **Department of the Treasury** (www.treas .gov) website for details (type the word 'Cuba' into the site search engine). Persons holding US passports will find agencies handling 'air-only' packages on p474 and tours for US-license holders following.

From the US

United States citizens eligible for a US government 'license' to visit Cuba should contact **Marazul Charters Inc** (☎ 305-263-6829, toll-free 800-223-5334; www.marazulcharters.com), which books charter flights direct from New York and Miami to Havana.

ABC Charters (☎ 305-871-1260, toll-free 866-422-2247; www.abc-charters.com), with flights from Miami to Havana, Santiago de Cuba or Holguín, has been recommended for its user-friendliness.

Since the people-to-people educational exchange license was revoked in 2003, some of the most rewarding tours from the US have been scuttled – for now. Contact the following for their current tour status:

Center for Cuban Studies (☎ 212-242-0559; www .cubaupdate.org) Arranges trips through universities.

Global Exchange (☎ 415-255-7296, 800-497-1994; www.globalexchange.org)

GETTING AROUND

AIR

Cubana de Aviación (www.cubana.cu) and its regional carrier Aerocaribbean have flights to Havana,

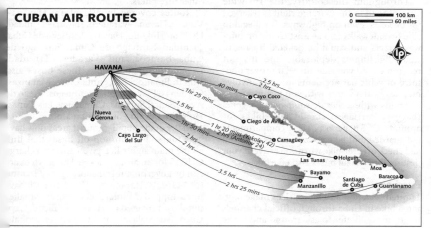

CUBAN AIR ROUTES

Baracoa, Bayamo, Camagüey, Cayo Largo del Sur, Ciego de Ávila, Guantánamo, Holguín, Isla de la Juventud, Manzanillo, Moa and Santiago de Cuba. One-way flights are half the price of round-trip flights and weight restrictions are strict (especially on Aerocaribbean's smaller planes). You can purchase tickets at most hotel tour desks and travel agencies for the same price as at the airline offices, which are often chaotic. Sol y Son is Cubana's own travel agency and is known for its customer service and efficiency.

Aerogaviota (☎ 7-203-0686; Av 47 No 2814 btwn Calles 28 & 34, Playa, Havana) runs more expensive charter flights to La Coloma (Pinar del Río province), Nueva Gerona, Cayo Largo del Sur, Varadero, Cayo Las Brujas, Cayo Coco, Playa Santa Lucía and Santiago de Cuba.

BICYCLE

Cuba is a cyclist's paradise, with bike lanes, bike workshops and drivers accustomed to sharing the road countrywide. Spare parts are difficult to find – you should bring important spares with you. Still, Cubans are grand masters at improvised repair and though specific parts may not be available, something can surely be jury-rigged. *Poncheros* fix flat tires and provide air; every small town has one.

Helmets are unheard of in Cuba except at upscale resorts, so you should bring your own. A lock is imperative as bicycle theft is rampant. *Parqueos* are bicycle parking lots located wherever crowds congregate (eg markets, bus terminals, downtown etc); they cost one peso.

Throughout the country, the 1m-wide strip of road to the extreme right is reserved for bicycles, even on highways. It's illegal to ride on sidewalks and against traffic on one-way streets and you'll be ticketed if caught. Road lighting is deplorable and it's not recommended you ride after dark (over one-third of vehicular accidents in Cuba involve bicycles); carry lights with you just in case.

Trains with *coches de equipaje* or *bagones* (baggage carriages) should take bikes for around CUC$10 per trip. These compartments are guarded, but take your panniers with you and check over the bike when you arrive at your destination. Víazul buses also take bikes.

Purchase

Limited selection and high prices make buying a bike in Cuba through official channels unattractive. Better to ask around and strike a deal with an individual to buy their *chivo* (Cuban slang for bike) and trade it or resell it when you leave. With some earnest bargaining, you can get one for around CUC$30 – although the more you pay, the less your bones are likely to shake. Despite the obvious cost savings, bringing your own bike is still the best bet by far.

Rental

At the time of writing, official bike-rental agencies existed only at El Orbe in Havana (for rates see p151), at the major beach resorts (CUC$3 per hour or CUC$15 per day) and in Viñales and Trinidad (CUC$6 to CUC$8 per day). Bikes are usually included as a perk in all-inclusive resort packages.

Don't worry if there are no official bike rental outlets; no matter where you are, you'll always find someone willing to arrange a private rental. The going rate is CUC$3 to CUC$7 per day.

BUS

Bus travel is a dependable way of getting around Cuba, at least in the more popular areas. **Víazul** (☎ 7-881-1413, 7-881-5652, 7-881-1108; www.viazul.com) is the only long-distance bus company available to non-Cubans, with punctual, (over)air-conditioned coaches going to destinations of interest to travelers. Víazul charges for tickets in Convertibles and you can be confident you'll get where you're going on these buses – and on time. They have daily departures and they're a good place to meet other foreigners.

Routes covered by Víazul are Havana–Viñales, Havana–Varadero, Havana–Trinidad, Havana–Holguín, Havana–Santiago de Cuba, Trinidad–Santiago de Cuba, Santiago de Cuba–Baracoa and Varadero–Trinidad. Depending on the route, these buses also stop in Pinar del Río, Santa Clara, Matanzas, Cárdenas, Playa Girón, Cienfuegos, Ciego de Ávila, Sancti Spíritus, Camagüey, Las Tunas, Holguín, Bayamo or Guantánamo.

Many of the popular tourist areas now have 'bus tours,' hop-on/hop-off buses that link all the main sights in a given area and charge CUC$5 for an all-day ticket. The services are run by government transport agency **Transtur** (☎ 7-831-7333). Havana and Varadero both have open-topped double-decker buses. Smaller minibuses are used in Viñales, Trinidad, Cayo Coco, Guardalavaca and Baracoa (seasonal

Cubans travel over shorter distances in provincial buses. These buses sell tickets in pesos and are a lot less comfortable or reliable than Víazul. They leave from the provincial bus stations in each province. Schedules and prices are usually chalked up on a board inside the terminal.

Reservations

Reservations with Víazul aren't always necessary, though it's advisable to check during peak travel periods (June to August, Christmas and Easter) and on popular routes (Havana–Trinidad, Trinidad–Santa Clara and Santiago de Cuba–Baracoa). Víazul out of Baracoa is almost always booked, so reserve an advance seat on this service when you arrive. It is now possible to make reservations online at www.viazul.com.

CAR

Renting a car in Cuba is easy but, once you've factored in gas, insurance, hire fees etc, it isn't cheap. Bank on paying CUC$70 per day minimum, even for a small car. It's actually cheaper to hire a taxi for distances of under 150km.

Driver's License

Your home license is sufficient to rent and drive a car in Cuba.

Fuel & Spare Parts

Gas sold in Convertibles (as opposed to peso gas) is widely available in stations all over the country (the north coast west of Havana being the notable exception). Gas stations are often open 24 hours and may have a small parts store on site. Gas is sold by the liter and comes in *regular* (CUC$0.95 per liter) and *especial* (CUC$1.15 per liter) varieties. Rental cars are advised to use *especial*. All gas stations have efficient pump attendants, usually in the form of *trabajadores sociales* (students in the process of studying for a degree).

While you cannot count on spare parts per se to be available, Cubans have decades of experience keeping old wrecks on the road without factory parts and you'll see them do amazing things with cardboard, string, rubber and clothes hangers to keep a car mobile.

If you need air in your tires or you have a puncture, use a gas station or visit the local *ponchero*. They often don't have measures so make sure they don't overfill them.

Insurance

Rental cars come with an optional CUC$10 per day insurance, which covers everything but theft of the radio (which you'll need to put in the trunk of the car at night). You can choose to decline the insurance, but then the refundable deposit you must leave upon renting the car (in cash if you don't have a credit card issued by a non-US bank) soars from CUC$200 to CUC$500. If you do have an accident, you must get a copy of the *denuncia* (police report) to be eligible for the insurance coverage, a process which can take all day. If the police determine that you are the

ROAD DISTANCES (KM)

	Bayamo	Camagüey	Ciego de Ávila	Cienfuegos	Guantánamo	Havana	Holguín	Las Tunas	Matanzas	Pinar del Río	Sancti Spíritus	Santa Clara
Camagüey	210											
Ciego de Ávila	318	108										
Cienfuegos	540	330	222									
Guantánamo	161	371	479	701								
Havana	744	534	426	254	905							
Holguín	71	209	317	539	182	743						
Las Tunas	82	128	236	458	243	662	81					
Matanzas	684	474	366	194	845	105	683	602				
Pinar del Río	906	696	588	416	1067	162	905	824	267			
Sancti Spíritus	394	184	76	151	555	354	393	312	294	516		
Santa Clara	473	263	155	67	634	276	472	391	217	438	590	
Santiago de Cuba	117	550	435	657	84	861	138	199	801	1023	511	590

TRANSPORT

party responsible for the accident, say *adiós* to your deposit.

Rental

Renting a car in Cuba is very straightforward and you can usually be signed up and fitted out in well under an hour. You'll need your passport, driver's license and refundable CUC$200 deposit (in cash or non-US credit card). You can rent a car in one city and drop it off in another for a reasonable fee, which is handy. If you're on a tight budget, ask about diesel cars – some agencies stock a few and you'll save bundles in gas money considering a liter of non-diesel is CUC$1.15 while a liter of *petróleo* (diesel) is CUC$0.65. Note that there are very few rental cars with automatic transmission.

If you want to rent a car for three days or fewer, it will come with limited kilometers, while contracts for three days or more come with unlimited kilometers. In Cuba, you pay for the first tank of gas when you rent the car (CUC$1.15 per liter) and return it empty (a suicidal policy that sees many tight-fisted tourists running out of gas a kilometer or so from the drop-off point). Just to make it worse, you will not be refunded for any gas left in the tank. Petty theft of mirrors, antennas, taillights etc is common, so it's worth it to pay someone a Convertible or two to watch your car for the night. If you lose your rental contract or keys you'll pay a CUC$50 penalty. Drivers under 25 pay a CUC$5 fee, while additional drivers on the same contract pay a CUC$15 surcharge.

Check over the car carefully with the rental agent before driving into the sunset, as you'll be responsible for any damage or missing parts. Make sure there is a spare tire of the correct size, a jack and lug wrench. Check that there are seatbelts and that all the doors lock properly.

We have received many letters about poor or nonexistent customer service, bogus spare tires, forgotten reservations and other car-rental problems. Reservations are only accepted 15 days in advance and are still not guaranteed. While agents are usually accommodating, you might end up paying more than you planned or have to wait for hours until someone returns a car. The more Spanish you speak and the friendlier you are, the more likely problems will be resolved to everyone's satisfaction (tips to the agent might help). As with most Cuban travel, always be ready to go to Plan B.

Road Conditions

You thought using a car in Cuba would be easy? Think again. Driving here isn't just a different ballpark, it's a different sport. The first problem is that there are no signs – almost anywhere. Major junctions and turnoffs to important resorts or cities are often not indicated at all. Not only is this distracting, it's also incredibly time-consuming. The lack of signage also extends to highway instructions. Often a one-way street is not clearly indicated or a speed limit not highlighted, which can cause problems with the police (who won't understand your inability to telepathically absorb the road rules), and road markings are nonexistent everywhere.

Repair-wise, the Autopista, Vía Blanca and Carretera Central are generally in a good state, but be prepared for roads suddenly deteriorating into chunks of asphalt and unexpected railroad crossings everywhere else (especially in the Oriente). Rail crossings are particularly problematic as there are hundreds of them and there are never any safety gates. Beware however overgrown the rails may look, you can pretty much assume that the line is still in use. Cuban trains, rather like its cars, defy all normal logic when it comes to mechanics.

While motorized traffic is refreshingly light, bicycles, pedestrians, oxcarts, horse carriages and livestock are a different matter. Many old cars and trucks lack rearview mirrors and traffic-unaware children run out of all kinds of nooks and crannies. Stay alert, drive with caution and use your horn when passing or on blind curves.

Driving at night is not recommended due to variable roads, drunk drivers, crossing cows and poor lighting. Drunk-driving remains a troublesome problem despite a government educational campaign. Late night in Havana is particularly dangerous, when it seems there's a passing lane, cruising lane and drunk lane.

Traffic lights are often busted or hard to pick out and right-of-way rules thrown to the wind. Take extra care.

Road Rules

Cubans drive how they want, where they want. It seems chaotic at first, but it has its rhythm. Seatbelts are supposedly required and maximum speed limits are technically 50km/h in the city, 90km/h on highways and 100km/h on the Autopista, but some cars can't even go that fast and those that can go faster still.

With so few cars on the road, it's hard not to put the pedal to the floor and just fly. Unexpected potholes are a hazard, however, as are police. There are some clever speed traps, particularly along the Autopista. Speeding tickets start at CUC$30 and are noted on your car contract; the fine is deducted from your deposit when you return the car. When pulled over by the cops, you're expected to get out of the car and walk over to them with your paperwork. An oncoming car flashing its lights means a hazard up ahead (usually the police).

The Cuban transport crisis means there are a lot of people waiting for rides by the side of the road. Giving a *botella* (a lift) to local hitchhikers has advantages aside from altruism. With a Cuban passenger you'll never get lost, you'll learn about secret spots not in any guidebook and you'll meet some great people. There are always risks associated with picking up hitchhikers; giving lifts to older people or families may reduce the risk factor. In the provinces, people waiting for rides are systematically queued by the *amarillos* (roadside traffic organizers; see boxed text, p368), and they'll hustle the most needy folks into your car, usually an elderly couple or a pregnant woman.

FERRY

The most important ferry services for travelers are the catamaran from Surgidero de Batabanó to Nueva Gerona, **Isla de la Juventud** (☎ 7-878-1841) and the passenger ferry from Havana to Regla and **Casablanca** (☎ 7-867-3726). These ferries are generally safe, though in 1997 two hydrofoils crashed en route to Isla de la Juventud. In both 1994 and 2003, the Regla/Casablanca ferry was hijacked by Cubans trying to make their way to Florida. The 2003 incident involved tourists, so you can expect tight security.

HITCHHIKING

The transport crisis, culture of solidarity and low crime levels make Cuba a popular hitchhiking destination. Here, hitchhiking is more like ride-sharing. Traffic lights, railroad crossings and country crossroads are regular stops for people seeking rides. In the provinces and on the outskirts of Havana, the *amarillos* (see boxed text, p368) organize and prioritize ride seekers and you're welcome to jump in line. Rides cost five to 20 pesos depending on distance. Travelers hitching rides will want a good map and some Spanish skills. Expect to wait two or three hours for rides in some cases. Hitchhiking is never entirely safe in any country in the world. Travelers who decide to hitchhike should understand that they are taking a small but potentially serious risk. People who do choose to hitchhike will be safer if they travel in pairs and let someone know where they are planning to go.

LOCAL TRANSPORT
Bici-taxi

Bici-taxis are big tricycles with a double seat behind the driver and are common in Havana, Camagüey, Holguín and a few other cities. In Havana they'll insist on a CUC$1 minimum fare (Cubans pay five or 10 pesos). Some bici-taxistas ask ridiculous amounts. The fare should be clearly understood before you hop aboard. By law, bici-taxis aren't allowed to take tourists (who are expected to use regular taxis) and they're taking a risk by carrying foreigners. Bici-taxi rules are more lax in the provinces and you should be able to get one for five pesos.

Boat

Some towns such as Havana, Cienfuegos, Gibara and Santiago de Cuba have local ferry services. Details of these are provided in the respective chapters.

Bus

Very crowded, very steamy, very challenging, very Cuban – *guaguas* (local buses) are useful in bigger cities. Buses work fixed routes, stopping at *paradas* (bus stops) that always have a line, even if it doesn't look like it. You have to shout out *¿el último?* to find out who was last in line before you showed up. You give this call when the next person arrives and then you know exactly where you fall in line, allowing you to go have a beer until the bus shows up.

Buses cost from 40 centavos to one peso. Havana and Santiago de Cuba have recently been kitted out with brand new fleets of Chinese-made metro buses. You must always walk as far back in the bus as you can and exit through the rear. Make room to pass by saying

TRANSPORT

permiso, always wear your pack in front and watch your wallet.

Colectivos & Máquinas

Colectivos are taxis running on fixed, long-distance routes, leaving when full. They are generally pre-1959 American cars that belch diesel fumes and can squash in at least three people across the front seat. State-owned taxis that charge in Convertibles hanging about bus stations are faster and usually cheaper than the bus. State-owned peso taxis and private peso taxis *(máquinas)* are prohibited from taking foreigners (except the *carnet*-carrying kind; see p462).

Horse Carriage

Many provincial cities have *coches de caballo* (horse carriages) that trot on fixed routes and cost one peso.

Taxi

Tourists are only supposed to take taxis that charge in Convertibles, including the little yellow coco-taxis (three-wheel, egg-shaped taxis that hold two to three people). Car taxis are metered and cost CUC$1 to start and CUC$1 per kilometer. Taxi drivers are in the habit of offering foreigners a flat, off-meter rate that usually works out very close to what you'll pay with the meter. The difference is that with the meter, the money goes to the state to be divided up; without the meter it goes into the driver's pocket. Coco-taxis are not metered and cost CUC$0.50 per kilometer.

TOURS

Of the many tourist agencies in Cuba, the following are the most useful:

Cubamar Viajes (☎ 7-833-2523/4; www.cubamar viajes.cu) Rents campismo cabins and mobile homes (caravans).

Cubanacán (☎ 7-873-2686; www.cubanacan.cu) General tour agency that also has divisions called Cubanacán Náutica (scuba diving, boating and fishing) and Turismo Y Salud (surgery, spas and rehabilitation).

Cubatur (☎ 7-835-4155)

Ecotur (☎ 7-204-5188)

Gaviota (☎ 7-204-4411; www.gaviota-grupo.com)

Havanatur (☎ 7-835-3720; www.havanatur.cu) Works with Marazul Tours in the US.

Paradiso (☎ 7-832-9538/9; paradis@paradiso.artex .com.cu) Multiday cultural and art tours.

San Cristóbal Agencia de Viajes (☎ 7-861-9171; fax 7-860-9585; www.viajessancristobal.cu)

TRAIN

Cuba was the sixth country in the world to get a railway (before Spain even) and, as a result, it is proud of its extensive network – however antiquated it might be. Public railways operated by Ferrocarriles de Cuba serve all of the provincial capitals and are a great way to experience Cuba if you have time and patience. As a Cuban traveler said, '80% of the trains are late and the other 20% are cancelled.' While train travel is safe, the departure information provided in this book is purely theoretical. Getting a ticket is usually no problem as there's a quota for tourists paying in Convertibles.

Foreigners must pay for their tickets in cash, but prices are reasonable and the carriages, though old and worn, are fairly comfortable, offering lots of local color. The toilets are foul. Watch your luggage on overnight trips and bring some of your own food. Only the Tren Francés has snack facilities although vendors often come through the train selling coffee (you supply the cup).

The Hershey Train is the only electric railway in Cuba and was built by the Hershey Chocolate Company in the early years of the 20th century; it's a fun way to get between Havana and Matanzas (see boxed text, p179).

Classes

Trains are either *especial* (air-conditioned, faster trains with fewer departures), *regular* (slowish trains with daily departures) or *lecheros* (milk trains that stop at every dinky town on the line). Trains on major routes such as Havana–Santiago de Cuba will be *especial* or *regular* trains.

Costs

Regular trains cost under CUC$3 per 100km, while *especial* trains cost closer to CUC$5.50 per 100km. The Hershey Train is priced like the *regular* trains.

Reservations

In most train stations, you just go to the ticket window and buy a ticket. In Havana, there's a separate waiting room and ticket window for passengers paying in Convertibles in La Coubre train station. Be prepared to show your passport when purchasing tickets. It's always wise to check beforehand at the station for current departures because things change.

Services

Cuba's best and fastest train (by a stretch) is the Tren Francés that runs between Havana and Santiago de Cuba on alternate days (1st/2nd class CUC$62/50, 12½ hours, 861km). Train 1 leaves Havana daily at 7pm, passing Santa Clara and Camagüey, before reaching Santiago de Cuba at 9am. Train 2 leaves Santiago de Cuba daily at 5:35pm and reaches Havana at 9:30am. The trains with recycled European carriages are comfortable and air-conditioned, but there are no sleeper compartments. At the time of writing the Tren Francés had been temporarily suspended for 'repairs.'

Other train routes that may be of interest to travelers include Pinar del Río–Sábalo, Havana–Matanzas, Havana–Cienfuegos, Havana–Sancti Spíritus, Havana–Holguín, Havana–Manzanillo, Santa Clara–Morón-Nuevitas, Cienfuegos–Santa Clara–Sancti Spíritus, Camagüey–Nuevitas, Camagüey-Bayamo, Bayamo–Manzanillo, Manzanillo-Bayamo–Santiago de Cuba and Santiago de Cuba–Holguín. Trinidad has been cut off from the main rail network since 1992 when a storm downed a bridge. The furthest east the line goes is Guantánamo – there is no line to Baracoa.

Many additional local trains operate at least daily and some more frequently. More information is provided in the regional chapters of this book.

TRUCK

Camiones (trucks) are a cheap, fast way to travel within or between provinces. Every city has a provincial and municipal bus stop with *camiones* departures. They run on a (loose) schedule and you'll need to take your place in line by asking for *el último* to your destination; you pay as you board. A truck from Santiago de Cuba to Guantánamo costs five pesos (CUC$0.20), while the same trip on a Víazul bus costs CUC$6.

Camion traveling is hot, crowded and uncomfortable, but is a great way to meet local people fast; a little Spanish will go a long way.

Sometimes terminal staff tell foreigners they're prohibited from traveling on trucks. As with anything in Cuba, never take the word 'no' as your final answer. Crying poor, striking up a conversation with the driver, appealing to other passengers for aid etc usually helps.

TRANSPORT

Health Dr David Goldberg

CONTENTS

Before You Go	**484**
Insurance	484
Medical Checklist	484
Internet Resources	485
Further Reading	485
In Transit	**485**
Deep Vein Thrombosis (DVT)	485
Jet Lag & Motion Sickness	485
In Cuba	**486**
Availability & Cost of Health Care	486
Infectious Diseases	486
Traveler's Diarrhea	487
Environmental Hazards	488
Traveling with Children	489
Women's Health	489
Traditional Medicine	489

From a medical point of view, the Caribbean islands are generally safe as long as you're reasonably careful about what you eat and drink. The most common travel-related diseases, such as dysentery and hepatitis, are acquired by the consumption of contaminated food and water. Mosquito-borne illnesses are not a significant concern on most of the islands within the Cuban archipelago.

Prevention is the key to staying healthy while traveling around Cuba. Travelers who receive the recommended vaccines and follow commonsense precautions usually come away with nothing more than a little diarrhea.

BEFORE YOU GO

Since most vaccines don't produce immunity until at least two weeks after they're given, visit a physician four to eight weeks before departure. Ask your doctor for an International Certificate of Vaccination (otherwise known as the 'yellow booklet'), which will list all the vaccinations you've received. This is mandatory for countries that require proof of yellow-fever vaccination upon entry. Cuba doesn't require yellow-fever vaccination, but it's a good idea to carry your yellow booklet wherever you travel.

Bring medications in their original, clearly labeled containers. A signed and dated letter from your physician describing your medical conditions and medications, including generic names, is also a good idea. If carrying syringes or needles, be sure to have a physician's letter documenting their medical necessity.

INSURANCE

If your usual health insurance doesn't cover you for medical expenses abroad, consider getting extra insurance; see p465 and check out the Travel Services/Insurance section at lonelyplanet.com for more information. Find out in advance if your insurance plan will make payments directly to providers or reimburse you later for overseas health expenditures. (In many countries, doctors expect payment in cash.)

Should you get into trouble health-wise and end up in hospital, call **Asistur** (☎ 7-866-8527; www.asistur.cu) for help with insurance and medical assistance. The company has regional offices in Havana, Varadero, Cienfuegos, Cayo Coco, Camagüey, Guardalavaca and Santiago de Cuba.

MEDICAL CHECKLIST

- acetaminophen (Tylenol) or aspirin
- adhesive or paper tape
- antibacterial ointment (eg Bactroban; for cuts and abrasions)
- antibiotics
- antidiarrheal drugs (eg loperamide)
- antihistamines (for hay fever and allergic reactions)

GOVERNMENT TRAVEL HEALTH ADVICE

It's usually a good idea to consult your government's travel health website before departure, if one is available:

Australia (www.smarttraveller.gov.au) Follow the link to Travel Health.

Canada (www.travelhealth.gc.ca)

UK (www.dh.gov.uk) Follow the links to Policy and Guidance and Health Advice for Travellers.

USA (www.cdc.gov/travel)

RECOMMENDED VACCINATIONS

No vaccines are required for Cuba, but a number are recommended:

Vaccine	Recommended for	Dosage	Side effects
Chickenpox	Travelers who've never had chickenpox	2 doses 1 month apart	Fever; mild case of chickenpox
Hepatitis A	All travelers	1 dose before trip; booster 6-12 months later	Soreness at injection site; headaches; body aches
Hepatitis B	Long-term travelers in close contact with the local population	3 doses over a 6-month period	Soreness at injection site; low-grade fever
Rabies	Travelers who may have contact with animals and may not have access to medical care	3 doses over a 3-4 week period	Soreness at injection site; headaches; body aches
Tetanus-diphtheria	All travelers who haven't had a booster within 10 years	1 dose lasts 10 years	Soreness at injection site
Typhoid	All travelers	4 capsules orally, 1 taken every other day	Abdominal pain; nausea; rash

- anti-inflammatory drugs (eg ibuprofen)
- bandages, gauze, gauze rolls
- DEET-containing insect repellent for the skin
- iodine tablets (for water purification)
- oral rehydration salts
- permethrin-containing insect spray for clothing, tents and bed nets
- pocketknife
- scissors, safety pins, tweezers
- steroid cream or cortisone (for poison ivy and other allergic rashes)
- sunblock
- syringes and sterile needles
- thermometer

INTERNET RESOURCES

There is a wealth of travel health advice on the internet. For further information, lonelyplanet.com is a good place to start. The World Health Organization publishes a superb book called *International Travel and Health*, which is revised annually and is available online at no cost (www.who .int/ith). Another website of general interest is **MD Travel Health** (www.mdtravelhealth.com), which provides complete travel health recommendations for every country and is updated daily.

FURTHER READING

If you're traveling with children, Lonely Planet's *Travel with Children* may be useful.

The *ABC of Healthy Travel,* by Eric Walker et al, is another valuable resource.

IN TRANSIT

DEEP VEIN THROMBOSIS (DVT)

Blood clots may form in the legs (deep vein thrombosis) during plane flights, chiefly because of prolonged immobility. The longer the flight, the greater the risk. Though most blood clots are reabsorbed uneventfully, some may break off and travel through the blood vessels to the lungs, where they could cause life-threatening complications.

The chief symptom of DVT is swelling or pain in the foot, ankle or calf, usually – but not always – on just one side. When a blood clot travels to the lungs, it may cause chest pain and difficulty breathing. Travelers with any of the symptoms noted above should immediately seek medical attention.

To prevent the development of DVT on long flights, you should walk about the cabin, perform isometric compressions of the leg muscles (ie flex the leg muscles while sitting), drink plenty of fluids and avoid alcohol and tobacco.

JET LAG & MOTION SICKNESS

Jet lag is common when crossing more than five time zones, resulting in insomnia, fatigue, malaise or nausea. To avoid jet lag, try to drink plenty of (nonalcoholic) fluids and eat

HEALTH

light meals. Upon arrival, get exposure to natural sunlight and readjust your schedule (for meals, sleep etc) as soon as possible.

Antihistamines such as dimenhydrinate (Dramamine) and meclizine (Antivert, Bonine) are usually the first choice for treating motion sickness. Their main side effect is drowsiness. A herbal alternative is ginger, which works like a charm for some people.

IN CUBA

AVAILABILITY & COST OF HEALTH CARE

The Cuban government has established a for-profit health system for foreigners called **Servimed** (☎ 7-24-01-41), which is entirely separate from the free, not-for-profit system that takes care of Cuban citizens. There are more than 40 Servimed health centers across the island, offering primary care as well as a variety of specialty and high-tech services. If you're staying in a hotel, the usual way to access the system is to ask the manager for a physician referral. Servimed centers accept walk-ins. While Cuban hospitals provide some free emergency treatment for foreigners, this should only be used when there is no other option. Remember that in Cuba medical resources are scarce and the local populace should be given priority in free healthcare facilities.

Almost all doctors and hospitals expect payment in cash, regardless of whether you have travel health insurance or not. If you develop a life-threatening medical problem, you'll probably want to be evacuated to a country with state-of-the-art medical care. Since this may cost tens of thousands of dollars, be sure you have insurance to cover this before you depart. See p465 for details.

There are special pharmacies for foreigners also run by the Servimed system, but all Cuban pharmacies are notoriously short on supplies, including pharmaceuticals. Be sure to bring along adequate quantities of all medications you might need, both prescription and over-the-counter. Also, be sure to bring along a fully stocked medical kit.

INFECTIOUS DISEASES
Dengue (Break-bone) Fever

Dengue fever is a viral and mosquito-borne infection found throughout the Caribbean. A major outbreak of dengue fever, centering on

Havana and resulting in more than 3000 cases, was reported from November 2001 through to March 2002. Since then, an aggressive government program has all but eradicated dengue from the island. See also p488 for information on avoiding mosquito bites.

Hepatitis A

Hepatitis A is the second most common travel-related infection (after traveler's diarrhea). It occurs throughout the Caribbean, particularly on the northern islands. Hepatitis A is a viral infection of the liver that is usually acquired by ingestion of contaminated water, food or ice, though it may also be acquired by direct contact with infected persons. The illness occurs throughout the world, but the incidence is higher in developing nations. Symptoms may include fever, malaise, jaundice, nausea, vomiting and abdominal pain. Most cases resolve without complications, though hepatitis A occasionally causes severe liver damage. There is no treatment.

The vaccine for hepatitis A is extremely safe and highly effective. If you get a booster six to 12 months after the first vaccine, it lasts for at least 10 years. You really should get this vaccine before you go to Cuba or any other developing nation. Because the safety of the hepatitis A vaccine has not been established for pregnant women or children under the age of two, they should instead be given a gamma globulin injection.

Hepatitis B

Like hepatitis A, hepatitis B is a liver infection that occurs worldwide but is more common in developing nations. Unlike hepatitis A, the disease is usually acquired by sexual contact or by exposure to infected blood, generally through blood transfusions or contaminated needles. The vaccine is recommended only for long-term travelers (on the road for more than six months) who expect to live in rural areas or have close physical contact with the local population. Additionally, the vaccine is recommended for anyone who anticipates sexual contact with the local inhabitants or a possible need for medical, dental or other treatments while abroad, especially if a need for transfusions or injections is expected.

The hepatitis B vaccine is safe and highly effective. However, a total of three injections are necessary to establish full immunity. Several countries added the hepatitis B vaccine to the list of routine childhood immunizations in the 1980s, so many young adults are already protected.

Malaria

In the Caribbean, malaria occurs only in Haiti and certain parts of the Dominican Republic. Malaria pills aren't necessary for Cuba.

Rabies

Rabies is a viral infection of the brain and spinal cord that is almost always fatal. The virus is carried in the saliva of infected animals and is usually transmitted through an animal bite, though contamination of any break in the skin with infected saliva may result in rabies. Rabies occurs in several Caribbean islands, including Cuba. Most cases in Cuba are related to bites from dogs, bats and wild animals, especially the small Indian mongoose.

The rabies vaccine is safe, but a full series requires three injections and is quite expensive. Those at high risk of rabies, such as animal handlers and spelunkers (cave explorers), should certainly get the vaccine. Those at lower risk of animal bites should consider asking for the vaccine if they are traveling to remote areas and might not have access to appropriate medical care if needed. The treatment for a possibly rabid bite consists of rabies vaccine with rabies immune globulin. It's effective but must be given promptly. Most travelers don't need the rabies vaccine.

All animal bites and scratches must be promptly and thoroughly cleansed with large amounts of soap and water, and local health authorities must be contacted to determine whether or not further treatment is necessary (see p488).

Typhoid

Typhoid fever is caused by ingestion of food or water contaminated by a species of salmonella known as *Salmonella typhi*. Fever occurs in virtually all cases. Other symptoms may include headache, malaise, muscle aches, dizziness, loss of appetite, nausea and abdominal pain. Either diarrhea or constipation may occur. Possible complications include intestinal perforation, intestinal bleeding, confusion, delirium or (rarely) coma.

The typhoid vaccine is usually given orally, but is also available as an injection. Neither vaccine is approved for use in children under two. If you get typhoid fever, the drug

of choice is usually a quinolone antibiotic such as ciprofloxacin (Cipro) or levofloxacin (Levaquin), which many travelers carry for treatment of diarrhea.

Other Infections
BRUCELLOSIS

Brucellosis is an infection of domestic and wild animals that may be transmitted to humans through direct animal contact or by consumption of unpasteurized dairy products from infected animals. In Cuba, most human cases are related to infected pigs. Symptoms may include fever, malaise, depression, loss of appetite, headache, muscle aches and back pain. Complications may include arthritis, hepatitis, meningitis and endocarditis (heart valve infection).

FASCIOLIASIS

This is a parasitic infection that is typically acquired by eating contaminated watercress grown in sheep-raising areas. Early symptoms may include fever, nausea, vomiting and painful enlargement of the liver.

HIV/AIDS

HIV/AIDS has been reported in all Caribbean countries. Be sure to use condoms for the purposes of safe sex.

LEPTOSPIROSIS

Acquired by exposure to water contaminated by the urine of infected animals. Outbreaks often occur at times of flooding, when sewage overflow may contaminate water sources. The initial symptoms, which resemble a mild flu, usually subside uneventfully in a few days, with or without treatment, but a minority of cases are complicated by jaundice or meningitis. There is no vaccine. You can minimize your risk by staying out of bodies of fresh water that may be contaminated by animal urine. If you're visiting an area where an outbreak is in progress, as occurred in Cuba in 1994, you can take 200mg of doxycycline once weekly as a preventative measure. If you actually develop leptospirosis, the treatment is 100mg of doxycycline twice daily.

TRAVELER'S DIARRHEA

To prevent diarrhea, avoid tap water unless it has been boiled, filtered or chemically disinfected (with iodine tablets); only eat fresh fruits or vegetables if cooked or peeled; be wary of dairy products that may contain unpasteurized milk; and be highly selective when eating food from street vendors.

If you develop diarrhea, be sure to drink plenty of fluids, preferably an oral rehydration solution containing lots of salt and sugar. A few loose stools don't require treatment, but if you start having more than four or five stools a day, you should start taking an antibiotic (usually a quinolone drug) and an antidiarrheal agent (such as loperamide). If diarrhea is bloody, persists for more than 72 hours or is accompanied by fever, shaking chills or severe abdominal pain, you should seek medical attention.

ENVIRONMENTAL HAZARDS
Animal Bites
Do not attempt to pet, handle or feed any animal, with the exception of domestic animals known to be free of any infectious disease. Most injuries are directly related to a person's attempt to touch or feed the animal.

Any bite or scratch by a mammal, including bats, should be promptly and thoroughly cleansed with large amounts of soap and water, followed by application of an antiseptic such as iodine or alcohol. The local health authorities should be contacted immediately for possible postexposure rabies treatment, whether or not you've been immunized against rabies (see p487). It may also be advisable to start an antibiotic, since wounds caused by animal bites and scratches frequently become infected. One of the newer quinolones, such as levofloxacin (Levaquin), which many travelers carry in case of diarrhea, would be an appropriate choice.

Spiny sea urchins and coelenterates (coral and jellyfish) are a hazard in some areas. Some stings (eg from a Portuguese man-of-war) can produce a bad reaction, and if you start to feel nauseous or faint you should seek medical treatment.

Heatstroke
To protect yourself from excessive sun exposure, you should stay out of the midday sun, wear sunglasses and a wide-brimmed sun hat, and apply sunscreen with SPF 15 or higher, with both UVA and UVB protection. Sunscreen should be generously applied to all exposed parts of the body approximately 30 minutes before sun exposure and should be reapplied after swimming or vigorous ac-

tivity. Travelers should also drink plenty of fluids and avoid strenuous exercise when the temperature is high.

Insect Bites & Stings
Because of an aggressive program of mosquito control, mosquito-borne illnesses are usually not a concern in Cuba. However, outbreaks of dengue fever (see p486) have occurred in the recent past, so you should be aware of the means of preventing mosquito bites, if necessary. If dengue or other mosquito-borne illnesses are being reported, you should keep yourself covered (wear long sleeves, long pants, a hat, and shoes rather than sandals) and apply a good insect repellent, preferably one containing DEET, to exposed skin and clothing. Do not apply DEET to eyes, mouth, cuts, wounds or irritated skin. Products containing lower concentrations of DEET are as effective, but for shorter periods of time. In general, adults and children over 12 should use preparations containing 25% to 35% DEET, which usually lasts for about six hours. Children between two and 12 years of age should use preparations containing no more than 10% DEET, applied sparingly, which will usually last about three hours. Neurologic toxicity has been reported from DEET, especially in children, but appears to be extremely uncommon and generally related to overuse. DEET-containing compounds should not be used on children under the age of two.

Insect repellents containing certain botanical products, including eucalyptus and soybean oil, are effective but last only for 1½ to two hours. Products based on citronella are not effective.

For additional protection, you can apply permethrin to clothing, shoes, tents and bed nets. Permethrin treatments are safe and remain effective for at least two weeks, even when items are laundered. Permethrin should not be applied directly to skin.

Water
Tap water in Cuba is not reliably safe to drink. Vigorous boiling for one minute is the most effective means of water purification.

You may also disinfect water with iodine pills. Instructions are included and should be carefully followed. Or you can add 2% tincture of iodine to 1L of water (five drops to clear water, 10 drops to cloudy water) and let it stand for 30 minutes. If the water is cold, longer times may be required. The taste of iodinated water may be improved by adding vitamin C (ascorbic acid). Iodinated water should not be consumed for more than a few weeks. Pregnant women, those with a history of thyroid disease, and those allergic to iodine should not drink iodinated water. See p72 for more treatment options.

A number of water filters are on the market. Those with smaller pores (reverse osmosis filters) provide the broadest protection, but they are relatively large and are readily plugged by debris. Those with somewhat larger pores (microstrainer filters) are ineffective against viruses, although they remove other organisms. Follow the manufacturers' instructions carefully.

TRAVELING WITH CHILDREN

In general, it's safe for children to go to Cuba. However, because some of the vaccines listed previously are not approved for use on children (or during pregnancy), travelers with children should be particularly careful not to drink tap water or consume any questionable food or beverage. Also, when traveling with children, make sure they're up to date on all routine immunizations. It's sometimes appropriate to give children some of their vaccines a little early before visiting a developing nation. You should discuss this with your pediatrician.

WOMEN'S HEALTH

You can get sanitary items in Cuba, but they are usually more expensive than in Europe, North America or Australia and they are not always readily available (eg easy to find in Varadero, but not quite so easy in Bayamo). Advice: bring a good supply of your own. If pregnant while traveling, see left.

TRADITIONAL MEDICINE

The following table lists some traditional remedies for common travel-related issues:

Problem	Treatment
Jet lag	Melatonin
Mosquito-bite prevention	Eucalyptus and/or soybean oil
Motion sickness	Ginger

HEALTH

Language

CONTENTS

Learning Spanish	490
Pronunciation	490
Gender & Plurals	492
Accommodation	492
Conversation & Essentials	492
Directions	493
Health	493
Language Difficulties	494
Numbers	494
Question Words	494
Shopping & Services	494
Time & Dates	495
Transport	495
Travel with Children	496

Spanish is the official language of Cuba, and some knowledge of it is a great help in traveling around the country. Away from the hotels and tourist centers, few people speak English and then only very poorly. Despite this, many Cubans have some knowledge of English, since it's taught in school from grade six. Almost all museum captions in Cuba are in Spanish only.

If you speak no Spanish at all, you can always ask directions simply by pointing to the name in this guidebook. Never hesitate to try out your Spanish on Cubans!

Words of Arawak Indian origin that have passed into Spanish and other European languages include *barbacoa* (barbecue), *canoa* (canoe), *cigarro* (cigarette), *hamaca* (hammock), *huracán* (hurricane), *maíz* (maize), *patata* (potato) and *tabaco* (tobacco). The only commonly used words of African origin are generally associated with the Afro-Cuban religions, but Afro-Cuban speakers have given Cuban Spanish its rhythmical intonation and soft accent.

LEARNING SPANISH

If you don't speak Spanish, don't despair. It's easy enough to pick up the basics, and courses are available in Havana (p125) and Santiago de Cuba (p421). Alternatively, you can study books, records and tapes while you're still at home planning your trip. These study aids are often available free at public libraries – or you might consider taking an evening or college course. For words and phrases for use when ordering at a restaurant, see Eat Your Words on p76.

Lonely Planet's *Latin American Spanish* phrasebook is a compact guide to the Spanish of the region. Another useful resource is the *University of Chicago Spanish–English, English–Spanish Dictionary*. It'll also make a nice gift for some friendly Cuban when you're about to leave the country.

PRONUNCIATION

Spanish spelling is phonetically consistent, meaning that there's a clear and consistent relationship between what you see in writing and how it's pronounced. The pronunciation guides included with all the words and phrases in this chapter should help you get the hang of it all.

Spanish-language soap operas (*telenovelas*) are probably the best vehicle for getting a grip on pronunciation – the actors tend to speak overdramatically and a lot slower than the Spanish speakers you're likely to meet on the street – it's also easy to follow the plot. Just be careful you don't get hooked!

Vowels

a	as in 'father'
e	as in 'met'
i	as in 'marine'
o	as in 'or', without the 'r' sound
u	as in 'rule'; the 'u' is not pronounced after **q** and in the letter combinations **gue** and **gui**, unless it's marked with a diaeresis (eg *argüir*), in which case it's pronounced as English 'w'
y	at the end of a word or when it stands alone, it's pronounced as the Spanish **i** (eg *ley*); between vowels within a word it's like the 'y' in 'yellow'

Consonants

While the consonants **ch**, **ll** and **ñ** are generally considered distinct letters, **ch** and **ll** are

CUBAN SPANISH

Cuban Spanish is rich, varied and astoundingly distinct. Slang and *dichos* (sayings) dominate daily conversation so much that even native Spanish-speakers sometimes get lost in the mix. Borrowing words from African languages, modifying English terms ('Spanglish') and adopting language from movies, marketing and sports, Cuban Spanish is constantly evolving, with new, invented words surfacing all the time. Indeed, the origins of some relatively new slang words seem to have been lost entirely. Ask a Cuban where *rickenbili* (the word for those motorized bicycles you see around town) comes from, for instance, and they'll laugh and shrug. Here are some of the most common slang terms and colloquialisms travelers are likely to hear; see also the Glossary (p497).

asere – man, brother
bárbaro – cool; literally 'killer'
barro – money (dollars or pesos)
brother – as in English
compay – brother, friend (frequently used in the Oriente)
¡Coño! – frequently used exclamation akin to 'Damn!'; used for good or bad things/situations
cubalse – plastic bag (in the Oriente); see also *nylon*
dame un chance – let me pass, excuse me; literally 'give me a chance'
está en llama – it's screwed/messed up
fiana – police cruiser
fula – dollars
güiro – party
jamaliche – food; also translates as 'food junkie'
kilo(s) – centavo(s)
la lucha – daily struggle
loca – homosexual, queer

mamey – mommy; used as term of endearment for females
nylon – plastic bag
papaya – vagina; the fruit itself is called *fruta bomba* everywhere except in the Oriente, where it's called *papaya*
papi – daddy; used as term of endearment for males
pepe – someone from Spain
pincha – job
pollito – pretty girl
por la izquierda – attained through the black market
prieto/a – dark-skinned
puto/a – gigolo/prostitute
¿Qué bolá asere? – What's happening, man/brother?
¿Qué es la mecánica? – What's the process here?, How does this work? (eg when buying bus tickets, entering a crowded club or renting a catamaran)
tortillera – lesbian, dyke
yuma – someone from the US

now often listed alphabetically under **c** and **l** respectively. The letter **ñ** is still treated as a separate letter, and it comes after **n** in dictionary listings.

b similar to English 'b,' but softer; referred to as *b larga*
c as in 'celery' before **e** and **i**; otherwise as English 'k'
ch as in 'church'
d as in 'dog'; between vowels and after **l** or **n**, it's closer to the 'th' in 'this'
g as the 'ch' in the Scottish *loch* before **e** and **i** ('kh' in our pronunciation guides); elsewhere, as in 'go'
h invariably silent; worth noting if your name begins with 'h' and you're waiting for public officials to call you
j as the 'ch' in the Scottish *loch* ('kh' in our pronunciation guides)
ll as the 'y' in 'yellow'
ñ as the 'ni' in 'onion'
rr very strongly rolled

v similar to English 'b,' but softer; referred to as *b corta*
x as in 'taxi' except for a few words, when it's pronounced as **j**
z as the 's' in 'sun'

Word Stress

In general, words ending in vowels or the letters **n** or **s** have stress on the second-last syllable, while those with other endings have stress on the last syllable. Thus *vaca* (cow) and *caballos* (horses) both carry stress on the second-last syllable, while *ciudad* (city) and *infeliz* (unhappy) are both stressed on the last syllable.

Written accents will almost always appear in words that don't follow the rules above, eg *sótano* (basement), *América* and *porción* (portion). When counting syllables, be sure to remember that diphthongs (vowel combinations, such as the 'ue' in *puede*) constitute only one. When a word with a written accent appears in capital letters, the accent is often not written, but is still pronounced.

GENDER & PLURALS

In Spanish, nouns are either masculine or feminine, and there are rules to help determine gender (there are, of course, some exceptions). Feminine nouns generally end with -**a** or with the groups -**ción**, -**sión** or -**dad**. Other endings typically signify a masculine noun. Endings for adjectives also change to agree with the gender of the noun they modify (masculine/feminine -**o**/-**a**). Where both masculine and feminine forms are included in this chapter, they are separated by a slash, with the masculine form first, eg *perdido/a*.

If a noun or adjective ends in a vowel, the plural is formed by adding **s** to the end. If it ends in a consonant, the plural is formed by adding -**es**.

ACCOMMODATION

I'm looking for ...	Estoy buscando ...	e-stoy boos-kan-do ...
Where is ...?	¿Dónde hay ...?	don-de ai ...
a boarding house	una pensión/ residencial/ un hospedaje	oo-na pen-syon/ re-see-den-syal/ oon os-pe-da-khe
a hotel	un hotel/ una villa	oon o-tel/ oo-na vee-ya
a youth hostel	un albergue juvenil	oon al-ber-ge khoo-ve-neel

I'd like a ... room.	Quisiera una habitación ...	kee-sye-ra oo-na a-bee-ta-syon ...
double	doble	do-ble
single	para una persona	pa-ra oo-na per-so-na
twin	con dos camas	kon dos ka-mas

How much is it per ...?	¿Cuánto cuesta por ...?	kwan-to kwes-ta por ...
night	noche	no-che
person	persona	per-so-na
week	semana	se-ma-na

Does it include breakfast?
¿Incluye el desayuno? een-kloo-ye el de-sa-yoo-no

May I see the room?
¿Puedo ver la habitación? pwe-do ver la a-bee-ta-syon

I don't like it.
No me gusta. no me goos-ta

It's fine. I'll take it.
OK. La alquilo. o-kay la al-kee-lo

I'm leaving now.
Me voy ahora. me voy a-o-ra

MAKING A RESERVATION	
To ...	A ...
From ...	De ...
Date	Fecha
I'd like to book ...	Quisiera reservar ... (see the list under 'Accommodation' for bed/ room options)
in the name of ...	en nombre de ...
for the nights of ...	para las noches del ...
credit card ...	tarjeta de crédito ...
number	número
expiry date	fecha de vencimiento
Please confirm ...	Puede confirmar ...
availability	la disponibilidad
price	el precio

full board	pensión completa	pen-syon kom-ple-ta
private/shared bath	baño privado/ compartido	ba-nyo pree-va-do/ kom-par-tee-do
all-inclusive	todo incluído	to-do een-klu-ee-do
too expensive	demasiado caro	de-ma-sya-do ka-ro
cheaper	más económico	mas e-ko-no-mee-ko
discount	descuento	des-kwen-to

CONVERSATION & ESSENTIALS

In their public behavior, Cubans are very informal. If you approach a stranger for information, however, you should always preface your question with a greeting like *buenos días* or *buenas tardes*. Cubans routinely address one another as *compañero/a* (comrade), but the traditional *señor* and *señora* are always used with foreigners. In addition, you should only use the polite form of address, especially with the police and public officials. Young people may be less likely to expect this, but it's best to stick to the polite form unless you're quite sure you won't offend by using the informal mode. The polite form is used in all phrases in this chapter; where both options are given, the abbreviations 'pol' and 'inf' indicate the different forms.

Hello.	Hola.	o-la
Good morning.	Buenos días.	bwe-nos dee-as
Good afternoon.	Buenas tardes.	bwe-nas tar-des
Good evening/ night.	Buenas noches.	bwe-nas no-ches
Goodbye.	Adiós.	a-dyos

LANGUAGE

See you soon.	Hasta luego.	as·ta lwe·go
Bye.	Chao.	chow (inf)
Yes.	Sí.	see
No.	No.	no
Please.	Por favor.	por fa·vor
Thank you.	Gracias.	gra·syas
Many thanks.	Muchas gracias.	moo·chas gra·syas
You're welcome.	De nada.	de na·da
Pardon me.	Perdón.	per·don
Excuse me.	Permiso.	per·mee·so
(used when asking permission)		
Forgive me.	Disculpe.	dees·kool·pe
(used when apologizing)		

How are things?
| ¿Qué tal? | ke tal |

What's your name?
| ¿Cómo se llama? | ko·mo se ya·ma (pol) |
| ¿Cómo te llamas? | ko·mo te ya·mas (inf) |

My name is ...
| Me llamo ... | me ya·mo ... |

It's a pleasure to meet you.
| Mucho gusto. | moo·cho goos·to |

The pleasure is mine.
| El gusto es mío. | el goos·to es mee·o |

Where are you from?
| ¿De dónde es/eres? | de don·de es/e·res (pol/inf) |

I'm from ...
| Soy de ... | soy de ... |

Where are you staying?
| ¿Dónde está alojado/a? | don·de es·ta a·lo·kha·do/a (pol) |
| ¿Dónde estás alojado/a? | don·de es·tas a·lo·kha·do/a (inf) |

May I take a photo?
| ¿Puedo sacar una foto? | pwe·do sa·kar oo·na fo·to |

DIRECTIONS

How do I get to ...?
| ¿Cómo puedo llegar a ...? | ko·mo pwe·do ye·gar a ... |

Is it far?
| ¿Está lejos? | es·ta le·khos |

Go straight ahead.
| Siga/Vaya derecho. | see·ga/va·ya de·re·cho |

Turn left.
| Voltée a la izquierda. | vol·te·e a la ees·kyer·da |

Turn right.
| Voltée a la derecha. | vol·te·e a la de·re·cha |

Can you show me (on the map)?
| ¿Me lo podría indicar | me lo po·dree·a een·dee·kar |
| (en el mapa)? | (en el ma·pa) |

north	norte	nor·te
south	sur	soor
east	este/oriente	es·te/o·ryen·te
west	oeste/occidente	o·es·te/ok·see·den·te

here	aquí	a·kee
there	allí	a·yee
by bus	en autobús	en ow·to·boos
by taxi	en taxi	en tak·see
on foot	a pie	a pye
avenue	avenida	a·ve·nee·da
block	cuadra	kwa·dra
street	calle/paseo	ka·ye/pa·se·o
beach	playa	pla·ya
bathing resort	balneario	bal·ne·a·ryo

HEALTH

I'm sick.
| Estoy enfermo/a. | es·toy en·fer·mo/a |

I need a doctor.
| Necesito un médico. | ne·se·see·to oon me·dee·ko |

Where's the hospital?
| ¿Dónde está el hospital? | don·de es·ta el os·pee·tal |

I'm pregnant.
| Estoy embarazada. | es·toy em·ba·ra·sa·da |

I've been vaccinated.
| Estoy vacunado/a. | es·toy va·koo·na·do/a |

I'm allergic	Soy alérgico/a	soy a·ler·khee·ko/a
to ...	a ...	a ...
antibiotics	los antibióticos	los an·tee·byo·tee·kos
peanuts	al maní	al ma·nee
penicillin	la penicilina	la pe·nee·see·lee·na

I'm ...	Soy ...	soy ...
asthmatic	asmático/a	as·ma·tee·ko/a
diabetic	diabético/a	dya·be·tee·ko/a
epileptic	epiléptico/a	e·pee·lep·tee·ko/a

I have ...	Tengo ...	ten·go ...
a cough	tos	tos
diarrhea	diarrea	dya·re·a
a headache	un dolor de	oon do·lor de
	cabeza	ka·be·sa
nausea	náusea	now·se·a

EMERGENCIES

Help!	¡Socorro!	so·ko·ro
Fire!	¡Incendio!	een·sen·dyo
I've been robbed.	Me robaron.	me ro·ba·ron
Go away!	¡Déjeme!	de·khe·me
Get lost!	¡Váyase!	va·ya·se
Call ...!	¡Llame a ...!	ya·me a ...
an ambulance	una ambulancia	oo·na am·boo·lan·sya
a doctor	un médico	oon me·dee·ko
the police	la policía	la po·lee·see·a

It's an emergency.
   Es una emergencia.   es oo·na e·mer·khen·sya
Could you help me, please?
   ¿Me puede ayudar, por favor?   me pwe·de a·yoo·dar por fa·vor
I'm lost.
   Estoy perdido/a.   es·toy per·dee·do/a
Where are the toilets?
   ¿Dónde están los baños?   don·de es·tan los ba·nyos

LANGUAGE DIFFICULTIES

Do you speak (English)?
   ¿Habla/Hablas (inglés)?   a·bla/a·blas (een·gles) (pol/inf)
Does anyone here speak English?
   ¿Hay alguien que hable inglés?   ai al·gyen ke a·ble een·gles
I (don't) understand.
   Yo (no) entiendo.   yo (no) en·tyen·do
How do you say ...?
   ¿Cómo se dice ...?   ko·mo se dee·se ...
What does ... mean?
   ¿Qué quiere decir ...?   ke kye·re de·seer ...

Could you please ...?	¿Puede ..., por favor?	pwe·de ... por fa·vor
repeat that	repetirlo	re·pe·teer·lo
speak more slowly	hablar más despacio	a·blar mas des·pa·syo
write it down	escribirlo	es·kree·beer·lo

NUMBERS

1	uno	oo·no
2	dos	dos
3	tres	tres
4	cuatro	kwa·tro
5	cinco	seen·ko
6	seis	says
7	siete	sye·te
8	ocho	o·cho
9	nueve	nwe·ve
10	diez	dyes
11	once	on·se
12	doce	do·se
13	trece	tre·se
14	catorce	ka·tor·se
15	quince	keen·se
16	dieciséis	dye·see·says
17	diecisiete	dye·see·sye·te
18	dieciocho	dye·see·o·cho
19	diecinueve	dye·see·nwe·ve
20	veinte	vayn·te
21	veintiuno	vayn·tee·oo·no
30	treinta	trayn·ta
31	treinta y uno	trayn·ta ee oo·no
40	cuarenta	kwa·ren·ta
50	cincuenta	seen·kwen·ta
60	sesenta	se·sen·ta
70	setenta	se·ten·ta
80	ochenta	o·chen·ta
90	noventa	no·ven·ta
100	cien	syen
101	ciento uno	syen·to oo·no
200	doscientos	do·syen·tos
1000	mil	meel
5000	cinco mil	seen·ko meel
10,000	diez mil	dyes meel
50,000	cincuenta mil	seen·kwen·ta meel
100,000	cien mil	syen meel
1,000,000	un millón	oon mee·yon

QUESTION WORDS

Who?	¿Quién?/¿Quiénes?	kyen/kye·nes (sg/pl)
What?	¿Qué?	ke
Which?	¿Cuál?/¿Cuáles?	kwal/kwa·les (sg/pl)
When?	¿Cuándo?	kwan·do
Where?	¿Dónde?	don·de
How?	¿Cómo?	ko·mo
How much?	¿Cuánto?	kwan·to

SHOPPING & SERVICES

I'm looking for (the) ...	Estoy buscando ...	es·toy boos·kan·do ...
ATM	el cajero automático	el ka·khe·ro ow·to·ma·tee·ko
bank	el banco	el ban·ko
bookstore	la librería	la lee·bre·ree·a
embassy	la embajada	la em·ba·kha·da
exchange office	la casa de cambio	la ka·sa de kam·byo
general store	la tienda	la tyen·da
laundry	la lavandería	la la·van·de·ree·a
market	el mercado	el mer·ka·do
pharmacy	la farmacia/ la droguería	la far·ma·sya/ la dro·ge·ree·a

post office	el correo	el ko·re·o
supermarket	el supermercado	el soo·per·mer·ka·do
tourist office	la oficina de turismo	la o·fee·see·na de too·rees·mo

What time does it open/close?
¿A qué hora abre/cierra?   a ke o·ra a·bre/sye·ra

I want to change some money/traveler's checks.
Quiero cambiar dinero/   kye·ro kam·byar dee·ne·ro/
cheques de viajero.   che·kes de vya·khe·ro

What is the exchange rate?
¿Cuál es el tipo de   kwal es el tee·po de
cambio?   kam·byo

I want to call ...
Quiero llamar a ...   kye·ro ya·mar a ...

airmail	correo aéreo	ko·re·o a·e·re·o
black market	mercado negro/ paralelo	mer·ka·do ne·gro/ pa·ra·le·lo
letter	carta	kar·ta
registered mail	certificado	ser·tee·fee·ka·do
stamps	estampillas	es·tam·pee·yas

I'd like to buy ...
Quisiera comprar ...   kee·sye·ra kom·prar ...

I'm just looking.
Sólo estoy mirando.   so·lo es·toy mee·ran·do

May I look at it?
¿Puedo mirarlo?   pwe·do mee·rar·lo

How much is it?
¿Cuánto cuesta?   kwan·to kwes·ta

That's too expensive for me.
Es demasiado caro   es de·ma·sya·do ka·ro
para mí.   pa·ra mee

Could you lower the price?
¿Podría bajar un poco   po·dree·a ba·khar oon po·ko
el precio?   el pre·syo

I don't like it.
No me gusta.   no me goos·ta

I'll take it.
Lo llevo.   lo ye·vo

less	menos	me·nos
more	más	mas
large	grande	gran·de
small	pequeño/a	pe·ke·nyo/a

Do you accept ...?	¿Aceptan ...?	a·sep·tan ...
credit cards	tarjetas de crédito	tar·khe·tas de kre·dee·to
traveler's checks	cheques de viajero	che·kes de vya·khe·ro
US dollars	dólares americanos	do·la·res a·me·ree·ka·nos

TIME & DATES
What time is it?	¿Qué hora es?	ke o·ra es
It's one o'clock.	Es la una.	es la oo·na
It's seven o'clock.	Son las siete.	son las sye·te
half past two	dos y media	dos ee me·dya
midnight	medianoche	me·dya·no·che
noon	mediodía	me·dyo·dee·a

now	ahora	a·o·ra
today	hoy	oy
tonight	esta noche	es·ta no·che
tomorrow	mañana	ma·nya·na
yesterday	ayer	a·yer

Monday	lunes	loo·nes
Tuesday	martes	mar·tes
Wednesday	miércoles	myer·ko·les
Thursday	jueves	khwe·ves
Friday	viernes	vyer·nes
Saturday	sábado	sa·ba·do
Sunday	domingo	do·meen·go

January	enero	e·ne·ro
February	febrero	fe·bre·ro
March	marzo	mar·so
April	abril	a·breel
May	mayo	ma·yo
June	junio	khoon·yo
July	julio	khool·yo
August	agosto	a·gos·to
September	septiembre	sep·tyem·bre
October	octubre	ok·too·bre
November	noviembre	no·vyem·bre
December	diciembre	dee·syem·bre

TRANSPORT
Public Transport
What time does ... leave/arrive?	¿A qué hora sale/llega?	a ke o·ra ... sa·le/ye·ga
the bus	el autobús/ guagua/ ómnibus	el ow·to·boos/ gwa·gwa/ om·nee·boos
the plane	el avión	el a·vyon
the ship	el barco/buque	el bar·ko/boo·ke
the train	el tren	el tren

airport	el aeropuerto	el a·e·ro·pwer·to
bus station/stop	la estación/ parada de autobuses	la es·ta·syon/ pa·ra·da de ow·to·boo·ses
luggage check room	guardería de equipaje	gwar·de·ree·a de e·kee·pa·khe
ticket office	la boletería	la bo·le·te·ree·a
train station	la estación de ferrocarril	la es·ta·syon de fe·ro·ka·reel

ROAD SIGNS	
Acceso	Entrance
Aparcamiento	Parking
Ceda el Paso	Give Way
Despacio	Slow
Dirección Única	One Way
Mantenga Su Derecha	Keep to the Right
No Adelantar/No Rebase	No Passing
Peaje	Toll
Peligro	Danger
Prohibido Aparcar/	No Parking
No Estacionar	
Prohibido el Paso	No Entry
Pare/Stop	Stop
Salida de Autopista	Exit Freeway

I'd like a ticket to ...
Quiero un boleto a ...   kye·ro oon bo·le·to a ...

What's the fare to ...?
¿Cuánto cuesta hasta ...? kwan·to kwes·ta as·ta ...

1st class	primera clase	pree·me·ra kla·se
2nd class	segunda clase	se·goon·da kla·se
single/one-way	de ida	de ee·da
student's	de estudiante	de es·too·dyan·te
return/round-trip	de ida y vuelta	de ee·da ee vwel·ta
taxi	taxi	tak·see

Private Transport

I'd like to	Quisiera	kee·sye·ra
hire a/an ...	alquilar ...	al·kee·lar ...
4WD	un todo terreno	oon to·do te·re·no
bicycle	una bicicleta	oo·na bee·see·kle·ta
car	un auto	oon ow·to
motorbike	una moto	oo·na mo·to
hitchhike	hacer botella	a·ser bo·te·ya
truck	camión	ka·myon

Is this the road to ...?
¿Se va a ... por   se va a ... por
esta carretera?   es·ta ka·re·te·ra

Where's a gas station?
¿Dónde hay una   don·de ai oo·na
gasolinera?   ga·so·lee·ne·ra

Please fill it up.
Llene, por favor.   ye·ne por fa·vor

I'd like (20) liters.
Quiero (veinte) litros.   kye·ro (vayn·te) lee·tros

diesel	petróleo	pe·tro·le·o
gas	gasolina	ga·so·lee·na

(How long) can I park here?
¿(Por cuánto tiempo)   (por kwan·to tyem·po)
puedo aparcar aquí?   pwe·do a·par·kar a·kee

Where do I pay?
¿Dónde se paga?   don·de se pa·ga

I need a mechanic.
Necesito un mecánico.   ne·se·see·to oon me·ka·nee·ko

The car has broken down (in ...).
El carro se ha averiado   el ka·ro se a a·ve·rya·do
(en ...).   (en ...)

The motorbike won't start.
No arranca la moto.   no a·ran·ka la mo·to

I have a flat tyre.
Tengo un pinchazo.   ten·go oon peen·cha·so

I've run out of gas.
Me quedé sin gasolina.   me ke·de seen ga·so·lee·na

I've had an accident.
Tuve un accidente.   too·ve oon ak·see·den·te

TRAVEL WITH CHILDREN

Do you have ...?	¿Hay ...?	ai ...
an (English-	una niñera	oo·na nee·nye·ra
speaking)	(de habla	(de a·bla
babysitter	inglesa)	een·gle·sa)
a car seat	un asiento de	oon a·syen·to de
for babies	seguridad	se·goo·ree·dad
	para bebés	pa·ra be·bes
a child-minding	un servicio de	oon ser·vee·syo de
service	cuidado de	kwee·da·do de
	niños	nee·nyos
a children's	una carta	oo·na kar·ta
menu	infantil	een·fan·teel
a day nursery	una guardería	oo·na gwar·de·ree·a
(disposable)	pañales (de	pa·nya·les (de
diapers	usar y tirar)	oo·sar ee tee·rar)
formula (milk)	leche en polvo	le·che en pol·vo
a high chair	una trona	oo·na tro·na
a stroller	un cochecito	oon ko·che·see·to

Do you mind if I breast-feed here?
¿Le molesta que dé   le mo·les·ta ke de
de pecho aquí?   de pe·cho a·kee

phrasebooks

Latin American
Spanish

with 3500-word two-way dictionary

Also available from
Lonely Planet:
Latin American Spanish
phrasebook

Glossary

agropecuario – vegetable market; also sells rice, fruit
aguardiente – fermented cane; literally 'firewater'
Altos – upstairs apartment (when following an address)
ama de llaves – housekeeper; see *camarera*
amarillo – a roadside traffic organizer in a yellow uniform
americano/a – in Cuba this means a citizen of any Western hemisphere country (from Canada to Argentina); a citizen of the US is called a *norteamericano/a* or *estadounidense*; see also *gringo/a* and *yuma*
Arawak – linguistically related Indian tribes that inhabited most of the Caribbean islands and northern South America
Autopista – the national highway that has four, six or eight lanes depending on the region

babalawo – a *Santería* priest; also *babalao;* see also *santero*
bahía – bay
Bajos – downstairs apartment (when following an address)
balseros – rafters; used to describe the emigrants who escaped to the US in the 1990s on homemade rafts
bárbaro – cool, killer
barbuda – name given to Castro's rebel army; literally 'bearded one'
barrio – neighborhood
batá – a conical two-headed drum
bici-taxi – bicycle taxi
bloqueo – Cuban term for the US embargo
bodega – stores distributing ration-card products
bohío – thatched hut
bolero – a romantic love song
botella – hitchhiking; literally 'bottle'

cabaña – cabin, hut
cabildo – a town council during the colonial era; also an association of tribes in Cuban religions of African origin
Cachita – popular name for the Virgin of El Cobre
cacique – chief; originally used to describe an Indian chief and today used to designate a petty tyrant
Cadeca – exchange booth
cafetal – coffee plantation
cajita – takeout meal; literally 'small box'
caliente – hot
calle – street
camarera – housekeeper or waitress (the Spanish term *criada*, which also means 'brought up,' is considered offensive in revolutionary Cuba); see also *ama de llaves*
cambio de turno – shift change (in shops)
camello – metro buses in Havana named for their two humps; literally 'camel'
camión – truck

campesinos – people who live in the *campo*
campismo – national network of 82 camping installations, not all of which are open to foreigners
campo – countryside
cañonazo – shooting of the cannons, a nightly ceremony performed at the Fortaleza de San Carlos de la Cabaña across Havana harbor
carnet – the identification document that allows foreigners to pay for museums, transport (including *colectivos*) and theater performances in pesos
carpeta – hotel reception desk
cartelera – culture calendar or schedule, entertainment brochure
casa de la cultura – literally 'culture house,' where music, art, theater and dance events happen
casa natal – birth house
casa particular – private house that lets out rooms to foreigners (and sometimes Cubans); all legal casas must display a green triangle on the door
casco histórico – historic center of a city (eg Trinidad, Santiago de Cuba)
cayo – a coral key
CDR – Comités de Defensa de la Revolución; neighborhood-watch bodies originally formed in 1960 to consolidate grassroots support for the Revolution; they now play a decisive role in health, education, social, recycling and voluntary labor campaigns
central – modern sugar mill; see *ingenio*
chachachá – cha-cha; dance music in 4/4 meter derived from the rumba and mambo
Changó – the *Santería* deity signifying war and fire, twinned with Santa Barbara in Catholicism
chequeré – a gourd covered with beads to form a rattle
chivo – Cuban slang for 'bike'
cimarrón – a runaway slave
circunvalación – a road that circumvents city centers, allowing you to drive on without plunging into the heart of urban hell
claves – rhythm sticks used by musicians
coche – cart, normally drawn by horses
coco-taxi – egg-shaped taxi that holds two to three people; also called *huevito* (literally 'little egg')
Cohiba – native Indian name for a smoking implement; one of Cuba's top brands of cigar
cola – line, queue
colectivo – collective taxi that takes on as many passengers as possible; usually a classic American car
comida criolla – Creole food
compañero/a – companion or partner, with revolutionary connotations (ie 'comrade')

conseguir – to get, obtain
Convertibles – Convertible pesos
creyente – believer
criadero – hatchery
criollo – Creole; Spaniard born in the Americas
c/u – *cada uno;* used in vegetable markets to denote price per unit
Cubanacán – soon after landing in Cuba, Christopher Columbus visited a Taíno village the Indians called Cubanacán (meaning 'in the center of the island'); a large Cuban tourism company uses the name
cuerpo guardia – emergency-services area at hospitals

daiquirí – rum cocktail made with crushed ice and other ingredients, named for the Río Daiquirí, near Santiago de Cuba, where it was invented in 1899
danzón – a traditional Cuban ballroom dance colored with African influences, pioneered in Matanzas during the late 19th century
décima – the rhyming, eight-syllable verse that provides the lyrics for Cuban *son*
diente de perro – jagged rock shelf that lines most of Cuba's southern shore
duende – spirit/charm; used in flamenco to describe the ultimate climax to the music

el imperio – 'the empire'; a term used in the official Cuban media to refer to the US, which is led by the *imperialistas*
El Líder Máximo – Maximum Leader; title often used to describe Fidel Castro
el último – literally 'the last'; this term is key to mastering Cuban queues (you must 'take' *el último* when joining a line and 'give it up' when someone new arrives)
Elegguá – the god of destiny in Cuban religions of African origin such as *Santería*
embalse – reservoir
encomienda – a section of land and an indigenous workforce entrusted to an individual by the Spanish crown during the early colonial era
entronque – crossroads in rural areas
espectacular – show/extravaganza
esquina caliente – where baseball fanatics debate stats, teams, history and who's up and who's down; literally 'hot corner'; also called a *peña*

fiesta campesina – country or rural fair
finca – farmhouse
flota – a fleet of Spanish ships

Gitmo – American slang for Guantánamo US Naval Base
Granma – the yacht that carried Fidel and his companions from Mexico to Cuba in 1956 to launch the Revolution; in 1975 the name was adopted for the province where the *Granma* arrived; also name of Cuba's leading daily newspaper
gringo/a – any Caucasian; see also *americano/a* and *yuma*
guagua – a bus
guajiro/a – a country bumpkin or hick
Guantanamera – a girl from Guantánamo province; the title of the popular song 'Guajira Guantanamera' means 'country girl from Guantánamo province'
guaracha – a satirical song for a single voice backed by a chorus
guarapo – fresh sugarcane juice
guayabera – a pleated, buttoned men's shirt; tropical formal-wear
guerillero – fighter, warrior

Habanero/a – someone from Havana
herbero – seller of herbs, natural medicines and concocter of remedies; typically a wealth of knowledge on natural cures

ingenio – an antiquated term for a sugar mill; see *central*
inmigración – immigration office

jardín – garden
jefe de turno – shift manager
jején – sand flea
jinetera – a woman who attaches herself to male foreigners for monetary or material gain; the exchange may or may not involve sex
jinetero – a male tout who hustles tourists; literally 'jockey'
joder – to mess up, spoil

kometa – hydrofoil

libreta – the ration booklet
loma – hill
luchar – literally 'to struggle/fight'; used in all sorts of daily situations

M-26-7 – the '26th of July Movement,' Fidel Castro's revolutionary organization, was named for the abortive assault on the Moncada army barracks in Santiago de Cuba on July 26, 1953
Mambís – 19th-century rebels fighting Spain
mamey – delicious fleshy tropical fruit that resembles a red avocado
maqueta – scale model
máquina – private peso taxi
maraca – a rattle used by musicians
mercado – market
merendero – outdoor bar; picnic spot
mirador – lookout or viewpoint

mogote – a limestone monolith found at Viñales
mojito – cocktail made from rum, mint, sugar, seltzer and fresh lime juice
Moncada – a former army barracks in Santiago de Cuba named for General Guillermo Moncada (1848–95), a hero of the Wars of Independence
moneda nacional – abbreviated to MN; Cuban pesos
mudéjar – Iberian Peninsula's Moorish-influenced style in architecture and decoration that lasted from the 12th to 16th centuries and combined elements of Islamic and Christian art
mulato/a – mixed race; dark color

nueva trova – philosophical folk/guitar music popularized in the late '60s and early '70s by Silvio Rodríguez and Pablo Milanés

Operación Milagros – the unofficial name given to a pioneering medical program hatched between Cuba and Venezuela in 2004 that offers free eye treatment for impoverished Venezuelans in Cuban hospitals
organopónico – urban vegetable garden
Oriente – the region comprised of Las Tunas, Holguín, Granma, Santiago de Cuba and Guantánamo provinces; literally 'the east'
orisha – a *Santería* deity

paladar – a privately owned restaurant
palenque – a hiding place for runaway slaves during the colonial era
palestino – a nickname given to people from the Oriente by those from the west
parada – bus stop
parque – park
parqueador – parking attendant
patria – homeland, country
PCC – Partido Comunista de Cuba; Cuba's only political party, formed in October 1965 by merging cadres from the Partido Socialista Popular (the pre-1959 Communist Party) and veterans of the guerrilla campaign
pedraplén – stone causeways connecting offshore islands to mainland Cuba
pelota – Cuban baseball
peninsular – a Spaniard born in Spain but living in the Americas
peña – musical performance or get-together in any genre: *son*, rap, rock, poetry etc; see also *esquina caliente*
período especial – the 'Special Period in Time of Peace' (Cuba's economic reality post-1991)
piropo – flirtatious remark/commentary
ponchero – a fixer of flat tires
pregón – a singsong manner of selling fruits, vegetables, brooms, whatever; often comic, they are belted out by *pregoneros/as*

presa – dam
puente – bridge

¿qué bola? – 'what's up?' (popular greeting, especially in the Oriente)
quinciñera – Cuban rite of passage for girls turning 15 *(quince),* whereby they dress up like brides, have their photos taken in gorgeous natural or architectural settings and then have a big party with lots of food and dancing

ranchón – rural farm/restaurant
reconcentración – a tactic of forcibly concentrating rural populations, used by the Spaniards during the Spanish-Cuban-American War
reggaetón – Cuban hip-hop
Regla de Ocha – set of related religious beliefs popularly known as *Santería*
resolver – to resolve or fix a problematic situation; along with *el último*, this is among the most indispensable words in Cuban vocabulary
río – river
rumba – an Afro-Cuban dance form that originated among plantation slaves during the 19th century; during the '20s and '30s, the term 'rumba' was adopted in North America and Europe for a ballroom dance in 4/4 time; in Cuba today, to *rumba* simply means to 'party'

sala polivalente – boxing arena
salsa – Cuban music based on *son*
salsero – *salsa* singer
Santería – Afro-Cuban religion resulting from the syncretization of the Yoruba religion of West Africa and Spanish Catholicism
santero – a priest of *Santería;* see also *babalawo*
Santiagüero – someone from Santiago de Cuba
sello – stamp (in a passport or on a letter)
SIDA – *síndrome de inmunodeficiencia adquirida;* AIDS
s/n – *sin número;* indicates an address that has no street number
son – Cuba's basic form of popular music that jelled from African and Spanish elements in the late 19th century
sucu-sucu – a variation of *son* music

Taíno – a settled, Arawak-speaking tribe that inhabited much of Cuba prior to the Spanish conquest; the word itself means 'we the good people'
tambores – *Santería* drumming ritual
taquilla – ticket window
telenovela – soap opera
telepunto – Etecsa (Cuban state-run telecommunications company) telephone and internet shop/call center

temporada alta/baja – high/low season
terminal de ómnibus – bus station
tinajón – large earthenware jar; particularly common in the city of Camagüey
tres – a guitar with seven strings and an integral part of Cuban *son* music
trova – traditional poetic singing/songwriting
trovador – traditional singer/songwriter

Uneac – Unión Nacional de Escritores y Artistas de Cuba (National Union of Cuban Writers and Artists)

vaquero – cowboy
vega – tobacco plantation
VIH – *virus de inmunodeficiencia humana;* HIV

Yanqui – someone from the US
Yoruba – an ethno-linguistic group from West Africa
yuma – slang for someone from the US; can be used for any foreigner; see *americano/a* and *gringo/a*

zafra – sugarcane harvest
zarzuela – operetta

Behind the Scenes

THIS BOOK

The 5th edition of Cuba was researched and written by Brendan Sainsbury. The Health chapter was written by Dr David Goldberg. The 4th edition of Cuba was researched and written by Brendan Sainsbury, the 3rd edition by Conner Gorry and the 1st and 2nd editions by David Stanley.

Commissioning Editor Catherine Craddock
Coordinating Editor Branislava Vladisavljevic
Coordinating Cartographer Valeska Cañas
Coordinating Layout Designer Carol Jackson
Managing Editor Bruce Evans
Managing Cartographer Alison Lyall
Managing Layout Designers Sally Darmody, Indra Kilfoyle
Assisting Editors Andrea Dobbin, Kate Evans, Victoria Harrison, Anne Mulvaney, Kristin Odijk, Helen Yeates
Assisting Cartographers Karen Grant, Mark Griffiths, Alex Leung, Marc Milinkovic, Andy Rojas, Sam Sayer, Peter Shields
Assisting Layout Designer Paul Iacono
Cover Designer Jane Hart
Project Manager Rachel Imeson

Thanks to Lucy Birchley, Jessica Boland, Nicholas Colicchia, Melanie Dankel, Ryan Evans, Brice Gosnell, Lisa Knights, Robyn Loughnane, Malcolm O'Brien, Wibowo Rusli

THANKS
BRENDAN SAINSBURY

Muchas gracias to Julio Roque in Havana (as always), Yoan Reyes and family in Viñales, Angel in Santa Clara, Nilson Guilaré in Baracoa, Mireya and Julio in Trinidad, my very understanding editor Catherine Craddock in Oakland, and my two vital accomplices: Liz (wife) and Kieran (son), without whom none of this would have been possible.

OUR READERS

Many thanks to the travelers who used the last edition and wrote to us with helpful hints, useful advice and interesting anecdotes:

A Albert Aixala, Thomas Albright, Matthew Alexander, Nassor Ali, Ester Almenar, Arian Alonso, Marko Andric, Florian Ansorge, Paul Appleton, Asa Arencrantz, Miguel Angel Arroyave Rios, Jules Atkins **B** Andrea Badalucco, Gavan Baddeley, A Bajo, Irena Batistic, Corinna Bayerlein, Nick Beddow, Kavita Bedford, Lina Bellou, Johan Benesch, Stephen Benjamin, Ron Berezan, Anna Bergman, Bengt Bergman, Norma Bernad Romeo, David Berry, Jessica Berube, Norbert Bessems, Barbara Best, Amina Bhai, Neo Bill,

---

THE LONELY PLANET STORY

Fresh from an epic journey across Europe, Asia and Australia in 1972, Tony and Maureen Wheeler sat at their kitchen table stapling together notes. The first Lonely Planet guidebook, *Across Asia on the Cheap*, was born.

Travelers snapped up the guides. Inspired by their success, the Wheelers began publishing books to Southeast Asia, India and beyond. Demand was prodigious, and the Wheelers expanded the business rapidly to keep up. Over the years, Lonely Planet extended its coverage to every country and into the virtual world via lonelyplanet.com and the Thorn Tree message board.

As Lonely Planet became a globally loved brand, Tony and Maureen received several offers for the company. But it wasn't until 2007 that they found a partner whom they trusted to remain true to the company's principles of traveling widely, treading lightly and giving sustainably. In October of that year, BBC Worldwide acquired a 75% share in the company, pledging to uphold Lonely Planet's commitment to independent travel, trustworthy advice and editorial independence.

Today, Lonely Planet has offices in Melbourne, London and Oakland, with over 500 staff members and 300 authors. Tony and Maureen are still actively involved with Lonely Planet. They're traveling more often than ever, and they're devoting their spare time to charitable projects. And the company is still driven by the philosophy of *Across Asia on the Cheap*: 'All you've got to do is decide to go and the hardest part is over. So go!'

Mike Billhardt, Per Bisgaard, Per Ole Bjonnes, Dana Boim Pelleg, Ann Bolton, Matias Bordaverri, David Boutier, Anna Boyiazis, Hilary Boyse, Liana Brazil, Kristin Brevik, Catherine Bristow, Martin Buehner, Jan Buijs, Andrew Butchers **C** Agustin Caballero, Sonya Calderbank, Thomas Caley, Pablo Alejandre Calviño, John Canty, Brad Carpenter, Rory Carroll, Natalia Casagrande, Juan Caunedo, Louis Chabot, Linda Chapman, Luisa Charytonow, Christine Chow, Greg Chronopolos, Hans Clemensen, Sabine Corpeleijn, Carlos Cortinas, Barbara Couturaud, Frederick Cowper-Coles, Murray Cox, Janet & John Croft, Ryan Czajkowskyj **D** Tom Dacey, Thomas Dahl, Susana Dancy, Alex Danilov, Kevin Darling, Jacqueline De Goede, Bert De Jong, Casper De Jong, Clare Jones De Rocco, Jan De Roeck, Ineke De Weerdt, Hermann Deierling, Arjan Dekker, Christian Diaz Doren, Yovierkys Diaz Torres, John Doe, Melania Domene, Madeleine Douglas, Katya Druzhinina **E** Bertha E, Dave E, Barbara Easteal, Corinna Edenharter, Maya & Meline Egli, Philippe Egli, Jose Angel Esteras **F** Kirsten Fairfax, Carol Fairhurst, John Farrington, Matilde Fassler, Sonia Feijoo Rodriguez, Christophe Feldmann, Marta Filipova, Katie Firster, Robert Fisher, Alex Flores, Jorge Flores, Esther Forster, Louise Foxe, Daniele Fraioli, Agnes Franko, Mikkel Franks, Sonja Fredriksen **G** Eva Garby, Aurore Gardès, Reg Gatenby, Giordano Ghiretti, Juan Manuel Gimenez, Luca Giovannini, Harry Goof, Stephany Grasset, Suzanne Grasso, Robin Gregory, Urs Gretler, Federica Grifi, Hanni Gross, Susan Grossey, Heidi Gryksa, Laura Gual **H** Chris Hafey, Thomas Hallinan, John Hamers, Niels Hansen, Glen Hansman, Louis F Hartung, Vassilis & Revekka Hatzimihail, Ellen Cathrine Haugen, Carolyn Havergal, Jochem & Bianca Havermans, Richard Hawkins, Clive Hewson, Stuart Hippach, Brian Hoffmann, Wilco Hogenaar, Jannine Howe, Miles Hubbard, Beatrice Huber, Frans Huber, Séguin Hugo, Laura Hurley, Christian Huss **I** Ole-Martin Ihle **J** Marleen Jager, Chris Jagger, Carmelle Jaitly, Marlen Jordi **K** Gabor Kallay, Ellen Kaptijn, Micheal Kazuhiro Nishitani, Susanne Kellermann, David Kerkhoff, Robert Kerr, Meindert & Katja Keuning, Sara Khoja, Angelos Kikeras, Elisabeth Koenraads, Andrey Kolybelnikov, Claudia Korsten, Lena Kreymann, Martin Krippl, Natalie Kuempel, Renate Kuhn, Peter Kukanja **L** Dolf L'Ortye, Cristina Lachert, Nicolas Le Carre, Lionel Leclerc, Jeremy Leggett, John Lehane, Peter Leong, Aleigh Lewis, Jean Pierre Lippens, Marijn Litjens, Zipi & Moshe Litvin, Valentina Lopez, Natalie Loughran, Carla Louro, Dave Lucas, Davide Lucchese, Cara Ludlow **M** Jacco Maan, Mark Macdonald, Robin Mackay, Fiona Mackenzie, Julia Mader, Manuel Madrid, Zuriñe Madrid, Olli Maenpaa, Iñigo Malumbres, Maurizia Mancini, Trudie Mansfield, Caracristi Marina, James Marsden, Terry Marsh, Fraser Mashiter, Jelena Mateos, Roger Mateos, Lucy Maugham, Janet Mckinlay, Bev Mclellan, Christine Mes, Véronique Mesmaekers, Johanna Meyer-Wolfbauer, Anette Molbech, Dino Moutsopoulos, Karin Mruhn, Lucy Mulloy, Julio Muñoz, Yannick Muriat, Michelle Murphy **N** Ina Elise Dale Narum, Benjamin Nassauer, Scherie Nicol, Roland Nilsson, Daniel Nisman **O** Ana Oblak, Miss Osbourne, Charles Owen **P** Daylin Padron, Pavel Paloncý, Kostas Papa, Nicola Parmeggiani, Louise Passchier, Losha Patlavsky, Stefan Pedersen, Andreas Pelz, Fabio Perez, Milena Persiani, Leonidas Petinatos, Elia Petrou, Michael Pierse, Jay Plata, Jacqui Pols, Patrick Pols, Chiara Polverini, Lukas Port, William Potter, Stephen Poulios, Flemming Poulsen, Paula Puranen **Q** Mirjam Quixtner **R** Emily R, Franco Ragazzi, Christian Rangen, Daniel Reiter, Roberti Renzo, Rosy Richardson, Heinrich Richter, Roksana Roksana, Derek Rosen, Salman Rosenwaks, Ricardo Ross, Alana Rosser, Jildou Rozestraten **S** Astrid San Martín, Victor Sánchez Maraña, Lisa Savage, Anna Schindler, Axel Schipers, Christan Schneider, Esther Schneider, Patricia Schneider, Simon Schoeler, Raphael Schoen, Lucas & Henriet Schreurs, Berenda Schutte, Philip Scott, Matthew Screech, Kevin Seely, Widmer Seraina, Alan Slavin, Alex Smith, Sam Smith, Stewart Smith, Sally Snadden, Piotr Sobczak, Diego Sogorb, Rafal Sokolowski, Clair Louise Spence, Eric Stark, Christoph Starker, Sandra Stendahl, Gae Stephenson, Les Stewart, Michael Stingl, Maria Francesca Strata, Katrin Strobelberger, David Stuewe, Jutta Verena Sturm, Ariana Svenson, George Swann, Anita Symonds, J Symons **T** Annelies Tack, Antonio Tassone, Jan Tegelaar, Robert Theuns, Jo Thornborrow, Gitte Thorup, Ciska Tillema, Egle Tiskevciute, Benjamin Treves, Eduardo Trilla Delgado, Mary Ellen Trueman, Linda Turck, Harry Turner, Charles Tyler **U** Claudia Unger **V** Zoltan Vajda, Roos Van Der Steeg, Max Varela, Ash Vargas, John Varley, Katharina Velan, Karolien Verheyen, Sylvie Vignon, Santiago Vila, Lise Villadsen, Barbara Villagrasa, Mariano Villagrasa, Jurgen Vogt, Robert Vonk, Karin Vos **W** Margaret & Anton Walker, Paul Wane, Eva Wasem, Ellen Weber, Bruno Wegmüller, Philipp Wendtland, Ruth Weston, Eric Westzaan, Terry Williams, Udo Winterhagen, Danielle Wolbers, Joan Wright, Brigitte Wüthrich, Nicolette Wykeman

ACKNOWLEDGMENTS

Many thanks to the following for the use of their content:

Globe on title page ©Mountain High Maps 1993 Digital Wisdom, Inc.

Internal Photographs by Brendan Sainsbury p4; © Adam Eastland/Alamy p13; © Hackenberg-Photo-Cologne/Alamy p15. All other photographs by Lonely Planet Images, and by Jerry Alexander p15; Christopher Baker p6, p8, p9, p12, p16; Frank Carter p6; Tom Cockrem p12; Rick Gerharter p11; Roberto Gerometta p8; Christopher Groenhout p7; Rhonda Gutenberg p11; Tim Hughes p14; Richard l'Anson p7, p10; Rachel Lewis p5; Alfredo Maiquez p9, p14.

All images are the copyright of the photographers unless otherwise indicated. Many of the images in this guide are available for licensing from Lonely Planet Images: www.lonelyplanet images.com.

Index

A

Academia de Ajedrez 389
accommodation 458-61, *see also individual locations*
    campismos 459-60
    casas particulares 55, 460
    hotels 460-1
activities 87-93, *see also individual activities*
Acuario Nacional 156
Afro-Cuban culture 231, 426
Agramonte, Ignacio 333, 338
agropecuarios 75, 335
Aguachales de Falla Game Reserve 325
AIDS 487
air travel
    air fares 474
    air routes **477**
    airlines 473-4
    airports 473
    to/from Cuba 473-7
    within Cuba 477-8
Alejandro Robaina Tobacco Plantation 206
Alonso, Alicia 64
amarillos 55, 368, 481
animal bites 488
animals 81-2, *see also* endangered species, *individual animals*
Antiguo Cafetal Angerona 183
architecture 62-3, **6-7**
    art deco 120
    walking tours 123-5
area codes 468-9, *see also inside front cover*
Arrechabala Rum Factory 253
art 59-64, *see also individual arts*
    courses 126, 303, 463-6
    exporting artwork 463, 468
    Indian art 195
art deco 120
art galleries, *see* galleries
Artemisa 183
Asociación Cultural Yoruba de Cuba 115
Asociación Hermanos Saíz 59

000 Map pages
000 Photograph pages

ATMs 466
Autopista Nacional 299

B

babalawos 59
Bacardí building 114
Bacardí dynasty 415
Bacardí Rum Factory 415
Baconao Biosphere Reserve 431, 433-5
Bahía de Cochinos, *see* Bay of Pigs
Bahía de Naranjo 375
Bahía Honda 218-19
ballet 64, 117
Balneario San Diego 219
balseros 51
Banes 378-80
Baños de Elguea 290
Baracoa 449-55, **450, 14**
    accommodation 452-3
    drinking 454
    eating 453-4
    entertainment 454
    festivals 452
    internet access 449
    medical services 449
    shopping 454
    sights 449-52
    tours 452
    travel to/from 454-5
    travel within 455
Barrio Chino 117
baseball 56-7, 116, 147
bathrooms 469
Batista, Fulgencio 43-5, 378
    assassination attempt 44, 45
    military coup 43
Bay of Pigs 46, 48, 259, 260, **258**
Bayamo 386-92, **387**
    accommodation 390
    drinking 391
    entertainment 391
    festivals 389
    food 390-1
    internet access 388
    medical services 388
    shopping 391
    sights 388-9
    travel to/from 391-2
    travel within 392

beaches
    Boca Ciega 170-5
    Cayo Jutías 217
    Cayo Levisa 218
    El Mégano 170-5
    itineraries 29, **29**
    María la Gorda 208-9
    nudist beach 196, 197
    Playa Ancón 308-10
    Playa Baracoa 184
    Playa Blanca (Baracoa) 452
    Playa Blanca (Playa Pesquero) 373
    Playa Caletones 371
    Playa Cazonal 434
    Playa Coral 233
    Playa Daiquirí 433
    Playa Esmeralda 377-80
    Playa Girón 258-60
    Playa Jibacoa 178-80
    Playa La Herradura 357
    Playa La Llanita 357
    Playa Larga 257-8
    Playa Las Bocas 357
    Playa Los Cocos (Playa Girón) 258
    Playa Los Cocos (Playa Santa Lucía) 346
    Playa Los Pinos 345
    Playa Maguana 456
    Playa Paraíso 196
    Playa Pesquero 373-4
    Playa Pilar 329
    Playa Salado 184
    Playa Santa Lucía 345-8
    Playa Siboney 429-30
    Playa Sirena 195-6
    Playas del Este 170-5
    Punta Covarrubias 356-7
    Santa María del Mar 170-5
    Tarará 170-5
begging 463-4
Bejucal 182-3
bici-taxis 481
bicycle travel, *see* cycling
biosphere reserves 81, *see also* national parks
    Baconao Biosphere Reserve 431, 433-5
    Buenavista Biosphere Reserve 288, 314
    Ciénaga de Zapata 256-7

Cuchillas de Toa 456
  Gran Parque Natural Montemar
    256-7
  itineraries 33, **33**
  Península de Guanahacabibes
    207-10
  Sierra del Rosario 15, 222-4
birds 81, *see also individual species*
bird-watching 91
  Boca de Guamá 256
  Ciénaga de Zapata 257
  Cueva de los Portales 219-20
  El Nicho 272
  itineraries 32, **32**
  La Hacienda la Belén 344
  Las Terrazas 222, 223
  Loma de Cunagua 325-6
  Parque Nacional Alejandro de
    Humboldt 456
  Parque Nacional Desembarco del
    Granma 401
  Parque Natural El Bagá 327
  Península de Guanahacabibes
    208, 209
Black Virgin 164, 435
bloqueo, see US embargo
boat tours
  Cayerías del Norte 289
  Cayo Guillermo 329
  Cienfuegos 266
  Marea del Portillo 402
  Varadero 243
boat travel, *see also* ferries
  to/from Cuba 477
  within Cuba 481
boating 92, 93
  Cayo Jutías 217
  Cayo Largo del Sur 196
  Ciénaga de Zapata 257
  Cienfuegos 266
  Florencia 326
  Playa Ancón 309-10
  Playa Jibacoa 179
  Playas del Este 171
  Río Canímar 233
  Río Toa 455
Boca de Guamá 255-6
Boca de Yumurí 447-9
Bolívar, Simón 38, 111
books, *see also* literature
  biographies 25
  health 485
  history 39
  itineraries 32, **32**
  travel 23

boxing 57, 93
brucellosis 487
Buenavista Biosphere Reserve 288,
  314
bus travel 478-9, 481-2
Bush, George W 51
business hours 461, *see also inside
  front cover*

C
Cabañas Los Pinos 219
cabaret 144-5, 160, 248, 427
cabildos 65, 231, 270
Cabrera Infante, Guillermo 58, 60, 61
cafetales 183, 222-3, 431
Caibarién 287-8
cajitas 74
Camagüey 7, 332-43, **336-7**
  accommodation 339-40
  drinking 341
  entertainment 341-2
  festivals 339
  food 340-1
  history 333
  internet access 333
  medical services 334
  shopping 342
  sights 335-9
  travel to/from 342-3
  travel within 343
Camagüey province 331-48, **332**
cámara oscura 112
camellos 55
camiones 483
campismos 459-60
cañonazo ceremony 169
canopy tours 93, 224
canyoning 93, 313
Capitolio Nacional 114
Capone, Al 42
car travel 479-81
  driver's license 479
  insurance 479-80
  rental 480
  road conditions 480
  road distances chart 479
  road rules 480-1
Cárdenas 251-4, **252**
Carnaval (Santiago de Cuba) 27,
  421, 12
Carpentier, Alejo 60, 121
carpintero real 456
cars 55, 111, 203
Carter, Jimmy 48, 184
Casa de África 111

Casa de Asia 111
Casa de Diego Velázquez 411
Casa de la Obra Pía 111
Casa de las Américas 59, 122
Casa de las Religiones Populares 417
Casa de las Tradiciones 414
Casa del Caribe 417
Casa Templo de Santería Yemayá 302
Casablanca 169-70
casas natales
  Casa de Estrada Palma 389
  Casa Finlay 338
  Casa Natal de Calixto García 365
  Casa Natal de Carlos Manuel de
    Céspedes 388
  Casa Natal de José María de
    Heredia 413
  Casa Natal Nicolás Guillén 338
  Casa Oswaldo Guayasamín 111
  Museo Casa Natal de Antonio
    Maceo 414
  Museo Casa Natal de José Antonio
    Echeverría 252
  Museo Casa Natal de José Martí 113
  Museo Casa Natal de Ignacio
    Agramonte 338
casas particulares 55, 460
cash 466-7
Castillo de la Real Fuerza 110
Castillo de los Tres Santos Reyes
  Magnos del Morro 167-8
Castillo de Nuestra Señora de los
  Ángeles de Jagua 272
Castillo de San Pedro de la Roca del
  Morro 419
Castillo de San Salvador de la Punta
  117
Castillo de San Severino 232
Castillo del Morrillo 233
Castro, Ángel 379
Castro, Fidel 382-3
  as music fan 68
  as political leader 46-52, 184,
    259, 379
  as revolutionary 43-6, 347, 400,
    416
  early life 378, 380-1, 397, 414
  imprisonment 193, 194
Castro, Raúl 20, 50, 52
cathedrals, *see* churches
Catholicism 58
  Black Virgin 164, 435
  La Milagrosa 121
  Olallo, José 335, 339
  visit of Pope John Paul II 50, 58, 339

caves
    Cueva de Aguas 452
    Cueva de Ambrosio 239
    Cueva de los Peces 260
    Cueva de los Portales 219-20
    Cueva de Musalmanes 239
    Cueva de Punta del Este 195
    Cueva de San Miguel 215
    Cueva del Indio 215
    Cueva Las Perlas 209
    Cueva Martín Infierno 273-4
    Cueva Saturno 234
    Cuevas de Bellamar 232
    Farallones de Seboruco 381
    Gran Caverna de Santo Tomás
        217
    La Batata 312
caving 93
Cayerías del Norte 288-90
Cayo Coco 326-9, **326**
Cayo del Rosario 196
Cayo Ensenachos 288
Cayo Granma 419
Cayo Guillermo 329-30
Cayo Iguana 196
Cayo Jutías 217
Cayo Largo del Sur 195-7, **196**
Cayo Las Brujas 288
Cayo Levisa 218
Cayo Piedras del Norte 239
Cayo Rico 196
Cayo Romano 347
Cayo Sabinal 345
Cayo Saetía 381-2
Cayo Santa María 288, **289**
cell phones 468
cemeteries
    Cementerio La Reina 266
    Cementerio Santa Ifigenia 418
    Necrópolis Cristóbal Colón 120-1
    Necrópolis Tomás Acea 266
Central Australia 255
Central Camilo Cienfuegos 178
Centro Cultural Africano Fernando
    Ortiz 417
Centro Cultural Cinematográfico 146
Centro Cultural Pablo de la Torriente
    Brau 112
Centro de Ingeniería Genética y
    Biotecnología 156
Centro Gallego 115

Centro Habana 114-17, 123-5, **106**,
    124
Centro Internacional de Restauración
    Neurológica 156
Centro Nacional de Investigaciones
    Científicas 156
Centro Wilfredo Lam 109
Céspedes, Carlos Manuel de 38, 110,
    363, 386, 388, 397, 411, 418
chachachá 66-7
Charangas de Bejucal 182-3
Chávez, Hugo 52
chess 57, 389
Chibás, Eduardo 121
children, travel with 461
    activities 126, 461
    food 75
    health 489
Chivirico 437
chocolate 138, 452
churches
    Basílica de Nuestra Señora del
        Cobre 435-6
    Catedral de la Inmaculada
        Concepción 253
    Catedral de las Santas Hermanas
        de Santa Clara de Asís 280
    Catedral de Nuestra Señora de la
        Asunción 411, 449
    Catedral de Nuestra Señora de la
        Candelaria 338
    Catedral de San Cristóbal de La
        Habana 109
    Catedral Ortodoxa Nuestra Señora
        de Kazán 113
    Iglesia de Nuestra Corazón de
        Sagrado Jesús 338
    Iglesia de Nuestra Señora de la
        Merced 338
    Iglesia de Nuestra Señora de la
        Soledad 338
    Iglesia de Nuestra Señora de
        Regla 164
    Iglesia de Nuestra Señora del
        Carmen (Camagüey) 338
    Iglesia de Nuestra Señora del
        Carmen (Santa Clara) 280
    Iglesia de San Cristo del Buen
        Viaje 338
    Iglesia de San Francisco de Paula
        113
    Iglesia del Sagrado Corazón de
        Jesús 115
    Iglesia del Santo Angel Custodio
        114

Iglesia Jesús de Miramar 156
Iglesia Parroquial de la Santísima
    Trinidad 302
Iglesia Parroquial del Espíritu
    Santo 113
Iglesia Parroquial Mayor del
    Espíritu Santo 295
Iglesia y Convento de Nuestra
    Señora de Belén 113
Iglesia y Convento de Santa
    Clara 113
Iglesia y Monasterio de San
    Francisco de Asís 111-12
Parroquia de San Juan Bautista de
    Remedios 286
Parroquial del Santo Cristo del
    Buen Viaje 113
Churchill, Winston 323
Ciego de Ávila 318-23, **319**
    accommodation 320-1
    drinking 321
    entertainment 321-2
    festivals 320
    food 321
    internet access 318
    medical services 318
    shopping 322
    sights 319-20
    tourist offices 319
    travel to/from 322
    travel within 322-3
Ciego de Ávila province 316-30, **317**
Ciénaga de Zapata 256-7
Cienfuegos 262-71, **264**, **272**, 6
    accommodation 267-8
    clubbing 269
    courses 266
    drinking 268-9
    emergency services 263
    entertainment 269-70
    festivals 266
    food 268
    internet access 263
    medical services 263
    shopping 270
    sights 265-6
    tours 266
    travel to/from 270
    travel within 270-1
Cienfuegos, Camilo 11, 44, 45, 46,
    314, 334
Cienfuegos province 261-74, **262**
cigar factories 114-15, 202, 207,
    279-80, 414
cigars 54, 206, 468

cinema, *see* movies
climate 21, 462
climate change 475
Clinton, Bill 50
Coche Mambí 112
cockfighting 57
Cocodrilo 195
coco-taxis 482
coffee 72, 83, 312, 431
coffee plantations 183, 222-3, 431
cohibas, see cigars
Cojímar 170
Cold War 47-50
colectivos 482
Columbus, Christopher 34, 253, 277, 373, 442, 449
Columbus, Diego 442
Comandancia La Plata 394
Comité Central del Partido Comunista de Cuba 120
Compay Segundo 419
congrí oriental 70
consulates 464
Cooder, Ry 69
Coppelia 139
costs 21-2, *see also inside front cover*
courses 462-3
    art 126, 303, 463-6
    culture 125, 303, 462-3
    dance 125, 303, 421, 462-3
    film 463-6
    language 125, 271, 421, 462
    music 125, 303, 421
credit cards 466
Criadero Cocodrilo 194
Criadero de Cocodrilos 255-6
cricket 323
crocodiles 82, 194, 255-6, 257, 327, 434, **15**
Cruz, Celia 67
Cuartel Moncada, *see* Moncada Barracks
Cuban Missile Crisis 46, 48
Cuban Revolution 43-6, 116-17, 400
Cuchillas de Toa Biosphere Reserve 456
Cueva de Aguas 452
Cueva de Ambrosio 239
Cueva de los Peces 260
Cueva de los Portales 219-20
Cueva de Musalmanes 239
Cueva de Punta del Este 195
Cueva de San Miguel 215
Cueva del Indio 215
Cueva Las Perlas 209

Cueva Martín Infierno 273-4
Cueva Saturno 234
Cuevas de Bellamar 232
Cuidad Nuclear, *see* Juragua
culture 53-64
    courses 125, 303, 462-3
    itineraries 28, **28**
customs regulations 463
cycling 89-90, 478
    Bahía Honda 218-19
    Boca de Yumurí 447-9
    Camagüey 343
    Cayo Largo del Sur 196
    Guardalavaca 375
    La Farola 455
    Las Terrazas 224
    Matanzas 236
    Parque Nacional Viñales 215
    Playa Jibacoa 179
    Soroa 220
    Trinidad 303
    Varadero 251

D

daiquirí 415
dance 64, 65, 66-7, 68, 426
    courses 125, 303, 421, 462-3
    Museo de Danza 119
dangers 463-4
    hitchhiking 368, 481
    scams 97
danzón 64, 65
deep vein thrombosis 485
Delfinario 239
dengue fever 486
Día de la Liberación 26
Día de la Rebeldía Nacional 26
Día de los Trabajadores 26
diarrhea 487-8
disabilities, travelers with 469
diving 87-9
    Bay of Pigs 260
    Cayerías del Norte 289
    Cayo Coco 327
    Cayo Guillermo 329
    Cayo Largo del Sur 196
    Cayo Levisa 218
    Chivirico 437
    Guardalavaca 375
    Havana 157
    Isla de la Juventud 190
    Jardines de la Reina 330
    Marea del Portillo 402-3
    María la Gorda 208-9
    Parque Baconao 434

Playa Ancón 309
Playa Jibacoa 179
Playa Santa Lucía 347
Playas del Este 171
Punta Covarrubias 356-7
Rancho Luna 271
Varadero 240-1
dolphins 239, 271, 375, 434
dominó 57
Dos Ríos 392
double economy 22, 53
drinks 71-2
driver's license 479
driving, *see* car travel

E

Echeverría, José Antonio 45, 252
economy 54-5
eco-resorts 223
Ediciones Vigía 230
Edificio Bacardí 114
Edificio Focsa 63, 119
Edificio Santo Domingo 113
Egrem 65
El Cobre 435-6
El Nicho 272-3
El Pedraplén 288
El Pinero 188
El Saltón 436
El Uvero 437-8
El Yunque 456
electricity 459
Embalse Hanabanilla 285
embargo 47-52
embassies 464
emergencies, *see inside front cover*
encomiendas 35
endangered species 82
    carpintero real 456
    crocodiles 82, 194, 255-6, 257, 327, 434, **15**
    jutías 81, 82
    manatees 80, 81, 82, 257
    turtles 81, 82, 195, 196, 208
entry permits 470-1
environmental issues 14-15, 84-6, 223, 327, 475, *see also* sustainable development
Escuela Nacional de Ballet 117
Estadio Panamericano 170
Estrada Palma, Tomás 389
ethnicity 57
events, *see* festivals, sporting events
exchange rates, *see inside front cover*
ExpoCuba 163

F

factories
    chocolate 452
    cigar 114-15, 202, 207, 279-80, 414
    rum 253, 415
Farallones de Seboruco 381
fascioliasis 487
fauna, *see* animals, birds, reptiles
Fernández, Joesito 445
ferries 481
festivals 26-7, 127, **12-13**
    Charangas de Bejucal 182-3
    Feria Internacional del Libro de La Habana 127
    Festival Internacional de Ballet de La Habana 64, 127
    Festival Internacional de Cine Pobre 13, 26, 372
    Festival Internacional del Nuevo Cine Latinoamericano 61, 127
    Festival Internacional 'Habana Hip-Hop' 127
    Fiesta de la Cubanía 13, 389
    Fiesta de la Toronja 190
    food & drink 72-3
    International Humor Festival 182
    Jazz Festival 27, 127, **13**
    Jornada Cucalambeana 353
    Las Parrandas 27, 285, 286, **12**
    Romerías de Mayo 366
    Santiago Carnival 27, 421, **12**
Figueredo, Perucho 388
film, *see* movies
Finca Fiesta Campesina 255
Finca Las Manacas 380
Finlay, Carlos 121, 156, 338
First War of Independence 38-9, 325
fishing 90
    Cayerías del Norte 289
    Cayo Coco 327
    Cayo Guillermo 329
    Cayo Largo del Sur 196
    Ciénaga de Zapata 257
    Cienfuegos 266
    Embalse Hanabanilla 285
    Guardalavaca 375
    Laguna de la Leche 324-5
    Laguna La Redonda 325
    María la Gorda 208-9
    Marina Hemingway 156

000 Map pages
000 Photograph pages

Parque Rocazul 373
Pinar del Río 206
Playa Ancón 309
Playa Jibacoa 179
Playa Santa Lucía 347
Playas del Este 171
Río Canímar 233
Varadero 241
flamingos 195, 257, 327, 347
flora, *see* plants
Florencia 326
Florida 343-4
Focsa building 63, 119
folklórico dance groups 426
food 70-9, 464
    customs 75-6
    festivals 72-3
    ice cream 70, 139
    language 76-9
    new Cuban cuisine 71
    takeout 74
    tipping 75
forts 62
    Castillo de la Real Fuerza 110
    Castillo de los Tres Santos Reyes Magnos del Morro 167-8
    Castillo de Nuestra Señora de los Ángeles de Jagua 272
    Castillo de San Pedro de la Roca del Morro 419
    Castillo de San Salvador de la Punta 117
    Castillo de San Severino 232
    Castillo del Morrillo 233
    Fortaleza de San Carlos de la Cabaña 168-9
    San Hilario 345
Fototeca de Cuba 112
Fuente de la India 115
Fuente de los Leones 111
Fuentes, Gregorio 90
Fundación Naturaleza y El Hombre 153

G

galleries 147-8
    Centro Raúl Martínez Galería de Arte Provincial 320
    Centro Wilfredo Lam 109
    Colección de Arte Cubano 116
    Colección de Arte Universal 116
    Estudio-Galería Jover 335
    Fototeca de Cuba 112
    La Casona Centro de Arte 112
    Sala Galería Raúl Martínez 110
    Taller Experimental de Gráfica 110

García, Calixto 122, 351, 365, 366
García, Guillermo 403
García, Vicente 353
gardens
    El Jardín de Caridad 212
    Jardín Botánico de Cienfuegos 272
    Jardín Botánico de Cupaynicu 392
    Jardín Botánico Nacional 163
    Jardín de Cactus 434
    Jardín de los Helechos 419-20
    Jungla de Jones 194
gay travelers 144, 464-5
geography 80
Gibara 370-3
Gitmo, *see* Guantánamo US Naval Base
glorieta 396, 397
golf 163, 242
Gómez, Máximo 38, 39, 117, 120
González, Elián 50, 51
Gran Caverna de Santo Tomás 217
Gran Parque Nacional Sierra Maestra 393-6, **394**
Gran Parque Natural Montemar 256-7
Gran Synagoga Bet Shalom 122
Gran Teatro de La Habana 115
Granjita Siboney 430
Granma (yacht) 44, 116-17, 386
Granma province 384-403, **385**
grapefruit steaks 55
Grito de Yara 38, 39, 393
guaguas 481
Guáimaro 344
Guanabacoa 166-7
Guanahatabey people 34, 200, 208
Guantánamo 442-6, **443**
    accommodation 444-5
    eating 445
    entertainment 445-6
    history 442
    internet access 442
    medical services 443
    shopping 446
    sights 444
    travel to/from 446
    travel within 446-7
Guantánamo province 440-57, **441**
Guantánamo US Naval Base 42, 446-8
Guardalavaca 374-8, **374**, **376**
guayabera 295
Guevara, Che 47, 277, 280-1, **10**
    as revolutionary 44, 46, 277
    death of 46, 49
    mausoleum 279
    museums 169, 279
    post-Revolution 47, 49, 219

Guillén, Nicolás 59, 60, 338
Gutiérrez Alea, Tomás 61

H
Habana, *see* Havana
Habana Vieja 108-14, 122-3, **100**, **123**
habanera 67
Haiti 37, 38
Hatuey 11, 393, 450
Havana 94-175, **95**, **99**, **7**, **16**
    accommodation 126-33, 157-8
    Barrio Chino 117
    Centro Habana 114-17, 123-5, **106**, **124**
    childrens' activities 126
    clubbing 143-4
    courses 125-6
    drinking 140-2
    emergency services 98
    entertainment 142-7, 160-1
    food 133-40, 158-60
    Habana Vieja 108-14, 122-3, **100**, **123**
    history 95-6
    internet access 98, 153
    Malecón 121-2, **16**
    Marianao 152-61, **154-5**
    medical services 107, 153
    Miramar 152-61, **154-5**
    old city wall 114
    Playa 152-61, **154-5**
    restoration projects 96, 109
    shopping 147-9, 161
    sights 108-22, 153-6
    tourist information 108, 153
    tours 125, 126
    travel to/from 149-50, 161
    travel within 150-2, 161
    Vedado 117-25, **102-3**
    walking tours 122-5, **123**, **124**
Havana province 176-84, **177**
health 484-9
    animal bites 488
    books 485
    insect bites 488
    insurance 484
    vaccinations 485
    water 488-9
    websites 485
heatstroke 488
Helms-Burton Act 50, 51
Hemingway, Ernest
    books 90, 436
    life in Cuba 318, 329, 347

Museo Hemingway 167
    tours 327
hepatitis A/B 486
Heredia, José María de 413
Hershey Electric Railway 178, 179
hiking 91-2
    Bahía de Naranjo 375
    Baracoa 452
    Cayo Jutías 217
    Cayo Largo del Sur 197
    Chivirico 437
    El Saltón 436
    El Yunque 456
    Embalse Hanabanilla 285
    Gran Parque Nacional Sierra
        Maestra 393-4, 395, **394**
    Las Terrazas 223
    Marea del Portillo 402
    Nueva Gerona 190
    Parque Nacional Alejandro de
        Humboldt 457
    Parque Nacional Desembarco del
        Granma 401
    Parque Nacional Viñales 215
    Península de Guanahacabibes
        209
    Pico Turquino 395, 438-9
    San Antonio de los Baños 182
    Sierra de Jatibonico 314
    Sierra del Cristal 381
    Soroa 220
    Topes de Collantes 312-13
    Trinidad 303
    Viñales 212
hip-hop, *see reggaetón*
history 34-52
    Bay of Pigs 46, 48, 259
    British rule 36, 38, 95
    Cold War 47-50
    Cuban Missile Crisis 46, 48
    Cuban Revolution 43-6, 116-17, 400
    developing-world affairs
        48-50, 49
    First War of Independence 38-9, 325
    French immigrants 37
    independence 41, 42
    pre-Columbian 34
    recent events 51-2
    Spanish-Cuban-American War
        39-40, 325, 430
    Spanish conquest 34-5, 95, 286
    Special Period 49, 50-1, 55, 368
hitchhiking 368, 481

HIV/AIDS 487
Holguín 361-70, **362**, **364**
    accommodation 366-7
    clubbing 369
    drinking 367-8
    entertainment 368-9
    food 367
    internet access 363
    medical services 363
    shopping 369
    sights 363-6
    travel to/from 369-70
    travel within 370-1
Holguín province 359-83, **360-1**
holidays 26, 465
Holmes, Antonio Guiteras 233
horse carriages 482
horseback riding 92
    Cayo Largo del Sur 196
    Chivirico 437
    El Saltón 436
    Florencia 326
    Guardalavaca 375
    Havana 163
    La Hacienda la Belén 344
    Las Terrazas 222
    Marea del Portillo 402-3
    Parque Baconao 434
    Parque Nacional Viñales 215
    Parque Rocazul 373
    Pinar del Río 206
    Playa Coral 233
    Playa Jibacoa 179
    Río Canímar 233
    Sierra del Cristal 381
    Soroa 220
    Trinidad 303
horses 92
Hotel Habana Libre 118-19
Hotel Inglaterra 115
Hotel Nacional 118
hotels 460-1
human rights 51, 52, 58, 59, 448
Humboldt, Alexander von 83
hurricanes 80, 86
hydrofoils, *see* ferries

I
Icaic 61, 146
ice cream 70, 139
Ídolo del Agua 401
Iglesia de Nuestra Corazón de Sagrado
    Jesús 338
Iglesia de Nuestra Señora de la
    Merced 338

Iglesia de Nuestra Señora de la Soledad 338
Iglesia de Nuestra Señora de Regla 164
Iglesia de Nuestra Señora del Carmen (Camagüey) 338
Iglesia de San Cristo del Buen Viaje 338
Iglesia de San Francisco de Paula 113
Iglesia del Santo Angel Custodio 114
Iglesia Parroquial de la Santísima Trinidad 302
Iglesia Parroquial del Espíritu Santo 113
Iglesia y Monasterio de San Francisco de Asís 111-12
iguanas 196
immigration 473
immigration offices 470
insect bites 488
Instituto Superior de Arte 156
insurance
    car 479-80
    health 484
    travel 465
International Humor Festival 182
internet access 465
internet resources, see websites
Isla de la Juventud 185-97, **187**, 14
    education campaign 193
    history 186
    travel to/from 186, 192
    travel within 186
Isla Turiguano 325-6
itineraries 4, 28-33, **4**
    beaches 29, **29**
    bird-watching 32, **32**
    books 32, **32**
    culture 28, **28**
    islands 33, **33**
    music 31, **31**
    off the beaten track 30, **30**
    parks & reserves 33, **33**

J
Jardín Botánico de Cienfuegos 272
Jardines de Hershey 178
Jardines de la Reina 330
Jaruco 180
jazz 67-8
Jazz Festival 27, 127, 13
Jefferson, Thomas 36, 38

000 Map pages
000 Photograph pages

jet lag 485-6
jineterismo 51, 54, 141, 301
Jornada Cucalambeana 353
Jungla de Jones 194
Juragua 274
jutías 81, 82

K
kayaking, *see* boating
Kennedy, John F 48, 207, 259
Khrushchev, Nikita 48
King Ranch 345
Korda, Alberto 45

L
La Farola 455
La Gran Piedra 430-3, **432**
La Habana, *see* Havana
La Hacienda la Belén 344
La Milagrosa 121
La Rusa 451
La Trocha 325
La Virgen de la Caridad (El Cobre) 435
La Virgen de la Caridad (Havana) 164
Ladas 55, 203
Laguna de la Leche 324-5
Laguna de las Salinas 257
Laguna del Tesoro 256
Laguna La Redonda 325
Lam, Wilfredo 63
language 490-6
    courses 125, 271, 421, 462
    food vocabulary 76-9
    slang 491
Las Parrandas 27, 285, 286, 12
Las Terrazas 15, 222-4
Las Tunas 351-6, **352**
    accommodation 353
    drinking 354-5
    entertainment 355
    festivals 353
    food 353-4
    internet access 351
    medical services 351
    shopping 355
    sights 351-3
    travel to/from 356
    travel within 356-7
Las Tunas province 349-58, **350**
legal matters 465
Lennon, John 118
leptospirosis 487
lesbian travelers 144, 464-5
Lezama Lima, José 60
licenses for US visitors 471-2

literature 25, 59-60, *see also* books
    itineraries 32, **32**
Loma de Cunagua 325-6
Loma de San Juan 417
Lonja del Comercio 111
López, Narciso 39, 251
López Serrano building 122
Los Aquáticos 215

M
M-26-7 44, 415
Maceo, Antonio 38, 39, 40, 121, 164, 200, 414, 11
Machado y Morales, Gerardo 43
Mafia 42-3, 96
magazines 459
malaria 487
Malecón 121-2, 16
Mambís 40
mambo 64, 66-7
Manaca Iznaga 310
manatees 80, 81, 82, 257
Mansión Xanadu 242
Manzanillo 396-8
maps 465-6
Maqueta de La Habana Vieja 111
máquinas 482
Marabana 27
Marea del Portillo 402-3
María la Gorda 208-9
Marianao 152-61, **154-5**
Mariel 183-4
Mariel Boatlift 48, 184
Márquez, Gabriel García 60
Martí, José 39, 40-1, 386, 392, 447
    early days 189
    literary work 59
    mausoleum 419
    museum 113
    statues 115, 120, 232, 265, 319, 353, 395, 438, 11
Matanzas 227-36, **228-9**, **233**
    accommodation 234
    drinking 235
    entertainment 235
    festivals 234
    food 234-5
    internet access 230
    medical services 230
    shopping 235
    sights 230-4
    travel to/from 235-6
    travel within 236
Matanzas province 225-60, **226**
Matos, Huber 333, 334

Matthews, Herbert 45
Mausoleo a los Mártires de Artemisa 183
measures 459, *see also inside front cover*
Media Luna 398
medical services 486, *see also* health
Mella, Julio Antonio 119
memorials, *see* monuments & memorials
Mercado Agropecuario El Río 335
metric conversions, *see inside front cover*
military zones 194-5, 447, 452
Minas 344
Ministerio del Interior 120
Miramar 152-61, **154-5**
Moa 382-3
mobile phones 468
Moncada Barracks 43, 416, 416-17
money 21-2, 466-7, *see also inside front cover*
monuments & memorials
  Celia Sánchez Monument 396
  Colina Lenin 166
  Memorial a José Martí 120
  Memorial a los Estudiantes de Medicina 117
  Memorial a los Mártires de Barbados 351
  Memorial to José Miguel Gómez 122
  Memorial Vicente García 353
  Monument to Celia Sánchez 161
  Monument to Lenin 161
  Monumento a Alfabetización 353
  Monumento a Antonio Maceo 121
  Monumento a Calixto García 122
  Monumento a Julio Antonio Mella 119
  Monumento a la Toma del Tren Blindado 279
  Monumento a las Víctimas del Maine 121
  Monumento al Cimarrón 436
  Monumento Ernesto Che Guevara 279
  Parque Rocazul 373
  Pavillón Granma 116-17
Moré, Benny 265, 270, 273
Morón 323-4
moros y cristianos 70
motion sickness 485-6
movies 24, 61, 372
  courses 463-6
Mural de la Prehistoria 214

museums, *see also casas natales*
  Casa Museo del Café 312
  Celia Sánchez Museum 398
  Finca Las Manacas 380
  Fundación Naturaleza y El Hombre 153
  Moncada Barracks 417
  Museo 28 Septiembre de los CDR 112
  Museo Antropológico Montané 119
  Museo Arqueológico (Baracoa) 451
  Museo Chorro de Maita 375
  Museo de Ambiente Histórico Cubano 411
  Museo de Arte Colonial 110
  Museo de Arte Religioso 112
  Museo de Artes Decorativas 119
  Museo de Batalla de Ideas 253
  Museo de Cera 389
  Museo de Ciencias Naturales Sandalio de Noda 202
  Museo de Comandancia del Che 169
  Museo de Danza 119
  Museo de Fortificaciones y Armas 168
  Museo de Historia Natural Felipe Poey 119
  Museo de Historia Provincial (Holguín) 365
  Museo de la Alfabetización 156
  Museo de la Cerámica Artística Cubana 110
  Museo de la Ciudad 110
  Museo de la Comandancia 255
  Museo de la Farmacia Habanera 113
  Museo de la Guerra Hispano-Cubano-Norteamericano 430
  Museo de la Imagen 417
  Museo de la Lucha Clandestina (Nueva Gerona) 188
  Museo de la Lucha Clandestina (Santiago de Cuba) 414
  Museo de la Orfebrería 112-13
  Museo de la Plata 433
  Museo de la Revolución 116-17
  Museo de la Ruta de los Esclavos 232
  Museo de las Parrandas Remedianas 286
  Museo de Naipes 112
  Museo de Numismático 112
  Museo de Pintura Mural 112-13
  Museo de Piratería 419
  Museo de Playa Girón 258
  Museo de San Juan de Dios 335

  Museo de Tabaco 111
  Museo del Aire 156
  Museo del Automóvil 111
  Museo del Carnaval 413
  Museo del Chocolate 138
  Museo del Ferrocarril 122
  Museo del Humor 182
  Museo del Ron 112
  Museo El Templete 110
  Museo Farmacéutico 232
  Museo Finca El Abra 189-90
  Museo Hemingway 167
  Museo Histórico La Demajagua 396-7
  Museo Histórico Municipal (Trinidad) 301-2
  Museo Histórico Naval Nacional 266
  Museo Indocubano Bani 379
  Museo Las Coloradas 401
  Museo Municipal (Guantánamo) 444
  Museo Municipal de Guanabacoa 166
  Museo Municipal de Regla 166
  Museo Municipal Emilio Bacardí Moreau 413
  Museo Nacional Camilo Cienfuegos 314
  Museo Nacional de Bellas Artes 116
  Museo Nacional de Historia Natural 111
  Museo Nacional de la Lucha Contra Bandidos 302
  Museo Nacional de Transporte Terrestre 433
  Museo Napoleónico 119
  Museo Oscar María de Rojas 252
  Museo Provincial Abel Santamaría 279
  Museo Provincial Ignacio Agramonte 335
  Museo Provincial Simón Reyes 320
  Railroad Museum 183
  Sitio Histórico de Birán 380-1
music 65-9, **8-9**
  courses 125, 303, 421
  itineraries 31, **31**

N
national parks & reserves 83-4, **85**, *see also* biosphere reserves
  Aguachales de Falla Game Reserve 325
  Gran Parque Nacional Sierra Maestra 393-6, **394**

INDEX

national parks & reserves *continued*
Gran Parque Natural Montemar 256-7
itineraries 33, **33**
Parque Nacional Alejandro de Humboldt 456-7
Parque Nacional Caguanes 314
Parque Nacional Desembarco del Granma 400-1
Parque Nacional La Mensura 381
Parque Nacional Península de Guanahacabibes 208-10
Parque Nacional Sierra Cristal 381
Parque Nacional Viñales 214-17
Parque Natural El Bagá 327
Reserva Ecológica Varahicacos 239
Sierra del Cristal 381
Necrópolis Cristóbal Colón 120-1
Necrópolis Tomás Acea 266
newspapers 57-8, 459
Niquero 398-400
Nixon, Richard 46
Nueva Gerona 188-93, **189**
accommodation 190-1
drinking 191
entertainment 191-2
festivals 190
food 191
internet access 188
medical services 188
shopping 192
sights 188-90
travel to/from 192
travel within 192-3
nueva trova 69, **8**
Nuevitas 344
Núñez Jiménez, Antonio 87, 295

O
Obama, Barack 20, 52, 448
Ocampo, Sebastián de 35
Olallo, José 335, 339
opening hours 461, *see also inside front cover*
Operación Milagros 52
organopónicos 75
Oriente 357
Orquideario Soroa 220
Ortiz, Fernando 36

000 Map pages
000 Photograph pages

P
Pabellón para la Maqueta de la Capital 153
Pabexpo 156
painting 63-4
País, Frank 44, 45
Palacio Cueto 112
Palacio de las Convenciones 156
Palacio de los Capitanes Generales 110
Palacio de los Condes de Casa Bayona 110
Palacio de los Condes de Santovenia 111
Palacio de los Marqueses de Aguas Claras 109
Palacio del Segundo Cabo 110
Palacio Velasco 117
paladares 55, 71, 73-4
palm trees 83
Palmar del Junco 232
Palmira 270
Parque Almendares 119
Parque Baconao 433-5
Parque Calixto García 365
Parque Central 115-16
Parque Céspedes 363-5, 388, 410-11
Parque de la Fraternidad 115
Parque de los Enamorados 117
Parque Escaleras de Jaruco 180
Parque Histórico Abel Santamaría 417
Parque Histórico Militar Morro-Cabaña 167-9, **168**
Parque Josone 239
Parque La Güira 219
Parque Lenin 161-4, **162**
Parque Lennon 118
Parque Nacional Alejandro de Humboldt 456-7
Parque Nacional Caguanes 314
Parque Nacional Desembarco del Granma 400-1
Parque Nacional La Mensura 381
Parque Nacional Monumento Bariay 373
Parque Nacional Sierra Cristal 381
Parque Nacional Viñales 214-17
Parque Rocazul 373
Parque Vidal 282
Parroquia de San Juan Bautista de Remedios 286
Paseo de Martí 117
passports 473
Pavillón Granma 116-17
pedraplén 85
pelota, see baseball

Península de Guanahacabibes 207-10
Península de Zapata 15, 254-60
período especial 49, 50-1, 55, 368
peso pizza 55
phone cards 469
Pico Turquino 15, 395, 438-9
Pilón 401-2
Pinar del Río 200-6, **201**
accommodation 204
eating 204-5
entertainment 205
festivals 203
internet access 202
medical services 202
shopping 205
sights 202-3
travel to/from 205-6
travel within 206
Pinar del Río province 198-224, **199**, 15
pirates 36, 95, 186, 419
planning 21-5, *see also* itineraries
plants 83
Platt Amendment 42, 186, 448
Playa 152-61, **154-5**
Playa Ancón 308-10
Playa Baracoa 184
Playa Blanca 373
Playa Caletones 371
Playa Cazonal 434
Playa Coral 233, 234
Playa Daiquirí 433
Playa Esmeralda 377-80
Playa Girón 258-60
Playa Jibacoa 178-80
Playa La Herradura 357
Playa La Llanita 357
Playa Larga 257-8
Playa Las Bocas 357
Playa Los Cocos 196, 346
Playa Los Pinos 345
Playa Maguana 456
Playa Pesquero 373-4
Playa Pilar 329
Playa Salado 184
Playa Santa Lucía 345-8, **346**
Playa Siboney 429-30
Playa Sirena 195-6
Playa Tortuga 196
Playas del Este 170-5, **172-3**
Plaza de Armas 110-11
Plaza de la Catedral 109-10
Plaza de la Revolución 119-20
Plaza de San Francisco de Asís 111-12

Plaza del Cristo 113
Plaza Tribuna Anti-Imperialista 121-2
Plaza Vieja 112
polymitas, see snails
Pope John Paul II 50, 58, 339
population 56
postal services 467
Prado 117
Prado de las Esculturas 431
Presidio Modelo 193
Puente Calixto García 230
Puente de Bacunayagua 178
Puente Yayabo 294
Puerto Esperanza 217-18
Puerto Padre 356
Punta Covarrubias 356-7
Punta de Maisí 447
Punta Francés 15, 190
puppet theater 64

Q
queuing 174
Quinta 120

R
rabies 487
radio 459
Radio Rebelde 45
Rafael Freyre 377
Railroad Museum 183
rainforests 83
Rancho La Guabina 206
Rancho Luna 271-2
Ranchón Gaviota 179
rap 68-9
Real Fábrica de Tabacos Partagás
    114-15
reggaetón 9, 68-9
Regla 164-6, **165**
religion 58-9, *see also* Catholicism,
    Santería
Remedios 285-7, 7
reptiles 81
Reserva Ecológica Varahicacos 239
responsible travel 23, 88, 475, *see also*
    sustainable travel
restaurants 73-4
Río Canímar 233
Río Toa 455
road distances chart 479
Robaina, Alejandro 206
rock climbing 92-3, 216
rodeos 206, 325-6, 345, 355, 434
Rodríguez, Silvio 182
Romerías de Mayo 366

Roosevelt, Theodore 42, 417
ropa vieja 72
rum 71-2
    Bacardí dynasty 415
    factories 253, 415
    Museo del Ron 112
rumba 64, 65, 66, 232, 9

S
safe travel 463-4
    hitchhiking 368, 481
    road conditions 480
    scams 97
sailing 309-10
Sala Galería Raúl Martínez 110
salsa 67-8, 8
Salto del Arco Iris 220
Salto del Caburní 312
Salto del Guayabo 381
San Antonio de los Baños 181-2
San Diego de los Baños 219-20
San Francisco de Paula 167
San Miguel de los Baños 250
Sánchez, Celia 44, 161, 396, 398
Sancti Spíritus 293-8, **294**
    accommodation 296-7
    eating 297
    entertainment 297-8
    internet access 293
    medical services 293
    shopping 298
    sights 294-6
    travel to/from 298
    travel within 298-9
Sancti Spíritus province 291-315, **292**
Santa Clara 277-85, **278**
    accommodation 281-2
    drinking 283
    eating 282-3
    entertainment 283-4
    internet access 277
    medical services 279
    shopping 284
    sights 279-80
    travel to/from 284
    travel within 285
Santa Cruz del Norte 178
Santa Isabel de las Lajas 270
Santa María del Rosario 167
Santamaría, Abel 43
Santería 58-9, 417, 435
    babalawos 59
    cabildos 65, 231, 270
    Casa Templo de Santería Yemayá
        302

La Virgen de la Caridad (Havana)
    164
La Virgen de la Caridad (El Cobre)
    435
Palmira 270
Santiago Carnival 27, 421, 12
Santiago de Cuba 407-29, **408-9**,
    412
    accommodation 421-3
    clubbing 426-7
    drinking 425
    eating 423-5
    emergency services 409
    entertainment 425-7
    festivals 421
    internet access 410
    medical services 410
    shopping 427-8
    sights 410-14
    tours 421
    travel to/from 428
    travel within 428-30
    walking tour 420-1, **420**
Santiago de Cuba province 404-39, **406**
Santiago de las Vegas 164
Santo Domingo 393
Sardiñas, Guillermo 188
scams 97
sculpture 63-4
Second War of Independence, *see*
    Spanish-Cuban-American War
serigraphy 63
Seven Years' War 36, 38
shopping 467-8
Siboney people 186
Sierra del Chorrillo 344
Sierra del Cristal 381
Sierra del Rosario 15, 222-4
Sitio Histórico de Birán 380-1
skydiving 93, 241-2, 375
slang 491
slavery 35-6, 37, 39, 40
smoking 54
snails 448, 452
snakes 81
snorkeling 90-1
    Bay of Pigs 260
    Cayerías del Norte 289
    Cayo Guillermo 329
    Cayo Jutías 217
    Cayo Largo del Sur 196
    Cayo Levisa 218
    Chivirico 437
    Cueva Saturno 234
    Guardalavaca 375

INDEX

snorkeling *continued*
    Marea del Portillo 402-3
    María la Gorda 208-9
    Playa Ancón 309
    Playa Coral 233, 234
    Playa Jibacoa 179
    Playa Santa Lucía 347
    Río Canímar 233
    Varadero 240-1
son 65, 66, **9**
Soroa 220, **221**
Sotomayor, Javier 57
Soviet-Cuban relations 45, 47, 48,
    274, 299
spa resorts
    Balneario San Diego 219
    Baños de Elguea 290
    San Miguel de los Baños 250
Spanish-Cuban-American War 39-40,
    325, 430
Special Period 49, 50-1, 55, 368
sport 56-7, *see also individual sports*
sporting events 27, 93
Stevenson, Teófilo 56
stretch Ladas 55, 203
sugar industry 36-7, 39, 51, 181, 299
sugar mills
    Central Australia 255
    Central Camilo Cienfuegos 178
Surgidero de Batabanó 180-1
sustainable development 82, 223, *see
    also* environmental issues
sustainable travel 23, 24, *see
    also GreenDex,* responsible travel
swimming 223-4, 215-19

T
Taíno people 34, 35, 256, 375, 451
Taller Experimental de Gráfica 110
taxis 482, *see also* bici-taxis, coco-
    taxis, *colectivos, máquinas*
Teatro Principal 342
Teatro Sauto 231
Teatro Tomás Terry 265
telenovelas 61
telephone services 468-9
television 61
terrorism 47, 351, 354
theater 64
theft 463-4
timba 67-8

000 Map pages
000 Photograph pages

time 469
tinajones 333, 342
tipping 75, 467
tobacco 54
    factories 114-15, 202, 207,
        279-80, 414
    Museo de Tabaco 111
    plantations 206
tocororos 311
toilets 469
Topes de Collantes 311-14, **312**
Torricelli Act 50
tourist cards 469-72
tourist information 469
tours 327, 477, 482, *see also* boat
    tours, walking tours
traditional medicine 489
train travel 482-3
travel insurance 465
travel restrictions 21, 22, 52, 474
travel to/from Cuba 473-7
travel within Cuba 477-83
trekking, *see* hiking
Trinidad 298-308, **300, 309,** 6
    accommodation 304-5
    drinking 306
    entertainment 306-7
    festivals 303-4
    food 305-6
    history 299-301
    internet access 301
    medical services 301
    shopping 307
    sights 301-3
    tours 303
    travel to/from 307-8
    travel within 308-9
Tropicana Nightclub 160
trovadores 68
truck travel 483
turtles 81, 82, 195, 196, 208
typhoid 487

U
Uneac 60
Unesco Biosphere Reserves, *see*
    biosphere reserves
Unesco World Heritage Sites, *see*
    World Heritage Sites
United Fruit Company 379
Universidad de La Habana 119
US-Cuba relations
    Bay of Pigs 46, 48, 259
    Cold War 47-50
    Cuban Missile Crisis 46, 48

early history 36-7, 39, 41, 42
    Elián González 50, 51
    Guantánamo US Naval Base 42,
        446-8
    Helms-Burton Act 50, 51
    immigration to US 47, 48, 51,
        184, 448
    Museo de Batalla de Ideas 253
    Platt Amendment 42, 186, 448
    post-Revolution 46-7
    Torricelli Act 50
    travel restrictions 21, 22, 52, 474
US embargo 47-52
US Interests Office 121
US Naval Base, *see* Guantánamo US
    Naval Base
US visitors licenses 471-2
USS *Maine* 41, 121

V
vaccinations 485
Valle de la Prehistoria 433
Valle de los Ingenios 310-11
Valle de Viñales 210-17
Varadero 236-51, **238-9, 240-1**
    accommodation 243-6
    clubbing 247-8
    drinking 247
    emergency services 237
    entertainment 247-8
    festivals 243
    food 246-7
    internet access 237
    medical services 237
    shopping 248-9
    sights 238-40
    tours 242-3
    travel to/from 249-50
    travel within 250-1
Vedado 117-25, **102-3**
vegetarian travelers 74-5
Velázquez de Cuéllar, Diego 35,
    405, 411
Versalles quarter 232
video systems 459
Villa Clara province 275-90, **276**
Viñales 210-14, **211**
    accommodation 212-13
    drinking 213
    entertainment 213-14
    food 213
    internet access 210
    medical services 210
    shopping 214
    sights 211-12

tours 212
travel to/from 214
travel within 214
visas 469-72, *see also* passports
  entry permits 470-1
  extensions 470
  immigration offices 470
  licenses for US visitors 471-2
volunteering 472

W
walking, *see* hiking
walking tours
  Centro Habana 123-5, **124**
  Habana Vieja 122-3, **123**
  Santiago de Cuba 420-1, **420**
water 488-9
waterfalls
  El Nicho 272-3
  Salto del Arco Iris 220

Salto del Caburní 312
Salto del Guayabo 381
weather 21, 462
websites
  Cuba 25, 34, 35, 53
  health 485
weights 459, *see also inside front cover*
wildlife, *see* animals, birds, plants, reptiles
women in Cuba 54
women travelers 472
women's health 489
World Heritage Sites 81, *see also* biosphere reserves
  Camagüey 7, 332-43, **336-7**
  Castillo de San Pedro de la Roca del Morro 419
  Cienfuegos 262-71, **264**, **272**, 6

First Coffee Plantations in the Southeast of Cuba 431
  Habana Vieja 108-14, 122-5, **100**, **123**
  Parque Nacional Alejandro de Humboldt 456-7
  Parque Nacional Desembarco del Granma 400-1
  Trinidad 298-308, **300**, **309**, 6
  Valle de los Ingenios 310-11
  Valle de Viñales 210-17

Y
Yara 393

Z
Zoológico de Piedras 447
zoos 163
zunzuncitos 81, 195

GreenDex

GOING GREEN

The following attractions, accommodation, cafes, pubs and restaurants have been selected by Lonely Planet authors because they demonstrate a commitment to sustainability. We've selected hotels, pubs and restaurants for their support of local producers – so they might serve only seasonal, locally sourced produce on their menus. We've also highlighted farmers markets and the local producers themselves. In addition, we've covered accommodation that we deem to be environmentally friendly, for example for their commitment to recycling or energy conservation. Attractions are listed because they're involved in conservation or environmental education or have been given an ecological award. For more tips about travelling sustainably in Cuba, turn to the Getting Started chapter (p23). We want to keep developing our sustainable-travel content. If you think we've omitted someone who should be listed here, email us at www.lonelyplanet .com/contact. For more information about sustainable tourism and Lonely Planet, see www.lonely planet.com/responsibletravel.

CAMAGÜEY PROVINCE
food
  Mercado Agropecuario
    El Río 341
sights
  La Hacienda la Belén 344

CIEGO DE ÁVILA PROVINCE
accommodation
  Sitio La Güira 328
sights
  Laguna La Redonda 324
  Loma de Cunagua 325
  Parque Natural El Bagá 327

CIENFUEGOS PROVINCE
accommodation
  Villa Guajimico 274
food
  Hacienda La Vega 273
sights
  El Nicho 272
  Jardín Botánico de Cienfuegos 272

GRANMA PROVINCE
accommodation
  Villa Santo Domingo 395
activities
  Sendero Arqueológico Natural El
    Guafe 401
information
  Villa Santo Domingo 393

sights
  Gran Parque Nacional Sierra
    Maestra 393
  Jardín Botánico de Cupaynicu 392
  Parque Nacional Desembarco del
    Granma 400
  Pico Turquino 395

GUANTÁNAMO PROVINCE
accommodation
  Villa Maguana 456
activities
  El Yunque 456
information
  Ecotur 449
sights
  Museo Arqueológico 451
  Parque Nacional Alejandro de
    Humboldt 456
  Rancho Toa 455

HAVANA
food
  Restaurante El Bambú 163
sights
  Acuario Nacional 156
  Castillo de los Tres Santos Reyes
    Magnos del Morro 167
  Fortaleza de San Carlos de la
    Cabaña 168
  Fundación Naturaleza y El Hombre
    153

  Jardín Botánico Nacional 163
  Parque Almendares 119

HAVANA PROVINCE
activities
  Ranchón Gaviota 179
sights
  Parque Escaleras de Jaruco 180

HOLGUÍN PROVINCE
accommodation
  Hotel Playa Pesquero 373
  Villa Cayo Saetía 382
  Villa Pinares del Mayarí 381
activities
  Las Guanas Eco-Archaeological
    Trail 375
  Parque Rocazul 373
information
  Ecotur 375
sights
  Parque Nacional La Mensura
    381
  Parque Nacional Sierra Cristal 381

ISLA DE LA JUVENTUD (SPECIAL MUNICIPALITY)
information
  Ecotur 188
sights
  Criadero Cocodrilo 194
  Cueva de Punta del Este 195

Granja de las Tortugas 196
La Jungla de Jone 194
Punta Francés 190
Sea Turtle Breeding Center 195

MATANZAS PROVINCE

activities
Acua Diving Center 240
Aquaworld Diving Center 241
Bar Cubamar 233
Barracuda Diving Center 240
Gran Parque Natural Montemar 256
International Scuba Center 260
Laguna de Maya 233
Playa Coral 233
information
Gran Parque Natural Montemar National Park Office 257
sights
Cayo Piedras del Norte 239
Cueva de Ambrosio 239
Cueva de Musalmanes 239
Reserva Ecológica Varahicacos 239

PINAR DEL RÍO PROVINCE

accommodation
Hotel Cayo Levisa 218
Hotel Moka 224
Rancho La Guabina 207
Villa Cabo San Antonio 209
activities
Baños del Bayate 224
Baños del San Juan 223

Centro Internacional de Buceo 208
Estación Ecológica Guanahacabibes 209
food
El Romero 224
Patio de María 224
Restaurante Cayo Jutías 217
information
Oficinas del Complejo 222
Parque Nacional Viñales Visitors Center 214
sights
Centro de Investigaciones Ecológicas 222
Cueva de los Portales 219
Gran Caverna de Santo Tomás 217
Jardín Unión 222
Orquideario Soroa 220
Parque La Güira 219
Parque Nacional Península de Guanahacabibes 208
Parque Nacional Viñales 214
Rancho La Guabina 206

SANCTI SPÍRITUS PROVINCE

accommodation
Villa de Recreo María Dolores 305
activities
Hacienda Codina 313
Ranchón El Cubano 303
food
Ranchón El Cubano 303

information
Topes de Collantes Carpeta Central Information Office 312
sights
Caguanes National Park 314
Casa Museo del Café 312
Fundación de la Naturaleza y El Hombre 295
Sierra de Jatibonico 314

SANTIAGO DE CUBA PROVINCE

accommodation
Campismo Caletón Blanco 437
Campismo La Mula 439
Hacienda El Indio – Villa Colibrí 434
Hotel Carrusel El Saltón 436
Villa La Gran Piedra 433
sights
Cafetal La Isabelica 431
Jardín Botánico 431
Jardín de Cactus 434
La Gran Piedra 431
Parque Baconao 433
Valle de Río Baconao 434

VILLA CLARA PROVINCE

accommodation
Villa Las Brujas 289
food
Casa del Campesino 285
sights
Embalse Hanabanilla 285

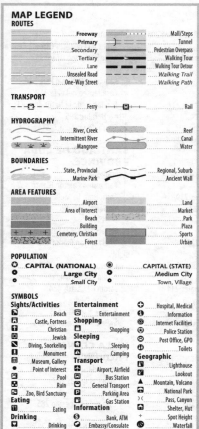

MAP LEGEND

ROUTES

Freeway	Mall/Steps
Primary	Tunnel
Secondary	Pedestrian Overpass
Tertiary	Walking Tour
Lane	Walking Tour Detour
Unsealed Road	Walking Trail
One-Way Street	Walking Path

TRANSPORT

Ferry	Rail

HYDROGRAPHY

River, Creek	Reef
Intermittent River	Canal
Mangrove	Water

BOUNDARIES

State, Provincial	Regional, Suburb
Marine Park	Ancient Wall

AREA FEATURES

Airport	Land
Area of Interest	Market
Beach	Park
Building	Plaza
Cemetery, Christian	Sports
Forest	Urban

POPULATION

CAPITAL (NATIONAL)	CAPITAL (STATE)
Large City	Medium City
Small City	Town, Village

SYMBOLS

Sights/Activities
- Beach
- Castle, Fortress
- Christian
- Jewish
- Diving, Snorkeling
- Monument
- Museum, Gallery
- Point of Interest
- Pool
- Ruin
- Zoo, Bird Sanctuary

Eating
- Eating

Drinking
- Drinking

Entertainment
- Entertainment

Shopping
- Shopping

Sleeping
- Sleeping
- Camping

Transport
- Airport, Airfield
- Bus Station
- General Transport
- Parking Area
- Gas Station

Information
- Bank, ATM
- Embassy/Consulate

- Hospital, Medical
- Information
- Internet Facilities
- Police Station
- Post Office, GPO
- Toilets

Geographic
- Lighthouse
- Lookout
- Mountain, Volcano
- National Park
- Pass, Canyon
- Shelter, Hut
- Spot Height
- Waterfall

LONELY PLANET OFFICES

Australia
Head Office
Locked Bag 1, Footscray, Victoria 3011
☎ 03 8379 8000, fax 03 8379 8111
talk2us@lonelyplanet.com.au

USA
150 Linden St, Oakland, CA 94607
☎ 510 250 6400, toll free 800 275 8555
fax 510 893 8572
info@lonelyplanet.com

UK
2nd fl, 186 City Rd
London EC1V 2NT
☎ 020 7106 2100, fax 020 7106 2101
go@lonelyplanet.co.uk

Published by Lonely Planet Publications Pty Ltd
ABN 36 005 607 983

Mixed Sources
Product group from well-managed forests and other controlled sources
www.fsc.org Cert no. SGS-COC-005002
© 1996 Forest Stewardship Council